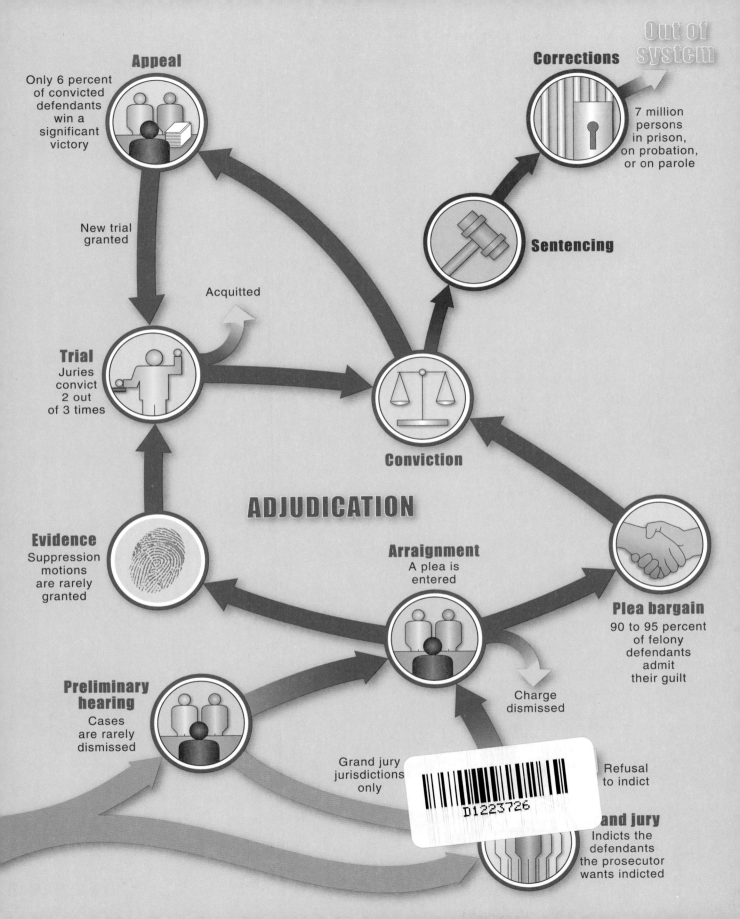

Appeal
Only 6 percent of convicted defendants win a significant victory

Corrections
7 million persons in prison, on probation, or on parole

Out of system

New trial granted

Acquitted

Sentencing

Trial
Juries convict 2 out of 3 times

Conviction

ADJUDICATION

Evidence
Suppression motions are rarely granted

Arraignment
A plea is entered

Plea bargain
90 to 95 percent of felony defendants admit their guilt

Charge dismissed

Preliminary hearing
Cases are rarely dismissed

Grand jury jurisdictions only

Refusal to indict

and jury
Indicts the defendants the prosecutor wants indicted

13e

AMERICA'S COURTS

AND THE CRIMINAL JUSTICE SYSTEM

David W. Neubauer, Ph.D.
University of New Orleans

Henry F. Fradella, J.D., Ph.D.
Arizona State University

CENGAGE

Australia • Brazil • Mexico • Singapore • United Kingdom • United States

America's Courts and the Criminal Justice System, Thirteenth Edition
**David W. Neubauer, Ph.D., and
Henry F. Fradella, J.D., Ph.D.**

Senior Product Director:
Marta Lee-Perriard

Senior Product Team Manager:
Carolyn Henderson-Meier

Content Developer: Julia White

Product Assistant: Megan Nauer

Senior Marketing Director: Mark Linton

Senior Content Project Manager:
Christy Frame

Senior Art Director: Helen Bruno

Production Service and Compositor:
Mary Stone, MPS Limited

Photo Development Editor: Kim Adams Fox

Photo Researcher: Venugopal Loganathan,
Lumina Datamatics

Text Researcher: Karthick Govinaraju,
Lumina Datamatics

Copy Editor: Chris Sabooni

Text and Cover Designer:
Michael Tanamachi

Cover Image: Brocreative/Shutterstock.com

For product information and technology assistance, contact us at
Cengage Customer & Sales Support, 1-800-354-9706.

For permission to use material from this text or product, submit all requests online at **www.cengage.com/permissions.**
Further permissions questions can be emailed to
permissionrequest@cengage.com.

Library of Congress Control Number: 2017953978

Student Edition:
ISBN: 978-1-337-55789-4

Loose-leaf Edition:
ISBN: 978-1-337-56043-6

Cengage
20 Channel Center Street
Boston, MA 02210
USA

Cengage is a leading provider of customized learning solutions with employees residing in nearly 40 different countries and sales in more than 125 countries around the world. Find your local representative at: **www.cengage.com.**

Cengage products are represented in Canada by Nelson Education, Ltd.

To learn more about Cengage platforms and services, visit **www.cengage.com**.

To register or access your online learning solution or purchase materials for your course, visit **www.cengagebrain.com.**

Printed in the United States of America
Print Number: 02   Print Year: 2018

Dedication

From David
To Jeff, Kristen, and Amy

From Hank
To the great mentors I have had, for
their friendship and guidance:
Henry F. Dressel, Esq.,
Robert L.K. Richardson, Ph.D.,
The Honorable Stephen M. McNamee,
and
John R. Hepburn, Ph.D.

DAVID WILLIAM NEUBAUER was born in Chicago. He grew up in Aurora, Illinois, graduating from West Aurora High School in 1962. After receiving a B.A. in political science from Augustana College in Rock Island in 1966, graduating *cum laude* and being elected to Phi Beta Kappa, he began graduate work at the University of Illinois, receiving a Ph.D. in 1971.

Neubauer has previously taught at the University of Florida and Washington University in St. Louis. He is now professor emeritus at the University of New Orleans, where he chaired the political science department from 1982 to 1986.

Neubauer served as a consultant to the Federal Judicial Center on two court management projects, and he worked with the American Judicature Society as principal investigator on a project (funded by the National Institute of Justice) concerning court delay reduction. Over the years he has served on review panels for the National Institute of Justice, the Bureau of Justice Statistics, the National Science Foundation, the National Institute of Mental Health, and the National Center for State Courts. He also served as a consultant to the Metropolitan Crime Commission of New Orleans.

Neubauer is the co-author of *Judicial Process: Law, Courts, and Politics in the United States*, Seventh Edition (2017), co-author of *Battle Supreme: The Confirmation of Chief Justice John Roberts and the Future of the Supreme Court* (2006), and editor of *Debating Crime: Rhetoric and Reality* (2001). All are published by Wadsworth/Cengage.

HENRY F. FRADELLA was born in New York City and grew up there and in its Monmouth Country, New Jersey, suburbs. After graduating with highest honors from the Searing School in Manhattan in 1986, Fradella earned a B.A. in psychology in 1990 from Clark University, graduating *summa cum laude* and as a member of Phi Beta Kappa. Fradella then earned a masters in Forensic Science and a law degree in 1993 from The George Washington University, and a Ph.D. in interdisciplinary justice studies from Arizona State University in 1997.

Prior to becoming a full-time academic, Fradella worked as an autopsy technician in the Office of the Chief Medical Examiner of Washington, D.C.; practiced law; and worked in the federal courts as a judicial law clerk. He began his career in academia as an assistant professor at The College of New Jersey (TCNJ). After having earned tenure and promotion to the rank of associate and then full professor over a 10-year period, Fradella resigned from TCNJ in 2007 to become a professor in, and chair of, the Department of Criminal Justice at California State University, Long Beach. He served in that position until August 2014, when he became a professor in, and associate director of, the School of Criminology and Criminal Justice at Arizona State University.

Fradella is the author of over 80 articles, reviews, and scholarly commentaries; three sole-authored books; and six additional books written with co-authors. Four of these books were published by Wadsworth/Cengage Learning. Dr. Fradella has guest-edited two volumes of the *Journal of Contemporary Criminal Justice*; served three terms as the legal literature editor of the *Criminal Law Bulletin*; and a three-year term as the co-editor of the Western Society of Criminology's official journal, *Criminology, Criminal Justice, Law & Society* (formerly *Western Criminology Review*).

Brief Contents

Contents

Juvenile Courts 106

The Dynamics of Courthouse Justice   138

Prosecutors   166

Defense Attorneys   196

CHAPTER 13

Trials and Juries   374

CHAPTER 15

Appellate and *Habeas Corpus* Review   466

Features Content

America's Courts and the Criminal Justice System, Thirteenth Edition, examines the history, traditions, and philosophy underlying our system of justice as it is played out in the criminal court. In a complex, sometimes contradictory, and often fragmented process, defendants are declared innocent or found guilty, and the guilty are fined, placed on probation, or sentenced to a period of incarceration. This book is about the defendants caught up in the process: the three-time losers; the scared, young, first-time offenders; and the business executives who are before the court to answer an indictment. But most of all, this book focuses on the prosecutors, judges, defense attorneys, and jurors who are involved in the daily decisions about guilt or innocence, probation or prison.

The impact of these decisions on crime and criminals is the subject of widespread controversy. Concern over how the courts handle criminal cases has been a staple of American political rhetoric for decades. The nature of this public debate and the solutions proposed to correct the problems are integral parts of this book. To be sure, the past few decades have witnessed significant deep-seated changes and readjustments in the criminal justice system—given all the public posturing, one would hardly expect less.

This book is written for undergraduate courses that deal with the criminal courts in the United States. Such courses (or parts of courses) are taught in various departments: criminal justice, criminology, administration of justice, political science, sociology, psychology, and social welfare. This book highlights not only the pivotal role of the criminal courts within the criminal justice system but also the courts' importance and impact on society as a whole.

America's Courts and the Criminal Justice System, Thirteenth Edition, focuses on the dynamics of the courthouse. Thus, it differs from casebooks, which use appellate court decisions to highlight the history, structure, and philosophy of courts. Although these are important matters, casebooks often project a rather sterile image of courthouse justice and omit what courts do in practice, how they do it, and, most important, why they do it.

This book's emphasis on the dynamics of courthouse justice grows out of our own research. During our professional careers, we have spent considerable time in state and federal courts in all parts of the nation. One of us worked in a federal courthouse; the other has conducted years of field research, interviewing numerous judges, jurors, prosecutors, defense attorneys, probation officers, jailers, police officers, and defendants. We have observed these officials in action and discussed with them their problems and their views of possible solutions. By the luck of the draw, one of us has also served on juries in state and federal court, while the other has appeared in court both as a lawyer and as an expert witness. Throughout this book, we have tried to convey to the reader the sense of being in the courthouse.

Central Themes

Law on the Books

The starting point of this text is to provide readers with a working knowledge of the major structures and basic legal concepts that underlie the criminal courts. In deciding guilt or innocence and determining the appropriate punishment, the courts apply the criminal law through a complicated process termed "criminal procedure." The structure of the courts, the nature of the criminal law they apply, and the procedures followed all have important consequences for how the courts dispense justice.

But to understand the legal system, one needs to know more than the formal rules. Also necessary is an understanding of the assumptions underlying these rules, the history of how they evolved, and the goals they seek to achieve. A discussion of the assumptions, history, and goals makes clear that America's criminal justice process is not monolithic but consists of a number of separate and sometimes competing units. It also points out conflicts over the goals the criminal courts are expected to achieve.

Law in Action

Many books leave the false impression that an understanding of the formal law and major structures of the court is all that one needs to know about the criminal courts. This kind of analysis provides only a limited view of how the courts administer justice. The law is not self-executing. It is a dynamic process of applying abstract rules to concrete situations.

In making decisions about charges to be filed, the amount of bail to be required, and the sentence a convicted person will receive, judges, prosecutors, and defense attorneys must make choices for which the formal law provides few precise guidelines. Thus, the second theme of this book is law in action, which emphasizes the dynamics of the criminal court process.

An examination of law in action reveals a gap between how the law is supposed to operate and how it is actually applied. For example, the law in theory suggests that the guilt of defendants should be decided by a jury trial. In practice, however, trials are rare. Most defendants plead guilty without a trial. Asking why there is a gap between the law on the books and the law in action is a big step toward understanding the dynamics of courthouse justice.

Law in Controversy

No treatment of the criminal courts would be complete without a discussion of the problems they are confronting. Are the courts too slow? Are judges too soft in sentencing? Does the criminal court process discriminate against the poor? These are just a few of the questions about the operations of the criminal courts that this book will consider. In turn, many organizations, groups, and individuals have probed the problems facing the criminal courts and proposed reforms. The third theme of this book is to discuss and analyze the controversies surrounding courthouse justice and to analyze the reforms that have been suggested for what ails the courts. Not everyone agrees on the types of

changes needed. Some argue that certain reforms will produce greater difficulties without solving the original problems. This book examines competing perspectives on the changes and reforms that are being proposed.

Key Features

Case Close-Up

Each chapter highlights an important court decision that has affected our nation's criminal justice system. Some, like *Miranda* and *Gideon*, are familiar names. Others are less well known. But each highlights the dynamic nature of courts in the United States.

Courts and Controversy

These boxed features provide multiple perspectives on the topics discussed in the chapter. To better focus on the wide-ranging debate surrounding the criminal courts in the United States, these controversies have been given an expanded subhead. Thus, throughout the book, these features will discuss controversies centering on judicial administration, crime reduction, gender equity, racial discrimination, and economic inequality.

New to This Edition

Writing the Thirteenth Edition was gratifying and stimulating. It was gratifying to learn from peer-reviewers that numerous colleagues in the professoriate and their students have found previous editions of the book useful. It was stimulating because it involved closely examining recent changes in both scholarship and public dialogue. The Thirteenth Edition offers a current perspective on a continually evolving subject: the criminal court process.

We significantly reorganized the book for the Thirteenth Edition. Notably, the 17 chapters in the past few editions of the book have been condensed so that the Thirteenth Edition contains 15 chapters. This, in turn, should allow instructors to adapt the book more easily for use in traditional 15-week semesters. To accomplish this, (1) the first two chapters in earlier editions have been condensed into a single introductory chapter that provides an overview of both courts and law in the United States; and (2) the two chapters on sentencing in earlier editions have been combined into a single chapter.

We have added several new topics in the Thirteenth Edition. We highlight questions and concerns regarding racial justice in police–citizen interactions, prosecutorial charging, jury deliberations, and criminal sentencing. We also expand our coverage of questionable forensic scientific evidence in criminal cases. And, the courts' role in reducing wrongful convictions has been highlighted throughout the book. Finally, we have made every effort to report the most up-to-date statistics available and to cite current empirical research throughout the Thirteenth Edition. To offset the additions to the book without expanding its length, we removed the former "Courts, Law, and Media" feature from each chapter that had been included in the last two editions of the book.

Chapter-by-Chapter Changes

Chapter 1—This chapter combines the introductory material in the first two chapters of earlier editions of the book. This chapter frames the study of courts using the racially charged case of Dylann Roof, who was convicted of the shooting deaths of nine African-American people in a South Carolina church. It also includes a new "Courts, Controversy, and Justice" feature on racial bias using the case of George Zimmerman, who was acquitted of killing unarmed teenager Travon Martin. Both Dylann Roof's and George Zimmerman's cases have been integrated throughout the chapter to illustrate several of the chapter's main points. The coverage of civil law has been reduced so that the chapter's introduction to law focuses on criminal law. The chapter also includes a new table on mass shootings, as well as updated examples of how the media can distort perceptions of the justice system by how they present information on high-profile criminal cases.

Chapter 2—Formerly Chapter 3, this chapter now includes the most up-to-date information and statistics on the federal judiciary and its caseload (including coverage of federal question jurisdiction, diversity jurisdiction, discrimination and civil rights cases, and prisoner petitions, some of which are presented in new figures). The chapter includes a new "Case Close-Up" feature on the federal court litigation surrounding stop-and-frisk activities in New York City, as well as information regarding new federalism concerns in the wake of *Taylor v. United States* (2016).

Chapter 3—Formerly Chapter 4, this chapter on state courts integrates new research on traffic cases (including DUI prosecutions), expands the discussion of community courts, presents updated caseload statistics for state courts, and includes new research on the effectiveness of various types of specialized courts.

Chapter 4—Formerly the last chapter in the book, this chapter on juvenile courts is now presented after the chapter on state courts. It includes many new citations, updated statistics on juvenile crime and transferring juveniles to adult court, and new tables and figures illustrating the latest trends in juvenile justice.

Chapter 5—In this chapter on the courthouse and the individuals who work there, we have included the latest research on court delay, information on the professionalization of court administration, and the recent decision in *Betterman v. Montana* (2016).

Chapter 6—Prosecutors are the focus of this chapter. We expanded coverage of prosecutorial misconduct, including the new move in select jurisdictions to hold prosecutors criminally responsible for misconduct that sends a wrongfully convicted person to prison.

Chapter 7—The chapter on the defense attorney includes up-to-date coverage on defenders' caseloads and of case law concerning the right to counsel, self-representation, and ineffective assistance of counsel, including *Luis v. United States* (2016).

Chapter 8—The chapter presents the most current research and data on judges. It also includes updated information on filibustering judicial nominees in the U.S. Senate; new examples of threats to judicial independence; new profiles of errant judges subjected to discipline; and the impact of *Williams v. Pennsylvania* (2016).

Chapter 9—The most current research on both victim and perpetrator demographic characteristics is presented in this revised chapter. The chapter has been reframed using the controversial case of Brock Turner, the Stanford University swim team member sentenced to only a short jail sentence for rape.

Chapter 10—This chapter on the processing of criminal cases explores the most current research on the pretrial processing of criminal felony cases. New tables and figures have been created to illustrate the most up-to-date data on criminal arrests, crime clearance rates, and case attrition statistics. The chapter also contains a new section on bail reform efforts across the United States that includes the use of risk assessment instruments in bail determinations.

Chapter 11—This chapter includes new content, including additional case law and expanded coverage of how seized property is accounted for and stored. The chapter now integrates *Cone v. Bell* (2009), *Utah v. Strieff* (2016), *Rodriguez v. United States* (2015), and *Birchfield v. North Dakota* (2016), as well as information on varying time lengths for obtaining search warrants, and updated requirements for recording custodial interrogations.

Chapter 12—The most up-to-date research on plea bargaining is integrated into this chapter.

Chapter 13—The chapter now includes expanded coverage of controversies surrounding the use of forensic scientific evidence at trial, including a new section on complex DNA mixture analysis. This chapter includes key recommendations from The President's Council of Advisors on Science and Technology (2016) report on "Forensic Science in Criminal Courts," as well as the critical responses to the report from criminal investigators and prosecutors. The chapter also includes a new section of "new technology as evidence" focusing on digital video evidence from police body-worn cameras. Finally, this chapter includes two recent U.S. Supreme Court decisions—*Warger v. Shauers* (2014) and *Foster v. Chatman* (2016)—as well as the controversial federal appeals court decision in *Smithkline Beecham Corp. v. Abbott Laboratories* (2014).

Chapter 14—This chapter on sentencing combines and streamlines two former chapters—one on sentencing options and another on sentencing decisions. New tables and figures have been created, presenting the latest sentencing statistics. The chapter offers expanded coverage of public safety realignment efforts: the U.S. Supreme Court cases of *Ross v. Blake* (2016) and *Glossip v. Gross* (2016).

Chapter 15—Formerly Chapter 16, this chapter has been updated to present the latest data on both state and federal appeals, as well as *habeas corpus* proceedings. The chapter includes new and expanded coverage of exonerations and wrongful convictions. And it includes information on aftermath of the death of Justice Antonin Scalia relevant to both law and politics, including the unacted-upon nomination of Merrick Garland and the battle over Neil Gorsuch's nomination and eventual confirmation to the U.S. Supreme Court.

Pedagogical Innovations

This edition contains an array of pedagogical aids to facilitate student learning. These include the following:

- Chapter learning objectives open each chapter and are revisited in the Chapter Review to facilitate student mastery of chapter concepts. The learning objectives are also linked to the text's supplements (test bank and website quizzes) to further advance learning.

- End-of-chapter critical thinking questions provide students with an opportunity to practice their skills in the chapter's key area.

- An end-of-chapter list of key terms with page references serves as a helpful study tool.

- Suggestions for further reading are offered so students can explore chapter concepts further.

- Numerous exhibits and figures amplify text coverage for easier understanding by students.

Supplements

MindTap Criminal Justice

MindTap from Cengage Learning represents a new approach to a highly personalized, online learning platform. A fully online learning solution, MindTap combines all of a student's learning tools—readings, multimedia, activities, and assessments—into a singular Learning Path that guides the student through the curriculum. Instructors personalize the experience by customizing the presentation of these learning tools for their students, allowing instructors to seamlessly introduce their own content into the Learning Path via "apps" that integrate into the MindTap platform. Additionally, MindTap provides interoperability with major learning management systems (LMS) via support for open industry standards and fosters partnerships with third-party educational application providers to provide a highly collaborative, engaging, and personalized learning experience.

Online Instructor's Manual

The instructor's manual contains a variety of resources to aid instructors in preparing and presenting text material in a manner that meets their personal preferences and course needs. It presents chapter-by-chapter suggestions and resources to enhance and facilitate learning. The instructor's manual includes learning objectives, key terms, a detailed chapter outline, a chapter summary, discussion topics, student activities, and media tools. The learning objectives are correlated with the discussion topics, student activities, and media tools.

Cengage Learning Testing Powered by Cognero

This assessment software is a flexible, online system that allows you to import, edit, and manipulate test bank content from the *America's Courts and the Criminal Justice System* test bank or elsewhere, including your own favorite test questions; create multiple test versions in an instant; and deliver tests from your LMS, your classroom, or wherever you want.

PowerPoint® Lectures

Helping you make your lectures more engaging while effectively reaching your visually oriented students, these handy Microsoft PowerPoint® slides outline the chapters of the main text in a classroom-ready presentation. The PowerPoint slides are updated to reflect the content and organization of the new edition of the text and feature some additional examples and real-world cases for application and discussion.

Acknowledgments

Writing the Thirteenth Edition was made easier by the assistance and encouragement of people who deserve special recognition. First and foremost, we are indebted to Megan Verhagen, a graduate student in Arizona State University's School of Criminology and Criminal Justice. During the 2016–2017 academic year, Megan served as Dr. Fradella's research assistant. In that capacity, she assisted the authors by identifying new research that needed to be integrated into the Thirteenth Edition. She also updated many tables and figures throughout the book to reflect the most up-to-date statistics available. We both thank Megan for her outstanding research.

Second, we appreciate the thoughtful and detailed feedback we received from Christine Scott-Hayward and Christopher D. Totten with regard to combining and streaming the two chapters on sentencing in prior editions of the book into one uniform sentencing chapter in this edition.

Third, we would like to thank the Cengage criminal justice team, especially Carolyn Henderson Meier (product team manager) and Julia White (content developer). We are also grateful to the gifted production team who turned raw manuscript into a polished book and dispensed good cheer along the way, especially Christy Frame (senior content project manager) and Mary Stone at MPS.

As always, David's wife and children deserve a special note of thanks for their love and support. He dedicates the book to his children, in response to their bemusement at the idea that Daddy was busy writing a book.

Hank thanks David for asking him to become a co-author on this most influential of books. Hank's husband Kyle also deserves special thanks for being supportive and putting up with his long hours of work on the book, even when it meant feeling neglected.

David W. Neubauer
Slidell, Louisiana

Henry F. Fradella
Cave Creek, Arizona

Reviewers of America's Courts and the Criminal Justice System

Special thanks are due to the reviewers of this and all previous editions.

James Alfini
American Judicature Society

Ruben Auger-Marchand
Indiana University; Purdue University

E. Stan Barnhill
University of Nevada-Reno

Barbara Belbot
University of Houston-Downtown

Larry Berkson
American Judicature Society

Patricia A. Binfa
Westwood College

Anita Blowers
University of North Carolina-Charlotte

Paula M. Broussard
University of Southwestern Louisiana

Mark S. Brown
University of South Carolina

Frank Butler
Temple University

Elizabeth Callahan
Lincoln University

Kathleen Cameron-Hahn
Arizona State University

Reynolds N. Cate
St. Mary's University

Bill Clements
Norwich University

Glenn S. Coffey
University of North Florida

George Cole
University of Connecticut

Beverly Blair Cook
University of Wisconsin-Milwaukee

Cathy Cowling
Campbell University

Mark Dantzker
Loyola University of Chicago

Erika Davis-Frenzel
Indiana University of Pennsylvania

Chris DeLay
University of Louisiana-Lafayette

Max Dery
California State University-Fullerton

Scott Donaldson
Tarrant County College

Thornton Douglas
University of Illinois-Chicago

Eugene J. Evans, Jr.
Camden County College

Mary Ann Farkas
Marquette University

Roy Flemming
Wayne State University

David O. Friedrichs
University of Scranton

James A. Gazell
San Diego State University

Marc Gertz
Florida State University

Gary S. Green
Minot State University

Pamela L. Griset
University of Central Florida

Joseph Hanrahan
Westfield State University

Peter Haynes
Arizona State University

Michael Hazlett
Western Illinois State University

Edward Heck
University of New Orleans

Ellen Hockstedler
University of Wisconsin-Milwaukee

Lou Holscher
Arizona State University

N. Gary Holten
University of Central Florida

Vincent R. Jones, Esq.
Governors State University

Kimberly Keller
University of Texas-San Antonio

Rodney Kingsnorth
California State University-Sacramento

Karl Kunkel
Southwest Missouri State University

Jim Love
Lamar University

Patricia Loveless
University of Delaware

David O. Lukoff
University of Delaware-Newcastle

James Maddex
Georgia State University

Stephen Meinhold
University of North Carolina-Wilmington

Larry Myers
Sam Houston State University

Elizabeth Pelz
University of Houston-Downtown

Richard Perry
San Jose State University

Eric Rise
University of Delaware

Linda Robyn
Northern Arizona University

John Paul Ryan
American Judicature Society

Joseph Sanborn
Glassboro State College

Jefferey M. Sellers
University of Southern California

William F. "Wic" Southern, Jr.
Carteret Community College

Jose Texidor
Penn State University

David O. Thysens
Saint Martin's College

Frederick Van Dusen
Palm Beach Community College

Donald Walker
Kent State University

Russell Wheeler
Federal Judicial Center

Paul Wice
Drew University

Sheryl Williams
Jersey City State College

Nancy Wolfe
University of South Carolina

AMERICA'S COURTS

AND THE CRIMINAL JUSTICE SYSTEM

REUTERS/Alamy Stock Photo

Dylann Roof appears by closed-circuit television at his bail hearing in Charleston, South Carolina, in June 19, 2015–two days after he gunned down nine people Emanuel African Methodist Episcopal Church in an attempt to start a race war.

Chapter Outline

On the evening of Wednesday, June 17, 2015, Dylann Roof entered the Emanuel African Methodist Episcopal Church in Charleston, South Carolina. Roof was 21-years-old at the time. He joined a group of people attending a Bible study at the historically Black church. After sitting with the group for about an hour, Roof, who is White, pulled a semiautomatic 45-caliber handgun from a fanny pack and opened fire while shouting racial epithets. One congregant tried to reason with Roof, but he responded, "No, you've raped our women and you are taking over the country. I have to do what I have to do" (as quoted in Drash, 2015, para. 19). In the end, Roof killed nine people, all of whom were African-American.

Roof was captured the morning after the mass shooting. He confessed to the crime, explaining that he had hoped to ignite a race war (Ellis, Botelho, & Payne, 2015). The investigation following the shooting revealed photos of Roof on Facebook, and photos on his website showed him wearing White supremacist paraphernalia. The website also contained a manifesto Roof authored in which he expressed his hatred of many racial and ethnic minority groups.

> I have no choice. . . . I am not in the position to, alone, go into the ghetto and fight. I chose Charleston because it is most historic city in my state, and at one time had the highest ratio of blacks to Whites in the country. We have no skinheads, no real KKK, no one doing anything but talking on the internet. Well someone has to have the bravery to take it to the real world, and I guess that has to be me. (Robles, 2015, para 4)

The state of South Carolina charged Roof with nine counts of capital murder, meaning

Learning Objectives

After reading this chapter, you should be able to:

LO1   Describe how the courts are related to the other components of the criminal justice system.

LO2   Discuss the major types of courts found in the United States.

LO3   Identify the most important actors in the courthouse.

LO4   List the steps in a typical felony prosecution.

LO5   List the four key elements defining law.

LO6   Identify the three key characteristics of common law.

LO7   Explain the importance of the adversary system.

LO8   Name the four amendments of the Bill of Rights that deal specifically with criminal procedure.

LO9   Identify the major elements of a crime.

LO10   Identify some of the most important legal defenses in American law.

LO11   Explain how a "law in action" perspective complements a "law on the books" approach to studying the criminal courts.

LO12   Distinguish between the crime control model of criminal justice and the due process model of criminal justice.

that prosecutors sought the death penalty. And the U.S. government also indicted Rood on federal charges, including nine counts of using a firearm to commit murder and 24 civil rights violations based on federal hate crime laws.

After Roof was found competent to stand trial, a federal judge granted Roof's request to represent himself at his federal trial (as is his constitutional right). It took the jury less than two hours to return guilty verdicts on all 33 charges. In January of 2017, he was formally sentenced to death.

Courts and Crime

Dylann Roof's case is atypical of most criminal cases for a number of important reasons. First, he was charged with capital murder. Contrary to their omnipresence in the media, murder and nonnegligent homicide cases account for less than 1/10 of 1 percent of all criminal arrests (Federal Bureau of Investigation, 2015). Moreover, the death penalty is sought in only a small fraction of murder cases. Second, the multiple counts of murder resulted from a mass shooting—an incident in which four or more people were killed. As Table 1.1 illustrates, these events are relatively rare, although they have increased in recent years. In 1982, one mass shooting occurred in which eight people were killed. By the end of 2016, 84 additional mass shootings had occurred in the United States, resulting in 672 more fatalities (Follman, Aronsen, & Pan, 2017).

Third, Roof faced parallel criminal proceedings in both state and federal courts, whereas the overwhelming majority of criminal cases are litigated exclusively in state courts. Similarly, criminal prosecutions for racially motivated killings are rare. Fourth, Roof was the first person in U.S. history to face both a federal and state death penalty at the same time (Kozlowska, 2016). Fifth, Dylann Roof's case went to trial, rather than being resolved via the plea-bargaining process like 90 to 95 percent of all felony cases. And finally, Roof opted to represent himself, rather than have an attorney represent him the way that 99.5 percent of all criminal defendants do (Hashimoto, 2007). In contrast to all these exceptions to the rule, one thing about Dylann Roof's case is quite typical: he was found guilty—just as

TABLE 1.1	U.S. Mass Shootings and Fatalities, 2007–2016	
Year	Incidents	Fatalities
2016	6	71
2015	7	46
2014	4	18
2013	5	35
2012	7	72
2011	3	19
2010	1	9
2009	4	39
2008	3	18
2007	4	53
10-Year Total	44	380

Source: Follman, Aronson, & Pan, 2017.

approximately 90 percent of all felony defendants who go to trial are convicted.

Dylann Roof's case also highlights the common disconnect between the way a case is perceived by those evaluating the evidence presented in a court of law and the ways in which a case is perceived in the court of public opinion. In a courtroom, defendants are presumed innocent until proven guilty beyond a reasonable doubt. In contrast, reporters, media pundits, and their audiences are not constrained by formal presumptions or the rules

Does the Criminal Law Inhibit Justice as a Function of Racial Biases?

On February 26, 2012, 17-year-old Trayvon Martin was walking back to a house at which he was a guest after purchasing Skittles and a fruit drink from a local 7-Eleven. George Zimmerman, a 28-year-old, mixed-race Hispanic male, who was a member of his local neighbor watch program, called 911 and reported Martin, an African-American teenager wearing a gray hoodie, as a "suspicious person." Although police instructed Zimmerman not to get out of his vehicle or otherwise engage the person he called to report, Zimmerman ignored these instructions. Armed with a 9-millimeter pistol, Zimmerman pursued Martin on foot. Within minutes, Zimmerman shot and killed Martin, who was unarmed. Zimmerman claimed he did so in self-defense after the unarmed teenager "knocked him to the ground, punched him, and slammed his head repeatedly against the sidewalk" (Alvarez & Buckley, 2013, p. A1). Zimmerman was eventually charged with second-degree murder and the lesser offense of manslaughter. The events following Martin's death and Zimmerman's acquittal set off a national debate on racial profiling, the scope of self-defense laws, and even gun rights.

The case against George Zimmerman for killing Trayvon Martin began as a routine homicide investigation. Police arrived at the scene within minutes of the shooting. Zimmerman was bleeding from the nose and the back of his head. These injuries supported Zimmerman's version of the events in question. Specifically, Zimmerman claimed that Martin "pounced" on him and, during the ensuing struggle, Martin made Zimmerman fear for his life. Thus, Zimmerman maintained that he shot Martin in self-defense after his repeated calls for help had gone unheeded. After questioning Zimmerman for nearly five hours, police decided that there was insufficient evidence to arrest Zimmerman on any charges. Apparently, Florida's "stand your ground" law played a significant role in that decision since that version of a self-defense law bars police from arresting anyone who uses force in self-defense "unless it determines that there is probable cause that the force that was used was unlawful" (Florida Stat. § 776.032(2), 2005). With no real evidence to contradict Zimmerman's version of the events, police decided to let him go.

However, investigators ultimately decided that Zimmerman could have avoided the encounter with Martin if he had listened to the police instructions to stay in his vehicle until law enforcement officers arrived. Indeed, the National Sheriffs' Association (2012) criticized Zimmerman's actions as "significantly contradict[ing] the principles of the Neighborhood Watch Program" (para. 2), which does not condone participants taking "the law into their own hands" (para. 3). Moreover, segments of the public, fueled, in large part, by the media, accused Zimmerman of having racially profiled an unarmed Black teenager wearing a hoodie as being someone up to no good in a nice, gated community in a Florida suburb.

At trial, prosecutors painted Zimmerman as a "wannabe cop" motivated, in part, by racial prejudice. But to prove second-degree murder, the prosecution needed to prove that Zimmerman shot Martin with a "'depraved mind' brimming with ill will, hatred, spite or evil intent" (Alvarez & Buckley, 2013, p. A1). To prove the lesser offense of manslaughter, the prosecution needed to prove that Zimmerman had recklessly placed himself in a situation that led to Trayvon Martin's death. But proving either charge is extremely difficult in a self-defense case. In fact, the law in Florida required

of evidence. This disparity often causes people to misperceive the criminal judicial process as unfair. This book seeks to correct the most common misperceptions about the role of the courts in the U.S. criminal justice system.

There can be no doubt that changes in popular culture affect America's legal institutions. For example, "changes in popular culture brought about by rapid scientific and technological advances and widespread dissemination of information about them" has "heightened juror expectations and demands for scientific evidence in almost every respect" (Shelton, Kim, & Barak, 2009, p. 2). Indeed, jurors expect sophisticated forensic evidence in even the most mundane cases (Shelton, 2008; Feeler, 2014). Some scholars and practitioners prosecutors to convince the jury, beyond a reasonable doubt, that Zimmerman did not act in self-defense. That high burden of proof is nearly insurmountable to overcome in cases, like this one, in which the parties clearly fought and no eyewitnesses or evidence contradict claims of self-defense.

> Even after three weeks of testimony, the fight between Mr. Martin and Mr. Zimmerman on that rainy night was a muddle, fodder for reasonable doubt. It remained unclear who had started it, who screamed for help, who threw the first punch and at what point Mr. Zimmerman drew his gun. There were no witnesses to the shooting. . . . The defense also had one piece of irrefutable evidence, photographs of Mr. Zimmerman's injuries—a bloody nose along with lumps and two cuts on his head. It indicated that there had been a fight and that Mr. Zimmerman had been harmed. . . . (Alvarez & Buckley, 2013, p. A1)

In addition, subsequent forensic analysis partially substantiated Zimmerman's claim that Martin was on top of him, preventing Zimmerman from escaping Martin's assault; in fact, a forensic pathologist concluded that, "the trajectory of the bullet was consistent with Mr. Martin leaning over Mr. Zimmerman when the gun was fired" (Alvarez & Buckley, 2013, p. A1). Thus, in the end, legal experts largely agreed that Zimmerman's acquittal was technically proper under the law even though he made a series of very bad choices on the night in question (Savage & Muskal, 2013). Nonetheless, scholars and civil rights activists argued that permissive gun laws and broad self-defense laws combined to create an unjust end to a case involving the tragic death of an unarmed teenager whose race and style of dress likely influenced both his killer and the jury who deliberated that gunman's fate (Fradella, 2013; Jones-Brown & Fradella, 2015; Megale, 2013).

According to the Pew Research Center (2013), nearly as many Americans were satisfied by the outcome (39 percent) as we dissatisfied with it (42 percent). But a closer look at the data reveals significant differences on perception by race and by age:

- 86 percent of Blacks were dissatisfied with Zimmerman's acquittal compared to 58 percent of Hispanics and 30 percent of Whites.
- 78 percent of Blacks, 47 percent of Hispanics, and only 28 percent of Whites said the case raised important issues about race that need to be discussed.
- 60 percent of Whites and 40 percent of Hispanics felt the issue of race in the case received more attention than it deserved, whereas only 13 percent of Blacks felt that way.
- Among Whites, 49 percent were satisfied with the verdict compared to 30 percent who were dissatisfied. But this difference varied by age. Whites under the age of 30 were roughly evenly split, whereas Whites over the age of 65 expressed satisfaction in the verdict by a nearly 2-to-1 ratio.
- Of those under the age of 30, 53 percent were dissatisfied with the verdict, whereas 29 percent were satisfied. In sharp contrast, 50 percent of people age 65 and older were satisfied with the case outcomes compared to 33 percent who were dissatisfied.
- 80 percent of Tea Party Republicans and 61 percent of mainstream Republicans expressed satisfaction with the verdict, compared with 42 percent of Independents and just 22 percent of Democrats.

Where do you stand on the outcome of the Zimmerman trial? Why?

call this phenomenon the **CSI effect**, even though forensic science on television appears to be only one factor in an overall social trend that embraces technology while discounting logical inference (see Chapter 13). But the widespread use of forensic evidence to convict guilty defendants at trial and exonerate the innocent on appeal is just one example of the dynamic nature of the legal system in the United States. But as the "Courts, Controversy, & Justice" feature illustrates, forensic evidence may not be conclusive; moreover, it must be considered in light of other evidence that reasonable people may interpret differently.

Although courts and law have a long history that provides stability, this does not mean that courts and law are static institutions. On the contrary, changes in society end up in courthouses in a variety of ways. At times, specific events are the catalyst for change. In the aftermath of the terrorist attacks of September 11, 2001, for example, courts wrestled with questions about the scope of electronic eavesdropping and whether alleged terrorists can be held indefinitely in military prisons without trials. Similarly, claims of racial profiling in who were stopped, questioned, and frisked by New York City Police Department officers led to the federal courts adjudicating several class action civil rights lawsuits that ultimately resulted in a settlement involving judicial oversight of police stop-and-frisk activities (White, Fradella, Morrow, & Mellom, 2016). And the acquittal of George Zimmerman for killing of Trayvon Martin gave rise to the Black Lives Matter movement. That movement grew exponentially in 2014 through 2016 in response to a series of incidents in which unarmed African-American citizens were shot and killed during encounters with police, including Michael Brown (Fergusson, MO), Eric Garner (New York City), Laquan McDonald (Chicago), Tamir Rice (Cleveland), and Freddie Gray (Baltimore), just to name a few. These events, in turn, not only caused prosecutors, judges, and juries to examine whether police use of force was legally justified under the facts of each case but also prompted the U.S. Department of Justice to investigate some local law enforcement agencies that, as a result, are now subject to judicial scrutiny or oversight (Childress, 2015). In short, there can be no doubt that the courts frequently play a significant role in the resolution of major social problems related to crime and responses to it.

At other times, courts have been forced to adapt to changes in other branches of government. Legislatures across the nation, for example, have launched wars on drugs that have flooded the courts with a growing number of cases even as the incidence of other crimes decreases. Likewise, changes in public opinion affect how justice is administered. Concerned about crime rates that are too high, the public has demanded that judges get tough with criminals.

Courts are independent from the other branches of government, but this does not mean that they are divorced from the society they serve. Rather, societal issues impact the kinds of cases brought to court and how they are handled. For example, concerns about gender equity prompted examination of how courts handle domestic violence and why district attorneys decline to prosecute many sexual assault cases. How courts adapt to social changes is important. And while change in society is inevitable, it is also unsettling. Simply stated, change produces controversy. A good deal of this book examines the controversy surrounding courts and crime.

Courts and the Criminal Justice System

The criminal justice system in the United States is large and complex. Indeed, fighting crime is a major societal activity. According to the U.S. Bureau of Justice Statistics (Kyckelhahn, 2015), every year, local, state, and federal governments spend approximately $265.16 billion on the criminal and civil justice system in the United States. These tax dollars support an enormous assortment of criminal justice agencies, which in turn employ a large (and growing) number of employees; approximately 2.5 million people earn their living working in the criminal justice system. These government officials are quite busy: Every year, the police make more than 13 million arrests, not including traffic violations. And every day, correctional personnel supervise approximately 7 million people—about 2.2 million of whom are in prisons or jails and the balance of whom are supervised in the community on probation or parole. Yet as large as these figures are, they still underestimate societal activity directed against crime. A substantial number of persons are employed in the private sector in positions either directly (defense attorneys and bail agents) or indirectly (locksmiths and private security) related to dealing with crime (Hakim, Rengert, & Shachmurove, 1996; Police Executive Research Forum, 2014; Ribovich & Martino, 2007).

The numerous public agencies involved in implementing public policy concerning crime are referred to as the **criminal justice system**. Figure 1.1 depicts

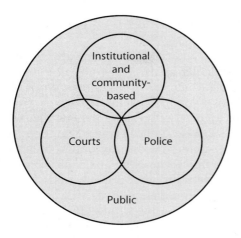

FIGURE 1.1 The Overlapping Circles of the Criminal Justice System

the criminal justice system as consisting of three overlapping circles: Police are responsible for apprehending criminals; the courts are responsible for deciding whether those arrested are legally guilty and, if so, determining the sentence; corrections is responsible for carrying out the penalty imposed on the guilty.

The major components of the criminal justice system do not make up a smoothly functioning and internally consistent organization. Rather, the criminal justice system is both interdependent and fragmented.

An Interdependent Criminal Justice System

Viewing the various components of criminal justice as a system highlights the fact that these different agencies are interdependent and interrelated. Police, courts, and corrections are separate government institutions with different goals, histories, and operating procedures. Though separate, they are also tied together because they must interact with one another. The courts play a pivotal role within the criminal justice system because many formal actions pertaining to suspects, defendants, and convicts involve the courts. Only the judiciary can hold a suspect in jail prior to trial, find a defendant guilty, and sentence the guilty person

to prison. Alternatively, of course, the courts may release the suspect awaiting trial, find the suspect not guilty, or decide to grant probation.

The decisions that courts make have important consequences for other components of the criminal justice system. Judges' bail policies, for example, immediately affect what happens to a person arrested by the police; likewise, corrections personnel are affected because the bail policies of the judges affect the size of the local jail population. If the decisions made by the courts have important consequences for police and prisons, the reverse is equally true: The operations of law enforcement and corrections have a major impact on the judiciary. The more felons the police arrest, the greater the workload of the prosecutors; and the more overcrowded the prisons, the more difficult it is for judges to sentence the guilty.

A Fragmented Criminal Justice Nonsystem

The system approach to criminal justice dominates contemporary thinking about criminal justice. But not everyone is convinced of the utility of this conceptualization. Some people point to a nonsystem of criminal justice. Although the work of the police, courts, and corrections must, by necessity, overlap, this does not mean that their activities are coordinated or coherent. From the perspective of the nonsystem, what is most salient is the fragmentation of criminal justice. Fragmentation characterizes each component of the criminal justice system. The police component consists of nearly 18,000 law enforcement agencies, with varying traditions of cooperation or antagonism. Likewise, the corrections component includes more than 1,820 state and federal correctional facilities, to say nothing of the thousands of local jails. But corrections also encompasses probation, parole, drug treatment, halfway houses, and the like.

The same fragmentation holds true for the courts. In many ways, talking about courts is misleading, because the activities associated with "the court" encompass a wide variety of actors. Many people who work in the courthouse—judges, prosecutors, public defenders, clerks, court reporters, bailiffs—are employed by separate government agencies. Others who work in the courthouse are private citizens, but their actions directly affect what happens in this governmental institution; defense attorneys and bail agents are prime examples. Still others are ordinary citizens who find themselves in the courthouse either because they are compelled to be there (defendants and jurors) or because their activities are essential to the disposition of cases (victims and witnesses).

The fragmentation within the three components of the nonsystem of criminal justice is compounded by the decentralization of government. American government is based on the principle of federalism, which distributes governmental power between national (usually referred to as federal) and state governments. In turn, state governments create local units of government, such as counties and cities. Each of these levels of government has its own array of police, courts, and corrections. This decentralization adds tremendously to the complexity of the American criminal justice system. For example, depending on the nature of the law allegedly violated, several different prosecutors may bring charges against a defendant, including the following: city attorney (local), district attorney (county), attorney general (state), U.S. attorney (U.S. district court), and U.S. attorney general (national).

Tensions and Conflicts

Criminal justice is best viewed as both a system and a nonsystem. Both interdependence and fragmentation characterize the interrelationships among the agencies involved in apprehending, convicting, and punishing wrongdoers. In turn, these structural arrangements produce tensions and conflicts within each component. For example, the prosecutor may loudly condemn the actions of a judge, or a defense attorney may condemn the jury for an unjust verdict.

Tensions and conflicts also occur among the components of criminal justice. The interrelationships among police, courts, and corrections are often marked by tension and conflict because the work of each component is evaluated by others: The police make arrests, yet the decision to charge

is made by the prosecutor; the judge and jury rate the prosecutor's efforts.

Tensions and conflicts also result from multiple and conflicting goals concerning criminal justice. Government officials bring to their work different perspectives on the common task of processing persons accused of breaking the law. Tensions and conflicts among police, courts, and corrections, therefore, are not necessarily undesirable; because they arise from competing goals, they provide important checks on other organizations, guaranteeing that multiple perspectives will be considered. The same holds true within the courts. Judges, prosecutors, and defense attorneys, for example, share the common task of processing cases but at the same time exhibit different perspectives on the proper outcome of the case. Understanding this complexity, in *America's Courts and the Criminal Justice System*, we examine the nation's judiciary in three complementary sections. Part I is about the basic organization of our court system; Part II concerns identifying the actors in the courthouse; and Part III focuses on following the steps of the judicial process from arrest through trial, as well as how the convicted are sentenced and how those convictions and sentences may be subsequently challenged.

An Overview of U.S. Courts

By rough count, 17,000 courthouses are operating in the United States. Some are imposing turn-of-the-century buildings noted for their elaborate architecture. Others are faceless modern structures marked by a lack of architectural inspiration. A few courts, you might be surprised to learn, are in the front of a funeral parlor or the back of a garage, where justices of the peace preside in rural areas. Buildings aside, courts are governmental organizations created to hear specific types of cases. Figure 1.2 offers a preliminary overview of different types of courts in the United States.

One distinction is between federal and state courts. The term *dual court system* refers to separate state and federal courts (rarely do cases move from one system to the other).

Another important difference between courts relates to function. Most courts are trial courts. As the

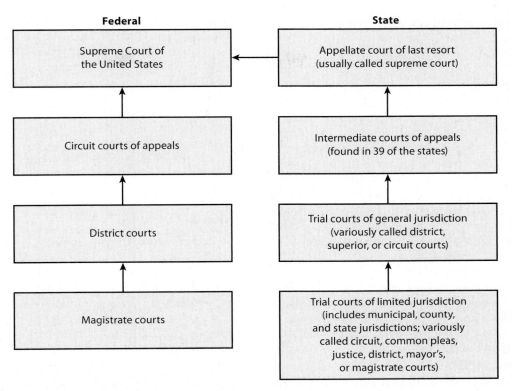

FIGURE 1.2 Overview of the Court Structure in the United States

name implies, this is where trials are held, jurors sworn, and witnesses questioned. Trial courts are noisy places resembling school corridors between classes. Amid the noisy crowd you will find lawyers, judges, police officers, defendants, victims, and witnesses walking through the building during working hours.

Trial courts, in turn, are divided between major and lower. Lower courts initially process felony cases (set bail, for example) but cannot find the defendant innocent or guilty and therefore cannot sentence. Their primary activity involves processing the millions of minor offenses such as public drunkenness, petty theft, and disorderly conduct. Major trial courts, on the other hand, are responsible for the final phases of felony prosecutions. In these courts, defendants charged with crimes such as murder, robbery, burglary, and drug dealing enter a plea of guilty (or occasionally go to trial), and the guilty are sentenced.

Other courts (fewer in number) are appeals courts that review decisions made by trial courts (usually only the major trial courts). Appeals courts review decisions made elsewhere, but no trials are held, no jurors employed, and no witnesses heard. Rather, appellate courts are places where lawyers argue whether the previous decision correctly or incorrectly followed the law. In many ways, appellate courts are like a monastery, where scholars pore over old books and occasionally engage in polite debates. Given the growing volume of cases, the federal government and most states have created two levels of appellate courts: intermediate courts, which must hear all cases, and supreme courts, which pick and choose the cases they hear.

Although the U.S. Supreme Court stands atop the organizational ladder, it hears only a handful of the cases filed each year (often fewer than 85 per year). Thus, its importance is measured not in terms of the number of cases decided but in the wide-ranging impact these few decisions have on all stages of the process.

Identifying the Actors in the Courthouse

Enter a trial courtroom, and you will observe numerous people either busily engaged in doing something or seemingly doing nothing. Some of the actors in the courthouse are easily identifiable by the clothes they wear. The person sitting high above everyone else and wearing the black robes is the judge. The person in handcuffs arrayed in a bright orange jumpsuit is the defendant. And the men and women dressed in uniforms are law enforcement officers. But the roles being performed by the others in attendance are not readily apparent. It is clear that those sitting in front of the railing are more important than those in back of it. Until court proceedings begin, the observer is never sure whether they are victims, defendants, family, witnesses, reporters, potential jurors, or retired citizens whose hobby is court watching. After the proceedings begin, the roles of those in back of the railing become more apparent.

Some participants are present on a regular basis; others, only occasionally. Many are public employees, but some are private citizens. Using the categories applied to the criminal justice system, Table 1.2 provides a chart of many of the actors one would expect to see in a courthouse on any given day. Some of the titles vary from place to place. Similarly, the participants vary depending on the type of case. In a murder case, for example, a scientist from the crime lab may be presenting evidence, but in a child sexual abuse case, the actors will more likely include a social worker or psychiatrist. A brief overview of the main actors will help set the stage.

Prosecutors

The organization of prosecutors in the United States is as fragmented as the courts in which they appear. To limit ourselves only to state courts and state prosecutions, in most states you find one prosecutorial office for the lower courts (typically the city attorney), another for the major trial court (typically called the district attorney or the state's attorney), and yet another at the state level (almost uniformly called the attorney general).

Regardless of the level, prosecutors are the most influential of the courthouse actors. Their offices

TABLE 1.2   Actors in the Courthouse

	Justice Professionals			Members of the Public	
Police	**Lawyers**	**Court Support Staff**	**Corrections Officials**	**Regular Participants**	**Irregular Participants**
Federal	Prosecutors	Clerks of Court	Probation Officers	Bail Agents	Defendants
State	Public Defenders	Court Reporters	Jail Employees	Reporters	Victims
Sheriff	Court-Appointed Defense Lawyers	Pretrial Services Personnel	Prison Employees	Social Services Personnel	Witnesses
Local	Private Defense Attorneys	Bailiffs	Drug Rehabilitation Program Personnel	Select Expert Witnesses	Jurors
Special Districts	Judges	Court Administrators			Victim Advocates
Private Security	Law Clerks	Victim-/Witness-Assistance Program Personnel			
		Rape Crisis Center			

decide which cases to prosecute, which cases to plea-bargain, and which cases to try. They may also be influential in matters such as setting bail and choosing the sentence.

Defense Attorneys

The U.S. Constitution guarantees defendants the right to counsel. But for most defendants, this abstract "right" collides with economic reality. Many defendants cannot afford to hire a lawyer, so the government must provide one at government expense, either a court-appointed lawyer or a public defender. Only a handful of defendants hire a private lawyer.

Our notions of defense attorneys have been shaped by fictional characters on television and in movies who are always able to show that their clients are innocent. Reality is strikingly different. Often defense attorneys urge their clients to plead guilty based on the assessment that a jury will find the defendant guilty beyond a reasonable doubt. Even when cases are tried, defense attorneys only occasionally are able to secure a not-guilty verdict for their clients.

Judges

Judges in state courts are by and large elected by the voters. Federal judges, on the other hand, are nominated by the president of the United States and confirmed by the U.S. Senate. Judges are the ultimate authority figures in the courthouse because only judges can set bail, only judges can instruct jurors about the meaning of the law, and only judges can impose sentences. Exercising this authority, though, is limited by the reality of high caseloads. The quickest way to dispose of cases is by a plea of guilty. Thus, judges must be responsive to prosecutors and defense attorneys if they are to achieve their principal goal of disposing of cases.

Defendants and Victims

Defendants are, by and large, young, poor, uneducated males. A large percentage stand accused of property crimes (theft and burglary) or low-level drug offenses. They are hardly the clever and sophisticated criminals portrayed in fiction. African-Americans and Latinos comprise a disproportionately large percentage of felony defendants, a fact that has placed race and ethnicity at the forefront of the politics of justice (Walker, Spohn, & DeLone, 2017).

The victims of crime are playing an increasingly important role in the criminal courts. Once banished to a bit part of testifying, they are increasingly demanding major roles in setting bail, agreeing to pleas of guilty, imposing sentences, and granting release from prison. Groups such as Mothers Against Drunk Driving (MADD) and the National Organization for Victim Assistance (NOVA) have become a potent political force.

An Overview of Criminal Judicial Processes

Both Figure 1.3 and Table 1.4 present an overview of the stages a felony case passes through from arrest to appeal. The specifics of criminal procedure vary from state to state, and federal requirements differ from state mandates. Rest assured that the remainder of the text will complicate this oversimplification. But for now, we focus on a defendant charged with a noncapital state felony.

Arrest

Every year the police make more than 12 million arrests for nontraffic offenses. Most are for minor crimes, but nearly 2.17 million involve serious crimes, such as murder, rape, assault, robbery, burglary, arson, and theft. The police are able to make an arrest in only 46.8 percent of violent crimes known to them and a mere 19 percent of property crimes known to them. As a result, only a fraction of the nation's major crimes ever reach the courts.

Initial Appearance

An arrested person must be brought before a judge without unnecessary delay. For felony

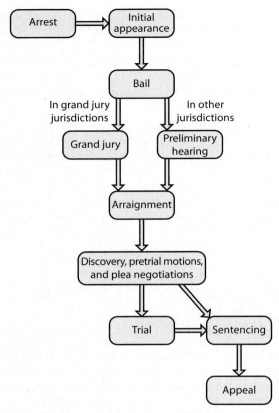

FIGURE 1.3 Flowchart of the Steps in the Criminal Judicial Process

defendants, the initial appearance is largely a formality because no plea may be entered. Instead, defendants are told what crime they are alleged to have committed and perfunctorily advised of their rights, and a date for the preliminary hearing is set. For misdemeanor defendants, the initial appearance is typically the defendant's only courtroom encounter; three out of four plead guilty and are sentenced immediately.

Bail

The most important event that occurs during the initial appearance is the setting of bail. Because a defendant is considered innocent until proven guilty, the vast majority of defendants have the right to post bail. But this legal right is tied to the defendant's economic status. Many defendants are too poor to scrounge up the cash to pay the bail agent's fee; thus, they must remain in jail awaiting trial. The overriding reality, however, is that U.S. jails are overflowing. As a result, pretrial detention is limited largely to defendants who are alleged to have committed serious crimes; judges set a very high bail because they do not want these defendants wandering the streets before trial. For defendants charged with less-serious crimes, judges and prosecutors may want to keep them in jail while awaiting trial, but the citizens are often unwilling to invest the tens of millions of dollars needed to build more jails.

Grand Jury

The grand jury is designed as a check on unwarranted prosecutions. Grand juries are required in all federal felony prosecutions, but only about half the states use them. In grand jury proceedings, a prosecutor must convince a simple majority of the grand jurors that a crime was committed and that there is probable cause that the defendant committed a crime. Probable cause is not a particularly high or exacting standard of proof. All that needs to be shown to meet this burden of proof is a "fair probability" that the defendant committed the crime.

If the grand jury finds probable cause to hold the defendant for trial, it returns an indictment (also called a "true bill") charging the defendant with a crime. On rare occasions, grand juries refuse to indict (such refusal is called a "no bill" or a "no true bill"). Legal theory aside, grand juries are dominated by the prosecutor, and they obligingly indict whomever the prosecutor wants indicted.

Preliminary Hearing

Like grand jury proceedings, preliminary hearings provide a check against unwarranted prosecutions. During a preliminary hearing, the prosecutor must prove to a judge (rather than to a grand jury) that a crime was committed and that there is probable cause to believe that the defendant committed the crime. Given the low burden of proof, most of the time a judge finds that probable cause is present and orders the defendant held for further proceedings. In most courthouses, few cases are dismissed at the preliminary hearing for lack of probable cause.

Arraignment

Although the two terms are often used interchangeably, an arraignment differs from the initial appearance. During arraignment, the defendant is given a copy of the formal charges, advised of his or her rights (usually more extensively than at the initial appearance), and for the first time is called upon to enter a plea. Not surprisingly, most defendants plead not guilty, but a few admit their guilt then and there and enter a plea of guilty. Overall, little of importance happens during arraignment.

Discovery

The term *discovery* refers to the exchange of information prior to trial. In some states, but not all, the prosecutor is required to turn over a copy of the police reports to the defense prior to trial. In general, however, the defense is required to provide the prosecutor with little, if any, information. The formal law aside, many prosecutors voluntarily give defense attorneys they trust extensive information prior to trial, anticipating that the defense attorney will persuade the defendant to enter a plea of guilty.

Pretrial Motions

Motions are simply requests for a judge to make a decision. Many motions are made during trial, but a few may be made beforehand. The most significant pretrial motions relate to how the police gathered evidence. Defense attorneys file motions to suppress evidence—that is, to prevent its being used during trial. Motions to suppress physical evidence contend that the police conducted an illegal search and seizure (*Mapp v. Ohio*, 1961). Motions to suppress a confession contend that the police violated the suspect's constitutional rights during questioning (*Miranda v. Arizona*, 1966).

Plea Negotiations

Most findings of guilt result not from a verdict at trial but from a voluntary plea by the defendant. Ninety percent of all felony convictions are the product of negotiations between the prosecutor and the defense attorney—and sometimes the judge as well (but not the police; officers are not permitted to negotiate plea bargains). Although the public thinks of plea bargaining as negotiating a lenient sentence, the reality is that each courthouse has an informal understanding of what a case is worth. Thus, plea bargaining is governed by informal understandings of what sentence is appropriate for a given type of defendant.

Trial

Trial by jury is one of the most fundamental rights granted to those accused of violating criminal law. A defendant can be tried either by a judge sitting alone (called a "bench trial") or by a jury. A jury trial typically begins with the selection of 12 jurors. Each side makes opening statements, indicating what they think the evidence in the case will show. Because the prosecutor has the burden of proving the defendant guilty beyond a reasonable doubt, he or she is the first to call witnesses. After the prosecution has completed its case, the defense has the opportunity to call its own witnesses. When all the evidence has been introduced, each side makes a closing argument to the jury, and the judge then instructs the jury about the law. The jurors retire to deliberate in secret. Though the details of trial procedure vary from state to state, one factor is constant: The defendant's chances for an acquittal are not good.

Sentencing

Most of the steps of the criminal process are concerned with determining innocence or guilt. In upwards of 90 percent of criminal cases, criminal trials end with convictions. But many defendants are often more concerned about how many years they will have to spend in prison than about the question of guilt, which partially explains why so many defendants plead guilty in exchange for a specific sentence.

Once guilt has been established by plea or conviction at trail, the members of the courtroom work group strive to help a judge determine what sentence to impose. Probation officers usually play a significant role at this junction, since they conduct a presentence investigation into a defendant's personal life (e.g., educational background, family ties, financial situation, etc.) and then present sentencing recommendation to a judge in a report.

The principal decision the judge must make is whether to impose a prison sentence or place the defendant on probation. Fines are rarely used in felony cases. The death penalty is hotly debated but in actuality is limited to only some first-degree murder cases. Prison overcrowding is the dominant reality of contemporary sentencing; roughly 1.56 million inmates are incarcerated in state and federal prisons (Carson, 2015). Only recently has attention begun to focus on the fact that the political rhetoric of "lock them up and throw away the key" has resulted in severe prison overcrowding, causing policy makers to consider a range of intermediate sanctions that provide alternatives to incarceration.

Appeal

Virtually all defendants found guilty during trial contest their fate, filing an appeal with a higher court in the hope that they will receive a new trial. Contrary to public perceptions, defendants are rarely successful on appeal; fewer than one in ten appellants achieve a victory in the appellate courts, and of those who do, most are reconvicted in a subsequent trial. Moreover, appeals are filed in only a small proportion of all guilty verdicts; defendants who plead guilty rarely appeal.

Appellate court opinions affect future cases because the courts decide policy matters that shape the operation of the entire criminal justice system. The "Case Close-Up" on *Brown v. Mississippi* (1936) illustrates this point.

The Basis of Law

The basis of law can be summarized in two words: human conflict. A controversy over how much money is owed, a quarrel between husband and wife, a collision at an intersection, and the theft of a television set are a few examples of the great number of disputes that arise and threaten to disrupt the normal activities of society. Business and everyday activities depend on mechanisms for mediating inevitable human conflicts. Without such mechanisms, individual parties might seek private, violent means of settlement. The legendary feud between the Hatfields and the McCoys illustrates the disruptiveness of blood feuds motivated by revenge—not only in the lives of the individual parties directly involved but also in the larger society.

Law is an everyday word, but as Professor Lawrence Friedman (1984, p. 2) suggests, "It is a word of many meanings, as slippery as glass, as elusive as a soap bubble." Although there are various approaches to defining the term, most scholars define **law** as a body of rules enacted by public officials in a legitimate manner and backed by the force of the state (Neubauer & Meinhold, 2017). This definition can be broken into four phrases, and each has important implications for how we think about law.

The first element—law is a body of rules—is self-evident. What is not immediately obvious, however, is the fact that these rules and regulations are found in a variety of sources, such as statutes, constitutions, court decisions, and administrative regulations.

The second element—law is enacted by public officials—is of critical importance. All organizations of any size or complexity have rules and regulations that govern their members. But these private rules are not law under our definition unless they are recognized by public officials—judges, legislators, and executives in particular.

The third element—law is enacted in a legitimate manner—means that it must be agreed upon ahead of time how the rules will be changed. Thus, legislatures have methods for passing new laws, bureaucrats have procedures for applying those laws, and judges follow a well-known process in interpreting those laws.

The final element—law is backed by the force of the state—says that these rules and regulations would be largely meaningless without sanctions. Thus, what differentiates law from other societal rules is that law has teeth to it—namely, the

CASE CLOSE-UP   *Brown v. Mississippi*

In April 1934, Ed Brown, Henry Shields, and Yank Ellington were indicted for murdering Raymond Stewart. Around 1:00 p.m. on March 30, 1934, Deputy Sheriff Dial discovered the body of Raymond Stewart. Later that evening, Dial and some colleagues went to the home of Yank Ellington and requested Ellington to accompany them to the house of the deceased. Ellington was a poor, uneducated Black man who complied with the deputy's request. Once they arrived at Stewart's home, a number of White men accused Ellington of having killed Stewart. When Ellington denied doing so, the group seized him and—with Deputy Dial's participation—hanged him by a rope from the limb of a tree. They let him down before he died, only to hang him again. After they let him down a second time, Ellington still maintained his innocence. So, the group tied him to a tree and whipped him, demanding that he confess. He continued to maintain his innocence. He was finally released and returned home in intense pain.

A day or two later, Deputy Dial, accompanied by another deputy, returned to Ellington's home and arrested him. While en route to the jail in a neighboring county, the two men again severely whipped Ellington, declaring that the whipping would continue until he confessed. To stop his torture, Ellington agreed to confess to whatever statement the deputy dictated. He then did so and was put in jail.

Two other Black men, Ed Brown and Henry Shields, were also arrested and taken to the same jail. Deputy Dial, again accompanied by a number of White men (one of whom was also an officer and one of whom was the jailer), came to the jail. They made Brown and Shields strip and then beat their bare backs with a leather strap with buckles on it. As had been done with Ellington, the men made it clear that the beatings would continue unless and until Brown and Shields confessed with all of the details demanded of them. The whippings continued until Brown and Shields adjusted their confessions to match the specific details demanded by their torturers.

After what was later described as a "solemn farce" of a hearing at which the three men's "free and voluntary confessions" were admitted into evidence, the men were tried and convicted of Stewart's death based on their confessions and then sentenced to death. The three men's cases were appealed to the U.S. Supreme Court, which wrote:

> [T]he trial court was fully advised by the undisputed evidence of the way in which the confessions had been procured.

The trial court knew that there was no other evidence upon which conviction and sentence could be based. Yet it proceeded to permit conviction and to pronounce sentence. The conviction and sentence were void for want of the essential elements of due process, and the proceeding thus vitiated could be challenged in any appropriate manner. It was challenged before the Supreme Court of the State by the express invocation of the Fourteenth Amendment. That court entertained the challenge, considered the federal question thus presented, but declined to enforce [the defendants'] constitutional right. The court thus denied a federal right fully established and specially set up and claimed, and the judgment must be reversed. (*Brown v. Mississippi*, 1936, p. 287)

Sadly, such brutal tactics were frequently used against criminal suspects prior to the decision in *Brown v. Mississippi*. In fact, the Wickersham Commission, a federal commission set up to investigate police conduct in the early 1930s, used the term *the third degree* to describe police tactics at the time (Penney, 1998, pp. 336–337). They defined the term as "the inflicting of pain, physical or mental, to extract confessions or statements" (Wickersham Commission, 1931, p. 19).

The Commission documented the use of a litany of sadistic practices, including beating with fists, blackjacks, rubber hoses, and telephone books; the use of hot lights; confinement in airless and fetid rooms; and hanging from windows. The Commission was also concerned with psychologically abusive tactics, such as incommunicado detention, prolonged relay questioning, stripping the suspect of clothing, and the deprivation of sleep and food (Penney, 1998, p. 336).

The Wickersham Commission's report facilitated widespread change in policing in the United States. Not only did the report set in motion many efforts to stop police corruption and brutality (see Skolnick & Fife, 1993), but also it affected the decision making of the U.S. Supreme Court. The Court began citing the Wickersham Commission's report on police brutality in obtaining confessions as evidence that confessions were often involuntary and/or unreliable.

In reversing the defendants' convictions in *Brown v. Mississippi*, the Supreme Court ruled that confessions beaten out of suspects were clearly inadmissible because they were involuntary. The Court did so using the Fourteenth Amendment's guarantee of "due process of law." As a result, several bedrock

(Continued)

(Continued)

principles of contemporary criminal procedure are attributable to the landmark decision in *Brown v. Mississippi*. Specifically:

1. An involuntary statement is considered to be inherently untrustworthy or unreliable, and convictions based on unreliable evidence violate due process.

2. Coercive police practices are a violation of "fundamental fairness," an essential element of due process. Therefore, a confession coerced by the police violates due process, even if that confession is otherwise reliable.

3. Free choice is an essential aspect of due process, and an involuntary confession cannot be the product of a person's free and rational choice.

Finally, note that *Brown v. Mississippi* marked the beginning of the Supreme Court's review of how police obtain confessions and when those confessions may be used as evidence in a court of law—a process that continues today (Chapter 11).

---

consequences of legal sanctions. As Daniel Oran's *Law Dictionary for Nonlawyers* (2000) puts it, law is "that which must be obeyed." In most instances, though, it is not necessary to apply legal sanctions, because the threat is enough to keep most people abiding by the law most of the time.

It is also important to stress what this working definition of law omits—namely, any mention of justice. In a representative democracy, public perceptions of law embody fundamental notions of justice, fairness, and decency. It is the potential linking of law and justice (in the form of unjust laws) that also makes law so difficult to define. But law and morality do not necessarily equate. Our working definition of law deliberately excludes any reference to justice because there is no precise legal or scientific meaning for that term. Furthermore, people use the term *justice* to support particular political and social goals. In the public arena, it is a catchall term used in several different ways (see Owen, Fradella, Burke, & Joplin, 2015).

The Common Law Heritage

The legal systems of the United States and other English-speaking nations that were once British colonies (including Australia, New Zealand, and Canada) trace their origins to England and its so-called **common law**. The common law first appeared in medieval England after the Norman Conquest in 1066. The new rulers gradually introduced central government administration,

including the establishment of courts of law. Initially, the bulk of the law was local and was administered in local courts. A distinct body of national law began to develop during the reign of Henry II (1154–1189), who was successful in expanding the jurisdiction of the royal courts. The king's courts applied the common customs of the entire realm rather than the parochial traditions of a particular village. Thus, the term *common law* meant "general law" as opposed to "special law"; it was the law common to the entire land.

Common law is used in many English-speaking nations, including England, Australia, New Zealand, Canada, and the United States. Because the common law of England forms the basis of law in all U.S. states other than Louisiana (which derives its civil law from the Napoleonic Code and the Continental legal heritage; the state's criminal law, however, derives from the common law), U.S. law is sometimes referred to as **Anglo-American law**.

During the development of the common law legal system, a distinctive way of interpreting the law gradually emerged. Three key characteristics of this common law heritage stand out: The law was judge-made, based on precedent, and found in multiple sources.

Judge-Made Law

One key characteristic of the common law is that it was predominantly **judge-made law** (rather than legislatively enacted). Until the late 19th century, no important body of statutory law existed in either England or the United States. Rather, judges organized social relationships through law. In the field of civil law, for example, the common law courts developed the rights and obligations of citizens in such important areas as property, contracts, and torts. Even today, American law in these areas is predominantly judge-made.

Similarly, in the field of criminal law, by the 1600s the English common law courts had defined felonies such as murder, arson, robbery, larceny, and rape. Moreover, the legal defenses of insanity and self-defense had also entered the common law. These English criminal law concepts were transplanted to America by the colonists. After the American Revolution, common law crimes considered applicable to local conditions were retained. Although legislative bodies, not the courts, now define crimes, contemporary statutory definitions often reflect their common law heritage.

Precedent

A second key characteristic of the common law is the use of **precedent**, often referred to as *stare decisis* (Latin for "let the decision stand"). The doctrine of precedent requires a judge to decide a case by applying the rule of law found in previous cases, provided the facts in the current case are similar to the facts in the previous cases. By following previous court decisions, the legal system promotes the twin goals of fairness and consistency. Exhibit 1.1 gives an example of the precedent-based citation system used in American law. For insight into the legal reasoning processes that judges use when applying precedent, see Appendix C.

The common law's reliance on precedent reflects a cautious approach to problem solving. Rather than writing a decision attempting to solve the entire range of a given legal problem, common law courts decide only as much of the case as is necessary to resolve the individual dispute. Broad rules and policy directives emerge only through the accumulation of court decisions over time. Unfortunately, many Americans make the mistake of translating the common law heritage, particularly the doctrine of precedent, into a static view of the courts and the law. The entire history of Anglo-American law emphasizes the importance of common law courts'

shaping old law to new demands. In the words of Justice Oliver Wendell Holmes (1920, p. 187): "It is revolting to have no better reason for a rule of law than that it was so laid down in the times of Henry IV. It is still more revolting if the grounds upon which it was laid down have vanished long since, and the rule simply persists from blind imitation of the past."

One way courts achieve flexibility is in adapting old rights to new problems. Another is the ability of courts to distinguish between precedents. Recall that the doctrine of precedent involves previous cases with a similar set of facts. Courts sometimes state that the present facts differ from those on which previous decisions were based and reach a different ruling. Finally, judges will occasionally (but very reluctantly) overturn a previous decision by stating that the previous court opinion was wrong. However, the common law is committed to gradual change to maintain stability; it is often said that the law and the courts are conservative institutions.

Multiple Sources of Law

The third key characteristic of the common law is that it is found in multiple sources (a concept sometimes expressed as "uncodified"). In deciding the legal meaning of a given crime (murder, for example), it is not sufficient to look only at the legislative act. One must also know how the courts have interpreted the statute. Depending on the issue, the applicable rules of law may be found in constitutions, statutes, administrative regulations, or court decisions.

Constitutions

Within the hierarchy of law, constitutions occupy the top rung. A **constitution** is the first document that establishes the underlying principles and general laws of a nation or state. The U.S. Constitution is the fundamental law of the land. All other laws—federal, state, and local—are secondary. Similarly, each state has a constitution that is the "supreme law of the state." State courts may use the state constitution to invalidate the actions of legislators, governors, or administrators.

EXHIBIT 1.1 | How to Read Legal Citations

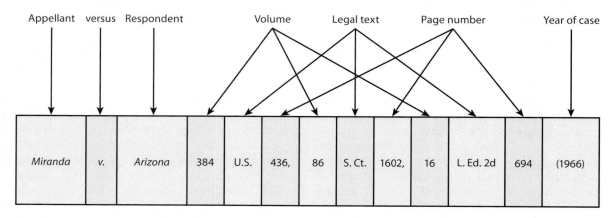

When first confronted with legal citations, students are often bewildered by the array of numbers. But with a few basics in mind, these citations need not be confusing; they are efficient aids in finding court decisions.

The full citation for *Miranda* is as follows: *Miranda v. Arizona*, 384 U.S. 436, 86 S. Ct. 1602, 16 L. Ed.2d 694 (1966). The lead name in the case usually refers to the party who lost in the lower court and is seeking to overturn that decision. That party is called the "appellant." The second name refers to the party (or parties) who won at the lower level (in this instance, the state of Arizona). The second party is called the "appellee," or more simply, the "respondent." Miranda is the appellant who is seeking to overturn his conviction. The state of Arizona is named as the respondent because criminal prosecutions are brought in the name of the state.

After the names of the parties come three sets of references. All decisions of the U.S. Supreme Court are reported in the *Supreme Court Reports*, which is published by the U.S. Government Printing Office. It is the official reporting system and is abbreviated U.S. In addition, decisions of the Supreme Court are reported in two private reporting systems: the *Supreme Court Reporter*, which is abbreviated S. Ct., and in *Lawyers Supreme Court Reports, Lawyers Edition*, which is abbreviated L. Ed. 2d. The numbers preceding the abbreviation for the volume refer to the volume number. Thus, *Miranda* can be found in volume 384 of the *Supreme Court Reports*. The number after the abbreviation refers to the page number. Thus, the Miranda decision in volume 384 begins on page 436; in volume 86 of the *Supreme Court Reporter*, it is on page 1602. A library usually carries only one of the reporting systems, so the multiple references make it easy to locate the given case, no matter which of the three reporting systems is available. The final number in parentheses is the year of the case.

Decisions of other courts at both the federal and state levels are reported in a similar manner in other volumes.

Constitutions define the powers that each branch of government may exercise. For example, Article III of the U.S. Constitution creates the federal judiciary (see Chapter 2). Constitutions also limit governmental power. Some limitations take the form of prohibitions. Thus, Article I, Section 9, states, "The privilege of the Writ of *Habeas Corpus* shall not be suspended." Other limitations take the form of specific rights granted to citizens. The clearest example is the first ten amendments to the U.S. Constitution, known collectively as the Bill of Rights. For example, the First Amendment begins, "Congress shall make no law respecting an establishment of religion, or prohibiting the free exercise thereof." State constitutions also contain bills of rights, many of which are modeled after their national counterpart.

Constitutions also specify how government officials will be selected. The U.S. Constitution provides that federal judges shall be nominated by the president, confirmed by the Senate, and serve during "good behavior." Similarly, state constitutions specify that state judges will be selected by election, appointment, or merit (see Chapter 8).

Statutes

The second rung of law consists of **statutes**. Laws enacted by federal and state legislatures are usually referred to as "statutory law." A statutory law enacted by a local unit of government is commonly called a **municipal ordinance**.

Until the latter part of the 19th century, American legislatures played a secondary role in the formulation of law. It was not until the 20th century that state legislatures became the principal source of law (Friedman, 1984). A fundamental reason for the growing importance of legislatively enacted statutes was that rapidly industrializing society was faced with new types of problems. Questions of how to protect the interests of workers and consumers were much broader in scope than those typically handled by the courts. The common law took decades to develop and refine legal rights and obligations, but the growing needs of an increasingly complex society could not afford the luxury of such a lengthy time frame. Legislators could enact rules of law that were not only much broader in scope than those adopted by judges but also were more precise and detailed. Thus, a great deal of law today is statutory.

Administrative Regulations

The third rung of American law consists of **administrative regulations**. Legislative bodies delegate rule-making authority to a host of governmental bureaucracies called by various names, such as agencies, boards, bureaus, commissions, and departments. All levels of government—federal, state, and local—authorize administrative agencies to issue specific rules and regulations consistent with the general principles specified in a statute or municipal ordinance. The Internal Revenue Service, by rule, decides what constitutes a legitimate deduction. State boards, by rule, set standards for nursing homes. Local zoning boards, by rule, decide where restaurants may be built.

Administrative regulations are the newest, fastest growing, and least understood source of law. The rules and regulations promulgated by government agencies are extensive. The federal bureaucracy alone issues thousands of pages of new rules and policy statements each year. These extensive regulations promulgated by government agencies must often be interpreted by courts.

Judge-Made Law

Court decisions remain an important source of law. According to the common law tradition, courts do not make law, they merely find it. But this myth, convenient as it was for earlier generations, cannot mask the fact that courts do make law. This tradition, though, suggests a basic difference between legislative and judicial bodies. Legislative bodies are free to pass laws boldly and openly. Moreover, their prescription of the rules is general and all-encompassing. Courts make law more timidly, on a piece-by-piece basis, and operate much more narrowly.

Although American law today is primarily statutory and administrative, vestiges of judge-made law persist. The law governing personal injury remains principally judge-made, as do procedural matters such as rules of evidence. The major influence of case law (another term for court decisions), however, is seen in interpreting the law of other sources. The Constitution is a remarkably short document—some 4,300 words—and it is full of generalizations such as "due process of law," "equal protection of the laws," and "unreasonable searches and seizures." The Founders left later generations to flesh out the operating details of government. Supreme Court decisions have been primarily responsible for adapting constitutional provisions to changing circumstances. Through an extensive body of case law, the Court has applied specific meaning to these vague phrases. (See Appendix C for more information on judge-made law.)

Judge-made case law is vital in determining the meaning of other sources of law as well. Statutes, for example, address the future in general and flexible language. The interpretations that courts provide can either expand or contract the statute's meaning. No lawyer is comfortable with his or her interpretation of an alleged violation of the criminal law without first checking to see how the courts have interpreted it.

The Adversary System

Law is both substantive and procedural. **Substantive law** creates legal obligations. Tort, contract, and domestic relations are examples of substantive civil law. Murder, robbery, and burglary are examples of substantive criminal law. **Procedural law**, on the other hand, establishes the methods of enforcing these legal obligations. Trials are the best-known aspect of American procedural law, but trials do not exist alone. Before trial there must be orderly ways to start, conduct, and end lawsuits. An important aspect of procedural law centers on the roles lawyers and judges play in the legal process.

In many nations, criminal investigations are conducted by a single government official whose function is to establish a unified version of what happened, seeking out facts that show the defendant's guilt as well as those that indicate his or her innocence. The Anglo-American legal system rejects such an approach. Its guiding premise is that a battle between two opposing parties will uncover more of the truth than would a single official, no matter how industrious and well meaning. Under the **adversary system**, the burden is on the prosecutor to prove the defendant guilty beyond a reasonable doubt, and the defense attorney is responsible for arguing for the client's innocence and asserting legal protections. The judge serves as a neutral arbitrator who stands above the fight as a disinterested party, ensuring that each side battles within the established rules. Finally, the decision is entrusted to the jury (although, in some instances, a judge alone may decide).

Safeguards

The guiding assumption of the adversary system is that two parties, approaching the facts from entirely different perspectives, will uncover more of the truth than would a single investigator, no matter how industrious and objective. Prior to any court appearances—indeed, even prior to an arrest—the U.S. Constitution provides numerous procedural safeguards to restrain the power of the police. For example, as explained in more detail

in Chapter 11, police must follow certain procedures before conducting searches and seizures. Similarly, before conducting any custodial interrogations, police are generally required to inform suspects of their *Miranda* rights.

In court, especially at certain hearings and trials, each side has the opportunity, through cross-examination, to probe for possible biases in witnesses and to test what witnesses actually know, not what they think they know. The right to cross-examination is protected by the Sixth Amendment: "In all criminal prosecutions, the accused shall enjoy the right . . . to be confronted with witnesses against him."

By putting power in the hands of several different parties, the adversary system creates another type of safeguard. Each actor is granted limited powers, and each has limited powers to counteract the others. If the judge is biased or unfair, the jury has the ability to disregard the judge and reach a fair verdict; if the judge believes the jury has acted improperly, he or she may set aside the jury's verdict and order a new trial. This diffusion of powers in the adversary system incorporates a series of checks and balances aimed at curbing political misuse of the criminal courts.

In diffusing power, the adversary system provides a third safeguard: It charges a specific actor—the defense attorney—with asserting the rights of the accused. Defense attorneys search out potential violations of the rights of the accused. They function as perpetual challengers in the criminal court process and are ready at every juncture to confront the government by insisting that the proper procedures be followed.

The Rights of the Accused

Procedural law in the United States places a heavy emphasis on protecting the individual rights of each citizen. A key feature of a democracy is the insistence that the prevention and control of crime be accomplished within the framework of law. The criminal process embodies some of society's most severe sanctions: detention before trial, confinement in prison after conviction, and, in certain limited situations, execution of the offender.

Because the powers of the criminal courts are so great, there is concern that those powers might be abused or misapplied.

Restrictions on the use and application of government power take the form of rights granted to the accused. One of the most fundamental protections is the privilege against self-incrimination. Another is the right to a trial by jury. These protections exist not to free the guilty but to protect the innocent (see Table 1.3). Basing the criminal justice process on the necessity of protecting individual liberties (of the innocent and guilty alike) obviously reduces the effectiveness of that process in fighting crime. To ensure that innocent persons are not found guilty, Anglo-American criminal law pays the price of freeing some of the guilty.

The primary justification for providing constitutional safeguards for those caught in the net of the criminal process is to ensure that innocent persons are not harassed or wrongly convicted. The American legal system is premised on a distrust of human fact finding. The possibility of wrongly convicting an innocent person arises when honest mistakes are made by honorable people. But it also arises when dishonorable officials use the criminal justice process for less-than-honorable ends. In countries without built-in checks, the criminal justice process provides a quick and easy way for government officials to dispose of their enemies. For example, a common ploy in a totalitarian government is to charge persons with the ill-defined crime of being an "enemy of the state." The possibility of political

TABLE 1.3	Provisions of the U.S. Constitution Dealing with Criminal Procedure
	Constitutional Language
Crime	Article I Section 9.3: No bill of attainder may be passed by the legislature. Article I Section 10.1: No state may pass any bill of attainder. Article I Section 9.3: The legislature may not pass an ex post facto law. Article I Section 10.1: No state may pass an ex post facto law.
Arrest	Amendment IV: Right against unreasonable search and seizures applies to arrest.
Initial appearance	Amendment VI: Right to know charges.
Bail	Amendment VIII: Right against excessive bail.
Preliminary hearing	Amendment VI: Right to assistance of counsel.
Charging	None
Grand jury	Amendment V: Right to a grand jury for a capital or otherwise infamous crime.
Arraignment	Amendment VI: Right to know charges.
Evidence	Amendment IV: Right against unreasonable search and seizures. Amendment V: Right against self-incrimination.
Plea bargaining	None
Trial	Amendment V: Right not to be tried twice for the same crime. Amendment VI: Right to a speedy trial; right to an impartial jury; right to a public trial; right to be confronted by witnesses against oneself; right to a jury from state or district where crime shall have been committed; right to obtain witnesses in one's favor; right to conduct cross-examination; right to speak at trial.
Sentencing	Amendment VIII: Right against excessive fines; right against cruel and unusual punishment. Amendment XIII: Right against involuntary servitude.
Appeal	Article I Section 9.2: Privilege of the writ of habeas corpus shall not be suspended.

misuse of the criminal justice process by a tyrannical government or tyrannical officials is a major concern in the Anglo-American heritage.

Another reason that democracies respect the rights of those accused or suspected of violating the criminal law is the need to maintain the respect and support of the community. Democratic governments derive their powers from the consent of the governed. Such support is undermined if power is applied arbitrarily. Law enforcement practices that are brutal or overzealous are likely to produce fear and cynicism among the people—lawbreakers and law abiders alike. Such practices undermine the legitimacy that law enforcement officials must have in order to enforce the law in a democracy.

Due Process

The principal legal doctrine for limiting the arbitrariness of officials is due process. Due process of law is mentioned twice in the Constitution:

- "No person shall . . . be deprived of life, liberty or property without due process of law." (Fifth Amendment)
- "No state shall deprive any person of life, liberty or property without due process of law." (Fourteenth Amendment)

The concept of **due process of law** has a broad and somewhat elastic meaning, with definitions varying in detail from situation to situation. The core of the idea of due process is fundamental fairness insofar as a person should always be given notice of any charges brought against him or her, that a person should be provided a real chance to present his or her side in a legal dispute, and that no law or government procedure should be arbitrary or capricious. The specific requirements of due process vary somewhat, depending on the Supreme Court's latest interpretations of the Bill of Rights.

Bill of Rights

The major obstacle to the ratification of the Constitution was the absence of specific protections for individual rights. Several of the most prominent leaders of the American Revolution opposed the adoption of the Constitution, fearing that the proposed national government posed as great a threat to the rights of the average American as had the king of England. Therefore, shortly after the adoption of the Constitution, ten amendments, collectively known as the **Bill of Rights**, were adopted. Many of these protections—particularly the Fourth, Fifth, Sixth, and Eighth Amendments—deal specifically with criminal procedure.

Originally, the protections of the Bill of Rights restricted only the national government. Through a legal doctrine known as **selective incorporation**, however, the Supreme Court ruled that the due process clause of the Fourteenth Amendment made some provisions of the Bill of Rights applicable to the states as well. Although not all the protections of the Bill of Rights have been incorporated into the Fourteenth Amendment, all of the major protections now apply to the states as well as to the national government (Exhibit 1.2). The major provisions of the Bill of Rights incorporated through the due process clause of the Fourteenth Amendment are protections against unreasonable searches and seizures (Fourth Amendment); protection against self-incrimination (Fifth); the right to counsel and trial by jury (Sixth); and the prohibition against cruel and unusual punishment (Eighth).

Introduction to Criminal Law

Most disputes that come to court involve private parties litigating **civil law** claims involving *contracts*—agreements between two or more persons involving a promise supported by mutual obligations; *torts*—legal wrong done to another person's rights, body, reputation, or property; *domestic relations*—matters of family law mainly involve divorce and related issues such as child custody, child support, and alimony; or *property*—ownership of real estate, tangible personal items, or ideas (e.g., patents, trademarks, and copyrights). *Plaintiffs* file civil lawsuits to resolve such disputes because the courts possess powers that private parties do not; courts can, for example, order a person to pay money owed under a contract or

EXHIBIT 1.2   Cases Incorporating Provisions of the Bill of Rights into the Due Process Clause of the Fourteenth Amendment

FIRST AMENDMENT

Establishment of religion: *Everson v. Board of Education* (1947)
Free exercise of religion: *Cantwell v. Connecticut* (1940)
Freedom of speech: *Gitlow v. New York* (1925)
Freedom of the press: *Near v. Minnesota* (1931)
Freedom to peaceably assemble: *DeJong v. Oregon* (1937)
Freedom to petition government: *Hague v. CIO* (1939)

SECOND AMENDMENT

Right to bear arms: *McDonald v. City of Chicago* (2010)

FOURTH AMENDMENT

Unreasonable search and seizure: *Wolf v. Colorado* (1949)
Exclusionary rule: *Mapp v. Ohio* (1961)
Warrant requirement: *Ker v. California* (1963) and
    Aguilar v. Texas (1964)

FIFTH AMENDMENT

Grand jury: Not incorporated
No double jeopardy: *Benton v. Maryland* (1969)
No self-incrimination: *Malloy v. Hogan* (1964)
Compensation for taking private property: *Chicago,*
    Burlington and Quincy Railroad v. Chicago (1897)

SIXTH AMENDMENT

Speedy trial: *Klopfer v. North Carolina* (1967)
Public trial: *In re Oliver* (1948)
Impartial jury: *Parker v. Gladden* (1966)
Jury trial: *Duncan v. Louisiana* (1968)
Venue: Not incorporated
Notice: *Cole v. Arkansas* (1948)

Confrontation of witnesses: *Pointer v. Texas* (1965)
Compulsory process: *Washington v. Texas* (1967)
Assistance of counsel in capital cases: *Powell v. Alabama*
    (1932)
Assistance of counsel in noncapital felony cases: *Gideon v.*
    Wainwright (1963)
Assistance of counsel in most misdemeanor cases:
    Argersinger v. Hamlin (1972)
Assistance of counsel during plea bargaining: *Missouri v.*
    Frye (2012) and *Lafler v. Cooper* (2012)

SEVENTH AMENDMENT

Jury trial in civil cases: Not incorporated

EIGHTH AMENDMENT

No excessive bail: Status unclear (possibly incorporated
    according to dicta in *McDonald v. City of Chicago* [2010],
    but no U.S. Supreme Court case has ever clearly stated
    that the excessive bail clause has been incorporated)
No excessive fines: *Cooper Industries v. Leatherman Tool*
    Group, Inc. (2001)
No cruel and unusual punishment: *Robinson v. California*
    (1962)

NINTH AMENDMENT

Privacy: *Griswold v. Connecticut* (1965). (Note that the
word *privacy* does not appear in the Ninth Amendment [nor
anywhere else in the Constitution], but in *Griswold*, several
justices viewed the Ninth Amendment as guaranteeing
that right.)

Source: Adapted from John Ferdico, Henry F. Fradella, and Christopher Totten. 2015. *Criminal Procedure for the Criminal Justice Professional.* 12th ed. Boston, MA: Cengage.

award monetary damages suffered for an injury received in an automobile accident.

In contrast to breaches of the civil law that are considered private matters involving only the individual parties, violations of the criminal law are considered public wrongs. As such, **criminal law** relates to actions that are considered so dangerous, or potentially so, that they threaten the welfare of society as a whole.

A second difference involves prosecution. Unlike civil law, in which plaintiffs (who are private

parties) file suit in court alleging particular *defendants* infringed some private rights, violations of public wrongs are prosecuted by the state.

The type of penalties imposed on law violators is a third difference. In civil law, the injured party generally receives some form of compensation. Violators of criminal law, however, are punished. In setting penalties, the law often makes a distinction based on the serious of the offense. The most serious crimes are called **felonies** and in most states, they are punishable by one year or more in prison. Less serious offenses are called **misdemeanors**, which are typically punishable by up to a one-year sentence in a local jail. And finally, the least serious offenses are called **violations**, which are subject to fines or very short jail terms.

It is important to recognize that criminal law is intended to supplement, not supplant, civil law. Thus, a person may be prosecuted criminally and the victim may also seek to recover civil damages for the same act. In automobile accidents involving drinking, for example, the drunk driver may be charged criminally with drunk driving and the injured party may also file a civil suit seeking monetary damages.

Elements of a Crime

In every criminal case, the prosecution must prove what is known as *corpus delicti*, a Latin phrase meaning "body of the crime." *Corpus delicti* refers to the essential **elements of a crime** that the prosecution must prove beyond a reasonable doubt. In defining the elements of a particular offense, criminal laws are based on five general principles. Most behavior cannot be called criminal unless:

• a guilty act, called an *actus reus*, is committed, with

• a particular level of criminal intent, called *mens rea*, and

• the guilty act and the criminal intent are related.

• In addition, a number of crimes also require the prosecution to prove additional elements, such as the presence of certain attendant circumstances and/or that the guilty act caused a particular result.

Actus Reus: The Guilty Act

Before there can be a crime, there must be a **guilty act (*actus reus*)**. Thus, criminal liability occurs only after a voluntary act that results in criminal harm. The requirement of a guilty act reflects a fundamental principle of American law: No one should be punished solely for bad thoughts. Depending on the crime, there are different types of guilty acts. Most crimes have a voluntary act as the *actus reus*. Thus, a person who strikes another

while suffering an epileptic seizure would not be guilty of battery, because the act (hitting) was not voluntary. An omission—a failure to act when there is a legal duty to act—can also qualify as an *actus reus*, such as failing to file income taxes, failing to yield the right of way, and failing to provide adequate care for one's children. The act of possession can also qualify as an *actus reus*, such as the offense of possession of an illegal drug. Differences in the nature of the guilty act account for many gradations of criminal offenses. To choose one obvious example, stealing property is considered separately from damaging property.

An important subdivision of the guilty act is a class of offenses labeled as **attempts** (for example, attempted burglary or attempted murder). The law does not want a person to avoid legal liability merely because someone or something prevented the commission of a crime. Typically, though, the penalties for attempt are less severe than if the act had succeeded. One result is that in some states, defendants often plead guilty in an attempt to reduce the possible severity of the prison sentence.

Mens Rea: Criminal Intent

Most crimes consist of two elements, the guilty act itself and the accompanying mental state. The rationale is that criminal sanctions are not necessary for those who innocently cause harm. As Justice Holmes (1881, p. 3) once pithily put it, "Even a dog distinguishes between being stumbled over and being kicked." The mental state, or **criminal intent**, required for a crime to have been committed is referred to as *mens rea* (Latin for "guilty mind").

Despite its importance in criminal law, guilty intent is difficult to define because it refers to a subjective condition, a state of mind. Some statutes require only general intent (intent to do something that the law prohibits), but others specify the existence of specific intent (intent to do the exact thing charged). Moreover, legislatively defined crimes have added new concepts of mental state to the traditional ones. Thus, crimes differ with respect to the mental state the prosecution must prove existed in order to secure a criminal conviction. Larceny (termed "theft" in some states), for example, typically requires proof of a very great degree of intent; the prosecutor must prove that the defendant intentionally took property to which he knew he was not entitled, intending to deprive the rightful owner of possession permanently. Negligent homicide, on the other hand, is an example of a crime involving a lesser degree of intent; the prosecution need only show that the defendant negligently caused the death of another. Most crimes require that the defendant knew he or she was doing something wrong. Also, the law assumes that people know the consequences of their acts. Thus, a person cannot avoid legal liability by later saying, "I didn't mean to do it."

Union of Act and Intent

Criminal law requires that the guilty act and the guilty intent occur together, a concept often referred to as the union of **actus reus** and **mens rea**. Suppose that you pick up another student's textbook, believing it to be your own. Although you take the book—an act that would constitute the *actus reus* for theft—you had no criminal intent; you made an honest and reasonable mistake. Thus, without the union of *actus reus* (the taking of the book) and *mens rea* (the intent to steal), you would not be liable for theft.

Attendant Circumstances

Some crimes require the presence, or absence, of **attendant (accompanying) circumstances**. Driving at a speed of 150 miles per hour would constitute a crime only if it occurred on a public roadway; it would not be a crime to drive at that speed on a racetrack. The location of the speeding is the attendant circumstance for the crime. Attendant circumstances may also be used to define the level or "degree" of crime. For example, most states differentiate between classes of theft on the basis of the amount stolen. The law might provide that a theft of less than $500 be treated as a misdemeanor and a theft of $500 or more be treated as a felony. The amount stolen is the attendant circumstance.

Results

In a limited number of criminal offenses, the **result** of the illegal act plays a critical part in defining the crime. The difference between homicide and battery, for example, depends on whether the victim died or lived. Similarly, most states distinguish between degrees of battery, depending on how seriously the victim was injured. Note that the concept of results differs from that of intent. In all of the preceding examples, the defendant may have had the same intent. The only difference was how hearty the victim was or perhaps how skillful the defendant was in carrying out his or her intentions.

Defining Crimes

Using the principles of *actus reus*, *mens rea*, attendant circumstances, and result, legislatures define the elements of crimes in penal codes. Because the particular elements combine to provide the technical (that is, legal) definition or *corpus delicti* of a crime, criminal statutes must be read closely; each clause in a penal statute usually constitutes a critical part of the offense.

Criminal Defenses

Individuals may have performed illegal acts but may nonetheless be not guilty of a crime because of the applicability of legally recognized defenses. **Criminal defenses** derive from the way crime is defined. In most criminal cases, the defense attempts to cast doubt on the defendant's guilt. This is usually accomplished by undercutting the prosecution's case such that the jury has reason to doubt whether the defendant committed all of the elements of the crime(s) charged.

In other cases, however, the defense may assert specific legal doctrines in an attempt to secure an acquittal. An **alibi defense**, for example, permits defendants to argue that they were somewhere else at the time the crime was committed. Witnesses may be called to testify that during the time in question the defendant was drinking beer at a local bar or shopping downtown with some friends. Most states and the federal system require that defendants provide a notice of an alibi defense prior to trial, along with a list of witnesses to be called to support this assertion. A notice of alibi defense gives the prosecution the opportunity to investigate the witnesses' stories before trial. Prosecutors who suspect that witnesses have carefully rehearsed their alibi testimony can use clever cross-examination to ask questions out of sequence, hoping to catch each witness in a series of contradictions. Prosecutors can also call rebuttal witnesses to suggest that the witnesses are longtime friends of the defendant, who may be likely to lie.

Defenses That Negate *Mens Rea*

Sometimes people engage in an act that at first blush might appear to be criminal, but they do so under circumstances demonstrating that they lacked true criminal intent. These defenses are said to negate *mens rea*. The two most common of these defenses include the mistake of fact defense and the defense of necessity.

When a person makes an honest and reasonable mistake regarding a factual matter that, if true, would have justified the act or omission that is the subject of a criminal prosecution, he or she may be able to assert the defense known as **mistake of fact** if the mistake negates the *mens rea* of the crime with which the defendant is charged. For example, if a student took a book that belonged to a classmate under the mistaken belief that the book was his own, the mistake would negate the crime of theft because there was no intent to steal.

Criminal law recognizes that there are times when someone acts not of his or her own free will, but rather because of the necessary circumstances of the moment or the coercion of another. When such situations exist, the law permits a defendant to argue that his or her conduct should either be excused entirely or mitigated to a less serious charge because *mens rea* was formed under extraordinary circumstances that render it unfair to hold the defendant responsible for the unlawful conduct. Consider the case of *State v. Cole* (1991). The defendant's wife was six months pregnant and had developed pains in her back and stomach. He did not have a telephone to call for help, and his only neighbor was not at home. The next closest phone was more than a mile and a half away. So, even though his driver's license had been suspended, he drove to the phone to call for help. The defense of **necessity** excused his conduct.

Defenses of Justification

Defenses of justification are based on the commission of an act under circumstances the criminal law does not seek to punish, such as using force in **self-defense**, defense of other persons, or defense of property. Note that it may even be legal to use deadly force to repel an unlawful and potentially deadly attack against oneself or another human being. In contrast, the criminal law never permits deadly force to be used strictly to defend property.

Procedural Defenses

There are a number of **procedural defenses** that the law recognizes for public policy reasons. These defenses are generally unconcerned with factual guilt. Rather, they focus on compliance with the rules and processes of the criminal justice system, such as the right to a speedy trial and the related defense of the passage of time specified in statutes of limitations (see Chapter 5), the bar against double jeopardy, immunity, and the use of the exclusionary rule to prevent illegally obtained evidence from being used to convict someone (see Chapter 11).

Defenses of Excuse

Defenses of excuse seek to excuse acts committed by defendants who should not be held criminally responsible for their actions because they were too young or because their mental state prevented them from understanding the consequences of their actions.

The law recognizes youthful age as a criminal defense under certain circumstances. In most states, children under the age of 7 are considered legally incapable of forming criminal intent and therefore cannot be held criminally responsible for their actions, a criminal defense referred to as **infancy**. After reaching this minimum age, but before becoming an adult, a child's criminal violations are treated as acts of **juvenile delinquency**. The premise of juvenile delinquency is that people under a certain age have less responsibility for their actions than adults do. The exact age at which a person is no longer considered a juvenile, and can thus be prosecuted as an adult, differs from state to state. As more and more youths are committing violent crimes, states are lowering the age for prosecuting a minor as an adult (see Chapter 4).

The most controversial defense of excuse is insanity. Contemporary discussions on the **insanity defense** show marked philosophical divergences within society concerning an individual's responsibility for his or her own acts. The lack of agreement is reflected in major differences among states concerning the extent to which a person's mental faculties must be impaired before he or she is considered legally insane. The standards for insanity vary, but most jurisdictions follow the modern federal formulation of the insanity defense (Fradella, 2007a; Schug & Fradella, 2015). That version of the insanity defense excuses criminal conduct if, as a result of a severe "mental disease or defect" at the time of the commission of the offense, the defendant was unable to substantially appreciate the wrongfulness of his or her conduct. Although the prosecution must still prove all of the elements of the crime in question, the defense bears the burden of persuasion to prove the defendant's insanity either by a preponderance of the evidence or by clear and convincing evidence, depending on the jurisdiction.

Law on the Books vs. Law in Action

The structure of the courts, the legal duties of the main actors, and the steps in the criminal process are all basic to understanding how the courts dispense criminal justice. These elements constitute *law on the books*—the legal and structural components of the judiciary. In essence, the starting point in understanding the legal system is knowing the formal rules.

Law on the books is found in constitutions, laws enacted by legislative bodies, regulations issued by administrative agencies, and cases decided by courts. Little doubt exists that decisions by the U.S. Supreme Court have far-reaching ramifications. To highlight the importance of court decisions, each chapter's Case Close-Up provides an in-depth look at some of the court decisions that have shaped our nation's criminal justice system.

But law on the books only partially explains how a criminal case unfolds. Although the formal law was certainly important, it cannot totally explain why the jury voted to acquit George Zimmerman.

Indeed, technology and media may both have played a role in the case outcome. Nor can law on the books explain why different judges looking at the same facts and reading the same law can reach opposite conclusions. And one need not be an expert in law and justice to know that laws alone do not account for the way that evidence is gathered by police, presented in courts of law, and evaluated by judges and juries, especially when issues like racism, sexism, and homophobia come into play. In other words, law on the books represents an idealized view of law—one that stresses an abstract set of rules that is so theoretical that it fails to incorporate real people. A *law in action* approach to courts and crime considers the human factors governing the actual application of the law. This view stresses the mutual interdependence of courtroom actors and the ways in which they devote considerable time to processing criminal cases from intake through plea bargaining and determining the appropriate sentence to impose on defendants found guilty. Table 1.4 presents a few differences between law on the books and law in action; many others are explored throughout this book.

The law in action perspective also stresses the importance of discretion. At virtually every step of the process a choice has to be made about whether to move the case to the next step or to stop it now. These decisions are made by the legal actors—police, prosecutors, and judges, for example. They are also made by ordinary citizens, whether in their role as victims, witnesses, or jurors.

A wide gap exists between legal theory (law on the books) and how that law is applied (law in action). Although some people find this gap shocking, actually it is not; after all, few, if any, human institutions ever live up to the high ideals set out for them. If you spend five minutes observing a stop sign on a well-traveled street, you will find that not all cars come to a complete stop, and some do not slow down much at all. Yet at the same time, the stop sign (the law on the books in this example) clearly does affect the behavior of drivers (law in action). The criminal process is filled with numerous detours. At each stage officials decide to advance the defendant's case to the next step, reroute it, or terminate it. The result is that many cases that enter the criminal court process are eliminated during the early stages.

TABLE 1.4	Examples of the Difference Between Law on the Books and Law in Action	
	Law on the Books	**Law in Action**
Crime	Any violation of the criminal law.	People report about 2.8 million violent crimes and 5.7 million property crimes to the police each year. Our best estimates suggest that 59% percent of crime is never reported to police.
Arrest	The physical taking into custody of a suspected law violator.	Every year, the police make more than 11.2 million arrests for nontraffic offenses. Most are for minor crimes, but nearly 0.5 million involve serious crimes.
Initial appearance	The accused is told of the charges, bail is set, and a date for the preliminary hearing is set.	This occurs soon after arrest, which means the judge and lawyers know little about the case.
Bail	Money or property is pledged as a form of guarantee that a released defendant will appear at trial.	Bail is tied to a variety of factors, including some that seemingly have little to do with the case. But whether someone is released on bail has a significant effect on the rest of the case.
Charging decision	Formal criminal charges against the defendant, stating what criminal law was violated.	Between arrest and appearance at the major trial court, half of cases are dropped.
Preliminary hearing or grand jury	Judicial proceedings to determine whether probable cause exists to make the accused stand trial on felony charges.	Cases are rarely dismissed at this stage.
Arraignment	The defendant is informed of the pending charges and is required to enter a plea.	Most defendants plead not guilty at this stage and then later change their pleas as part of a plea bargain.
Discovery	Formal and informal exchange of information before trial.	Prosecutors turn over evidence of guilt in hopes of obtaining a plea of guilty.
Pretrial motions	Defense may seek to have evidence suppressed because it was collected in a way that violates the Constitution.	Suppression motions are rarely granted but are at the heart of a major debate.
Plea negotiations	The defendant pleads guilty with the expectation of receiving some benefit.	About 90 to 95 percent of felony defendants plead guilty.
Trial	A fact-finding process using the adversarial method before a judge or a jury.	Most likely only in serious cases; defendant is likely to be convicted.
Sentencing	Punishment imposed on a defendant found guilty of violating the criminal law.	Seven million persons in prison, on probation, or on parole.
Appeal	Review of the lower-court decision by a higher court.	The overwhelming majority of criminal cases are affirmed on appeal.

A law in action perspective helps us understand the dynamics of courthouse justice. High caseloads are the reality in courthouses across the nation. As a result, judges are under pressure to move cases lest a backlog develop. Similarly, in most cases the formal rules found in law on the books fail to provide answers to all the questions that arise in a case. As a result, prosecutors must make discretionary choices about matters such as what sentencing recommendation to make to the judge. Finally, cooperation, rather than conflict during trial, often characterizes the behavior of courthouse actors. As a result, defense attorneys often find that negotiating a plea of guilty, rather than going to trial, is in the best interest of their client.

Courts and Controversy

The trial of George Zimmerman illustrates some of the controversies surrounding courts and crime in the United States. For some, the verdict represented the appropriate outcome in a self-defense case; for others, Zimmerman's acquittal sparked great outrage that the killer of an unarmed teenager had gone free (Jones-Brown & Fradella, 2015).

As previously discussed, many experts explained the Zimmerman verdict as a result of lack of evidence. But the fine points of law, such as the prosecution having to prove—beyond a reasonable doubt—that Zimmerman had not acted in self-defense, rarely sways public opinion when cases involve controversial topics such as racial perceptions.

At the heart of the public's concern about crime has been a debate over the actions and inactions of the criminal courts. What the courts do (and do not do) and how they do it occupies center stage in the nation's continuing focus on crime. Numerous reforms have been suggested, but no agreement has been reached as to what types of change are in order. Throughout this book, the "Courts and Controversy" boxes, such as the one on page 6, highlight many issues being debated by the courts today.

In the public dialogue on the issues facing the criminal courts, conservatives square off against liberals, and hard-liners against those said to be soft on crime. This sort of terminology is not very helpful. Such phrases as "soft on crime" attract our attention to questions about the goals of the criminal courts, but they are not useful for systematic inquiry because they are ambiguous and emotional (Neubauer, 2004).

More constructive in understanding the controversy over the criminal courts are the crime control and due process models developed by Herbert Packer (1968) and discussed by Samuel Walker (2006). In an unemotional way, these two models highlight competing values concerning the proper role of the criminal courts. The conservative crime control model proposes to reduce crime by increasing the penalties on criminals. The liberal due process model advocates social programs aimed primarily at reducing crime by reducing poverty. Table 1.5 summarizes the two views.

Crime Control Model

The most important value in the **crime control model** is the repression of criminal conduct. Unless crime is controlled, the rights of law-abiding citizens will not be protected, and the security of society will be diminished. Conservatives see crime as the product of a breakdown of individual responsibility and self-control. To reinforce social values of discipline and self-control, and to achieve the goal of repressing crime, the courts must process defendants efficiently. They should rapidly remove defendants against whom inadequate evidence exists and quickly determine guilt according to evidence. The crime control model holds that informal fact-finding—initially by the police and later by the prosecutor—not only is the best way to determine whether the defendant is in fact guilty but also is sufficiently foolproof to prevent the innocent from being falsely convicted. The crime control model, therefore, stresses the necessity of speed and finality in the courts to achieve the priority of crime suppression.

According to the crime control model, the courts have hindered effective law enforcement and therefore have produced inadequate protection of society. Advocates of this model are concerned that criminals "beat the system" and "get off easy." In their view, the cure is to eliminate legal loopholes by curtailing the exclusionary rule, abolishing the insanity defense, allowing for preventive detention of dangerous offenders, and increasing the certainty of punishment.

TABLE 1.5	Competing Values in the Criminal Justice System	
	Crime Control Model	**Due Process Model**
Key goal	Repression of criminal conduct.	Respect for and protection of individual rights.
Focus	Apprehend, convict, and punish offenders.	Protect the innocent/wrongfully accused; limit governmental power.
Values	Expeditious processing of offenders to achieve justice for victims and society as a whole.	Dignity and autonomy of both the accused and the system are to be preserved.
Mood	Certainty; focuses on factual guilt. Assumes that someone arrested and charged is probably guilty. Relies on informal, nonadjudicative fact-finding—primarily by police and prosecutors.	Skepticism; focuses on legal guilt. Assumes that someone is innocent until proven guilty beyond a reasonable doubt. Relies on formal, adjudicative, adversarial fact-finding processes.
Goal of courts	Assembly-Line Justice: Process cases quickly and efficiently to promote finality of convictions.	Obstacle Court Justice: Presents numerous obstacles to prevent errors and wrongful convictions by ensuring careful consideration of each case.
Attitude toward defendants' rights	Technicalities permit the guilty go free.	Technicalities prevent abuses of governmental authority to foster freedom in a constitutional democracy.
Sentencing	Punishment deters crime and incapacitates offenders.	Rehabilitation prevents crime.

Due Process Model

In contrast, the **due process model** emphasizes protecting the rights of the individual. Its advocates are concerned about lawbreaking; they see the need to protect the public from predatory criminals. At the same time, however, they believe that granting too much leeway to law enforcement officials will only result in the loss of freedom and civil liberties for all Americans. This alternative diagnosis stresses different causes of crime. Liberals see crime not as a product of individual moral failure but rather as the result of social influences (Currie, 1985). In particular, unemployment, racial discrimination, and government policies that work to the disadvantage of the poor are the root causes of crime; only by changing the social environment will crime be reduced (Currie, 1989).

Although adherents of the due process model do not downgrade the need for controlling crime, they believe that single-minded pursuit of such a goal threatens individual rights and poses the threat of

a tyrannical government. Thus, the key function of the courts is not the speed and finality projected in the crime control model but an insistence on careful consideration of each case. The dominant image is one of the courts as an obstacle course. The due process model stresses the possibility of error in the informal fact-finding process and therefore insists on formal fact-finding to protect against mistakes made by the police and prosecutors.

Proponents of the due process model believe that the courts' priority should be to protect the rights of the individual. Any resulting decrease in the efficiency of the courts is the price we must pay in a democracy based on individual liberties. The due process model emphasizes the need to reform people through rehabilitation. Community-based sentencing alternatives are considered preferable to the extensive use of prison sentences. Advocates of this approach are concerned that the court system is fundamentally unfair to poor and minority defendants; they therefore support leading court decisions protecting the rights of those accused of crimes.

Shifting the Balance

The U.S. justice system strives to achieve control crime while simultaneously honoring the constitutional rights of the accused. At different stages in our nation's history, we have clearly focused more on the underlying values of one model over the other. Consider that in the first half of the 20th century, increased urbanization, immigration, and industrialization contributed to an increase in criminal activity. The increase in crime combined with fears of people from different backgrounds and cultures led to increases in police power with a focus on "law and order" crime control.

In the 1950s and 1960s, social consciousness began to focus on social equality and equal justice under law. Part of this new consciousness brought to light abuses of police power. Led by Chief Justice Earl Warren, a former public defender, the U.S. Supreme Court began to "constitutionalize" criminal procedure with a focus on due process and individual rights and liberties. Since the 1970s, though, and continuing through today, "wars" on crime, drugs, and terrorism have contributed to a renewed emphasis on crime control. Thus, the pendulum can swing. The law, however (especially constitutional law), helps to provide a certain level of stability even as society places changing levels of value on crime control and due process. Still, as controversies like the war on drugs illustrate, reasonable people can differ as to the proper scope of the law in crime control efforts.

Media Depictions and Distortions of Criminal Courts

Most people in the United States learn about the ways in which criminal cases are processed through the courts from the media (Surette, 2015). Sometimes this media coverage takes the form of intensive news coverage, just as it did in the cases

of Dylann Roof and George Zimmerman. Other times this media coverage comes from dramatized or even completely fictionalized portrayals of criminal trials on television and in the movies. From the perspective of *America's Courts and the Criminal Justice System*, the extensive media attention to law has major advantages. Media coverage of real trials and portrayals of fictitious ones provide dramatic illustrations that the outcome is influenced by the law (law on the books), the actions of people (law in action), and the disagreements that result (law in controversy). The same can be said for police drug busts, prosecutors' decisions to seek the death penalty, defense attorneys cross-examining witnesses, and judges' decisions to admit evidence. But there are disadvantages as well. In trying to dramatize occasionally dull legal proceedings, the media coverage can distort reality (Surette, 2015; Donovan, 2013). This is especially a concern when jurors expect to be dazzled with forensic scientific evidence, as they see on television. Media coverage can provide caricatures, not pictures, of courts and the criminal justice system. Thus, at times, a principal task of a book on courts and the criminal justice system is to encourage readers to "unlearn" what they think they know.

The task of thinking critically about how the media both portray and distort the justice system is to focus on the contrasting caricatures offered by fictional treatments. Depending on the dramatic needs of the movie or TV show, the police may be portrayed as diligent or brutal, prosecutors pictured as crusaders of justice or preventers of justice determined to convict the suspect who is easiest to try, judges presented as insightful masters of the system or politically motivated hacks, defense attorneys projected as crusaders for their clients' interests or corrupters of the justice system, and prison guards presented as understanding human beings or brutal sociopaths. Even the news distorts the criminal justice process, often unintentionally, but sometimes purposefully. Consider how *Fox News* presented the Dylann Roof shooting as an attack on faith because it happened in a church, rather than a racially motivated hate crime as evidenced by Roof's statements at the time of the shooting and those contained his written manifesto. Also consider how the *Today* show presented George Zimmerman's comments to a police dispatcher on the night he shot Trayvon Martin. Their edited version of the recorded conversation relayed Zimmerman saying, "This guy looks like he's up to no good. He looks Black." But the actual police recording went like this:

Zimmerman: This guy looks like he's up to no good. Or he's on drugs or something. It's raining and he's just walking around, looking about.

Dispatcher: OK, and this guy—is he Black, White, or Hispanic?

Zimmerman: He looks Black. (Wemple, 2013, para. 5)

Conclusion

"Why did the defendant do it?" is the dominant question the public asks in a murder case. Alas, trials do not always provide an answer to the question of why, especially when the defendant fails to take the stand in her or his own defense, as was the case in the George Zimmerman trial (Turley, 2012). When a defendant, on the advice of counsel, decides not to explain their side of the story, the public often looks elsewhere for an answer. In the George Zimmerman trial, some may have resorted to judgments that are intertwined with complex considerations of race. In other cases, science helps provide answers. Indeed, the public expectation that scientific evidence will provide the answers seems to continue growing. And the modern media is able to provide its attentive audience with even more information, always on the lookout for the next trial of the century, even if the question of why the defendant may have committed the crime remains unanswerable.

Ours is a law-drenched age. Voters and elected officials alike see the solution to pressing social problems in terms of passing a law. It seems we are not serious about an issue unless we have a law regulating it, and we are not really serious unless

we have criminal laws. But laws are not self-enforcing. Some people delude themselves by thinking that passing a law solves the problem. This is not necessarily so. Indeed, if the problem persists, frustration sets in. Thus, legislatures mandate that drivers purchase automobile insurance, but accident victims become frustrated when they discover the other party has no insurance. Similarly, judges require defendants to pay restitution, but crime victims discover that impoverished defendants (particularly those in prison) have no ability to pay. In the same vein, conservatives call for preventive detention, but jailers have no jail cells available.

Although most people know something about the law, they also "know" much that is contrary to fact. Some of these public understandings and misunderstandings about law are the product of education. High-school level American government and history textbooks, for example, offer a simplified, formal picture of law and the courts, lawyers, and trials. Americans also learn about the legal system by going to the movies, watching television, and reading fiction. At times, people who rely on these sources are badly misled. Entertainment programs misrepresent the nature and amount of crime in the United States. Because murder makes a much better show than embezzlement or burglary, entertainment media rarely show street crime other than drug offenses.

Television also offers a number of false or doubtful propositions. It tells us, for example, that criminals are white males between the ages of 20 and 50, that bad guys are usually businesspeople or professional criminals, and that crime is almost always unsuccessful in the end. Television and film also often misrepresent the roles of the actors in the legal system. For example, with few exceptions, police are in constant action, chasing crooks in cars, running after them on foot, and capturing them only after exchanging gunfire. In addition, entertainment media distort important issues of civil liberties. As soon as we know who did it and that the guilty crook has been apprehended, the case is solved, with no need for the prosecutor to prove the defendant guilty. These understandings and misunderstandings form the backdrop for this book.

CHAPTER REVIEW

LO1   1.   Describe how the courts are related to the other components of the criminal justice system.

Law enforcement, courts, and corrections are separate sets of organizations, but they are also interdependent. The courts process cases after suspects are arrested, and corrections handles defendants who are found guilty by the courts.

LO2   2.   Discuss the major types of courts found in the United States.

In the United States, separate systems of federal courts and state courts exist. Within each system one or two levels of trial courts and one or two levels of appellate courts hear cases.

LO3   3.   Identify the most important actors in the courthouse.

Judges, prosecutors, and defense attorneys are the most important actors in the courthouse. Defendants and victims are also important because they are the source of cases for the courts.

LO4   4.   List the steps in a typical felony prosecution.

A typical felony prosecution begins with an arrest, followed by an initial appearance, the setting of bail, and either grand jury proceedings or a preliminary hearing. If a case survives these hurdles, it proceeds to a formal arraignment, after which decisions about evidence discovery, pretrial motions, and plea negotiations may occur. Cases that are not resolved by plea bargain go to trial. Those convicted at trial are then sentenced and have the right to file an appeal.

LO5   5.   List the four key elements defining law.

Law is defined as: (1) a body of rules, (2) enacted by public officers, (3) in a legitimate manner, and (4) backed by the force of the state.

LO6   6.   Identify the three key characteristics of common law.

The three key characteristics of the common law are: (1) judge-made law, (2) precedent, and (3) multiple sources of law.

LO7   7.   Explain the importance of the adversary system.

The adversary system seeks to protect individual rights by diffusing governmental power in several actors and insisting that the defendant is presumed innocent until proven guilty.

LO8   8.   Name the four amendments of the Bill of Rights that deal specifically with criminal procedure.

Of the first ten amendments to the U.S. Constitution—collectively known as the Bill of Rights—the Fourth, Fifth, Sixth, and Eighth deal specifically with criminal procedure.

LO9   9.   Identify the major elements of a crime.

Most behavior cannot be criminal unless: (1) an *actus reus* (a guilty act) is committed, (2) with accompanying *mens rea* (criminal intent), and (3) the guilty act and the criminal intent are related. In addition, a number of crimes are defined on the basis of (4) attendant circumstances, and/or (5) specific results.

LO10 10. Identify some of the most important legal defenses in American law.

Some of the most important legal defenses in American law include alibi, necessity, mistake of fact, self-defense, procedural defenses, infancy, and insanity.

LO11 11. Explain how a "law in action" perspective complements a "law on the books" approach to studying the criminal courts.

The law on the books approach to studying the criminal courts stresses the

importance of examining the formal law and how courts interpret that law. The law in action approach is complementary because it stresses the importance of discretion throughout a criminal prosecution.

LO12 12. Distinguish between the crime control model of criminal justice and the due process model of criminal justice.

The crime control model emphasizes the need to repress crime and efficiently process the large number of guilty defendants. The due process model of criminal justice emphasizes the importance of protecting the rights of citizens and providing careful consideration for each case.

CRITICAL THINKING QUESTIONS

1. On a sheet of paper, apply the general overview of court structure in the United States (Figure 1.2) to your local community.

2. On a sheet of paper, apply the list of actors in the courthouse (Table 1.2) to your local community. If you live in a rural area, how does your list differ from that of someone who lives in a larger community? If you live in a large metropolitan area, how does your list differ from that of someone living in a more rural area?

3. Constitutional rights of the accused is, of course, a controversial topic. The crime control model, in particular, decries letting the obviously guilty go free on "technicalities," whereas the due process model emphasizes basic rights. What common ground do these two approaches share? Where do they disagree most?

4. Nearly all non–English-speaking industrial democracies use the inquisitorial system rather than the adversary system. In this system, the judge, not the prosecutor and not the defense attorney, calls witnesses and questions them. Would you prefer being tried under the adversary system or the inquisitorial system? Would you have confidence in the willingness of the judge to search out equally evidence for conviction and evidence for acquittal?

5. Use newspapers, radio, and criminal justice discussion lists or chat groups to monitor discussions concerning the criminal justice system. Do citizens make distinctions among police, courts, and corrections, or do they lump everything under the general rubric of the criminal justice system?

6. One of the biggest societal changes in recent years has been the rapid expansion of computer technology. How have legislatures responded to crimes involving the use of computers? How has the Internet changed the debate over pornography?

KEY TERMS

administrative regulations   21

adversary system   22

alibi defense   27

Anglo-American law   18

attempt   26

attendant (accompanying)
   circumstances   27

Bill of Rights   24

civil law   24

common law   18

constitution   19

corpus delicti   26

crime control model   31

criminal defense   27

criminal intent (*mens rea*)   26

criminal justice system   8

criminal law   25

CSI effect   7

defenses of excuse   28

defenses of justification   28

due process model   32

FOR FURTHER READING

Bogira, Steve. 2005. *Courtroom 302*. New York: Vintage.

Ferdico, John, Henry F. Fradella, and Christopher Totten. 2015. *Criminal Procedure for the Criminal Justice Professional*. 12th ed. Boston, MA: Cengage.

Fox, Richard, Robert Van Sickel, and Thomas Steiger. 2007. *Tabloid Justice: Criminal Justice in an Age of Media Frenzy*. 2nd ed. Boulder, CO: Lynne Rienner.

Garland, David. 2002. *The Culture of Control: Crime and Social Order in Contemporary Society*. Chicago: University of Chicago Press.

Marion, Nancy. 2007. *A Primer in the Politics of Criminal Justice*. 2nd ed. Monsey, NY: Criminal Justice Press.

Neubauer, David. 2001. *Debating Crime: Rhetoric and Reality*. Belmont, CA: Wadsworth.

Neubauer, David, and Stephen Meinhold. 2017. *Judicial Process: Law, Courts, and Politics in the United States*. 7th ed. Boston, MA: Cengage.

Owen, Stephen S., Henry F. Fradella, Tod W. Burke, and Jerry Joplin, 2015. *The Foundations of Criminal Justice*. 2nd ed. New York: Oxford University Press.

Pollock, Joycelyn. 2016. *Ethical Dilemmas and Decisions in Criminal Justice*. 9th ed. Boston, MA: Cengage.

Reddington, Frances P., and Gene Bonham, Jr. 2011. *Flawed Criminal Justice Policies: At the Intersection of the Media,* *Public Fear and Legislative Response*. Durham, NC: Carolina Academic Press.

Robinson, Matthew B. 2015. *Media Coverage of Crime and Criminal Justice*. 2nd ed. Durham, NC: Carolina Academic Press.

Schug, Robert, and Henry F. Fradella. 2014. *Mental Illness and Crime*. Thousand Oaks, CA: Sage.

Shelton, Donald E., Young S. Kim, and Gregg Barak. 2009. "An Indirect-Effects Model of Mediated Adjudication: The CSI Myth, the Tech Effect, and Metropolitan Jurors' Expectations for Scientific Evidence." *Vanderbilt Journal of Entertainment and Technology Law*, 12(1), 1–43.

Stevens, Dennis J. 2009. *Media and Criminal Justice: The CSI Effect*. Sudbury, MA: Jones and Barlett.

Surette, Ray. 2015. *Media, Crime, and Criminal Justice*. 5th ed. Stamford, CT: Cengage.

Walker, Samuel E., and Carol A. Archbold. 2014. *The New World of Police Accountability*. 2nd ed. Thousand Oaks, CA: Sage.

White, Michael D., and Henry F. Fradella. 2016. *Stop and Frisk: The Use and Abuse of a Controversial Police Tactic*. New York: New York University Press.

Richard Levine/age fotostock/Superstock

Thousands of demonstrators marched down Fifth Avenue in New York City, protesting the NYPD stop-and-frisk policy. The protesters maintained that the policy targeted people of color and created an atmosphere of fear and hostility between communities and the police.

Chapter Outline

Alfonso Lopez, Jr., a 12th grader at Edison High School in San Antonio, Texas, thought he had found an easy way to make a quick buck. "Gilbert" would pay him $40 to take a .38-caliber pistol to school and deliver it to "Jason," who planned to use it in a "gang war." Based on an anonymous tip, school officials confronted Lopez, who admitted carrying the unloaded weapon (but he did have five bullets on his person). Lopez was charged in federal court with violating the Gun-Free School Zones Act of 1990. After a bench trial, Lopez was found guilty and sentenced to six months in prison. The Supreme Court reversed the conviction, however, concluding that the U.S. Congress had no authority to outlaw guns in schools.

The Supreme Court's decision in *United States v. Lopez* first attracts our attention because it deals with gun control—one of the truly hot button issues of American politics. But a closer probing raises other, even more important questions. What should be a federal crime? After all, weapons offenses are usually violations of state law, and indeed Mr. Lopez was initially charged in state court; but these charges were dropped after federal officials stepped in. How is it that five conservative judges, appointed by Republican presidents and pledged to get tough on crime, reversed a conviction that was certainly popular with the American public?

The issues, both direct and indirect, raised in *United States v. Lopez* trace their origins to the early days of the Republic. The founding fathers were deeply divided over which cases federal courts should hear. Indeed, the drafters of the U.S. Constitution were deeply divided over whether there should be any federal courts besides the U.S. Supreme Court. A principal task of this chapter, therefore, is

Learning Objectives

After reading this chapter, you should be able to:

LO1 Define the four primary types of jurisdiction: geographical, subject matter, personal, and hierarchical.

LO2 Compare and contrast the tasks of trial and appellate courts.

LO3 Explain the historical evolution of the federal courts into their present structure and operations.

LO4 Analyze the different responsibilities and workloads of U.S. magistrate judges, district judges, circuit judges, and Supreme Court justices.

LO5 Analyze the impact the federal courts have on the administration of criminal justice at the state and local levels through their federal question jurisdiction.

LO6 Differentiate the jurisdiction and functions of Article III courts from those of Article I courts and other specialized federal courts.

LO7 Distinguish the various agencies and their hierarchical responsibilities for the administration of the federal court system.

LO8 Evaluate the major problems facing the federal courts and the strengths and weaknesses of the major solutions that have been proposed to address these problems.

to discuss how the current federal judicial structure—magistrate, district, and appellate courts and the Supreme Court—is a product of more than 200 years of political controversy and compromise about the proper role of the federal judiciary. The remainder of the chapter focuses on the specialized courts and their administrative structures. Most important, we will discuss the contemporary debate over how many cases are too many for the federal courts to handle, thus illustrating that the controversies continue. But first, to establish some common ground about the often confusing topic of court organization, we begin this chapter by examining some basic principles.

Basic Principles of Court Organization

Even lawyers who regularly use the courts sometimes find the details of court organization confusing. Court nomenclature includes many shorthand phrases that mean something to those who work in the courts daily but can be quite confusing to the outsider. Learning the language of courts is like learning any foreign language—some of it can come only from experience. Before studying the specifics of federal courts in this chapter and state courts in Chapter 4, it is helpful to understand the basic principles of court organization within the dual court structure that exists in the United States.

Dual Court System

The United States has a **dual court system**: one national court system plus separate court systems in each of the 50 states and the District of Columbia. The result is more than 51 separate court systems. Figure 2.1 illustrates the structure of the dual court system in the United States. The division of responsibilities is not as clear-cut as it looks, however. State and federal courts sometimes have **concurrent jurisdiction** (meaning that they share some judicial powers) over certain types of cases. For example, selling drugs or robbing banks are crimes under federal law and under the laws of most states, which means the accused could be tried in either federal court or state court. Moreover, litigants in purely state court proceedings may appeal to the U.S. Supreme Court, a federal court, if a federal question is presented, such as a question of federal constitutional law.

One of the most immediate consequences of the dual court system is the complexity it adds to the criminal justice system. In essence, the framers of the U.S. Constitution created two parallel criminal justice systems consisting of their own law enforcement, court structure, and correctional systems. Of all the levels of complexity created by the dual court system, perhaps the most confusing is the application of the constitutional prohibition against double jeopardy (see "Courts, Controversy, & the Administration of Justice: Should the Double Jeopardy Clause Prohibit Parallel State and Federal Prosecutions?").

Jurisdiction

Court structure is largely determined by limitations on the types of cases a court may hear and decide. **Jurisdiction** is the power of a court to decide on a dispute. A court's jurisdiction can be further classified according to four subcomponents: geographical jurisdiction, subject matter jurisdiction, personal jurisdiction, and hierarchical jurisdiction.

Geographical Jurisdiction and Venue

Courts are authorized to hear and decide disputes arising within a specified **geographical jurisdiction** (sometimes referred to as "territorial jurisdiction"). Geographical jurisdiction in criminal cases is primarily concerned with a sovereign's power to punish conduct that violates its criminal laws.

United States Supreme Court
The High Court of Last Resort in the United States
The most powerful court in the world. It has virtually complete control of the cases it hears by exercising its discretionary appellate jurisdiction over decisions of the U.S. Courts of Appeals and the decisions of the highest courts in the state systems if a question of federal law (including federal constitutional law) is presented. Usually hears fewer than 90 cases each term, less than third of which typically involve criminal cases.

The Federal Courts
Hears cases throughout the United States. Decides roughly 78,000 criminal cases and 13,500 criminal appeals each year.

The State Courts
Important variations from state to state. Decides roughly 6.6 million adult criminal cases each year.

United States Courts of Appeals
Mandatory appellate jurisdiction over the decisions of the U.S. District Courts.
12 Regional Circuits and 1 Federal Circuit that hears appeals from specialized trial courts like the U.S. Court of International Trade, the U.S. Claims Court, and the U.S. Court of Veterans' Appeals.
The last stop for the vast majority of defendants convicted in federal court, very few of which win a significant victory.

State High Courts of Last Resort
Mandatory and discretionary appellate jurisdiction over decisions rendered by lower state courts. Major policymaker for the state. Final decider for questions of state law. Typically decides a handful of criminal appeals each year.

State Intermediate Appellate Courts
(40 out of 50 states)
Mandatory appellate jurisdiction over decisions by the state's major trial courts. Few criminal appellants win a significant victory.

United States District Courts
Trial courts of original jurisdiction over federal cases.
94 federal districts (including territorial ones in the District of Columbia, Puerto Rico, Guam, the U.S. Virgin Islands, and the Northern Mariana Islands).
Mandatory appellate jurisdiction over decisions by non-Article III courts.
Adjudicates all federal crimes like drug smuggling, mail fraud, robbery of FDIC-insured banks. Also adjudicates civil lawsuits like civil right cases, claims of federal civil law (e.g., copyright and trademark infringement), and state civil law claims involving diversity of citizenship, such as torts.
U.S. Magistrate Judges are responsible for preliminary stages of all federal felony cases. Magistrates also hear many minor criminal cases and assist with the processing of *habeas corpus* petitions and other civil lawsuits.

State Major Trial Courts
Superior Courts/Courts of Common Pleas/District Courts
Trial courts of general jurisdiction that are usually arranged by county or groups of counties to hear felonies (murder, rape, robbery) and civil cases that do not involve small claims (accident cases, contract disputes). Sometimes they have appellate jurisdiction over state's minor trial courts.

Non-Article III Courts
U.S. Bankruptcy Courts, U.S. Tax Court, decisions of U.S. Magistrate Judges, and Administrative Law Judges (ALJ) in various federal agencies like the FCC, Social Security Administration, EEOC, NLRB, FTC, etc.

State Minor Trial Courts
Municipal Courts/Justice of the Peace Courts/ Magisterial District Courts
Limited original jurisdiction to hear misdemeanor cases (petty theft, public drunkenness, disorderly conduct), civil and criminal traffic violations, local ordinance violations, and small claims of a civil nature.

FIGURE 2.1 Overview of the Dual Court Structure of the United States

Thus, the courts of California have no jurisdiction to try a person accused of committing a crime in Oregon; Oregon has such power, since the accused is alleged to have violated its criminal law. But which courts within the state of Oregon would hear the case? That is a matter of venue.

Venue is the particular location or area in which a court having geographic jurisdiction may hear a case. Proper venue is based on statutorily defined geographic subdivisions. These subdivisions are often determined by city or county boundaries, although other boundaries can be set that are unrelated to city or county lines. Divisions in the federal system are a good example of this. Washington is a large and populous state. Instead of having one federal district coterminous with the boundaries of the state, there are two federal districts in Washington, the eastern district and the western district. Larger states are subdivided even further; California, for example, has a northern, eastern, central, and southern district. A federal case that arises from an act in Sacramento is properly tried in the northern district of California; the other districts in California would lack proper venue.

A defendant can waive venue in the district or county where a crime was committed by consenting to be tried in a venue in another district or county. In state courts, venue can generally be transferred only to another district or county within a particular state, since only the courts of that particular state would have geographic jurisdiction over alleged violations of its own criminal law. In contrast, venue can be changed between districts of the federal system since the offense is against the United States—the same sovereign in federal courts across the country.

Changes of venue in the federal courts are typically granted for one of two reasons. First, venue may be transferred to another location that is much more convenient for the parties and witnesses than the intended place of trial. Second, a change of venue is appropriate when a defendant is unlikely to get a fair and impartial trial in the federal district where the crime is alleged to have taken place. Intense pretrial publicity, for example, may have prejudiced the local jury pool. Since the right to a fair trial is guaranteed by the Sixth Amendment, a federal court should transfer venue to another federal

district where the jury pool is less affected by pretrial publicity. For example, Timothy McVeigh, the defendant in the Oklahoma City bombing case, was tried for his crimes outside Oklahoma, even though that is where he committed the offenses. The extensive pretrial publicity and the intense personal connection to the case of the potential jurors in Oklahoma City made it very likely that the defendant could not get a fair and impartial trial in Oklahoma. The case was therefore transferred to Denver, Colorado, where the jury pool was less personally involved and more likely to meet the constitutional due process guarantees of a fair and impartial jury.

One major complication arising from geographical jurisdiction occurs when a person is arrested in one state for committing a crime in another state. **Extradition** involves the surrender by one state of an individual accused of a crime outside its own territory and within the territorial jurisdiction of the other state. If an American fugitive has fled to a foreign nation, the U.S. Secretary of State will request the return of the accused under the terms of the extradition treaty the United States has with that country (a few nations of the world do not have such treaties).

Subject Matter Jurisdiction

Court structure is also determined by **subject matter jurisdiction**. Trial courts of *limited or special jurisdiction* are restricted to hearing a limited category of cases, typically misdemeanors and civil suits involving small sums of money. State courts typically have traffic courts or juvenile courts, both of which are examples of subject matter jurisdiction. The federal courts are all courts of limited jurisdiction, since they are limited to adjudicating certain types of cases (to be discussed later in this chapter). In contrast to trial courts of limited/special jurisdiction, trial courts of *general jurisdiction* are empowered to hear all other types of cases within the geographical jurisdiction of the court. In the state court systems (to be discussed in the next chapter), the county trial court fits here.

Personal Jurisdiction

Personal jurisdiction (sometimes called "*in personum* jurisdiction") refers to a court's power over an individual person or corporation. A court gains

Should the Double Jeopardy Clause Prohibit Parallel State and Federal Prosecutions?

On May 7, 1985, 27-year-old U.S. Army Sergeant Timothy Hennis responded to a classified ad placed by a North Carolina woman who was trying to sell a dog. A few days later, authorities found the bodies of the woman and two of her three children in their home. The woman had been raped and was stabbed 15 times.

A community member told police that a few days earlier, he had seen a man (whom he later identified as Hennis) wearing a black "Members Only" jacket leaving the family's driveway with a garbage bag slung over his shoulder. The Friday after the murders, Hennis had taken a black "Members Only" jacket to a local dry cleaner. The following day, Hennis's neighbors saw him burning a bonfire in a 55-gallon drum for at least five hours. Fingerprints and pubic hair were found at the crime scene; none of them belonged to the family members. And none of evidence or the semen found in the victim were a match with Hennis.

Hennis was charged with three counts of murder and one count of rape. He was convicted and sentenced to death. His conviction was set aside on appeal because of evidentiary rulings that may have inflamed and biased the jury at Hennis's trial. Hennis was acquitted on all counts at this second trial, due, in large part, to two factors. First, the unduly prejudicial evidence erroneously used in the first trial was excluded from the second trial. Second, defense attorneys were able to discredit the testimony of the community member who had previously identified Hennis. This witness first described the man he had seen as one shorter and slighter than himself, but then revised his description to match Hennis's build—one considerably taller and heavier than the witness's own. After his acquittal, Hennis reenlisted in the army, apparently serving exemplarily until he retired in July 2005.

In the mid-1980s, forensic science was much less precise than it is today, and DNA technology had not yet been used for law enforcement purposes. In the spring of 2005, however, 20 years after the murders, a homicide detective sent the semen sample recovered from the crime scene for DNA testing. It was a match for Tim Hennis. The Double Jeopardy Clause of the Fifth Amendment to the U.S. Constitution prevents the same sovereign from trying a criminal defendant on the same charges after acquittal. Thus, North Carolina could not try Hennis again for either the rape or the murders. But the federal government is a different sovereign and, therefore, is not technically bound by double jeopardy in the Hennis case. With that in mind, the army recalled Hennis to active service in September 2006. His court martial trial in a federal, military court began in March 2010. The following month, and after only three hours of deliberation, a jury convicted Hennis. He was sentenced to death and currently has appeals pending. According to the Death Penalty Information Center, Hennis is the only person in U.S. history to have been exonerated after a capital conviction and then returned to death row for the same crime.

Some scholars have argued that the army violated the spirit—if not the precise letter—of the Constitution's prohibition on double jeopardy. Recall from Chapter 1 that Dylann Roof faced state criminal charges for the nine murders he committed during his shooting massacre at Emanuel African Methodist Episcopal Church in South Carolina. He also faced federal criminal prosecution for using a firearm to commit murder and 24 civil rights violations—12 counts charged under a law targeting racially motivated killings (among other types) and 12 more counts under a different statute that prohibits using force or threatening the use of force to obstruct a person's free exercise of religious beliefs.

What do you think? Are federal prosecutions after failed state prosecutions a good way to remedy miscarriages of justice, or are the rights of defendants unnecessarily placed in jeopardy?

power over a particular defendant by virtue of the defendant's having done some act within the place where the court is located or having had some contact with the place in which the court is located. In criminal cases, personal jurisdiction refers to a court's authority to try a defendant for violating the state's criminal law. While a bit of an oversimplification, courts obtain personal jurisdiction over a defendant by the defendant having violated the law of the particular sovereign while within the forum state. This is relatively straight-forward for traditional crimes against a person such as assault, rape, or murder. In contrast, establishing personal jurisdiction over a criminal defendant accused of fraud or cybercrimes who was not physically present in the forum state at the time the alleged crime occurred can be quite complicated (see Kerr, 2008; Brown, 2015).

Hierarchical Jurisdiction

The third subcomponent of jurisdiction is **hierarchical jurisdiction**, which refers to differences in the courts' functions and responsibilities. **Original jurisdiction** means that a court has the authority to try a case and decide it. **Appellate jurisdiction** means that a court has the power to review cases that have already been decided by another court. Trial courts are primarily courts of original jurisdiction, but they occasionally have limited appellate jurisdiction—for example, when a trial court hears appeals from lower trial courts such as a municipal court or a justice of the peace court (Chapter 4). Appellate courts often have very limited original jurisdiction. The U.S. Supreme Court has original jurisdiction involving disputes between states, and state supreme courts have original jurisdiction in matters involving disbarment of lawyers.

Differentiating Trial and Appellate Courts

Virtually all cases begin in a **trial court** that has original jurisdiction. In a criminal case, the trial court arraigns the defendant, conducts a trial (or takes a guilty plea), and, if the defendant is found guilty, imposes sentence. In a civil case, the trial court operates in much the same way, ensuring that each party is properly informed of the complaint and conducting a trial or accepting an out-of-court settlement. Because only trial courts hear disputes over facts, witnesses appear only in trial courts. Trial courts are considered finders of fact, and the decision of a judge (or jury) about a factual dispute is very difficult to challenge on appeal (Chapter 15).

The losing party in the trial court generally has the right to request an appellate court to review the case. The primary function of the **appellate court** is to ensure that the trial court correctly interpreted the law. But appellate courts may also make new law.

Appellate and trial courts operate very differently because their roles are not the same. Appellate courts exercising appellate jurisdiction do not hear testimony from witnesses, conduct trials, or use juries. Those actions occur in a trial court exercising original jurisdiction. Moreover, instead of a single judge deciding, as in trial courts, a group of judges makes appellate court decisions; there may be as few as 3 or as many as 28 judges. (For more details on appellate courts and the appeals process, see Chapter 15.)

History of the Federal Courts

At first glance, the history of the federal courts appears to be a debate over details of procedure. But a closer look reveals that the political controversies that have shaped the federal judiciary go to the heart of the federal system of government, often involving the allocation of power between the national and state governments. Thus, any discussion of the federal courts in the early 21st century must begin with two 18th-century landmarks—Article III of the U.S. Constitution and the Judiciary Act of 1789. Although there have been important changes since, the decisions made at the beginning of the Republic about the nature of the federal judiciary have had a marked impact on contemporary court structure.

The Constitutional Convention

One major weakness of the Articles of Confederation was the absence of a national supreme court to enforce federal law and resolve conflicts and disputes between courts of the different states. Thus, when the delegates gathered at the Constitutional Convention in Philadelphia in 1787, a resolution was unanimously adopted that "a national judiciary be established." There was considerable disagreement, however, on the specific form that the national judiciary should take. Article III was one of the most hotly debated sections of the Constitution.

The dominant question of whether there should be a federal court system separate from the state systems produced two schools of thought. Advocates of states' rights (later called Anti-Federalists) feared that a strong national government would weaken individual liberties. More specifically, they saw the creation of separate federal courts as a threat to the power of state courts. As a result, the Anti-Federalists believed that federal law should be adjudicated first by the state courts; the U.S. Supreme Court should be limited to hearing appeals only from state courts. On the other hand, the Nationalists (who later called themselves "Federalists" because they favored ratification of the Constitution) distrusted the provincial prejudices of the states and favored a strong national government that could provide economic and political unity for the struggling new nation. As part of this approach, the Nationalists viewed state courts as incapable of developing a uniform body of federal law that would allow businesses to flourish. For these reasons, they backed the creation of lower federal courts.

The conflict between Federalists and Anti-Federalists was resolved by one of the many compromises that characterized the Constitutional Convention. **Article III** is brief, providing only an outline of a federal judiciary: "The judicial Power of the United States, shall be vested in one Supreme Court, and in such inferior Courts as the Congress may from time to time ordain and establish." The brevity of this provision left Congress with the task of filling in much of the substance of the new judicial system.

The Judiciary Act of 1789

Once the Constitution was ratified, action on the federal judiciary came quickly. Indeed, the first bill introduced in the Senate dealt with the unresolved issue of inferior federal courts. The congressional debate included many of the same participants, who repeated all the arguments involved in the judiciary debates at the Constitutional Convention. After extensive debate, Congress passed the

Judiciary Act of 1789, which laid the foundation for our current national judicial system. The Judiciary Act of 1789 represented a major victory for the Federalists; they were successful in creating separate federal district courts. At the same time, the act was a compromise that allayed some of the Anti-Federalists' fears. The organization of the federal judiciary supported state interests in three ways (LaCroix, 2007, 2012; Richardson & Vines, 1970).

First, the boundaries of the district courts were drawn along state lines; no district encompassed more than one state. Thus, from the outset, the federal judiciary was "state-contained." Even though district courts enforced national law, they were organized along local lines, with each district court responsible for its own work under minimal supervision.

Second, by custom the selection process ensured that federal district judges would be residents of their districts. Although nominated by the president, district judges were to be (and are today) local residents, presiding in their home area, and therefore subject to the continuing influence of the local social and political environment (see Chapter 8).

Third, the act gave the lower federal courts only limited jurisdiction. The Federalists wanted the full range of federal jurisdiction granted by the Constitution to be given to district and circuit courts. However, to achieve a lower federal court system, they were forced to reduce this demand greatly. But this issue would reappear repeatedly over the next 100 years.

1789–1891

The Judiciary Act of 1789 provided only a temporary compromise on the underlying disagreements between Federalists and Anti-Federalists. The Federalists immediately pushed for expanded powers for the federal judiciary. These efforts culminated in the passage of the Judiciary Act of 1801, which created many new judgeships and greatly extended the jurisdiction of the lower courts. The Federalist victory was short-lived, however. With the election of Thomas Jefferson as president, the Anti-Federalists in Congress quickly repealed the act and returned the federal judiciary to the basic outlines of the previous court system. The 1801 law is best remembered for the resulting lawsuit of *Marbury v. Madison* (1803), in which Chief Justice John Marshall declared that the U.S. Constitution granted courts the power of judicial review—the authority to invalidate acts of Congress as unconstitutional (for more on judicial review, see Appendix C).

Between 1789 and 1891, there was general agreement on the inadequacy of the federal judicial system, but the underlying dispute persisted. Congress passed numerous minor bills modifying the system in a piecemeal fashion. Dissatisfaction centered on two principal areas: circuit riding and the appellate court workload.

One of the most pronounced weaknesses of the 1789 judicial structure was circuit riding. The Supreme Court justices, many of them old and ill, faced days of difficult and often impossible travel. In 1838, for example, the nine justices traveled an average of 2,975 miles. There were numerous complaints from the justices about the intolerable conditions that circuit-riding duties imposed on them.

Beyond the personal discomforts some justices encountered, the federal judiciary confronted a more systemic problem—mounting caseloads. Initially, the federal judges of the newly created trial courts had relatively little to do because their jurisdictions were very limited. The Supreme Court likewise had few cases to decide. But the initially sparse workload began to expand as the growth of federal activity, the increase in corporate business, and the expansion of federal jurisdiction by court interpretation created litigation for a court system that was ill equipped to handle it. From the end of the Civil War until 1891, it was not uncommon for an appeal to wait two or three years before it was argued before the Supreme Court. This was because the high court had to decide every case appealed to it.

Court of Appeals Act of 1891

At first glance, the creation of the court of appeals in 1891 appears to have been an automatic response to increased federal litigation resulting from a rapidly expanding population and the growth of business following the Civil War. A closer look indicates that it was the culmination of "one of the most enduring struggles in American political history" (Richardson & Vines 1970, p. 26). There was no debate over the difficulties facing the federal court system. All parties to the controversy agreed that the federal judiciary needed relief; what was in dispute was the nature of the relief.

To solve the burden of mounting litigation in the federal courts, the supporters of states' rights wanted to return cases to the state level by reducing the jurisdiction of federal courts. The supporters of national power, on the other hand, argued for expanding the jurisdiction of federal courts by creating a system of federal appellate courts that would take a great deal of the burden off the high court and also allow the trial courts to function as true trial courts.

The landmark Court of Appeals Act of 1891 represented the climactic victory of the Nationalists' interests. The law created new courts known as circuit courts of appeals. Under this new arrangement, most appeals of trial decisions went to a circuit court of appeals. In short, the creation of the circuit courts of appeals released the high court from hearing many types of petty cases. The high court now had much greater control over its workload and could concentrate on deciding major cases and controversies.

Federal Courts Today

In 1925, Congress passed the Judges Bill, which among other things gave the Supreme Court much greater control over its docket. In 1988, Congress eliminated even more mandatory appeals to the high court. Other important changes that have shaped the development of the federal courts are presented in the box, "Key Developments in the Federal Judiciary."

The current structure of federal courts is best understood in terms of four layers of courts: magistrate, district, appellate, and Supreme Court. In addition, the federal judiciary includes specialized courts and administrative structures.

KEY DEVELOPMENTS IN THE FEDERAL JUDICIARY

U.S. Constitution	1787	Article III creates U.S. Supreme Court and authorizes lower federal courts.
Judiciary Act of 1789	1789	Congress establishes lower federal courts.
Marbury v. Madison	1803	The Court has the authority to declare an act of Congress unconstitutional.
Courts of Appeals Act	1891	Modern appellate structure is created.
Judges Bill	1925	Supreme Court is given control over its docket.
Court Packing Plan	1937	FDR's attempt to pack the Court is defeated.
Administrative Office Act	1939	Current administrative structure is created, including judicial conference and judicial councils.
Federal Judicial Center	1967	Research and training unit is created.
Federal Magistrate Act	1968	Commissioners are replaced by U.S. magistrates (later, the name is changed to "magistrate judges").
Multidistrict Litigation Act	1968	Created the Judicial Panel on Multidistrict Litigation and gave it the power to transfer to a single district court the pretrial proceedings for civil cases involving common questions of fact, such as litigation regarding airplane crashes, product liability, patent infringements, and securities fraud.
Bankruptcy Reform Act	1978	Conferred original bankruptcy jurisdiction on the U.S. district courts and established a bankruptcy court in each judicial district to exercise bankruptcy jurisdiction.
Foreign Intelligence Surveillance Act	1978	Authorized the chief justice of the United States to designate seven federal district court judges to review applications for warrants related to national security investigations on a special court named the Foreign Intelligence Surveillance Court. The Act also created the U.S. Foreign Intelligence Surveillance Court of Review, a special appellate court whose only function is to review denials by the Foreign Intelligence Surveillance Court of applications for electronic surveillance warrants.
Federal Courts Improvement Act	1982	Congress combined the jurisdictions of the U.S. Court of Customs and Patent Appeals and the U.S. Court of Claims into one court, the U.S. Court of Appeals for the Federal Circuit.
Sentencing Commission	1984	Commission is charged with developing sentencing guidelines.
Congressional Act of 1988	1988	Some mandatory appeals to the Supreme Court are eliminated.
Antiterrorism and Effective Death Penalty Act (AEDPA)	1996	Right of state prisoners to file **habeas corpus petitions** in federal court is severely limited.
USA PATRIOT Act	2001	The government's ability to gather domestic antiterrorism intelligence is expanded, allowing for less court scrutiny and closing some court proceedings to the public.
Military Trials for Enemy Combatants Act	2006	The president was empowered to identify enemy combatants and detain them indefinitely without their being able to obtain federal court review of their detentions through *habeas corpus* proceedings, a right traditionally afforded to prisoners.
House v. Bell	2006	Created a narrow exception to the AEDPA by allowing prisoners with evidence of actual innocence to obtain *habeas corpus* review if a "miscarriage of justice" would occur with the court's review.
Boumediene v. Bush and Al Odah v. United States	2008	The Supreme Court invalidated the provision of the Military Trials for Enemy Combatants Act that deprived the detainees of their constitutional right to *habeas corpus* review in the federal courts.

U.S. Magistrate Judges

Congress created **U.S. magistrate judges** in 1968 to replace the former position of U.S. commissioners. The purpose was to provide a new type of judicial officer in the federal judicial system to alleviate the increased workload of the U.S. district courts (Anderson, 2007). Technically, magistrate judges and their courts are a subcomponent of federal district courts; their duties and workload, however, merit separate discussion.

Magistrate judges perform quasi-judicial tasks and work within the judicial branch of government. They are not, however, Article III judges. Magistrate judges are selected by district court judges. Full-time magistrate judges are appointed for eight-year terms, and part-time magistrate judges for four-year terms. They may, however, be removed for "good cause." Except in special circumstances, all must be lawyers. According to the Administrative Office of the U.S. Courts (2016), there are currently 536 full-time magistrate judges and 34 part-time magistrate judges.

Magistrate judges are authorized to perform a wide variety of duties. In felony cases, they are responsible for preliminary proceedings, including holding initial appearances, conducting preliminary hearings, appointing counsel for indigents, setting bail, and issuing search warrants. In misdemeanor and petty offense cases, the jurisdiction of magistrate judges is more extensive; they may preside over trials, accept pleas of guilty, and also impose sentences. On the civil side, they supervise discovery, review Social Security disability benefit appeals, and even conduct full civil trials with the consent of the litigants. In short, under specified conditions and controls, magistrate judges may perform virtually all tasks carried out by district court judges, except trying and sentencing felony defendants (*Gonzales v. United States*, 2008).

Caseload of U.S. Magistrate Judges

Magistrate judges play an increasingly important role in helping district court judges dispose of their growing caseloads. In 2015, for example, magistrate judges handle approximately 1.09 million matters for the federal courts, including being involved in some way in roughly 350,000 felony preliminary proceedings. In addition, they dispose of approximately 95,000 misdemeanor and petty offenses and roughly 26,000 prisoner litigation cases. Magistrate judges are also involved in assisting with nearly 349,000 civil matters.

U.S. District Courts

Congress has created 94 **U.S. district courts**, of which 89 are located within the 50 states. There is also a district court in the District of Columbia and four territorial district courts located in Guam, Puerto Rico, the Virgin Islands, and the Northern Mariana Islands.

There is at least one district court in each state; moreover, based on the compromise that produced the Judiciary Act of 1789, no district court crosses state lines. Some states have more than one district court: California, New York, and Texas, for instance, each have four. Because district courts often encompass large geographical areas, some hold court in various locations, or divisions. Some districts have only one division, while others have several.

Congress has created 677 district court judgeships for the 94 districts. The president nominates district judges, who must then be confirmed by the Senate (see Chapter 8). Once they take the oath of office, they serve during "good behavior," which for practical purposes means for life. The number of judgeships in each district depends on the amount of judicial work as well as the political clout of the state's congressional delegation; the number ranges from two district judges in Idaho, North Dakota, and Vermont to 28 in densely inhabited Manhattan, officially called the U.S. District Court for the Southern District of New York (Administrative Office of the U.S. Courts, 2016b).

Judges are assisted by an elaborate supporting cast of clerks, secretaries, law clerks, court reporters, probation officers, pretrial services officers, and U.S. marshals. The larger districts also have a federal public defender. Another important actor at the district-court level is the U.S. attorney. There is one U.S. attorney (see Chapter 6) in each district, nominated by the president and confirmed by the Senate, but unlike the judges, he or she serves at the pleasure of the president.

The work of the district judges is significantly assisted by approximately 350 **bankruptcy judges**. Although bankruptcy judges are adjuncts of the district courts, they are appointed for 14-year terms by the court of appeals in which the district is located. In 2005, bankruptcy filings reached an astonishing level, with more than 1.78 million petitions filed. The vast majority of these bankruptcy filings were non–business-related, typically involving consumers who cannot pay their bills; the others were filed by businesses big and small. That same year, however, Congress passed the Bankruptcy Abuse Prevention and Consumer Protection Act of 2005. The law made it more difficult for consumers to discharge debts that they were having trouble paying. As a result, the number of bankruptcy petitions filed dropped to around 800,000 per year by 2007. In the wake of the economic downturn since then, however, bankruptcy filings rose again, to nearly 1.6 million petitions in 2010. By 2013, bankruptcy filings dropped to approximately 1.1 million petitions. By 2015, that number dropped to 860,182, the lowest number since 2007.

Caseload of U.S. District Courts

In the federal system, the U.S. district courts are the federal trial courts of original jurisdiction. Table 2.1 provides an overview of case volume

in the federal courts. The volume of cases is large and growing in complexity.

The district courts are the trial courts for all major violations of federal criminal law. Each year, U.S. attorneys file approximately 80,000 criminal cases, primarily for drug violations, embezzlement, and fraud. For many years, federal prosecutions remained fairly constant (roughly 30,000 per year), only to shoot up beginning in 1980. A major part of this upsurge has been the dramatic increase in drug prosecutions, which, as Figure 2.2 illustrates, account for more than 31 percent of all federal criminal cases. Moreover, trials of criminal cases are now more frequent (and also longer) than in years past. Thus, although civil, not criminal, cases account for most of the work of the district courts, in some districts criminal filings are limiting the ability of these courts to decide civil cases.

Civil lawsuits consume considerably more of the federal courts' time than criminal cases do. Although only a small number of all civil cases are filed in federal courts as compared with state courts, federal civil cases typically involve considerably larger sums of money than the cases filed in state court. This is due, in part, to the types of cases over which the federal courts have jurisdiction. Federal courts are permitted to hear only civil cases involving diversity of citizenship and several types of cases that involve questions of federal law, including prisoner petitions.

TABLE 2.1	Case Filings in the U.S. Courts		
	2002	**2007**	**2015**
U.S. Supreme Court	8,255	8,241	7,033
U.S. Circuit Courts of Appeals	57,555	58,410	52,698
U.S. District Courts	341,841	325,920	340,238
U.S. Bankruptcy Courts	1,547,669	801,269	860,182

Diversity Jurisdiction

Diversity of citizenship cases involve suits between citizens of different states or between a U.S. citizen and a foreign country or citizen. For example, a citizen from California claims to be injured in an automobile accident in Chicago with an Illinois driver and sues in federal court in Illinois because the parties to the suit are of "diverse citizenship." Pursuant to the Supreme Court's decision in *Erie Railroad Co. v. Tompkins* (1938), federal courts apply state—not federal—law when adjudicating state claims in federal court under their diversity of citizenship jurisdiction.

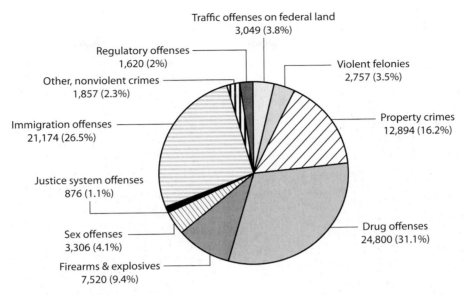

FIGURE 2.2 Federal Criminal Prosecutions

Source: Federal Judicial Center. *Caseload Statistics* 2015, Table D-2. Washington, DC: Administrative Office of the U.S. Courts.

From the 1980s through the mid-1990s, diversity cases constituted approximately 25 percent of the civil docket of the district courts, thus making a significant contribution to the workload of the district courts. In an effort to restrict the types of minor disputes that may be filed in federal court, Congress in 1996 raised the amount-in-controversy to $75,000 under 28 U.S.C. § 1332(a). At first, this change in jurisdictional amount decreased the number of diversity cases filed in federal courts each year such that diversity cases were reduced to 18.7 percent of the federal civil caseload in 2000. However, the effects of the change in the amount-in-controversy were short-lived. Since 2005, diversity filings have constituted between 25 and 36 percent of the federal civil case load. Given the burdensome workload that diversity jurisdiction brings to the federal courts, combined with the fact that the exercise of diversity jurisdiction requires the federal courts to apply state law—a task that is arguably better performed in state courts—both judges and legal scholars have called for the abolition of diversity of citizenship jurisdiction in the federal courts. If that were to occur, the federal courts would be able to focus on federal questions. However, Congress has not heeded such calls. Rather, Congress may

have decided to maintain the status quo because it agreed with the overwhelming sentiment of lawyers in private practice that state courts are biased against out-of-state defendants (Underwood, 2006; Mask & MacMahon, 2015). Alternatively, Congress may simply have opted to continue using the federal courts to resolve interstate disputes.

Federal Questions

Article III provides that federal courts may be given jurisdiction over "Cases, in Law and Equity, arising under this Constitution, the Laws of the United States, and Treaties made, or which shall be made under their authority." Cases that fall under this type of jurisdiction are generally referred to as involving a **federal question**. Although some federal question cases present issues concerning the interpretation or application of the U.S. Constitution, most federal question cases concern the application or interpretation of a statute enacted by Congress, as illustrated in Exhibit 2.1. Some of these laws—and the decisions of the federal courts interpreting them—significantly affect the operation of the criminal justice system.

EXHIBIT 2.1	Federal Question Jurisdiction Cases

- Suits between states—Cases in which two or more states are parties.

- Cases involving ambassadors and other high-ranking public figures—Cases arising between foreign ambassadors and other high-ranking public officials.

- Federal crimes—Crimes defined by or mentioned in the U.S. Constitution or those defined and/or punished by federal statute. Such crimes include treason against the United States, piracy, counterfeiting, crimes against the law of nations, and crimes relating to the federal government's authority to regulate interstate commerce. However, most crimes are state matters.

- Bankruptcy—The statutory procedure, usually triggered by insolvency, by which a person is relieved of most debts and undergoes a judicially supervised reorganization or liquidation for the benefit of the person's creditors.

- Patent, copyright, and trademark cases:

    1. Patent—The exclusive right to make, use, or sell an invention for a specified period (usually 17 years), granted by the federal government to the inventor if the device or process is novel, useful, and non-obvious.

    2. Copyright—The body of law relating to a property right in an original work of authorship (such as a literary, musical, artistic, photographic, or film work) fixed in any tangible medium of expression, giving the holder the exclusive right to reproduce, adapt, distribute, perform, and display the work.

    3. Trademark—A word, phrase, logo, or other graphic symbol used by a manufacturer or seller to distinguish its product or products from those of others.

- Admiralty—The system of jurisprudence that has grown out of the practice of admiralty courts: courts that exercise jurisdiction over all maritime contracts, torts, injuries, and offenses.

- Antitrust—The body of law designed to protect trade and commerce from restraining monopolies, price fixing, and price discrimination.

- Securities and banking regulation—The body of law protecting the public by regulating the registration, offering, and trading of securities and the regulation of banking practices.

- Other cases specified by federal statute—Any other cases specified by an applicable federal statute, such as of civil rights, labor relations, environmental cases, and cases arising under the Americans with Disabilities Act.

Source: "Understanding Federal and State Courts." Available online at http://www.uscourts.gov/EducationalResources/FederalCourtBasics /CourtStructure/UnderstandingFederalAndStateCourts.aspx

The Constitutionalization of Criminal Procedure

Under Chief Justice Earl Warren, the U.S. Supreme Court sparked a due process revolution, giving defendants the right to counsel (Chapter 7), broadening notions of a fair trial (Chapter 13), and expanding the right to appeal (Chapter 15). The federal courts have also set standards regulating how local and state law enforcement officers gather evidence and interrogate suspects (Chapter 11). And the federal courts continue to impact greatly the sentencing and punishment of criminal offenders (Chapter 14). Violations of these constitutional rights as interpreted in relevant federal court precedent can lead to a conviction being overturned either on direct appeal or collaterally in *habeas corpus* proceedings (Chapter 15).

Discrimination Laws and Civil Rights Cases

Federal laws prohibit discrimination on the basis of race, religion, sex, age, or national origin in domains such as employment, welfare, housing, and voting. For example, except in rare instances, employers are required to ignore gender when hiring or promoting, provide equal pay to all employees, and treat pregnancy like any other temporary disability (Kruger, 2007; Ziegler, 2015). Bona fide occupational qualifications, however, are exempt. Thus, valid job-related requirements necessary to normal business operations are allowed.

Criminal justice agencies, though, should avoid height and weight requirements that are not legitimately related to job performance.

Similarly, the millions of people with disabilities in the United States are protected against discrimination in employment and in their use of public facilities and services under the Americans with Disabilities Act. These protections affect the design and functionality of police departments, courthouses, and correctional facilities to accommodate the special needs of the disabled. In *Yeskey v. Pennsylvania Department of Corrections* (1998), the U.S. Supreme Court held that the Americans with Disabilities Act applies to the ways in which police officers and correctional officials interact with people with disabilities. As a result, police may be civilly liable for arresting someone because they confuse the effects of a disability with criminally aggressive behavior or because they fail to accommodate a person's disability during investigation, interrogation, or arrest (Osborn, 2008; Douglas & Cuskelly, 2012). Similarly, the Court held in *United States v. Georgia* (2006) that states and municipalities can be held civilly liable for failing to maintain correctional facilities that accommodate the special needs of disabled prisoners.

Prisoner Petitions

In spite of a criminal conviction, inmates in local, state, and federal custody all retain certain constitutional rights. The Supreme Court emphasized this point in *Wolff v. McDonnell* (1974), when it said, "There is no iron curtain drawn between the Constitution and the prisons of this country" (pp. 555–556). To enforce their rights, prisoners are permitted to file several types of civil lawsuits, which are collectively referred to as **prisoner petitions**. The four primary types of prisoner petitions that the federal courts adjudicate are summarized in Table 2.2.

Prisoner petitions have grown steadily and now account for a considerable portion of the workload of the federal courts. Collectively, civil rights cases from state and federal inmates have increased significantly, from about 3,500 filings in 1960 to a record high of more than 68,235 cases in 1996. These numbers were driven, in large part, by the sharp increase in the prison population over the corresponding period. The following year, prisoner petitions began to decrease as a result of Congress enacting the Prison Litigation Reform Act (PLRA) of 1996. The PLRA made it more difficult for prisoners to file Section 1983 cases by requiring them to exhaust administrative remedies before filing a federal case, by making them pay certain fees from which they had previously been exempt, and by barring them from filing subsequent cases if they had prior Section 1983 cases dismissed for being frivolous or malicious.

U.S. magistrate judges greatly assist federal district judges with *habeas* petitions and prisoner civil rights. But, because they are not Article III judges, magistrates generally write a report to the U.S. district judge to whom the case is formally assigned. The report concludes with a recommendation for how to rule in the case. The report and recommendation are usually adopted by the district judge who ultimately orders the final judgment in the case.

Discrimination and Civil Rights Caseload in the Federal Courts

Nonprisoner civil rights filings doubled in U.S. district courts from 1990 (18,922 filings) to 1997 (43,278 filings). This increase in the civil rights caseload of the federal courts was due, in large part, to the major expansion of federal civil rights by various acts of Congress, most especially the passage of the Americans for Disabilities Act of 1990 and the Civil Rights Act of 1991, which amended several older employment discrimination laws, including, among others, Title VII of the Civil Rights Act of 1964 and the Age Discrimination in Employment Act of 1973. In the early 2000s, civil rights filings stabilized at around 40,500 cases per year. Since then, however, they have declined to around 37,384 filings, thereby accounting for approximately 13.4 percent of all civil cases filed in the federal courts.

U.S. Courts of Appeals

As mentioned previously, Congress created the **U.S. courts of appeals** in 1891 to relieve the Supreme Court from hearing the growing number of appeals. The courts of appeals are the intermediate appellate courts of the federal system. Originally

TABLE 2.2	Prisoner Petitions in U.S. District Courts in 2015			

Type	Prisoner Petition Description	Number Filed	Percent of Prisoner Petitions	Percent of Total Civil Docket
Habeas corpus	Typically filed under 28 U.S.C. § 2254, *habeas corpus cases* are those in which inmates may collaterally challenge their convictions (after exhausting all available state remedies to do so) by arguing that their trial was constitutionally defective.	19,614	35.27%	6.97%
Motions to Vacate Sentence	Allow a federal prisoner to try to get a sentence set aside or corrected because the sentence was imposed contrary to law. Such motions might allege that the court lacked jurisdiction to impose a criminal sentence or that the sentence was in excess of that allowed under the law.	6,504	11.69%	2.31%
Mandamus Petitions	Seeks a court order to compel a public entity or official to do something that is owed to the plaintiff as a matter of constitutional or statutory right.	917	1.65%	0.33%
Section 1983 and *Bivens* Civil Rights actions	Against state actors: 42 U.S.C. § 1983 allows individual persons to sue those who act under color of state law to redress alleged deprivations of constitutional rights. Typical claims are use of excessive force, illegal searches and seizures, interference with Fifth and/or Sixth Amendment rights to counsel during interrogations (Chapter 11), denials of First Amendment rights, interference with the Sixth Amendment right to access the courts, and violations of the Eighth Amendment's guarantee against cruel and unusual punishment based on claims of excessive force, lack of medical care, or inhumane conditions of confinement.	28,580	51.39%	10.15%
	Against federal actors: *Bivens v. Six Unknown Agents of the Federal Bureau of Narcotics* (1971), permits private persons to sue those who act under color of federal authority (e.g., federal law enforcement or correctional officers) for alleged deprivations of constitutional rights.			

Source: Federal Judicial Center. *Caseload Statistics* 2015, Table C-2A. Washington, DC: Administrative Office of the U.S. Courts.

called "circuit courts of appeal," they were renamed and are each now officially known as the U.S. Court of Appeals for the ___ Circuit. Each circuit hears appeals from specific district courts. At present, there are 14 circuits: 11 numbered circuits (each containing at least three states); a Circuit Court of Appeals for the District of Columbia; the Court of Appeals for the Federal Circuit; and the Court of Appeals for the Armed Forces.

As illustrated in Figure 2.3, the numbered circuits and the Circuit Court of Appeals for the District of Columbia are geographically arranged. All 12 of these circuit courts are empowered to review all final decisions of U.S. district courts, as well as certain interlocutory decisions of district courts (see Chapter 15). They also have the power to review and enforce orders of many federal administrative bodies. In contrast, the Federal Circuit is

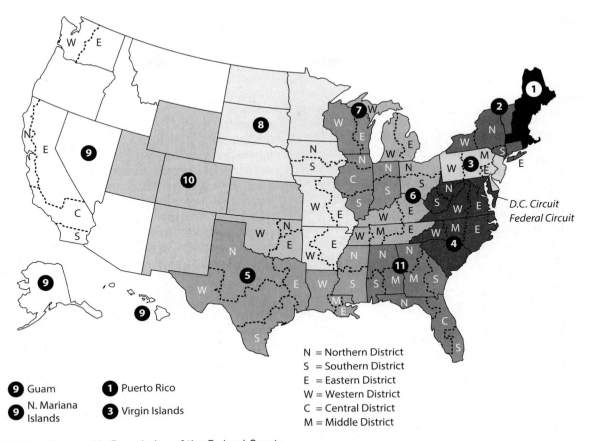

FIGURE 2.3 Geographic Boundaries of the Federal Courts

Source: Russell Wheeler and Cynthia Harrison. *Creating the Federal Judicial System*. 2nd ed. Washington, DC: Federal Judicial Center, 1994, p. 26.

the only civilian judicial circuit whose jurisdiction is based on subject matter rather than geographical boundaries. It was created by an act of Congress in 1982 and granted nationwide jurisdiction to hear specialized appeals concerning certain types of government contracts, patents, trademarks, certain nontort money claims against the U.S. government, federal personnel, and veterans' benefits. Finally, the Court of Appeals for the Armed Forces hears appeals only from cases decided in military courts and tribunals concerning members of the U.S. armed forces on active duty and other persons subject to the Uniform Code of Military Justice.

The courts of appeals are staffed by 179 judges nominated by the president and confirmed by the Senate. As with the district courts, the number of judges in each circuit varies, from 6 (the First

Circuit) to 29 (the Ninth Circuit), depending on the volume and complexity of the caseload (Administrative Office of the U.S. Courts, 2016c). Each circuit has a chief judge who performs administrative duties in addition to hearing cases. As a rule, the judge who has served on the court the longest and who is under 65 years of age is designated as the chief judge. Several staff positions aid the judges in conducting the work of the courts of appeals. A circuit executive assists the chief judge in administering the circuit. The clerk's office maintains the records. Each judge is also allowed to hire three law clerks. In addition, each circuit has a central legal staff that screens appeals and drafts memorandum opinions.

In deciding cases, the courts of appeals normally use rotating three-judge panels. Along with active judges in the circuit, these panels often include visiting judges (primarily district judges from the same circuit) and senior judges. By majority vote, all the judges in the circuit may sit together to decide a case or rehear a case already decided by a panel. Such *en banc* hearings are relatively rare, however; in a typical year fewer than 100 are held throughout the entire nation.

Caseload of U.S. Courts of Appeals

Over the past five decades, the caseload of the courts of appeals has skyrocketed. This dramatic increase in caseload has not been matched by an equivalent increase in judgeships, however. In 1960, there were 68 judgeships whose workload involved hearing 172 cases per three-judge panel. Today, there are 179 circuit court judges who hear more than 1,000 cases per three-judge panel.

The number of appeals filed annually in the federal courts has varied between 54,679 in 2000 and a high of 68,473 in 2005. That number has fallen, as 52,698 appeals were filed in 2015, the most recent year for which statistics are available. Appeals from criminal convictions in the U.S. district courts constitute about 22 percent of the workload of the courts of appeals. Appeals from decisions in prisoner petition cases comprise approximately 26.4 percent of the federal appellate caseload. Thus, criminal and prisoner petitions account for nearly 48 percent of the appeals filed each year, while civil appeals, including bankruptcy appeals and appeals from administrative agencies, account for the remainder.

A decision by a U.S. Court of Appeals exhausts the litigant's right to one appeal. The losing party may request that the U.S. Supreme Court hear the case, but such petitions are rarely granted. As a result, the courts of appeals are the "courts of last resort" for virtually all federal litigation. Their decisions end the case; only a tiny percentage will be heard by the nation's highest court.

U.S. Supreme Court

The **U.S. Supreme Court** is the court of last resort in the federal court system, meaning that it is a court from which no appeal is possible. The Supreme Court has one chief justice and a number of associate justices fixed by Congress. By act of Congress in 1948, the number of associate justices is eight. Power to nominate the justices is vested in the president of the United States, and appointments are made with the advice and consent of the Senate. Once confirmed to the Supreme Court, there is no mandatory retirement age for Supreme Court justices; so as long as they maintain "good behavior," the justices may remain on the court until their death or until they voluntarily choose to retire.

The Constitution grants the Supreme Court original jurisdiction in a limited number of cases. In other words, the Supreme Court acts as a trial court in certain types of cases, such as controversies between the United States and a state, between two states, or between foreign ministers or ambassadors. Such cases are quite rare; so in the overwhelming majority of cases, the Supreme Court exercises its appellate jurisdiction, reviewing the decisions of the lower federal courts and the highest state courts.

With a few limited exceptions, the appellate jurisdiction of the Supreme Court is discretionary rather than mandatory. In other words, the Court has great discretion with regard to the appeals it elects to hear and decide. The Supreme Court exercises this discretion through the granting of a **writ of *certiorari***, which means that the Court, upon petition by a party, agrees to review a case decided by one of the circuit courts of appeals or the highest court of a state. The writ of *certiorari* is an order issued by the Supreme Court to a lower court to send the case records so that the Supreme Court can determine whether the law has been correctly applied.

Granting Cert: The Rule of Four

A vote of four Supreme Court justices is required to grant *certiorari* to review a case. This is often referred to as the **rule of four**. The rule of four is not contained in any law or formal rule of the Court; rather, it is a custom that has been observed since the Supreme Court gained the ability to control its own docket with the creation of the circuit courts of appeal in 1891 (Fang, Johnson, & Roberts, 2007). The rule of four is remarkable in that it is a device through which "a minority of the Court can impose on the majority a question that the majority does not think it appropriate to address" (Kurland & Hutchinson, 1983, p. 645). This power of a minority of justices appears to make a difference in about 25 percent of the Court's cases; for the other three-quarters of their caseload, a majority of justices agree that a case presents an issue that the Court should address through plenary review (Fang et al., 2007).

Whether *certiorari* is granted by four justices or more, the Court's discretion is always guided by whether a case presents questions that have some general "importance beyond the facts and parties involved" (*Boag v. MacDougall*, 1982, p. 368, Rehnquist, J., dissenting). For example, the Court may grant *certiorari* in cases involving important and unsettled questions of federal law or in situations involving a conflict among state high courts or the federal circuits concerning the interpretation of federal law, most especially one ruling on a question of interpretation of the U.S. Constitution. Note that failure to grant *certiorari* is not an affirmation in disguise of the lower court's decision. It simply means that the petitioner failed to persuade four of the nine justices to hear the appeal.

Caseload of U.S. Supreme Court

Only a small percentage of the requests for a *writ of certiorari* (or *cert,* as it is often called) is granted. In particular, the legal issue must involve a "substantial federal question." This means state court interpretations of state law can be appealed to the Supreme Court only if there is an alleged violation of either federal law or the U.S. Constitution. For example, a suit contending that a state supreme court has misinterpreted the state's divorce law would not be heard because it involves an interpretation of state law and does not raise a federal question. The same is true for decisions of state high courts recognizing controversial rights, such as the right for same-sex couples to marry, when the decisions are based entirely on their state constitutions. As a result of this limitation that cases must raise a substantial federal question, the vast majority of state cases are never reviewed by the Supreme Court.

By statute, the Supreme Court begins its annual term on the first Monday in October and it continues until late June or early July of the following year. Each term is comprised of rotating intervals of sittings and recesses, each of which lasts approximately two weeks. During *sittings,* the justices hear cases and deliver opinions. During *recesses,* they study the cases on their docket and work on researching and writing their opinions. In addition, each week, the justices evaluate roughly 130 petitions for writs of *certiorari.*

Through its discretionary powers to hear appeals, the Supreme Court limits itself to deciding about 80 cases a year. With the exception of capital cases, the Court does not really act as an error-correction court. Rather, the Court marshals its time and energy to decide the most important policy questions of the day (see Chapter 15).

Circuit Justices

Each justice on the Supreme Court is assigned to serve as a **circuit justice**. While the function of circuit justices has varied over time, their role today is concerned primarily with addressing certain requests for extension of time and ruling on requests for stays in cases coming from the circuit (or circuits) to which the justice is assigned. A **stay** is a court order that temporarily suspends activity in a case. If the circuit justice thinks that there is merit in a case such that the full Supreme Court should have an opportunity to decide whether to hear the case, the circuit justice may grant the stay. This is particularly important in capital cases, in which a stay of execution can keep a death-row prisoner alive until the full Court can review the case.

Specialized Federal Courts

The magistrate, district, appeals courts, and Supreme Court handle the bulk of federal litigation and therefore are a principal focus of this book. To round out our discussion of the federal judicial system, however, we also need to discuss briefly several additional courts that Congress has periodically created. These courts are called "specialized federal courts" because they are authorized to hear only a limited range of cases—taxes or

TABLE 2.3	Specialized Federal Courts		
Court	**Authority**	**Level**	**Jurisdiction**
Courts with Permanent Judges			
Tax Court	Article I	Trial	Tax disputes
Court of Federal Claims	Article I	Trial	Monetary claims against the federal government
Court of Veterans Appeal	Article I	Trial	Federal veterans' benefits
U.S. Court of International Trade	Article III	Trial	Imports of foreign goods
U.S. Court of Appeals of the Armed Forces	Article III	Appellate	Uniform Code of Military Justice
Court of Appeals for the Federal Circuit	Article III	Appellate	Trademarks, patents, foreign trade, claims against the federal government
Courts with Judges Borrowed from Other Federal Courts			
Alien Terrorist Removal Court	Article I	Trial	Decides whether an alien should be removed from the United States on the grounds of being an alien terrorist
Foreign Intelligence Surveillance Court	Article III	Trial	Electronic surveillance of foreign intelligence agents
Foreign Intelligence Surveillance Court of Review	Article III	Appellate	Electronic surveillance of foreign intelligence agents

Source: Adapted from Lawrence Baum, *Specializing the Courts*. Chicago: University of Chicago Press, 2011. For further details on these courts visit the Federal Judicial Center at http://www.fjc.gov/history/home.nsf/page/courts.html.

patents, for example. They are created for the express purpose of helping administer a specific congressional statute.

Table 2.3 gives an overview of the specialized federal courts and highlights two important distinctions. First, most specialized courts have permanent, full-time judges appointed specifically to that court. A few specialized courts, however, temporarily borrow judges from federal district courts or courts of appeals as specific cases arise (Baum, 2011; Solimine, 2014).

The second distinction relates to the specialized courts' constitutional status. Judicial bodies established by Congress under Article III are known as **constitutional courts**. The Supreme Court, courts

of appeals, and district courts are, of course, constitutional courts. Judicial bodies established by Congress under **Article I** are known as **legislative courts**. Courts presided over by bankruptcy judges and U.S. magistrate judges are examples of legislative courts. The constitutional status of federal courts has important implications for judicial independence. Article III (constitutional court) judges serve for a period that amounts to a lifetime appointment, but Article I (legislative court) judges are appointed for a specific term of office. Moreover, Article III judges are protected against salary reductions while in office. Article I judges enjoy no such constitutional protection. In short, constitutional courts have a greater degree of independence from the other two branches of government than do the legislative courts. The specialized federal courts are overwhelmingly civil in their orientation, handling such matters as patents and tariffs on imported goods. But three specialized courts bear directly on criminal matters, the military courts, the Foreign Intelligence Surveillance Act Court, and immigration courts. In addition, a murky legal area has arisen because of the capture of those who are called "military noncombatants"; it is not clear in which courts they will be tried.

Military Justice

Congress adopted the Uniform Code of Military Justice in 1950, extending significant new due process rights in courts-martial. Congress also created the U.S. Court of Appeals for the Armed Forces, composed of five civilian judges appointed by the president for 15-year terms. The intent was clearly to extend civilian influence to military law. The Military Justice Act of 1968 contributed to the further civilianization of courts-martial. The code covers criminal acts, but can also punish acts that are not criminal for civilians (for example, disrespect of an officer). Moreover, on a military base, military justice applies not only to members of the armed services but also to civilian employees, and it covers acts committed by military personnel on and off a military base (Fidell, 2016).

As with other systems of criminal law, the objective of military justice is to provide a forum for determining guilt or innocence. In addition, however, courts-martial serve the purpose of enforcing order and discipline in the military. In the words of the U.S. Military (U.S. Joint Service Committee on Military Service, 2008), "The purpose of military law is to promote efficiency and effectiveness in the military establishment, and thereby to strengthen the national security of the United States." Thus, although military justice is not exempt from the Constitution, it is certainly distinctive. Military justice differs from state and federal justice in the following ways:

- Proceedings are open to military society.
- The burden of proof is less demanding.
- Three- and five-person juries are used.
- The jurors are military personnel.

- A two-thirds majority is sufficient to convict.
- Convictions are automatically appealed to a higher military court.

The principal concern with military courts is that jurors may be unduly influenced by military commanders.

In recent years, a few high-profile cases have thrust military justice into the news. Some of the more prominent cases include these:

- Several Army personnel were found guilty of abusing inmates in Iraq's notorious Abu Ghraib prison.
- Seven U.S. soldiers from an elite Airborne division were charged with knowingly engaging in sex for money on a public website.
- At the age of 39, psychiatrist and Army Major Nidal Malik Hasan went on a shooting rampage at Fort Hood, killing 13 people and wounding 29 others. Hasan acted as his own attorney during this court-martial. He was found guilty of 45 charges and sentenced to death.
- Chelsea Manning, formerly known as Pfc. Bradley Manning, was accused of leaking classified government documents, including a classified military video of an attack in Iraq that was posted online by WikiLeaks. Manning's actions allegedly formed the largest ever intelligence leak in American history. Manning was convicted in 2013 and sentenced to 35 years in prison. In the last days in his office term, President Obama commuted Manning's sentence to 7 years.
- Several trials involving charges of sexual assault, including one against Brigadier General Jeffrey Sinclair, brought national attention to the problems the military has with preventing and punishing sex crimes within the ranks. In 2014, the U.S. Senate passed a bill making it easier to prosecute sexual assaults in the military, but the Pentagon strongly objects to removing such cases from the chain of command (Cassata, 2014).

Enemy Combatants

In response to the attacks of September 11, 2001, the United States invaded Afghanistan, capturing hundreds of persons suspected of being members of the al-Qaeda terrorist organization. The military decided that those captured did not qualify as prisoners of war (and therefore would be subject to the Geneva Conventions) but instead would be considered **enemy combatants**. Since the War on Terrorism began, nearly 780 people from nearly 50 countries have been imprisoned as enemy combatants at the U.S. Navy base in Guantanamo Bay, Cuba; thousands more have been held in military installations in Afghanistan, Iraq, and elsewhere.

The George W. Bush administration asserted that international law did not require any legal process for enemy combatants. Rather, the president, as commander-in-chief, could detain enemy combatants until the War on Terrorism was over. The U.S. Supreme Court rejected this view in *Rasul v. Bush* (2004), ruling that federal courts have jurisdiction to hear the detainees' *habeas corpus* petitions challenging their indefinite detentions.

Less than two weeks after the *Rasul* decision, the Department of Defense established Combatant Status Review Tribunals (CSRTs) to review evidence in secret proceedings to determine whether a detainee had been properly classified as an enemy combatant. Within six months, over 550 CSRTs were held. Ultimately, the U.S. Supreme Court rejected the legality of these military commissions, ruling in *Hamdan v. Rumsfeld* (2006) that they had not been authorized by an act of Congress and that they violated both the Uniform Code of Military Justice and the Geneva Conventions.

Congress responded to the *Hamdan* decision by enacting the Military Commissions Act of 2006 (MCA), which authorized the president to identify enemies, imprison them indefinitely, try them in military commissions, and deprive the federal courts of jurisdiction to hear any *habeas corpus* cases filed by detainees. In doing so, Congress sanctioned past and future decisions of CSRTs and attempted to place enemy combatants beyond the reach of federal courts, processes afforded to criminal defendants and ordinary prisoners. The Supreme Court declared the MCA unconstitutional in *Boumediene v. Bush* (2008). As a result, a number of enemy combatants have been released by order of the courts reviewing their detention in Guantanamo Bay. In fact, nearly three-quarters of the cases

reviewed by federal judges concluded that there was insufficient evidence to hold the petitioners as enemy combatants and, therefore, ordered their release (Cole, 2010, as quoted in Walsh, 2010). By the end of President Barack Obama's second term, 55 detainees remained in U.S. custody in Guantanamo Bay (American Civil Liberties Union, 2017).

Foreign Intelligence Surveillance Court

The Foreign Intelligence Surveillance Court has authority over electronic surveillance of foreign intelligence agents. Because it was created by the Foreign Intelligence Surveillance Act (FISA), it is popularly referred to as the FISA Court. This court has no permanent judges; rather, the chief justice appoints 11 judges who hear requests for warrants as needed (Savage, 2013; Seabrook & Cole, 2016). The courtroom is inside the U.S. Department of Justice, and only the FISA judges are allowed to review the requests submitted by the Justice Department. By statute, a FISA judge is authorized to sign a search warrant for electronic eavesdropping based on "clear and convincing evidence," a legal standard that is less stringent than that required for a normal search warrant.

For years, the FISA Court labored in obscurity. Indeed, the only visible public role came in year-end reports, which invariably indicated that the court had approved all warrant requests. This lack of public attention changed greatly with the revelation in late 2005 that the National Security Agency was conducting warrantless surveillance of domestic phone conversations of suspected foreign terrorist groups like al-Qaeda. The Bush administration contended that the president had inherent war powers under the Constitution to order eavesdropping without warrants, even though some in Congress disputed this interpretation. In the wake of controversy, a Republican-controlled Congress enacted the Protect America Act of 2007. The law mandated that telecommunications providers assist the government in intercepting international phone calls and e-mails for national security purposes. The law was upheld in 2008 over a Fourth Amendment challenge (see Chapter 11) by a decision of the Foreign Intelligence Surveillance Court of Review (which has appellate review over decisions of the

Foreign Intelligence Surveillance Court), although the decision was not made public until early 2009. The court reasoned that requiring the government to obtain a warrant would impair its ability to gather time-sensitive information, thereby potentially putting national security interests at risk. The opinion concluded by saying that as long as the executive branch has "several layers of serviceable safeguards to protect individuals against unwarranted harms and to minimize incidental intrusions, its efforts to protect national security should not be frustrated by the courts" (*In re Directives Pursuant to Section 105B of the Foreign Intelligence Surveillance Act* 2008, p. 29). But the rulings, some over 100 pages long, remain classified, which means that the FISA Court has secretly expanded the government's ability to collect electronic data, not only on suspected terrorists but ordinary citizens as well (Lichtblau, 2013; Seabrook & Cole, 2016). The virtually secret operations of the FISA Court became highly visible in 2013 when Edward Snowden leaked thousands of documents exposing massive government spying programs, including the collection of phone-tracing data from Verizon cell phone customers. Federal judges, who have served on the court, have responded by publicly calling the process flawed (Braun, 2013). Indeed, the presiding judge of the FISA Court says the court's ability to oversee the government's vast electronic spying programs is limited (Leonnig, 2013). Amidst calls to impose accountability on electronic surveillance, Congress remains deadlocked, and Snowden remains in Russia beyond the reach of U.S. law.

Immigration Courts

The contentious debate over immigration reform has focused renewed attention on the overburdened immigration courts in the United States. Although the number of people illegally entering or remaining in the United States has stabilized in recent years, researchers estimate that there are nonetheless roughly 11 million undocumented immigrants in the United States (Warren, 2016), despite the fact that the country spends approximately $12.8 billion each year to finance the operations of the U.S. Customs and Board Protection Agency and another $5.4 billion on the U.S.

Immigration and Customs Enforcement Agency. Roughly 1,000 undocumented immigrants are removed from the United States each day (Taxin, 2014). Although some of these cases are handled as criminal prosecutions in federal court, the vast majority are disposed of by specialized immigration courts that currently have a backlog of nearly a half-million (Solis, 2016).

Immigration courts are not part of the Article III federal judiciary, but rather are housed in the U.S. Department of Justice, an administrative agency. The official title is the Executive Office for Immigration Review (EOIR), with appeals heard by the Board of Immigration Appeals. The chief function is to conduct administrative hearings to decide if a foreign-born individual should be removed from the country or granted protection from removal. At this writing, approximately 250 immigration judges conduct administrative court proceedings in 57 immigration courts nationwide (U.S. Department of Justice, 2016).

During the most recent year for which data is available, the immigration courts received nearly 262,300 matters. Of the roughly 181,600 case dispositions, approximately 170,000 of the cases concerned either deportations or other removals from the county (EIOR, 2016). To process the large number of cases, immigration court judges decide cases in rapid succession. Perhaps typical is a judge in Arlington, Virginia, who spends an average of seven minutes per case (Saslow, 2014), a clear example of assembly line justice (see Chapter 5). These numbers though underestimate how backlogged immigration courts really are; a typical case takes three years to be heard, and not surprisingly a significant number of illegal immigrants do not appear.

Federal Judicial Administration

The Administrative Office Act of 1939, which largely created the current administrative structure of the federal judiciary, illustrates the interplay between judicial administration and politics. During the mid-1930s, the conservative majority on the Supreme Court declared many pieces of New Deal legislation unconstitutional. After his reelection in 1936, President Franklin Delano Roosevelt put forth his Court-packing plan: The Court would be expanded from 9 to 15 justices, thus allowing FDR to pack the Court with justices more sympathetic to his policies. There was no legal barrier to such an action because the Constitution fails to specify how many justices shall serve on the Court. But the political obstacles proved insurmountable; many of Roosevelt's backers felt that tampering with the Court was a bad idea. The Court-packing plan never passed, but it did call attention to the president's complaints that the administration of federal courts was inefficient. At the same time, some judges were dissatisfied with the old system of court management because it was located in the Department of Justice, an executive agency. Thus, a movement arose among federal judges and national court reformers to clean their own house. The result was a compromise plan—the Administrative Office Act of 1939. The act expanded the responsibilities of the Judicial Conference, created the Administrative Office of the U.S. Courts, and established the judicial councils. These agencies, along with the office of the chief justice, the Federal Judicial Center, and the more recently created U.S. Sentencing Commission, are the main units involved in administering the federal courts. A summary of their functions, composition, and hierarchical structure is presented in Figure 2.4.

Chief Justice

The Chief Justice of the United States is the presiding officer of the U.S. Supreme Court and has supervisory authority over the entire federal judicial system. To fulfill these duties, the chief justice hires a fifth law clerk (one more than the four law clerks allotted to each associate justice) and an administrative assistant to help with the administrative tasks for the Court and for the judicial system as a whole.

At the Supreme Court itself, the chief justice presides over all courtroom proceedings as well as the private conferences in which the justices discuss and vote on cases. As a matter of tradition, the chief justice normally speaks either first or last in these conferences, thereby having significant influence on the discussion. The chief justice assigns associate justices (and himself) to serve as the circuit justice for the various federal circuits. While the chief justice's vote in a case carries no more or less weight than the vote of any of the associate justices, the most senior justice always decides who will write the opinion of the Court in a given case. Since the chief justice is the most senior position on the court (regardless of the number of years the chief justice has actually served on the Court), that means that when the chief justice votes with the majority of justices in a given case, he possesses the important power to assign the authorship of the majority opinion. This includes the ability to keep important constitutional cases for himself.

Other administrative tasks at the Supreme Court for the chief justice include regulating attorney admissions to the Supreme Court bar; formally opening and closing each court term; supervising and working with the Court's clerk, librarians, and reporter of decisions; budgeting; advocating for the courts before Congress; and serving as a spokesperson not only for the Supreme Court but also for all of the federal courts. For example, former Chief Justice William Rehnquist often spoke about the need for Congress to increase the number of federal judges, increase the salaries of judges to be competitive with the private practice of law, reduce the workload of the courts, and protect judicial independence. Chief Justice John Roberts has continued to echo all of these sentiments. For example, in an *Annual Report*, Chief Justice Roberts pointed out that the entire judicial system of the United States received only two-tenths of 1 percent of the total federal budget, a figure that causes the courts to "continuously look . . . for ways to do more with less" (2008, p. 4). This chronic underfunding of the courts has led to federal judges' pay being steadily eroded, since they have not been provided with cost-of-living increases for several years, even though Congress has given such increases to all other federal employees (including all members of Congress).

Outside the walls of the Supreme Court, the chief justice has many other ceremonial and administrative responsibilities. By mandate of Article I, Section 3 of the U.S. Constitution, the chief justice presides over impeachment trials of the president of the

Executive Branch
Participates in legislative process. Transmits appropriations requests. Provides buildings and security. Is represented on rules committees.

Congress
Appropriates funds. Enacts legislation on court organization and jurisdiction. Reviews procedural rule amendments.

Supreme Court
Approves rule amendments.

Chief Justice of the United States

Administrative Office of the U.S. Courts
The chief justice appoints the director and deputy director after consultation with Judicial Conference.
Functions: Provides, under Conference supervision, administrative support to courts (including budget, personnel, space and facilities), staff to Judicial Conference and its committees, legislative coordination, other functions.

Judicial Conference of the United States
Members: Chief justice (chair); chief judge and district judge from the twelve regional circuits; chief judge, Court of Appeals for the Federal Circuit; chief judge, Court of International Trade.
Functions: Sets national administrative policy for the federal judiciary; approves appropriations requests for submission to Congress; recommends changes in rules of procedure to the Supreme Court for submission to Congress; other statutory functions.

Federal Judicial Center
Board: Chief justice (chair); seven judges elected by the Judicial Conference; Administrative Office director. Board appoints Center director and deputy director.
Functions: Provides orientation and continuing education to judges and personnel of courts, research support to courts and Judicial Conference committees.

Committees of the Judicial Conference
Members: Judges, practicing lawyers, and legal scholars appointed by the chief justice, and ex officio government officials.
Functions: Make recommendations to the Conference and, in a few cases, exercise statutory responsibilities.

U.S. Sentencing Commission
Members: Seven voting members appointed by the president (no more than three of whom may be federal judges) and two nonvoting ex officio members.
Functions: Promulgates sentencing guidelines and otherwise establishes federal sentencing policies as directed by the 1984 Sentencing Reform Act.

Chief Judges of the Circuits

Judicial Conferences of the Circuits
Optional circuit-wide meetings, called no more than once a year by the chief circuit judge, about various topics related to the administration of justice. All federal judges may attend, and each court of appeals must adopt rules to provide for participation by members of the bar.

Judicial Councils of the Circuits
Members: Chief judge (chair); circuit and district judges in equal numbers; council size determined by majority vote of all active circuit and district judges.
Functions: (1) Make necessary orders for administration of justice within the circuit (all judges and employees of the circuit are statutorily directed to give effect to council orders); (2) consider complaints of judicial misconduct or disability under if referred by the chief circuit judge; (3) review district court plans in various administrative areas, as required by statute or Judicial Conference.

Courts of Appeals, District Courts, and Bankruptcy Courts
Courts, each with a chief judge and clerk of court, also develop and implement administrative policy in numerous areas within the framework depicted above.

FIGURE 2.4 Organization of Federal Judicial Administration

Source: Russell Wheeler. *A New Judge's Introduction to Federal Judicial Administration.* Washington, DC: Federal Judicial Center, 2003.

United States in the U.S. Senate. The chief justice normally administers the oath of office to the president and vice president at inaugurations. He supervises the acquisitions of the law department at the Library of Congress. The chief justice also possesses the significant authority to appoint judges to special tribunals and courts, such the U.S. Foreign Intelligence Surveillance Court and the Judicial Panel on Multidistrict Litigation (a group of seven federal judges who select the venue for the district that coordinates all pretrial proceedings for multiple cases across the country concerning the same basic cause of action with common questions of face, such as mass tort actions resulting from a plane crash or a product-liability case). And the chief justice serves on the boards of three cultural institutions: The Smithsonian (often serving as its Chancellor), the Hirshhorn Museum, and the National Gallery of Art.

In the role of leader of the federal courts system, the chief justice serves as the chair of the Judicial Conference of the United States, supervises the Administrative Office of the U.S. Courts, and serves as the chair of the Federal Judicial Center. All three of these organizations are discussed in greater detail in the following sections.

Judicial Conference of the United States

The Judicial Conference of the United States is the administrative policy-making organization of the federal judicial system. It is comprised of 26 members, including the chief justice, the chief judges of each of the courts of appeals, one district judge from each circuit, and the chief judge of the Court of International Trade. The conference meets semiannually for a two-day session. Because these short meetings are not sufficient to accomplish a great deal, most of the work is done by about 25 committees. The chief justice of the United States has the power to appointment members to the committees, all of which contain not only members of the Judicial Conference itself but also other judges, law professors, and practicing attorneys selected by the chief justice.

One of the most important responsibilities of the Judicial Conference is drafting proposed amendments to the rules that govern proceedings in the federal courts. These include the Federal Rules of Civil Procedure, Federal Rules of Criminal Procedure, Federal Rules of Bankruptcy Procedure, Federal Rules of Appellate Procedure, and the Federal Rules of Evidence. Other committees of the Judicial Conference oversee judicial codes of conduct, information technology in the federal courts, and court administration and case management.

The Judicial Conference directs the Administrative Office of the U.S. Courts in administering the judiciary budget and makes recommendations to Congress concerning the creation of new judgeships, increases in judicial salaries, and budgets for court operations. The Judicial Conference also plays a major role in discipline (including impeachment) of federal judges (a topic discussed in greater depth in Chapter 8). In short, the Judicial Conference is a vehicle through which federal judges play a major role in developing policy for the federal judiciary.

Administrative Office of the U.S. Courts

Since its establishment in 1939, the Administrative Office (AO) of the U.S. Courts has been responsible for implementing the policies established by the Judicial Conference by handling the day-to-day administrative tasks of the federal courts. The director of the AO is appointed by the chief justice and reports to the Judicial Conference. Acting as the Judicial Conference's official representative in Congress, the AO's lobbying and liaison responsibilities include presenting the annual budget requests for the federal judiciary, arguing for the need for additional judgeships, and transmitting proposed changes in court rules. The AO also serves as the housekeeping agency of the judiciary, responsible for allotting authorized funds and supervising expenditures. Throughout the year, local federal court staff send the AO a vast array of statistical data on the operations of the federal courts, ranging from the number of filings to the speed of the disposition of cases. The data are published in three separate volumes. The heftiest is the *Annual Report,* which runs to hundreds of pages and is now available on the Internet.

Federal Judicial Center

The Federal Judicial Center is the research and training arm of the federal judiciary. Its activities are managed by a director appointed by a board that consists of the chief justice, the director of the Administrative Office, and judges from the U.S. district court, courts of appeals, and bankruptcy court. One of the principal activities of the Federal Judicial Center is education and training of federal judicial personnel, including judges, probation officers, clerks of court, and pretrial service officers. The center also conducts research on a wide range of topics, including the work of the magistrate judges, ways of measuring the workload of the courts, and causes of delay.

Judicial Councils

The judicial council (sometimes referred to as the "circuit council") is the basic administrative unit of a circuit. The membership consists of both district and appellate judges of the circuit. A judicial council is given sweeping authority to "make all necessary and appropriate orders for the effective and expeditious administration of justice within its circuit." Working within this broad mandate, the councils monitor district court caseloads and judicial assignments. Although the law specifies that "all judicial officers and employees of the circuit shall promptly carry into effect all orders of the judicial council," the councils' actual enforcement powers are limited. The major weapons at their disposal are persuasion, peer group pressure, and publicity directed at the judge or judges who are reluctant to comply with circuit policy. At times, for example, circuit councils have ordered that a district judge receive no new cases until his or her docket has been brought up to date. Judicial councils are also authorized to investigate complaints of judicial disability or misconduct (a topic probed in greater detail in Chapter 8).

U.S. Sentencing Commission

The U.S. Sentencing Commission is an independent agency in the judicial branch of government. It consists of seven members—a chairperson, three vice chairs, and three commissioners appointed by the president of the United States. The Sentencing Commission was created by the Sentencing Reform Act of 1984. Its original purpose was to develop federal sentencing guidelines. Today, the Commission is also charged with evaluating the effects of the sentencing guidelines on the criminal justice system, recommending to Congress appropriate modifications of substantive criminal law and sentencing procedures, establishing a research and development program on sentencing issues, and monitoring the performance of federal probation officers with respect to their roles in recommending sentences to federal judges (see Chapter 14).

Caseloads in the Federal Courts

The onset of the Industrial Revolution increased the caseload of the federal courts, a trend that was later accelerated by Prohibition, then the New Deal, and even further by federal lawmaking often associated with President Lyndon Johnson's "Great Society" programs. Growing caseloads, in turn, prompted changes and additions to the federal judiciary; appellate courts have been added and specialized courts created.

What is new is the pace of that expansion. For most of our nation's history, the growth in federal cases was gradual. No longer—over the past 50 years, district court filings have increased more than sixfold, and court of appeals cases have increased more than tenfold. According to the Administrative Office of the U.S. Courts, federal judges today are faced with unprecedented levels of work. By and large, federal judges across the country face a greater number of cases each year and, in some instances, are encountering record levels of work.

The caseload problem is particularly acute in some metropolitan jurisdictions, where federal judges must postpone civil trials for months and even years to accommodate criminal trial schedules (particularly of major drug dealers) in accordance with the Speedy Trial Act (see Chapter 5). The solutions most often suggested for the problem of rising federal court caseloads are increasing the number of federal judges and reducing federal jurisdiction.

Increase the Number of Federal Judges?

Through the years, increases in the number of cases filed in federal court have been followed by an increase in the number of federal judgeships. More recently, however, the dramatic increases in federal court cases have not been accompanied by a corresponding increase in the number of federal judgeships. Particularly at the appellate level, the creation of new judgeships has lagged far behind the increase in filings.

It is unlikely that in the short term the number of federal judgeships will be increased. Only Congress can authorize additional judgeships, and Congress has been locked in a decades-long partisan battle over the federal judiciary. Chapter 8 will explore ongoing political battles between Republicans and Democrats over who should fill existing vacancies on the federal bench. Given this partisan divide, it is unlikely that additional judgeships will be created until one party controls a filibuster-proof majority of the United States (and the president is a member of that party) because new judgeships would become political spoils for the party in control at that time.

Reduce Federal Jurisdiction?

To cope with rising caseloads, federal judges have proposed not only creating more judgeships but also reducing the types of cases that can be filed in federal court. According to the *Report of the Federal Courts Study Committee* (1990), Congress created most of these problems by unwisely expanding federal court jurisdiction, and therefore Congress should enact remedial legislation. Specifically, the report advocated several jurisdictional reforms. Some of the proposals to limit the ability of prisoners to file civil rights lawsuits under 42 U.S.C. § 1983 until after having exhausted certain state administrative remedies were adopted by Congress as part of the Prisoner Litigation Reform Act of 1996.

But no action has been taken with respect to some of the more dramatic recommendations in the 1990 report:

1. Federal diversity jurisdiction should be abolished except in cases by or against citizens of foreign countries, and in complex, multistate cases arising primarily from large disasters.

2. The crime of illicit drug trafficking is punishable under both state law and federal law. This concurrent jurisdiction should be abolished such that offenses arising out of trafficking on a local basis should be the exclusive province of state criminal law (tried in state courts), leaving the federal courts to handle only large multistate or even multinational drug trafficking cases.

3. Congress should create several new Article I legislative courts, such as a Court of Disability Claims, which would hear appeals from decisions by administrative law judges denying claims for disability benefits under the Social Security Act and possibly under other disability statutes as well. The Committee even proposed an Article I court to adjudicate small claims under the Federal Tort Claims Act in which the amount sought in good faith by the plaintiff is $10,000 or less.

Perhaps because Congress was labeled the primary culprit, it is hardly surprising that Congress gave the report a chilly reception (Biskupic, 1993; Underwood, 2006; Miner, 2013). In short, the nation's top elected lawmakers have been at odds with the nation's top appointed law interpreters for most of the past century, and this disagreement is not likely to be resolved.

Arguments based on numbers of cases stress issues of efficiency, but typically need to be understood within a broader framework of political winners and losers. Thus, some disagreements reflect divisions along the lines of the due process versus crime control models of justice. But other disagreements reflect institutional differences: The views of federal judges (whether appointed by Republican or Democratic presidents) contrast with the views of federal lawmakers. Concurrent federal and state jurisdiction over certain drug-related offenses, to name just one example, illustrates the political nature of the debate over the appropriate scope of federal criminal law.

Consequences of Federal Involvement in the Criminal Justice System

Crime has been a pressing national concern for decades. As a result, national elected officials, whether members of Congress or the president, have often made crime a key campaign issue. In turn, the crime policies of nonelected officials, whether bureaucrats or judges, have been closely scrutinized. Despite all this clamor at the national level, the role of the federal government in the criminal justice system is limited. Crime remains primarily the responsibility of state and local governments. This imbalance between federal officials' need to be seen as doing something about the crime problem and their limited jurisdiction to do anything explains a good deal of the political dynamics surrounding the role of the federal government (and the federal judiciary) in the criminal justice system.

Forum for Symbolic Politics

In spite of the limited scope of its involvement in crime, the federal government remains the focal point of the national debate. Crime is a powerful issue and therefore has attracted a variety of interest groups. Some focus on crime issues directly—for example, the American Correctional Association (ACA), the Police Executive Research Forum (PERF), and Mothers Against Drunk Driving (MADD). Other interest groups, such as the American Civil Liberties Union (ACLU), Lambda Legal, and the National Organization for Women (NOW), find that crime and crime issues are related to other concerns.

Interest groups have a major impact on public policy. Most directly, they lobby on behalf of their members for favorable government policies. They can also mount campaigns encouraging their members to write federal officials in favor of (or in opposition to) specific proposals. Some organizations likewise make campaign contributions to selected officials. The National Rifle Association (NRA), for instance, contributes to officials who are dubious about gun control, whereas the Brady Campaign to Prevent Gun Violence supports candidates who favor gun control. Other times, interest groups file civil lawsuits, often in the federal courts, to facilitate social change, as the "Case Close-Up" feature on *Floyd v. City of New York* (2013) illustrates.

Federal Dollars

A basic rule of American politics is that citizens' demands for services exceed the willingness of voters to raise taxes to pay for those services. Those who one day vocally demand a tax reduction are quick to demand expanded government services the next day. Funding the criminal justice system illustrates this rule. Citizens demand that courts "get tough with criminals" but are unwilling to raise taxes to build new prison cells. Likewise, pleas for more cops on the beat are seldom followed by requests for increased taxes to pay for such increased hiring. Faced with these limitations, local and state officials often turn to Washington as a source of "free" money (with *free* defined as "no local taxes"). In turn, federal officials find that appropriating federal money is one way of assuring voters that they take the crime problem seriously.

Congress has authorized spending for a variety of anticrime programs. Some are general in nature—for example, block grants for local projects that reduce crime and improve public safety. Similarly, 60 percent of the research budget of the National Institute of Justice—the principal federal agency involved in the war on crime—is spent on developing new technology for law enforcement and the criminal justice system. Other spending programs are targeted toward specific concerns—for example, domestic violence and victim assistance programs (see Chapter 9).

Overall, though, the amount of federal dollars is small compared to what local and state governments spend. Moreover, federal money is often limited to a short period of time (typically three years).

Criminal justice officials must defend themselves against a variety of civil lawsuits. Perhaps the best known of these cases are filed under 42 U.S.C. § 1983 (often called "Section 1983 cases") alleging that law enforcement officials violated the rights guaranteed to all people under the U.S. Constitution. One of the most controversial of such cases, *Floyd v. City of New York*, stemmed from the New York City Police Department (NYPD) aggressive use of their legal authority to stop, question, and frisk (SQF) "suspicious" people.

Although policy authority to stop suspicious people can be traced back hundreds of years under English common law, it was the landmark decision in *Terry v. Ohio* (1968) that set the modern constitutional parameters governing the use of the tactic (White & Fradella, 2016). The U.S. Supreme Court held in *Terry* that police may temporarily detain and question a citizen if the officer has reasonable, articulable suspicion that a person may be involved in criminal activity (see Chapter 11). The Court also held that officers may superficially search (frisk) a detained person if there is reasonable, articulable suspicion that the person may be armed and dangerous. But the law governing SQF authority "illustrates the discrepancy between law in the books and the law in action" (Warner, 1942, p. 315). Especially since the early 1990s, this discrepancy has grown into a highly divisive controversy as a function of a strong disconnect between how SQF authority is supposed to work in principle, and how it has actually worked in practice. Nowhere has this controversy been more pronounced than in New York City.

New York, like many cities across the United States, experienced a major spike in violence, crime, and disorder in the 1980s. Much of the violence in New York was driven by the emergence of crack cocaine and competition for the drug market (White, 2014). At the same time, the city and subway system were struggling with rampant social and physical disorder. Marijuana, heroin, cocaine, and crack cocaine were regularly and openly being sold on street corners, blocks, and city parks, and upwards of 2,000 people slept on city subways each night (Kelling & Coles, 1996).

In 1993, New York City Mayor Rudolph Giuliani appointed William Bratton as the Commissioner of the NYPD. As part of his crime-control strategy, Bratton targeted disorder and quality-of-life offenses, used crime data to place police in crime "hot spots," and ordered police to focus on the seizure of illegal firearms and through the intensive investigation of

gun-related incidents. A particularly aggressive form of SQF emerged as the primary tactic to meet some of these policy objectives (White, 2014). But rather than focusing on the "amelioration of physical disorder" in partnership with the community in accordance with the tenant of Broken Windows theory (Kelling & Wilson, 1982), the NYPD employed an aggressive zero-tolerance interdiction approach to social disorder such as public drunkenness, vandalism, loitering, panhandling, prostitution, and the like. Put different, police used quality-of-life offenses "as excuses to fish for drugs, guns, or evidence of a more serious crime" (Waldeck, 1999, p. 1282).

At its height, SQF activity by the NYPD resulted in more than 685,000 stops in 2011 (White & Fradella, 2016). But fewer than 6.5 percent of these stops resulted in the issuance of a summons or an arrest, and less than 1 percent of stops resulted in a firearm being confiscated (Jones-Brown, Gill, & Trone, 2010). In other words, roughly 94 percent of the people NYPD stopped were innocent of any wrongdoing. Moreover, these "innocent stops" were not evenly distributed throughout the city. Stops in predominantly Black and Hispanic neighborhoods occurred "at rates in excess of what would be predicted from the separate and combined effects of population demography, physical and social conditions, and the crime rate" (Fagan, Geller, Davies, & West, 2010, p. 337).

Proponents of SQF claimed it was an effective crime-control strategy because street crime in New York City declined approximately 75 percent—a decrease roughly twice the national average and homicides dropped even more dramatically (see Zimring, 2012). But the empirical evidence calls this conclusion into question for three important reasons. First, there are a number of studies indicating that the relationship between SQF and the crime decline in New York City is modest, at best (Cerdá et al., 2010; McDonald, Fagan, & Geller, 2016; Rosenfeld, Fornango, & Rengifo, 2007). Second, SQF was just one of the strategies the NYPD used to combat crime during these years, so it is difficult, if not impossible, to tease out the effects of SQF separate from other tactics, like policing crime hot spots. And third, crime decreased dramatically across the United States through the 1990s and 2000s, including in many cities that did not employ an aggressive form of SQF to the policing crime and disorder.

Regardless of its impact on crime, there is considerable evidence demonstrating that the NYPD's SQF program exacted

(Continued)

(Continued)

significant social costs that were disproportionately experienced by members of racial and ethnic minority groups. After years of complaints failed to change the racially disparate ways in which the NYPD implemented SQF, civil rights advocates filed several federal lawsuits alleging that NYPD officers selectively targeted people on the basis of their race and national origin, without reasonable suspicion, in violation of the Fourth and Fourteenth Amendments to the U.S. Constitution. *Floyd* was one of these cases. In August 2013, a federal judge ruled that the NYPD was engaging in unconstitutional SQF practices that targeted predominately Black and Latino New Yorkers. That decision was appealed, but the case was settled while the appeal was pending when Bill de Blasio was elected as the new mayor of New York largely on the basis of a platform to curb the abuses of aggressive SQF tactics (White & Fradella, 2016).

The de Blasio administration's abandonment of aggressive SQF activity in 2012 did not result in an increase in criminal activity in the city. In fact, although the NYPD recorded just 45,788 stops in 2014 (a 93 percent decrease from 2011), frisks increased from approximately 55.7 percent to 66.3 percent; searches increased from 8.5 percent to 15.9 percent; arrests more than doubled from 6.0 percent in 2011 to 15.1 percent in 2014; seizures of guns increased 267 percent; seizures of other weapons increased by 104 percent; and seizures of drugs and other contraband increased by 185 percent (White, Fradella, Morrow, & Mellom, 2016). These data demonstrate that the quality of stop-and-frisk activity notably improved in terms of efficiency and accuracy from 2011 to 2014. Perhaps even more importantly, the rates of both violent and property crimes in New York City continued to decrease. "In short, there is no evidence to suggest that reforms to stop-and-frisk compromised the NYPD's ability to effectively fight crime" (White et al., 2016).

After federal funding ends, state or local units of government are expected to take over funding, but often these agencies are strapped for cash, leading to the cancellation of successful programs.

Conclusion

Offenders like Alfonso Lopez were no doubt on Justice Scalia's mind when he condemned what he called the deterioration of the federal courts. In the 1960s, the federal courts had few judges and small caseloads, but the cases they did hear were "by and large . . . cases of major importance." In contrast, Justice Scalia argued that while the federal courts now have more judges and larger caseloads, many of these cases are "minor" and "routine," concerning "mundane" matters of less import or even "overwhelming triviality" (quoted in Galanter, 1988). Thus, according to one of the Court's leading conservatives, the federal courts should be returned to their rightful role of deciding major controversies; lesser ones would be banished to state courts.

In the more than two decades since Justice Scalia made those comments, other judges, scholars, and commentators with diverse political viewpoints have echoed his sentiments that the federal courts handle too many routine cases that ought to be handled in state courts so that the federal courts could focus on more important federal questions (*Report of the Federal Courts Study Committee,* 1990). Such concerns are most evident with regard to the seemingly ever-expanding federalization of crimes—most especially drug cases (Husak, 2008; Luna, 2005; Miner, 2013). Consider *Taylor v. United States* (2016).

The defendant in *Taylor* was convicted of violations of a federal law known as the Hobbs Act arising out of conduct by gang members involving the robbery of marijuana dealers' homes. At trial, the defendant was prevented from offering evidence that the drug dealers he targeted only dealt in locally grown marijuana, and thus the interstate commerce element of the Hobbs Act could not be satisfied. On appeal, the Fourth Circuit affirmed the conviction, ruling that given the aggregate effect of drug dealing on interstate commerce, the prosecution only needed to prove the robbery or attempted robbery of a drug dealer to satisfy the commerce element of a Hobbs Act violation.

The Supreme Court agreed, reasoning that drug dealing—even if entirely within one state—constitutes interstate commerce because prior decisions of the Court held that Congress had the authority to regulate the national market of marijuana, including the production, possession, and sale of the drug within a state (see *Gonzales v. Raich*, 2005).

Taylor suggests that in spite of concerns about federalism, in an era when crime remains a major political issue, rolling back federal jurisdiction to the "good old days" (whenever that might have been) is unlikely to happen. What we learn ultimately is that the jurisdiction of federal courts is determined in no small measure by decisions of elected officials in Congress. In an earlier era, federal officials decided that federal law should cover matters such as prostitution, consumption of alcoholic beverages, gambling, and organized crime. Today they focus more on drug dealers, crooks who use guns, and intimate-partner-violence offenders.

Federal prosecutions often grab the headlines because the crimes are large or audacious or because the accused are people of prominence. In turn, the public by and large identifies the judiciary with federal courts. But we should not be misled. The federal courts are a relatively small part of the nation's judicial system. A major city such as Chicago or Los Angeles prosecutes more felons in a year than the entire federal judiciary. The nature of the crimes brought to federal court differs strikingly from those appearing in state judiciaries, though. State courts handle primarily street crimes that require immediate action—burglary, armed robbery, and murder, for example. By contrast, with the exception of drug-related offenses, federal crimes largely concern immigration offenses, fraud cases, firearms violations, and money laundering. It is to the more common state courts that we turn our attention in the next chapter.

CHAPTER REVIEW

LO1   1. Define the four primary types of jurisdiction: geographical, subject matter, personal, and hierarchical.

Geographical jurisdiction limits the power of courts to adjudicate disputes arising within certain geographic boundaries. Subject matter jurisdiction concerns the types of cases a court may hear and decide. Personal jurisdiction refers to a court's power over a specific person or legal entity (such as a partnership or corporation). Hierarchical jurisdiction concerns whether the court has the power to originally decide a case or to review it on appeal.

LO2   2. Compare and contrast the tasks of trial and appellate courts.

Trial courts are primarily concerned with considering evidence to resolve factual decisions within the bounds of the law. Appellate courts primarily review the legal decisions made by trial courts. In doing so, they serve dual purposes: error correction and policy formation (see Chapter 15).

LO3   3. Explain the historical evolution of the federal courts into their present structure and operations.

Article III of the U.S. Constitution established the U.S. Supreme Court and gave Congress the power to create lower courts. Congress has exercised its authority under Article III to create inferior courts at different times in U.S. history. Today, the trial courts that primarily exercise original jurisdiction in the federal system are the U.S. District Courts, whereas most appeals are resolved by the U.S. Courts of Appeals.

LO4   4. Analyze the different responsibilities and workloads of U.S. magistrate judges, district judges, circuit judges, and Supreme Court justices.

U.S. magistrate judges assist U.S. district judges by conducting pretrial criminal matters, supervising discovery in civil cases, and making reports and recommendations concerning the disposition of motions and prisoner petitions. District

court judges preside over trials and write opinions adjudicating many types of civil disputes. Typically sitting in panels of three, circuit judges review the records in cases appealed from district courts and write opinions ruling on the merits of legal arguments raised in those appeals.

LO5 5.   Analyze the impact the federal courts have on the administration of criminal justice at the state and local levels through their federal question jurisdiction.

By interpreting the requirements of federal law—especially the U.S. Constitution—the federal courts set the parameters for the operation of the criminal justice system so that police, prosecutors, defense attorneys, and judges honor the individual rights and liberties guaranteed in Constitution.

LO6 6.   Differentiate the jurisdiction and functions of Article III courts from those of Article I courts and other specialized federal courts.

Article III courts are empowered to adjudicate "cases and controversies" arising under the U.S. Constitution, federal law, and certain cases between citizens of different states or different counties. Article I courts are tribunals created by Congress to handle specialized types of cases, especially those that arise under the regulatory law of federal agencies. The decisions of Article I courts are generally reviewable in Article III courts. Article III judges are nominated by the president and confirmed to office by the U.S. Senate. Article I judges are not; they are appointed for fixed terms. Article I judges enjoy two protections to foster their independence: life-tenure (unless impeached) and a guarantee that

their salaries can never be decreased. Article I judges do not have these protections.

LO7 7.   Distinguish the various agencies and their hierarchical responsibilities for the administration of the federal court system.

The Judicial Conference of the United States sets national administrative policy for the federal judiciary. Under the supervision of the Judicial Conference, the Administrative Office of the U.S. Courts provides administrative support to courts (including budget, personnel, space, and facilities). The Federal Judicial Center provides orientation and continuing education to judges and personnel of courts, as well as research support for courts and Judicial Conference committees. The U.S. Sentencing Commission promulgates sentencing guidelines and otherwise establishes federal sentencing policies as directed by the 1984 Sentencing Reform Act.

LO8 8.   Evaluate the major problems facing the federal courts and the strengths and weaknesses of the major solutions that have been proposed to address these problems.

Heavy caseloads are the major problem facing the federal courts. Not only does the heavy workload burden those who work in the courts, but it also affects litigants whose cases may be delayed because of a backlog. Adding more staff, especially more federal judges, could help, but is cost-prohibitive. Reducing the jurisdiction of the federal courts, especially by eliminating diversity of citizenship jurisdiction, could also help, but this has not gained sufficient political support for Congress to have acted on the proposal.

CRITICAL THINKING QUESTIONS

1.   To what extent are contemporary debates over the role of the federal government similar to, but also different from, the debates in the late 18th century?

2.   How would the criminal justice system be different today if the founding fathers had decided not to create a separate system of federal courts and instead allowed federal laws to be enforced in state courts?

3. How would you reduce the federal court case-load? In considering where you would reduce federal court jurisdiction, also consider where you might increase it. What do your choices reflect about your political values?

4. To what extent does the debate over federal-ization of state crimes cut across traditional ideological values as represented in the due process model and the crime control model?

5. Federal law enforcement is limited in scope but subject to considerable public attention. Why?

KEY TERMS

appellate court   45

appellate jurisdiction   45

Article I   58

Article III   46

bankruptcy judge   50

Bivens actions   54

concurrent jurisdiction   41

constitutional courts   58

circuit justice   57

diversity of citizenship   50

dual court system   41

en banc   56

enemy combatants   60

extradition   43

federal question   51

geographical jurisdiction   41

habeas corpus   54

habeas corpus petitions   48

hierarchical jurisdiction   45

jurisdiction   41

legislative courts   58

mandamus petitions   54

motions to vacate sentences   54

original jurisdiction   45

personal jurisdiction   43

prisoner petitions   53

rule of four   56

Section 1983   54

subject matter jurisdiction   43

stay   57

trial court   45

U.S. courts of appeals   53

U.S. district courts   49

U.S. magistrate judges   49

U.S. Supreme Court   56

venue   43

writ of *certiorari*   56

FOR FURTHER READING

Ball, Howard. 2007. *Bush, the Detainees and the Constitu-tion: The Battle over Presidential Power in the War on Terror.* Lawrence: University of Kansas Press.

Bowie, Jennifer Barnes, Donald R. Songer, and John Szmer. 2014. *The View from the Bench and Chambers: Exam-ining Judicial Process and Decision Making on the U.S. Courts of Appeals.* Charlottesville: University of Virginia Press.

Brody, David. 2002. "The Misuse of Magistrate Judges in Federal Criminal Proceedings: A Look at the Non-Ministerial Nature of Sentencings." *Justice System Journal* 23: 259–262.

Hoffer, Peter Charles, William James Hull Hoffer, and N. E. H. Hull. 2016. *The Federal Courts: An Essential History.* New York: Oxford University Press.

Luna, Erik. 2005. "The Overcriminalization Phenomenon." *American University Law Review* 54: 703–746.

Lurie, Jonathan. 2001. *Military Justice in America: The U.S. Courts of Appeals for the Armed Forces, 1775–1980.* Lawrence: University of Kansas Press.

White, Michael D., and Henry F. Fradella. 2016. *Stop and Frisk: The Use and Abuse of a Controversial Police Tactic.* New York: New York University Press.

3 State Courts

OSWALDO PAEZ/AP Images

Suspected drug traffickers, arrested and handcuffed by the police, walk past packages containing cocaine in Cali, 185 miles southwest of Bogota, Colombia. The cocaine, destined for the United States, was found in brick form, wrapped in brown paper, and hidden in a Cali apartment. Although this arrest occurred in Colombia, the world's leading cocaine exporter, similar "drug busts" occur in the United States, especially in cities and towns along the United States–Mexico border.

Chapter Outline

After attending several judicial conferences around the nation, two judges had little trouble identifying the major problem facing the Los Angeles County municipal courts: Soaring drug prosecutions were further crowding jails that were already full. Implementing a solution, however, proved a more troublesome and time-consuming process. To establish a drug court, the judges needed the active cooperation of other judges, the district attorney, the public defender, treatment providers, and the sheriff. To ensure that these agencies had a voice in the process, a coordinating council was formally established. Finally, after months of meeting and planning, two drug courts were created (Torres & Deschenes, 1997).

Discussions of state courts usually contain references to major cases, such as armed robberies and automobile accidents. But this is only part of their workload. State judges must also adjudicate cases involving wives who want divorces from unfaithful husbands and husbands who physically abuse their wives; juveniles who rob liquor stores and juveniles who simply drink liquor.

The contemporary realities reflect an increase in the number of cases placed on the dockets of state courts and rising societal expectations about the administration of justice—while staffing levels remain constant. Thus, although an earlier generation viewed court reform in terms of a neater organizational chart, contemporary discussions are more likely to focus on topics such as finding a better way to handle drug cases.

This chapter examines the structure and functions of state courts. We begin with a discussion of the development of courts in the United States and then divide the somewhat confusing array of state courts into four levels: trial courts of limited jurisdiction, trial courts of general jurisdiction, intermediate courts of appeals, and courts of last resort.

Learning Objectives

After reading this chapter, you should be able to:

LO1   Outline the four layers of a typical state court system.

LO2   Describe the types of cases handled by the trial courts of limited jurisdiction.

LO3   Discuss the similarities and differences between justice of the peace courts and municipal courts.

LO4   List the four primary problems confronting the lower courts in the United States.

LO5   Identify the types of civil and criminal cases filed in trial courts of general jurisdiction.

LO6   Explain briefly the differences between a state high court of last resort in states with and without intermediate courts of appeals.

LO7   List the key components of court unification.

LO8   Identify how problem-solving courts using therapeutic jurisprudence handle cases.

LO9   Discuss the consequences of court organization.

(We discuss juvenile courts in Chapter 4 and examine appellate courts in depth in Chapter 15.) We will examine the efforts of court reformers to reorganize state court structure as well as the consequences of court organization for the administration of justice.

History of State Courts

Just as U.S. law borrowed heavily from English common law, the organization of U.S. courts reflects their English heritage. But the colonists and later the citizens of the fledgling new nation that called itself the United States of America adapted this English heritage to the realities of the emerging nation. Issues such as the clash of opposing economic interests, the debate over state versus national power, and outright partisanship have shaped America's 50 diverse state court systems.

Colonial Courts

Early colonial courts were rather simple institutions whose structure replicated English courts in form but not in substance. The numerous, complex, and highly specialized English courts were ill suited to the needs of a small group of colonists trying to survive on the edge of the wilderness, so the colonists greatly simplified the English procedures. As towns and villages became larger, however, new courts were created so that people would not have to travel long distances to have their cases heard. Moreover, a notion of separation of governmental powers began to emerge. In the early days, the same governmental body often held executive, legislative, and judicial powers. The county courts, for example, stood at the heart of American colonial government. In addition to adjudicating cases, they performed important administrative functions. Gradually, different institutions began to perform these tasks.

Diversity was the hallmark of the colonies, with each colony modifying its court system according to variations in local customs, different religious practices, and patterns of commercial trade. Some of these early variations in legal rulings and court structures have persisted and contribute to the great variety of U.S. court systems today (Glick & Vines, 1973).

In the northern colonies, biblical codes were often adopted. In the South, laws governing slavery were enacted. Overall, public punishments like the pillory and the stocks were commonly used, but the death penalty was used less often than in England.

Early American Courts

After the American Revolution, the functions of state courts changed markedly. Their governing powers were drastically reduced and taken over by the legislative bodies. The former colonists distrusted lawyers and harbored misgivings about English common law. They were not anxious to see the development of a large, independent judiciary. Thus, state legislatures often responded to unpopular court decisions by removing some judges or abolishing specific courts all together.

A major source of political conflict between legislatures and courts centered on the issue of monetary debtors. Legislators were more responsive to policies that favored debtors, usually small farmers. Courts, on the other hand, reflected the views of creditors, often merchants. Out of this conflict over legislative and judicial power, the courts gradually emerged as an independent political institution.

In the northern states, European immigration generated cultural and religious tensions between new arrivals and current residents. In the South, the justice system focused on tracking down escaped slaves. Meanwhile, the nation was steadily moving west, and a unique form of frontier justice emerged.

Courts in a Modernizing Society

Rapid industrialization following the Civil War produced fundamental changes in the structure of the American judiciary. Increases in population led to a higher volume of litigation. Just as important, the growing concentration of people in the cities (many of whom were immigrants) meant

| TABLE 3.1 | Case Filings in State Trial Courts in 2013 (in millions) |

Type of Case	Single-Tiered, Unified Courts (9 States)	Two-Tiered Court Systems (43 States)		Grand Total	Percent of Total
		General Jurisdiction	Limited Jurisdiction		
Traffic	9.3	2.9	38.9	51.1	54.3%
Criminal	2.4	3.5	13.6	19.5	20.7%
Civil	2.2	5.9	8.8	16.9	18.0%
Domestic relations	0.7	3.8	0.7	5.2	5.5%
Juvenile	0.2	1.0	0.2	1.4	1.5%
Total	14.8	17.1	62.2	94.1	100.0%

Source: Robert C. LaFountain, Shauna M. Strickland, Richard Y. Schauffler, Katherine A. Holt, and Kathryn J. Lewis. 2015. *Examining the Work of State Courts: An Analysis of 2013 State Court Caseloads*. Williamsburg, VA: National Center for State Courts.

the courts were faced with a new set of problems. Thus, by the end of the 19th century, the nation had to respond to a new type of social problem—crimes committed by juveniles (see Chapter 4).

The U.S. courts, still reflecting the rural agrarian society of the early 19th century, were inadequate in the face of rising demands for services (Colburn, 2006; Jacob, 1984). States and localities responded to societal changes in a number of ways. City courts were created to deal with new types of cases in the urban areas, including public drunkenness, gambling, and prostitution. Specialized courts were formed to handle specific classes of civil cases (for example, small claims courts and family courts). Additional courts were created, often by specifying the court's jurisdiction in terms of a geographic boundary within the city.

The development of courts in Chicago illustrates the confusion, complexity, and administrative problems that resulted from this sporadic and unplanned growth. In 1931, Chicago had 556 independent courts; the majority were justice of the peace courts, which handled only minor offenses (Glick & Vines, 1973). The jurisdiction of these courts was not exclusive; that is, a case could be brought before a variety of courts, depending on the legal and political advantages that each offered. Moreover, each court was a separate entity: each had a judge and a staff.

Such an organizational structure meant that cases could not be shifted from an overloaded court to one with little to do. Each court also produced patronage jobs for the city's political machines.

The sporadic and unplanned expansion of the American court system has resulted in an often-confusing structure. Each state system is different. Although some states have adopted a unified court structure, others still have numerous local courts with overlapping jurisdictions. To reduce confusion, we will examine state courts at four levels: trial courts of limited jurisdiction, trial courts of general jurisdiction, intermediate appellate courts, and courts of last resort. Table 3.1 summarizes the tremendous volume of cases decided each year by state courts.

Trial Courts of Limited Jurisdiction: Lower Courts

At the first level of state courts are **trial courts of limited jurisdiction**, sometimes referred to as **inferior courts**, or more simply, **lower courts**. The United States has more than 11,880 trial courts of limited jurisdiction, staffed by approximately 27,179 judicial officers (Strickland, Schauffler, LaFountain, & Holt, 2015). The lower courts constitute 85 percent of all judicial bodies in the United States. Nine U.S. jurisdictions—California, Idaho, Illinois, Iowa, Maine, Minnesota, Missouri, the District of Columbia, and Puerto Rico—have unified court systems that do not use trial courts of limited jurisdiction. On the other hand, New York has nearly 1,500 and Texas has over 2,250 courts of limited jurisdiction.

Variously called district, justice, justice of the peace, city, magistrate's, or municipal courts, the lower courts decide a restricted range of cases. Most of these courts are created by city or county governments and therefore are not part of the state judiciary. Thus, lower courts are typically controlled only by the local governmental bodies that create them and fund them.

Cases in the Lower Courts

The caseload of the lower courts is staggering—more than 62 million cases a year, the overwhelming number of which are traffic cases (nearly 39 million in any given year—see Table 3.1). Thus, these are the courts with which the average citizen is most likely to come into contact.

Lower-court judges typically authorize search warrants. In addition, the lower courts are primarily responsible for handling the early stages of felony criminal cases. Thus, after an arrest, a judge in a trial court of limited jurisdiction will hold the initial appearance, appoint counsel for indigent defendants, and conduct the preliminary hearing, if applicable. Later, the case is transferred to a trial court of general jurisdiction for trial (or plea) and sentencing. But the bulk of the work in the lower courts involves several types of nonfelony criminal cases and small claims of a civil nature.

Lower courts typically adjudicate two types of nonfelony criminal cases: misdemeanors and ordinance violations. Lower courts also adjudicate all of the traffic offenses in a jurisdiction.

Nonfelony Criminal Cases

A **misdemeanor** is a crime punishable by a fine, imprisonment (usually in a local jail, for a period of less than one year), or both. Misdemeanors are enacted by state legislative bodies and cover the entire state.

Most legislatures also designate certain minor offenses as **violations** (referred to as *infractions* or *petty offenses* in some states). Violations are usually punishable only by a fine, although some jurisdictions authorize short jail sentences of fewer than 10, 15, or 30 days for certain violations. In most states, violations are quasi-criminal, meaning that they are not considered true crimes for the purposes of a criminal record.

Laws passed by a local governing body, such as a city council, are called **ordinances**. They are similar in effect to a legislative statute, but they apply only to the locality, and any fine that is assessed for violations goes to the local government, not to the state. It is typical for ordinances to prohibit the same types of conduct (for example, disorderly conduct and public drunkenness) as state misdemeanors. Ordinance violations are technically noncriminal, which means that they are easier to prosecute. At times, police prefer to arrest a suspect for an ordinance violation because it presents fewer legal obstacles to gaining a conviction.

Traffic Offenses

Traffic offenses refer to a group of offenses involving self-propelled motor vehicles. These violations range from parking violations to improper equipment. Speeding is the most common traffic offense, followed by driving without a license, and driving while a license is suspended or revoked.

For a time, the number of traffic cases heard in the lower courts was declining, but no longer. During the past decade, the volume of traffic cases has increased (LaFountain et al., 2015). Although Texas leads the nation in terms of the number of traffic cases each year (roughly 8.1 million), that translates into approximately 30,036 traffic cases per 100,000 people. In contrast, approximately 5.4 million traffic cases are filed each year in New Jersey, representing a national high of roughly 60,821 traffic cases per 100,000 people. Overall, as Table 3.1 illustrates, traffic cases constitute nearly 55 percent of lower-court caseloads.

Traffic offenses are typically punishable by fines. But because the volume of these cases is quite large, traffic tickets can be big moneymakers for local governments. Indeed, traffic fines and fees are a multibillion-dollar business in the United States.

The money a driver pays for a typical traffic ticket includes both fines and fees. Revenue generated from fines usually goes to the government that has created the court, either the city, the county, or the state. Typically, this revenue stream is then used to pay the expenses of the court itself (judges, clerks, and the like) as well as the prosecutor's office and the public defender, but not necessarily. Revenue generated from court-imposed fees, on the other hand, goes to the court itself. In some jurisdictions, these fees are used to support important court matters, such as expenses of the public defender's office and reimbursing jurors. These revenues may also be dedicated to programs we have discussed throughout this book, including specialized courts, alternative dispute resolution (ADR) programs, driver education programs, victim compensation funds, and domestic violence facilities.

In some jurisdictions, the government makes a considerable profit from court-imposed fines. Over the years, some localities have become known as speed traps. Although this appears to be less true today, there are still some small towns that finance a considerable part of their expenses, including the police department, from tickets issued to out-of-town motorists. In Oklahoma, for example, revenue from traffic fines and fees fund upward of one-third of the budgets for a number of small towns with populations of fewer than 2,200; some of these small towns reported more revenue from traffic fines and fees than from local sales, use, alcohol, and tobacco taxes combined (Schammert, 2015).

When governments, whether state or local, are faced with a budget crisis, one place they often look for additional revenue without having to take the unpopular step of raising taxes is to increase fines and fees on traffic offenses. Florida, for example, facing a major budget shortfall during the Great Recession, increased traffic fines by a projected $63 million a year, sparing further budget cuts for courts, prosecutors, and public defenders (Dunkelberger, 2009). At the local level, in 2009 El Paso County, Colorado, reaped 147 percent more from moving violations than the year before thanks to an increase in traffic fines voted by the state legislature (Zubeck, 2009). Legislatures in more than 40 states likewise looked to solve some of their fiscal crises in a similar manner (Schwartz, 2009b).

Modern technology is making it even easier for local governments to generate more revenue through traffic enforcement. Across the nation, cities are installing cameras at traffic lights that take pictures of cars that run red lights. The result is often a significant increase in the citations generated by the computer and fines billed. In New Orleans, for example, traffic cameras generated more than 1.45 million tickets and $106.5 million in fines between 2008 and 2016 (Ferrand, 2016). If supporters say traffic cameras increase safety, critics say the red-light system is all about seeing green (Waller, 2008; Wessell, 2016). The use of traffic cameras to collect fines has been challenged in court (Ferrand, 2016; Roesler, 2009; Samuels, 2016). One such lawsuit alleged that using photographic evidence to nab speeders and red-light runners violates basic constitutional rights to due process, including the rights to be presumed innocent, to have a hearing before an impartial judicial official, and to have the opportunity to challenge the evidence. But the Ohio Supreme Court unanimously ruled that there were no constitutional violations, because these infractions are civil and not criminal (*Mendenhall v. Akron*, 2008).

On the other hand, some driving-related offenses, like driving under the influence (DUI), are serious enough that they are prosecuted as misdemeanors. Repeat or extreme cases of DUI are routinely classified as felonies today (see "Courts, Controversy, & Reducing Crime" on page 81).

Small Claims Civil Cases

On the civil side, the lower courts decide disputes under a set dollar amount; these cases are often referred to as "small claims." **Small claims courts** handle cases involving maximum amounts that range from a low of $2,500 in Kentucky and Rhode Island, to a high of $25,000 in Tennessee (NOLO, 2015). The trend is clearly in an upward direction. The largest number of cases falling under these dollar amounts is debt collection, primarily involving nonpayment for goods purchased or services rendered. Another major category includes landlord-tenant disputes—mostly claims by landlords against tenants concerning past-due rent, evictions, and property damage. A smaller number of

COURTS, CONTROVERSY, & REDUCING CRIME

Should DUI and Distracted Driving Prosecutions Be Increased?

Drinking and driving has been a problem since the invention of the automobile, but it did not gain recognition as a prominent social concern until the 1980s (Applegate, Cullen, Link, Richards, & Lanza-Kaduce, 1996). The group most responsible for focusing public attention on drinking and driving is Mothers Against Drunk Driving (MADD). Depending on the state, offenses related to driving while under the influence of alcohol or drugs is termed "driving under the influence" (DUI) or "driving while intoxicated" (DWI).

MADD is victim-oriented, with many leaders having themselves experienced a family death due to DUI violations. They are closely related to the victims' rights movement (see Chapter 9). Publicly, they are recognized as the leading proponents of increasing the criminal penalties for DUI. The almost sole emphasis on enforcement and punishment differs from other approaches, which stress the prevention of early alcohol use and treatment of alcohol dependence as better approaches to prevent drug and alcohol-related crashes (Powers-Jarvis, 2013; Hingson, Heeren, & Edwards, 2008).

For almost three decades, legislatures—under considerable pressure from MADD and other groups like it—have passed a variety of "get tough with drunk drivers" laws, including

- Increasing the drinking age to 21
- Lowering from 0.15 to 0.08 the blood alcohol content (BAC) level at which a person is presumed legally intoxicated
- Increasing jail penalties for DWI, particularly for repeat offenders
- Mandating that drivers who refuse to take a breathalyzer test will automatically lose their driver's license

But somehow the get-tough laws recently passed never seem to be harsh enough, so in subsequent years, legislatures are called upon to crack down even harder on DUI offenders. And when the threats of even more arrests and harsher punishments do not seem to be working, the agenda is shifted to technology—mandating that even first offenders be required to install a device that tests drivers and shuts down the car if it detects alcohol (MADD, 2015; Wald, 2006). Evolving

legislative agendas are crucial for organizations like MADD because they need to constantly motivate their constituents lest the organization lose momentum and also lose members.

To sociologist Joseph Gusfield, groups like MADD engage in symbolic politics, portraying DUI offenders as villains. The difficulty with this approach is that DUI arrestees reflect a range of social backgrounds, including ordinary citizens and at times even prominent members of the community. Moreover, the range of behavior varies greatly from a person barely at 0.08 and having caused no accident to those measuring near 0.30 (comatose for most people) who have killed several people. This analysis of MADD is reinforced by the organization's refusal to even discuss lowering the legal drinking age. MADD has long cast underage drinking in black-and-white terms, whereas many college officials see it as impossible gray. Raising the legal drinking age has not stopped student drinking, only displaced it, driving such activity off campus and behind doors, making it even more difficult to deal with (Hoover, 2008; Minton, 2013).

The absence of criminal stereotypes is compounded by the pervasive role of alcoholic beverages in American social and economic life. As a result, there is considerable societal ambivalence toward drinking and driving. Society is quick to condemn impaired drivers involved in serious accidents, but those who drive after a few drinks often evoke the attitude of "There but for the grace of God go I" (Gusfield, 1981).

The contradictions in societal attitudes toward drinking and driving explain why the enforcement of DUI laws is riddled with loopholes. These contradictions help us understand why actual enforcement of DUI laws blunts the cutting edge of the harsh penalties. Law on the books treats drinking and driving as a serious problem, but law in action sees DUI not as a criminal offense but as a traffic violation. The end product is not a series of absolutes propounded by MADD but rather a negotiated reality (Homel, 1988). With the imposition of tougher laws

- Police do not necessarily make more arrests. Faced with serious crime problems, big-city police forces assign higher priority to violent offenders than to DUI offenders (Mastrofski & Ritti, 1996).
- Prosecutors are pressured to plea-bargain. Given that local jails are already overcrowded and most defendants

(Continued)

(Continued)

are not as villainous as public images suggest, pleas to lesser charges such as reckless driving are often arranged.

- Juries are reluctant to convict. As discussed in Chapter 13, if jurors think the penalty is too harsh for the crime, they are less likely to convict.
- As more people go to jail for longer times following DUI convictions, the prisons become overcrowded, which necessitates shortening actual sentences (Vermont Center for Justice Research, 1995).
- Those who lose their licenses may continue to drive, and those previously convicted may continue to drive while impaired. Indeed, one survey found that more than half the persons in local jails charged with DUI had prior sentences for DUI offenses (Cohen, 1992).

Overall, studies of DUI laws tend to be skeptical of a deterrent effect of get-tough legislation (Fradella, 2000; Pinto, 2011). Typically, new, tougher laws are ushered in with announcements of a major crackdown followed by increased arrests for DWI. But over time, levels of drinking and driving return to previous levels as the perceived certainty of punishment declines with experience (Homel, 1988; Ross, 1992). For example, one study found "no evidence that lowering the BAC to 0.08 reduced fatality rates but other approaches like seat belt laws have been effective" (Freeman, 2007).

What works and what does not in reducing DUI fatalities is now being applied to a major new highway safety threat—texting while driving (Lowy, 2009). The National Transportation Safety Board has declared that texting, e-mailing, or talking on a cell phone while driving is simply too dangerous to be allowed. Indeed, cell phone use while driving is estimated to cause at least 26% of all car accidents each year in the United States (Ziv, 2015). Yet efforts to curb such dangerous practices quickly run into a basic problem—people engage in such behavior because they like to and because they do not think it is dangerous. Thus, these so-called driver distraction laws are often unpopular. And in a democracy, governmental efforts to enforce unpopular laws (which requires expenditures of tax dollars) often prove difficult.

What do you think? Should there be tougher punishments for DUI, or are current punishment levels about right? Should more efforts be made to arrest and prosecute impaired drivers, or is the current level of effort about right? And what should be done about drivers who operate vehicles while distracted by their cell phones? Overall, how do punishment and enforcement levels of DUI and distracted-driver laws compare with other social problems, such as domestic violence and drug abuse?

small claims cases involve alleged property damage, largely stemming from automobile accidents.

In most states, streamlined procedures have been adopted to provide quick, inexpensive processing by dispensing with strict rules of evidence and the right to trial by jury. Accordingly, small claims cases are less formal and less protracted than other civil cases. Yet, as Table 3.1 illustrates, small claims that are filed in the courts of limited jurisdiction comprise roughly 52 percent of the civil cases filed each year in the nation's state courts.

Justice of the Peace Courts

The legal system in the United States is largely county-based, and approximately 80 percent of U.S. counties are rural. In most rural areas, the lower courts are collectively called **justice of the peace courts**. The officeholder is usually referred to simply as a **JP**. This system of local justice traces its origins to 14th-century England, when towns were small and isolated. The JP system developed as a way to dispense simple and speedy justice for minor civil and criminal cases. The emphasis was decidedly on the ability of local landowners, who served as part-time JPs, to decide disputes on the basis of their knowledge of the local community.

The small-town flavor of the JP system persists today (even in large urban places such as Harris County, Texas, which includes Houston, and Maricopa County, Arizona, which includes Phoenix). In the past, the vast majority of JPs were part-time non-lawyers who conducted court at their regular places of business—the back of the undertaker's parlor, the front counter of the general store, or next to the grease rack in the garage.

> Americans, particularly in rural Western areas, disfavored judges with formal legal training. Lawyers were viewed as obfuscators and oppressors because of their ability to interpret a complex web of common law decisions. Frontier justices themselves eschewed legal training, believing that ordinary people were just as capable of resolving disputes as lawyers. (Newton, Welch, & Hamilton, 2012, p. 33)

JPs were criticized for their legal incompetence and their broad discretion, which was often exercised in a politically biased manner. Reformers led efforts to disband JP courts with great success in most of the country, especially in areas with growing populations. The increased workloads and broader tax bases in these areas allowed for hiring legally trained judges to staff more formal courts. Today, in states in which JP courts survived, JPs tend to be more professional and hold court in a courthouse or another government building. Nonetheless, around 14 states still do not require that JPs be trained lawyers, and, as a result, they often fail to abide by the rules that are supposed to bind them (Mansfield, 1999; Newton, Welch, & Hamilton, 2012).

Many JPs are locally elected officials or mayors of small towns who serve *ex officio.* Other than U.S. citizenship and a local residency requirement, the only other qualifications to serve as a JP in many jurisdictions is to be over the age of 18, mentally competent, and be free of certain types of criminal convictions. In other words, JPs in some states not only do not have to be lawyers; they do not necessarily even need to be college or even high school graduates.

Critics argue that the JP system has outlived its purpose. It may have met the needs of the small, isolated towns of a century ago, but it is out of step with the modern era (Newton, Welch, & Hamilton, 2012). The ultimate goal of judicial reformers is to abolish the JP system altogether. A major defect is that JP courts are not part of the state judiciary; they are controlled only by the local government bodies that create and fund them. Only recently have judicial conduct commissions (see Chapter 8) been granted the authority to discipline or remove local judges who abuse their offices.

Nor are the activities of the lower courts subject to appellate scrutiny. Rarely are trial courts of limited jurisdiction courts of record; no stenographic record is kept of the witnesses' testimony or the judges' rulings. When a defendant appeals, the appeal is heard by a trial court of general jurisdiction. This court must conduct an entirely new trial, taking the testimony of the same witnesses and hearing the same attorneys' arguments as the lower court did. This is called a **trial** *de novo.*

Today, many JPs have been replaced with magistrates, who assume the same kinds of responsibilities as traditional JPs, but do not use that title. Magistrates are more likely to be appointed than elected and tend to have better training than JPs. For example, North Carolina has phased out its JPs and replaced them with magistrates, who are required to have more education and are appointed by the district court (Neubauer & Meinhold, 2017).

Overall, the issues facing rural courts are qualitatively different from those faced by urban courts (Baehler & Mahoney, 2005; Nugent-Borakove, Mahoney, & Whitcomb, 2011). Compared to their big-city counterparts, rural courts exhibit three special features: lower caseloads, lack of resources, and greater familiarity (Bartol, 1996; see also McKeon & Rice, 2009; Nurgent-Borakove et al., 2011).

Lower Caseloads

Caseloads in rural courts are lighter than those in suburban or urban courts, largely because of higher crime rates in urban areas as compared with rural ones. This is particularly true of violent offenses, which are more than four times more likely to occur in urban as opposed to rural areas (Lee, 2008; Thompson, 1996; Weisheit, Falcone, & Wells, 2006). But this does not mean that rural citizens do not experience crime. Over the past decades, rural crime rates have increased significantly. In fact, the rates of certain violent crimes, such as rape, have risen in rural areas such that they exceed those in big cities (National Center for Victims of Crime, 2015; see also Berg & Lauritsen, 2016). And some types of crime—DUI and fraud, for example—are more prevalent in rural areas. Moreover, illegal drug use is increasingly common in rural areas, so much so that the "scourge of social and criminal problems associated with the methamphetamine epidemic" is putting a stress on rural courts (White, 2008).

Treating drug addiction is more difficult in rural areas because of the lack of public transportation, the shortage of treatment facilities, and the additional resources necessary to treat the medical conditions of addicts (Cooper, 2003).

Rural settings present unique problems for domestic violence cases (Benson, 2016; Pruitt, 2008). And rural areas also tend to harbor hate groups, militia, and others who bill themselves as antigovernment.

Lack of Resources

Although rural courts have lower caseloads, this does not mean that they do not face problems processing their workloads. Rural courts receive less federal money and have a lower local tax base than larger counties (McDonald, Wood, & Pflug, 1996; McKeon & Rice, 2009). As a consequence, court facilities are often outmoded and salaries are low.

Lack of resources is a particular problem in criminal cases in which defendants are indigent (Chapter 7). Because few attorneys practice law in rural areas, the defense pool is limited. These built-in limitations have been compounded in recent years by cutbacks in federal funding. Rural areas have been hardest hit by drastic reductions in publicly funded legal services for the poor, resulting in ever dwindling access to justice for nonurban residents (Pruitt, McKinney, Fehrenbacher, & Johnson, 2015; Kerrigan, 2008).

Familiarity

Whereas big-city courts are characterized by the interface of numerous bureaucracies, in rural areas contacts are invariably one-on-one (Pruitt & Showman, 2014; Weisheit et al., 2006). The active bar consists of a dozen or fewer members, including the prosecutor, the judge, and the lawyer who represent the local government. Often, there are five or fewer sheriff's deputies and a single probation officer, each of whom is known to the judge. The clerk's office typically consists of two or three long-term employees.

Not only is the number of actors in rural courts small, but their interactions are frequent and long term. By and large, justice is administered by those who grew up in the community, and they are bound together by long-standing social and family networks. As a result, rural courts place greater emphasis on informal mechanisms of social control, whereas urban courts are more legalistic and formal (Pruitt & Showman, 2014; Weisheit et al., 2006).

Although such comity generally creates a friendly social atmosphere, it also can mean "You scratch my back, and I'll scratch yours." It's not always a conscious thing. The members of the courtroom work group are friends; some may even be related. Thus, some point to a lack of an independent judiciary and a weak adversarial process in many parts of rural America. The danger is that community knowledge is substituted for the Constitution. Some specific types of injustices include capricious arrests, unduly high bonds, rubber-stamping prosecutorial decisions, and pressuring defendants into pleading guilty (Glaberson, 2006; Sitomer, 1985; Waldron, 2008). Defendants who are not part of the community (either socially or geographically) may be at a disadvantage. These courts want to preserve the peace and their community's traditional values; however, doing so sometimes comes at the expense of minorities, the poor, and those considered "outsiders" (Sitomer, 1985; see also Pruitt, 2006).

Reforming JP Courts

Some reformers would unify state courts into a three-tier system, consisting of a single trial court that handles both major and minor cases, an intermediate appellate court, and a state high court of last resort. This reform would abolish the office of justice of the peace, require all judges to be lawyers, and eliminate the trial *de novo* system. The biggest change occurred in California, which began phasing out its JPs after a landmark 1974 decision in which the Supreme Court of California unanimously held that it was a violation of federal due process to allow a non-lawyer to preside over a criminal trial that could result in incarceration of the defendant (*Gordon v. Justice Court*, 1974). The remaining justice courts (as well as municipal courts) were eliminated by the passage of Proposition 220 in June 1998, which merged all lower courts within the state judicial branch into the superior courts (the courts of general jurisdiction). Under current California law, all California judges must be licensed attorneys. Notably, the U.S. Supreme Court disagreed with California's analysis of the Fourteenth Amendment in the landmark case of *North v. Russell* (1976), which is why JPs still exist in numerous states.

One major obstacle to abolition is the powerful influence of non-lawyer judges, who do not want their jobs abolished. Another is some people's belief that JPs are easily accessible, whereas more formal courts are miles away. For example, JPs are readily available to sign arrest warrants for the police or to try a motorist accused of driving too fast. JP courts are often viewed as people's courts, forums where people without much money can go to resolve their problems without the necessity of having a lawyer.

Historically, the low pay and equally low status of the JP did not attract highly qualified personnel. One survey showed that between a third and a half of California's lower-court judges were not even high school graduates (Ashman & Chapin, 1976). Perhaps most shocking of all, the assistant attorney general of Mississippi estimated that "33 percent of the justices of the peace are limited in educational background to the extent that they are not capable of learning the necessary elements of law" (*North v. Russell,* 1976). Although some states have moved to upgrade the quality of the personnel, others have not. In the state of New York, 75 percent of the JPs are not lawyers, and over the past three decades over 1,100 have been reprimanded by the Commission on Judicial Conduct. The problems that arise are perhaps best summed up in a quote from a JP who, after threatening to jail a woman because her dog was running loose, said: "I just follow my own common sense. And the hell with the law" (Glaberson, 2006). And the problems persist. A rural judge has been cited for levying over $11,000 in illegal fines and at least created the appearance he was doing so to provide additional revenue for the city (Gorman, 2009).

High on the judicial reformers' list of priorities has been upgrading the quality of lower-court judges, and they have made major strides. Many states have instituted training programs for lay judges. For example, Texas requires all newly selected JPs to attend a training seminar and provides ample opportunities for continuing judicial education. Indeed, most states now require judges

of limited jurisdiction courts to have graduated from law school and passed the state bar. But at least 18 states—Arizona, Colorado, Delaware, Georgia, Indiana, Kansas, Louisiana, Mississippi, Montana, Nevada, New Mexico, New York, South Carolina, Texas, Utah, West Virginia, Wisconsin, and Wyoming—allow non-lawyers to hold lower-court judgeships (Strickland et al., 2015).

Municipal Courts

The urban counterparts of the justice of the peace courts are **municipal courts**. The overriding reality of municipal courts in the nation's big cities is the press of cases. Accordingly, "obstacles" to speedy disposition—constitutional rights, lawyers, trials—are neutralized. In a process some have labeled an assembly line, shortcuts are routinely taken to keep the docket moving. Thus, the municipal courts more closely resemble a bureaucracy geared to mass processing of cases than an adjudicative body providing consideration for each case.

The emphasis on moving cases begins when the defendant is arraigned. Instead of addressing defendants individually—a time-consuming process—municipal court judges often open court by advising defendants of their constitutional rights as a group. Notification of rights is treated by the court as a clerical detail to be dispensed with before the taking of guilty pleas can begin.

Defense attorneys constitute another potential obstacle to the speedy disposition of cases. Although defendants have a theoretical right to be represented by an attorney, in practice the presence of an attorney in the lower courts is rare except for DUI prosecutions, for which defendants face potentially severe penalties. The general absence of defense attorneys reinforces the informality of the lower courts and the lack of attention to legal rules and procedures.

What of those too poor to hire a lawyer? In *Argersinger v. Hamlin* (1972), the Supreme Court ruled that "absent a knowing and intelligent waiver, no person may be imprisoned for any offense, whether classified as petty, misdemeanor, or felony unless he was represented by counsel." Thus, an indigent defendant may be fined without having a lawyer, but a judge considering imposing a jail term must give the impoverished defendant the opportunity to have a court-appointed counsel at state expense. Compliance, however, has generally been token in nature, meaning that the legal right to counsel in lower courts remains an empty right for many defendants.

In municipal courts, the defendant's initial appearance is usually the final one. Most people charged with a traffic violation or a minor misdemeanor plead guilty immediately. The quick plea represents the fatalistic view of most defendants: "I did it—let's get it over with." Realistically, a defendant charged with crimes such as public drunkenness and disorderly conduct probably cannot raise a valid legal defense. What has struck all observers of the lower courts is the speed with which the pleas are processed.

Few trials are held in the lower courts. A defendant has a right to a jury trial only if the offense can be punished by imprisonment for more than six months (*Baldwin v. New York*, 1970). The absence of attorneys and the minor nature of the offenses combine to make requests for jury trials rare. If there is a trial, it is a bench trial often conducted in an informal manner.

Assembly-Line Justice and the Courtroom Work Group

The courtroom work group often toils together to keep cases moving quickly. Some courts manipulate bail to pressure defendants into an immediate disposition. During arraignment, each defendant is informed of the right to a full hearing with a court-appointed attorney. But, if the hearing cannot be held for two or three weeks, during which time the defendant will have to be in jail, it is not surprising that the majority of defendants choose to waive their right to counsel in favor of a speedy disposition.

The routines of the lower courts are threatened, however, by uncooperative defendants. Judges and prosecutors dislike defendants who "talk too much." The accused who unreasonably take up too much of the court's time can expect sanctions. Consider the case of a young, middle-class, white man who made a detailed inquiry into his rights and then gave a relatively lengthy account (roughly two minutes) of his alleged offense of vagrancy. Although the defendant was polite, the judge interrupted him with "That will be all, Mr. Jones" and ordered him to jail. Other defendants who "talked too much" received sentences that were longer than normal (Mileski, 1971; see also Mack & Anleu, 2007).

Sentencing in the Lower Courts

Because few defendants contest their guilt, the lower courts are more sentencing institutions than true trial courts. The courtroom encounter is geared to making rapid decisions about which sentence to impose. The punishments imposed by lower-court judges include many of those found in the major trial courts—fines, probation, and jail. In the misdemeanor courts, however, judges can choose alternative sanctions, including community service, victim restitution, placement in substance-abuse treatment programs, mandatory counseling, and required attendance in education programs such as driver clinics (Meyer & Jesilow, 1997). Despite the diversity of potential sanctions, fines play a predominant role. Few misdemeanor defendants are sentenced to jail.

The sentencing process in the lower courts involves elements of both routinization and individualization. Lower-court judges define their role as "doing justice"; rather than merely being bound by rules of law, judges use their discretion to achieve what they believe to be a fair and just result (Meyer & Jesilow, 1997). In attempting to achieve justice, lower-court judges use readily identifiable characteristics to sort defendants into categories. In the lower courts, sentencing involves a process of quickly determining group averages. The result is a high degree of uniformity; by and large, a defendant gets the same sentence as all others in the same category. To the casual observer, the process appears to be an assembly line, but sentences can also be fitted to the specific defendant. During plea negotiations, there is some individual attention to cases. Despite sentencing consistencies, exceptions are made (Ragona & Ryan, 1983). The most important factors in both the routinization and the individualization of sentencing in the lower courts are the nature of the event and the defendant's criminal record.

The defendant's prior criminal record is also a key factor in sentencing. First offenders rarely receive a jail term. Indeed, for petty offenses, first offenders may be released without any penalty whatsoever. Repeaters are given more severe sanctions (Mileski, 1971). For example, a study of DUI dispositions in Sacramento, California, highlights the importance of a prior record and the nature of the event (Kingsnorth, Barnes, & Coonley, 1990). For defendants with no prior convictions, the likelihood of a reduction to a charge of reckless driving increased three to four times. Similarly, the probability of receiving a jail sentence increased dramatically for those with a prior record. The nature of the event (measured by the level of blood alcohol) also played a role. A low level of blood alcohol was of primary importance in the decision to reduce charges from DUI to reckless driving. Similarly, for defendants with a high level of alcohol in their systems, not only was a jail sentence much more likely, but also that jail term was probably lengthy. These two factors, of course, operate together. Defendants with no priors and low levels of blood alcohol fared much better than those with prior convictions and high levels of alcohol in their system. Studies like this one, however, rarely enter the public discourse.

Problems of the Lower Courts

For decades, reformers have criticized the lower courts, highlighting a variety of problems. Only a shadow of the adversary model of criminal justice can be found in these courts. Few defendants are represented by an attorney. Trials are rare. Rather than the rules of courtroom procedure, informality predominates. And some defendants have been denied fundamental legal rights, including the right to a trial, an impartial judge, and the presumption of innocence (Epstein, 2015; Glaberson, 2006). Jail sentences are imposed, sometimes with lightning speed and not always in accordance with law (Ashman, 1975; Glaberson, 2006). In short, practices that would be condemned if they occurred in higher courts are commonplace in the lower courts. Is this justice?

Research over the years has focused on four problem areas: inadequate financing, inadequate facilities, lax procedures, and unbalanced caseloads.

Inadequate Financing

In general, lower courts are funded locally. Sparsely populated counties and small municipalities often lack funds to staff and equip their courts adequately. Even when funds are available, there is no guarantee that local governments will spend money on the lower courts. In many cities, these courts are expected to produce revenue for local governments. Indeed, some lower courts generate revenues much greater than their operating expenses, yet they still lack adequate courtrooms and other facilities. Rather, the funds go to pay for city services.

Inadequate Facilities

Lower-court courtrooms are often crowded and noisy, with 100 or more people forced to spend hours waiting for their minute before the judge. Some are makeshift, hastily created in the side of a store or the back of a garage. In the state of New York, "Some of the courtrooms are not even courtrooms: tiny offices or basement rooms without a judge's bench or jury box" (Glaberson, 2006). Such courtroom conditions lack dignity and leave a bad impression, suggesting that the judiciary is more interested in collecting the fine for speeding than bothering to do justice. Such inadequate facilities are detrimental to the attitudes of the defendant, prosecutor, judge, and all others involved in the justice process.

Lax Court Procedures

Besides singling out inadequate facilities, critics of lower courts often cite lax procedures in the day-to-day administration of these courts. Many trial courts of limited jurisdiction do not have written rules for the conduct of cases. Conventional bookkeeping methods are often ignored. How much fine money was collected and how it was spent is often impossible to determine. You can find some information in the city budget but not in the court records; this frustrates any attempts to assess the effectiveness of these courts.

Unbalanced Caseloads

Many lower courts are characterized by moderate to heavy caseloads, but others appear to have little to do. Because of unbalanced caseloads, some courts have huge backlogs that they are ill equipped to handle. But because these courts are locally controlled, there is no way to equalize the workload.

Unbalanced caseloads are the clearest indication that any generalizations about the problems of the lower courts must be coupled with the observation that the nation's lowest tribunals are tremendously varied. From state to state, between one county and its neighboring county, and even within a city, wide discrepancies exist in the quality of justice rendered. There is no easy way to determine what is wrong (or even what is right) about these courts. Because of the wide disparity, it is best to examine rural justice of the peace courts separately from urban municipal courts. Although they share many problems, they are also sufficiently different to warrant separate treatment.

Community Justice

As court activities have been consolidated and streamlined, some of the qualities of locally dispensed justice have been lost. As a result, some court reformers continuously seek ways to reestablish court–community cooperation.

The central target of these community justice efforts is minor disputes between parties in ongoing relationships (domestic partners, neighbors, consumers–merchants, landlords–tenants, employees–employers). Examples include unruly children who annoy neighbors, dogs who defecate on the wrong lawns, owners who neglect their property, and acquaintances who dispute small debts. It is not clear what role the criminal justice system can play in resolving such private disputes. Yet private disagreements between friends, neighbors, and significant others are the steady diet of the police and the lower courts. A trial would only obscure the underlying issues because the problem is either irrelevant or immaterial to the legal action. In such interpersonal disputes, the person who files a complaint may be as "guilty" as the defendant. Many of these private disputes are essentially civil matters, yet criminal justice agencies must deal with them to head off the commission of a more serious crime. In addressing problems such as these, mediation programs seek

solutions not in terms of a formal finding by a judge but rather through compromise and bargaining. The goal is to seek long-term solutions in the hope the disputants will not return. The two most commonly mentioned types of programs are alternative dispute resolution and community courts.

Alternative Dispute Resolution

Efforts at court–community collaboration are but one example of a broader movement termed **alternative dispute resolution (ADR)**, which seeks to settle disputes by less adversarial means than the traditional legal processes (Coltri, 2009; Goldberg, Sander, Rogers, & Cole, 2012; Nolan-Haley, 2013). Many ADR programs function as alternatives to going to court. Others involve efforts to settle court cases after they have been filed but before they are tried by a judge. ADR efforts, such as **arbitration** and **mediation**, most often focus on civil matters, but nonserious criminal matters may also be included.

The rapid growth of ADR programs has produced a second-generation wave of reforms aimed at improving the qualifications of those who serve in these programs, often through the use of specialized community courts (Brown, 2005; Pou, 2005; Saini, 2016).

Community Courts

Courts across the nation are searching for ways to reach out in order to be more responsive to the needs of specific communities within their geographical jurisdictions. The phrase "justice community" refers to the range of organizations and people within any specific locale who have a stake in the justice system. It includes judges, court personnel, district attorneys, public defenders, private attorneys, probation departments, law enforcement personnel, community organizers, business groups, and others (Atherton, 2015; Borys, Banks, & Parker, 1999; Williams, 2007).

Often these outreach efforts lead to an emphasis on mediation of minor disputes. There are important organizational differences, though, between court-based mediation and community courts. **Community courts**, or community mediation programs, as they have sometimes been called, are government-sponsored (by either court or prosecutor), and as a result, these programs receive the bulk of their cases as referrals from criminal justice agencies. The dominant goal is to improve the justice system by removing minor cases from the court. In their view, cases such as simple assault, petty theft, and criminal trespass are prime candidates for mediation and not formal processing in the lower courts.

The community courts of today were initially termed "criminal justice–based mediation programs," also known as multidoor courthouses or neighborhood justice centers. Many of these dispute-resolution programs began with a primary emphasis on misdemeanor criminal cases and later added civil matters from the local small claims court and other sources. In a sense, they convert criminal matters to civil ones by treating the cases as matters for discussion between the individual disputants and not for processing between the state and the defendant. The Center for Court Innovation (2016) stresses that community courts are neighborhood-focused courts that attempt to harness the power of the justice system to address local problems.

The best-known community court in the nation is the Midtown Community Court in New York City. The Midtown experience was born of a profound frustration with quality-of-life crime in the neighborhood, particularly prostitution, graffiti, illegal vending, vandalism, and low-level drug offenses (Center for Court Innovation, 2009). Offenders are sentenced to make restitution to the community through work projects in the neighborhood: removing graffiti, cleaning subway stations, and sorting cans and bottles for recycling. But at the same time, the court attempts to link offenders with drug treatment, health care, education, and other social services. Perhaps one of the most distinctive features is that the courthouse includes an entire floor of office space for social workers to assist offenders referred by the judge in the courtroom a few floors below. Thus, instead of sending an offender to a distant bureaucracy, the courthouse now incorporates helping institutions within its midst. The Midtown Community Court is serving as a prototype for other jurisdictions as well (Clear, Hamilton, & Cadora, 2011).

Trial Courts of General Jurisdiction: Major Trial Courts

At the second level of state courts are the **trial courts of general jurisdiction**, usually referred to as *major trial courts.* An estimated 3,109 major trial courts in the 50 states and the District of Columbia are staffed by nearly 10,740 judges (Strickland, Schauffler, LaFountain, & Holt, 2015). The term *general jurisdiction* means that these courts have the legal authority to decide all matters not specifically delegated to lower courts. The specific division of jurisdiction between the lower courts and the major trial courts is specified by law—statutory, constitutional, or both. The most common names for these courts are district, circuit, and superior. The specific names used in all states are listed in Table 3.2.

The geographical jurisdictions of the major trial courts are defined along existing political boundaries, primarily counties. Each court has its own support staff consisting of a clerk of court, a sheriff, and others. In most states, the trial courts of general jurisdiction are also grouped into judicial districts or circuits. In rural areas these districts or circuits encompass several adjoining counties. Here, the trial court judges are true generalists who hear a wide variety of cases as they literally ride circuit, holding court in different counties on a fixed schedule. More populated counties have only one circuit or district for the area. Here, judges are often specialists assigned to hear only certain types of cases, such as criminal, family, juvenile, or civil. Refer to Table 3.1 for some basic workload data on the major trial courts.

As discussed in Chapter 2, the lion's share of the nation's judicial business takes place at the state, not the federal, level. As Table 3.1 specifies, about 31.9 million cases are filed each year in the major trial courts of the states, just shy of 89 times the number of similar filings in the federal district courts. Moreover, the types of cases filed in the state courts differ greatly from those filed in the federal courts. Litigants in federal courts are most often big businesses and governmental bodies. In sharp contrast, litigants in state courts are typically individuals and small businesses.

TABLE 3.2   Major Trial Courts in Different States

Circuit Court

Alabama, Arkansas,[a] Florida, Hawaii, Illinois, Indiana,[b] Kentucky, Maryland, Michigan, Mississippi,[a] Missouri, Oregon, South Carolina, South Dakota, Tennessee,[a] Virginia, West Virginia, Wisconsin

Court of Common Pleas

Ohio, Pennsylvania

District Court

Colorado, Idaho, Iowa, Kansas, Louisiana, Minnesota, Montana, Nebraska, Nevada, New Mexico, North Dakota, Oklahoma, Texas, Utah, Wyoming

Superior Court

Alaska, Arizona, California, Connecticut, Delaware,[a] District of Columbia, Georgia, Maine, Massachusetts, New Hampshire, New Jersey, North Carolina, Rhode Island, Vermont,[c] Washington

Supreme Court

New York[d]

[a]Arkansas, Delaware, Mississippi, and Tennessee have separate chancery courts with equity jurisdiction.
[b]Indiana uses superior and circuit courts.
[c]Vermont also uses district courts.
[d]New York also uses county courts.

Source: Based on data from Court Statistics Project. 2013. State Court Structure Charts. Williamsburg, VA: National Center for State Courts. Available online at http://www.courtstatistics.org/Other-Pages/State_Court_Structure_Charts.aspx.

Whereas federal courts hear a high percentage of cases dealing with white-collar crimes and major drug distribution, state courts decide primarily street crimes. The more serious criminal violations (felonies) are heard in the trial courts of general jurisdiction. Most of these criminal cases, however, do not go to trial, but rather are resolved by plea bargain (Chapter 12). Thus, the dominant issue in the trial courts of general jurisdiction is not guilt or innocence, but what penalty to apply to the guilty.

The public associates most of the felony cases in state courts of general jurisdiction with crimes of violence, such as murder, robbery, and rape. But as Chapter 10 explains, 90 percent of criminal violations involve nonviolent crimes (especially property crimes such as burglary and theft) and drug offenses. Drug-related offenses range from simple possession of small amounts of illicit drugs to the sale of large quantities of cocaine and heroin. The Bureau of Justice Statistics reports that drug offenses account for nearly one-third of all arrests, and nontrafficking drug offenses account for the largest percentage of all state court felony prosecutions (Reaves, 2013). The largest percentage of these cases involves marijuana.

In 2014, nearly 620,000 people were arrested for marijuana law violations, representing 40 percent of all drug arrests in the United States (FBI, 2015). Recently, however, some states have begun to decriminalize the possession of small amounts of marijuana, handing such possession as a violation, rather than a crime. Two states—Colorado and Washington—have even legalized recreational use of marijuana. The impact on the court systems of these states has yet to be seen, but presumably these changes in drug possession laws will reduce the volume of cases in state trial courts.

Intermediate Courts of Appeals

A century ago, state court systems included only a single appellate body—the state court of last resort. Like their federal counterparts, however, state courts have experienced a significant growth in appellate cases that threatens to overwhelm the state high court of last resort. State officials in 39 states have responded by creating **intermediate courts of appeals (ICAs)** (Exhibit 3.1). The only states that have not followed suit are sparsely populated ones with a low volume of appeals. The ICAs must hear all properly filed appeals. Subsequent appeals are at the discretion of the higher court. Thus, a decision by the state's intermediate appellate court is the final one for most cases.

The structure of the ICAs varies in several ways. Twenty-four states organize their ICAs on a statewide basis and the rest on a regional basis. In most

| EXHIBIT 3.1 | Intermediate Courts of Appeals (Number of Judges in Different States) |

APPEALS COURT

Massachusetts (28)

APPELLATE COURT

Connecticut (9), Illinois (51)

APPELLATE DIVISION OF SUPERIOR COURT

New Jersey (35)

APPELLATE DIVISIONS OF SUPREME COURT

New York (49)

APPELLATE TERMS OF SUPREME COURT

New York (13)

COMMONWEALTH COURT

Pennsylvania (9)

COURT OF APPEALS

Alaska (3), Arizona (22), Arkansas (12), Colorado (22), Georgia (12), Idaho (4), Indiana (15), Iowa (9), Kansas (14), Kentucky (14), Michigan (28), Minnesota (19), Mississippi (10), Missouri (32), Nebraska (6), New Mexico (10), North Carolina (15), Oregon (13), South Carolina (10), Tennessee[a] (12), Utah (7), Virginia (11), Washington (22), Wisconsin (16)

COURTS OF APPEAL

California (105), Louisiana (53), Ohio (69)

COURTS OF APPEALS

Texas (80)

COURT OF CIVIL APPEALS

Alabama (5), Oklahoma (12)

COURT OF CRIMINAL APPEALS

Alabama (5), Tennessee (12)

COURT OF SPECIAL APPEALS

Maryland (12)

DISTRICT COURT OF APPEALS

Florida (61)

INTERMEDIATE COURT OF APPEALS

Hawaii (6)

SUPERIOR COURT

Pennsylvania (23)

TEMPORARY COURT OF APPEALS

North Dakota (3)[b]

NONE

Delaware, District of Columbia, Maine, Montana, Nevada, New Hampshire, Rhode Island, South Dakota, Vermont, West Virginia, Wyoming

[a]Civil only

[b]This temporary court was created in 1987 to hear cases specifically assigned to it by the North Dakota Supreme Court. It continues to operate as of the writing of this edition.

Source: Malega, Ron, and Thomas H. Cohen. 2013. *State Court Organization, 2011.* Washington, DC: U.S. Department of Justice, Office of Justice Programs, Bureau of Justice Statistics.

states, these bodies hear both civil and criminal appeals. Alabama and Tennessee, however, have separate courts of appeals for civil and criminal cases. Like their federal counterparts, these courts typically use rotating three-judge panels for deciding cases.

The ICAs handle the bulk of the caseload in the appellate system, and their workload has increased dramatically in the past decade. States have created these courts and given them additional judgeships in hopes of relieving the state high courts of last resort of crushing caseloads, only to find that the ICAs experience the same problems.

ICAs will be covered in more detail in Chapter 15, but in general, intermediate courts of appeals engage primarily in error correction; they review trials to make sure that the law was followed. The overall standard is one of fairness—the defendant is entitled to a fair trial but not a perfect one. As a result, defendants find that appellate courts are markedly unsympathetic to their legal arguments; only a small percentage of such appeals results in a victory. Moreover, those victories are often temporary ones, since the handful of defendants who win the right to a new trial are often reconvicted during their second trial. Thus, although the public perceives that appellate courts are prone to release defendants on technicalities, the opposite is true.

As we will shortly see, the intermediate courts of appeals represent the final stage of the process for most litigants. Very few cases make it to the appellate court in the first place, and of those cases, only a handful will be heard by the state's highest appellate court.

State High Courts of Last Resort

The court of last resort is generally referred to as the **state high court of last resort**. The specific names vary from state to state, and to further complicate the picture, Texas and Oklahoma have two courts of last resort—one for civil appeals and another for criminal appeals. The number of state high court judges varies from a low of five to as many as nine (see Exhibit 3.2). Unlike the intermediate appellate courts, these courts do not use panels in making decisions; rather, the entire court participates in deciding each case. All state high courts of last resort have a limited amount of original jurisdiction

in dealing with matters such as disciplining lawyers and judges.

In states without an intermediate court of appeals, however, state high courts of last resort have no power to choose which cases will be placed on its docket; in most other states, the high court has a purely discretionary docket. As with the U.S. Supreme Court, the state high courts of last resort select only a few cases to hear, but these cases tend to have broad legal and political significance. The ability of most state high courts of last resort to choose which cases to hear and which cases not to hear makes them important policy-making bodies. Whereas intermediate appellate courts review thousands of cases each year looking for errors, state high courts of last resort handle a hundred or so cases that present the most challenging legal issues arising in that state.

Nowhere is the policy-making role of state high courts of last resort more apparent than in deciding death penalty cases. In most states with death penalty laws, if the judge imposes the death penalty, then the case is automatically appealed to the state's highest court, thus bypassing the intermediate courts of appeals. Because of the high stakes, state high courts of last resort expend considerable time and energy in reviewing these cases.

EXHIBIT 3.2   Courts of Last Resort in Different States (Number of Judges)

SUPREME COURT

Alabama (9), Alaska (5), Arizona (5), Arkansas (7), California (7), Colorado (7), Connecticut (7), Delaware (5), Florida (7), Georgia (7), Guam (3), Hawaii (5), Idaho (5), Illinois (7), Indiana (5), Iowa (7), Kansas (7), Kentucky (7), Louisiana (7), Michigan (7), Minnesota (7), Mississippi (9), Missouri (7), Montana (7), Nebraska (7), Nevada (7), New Hampshire (5), New Jersey (7), New Mexico (5), North Carolina (7), North Dakota (5), Northern Mariana Islands (3), Ohio (7), Oklahoma[a] (9), Oregon (7), Pennsylvania (7), Puerto Rico (9), Rhode Island (5), South Carolina (5), South Dakota (5), Tennessee (5), Texas[a] (9), Utah (5), Vermont (5), Virgin Islands (3), Virginia (7), Washington (9), Wisconsin (7), Wyoming (5)

COURT OF APPEALS

District of Columbia (9), Maryland (7), New York (7)

SUPREME JUDICIAL COURT

Maine (7), Massachusetts (7)

COURT OF CRIMINAL APPEALS

Oklahoma[a] (5), Texas[a] (9)

SUPREME COURT OF APPEALS

West Virginia (5)

---

[a]Two courts of last resort in these states.

Source: Malega, Ron, and Thomas H. Cohen. 2013. *State Court Organization, 2011.* Washington, DC: U.S. Department of Justice, Office of Justice Programs, Bureau of Justice Statistics.

The outcomes of these reviews, though, vary greatly from state to state; some state high courts of last resort rarely overturn a death penalty decision, but others are very prone to reverse it.

The state high courts of last resort are the ultimate review board for matters involving interpretation of state law. The only other avenue of appeal for a disgruntled litigant is the U.S. Supreme Court, but successful applications are few and must involve important questions of federal law. Chapter 15 will probe why many state high courts of last resort have in recent years emerged as significant governmental bodies. In state after state, the supreme courts are deciding issues that have a major impact on the law and government of their jurisdiction.

Court Unification

Historically, court reform focused on organizational structure. To court reformers, the multiplicity of courts is inefficient (because judges cannot be shifted to meet the caseload needs of other courts) and also inequitable (because the administration of justice is not uniform). Thus, traditional court reform has most often identified with implementing a unified court system. Figure 3.1 provides a diagram of a state (Florida) with a unified court system; Figure 3.2 offers a contrasting diagram of a state (Texas) with limited unification.

Key Components

The principal objective of a **unified court system** is to shift judicial administration from local control to centralized management. The loose network of independent judges and courts is replaced by a coherent hierarchy with authority concentrated in the state capital. Although court reformers differ about the exact details of a unified court system, their efforts reflect five general principles: a simplified court structure; centralized administration, rulemaking, and judicial budgeting; and statewide financing (Berkson & Carbon, 1978).

Simplified Court Structure

Court reformers stress the need for a **simplified court structure** with a simple, uniform court structure for the entire state. In particular, the multiplicity of minor and specialized courts, which often have overlapping jurisdiction, would be consolidated in one county-level court. This would mean that variations between counties would be eliminated and replaced by a similar court structure throughout the state. Overall, the court reformers envision a three-tier system: a state court of last resort at the top, intermediate courts of appeal where the volume of cases makes it necessary, and a single trial court.

Centralized Administration

Reformers envision **centralized administration**, with the state high court of last resort, working through court administrators, providing leadership for the state court system. The state court system would embody a genuine hierarchy of authority, in which local court administrators would be required to follow the policy directives of the central office and would in turn be held accountable by the state high court of last resort. Thus, a centralized state office would supervise the work of judicial and nonjudicial personnel.

Centralized Rule Making

Reformers argue that the state high courts of last resort should have the power to adopt uniform rules to be followed by all courts in the state. Examples of **centralized rule making** include procedures for disciplining errant attorneys and time standards for disposing of cases. In addition, judges could be temporarily assigned to other courts to alleviate backlogs and reduce delay. Centralized rule making would shift control from the legislature to judges and lawyers.

Centralized Judicial Budgeting

Centralized judicial budgeting would give the state judicial administrator (who reports to the state high court of last resort) the authority to prepare a single budget for the entire state judiciary and send it directly to the legislature. The governor's power to recommend a judicial budget would be eliminated. Likewise, lower courts would be dependent on the state high court of last resort for their monetary needs and unable to lobby local representatives directly. Thus, decisions about allocating funds would be made at the state and not the local level.

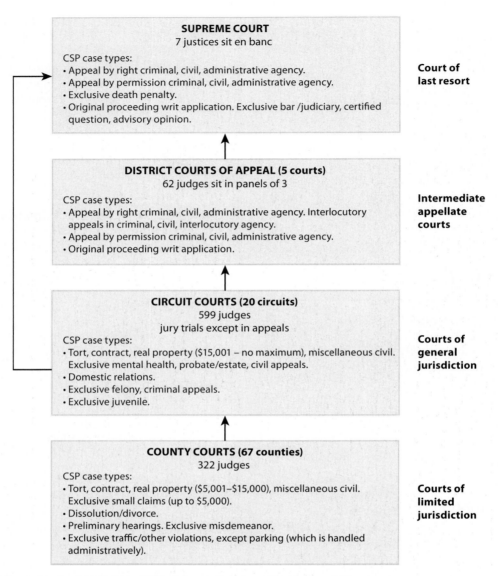

FIGURE 3.1 Example of a State with a Unified Court Structure: Florida Court Structure

Statewide Financing

Along with centralized judicial budgeting, reformers argue for the adoption of **statewide financing** of the judiciary. Although courts are mandated by state law, they are often financed in whole or in part by local governments. Given that courts are often not a high priority for local government, they end up with less-than-adequate local financing. State government, in contrast, has more money and could better support necessary court services. But budgetary woes caused by the Great Recession caused many states to experience significant budget deficits which, in turn, led to reductions in critical funding for the courts. Yet at the same time, public demands for court services are increasing. Faced with these realities, court leaders are being encouraged to examine zero-cost or very-low-cost innovations (Broccolina & Zorza, 2008).

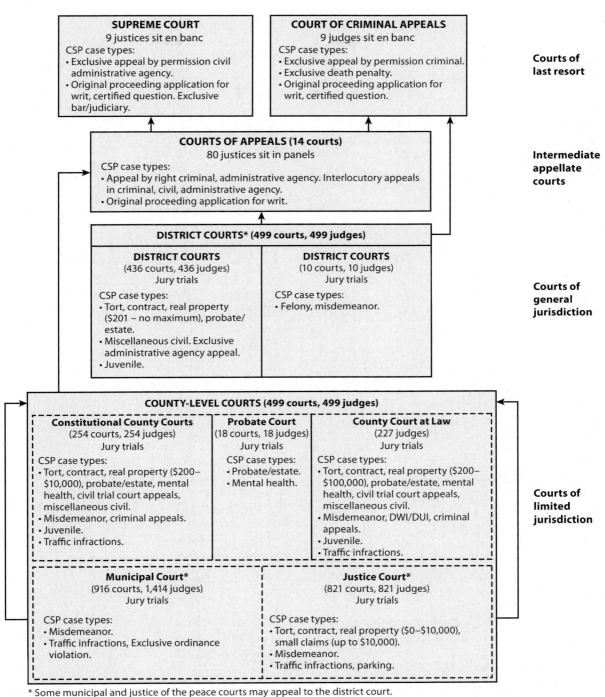

FIGURE 3.2 Example of a State with Limited Court Unification: Texas Court Structure

Analysis

The assumptions and philosophy of traditional notions of court reform have been called into serious question. Some scholars believe that the old principles of court reorganization hamper creative thinking about the direction court reform should take (Flango, 1994; Lamber & Luskin, 1992). One concern is that the concept of a unified court system does not allow for a desirable diversity. The standard blueprint of court organization fails to consider, for example, important differences in the working environment of courts in densely populated cities as opposed to those in sparsely inhabited rural areas.

Critics have also charged that traditional concepts of court reform stress abstract ideals of court organization (law on the books) to the neglect of the realities of the courthouse (law in action) (Baar, 1980). As a result, court reformers suffer from elite bias. Their perceptions of the problems of the courthouse extend only to cases with policy significance involving major community actors and rarely extend to ordinary cases affecting average citizens. In the biting words of Laura Nader (1992), court reformers talk about ridding the courts of "garbage cases," which include domestic violence, substance abuse, and neglected children. The solutions proposed by lawyer elites seem unresponsive to the realities of ordinary cases heard in the nation's trial courts. A judiciary with a clearly delineated organizational structure staffed by judges selected on the basis of merit (see Chapter 8) will face the same problems of large caseloads and types of cases—juvenile delinquency, for example—that are difficult to decide. Moreover, courts, no matter how well organized, must cope with public sentiments demanding getting tough with crime (see "Case Close-Up: *Ewing v. California* and Three Strikes Laws").

Problem-Solving Courts

Contemporary court reform in the United States concentrates more on improving the quality of justice meted out by courts and less on providing a neat organizational chart. The modern agenda of court reform includes topics such as reducing trial court delay (Chapter 5), improving the efficiency of the appellate courts (Chapter 15), creating alternative dispute resolution, and establishing community courts.

Contemporary court reform is often identified with problem-solving courts (Boldt, 2014; Wolf, 2007). Although problem-solving courts vary considerably from place to place, they all emphasize addressing the underlying issue of the individual appearing in court. Moreover, these judicial bodies actively collaborate with service providers (Boldt, 2014; Casey & Rottman, 2004).

Contemporary court reform involves the creation of specialized courts to deal with specific types of cases. Initially, these were called "designer courts" or "boutique courts," indicating their specialized nature. Today, drug courts represent the most numerous and widely adopted type of problem-solving court. In addition to the roughly 3,150 drug courts in operation in the United States and its territories today, as Table 3.3 illustrates, there are approximately 1,310 other problem-solving courts, including mental health courts, domestic violence court, child support court, prisoner reentry court, prostitution court, gun court, and other specialized courts that include courts for people of certain ages, such as teen court or elder court (National Institute of Justice, 2017). Many of these specialized courts rely on **therapeutic jurisprudence** (Amendola, 2010; Boldt, 2014; Rosenthal, 2002; Wexler & Winick, 1996), which is characterized by five essential elements:

1. Immediate intervention
2. Nonadversarial adjudication
3. Hands-on judicial involvement
4. Treatment programs with clear rules and structured goals
5. A team approach that brings together the judge, prosecutors, defense counsel, treatment provider, and correctional staff (Rottman & Casey, 1999)

Drug courts, domestic violence courts, and mental health courts are prime examples of courts based on the concept of therapeutic jurisprudence.

CASE CLOSE-UP   *Ewing v. California* and Three Strikes Laws

Forty-year-old Gary Ewing was caught moments after he attempted to steal three golf clubs, which he had hidden in his pants leg. Under normal circumstances Ewing would have been prosecuted for a misdemeanor violation. But his background of several previous convictions marked the case as unusual. Thus, the Los Angeles District Attorney decided to prosecute Ewing under California's "three strikes and you're out" law; as a result, he was sentenced to 25 years in prison without parole.

Three Strikes laws have become an increasingly popular reaction to citizen frustrations over crime. As discussed further in Chapter 14, these laws systematically increase potential prison sentences for defendants who have been convicted of violent offenses. In California, however, only one of the convictions must be for a violent crime, thus adding to the controversy in the nation's most populous state. Critics argue that such laws are fundamentally unfair because the sentence is disproportionate to the actual crime committed. However, in *Ewing v. California* a majority of the U.S. Supreme Court rejected this argument, holding that the sentence was not disproportionate and hence not a violation of the Eighth Amendment prohibition against cruel and unusual punishment.

Justice O'Connor's opinion for the majority stressed that in enacting Three Strikes laws, the California legislature had made a deliberate policy choice that individuals who repeatedly engage in serious or violent criminal behavior have not been deterred by conventional punishments, and therefore society can protect itself by isolating the defendant. Justice Stevens and three other justices dissented, arguing that a 25-year sentence for such a petty offense was "grossly disproportionate" and therefore constituted cruel and unusual punishment.

These laws increase the volume of criminal prosecutions. Note that Gary Ewing would normally have been tried in a misdemeanor court, where costs are low and trials are few. Instead, he was prosecuted in a more costly felony court, where trials are more likely and also more time consuming.

In California, for example, felony jury trials increased by nearly 10 percent after the state enacted its Three Strikes law (Brown & Jolivette, 2005; Chen, 2014). The felony trial rate more than quintupled in Los Angeles (Schultz, 2000).

Ample evidence shows that such get-tough policies have resulted in uneven application of the laws. According to a study by the nonpartisan California Legislative Analyst's Office (Brown & Jolivette, 2005), in some counties, California prosecutors "seek Three Strikes enhancements only in certain cases, such as for certain types of crimes that are particular problems in their county or when the current offense is serious or violent. In other counties, prosecutors seek Three Strikes enhancements in most eligible cases" (para. 36). Three Strikes laws also give prosecutors enormous leverage in forcing a defendant to accept a plea bargain (Chen, 2014; Ryan, 2002). The risk of conviction at trial may even lead an innocent person facing a third strike to plead guilty.

In addition, Three Strikes laws contribute to great variations in sentencing. For example, California's Kern County is 13 times more likely to send someone to state prison with a strike enhancement than San Francisco County is (Brown & Jolivette, 2005). Finally, these laws have had a tremendous impact on corrections. Not only have Three Strikes laws increased the number of pretrial inmates being detained in local jails, but also they have resulted in a growing and aging prison population (Brown & Jolivette, 2005; see also Chapter 14).

Supporters of Three Strikes laws point to falling crime rates as evidence of the law's effectiveness. But there is little agreement among researchers about these laws' impact on crime and public safety. Consider that the "violent crime rate in those counties least likely to send strikers to prison declined by an average of 45 percent, while the violent crime rate in the counties most likely to send strikers to prison declined by an average of 44 percent" (Brown & Jolivette, 2005, para. 50).

Drug Courts

The emergence of **drug courts** illustrates how the judiciary is responding both to increases in caseload and changes in the types of cases being brought to court. In the mid-1980s, drug caseloads increased dramatically in courts throughout the country. As a centerpiece of the so-called war on drugs, elected officials across the nation backed efforts to arrest, prosecute, and imprison persons possessing or selling illegal drugs. As a result, arrests for drug-related violations represent the largest single category of police activity, particularly in the nation's major urban areas.

TABLE 3.3	Number and Types of Specialized Courts

Specialized Courts

Type of Court	Number
Drug Courts	
Adult	1,558
Juvenile	409
Family	312
Veterans	306
DWI	284
Tribal	138
Co-occurring	70
Reentry	29
Federal district	27
Federal veterans	6
Campus	3
Total drug courts	3,142

Other Specialized Courts

Mental health courts	427
Truancy courts	267
Domestic violence courts	176
Other problem-solving courts	168
Child support courts	68
Community courts	57
Federal reentry courts	44
Reentry courts	33
Prostitution courts	30
Homelessness courts	22
Sex offender courts	8
Parole violation courts	6
Gun courts	2
Federal problem-solving courts	2
Total of other problem-solving courts	1,310

Source: National Institute of Justice, Office of Justice Programs. 2017. *Specialized Courts.* Available online at https://www.nij.gov/topics/courts /pages/specialized-courts.aspx

Faced with a rapidly increasing caseload of types of cases that did not seem to fit the traditional criminal court model, courts began to experiment with new ways of processing cases by creating drug courts. Rather than viewing these defendants as criminals, they saw them as persons with an addiction problem. Drug courts emphasize treatment. The assumption was that treatment would reduce the likelihood that convicted drug offenders would be rearrested.

The first drug court was created in 1989 in Dade County, Florida Circuit Court (in which the city of Miami is located). To be eligible, defendants must have had no prior felony convictions, must have been charged with possession only (not sale), and must have admitted their drug problem and requested treatment. Such offenders were diverted into treatment. A judge, in addition to probation officers, monitored offenders' progress by requiring participants to report periodically to the court. The judge assessed offenders' progress and moved them through the phases of the program.

Since the advent of the first drug court, these specialized courts have grown to become an important part of the criminal justice system (Belenko, 2001; Shomade, 2012; Winick, 2013). There are approximately 3,150 drug courts operating in the 50 states today (National Drug Court Resource Center, 2015). Early drug courts had the simple goal of reducing drug use and recidivism by monitoring offenders through weekly court visits, drug testing, and supervision by probation officers and judges alike. It soon became clear that offenders needed more indepth treatment in order to change behavior patterns so that long-term goals of reduced criminal activities and drug use could be maintained after the offender was out of the program (Belenko, 2001; Gallagher, Nordberg, & Kennard, 2015).

The Effectiveness of Drug Courts

Initial evaluations of early drug courts found favorable rates of success. For example, as compared with defendants not in the program, offenders in the Dade County drug court treatment program had lower incarceration rates, less frequent rearrests, and longer times to rearrest (Goldkamp & Weiland, 1993). More sophisticated evaluations, however, have highlighted the complex impact of drug courts. In Washington, D.C., participation in a drug court treatment program has been relatively poor—only 41 percent of those eligible chose to participate. Moreover, completion of the program took much longer than anticipated; cases were open an average of 11 months as opposed to the 6 months estimated (Harrell, Cavanagh, & Roman, 2000).

More recent studies support the earlier conclusions that drug courts have a positive impact (Downey & Roman, 2010; Huddleston & Marlowe, 2011; Cheesman, Scott, Holt, Kunkel, Lee, & White, 2016). Most drug court studies have found:

- that overall treatment retention is substantially better than in other community-based treatment programs for offenders (Belenko, 2001; Springer & Roberts, 2007; Goldkamp, White, & Robinson, 2001; U.S. Government Accountability Office, 2005; Marlowe, 2016);

- lower recidivism rates from drug court participants than for comparison groups (Banks & Gottfredson, 2004; Belenko, 2001; Gottfredson, Najaka, & Kearley, 2003; Springer & Roberts, 2007; Marlowe, 2016); and

- a net cost savings to the criminal justice system by providing offenders with treatment that is much less expensive than incarcerating them (Aos, Miller, & Drake, 2006; Belenko, 2001; Carey, Finigan, & Pukstas, 2008; Logan, Hoyt, McCollister, French, Leukefeld, & Minton, 2004; Springer & Roberts, 2007; Marlowe, 2016).

But the impact of drug courts varies by time, manner, and place (Goldkamp, 2002). Moreover, the drug court model appears to be relatively ineffective when applied to drunk drivers (Bouffard & Richardson, 2007; Eckberg & Jones, 2015). Completion of drug court reduced recidivism among non-DUI offenders, but there was no significant reduction in recidivism among chronic DUI offenders (Bouffard, Richardson, & Franklin, 2010).

Juvenile Drug Courts

Some jurisdictions have extended the therapeutic jurisprudence model of drug courts to youthful offenders (Belenko, 2001; Henggler, McCart, Cunningham, & Chapman, 2012). Although dramatically fewer in number than adult drug courts, juvenile drug courts quickly emerged "as one of the most popular means of diversionary treatment within the juvenile justice system" (Miller, Ventura-Miller, and Barnes, 2007, pp. 246–247).

Juvenile drug courts use judicial and multiagency teams (e.g., prosecutors, defense attorneys, treatment providers, school officials) to provide intensive and continuous supervision of participants to ensure "compliance with the court-imposed conditions of participation," such as "treatment program participation, school attendance, drug testing, community service, court appearances" (Cooper, 2001, p. 6). Frequent court appearances for active judicial involvement in case management, juvenile accountability, and a behaviorally based system of rewards and sanctions (especially using community service and curfews) are all key differences from regular juvenile courts. In addition, juvenile drug courts offer earlier and "far more comprehensive assessments of offenders based on an integration of cumulative information, a heavy concentration on family functioning, and highly coordinated services for offenders and their families" (Gilmore, Rodriguez, & Webb, 2005, p. 289; see also Chassin, 2008).

Most studies have reported that juvenile drug-court participation reduced recidivism (Applegate & Santana, 2000; Shaffer, 2006; Shaw & Robinson, 1998; Stevens et al., 2016). However, the positive effects of participation in juvenile drug courts appear to "decline when court supervision ends" (Chassin, 2008, p. 170; see also Belenko & Dembo, 2003; Flanzer, 2005). And, the efficacy of drug-court interventions for juveniles is significantly affected by the length of drug use, whether the juvenile is involved in other types of criminal offenses, and the presence of co-occurring psychiatric disorders (Fradella, Fischer, Kleinpeter, & Koob, 2009; Sullivan, Blair, Latessa, & Sullivan, 2016).

Domestic Violence Courts

Domestic violence courts comprise another type of problem-solving court being created in a growing number of communities across the nation.

Domestic violence was once considered a private family matter but is now viewed as a significant social problem (Chapter 9). Changes in how police and prosecutors respond to domestic violence cases have produced changes in how courts respond as well.

In domestic violence courts, the emphasis is on integration. These courts respond to a historical problem in the court system, which required domestic violence victims and their families to appear in different courts before multiple judges, often located in different courthouses in different parts of the county. As a result, a single family could be involved in several courts before several different judges and face the possibility of conflicting court orders (Casey & Rottman, 2004; Koshan, 2014).

Today, practices of domestic violence courts typically include the following:

- A dedicated judge presides over all phases of domestic violence cases, and related cases are consolidated.

- Ongoing monitoring by judge and staff enables the court to hold offenders accountable.

- A resource coordinator prepares information for the judge and is the court's primary liaison with the community.

- On-site victim advocates serve as the primary linkage to social service agencies.

- The emphasis is on a coordinated community response that includes information sharing, education, and coordination across the criminal justice system (Center for Court Innovation, 2014).

Operating within this general framework, more than 225 specialized domestic violence courts have been created across the nation and a similar number internationally (Labriola, Bradley, O'Sullivan, Rempel, & Moore, 2009; National Drug Court Resource Center, 2014). One example is Manhattan's Specialized Domestic Violence Court (Center for Court Innovation, 2009). By removing domestic violence cases from mixed-docket courts, this specialized court seeks to increase defendant accountability, promote victim safety, and better coordinate the activities of governmental agencies that respond to domestic violence. Also called "integrated domestic violence courts," they are dedicated to the one-family-one-judge concept. Thus, a single judge handles multiple criminal, family court, and divorce cases involving the same defendant (Koshan, 2014; Peterson, 2004).

Most evaluations of domestic violence courts suggest that they are successful in reducing re-offenses of domestic violence. For example, an evaluation of a California domestic violence court found a 62 percent completion rate for a yearlong program and lower recidivism rates among program completers versus noncompleters—specifically 15 percent versus 25 percent for domestic violence arrests (Petrucci, 2010). Other evaluations of domestic violence court programs in Albuquerque, New Mexico (Pitts, Givens, & McNeeley, 2009) and Lexington County, South Carolina (Gover, McDonald, & Alpert, 2003) similarly found that program completers were significantly less likely to receive subsequent charges for domestic violence, other violent offenses, or any other criminal offense. In contrast, an evaluation of Manhattan's Specialized Domestic Violence Court showed mixed results: Conviction rates did not increase, cases were disposed of more quickly, defendants were more likely to be placed in a batterer-intervention program, and rearrests increased (Koshan, 2014; Peterson, 2004). The mixed results from evaluations of different domestic violence courts may be because completion rates vary dramatically, often as a function of the length of the program (Petrucci, 2002). Still, the evidence indicates that these courts enhance victims' and defendants' satisfaction with the court process and deliver more services to victims and their families (Casey & Rottman, 2004; Koshan, 2014).

Mental Health Courts

Mental health courts (MHCs) are a third type of problem-solving court using the concept of therapeutic jurisprudence. Over the past several years there has been a growing awareness that the mentally ill are overrepresented in the criminal justice system. It is estimated that anywhere from 14.5 percent to 31 percent of those in jail suffer from serious mental illness, a rate that is many times that of the general adult population (Steadman, Osher, Robbins, Case, & Samuels,

2009; Treatment Advocacy Center, 2014). Indeed, Los Angeles County Jail and New York's Rikers Island held more people with mental illness than the largest psychiatric hospital inpatient facilities in the United States (AbuDagga, Wolfe, Carome, Phatdouang, & Torrey, 2016; Council of State Governments Justice Center, 2008). Not only do mentally ill defendants present special security risks in courts and jails, but they are also more likely to repeatedly recycle through the criminal justice system (AbuDagga et al., 2016; Mental Health America, 2012).

The first MHC was established in 1997; since then, a growing number of courts across the nation are establishing MHCs that are remarkably diverse. For example, Mann (2011) found that 85 percent of MHCs accept misdemeanor cases; 75 percent of MHCs handled felony cases (although only 20 percent accepted violent felony cases and only 1 percent handled seriously violent felony cases); and the eligible clinical diagnoses for participation varied significantly across MHCs. Nonetheless, these courts exhibit several key features:

- A specialized court docket is created.
- Mental health screening is available for acceptable candidates.
- Mentally ill defendants voluntarily enroll in the specialized court, which, in turn, processes their cases on the basis of therapeutic jurisprudence rather than the adversary style of justice.
- Judges supervise a community-based treatment plan for each defendant, involving a team of court staff and mental health professionals.
- The judge and probation officials periodically review the progress of each defendant and use a system of incentives for compliance and sanctions for noncompliance with the conditions imposed by the court.
- Criteria define a participant's completion (sometimes called "graduation form") of the program (Council of State Governments Justice Center, 2012; Mann, 2011).

The few empirical evaluations of MHCs to date generally found that these specialized courts are effective (Herinckx, Swart, Ama, Dolezal, & King, 2005; Hiday, Ray, & Wales, 2015; McNiel & Binder, 2007; Moore & Hiday, 2006; Rossman et al., 2012; Trupin & Richards, 2003). For example, Dirks-Linhorst and Linhorst (2012) found that the rearrest rate of 351 defendants who successfully completed an MHC program was 14.5 percent, as compared with 38 percent among defendants negatively terminated from the program and 25.8 percent among defendants who chose not to participate. But at least two studies have concluded that there is little difference in reoffending levels between MHC graduates and those who do not complete such a program (Christy, Poythress, Boothroyd, Petrila, & Mehra, 2005; Cosden, Ellens, Schnell, & Yamini-Diouf, 2005). The intense variations in the MHC programs, ranging from critical difference in program structure to participant-level differences (such as demographics, criminal history, and drug use history), may be responsible for these divergent findings (see Rossman et al., 2012).

Technology Shapes the Courtrooms of the Future

From the outside looking in, Courtroom 23 in Orange County, Florida, looks like your typical courtroom—a jury box, tables for the lawyers, the judge's bench, and the like. But from the inside looking out, Courtroom 23 hardly resembles a traditional courtroom—computer monitors are everywhere, microphones are located around the courtroom, and video monitors are in plain view. Welcome to the modern courtroom, where technology is an integral part of the design, not a retrofitted feature.

Courtroom 23 is billed as the courtroom of the future and is the outgrowth of an earlier effort known as Courtroom 21. Launched in 1993 as a joint effort of the National Center for State Courts and the William and Mary School of Law, Courtroom 21 was the most technologically advanced courtroom in the world (National Center for State Courts, 2012). As technology has evolved, so has the notion of a high-technology courtroom. In the words of DC Superior Court Judge Herbert Dixon (2011), these changes have not always been easy. "Traditional litigators and judges whose skills were honed without the newfangled gadgets were not the fastest to embrace new technologies." As time passed, however, the number of old-time litigators diminished and interest in using new technologies increased.

Based on conducting several complex criminal trials, Judge Dixon highlights several important features of the courtrooms of the future. Evidence cameras, which project images of paper documents and the like, he labels as essential. Witnesses can readily mark vital aspects of the evidence and jurors can easily see it as well. Laptop connections are likewise of key importance. Lawyers can present digital images and sounds without carrying the evidence physically to the courtroom. Overall, jurors rated the use of courtroom technology very positively (Dixon, 2011; Womer, 2016).

Beyond trials, technology is shaping the future of courts in another important way, through electronic communications. Termed cyber-courts or virtual courts, judges can resolve disputes through electronic communications without the lawyers and parties being physically present. And at the discretion of the judge, proceedings of the cyber-court may be open to the public on the Internet (Global Courts, 2012; Womer, 2016). In the not-too-distant future, bail hearings and routine arraignments may be routinely conducted in a virtual court.

Consequences of Court Organization

What activities legislatures define as illegal has a major impact on the courts. In turn, how the courts are organized and administered has a profound effect on the way cases are processed and on the type of justice that results.

Decentralization and Choice of Courts

Although people often talk about the American legal system, no such entity exists. Instead, the United States has more than 51 legal systems—the federal courts and separate courts in each of the 50 states and many U.S. territories, such a Guam, the Northern Mariana Islands, and Puerto Rico. As a result, lawyers sometimes try to maneuver cases so that they are heard in courts that are perceived to be favorable to their clients. For example, some criminal offenses violate both state and federal laws. As a general rule, federal officials prosecute major violations, leaving more minor prosecutions to state officials.

The prosecution of the DC-area snipers illustrates the importance of the choice of courts. During a three-week shooting spree in 2002, John Muhammad and Lee Malvo engaged in 13 shootings, killing 10 people and wounding 3. The U.S. attorney general decided to transfer the defendants to Virginia because that state's law makes the death penalty more likely than in the other jurisdictions where murders occurred—Maryland and the District of Columbia. After both were convicted, Muhammad was sentenced to death, but Malvo (because he was young) was sentenced to life imprisonment.

Local Control and Local Corruption

The 50 state court systems are in actuality often structured on a local basis. The officials who staff these courts—judges and lawyers, prosecutors and defense attorneys—are recruited from the local community they serve and thus reflect the sentiments of that community. As a result, the U.S. system of justice has close ties to local communities, and the application of "state" law often has a local flavor. Jurors in rural areas, for example, often have markedly different attitudes toward guns than jurors in suburban areas.

Local control of justice has the obvious advantage of closely linking courts to the people they serve. But local control has also been an incubator of corruption and injustice. Every state invariably has a town or two where gambling and prostitution flourish because the city fathers agree to look the other way. Not surprisingly, they often receive monetary benefits for being so nearsighted. Increasingly, though, such activities attract the attention of state police, state attorneys general, and federal prosecutors.

The locally administered criminal justice system has also been marked by pockets of injustice. At times, the police and the courts have been the handmaidens of the local economic elite. In the South, historically, the police and the courts hindered efforts to exercise civil rights by arresting or harassing those who sought to register to vote, to eat at whites-only lunch counters, or to simply speak up to protest segregation. The dual court system has provided a safety valve for checking the most flagrant abuses of local justice. Often, it is federal—not state or local—officials who prosecute corrupt local officials.

Uneven Court Financing

The combination of court decentralization and local control of the judiciary results in uneven court financing. As discussed earlier, only a few states have adopted statewide financing of courts. Thus, in most states, courts are financed by a sometimes bewildering array of state taxes, local taxes, court fees, and fines. During normal times, this patchwork system of financing courts provides limited funding for the judiciary. In the words of David Boies, co-chair of a commission formed by the American Bar Association to study court budget issues, "The justice system's funding has been decreasing in constant dollars for at least two decades" (Schwartz, 2011, p. A18).

During a nationwide financial crisis, like the one that began in 2008, cutbacks in funding the courts have resulted in major reductions in services. A 30 percent reduction in state general funds over a three-year period in California meant that citizens of the nation's largest state faced delays in finalizing divorces, prolonged custody battles, and extended waits for lawsuits to go to trial (Dolan & Kim, 2011). This situation has not significantly improved with the economic recovery during much of the 2010s, especially since small reinvestments in the civil justice system have come at the cost of increased fees that many cannot afford (Lagos, 2015). Steep reductions in overtime pay for court employees in the state of New York meant that a three-day trial will now take four days, thus backing up the justice system even further (Caher & Keshner, 2011). Across the nation, getting cases, civil or criminal, to trial will prove to be a struggle.

Economic downturns not only reduce court funding but also increase demands for court services. Financial crises, for example, typically result in increased filings of bankruptcy petitions in federal courts (Chapter 2) and mortgage foreclosure cases in state courts (Sommer & Li, 2011; Task Force on Judicial Budget Cuts, 2014).

Beyond the immediate problems of trying to provide the same services with less funding, courts also face long-term limitations in designing new programs to respond to changing social problems. Citizen demands to create or expand problem-solving courts—like drug courts, domestic violence courts, and mental health courts—are stymied because of a lack of funding. Other sectors of the criminal justice system face similar frustrations. Budget cuts, for example, often force prosecutors to provide fewer services for crime victims (Chapter 9) and public defenders to reduce services (Chapter 7).

Conclusion

The implementation of drug courts across the nation illustrates a major shift in thinking about court reform in the United States. Whereas traditional court reform emphasized consolidating various judicial bodies, the emerging agenda encourages the creation of specialized courts. Modern court reform also actively encourages working with members of the community, whereas the older tradition stressed notions of professionalism that disdained popular input. Likewise, court reform in the contemporary context stresses the importance of working with other agencies rather than viewing the judge as a lone authority figure. The next chapter focuses on these other agencies, elaborating on the concept of the courtroom work group.

What is perhaps most striking is that the ideas that have dominated discussion of court reform for most of this century are now being quietly buried. Instead of stressing organizational charts and other abstract notions, most efforts to reform the judiciary now focus on more specific matters—reducing court delay and targeting drug cases for special treatment, for example. Thus, today's court reform is marked by tremendous experimentation at the local level. Judges and other court actors identify a problem and seek solutions, adapting local resources and local understandings in the process. This adaptation to change has always been the hallmark of the American judiciary. Perhaps the only differences today are the rapid pace of change and the public attention paid to these ongoing efforts at judicial reform.

CHAPTER REVIEW

LO1 1. Outline the four layers of a typical state court system.

A typical state court system includes lower courts (trial courts of limited jurisdiction), major trial courts (trial courts of general jurisdiction), intermediate appellate courts, and the state high court of last resort.

LO2 2. Describe the types of cases handled by the trial courts of limited jurisdiction.

The lower courts handle the preliminary stages of felony cases and also decide a large number of misdemeanor, traffic, and small claims cases.

LO3 3. Discuss the similarities and differences between justice of the peace courts and municipal courts.

Both justice of the peace (JP) courts and municipal courts are considered lower courts. They differ primarily in terms of caseloads. The rurally based JP courts have relatively low caseloads, whereas the urban-based municipal courts have very large caseloads. Different urban and rural tax bases also affect their funding levels.

LO4 4. List the four primary problems confronting the lower courts in the United States.

The four major problems confronting the lower courts are inadequate financing, inadequate facilities, lax court procedures, and unbalanced caseloads.

LO5 5. Identify the types of civil and criminal cases filed in trial courts of general jurisdiction.

The major trial courts decide felony cases and civil cases including domestic relations, estate, personal injury, and contract cases.

LO6 6. Explain briefly the differences between a state high court of last resort in states with and without intermediate courts of appeals.

In states without intermediate appellate courts, state courts of last resort must hear all criminal appeals. In states without intermediate courts of appeals, state courts of last resort have discretion to hear only the cases they decide are the most important.

LO7 7. List the key components of court unification.

The key components of court unification include simplified court structure, centralized administration, centralized rule making, centralized judicial budgeting, and statewide financing.

LO8 8. Identify how problem-solving courts using therapeutic jurisprudence handle cases.

Courts using therapeutic jurisprudence have five essential elements: (1) immediate intervention, (2) nonadversarial adjudication, (3) hands-on judicial involvement, (4) treatment programs with clear rules, and (5) a team approach to treatment.

LO9 9. Discuss the consequences of court organization.

The organization of courts in the United States impacts the processing of cases in several ways, including the decentralization of justice, which at times can mean that there is a choice of courts and that local control has at times resulted in local corruption.

CRITICAL THINKING QUESTIONS

1. Although we typically talk of state courts (as opposed to federal courts), would it be better to talk about local courts? To what extent are there major variations within your state?

2. Compare your state's court structure to those in Figures 3.1 and 3.2. How unified is your state court structure?

3. Have there been discussions in your state of court reorganization? What major interest groups are urging court reform, and what advantages do they suggest? What interest groups are opposing court reform, and what disadvantages do they cite?

4. Why do crime control advocates often oppose drug courts, and why do due process proponents support drug courts?

5. Make a list of state and local politicians who have been tried in federal court. Were there parallel state investigations or prosecutions? To what extent would corrupt local officials be better off if federal court jurisdiction were limited?

KEY TERMS

alternative dispute resolution (ADR) 88

arbitration 88

centralized administration 93

centralized judicial budgeting 93

centralized rule making 93

community courts 88

drug courts 97

inferior court (lower court) 78

intermediate courts of appeals (ICAs) 90

JP 82

justice of the peace courts 82

mediation 88

misdemeanor 79

municipal court 85

ordinance 79

simplified court structure 93

small claims court 80

state high court of last resort 92

statewide financing 94

therapeutic jurisprudence 96

traffic offenses 79

trial court of general jurisdiction 89

trial court of limited jurisdiction (lower court/inferior court) 78

trial *de novo* 83

unified court system 93

violations 79

FOR FURTHER READING

Abadinsky, Howard. 2014. *Drug Use and Abuse: A Comprehensive Introduction*. 8th ed. Belmont, CA: Wadsworth.

Adler, Patricia, Peter Adler, and Patrick O'Brien. 2012. *Drugs and the American Dream: An Anthology*. Hoboken, NJ: Wiley-Blackwell.

Almquist, Lauren, and Elizabeth Dodd. 2009. *Mental Health Courts: A Guide to Research Informed Policy and Practice*. Council of State Governments Justice Center.

Council of State Governments. 2016. "Mental Health Consensus Project." Available online at http://consensusproject.org.

Federal Judicial Center. "Resources on Courtroom Technology." Available online at http://www.fjc.gov/public/home.nsf/autoframe?openagent&url_l=/public/home.nsf/inavgeneral?openpage&url_r=/public/home.nsf/pages/1100

Feeley, Malcolm M., and Greg Berman. 2013. *Court Reform on Trial: Why Simple Solutions Fail*. New Orleans, LA: Quid Pro Books.

Fell, James, Deborah Fisher, Robert Voas, Kenneth Blackman, and Scott Tippetts. 2009. "The Impact of Underage Drinking Laws on Alcohol-Related Fatal Crashes of Young Drivers." *Alcoholism, Clinical, and Experimental Research* 33: 1208–1219.

Lederer, Fredic. 2010. "Wired: What We've Learned about Courtroom Technology." *Criminal Justice* 24: 18–25.

Marion, Nancy E., and Joshua B. Hill. 2015. *Legalizing Marijuana: A Shift in Policies Across America*. Durham, NC: Carolina Academic Press.

Schug, Robert A., and Henry F. Fradella. 2015. *Mental Illness and Crime*. Thousand Oaks, CA: Sage.

Slate, Risdon, Jacqueline K. Buffington-Vollum, and W. Wesley Johnson. 2003. *The Criminalization of Mental Illness: Crisis and Opportunity for the Justice System*. 2nd ed. Durham, NC: Carolina Academic Press.

Winick, Bruce, and David Wexler (Eds.). 2003. *Judging in a Therapeutic Key: Therapeutic Jurisprudence and the Courts*. Durham, NC: Carolina Academic Press.

4 Juvenile Courts

Shelley Gazin/The Image Works

A lawyer meets with her young client in a juvenile detention facility. The bleakness of the wire divider suggests not just a physical separation (perhaps he is a violent offender) but also a societal separation. Juvenile courts were created about 100 years ago to separate youthful from adult offenders, but some argue that the current juvenile justice system does not deal effectively with contemporary problems.

Chapter Outline

Gerald Gault was charged with making a lewd phone call. If he had been an adult, the maximum sentence was on the lenient side—a fine of $50 and two months in jail. But because he was 15 years old, the sentence was potentially much stiffer—up to six years in the state industrial school. These substantive differences mirrored important procedural contrasts as well. If he had been an adult, Gerald Gault would have had the right to confront the witness making the accusation and also the right to have a lawyer present. But because he was a juvenile, none of these basic legal protections applied.

In re Gault (1967) highlights the duality of juvenile court, which is part court of law and part social welfare agency. It sometimes operates formally, but more often its procedures are informal. These contrasts produce a series of contradictions, which are highlighted in the words of a former judge of the Denver Juvenile Court:

> It is law, and it is social work; it is control, and it is help; it is the good parent and, also, the stern parent; it is both formal and informal. It is concerned not only with the delinquent, but also with the battered child, the runaway, and many others. . . . The juvenile court has been all things to all people. (Rubin, 1989, pp. 79–80)

The historic mandate of juvenile court was to rescue children from a criminal life by providing the care and protection normally afforded by the natural parents. Thus, helping a child was far more important than protecting constitutional rights. But in certain instances, helpful benevolence has been replaced by harsh punishments.

In deciding *In re Gault*, the Supreme Court confronted the difficult task of determining

Learning Objectives

After reading this chapter, you should be able to:

LO1 Describe the child-saving movement and its relationship to the doctrine of *parens patriae*.

LO2 List the five ways in which juvenile courts differ from adult courts.

LO3 Discuss how states vary in terms of when a juvenile may be transferred to adult court for prosecution.

LO4 Contrast the three major types of cases that are heard in juvenile court.

LO5 Identify and briefly describe the single most important Supreme Court case with respect to juvenile justice.

LO6 Explain the difference between a juvenile case that is petitioned and one that is nonpetitioned.

LO7 Compare and contrast how adherents of the crime control model and proponents of the due process model of criminal justice see the future of juvenile courts.

the relationship between the social welfare functions of juvenile court and basic due process so important to the American court system. The best starting point in unraveling these dualities is an examination of the past 100 years of juvenile court.

Juvenile Courts 100 Years Ago

Juvenile courts are a distinctly 20th-century development. The major economic and social changes of the late 19th century prompted a rethinking of the role of youth. The result was the creation of specialized courts to deal with what were thought to be distinctly youth-oriented problems. Many of the issues that arose 100 years ago remain with us today, shaping the thinking that will affect juvenile courts for years to come.

Industrialization, Cities, and Crime

By the last third of the 19th century, the United States was well on its way to becoming the world's greatest industrial nation. What had once been a nation of small farmers was rapidly becoming a nation of city dwellers. The factories were located in the cities, and the workers for these factories were partially drawn from those who wished to escape the hard work of farming. But most of the new jobs were filled by immigrants from foreign lands who sought freedom from political oppression or economic want in their home countries. The result was a tremendous growth in cities. Indeed, the population of the nation almost doubled, growing from 40 million in 1870 to 76 million in 1900.

America's emerging big cities were truly diverse. The residents spoke different languages, ate strange foods, dressed differently, and worshiped in a variety of churches. The White Anglo-Saxon Protestants who controlled the institutions of the United States at the time did not extend a cordial welcome to these new immigrants. On the contrary, the immigrant urban masses were associated with the poverty, social disorder, and crime of the emerging big cities. Protecting society from the "dangerous poor" became a pressing social concern. Then, as now, there was confusion over what was poverty and what was crime.

The Child Savers and the Progressive Movement

Beginning around 1890, members of the Progressive movement advocated a variety of political, economic, and social reforms. They were genuinely concerned about the economic disparities, social disorders, and excesses of industrialization, particularly as they affected children.

Progressives denounced the evils of child labor and pushed for legislation banning the practice. They were likewise appalled by the violent and exploitive conditions of reform schools. The fact that orphans were thrown into reform schools for the uncontrollable circumstance of having no parents shocked the Progressives' moral values. Taking up the plight of the children of the urban immigrant poor, they argued that these children were not bad, but were corrupted by the environment in which they grew up.

The Progressives' concern for the plight of the urban masses was also motivated by self-interest. They were largely middle class, and their position in society was threatened by the growth of a competing urban class composed of the poor and the working poor. These Anglo-Saxon Protestants found the culture of the Southern European Catholics shocking. Anthony Platt's (1969) classic study, *The Child Savers*, notes the types of behavior the Progressives sought to punish—drinking, fighting, begging, frequenting dance halls, staying out late at night, and sexual license. Within a generation, many of the social forces unleashed by the Progressive movement would lead to Prohibition, which was directed squarely at the growing political power of big-city Catholic immigrants, whose power base was the neighborhood tavern.

Thus, from its origins, the juvenile court movement reflected class distinctions: The children of the poor were processed through the system, but those of the more well-to-do were handled informally. These class differences would mark juvenile court activities throughout the century. Then, as now, there was confusion over what was genuine social concern and what was self-serving class interest.

Parens Patriae

The Progressives' efforts to save the children of the urban masses reflected a major shift in thinking about children. Historically, children had been viewed as miniature adults. Children under the age of 7 were presumed to be incapable of criminal intent and were therefore exempt from prosecution. Those 8 or older were considered adults in the eyes of the law, prosecuted as adults, convicted as adults, and served their sentences in the same prison cells as adults.

By the end of the 19th century, the notion of children as miniature adults was giving way to a very different conceptualization—children as persons with less than fully developed moral and cognitive capacities. This shift in thinking was reflected in the emerging legal doctrine of *parens patriae* (state as parent). No longer were parents considered to have sole and exclusive legal responsibility over their children. If the parents failed in their responsibility to raise a child properly, the state could intervene to protect children's welfare. This doctrine also meant that in extreme circumstances parents' rights over their children could be terminated altogether.

Then, as now, there was confusion over the right of parents to raise their children in their own image and the need of the state to limit social disorder.

How Juvenile Courts Differ from Adult Courts

The juvenile court is a continuing legacy of the Progressive movement. Not content to tinker with existing procedures, the Progressives insisted on a radical departure from past practices. Adopting the legal doctrine of *parens patriae* resulted in juvenile judicial proceedings that differed greatly from those used in adult courts. The juvenile court movement began with the philosophy of "what is in the best interest of the child, a doctrine that over the years evolved into a mixed bag of philosophies" (Silva, 2014a).

The unique legal dimensions of **juvenile court** are reflected in the legal terms used. Whereas adults are arrested, tried, and sentenced to prison, juveniles are taken into custody, have an adjudicatory hearing, and are committed to residential placement. For additional coverage of the legal terms used to distinguish juvenile and adult criminal court processes, see the "Law on the Books vs. Law in Action" feature later in this chapter on page 128.

Juvenile courts differ from adult courts in five important ways: They emphasize helping the child, they are informal, they are based on civil law, they are secret, and they rarely involve a jury.

Emphasis on Helping the Child

Prosecution of adults at the turn of the 20th century sought to achieve punishment. By contrast, the newly created juvenile courts emphasized helping the child. Benevolence and rehabilitation, not punishment, were of paramount importance.

The doctrine of *parens patriae* became the underlying philosophy of juvenile court; the state should deal with a child who broke the law much as a wise parent would deal with a wayward child. The Progressives sought to use the power of the state to save children from a life of crime. Juvenile courts would provide flexible procedures for the treatment of the underlying social problems that were seen as the basis of juvenile crime. Guidance would be the norm.

Informal Proceedings

Criminal prosecutions involving adults are formal and adversarial in nature. By contrast, juvenile court proceedings emphasize informality. Although key elements of due process have been integrated into juvenile court in recent years, juvenile proceedings nonetheless retain their informal nature. As a result, rules of evidence and rules of procedure, so important in adult criminal courts, have little relevance in juvenile proceedings.

Flowing from the premise that juvenile courts are meant to help the child, the creators of juvenile court viewed procedural safeguards not only as unnecessary, but also as harmful. The concern was that a legal technicality might allow a child to avoid getting help (Sanborn, 1993). In essence, the substance of the decision (helping the child) was more important than the procedures used to reach that decision.

Proceedings Based on Civil Law

Prosecutions of adults are based on the criminal law. In contrast, juvenile court proceedings are based on the civil law. This is why the legal terminology used in adult and juvenile courts differs so greatly. The terms *summons* and *commitment*, for example, are borrowed directly from civil practice.

Using civil rather than criminal law reinforced the key notion that juvenile courts were intended to rehabilitate, not punish. It is for this reason, for example, that a child's juvenile court record is not admissible in adult court. Regardless of the frequency or severity of the offenses committed by a juvenile, once he or she becomes an adult in the eyes of the criminal law, the person starts over with no prior record.

Over the years, the U.S. Supreme Court, state courts, and legislatures have added some procedural due process features of adult courts to juvenile proceedings. And, over the years, both punishment and protection of the community have joined rehabilitation as objectives of juvenile delinquency proceedings. Thus, today it is probably best to view juvenile proceedings as quasi-criminal—a blend of civil and criminal law quite different from the original ideals of the early juvenile courts (Moriearty, 2008).

Secret Proceedings

Criminal proceedings involving adults are open to the public (except grand jury proceedings, and, on the rarest of rare occasions, part of jury selection in ultrasensitive cases). By contrast, juvenile court proceedings have historically been secret. This means that crime victims who are interested in what happens in their case, or ordinary citizens who are simply curious about what goes on in the courthouse, may freely attend sessions involving adults but not those involving juveniles. In most jurisdictions, it is illegal for law enforcement personnel or juvenile court officials to release the names of juveniles to the media. Moreover, even if the media are able to find out the names, journalistic ethics prohibit that information from being printed or broadcast.

The secrecy of juvenile proceedings is changing in some jurisdictions. Currently, 18 states open delinquency hearings to the general public, and 20 others have passed statutes that open such hearings for certain types of cases. However, judges often retain the authority to close hearings at their discretion (Sickmund & Punzzanchera, 2014).

To its supporters, the secrecy of juvenile court proceedings is essential in meeting the key goal of working with children in trouble to prevent future criminal behavior. To critics, this secrecy merely reinforces the informality of the process and prevents much-needed public scrutiny.

Absence of Jury Trials

Adults accused of violating the criminal law have the right to a trial by a jury of their peers. By contrast, juveniles have no such constitutional right. To be sure, a few states have created, often by statute, an extremely limited right to a trial by jury in some matters concerning juveniles. Nonetheless, the central point is clear: Whereas the possibility of a jury trial structures the disposition of adult offenders, the likelihood of a jury trial almost never enters into the discussion in juvenile court.

The absence of jury trials reinforces the informal nature of the proceedings. It also strengthens the control of juvenile court personnel—both judges and probation officers. In adult courts, the views of ordinary citizens may prove to differ from those of judge or prosecutor, but there is no such possibility in juvenile court.

The Organization of Juvenile Courts

Today, all states have juvenile courts, but their organizational relationship to other judicial bodies varies greatly. In some ways, the term *juvenile court* is a misnomer. Only a few states have created juvenile courts that are completely separate from other judicial bodies.

As Chapter 3 emphasized, important variations exist in state court organization. Nowhere is this diversity more apparent than in the organization of juvenile courts. Along a continuum from the most to the least distinctive, juvenile courts are organized in one of three ways: a separate court, part of family court, or a unit of the trial court.

Juvenile Court as a Separate Court

In a few jurisdictions, juvenile court is completely separate from other judicial bodies. This is the case in the states of Connecticut, Rhode Island, and Utah. A juvenile court as a separate statewide entity means that it has its own administration, judges, probation officers, clerks of court, and other employees. Stated another way, matters concerning juveniles are its exclusive jurisdiction. A few large cities, such as Boston and Denver, also separate juvenile courts from other judicial bodies.

Juvenile Court as Part of Family Court

A second organizational arrangement is for juvenile court to be a part of family court, which has broad responsibility over family matters. One major type of case is divorce and related issues, including child custody, child support, alimony, and property settlement. In addition, the jurisdiction of family courts encompasses paternity matters and adoption of children. Most important for our purposes, family-court jurisdiction also typically includes matters concerning juveniles (delinquency, status offenses, and child-victim cases).

Six states and the District of Columbia have authorized family courts on a statewide basis. In Delaware, New York, Rhode Island, and South Carolina, family courts are separately organized. In the District of Columbia, Hawaii, and New Jersey, family courts are a separate division of the trial court of general jurisdiction.

Juvenile Court as a Unit of Trial Court

The third place that juvenile courts are housed organizationally is as part of a trial court. Typically, juvenile court is part of the jurisdiction of the major trial court, but on occasion it is in the minor trial court.

Beyond the legal considerations of jurisdiction, the question of where matters concerning juveniles are heard is largely a function of case volume. In rural areas with few cases, they most often are a type of case on the judge's calendar, much like tort and contract. But most areas have sufficient cases to justify one or more judges who devote themselves full-time to matters concerning juveniles. This specialization is dictated partly by case volume, but also by the requirement that juvenile proceedings be conducted in secret. Administratively, therefore, a separate section of court (sometimes in a different courthouse) makes it easier to keep juvenile proceedings closed to the public.

Law in Action: The Impact of Structure

Since juvenile courts were first established, there has been a debate over the appropriate place in the judicial hierarchy for this new judicial body. Where a state ended up placing its juvenile court was largely determined by broader debates over court organization.

Court reformers recommend that juvenile court be part of family court. But whether this structural arrangement results in "better" justice is, at best, hard to document. There is some evidence, for example, that the more the judge is a juvenile court specialist, the more likely the judge will handle cases informally rather than conduct a full hearing (Sosin, 1978). Similarly, specialists are less likely to find a youth to be a delinquent (Johnson & Secret, 1995). The structural differences, however, appear to be far less important than the social environment in which the juvenile court operates; juvenile courts in big cities march to a different drummer than those in rural or suburban areas (Sanborn, 1994).

Juvenile Court Jurisdiction: Subject Matter

Of the children brought before juvenile court, there is enormous variation in the types of cases. Felons and misdemeanants, petty offenders, and truants are all under the jurisdiction of the juvenile court because of their age. And to complicate matters even further, some juveniles are before the court because of neglect or abuse by their parents (Karatekin, Gehrman, & Lawler, 2014; Lawler, Gehrman, & Karatekin, 2016).

Juvenile court matters fall into three major categories: delinquency, status offenses, and children in need of supervision (sometimes called "child-victims"). The distribution of cases across these three categories is presented in Figure 4.1.

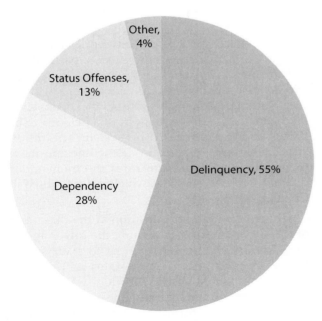

FIGURE 4.1 Caseload of the Juvenile Courts

Source: LaFountain, Robert C., Richard Y. Schauffler, Shauna M. Strickland, and Kathryn A. Holt. 2012. *Examining the Work of State Courts: An Analysis of 2010 State Court Caseloads*. Williamsburg, VA: National Center for State Courts.

Juvenile Delinquency

Delinquency is a violation of a criminal law that would be a crime if the act were committed by an adult. Common examples include theft, burglary, sale or possession of drugs, and criminal damage to property. Thus, in a juvenile delinquency matter, there is no age difference in the substance of the criminal law, but the procedures are considerably different.

A juvenile delinquent may be placed on probation or committed to a juvenile institution. The period of confinement may exceed that for an adult charged with the same act.

Status Offenses

Status offenses involve acts that are illegal only for juveniles. Common examples include running away from home, truancy, possession of alcohol, incorrigibility/ungovernability, and curfew violations. Each year, these types of cases account for roughly 13 percent of the overall juvenile court docket (La Fountain et al., 2012). Traditionally, juveniles found to be status offenders could be sent to the same juvenile correctional institutions as those found to be delinquent, but this is changing. In recent years, some states have decriminalized some of these behaviors; offenders are now treated as dependent children, and child protective service agencies are given the primary responsibility for addressing the problem.

Children in Need of Supervision

Juvenile courts also deal with **children in need of supervision**, sometimes referred to as **child-victims**. Such children are before the court through no fault of their own. These types of cases generally involve issues of child abandonment, child abuse (such as battered children), or child neglect (such as children who are not receiving proper education or medical care).

Clearly, the types of issues in cases concerning children in need of supervision present different issues from those in which juveniles are before the court because of their own actions. For example, children in need of supervision are not placed in juvenile detention facilities. Rather, juvenile courts have a broad mandate to order social services, foster home or group home care, or medical or mental health services for abused or neglected children (DiPietro, 2008). Because of the complexities inherent in the distinctive nature of these cases, further discussion of these cases is beyond the scope of this book.

Law in Action: One-Pot Jurisdiction

The broad subject-matter jurisdiction of juvenile courts complicates the task of addressing the problems facing juvenile justice. At any given time in juvenile court, the judge, prosecutor, probation officer, and police officer are simultaneously dealing with a wide variety of problems. This has been called the "one-pot" jurisdictional approach, in which youths who commit serious crimes, status offenders, and deprived children are put into the same "pot" (Springer, 1986).

Consider the following three hypothetical cases, all of which would meet a given state's age criteria:

- A juvenile who has burglarized a liquor store
- A juvenile who has been stopped by the police for possessing liquor
- A juvenile whose parents drink so heavily that they have given up any efforts to raise their child

The first is a delinquent, the second a status offender, and the third a child-victim. Yet, all three kinds of children were thought to be the products or victims of bad family and social environments; consequently, it was thought that they should be subject, as the wards of the court, to the same kind of solicitous, helpful care (Springer, 1986, pp. 62–63).

It is this broad diversity of juvenile problems that members of the courtroom work group must confront in trying to dispense juvenile court's version of justice.

Juvenile Court Jurisdiction: Age

For adults, court jurisdiction is largely determined by the nature of the criminal offense. For **juveniles**, on the other hand, jurisdiction is normally

determined by their age. But different states provide complex sets of criteria relating to the age at which juvenile courts have jurisdiction over children and young adults.

Age Limits for Original Jurisdiction over Delinquency Matters

In most states, the juvenile court has original jurisdiction over all youth charged with a violation of criminal law who were younger than age 18 at the time of the offense, arrest, or referral to court. Age 18, however, hardly constitutes a consensus among the states for the **upper age of jurisdiction** (when a child becomes an adult, at least in the eyes of the criminal law). For the purpose of establishing juvenile court jurisdiction over delinquency matters, two states establish the upper age of juvenile court jurisdiction at 15, nine others at age 16, and the remaining states at 17 (see Figure 4.2). Note, however, that many states have higher upper ages of juvenile court jurisdiction for other types of cases, such as in abuse, neglect, or dependency matters—typically through age 20.

The adjoining states of New York and Pennsylvania illustrate this complex national pattern. In New York, a 16-year-old is considered an adult and is prosecuted in the adult criminal justice system. But move across the border, and Pennsylvania treats that same 16-year-old as a juvenile to be processed in the juvenile court system. This difference in laws of jurisdictions sometimes no more than a few feet apart illustrates the tremendous diversity of American law, which is highlighted in Chapter 4.

There is even more variation at the other end of the spectrum for establishing the **lower age of jurisdiction** for a juvenile court to exercise delinquency jurisdiction. Most states rely on case law or the common law tradition, which holds that children under a certain age (usually 7 or 8) are incapable of forming criminal intent and, therefore, are exempt from prosecution, even in delinquency proceedings. But, as Table 4.1 illustrates, 18 states have statutorily established a minimum age for juvenile court jurisdiction over delinquency matters.

FIGURE 4.2 Upper Age of Juvenile Court Jurisdiction over Delinquency Matters

Source: Office of Juvenile Justice and Delinquency Prevention. 2016. *OJJDP Statistical Briefing Book*, 2015. Available online at https://www.ojjdp.gov/ojstatbb/structure_process/qa04102.asp?qaDate=2015&text=

Age Limits Beyond Original Jurisdiction

In most states, once original jurisdiction over delinquency proceedings has been established, juvenile courts may retain jurisdiction over youth who have reached the age at which original juvenile court jurisdiction ends. In fact, as Table 4.2 illustrates, legislation in more than two-thirds of the states permits juvenile courts to continue exercising jurisdiction over young adults "to provide sanctions and services for

TABLE 4.1	Lowest Age of Juvenile Court Jurisdiction over Delinquency Matters
Youngest Age	**State**
6	North Carolina
7	Connecticut, Maryland, Massachusetts, New York, North Dakota
8	Arizona
10	Arkansas, Colorado, Kansas, Louisiana, Minnesota, Mississippi, Pennsylvania, South Dakota, Texas, Vermont, Wisconsin

Source: Office of Juvenile Justice and Delinquency Prevention. 2016. *OJJDP Statistical Briefing Book*, 2015. Available online at https://www.ojjdp.gov/ojstatbb/structure_process/qa04102.asp?qaDate=2015&text=

TABLE 4.2	Oldest Age of Juvenile Court Jurisdiction over Delinquency Matters

Oldest Age	State
18 (n = 2)	Oklahoma, Texas
19 (n = 4)	Alaska, Connecticut, Mississippi, North Dakota
20 (n = 36)	Alabama, Arizona,[a] Arkansas, Delaware, District of Columbia, Florida, Georgia, Idaho, Illinois, Indiana, Iowa, Kentucky, Louisiana, Maine, Maryland, Massachusetts, Michigan, Minnesota, Missouri, Nevada,[b] New Hampshire, New Mexico, New York, North Carolina, Ohio, Pennsylvania, Rhode Island, South Carolina, South Dakota, Tennessee, Utah, Virginia, Washington, West Virginia, Wyoming
21 (n = 1)	Vermont
22 (n = 1)	Kansas
24 (n = 4)	California, Montana, Oregon, Wisconsin
Until the full term of the disposition order (n = 3)	Colorado, Hawaii, New Jersey

[a]Arizona statute extends jurisdiction through age 20, but a 1979 state supreme court decision held that juvenile court jurisdiction terminates at age 18.
[b]Nevada extends jurisdiction until the full term of the disposition order for sex offenders.

Source: Office of Juvenile Justice and Delinquency Prevention. 2016. *OJJDP Statistical Briefing Book*, 2015. Available online at https://www.ojjdp.gov /ojstatbb/structure_process/qa04106.asp?qaDate=2015&text=

a duration of time that is in the best interests of the [youth] and the public," at least for certain types of offenses (Snyder & Sickmond, 2006, p. 103).

Transfers to Adult Court

Although a fairly uniform upper age limit for the exercise of original juvenile court jurisdiction in delinquency proceedings has been established in the United States, there is far less uniformity involving lower age limits for juveniles charged with serious offenses, or who have a history of repeated offenses, who may be tried as adults. **Transfer to criminal court** (alternatively referred to as *certification* or *waiver*) refers to the process whereby the jurisdiction over a juvenile delinquent is moved to adult court.

Types of Transfers

There are four primary mechanisms for juvenile transfers to adult criminal courts: judicial waivers, prosecutorial waivers, statutory/legislative waivers, and automatic waivers.

Judicial Waivers

Judicial waiver laws permit—and sometimes even require—juvenile court judges to transfer a juvenile to adult court for criminal prosecution. Cases are filed in juvenile court pursuant to their original jurisdiction. At a special transfer hearing, though, the juvenile court judge can waive jurisdiction based on the facts and circumstances of a particular case, thereby transferring jurisdiction in the case to criminal court (House, 2013).

Judicial waivers are the oldest form of transfers. They are also the most common type of waiver, as 45 states use some form of judicial waiver (Griffin, Addie, Adams, & Firestine, 2011). Only 15 states, however, rely exclusively on judicial waivers; thus, 30 states use more than one mechanism to transfer juveniles to adult courts.

In most states that use judicial waivers, transfers to adult court are discretionary. When judicial waivers are discretionary, the discretion exercised by juvenile court judges is guided by certain standards set forth in statutory law. For example, most states with juvenile waiver laws set a minimum age and a specified type of offense (see Table 4.3). In contrast, a handful of states—Alaska and Washington, for example—allow judicial waiver of juvenile court jurisdiction in nearly all types of delinquency cases.

In 15 states, judicial waivers are presumptive for certain types of offenses (OJJDP "Statistical

TABLE 4.3   Minimum Ages and Offenses for Judicial Transfers to Adult Criminal Court

State	Minimum Age for Judicial Waiver	Judicial Waiver Offense and Minimum Age Criteria							
		Any Criminal Offense	Certain Felonies	Capital Crimes	Murder	Certain Person Offenses	Certain Property Offenses	Certain Drug Offenses	Certain Weapon Offenses
Alabama	14	14							
Alaska	NS	NS				NS			
Arizona	NS		NS						
Arkansas	14		14	14	14	14			14
California	14	16	14		14	14	14	14	
Colorado	12		12		12	12	12		
Connecticut	14		14	14	14				
Delaware	NS	NS	15		NS	NS	16	16	
District of Columbia	NS	15	15		15	15	15		NS
Florida	14	14							
Georgia	13		15	13		13			
Hawaii	NS		14		NS				
Idaho	NS	14	NS		NS	NS	NS	NS	
Illinois	13	13	15					15	
Indiana	NS		NS		10			16	
Iowa	14	14							
Kansas	12	12	14				14	14	
Kentucky	14		14	14					
Louisiana	14				14	14			
Maine	NS		NS		NS	NS			
Maryland	NS	15		NS					
Michigan	14	14							
Minnesota	14	14							
Mississippi	13	13							
Missouri	12		12						
Nevada	13	16	14		13	16			
New Hampshire	13		15		13	13		15	

(Continued)

TABLE 4.3   (Continued)

State	Minimum Age for Judicial Waiver	Judicial Waiver Offense and Minimum Age Criteria							
		Any Criminal Offense	Certain Felonies	Capital Crimes	Murder	Certain Person Offenses	Certain Property Offenses	Certain Drug Offenses	Certain Weapon Offenses
New Jersey	14	14	14		14	14	14	14	14
North Carolina	13		13	13					
North Dakota	14	16	14		14	14		14	
Ohio	14		14		14	16	16		
Oklahoma	NS		NS						
Oregon	NS		15		NS	NS	15		
Pennsylvania	14		14		14	14			
Rhode Island	NS		16	NS	17	17			
South Carolina	NS	16	14		NS	NS		14	14
South Dakota	NS		NS						
Tennessee	NS	16			NS	NS			
Texas	14		14	14				14	
Utah	14		14		16	16	16		16
Vermont	10				10	10	10		
Virginia	14		14		14	14			
Washington	NS	NS							
West Virginia	NS		NS		NS	NS	NS	NS	
Wisconsin	14	15	14		14	14	14	14	
Wyoming	13	13							

Note: Ages in the minimum age column may not apply to all offense restrictions, but represent the youngest possible age at which a juvenile may be judicially waived to criminal court. "NS" indicates that no minimum age is specified.

Source: Office of Juvenile Justice and Delinquency Prevention. 2015. *OJJDP Statistical Briefing Book*, 2014. Available online at https://www.ojjdp.gov /ojstatbb/structure_process/qa04110.asp?qaDate=2014

Briefing Book," 2015). This means that for a class of offenses, the juvenile court judge is expected to transfer cases to adult court barring exceptional circumstances. Often, the burden of proof to show those exceptional circumstances lies with the juvenile, who (usually through counsel) must rebut the presumption that the case should be tried in criminal court (Griffin et al., 2011).

In 14 states, however, juvenile court judges are deprived of discretion over whether to waive certain types of cases because waivers are mandatory for certain offenses (OJJDP "Statistical Briefing Book," 2015). Mandatory judicial waivers function just like statutory waivers (see the section following), but the juvenile court handled preliminary matters such as appointing counsel and deciding whether the juvenile should be held in detention pending adjudication of the case in criminal court.

Prosecutorial Waivers

For certain offenses in 14 states and the District of Columbia, prosecutors have the option of filing delinquency petitions in juvenile court or filing criminal charges in adult court (OJJDP "Statistical Briefing Book," 2015). Since either the juvenile courts or the criminal courts may handle such cases depending on the court in which the prosecutor elects to file the case, **prosecutorial waivers** are sometimes called "concurrent jurisdiction waivers."

Because this decision to waive juvenile court jurisdiction is vested within the discretion of the prosecutor, no hearings are held on this determination. And unlike laws that set forth factors to guide the exercise of judicial discretion in judicial waivers, "prosecutorial discretion laws are usually silent regarding standards, protocols, or appropriate considerations for decisionmaking" (Griffin et al., 2011, p. 5). Rather, as with other charging decisions (see Chapter 10), prosecutorial discretion is largely unfettered.

Statutory Exclusion/Legislative Waivers

Nearly 30 states have enacted laws that grant exclusive jurisdiction over certain crimes to adult court regardless of the age of the offender (OJJDP "Statistical Briefing Book," 2015). These laws are known as **statutory exclusion/legislative waivers**. As with mandatory judicial waivers, juvenile courts have no power to hear such cases. However, unlike with mandatory judicial waiver cases, even the preliminary aspects of a case are handled in criminal courts. Murder is the most frequent offense subject to statutory waiver, although other violent felonies are included under the laws of some states.

Automatic Waivers

A special form of automatic transfer operates in about 34 states for youth who have already been prosecuted as adults in the past. These so-called **automatic waivers** are built on the premise of "once an adult, always an adult" (OJJDP "Statistical Briefing Book," 2015). Automatic waiver laws are generally comprehensive in nature in that they typically require criminal courts to handle all subsequent offenses allegedly committed by a juvenile after an initial transfer to adult court. But some states limit the application of these automatic transfers only to subsequent felonies or to juveniles who have reached the age of 16 (Griffin et al., 2011).

Corrective Mechanisms

At first blush, mandatory judicial waivers, statutory waivers, and automatic waivers may seem particularly harsh insofar as they seemingly prevent any individualized judicial consideration of the transfer decision. About half the states have attempted to compensate for this by enacting some mechanisms that can mitigate the one-size-fits-all approach of such waivers. The most common of these are called **reverse waivers**. This process, which has been adopted in some form in about half the states, allows a juvenile to petition the criminal court to transfer jurisdiction to a juvenile court (OJJDP "Statistical Briefing Book," 2015).

Another corrective mechanism some states have enacted is called **blended sentencing**. In the nearly 20 states that have enacted such laws, criminal court judges can impose juvenile dispositions under certainly circumstances, rather than imposing standard criminal sentences (OJJDP "Statistical Briefing Book," 2015). Blended sentencing offers some of the benefits of both adult and juvenile courts insofar as youthful offenders "can be held accountable for the serious offenses they have committed, but are also offered the possibility of rehabilitation and redemption" (Brown & Sorensen, 2014, p. 238).

Use of Waivers

Every year, only a very small proportion of juveniles are transferred to adult court. Indeed, as Figure 4.3 depicts, only about 1 percent of all juvenile delinquency cases are waived to criminal court. The cases that are transferred generally involve juveniles accused of murder, armed robbery, or another particularly violent felony. Nonetheless, Black and Hispanic juveniles are about three times more likely to be transferred to adult criminal court as a White juvenile (Brown & Sorensen, 2014; Lehmann, Chiricos, & Bales, 2017).

The number of juveniles transferred to criminal court peaked in 1994 at 13,700 cases but since then has declined to about 4,000 cases a year (Puzzanchera & Hockenberry, 2015). The decrease in violent crime by juveniles has driven much of this decline (Adams & Addie, 2011). A disproportionate number of juveniles transferred to adult criminal court are male African-Americans (Puzzanchera &

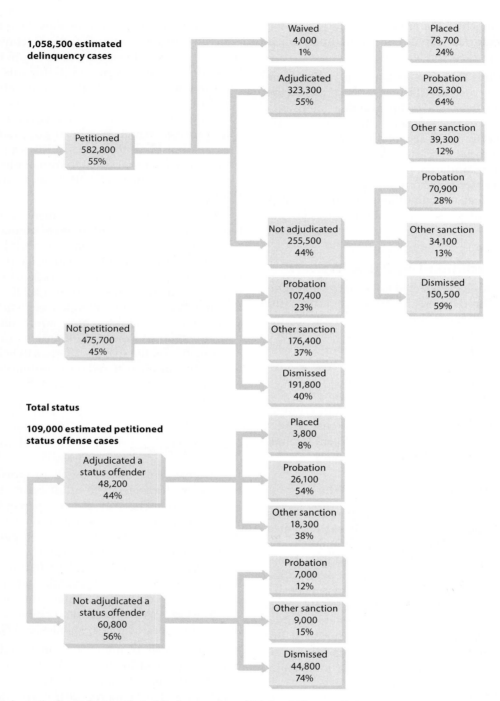

FIGURE 4.3 Juvenile Court Processing of Delinquency and Status Offenses Cases

Note: Cases are categorized by their most severe or restrictive sanction. Numbers may not add to totals because of rounding.

Source: Hockenberry, Sarah, and Charles Puzzanchera. 2015. *Juvenile Court Statistics, 2013*. Pittsburgh, PA: National Center for Juvenile Justice.

Hockenberry, 2013). Figures like these lead youth advocacy groups like the Center for Children's Law and Policy (2012) to conclude that young people of color are overrepresented and that states have not done enough to address racial disparities.

How juvenile transfer laws actually operate is complex (Verrecchia, 2011). For example, transferred juveniles, particularly those convicted of violent offenses, typically receive longer sentences than those sentenced in the juvenile court for similar crimes. However, they may be released on bail for a considerable period of time while they await trial in the criminal court (Meyers, 2005; Redding, 2008; Steiner, 2009).

The Office of Juvenile Justice and Delinquency Prevention evaluated changes in Wisconsin, New Mexico, and Minnesota (Torbet, Griffin, Hurst, & MacKenzie, 2000). The final report highlights the following lessons learned:

- A disconnect exists between legislative intent and the actual implementation of new laws.
- The new sentencing laws encourage plea bargaining.
- Judicial and prosecutorial discretion expand.
- Local application of new laws varies widely.
- New sentencing laws have a disproportionate impact on minorities.

Recent research tends to confirm these findings (Shook, 2014; Griffin et al., 2011). Stated another way, alterations of laws on the books do not necessarily produce the intended changes in law in action.

Public pressure to try juveniles as adults is spawned by concerns over violent juvenile crimes. Reality, though, does not match the expectations of elected officials or the public. (See "Courts, Controversy, & Reducing Crime: Should Juveniles Be Tried as Adults?")

Due Process in Juvenile Courts

Juvenile court statutes set forth two standards for deciding the appropriate disposition for a child: the best interests of the child and the best interests of the community. Because the concept of the juvenile court was to aid—not punish—children, the due process guarantees of the adult criminal court were absent. Procedures were more administrative than adversarial, stressing the informal, private, and noncombative handling of cases. It is for this reason that juvenile cases are often captioned *In re*, a Latin phrase meaning "in the matter of." But at what point do juveniles obtain benefits from the special procedures applicable to them that offset the disadvantage of denial of due process?

Key Court Decisions

The nature of the juvenile court process remained unchanged until the 1960s. When the Warren Court began to scrutinize procedures in adult criminal courts, its attention turned also to juvenile courts. In a groundbreaking decision, the Supreme Court held in *In re Gault* (1967) that the due process clause of the Fourteenth Amendment applied to juvenile court proceedings. The court emphasized that "under our Constitution the condition of being a boy does not justify a kangaroo court." The opinion specified that juveniles have: (1) the right to notice, (2) the right to counsel, (3) the right to confront witnesses, and (4) privilege against self-incrimination. (See "Case Close-Up: *In re Gault* and Due Process in Juvenile Courts.") Three years later, the Court ruled that when a juvenile is charged with an act that would be a crime if committed by an adult, then every element of that criminal act must be proved beyond a reasonable doubt (*In re Winship*, 1970).

The *Gault* and *Winship* decisions point to the constant tension within the juvenile court system between those who think that children should be given all the due process guarantees accorded adults and those who reason that children must be handled in a less adversarial, more treatment-oriented manner so that legal procedures will not interfere with efforts to secure the justice that is in the children's best interests.

Gault and *Winship* signaled that the juvenile court must become a real court and its procedures must be regularized in accordance with

Should Juveniles Be Tried as Adults?

Public concerns about juvenile crime, particularly violent crimes committed by juveniles, are often fueled by headlines about juveniles committing brazen or senseless crimes. And at one time, the crime statistics seemed to bear out this public concern. Beginning in the mid-1980s the juvenile crime rate increased, with juvenile arrests more than doubling in the span of a decade or so (Cannon, 1997). What attracted the most public attention is the increase in violent juvenile crime, which shot up 93 percent (as compared with a 22 percent increase in property crimes).

To some observers, a juvenile crime wave was on the horizon. Newspaper headlines proclaimed, "Youth Violence Explosion Likely to Worsen" (Bass, 1995) and "Violent Children Straining Limit of Justice System" (Hallinan, 1993). These concerns were bolstered by the realization that the juvenile population would increase from 27 million to 39 million by 2010.

But these dire predictions failed to materialize. Beginning in 1995, arrests for violent juvenile crimes declined significantly (Puzzanchera & Adams, 2011; "OJJDP Statistical Briefing Book," 2015). Thus, what some had predicted to be a juvenile crime wave now appears to have been only a ripple.

The commonly held belief that juvenile delinquents are becoming younger as a group and committing more serious crimes at earlier ages than in the past does not hold up to scrutiny. The Office of Juvenile Justice and Delinquency Prevention (1996) compared the characteristics of young offenders arrested in the 1990s with those arrested in 1980 and concluded that serious and violent juvenile offenders were not significantly younger than those of 10 or 15 years earlier.

But downward trends in juvenile crime have apparently had little impact on the public dialogue. The U.S. Congress and numerous states have responded to public perceptions that violent juvenile crime is a growing menace. The typical legislative response has been to make it easier to transfer juveniles. Consider that between 1992 and 1999, 48 states and the District of Columbia changed their transfer statutes to make it easier to waive juveniles to adult courts (Griffin et al., 2011; "Statistical Briefing Book," 2009). Some of these efforts involve lowering the age of transfer. Others involve increasing the list of crimes for which juveniles may be transferred. Others seek to mandate transfers in certain situations.

But do these laws work? A review of the major studies on this topic concludes that the answer is no. In terms of specific deterrence (stopping a particular person from committing another crime), several major studies find higher recidivism rates among juveniles convicted for violent offenses in criminal court as compared with similar offenders tried in juvenile court. The limited literature on general deterrence (deterring others from committing crime) is somewhat inconsistent but tentatively suggests that transfer laws do not deter crime (Redding, 2008).

Even though the number of juveniles in the United States is increasing, the percentage of cases being transferred to adult court is declining. One reason is cost—faced with a major budget deficit linked to the 2008 recession, many states are saving money by closing older, razor-wire juvenile detention centers (Richmond, 2010). Another is the 2005 Supreme Court decision in *Roper v. Simmons* that highlighted the general difference between young juveniles and older ones (Secret, 2011).

What do you think? Should juveniles be prosecuted as adults? If you answer yes, under what conditions should juveniles be prosecuted as adults, and for what crimes? In what ways are your standards similar to or different from existing practices? If you answer no, what would you suggest to strengthen rehabilitative efforts in juvenile court? In what ways are your recommendations similar to or different from existing practices? In forming your answer, also consider the following question: Do you think that the recent decrease in juvenile crime, particularly violent crime, is temporary or long term?

constitutional requirements. Juvenile courts, however, afford far fewer due process rights than their adult counterparts. Following the two landmark cases, however, the more conservative Burger and Rehnquist Courts were less enthusiastic about extending due process (see the following "Key Developments" feature). Juvenile delinquents, for example, have no constitutional right to a trial by jury (*McKeiver v. Pennsylvania*, 1971), and preventive detention is allowed (*Schall v. Martin*, 1984).

The sheriff of Gila County, Arizona, took 15-year-old Gerald Francis Gault into custody for making a lewd phone call to a neighbor. As to what was actually said, the Supreme Court would only say, "It will suffice for purposes of this opinion to say that the remarks or questions put to her were of the irritatingly offensive, adolescent, sex variety."

Gault was transported to the Children's Detention Home, and no effort was made to contact his parents. Over the next couple of weeks, several brief hearings were held, but no record exists of what happened. What is known, though, is that there is some dispute about whether Gerald Gault actually made the phone call. According to one version, he dialed the number, but his friend did the talking. Whatever may have transpired, the hearing would not be able to determine, because the witness was never present.

After another brief hearing, Gerald was found to be a juvenile delinquent and committed to the State Industrial School "for the period of his minority [that is, until 21] unless sooner discharged by due process of law." This harsh sentence was probably influenced by the fact that at the time he was on six months' probation as a result of having been in the company of another boy who had stolen a woman's purse.

It was the lack of procedural regularity in cases like this one that concerned the American Civil Liberties Union (ACLU). Through a series of complex maneuvers, the ACLU was able to get the case before the Arizona Supreme Court and then the U.S. Supreme Court (Manfredi, 1998).

In deciding *Gault*, the Court was essentially writing on a blank slate concerning juveniles. A year earlier, the Court had ever so tentatively imposed some due process requirements for juveniles accused of serious felonies (*Kent v. United States*, 1966). But now the Court was ready to confront head-on the basic question about juvenile courts: Does the Bill of Rights apply to juveniles, or are children's best interests protected by informal and paternalistic hearings? Justice Abe Fortas's opinion underscored the lack of procedural regularity, stressing that "Due process of law is the primary and indispensable foundation of individual freedom."

At the same time, the opinion in *Gault* supports the purposes of the juvenile court: A juvenile court proceeding is one "in which a fatherly judge touched the heart and conscience of the erring youth by talking over his problems, by paternal advice and admonition" to save him from a downward career. The goodwill and compassion of the juvenile court will not, however, be diminished by due process of law. In one bold stroke, *In re Gault* carved out the following four new constitutional rights in juvenile proceedings:

- Juveniles have the right to timely notice of charges. In the future, parents must be informed that their child has been taken into custody, and written charges must be filed.

- Juveniles have the right to counsel. Following *Gideon*, the Court held that juveniles, like adults, have the right to have an attorney present during the proceedings, and if they are indigent, to have a lawyer appointed.

- Juveniles have the right against self-incrimination. *Miranda*, decided by the Court just a year before, greatly extended the right for adults, and many of the same strictures were now extended to juveniles.

- Juveniles have the right to confront and cross-examine complainants and other witnesses.

The Court's opinion in *Gault* was supported by seven justices and partially by an eighth. Only Justice Potter Stewart dissented outright. He viewed the decision as "a long step backwards into the 19th century." The danger he saw was that abolishing the flexibility and informality of the juvenile courts would cause children to be treated as adults in courts.

In recent years, the Court has wrestled with the difficult question of the appropriate punishment for juveniles who commit serious crimes. In a path-breaking decision the Court held that the death penalty may not be imposed on offenders who commit crimes before they are 18 years old (*Roper v. Simmons*, 2005). Applying the same logic, the Court held that sentencing juvenile offenders to life without the possibility of parole violates the Eighth Amendment's ban on cruel and unusual punishment, but only for crimes that did not involve killings (*Graham v. Florida*, 2010). Two years later, in the companion cases of *Miller v. Alabama* (2012) and *Jackson v. Hobbs* (2012), the Court extended *Graham* by holding that that mandatory life without parole sentences for those under the age of 18 at the time of their crimes violates the Eighth Amendment's prohibition on cruel and unusual punishments.

> Mandatory life without parole for a juvenile precludes consideration of his chronological age and its hallmark features—among them, immaturity, impetuosity, and failure to appreciate risks and consequences. It prevents taking into account the family and home environment that surrounds him—and from which he cannot usually extricate himself—no matter how brutal or dysfunctional. (*Miller v. Alabama*, 2012, p. 2468)

Important Congressional Acts

Congress has also imposed key mandates on the juvenile justice process. The Juvenile Justice and Delinquency Prevention Act of 1974 mandated deinstitutionalization of status offenders by stating that juveniles not charged with acts that would be crimes for adults shall not be jailed. Similarly, the law specifies that juveniles charged with criminal acts shall not be detained in any institution in which they have contact with adult inmates (Snyder & Sickmund, 2006). There is little doubt that this law has fundamentally changed the way our nation deals with troubled youth.

Congressional mandates, coupled with *Gault* and other Supreme Court rulings, have had a marked effect on juvenile-court procedures. "Today's juvenile court is constantly discarding many of its traditional and fundamental characteristics, and it is adopting many of the features customarily associated with criminal court" (Sanborn, 1993; see also Moriearty, 2008). Indeed, as juvenile courts have become more formal institutions of law, the benevolent *parens patriae* character that distinguished it from the adult criminal system has eroded. In recognition of this fact, the highest court in the state of Kansas took a radical step in 2008 by declaring that the rationale upon which the U.S. Supreme Court's decision in *McKeiver* was premised (namely benevolence, parental concern, rehabilitation, and sympathy) was no longer valid. Thus, the Kansas Supreme Court ruled that juveniles have a constitutional right to a trial by jury not only under their own state constitution, but also under the Sixth and Fourteenth Amendments to the U.S. Constitution (*In re L.M.*, 2008). It remains

to be seen whether other states or the U.S. Supreme Court will follow Kansas's lead or whether the *In re L.M.* decision will be invalidated. Regardless of which path is ultimately taken, it is clear that the juvenile court system in the United States has changed dramatically in philosophy and operation from its original form.

Courtroom Work Group

At first glance, members of juvenile courtroom work groups are similar to those found in adult courts—prosecutors bring charges, defense attorneys attempt to get the best deal possible for their clients, and judges decide matters that others have not successfully negotiated. These parallels, though, can be deceiving because the tasks of juvenile and adult courts are not the same. More so than courts dealing with adults accused of violating the law, juvenile courts grant judges and other officials unusually wide latitude in making discretionary decisions intended to "individualize justice." Moreover, although the Supreme Court has imposed minimal due process requirements, juvenile courts remain judicial bodies in which informal processing still dominates.

As will be explained in more detail in Chapter 5, shared norms are the hallmark of courtroom work groups. In assessing the worth of a case, members of the juvenile court work group incorporate many of the same factors as those in adult courts—the severity of the offense and the prior record of the offender. The juvenile-court tradition of individualized treatment, though, encourages the consideration of another important factor—the characteristics of the family. The control the parent or parents have over the youth is a major consideration in deciding the disposition of the case (Fader, Harris, Jones, & Poulin, 2001). Similarly, members of the juvenile-court work group also consider family structure. Youths whose families are perceived to be dysfunctional were much more likely to receive an out-of-home placement than youths whose families were not perceived to be dysfunctional (Rodriguez, Smith, & Zatz, 2009).

KEY DEVELOPMENTS CONCERNING JUVENILE COURTS

Ex parte Crouse (1839)	Philadelphia Supreme Court uses term *parens patriae*.
Illinois Juvenile Court Act (1899)	First juvenile court created in Cook County, Illinois.
Juvenile Court Act (1938)	Federal government adopts principles of juvenile court movement.
Wyoming (1945)	Last state to create a juvenile court.
Kent v. United States (1966)	Court establishes conditions of waiver to criminal court.
In re Gault (1967)	Juveniles are entitled to due process guarantees.
In re Winship (1970)	Proof must be established "beyond a reasonable doubt" in classifying juveniles as delinquent.
McKeiver v. Pennsylvania (1971)	Juvenile delinquents are not entitled to a jury trial.
Juvenile Justice and Delinquency Prevention Act (1974)	Mandates deinstitutionalization of status offenders.
Schall v. Martin (1984)	Court departs from trend of increasing juvenile rights, upholding the general notion of *parens patriae*.
Thompson v. Oklahoma (1988)	Execution of a person under the age of 16 at the time of his or her crime is unconstitutional.
Stanford v. Kentucky (1989)	It is not unconstitutional to apply the death penalty to persons who were convicted of murder when they were 17.
Roper v. Simmons (2005)	The Eighth Amendment forbids the imposition of the death penalty on offenders who were under the age of 18 when their crimes were committed (reversing *Thompson v. Oklahoma* and *Stanford v. Kentucky*).
Graham v. Florida (2010)	Sentencing juvenile offenders to life without the possibility of parole violates the Eighth Amendment's ban on cruel and unusual punishment, but only for crimes that did not involve killings.
J.D.B. v. North Carolina (2011)	A child's age is part of the custody analysis of *Miranda*.
Miller v. Alabama (2012) and *Jackson v. Hobbs* (2012)	Imposing a mandatory sentence of life without parole on an offender who committed capital murder when under the age of 18 violates the Eighth Amendment's Cruel and Unusual Punishment Clause.

The legally trained members of the courtroom work group rely heavily on the professional judgments of non-lawyers in assessing both the background of the youth and the characteristics of the family. This affects the juvenile court work group in a critical way. Whereas in adult court the skills of lawyers are of fundamental importance, in juvenile court they are secondary. Judges, lawyers, and defense attorneys have been trained to interpret and apply the law, but these skills provide little help in making the key decisions in juvenile court cases. Instead, social workers, psychologists, and counselors have been trained to assess the child's problem and devise a treatment plan.

Judges

Judges are the central authority in the juvenile court system. More so than their counterparts in criminal court, they have wide discretion over detention, the adjudicatory hearing, disposition, and other matters. Depending on the size of the court and the rotation system, an individual judge may spend only a little time or a great deal of time in juvenile court.

In many jurisdictions, assignment to the juvenile court is not a highly sought-after appointment. Although some judges like the challenges of juvenile court, to others it is a dead-end assignment. Judges who specialize in juvenile-court matters are often those who enjoy the challenges of working with people rather than those who are intrigued by nuances of legal interpretations. But even judges deeply committed to the juvenile system may seek rotation to other sections to advance their judicial careers (Krisberg & Austin, 1993).

Hearing Officers

In many jurisdictions, judges are assisted by *hearing officers* (sometimes known as *referees, masters,* or *commissioners*). Typically, hearing officers are attorneys appointed by the court to serve on a full- or part-time basis to hear a range of juvenile-court matters. These hearing officers enter findings and recommendations that require confirmation by the judge to become an order.

Prosecutors

Over the past several decades, the power and influence of the prosecutor have grown in U.S. courthouses (see Chapter 6). Rising crime rates, coupled with U.S. Supreme Court decisions requiring more due process, have contributed to the growing role of the prosecutor in juvenile courts (Kupchik, 2006; Shine & Price, 1992).

Prosecutors now dominate the intake-processing stage in most jurisdictions. At times, intake officers make the initial decision and the prosecutor later reviews that determination. But increasingly, prosecutors are the chief decision makers (with input from others, of course). Similarly, prosecutors, more so than judges, are typically the ones who negotiate the disposition of all but the most serious juvenile delinquency cases.

Although the role of the prosecutor's office has increased in juvenile court, an assignment to a section of juvenile court is not a sought-after promotion. On the contrary, it is the newly hired assistant DAs fresh out of law school who tend to be assigned to juvenile court. Thus, much like judges, assistant DAs typically hope for a promotion to a felony unit, where they can practice "real law," trying and convicting "real criminals" (Kupchik, 2006).

Defense Attorneys

In re Gault (1967) held that juveniles were entitled to representation by defense counsel in delinquency proceedings. Yet, defense attorneys play a secondary role in the juvenile court (Burruss & Kempf-Leonard, 2002). Studies reveal great disparities in the number of juveniles who are actually represented by a lawyer, ranging from a low of 15 percent to a high of 95 percent (Guevara, Herz, & Spohn, 2008). Contrary to what some may intuitively believe, studies reveal that youths represented by counsel actually receive a harsher disposition than those who appear in court without an attorney (Guevara et al., 2008), a fact that might explain why so many juveniles waive their right to counsel, thereby keeping proceedings more informal. Yet, being unrepresented by counsel may compromise the due process rights guaranteed by *Gault* (Puritz, Burrell, Schwartz, Soler, & Warboys, 1995; Young, 2000). The American Bar Association has been working with other advocacy groups to ensure that juvenile offenders are competently represented by attorneys with "particularized training in youth development and juvenile law" and who are assisted by interdisciplinary support services (Shepherd, 2003, p. 27). Minnesota has mandated appointment of counsel in juvenile cases, but law in action lags significantly behind law on the books (Feld & Schaefer, 2010).

Lack of representation by a lawyer partially reflects the nature of the caseload—many of the cases are minor. As we saw with adults in misdemeanor court, few have lawyers because the penalties are so light. The same holds true for juveniles—most cases will receive some form of probation, supervision, and/or restitution irrespective of whether a lawyer is, or is not, present.

The role of the defense attorney is further limited by the informality of juvenile courts. In contrast to adult court, juvenile court proceedings place little emphasis on the privilege against self-incrimination. From the initial police contact (and often arrest) through the intake proceedings, juveniles are urged to tell the truth. It should be no surprise, therefore, to learn that fewer than 10 percent of juveniles assert their right to remain silent (Grisso, 1981).

Defense attorneys, when they are present at all, become involved after their client has cooperated with police and prosecutor, and perhaps the probation officer and judge as well. For the cases in which there is only weak evidence, the defense strategy is to seek a dismissal. For the vast majority of cases in which there is strong evidence, defense attorneys negotiate, based on the norms of the work group, the best possible deal for their client. Since most of the cases are, by adult standards, relatively minor, the dispositions reached tend to be on the lenient side—primarily probation, restitution, and community service.

Probation Officers

From the beginning, **probation officers** were a key part of juvenile court. In fact, probation in adult court traces its heritage to these developments. Juvenile probation takes several forms. In some states, probation officers are part of the judicial branch (either locally or statewide); in other jurisdictions, they are part of the executive branch (either locally or statewide).

As in adult court, probation officers in juvenile court conduct background reports and supervise those placed on probation. What is strikingly different, though, is the stage at which they become involved. In adult courts, probation officers are brought into the process after the defendant has entered a plea of guilty or been found guilty. In juvenile courts, they become involved at the early stages of the process. Thus, the probation officer, not a judge or prosecutor, is often the first court official to have contact with the child. Indeed, it is often the probation officer who recommends an informal disposition to the case. Moreover, in more serious cases, the probation officer's recommendation, along with the social worker's, most often becomes the order of the court.

Steps of the Juvenile Court Process

From the perspective of law on the books, the steps of the juvenile court process resemble those for adult courts. Although the terminology is slightly different, juveniles accused of violating the law appear to be treated the same as adults in the same situation. From the perspective of law in action, however, the steps of the juvenile court process are strikingly different from their adult counterparts. More than mere differences in terminology, what makes the processing of juveniles so distinctive is the heavy emphasis on informal decision making. The vast majority of decisions are reached not by lawyers and defendants standing before a judge in open court but rather by a juvenile, a parent, and a probation officer sitting around a desk discussing what will happen next.

Delinquency (Crime)

How many crimes are committed by juveniles (as opposed to adults) is impossible to determine with any great precision. As discussed in Chapter 10, the FBI's Uniform Crime Reports are based on crimes reported to the police, and most crime victims have no way of knowing the age of the person responsible. Juvenile crime increased steadily beginning in 1985, but this increase declined dramatically after 1995. Two important features related to juvenile crime are worth noting:

- Crimes against juveniles are less likely to be reported to the police.
- Juveniles are 2.2 times as likely as adults to be victims of serious violent crime (Sickmund & Puzzanchera, 2014).

Summons (Arrest)

A **summons** is a legal document requiring an individual (in this case, a juvenile) to appear in court

LAW ON THE BOOKS VS. LAW IN ACTION

Steps of the Juvenile Court Process

	Law on the Books	Law in Action
Crime	*Delinquency:* Acts or conduct in violation of criminal laws. *Status offense:* Behavior that is considered an offense only when committed by a juvenile.	Juveniles are more likely than adults to be victims of violent crime. Poor, young, minority males are disproportionately at risk of being victims of violent crime.
Arrest	*Summons:* A legal document ordering an individual to appear in court at a certain time on a certain date.	Around 650,000 juveniles are arrested yearly. Juveniles are arrested primarily for property offenses.
Initial appearance	*Initial hearing:* An often informal hearing during which an intake decision is made.	There are roughly 1.4 million juvenile cases a year. Fifty-seven percent of juvenile filings involve delinquency.
Bail	*Detention:* Holding a youth in custody before case disposition.	There are nearly 51,000 offenders in public and private juvenile detention facilities, less than half the number who were incarcerated in the early 2000s.
Charging	*Intake decision:* The decision made by juvenile court that results in the case being handled either informally at the intake level or more formally and scheduled for an adjudicatory hearing. *Nonpetitioned:* Cases handled informally by duly authorized court personnel. *Petition:* A document filed in juvenile court alleging that a juvenile is delinquent or a status offender and asking that the court assume jurisdiction over the juvenile.	Intake decisions are often informal. Courtroom work-group norms govern decision making. Forty-five percent of juvenile delinquency cases are handled informally (nonpetitioned). Older juveniles with more serious charges are more likely to be handled formally.
Preliminary hearing	*Conference:* Proceeding during which the suspect is informed of rights and a disposition decision may be reached.	In the vast majority of petitioned cases, the juvenile admits guilt during the conference.
Grand jury	Not applicable in juvenile proceedings.	Few juvenile cases are transferred to adult court, where grand jury right may attach.
Arraignment	Occurs during the conference.	Fifty-five percent of juvenile delinquency cases are handled formally (petitioned).
Evidence	Juveniles have the same constitutional protections as adults with regard to interrogation and unreasonable search and seizure.	Police gathering of evidence is very rarely contested.
Plea bargaining	*Plea bargaining:* Formal and informal discussions resulting in juvenile's admitting guilt.	Even more than in adult court, dispositions in juvenile court are the product of negotiations.
Trial	*Adjudicatory hearing:* Hearing to determine whether a youth is guilty or not guilty.	Adjudicatory hearings are more informal than adult trials.

| Sentencing | *Disposition:* A court decision on what will happen to a youth who has not been found innocent. *Placement:* Cases in which juveniles are placed in a residential facility or otherwise removed from their homes. *Probation:* Cases in which youths are placed under informal/voluntary or formal/court-ordered supervision. *Dismissal:* Cases dismissed (including those warned, counseled, and released) with no further disposition anticipated. *Other:* Miscellaneous dispositions including fines, restitution, and community service. | The disposition is often referred to as a treatment plan. Approximately 83,500 juveniles are placed in residential facilities each year. More than 231,400 youths each year receive court supervision. Even case dismissals may include a treatment plan or restitution. Teen courts are a modern version of other dispositions. |
| Appeal | *Appeal:* Request that a higher court review the decision of the lower court. | Appeals are very rare in juvenile proceedings. |

at a certain time and on a certain date. Although the summons is the official term used in juvenile court, it is informally referred to as an arrest. In the latest year for which data are available (FBI, 2016), law enforcement agencies in the United States made an estimated 649,970 arrests of persons under 18, a number that has deceased over the years. Overall, juveniles were involved in 10.3 percent of all violent-crime index arrests and 14.2 percent of all property-crime index arrests. Juvenile arrest statistics include three noteworthy features:

- Nearly 30 percent of juvenile arrests were of females, and the female proportion of arrests has grown in recent years (OJJDP "Statistical Briefing Book," 2015; Zahn, Hawkins, Chiancone, & Whitworth, 2008).

- Just over one-quarter of juvenile arrests involve arrestees younger than 15 years of age (OJJDP "Statistical Briefing Book," 2015).

- Juvenile arrests disproportionately involve minorities, especially for violent crimes (OJJDP "Statistical Briefing Book," 2015).

Intake (Initial Hearing)

Delinquency cases begin with a **referral**. Roughly four out of five referrals are a result of arrests made by law enforcement personnel. Referrals, though, may originate from several other sources; for example, some juvenile court cases stem from petitions filed by teachers, neighbors, merchants, or even parents unable to control their children. But mainly they follow after a juvenile has been arrested by the police.

These arrests and other referrals produce approximately 1.4 million juvenile court cases every year. Best estimates indicate that 55 percent of juvenile filings involve delinquency, 28 percent involve dependency cases, and 13 percent status offenses (see Figure 4.1).

Juvenile court cases have decreased significantly in recent years even though the juvenile population is growing. Indeed, the National Center for State Courts estimates that over the past decade juvenile caseloads decreased by 17 percent in the population adjusted rate (LaFountain et al., 2011).

Soon after referral to juvenile court, an **initial hearing** (sometimes called a *"preliminary inquiry"*) is held. As with much of the terminology of juvenile court, *hearing* is often a misnomer. A hearing implies a formal setting in front of a judge, but more typically it is an informal exchange involving the police officer, probation officer, child, and parent.

Detention Hearing

Police make the first **detention** decision shortly after taking the juvenile into custody. Typically, the police release the youth to the custody of his or her parents (or guardians). If the crime is serious, however, the police may detain the youth in a police lockup or local jail. In an earlier era, juveniles were held in the same facilities as adult offenders, but no longer. Federal law mandates that juveniles be held in facilities separated by sight and sound from detention facilities for adults. In many communities, the number of cells is limited, so even serious violators may be returned to the streets.

A second detention decision may occur after the juvenile has been referred to the juvenile court. Intake personnel review the case and determine whether the youth should be released to the parents or detained. Juveniles may be detained if they are thought to be dangerous to themselves or others if released. Statutes in most states now mandate that if the juvenile is to be detained, a detention hearing must be held before a judge or other hearing officer within 24 to 48 hours of arrest.

In a typical year, one out of five juveniles is detained prior to the adjudicatory hearing (Puzzanchera & Hockenberry, 2013; Sickmund & Puzzanchera, 2014; Snyder & Sickmund, 2006). On any given day, 81,000 youths are held in public and private juvenile detention facilities (Hockenberry, Sickmund, & Sladky, 2011). Overall non-Whites are more likely to be detained (Armstrong & Rodriguez, 2005; Sickmund & Puzzanchera, 2014).

Petition

During the initial hearing, a decision is made not only about detention but also about whether the case will be handled formally (petition) or informally (nonpetitioned). This decision is most often referred to as the **intake decision** (the juvenile equivalent of the charging decision for adults accused of violating the criminal law).

As Figure 4.3 shows, about 46 percent of delinquency cases are handled informally (termed **nonpetitioned cases**). An informal process is used when the decision makers (police, probation officers, intake workers, and prosecutors) believe that accountability and rehabilitation can be achieved without the use of formal court intervention. Informal sanctions are voluntary. At times, they involve

no more than a warning and counseling, but more often they consist of voluntary probation, restitution, and community service.

Juvenile cases that are handled formally are referred to as **petition** cases (or petitioned). Figure 4.3 indicates that approximately 54 percent of delinquency cases receive such treatment. Intake officers are more likely to petition in delinquency cases if:

- Juveniles are older and have longer court histories
- The delinquency is serious (involves violence, for example)

The limited research on petition decisions in juvenile courts suggests that the same *focal concerns* that guide charging decisions in adult criminal cases—blameworthiness, protection of the community, and the practical constraints and consequences of the charging decision (see Chapter 6)—are related to petition decisions in the juvenile context (Higgins, Ricketts, Griffith, & Jirard, 2013). A recent study of over 71,000 juvenile cases in Florida concludes that true juveniles (youth in the middle age range of the court's jurisdiction) were more likely to receive informal processing (Mears et al., 2014).

Conference

The **conference** is roughly equivalent to a preliminary hearing in an adult proceeding. The more minor the transgression, the more likely the conference will be held at the same time as the initial hearing and the detention hearing. In more serious matters, particularly if the decision has been made to file a petition, the conference is more likely to be held in closed court.

During the conference, the judge informs the respondent of the charges in the petition. The person is also informed of constitutional protections, including the right to counsel, the right to free counsel, the right to subpoena witnesses for the defense, and the opportunity to cross-examine prosecution witnesses.

Vast numbers of juveniles admit to their offense during the conference, waiving the right to counsel and the right to trial. Others request counsel, adjourn to the hallway of the courthouse, and after

5 or 10 minutes with an attorney come back before the judge and admit their offense (Rubin, 1989).

Evidence: Gathering and Suppressing

Challenges to how the police gathered evidence play a very minor role in juvenile cases. The presumption is that the child is in trouble (with the juvenile delinquency charge an indicator of that trouble). This presumption makes it difficult to challenge evidence gathering—the judge might conclude that there is insufficient evidence to find the child a delinquent but still enough to conclude that the child is in need of supervision. Moreover, the informal nature of the entire proceeding discourages legal challenges. The general absence of defense attorneys likewise discourages raising issues associated with *Mapp* and *Miranda*. However, as Chapter 11 should make clear, the protections of the Fourth, Fifth, and Sixth Amendments certainly apply to juveniles. Moreover, as cases like *J.D.B. v. North Carolina* (2011) illustrate, law enforcement officers must take special care to make sure that they are honoring the constitutional rights of juvenile suspects.

Plea Bargaining

The informality of juvenile court makes it somewhat difficult to focus on plea bargaining as a distinct phase, because often it is not. Rather, the discretion that runs throughout the juvenile court process is really plea bargaining by a different name (Dougherty, 1988; Kupchik, 2006).

Efforts to negotiate the matter typically begin during the intake process. Parent, child, and probation officer discuss the matter and often arrive at a solution satisfactory to all parties. Thus, a significant proportion of the 46 percent of juvenile delinquency cases that are nonpetitioned clearly represent what in adult court would be labeled as plea bargaining.

Efforts to negotiate a settlement continue after a petition is filed. As Figure 4.3 underscores, 44 percent of petitioned delinquency cases are in the "nonadjudicated" category. Yet, approximately 41 percent of juveniles not adjudicated delinquent

are nonetheless sanctioned, representing another substantial percentage of cases that are plea bargaining. Figure 4.3 demonstrates that similar resolutions by plea bargains (albeit involving lower numbers) occur in status offense cases.

Adjudicatory Hearing

The **adjudicatory hearing** is equivalent to the trial in adult court. The purpose is to determine whether the allegations contained in the petition are supported by a "preponderance of the evidence" (for status offenses) or "beyond a legal doubt" (for juvenile delinquency).

One of the key changes growing out of the due process revolution associated with *In re Gault* is that juveniles have the right to present evidence in favor, which includes cross-examining the government's witnesses and subpoenaing defense witnesses. The juvenile also maintains the privilege against self-incrimination.

Figure 4.3 illustrates that 55 percent of petitioned delinquency cases and 44 percent of status offense cases are **adjudicated**. This seems like a high "trial" rate, but a closer look indicates that this is not the case. Adjudicatory hearings are much less formal than adult trials. This is due in part to the lack of juries (except in a few exceptional cases in a handful of states). The rules of evidence (see Chapter 13) are designed to keep certain information from lay jurors lest they place undue emphasis on some information. But since there are usually no juries, these rules have considerably less applicability. Of course, if the holding of *In re L.M.* (2008) is adopted beyond the state of Kansas, the formality of juvenile proceedings across the county will grow exponentially.

Disposition

The more serious the crime and/or the longer the juvenile has been in trouble with the law, the more likely it is that a formal probation report will be prepared. Like its adult counterpart, the probation report (sometimes called the "predisposition report") is prepared by the probation officer; it is based on interviews with the juvenile, the parents, school officials, and others. The report chronicles the juvenile's prior history with the court and also may estimate the economic harm suffered by the victim. Finally, the report makes a **disposition** recommendation.

The most common disposition is a **dismissal**. Cases dismissed (including those warned, counseled, and released), with no further disposition anticipated, are most likely to occur among cases that are handled informally.

The second most common disposition is **probation**. Probation allows the juvenile to be released into the custody of a parent or guardian while being placed under the supervision of a juvenile probation officer. The range of probation dispositions is quite broad. Some youths participate in informal/voluntary probation with low levels of monitoring, while others are monitored more closely under terms of formal, court-ordered supervision. Many juveniles on probation are ordered to undergo some form of training, education, or counseling as part of the terms of their probation.

As depicted in Figure 4.3, in approximately 8 percent of status offenses cases and 24 percent of cases in which the juvenile is adjudicated a delinquent, the youth is ordered into some formal **placement**. Consistent with the nonpunishment orientation of the juvenile process, juveniles are not sentenced to prison but rather are placed in a residential facility for delinquents or status offenders, or otherwise removed from their homes and placed in a training school, camp, ranch, or group home. However, life in a juvenile correctional facility has come to resemble life in prisons in spite of the supposed different philosophy of the juvenile justice system.

The most recent statistics indicate that 70,793 juvenile offenders are serving placements in juvenile residential facilities (Sickmund & Puzzanchera, 2014). This figure represents a significant decline from just a few years before. Consider that residential placements topped 92,721 in 2006 and 107,493 in 1999 (Sickmund & Puzzanchera, 2014). Consistent with most sentencing research on adults (Chapter 14), legal factors, such as the severity of the crime and prior delinquency adjudications, drive decisions about juvenile placements. But extra-legal factors

also play an important role. As with adult sentencing decisions and the focal concerns perspective, race appears to serve as a perceptual shorthand in the disposition process for juveniles such that African-Americans are often viewed as threatening and are, therefore, more likely than Whites to receive institutional placements (Higgins, Ricketts, Griffith, & Jirard, 2013; Lieber, 2013; Sickmund & Puzzanchera, 2014).

Finally, a significant number of dispositions that do not fall under the previous three categories are referred to simply as **other dispositions**. These include fines, restitution, community service, and referrals outside the court for services with minimal or no further court involvement anticipated.

In making disposition decisions, juvenile-court judges focus primarily on offense characteristics and are influenced only marginally by the offender's social characteristics. These findings are more consistent with the view that juvenile courts are becoming more like adult criminal courts than with the view that individualized justice is the goal (Applegate, Turner, Sanborn, Latessa, & Moon, 2000).

Juvenile courts in urban areas tend to send proportionally fewer delinquents to state detention facilities than do courts serving less populous areas (Rubin, 1989). Officials in rural areas are sometimes quicker to "pull the string" and send less serious delinquency cases to state placement—partially because they have fewer institutional resources to deal with these youths, but also because the equivalent event is viewed as more harmful in small towns than in big cities.

Appeal

Juveniles have a right to appeal in nearly all states. The opinion in *Gault* discussed the importance of appeals for due process rights, but declined to make it a constitutional requirement. Prompted, however, by the possibility that the Supreme Court might indeed make it a constitutional right, state legislatures have passed laws granting juveniles the right to appeal. Thus, today the common practice is to give juveniles the same rights to appeal that apply to adults. By statute, juveniles also have the right to a transcript and a right to counsel for the first appeal.

The right to appeal is primarily limited to juveniles (and their parents). The state may appeal only in limited circumstances, and this right is seldom exercised.

The Future of Juvenile Courts

Juvenile courts, which were once virtually invisible judicial bodies, have in recent years become a major focus in the debate over crime. Amid the constantly evolving war on crime (Chapter 1), there are cross-cutting pressures to change the nature of juvenile court justice. Indeed, some critics argue that this grand experiment has been a failure and should be scrapped.

More than a century after the founding of juvenile courts, it is appropriate to ask, what will juvenile courts be like 50 or 100 years from now? The debate over the future reflects basic disagreements along the lines of the crime control versus due process models.

Crime Control Model: More Adult Penalties

The crime control model begins with the premise that crime is the product of moral breakdown. This is clearly the theme sounded by Darlene Kennedy (1997) of the National Center for Public Policy Research. "Let's hold juveniles responsible for their crimes," she argued, blaming undue leniency of juvenile court for violent juvenile crimes. "The solution is greater deterrence through expected punishments. Children who commit crimes should be punished like adults."

One version of more adult penalties for juvenile offenders involves increasing the number of transfers to adult court. According to the National District Attorneys Association (2007): "Very few juveniles are prosecuted and sentenced as adults in America. . . . In those cases where adult court prosecution does

occur, the simple fact of the matter is that adult court prosecution is clearly warranted. . . ."

Some go so far as to argue that it is time to abolish juvenile court altogether. As far back as 1990, Marvin Wolfgang argued that: "The dual system of juvenile and criminal justice that prevents the sharing of information and permits a serious, chronic violent juvenile to become a virgin offender after his 19th birthday is a strange cultural invention" (quoted in Bureau of Justice Statistics, 1990, p. 18). This line of thought led Peter Reinharz, chief of New York City's juvenile prosecution unit, to argue, "It's time to sell everything off and start over" (quoted in Butterfield, 1997). Chronic overcrowding of juvenile justice facilities is one problem often mentioned, but it is unclear how merely shuffling the overcrowding problems of juvenile facilities to already overcrowded adult courts and adult prisons will alleviate the problem. Public opinion, however, supports the continued operation of a separate juvenile justice system in the United States, although there are disagreements about the details of its operation, ranging from the age at which juveniles should be treated as adults to the appropriateness of harsh punishments over more rehabilitative efforts (Mears, Hay, Gertz, & Mancini, 2007).

In short, a sharp increase in the public's fear of juvenile crime, particularly gangs, drugs, and violence, has added impetus to a get-tough attitude toward juvenile criminals.

Due Process Model: More Youth Crime Prevention

The due process model starts with the premise that crime is a reflection of social problems. Punishment alone, therefore, is not necessarily the answer and might even be counterproductive. Placing juveniles in the same prisons as adults, for example, might simply make the youths more hardened and more accomplished crooks.

Amid numerous voices arguing that the juvenile court created more than 100 years ago is now outmoded, some respond that the nation should return to those roots. The Progressive movement was concerned about mistreatment of juveniles at the turn of the previous century, and we should have the same concern today, argue groups like the American Civil Liberties Union. The core of the argument is that crime prevention works. Instead of pouring increasing amounts of public dollars into prisons (both adult and juvenile), we need to put more into education and prevention.

In "A Call to Action for Juvenile Justice," the American Civil Liberties Union (2008) outlined three priorities for the juvenile court system. Priority one is to keep children out of the criminal justice system. In particular, end the disparity in punitive sentences given to youths of color. Priority two is to protect the rights of incarcerated children. Ensuring access to counsel and the courts is very important (Quinn, 2014). Priority three is reintegrating children into communities. All too often juvenile adjudications can follow children for decades, hampering their ability to find employment.

Conclusion

The charge against Gerald Gault—making a lewd telephone call—seems tame compared with today's concerns about preteens committing violent crimes. Nonetheless, this irritating but hardly life-threatening behavior was to usher in a new era. Whereas the Progressives saw procedural rights as an impediment to helping children in need, a later generation viewed due process as providing an important safety net against high-handed behavior by government officials.

Court decisions like *In re Gault* and changing patterns of youthful behavior—to say nothing of the types of crimes committed by youths today—could not have been foreseen by the Progressive movement. Whether the founders of juvenile court would recognize their innovation more than 100 years later is debatable. Initially, juvenile court was supposed to make decisions based on the "best interests" of the child. Today, a get-tough attitude has come to dominate discussions of juvenile court. Holding the youth accountable to community standards now plays a major role in the dispositions reached.

The future of juvenile courts is rapidly unfolding. To some observers, juvenile courts need to provide more adult-like due process. To others, juvenile courts need to provide more adult-like sentences. Still others would stress the need for new and creative ways of dealing with contemporary problems of American youth. The Progressive movement, after all, responded to changing conditions in society produced by the Industrial Revolution. To many, the current challenge is to respond to the changing conditions of society produced by the information age.

CHAPTER REVIEW

LO1   1.   Describe the child-saving movement and its relationship to the doctrine of *parens patriae*.

Under the legal doctrine of *parens patriae* (state as parent), the government can intervene to protect the child if the parents are failing in their responsibilities. The child-saving movement, which began around 1890, believed that juvenile offenders required treatment, not punishment.

LO2   2.   List the five ways in which juvenile courts differ from adult courts.

Juvenile courts emphasize helping the child; the proceedings are informal, the process is based on civil law, the proceedings are secret, and jury trials are not allowed.

LO3   3.   Discuss how states vary in terms of when a juvenile may be transferred to adult court for prosecution.

Most states consider children to be juveniles until they reach their 18th birthday but some set this upper age as low as 15. Juveniles accused of serious offenses, or who have a history of repeated offenses,

may be tried as adults. Some states set no lower age for transfer, while others set the lower limit at 14 or 16.

LO4 4.   Contrast the three major types of cases that are heard in juvenile court.

In juvenile delinquency cases, the child is charged with a violation of the criminal law that is not based on age. In status offenses, the child is charged with an activity that is illegal only for juveniles. In child-victim cases, the child has committed no crime but the parents are accused of neglect or the like.

LO5 5.   Identify and briefly describe the single most important Supreme Court case with respect to juvenile justice.

The Supreme Court decided *In re Gault* in 1967. Gault was arrested for making an obscene phone call, but his parents were not notified of his arrest or told of the court hearing. The Supreme Court held that juveniles are entitled to many of the same due process rights of adults, including the right to notice, the right to counsel, the right to confront witnesses, and the privilege against self-incrimination.

LO6 6.   Explain the difference between a juvenile case that is petitioned and one that is nonpetitioned.

In juvenile court, charging occurs during the intake decision. Less serious cases are nonpetitioned and handled informally. Petition cases are handled formally and often result in a finding of juvenile delinquency.

LO7 7.   Compare and contrast how adherents of the crime control model and proponents of the due process model of criminal justice see the future of juvenile courts.

Adherents of the criminal control model of criminal justice stress that juveniles should face more adult-like penalties and that the juvenile courts should either be abolished or more juveniles transferred to adult court for prosecution. Proponents of the due process model of criminal justice stress that juveniles need more crime prevention programs and that juvenile courts should be less punishment-oriented.

CRITICAL THINKING QUESTIONS

1.   In what ways do juvenile courts differ from courts that process adults accused of violating the criminal law? In what ways are juvenile courts similar?

2.   What are the key features of the juvenile courts in your state? How are they organized, what is the upper age limit, and what is the lower age limit?

3.   What advantages do you see in adding due process rights to juvenile court? What disadvantages do you see? To what extent are discussions over this matter influenced by atypical cases?

4.   Compare the courtroom work groups of adult court and juvenile court. Which actors are the same? Which actors are different? Do the members of the courtroom work group function the same way in juvenile court as in adult court?

5.   Compare the steps of the adult court process with the steps of juvenile court. In what ways are they similar? In what ways are they different?

6.   What do you think juvenile courts will look like 100 years from now? Will they incorporate more adult due process? Will they stress more adult penalties? Or will they develop more innovative helping programs?

KEY TERMS

adjudicated   131

adjudicatory hearing   131

automatic waiver   119

blended sentencing   119

child-victims   113

children in need of
    supervision   113

conference   130

delinquency   113

detention   129

dismissal   132

disposition   132

initial hearing   129

intake decision   130

judicial waiver   116

juvenile   114

juvenile court   110

lower age of jurisdiction   114

nonpetitioned case   130

other dispositions   132

parens patriae   110

petition   130

placement   132

probation   132

probation officer   127

prosecutorial waiver   119

referral   129

reverse waivers   119

status offense   113

statutory/legislative waiver   119

summons   127

transfer to criminal court   116

upper age of jurisdiction   114

FOR FURTHER READING

Bechtold, Jordan, and Elizabeth Cauffman. 2014. "Tried as an Adult, Housed as a Juvenile: A Tale of Youth from Two Courts Incarcerated Together." *Law and Human Behavior* 38(2): 126–138.

Bernstein, Nell. 2014. *Burning Down the House: The End of Juvenile Prison*. New York, NY: New Press.

Conrad, Shelby, Christie Rizzo, Nicole Placella, and Larry Brown. 2014. "Gender Differences in Recidivism Rates for Juvenile Justice Youth: The Impact of Sexual Abuse." *Law & Human Behavior* 38(4): 305–314, 2014.

Davis, Carla P. 2017. *Girls and Juvenile Justice: Power, Status, and the Social Construction of Delinquency*. New York, NY: Palgrave.

Feld, Barry. 2017. *The Evolution of the Juvenile Court: Race, Politics, and the Criminalizing of Juvenile Justice*. New York, NY: New York University Press.

Greenwood, Peter. 2006. *Changing Lives: Delinquency Prevention as Crime-Control Policy*. Chicago, IL: University of Chicago Press.

Krisberg, Barry A. 2018. *Juvenile Justice and Delinquency*. Thousand Oaks, CA: Sage.

Kupchik, Aaron. 2006. *Judging Juveniles: Prosecuting Adolescents in Adult and Juvenile Courts*. New York, NY: New York University Press.

Paik, Leslie. 2011. *Discretionary Justice: Looking Inside a Juvenile Drug Court*. New Brunswick, NJ: Rutgers University Press.

Richardson, Joseph, Waldo Johnson, and Christopher St. Vil. 2014. "I Want Him Locked Up: Social Capital, African American Parenting Strategies, and the Juvenile Court." *Journal of Contemporary Ethnography* 43: 488–522.

Shelden, Randall, Sharon Tracy, and William Brown. 2012. *Youth Gangs in American Society*. 4th ed. Belmont, CA: Cengage.

Siegel, Larry, and Brandon Welsh. 2012. *Juvenile Delinquency: Theory, Practice, and Law*. 11th ed. Belmont, CA: Cengage.

Tapia, Mike. 2012. *Juvenile Arrest in America: Race, Social Class, and Gang Membership*. El Paso: LFB Scholarly Press.

© dcdebs/E+/Getty Images

A judge watches as a sheriff's deputy answers a question posed to him by a lawyer. While such a scene is typical, the courtroom work group is composed of many people who rarely are depicted in news photos or on television. Rather, the courtroom work group works together "behind-the-scenes" out of shared norms and their mutual interdependence on each other.

Chapter Outline

Sixteen times, Willie Barker's murder case was set for trial, and 16 times it was continued. At first the defense readily agreed, gambling that Barker's codefendant would be found not guilty. Thus, some of the continuances were caused by the six separate trials before the codefendant was finally convicted. Other continuances were granted because of the illness of the police investigator. It was not until five years after his arrest that Barker was convicted of murder. To Barker's lawyer, this lengthy delay clearly violated the Sixth Amendment's right to a speedy trial. The Kentucky prosecutor replied that the delay did not jeopardize Barker's right to a fair trial.

Barker v. Wingo (1972) underscores three key points about criminal-case processing in contemporary courts. First, courts deal with lots of cases. From the perspective of victims and defendants, criminal cases are discrete life events, but from the vantage point of judges, prosecutors, and defense attorneys, the docket consists of numerous cases, each demanding the court's time. The pressure to move cases, often referred to as assembly-line justice, is the first concept discussed in this chapter.

Second, the problems in prosecuting and convicting Barker indicate that discretion is often needed in interpreting the law. After all, the meaning of "speedy trial" is not self-evident. As we shall see, the concept of discretion begins to grapple with the day-to-day realities of courthouse dynamics.

Third, the *Barker* case shows that case dispositions involve far more than the isolated actions of individual judges. From arrest through trial and sentencing, case dispositions require mutual activity on the part of prosecutors and defense attorneys, to say nothing of police officers and probation officers, bail agents, and bailiffs. This chapter

Learning Objectives

After reading this chapter, you should be able to:

LO1 Have a general sense of who works where in the courthouse.

LO2 Analyze the importance of assembly-line justice.

LO3 Describe why discretion is found in the criminal courts.

LO4 Identify the principal actors in the courtroom work group.

LO5 Indicate why ethics is important to the American legal system.

LO6 Contrast differing understandings of why delay is a problem in the courts.

LO7 Discuss the strengths and weaknesses of speedy-trial laws.

LO8 Explain why law in action approaches to court delay are more effective than law on the books approaches.

uses the concept of the courtroom work group to analyze the complexities of interaction among courthouse regulars.

This chapter examines the dynamics of courthouse justice by analyzing three major explanations for the great difference between textbook images of criminal procedure and the realities of the courtroom. We will then apply these concepts to one of the most often mentioned problems of American justice—delay. As in the *Barker* case, though, we will see that deciding how long is too long is a knotty question. But first let us begin with a tour of a typical U.S. courthouse.

The Courthouse and the People Who Work There

Court jurisdiction and court structure are admittedly intangible concepts. Courthouses, on the other hand, are concrete. From the outside, courthouses appear to be imposing government buildings, but on the inside they are beehives of activity. Most immediately, courthouses are places where you find lawyers arguing before juries, talking to their clients, and conversing with one another. But courthouses also employ numerous non-lawyers who perform vital roles; without clerks and probation officers, bail agents and bailiffs, courthouses could not function. Not to be overlooked, ordinary citizens (whether victims or defendants, witnesses or jurors) also perform important roles in the courthouse.

In trying to understand how lawyers and non-lawyers, regular participants and occasional ones, dispense courthouse justice on a daily basis, it is helpful to start with a walking tour of a courthouse. What goes on inside different courthouses, of course, varies in important ways. In the courthouses of small towns, for example, one finds only a few courthouse regulars who handle many different types of matters. By contrast, in the courthouses of major cities you will find numerous courthouse regulars who specialize in specific duties. Moreover, in some courthouses, civil and criminal cases are heard in the same courtroom at the same time; in other jurisdictions, civil and criminal cases are separated by time and place. These variations aside, the following provides an overview of a typical day in a medium-sized courthouse in the United States.

The Courthouse

Early American courthouses were simple structures with "plain furnishings and finishes" (Sahoo, 2006, p. 9). But by the mid-1800s, major courthouses were designed to be "imposing, grandiose" structures that incorporated "formal architectural elements such as columns, domes, clock towers, and grand entrances" (Sahoo, 2006, p. 9). Today, courthouses in the United States "come in a myriad of designs, from centuries-old stone fortresses to modern-day, multifloor monolithic towers, from the one-room council chambers to the abstract designs of the creative architect" (Zaruba, 2007, p. 46).

The locations of courthouses vary dramatically as well. In some cities, courthouses are landmarks in the center of downtown areas. Such courthouses have served as anchors "for many commercial and community activities" (Sahoo, 2006, p. 9). In sharp contrast, for security reasons, criminal courts of other cities were purposefully constructed near pretrial detention facilities in isolated and inconvenient locations. Clustered nearby are older buildings, occupied by bail agents and defense attorneys. Garish neon signs proclaiming "Bail Bonds, 24-Hour Service" compete with unpainted wooden structures to provide a general sense of urban decay. The courthouse building likewise often has a haggard and unkempt look about it. Beneath the veneer of decades of grime, though, one sees a once grand building built during an era when citizens took great pride in their public buildings. Although criminal court buildings are constructed in a variety of architectural styles, they nevertheless all seem to present an image of solidity and unyielding strength.

In the modern era, court security concerns drive courthouse design, renovation, and function. Entrance is usually gained by climbing an excessive number of steps that lead to a single set of doors through which all people must enter.

> Visitors or employees entering the courthouse are met by CSOs [Court Security Officers] and screened as they pass through a metal detector. Persons setting off a metal detector are scanned by a CSO using a handheld detector. Briefcases, packages, and other items in which dangerous or prohibited items might be stored are X-rayed. The CSOs also hand-check any item deemed suspicious or problematic. Policies regarding the use, or even the presence, of cellular and digital phones, personal digital assistants, or other electronic devices are set by each individual courthouse. (Novak, 2003, p. 24)

In older courthouses, prisoners used the same entrances and circulation paths as judges, jurors, and members of the public. Modern courthouses, however, are designed to transfer prisoners securely from holding facilities into courthouses using different entrances and restricted internal routes so that they are kept separated from the public and courthouse personnel (Novak, 2003; Rowden & Jones, 2015; Zaruba, 2007).

Once inside a courthouse, visitors may find themselves in an austere, small area or in a massive lobby with an impressive, high-arched ceiling. Either way, the lobby and hallways typically resound with animated conversations among lawyers, bail agents, bailiffs, defendants, family members, witnesses, and a variety of other interested parties. Indeed, for many bail agents and private criminal lawyers, these hallways are their daytime offices.

The Courtroom

After some difficulty, most first-time visitors manage to locate their courtroom of interest, entering through heavy double doors, which suggests that this is not an ordinary public building. This initial impression of orderliness under law quickly gives way to a sense of social anarchy. One is immediately confronted with a visual and audio reality far different from that portrayed on television or in the movies (Figure 5.1). What is happening inside the courtroom is best viewed in terms of the actors who congregate in different locations.

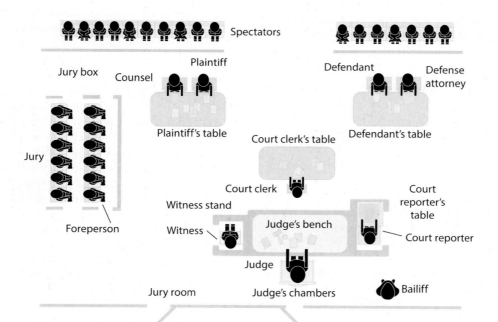

FIGURE 5.1 Courtroom

In the front is an imposing bench that dominates the courtroom, literally elevating the black-robed judge on a pedestal. Court begins by the customary call of the crier: "All rise, the court for ___ County is now in session, the Honorable ___ presiding." On cue, the judge strides mindfully from behind a hidden door, with a law book or case folder tucked under one arm. Just below the bench sits a deputy clerk of court (sometimes called the calendar clerk or courtroom deputy), who controls the scheduling of cases, marks and maintains exhibits, and keeps the judge apprised of the relevant details of the case.

A *court reporter* (sometimes called a court stenographer) typically sits to one side of the bench. Court reporters are specially trained to record and transcribe what is said in many types of legal proceedings. The judge's staff also may include a *judicial law clerk*—typically a recent law school graduate who assists the judge with conducting legal research and drafting judicial opinions. Most judges also have a *judicial secretary* who, in addition to usual secretarial tasks, also maintains the judge's calendar and controls access to the judge when he or she is not presiding in the courtroom.

Bailiffs are present in most courtrooms, although their roles vary significantly in different courts. In the federal system, many judges use their deputy clerks and judicial law clerks to announce that court is in session; escort the jury to and from the jury room; mark evidence; maintain supplies of water, paper, and pencils in the courtroom; relay messages to and from the jury; operate courtroom equipment; and lock and unlock the courtroom. In many state courts, these duties are performed by designated court employees known as *bailiffs*. In some states, bailiffs have additional duties, such as serving court orders; preparing bond forms; and even conducting some security duties, such as staffing metal detectors and x-ray machines.

About 10 to 20 feet from the front of the bench are two tables reserved for the defense and prosecution, respectively. The district attorney's (DA) table is piled high with case folders needed for the day's activities. Somehow, no matter how high the pile of case folders, a file or part of a file is invariably missing, resulting in last-minute scurrying by frantic assistant DAs trying to rectify the periodic lapses of the prosecutorial bureaucracy. The mountain of files on the public defender's (PD) table usually matches that of the prosecutor's. The PD likewise finds that files are missing or incomplete, resulting in scurrying around, looking for missing pieces of paper. When a case involving a private criminal lawyer is called, the PD temporarily gives up the seat at the defense table, but the files remain, an indication that it is really the PD who dominates. Between the bench and the lawyers' tables stands a battered wooden podium, which is typically used only for ceremonial occasions—most notably, when the defendant enters a plea of guilty or the lawyers argue before a jury. Otherwise, lawyers typically argue while sitting behind the table.

To the side of the bench is the jury box. On trial day, jurors occupy these seats; when no jury trial is being conducted, a variety of folks can be found in and around the jury box, waiting, socializing, and occasionally conducting business. Often the easiest to identify are police officers who are in court to provide testimony. Also in attendance are probation officers, substance-abuse counselors, and pretrial services representatives. Bail agents also often drop in to make sure that the persons for whom they have posted bail have indeed arrived as scheduled.

Often sitting in the jury box, too, are defendants who have been detained before trial. Defendants out on bail sit in the public sector, but those in jail sit in brightly colored uniforms with the name of the county jail readily displayed. Often they are manacled together and are temporarily unchained when their cases are called. Surrounding the defendants, hovering like brooding hens, are the sheriff's deputies or other courtroom security officers. The number of deputies in court provides a pretty good indication of the perceived threat of the defendants; the higher the ratio of guards to prisoners, the more serious the crime and the criminal.

A railing separates the courthouse regulars from the occasional participants. The first row or two are reserved for lawyers waiting for their cases to be called. Sitting in the remaining rows are the defendants (those who have been freed on bond or released on their own recognizance), family members, and perhaps a variety of other observers—for example, senior citizens, who enjoy rooting for the prosecutor.

Increasingly in contemporary courthouses, one will also find victim advocates affiliated with organizations such as victim/witness-assistance programs, Mothers Against Drunk Driving, child advocates, and rape crisis centers. Like senior citizens, these people make known their desire for harsh punishments. Table 5.1 summarizes the courthouse actors and their main activities.

TABLE 5.1	Courthouse Actors	
	Actors	**Main Activities**
Law enforcement	Court security staff	Provide security throughout the courthouse
	Sheriff's deputy	Transports prisoners to and from jail
	Bailiff	Maintains order in the courtrooms; handles evidence
Lawyers	Prosecutor	Government official who prosecutes criminal cases
	Public defender	Government attorney who represents indigent defendants
	Private defense attorney	Lawyer paid by a defendant for representation
Court personnel	Judge	Officer who presides in a court of law
	Law clerk	Performs legal research for the judge
	Clerk of court	Record keeper, often responsible for summoning potential jurors to participate in the jury-selection process
	Court reporter	Makes verbatim transcript of proceedings
	Secretary	Handles routine work of judge's office, including keeping the judge's calendar
	Translator	Renders another language into English and vice versa
	Court administrator	Supervises and performs administrative tasks for the court
	Docket clerk	Prepares and assembles case files; distributes legal documents to attorneys and judges; maintains files and records, including entry of data into computer records
Corrections	Probation officer	Recommends defendants for probation and monitors their activities while on probation
	Pretrial services representative	Handles release of qualified pretrial detainees
	Diversion program representative	Recommends defendants for diversion programs such as drug rehabilitation and anger management programs and monitors progress in them
Public	Bail agent	Secures pretrial release of defendants for a fee
	Reporter	Provides media coverage of key events
	Defendant	Person accused of violating the law
	Victim	Person who has suffered a loss due to crime
	Witness	Anyone who will testify in court
	Jurors	Citizens who will decide whether the defendant is guilty or not guilty
	Rape crisis center representative	Provides counseling and support services for sexual assault victims; provides counseling to rape victims
	Child advocate	Person who speaks up for a child's best interest
	Court watchers	Reporters, researchers, students, retirees, and others who go to court to observe proceedings
	Victim/witness assistance	Public or private agency seeking to improve treatment program of victims and witnesses

What is disconcerting to the newcomer to the courtroom is that these actors seem in constant motion. Small groups form and re-form as cases are called and defendants are summoned before the bench. In one corner, an assistant DA can be seen conversing with an assistant PD, while in the back of the room a private defense attorney is engaged in whispered conversations with a defendant and his mother. Moreover, the cast of characters is ever changing. Many actors are in court for a specific case, and when that case has finished, they leave, often walking to another courtroom where they have other cases to attend. Most exasperating of all, the courtroom alternates between bursts of energy and periods of lethargy. Cases are called, only to be put on hold because one of the needed participants is temporarily busy elsewhere in the courthouse.

Behind the Scenes

Outside the great hall of the courthouse and behind the individual courtrooms are areas where visitors seldom venture. What is immediately obvious is that the steady march of people and the accompanying din are absent. Behind the scenes work the actors who provide essential support for courtroom activities.

Courts are paperwork bureaucracies. Even the simplest case requires sheets and sheets of paper: the initial charge, and later, the indictment, bail release forms, pretrial motions, notice of appearance of counsel, and so on. Most of the behind-the-scenes people process this paperwork. Their actions are almost never visible, but their inaction can make headlines.

Other behind-the-scenes actors are managers. A constant complaint is that the courts are mismanaged. Alas, the definition of management in a court setting is elusive. Part of the difficulty is that in many jurisdictions, three distinct sets of court managers—clerks of court, chief judges, and court administrators—are often in competition. Just as important, it is difficult to define what the managers should be doing. A fundamental conflict exists between management (standardized work processes and standard outputs) and the profession of law (individual attention to cases that are fundamentally different). Thus, at the heart of the problem of managing the courthouse is the tension between the rationality of bureaucracy and the anti-bureaucratic philosophies of judges (DuPont-Morales, Hooper, & Schmidt, 2000; Lens, 2015; Saari, 1982).

The **clerk of court**, variously referred to as *prothonotary*, *register of probate*, and *clerk*, is pivotal in the administration of local judiciaries. They are responsible for docketing cases, collecting fees, overseeing jury selection, and maintaining court records. These local officials have enormous power. Since they are elected officials in all but six states, they can operate semiautonomously from the judge. Thus, they have traditionally competed with judges for control over judicial administration (Aikman, 2006; Mays & Taggart, 1986).

Judges are responsible for court administration, but they have most often been ineffective managers. This is primarily due to the unique environment in which the courts operate. Judges may be held responsible, but they seldom have the necessary authority to implement systemic change in a courthouse (Aikman, 2006; Jacob, 1997). Moreover, they are not usually trained in management. The end result is that the lawyers who become judges are not accustomed to analyzing patterns of case dispositions or managing large dockets—the essential skills a manager needs. These problems are reflected in the position of chief judge. Although the chief judge has general administrative responsibilities, the position is really one of "first among equals." Particularly when the chief judge assumes the position by seniority, as many do, there is no guarantee that the person will be interested in management or will be effective at it.

One of the most innovative approaches to court problems has been the creation of a professional group of trained administrators to assist judges in their administrative duties. In short, management—like law—is a profession; therefore, well-trained managers can give the courts what they have often lacked—managerial skill and bureaucratic knowledge. The development of the professional position of court administrator has been sporadic (Flanders, 1991; Lawson & Howard, 1991). However, by the 1980s, every state had established a statewide court administrator. In the years since then, court administration has become increasingly professionalized (Aikman, 2006). Moreover, the profession has expanded significantly; today, most courts (even at the trial court level) routinely employ professional court administrators (Aikman, 2006). The primary duties of these officials are preparing annual reports, summarizing caseload data, preparing budgets, and troubleshooting. Usually, they report to the state supreme court or the chief justice of the state supreme court.

Tension between judges and the court administrator may arise. Some judges are reluctant to delegate responsibility for important aspects of the court's work, such as case scheduling (Aikman, 2006; Bijlsma-Frankema, Sitkin, & Weibel, 2015; Mays & Taggart, 1986). In practice, the distinction between administration and adjudication is not clear-cut. A court administrator's proposal to streamline court procedures may be viewed by the judges as an intrusion on his or her role in deciding cases. For example, it is not easy to determine whether transferring a judge from one assignment to another is a judicial or nonjudicial responsibility (Aikman, 2006; Hoffman, 1991; Stott, 1982).

Courthouse Security and Changing Technologies

Upset with the way his divorce and child custody case had been handled, James Ray Palmer, 48, headed back to the Crawford County Courthouse in Van Buren, Arkansas. When the secretary politely informed Palmer that the judge was not available, he pulled out a semiautomatic weapon and began firing. The secretary was wounded in the leg but escaped life-threatening injuries. Before he was shot by a sheriff's deputy, Palmer managed to fire 70 rounds from some of the four weapons in his possession (CNN, 2011).

The shooting in rural Arkansas is but one incident of violence in courthouses, and such attacks have greatly changed courthouse security. On a typical morning, you will find long lines of jurors, witnesses, defendants, and litigants waiting to enter the courthouse. Not too long ago, entering a courthouse often meant little more than walking through the door past a bored security officer. No longer. Now metal detectors guarding courthouse doors are an ever-present reminder of how threats of violence have altered American society, courthouses included. Metal detectors and surveillance cameras hardly qualify as modern technologies, because they have been in use for a long time. But what has changed dramatically is how widespread they have become in courthouses in recent years. And changes in airport security are certain to affect courthouse security as well.

Targeted Acts of Violence in Courts

In 2010, the Center for Judicial and Executive Security (CJES) released a study entitled "Court-Targeted Acts of Violence." The report examined "185 incidents of courthouse and judicial shootings, bombings, and arson attacks" during the 40-year period between 1970 and 2009 (Fautsko, 2013, p. ii). CJES and the National Center for State Courts examined other forms of violence against court actors, such as "knifings, murder-for-hire and bomb plots, violent assaults, etc.," and found 406 such incidents occurred between 2005 and 2012 (Fautsko, 2013, p. ii). The study concluded that although violence against people who work in the courts increased dramatically in recent years, needed improvements in court security has lagged:

- 86 percent of courts did not have a security committee, or at least one that was deemed to be fully functioning
- 84 percent of courts did not have an incident reporting system, or had one that was rudimentary at best
- 79 percent of the courts provided some training for their security officers, but the training did not include court-specific courses
- 92 percent of courts assessed had less than adequate or no exterior CCTV cameras at all
- 74 percent of courts had entryway screening, although some needed more equipment such as magnetometers and x-ray machines
- 26 percent or a quarter of respondents had no screening station at all

- 96 percent of courtrooms had some type of duress alarm
- 55 percent of courts had no security officers in courtrooms during proceedings
- 62 percent had duress alarms in judges' chambers (Fautsko, 2013, p. iv)

Clearly, operating a court building today is, by its very nature, a risky business for a number of reasons. First, governmental buildings, courthouses included, represent important symbolic targets for terrorist groups, whether of domestic or international origin. The bombing of the federal courthouse in downtown Oklahoma City in 1995 exposed external threats to buildings like these. Protecting older courthouses is difficult because they were built for ready access, not protection. But newer courthouses are constructed with safety as a primary focus.

Second, every day, court buildings are visited by a large volume of disgruntled and even lawbreaking citizens. Gang members trying to intimidate witnesses, defendants charged with domestic violence, and disgruntled spouses litigating a divorce are but three examples of types of people who might explode into violence in the courtroom. No wonder there is often extra security in a courtroom when the judge or jury reaches a verdict.

In some ways security at courthouses is more restrictive than its better-known counterpart at airports. Weapons of course are strictly off-limits in both places. But depending on the courthouse, one may not be able to carry in cameras, cell phones, laptop computers, or knitting needles. Moreover, courthouse security is also very concerned about persons smuggling contraband to prisoners.

Beyond the changing technology of courthouse security is a changing mind-set of what *courthouse security* means. Security is no longer merely protecting the people who work in the courthouse, judges and lawyers primarily. Notions of courthouse security have expanded to protecting the citizens in the courthouse as well. According to the National Sheriff's Association (2011), courthouses and their immediate areas now need a security component that can only best be described as a police district in and of itself. Thus, courthouse security needs to be concerned about the possibility of physical disagreements between litigants, civil or criminal, in

the courthouse and outside as well. And it needs to take into account that courthouse disagreements may lead to retaliation in other places.

Consistent with the theme of this chapter, courthouse actors like the sheriff, court administrator, chief judge, and county boards at times disagree about the adequacy of security. Increasing security sounds good in the abstract but takes on a different tone when the issue turns to who will pay. Sheriffs have been known to plead poverty when it comes to requests for even more deputies assigned to courtroom duty rather than patrol, investigation, or jail duties. There are also important policy disagreements among courthouse actors. Some judges express concerns that too much security lessens public access to the courthouse and often causes major inconvenience to jurors.

Courthouse security varies from place to place, with rural areas like Van Buren, Arkansas, less restrictive than big cities. The courthouse in Van Buren had no metal detector, and an armed deputy was on duty only when the court was in session. But the trend for even more costly and expansive security is sure to continue. On occasion, the news media carry stories about violence in the courthouse, which inevitably leads to even tighter security.

Security Beyond the Courthouse

Sadly, courthouse employees—especially judges, prosecutors, and defense attorneys—need to worry about their safety even when they are not at work. Consider that, according to a 2009 report from the U.S. Department of Justice, 5,744 threats were made to federal judges and prosecutors between 2003 and 2008. That study was prompted, in large part, by the murder in 2005 of the husband and mother of Judge Joan H. Lefkow, a U.S. District Court judge for the Northern District of Illinois. State court employees face identical concerns. In a single year, there were nearly 300 security threats to California state judges and their family members (Franklin, 2008). Given such risks, key court staff needs to take a number of steps to mitigate their chances of victimization. Leading recommendations for doing so include

- Installing a monitored home security system;
- Locking all doors and windows when not in use;

- Not listing their home address on any public documents (which may mean holding title to homes, cars, and other property in the name of a trust);

- Only using the courthouse address and phone number as one's mailing address and contact phone, including on bills, personal checks, and subscriptions to periodicals;

- Applying for confidentiality on drivers' licenses and vehicle registrations; and

- Making sure that telephone numbers and addresses are unlisted (Franklin, 2009; National Center for State Courts, 2014).

Dynamics of Courthouse Justice

A brief tour of a courthouse indicates that justice is very unlike the dramatizations one sees on TV or in the movies. First-time observers find scant relationship between the dynamics of courthouse justice (law in action) and widely held cultural images (law on the books).

- Expecting to see individual trials, they instead witness a parade of defendants and their cases. In particular, newcomers to the courthouse are often struck by the sheer volume of cases.

- Expecting the law to provide guidance, they instead find that decisions are not necessarily clear-cut and that some leeway is available. How else can one explain disagreements over lengths of prison sentences and terms of probation?

- Expecting to observe the conflict (and perhaps even hostility) projected by the adversarial model, courthouse watchers discover cooperation among judges, prosecutors, and defense attorneys. At times, conversations become animated, but by and large, the verbal exchanges reflect a good amount of badinage.

In exploring these differences, practitioners and scholars have used three concepts—assembly-line justice, discretion, and the courtroom work group (see Table 5.2).

- Assembly-line justice explains why few cases receive individual treatment.

- Discretion emphasizes that decisions, although guided by law, are not totally determined by rules found in statutes or court decisions.

- The courtroom work group concept stresses the importance of the patterned interactions of judges, prosecutors, and defense attorneys.

As we shall see, each of these explanations is useful in understanding the dynamics of courthouse justice.

TABLE 5.2	Three Concepts Explaining the Dynamics of Courthouse Justice	
Concept	**Definition**	**Examples**
Assembly-line justice	The operation of any segment of the criminal justice system with such speed and impersonality that defendants are treated as objects to be processed rather than as individuals.	The War on Drugs has greatly increased case volume. Judges feel pressure to move cases.
Discretion	The authority to make decisions without reference to specific rules or facts.	Prosecutors decide whether to file criminal charges. Judges choose between prison or probation.
Courtroom work group	The regular participants in the day-to-day activities of a particular courtroom; judge, prosecutor, and defense attorney interacting on the basis of shared norms.	Cooperation more than conflict governs the working relationships of courtroom actors. Case disposition requires joint actions of judge, prosecutor, and defense attorney. Rules of thumb guide bail release and sentencing.

Assembly-Line Justice

The most commonly advanced reason that criminal courts do not administer justice according to the textbook image is **assembly-line justice**. This explanation was put forth by the President's Commission on Law Enforcement and Administration of Justice (1967, p. 31): "The crux of the problem is that there is a great disparity between the number of cases and the number of judges." Not only judges but also prosecutors, defense attorneys, and probation officers are in short supply. The deluge of cases is reflected in every aspect of the courts' work, from overcrowded corridors and courtrooms to the long calendars that judges, prosecutors, and defense attorneys face each day. Although this report was written nearly 50 years ago, sadly, these facts have not changed, as the court system remains grossly underfunded and understaffed today (Berman & Feinblatt, 2015; Broccolina & Zorza, 2008).

Strengths of the Explanation

The assembly-line justice explanation highlights some important features of the contemporary courthouse. No one disputes that the volume of cases is large. For the last decade or so, between 12 and 14 million persons have been arrested each year. Because of the large volume, overworked officials are often more interested in moving the steady stream of cases along than in individually weighing each case on the scales of justice. Particularly in large cities, tremendous pressures exist to move cases and keep the docket current lest the backlog becomes worse and delays increase. In short, law on the books suggests a justice process with unlimited resources, whereas law in action stresses an administrative process geared toward disposing of a large volume of cases.

To cope with large caseloads, prosecutors, defense attorneys, and judges often apply several mass-production techniques. Thus, actors often specialize in specific tasks. In big-city public defender's offices, for example, one assistant will conduct the initial interview with the defendant, another will represent him or her at the initial appearance, and still another will negotiate the plea. Another mass-production technique is group processing. During the initial appearance, felony defendants are often advised of their rights in one large group rather than individually. Moreover, in the lower courts, sentences are often fixed on the basis of the defendant's membership in a given class rather than on detailed consideration of the individual case.

Weaknesses of the Explanation

Although the assembly-line justice explanation draws our attention to some important aspects of the criminal courts, it also obscures many important considerations. First of all, this orthodox explanation stresses that excessive caseloads are a modern problem. Repeated references are made to the "rise" of plea bargaining and the "decline" of the trial. However, these vivid metaphors distort history. American courts have been faced with caseload pressures for more than a century. Even more important, plea bargaining predates any of the "modern" problems of the courthouse. Indeed, plea bargaining "began to appear during the early or mid-nineteenth century and became institutionalized as a standard feature of American urban criminal courts in the last of the nineteenth century" (Haller, 1979, p. 273; see also Fisher, 2003). In short, those who try to explain how justice is administered in the courthouse simply in terms of too many cases resulting from the growth of big cities are ignoring the historical evidence.

Emphasizing excessive caseloads also fails to consider the types of cases trial courts must decide. Most trial court cases, criminal or civil, present no disputed questions of law or fact. Rather, most case dispositions reflect **routine administration**: "A matter is routine when a court has no disputed question of law or fact to decide. Routine administration means the processing or approving of undisputed matters" (Friedman & Percival, 1976, p. 267). Most cases, therefore, end with a plea of guilty (rather than a trial), not because the courthouse has too many cases but because the courts are confronted with a steady stream of routine cases in which the only major question is the sentence to be imposed.

This has led some commentators to conclude that the emphasis on due process procedures that "dominated the era between the 1930s and the 1970s, [has been] supplanted by a model . . . in which the focus (both in criminal and civil cases) is on how to achieve resolution without or with little adjudication" (Resnik, 2006, p. 1140).

Although heavy caseloads are part of the conventional wisdom surrounding the operations of criminal courts, several studies cast serious doubt on this proposition. A 1979 study in Connecticut compared two courts—one with a heavy caseload, another with a light one. It would be logical to expect major differences in how cases were processed and in the substance of justice handed out, but the results indicated that the courts were remarkably similar. Neither court had many trials. In neither did the defense attorneys engage in a pitched battle with the prosecution. Both courts set bail in approximately the same amounts and imposed roughly similar sentences. Each court spent the same amount of time per case, moving through its business "rapidly and mechanically." The only difference was that the busier court was in session longer than the court that had fewer cases (Feeley, 1979). This and other studies clearly suggest that the criminal court process cannot be understood solely on the basis of excessive caseloads, because such an explanation omits too many important considerations—most especially organizational relationships and local legal culture (Heumann, 1975; Lynch, 1994; Nardulli, 1979; Roach-Anleu, 2009).

Discretion

Law on the books projects an image of a legal system that seemingly runs by itself—a mechanical process of merely applying rules of law to given cases. Law in action, however, emphasizes a legal system in which the legal actors exercise discretion because choices must be made.

Discretion lies at the heart of the criminal justice process. From the time a crime is committed until after a sentence is imposed, discretion is exercised every time key decisions are made. Police exercise discretion when they decide whether to make an arrest. After arrest, the prosecutor may decide not to prosecute. Once charges have been filed, a lower-court judge must set the amount of bail and decide whether sufficient probable cause exists to hold the defendant for the grand jury. In turn, grand juries have discretion over indictments, trial juries over conviction, and judges over sentencing when the legislative scheme permits them some latitude in deciding what punishments to impose.

Discretion is best defined as the lawful ability of an agent of government to exercise choice in making a decision. Viewed from this perspective, discretion has three major subcomponents: legal judgments, policy priorities, and personal philosophies (Cole, 1970; Kim, Spohn, & Hedberg, 2015; Stith, 2008).

Many discretionary decisions in the criminal court process are made on the basis of legal judgments. An example would be a prosecutor who refuses to file a criminal charge because in her legal judgment, the evidence is insufficient to prove all the elements of the offense. Some legal judgments stem from a prediction about the likely outcome of a case at a later stage in the proceedings. The prosecutor, for example, may believe that the defendant did violate the law but that no jury would convict.

Other discretionary decisions reflect policy priorities. Because criminal laws are so broad and general, they must be selectively enforced. The number of crimes that could be charged is virtually unlimited, but the resources devoted to detecting wrongdoers and processing them through the courts (and later incarcerating them) are limited. Thus, discretionary decisions are often made on the basis of policy priorities. Through policy priorities, court officials try to devote more resources to prosecuting serious crimes, such as murder, rape, and armed robbery, rather than minor offenses.

Other discretionary decisions reflect the decision makers' personal values and attitudes—their personal philosophies. Judges and prosecutors have varying views of what offenses are serious and deserving of a high priority. Differences among judges in the same courthouse are readily apparent. Some differences center on the purpose of the criminal law. Those who believe that the courts can deter crime (through heavy sentences, for example) behave differently from those who discount the role the courts can play in deterrence. Stated another way, the same differences of opinion about crime that characterize society as a whole likewise divide courthouse actors.

The Downside of Discretion

The exercise of discretion by various criminal justice actors can be used effectively to improve the functioning of the criminal justice system (Gottfredson & Gottfredson, 1988). On the other hand, discretion, especially when broadly authorized, invites the potential for abusing it. Police may "solicit or accept of bribes in exchange for failure to either report consensual crimes or make arrests in such cases, and in the falsification of evidence to make arrests and secure convictions of suspects" (Bushway & Forst, 2013, p. 212). Prosecutors might dismiss or undercharge in a case as a favor; overcharge; electively or vindictively prosecute; fail to disclose evidence to the defense; make misleading arguments in court; or even solicit perjurious (false) testimony (see Chapter 11; see also Cass, 2015; Schoenfeld, 2005). And judges might engage in an array of misconduct that can unfairly impact nearly all phases of case processing and outcomes (see Chapter 8).

Most of the time, however, justice actors do not exercise their discretion in a corrupt manner. Rather, their discretionary decision making can allow certain factors to influence case processing and outcomes that are not supposed to be a part of the criminal justice process. For example, legal factors, such as the nature of the criminal offense and the defendant's criminal history, are the most salient determinants of criminal sentences (Albonetti, 1997; Kim, Spohn, & Hedberg, 2015; Spohn, 2009; Spohn & DeLone, 2000; Steffensmeier, Ulmer, & Kramer, 1998; Ulmer, 1997). Yet, as explored in greater detail in Chapter 15, the race, ethnicity, gender, age, sexual orientation, socio-economic status, and similar personal characteristics of both defendant and the victim produce disparities in both the likelihood and type of incarceration, as well as sentence length (Johnson, 2006; Johnson, Ulmer, & Kramer, 2008; Kim, Spohn, & Hedberg, 2015; Kramer &

Ulmer, 2009; Spohn & DeLone, 2000). And similar disparities across various personal characteristics have been demonstrated in decisions involving charging, bail, and plea bargaining (see Chapters 10 and 12).

The Courtroom Work Group

Every day, the same group of courthouse regulars assembles in the same courtroom, sits or stands in the same places, and performs the same tasks as the day before. The types of defendants and the nature of the crimes they are accused of also remain constant. Only the names of the victims and defendants are different. Whereas defendants come and go, the judges, prosecutors, defense attorneys, clerks, and probation officers remain the same. To even the most casual observer, the courthouse regulars occupy a special status. They freely issue instructions to the temporary visitors to the courthouse (don't smoke, don't talk, don't read the newspaper), although they smoke, talk, and read the newspaper themselves. The ordinary citizens sit on hard benches in the rear of the courtroom and may approach the bench only when specifically requested to. The courthouse regulars, on the other hand, enjoy easy access to the front part of the courtroom.

The activities of the courthouse regulars represent a complex network of ongoing social relationships (Blumberg, 1970; Flemming, Nardulli, & Eisenstein, 1992; Guzik, 2007; Metcalfe, 2016; Neubauer, 1974b; Sarat & Felstiner, 1995). These relationships are as important as they are complex. James Eisenstein and Herbert Jacob (1977) have proposed that the best way to analyze the network of ongoing relationships among the courthouse actors is through the concept of the **courtroom work group**.

Judges, prosecutors, and defense attorneys are representatives from separate, independent sponsoring institutions. They are drawn together by a common task: Each must do something about a given case. As a result, courthouse regulars work together cooperatively on a daily basis in ways not envisioned by the formal adversary model

(Jacob, 1991; Lichtenstein, 1984; Lynch & Evans, 2002; Metcalfe, 2016). Indeed, in problem-solving courts (especially those subscribing to a therapeutic jurisprudence model) such cooperation forms the philosophical backbone for the courts' existence (Berman & Feinblatt, 2015; Worrall & Nugent-Borakove, 2008). To understand the extent as well as the limits of this cooperation, we need to examine why courtroom work groups form in the first place and their impact on the administration of justice.

Mutual Interdependence

The criminal courthouse is not a single organization but rather a collection of separate institutions that gather in a common workplace. Whereas most large organizations consist of distinct divisions operating under a central leadership, the criminal courthouse consists of separate institutions without a hierarchical system of control. For instance, a judge cannot reward a prosecutor or a public defender who performs well. Rather, each of the courthouse regulars is a representative of a sponsoring institution, which hires and fires them, monitors their activities, and rewards their performance.

None of these actors can perform his or her tasks independently; they must work together. These interactions are critical because none of the courthouse regulars can make decisions independently; each must consider the reactions of others. This is most readily seen in the work of the defense attorney. In representing his or her client, the defense attorney must consider the type of plea agreement the prosecutor may offer, the sentencing tendencies of the judge, and the likelihood of a jury verdict of guilty. Prosecutors and judges are interdependent in similar ways.

Each member of the work group can achieve individual goals and accomplish separate tasks only through work-group participation. The actors come to share common interests in disposing of cases. Hence, cooperation—mutual interdependence—within the work group is viewed to lead to mutual benefits. Assistant prosecutors, for example, are judged by their superiors not so much on how many cases they win but on how few they lose. Thus, to secure their primary goal of gaining convictions, they must depend on defense attorneys to sell their clients on the advantages of the bargain offered and also on judges to impose the agreed-upon settlement.

Shared Decision Making

Courtroom work groups reflect shared decision making. Judges retain the legal authority to make the major decisions, such as setting bail and imposing sentences, but they often rely on others. They routinely follow the bail recommendations of the prosecutor and accept guilty-plea agreements reached by the defense and prosecution. This does not mean that the judge is without power; the other actors must be sensitive to what the judge might do. Prosecutors (and defense attorneys) know the amount of bail a particular judge has set in past situations, so that is what they recommend in the current case.

This shared decision making is highly functional because it diffuses responsibility. Judges, prosecutors, defense attorneys, and others are aware that the decisions they make could turn out to be wrong. Since such dire results cannot be predicted, the members of the courtroom work group share a sense that when one of their members looks bad, they all look bad. Decisions, therefore, are made jointly. If something later goes wrong, work-group members have protected themselves because everyone thought it was a good idea at the time (Clynch & Neubauer, 1981; Wandall, 2016).

The hallmark of work groups is regularity of behavior. This regularity is the product of shared norms about how each member should behave and what decisions are desirable. Courthouse workers can make their common worksite a fractious and unpredictable place for carrying out assigned tasks or, through cooperation, a predictable place to work. The greater the certainty, the less time and resources they need to spend on each case. Newcomers learn these important informal norms of cooperation through a process referred to as "socialization."

Socialization

A problem common to all organizations, courts included, is the need to break in new members, a process known as **socialization**. Through socialization, newcomers are taught not only the formal requirements of the job (how motions are filed and so on) but also informal rules of behavior. In other words, veteran members of the courtroom work group have to "break in" new members so that they understand the ways things are done (Haynes, Ruback, & Cusick, 2010; Wiseman, 1970; Wolfe, McLean, & Pratt, 2017).

Thus, newcomers learn not only from their peers but also from other members of the social network. One of the most important things they learn is the importance of shared norms. It is the shared norms that provide structure to what otherwise would appear to be an unstructured, almost chaotic, process. These shared norms allow the members of the courtroom work group to routinely process what are known as "normal crimes."

Normal Crimes

As discussed earlier, most of the matters before the courts are routine. Although each case is unique, most fall into a limited number of categories. Based on similarities among cases, members of the work group develop certain ideas about types of crimes and criminals. A landmark study in 1965 by Sudnow aptly labeled this phenomenon the **normal crime**, a term still used today. The legal actors categorize crimes on the basis of the typical manner in which they are committed, the typical social characteristics of the defendants, and the types of victims. Once a case has been placed into one of these categories, it is usually disposed of on the basis of a set pattern. In essence, normal crimes represent a group sense of justice.

Rewards and Sanctions

Actors who violate these rules of personal and professional conduct can expect sanctions from the other members of the work group. A variety of rewards (carrots) are available as benefits to those who follow the rules. For example, defense attorneys who do not unnecessarily disrupt routines are able to negotiate a sentence that is slightly less severe than normal. In turn, some sanctions (sticks) may be applied to those who do not cooperate. Judges can sanction uncooperative private defense attorneys, for instance, by making them wait for their case to be called. By far the more effective approach is the carrot, because it operates indirectly and is less disruptive. The imposition of sanctions can lead to countersanctions, with the result that the network is disrupted even further.

Variability in Courtroom Work Groups

Virtually all criminal courts studied to date exemplify the patterns that were just discussed of how courtroom work groups operate, but some important variations need to be considered. For example, the stability of the work groups varies—low turnover in some courts promotes stability in the work group, whereas high turnover in others produces ongoing disruptions of the relationships in the courthouse.

Mavericks can be found in most courthouses. Some defense attorneys engage in hostile relations with prosecutors and exhibit many attributes of adversarial behavior. They do so at a price, however: They are seldom able to negotiate effectively for good deals during plea bargaining (Covey, 2007).

The policy norms vary from community to community. Property crimes are viewed as more threatening in rural areas than in urban ones, so the appropriate penalty for a defendant convicted of burglary in a rural area is more severe than that for a defendant convicted in a big city. In recent years, one set of major concerns about the policy norms relates to gender equity (see "Courts, Controversy, & Gender Equity: Is Gender Bias a Significant Problem in the Courts?").

To the general public, perhaps the most visible variation between work groups concerns delay. Each courthouse has, over time, evolved a set of expectations about the proper pacing of case dispositions. Some courthouses process cases in a timely fashion; others do not.

Is Gender Bias a Significant Problem in the Courts?

The past several decades have witnessed a monumental change in the gender composition of the American workforce. Not only are a higher percentage of women working outside the home, but women are also increasingly working in what were once considered male professions. Law most certainly is a case in point. Today, women constitute between 40 and 55 percent of all law students and make up approximately 30 percent of the nation's judges (National Association of Women Judges, 2016).

One of the areas of most concern to the women's rights movement is gender bias. Thirty-six states have created task forces to investigate gender bias in the legal system. Some state task forces define gender bias as making decisions based on stereotypes about men and women; others stress insensitivity toward certain aspects of men's and women's lives; still others emphasize intentional bias and ill will. Regardless of the precise definition, a team of researchers found these reports to be remarkably consistent. The state task forces consistently found gender bias in four areas of the legal system: domestic violence, sexual assault, divorce, and behavior toward female workers and domestic violence (Agnew-Brune, Moracco, Person, & Bowling, 2015; Belknap, Hartman, & Lippen, 2010; Hemmens, Strom, & Schlegel, 1997).

Sexual assault is one area in which women experience gender bias. Sexual assaults are underreported for a number of reasons, ranging from the stigma and internalized sense of shame that sexual assault victims often experience (Koss, 2000; Weiss, 2010) to concerns about whether victims will be believed and whether they will be blamed (see James & Lee, 2015; Russell, Oswald, & Kraus, 2011). Moreover, many victims fear that reporting their sexual assault will result in re-victimization by the justice system when its actors make judgments about the case based on their own attitudes (including sexism and belief in rape myths) and their perceptions of victim credibility, attractiveness, sexual history, attire, and level of intoxication (for a review, see Grubb & Harrower, 2009; Morabito, Pattavina, & Williams, 2016).

Divorce cases are another area in which the possibility of gender bias looms. State task force reports unanimously found that women suffer from gender bias in terms of awarding alimony, division of property, and child support. The courts, on the other hand, appear to be biased against fathers in child custody awards.

Finally, all the state task force reports found gender bias against female lawyers and court employees. Of principal concern were offensive and intolerable actions toward female participants in the legal system. The most common form of gender bias mentioned was the practice of judges and attorneys addressing female lawyers in a demeaning manner. Female lawyers, more so than their male counterparts, were addressed by their first names. Moreover, terms like "sweetie," "little lady lawyer," "pretty eyes," and "dear" were used. Another common form of gender bias suffered by female attorneys (and judges) is sexist remarks or jokes. Gender bias also affects hiring and promotion. Female lawyers perceive that it is harder to get hired, and once hired they are paid less and have fewer opportunities for promotion.

It is important to underscore that these findings are based on reports of specific events ("Have you ever had remarks made about your looks?") as well as perceptions of gender bias or problems. Women consistently reported problem areas at higher levels than men. Answers to questions like those asked in surveys, of course, can be understood in different ways. Perhaps women are oversensitive to these issues (or alternatively, males are oblivious). Another stumbling block is the difficulty in estimating the true extent of the gender-bias problem. Perceptions of bias could be the product of an isolated few who have contact with many female lawyers and judges, or they could be the result of persistent practices by numerous male lawyers and judges.

Perceptions of gender bias are a serious matter because they affect litigants' perceptions of the fairness of justice. If litigants and/or their lawyers perceive that they are treated differently, they have less confidence in the process of justice, irrespective of the outcome of the case. It is also important to underscore that the gender-bias issues investigated must be taken seriously because they directly affect the lives of many women and their children as well. Moreover, the issues are some of the most explosive facing the justice system and have become, in a relatively few years, important public issues.

Gender bias is not a problem created by the court system; rather, it is a reflection of prevailing attitudes in society. Although "current laws and affirmative action plans have furthered women's equality, they cannot by themselves change the attitudes of individuals. It is the individual attitudes that require change if gender bias is to be eradicated" (Hemmens et al., 1997, p. 31).

What do you think? Is gender bias a serious problem in the nation's courthouses? Have you seen or experienced biased behavior by lawyers, judges, or other court personnel? If you are troubled by using individual reports to make the case for gender bias, what alternative methods would you use to study the problem?

The Problem of Delay

A commonly mentioned problem affecting many of the nation's courts is that too many cases take too long to reach disposition. The magnitude of the backlog and the length of the delay vary greatly, however, depending on the court involved.

In a general sense, the term **delay** suggests abnormal or unacceptable time lapses in the processing of cases (Neubauer, Lipetz, Luskin, & Ryan, 1981; Melcarne & Ramello, 2015). The inherent subjectivity of the term becomes apparent when we try to define *unnecessary delay* (Neubauer, 1983; Steelman, 1997). Although the question "How long is too long" varies by both jurisdiction and the complexity of cases, the American Bar Association (ABA) and the Conference of State Court Administrators (COSCA) have both developed standards that establish nonbinding expectations for the reasonable processing of cases (Figure 5.2).

Most courts, however, fall short of these aspirations. Consider that in 2009, the most recent year for which the Bureau of Justice Statistics has complied data, only 67 percent of felony cases were adjudicated within the 180-day goal. "The median time from arrest to adjudication for felony defendants in 2009 was 111 days. This was the highest median recorded in any . . . year and was about a month longer than the low of 79 days recorded in 1998" (Reaves, 2013, p. 22).

Over three-quarters of the states have adopted their own case-disposition targets, some of which aspire to meet the ABA or COSCA standards (Van Duizend, Steelman, & Suskin, 2011). And, many courts are, in fact, meeting these model time standards, as 85 percent of felony defendants in large urban counties have their cases disposed within one year. More than 80 percent of felony assaults, nontrafficking drug offenses, weapons offenses, and property offense other than fraud are adjudicated within a year. In contrast, only

COSCA Case Processing Standards	ABA Case Processing Standards
Civil • Non-jury trial – 100% within 12 months • Jury trial – 100% within 18 months	**Civil** • 90% within 12 months • 98% within 18 months • 100% within 24 months

Criminal
 • Felony – 100% within 180 days
 • Misdemeanor – 100% within 90 days
	Criminal
	 • Felony
	   • 90% within 120 days
	   • 98% within 180 days
	   • 100% within 1 year
	 • Misdemeanor
	   • 90% within 30 days
	   • 100% within 90 days

Juvenile • Detention and shelter hearings – 100% 24 hours • Adjudicatory or transfer hearings • Concerning a juvenile in a detention or shelter facility – 100% within 15 days • Concerning a juvenile not in a detention or shelter facility – 100% within 30 days	**Juvenile** • Detention and shelter hearings – 100% 24 hours • Adjudicatory or transfer hearings • Concerning a juvenile in a detention or shelter facility – 100% within 15 days • Concerning a juvenile not in a detention or shelter facility – 100% within 30 days
Domestic • Uncontested – 100% within 3 months • Contested – 100% within 6 months	**Domestic** • 90% within 3 months • 98% within 6 months • 100% within 1 year

FIGURE 5.2 Case-Processing Standards

Source: *Model Time Standards for State Trial Courts.* Williamsburg VA: National Center for State Courts, 2011. Available online at http://www.ncsconline .org. Reprinted by permission.

about a third of murder cases are completed within a year of arrest (Reaves, 2013). But, as Figure 5.3 illustrates, there is great variability by jurisdiction.

From one perspective, the data presented in Figure 5.3 suggest that some courts are not currently meeting the recommended standards. But from a different perspective, perhaps they are, because the data measure time from arrest to disposition, thus including the time that passes in the prosecutor's office as well as in the courts.

Consequences of Delay

Concern that "justice delayed is justice denied" is as old as the common law itself. In the 13th century, the nobles forced King John to sign the Magna Carta and promise not to "deny or delay right or justice." In the 19th century, the novelist Charles Dickens condemned the tortuous process of litigation in the English courts. Today, judicial reformers and critics argue that case delay undermines the values and guarantees associated with the legal system.

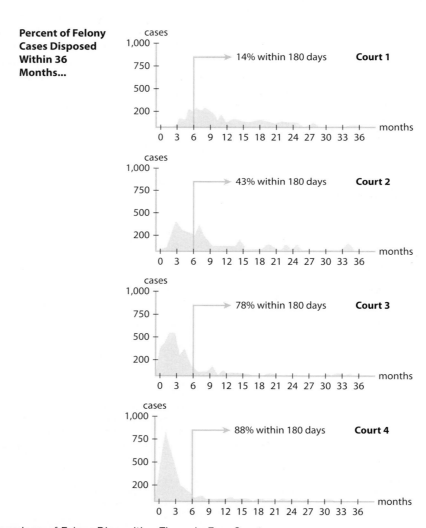

FIGURE 5.3 A Comparison of Felony Disposition Times in Four Courts

Source: *CourTools: Trial Court Performance Measures.* Williamsburg VA: National Center for State Courts, 2013. Available online at http://www.courtools.org /Trial-Court-Performance-Measures.aspx

The three most often cited negative consequences of delays in the courthouse center on defendant, society, and citizen.

Historically, court delay was considered a problem because it jeopardized the defendant's right to a speedy trial. The Sixth Amendment provides that "in all criminal prosecutions, the accused shall enjoy the right to a speedy and public trial. . . ." Defendants may languish in jail for a number of months before guilt or innocence is determined. A number of states have enacted speedy-trial laws premised on the need to protect the defendant's rights.

More recently, delay has been viewed as hampering society's need for a speedy conviction. This view stresses harm done to the prosecution's case. As the case becomes older and witnesses' memories diminish, the defendant's chances of acquittal increase. In short, the state is also viewed as possessing the right to a speedy trial. Thus, in recent years some jurisdictions have enacted speedy-trial laws to try to increase conviction rates.

Regardless of the costs or benefits to either the defense or the prosecution, a third perspective emphasizes that delay erodes public confidence in the judicial process. Citizens lose confidence in the swiftness or certainty of punishment for those who are found guilty. In addition, victims and witnesses may be forced to make repeated, needless trips to the courthouse. Such appearances can cost citizens time and money and ultimately discourage them from prosecuting. Overall, delay in disposing of cases wastes the resources of the criminal justice system.

Assessing the Costs of Delay

Assertions about the costs of delay require careful scrutiny. A general consensus has emerged that delay is a problem facing the courts, with no agreement about the particulars. The three perspectives just described stress the different reasons that delay is a problem. Some perceive that lengthy pretrial incarceration forces defendants to enter into detrimental plea bargains. Others, however, portray caseload pressures as forcing prosecutors into offering unduly lenient negotiated agreements.

In 1978, the National Center for State Courts sponsored a landmark study on the problem of delay in criminal cases (Church & McConnell, 1978). The report noted that few of the assertions about the social costs of delay have been subjected to empirical examination. While there was some evidence to indicate that jail overcrowding and defendants' skipping court appearances (Chapter 10) were related to case delay, the report did not find support for the assertions that case delay causes deterioration of cases or pressures prosecutors to offer lenient plea bargains. Over the decades since then, we have learned more about the problems of court delays. Although improved case-flow management implemented in the 1980s and 1990s shortened the median time from arrest to disposition, it is clear that such techniques "can probably never be viewed as a full and final solution to court delay" (Steelman, 1997, p. 158).

Law on the Books Approach to Court Delay

The law on the books approach to court delay focuses on resources and procedures. It is an article of faith among many commentators that the problem of delay results from an imbalance between available resources and mounting caseloads (Church & McConnell, 1978). A common response is to supplement resources—add judges, prosecutors, clerks, and so on—although the realities of today's austere budgets often prevent doing so. Beyond adding more resources when financially feasible, traditional court reformers emphasize streamlining procedures. They view procedural stages such as preliminary hearing, grand jury indictment, and pretrial motions as sources of delay. But this conventional wisdom about court delay has been called into serious question (Church, 1982; Gallas, 1976).

In *Justice Delayed* (Church, Carlson, Lee, & Tan, 1978), the National Center for State Courts studied 21 courts across the nation and found that the level of court resources was not associated with court delay. The relative size of court caseloads, for example, bore little relationship to case-processing time. Similarly, court procedures were poor predictors

The police arrested two suspects—Willie Barker and Silas Manning—for beating an elderly couple to death with a tire iron in Christian County, Kentucky. The district attorney had a stronger case against Manning and believed that Barker could not be convicted unless Manning testified against him. Thus, the district attorney first sought a conviction against Manning. The court-appointed lawyer initially had no objection to continuing the trial; after all, an acquittal could only help Barker.

The Commonwealth of Kentucky, however, encountered more than a few difficulties in its prosecution of Manning. Altogether, six trials were conducted. Two ended in hung juries and two others in convictions that were reversed on appeal. Finally, Manning was convicted of murdering one victim, and a sixth trial resulted in a conviction for the other murder.

During these legal maneuverings, Barker was in jail for 10 months, which largely explains why at the time the 12th continuance was requested, the defense filed a motion to dismiss the charges. By the time the Commonwealth was ready to try Barker (after two more continuances), another problem arose: The chief investigator on the case was ill, resulting in two additional continuances. Eventually, the judge announced that the case would be dismissed if it were not tried at the next scheduled date. The trial finally commenced, with Manning as the chief prosecution witness; Barker was convicted and given a life sentence.

In assessing these lengthy delays, the opinion of the Court notes that "the right to speedy trial is a vaguer concept than other procedure rights. It is, for example, impossible to determine with precision when the right has been denied. We cannot definitely say how long is too long in a system where justice is supposed to be swift but deliberate" (*Barker v. Wingo*, 1972, p. 522). In essence, the right to a speedy trial is relative, not absolute. The test would be a balancing test, in which the conduct of both the prosecution and the defendant are weighted. Calling the delay "extraordinary," the Court nonetheless ruled that Barker's case was not seriously prejudiced by the more than five-year delay.

Only in extraordinary circumstances has the Court ordered criminal charges dismissed for lack of a timely trial. One such situation involved an eight-year gap between indictment and arrest. The government was negligent in making any effort to track down the defendant, and the defendant was entitled to go free without a trial (*Doggett v. United States*, 1992).

---

of delay. Courts that emphasized plea bargaining (as opposed to trying cases) were as fast (or as slow) as their opposite numbers (see also Steelman, 1997).

These findings explain why the law on the books approach—issuing more and more rules and regulations—is often ineffective in speeding up case dispositions and reducing excessive caseloads. Speedy-trial laws are a case in point.

Speedy-Trial Laws

Speedy-trial laws are federal or state statutes that specify time limits for bringing a case to trial after arrest. Some speedy-trial laws specify precise time standards for periods from arrest to arraignment, trial, and or sentencing. These laws supplement the provisions of the U.S. Constitution and 35 state constitutions that have speedy-trial guarantees. These provisions, however, apply only when the delay has been "extensive." What constitutes unnecessary delay, however, is difficult to pinpoint (see "Case Close-Up: *Barker v. Wingo* and the Right to a Speedy Trial"). But it is clear that whatever might qualify as unnecessary delay, raising a Sixth Amendment speedy-trial claim is limited to the time it takes to bring a case to trial, not what happens after a conviction. In *Betterman v. Montana* (2016), the Supreme Court made it clear that the Sixth Amendment right to a speedy trial does not extend into a guarantee of a right to a speedy sentencing after conviction.

Given the vagueness of constitutional standards regarding "extensive" and "unnecessary" delays, legislatures have shown considerable interest in putting some teeth into the guarantee of a speedy trial. The best-known such effort is the Speedy Trial Act of 1974 (amended in 1979), which specifies time standards for the two primary stages in the federal court process. A span of 30 days is allowed from arrest to indictment, and 70 days from indictment to trial. Certain time periods, such as those associated with hearings on pretrial motions and the mental competency of the defendant, are considered excludable time.

Speedy-trial statutes exist in all 50 states (Herman & Chemerinsky, 2006), but they have a different orientation from their federal counterpart. Most state laws are defendant-centered; that is, they are designed to protect defendants from suffering extensive delay, particularly if they are incarcerated prior to trial. By contrast, the federal law is designed to protect the interests of society; that is, a speedy trial is viewed as an important objective irrespective of whether the defendant's interests are in jeopardy.

Limits of Speedy-Trial Laws

Efforts to mandate speedy trials are striking in their lack of specifics. These laws are not based on an analysis of why delay occurs. Moreover, they do not provide for any additional resources (more judges or prosecutors) to aid the courts in complying. This can produce unforeseen consequences. In a number of federal courts, compliance has come at the price of delaying civil cases. Potential difficulties also arise because not all cases fit easily into the mandated time frames. A major murder case or a large drug-smuggling case takes longer to prepare than an ordinary burglary prosecution.

Researchers approach speedy-trial laws with considerable skepticism. Various studies find that such laws have had limited impact in speeding up the flow of cases through the state criminal court process (Church et al., 1978; Hamburg, 2015; Mahoney et al., 1988; Nimmer, 1978). The primary reason is that most state laws fail to provide the court with adequate and effective enforcement mechanisms. As a result, the time limits specified by speedy-trial laws are seldom a guide to actual practice. One study found that North Carolina's speedy-trial law did indeed speed up the criminal docket, but Connecticut's law did not (Marvell & Luskin, 1991). The federal speedy-trial law has proven effective. The average criminal case filed in the federal courts in

the early 1970s took seven months to reach a disposition. By the early 1980s, the average case was disposed of in less than three months. Thus, the federal approach of court planning followed by fixed standards works to reduce delay (Garner, 1987).

Without adequate resources, however, speedy trials are doomed to failure. Recent budget cuts have increased court delays in California. Officials predict extended waits for lawsuits to reach court, longer custody fights, and even lengthy battles to challenge traffic citations (Dolan & Kim, 2011).

Overall, researchers stress that law in action approaches to reducing court delay are ultimately more effective.

Law in Action Approach to Court Delay

Law on the books approaches to reducing court delay are ineffective because they ignore the dynamics of courthouse justice. All too often, the impression conveyed is that case-flow management is somehow removed from other issues in the criminal court process. Delay is related not to how many cases a court must process but to the choices that the actors make in how they process these cases. Defense attorneys, for example, may seek continuances to avoid harsh judges, to obtain more time to prepare a defense, or even to pressure the client to pay the agreed-upon fee. Prosecutors may use delay to increase the stakes of plea bargaining or to postpone weak cases they are likely to lose. Judges acquiesce to requests for continuances so as not to disrupt the dispositional process (Flemming et al., 1987).

For these reasons, lawyers and judges are generally content with the existing pace of litigation in their courts. Practitioners were asked to provide appropriate case-processing times for typical cases. Within the four courts studied—the Bronx, Detroit, Miami, and Pittsburgh—there was little systematic disagreement among judges, defense counsel, and prosecutors on the appropriate pace of case dispositions (Church et al., 1978). More recent studies have similarly concluded that it is "pervasive local legal culture that transcends court jurisdiction, court size, judicial resources, court rules, or calendaring systems as the explanation of differences in the pace of litigation in fast and slow courts" (Gallas, 2005, p. 23). Findings like these show why law in action approaches to court delay seek to alter practitioners' attitudes regarding proper case-disposition times. Improving case scheduling and trying to achieve better coordination among courtroom work-group members are two such approaches.

Case Scheduling

Waiting is one activity in which people at the courthouse inevitably become engaged. A busy courtroom can grind to a halt because an important witness fails to show up or a lawyer is detained in another courtroom. From an administrative perspective, the courts are extremely complex institutions. The disposition of a case often requires the presence of the following individuals: judge, clerk, court reporter, bailiff, defendant, prosecutor, defense attorney, police officer, victim, and witness. Depending on the procedural stage, jurors, a probation officer, a pretrial services representative, and an interpreter may also need to appear.

Many of these people have several different courts to appear in during a single day. For example, defense attorneys, prosecutors, and probation officers may have several cases set for the same time. There can be administrative problems, too. Because of an illegible address, the defendant never receives a notice. Or the jailer may forget to include the needed defendant on the day's list. If just one person is late, the others must wait, and if one person never shows up at all, the hearing must be rescheduled.

Efforts at Coordination

As we have noted previously, the court is actually a collection of agents from separate and independent organizations: judge, police officer, prosecutor, sheriff, clerk, and probation officer. Most of these organizations are headed by elected officials or, like the police, report to elected officials. They have their own bases of power, their own separate legal mandates, and their own scheduling problems. Judges and court administrators, therefore, have only limited control over coordinating interagency schedules and cooperative efforts (although they are often held responsible when something goes wrong).

Variability in Courtroom Work Groups Revisited

The variability in courtroom work groups (discussed earlier in this chapter) has major consequences for how long it takes courts to dispose of cases. A team of researchers associated with the National Center for State Courts studied a blend of urban and rural courts (Ostrom, Ostrom, Hanson, & Kleiman, 2007). In each courthouse, they interviewed the wide range of officials discussed in this chapter. They focused on how cases were managed and how court actors interacted and found four distinctive ways of doing things.

Some courts were characterized as hierarchical because there was a clear chain of command among judges, administrative staff, and courtroom staff. Courts with a hierarchical culture processed felony cases significantly faster than other courts. Other courts were characterized as communal because they valued communication, cooperation, and compromise. Courts with a communal culture processed felony cases more slowly than other courts. The authors caution that no cultural type is necessarily good or bad. Rather, variations in courtroom work groups reflect responses to multiple goals as well as differing ways of managing relations between a diverse set of courthouse actors (Ostrom et al., 2007).

Legal Ethics

Lawyers often suffer from a negative public image, which is one reason the legal profession places considerable emphasis on **legal ethics**. *Ethics* refers to the study and analysis of what constitutes good or bad conduct (Pollock, 2012). Legal ethics represents a specific type of ethics. First, it is an example of applied ethics, in which ethical principles are applied to specific issues. Legal ethics is also an example of professional ethics, because it involves the behavior of a profession, in this case the legal profession. All ethical systems, legal ethics included, have a moral component. But morality and ethics are different. Whereas morality emphasizes a set of moral absolutes, legal ethics involves the difficult task of helping lawyers sort out the best option when perhaps no good options exist.

Legal ethics is of critical importance because the American legal system is based on the adversarial system, which stresses verbal combat. At its basis, this system represents a fight between opposing viewpoints, and the use of legal ethics is one way to regulate this verbal combat to ensure, in essence, a fair fight. At heart, legal ethics emphasizes protecting clients by ensuring that they have competent attorneys to forcefully present their cases. Legal ethics also seeks to promote public respect for the legal system. Thus, lawyers are not allowed to mislead the court, nor can they knowingly allow witnesses for their side to perjure themselves.

Regulation of the legal profession begins with codes of legal ethics and professional responsibilities. The American Bar Association (ABA) adopted the *Model Rules of Professional Conduct* in 1983, which it updates periodically. These rules serve as models for the ethics rules of most states. But, consistent with federalism (see Chapter 2), each state has adopted its own code. Thus, state bar associations, not the national association of lawyers, enforce these codes. Law students are required to take a course in legal ethics, and before they can be admitted to the bar, they must pass a separate test on legal ethics.

The codes of legal ethics promulgated by the legal profession are increasingly supplemented by statutes and court decisions. Most important, the Supreme Court has made significant rulings on when prosecutors must disclose exculpatory information to the defense (Chapter 11) and when prosecutors may not use race as a factor in jury selection (Chapter 13).

The primary responsibility for establishing and enforcing professional standards of conduct for the legal profession rests with the highest court of each state. In turn, state courts of last resort have delegated enforcement to the state bar association, which establishes a specific committee to enforce the provisions. Disciplinary proceedings typically begin with the filing of a complaint by a disgruntled client, although judges, other lawyers, or the committee itself can initiate action. Complaints about attorney misconduct are typically investigated in secret, although a few states mandate a more public process. Most complaints are dismissed because of insufficient evidence. But when evidence of an ethical violation exists, the committee files charges and conducts a private hearing. If the charges are proved, the committee recommends disciplinary actions, which can range from a reprimand (either private or public) to a suspension of the license to practice law for a given period of time to restitution to the client. The most severe sanction is disbarment, which permanently revokes a lawyer's right to practice law. These recommendations may be appealed to the state supreme court, which, after a public hearing, may accept, modify, or reject them. Bar association sanctions against lawyers are relatively rare, however.

The typical remedy for legal mistakes made during the trial is an appellate court reversal (Chapter 15). Legal ethics is enforced in other ways, as well, including sanctions meted out by judges (Chapter 8) and civil lawsuits for legal malpractice (Chapter 7). Typically though, lawyers working in the criminal justice system enjoy legal immunity, which is to say you cannot sue a prosecutor, defense attorney, or a judge just because you lost your case.

The ethical issues surrounding the three types of lawyers who appear in court vary greatly, depending on the role they play. In the next chapters, we will examine some of the legal issues facing prosecutors, defense attorneys, and judges.

Conclusion

Discussions of court delay and its consequences all too often are conducted in abstract terms. *Barker v. Wingo*, however, forces one to deal with some of the realities. The Court's opinion is clearly mindful of the fact that to interpret the right to a speedy trial in a manner understood by the drafters of the Constitution would, in all likelihood, result in brutal murderers being set free.

Barker v. Wingo and our discussion of the problem of delay show that the actual operations of the criminal courts differ greatly from official expectations. Three concepts—excessive caseloads, discretion, and the courtroom work group—have been used to explain this gap between the law in action and the law on the books. Although courts are burdened with too many cases, an excess of cases is at best only a partial explanation for the behavior of the criminal courts. More important is the role that discretion plays in the court system, shaping the dictates of formal law to the actual cases and defendants that come to the criminal courts. The courtroom work-group concept emphasizes the interactions among the key actors in court. The next three chapters will examine in greater depth how prosecutors, defense attorneys, and judges work within the courtroom work group, and why.

CHAPTER REVIEW

LO1 1. Have a general sense of who works where in the courthouse.

Bail bondsmen have their offices outside courthouses. Judges, lawyers, clerks, court stenographers, law clerks, and bailiffs work inside the courtroom. Clerks of court and court administrators work behind the scenes.

LO2 2. Analyze the importance of assembly-line justice.

The concept of assembly-line justice stresses the high volume of cases in courthouses and the emphasis on moving the docket.

LO3 3. Describe why discretion is found in the criminal courts.

At every key stage of the criminal court process, humans must apply the law. Choices are made on the basis of legal judgments, policy priorities, and values and attitudes of the actors.

LO4 4. Identify the principal actors in the courtroom work group.

The courtroom work group refers to the regular participants, such as judges, prosecutors, and defense attorneys, who interact on a daily basis.

LO5 5. Indicate why ethics is important to the American legal system.

Legal ethics are important because they provide necessary boundaries on conflict represented by the adversary system and also seek to ensure clients that their lawyers are working in their best interests.

LO6 6. Contrast differing understandings of why delay is a problem in the courts.

Some see delay as a problem because it works to the disadvantage of the prosecutor, others see delay as a problem because it jeopardizes the rights of defendants, and still others see delay as a problem because it reflects a waste of resources.

LO7 7. Discuss the strengths and weaknesses of speedy-trial laws.

Speedy-trial laws reflect a law on the books approach to problem solving. Although these laws have the advantage of calling attention to delay as a problem, they are limited because they provide no mechanisms to deal with discretion.

LO8 8. Explain why law in action approaches to court delay are more effective than law on the books approaches.

Law in action approaches to solving the problem of delay can prove effective because they focus on coordinating the activities of the key actors in the courthouse. Without such coordination, the local legal culture is unlikely to be changed.

CRITICAL THINKING QUESTIONS

1. Take a tour of your local courthouse. How does your perception of it match the description at the beginning of this chapter? Compare notes with other classmates; perhaps they focused on features that you did not.

2. Place yourself in the position of a felony court prosecutor. In what ways does the cooperation of other members of the courtroom work group work to your benefit? How would your answer be different if you approached the question from the vantage point of the judge or the defense attorney?

3. Of the several consequences of delay, which one do you think is the most important? Which one is the least important?

4. In *Barker v. Wingo*, the U.S. Supreme Court stressed the legitimate reasons for the 16 trial continuances. But is there a danger that prosecutors might illegitimately seek continuances?

KEY TERMS

assembly-line justice   149

clerk of court   145

courtroom work group   151

delay   155

discretion   150

legal ethics   160

normal crime   153

routine administration   149

socialization   153

speedy-trial laws   158

FOR FURTHER READING

Aikman, Alexander. 2006. *The Art and Practice of Court Administration*. Boca Raton, FL: CRC Press.

Bach, Amy. 2009. *Ordinary Injustice: How America Holds Court*. New York: Holt Paperbacks.

Barrett, Jimmie. 2009. *Protecting Court: A Practitioner's Guide to Court Security*. Minneapolis, MN: Mill City Press.

Braswell, Michael, Belinda McCarthy, and Bernard McCarthy. 2011. *Justice, Crime and Ethics*. 7th ed. Burlington, MA: Anderson/Elsevier.

Burke, Kevin, and Frank Broccolina. 2005. "Another View of Local Legal Culture: More than Court Culture." *Court Manager* 20: 29.

Castellano, Ursula. 2009. "Beyond the Courtroom Workgroup: Caseworkers as the New Satellite of Social Control." *Law and Policy* 31: 429–462.

Gould, Jon, Roger Hartley, William Raftery, Linda Merola, and James Oleson. 2011. "The Challenges and Opportunities of Evidence-Based Management in the Courts." *Judicature* 95: 61–67.

Haynes, Stacy, Barry Ruback, and Gretchen Cusick. 2008. "Courtroom Workgroups and Sentencing: The Effects of Similarity, Proximity, and Stability." *Crime & Delinquency* 56: 126–161.

Lipetz, Marcia. 1980. "Routines and Deviations: The Strength of the Courtroom Workgroup in a Misdemeanor Court." *International Journal of the Sociology of Law* 8: 47–60.

Merritt, Nancy. 2006. *Sentencing Reform and the Influence of Courtroom Communities: Oregon's Measure 11*. Newark: Rutgers, The State University of New Jersey–Newark.

National Association for Court Management. 2011. "Visioning and Strategic Planning." Available online at http://www.nacmnet.org/CCCG/strategic-planning.html

Olin, Dirk, and Rebecca Kourlis. 2011. *Rebuilding Justice: Civil Courts in Jeopardy and Why You Should Care*. Golden, CO: Institute for the Advancement of the American Legal System.

Orlik, Deborah K. 2013. *Ethics for the Legal Professional.* 8th ed. Upper Saddle River, NJ: Pearson.

Peak, Kenneth. 2012. *Justice Administration: Police, Courts and Corrections Management.* 7th ed. Upper Saddle River, NJ: Pearson.

Robson, Peter, and Jessica Silbey (Eds.). 2012. *Law and Justice on the Small Screen.* Oxford, England: Hart Publishing.

Rudes, Danielle S., and Shannon Portillo. 2012. "Roles and Power within Federal Problem-Solving Courtroom Workgroups." *Law and Policy* 34(4): 402–427.

Souryal, Sam S. 2011. *Ethics in Criminal Justice: In Search of the Truth.* 5th ed. Burlington, MA: Anderson/Elsevier.

Stojkovic, Stan, John Klofas, and David Kalinich. 2010. *The Administration and Management of Criminal Justice Organizations.* Long Grove, IL: Waveland Press.

Wendel, Bradley. 2014. *Professional Responsibility: Examples and Explanations.* 4th ed. New York: Aspen/Wolters Kluwer.

Young, Richard. 2013. "Exploring the Boundaries of the Criminal Courtroom Workgroup." *Common Law World Review* 42: 203–229.

Raleigh News & Observer/Getty Images

Former District Attorney Mike Nifong, left, speaks while Duke lacrosse player Reade Seligmann, right, listens in the courtroom at a Durham County, North Carolina, court building in 2006. Instead of trying to find the truth about what happened on March 13, 2006, Nifong set out to prove that three Duke University lacrosse players had raped an exotic dancer. Nifong's conduct led to his being disbarred from the practice of law by the State Bar of North Carolina. But the result of the disciplinary action against Nifong may never be able to erase the stain left by a case that went wrong from the start for Duke lacrosse players Dave Evans, Collin Finnerty, and Reade Seligmann.

Chapter Outline

"I wouldn't allow Durham to become known for 'a bunch of lacrosse players from Duke raping a black girl,'" proclaimed Mike Nifong, candidate for district attorney. After a 30-year career as an assistant prosecutor in Durham County, North Carolina, Nifong was running for election as district attorney. His comments fanned the fires of what quickly became a sensational national case.

Following a party thrown by the Duke lacrosse team, three team members were accused of sexually assaulting a woman who had been hired as a stripper. While the case was being investigated and while charges were pending, Nifong made nearly 50 pretrial statements to the press.

Among the statements, ten were alleged to be improper commentary on the team members' failure or refusal to give information to law enforcement authorities and their invocation of their constitutional rights. Another ten were alleged to be "improper commentary on [his] opinion about the guilt of the accused and/or about his opinion that a crime had occurred." Finally, the bar listed statements that particularly heightened public condemnation of the accused, many of which asserted a racial motivation for the attack. (Mosteller, 2007, p. 1349)

Nifong was apparently motivated to appear in the media as a crusader for racial justice while he was locked in a tight reelection battle. He represented himself as someone fighting to vindicate a young, African-American woman's sexual victimization by White student athletes of socio-economic privilege. And his plan worked; Nifong was reelected with strong support from the Black community in the Durham area even though one of his opponents, a Black man, had won some major community endorsements that would typically sway the larger community (Mosteller, 2007; Phillips & Griffin, 2015).

Learning Objectives

After reading this chapter, you should be able to:

LO1   Discuss the two major characteristics of prosecutors in the United States.

LO2   Describe the three most important entities in federal prosecution.

LO3   Identify the three somewhat overlapping agencies involved in prosecution in state courts.

LO4   Explain the major factors affecting the work life of assistant district attorneys.

LO5   Analyze the principal factors affecting prosecutorial ethics.

LO6   Outline two major examples of the expanding domain of the prosecutor.

Nifong would win the election, but the rape charges would eventually be dismissed for lack of evidence.

In addition to filing politically motivated charges that were allowed to continue for months even though it had become clear that the defendants were innocent, Nifong concealed exculpatory DNA evidence and made deceptive and misleading statements to the press, the trial court, fellow attorneys, and the state bar. This unethical conduct ultimately resulted in Nifong being hauled before the State Bar of North Carolina for disciplinary proceedings. The State Bar concluded that Nifong violated several provisions of the North Carolina Revised Rules of Professional Conduct, including two parts of Rule 3, which concern pretrial publicity. (These rules are based on the Model Rules of the American Bar Association, which have been adopted in more than 40 states.)

- Rule 3.6(a) prohibits a lawyer from making an "extrajudicial statement that the lawyer knows, or reasonably should know, will be disseminated by means of public communication and will have a substantial likelihood of materially prejudicing an adjudicative proceeding in the matter."
- Rule 3.8(f) prohibits prosecutors from making out-of-court statements that have a substantial likelihood of heightening public condemnation of the accused.

Nifong's violation of these rules, among others, ultimately caused him to lose his license to practice law, because the rules are designed to protect criminal defendants' Sixth Amendment right to a fair trial from being eroded by unfair media coverage from a seemingly reliable source (see Chapter 13). But Nifong made some outrageous statements in spite of these ethics rules when he said things like, "The guilty will stand trial" and "I am convinced there was a rape."

Nifong also improperly commented on the lacrosse players' invocation of the right to remain silent and the right to counsel as evidence of their guilt when he said to the media, "If it's not the way it's been reported, then why are they so unwilling to tell us what, in their words, did take place that night?" Nifong also said, "And one would wonder why one needs an attorney if one was not charged and had not done anything wrong."

Although the Duke lacrosse sexual assault case was highly unusual, it illustrates the influential role prosecutors play in the criminal justice system. More so than judges and defense attorneys, the prosecutor is the most powerful official in the criminal courts. From initial arrest to final disposition, how the prosecutor chooses to exercise discretion determines to a large extent which defendants are prosecuted, the type of bargains that are struck, and the severity of the sentence imposed.

This chapter discusses several factors involved in the work of the prosecutor. We begin by examining the prosecutor's role in the criminal justice system and then consider separately the structure of federal and state prosecutors' offices. Our focus then shifts to actual courtroom behavior, looking at prosecutors at work. But prosecutors do not work in isolation. Thus, the later parts of this chapter look at prosecutors within the context of the courtroom work group and their expanding domain in the criminal justice system.

Origin of the Public Prosecutor

Most modern prosecutors in the United States hold a public office. They are government employees in civil service. But the public prosecutor of today evolved from private prosecutions at English common law "where the legal system primarily relied upon the victim or the victim's relatives or friends to bring a criminal to justice" (Bessler, 1994, p. 515).

From Private to Public Prosecutions

Private citizens were permitted to institute criminal proceeding in Great Britain "as means of facilitating private vengeance" (Bessler, 1994, p. 515). This tradition of private prosecution carried over to the American colonies, even though a few public prosecution offices had existed since at least the 1640s, when Virginia created an office of the attorney general to prosecute select cases on behalf of the British monarchy (Bessler, 1994). In 1704, Connecticut enacted the first statutory scheme for public prosecutions. And in 1711, "Virginia established a formal system of county prosecuting attorneys" (p. 516). Nonetheless, private prosecution remained the norm in the United States until the late 1800s. Victims who could afford to retain private counsel to prosecute on their behalf hired lawyers to present their cases before grand juries and at trials. Victims who lacked the funds to hire a lawyer prosecuted cases for themselves.

Perhaps surprisingly to some, some states still permit private criminal prosecutions today (Fairfax, 2009). In most of these jurisdictions, crime victims can hire their own lawyers to criminally prosecute a case, so long as the local public prosecutor (usually the district attorney, as described later in the chapter) retains the ultimate control of the case. But a handful of states still allow private prosecutors to litigate certain types of criminal cases with "unbridled discretion" (Bessler, 1994, p. 521; see also Fairfax, 2009).

Due process concerns about private prosecutions—especially potential conflicts of interest, vindictive prosecutions, corruption, accountability, and the non-delegable sovereign act of exercising prosecutorial discretion—eventually led to the overwhelming number of U.S. jurisdictions moving to the public prosecutor model described in the remainder of this chapter. Indeed, in *Young v. United States ex rel. Vuitton et Fils S.A.* (1987), the U.S. Supreme Court overturned a federal conviction for criminal contempt of court that was privately prosecuted by counsel appointed by a federal district court. Key to the Court's decision was that the lawyers appointed to prosecute the contempt case had a conflict of interest. But it is worthy to note, Justice Blackman's concurrence in the case stated that "due process requires a disinterested prosecutor with the unique responsibility to serve the public, rather than a private client, and to seek justice that is unfettered" (p. 816).

Quasi-Public Prosecutions

Due to the small size or budgetary restrictions (both of which are typically applicable in rural areas), some U.S. jurisdictions have adopted one of two models of quasi-public prosecution. Under the *prosecution outsourcing model*, the jurisdiction might contract with a nongovernmental lawyer in private practice or a law firm to prosecute cases on behalf of the state either on a fixed time basis (e.g., for a year) or on an *ad hoc* basis when the need arises. Under the *part-time prosecutor model* that is used in approximately 25 percent of the states, lawyers are hired or elected to serve as part-time government prosecutors, but they are simultaneously permitted to maintain a private law practice. In both of these models, "private or semiprivate actors are given the tremendous discretion and power associated with the public prosecution of criminal offenses" (Fairfax, 2009, p. 413).

Although due process concerns are lessened by quasi-public prosecutions in comparison to true private prosecutions, problems with conflicts of interest remain a real concern with both part-time and outsourced prosecutors. For example, "allegations of at least the appearance of impropriety were made when it was revealed that the part-time prosecutor in Surry County, Virginia, investigating dogfighting charges against NFL superstar quarterback Michael Vick had represented, at one time, Vick's father in the prosecutor's private civil law practice" (Fairfax, 2009, p. 438 n. 95). Nonetheless, some jurisdictions are so small that "the outsourcing of the prosecution function is not a choice among alternatives; it is the recognition of the reality that a public prosecutor is a cost-prohibited luxury" (Fairfax, 2009, p. 418).

Role of the Prosecutor

The prosecutor is of critical importance because of the office's central position in the criminal justice system. Whereas police, defense attorneys, judges, and probation officers specialize in specific phases of the criminal justice process, the duties of the prosecutor bridge all of these areas. This means that on a daily basis, the prosecutor is the only official who works with all actors of the criminal justice system. As Justice Robert Jackson (1940, p. 18) once remarked, "The prosecutor has more control over life, liberty, and reputation than any other person in America."

Prosecutors stand squarely in the middle of the fragmented nonsystem of criminal justice discussed in Chapter 1. Naturally, the various actors have conflicting views about how prosecutorial discretion should be used—the police push for harsher penalties; defense attorneys, for giving their clients a break; and judges, to clear the docket. Thus, prosecutors occupy a uniquely powerful and highly visible position in a complex and conflict-filled environment. Amid the diffusion of responsibility that characterizes the criminal justice system, power has increasingly been concentrated in the hands of the prosecutor (Misner, 1996; Sklansky, 2016; Worrall & Borakove, 2008). The "Law on the Books vs. Law in Action" feature provides an overview of the role of the prosecutor throughout the criminal justice process.

Broad Discretion

A key characteristic of the American **prosecutor** is broad discretion. Although the prosecutor works in the courthouse, the office of prosecutor is part of the executive branch of government. This independence from the judiciary is vital for the proper functioning of the adversary system, since prosecutors at times challenge judicial decisions. The breadth of prosecutorial power stems from numerous court cases since 1833. Typical is *People v. Wabash, St. Louis, and Pacific Railway,* an 1882 decision in which the Illinois Court of Appeals stated that the district attorney (DA) "is charged by law with large discretion in prosecuting offenders against the law. He may commence public prosecutions . . . and may discontinue them when, in his judgment the ends of justice are satisfied." In decisions like this one, appellate courts have allowed the modern prosecuting attorney to exercise virtually unfettered discretion relating to initiating, conducting, and terminating prosecutions (Albonetti, 1987; Jacoby, 1980; Sarat & Clarke, 2008; Sklansky, 2016).

Even though the "Law on the Books" vests prosecutors with almost unlimited discretion with regard to charging decisions, the reality of "Law in Action" is that prosecutors are not insulated to pressure from politicians, the media, and the public at large. Consider the facts of how George Zimmerman came to be charged for shooting and killing Trayvon Martin (Chapter 1). The initial decision not to charge Zimmerman was presumably based on prosecutors' view of the evidence that

LAW ON THE BOOKS VS. LAW IN ACTION

Role of the Prosecutor in Steps of Criminal Procedure

	Law on the Books	Law in Action
Crime	Must enforce all laws to the fullest.	The impossible legal mandate means that priorities must be established.
Arrest	Little involvement.	In major crimes, may advise the police whether sufficient evidence of probable cause exists to arrest.
Initial appearance	Represents the government.	Manages the chaos in the lower court, where there are many cases and little is known about the crime or the defendant.
Bail	Can make a bail recommendation to the judge.	Typically recommends a high bail amount to the judge.
Charging	Exclusive domain of the prosecutor.	Often decides which defendants will be charged with what crime.
Preliminary hearing	Dominates this step because of the authority to call witnesses.	Highly successful in having defendants bound over for further proceedings.
Grand jury	Acts as legal adviser to the grand jury.	The prosecutor largely decides which cases will be heard; the grand jury tends to "rubber stamp" prosecutorial requests for indictments.
Arraignment	Formally presents the charges against the defendant in open court.	By taking the case this far, the prosecutor has indicated his or her willingness to move forward on a case.
Discovery	Important variations in state law regarding how much information must be disclosed prior to trial.	Informally provides trusted defense attorneys with information to induce a plea of guilty.
Suppression motions	Argues that police acted legally in searching and/or interrogating the suspect.	Argues that police acted legally in searching for evidence to be admitted.
Plea bargaining	District attorneys have considerable discretion in plea bargaining.	Based on normal penalties, dictates the terms under which defendant pleads guilty.
Trial	Presents witnesses proving defendant guilty and urges jury to return a verdict of guilty.	Very successful in gaining convictions.
Sentencing	In many jurisdictions, the district attorneys can make a sentencing recommendation to the judge.	Judge is more likely to follow the district attorney's sentencing recommendation than the defense attorney's.
Appeal	Argues before the appellate court why the lower court conviction should stand, and often wins.	Wins a significant victory in most appeals.

they could not prove a homicide charge beyond a reasonable doubt in light of Zimmerman's claim of self-defense. In the wake of that decision, though, social justice activists, the media, and many members of the community vocally decried the decision not to prosecute Zimmerman, arguing that it was the product of racism. The political firestorm that ensued eventually led Florida Governor Rick Scott to appoint Angela Corey, a state attorney with a tough-as-nails reputation, as a special prosecutor to examine the case. She, however, charged Zimmerman with second degree murder, a charge for which Zimmerman was acquitted. Several notable legal experts questioned the wisdom of the second-degree murder charge, arguing that she overcharged Zimmerman. Law Professor Bennett Gershman (2013), for example, asked, "Why did Corey overcharge Zimmerman, knowing that the proof would support at most a charge of manslaughter?" (para. 7). He speculated that she may have done so in the hopes of pressuring Zimmerman into accepting a plea bargain on a lesser charge. But he also noted that Corey was under intense presume to charge Zimmerman with murder:

> Given the national and even international notoriety of the case, Corey's announcement of the murder charge, whether or not based on the evidence, and whether or not motivated by personal or political considerations, appeared to be a hugely popular decision. Since it was preliminary to a trial, and appeared to be a reasonable exercise of prosecutorial discretion, there was no excessive criticism. (Gershman, 2013, para. 9)

Limits on Discretion During Trial

Appellate courts have placed restrictions on the exercise of prosecutorial power during the trial itself. In the context of the adversary system, the prosecutor is expected to advocate the guilt of the defendant vigorously. But the prosecutor is also a lawyer and is therefore an **officer of the court**; that is, he or she has a duty to see that justice is done. Violations of the law must be prosecuted, but in a way that guarantees that the defendant's rights are respected and protected. In 1935, the Supreme Court spelled out the limitations imposed on prosecutors by their obligation as officers of the court: "He may prosecute with earnestness and vigor—indeed, he should do so. But while he may strike hard blows, he is not at liberty to strike foul ones. It is as much his duty to refrain from improper methods calculated to produce a wrongful conviction as it is to use every legitimate means to bring about a just one" (*Berger v. United States*, 1935, p. 88).

Prosecutorial Misconduct

As the quote from *Berger v. United States* (1935) indicates, prosecutors are supposed to play by the rules. They are expected to be tough, but fair. As

Mike Nifong's conduct the Duke lacrosse case illustrates, however, prosecutors do not always live up to this duty. And sometimes such misconduct results in horrible miscarriages of justice. Consider what happened to Michael Morton. He served 25 years in prison for murdering his wife until DNA evidence demonstrated that he had been wrongfully convicted of the crime. Importantly, though, the prosecutor, Ken Anderson, had evidence that Morton's 3-year-old son witnessed the murder and said his dad was not home at the time. But Anderson kept that information from the defense. While Morton spent 25 years in prison for a crime he did not commit, Anderson's career flourished, eventually landing him a judgeship in Texas. Anderson was eventually criminally charged with tampering with evidence. He agreed to surrender his license to practice law in exchange for having the charges dropped. And he was sentenced to serve 10 days in jail on a contempt of court charge for telling the judge in a pretrial hearing during Morton's prosecution that he had no favorable evidence to give to Morton's lawyers. He was released after five days for good behavior.

Although some commenters hailed the prosecution of Ken Anderson's misconduct, others decried it; the *New York Times* called it "insultingly short" in comparison to the years Morton spent behind bars from a crime he did not commit ("A Prosecutor Is Punished," 2013, para. 1). Even though the consequences Mike Nifong and Ken Anderson ultimately faced may seem minor in comparison to the harms their misconduct caused, their cases are remarkable because they were actually punished. The same cannot be said for most acts of prosecutorial misconduct. Consider the following results of three studies.

One study found 707 cases in which state appellate courts determined prosecutorial misconduct had occurred in California between 1997 and 2009; yet, of the more than 4,740 lawyers that the state bar disciplined over those same years, only 10 were prosecutors (Ridolfi & Possley, 2010). That same year, *USA Today* published the results of a six-month investigation into 201 cases involving misconduct by federal prosecutors. Of those, only one prosecutor "was barred even temporarily from practicing law for misconduct" (Heath & McCoy,

2010, para. 15). And a 2013 study of New York City cases found 30 cases in which prosecutorial misconduct was so significant that criminal conviction was overturned. Yet, only of the prosecutors was significantly disciplined (Sapien & Hernandez, 2013).

The permissive attitude toward prosecutorial misconduct in the states may be changing. In late 2016, California enacted a law making it a felony punishable by up to three years in prison for a prosecutor to intentionally withhold or tamper with evidence.

In recent years, the Supreme Court has expressed repeated concern about prosecutorial misconduct. Convictions have been reversed because prosecutors were too zealous in their advocacy. But at the same time, the nation's highest tribunal has also decided that prosecutors enjoy absolute immunity from civil lawsuits when acting as courtroom advocates. However, under other conditions, prosecutors may be sued civilly (see "Case Close-Up: *Connick v. Thompson* and Prosecutorial Misconduct").

Charging Decisions

Of all the discretionary decisions prosecutors routinely make, perhaps none is more important than the decision of whether to file charges, thereby transforming a suspect into a criminal defendant. There are few, if any, legislative or judicial guidelines to guide prosecutors in the exercise of their discretion in this domain. Indeed, the Supreme Court has made it clear that, "So long as the prosecutor has probable cause to believe that the accused committed an offense defined by statute, the decision whether or not to prosecute, and what charge to file or bring before a grand jury generally rests entirely in his discretion" (*Bordenkircher v. Hayes*, 1975, p. 364). Scholars posit that prosecutorial discretion in charging decisions is guided by a set of *focal concerns* on the practical constraints and consequences regarding both organizational efficiency and the certainty of conviction (Beichner & Spohn, 2005; Ulmer, Kurlychek, & Kramer, 2007; O'Neal & Spohn, 2016).

Overview of Focal Concerns Theory

Steffensmeier (1980) originated **focal concerns theory** as a way of explaining judicial decision making,

primarily as it relates to criminal sentencing (Steffensmeier, Ulmer, & Kramer, 1998; Ulmer, 1997). This framework maintains that sentencing decisions are shaped by three primary *focal concerns*: blameworthiness, protection of the community, and the practical constraints and consequences of the sentencing decision.

Blameworthiness generally refers to the offender's culpability and the severity of harm caused. The *protection of the community* factor primarily concerns preventing future crime through deterrence and incapacitation. This, in turn, requires judges to examine the defendant's dangerousness and likelihood that he or she will reoffend in the future (Albonetti, 1991; Helms & Jacobs, 2002; Johnson, Klahm, & Maddox, 2015). Finally, the *practical constraints and consequences* concerns both the organizational and social costs associated with sentencing certain individuals (e.g., mothers, the elderly, etc.), as well as those facing courts and correctional facilities (such as overcrowding).

According to the focal concern perspective, because they are frequently constrained by time, resources, and limited information about the defendant, judges often rely on social stereotypes as part of a "perceptual shorthand" that connects these stereotypes to key offender characteristics, such as their blameworthiness and their future dangerousness (Steffensmeier, Ulmer, & Kramer, 1998). As a result, conduct and characteristics that are stereotypically associated with specific social groups—especially on the basis of race, ethnicity, gender, and age—can result in defendants being treated with greater leniency or severity, depending on whether offenders fit into positive or negative schemas ascribed to the larger social stereotype (Cochran & Mears, 2014; Huebner & Bynum, 2008; Johnson & Betsinger, 2009).

Focal Concerns Theory Applied to Charging

Research has extended focal concerns theory to explain, in part, how prosecutors make charging decisions (Beichner & Spohn, 2005; O'Neal & Spohn, 2016; Ulmer, Kurlychek, & Kramer, 2007). Prosecutorial charging decisions share many of the

CASE CLOSE-UP   *Connick v. Thompson* and Prosecutorial Misconduct

John Thompson spent 14 years on death row because a prosecutor deliberately withheld evidence that might have led to his acquittal. Should the district attorney's office have to pay for such egregious prosecutorial misconduct? A six-person federal jury decided that the district attorney's office was liable and calculated damages at $1 million per year. Five justices of the Supreme Court reached a very different decision.

John Thompson was charged with the murder of a New Orleans hotel executive, and the extensive publicity surrounding that case resulted in Thompson being charged with an unrelated armed robbery that occurred after the murder. To enhance their chances of getting a guilty verdict in the murder case, the Orleans Parish district attorney's office tried Thompson first on the armed robbery charge and secured a conviction. During the subsequent murder trial, the defendant declined to testify because he didn't want the jury to know of his prior felony conviction. Thompson was convicted and sentenced to death.

A month before the scheduled execution, a private investigator found a lab report that clearly showed that Thompson could not have committed the armed robbery—the robber had type B blood; Thompson's blood was type O. Assistant District Attorney Gerry Deegan had checked out the lab report from the police evidence locker but never placed it in the courthouse property room. On his death bed, Deegan confessed to a friend and former prosecutor that he had deliberately withheld the evidence. Under *Brady v. Maryland* (1963), prosecutors must disclose evidence favorable to the defense (see Chapter 11).

Thompson's attempted armed robbery conviction was dismissed, and he was retried on the murder charge. This time he took the stand in his own defense, and after only 30 minutes of deliberation, the jury acquitted. Thompson filed a Section 1983 civil rights suit in the U.S. District Court for the Eastern District of Louisiana. The $14 million verdict was upheld by the U.S. Fifth Circuit before the Supreme Court decided to hear the appeal from the district attorney's office.

Writing for the five-judge conservative majority, Justice Thomas overturned the jury verdict, arguing that one cannot sue for civil rights violations under Section 1983 for failure to train prosecutors based on a single *Brady* violation. Assistant District Attorney Deegan was viewed as a rogue prosecutor and not typical of prosecutors in the office. Justice Ginsburg's dissent scoffed at such notions of an isolated act, writing that under *Connick* "long-concealed prosecutorial transgressions were neither isolated nor atypical."

The current Orleans Parish district attorney reacted positively to the decision, noting that the $14 million verdict would have crippled his office (Maggi, 2011). Others, however, feared the decision would lead to prosecutorial impunity (Appleton, 2011). An influential article in the online edition of *The Yale Law Journal* argues that this decision means that prosecutors cannot be held accountable. The Court based its decision in part on the availability of other measures to check prosecutorial misconduct, but these are ineffective (Keenan, Cooper, Lebowitz, & Lerer, 2011).

Connick v. Thompson is but the latest in a somewhat tortured line of prosecutorial misconduct decisions. Prosecutors are immune from civil lawsuits when they are performing their prosecutorial role, but they enjoy only qualified immunity outside the judicial arena, in particular when they provide faulty legal advice to the police (*Burns v. Reed*, 1991). The Court revisited the issue two years later and laid down a slightly more discernible line of permissible and impermissible conduct. The Court restated that prosecutors have absolute immunity from civil damage suits for actions in connection with the traditional role of courtroom advocacy, but DAs enjoy only "qualified immunity" for other actions. The Court unanimously held that statements made in a news conference were not protected by absolute immunity. But the justices split 5 to 4 on whether investigative actions by the DA were subject to suit (*Buckley v. Fitzsimmons*, 1993).

The Duke lacrosse players sued Mike Nifong and the city for which he had been employed. After the *Connick* decision, part of the lawsuit was allowed to proceed. In May 2014, the city of Durham settled the long-running lawsuit. The plaintiffs received no money, but the city donated $50,000 to the North Carolina Innocence Inquiry Commission, and Nifong agreed to give the commission $1,000, settling the case against him.

same concerns presented by judicial sentencing decisions, especially with regard to a defendant's blameworthiness and the risks the defendant poses to the community. Although there is overlap, prosecutors weigh some practical constraints and consequences when making charging decision that are different from those considered by judges. For example, prosecutors have to carefully consider how their charging decisions affect organizational efficiency and resources both in their own offices and in court (Goelzhauser, 2013; Ulmer & Johnson, 2004).

Focal concerns about organizational efficiency require prosecutors to evaluate the consequences of their charging decisions with the contexts of media scrutiny and its accompanying political consequences, their relationships with law enforcement, their relationships with other members of the courtroom work group, and the limitations of budgets, personnel, and time (Gershman, 2011; Stemen & Frederick, 2013). Prosecutors also have to consider the certainty of conviction as one of their focal concerns (Albonetti & Hepburn, 1996). In doing so, prosecutors need to consider the *legally relevant factors* of the case when making charging decisions, including

- the seriousness of the offense (Albonetti, 1987; Jacoby, Mellon, Ratledge, & Turner, 1982; Kim, Spohn, & Hedberg, 2015; Neubauer, 1974a; Spears & Spohn, 1997)

- the strength of the evidence, such as valid eyewitness identifications, victims who are cooperative and willing to testify, and the corroborating physical or forensic evidence (Albonetti, 1987; Jacoby et al., 1982; O'Neal, Tellis, & Spohn, 2015; Spohn & Holleran, 2001)

- the culpability of the defendant, including the number of charges, the accused person's prior criminal history, and the accused person's motives for the offense (Albonetti, 1987; Gershman, 2011; Kim, Spohn, & Hedberg, 2015; Neubauer, 1974a; Spohn & Holleran 2001)

- the degree of harm caused by the offense and the corresponding proportionality of the potential punishment (Gershman, 2011; O'Neal, Tellis, & Spohn, 2015)

- the degree to which the accused cooperates in prosecuting others (Gershman, 2011)

- the availability and likelihood of prosecution by another jurisdiction (Gershman, 2011)

Taken as whole, these legally relevant focal concerns lead prosecutors to decline prosecution of a large number of arrests so that they can focus time and resources on "cases involving more serious crimes (e.g., Mather, 1979), with stronger evidence (e.g., Albonetti, 1987), and more culpable defendants (e.g., Spohn & Holleran, 2001)" (O'Neill-Shermer & Johnson, 2010, p. 399).

But prosecutors also consider *extra-legal* case characteristics—factors that are not supposed to be legally relevant—in much the same way judges rely on social stereotypes as part of a "perceptual shorthand" that connects these stereotypes to key offender characteristics (Cochran & Mears, 2014; Spohn & Holleran, 2000; Ulmer, Kurlychek, & Kramer, 2007). Most of the *extralegal factors* concern the personal characteristics of the offender, the victim, and key witnesses, such as race, ethnicity, sex, age, socio-economic status, educational level, employment status, and so on. Research is inconclusive whether such extra-legal factors play a significant role in the charging decision.

- Some studies conclude that race does not influence the decision to prosecute or dismiss a case or to reduce charges (e.g., Albonetti, 1986, 1987; Baumer, Messner, & Felson, 2000; Johnson & Klahm, 2015; O'Neill-Shermer & Johnson, 2010; Spears & Spohn, 1997). Other studies disagree, finding that the race of the suspect or the racial differences in the victim–offender dyads (especially if the defendant is Black or Hispanic and the victim is White) significantly affect the charging and dismissal decisions (Baumer, Messner, & Felson, 2000; Cochran & Mears, 2014; LaFree, 1980; Spohn, Gruhl, & Welch, 1987; Spears & Spohn 1997). And still others report findings that advantage racial and ethnic minorities over Whites, especially in misdemeanor shoplifting (Myers, 1982) and felony drug cases (Barnes & Kingsnorth, 1996; Franklin, 2010; Wooldredge & Thistlethwaite, 2004).

- Researchers have demonstrated that prosecutors are more likely to charge defendants who are male (Nagel & Hagan, 1983; Spohn, Gruhl, & Welch, 1987; Spohn & Spears, 1997; Ward, Hartley, & Tillyer, 2016) or unemployed (Schmidt & Steury, 1989) and are less likely to reduce initial charges against males compared to females (O'Neill-Shermer & Johnson, 2010; Ward, Hartley, & Tillyer, 2016).

- O'Neill-Shermer and Johnson (2010) found "no evidence that young minority males were particularly disadvantaged in overall charging decision" (p. 421). Other research found that the interplay of certain demographic characteristics affects charging decision, albeit not in the direction most people would assume. For example, even though Franklin (2010) found that "young, Black males were treated no more harshly than any of the race-gender-age categories examined" in charging decisions in felony drug cases, "White defendants between thirty and thirty-nine years old were significantly less likely to have their cases dismissed as compared to young, Black defendants" (p. 190). Barnes and Kingsnorth (1996) reported similar findings and hypothesized that the rather surprising data might be a function of the fact that "Black defendants were likely arrested with poorer quality evidence when compared with White defendants, forcing prosecutors to dismiss their cases more frequently" (Franklin, 2010, p. 190).

Few people assume that racism, sexism, and other forms of intentional bias are, in and of themselves, responsible for invidious discrimination in charging decisions. Rather, most researchers believe these factors influence prosecutors' predictions of how judges and jurors might assess the background, behavior, and motivations of both suspects and victims (Frohmann, 1997). Indeed, there is ample evidence that prosecutors are more likely to file charges when there is a "stand-up" victim—someone whose personal characteristics align with societal stereotypes concerning who is credible and undeserving of victimization (see LaFree, 1980; Stanko, 1988). These factors are particularly salient in sexual assault cases (see "Courts, Controversy, & Gender Equity: Are Sexual Assaults Against Women Underprosecuted?").

Decentralization

Another characteristic of the office of prosecutor is decentralized organization. Although the American prosecutor represents the state in the prosecution of criminal cases, the office is not centralized, as it is in England and most of Europe (Flemming, 1990; Jehle & Wade, 2006; Sklansky, 2016). Instead, prosecution is highly decentralized, with more than 8,000 federal, state, county, municipal, and township prosecution agencies.

Commensurate with the nation's often confusing dual court system, separate prosecutors are found in federal and state courts. The structure, however, is not parallel with court structure; that is, each court does not have attached to it a specific prosecutor. DAs, for example, often conduct the trial in the trial court of general jurisdiction and then appeal through both layers of state courts and, on rare occasions, even to the U.S. Supreme Court (a federal judicial body). Moreover, different prosecutors' offices may handle the same case; sometimes, the city attorney conducts the preliminary stages of a felony case in the lower courts, and the district attorney prosecutes in the trial court of general jurisdiction.

Table 6.1 provides a rough overview of typical state and federal prosecutorial structure. Be aware, however, that the apparent hierarchy of prosecutorial structure is an illusion. In the federal courts, the U.S. attorneys enjoy considerable autonomy from the U.S. Justice Department, and in the states, local district attorneys are totally separate from state attorneys general. We will begin with prosecution in federal courts and then turn to the more complex realities of state prosecutions.

Prosecution in Federal Courts

Prosecutions in federal courts are conducted by the U.S. Department of Justice. Billed as the world's largest law firm, the Department of Justice represents the U.S. government in all legal matters not specifically delegated to other agencies.

Are Sexual Assaults Against Women Underprosecuted?

To many critics, the criminal justice system does not take allegations of rape/sexual assault seriously enough. On the other hand, the Duke lacrosse player sexual assault prosecution serves as a cautionary tale, because in these types of cases, stories of victims can change and the physical evidence does not always corroborate the victim's version of the truth. Similarly, a New York prosecutor was quick to prevent Dominique Strauss-Kahn, the powerful head of the International Monetary Fund, from leaving the country after he was accused of sexual assault by a hotel maid. Three months later, the criminal charges were dropped because the victim told too many inconsistent stories to prosecutors. But Strauss-Kahn's chance to be elected president of France was over (Smith-Spark, 2011).

Sexual assault is one of the most visible gender equity controversies in the criminal justice system. Along with domestic violence (see Chapter 9) and gender bias in the courtroom (Chapter 5), it is the topic that feminists have most identified as involving systematic bias throughout the criminal justice system. A report of the U.S. Senate Judiciary Committee—*The Response to Rape: Detours on the Road to Equal Justice* (1993)—forcefully concludes that the justice system creates serious barriers to women who are sexually assaulted. Assessing the continuing validity of these arguments approximately 20 years later is difficult because the statistics on the number of sexual assaults each year, the percentage of them reported to the police, the number resulting in criminal charges, and how many cases result in conviction vary widely.

When testifying before a subcommittee of the U.S. Senate's Judiciary Committee, Michelle Dempsey, a professor at Villanova Law School, argued that rape "is one of the most underreported offense in the United States with empirical studies estimating that merely 15–20 percent of cases are reported" (*Financial Express*, 2010). Professor Dempsey cited the findings of a major study using data collected from the National Violence Against Women Survey (Tjaden & Thoennes, 2006). Official statistics suggest that the reporting rate for the crime of rape has increased by nearly 35 percent in recent years (Truman, 2011). Consider that in 2010,

a total of 188,380 rapes were reported in the National Crime Victimization Survey, 84,767 (45 percent) of which were reported to police according to the FBI in its annual publication, *Crime in the United States* (2011). Of course, these statistics are based on official data which, in turn, are affected by police actions.

The reporting rate for rape does not tell the whole story. According to the FBI (2011), only 40 percent of rapes reported to police are cleared by arrest. Prosecutors, in turn, file charges in only about half of the cases in which arrests are made (O'Neal, Tellis, & Spohn, 2015; Spohn, Beichner, Frenzel, & Holleran, 2002). And, of the cases prosecuted, only half result in a felony conviction (Cohen & Kyckelhahn, 2010). Critics argue that these figures support the conclusion that sexual assaults are underprosecuted. Some research supports this position, while other research does not.

- McCahill, Meyer, and Fischman (1979) and Kerstetter (1990) found that police tend to take reported rapes by strangers more seriously than reports of rapes by people known to the victim. Prosecutors evidence the same bias when deciding whether to prosecute cases (Battelle Memorial Institute Law and Justice Center, 1977; Vera Institute of Justice, 1981). Other researchers, however, have not found support for these propositions (see Spohn & Holleran, 2000).

- Police or prosecutorial discretion in rape cases is often guided by whether the victim is someone whom a judge or jury would find credible. But in assessing credibility, some researchers argue that the character of the victim (and sometimes the accused as well) is assessed using stereotypes (Stanko, 1988). Similarly, unfair judgments about victims' moral character are often made on the bases of their behavior just prior to the alleged sexual assault, including factors such as how the victim was dressed or whether the victim consumed alcohol or drugs (McCahill et al., 1979). In contrast, other researchers find little support for victim characteristics influencing prosecutorial charging decisions (Spohn & Holleran, 2000). Rather, legally relevant evidentiary factors, such as the victim's ability to identify the assailant and the presence of physical or medical evidence to corroborate the victim's accusation, are the salient factors that explain prosecutorial decisions whether to file or drop charges (Holleran, Beichner, & Spohn, 2010; Horney & Spohn, 1996; O'Neal, Tellis, & Spohn, 2015).

The often ideological debate aside, a new program shows how the legal and medical community can do a better job in sexual assault cases. The SANE (Sexual Assault Nurse Examiners) program began by training hospital nurses in evidence collection, injury-detection methods, and ways of avoiding re-traumatizing a victim during the examination.

Researchers found statistically significant increases in guilty pleas or convictions. According to one detective, the program was successful because the quality of the medical forensic exams improved (Bulman, 2009; Campbell et al., 2014).

What do you think? Are sexual assaults underprosecuted? If so, is the reason because criminal justice officials fail to adequately consider the plight of the victim or because these cases are more likely to have evidence problems?

The department is headed by the **U.S. attorney general**, who is a member of the president's cabinet. Top-level officials are presidential appointees who reflect the views of the administration on important policy issues. Day-to-day activities are carried out by a large cadre of career lawyers, who enjoy civil service protection and have, over the years, developed invaluable expertise in particular areas of law (Landsberg, 1993; Sisk, Noone, Steadman, & Lester, 2006).

The Department of Justice is a sprawling series of bureaucracies including investigatory and law enforcement offices such as the Federal Bureau of Investigation, the Drug Enforcement Administration, the U.S. Marshals Service, and the Federal Bureau of Prisons. Also in the Department of Justice is the Office of Justice Programs, which oversees the Bureau of Justice Assistance and other entities.

In terms of prosecution, three entities—solicitor general, criminal division, and U.S. attorneys—are particularly important. We will examine them from the top down, although, as we shall see, the hierarchy does not prevent the exercise of considerable autonomy.

TABLE 6.1 Overview of Prosecutors in the Dual Court System

Federal	State
Solicitor General • Represents the U.S. government before the U.S. Supreme Court in all appeals of federal criminal cases. • Often appears as amicus in appeals involving state criminal convictions.	**Attorney General** • Chief legal officer of the state. • Civil duties more extensive than criminal duties. • Has limited authority in criminal prosecutions.
Criminal Division • Prosecutes a few nationally significant criminal cases. • Exercises nominal supervision over U.S. attorneys.	**Chief Prosecutors and Their Assistants** • Have great autonomy in prosecuting felony cases. • Typically argue cases on appeal.
U.S. Attorneys and Their Assistants • Prosecute the vast majority of criminal cases in federal courts. • Enjoy great autonomy in actions.	**Local Prosecutors** • Often handle preliminary stages of felony cases. • Prosecute the large volume of cases in the lower courts.

Note: To learn more about the vast bureaucracies included in the U.S. Department of Justice, go to http://www.usdoj.gov.

Solicitor General

The **U.S. Solicitor General** is the third highest-ranking official in the Justice Department. The solicitor general's principal task is to represent the executive branch before the Supreme Court. But at the same time, the justices depend on the solicitor general to look beyond the government's narrow interests. Because of the solicitor general's dual responsibility to the judicial and executive branches, the officeholder is sometimes called the Tenth Justice, an informal title that underlines the special relationship with the Supreme Court (Aberbach & Peterson, 2006; Caplan, 1988; Curry, 2015; Meinhold & Shull, 1993).

The office of the solicitor general is in essence a small, elite, very influential law firm whose client is the U.S. government. As the representative of the United States in litigation before the U.S. Supreme Court, the solicitor general's office argues all government cases before the Court. For example, the assistant solicitor general argued the major issues in *Burns v. Reed* (1991). But the influence of the office extends further.

Roughly half of the work of the solicitor general's office involves coordinating appeals by the federal government. With few exceptions, all government agencies must first receive authorization from the solicitor general to appeal an adverse lower court ruling to the Supreme Court. The office requests Supreme Court review only in cases with a high degree of policy significance and in which the government has a reasonable legal argument. In turn, the solicitor general has a high rate of success in petitioning the Supreme Court and in winning cases argued on their merits.

Criminal Division of the Justice Department

The criminal division formulates criminal law enforcement policies over all federal criminal cases, except those specifically assigned to other divisions. The criminal division, with the U.S. attorneys, has the responsibility for overseeing criminal matters under thousands of statutes, as well as certain civil litigation. The criminal division is organized into a number of units that handle matters such as fraud, organized crime, and public integrity. Several of the units deal with international matters and have become more visible with the U.S. efforts to fight terrorism.

Criminal division attorneys prosecute many nationally significant cases, especially for acts of domestic terrorism, such as those perpetrated by Dylann Roof (Chapter 1), Ted Kaczynski (the Unabomber), and Timothy McVeigh (for bombing a federal building in Oklahoma City). Additionally, the criminal division has directed prosecutions of several alleged international terrorists and overseen the detainment of enemy noncombatants on federal military bases. Through the years, the criminal division has also received extensive press coverage for cases involving corrupt government officials, alleged members of organized crime, and major drug-dealing enterprises.

U.S. Attorneys

The **U.S. attorneys** serve as the nation's principal litigators under the direction of the attorney general. Ninety-four U.S. attorneys are stationed throughout the United States, Puerto Rico, the Virgin Islands, Guam, and the Northern Mariana Islands.

U.S. attorneys are appointed by, and serve at the discretion of, the president of the United States, with the advice and consent of the Senate. One U.S. attorney is assigned to each of the judicial districts, with the exception of Guam and the Northern Mariana Islands, where one U.S. attorney serves both districts. Each U.S. attorney is the chief federal law enforcement officer of the United States within his or her particular jurisdiction. The 94 U.S. attorneys are assisted by over 6,000 assistant U.S. attorneys, who increasingly have become career employees.

U.S. attorneys represent the federal government in court in many matters. They have three statutory responsibilities:

- Prosecution of criminal cases brought by the federal government
- Initiation and defense of civil cases in which the United States is a party
- Collection of certain debts owed the federal government

The volume of litigation varies considerably among the districts. U.S. attorneys along the Mexican border, for example, initiate a large number of drug prosecutions. Nonetheless, each district handles a mixture of simple and complex litigation.

U.S. attorneys enjoy full authority and control in the areas of personnel management, financial management, and procurement. They exercise wide discretion in the use of their resources to further the priorities of local jurisdictions and the needs of their communities.

Although the criminal division of the U.S. Department of Justice supervises all federal prosecutions, in practice U.S. attorneys enjoy considerable autonomy. This is partly because of their remoteness from Washington, D.C.—the 93 U.S. attorneys are widely dispersed geographically. The selection process also plays a role. Many U.S. attorneys owe their appointments primarily to persons other than the U.S. attorney general or, in some cases, even the U.S. president (Bell, 1993). Thus, in the vast majority of cases, the decisions are made by U.S. attorneys scattered across the nation rather than by the central office based in Washington, D.C.

Prosecution in State Courts

Decentralization and local autonomy characterize prosecution in state courts. The result is divided responsibility, with state prosecution authority typically found in three separate offices: state, county (or district), and local. At times, the relationship among these separate agencies is marked by competition; various prosecutors jockey to be the first to prosecute a notorious defendant. We will examine the three major state prosecutors from the top down, but bear in mind that each office is separate and not necessarily subject to the dictates of the office above it.

State Attorneys General

The position of attorney general, the state's chief legal officer, is typically spelled out in the state's constitution. Among the most important duties are providing legal advice to other state agencies and representing the state in court when state actions are challenged. In recent years, attorneys general have focused on their civil responsibilities by emphasizing their role in protecting consumers from various forms of fraud. Thus, the typical home page of the attorney general of a state proclaims how many individual consumer complaints (many of which involve motor vehicle and home repair fraud) are handled annually. Many state attorneys general have also been visible in filing consumer lawsuits against major U.S. businesses. The biggest of all involves the suits by more than 30 states against the tobacco industry.

State attorneys general have chosen to emphasize their civil responsibilities because they typically have limited authority over criminal matters. Local autonomy is a key characteristic of the office of prosecutor. In general, state officials do not monitor the activities of local prosecutors. Although the **state attorney general** is the state's chief law enforcement official, his or her authority over local criminal procedures is quite limited. Indeed, in a handful of states, the attorney general has no legal authority to initiate or intervene in local prosecutions. In other states, this authority is limited to extreme situations.

Thus, the state attorney general exercises virtually no control or supervision over chief prosecutors at the county level. This lack of supervisory power, coupled with the decentralization of the office, means that local prosecutors enjoy almost total autonomy. Only the local voters have the power to evaluate the prosecutor's performance, by means of their votes.

Chief Prosecutor

The American prosecutor has few direct parallels elsewhere in the world (Flemming, 1990; Jehle & Wade, 2006; Sklansky, 2016). Compared with their counterparts in England and Europe, American prosecutors enjoy unmatched independence and discretionary powers (Albonetti, 1987; Sklansky, 2016). Moreover, the United States is the only country in the world where voters elect prosecutors (Ellis, 2012).

Variously called the "district attorney," "county attorney," "commonwealth attorney," "state's attorney," or "prosecuting attorney" (among other, less common titles), the prosecutor is the chief law enforcement official of the community. Altogether, 2,330 chief prosecutors are employed across the nation, with a staff of almost 80,000. Structure and workload differ according to the size of the population. The typical office serves a population of 36,000 people, with 400 adult felony cases in the district, a staff of 10, and a budget of $526,000. But deviations are readily apparent (Perry & Banks, 2011). The great majority of the nation's prosecutors' offices are small ones (Table 6.2). Frequently, rural prosecutors are part-time officials who also engage in private law practices.

Elections are a key characteristic of the office of prosecutor, as 95 percent of chief prosecutors are locally elected officials who typically serve four-year terms. The exceptions are Alaska, Connecticut, Delaware, the District of Columbia, New Jersey, and Rhode Island, where chief prosecutors are either appointed or are members of the state attorney general's office.

Because of elections, the work of the American prosecutor is deeply set within the larger political process. For a lawyer interested in a political career, the prosecutor's office offers a launching pad. Indeed, prosecutors "virtually own the politically potent symbols of 'law and order' politics" (Flemming, Nardulli, & Eisenstein, 1992, p. 23).

Numerous government officials—governors, judges, and legislators—have begun their careers as crusading prosecutors. Many prosecutors, however, do not plan to enter politics. Studies in Wisconsin and Kentucky, for example, indicated that more than half of the prosecutors had no further political ambitions.

TABLE 6.2	State Court Prosecutors' Offices					
		Full-Time Offices (By Population Served)				
	All Offices	**1 Million or More People**	**250,000 to 999,999 People**	**100,000 to 249,999 People**	**Under 99,999 People**	**Part-Time Offices**
Number of offices	2,330	43	211	341	1,389	346
Mean population served	299,567,000	2,025,000	496,000	158,000	36,000	13,000
Full-time equivalent employees	34,288 attorneys 43,640 staff 77,928 total	244 attorneys 291 staff 535 total	57 attorneys 74 staff 131 total	17 attorneys 22 staff 39 total	4 attorneys 6 staff 10 total	2 attorneys 1 staff 3 total
Felony cases closed	2,906,795 3% by jury verdict	759,057 2% by jury verdict	934,884 3% by jury verdict	622,073 3% by jury verdict	555,050 3% by jury verdict	35,731 3% by jury verdict
Mean budget	$5.8 billion	$49.2 million	$9.9 million	$2.3 million	$562,000	$157,000
Mean salary of chief prosecutor	$98,024	$165,732	$138,017	$121,777	$96,956	$44,981
Entry-level assistant prosecutor salary	$46,330 (full-time) to $55,885 (full-time)	$51,354 to $64,517	$47,580 to $57,759	$44,007 to $55,263	$42,380 to $46,000	$33,460 to $36,712

Source: Steven W. Perry and Duren Banks. 2011. *Prosecutors in State Courts, 2007—Statistical Tables.* Washington, D.C.: Bureau of Justice Statistics. Available online at http://bjs.ojp.usdoj.gov/content/pub/pdf/psc07st.pdf.

They viewed the office as useful for gaining visibility before establishing a private law practice (Engstrom, 1971; Jacob, 1966). Thus, after serving one or two terms in office, former DAs typically practice private law or assume other positions in the public sector—primarily judges (Jones, 1994).

The tremendous power of the prosecutor means that political parties are very interested in controlling the office. The chief prosecutor has numerous opportunities for patronage. In some communities, partisan considerations play a large role in the hiring of assistant district attorneys (Eisenstein, Flemming, & Nardulli, 1988). Political parties may also want one of their own serving as district attorney to guarantee that their affairs will not be closely scrutinized and to act as a vehicle for harassing the opposition.

Local Prosecutor

Little is known about the activities of local prosecutors—variously called "city attorneys," "solicitors," or the like. In some jurisdictions, local prosecutors are responsible for the preliminary stages of felony cases as they are processed in the lower courts. In these jurisdictions, it is the **local prosecutor** (not the chief prosecutor) who represents the government at the initial appearance, argues bond amounts, and conducts the preliminary hearing. These decisions may have important consequences for later stages of the felony prosecution, but the chief prosecutor's office has no direct control over these matters.

Local prosecutors, however, are primarily responsible for processing the large volume of minor criminal offenses disposed of in the lower courts. As explained in Chapter 4, public drunkenness, petty theft, disorderly conduct, and minor assaults are the staple of these judicial bodies.

The Prosecutor's Office at Work

In the courtroom, one's attention normally gravitates toward the individual lawyers as they call witnesses, ask questions, and cross-examine the opponent's witnesses. These individual activities, however, must be understood within the larger context in which they occur. As Table 6.2 illustrates, the day-to-day work of the prosecutor's office is executed by nearly 78,000 people—approximately 34,288 attorneys and 43,640 investigators, legal services personnel, victim advocates, and support staff. How these persons are hired, trained, and supervised has a major bearing on the exercise of prosecutorial discretion.

Assistant District Attorneys

Most assistant district attorneys (sometimes called deputy district attorneys) are hired immediately after graduation from law school or after a short time in private practice. Traditionally, these young attorneys attend local or regional law schools, rather than the nation's most prestigious law schools (whose graduates are usually able to obtain higher-paying jobs in private practice with prestigious law firms). This has changed somewhat in the past decade or two, as competition for positions in major prosecutor's offices has increased significantly, especially since new prosecutors gain valuable trial experience that new lawyers in law firms typically cannot.

In the past, many prosecutors hired assistants on the basis of party affiliation and the recommendations of elected officials. Increasingly, however, greater stress is being placed on merit selection, a trend exemplified by the Los Angeles prosecutor's office—the nation's largest, with more than 1,000 lawyers—where hiring is done on a civil service basis.

The turnover rate among assistant DAs is high. Most serve an average of three to six years before leaving prosecution to enter private practice, politics, business, or another field. Thirty-five percent of all prosecutors' offices nationwide report significant problems retaining assistant DAs, with low salaries cited as the leading reason for the high turnover (Perry, 2006). Indeed, low salaries were "the primary obstacle cited by prosecutors' offices with recruitment problems (83%) and offices with retention problems (71%)," especially when compared to the higher salaries lawyers earn in private law practice—a disparity that seems to grow over time (Perry, 2006, p. 3).

Turnover is also a product of assistants growing tired of the job. With its never-ending stream of society's ills, the criminal courthouse can become a depressing place to work. Moreover, regular trial work creates numerous physical and psychological pressures. In the words of a former New Orleans prosecutor, "The average trial assistant leaves work every day with a huge stack of papers under his arm. The grind can really wear you down. There's just too much work" (Perlstein, 1990). In *Bronx D.A.*, Sarena Straus (2006) discussed the day she reached her breaking point. She was a felony prosecutor in the Domestic Violence and Sex Crimes Unit. She had just interviewed a six-year-old autistic boy who watched his sister get stabbed to death that morning. "When I finished the interview, I went back to my office. It was 7 pm. Everyone else had gone home for the evening. I sat in my office and cried." Realizing she could no longer separate herself from her work, she left the job.

Although many assistants view their job as a brief way station toward a more lucrative and varied private practice, some see it as a permanent career position. In Wisconsin, the average tenure is about six years, and perhaps just as important, some assistants advance to become the elected DA in their county, run for the position in a neighboring county, or make other lateral moves (Jones, 1994). Across the nation, a marked trend toward a prosecutorial "civil service" has become obvious, with assistants moving from office to office (Jones, 2001).

Learning the Job

Law schools provide an overview of law on the books—criminal law, criminal procedure, evidence, and constitutional law, to name just a few. But most law schools give their students very little exposure to law in action. Thus, the typical assistant DA comes to the job having little familiarity with the day-to-day realities of the profession. Here is how one lawyer described his first days on the job:

> For the first week or two, I went to court with guys who had been here. Just sat there and watched. What struck me was the amount of things he [the prosecutor] has

to do in the courtroom. The prosecutor runs the courtroom. Although the judge is theoretically in charge, we're standing there plea-bargaining and calling the cases at the same time and chewing gum and telling the people to quiet down and setting bonds, and that's what amazed me. I never thought I would learn all the terms. What bothered me also was the paperwork.

> Not the Supreme Court decisions, not the *mens rea* or any of this other stuff, but the amount of junk that's in those files that you have to know. We never heard about this crap in law school. (Heumann, 1978, p. 94)

For decades, training in prosecutors' offices was almost exclusively on the job; it was not unusual for recent law school graduates with no experience to be sent into court on their first day on the job. One assistant summed up the office tradition as follows: "They have a very unique way of breaking people in. They say, 'Here's a file. There's the jury. Go try it'" (Flemming, Nardulli, & Eisenstein, 1992). More recently, large prosecutors' offices have begun to train new employees more systematically. After a week of general orientation to the different divisions of the office, new assistants are allowed to watch various proceedings and observe veteran trial attorneys at work.

Law schools have been under increasing pressure to teach their students more about the actual practice of law. Many have responded by adding more skills-oriented classes to their curricula, problem-based learning within classes, and a host of community-engaged learning activities (such as legal practice clinics and internship placement programs) that are aimed at helping students become more prepared to enter the legal workforce (Bard, 2011). Still, even if one graduates from law school with a more applied than theoretical legal education, there is still much to learn upon entering prosecutorial practice. For example, an important part of learning law in action involves working with the office clientele. Here is how journalist Gary Delsohn (2003b, p. 13) described the reality of the prosecutor's office in Sacramento, California:

> In an urban prosecutor's office, witnesses you build a case around are often just a shade less unsavory than the defendants you're trying to put away. It's blue-collar law. To succeed, a prosecutor has to be willing and able to deal with all kinds of people.

New assistants quickly learn to ask questions of more experienced prosecutors, court clerks, and veteran police officers. Through this socialization process, assistants learn important unwritten rules about legal practice relating to what types of violations should be punished and the appropriate penalties to be applied to such violations. Assistants also learn that their performance and chances for promotion are measured by how promptly and efficiently they dispose of cases. They become sensitive to hints—for example, if a judge complains that a backlog is developing because prosecutors are bringing too many minor cases, the new assistant usually gets the message that his or her plea-bargaining demands are too high.

Promotions are also related to the candidate's reputation as a trial attorney. Assistants are invariably judged by the number of convictions they obtain. In the courthouse environment, however, not losing a case has a higher value than winning. Thus, assistants learn that if the guilt of the defendant is doubtful or the offender is not dangerous, it is better to negotiate a plea than to disrupt the courtroom routine by attempting to gain a jury conviction.

Interestingly, as prosecutors become more experienced, their attitudes change. In a study of more than 200 state prosecutors in eight different offices across the United States, Wright and Levine (2014) found that experienced prosecutors regret the highly adversarial stances they took early in careers "They even give a name to this early collection of beliefs and attitudes about the importance of every case, the constant quest for trials, and the aggressive posturing with defense attorneys: 'young prosecutors' syndrome'" (p. 3).

Because roughly half of all state prosecutors fall into category of being "junior" enough to routinely exhibit young prosecutors' syndrome, their lack of experience leads them to make nonpragmatic decisions, often because they haven't yet had the chance to learn from their mistakes. Moreover, they haven't had sufficient time or experience to develop a "sense of compassion and restraint as a prosecutor" (p. 5). Such overly adversarial attitudes have real impact on the courts:

> Prosecutors who lack judgment about which cases to try, or those who are inclined to goad defendants into trials to prove their professional worth, aggravate already overcrowded trial dockets. They subject defendants, victims and witnesses to unnecessary courtroom drama and delay just to test their skills. Lastly, junior prosecutors who distrust defense attorneys may be more inclined to skirt the edges of their disclosure obligations, in violation of their constitutional and statutory duties. (pp. 3–4)

Wright and Levine suggest that new prosecutors can be helped to grow out of young prosecutors' syndrome more quickly by spending more time with more senior prosecutors who can mentor them "much in the way that rookie police officers learn from riding on patrol with veterans" (p. 5). They also recommend that law schools could do a better job developing a more balanced approached to criminal prosecution by instilling "a professional commitment to flexibility" and emphasizing "the value of negotiation as an alternative to litigation" (p. 59).

Promotions and Office Structure

As assistants gain experience and settle into the courthouse routine, they are promoted to more demanding and also more interesting tasks. Promotions are related to office structure (Flemming, Nardulli, & Eisenstein, 1992). Small prosecutors' offices usually use *vertical prosecution*, in which one prosecutor is assigned responsibility for a case from intake to appeal (Nugent & McEwen, 1988). In these offices, assistants are promoted by being assigned more serious cases. However, such an assignment system is administratively burdensome in large courthouses; assistants would spend much of their time moving from one courtroom to another and waiting for their one or two cases to be called. Therefore, most big-city prosecutors' offices use *horizontal prosecution*, in which prosecutors are assigned to specific functions, such as initial appearance, charging, preliminary hearing, grand jury, trial, or appeal. On a regular basis, one or two attorneys are systematically assigned to one courtroom with a given judge. Over time, prosecutors come to know the judge's views on sentencing and the like. Under horizontal prosecution, assistants spend a year or more handling misdemeanor offenses before they are promoted by being assigned to courtrooms with felonies.

Over the past decades, specialization has become increasingly common in chief prosecutors' offices, particularly in densely populated jurisdictions. Often it is the most experienced trial attorneys who staff these positions. Specialized units dealing with murder, sexual assault, armed robbery, and major drug crimes are the most prestigious, mainly because trial work is both plentiful and challenging.

Supervision

Assistant district attorneys are supervised by a section head, who is supposed to ensure that they follow office policies. However, for several reasons, assistant DAs enjoy fairly broad freedom.

Office policies are often general and somewhat vague. In small offices, they are seldom even put in writing. Official and unofficial policies are simply part of what the assistant learns informally; for this reason, it is hard for the bureau chief to enforce them. In large offices, decentralized work assignments mean that supervisors can exert only limited control over specific cases or individual assistants. Assistant DAs spend most of their time not in the central office but in the courtroom. Indeed, in crowded courthouses, trial assistants often have offices adjoining the judge's chambers and only rarely appear in the prosecutor's office at all. It is therefore difficult for supervisors to observe and monitor the assistant district attorney's activities. Each assistant has dozens of cases that require individual decisions on the basis of specific facts, unique witness problems, and so on. A supervisor has no way to monitor such situations except on the basis of what the assistant reports orally or writes in the file. Here, as elsewhere, information is power. Assistants can control their supervisors by selectively telling them what they think they should know (Neubauer, 1974b).

Attempts at Greater Supervision

The traditional form of prosecutorial management is centered on autonomy; each individual assistant DA is granted a great deal of freedom to make his or her own decisions. The Erie, Pennsylvania, DA's office is typical; it "promulgated few formal written policies, gave most of its assistants fairly wide latitude to dispose of cases in ways consistent with the general aim of the office, and relied on informal supervision" (Eisenstein, Flemming, & Nardulli, 1988, p. 215).

Concerned that autonomy allows too much unchecked discretion, some prosecutors have attempted to exert greater supervision by adopting a rigid system of office policies. Some forbid any charge reductions whatsoever for some types of defendants (habitual offenders) and for serious charges such as violent offenses and major drug dealing (Eisenstein, Flemming, & Nardulli 1988). To ensure compliance with these detailed office policies, formal, detailed, bureaucratic enforcement mechanisms are imposed. Typical is DuPage County, Illinois, where the DA's office "was highly centralized, rigidly enforcing the 'bottom-line' pleas established by the indictment committee. The DA's office relied on a formally structured hierarchy to administer its policies" (Eisenstein, Flemming, & Nardulli, 1988, p. 215). Chief prosecutors believe that these management systems monitor prosecutorial discretion, minimize differences among individual assistants, and concentrate scarce crime-fighting resources (Jacoby, 1980).

Attempts by supervisors to control the work of the assistants tend to erode the morale of the office, as the following account from the Sacramento, California, DA's office illustrates. According to one of the top supervisors in the office, second-guessing is rarely worth the trouble, because the deputies tend to "stay pissed" forever. Indeed, one assistant is still furious seven years after his boss refused to allow him to participate in a meeting involving his case (Delsohn, 2003a, 2003b). Overall, office review of all case files (to ensure that policies have been followed) makes some assistants uncomfortable because they think this means that they are not completely trusted. Reductions in individual discretion increase the general level of tension in the office. One trial assistant related how a colleague was summarily fired on the same day he violated office policy on plea bargaining. All the assistants resented and feared the administrator who fired him (Eisenstein, Flemming, & Nardulli, 1988, p. 215).

Prosecutorial Ethics

The Duke lacrosse team rape case has become the contemporary poster child for prosecutorial misconduct. But this was a truly exceptional case and needs to be analyzed within an array of legal issues that limit prosecutorial power.

Ethical issues facing prosecutors are very different from those confronting defense attorneys because prosecutors do not represent individual clients. Prosecutors often define their jobs as representing victims of crime (Chapter 9), but these are not typically considered to fit under the attorney–client relationship. Rather, the client of the prosecutor is the government, and for this reason, prosecutors are given special responsibilities. In the words of the Criminal Justice Standards: "The duty of the prosecutor is to seek justice, not merely to convict" (Standard 3-1.2c, American Bar Association, 2012). And, because prosecutors represent the government, they enjoy a great deal of protection from civil lawsuits.

Prosecutorial Immunity

Prosecutors enjoy **absolute immunity**—complete freedom from civil liability—for everything they do with regard to the core prosecutorial functions of initiating criminal charges and pursuing criminal convictions as the government's advocate (*Imbler v. Pachtman*, 1976). Such absolute immunity extends to all actions, even those motivated by ill will or bad faith, concerning filing or declining to file criminal charges, plea bargaining, and presenting arguments or evidence in court (whether before a grand jury, at bail hearings, at preliminary hearings, at trials, or on appeal). Thus, for example, a defendant whose conviction is overturned on appeal (and is later found not guilty) cannot sue the prosecutor for malpractice. The appellate court reversal is viewed as a sufficient remedy.

In contrast, when prosecutors are not acting as the government's advocate in some judicial phase of the criminal justice process, they enjoy only **qualified immunity** for their actions. Qualified immunity shields prosecutors from civil liability for acts beyond those associated with courtroom advocacy but still within the scope of their professional duties (such as when advising the police or speaking to the media). However, qualified immunity applies only if prosecutors are acting in good faith that they are not violating any law or ethical rule of which a reasonable person in his or her position would be aware. Examples of situations in which prosecutors enjoy only qualified immunity are presented in the "Key Developments" feature.

KEY DEVELOPMENTS CONCERNING THE PROSECUTOR

Berger v. United States (1935)	The prosecutor's primary interest is in doing justice, not simply winning cases.
Imbler v. Pochtmon (1976)	Prosecutors enjoy absolute immunity from civil liability when initiating and pursuing a criminal prosecution.
Morrison v. Olson (1988)	Independent counsel law is constitutional.
Burns v. Reed (1991)	Prosecutors enjoy only qualified immunity from lawsuits concerning advice given to the police.
Buckley v. Fitzsimmons (1993)	Prosecutors enjoy only qualified immunity from civil lawsuits for actions during criminal investigations and statements made during news conferences.
Kalino v. Fletcher (1997)	A prosecutor may be sued for making false statements of fact in an affidavit in support of an arrest warrant.
Connick v. Thompson (2011)	A district attorney's office may not be held liable under Section 1983 for failure to train prosecutors based on a single *Brady* violation (or perhaps, even a handful of *Brady* violations).

Ethical Duties of Prosecutors

Prosecutors have a number of specific ethical obligations in addition to the overarching prosecutorial duty to seek justice, such as disclosing exculpatory evidence, avoiding conflicts of interest, and refraining from any behavior that would interfere with the fair administration of justice. This section highlights only a few of prosecutors' major ethical responsibilities.

Chapter 11 discusses a series of Supreme Court cases that, like *Brady v. Maryland* (1963), require the prosecutor to hand over to the defense *exculpatory evidence* (evidence that tends to show the innocence of the defendant). But this can be a vague mandate that leads some prosecutors to hand over as little evidence as possible. One result is that appellate courts find that prosecutors sometimes improperly withhold evidence from the defense, and therefore the guilty verdict is reversed and a new trial ordered. Note that this is the typical remedy—appellate reversal—and does not sanction the erring prosecutor. Only on rare occasions do prosecutors face sanctions from the bar association for failure to disclose evidence to the defense.

Conflict of interest is another ethical issue facing prosecutors (and defense attorneys as well). Prosecutors employed part-time, for example, may confront a host of ethical issues. In private practice, a lawyer may represent an individual, but if that person runs afoul of the law, then the prosecutor must recuse himself or herself. Conflicts of interest may also arise when the prosecutor leaves the office for private practice. As a general rule, the now-private lawyer may not represent anyone who was prosecuted while the lawyer was working for the prosecutor's office. Even if he or she had no contact with the case, the lawyer may not represent that individual defendant.

As explained above, prosecutors exercise a tremendous amount of discretion in the charging decision, and several ethical standards relate to how this discretion should be used. Prosecutors are not supposed to institute any criminal charges that are not supported by probable cause, although many prosecutors charge only cases they feel they can win by proving guilt beyond a reasonable doubt. The ambiguous nature of varying legal standards may lead to criticism that prosecutors unfairly failed to prosecute a case. Conversely, prosecutors may be criticized for unfairly prosecuting a defendant based on political motives.

The ethical issues surrounding prosecutors' discretion to seek the death penalty are often debated. Although only a few homicides are eligible for sentence of death (Chapter 14), prosecutors often must make a series of close calls in these cases to decide which defendants should face capital punishment. To ensure that these decisions are made in an even-handed manner, many big-city prosecutors' offices have a special review process. Moreover, the courts have imposed a proportionality requirement—that is, they seek information that the decision to seek the death penalty in a specific case is proportional to the decision in other cases. Although ethical issues like this one are at the forefront of the debate over capital punishment, appellate courts rarely find that prosecutors abused their discretion.

How much information to release to the public presents another ethical issue for prosecutors (Pollock, 2012). In the modern era, both the prosecution and the defense often try their cases in the press before a jury is picked. For this reason, judges often impose a gag order on high-profile cases (Chapter 13), prohibiting either side from releasing information to the press. In ordinary cases, only on rare occasions have judges found that prosecutors went too far in seeking to convince the public (meaning potential jurors) of the overwhelming guilt of the defendant. But even without prosecutorial misconduct, the media can inflame public sentiments through less-than-objective news coverage.

Prosecutors and Courtroom Work Groups

Prosecutors spend most of their time working directly with other members of the courtroom work group. Even when interviewing witnesses or conducting legal research, the prosecutor is anticipating the reactions of judges and defense attorneys. Thus, the activities of prosecutors can be understood only within the setting of the courtroom work group (Worden, 1990).

The prosecutor is the most important member of the work group. Prosecutors set the agenda for judges and defense attorneys by exercising discretion over the types of cases filed, the nature of acceptable plea agreements, and the sentences to be handed out. Prosecutors also control the flow of information about cases by providing access to police arrest reports, laboratory tests, and defendants' criminal histories. By stressing certain information or withholding facts, prosecutors can influence the decisions of judges and defense attorneys.

As the dominant force in the courtroom work group, prosecutors clearly set the tone for plea bargaining. This is how one veteran explained his perspective:

> I get so damned pissed off and tired of these guys who come in and cry, "My guy's got a job" or "My guy's about to join the army," when he's got a rap sheet as long as your arm. His guy's a loser, and he's wailing on my desk about what a fine man he is. What really wins me is the guy who comes in and says, "O.K., what are we going to do with my criminal today? I know he has no redeeming social value. He's been a bad son of a bitch all his life, so just let me know your position. But frankly, you know, my feeling is that this is just not the case to nail him on. We all know if he does something serious, he's going." And before long the guy who approaches it this way has you wrapped around his little finger. (Carter, 1974, p. 87)

Prosecutors' actions, in turn, are influenced by other members of the courtroom work group.

Through the socialization process, assistant district attorneys internalize the accepted ways of doing things in the courthouse, learning to plead cases out on the basis of normal crimes (discussed in Chapter 5). Prosecutors who stray too far from the shared norms of the courtroom work group can expect sanctions. The judge may informally indicate that the state is pushing too hard for a harsh sentence or may publicly chastise a district attorney in open court, thus threatening the attorney's status among peers. The defense attorney may not agree to a prosecutor's request for a continuance or may use delaying tactics to impair the state's efforts to schedule cases, thus further disrupting the prosecutor's efforts to move cases. (The prosecutor, of course, is not without countersanctions. These will be discussed in the next two chapters.)

Operating within the constraints of the courtroom work group, effective assistant DAs are those who make tactical decisions that maximize their objectives. Experienced prosecutors, for example, know which defense attorneys can be trusted, granting these people greater access to information about the case and listening to them more when the case involves unusual circumstances. Prosecutors also quickly learn the tendencies of the judge. No prosecutor can afford to ignore how the judge wishes the courtroom to be run.

Although the prosecutor is generally the most important member of the courtroom work group, work groups show considerable variability. Differences between one community and the next abound, and in big-city courthouses, these differences often exist from courtroom to courtroom. Conflicting goals and varying political styles are two factors that account for contrasting work groups.

Conflicting Goals and Contrasting Work Groups

On the surface, the goals of prosecutors seem the model of simplicity: Their job is to convict the guilty. But a closer examination shows that the goals are not as clear-cut as they first appear. Prosecutors define their main job in different ways. Some stress working closely with law enforcement agencies. Thus, they serve as police advocates in court and stress punishing the guilty. Others emphasize their role as court-based officials. Thus, they define their job as impartially administering justice and emphasize securing convictions (Delsohn, 2003a, 2003b; Eisenstein, 1978; LaFave, 1965). The uncertainties about which goals should come first have historically produced marked diversity among prosecutors, with some prosecutors' offices focusing on the administration of justice, and others focusing on an adversarial model (McDonald, 1979; Utz, 1979). Such differences in philosophies still exist today (Baker, 1999; Delsohn, 2003a, 2003b), although media attention has often focused on prosecutors whose "win at all costs" mentality has eroded public confidence in those who are supposed to advocate for justice (Roberts & Stratton, 2008).

Political Styles and Contrasting Work Groups

The prosecutor's role within the courtroom work group also needs to be understood within the broader political context in which the office functions. This was the conclusion of Roy Flemming's (1990) study of nine prosecutors' offices in three states. Because they exercise broad discretion (in the context of decentralization and local autonomy), elected prosecutors choose political styles. This choice is both personal and strategic. It depends first on the prosecutor's satisfaction or dissatisfaction with the office's status within the courthouse community. It also depends on the prosecutor's perception of the value of conflict as a means of changing the office's status.

Prosecutors satisfied with the status of the office adopt an "office conservator" style. Office conservators accept the status quo. Continuity is often a key consideration; former assistants are elected with the blessings of the previous officeholder and the support of the local political establishment. Once in office, conservators do not deliberately step on toes; if they push for change, it generally comes as a response to the requests of others. Montgomery County, Pennsylvania, provides an example. The newly elected DA retained the preexisting staff intact. He did fashion some guidelines regarding guilty pleas, but they were flexible, symbolic gestures—signals that a changing of the guard had taken place, not a revolution. Most important, however, the DA tolerated the judges' traditional dominance of the courthouse community.

Prosecutors who are less content with the status of their offices face a more complicated set of choices. They must decide whether conflict is an effective tool for them to use. These "courthouse insurgents" are very dissatisfied with the status quo and are prepared to do battle to change it. They do not shy away from open conflict, nor do they hesitate to challenge the courthouse community in pursuit of their goals. DuPage County, Illinois, is an example. The state's attorney was an outsider to the county who won the office by narrowly defeating the Republican Party's favored candidate in a bitterly fought, mudslinging

primary. Perceiving that the office failed to stand up to defense attorneys, the new state's attorney turned the office inside out. Immediately after election, he eliminated the part-time staff, hired aggressive assistants, and instituted policies severely restricting plea bargaining. Moreover, the insurgent DA minced no words in publicly criticizing judges and defense attorneys.

"Policy reformers" are also dissatisfied with the status quo, but unlike courthouse insurgents, they are cautious, often conciliatory, in their approach. Upon taking office, they gradually move to tighten their offices' guilty-plea policies, encourage more assertive attitudes among their assistants, and try to develop innovative approaches to prosecutorial work. They do not shrink from trying to alter their relationships with judges. Erie, Pennsylvania, provides a case in point. Embittered by the decline of the office when he left as an assistant to enter private practice, the new Erie prosecutor bucked the political establishment and decisively trounced the incumbent in the Democratic Party primary to win the office. However, his plans to restore the respect of the office clashed with the docket policies of the court. Rather than fighting openly, the Erie DA mounted an indirect campaign to wrest control of the docket from the judges.

Flemming's study highlights two aspects of prosecutorial behavior that are not immediately obvious. First, differences in political styles cross party lines; these are not Republican or Democratic styles. Second, differences in political styles are not necessarily constant through time. In several communities, a district attorney was initially elected as an insurgent or a policy reformer but through the years came to adopt a conservator style.

The Expanding Domain of the Prosecutor

The domain of the prosecutor has been expanding throughout the past century, and pressures to place greater authority in the hands of the prosecutor are likely to continue (Davis, 2009; Worrall &

Borakove, 2008). Within the fragmented, sometimes nonsystem of criminal justice, the prosecutor is in the best position to provide coordination. Moreover, with crime as a dominant issue in elections, the prosecutor is uniquely able to capitalize on his or her role as the community's chief law enforcement official and to promise the voters to expand crime-fighting efforts.

We will examine two types of programs that exemplify the contemporary expansion of the domain of the prosecutor: improving police–prosecutor relationships and community prosecution.

Improving Police–Prosecutor Relationships

Police and prosecutors are commonly viewed as members of the same crime-fighting team, but a closer look reveals a more complex reality (Harris, 2011; Rowe, 2015). Police and prosecutors have differing perspectives on the law. To the police, the case is closed when the suspect is arrested, but prosecutors stress that they often need additional information to win in court (Stanko, 1981).

Inadequate police reports present a classic illustration of noncoordination within the criminal justice system. The thoroughness of police investigations and the quality of their arrests directly affect the likelihood of the prosecutor's obtaining a conviction. In a survey of 225 (mostly big-city) prosecutors, 66 percent cited inadequate police preparation of crime reports as a major problem in their offices (Nugent & McEwen, 1988). Commonly mentioned problems were that names and addresses of victims and witnesses were lacking, full details of how the crime was committed were missing, and vital laboratory reports were not forwarded on time. Faced with incomplete or inaccurate police reports, the prosecutor may be forced to drop charges (see Chapter 10).

Police and prosecutors in several jurisdictions have adopted strategies to improve coordination and communication between the two groups (Buchanan, 1989). In Indianapolis, for example, the prosecutor has funded a computer messaging system that enables attorneys in the office to transmit notes, case dispositions, and subpoenas directly to police officers at their work locations. In Alameda County, California, and Montgomery County, Maryland, "street jump" narcotics officers and prosecutors consult frequently, both in person and over the telephone, to build cases that meet the requirements of the search-and-seizure law.

A few agencies have gone further, institutionalizing teamwork and making communication between investigators and prosecutors a top priority. In Multnomah County, Oregon, the Organized Crime/Narcotics Task Force has brought together 12 investigators from several area agencies and two prosecutors from the district attorney's office, instituting daily informal contact about the progress of pending cases. Moreover, prosecutors act as consultants to the police during the investigative phase. Thus, investigators can get answers to difficult legal questions in a few minutes just by walking down the hall.

Programs like these indicate that, despite a long history of difficulties, some agencies apparently are bridging the gap. But a word of caution is in order. No research to date has systematically evaluated these programs to indicate their overall effectiveness. Until such research is conducted, no predictions can be made about which programs are likely to be effective in other communities.

Community Prosecution

The historic image of the district attorney stresses case processing: The DA files charges and doggedly pursues a conviction. But this traditional image is becoming blurred as locally elected prosecutors respond to a wide variety of social problems such as domestic violence, drug abuse, disorder on city streets, and growing numbers of juvenile offenders. In responding to these types of social problems, which often reflect disintegrating neighborhoods, prosecutors today are more likely to stress problem-oriented approaches (Center for Court Innovation, 2012b). At times, the specifics are hard to pin down because the approaches are truly shaped to local needs rather than to national program guides (Coles, 2000; Porter, 2011; Williams & Steward, 2013). But these new approaches have three elements in common (Center for Court Innovation, 2012b; Jacoby, 1995):

- Prosecutors have the responsibility not only to prosecute cases but also to reduce crime.

- The most effective results are obtained within small, manageable geographic areas, which often means working out of neighborhood offices.

- Change is more likely to occur through cooperative efforts or partnerships rather than through prosecutorial dictates. In many instances, community stakeholders help set the crime-fighting agenda.

The Neighborhood District Attorney approach in Multnomah County (Portland, Oregon) provides a case in point. Business leaders in the Lloyd District (an inner-city neighborhood) called for more police protection as well as the assignment of a special prosecutor to the district (for which they provided one-year's funding). Citizen demands were invariably expressed in traditional law enforcement terms—more police, more arrests, and more convictions, particularly of repeat offenders. The Lloyd District special prosecutor, however, quickly saw that people's concerns were more immediate than he had imagined. "They wanted something done about prostitution, public drinking, drug use, vandalism, [minor] assaults, littering garbage, and 'car prowls' (thefts from cars)" (Boland, 1996, p. 36). Although none of these problems (except thefts from cars) fit traditional notions of serious crime, they nonetheless raise serious concern among citizens. (This approach clearly emphasizes the activities of the local courts, discussed in Chapter 3.)

As the program developed, several distinctive features became apparent. For one, the assistant DA used the laws in new ways, including using civil remedies to fight crime. Perhaps most important, the program was problem-oriented: Rather than focusing on individual arrestees, the neighborhood district attorney addressed problems from a larger perspective, with long-term goals in mind. Ultimately, what emerged was an approach, not a program. Rather than being guided by clear-cut procedures, Portland has adopted a highly flexible organization that can meet the different needs of different neighborhoods (Boland, 1996).

Overall, community prosecution stresses a proactive approach: Rather than reacting to crime through prosecution, these programs stress crime prevention (Coles & Kelling, 1999; Miles, 2013). And often the crimes stressed are minor ones that are nonetheless serious irritants to local residents (Goldkamp, Irons-Guynn, & Weiland, 2002; Green, 2012).

Conclusion

Prosecutors in the United States are powerful, but, as with all other governmental officials, there are limits. In the Duke lacrosse case, the state's attorney general took over the case and eventually dismissed all charges because of a lack of evidence. Moreover, the North Carolina Bar Association charged Nifong with lying to the judge, withholding key DNA evidence from the defense, and making inflammatory statements to the public. The North Carolina Supreme Court agreed and disbarred him.

What happened to Mike Nifong and Ken Anderson may represent a new willingness to confront prosecutorial misconduct. Certainly, the Supreme Court's decision in *Connick v. Thompson* and California's 2016 law making it a felony for prosecutors to tamper with or withhold evidence represent efforts to control prosecutorial abuses. But these examples must be assessed within the broader context. For years, courts have granted prosecutors wide-ranging discretionary powers. The exercise of this discretion shapes the dynamics of the courthouse. In effect, all others involved in the criminal courts—judges, defense attorneys, probation officers, juries, witnesses, and so on—must react to the decisions made by the prosecutor. But the law imposes few formal restrictions on the use of these discretionary powers. Prosecutors' offices are decentralized, autonomous, and headed by locally elected officials.

This does not mean that prosecutorial discretion is uncontrolled; rather, it is influenced by other members of the courtroom work group. Through the socialization process and the occasional application of sanctions, new prosecutors are educated in the norms of the courtroom work group.

CHAPTER REVIEW

LO1 1. Discuss the two major characteristics of prosecutors in the United States.

The role of the prosecutor involves broad discretion and decentralization.

LO2 2. Describe the three most important entities in federal prosecution.

The three most important entities in federal prosecution are the U.S. solicitor general, the Criminal Division of the U.S. Department of Justice, and the offices of 94 U.S. attorneys.

LO3 3. Identify the three somewhat overlapping agencies involved in prosecution in state courts.

The three major agencies involved in prosecution in state courts are the state attorney general, the chief prosecutor, and the local prosecutor.

LO4 4. Explain the major factors affecting the work life of assistant district attorneys.

Assistant district attorneys are typically young lawyers who must learn how law in action is practiced, seek promotions to prosecuting more serious crimes, and are often loosely supervised.

LO5 5. Analyze the principal factors affecting prosecutorial ethics.

As governmental officials, prosecutors are largely immune from civil lawsuits, and if an error is made, an appellate court reversal is the typical remedy.

LO6 6. Outline two major examples of the expanding domain of the prosecutor.

Programs aimed at improving police–prosecutor relationships and community prosecution are two contemporary examples of the expanding domain of the prosecutor.

CRITICAL THINKING QUESTIONS

1. Robert Misner (1996) argued that given the fragmented nature of the criminal justice system (see Chapter 1), over the past 30 years responsibility has increasingly been centralized in the hands of the district attorney. What factors support this assessment?

2. Should state attorneys general be given authority to supervise locally elected district attorneys? How would such increased authority alter the criminal justice system?

3. How much authority should assistant district attorneys be given? As licensed attorneys, should they be given a large amount of discretion to dispose of cases according to their best judgment, or should they have more limited authority so that the office has a uniform policy?

4. Of the three political styles—office conservator, courthouse insurgent, and policy reformer—which best describes your local prosecutor?

5. Community prosecution stresses the need for the prosecutor to reach out to the community, but what does "community" mean? Is this reform based on a naive assumption that all members of the same geographic entity share similar views? How might different communities within the same city (or perhaps county) stress different law-enforcement priorities?

KEY TERMS

FOR FURTHER READING

Banks, Cyndi. 2013. *Criminal Justice Ethics: Theory and Practice.* 3d ed. Thousand Oaks, CA: Sage.

Davis, Angela. 2009. *Arbitrary Justice: The Power of the American Prosecutor.* New York: Oxford University Press.

Delsohn, Gary. 2003. *The Prosecutors: Kidnap, Rape, Murder, Justice: One Year behind the Scenes in a Big-City DA's Office.* New York: Plume.

Delsohn, Gary. 2003. *The Prosecutors: A Year in the Life of a District Attorney's Office.* New York: Dutton/Penguin.

Markovits, Daniel. 2008. *A Modern Legal Ethics: Adversary Advocacy in a Democratic Age.* Princeton, NJ: Princeton University Press.

Mason, Caleb. 2010. "The Police-Prosecutor Relationship and the No-Contact Rule: Conflicting Incentives after *Montejo v. Louisiana* and *Maryland v. Shatzer*." *Cleveland Law Review*, 58: 747–780.

Senjo, Scott. 2011. *Sexual Deviancy and the Law: Legal Regulation of Human Sexuality.* Dubuque, IA: Kendall Hunt.

Stemen, Don, and Bruce Frederick. 2013. "Rules, Resources, and Relationships: Contextual Constraints on Prosecutorial Decision Making." *Quinnipiac University Law Review* 31: 1–83.

Straus, Sarena. 2006. *Bronx D.A.: True Stories from the Sex Crimes and Domestic Violence Unit.* Fort Lee, NJ: Barricade Books.

Suthers, John. 2008. *No Higher Calling, No Greater Responsibility: A Prosecutor Makes His Case.* Goldon, CO: Fulcrum.

Taslitz, Andrew. 2012. "Information Overload, Multi-tasking, and the Socially Networked Jury: Why Prosecutors Should Approach the Media Gingerly." *Journal of the Legal Profession* 37: 89–138.

Train, Arthur. 2010. *True Stories of Crime from the District Attorney's Office.* Charleston, SC: BiblioBazar, 2010.

Worrall, John, and M. Elaine Nugent-Borakove (Eds.). 2008. *The Changing Role of the American Prosecutor.* Albany, NY: SUNY Press.

Defense attorney Alan Konop addresses the jury with his hand on the shoulder of the Reverend Gerald Robinson, who was accused of killing a nun in a hospital chapel 26 years before his trial date. He was convicted at the age of 68 and sentenced to 15 years to life in prison. His conviction was affirmed by an Ohio appeals court.

Chapter Outline

Clarence Earl Gideon had been in and out of prison since the age of 14. His brushes with the law had been minor—public drunkenness and petty theft, primarily—but now he faced a much more serious charge: burglarizing a poolroom in Bay Harbor. As he stood before the judge, he appeared to be a shipwreck of a man; his wrinkled face and trembling hands suggested a person much older than 51. Yet "a flame still burned inside Clarence Earl Gideon . . . he had a fierce feeling that the State of Florida had treated him wrongly" (Lewis, 1989, p. 6). He demanded that the court appoint a lawyer to defend him. The trial judge flatly refused; unrepresented by counsel, Gideon was found guilty. But on appeal, he was luckier. The Supreme Court plucked this obscure case from the bowels of the criminal justice system to issue a landmark decision: all indigent defendants were entitled to court-appointed counsel in felony trials. *Gideon v. Wainwright* (1963) was not only a victory for Clarence Earl Gideon but, more important, it sent shock waves through the criminal justice system.

The Court's decision in *Gideon* underscores the importance of lawyers in the criminal justice system. But what role do defense attorneys play in representing their clients? Some view defense attorneys as fighting to free falsely accused clients. Others, though, often contrast this favorable image with a less complimentary one of the defense attorney as a conniver who uses legal technicalities to free the guilty.

This chapter assesses these conflicting images in terms of the daily realities of the small proportion of the legal profession who represent defendants accused of violating the criminal law. The picture is a complicated one. Some defense attorneys suffer from the shortcomings mentioned by their critics; others do not. But all face day-to-day problems and challenges not usually encountered by the bulk of American lawyers who represent higher-status clients. The key topics of this chapter are the factors influencing the type of legal assistance available to those who appear in criminal courts: the legal right to counsel, the tasks defense attorneys perform, their relationship with courtroom work groups, the nature of the criminal bar, the relationship between lawyer and client, and finally, the various systems for providing legal assistance to the poor.

The Right to Counsel

Like many other provisions of the U.S. Constitution, the Sixth Amendment has a different meaning today than it did when it was first ratified. In a landmark decision, the U.S. Supreme Court held that, based on the Sixth Amendment's provision of **right to counsel**, indigent defendants charged with a felony are entitled to the services of a lawyer paid for by the government (see "Case Close-Up: *Gideon v. Wainwright* and the Right to Counsel"). Later, the Sixth Amendment right to counsel was extended to juvenile court proceedings as well (*In re Gault*, 1967). But as so often happens, answering one question raised several new ones. In the wake of the *Gideon* decision, the Court wrestled with issues involving the right to counsel with regard to (1) nonfelony criminal prosecutions, (2) stages of the criminal process, (3) ineffective assistance of counsel, and (4) self-representation. The following "Key Development" feature summarizes key cases affecting the Sixth Amendment right to counsel.

Nonfelony Criminal Prosecutions

The *Gideon* ruling was limited to state felony prosecutions. In *Argersinger v. Hamlin* (1972), the Court refused to extend the newly discovered constitutional right to court-appointed counsel to those accused of minor violations (misdemeanor or ordinance violations), holding that "absent a knowing and intelligent waiver, no person may be imprisoned for any offense, whether classified as petty, misdemeanor, or felony, unless he was represented by counsel." Later, the justices narrowed the *Argersinger* decision, ruling that a defendant is guaranteed the right to legal

counsel, paid by the state if necessary, only in cases that actually lead to imprisonment, not in all cases in which imprisonment is a potential penalty (*Scott v. Illinois*, 1979). *Scott* clearly had a chilling effect on an indigent person exercising his or her right to counsel (Christopher, 2014; Hashimoto, 2015). The net effect of the *Scott* case was to limit the right to counsel in nonfelony prosecutions, particularly if the guilty faced only paying a fine. Nonetheless, indigents are entitled to a court-appointed attorney even if facing only a suspended jail term for a minor charge (*Alabama v. Shelton*, 2002).

We know very little about how local courts actually provide indigents in nonfelony prosecutions with court-appointed counsel, but there is every indication that compliance is less than full. The National Association of Criminal Defense Lawyers (2009) examined seven states and reported that counsel was not being appointed in some cases. Lack of legal representation in spite of the Sixth Amendment right to counsel poses a particularly vexing problem in the lower courts in which misdemeanor offenses are processed in an assembly-line fashion (Chapter 4). Hashimoto (2013) found that 30 percent of misdemeanor defendants who were sentenced to incarceration reported that they were not represented by counsel. And in a comprehensive study conducted by Smith and Maddan (2011) in which they observed 1,649 initial appearances in the municipal courts of 21 different counties in Florida, lower trial court judges

> failed to advise defendants of their right to counsel almost 28% of the time, and neglected to ask defendants if they wanted appointed or hired counsel in half of the cases. Fewer were told about the benefit of counsel (38%), the importance of counsel (33%), and the disadvantages of proceeding without counsel (35%), or asked whether they could afford an attorney (38%). (p. 22)

KEY DEVELOPMENTS IN THE RIGHT TO COUNSEL

Sixth Amendment (1791)	"In all criminal prosecutions the accused shall enjoy the right . . . to have the assistance of counsel for his defence."
Powell v. Alabama (1932)	Indigent defendants in a capital case in state court have a right to court-appointed counsel.
Johnson v. Zerbst (1938)	Indigent felony defendants in federal court are entitled to court-appointed counsel.
Betts v. Brady (1942)	Indigent defendants in a noncapital case in state court have no right to appointed counsel.
Gideon v. Wainwright (1963)	Indigent felony defendants have the right to appointed counsel (*Betts* overruled).
Douglas v. California (1963)	Indigents have a right to court-appointed counsel during the first appeal.
In re Gault (1967)	Juveniles are covered by the Sixth Amendment's right to counsel.
Argersinger v. Hamlin (1972)	Indigent nonfelony defendants have the right to appointed counsel if they are facing jail time.
Faretta v. California (1975)	Defendants have the right to self-representation.
Scott v. Illinois (1979)	Although no indigent criminal defendant may be sentenced to a term of imprisonment unless he or she was afforded the right to assistance of appointed defense counsel, trial courts are not required to appoint counsel for a defendant charged with a statutory offense for which imprisonment upon conviction is authorized, but will not actually be imposed.
Strickland v. Washington (1984)	A defense attorney is ineffective only if proceedings were unfair and the outcome would have been different.
Wiggins v. Smith (2003)	The failure of an inexperienced defense attorney to conduct a reasonable investigation of the defendant's troubled personal background constituted ineffective assistance of counsel.
Halbert v. Michigan (2005)	Indigent defendants who plead guilty are entitled to state-paid legal help on appeal.
Schriro v. Landrigan (2007)	During the penalty phase of a death penalty trial, the defendant refused to allow his attorney to present mitigating evidence about organic brain damage. The defendant was not denied effective assistance of counsel under *Strickland*.
Indiana v. Edwards (2008)	A mentally ill defendant who is nonetheless competent to stand trial is not necessarily competent to dispense with a lawyer and represent himself.
Padilla v. Kentucky (2010)	Failing to inform one's client that a plea carries a risk of deportation constitutes ineffective assistance of counsel under *Strickland*.
Missouri vs. Frye and Lafler vs. Cooper (2012)	Defense counsel has the duty to communicate formal offers from the prosecution to accept a plea on terms and conditions that may be favorable to the accused, and defendants have a right to competent advice from a lawyer on whether to accept or reject such an offer.
Luis v. United States (2016)	The pretrial freeze of a criminal defendant's legitimate assets—those untainted by any connection to alleged crimes—violates the Sixth Amendment right to counsel since those funds must be available to a defendant to hire defense counsel of choice.

CASE CLOSE-UP   *Gideon v. Wainwright* and the Right to Counsel

From his prison cell, Clarence Earl Gideon drafted a petition that, despite the garbled prose of a man with no real education, nonetheless raised a major legal principle:

> When at the time of the petitioner's trial he ask the lower court for the aid of counsel, the court refused this aid. Petitioner told the court that this [Supreme] Court made decision to the effect that all citizens tried for a felony crime should have aid of counsel. The lower court ignored this plea. (Lewis, 1972)

Every year thousands of pauper petitions like this are sent to the Supreme Court; few are ever heard. But this petition struck a responsive chord. The Court signaled the importance of the issue when it appointed Abe Fortas, one of the best-known lawyers in Washington, D.C., to represent Gideon. (Fortas would later be appointed to the Court.)

In what became officially known as *Gideon v. Wainwright*, the Court forcefully noted that "in our adversary system of criminal justice, any person, hauled into court, who is too poor to hire a lawyer, cannot be assured a fair trial unless counsel is provided for him. This seems to us to be an obvious truth . . ." (p. 344).

The Sixth Amendment states that "in all criminal prosecutions, the accused shall enjoy the right . . . to have the assistance of counsel for his defence." As written by the framers more than 200 years ago, this constitutionally protected right to counsel meant only that the judge could not prevent a defendant from bringing a lawyer to court. (In England, defendants had been convicted despite requests to have their lawyers present.) Thus, the Sixth Amendment affected only those who could afford to hire their own lawyers.

Beginning in the 1930s, the Supreme Court took a more expansive view of the right to counsel. Criminal defendants in federal cases were entitled to a court-appointed lawyer if they were too poor to hire their own. But a different rule prevailed in the state courts. Only defendants accused of a capital offense were entitled to court-appointed counsel; indigent defendants charged with ordinary felonies or misdemeanors were not (*Betts v. Brady*, 1942). Thus, a significant number of defendants in state courts had to face the legal maze of criminal proceedings by themselves.

Gideon v. Wainwright (1963) significantly expanded the legal meaning of the right to counsel. As occasionally happens, the Court reversed its earlier precedent in *Betts*:

> That the government hires lawyers to prosecute and defendants who have the money hire lawyers to defend are the strongest indications of the widespread belief that lawyers in criminal courts are necessities, not luxuries. The right of one charged with crime to counsel may not be deemed fundamental and essential for fair trials in some countries, but it is in ours.

Now, all indigent defendants charged with a felony were entitled to the services of a lawyer paid by the government, irrespective of whether they were on trial in state or federal court.

Gideon proved to be a major transforming event in the American criminal justice system. It was the first major decision of the Warren Court's revolution in criminal justice. But unlike other decisions, it proved not to be controversial. The Court's rationale, focusing on basic fairness and the importance of lawyers, gave it widespread legitimacy. Moreover, *Gideon* focused on the need for a lawyer at the trial itself. Later decisions—*Miranda* in particular—restricted police gathering of evidence and proved to be highly contentious.

Moreover,

- 13 percent of defendants appeared with retained counsel prior to their initial appearance.
- 21 percent of defendants were advised of their right to counsel at the initial appearance and received appointed counsel at that time.
- The remaining 66 percent of defendants were without legal representation at this critical stage of the criminal prosecution. Of these defendants who were unrepresented by counsel, only one in five pled not guilty. The remaining 80 percent either pled guilty or no contest.

Stages of the Criminal Process

The *Gideon* ruling spawned another important question: When in the criminal process does the right to counsel begin (and end)? Note that the

Sixth Amendment provides for the right to counsel in "all criminal prosecutions," so it is not limited to the trial itself. The Supreme Court adopted a "critical stages" test, under which a defendant is entitled to legal representation at every stage of prosecution "where substantial rights of the accused may be affected," requiring the "guiding hand of counsel" (*Mempa v. Rhay*, 1967). As Table 7.1 summarizes, indigent defendants have a right to court-appointed counsel from the time they first appear before a judge until sentence is pronounced and the first appeal concluded. (The only exception is the grand jury, whose peculiar practices will be examined in Chapter 10.) As a general rule, defendants have a Sixth Amendment right to the assistance of counsel once any adversarial proceedings have begun (*Brewer v. Williams*, 1977; *Rothgery v. Gillespie County*, 2008).

The right to counsel in the pretrial stage is much more limited, however. Applying the critical-stages test, subsequent decisions held that defendants have the right to court-appointed counsel during custodial interrogations (*Miranda v. Arizona*, 1966) and police lineups (*Kirby v. Illinois*, 1972; *United States v. Wade*, 1967). However, merely being detained by the police is not sufficient grounds to guarantee a right to counsel (*United States v. Gouveia*, 1984).

TABLE 7.1	Right to Counsel During Steps in Felony Prosecutions		
	Extent of Right		**Supreme Court Case**
Arrest	No lawyer required		
Initial appearance	Lawyer required if critical stage		*Rothgery v. Gillespie County* (2008)
Bail	Lawyer required if critical stage		*Coleman v. Alabama* (1970)
Charging	No lawyer required		
Preliminary hearing	Lawyer required		*Coleman v. Alabama* (1970)
Grand jury	No lawyer allowed		
Arraignment	Lawyer required		*Hamilton v. Alabama* (1961)
Interrogation (preindictment)	Lawyer on request		*Miranda v. Arizona* (1966)
Interrogation (postindictment)	Lawyer required		*Massiah v. United States* (1964)
Lineup (preindictment)	No lawyer required		*Kirby v. Illinois* (1972)
Lineup (postindictment)	Lawyer required		*United States. v. Wade* (1967)
Plea bargaining	Lawyer required		*Brady v. United States* (1970); *Tollett v. Henderson* (1973); *Missouri v. Frye* (2012)
Trial	Lawyer required		*Gideon v. Wainwright* (1963)
Sentencing	Lawyer required		*Mempa v. Rhay* (1967)
Probation revocation	Lawyer at court's discretion		*Gagnon v. Scarpelli* (1973)
Parole revocation	Lawyer at board's discretion		*Morrissey v. Brewer* (1972)
First appeal	Lawyer required		*Douglas v. California* (1963)
Discretionary appeal	No lawyer required		*Ross v. Moffitt* (1974)

(The controversy surrounding the extension of the right to counsel in the police station will be examined in Chapter 11.)

In the companion cases of *Missouri v. Frye* (2012) and *Lafler v. Cooper* (2012), the Court held that defendants have a right to competent advice from a lawyer on whether to accept an offer to plead guilty in exchange for a lighter sentence. Specifically, defendants must be told of any formal plea offers from prosecutors that would result in a favorable deal and then be given competent advice about the consequences of rejecting a favorable offer.

The right to counsel also extends to certain posttrial proceedings, but as in pretrial proceedings, the right to counsel is more limited. Working on the assumption that a person's right to an appeal can be effective only if counsel is available, the Court held that indigents have the right to court-appointed counsel for the appeal (*Douglas v. California*, 1963), as well as free trial transcripts (*Griffin v. Illinois*, 1956). The Burger Court, however, rejected attempts to extend the *Douglas* ruling beyond the first appeal. Thus, in discretionary appeals and appeals to the Supreme Court, indigent defendants have no right to court-appointed counsel (*Ross v. Moffitt*, 1974).

The *Ross* decision has major consequences in death penalty cases (Chapter 14). The right to court-appointed counsel typically extends only to the first appeal (Chapter 15). But death penalty cases also undergo numerous post-appeal proceedings termed "postconviction remedies." Under *Ross*, defendants sentenced to death often must rely on voluntary counsel in pursuing these postconviction remedies. Some state supreme courts, however, have gone considerably further in mandating counsel for situations in which the U.S. Supreme Court has not required counsel under the Sixth Amendment. In fact, all states except Alabama provide some level of taxpayer-funded legal assistance to litigate such appeals (Mears, 2012). And even in Alabama, the decision in *Maples v. Thomas* (2012) clearly raised the bar in terms of the right to counsel during postconviction appeals in death cases (Steiker, 2013). The *Maples* Court reversed the conviction of a capital defendant who procedurally defaulted on his appeals after lawyers left the law firm that had agreed to represent Maples in

his appeal *pro bono* (free of charge) and no one had notified Maples.

Ineffective Assistance of Counsel

Is it enough to have a lawyer? Must the lawyer also be competent and effective? The Supreme Court has recognized the effective assistance of counsel as essential to the Sixth Amendment guarantee (*McMann v. Richardson*, 1970). The Court's most significant holding came in 1984 in *Strickland v. Washington*, in which an "objective standard of reasonableness" was set forth as the proper criterion to be applied in making a determination of the ineffectiveness of counsel. Speaking for the Court, former Justice Sandra Day O'Connor emphasized that the "benchmark for judging any claim of ineffectiveness must be whether counsel's conduct so undermined the proper functioning of the adversarial process that the trial cannot be relied on as having produced a just result." It is important to note that an attorney's decisions regarding trial strategy and tactics—such as the order of presentation of evidence; whether to cross-examine an adverse witness; whether to make an objection—all carry a strong presumption of competent performance. Indeed, the Supreme Court has said, "Strategic choices made after thorough investigation of law and facts relevant to plausible options are virtually unchallengeable" (*Knowles v. Mirzayance*, 2009). In short, appellate courts must reverse only if the proceedings were fundamentally unfair and the outcome would have been different if counsel had not been ineffective.

This standard places a heavy burden on the claimant; few appellate courts reverse decisions on these grounds. Indeed, the Court held that a lawyer's failure to file an appeal did not necessarily constitute ineffective assistance of counsel (*Roe v. Flores-Ortega*, 2000). However, the Court appears to have a higher *Strickland* threshold in death penalty cases. The Court ordered a new sentencing hearing in a death penalty case because the inexperienced defense attorney failed to conduct a reasonable investigation of the defendant's troubled personal background (*Wiggins v. Smith*, 2003). Similarly, the Court overturned a Pennsylvania death sentence because the defense attorney failed to search the record for evidence that could have persuaded the jury to spare the defendant's life (*Rompilla v. Beard*, 2005). But not all appeals on these grounds are successful. During the penalty phase of a death penalty trial, the defendant refused to allow his attorney to present mitigating evidence about organic brain damage. The Court held that the defendant was not denied effective assistance of counsel under *Strickland* (*Schriro v. Landrigan*, 2007).

The dual 2012 U.S. Supreme Court decisions of *Missouri v. Frye* and *Lafler v. Cooper* signaled a major shift in Sixth Amendment jurisprudence (Alkon, 2016; Silva, 2014). Prior to these cases, the *Strickland* standard was largely limited to cases litigated through trial. But *Frye* and *Lafler* recognized that since upwards of 90 to 95 percent of cases are resolved by plea bargain (Chapter 12), the reality of the modern criminal justice system is "front-loaded such that the trial is no longer the main event" (Marceau, 2012, p. 1162). Indeed, the Court said, "The reality is that plea bargains have become so central to the administration of the criminal justice system" it is no longer accurate to describe pretrial proceedings such as plea bargaining as an "adjunct to the criminal justice system; it *is* the criminal justice system" (*Missouri v. Frye*, 2012, p. 1407). As a result, it is now clear that the right to effective assistance of counsel is not limited to preserving the right to a fair trial; it also encompasses the pretrial stages of a criminal prosecution leading up to resolution of the case by plea bargain (see Chapter 12).

Self-Representation

Can defendants represent themselves if they wish? An important qualification was added to *Gideon* when the Supreme Court ruled that defendants have a constitutional right to self-representation. This means that criminal defendants have the right to proceed *pro se* (Latin for "on his or her own behalf").

The Court, however, did establish limits. Defendants who wish to represent themselves must show the trial judge that they have the ability to conduct the trial. The defendant need not have the skills and experience of a lawyer, and the judge may not deny

self-representation simply because the defendant does not have expert knowledge of criminal law and procedure (*Faretta v. California*, 1975). This decision has been qualified by the Court's recognition that the trial judge may appoint standby counsel when defendants choose to represent themselves (*McKaskle v. Wiggins*, 1984). Standby counsel is available during the trial to consult with the defendant, but it is the defendant, not the standby lawyer, who makes the decisions.

Although self-representation occurs rarely, these cases have the potential to become media spectacles. In 1970, Charles Manson unsuccessfully represented himself in his infamous trial for the killings of Sharon Tate and Leno and Rosemary LaBiaca. He primarily used his trial to espouse his bizarre beliefs, rather than offer any meaningful criminal defense. He was convicted and sentenced to death, although his sentence was subsequently reduced to life in prison. Infamous serial killer Ted Bundy represented himself, but in doing so, he revealed certain aspects of his crimes that ultimately led to his conviction and execution.

One of the oddest cases of self-representation was that of Colin Ferguson. Ferguson fired into a crowded Long Island Railroad commuter train, killing 6 passengers and wounding 19 others. Ferguson claimed that he acted out of a sense of "Black rage"; his lawyer argued he was insane. Ferguson then dismissed his court-appointed lawyer, who objected that the trial would become a complete circus because "a crazy man cannot represent himself." The prediction proved accurate (McQuiston, 1995). Broadcast nationwide, the trial, with its inevitable guilty verdict, was perceived as not a trial but a spectacle and underscored the limits of self-representation.

Dr. Jack Kevorkian represented himself in an assisted suicide case in Michigan, and Zacarias Moussaoui represented himself against charges that he was the 20th participant in the terrorist attack of September 11, 2001. Both were convicted. More recently, Major Nidal Malik Hasan represented himself at his trial for 13 counts of murder and 32 counts of attempted murder for opening fire on Fort Hood military base near Killeen, Texas, in 2009. He stunned the courtroom during the first day of trial by admitting, "I am the shooter."

He then spent the balance of the trial attempting to justify the killings by arguing he was defending his Islamic faith from U.S. war efforts. Since no defense of justification was legally applicable in the case (see Chapter 1), he was unsurprisingly convicted. In fact, he was sentenced to death. And, recall from Chapter 1 that Dylann Roof's unsuccessful self-representation without any defense of justification or excuse caused him to face the same fate.

A recent case proved that the Court appears ready to limit self-representation in bizarre situations. The Court held that a mentally ill defendant who is nonetheless competent to stand trial is not necessarily competent to dispense with a lawyer and represent himself (*Indiana v. Edwards*, 2008).

An empirical study, however, challenges the conventional wisdom that there is no good reason for a defendant to choose self-representation. *Pro se* defendants fare as well as represented defendants 80 percent of the time, and most do not suffer from mental illness (Hashimoto, 2007).

Defense Attorneys and Courtroom Work Groups

Lawyers are expected to be advocates for their clients' cases, arguing for legal innocence. As one defense counsel phrased it, "If the attorney does not appear to be taking the side of the defendant, then no one will" (Neubauer, 1974b, p. 73). But the zealous advocacy of a client's case is not the same thing as winning at all costs. As a member of the legal profession, a lawyer's advocacy of a client's case is limited by professional obligations. Like prosecutors, defense attorneys are officers of the court, who must fulfill their responsibilities within the framework established by legal ethics. They cannot deliberately mislead the court by providing false information. Nor can they knowingly allow the use of perjurious testimony.

Assessing how well lawyers represent their clients is difficult because of different ways of assessing the work performed. How do we define winning? Our popular culture suggests that winning means an acquittal. But experienced lawyers

reject such simplistic notions. A veteran Los Angeles public defender explained:

> What is our job as a criminal lawyer in most instances? Number one is . . . no kidding, we know the man's done it, or we feel he's done it, he may deny it, but the question is: Can they prove it? The next thing is: Can we mitigate it? Of course you can always find something good to say about the guy—to mitigate it. Those are the two things that are important, and that's what you do. (Mather, 1974b, p. 278)

Thus, many defense attorneys define winning in terms of securing probation, or accepting a plea to a misdemeanor charge. One attorney put it this way: "Given the situation, what is the best that can be done for my client?" (Neubauer, 1974b, p. 74). At virtually all stages of the criminal justice process, defendants may have the guiding hand of counsel (see "Law on the Books vs. Law in Action" feature on page 206).

How defense attorneys seek to reach the best solution possible for their client is directly related to their relationship with other members of the courtroom work group. Usually, assistant public defenders are permanently assigned to a single courtroom and work every day with the same judge, the same prosecutor(s), the same court reporter, and the same clerk of court. Similarly, private defense attorneys—although they practice before several judges—are a permanent fixture in the criminal courts, for a handful of lawyers dominate the representation of fee-paying criminal defendants in any city. This daily interaction of the criminal bar with the court community shapes the type and quality of legal representation received by those accused of violating the law. Whereas the adversary system stresses the combative role of the defense attorney, the day-to-day activities of the courtroom work group stress cooperation.

The legal system, civil and criminal, is based on controversy. Norms of cooperation work to channel such controversy into constructive avenues. All too often, advocacy is falsely equated with antagonism. Although defense attorneys exchange pleasantries with judges and prosecutors, their personal contacts with these officials outside the courtroom are limited.

Another qualification to bear in mind is that cooperative attorneys do not bargain every case; they also take cases to trial. If the defense attorney thinks

LAW IN ACTION VS. LAW ON THE BOOKS

The Role of Defense Attorneys in a Typical Felony Case

	Law on the Books	Law in Action
Crime		Counsels the client about the crime charged.
Arrest		Rarely present.
Initial appearance	Allowed to be present.	Typically advises client to say nothing during the court proceedings.
Bail	Argues for client's release on bail.	Judge more likely to listen to the district attorney's (DA's) recommended bail.
Charging		May urge the prosecutor to charge the client with a less serious offense.
Preliminary hearing	Allowed to be present but typically cannot call witnesses.	Good opportunity to find out what really happened in the case.
Grand jury	Only in some states may defense attorney be present.	Grand jury transcripts may be useful for discovery.
Arraignment	Allowed to be present.	Chance to talk to the client; may suggest entering a plea of guilty.
Evidence	Requests discovery information from the prosecutor; files motions to suppress confession and/or search and seizure.	Cooperative defense attorneys receive greater discovery information from the DA. Rarely successful in winning suppression motions.
Plea bargaining	Often a direct participant in plea discussions.	Negotiates for most beneficial deal possible.
Trial	Advocate for defendant's rights.	Typically stresses that the prosecutor has not proved the defendant "guilty beyond a reasonable doubt."
Sentencing	Makes a sentencing recommendation to the judge.	Argues for sentence at the low end of the normal penalty scale.
Appeal	Files notice of appeal and writes appellate brief.	Rarely successful on appeal.

the prosecutor is driving too hard a bargain or that the state cannot prove its case to the jury, a trial will be recommended. Furthermore, no evidence exists to show that cooperative attorneys do not argue the case to the best of their abilities during a trial.

Rewards and Sanctions

Defense attorneys who maintain a cooperative stance toward judges, prosecutors, and clerks can expect to reap some rewards. Defense attorneys have limited (in some instances, nonexistent) investigative resources. Prosecutors can provide cooperative defense attorneys with information about the cases by letting them examine the police reports, revealing the names of witnesses, and so on.

The court community can also apply sanctions to defense attorneys who violate the norms. Some sanctions work indirectly, by reducing a lawyer's income-generating ability. The clerk may refuse to provide beneficial case scheduling, or the judge may drag out a trial by continuously interrupting it for other business. Other sanctions are more direct. A judge can criticize a lawyer in front of his or her client (thus scaring away potential clients in the courtroom) or refuse to appoint certain attorneys to represent indigents—a significant source of income for some lawyers (Nardulli, 1978). A final category of sanctions involves the prosecutor's adopting a tougher stance during bargaining by not reducing charges or by recommending a prison sentence that is longer than normal.

Sanctions against defense attorneys are seldom invoked, but when they are, they can have far-reaching effects. Every court community can point to an attorney who has suffered sanctions, with the result that the attorney either no longer practices criminal law in the area or has mended his or her ways.

Variations in Cooperation

Defense attorneys are the least powerful members of the courtroom work group. Because of the numerous sanctions that can be applied to defense attorneys, they are forced into a reactive posture.

Prosecutors assess a defense attorney in terms of "reasonableness"—that is, the ability to "discern a generous offer of settlement and to be willing to encourage his client to accept such an offer" (Skolnick, 1967, p. 58). Based on this criterion, Skolnick put attorneys into three categories. One category consisted of defense attorneys who handled few criminal cases. One might suppose that prosecutors would prefer dealing with such inexperienced attorneys, but they did not. Because these attorneys did not know the ropes, they were too unpredictable and often caused administrative problems. In another category were attorneys who had active criminal practices and maintained a hostile relationship with the prosecutor's office. Known as "gamblers," these attorneys exemplified the aggressive, fighting advocate, but because they either won big or lost big, they also served to show the other attorneys the disadvantage of this posture. The final category of attorneys consisted of public defenders and private attorneys who represented large

numbers of defendants. These attorneys worked within the system.

An Assessment

Are criminal defense attorneys, especially public defenders and regular private attorneys, the co-opted agents of a court bureaucracy or simply calculating realists? This question has been a preoccupation of research on defense attorneys for decades (Flemming, 1986b).

Some studies argue that defense attorneys' ties to the court community mean that defendants' best interests are not represented. David Sudnow (1965) argued that public defenders became co-opted when public defenders and prosecutors shared common conceptions of what Sudnow called "normal crimes." Public defenders were more interested that a given case fit into a sociological cubbyhole than in determining whether the event met the proper penal code provisions. As a result, the public defenders seldom geared their work to securing acquittals for their clients. Thus, from the beginning, the presumption of guilt permeated the public defenders' assessment of cases. Similarly, Abraham Blumberg (1967b) concluded that all defense attorney regulars were double agents, working for both their client and the prosecutor. His study of a large New York court likened the practice of law to a confidence game, in which both the defendant and the defense attorney must have larceny at heart; a con game can be successful only if the "mark" is trying to get something for nothing. Judges and prosecutors depended on the defense attorneys to pressure defendants to plead guilty. In short, both Sudnow and Blumberg portray defense attorneys as ideological and as economic captives of the court rather than aggressive advocates.

However, other studies have concluded that defendants' best interests are not eroded when their attorneys adopt a cooperative posture within the courtroom community. Indeed, Jerome Skolnick (1967) suggested that clients do better as a result of a cooperative posture. Working within the system benefits the client because the prosecutor will be more amenable to disclosing information helpful to the defense, the bargains struck will be more favorable, and the defendant will not be penalized for the hostility of the defense attorney. Furthermore, attorneys identified as agitators may harm their clients' causes because prosecutors and judges will hand out longer sentences. Neubauer's (1974a) study of Prairie City, Illinois, also found that attorneys who remained on good terms with other members of the courtroom work group functioned better as counselors, because they were better able to predict the reactions of the court community to individual cases. In short, the studies by Skolnick (1967), Neubauer (1974a), and Mather (1974b) concluded that attorneys who work within the system are better able to develop a realistic approach to their work, based on experience and knowledge of how their clients will fare.

Little evidence exists, then, that defense lawyers have been co-opted by the criminal justice system. Indeed, a study of what motivates public defenders reached the opposite conclusion. Based on a study of 48 public defenders in three offices, Weiss (2005) concluded that public defenders are cynical about police, prosecutors, and judges. In the end, skepticism about justice being done motivates public defenders to vigorously defend their clients.

The Criminal Bar

Law offices of solo practitioners are a permanent feature of urban architecture. They can be found huddled around the stone edifice of the criminal courts and near the neon lights proclaiming "Harry's 24-Hour Bail Bonds." In Detroit, they are called "the Clinton Street Bar," and in Washington, D.C., "the Fifth Streeters"—titles that are not meant to be complimentary. These lawyers spend little time in their offices; they are most often at the courthouse, socializing with other members of the courtroom work group. Their proximity to the criminal courts and the sparseness of the law books in their offices are good indicators that the law practiced from these offices bears little resemblance to images of defense attorneys presented on television. A number of factors account for the low economic and professional status of the criminal bar.

Diversity and Stratification of the Legal Profession

Law is a diverse profession based partially on the law school attended and the place of work (Mather & Levin, 2012; Wilkins, 2012). Based on extensive interviews with practicing attorneys, Heinz and Laumann (1982), in *Chicago Lawyers: The Social Structure of the Bar*, reported dramatic differences among several sorts of lawyers, and these differences persist (Heinz, Nelson, Sandefur, & Laumann, 2005).

The most important differentiation within the legal profession involved which clients were served. Some lawyers represent large organizations (corporations, labor unions, or government). Others represent mainly individuals. By and large, lawyers operate in one of these two hemispheres of the profession; seldom, if ever, do they cross the line separating these very different types of legal work. The corporate client sector involves large corporate, regulatory, general corporate, and political lawyers. The personal client sector is divided into personal business and personal plight lawyers (divorce, tort, and so on).

Most of the attorneys who appear in criminal court are drawn from the personal-client sector. They are often referred to as "solo practitioners," because they practice alone or share an office with one or more other attorneys who are also in solo private practice. For this group of courtroom regulars, criminal cases constitute a dominant part of their economic livelihood. Thus, studies of private attorneys in different cities report that the bulk of nonindigent defendants are represented by a handful of attorneys (Nardulli, 1986; Neubauer, 1974a).

Environment of Practice

It is no accident that in many large cities, a distinct criminal bar exists. Low status, difficulty in securing clients, and low fees are three factors that affect the availability of lawyers to represent those accused of violating the law.

Most lawyers view criminal cases as unsavory. Representing criminal defendants also produces few chances for victory; most defendants either plead guilty or are found guilty by a judge or jury. Also, despite the legal presumption of innocence, once defendants are arrested, the public assumes they are guilty. As a result, the general public perceives criminal defense attorneys as freeing known robbers and rapists to return to the streets. To earn a living, lawyers first need clients. Attorneys working in the personal-client sector of the legal profession seldom have a regular clientele. Accordingly, a part of their time is spent securing clients. The criminal lawyer's most important commodity in securing clients is his or her reputation, which often develops on the basis of the lawyer's handling of a specific case. A lawyer's reputation is important in several ways. First, defendants want a specific attorney to represent them, not a firm of lawyers. Second, attorneys who do not practice criminal law often refer clients to a specific lawyer who does. Finally, a repeat offender may seek out the previous attorney, if he or she felt the lawyer provided good representation in the past. In securing clients, some defense attorneys rely on police officers, bail agents, and court clerks to give their names to defendants who need counsel (Wice, 1978).

Obtaining clients is only half the problem facing private attorneys who represent criminal clients. The second half is getting paid. "Criminal lawyers are more concerned than other lawyers with collection of the fee—after all, their clients are mostly criminals" (Lushing, 1992, p. 514). The lawyer's fee in a criminal case is generally a flat fee paid in advance. The three most important considerations in setting the fee are the seriousness of the offense, the amount of time it will take the lawyer to deal with the case, and the client's ability to pay. Well-known criminal lawyers, for example, often charge their prosperous clients considerable fees. In the words of a prominent New York City defense attorney, "Reasonable doubt begins with the payment of a reasonable fee" (Gourevitch, 2001, p. 111). The myth that criminal lawyers receive fabulous salaries is mostly untrue; although a few have become quite wealthy, most earn a modest middle-class living (Wice, 1978). Of course, many defendants are so impoverished that they cannot afford to hire a private attorney at all.

Providing Indigents with Attorneys

Indigents are defendants who cannot afford to pay a lawyer and, therefore, are entitled to a lawyer for free. Three-quarters of state prison inmates had court-appointed lawyers to represent them for the offense for which they were serving time. In urban courthouses, the indigency rate is a little higher: 82 percent of felony defendants cannot afford to hire their own lawyer (Bureau of Justice Statistics, 2012; Council of Economic Advisers, 2015). Obviously, the Supreme Court's decision in *Gideon*, requiring the state to provide attorneys for indigents, applies to a substantial number of criminal defendants.

Although the Supreme Court has essentially mandated the development of indigent-defense systems, it has left the financing and type of delivery system up to states and counties, which have considerable discretion in adopting programs (Worden & Worden, 1989). As with other aspects of the dual court system in the United States, the characteristics of defense systems for the indigent vary considerably, with some state governments funding virtually all indigent criminal defense services, other state governments sharing the financial costs of providing counsel with counties, and still other jurisdictions in which county funds are used exclusively (Farole & Langton, 2010; Langton & Farole, 2010; Owens, Accetta, Charles, & Shoemaker, 2015).

How best to provide legal representation for the poor has been a long-standing issue for the courts and the legal profession. In the United States, the three primary methods are assigned counsel (attorneys appointed by the judge on a case-by-case basis), contract systems (attorneys hired to provide services for a specified dollar amount), and public defender (a salaried public official representing all indigent defendants). The ongoing debate over the advantages and disadvantages of these three systems highlights some important issues about the quality of legal representation provided for the poor.

Assigned Counsel

The assigned counsel system reflects the way professions such as law and medicine traditionally responded to charity cases: Individual practitioners provide services on a case-by-case basis. **Assigned counsel systems** involve the appointment by the court of private attorneys from a list of available attorneys on an as-needed basis. The list may consist of all practicing attorneys in the jurisdiction or, more commonly, the attorneys who volunteer. There is great variability in how lawyers on the list are actually appointed to represent a particular client.

Under the ad hoc appointment method, the oldest and still the most common method, "the court appoints attorneys at random, with a minimum of consideration for the qualifications of the attorney or equitable distribution of cases among members of the private bar" (Allison, 1976, p. 403). Most jurisdictions have improved the coordination of their assigned counsel systems in the past 40 years so that case assignments are made by systematic rotations through the list of lawyers (Ogletree & Sapir, 2004). Some jurisdictions even maintain a few specialized lists of lawyers skilled to handle particular types of cases, but that is the exception, not the rule.

The assigned counsel system is used in half of all U.S. counties, but serves less than one-third of the nation's population. It predominates in small counties, those with fewer than 50,000 residents, where an insufficient volume of cases exists to support the costs of a public defender system.

Critics contend that the assigned counsel system results in the least-qualified lawyers being appointed to defend indigents (Buller, 2015; Iyengar, 2007). In most counties, the only attorneys who volunteer are either young ones seeking courtroom experience or those who seek numerous appointments to make a living. Even where appointments are rotated among all members of the practicing bar (as in New Jersey and in Houston, Texas), no guarantee exists that the lawyer selected is qualified to handle the increasing complexity of the criminal law; the appointee may be a skilled real estate attorney or a good probate attorney, but these skills are not readily transferable to the dynamics of a criminal trial.

The availability of lawyers willing to serve as assigned counsel is directly related to financial compensation. In the past, a number of jurisdictions expected attorneys to represent indigents as part of their professional responsibility, without being paid (*pro bono*). Today, however, attorneys assigned to represent indigent defendants are paid. Most commonly, lawyers are compensated for such defense work on the basis of separate hourly rates for out-of-court and in-court work. However, hourly fees for in-court felony work usually range far below the fees charged in private practice. Indeed, a study by the National Association of Criminal Defense Lawyers (Gross, 2013) revealed "staggeringly low rates of compensation for assigned counsel across the nation" averaging $65 per hour for felony cases, "with some states paying as little as $40 an hour" (p. 8). No state compensates assigned counsel near anything approximating the federal rate of $125 per hour (which is still quite low compared to what attorneys in private practice charge). Notably, many states' rates have been stagnant for years. Such low rates of compensation do not even cover overhead such as rent, office equipment, secretarial support, or access to reference materials (which can cost between $9 and $20 *per minute* under certain pricing packages; flat-rate plans can cost thousands of dollars per month, depending on the robustness of the subscription package). And few states allow for any adjustments based on geography, meaning that attorneys in practice in a metropolitan area with high overhead are compensated at the same rates at which their counterparts are paid in rural parts of a state in which overload is dramatically lower.

Critics of the assigned counsel system contend that inadequate compensation pressures attorneys to dispose of such cases quickly in order to devote time to fee-paying clients. And most research supports this contention (Brennan, 2015; Cohen, 2014). The widely held assumption that rates of compensation are directly related to the quality of criminal defense representation has been challenged by one study. The extent of effort of lawyers in Michigan who handled appellate representation did not vary significantly in relation to the rate of compensation. Overall, professional role expectations of lawyers may have a greater influence on their work than financial considerations (Priehs, 1999).

Contract Systems

Contract systems involve bidding by private attorneys to represent all criminal defendants found indigent during the term of the contract, in return for a fixed payment (Cohen, 2014; Priumu, 2016; Worden, 1991, 1993). Contract systems are most often found in counties with populations of fewer than 50,000, where the key feature is that they place an absolute budget limit on defense services for the indigent.

The primary advantage of contract systems is that they limit the costs government must pay for indigent defense. Critics counter with two types of concerns. The first is that contract programs will inevitably lead to a lower standard of representation through the bidding system, which emphasizes cost over quality. The second is that the private bar will no longer play an important role in indigent defense (Spangenberg Group, 2000; Toone, 2015).

The contract system was held unconstitutional in Arizona when the Arizona Supreme Court held that the Mohave County contract system, which assigned defense representation of the indigent to the lowest bidder, violated the Fifth and Sixth Amendments because the system (1) did not take into account the time the attorney is expected to spend on a case, (2) did not provide for support staff costs, (3) failed to take into account the competence of the attorney, and (4) did not consider the complexity of the case (*Smith v. State*, 1984). Likewise, courts in several other states have found legal defects in contract systems that result in inadequate funding levels (Spangenberg Group, 2000).

Skepticism that contract systems actually save money is growing. Several jurisdictions have been frustrated by contract firms submitting increasingly higher budgets after their initial low bids (Wice, 2005). Moreover, in some markets, contract systems have failed to reduce the costs of indigent defense, and may actually increase such costs, because there are too few attorneys to generate a competitive market (Cohen, 2014; Spangenberg & Beeman, 1995).

Public Defender

The **public defender** is a 20th-century response to the problem of providing legal representation for the indigent. Public defender programs are public or private nonprofit organizations with full- or part-time salaried staff who represent indigents in criminal cases in a jurisdiction.

Started in Los Angeles County in 1914, public defender offices spread slowly. By 1965, the National Legal Aid and Defender Association—the national organization that promotes better legal representation for indigents in civil as well as criminal cases—reported programs in only 117 counties. Since 1965, public defender programs have spread rapidly because of Supreme Court decisions (*Gideon* and later *Argersinger*), as well as increased concern for more-adequate representation of indigents. Today, the public defender system represents approximately 70 percent of all indigents nationwide. It predominates in most big cities and has also been adopted in numerous medium-sized jurisdictions.

The administration and funding of public defender programs occurs at either the state or local level. Twenty-two states have a state public defender program that oversees the policies and practices of the 427 public defender offices located in these states (Langton & Farole, 2010). In another 27 states and the District of Columbia, public defender offices were funded and administered at the local level (Farole & Langton, 2010). Maine is the only state that does not have a public defender office.

Proponents of the public defender system cite several arguments in favor of its adoption. One is that a lawyer paid to represent indigents on a continuous basis will devote more attention to cases than a court-appointed attorney who receives only minimal compensation. Moreover, many members of the practicing bar like the idea that they no longer have to take time away from fee-paying cases to meet their professional obligations.

A second advantage often claimed for the public defender system is that it provides more experienced, competent counsel. Because public defenders concentrate on criminal cases, they can keep abreast of changes in the law, and the day-to-day courtroom work keeps their trial skills sharp. The public defender is also likely to be more knowledgeable about informal norms and is therefore in a better position to counsel defendants and negotiate the best possible deal.

Are We Spending Too Little or Too Much on Indigent Defense?

Is *Gideon*'s promise broken? Fifty years after the Court's landmark right-to-counsel decision, some argue that the promise of equal justice under law has given way to a two-tiered system of criminal representation—one for those with money and another for those without it. Still others contend that the way *Gideon* has been implemented is way too costly.

From the perspective of the due process model, unmanageable caseloads are the single greatest obstacle to effective representation of the indigent (Brennan, 2015; Lefstein, 2011; National Right to Counsel Committee, 2009). In 1973, the National Advisory Commission on Criminal Justice Standards and Goals recommended that a maximum effective felony caseload for a public defender is 150 cases per year. Today, most states have workload standards that recommend a felony caseload of between 50 and 300 cases, with most states continuing to embrace the figure of 150 cases recommended by the National Advisory Commission in 1973 (Spangenberg Group, 2001). Yet, in many jurisdictions, it is typically much higher—sometimes approaching 1,000 clients per year (Brennan, 2015; Cauchon, 1999; Lefstein, 2011). "No more. We can't ethically handle this many cases," argues David Carrol of the National Legal Aid and Defender Association. Typical is Florida's Miami–Dade County, where the public defender's office refused to accept any new lesser-felony cases so they could concentrate on defending current clients (Eckholm, 2008). "Too many clients and too little time" seems to characterize many public defender offices, particularly after the deep recession that began in 2008 (Baxter, 2012, p. 91).

The short-term failure to adequately fund indigent defense can prove to be expensive in the long run. The advent of DNA evidence (Chapter 13) has led to the freeing of hundreds of the wrongfully convicted (Chapter 15), but only after major expenditures for lawyers and the like, to say nothing of damage to the reputation of the criminal justice system. Likewise, the lack of attorneys available to defend death row inmates is a major point of contention regarding the death penalty (see Chapter 14). And some state and local governments now face paying sometimes large amounts of money to prisoners who were wrongfully convicted (Chapter 15).

For many years, federal courts largely avoided the problem of out-of-control caseloads, but no longer (American Civil Liberties Union, 2013; Lefstein, 2011). Congressional mandated budget cuts have hit federal courts, particularly federal public defenders. In New Orleans, for example, the head federal public defender fired herself, rather than cutting another

Finally, a public defender system ensures continuity and consistency in the defense of the poor (Silverstein, 1965). Public defenders are usually able to provide early representation, entering the case at the initial appearance. Moreover, issues that transcend individual cases—criteria for pretrial release, police practices, and so forth—are more likely to be considered by a permanent, ongoing organization than under appointment systems.

Assessing the Merits of Public Defenders

Critics contend that public defenders—as paid employees of the state—will not provide a vigorous defense because they are tied too closely to the courtroom work group. Several studies have investigated this concern by comparing the adequacy of representation provided by assigned counsel to that by public defenders' offices. The dominant conclusion is that there is not much difference (Buller, 2015; Eisenstein, Flemming, & Nardulli, 1988; Flemming, 1989; Hartley, Miller, & Spohn, 2010; Wice, 1985). One recent study, however, reports that Florida defendants represented by public defenders fare less well than those represented by retained attorneys (Williams, 2013).

Several studies, however, find that defendants represented by assigned counsel attorneys fare less well (Buller, 2015; Cohen, 2014; Iyengar, 2007; Roach, 2010). In Philadelphia, for example, murder defendants represented by public defenders lawyer (Linderman, 2013). Across the nation federal public defenders must reduce spending by 14 percent (Johnson, 2013).

In the wake of the economic downturn of the early 21st century, state after state has often been forced to reduce funding for indigent defense. An issue is who should pay for public defenders. County boards believed that it is the state's responsibility to pay these expenses. But officials of the state countered that its budget was in dire straits, and therefore it was unable to afford such services (Liptak, 2003). The result is a new wave of litigation over who should finance legal representation for the indigent (Costello, 2014; Woods, 2014).

Crime control proponents, on the other hand, have long been concerned that the government is paying too much for indigent defense. As expenditures for defense services for the indigent have risen dramatically (DeFrances, 2001), there has been a noticeable trend toward containing the costs. One technique is the adoption of stringent indigency standards. Traditionally, big-city judges rarely inquired into the financial capabilities of defendants to determine whether they satisfy the court's definition of indigency. However, a report funded by the National Institute of Justice stresses that courts should screen applications "to ensure that only the truly indigent are provided representation at public expense" (Spangenberg, Wilson, Smith, & Lee, 1986, p. 69). However, indigency standards set too high obviously deprive defendants of their constitutional right to court-appointed counsel. This is particularly true in counties that consider making bail in determining indigency—the bail bonds person's fee may exhaust the financial resources to hire a lawyer (Hashimoto, 2013).

Another way of containing government expenses is cost recovery. In screening applications for defense services for the indigent, many courts now distinguish between defendants so poor that they are exempt from paying any costs of their defense and a new category of "partially indigent" defendants who may be able to pay a portion of the costs (Lee, 1992; Spangenberg et al., 1986). Defendants in many jurisdictions may be required to pay application fees for court-appointed counsel (Hashimoto, 2013). It "seems only fair" that defendants be required to pay, argues Jim Rams, president of the National District Attorneys Association. "Since the vast majority of criminal defendants do not get sentenced to jail . . . their job status and economics can and should change relatively quickly allowing repayment" (as quoted in Johnson, 2010, para. 11). The Brenan Center for Justice counters that in practice these fees often discourage individuals from exercising their constitutional rights, leading to wrongful convictions (Bannon, Nagrecha, & Diller, 2010).

(as opposed to assigned counsel) are convicted less often and are also less likely to receive a life sentence if convicted (Anderson & Heaton, 2012). Most importantly, though, the research continues to report that clients of private attorneys and public defenders receive similar case outcomes. Indeed, one study found that defendants represented by private counsel in "Three Strikes" cases in California (see Chapter 15) receive on average 16 percent longer sentences than those represented by public defenders, illustrating how members of the courtroom work group cooperate even in felony cases with particularly serious outcomes (Sutton, 2013).

The National Center for State Courts drew the following conclusions from the nine jurisdictions it studied:

1. Appointed counsel resolved the cases of their indigent defendants more expeditiously than did privately retained counsel.

2. Appointed criminal defense counsel gained as many favorable outcomes (acquittals, charge reductions, and short prison sentences) for their indigent clients as privately retained attorneys did for their clients.

3. Appointed criminal defense counsel prosecuting attorneys were equally experienced (Hanson, Hewitt, & Ostrom, 1992).

Likewise, the outcomes of criminal appeals do not vary between public defenders and privately retained counsel (Williams, 1995).

The Public Defender: The Practice of Law in the Shadows of Repute offers a radically different view of public defense attorneys. In this book, Lisa McIntyre (1987) demonstrated that public defense lawyers are indeed free to defend their clients zealously. She found that in the courts of Cook County, Illinois, public defenders are adversarial and even combative opponents of the state's prosecutorial apparatus. McIntyre argues, in fact, that the office of the public defender survives because its effective advocacy for its clients bolsters the legitimacy of the court system.

Why, then, does the public defender's image not reflect this? The freedom to defend against the state cannot include the freedom to embarrass it. Hence, the complexity of the public defender's institutional role requires that the office not advertise its successes. McIntyre shows that the public defender's office deliberately retains its image of incompetency in order to guarantee its continued existence. Public defenders may practice good law, but they must do it in the darker shadows of repute.

The long-standing debate over the adequacy of court-appointed counsel is beginning to give way to a new reality—large governmental expenses. Images and myths play a central role in the debate over funding levels for court-appointed lawyers (see "Courts, Controversy, and Economic Inequality: Are We Spending Too Little or Too Much on Indigent Defense?"). The reality of life for defense attorneys who represent indigent clients is not pretty.

> Low salaries for indigent[s'] defense attorneys often coexist with crushing caseloads. The focus in the modern criminal justice system values efficiency over justice. Criminal defense attorneys sometimes act as mere cogs in the conviction machine. "We wax poetically about justice for all, . . . and yet you go into courthouses all over the country, and what you see is not at all what is being celebrated. What you see is people being processed like widgets on an assembly line." The crushing caseload somewhat explains the lack of individualized attention to a client's case. One chief public defender explained, "We had an attorney last year who blew through 500 cases in a year, most of them felonies. . . . You can't confidently represent these folks [with that kind of caseload]." (Davoli, 2012, pp. 1155–1156 [internal citations omitted])

The vast majority of public defender agencies attempt to survive from one crisis to the next amid a perpetual flux of inexperienced lawyers. In response to the ongoing problems of the traditional agencies, some reform defender agencies have emerged. *Public Defenders and the American Justice System* by Paul Wice (2005) focuses on one reform defender system—Essex County (Newark), New Jersey. These reform agencies strive to maintain a group of experienced lawyers by emphasizing their independence from any political or judicial influence. One of their hallmarks is stressing the importance of one-on-one representation for each client.

Lawyers and Clients

One of the most important tasks of defense attorneys is counseling. As advocates, defense attorneys are expected to champion their clients' cases. But as counselors, they must advise their clients about the possible legal consequences involved. Lawyers must fully and dispassionately evaluate the strengths and weaknesses of the prosecutor's case, assess the probable success of various legal defenses, and—most important—weigh the likelihood of conviction or acquittal. In appraising risks and outlining options, lawyers interpret the law to their clients, who are often unversed in what the law considers important and what the law demands.

To be an effective advocate and counselor, the lawyer must know all the facts of a case. For this reason, the American legal system surrounds the attorney–client relationship with special protections. Statements made by a client to his or her attorney are considered **privileged communication**, which the law protects from forced disclosure without the client's consent. The attorney–client privilege extends not only to statements made by the client but also to any work product developed in representing the client.

Based on trust and a full exchange of information, the attorney assumes the difficult task of advocating a client's case. In civil litigation, the relationship between lawyer and client is often (but not always) characterized by trust and full disclosure (Cox, 1993). In criminal cases, however, the relationship is more likely to be marked by distrust and hostility. Indeed, more than half of defendants are described by their attorneys as passive participants in the overall defense, and 10 percent are described by their attorneys as recalcitrant—that is, rarely or never accepting the attorney's advice (Bonnie, Poythress, Hoge, Monahan, & Eisenberg, 1996).

In the modern era, high caseloads clearly complicate the ability of lawyers, particularly those appointed by the court to represent indigents, to find time to talk with clients. In the book *Indefensible: One Lawyer's Journey into the Inferno of American Justice*, David Feige (2006) reflected on days in court when he was unable to make court appearances because he was busy elsewhere. Given a caseload ranging from 75 to 120 active cases, "the simple matter of where to be when becomes one of the most complicated and taxing puzzles we face. It's not unusual to have six, eight, or even ten different courtrooms to go to in a single day" (p. 87). And on some days, an unexpectedly lengthy appearance in one courtroom means that a lawyer will be unable to meet with a client in another courtroom. In short, becoming a good client manager is something that every public defender has to learn.

Lawyers' Views on Their Clients

Getting along with clients is one of the most difficult tasks of public defenders. One veteran New York City public defender recounts the lecture he received from his boss early on. "If you're working this job looking for appreciation, you're never gonna last," she said. Instead it has to come from inside "even though we lose and lose, and we get creamed every day . . . you have to wake up the next morning and fight your heart out, looking for those few times we can stop it" (Feige, 2006, p. 33). Nonetheless, client disrespect irritates attorneys and sours their associations with clients. As one public defender complained, "It is frustrating to have to constantly sell yourself" to clients. "The standard joke around this county is, 'Do you want a public defender or a real attorney?'" (Flemming, 1986a, pp. 257–258). Many eventually leave the job because of the difficulty of dealing with their clients (Platt & Pollock, 1974).

Refusal to cooperate, deception, and dishonesty are serious problems public attorneys face in dealing with their clients (Flemming, 1986a). At times, defendants tell their attorneys implausible stories, invent alibis, or withhold key information. A veteran public defender observed that in drug cases, the clients all had the same defense—they left home to buy milk or Pampers for the baby. In the end, "when you've heard every defense a thousand times, true or not, they can all start to sound like bullshit" (Feige, 2006, p. 228). The defendant's lack of candor greatly complicates the job of the attorney in representing him or her. Evasions and deceptions can affect tactical and strategic decisions.

Lynn Mather (1974b) described a case in which a public defender went to trial at the request of a client who claimed she had no prior record. To the attorney's surprise, the defendant's pre-sentence report revealed that she had a five-year history of similar crimes. She was sentenced to prison. The public defender said that his client "fooled everyone." The lack of trust in the attorney–client relationship may stem from the necessity for the lawyer to prepare the client for less than total victory. The defense attorney may at some point have to inform the defendant that imprisonment is a likely result, given the crime, prior record, facts of the case, and so forth. Since defendants involved in the criminal process often do not look beyond the present, postponing bad news from day to day, such statements are not to their liking. Preparing the client for the possibility of conviction clashes with traditional notions that the attorney should always win.

Ultimately, it is the defendant's choice whether to accept the attorney's advice to plead guilty or to go to trial. Lawyers differ in their ability to influence their clients. Private attorneys find their advice accepted more readily than court-appointed lawyers do. This difference in part reflects the type of commitment the defendant has made. The indigent defendant has no choice in receiving the services of a public defender or assigned counsel, whereas defendants with private attorneys have a choice and have shown their commitment by paying a fee.

Defendants' Views on Their Lawyers

Public clients are skeptical about the skills of their lawyers and are worried about whose side the lawyers are on. Thus, many defendants view their lawyers, whether public or private, with suspicion, if not bitterness. This is particularly the case with court-appointed attorneys, whom many defendants consider the same as any other government-paid attorney. Some defendants think that public defenders will not work hard on their cases because they are paid whether or not they win. To others, the defense attorney has ambitions to become a judge or prosecutor and therefore does not want to antagonize the court system by fighting too hard. Overall, then, many defendants view the public defender as no different from the prosecutor. In prison, PD stands not for "public defender" but for "prison deliverer." In what has become a classic statement, a Connecticut prisoner responded to Jonathan Casper's (1970–1971) question as to whether he had a lawyer when he went to court with the barbed comment, "No, I had a public defender."

A classic study of public clients' opinions of their appointed counsel revealed that only 22 percent of prisoners were satisfied with their lawyers' performance even though nearly half held generally favorable views of criminal defense attorneys as a group (Atkins & Boyle, 1976; see also O'Brien, Pheterson, Wright, & Hostica, 1977). Two other studies from the same era found that privately retained defense lawyers were viewed more positively than those who were court appointed (Alpert & Hicks, 1977; Casper, 1970–1971), although Atkins and Boyle's study found that prisoners who had been represented by public defenders were generally more satisfied with their lawyers than those who had been represented by retained counsel. This result may have been a function of the fact that the study participants reported that public defenders were generally more skilled at plea bargaining than their counterparts in private practice—a finding that has been replicated in other studies (O'Brien, Pheterson, Wright, & Hostica, 1977).

A partial explanation for a breakdown of trust between the client and public defender involves the absence of one-to-one contact. Many public defenders' offices are organized on a zone basis. Attorneys are assigned to various courtrooms and/or responsibilities—initial appearance, preliminary hearing, trial sections, and so on. Each defendant sees several public defenders, all of whom are supposed to be working for him or her. This segmented approach to representation for indigents decreases the likelihood that a bond of trust will develop between attorney and client. It also increases the probability that some defendants will be overlooked—that no attorney will work on their cases or talk to them. One can certainly understand the frustration of this 33-year-old accused murderer with no previous record:

> "I figured that with he being my defense attorney, that as soon as that grand jury was over—because he's not allowed in the hearing—that he would call me and then want to find out what went on. After that grand jury I never saw him for two months." "You stayed in jail?" "Yeah." (Casper, 1972, p. 8)

Clearly, not all defendants' criticisms of their attorneys are valid. But valid or not, defendants' lack of trust and confidence in their lawyers is a major force in shaping the dynamics of courthouse justice. Defendants try to con their attorneys, and the lawyers respond by exhibiting disbelief when defendants state unrealistic expectations or invent implausible alibis. For an attorney, failure to gain "client control" can lead to a bad reputation in the courthouse and jeopardize his or her own position within the courtroom work group (Eisenstein, Flemming, & Nardulli, 1988).

Defense Attorney Ethics

Lawyers occupy an ambiguous position in American society. They are admired and respected and at the same time distrusted. These contradictory assessments are reflected in myths about lawyers as either heroes or villains (Wolfram, 1986). Popular culture often portrays lawyers as heroes who valiantly protect clients falsely accused or depicts attorneys as villains for going too far in defending the obviously guilty. Discussions of good lawyers and bad lawyers invariably focus on legal ethics.

But this focus often reflects considerable misunderstanding about what lawyers do and what legal ethics is all about.

Years ago, one of the authors was in an Illinois courtroom talking with a top police official. When asked what was wrong with the criminal justice system, he singled out a specific defense attorney. "We arrest the guilty, but he [pointing to a defense attorney] gets them off on a technicality," he opined. Less than a week later, a police officer in his department was accused of manslaughter for shooting an unarmed youth. The police association immediately hired that same lawyer to defend the indicted officer. This saga illustrates the duality of viewpoints about attorneys and perceived ethical problems. More so than the other lawyers in the criminal justice process, defense attorneys are most often identified as having ethical issues.

Defending unpopular clients is the basis for a great deal of criticism of lawyers. People often ask, "How can you defend a person like that?"—a question that implies that lawyers' actions are an offense to morality. But at the core of legal ethics is the notion that every party is entitled to legal representation, even unpopular defendants who have committed heinous crimes or defendants whose guilt is overwhelming.

Each state has adopted its own code of professional responsibility for lawyers licensed within it. All 50 U.S. states, however, have adopted some variation of the American Bar Association's **Model Rules of Professional Conduct**. These rules impose ethical obligations on lawyers to their clients, as well as to the courts, since all attorneys are officers of the court.

The *duty of candor to the tribunal*, as it is known, is the most important responsibility that all lawyers owe to the courts. This ethical rule prohibits lawyers from knowingly making false statements to the court, failing to disclose adverse legal precedents, obstructing access to or tampering with witnesses or evidence, making frivolous discovery requests, and offering any evidence known to be false—including perjurious or misleading testimony. This last restriction can pose a serious ethical issue for defense attorneys, since they are often reluctant to refuse clients' efforts to present their defense. But, as officers of the court, they may not knowingly allow the use of perjured testimony. So, if defense attorneys cannot talk their clients out of taking the stand (particularly if they think that a client is now making the situation worse because the jury will not believe the testimony), the lawyers' duty of candor to the tribunal may require defense attorneys to tell a judge in chambers about such a situation and then let the client testify without the lawyer's help.

Another key responsibility all lawyers owe to the court, including prosecutors and criminal defense attorneys, is refraining from making any out-of-court statements that an attorney knows or reasonably should know will be disseminated to the public and would have a substantial likelihood of prejudicing any judicial proceeding. Recall from Chapter 6 that Mike Nifong, the prosecutor in the Duke lacrosse rape case, was disbarred for violating this duty.

The duties that defense attorneys owe to their clients include

- zealously representing the client's interests within the bounds of the law

- abiding by a client's decisions concerning the objectives of representation

- avoiding providing any counsel that would encourage or assist a client in conduct that the lawyer knows is criminal or fraudulent (although a lawyer may discuss the legal consequences of any proposed course of conduct with a client and may counsel or assist a client to make a good faith effort to determine the validity, scope, meaning, or application of the law)

- acting with reasonable diligence and promptness in representing a client

- keeping the client reasonably informed about the status of his or her case

- maintaining client confidentiality

- avoiding conflicts of interest

The duty of zealous advocacy forms the bedrock of legal ethics. Lawyers are expected to be diligent in asserting valid defenses for their clients.

However, this ethical standard does not mean that the lawyers must always do what their clients say. Lawyers are professionals bound by ethical rules of the profession. Within these parameters, people often support the zealous advocacy of their own lawyers, while objecting that the advocacy of opposing counsel goes too far. Conversely, defendants often complain that they lacked competent counsel, which typically translates into a complaint that they were convicted.

Confidentiality is another key component of legal ethics. Based on the attorney–client privilege, the lawyer may not voluntarily disclose what the client confided. Nor may judges, prosecutors, or other officers of the court typically force such disclosure. Holding to this principle may expose the lawyer to charges of obstruction of justice. Consider the case of a client who provided his lawyer a diagram of where he buried the kidnapped baby: The lawyer was severely criticized for failing to show the police where the body was buried. Eventually, a Texas judge ruled that the facts of the case constituted a valid exception to attorney–client privilege (Dzien-kowski & Burton, 2006).

Potential conflict of interest is a key ethical issue facing lawyers. Attorneys are prohibited from engaging in representation that would compromise their loyalty to their clients. The most common problem found in the day-to-day practice of law in the criminal courts involves representing two clients who have opposing interests. In a murder case involving more than one defendant, for example, a lawyer may represent only one defendant because the defense might seek to lay the blame solely on another defendant. On the civil side, a lawyer who has represented a couple in various legal matters may be ethically prohibited from representing either party in a divorce proceeding because the lawyer may have learned important details of the couples' finances or other confidential matters.

Lawyers who fail to properly represent their clients may be sued for civil damages (Chapter 2). For this reason, lawyers carry legal malpractice insurance. It is important to stress, though, that lawyers are liable only in very limited situations. Just because a lawyer loses a case does not mean that the lawyer is incompetent.

Conclusion

From the bleak perspective of his prison cell, Clarence Gideon had no way of knowing that his petition to the Supreme Court would have the impact it did. Overnight, Gideon went from defending himself to having Abe Fortas—one of the nation's most prestigious lawyers—represent him. Following the Supreme Court reversal of his conviction, Clarence Earl Gideon was given a new trial. His court-appointed lawyer discovered evidence suggesting that the man who had accused Gideon of burglarizing the poolroom had himself committed the crime. Moreover, as a result of the *Gideon* decision, thousands of other prison inmates in Florida and elsewhere were freed.

Nor could Gideon have realized that his name would become associated with a landmark Supreme Court decision. He achieved no small degree of legal immortality. His case was chronicled by *New York Times* reporter Anthony Lewis (1964) in the book *Gideon's Trumpet. Gideon v. Wainwright* transformed the law, signaling a due process revolution in the rights of criminal defendants. Gideon himself was not transformed, however. He avoided any more major brushes with the law, but he died penniless on January 18, 1972, in Fort Lauderdale, Florida.

The travails of Clarence Earl Gideon illustrate the importance of legal access to the justice system. Perhaps nowhere else is there a greater contrast between the images and the realities of the criminal court process than in the activities of the defense attorney. Unlike fictional defense attorneys, who always defend innocent clients successfully, most defense attorneys deal with a steady stream of defendants who are in fact guilty, and their representation focuses on plea bargaining.

CHAPTER REVIEW

LO1   1.   Interpret the four major legal issues surrounding the right to counsel.

After *Gideon v. Wainwright* established
a right to counsel for indigent felony
defendants, courts have wrestled with
four areas: (1) right to counsel in nonfelony prosecutions, (2) stages of the criminal
process, (3) ineffective assistance of counsel, and (4) self-representation.

LO2   2.   Discuss how the courtroom work group
affects how defense attorneys represent their
clients.

Lawyers who work within the parameters of the courtroom work group receive
benefits for their clients, including more
case information from prosecutors and
perhaps better plea bargains. Lawyers
who are less cooperative find that they do
not get favorable case-scheduling considerations and get less favorable plea
bargains.

LO3   3.   Explain why most lawyers do not represent criminal defendants.

Most lawyers practice civil law because
it is more lucrative, they have higher
prestige, and they have fewer problems
dealing with clients.

LO4   4.   Compare and contrast the three systems
of providing indigents with court-appointed
attorneys.

The three major ways of providing indigents with court-appointed attorneys are:
(1) assigned counsel, (2) contract systems,
and (3) public defender. Studies find no
major differences between these three
systems in the results achieved.

LO5   5.   Recognize possible tensions between lawyers and clients.

Lawyers sometimes view their clients as
not telling them the whole truth about a
case and at times seeking to manipulate
their lawyers. Defendants may view their
attorneys as not fighting hard enough for
them and seeking to accommodate the
judge and prosecutor.

LO6   6.   Analyze the importance of legal ethics to
the defense of criminal defendants.

Legal ethics seek to ensure that lawyers
will zealously advocate for their clients.
Lawyers must assert a valid defense and
ensure confidentially. But legal ethics
places professional limits on how far that
advocacy may go, including not using
perjured or misleading testimony.

CRITICAL THINKING QUESTIONS

1.   The public generally views defense attorneys
as too zealous in their advocacy of obviously
guilty clients, while many scholars portray an
image of defense attorneys, particularly public
defenders, as too willing to plead their clients
guilty. What do you think? What evidence
would you cite for either position?

2.   In what ways have contemporary decisions
by the U.S. Supreme Court modified the
original meaning of the Sixth Amendment?

Is the original intent of the Sixth Amendment
relevant in today's world?

3.   What factors hinder a defense attorney in
his or her attempt to protect the rights of the
defendant? Think of both system factors and
individual ones.

4.   What are the major contrasts in the workaday world of private defense attorneys and
court-appointed lawyers?

5. Should all attorneys be required to provide pro bono defense for indigents? Would such activities improve the image of the bar? Would such activities be in the best interests of the defendants?

6. If you were arrested, which would you rather have: a private lawyer or a public defender?

KEY TERMS

FOR FURTHER READING

Davis, Kevin. 2007. *Defending the Damned: Inside Chicago's Cook County Public Defender's Office.* New York: Atria.

Etienne, Margareth. 2005. "The Ethics of Cause Lawyering: An Empirical Examination of Criminal Defense Lawyers as Cause Lawyers." *Journal of Criminal Law and Criminology* 95: 1195–1260.

Gould, Jon. 2008. "Indigent Defense—A Poor Measure of Justice." *Judicature* 92: 129–130, 136.

Hashimoto, Erica. 2013. *Assessing the Indigent Defense System.* Washington, D.C.: The American Constitution Society for Law and Policy.

Klebanow, Diana, and Franklin Jonas. 2003. *People's Lawyers: Crusaders for Justice in American History.* Armonk, NY: Sharpe.

Mayeux, Sara. 2014. "Ineffective Assistance of Counsel before *Powell v. Alabama*: Lesson from History for the Future of the Right to Counsel." *Iowa Law Review* 99: 2161–2184.

Mossman, Mary Jane. 2006. *The First Women Lawyers: A Comparative Study of Gender, Law, and the Legal Profession.* Oxford, UK: Hart.

Smith, Abbe. 2008. *Case of Lifetime: A Criminal Defense Lawyer's Story.* New York: Palgrave.

The Spangenberg Group. 2001. *Keeping Defender Workloads Manageable.* Washington, D.C.: Bureau of Justice Statistics.

Patton, David. 2013. "Federal Public Defense in an Age of Inquisition." *Yale Law Journal* 122: 2578–2602.

Williams, Marian. 2002. "A Comparison of Sentencing Outcomes for Defendants with Public Defenders versus Retained Counsel in 'Florida Circuit Court.'" *Justice System Journal* 23: 249–258.

8 Judges

AP Photo/David Kidwell, File

Former Luzerne County, Pennsylvania, Judge Mark Ciavarella, Jr., was sentenced to 28 years in prison after being convicted of taking more than $1 million in bribes in what came to be known as the "kids-for-cash" scandal. In exchange for kickbacks, Ciavarella sentenced juvenile offenders to a for-profit juvenile detention center, thereby increasing the number of residents in these centers. Notably, many of the youths committed to custody had engaged in very minor offenses, such as trespassing a vacant building or shoplifting a DVD, that normally would have resulted in a small fine, community service, or a short term on juvenile probation.

Chapter Outline

F act or fiction?

- Facing a $50 million verdict for fraudulent business practices, a coal executive spends $3 million to support a candidate for a seat on the West Virginia Supreme Court; the candidate wins and then casts the deciding vote to overturn the verdict.

- Facing a multi-million-dollar verdict in a toxic waste case, a large chemical company secretly finances a candidate for the Mississippi Supreme Court who is likely to rule in its favor.

One of these cases is based on a recent U.S. Supreme Court decision (*Caperton v. Massey Coal Company*, 2009); the other is based on the plot of the novel *The Appeal* by popular fiction writer John Grisham (2008), who is also a lawyer. And Grisham admits that his novel is at least partially inspired by the real case. This blending of fact and fiction, life imitating art, offers a very public example of the long-standing debate in the United States over how best to select judges. Should judges be elected directly by the voters, appointed by an elected official (president or governor), or selected by a hybrid system that gives lawyers a direct role in the process?

The debate over how to select judges underscores the important role of the judge in the American legal system. The purpose of this chapter is to untangle the conflicting notions about what judges do and how they do it. The chapter begins by examining the position of judge and how various pressures (the large number of cases, for example) have eroded the ideal image of a judge's power. Next, the judge will be considered as a member of the courtroom community. A judge's actions are shaped and influenced by the actions of prosecutors and defense attorneys,

Learning Objectives

After reading this chapter, you should be able to:

LO1 Discuss the role of the judge within the courtroom work group.

LO2 Name the three major ways that judges are selected in the United States.

LO3 Analyze the consequences of different methods of judicial selection.

LO4 Recognize major changes in the composition of the bench over the past several decades.

LO5 Describe the activities of state judicial conduct commissions.

LO6 Explain the difference between the impeachment and the removal of a federal judge.

among others. At the same time, the type of justice handed out varies from one judge to another. A persistent concern is whether judges are as qualified as they should be. Therefore, two suggestions for improving the quality of the judiciary will be examined: merit selection and mechanisms for removing unfit judges. The role of judicial ethics will also be examined.

The Position of Judge

For most people in the United States, the judge is the symbol of justice. Of all the actors in the criminal justice process, the public holds the judge most responsible for ensuring that the system operates fairly and impartially. And most certainly the trappings of office—the flowing black robes, the gavel, and the command "All rise!" when the judge enters the courtroom—reinforce this mystique. As important as these symbols are, they sometimes raise obstacles to understanding what judges actually do and how they influence the criminal justice process.

The vast array of legal powers often causes us to overestimate the actual influence of the judge by ignoring the importance of the other actors in the courtroom work group. At the same time, the mystique of the office often results in an underestimation of the role of the judge. Judges are not merely impartial black-robed umpires who hand down decisions according to clear and unwavering rules. "This view of the judge as an invisible interpreter of the law, as a part of the courtroom with no more individual personality than a witness chair or a jury box, is a fiction that judges themselves have done much to perpetuate" (Jackson, 1974, p. vii).

Powers of the Judge

The formal powers of judges extend throughout the criminal court process. From arrest to final disposition, the accused face judges whenever decisions affecting their futures are made (Table 8.1). Judges set bail and revoke it; they determine whether sufficient probable cause exists to hold defendants; they rule on pretrial motions to exclude evidence; they accept pleas of guilty; if a trial takes place, they preside; and after conviction, they set punishment.

Although we tend to think of judges primarily in terms of presiding at trials, their work is much more varied. In the course of their workday, they conduct hearings, accept guilty pleas, impose sentences, or work in their offices (called **chambers**). In carrying out the responsibilities of the office, judges mainly react to the work of prosecutors and defense attorneys.

Benefits of the Job

In discharging their duties, judges enjoy some distinct benefits of the office. Traditionally, they have been given a high level of prestige and respect. Lawyers address the judge as "your honor," and everyone rises when the judge enters or leaves the courtroom. Judges also enjoy other trappings of the office. Federal judges enjoy life terms, as do judges in a handful of states. More commonly, terms of office for state judges range from six to ten years, considerably longer than those of other public officeholders—a reflection of the independence of the American judiciary.

For many lawyers, a judgeship is the capstone to a successful career. Judicial salaries are not the highest incomes in the legal profession, but they are higher than the average of other criminal justice personnel. Annual salaries of general jurisdiction trial judges range from $118,385 to $201,100 (National Center for State Courts, 2016). The average is about $139,000. For some lawyers, a judicial salary represents an increase over that received in private practice, and it is certainly more secure. For the majority of lawyers, however, a judgeship represents a significant decrease in earning power (Jensen, 2011). For example, it is not at all unusual to find lawyers in federal court who earn much more than the judges before whom they appear in court.

TABLE 8.1	Role of Judges in the Steps of Criminal Procedure (Typical Felony Case)		
	Lower Court	**Major Trial Court**	**Appellate Court**
Crime			Appellate court opinions are the final word on interpreting criminal laws passed by the legislature.
Arrest	Signs arrest warrants.		Wrestles with legality of police arrest in context of question of illegal search and seizure.
Initial appearance	Informs defendant of pending charges; appoints counsel for indigents.		
Bail	Sets initial bail amount.	May alter bail amount.	Rarely decides that bail is excessive.
Charging	No authority to intervene.	No authority to intervene.	No authority to intervene.
Preliminary hearing	Presides over preliminary hearing.		
Grand jury		Chief judge has nominal supervision over the grand jury.	
Arraignment		Informs defendant of pending charges and enters defendant's plea.	
Evidence	Reviews and authorizes search warrants.	Rules on suppression motions involving illegal search and seizure and custodial interrogation.	Rulings establish boundaries for search and seizure and custodial interrogation.
Plea bargaining	Judges rely on pleas to dispose of items on large dockets.	Some judges actively participate, whereas others are passive.	Rarely rules that plea of guilty was not voluntary.
Trial	Rarely held.	Presides at trial. Rules on admissibility of evidence. Instructs jury as to the law applicable to the case.	Decides whether evidence was properly admitted. Decides whether trial judge properly instructed jury as to the law.
Sentencing	Typically imposes "normal penalties."	Increasingly difficult and controversial task.	In some jurisdictions, must interpret sentencing guidelines.
Appeal	Rare, except in some driving under the influence convictions.	Notice of appeal filed in trial court.	Rarely reverses trial judge.

Many judgeships carry with them considerable patronage powers. Court positions—bailiffs, clerks, court reporters, probation officers, and secretaries—must be filled. Because these positions are usually not covered by civil service, judges can award jobs to friends, relatives, campaign workers, and party leaders. In some cities, judicial staff positions are significant sources of party patronage.

Frustrations of the Job

Because of the pressures of today's criminal justice system, the ideals surrounding the judge are not always borne out by the reality. One of the most frustrating aspects of being a judge is the heavy caseload and corresponding administrative problems (Rosen, 1987). Thus, instead of having time to reflect on challenging legal questions or to consider the proper sentence for a convicted felon, trial judges must move cases, acting more like administrators in a bureaucracy than as judicial sages. As a New York judge put it:

> It is clear that the "grand tradition" judge, the aloof brooding charismatic figure in the Old Testament tradition, is hardly a real figure. The reality is the working judge who must be politician, administrator, bureaucrat, and lawyer in order to cope with a crushing calendar of cases. A Metropolitan Court Judge might well ask, "Did John Marshall or Oliver Wendell Holmes ever have to clear a calendar like mine?" (Blumberg, 1967a, p. 120)

Although this quote is roughly 50 years old, the same judicial frustrations affect judges today (Mayer, 2007).

Moreover, the judge's actions are limited by the system—lawyers are late, court documents get lost, jails are crowded. Added to these general constraints is the overall low prestige of criminal court judges, who occupy the lowest rung within the judicial system. Like the other actors in the criminal justice system, the judge becomes tainted by close association with defendants who are perceived as society's outcasts.

Thus, the frustrations of the criminal trial court judge are many. Some judges prefer the relative peace of civil court, where dockets are less crowded, courtrooms quieter, legal issues more intriguing, and witnesses more honest than in the criminal court atmosphere of too many cases, too much noise, too many routine (and often dull) cases, and too many fabricated stories (Rothwax, 1996). Other judges, however, like the camaraderie of the criminal court.

Despite these frustrations, judges appear to be very satisfied with their jobs. A recent study of trial court judges in New York reports that they were very satisfied with their jobs, enjoyed the activity of judging, and found the work substantively interesting. Their major complaint was the lack of regular pay raises—an overwhelming 94 percent stated they were very dissatisfied with the regularity of pay raises (Jensen, 2011).

Judges Within the Courtroom Work Group

The public believes that judges are the principal decision makers in courts. Often, they are not. Instead, they are constrained by the actions of other members of the courtroom work group—prosecutors, defense attorneys, and probation officers. Thus, judges often accept bail recommendations offered by prosecutors, plea agreements negotiated by defense attorneys, and sentences recommended by the probation officer. In short, although judges still retain the formal legal powers of their office, they often informally share these powers with other members of the courtroom work group.

Sanctions can be applied against judges who deviate from the consensus of the courtroom work group. Defense attorneys and prosecutors can foul up judges' scheduling of cases by requesting continuances or failing to have witnesses present when required. Particularly in big-city courts, judges who fall too far behind in disposing of the docket feel pressure from other judges, especially the chief judge. Judges who fail to move their docket may be transferred to less desirable duties (for example, traffic court or juvenile court).

By no means are judges totally controlled by the courtroom work group. As the most prestigious members of the group, they can bring numerous pressures to bear on prosecutors, defense attorneys, and others. A verbal rebuke to a defense attorney in open court or an informal comment to the head prosecutor that the assistant is not performing satisfactorily are examples of judicial actions that can go a long way toward shaping how the courtroom work group disposes of cases.

The amount of influence judges actually exert on the other members of the courtroom work group varies. Some judges are active leaders of the courtroom work group; they run "tight ships," pressuring attorneys to be in court on time, for example. These judges participate fully in courthouse dynamics. On the other hand, some judges have a laissez-faire attitude, allowing the attorneys as many continuances as they request.

In large courts, "judge shopping" is a common practice. Through the strategic use of motions for continuances and motions for a change of judge, defense attorneys maneuver to have their clients' cases heard by the judge they perceive as most favorable for their particular cases. Such judge shopping is the most direct evidence of variations among judges. Although organizational pressures work to provide a certain degree of consistency among judges, any examination of a multi-judge court immediately shows that judges differ in terms of the sentences they hand out, the way they run their courtroom, and the number of cases they have pending. Knowledge of these judicial differences is often as necessary for the practicing attorney as mastery of the law and rules of procedure.

Varying Roads to a Judgeship

Which lawyers are selected to be judges is determined by both formal selection methods and informal procedures. Table 8.2 presents the major formal selection methods used in the states, including partisan elections, nonpartisan elections, merit selection (sometimes referred to as the *Missouri Bar Plan*), and appointment.

Formal selection methods (law on the books) are far less important than informal methods (law in action) in determining which lawyers reach the bench. How selection is conducted establishes the formal routes to who becomes a judge; however, when a judicial vacancy occurs, interim selection methods are needed. And though appointment by governors and merit selection predominate in filling temporary vacancies, who is ultimately selected to serve on an interim basis significantly affects the final outcome for filling a vacancy permanently (Holmes & Emrey, 2006; Johnsen, 2017). We will examine the three major methods of judicial selection—executive appointment, popular election, and merit selection—and explore the influence of both formal and informal selection practices.

Executive Appointments

In the early years of the Republic, judges were selected by executive appointment or elected by the legislature. Today, these methods of judicial selection are used in only a handful of jurisdictions. Only two states currently use election by the legislature, and only three others still use appointment by the governor. In contrast, all Article III federal judges are selected by executive appointment.

Nominations to the Federal Bench

The U.S. Constitution specifies that the president has the power to nominate judges with the advice and consent of the Senate. Based on this constitutional authorization, both the president and the Senate have a voice in the selection process (Goldman, 1997; Holmes & Savchak, 2003). When district or circuit court judgeships become vacant, the Office of Legal Policy in the U.S. Department of Justice and the White House Counsel search for qualified lawyers by consulting party leaders of the state in which the vacancy has occurred, campaign supporters, U.S. senators, and prominent members of the bar. This initial private screening has been known to take a year or longer because of conflicts within the president's party regarding who should be selected (Goldman, Slotnick, & Schiovania, 2011; Tobias, 2015).

After the president has submitted a nomination for a vacant judicial post, the process shifts to the Senate. Most nominations are routine. After a hearing by the Senate Judiciary Committee, the full Senate usually confirms. If the nomination is controversial, the committee hearings and Senate vote become the focus of great political activity. Over the past decade, major partisan wrangling has surrounded nominations to the federal bench. Although most of President George W. Bush's nominees to the federal bench were confirmed, Democrats filibustered some nominations to the Courts of Appeals, thus preventing confirmation (Neubauer & Meinhold, 2016). Republicans in the U.S. Senate held up so many of President Obama's nominations to the federal bench, resulting in a rising number of vacancies as caseloads were also rising (Wheeler, 2012; Tobias, 2015), that a Democratic-controlled Senate changed its rules to prevent the

| TABLE 8.2 | Methods of Judicial Selection and Retention in the States |

Jurisdiction	Initial or Subsequent Selection	Level of Court		
		High Court of Last Resort	Intermediate Appellate Court	Trial Court of General Jurisdiction
Alabama	Initial Selection	Partisan Election	Partisan Election	Partisan Election
	Retention	Reelection	Reelection	Reelection
Alaska	Initial Selection	Merit Selection	Merit Selection	Merit Selection
	Retention	Retention Election	Retention Election	Retention Election
Arizona	Initial Selection	Merit Selection	Merit Selection	Varies[1]
	Retention	Retention Election	Retention Election	Varies[1]
Arkansas	Initial Selection	Nonpartisan Election	Nonpartisan Election	Nonpartisan Election
	Retention	Reelection	Reelection	Reelection
California	Initial Selection	Gubernatorial Appointment with judicial commission confirmation	Gubernatorial Appointment with judicial commission confirmation	Nonpartisan Election
	Retention	Retention Election	Retention Election	Reelection
Colorado	Initial Selection	Merit Selection	Merit Selection	Merit Selection
	Retention	Retention Election	Retention Election	Retention Election
Connecticut	Initial Selection	Merit Selection	Merit Selection	Merit Selection
	Retention	Governor Renominates; Legislature Reappoints	Governor Renominates; Legislature Reappoints	Governor Renominates; Legislature Reappoints
Delaware	Initial Selection	Merit Selection	Merit Selection	Merit Selection
	Retention	Merit Selection	Merit Selection	Merit Selection
District of Columbia	Initial Selection	Merit Selection	N/A	Merit Selection
	Retention	Merit Selection		Merit Selection
Florida	Initial Selection	Merit Selection	Merit Selection	Nonpartisan Election
	Retention	Retention Election	Retention Election	Reelection
Georgia	Initial Selection	Nonpartisan Election	Nonpartisan Election	Nonpartisan Election
	Retention	Reelection	Reelection	Reelection
Hawaii	Initial Selection	Merit Selection	Merit Selection	Merit Selection
	Retention	Merit Selection	Merit Selection	Merit Selection
Idaho	Initial Selection	Nonpartisan Election	Nonpartisan Election	Nonpartisan Election
	Retention	Reelection	Reelection	Reelection
Illinois	Initial Selection	Partisan Election	Partisan Election	Partisan Election
	Retention	Retention Election	Retention Election	Retention Election
Indiana	Initial Selection	Merit Selection	Merit Selection	Varies[2]
	Retention	Retention Election	Retention Election	Reelection

(Continued)

TABLE 8.2 (Continued)

Jurisdiction	Initial or Subsequent Selection	Level of Court		
		High Court of Last Resort	Intermediate Appellate Court	Trial Court of General Jurisdiction
Iowa	Initial Selection	Merit Selection	Merit Selection	Merit Selection
	Retention	Retention Election	Retention Election	Retention Election
Kansas	Initial Selection	Merit Selection	Merit Selection	Varies[3]
	Retention	Retention Election	Retention Election	Varies[3]
Kentucky	Initial Selection	Nonpartisan Election	Nonpartisan Election	Nonpartisan Election
	Retention	Reelection	Reelection	Reelection
Louisiana	Initial Selection	Partisan Election	Partisan Election	Partisan Election
	Retention	Reelection	Reelection	Reelection
Maine	Initial Selection	Gubernatorial Appointment with state senate confirmation	N/A	Gubernatorial Appointment with state senate confirmation
	Retention	Gubernatorial Reappointment with state senate confirmation		Gubernatorial Reappointment with state senate confirmation
Maryland	Initial Selection	Merit Selection	Merit Selection	Varies[4]
	Retention	Retention Election	Retention Election	Varies[4]
Massachusetts	Initial Selection	Merit Selection	Merit Selection	Merit Selection
	Retention	N/A; appointment until mandatory retirement at age 70		
Michigan	Initial Selection	Nonpartisan Election	Nonpartisan Election	Nonpartisan Election
	Retention	Reelection	Reelection	Reelection
Minnesota	Initial Selection	Nonpartisan Election	Nonpartisan Election	Nonpartisan Election
	Retention	Reelection	Reelection	Reelection
Mississippi	Initial Selection	Nonpartisan Election	Nonpartisan Election	Nonpartisan Election
	Retention	Reelection	Reelection	Reelection
Missouri	Initial Selection	Merit Selection	Merit Selection	Merit Selection
	Retention	Retention Election	Retention Election	Varies[5]
Montana	Initial Selection	Nonpartisan Election	N/A	Nonpartisan Election
	Retention	Reelection		Reelection
Nebraska	Initial Selection	Merit Selection	Merit Selection	Merit Selection
	Retention	Retention Election	Retention Election	Retention Election
Nevada	Initial Selection	Nonpartisan Election	N/A	Nonpartisan Election
	Retention	Reelection		Reelection
New Hampshire	Initial Selection	Merit Selection	N/A	Merit Selection
	Retention	N/A; appointment until mandatory retirement at age 70		

(Continued)

New Jersey	Initial Selection	Gubernatorial Appointment with state senate confirmation	By assignment of chief justice from superior court judges	Gubernatorial Appointment with state senate confirmation
	Retention	Gubernatorial Reappointment with state senate confirmation	By assignment of chief justice from superior court judges	Gubernatorial Reappointment with state senate confirmation
New Mexico	Initial Selection	Hybrid[6]	Hybrid[6]	Partisan Election
	Retention	Hybrid[6]	Hybrid[6]	Retention Election
New York	Initial Selection	Merit Selection	Hybrid[7]	Partisan Election
	Retention	Merit Selection	Hybrid[7]	Reelection
North Carolina	Initial Selection	Nonpartisan Election	Nonpartisan Election	Nonpartisan Election
	Retention	Reelection	Reelection	Reelection
North Dakota	Initial Selection	Nonpartisan Election	Supreme Court Appointment[8]	Nonpartisan Election
	Retention	Reelection	N/A	Reelection
Ohio	Initial Selection	Partisan Primary; Nonpartisan Election	Partisan Primary; Nonpartisan Election	Partisan Primary; Nonpartisan Election
	Retention	Reelection	Reelection	Reelection
Oklahoma	Initial Selection	Merit Selection	Merit Selection	Nonpartisan Election
	Retention	Retention Election	Retention Election	Reelection
Oregon	Initial Selection	Nonpartisan Election	Nonpartisan Election	Nonpartisan Election
	Retention	Reelection	Reelection	Reelection
Pennsylvania	Initial Selection	Partisan Election	Partisan Election	Partisan Election
	Retention	Retention Election	Retention Election	Retention Election
Rhode Island	Initial Selection	Merit Selection	N/A	Merit Selection
	Retention	Life Appointments		Life Appointments
South Carolina	Initial Selection	Legislative Election	Legislative Election	Legislative Election
	Retention	Legislative Reelection	Legislative Reelection	Legislative Reelection
South Dakota	Initial Selection	Merit Selection	N/A	Nonpartisan Election
	Retention	Retention Election		Reelection
Tennessee	Initial Selection	Merit Selection	Merit Selection	Partisan Election
	Retention	Retention Election	Retention Election	Reelection
Texas	Initial Selection	Partisan Election	Partisan Election	Partisan Election
	Retention	Reelection	Reelection	Reelection
Utah	Initial Selection	Merit Selection	Merit Selection	Merit Selection
	Retention	Retention Election	Retention Election	Retention Election
Vermont	Initial Selection	Merit Selection	Merit Selection	Merit Selection
	Retention	Vote of General Assembly	Vote of General Assembly	Vote of General Assembly

(Continued)

| TABLE 8.2 | (Continued) | | | |

Jurisdiction	Initial or Subsequent Selection	Level of Court		
		High Court of Last Resort	Intermediate Appellate Court	Trial Court of General Jurisdiction
Virginia	Initial Selection	Legislative Election	Legislative Election	Legislative Election
	Retention	Legislative Reelection	Legislative Reelection	Legislative Reelection
Washington	Initial Selection	Nonpartisan Election	Nonpartisan Election	Nonpartisan Election
	Retention	Reelection	Reelection	Reelection
West Virginia	Initial Selection	Partisan Election	N/A	Partisan Election
	Retention	Reelection		Reelection
Wisconsin	Initial Selection	Nonpartisan Election	Nonpartisan Election	Nonpartisan Election
	Retention	Reelection	Reelection	Reelection
Wyoming	Initial Selection	Merit Selection	N/A	Merit Selection
	Retention	Retention Election		Retention Election

1. Unless merit selection has been adopted by ballot initiative in counties with populations less than 250,000 people, partisan primaries lead to nonpartisan elections. Counties with populations over 250,000 people are required to use merit selection with retention elections.
2. Different counties use a variety of approaches, including merit selection, partisan elections, and nonpartisan elections.
3. Merit selection (with retention election) in some districts; partisan election (with reelection) in other districts.
4. Merit selection (with retention election) in some districts; nonpartisan election (with reelection) in other districts.
5. Retention election in some counties; nonpartisan reelection in other counties.
6. Judicial vacancies on appellate courts are filled by merit selection initially, but then the judge must compete in a partisan election to serve the remainder of an unexpired term. After winning a partisan election, judges then stand for retention election at regular intervals to retain judicial office.
7. Gubernatorial appointment and reappointment from elected sitting trial court justices recommended by appellate court assignment by a nominating commission.
8. Temporary court of appeals judges are assigned by the state supreme court for up to one year.

Source: National Center for State Courts. 2017. *Methods of Judicial Selection*, http://www.judicialselection.us/judicial_selection/methods/selection _of_judges.cfm

filibustering of nominations to federal district and circuit court judgeships. Judicial confirmations did not become any more expeditious after republicans gained control of the Senate in 2015. Indeed, some senators view the lack of action on the judicial nominations from a Democratic president as payback for the changes to the filibuster rules (Everett & Kim, 2015; Tobias, 2016). Yet, Republicans continued the Democrats' policy of preventing filibusters of nominees to all lower-court judgeships at the start of the Trump administration. Indeed, Republicans expanded this practice when they voted at the start of the Trump administration to eliminate filibusters of nominees for the U.S. Supreme Court, thereby upending a century of a tradition that was designed to promote compromise between the parties when staffing the nation's highest court.

Senators also influence federal judicial selections through the informal power of *senatorial courtesy*. Senators expect to be consulted before the president nominates a person for a judicial vacancy from their state if the president belongs to the same party. A senator who is not consulted may declare the nominee personally unacceptable, and senators from other states—finding strength in numbers—will follow their colleague's preferences and not approve the presidential nomination. Through this process, senators can recommend persons they think are qualified (former campaign managers come to mind) or exercise a direct veto over persons they find unacceptable (political enemies, for example). But the influence of senators in general over judicial nominations has been declining (Binder & Maltzman, 2004).

The Role of the American Bar Association and Other Interest Groups

Although the **American Bar Association (ABA)**, the national lawyers' association, enjoys no formal role in the screening of nominees for the federal bench, it has historically played an influential role through its Standing Committee on the Federal Judiciary. The committee traditionally investigated potential judicial nominees by consulting with members of the legal profession and law professors. It then ranked the candidates as "exceptionally well qualified," "well qualified," "qualified," or "unqualified." Although the president has the sole power to nominate, most presidents did not wish to name someone who would later be declared unqualified. Therefore, the deputy attorney general usually sought the ABA's recommendations prior to nomination, and some potential nominees were eliminated in this way. However, the role of the ABA has diminished over the past decade or so in light of alleged political biases in the ABA's ratings of candidates, as well as criticisms against its "special access" in the nomination process because of the ABA's positions on controversial issues:

> In 1997, Senator Hatch ended the ABA's "quasi-official" role in the Committee process, though ABA representatives continued to testify in confirmation hearings. In 2001, President George W. Bush ended the process of giving the ABA special access to proposed nominees' names in advance of nomination or awaiting its evaluation before making nominations. Although it may be more difficult to elicit candid comments once a nominee is announced, the ABA continues to provide evaluations of whether nominees are professionally qualified, and at least some members of the Senate Judiciary Committee continue to consider the ABA evaluation. (*Georgetown Law Journal*, 2007, pp. 1037–1038)

President Obama restored the traditional role of the ABA and sought its rankings prior to making a public announcement of a candidate (Smelcer, Steigerwalt, & Vining, 2014). But the return of this practice was short-lived. President Donald Trump ended the ABA's role in vetting judges approximately two months after he took the office (Liptak, 2017).

In recent years, the role of the ABA has been eclipsed by that of other interest groups (Scherer, Bartels, & Steigerwalt, 2008; Neubauer & Meinhold, 2016). The Federalist Society, Common Cause, NAACP, and the National Women's Political Caucus are examples of interest groups that seek to influence who is selected and confirmed for a federal judgeship. Interest groups from both sides of the ideological spectrum appear to have decided that federal judgeships are critical to their policy agenda and have begun pulling out all the stops to try to influence who is nominated and who is confirmed (Bannon, 2016; Bell, 2002; Scherer, 2005; Steigerwalt, 2010). Despite the rancorous debate, President Bush was generally successful, as were his predecessors, in securing the confirmation of his nominees to the federal bench (Dancey, Nelson, & Ringsmuth, 2011). Indeed, his two nominations to the U.S. Supreme Court were confirmed after threats of filibusters dissipated. Likewise, President Obama was successful, at least during the first seven years of his presidency, in securing the confirmation of his nominees to the Supreme Court and most of his other nominations to the federal bench, especially after the change in Senate rules regarding filibustering judicial nominees for most federal judgeships. The ideological debates in the U.S. Senate aside, a recent study finds that President Obama's district court appointees are not as liberal as many of his critics contend. Indeed, the Obama trial judges appear to be deciding cases as moderate, mainstream Democrats (Carp, Manning, & Stidham, 2013). Appointees to the courts of appeal exhibit a similar pattern (Haire, Edwards, & Hughes, 2013).

In an unprecedented move, however, the U.S. Senate refused to hold confirmation hearings for President Obama's nominee to fill the vacancy on the U.S. Supreme Court created when Justice Antonin Scalia unexpectedly passed away in February of 2016. In spite of the fact that Obama had roughly 11 months left in office when Scalia died, the Republican-controlled Senate argued that U.S. voters should decide the next justice by virtue of the candidate they chose to succeed Obama, even though one-third of all U.S. presidents appointed a U.S. Supreme Court justice in a presidential election year (Perry, 2016). As with many of his other judicial nominees, Obama nominated someone widely considered to be a moderate, U.S. Circuit

Court of Appeals Judge Merrick Garland. But the Republicans held steady in their refusal to even hold hearings on Garland's nomination. As a result, his nomination lasted for a total of 293 days—the longest period in Supreme Court history. The nomination expired when Obama left office at the conclusion of his second term of office.

Nominations to the U.S. Supreme Court

In theory (a "law on the books" approach), nominations to the U.S. Supreme Court do not differ from other nominations to the federal courts insofar as the president nominates a potential justice and the U.S. Senate must confirm the nomination before the candidate is appointed to the Court. But given the power and prestige of an appointment to the highest court in the land, the politics of U.S. Supreme Court nominations eclipses those of nominations to lower court vacancies.

Recall from Chapter 2 that all federal judges, including U.S. Supreme Court justices, enjoy life tenure. In order words, they serve until they voluntarily retire, die, or, in rare instances, are impeached from office. When a vacancy opens on the U.S. Supreme Court, a team of high-ranking officials—primarily from the executive branch—work to present the president with a list of potential nominees. The people who make the "short list" need to meet a number of important criteria, the most important of which is suitable experience. Although reasonable people may disagree on what constitutes suitable experience, U.S. Supreme Court justices overwhelming come from very similar backgrounds.

- Most attended Ivy League universities and elite law school, with Harvard, Yale, and Columbia collectively accounting for more than 25 justices. Indeed, all 9 of the justices currently sitting on the Court graduated from one of these three law schools.

- In spite of the fact that the Constitution places no restrictions on who may serve on the Supreme Court, all 114 justices have been attorneys, although not all held law degrees. (Prior to the advent of the modern law school, many justices during the 18th and 19th centuries studied law under a mentor.)

- All but 2 of the 114 justices spent at least some time in private law practice; many (approximately 44 percent) also spent time as a government lawyer (Barton, 2012; Smelcer, 2010).

- Nearly two-thirds of the justices had been judges on lower courts prior to being nominated to the U.S. Supreme Court (Segal & Spaeth, 2002; Smelcer, 2010).

- Half of all justices had been elected to a legislative position prior to their nomination, although that number is inflated due to the early appointments. Since 1953, only 3 justices have had any legislative experience (Smelcer, 2010).

- Just over one-third of justices have been military veterans (Smelcer, 2010).

Another important criterion is the political ideology of the potential nominee. More liberal presidents tend to nominate people whom they believe will be liberal justices. Conversely, more conservative presidents tend to nominate people they believe will be conservative justices. But predicting how a nominee will vote if confirmed to the Court is fraught with the possibility of error. Consider that, on the advice of his conservative chief of staff, Republican President George H. Bush nominated David Souter to the Supreme Court, and Souter turned out to be a reliable member of the Court's more liberal bloc. (The political and public policy impact of the Court is discussed in more detail in Chapter 15.)

Other factors also enter into the nomination process. For example, as discussed in more detail later in this chapter, presidents since Jimmy Carter have paid attention to diversifying the bench by nominating more women and people of differing racial and ethnic backgrounds. By an overwhelming majority, most U.S. Supreme Court justices have been White men. Only four women have ever served on the Court, one of whom, Sonia Sotomayor, is also the only person of Hispanic descent to have ever served. Only 2 justices have been African-American and none have been Asian, Native-American, or of Pacific Islander decent. All but 5 justices in history have been married. None has been openly gay. Of the 114 justices in history, 91 have been from mainline Protestant faiths. The remainder has been either Jewish or Catholic. No other religions have ever been represented on the Court. With few exceptions, most justices have come from either a wealthy or upper-middle class socio-economic background?

Finally, presidents also need to consider whether the person ultimately nominated will be able to win a confirmation vote in the U.S. Senate. Nominees undergo intensive background checks by the FBI and a thorough evaluation by the American Bar Association. Other interest groups also weigh in, as does the media. The U.S. Senate Judiciary Committee conducts several days of hearings, during which the nominee is subjected to intense questioning and scrutiny, much of which can be intensely partisan today (Stone, 2010; Ringhand, 2011). The entire Senate then votes on whether to confirm the nominee to the Court.

Commentators often examine the politics of U.S. Supreme Court nominations by analyzing confirmation votes. But this methodology "fails to account for the silent operation of the confirmation process" (Chabot, 2013, p. 1235). That is to say that behind the scenes, White House officials, senators, and members of their respective staffs discuss the "confirmability" of people who are under consideration and, most of the time, those who are unlikely to be confirmed are simply not nominated. President Obama's nomination of Merrick Garland to the Supreme Court stands as a notable exception to this rule since Garland had already been confirmed to the U.S. Court of Appeals for the D.C. Circuit by a Republican-controlled Senate in 1997 by a vote of 76 to 23 when President Bill Clinton nominated him. The fact that Garland was considered to be imminently qualified for both courts clearly suggests that politics, and not his qualifications, resulted in him not receiving a hearing in 2016.

Executive Appointments in the States

State appointive systems resemble the presidential system for selecting federal judges, except that with **gubernatorial appointments** no equivalent of senatorial courtesy exists at the state level. As with federal appointees, governors tend to nominate those who have been active in their campaigns. At times, governors have been known to make appointments to strengthen their position within a geographical area or with a specific group of voters. In recent years, some governors have allowed bar associations to examine the qualifications of potential nominees. State bar associations are gaining influence, much like the ABA influence on federal judicial appointees. However, governors have greater independence to ignore bar association advice.

Election of Judges

None of the original 13 states elected its judges (Phillips, 2009). Today, however, the majority of states use some sort of election mechanism to select at least some of their judges (see Table 8.2). The concept of an elected judiciary is a uniquely American invention for democratizing the political process, one that arose during Andrew Jackson's presidency. It is based on the notion that an elitist judiciary does not square with the ideology of a government controlled by the people (Dubois, 1980; Gerhardt & Stein, 2014; Streb, 2007). According to this philosophy, there should be no special qualifications for public office; the voters (not the elites) should decide who is most qualified.

In a few states, judges are selected using partisan elections (the nominee's political party is listed on the ballot). Historically, this approach enabled party bosses to use judicial posts as patronage to reward the party faithful. The Supreme Court ruled that party control is constitutional (*New York State Board of Elections v. Lopez Torres*, 2008). But in the majority of states that elect their judges, nonpartisan elections (no party affiliations are listed on the ballot) are used. Nevertheless, even where nonpartisan elections are used, partisan influences are often present ("law in action"); judicial candidates are endorsed or nominated by parties, receive party support during campaigns, and are readily identified with party labels.

Traditionally, campaigns for American judgeships have been low-key, low-visibility affairs marked by the absence of controversy and low voter turnout (Streb, 2007). Judicial candidates often stressed general themes in their campaigns, such as doing justice and being tough on criminals, thus providing voters few guides to possible differences between the candidates. The general lack of information and the low levels of voter interest give incumbent judges important advantages in running for reelection. The prestigious title "judge" is often listed on the ballot in front of the judge's name. For this reason, few local lawyers wish to challenge a sitting judge. Once a judge is selected, either through an election or an appointment to fill a midterm vacancy, the chances of being voted out of office are small. Few sitting judges are even opposed for reelection; of those challenged, few are ever voted out of office (Dubois, 1984; Johnsen, 2016; Streb, Frederick, & Lafrance, 2007). Indeed, one study found that over three-quarters of elections fail to provide voters a choice (Nelson, 2011). More broadly, however, a major study by James Gibson (2012) titled *Electing Judges* finds that elections increase institutional support of courts. In short, elections increase the legitimacy of the bench (compare Benesh, 2013).

Times are changing, however. In recent years, some **judicial elections** have become nastier, noisier, and costlier (Barnes, 2007; Bonneau, 2007; Johnsen, 2016; Schotland, 1998). Mudslinging and attack advertising have become common in some states (Arbor & McKenzie, 2011; Hall, 2014). Interest groups backed by business or plaintiff lawyers are spending millions to back their candidates (Bannon, 2016; Eckholm, 2014; Goldberg, Holman, & Sanchez, 2002). Thus, today's races, particularly at the state high-court level, are hard-fought affairs (Chokshi, 2014; Bonneau & Hall, 2003; Hall, 2014; Peters, 2009). Moreover, the U.S. Supreme Court ruled that candidates for judicial office are free to announce their views on key issues (*Republican Party v. White*, 2002). One consequence is that incumbent appellate judges are now being defeated for reelection at a higher rate than in the past, although at the trial level, incumbents still often win. But moving beyond the anecdotes of individual races, researchers find that concerns about *Republican Party v. White* (2002) are unfounded (Streb, 2013).

Merit Selection

"Remove the courts from politics" has been the long-standing cry of judicial reformers, who oppose popular election of judges because voters have no way to know which lawyers would make good judges. Moreover, an election suggests the appearance of impropriety because it provides an incentive for judges to decide cases in a popular manner. To cure these ills, legal reformers advocate merit selection, also known as the **Missouri Bar Plan**, because that state was the first to adopt it in 1940.

Merit plans are actually hybrid systems incorporating elements from other judicial selection methods: gubernatorial appointment, popular election, citizen involvement, and—most important—a formalized role for the legal profession. Merit selection involves the establishment of a judicial nominating commission composed of lawyers and laypersons who suggest a list of qualified nominees (usually three) to the appointing authority, who is usually the governor. The state's chief executive makes the final selection but is limited to choosing from those nominated by the commission.

After a fixed, probationary period of service on the bench, the new judge stands uncontested before the voters in a **retention election**. The length of the initial, probationary appointment varies greatly from state to state, from 1 year in some states to 10 or 12 years in others (American Judicature Society, 2013b). The sole question in such a retention election is, "Should Judge X be retained in office?" The options are "yes" and "no." If the incumbent judge wins the statutorily required majority of affirmative votes (a simple majority of more than 50 percent in some states; higher levels of up to 60 percent of the votes are required in other states), he or she earns a full term of office (usually 6, 8, or 10 years). Each subsequent term is secured through another uncontested retention ballot.

Most judges are returned to the bench by a healthy margin, often receiving 70 percent of the vote. Only a handful of judges have been removed from office (Aspin, 2011). Over a 30-year period, for example, 50 court judges from trial and appellate courts were defeated in 3,912 retention elections in 10 states (meaning that only 1.3 percent were not retained); 28 of these defeats occurred in Illinois, which requires a judge to receive a minimum of 60 percent of the popular vote to remain on the bench (Aspin, Hall, Bax, & Montoya, 2000; see also, Brody, 2008).

Although backers of the Missouri Bar Plan contend that it will significantly improve the judges selected and remove the courts from politics, studies of the merit selection system in operation have reached different conclusions. The politics of judicial selection has been altered but not removed; in fact, removing politics does not seem possible. What the reformers presumably mean is the removal of "partisan" politics. In operation, the Missouri Bar Plan has reduced the influence of political parties while at the same time greatly increased the power of the legal profession (Taylor, 2009; Watson & Downing, 1969).

Merit selection won increasing acceptance between 1940 and 1988, during which 15 states adopted some type of merit selection system for one or more levels of their state court system. As a result, approximately half the states use a merit selection today to fill at least some of their judicial vacancies (see Table 8.2). Since 1988, however, only one state—New Mexico—has adopted some form of merit selection (Anderson, 2004). Florida voters rejected a move to merit selection in 2000. Even in states that have not formally adopted merit selection, governors often use "voluntary merit plans" to fill temporary vacancies (Dubois, 1980; Holmes & Emrey, 2006). Typically, though, adoption of merit selection requires a difficult statewide constitutional amendment, which explains why few jurisdictions have adopted merit selection in recent years (Anderson, 2009).

Consequences of Judicial Selection

The debate over the best method for selecting state judges has raged for decades. Partisan and nonpartisan elections, used in a majority of states, are supported by those who believe elections are the most appropriate method for guaranteeing the popular accountability of state judicial policymakers. Critics, on the other hand, assert that elections are fundamentally inconsistent with the principle of judicial independence, which is vital for neutral and impartial judicial decision making. Less philosophically, these competing perspectives

find expression in tension between the legal profession and political parties over influencing judicial selections. The different methods of judicial selection heighten or diminish the influence of the bar or the influence of political parties. This debate indicates that methods of judicial selection are perceived to have important consequences. Three topics stand out. One centers on which system is "best." The second relates to similarities in judges' backgrounds. The third involves efforts to produce a more diverse judiciary.

Which System Is Best?

In evaluating which selection system is best, a key criterion is whether one system produces better judges than another. Judicial folklore has long held that particular systems may produce superior judges. Several studies have systematically analyzed this folklore. Because it is impossible to evaluate a normative concept such as "best," it is necessary to rephrase the question empirically. That is, do judges selected by one method differ from those selected by others? Researchers use measurable judicial credentials, such as education and prior legal experience, as indicators of judicial quality. These studies point to two different types of conclusions.

From the standpoint of individuals who wish to become judges, methods of judicial selection make a difference, but not much. When legislators appoint judges, it is quite clear that former legislators are more likely to be selected than in other systems. Similarly, when the governor appoints judges, the system benefits those who have held state office (such as legislators) but also may include those candidates favored by major campaign donors. By contrast, elective systems elevate to the bench a higher proportion of persons who have held local political office—which typically means the district attorney (DA). Under the Missouri Bar Plan and elective systems, former DAs are more often selected as judges. When the executive or legislature makes the selection, fewer DAs become judges.

From a broader perspective, methods of judicial selection have only a marginal influence on the types of lawyers who become judges. Whether elected by the voters, appointed by the governor, or selected through merit plans, state judges are more alike than different. In terms of personal background characteristics such as prior political experience, ties to the local community, political party affiliation, and quality of legal education, the systems of judicial selection do not appear to produce very different types of judges (Flango & Ducat, 1979; Goldschmidt, Olson, & Eckman, 2009; Hurwitz & Lanier, 2003).

But what of the quality of judging? Does one method of judicial selection produce higher-quality judges than another? Before it dissolved, the American Judicature Society (n.d.) asserted that merit selection is the best way of selecting judges for a number of reasons:

- Merit selection not only sifts out unqualified applicants, it searches out the most qualified.

- Judicial candidates are spared the potentially compromising process of party slating, raising money, and campaigning. Indeed, to avoid this situation, judges in 29 of the states that use judicial elections are barred from making personal solicitations for money. In *Williams-Yulee v. Florida Bar* (2015), the Supreme Court upheld such a rule prohibiting judicial candidates from personally asking their supporters for money.

- Professional qualifications are emphasized and political credentials are de-emphasized.

- Judges chosen through merit selection don't find themselves trying cases brought by attorneys who gave them campaign contributions.

- Highly qualified applicants will be more willing to be selected and to serve under merit selection because they will not have to compromise themselves to get elected. (pp. 2–3)

Scholars, however, are divided on this question. Some maintain that no systematic evidence proves that one selection system produces better judges than another (Choi, Gulati, & Posner, 2008; Emmert & Glick, 1987; Johnsen, 2016). Others argue that "judicial quality is lower in states that utilize elections to select their judges" (Sobel & Hall, 2007; Lim, 2013). This finding is partially supported by a study that found that merit selection produces fewer unfit judges than elections do as evidenced by the fact that "merit-selected judges are disciplined

less often than elected judges" (Reddick, 2010, p. 6). But putting aside the issue of "quality" in light of its subjective nature, it is important to note the evidence that judges who were selected in partisan elections react to public opinion with an eye toward their own reelections, whereas those appointed to office are free of this constraint (Brooks & Raphael, 2003; Lim, 2013; Pinello, 1995). This difference may play a critical role in whether judges are willing to overturn capital convictions (Brace & Boyea, 2007).

Evidence also exists that judicial-selection methods may influence case outcomes in particular types of cases. For example, Gryski, Main, and Dixon (1986) reported that decisions upholding sex-discrimination claims occurred far more frequently in states with appointive systems than in those with election systems. Pinello (1995) found that appointed judges reversed criminal convictions for constitutional violations at a significantly higher rate than did elected judges (see also, Epstein, Knight, & Shvetsova, 2002). And Helland and Tabarrok (2002), using a large sample from cases across the country, found that tort awards for in-state plaintiffs against out-of-state defendants were larger in jurisdictions in which judges were elected. Thus, it does appear that the method of judicial selection matters. Which is "best," however, is a matter of interpretation.

Similarities in Judges' Backgrounds

Although the United States uses a variety of methods for selecting judges, it is important to note that judges share some important similarities, which may be of even greater importance than the differences. In general, judges are men from the upper-middle class, and their backgrounds reflect the attributes of that class: They are more often White and Protestant, and they are better educated than the average American. Increasingly, though, judges are beginning to more closely resemble the American electorate. Judicial officers on state high courts of last resort, for example, are increasingly women and less likely to be high-status Protestants (Bonneau, 2001).

Another similarity among judges is that most were born in the community in which they serve. Trial court judges are usually appointed from particular districts; the persons appointed were often born in that area and attended local or state colleges before going on to a law school within the state.

Finally, judges are seldom newcomers to political life. Almost three out of four state high court judges have held a nonjudicial political office. Trial court judges also have held prior office—most often district attorney or state legislator. Eighty percent of federal judges had prior government experience. Before becoming judges, they had some familiarity with the range of public issues that government as well as courts must address. Because of these factors, few political mavericks survive the series of screens that precede becoming a judge. The process tends to eliminate those who hold views and exhibit behavior widely different from the mainstream of local community sentiment.

Diversity and the Judiciary

The United States is experiencing a revolutionary change in the composition of the bench. The dominant profile of judges as White males has begun to change. Since the presidency of Jimmy Carter, an increasing number of federal court vacancies have been filled with female judges, a pattern evident during both Republican and Democratic administrations (Goldman & Saronson, 1994; Goldman & Slotnick, 1999; Goldman, Slotnick, Gryski, & Schiavoni, 2007; Johnsen, 2016). Eighteen percent of President Clinton's nominations to the federal bench were women (Spill & Bratton, 2005). Republican President George W. Bush was also particularly vocal about his goal of diversity (Diasco & Solberg, 2009). And Democrat Barack Obama demonstrated his commitment to judicial diversity early in his presidency by nominating the first Latina to the U.S. Supreme Court, Sonia Sotomayor. Later he nominated Elena Kagan, bringing the number of women on the nation's highest court to three. And nearly three-quarters of President Obama's nominees to the federal bench who have been confirmed by the Senate have been women or minorities. According to the Federal Judicial Center (2017), by the end of the Obama presidency, 351 (26.2 percent) of the 1,338 sitting federal judges (on active or senior status) were women. The racial and ethnic breakdown of the federal judicial is presented in Table 8.3.

TABLE 8.3	Racial and Ethnic Composition of the Federal Judiciary		
	Active	**Senior**	**Total**
African-American	107 13.90%	42 7.39%	149 11.14%
Asian-American	25 3.25%	4 0.70%	29 2.17%
Hispanic	79 10.26%	16 2.82%	95 7.10%
Native-American	1 0.13%	1 0.18%	2 0.15%
Pacific Islander	1 0.13%	0 0.00%	1 0.07%
White	557 72.34%	505 88.91%	1,062 79.37%
Total	770	568	1,338

The Federal Judicial Center does not report any information about judges' sexual orientation, but news reports suggest that at least 12 federal judges are openly gay, 11 of whom were appointed by President Obama (Johnson, 2014; "Judicial Firsts under Obama," 2015). Moving beyond specific judicial attributes, a study of the federal judiciary over 200-plus years concludes that the composition of federal courts has changed to reflect large-scale social movements, but at a pace limited by structural considerations (Hurwitz & Lanier, 2012).

The picture with regard to state judges is significantly more complicated. Until the 20th century, the number of women judges in America was so small that they could be counted on the fingers of one hand. The 20th century began witnessing changes, though not very quickly. By 1950, women had achieved at least token representation on the bench (Carbon, 1984). Today, the National Association of Women Judges (2016) reports that of the roughly 18,006 state court judges in the United States, 5,596 (31 percent) are women. As the number of women serving on the state and federal benches has risen, there has been an understandable interest in probing the "difference" women may bring to the bench (Martin, 1993). Speculation by some has suggested that female judges are likely to be more liberal than male jurists. Some studies reported gender differences in areas like women's rights claims (Palmer, 2001), self-defense by women in homicide cases, and whether to award alimony (Coontz, 2000). But often the differences are small at best.

But other studies find no gender differences among judges (Miller & Maier, 2008; Rivera, 2015). A study of Justice Sandra Day O'Connor, the first woman to serve on the U.S. Supreme Court, concludes, "Overall, the findings presented here do very little to support the assertion that O'Connor's decision making is distinct by virtue of her gender" (Davis, 1993, p. 139). Similarly, an analysis of more than 2,100 written opinions indicated that male and female federal district court judges were not significantly different when it came to their decisions (Stidham & Carp, 1997). These findings have been supported by a study of judicial voting in thousands of cases that show that in most areas of law, the decisions of female and male judges are rarely different. In 12 out of 13 areas of law (sex discrimination is the only exception), male and female judges do not differ in their decisions (Boyd, Epstein, & Martin 2010; Rivera, 2015). Beyond patterns of judicial decisions, Sally Kenney (2012) argues in her book *Gender and Justice: Why Women in*

the Judiciary Really Matter that having women on the bench adds legitimacy to the institution.

In 1973, slightly more than 1 percent of state judges were African-American; by the mid-1980s, the percentage had increased to 3.8 percent (Graham, 1990). Today, that figure stands at roughly 7.2 percent (George & Yoon, 2016). The underrepresentation of African-Americans on the bench is partially a reflection of the paucity of African-American attorneys. But underrepresentation is also a product of how judges are selected. African-American judges are more likely to be found in states using appointment by either the governor or the legislature; they are less likely to be selected in states using elections (American Judicature Society, 2013a; Graham, 1990). In 1991, the Supreme Court held that the Voting Rights Act of 1965, as amended in 1982, applies to judicial elections (*Chisom v. Roemer* and *Houston Lawyers' Association v. Attorney General of Texas*). These rulings pave the way for major changes in the 41 states, particularly in the South, that use elections for at least some of their judges (Smith & Garmel, 1992). Table 8.4 presents data on the racial and ethnic diversity across the major trial and appellate courts of the states. The feature "Case Close-Up: *Chisom v. Roemer* and Diversity on the Bench" explores judicial diversity.

TABLE 8.4   Diversity on the Benches of State Court

	High Courts of Last Resort	Intermediate Appellate Courts	Major Trial Courts	Total
African-American/Black	28	84	679	791 6.44%
Asian-American/Pacific Islander	6	14	140	160 1.30%
Hispanic/Latino	12	32	358	402 3.27%
Native-American	1	1	13	15 0.12%
Total Judgeships	342	971	10,972	12,285

Note that the figures in Table 8.4 were compiled using data sources from 2008 through 2010. Data are limited to the appellate and major trial courts of the 50 states and the District of Columbia.

Source: National Center for State Courts. 2014a. *Diversity on the Bench*. http://www.judicialselection.us/judicial_selection/bench_diversity/index.cfm?state

CASE CLOSE-UP   *Chisom v. Roemer* and Diversity on the Bench

Janice Clark had always wanted to be a judge. As a practicing lawyer, she seemed to possess the education and experience necessary to don the black robes, but she still faced an insurmountable barrier. The problem was not gender—after all, women are being elected to the bench on a regular basis all over the United States. Rather, the insurmountable barrier was race. White voters rarely vote for African-American candidates; indeed, as an African-American candidate for a judgeship, Clark received only 3.2 percent of the White vote. So, as lawyers often do, she filed suit in the U.S. District Court for the Middle District of Louisiana. Joined by African-American voters and lawyers throughout Louisiana, her class action lawsuit alleged that electing judges from multimember districts diluted African-American voting strength in violation of the Voting Rights Act.

The lawsuit was joined by local civil rights groups as well as several national organizations, including the Voter Information Project and the Lawyer's Committee for Civil Rights Under Law. The nominal defendant was the governor of the state and all other government officials connected with judicial elections. Also appearing for the defendants were attorneys representing the Louisiana District Judges Association and the Orleans Trial Judges Association (*Clark v. Edwards*, 1988).

U.S. District Judge John Parker's opinion stressed that of the 156 district court judgeships in Louisiana, only 2 were held by African-Americans. The reason was that judgeships were elected from the entire judicial district, which had the effect of "diluting Black voting strength," a violation of the Voting Rights Act.

This case was one of several filed in the federal courts, and the underlying legal issue was eventually settled at the appellate level in *Chisom v. Roemer* (1991) and *Houston Lawyers' Association v. Attorney General of Texas* (1991). The basic legal issue hinged on an interpretation of the Voting Rights Act of 1965 as amended in 1982. The Voting Rights Act covers representatives. Clearly, legislators are considered representatives, but what of judges? The Fifth Circuit said no, but *Chisom* held otherwise, finding that judges were indeed covered by the Voting Rights Act.

Crossing this important threshold means that, in drawing election districts (either for legislatures or judges), the lines may not dilute minority voting. This conclusion was based on repeated findings of the existence of racially polarized voting, which in an election contest pitting an African-American candidate against a White one, White voters were very unlikely to cast their ballot for the African-American candidate (Engstrom, 1989). But the future of this line of decisions is cloudy. In a 5-to-4 decision, the Supreme Court ruled that race is an impermissible consideration in drawing congressional voting districts (*Miller v. Johnson,* 1995). Nonetheless, challenges to judicial election and selection procedures under the Voting Rights Act have been mounted in 15 states (Scruggs, Mazzola, & Zaug, 1995).

Janice Clark's legal argument eventually became the law of the land. The series of U.S. Supreme Court cases firmly established the principle that judges cannot be elected in ways that place minority candidates at an unfair disadvantage. But the eventual impact is far from certain. Each of the states with a significant minority population differs somewhat in tradition and method of judicial selection, factors that shape the emerging systems of judicial selection. But for Janice Clark, the outcome was both immediate and positive. She ran again for the major trial court bench in Baton Rouge and won, taking the oath of office on January 1, 1993. When a high-ranking state police official publicly complained about one of her decisions, she took to the bench and scolded the official, explaining that the problem was not her interpretation of the law, but how poorly the legislature had written the state's gaming law in the first place. Her unusual candor aside, it will be many years before we know whether minority judges have a long-term impact on the type of justice meted out in courthouses across America.

Judging the Judges

Judicial-selection techniques attempt to recruit Solomon-like figures to the bench. Judicial-education programs help beginning judges learn their new roles and keep veteran judges abreast of changes in the law. The troublesome problem remains, however: What should be done about unfit judges? Despite the lack of clarity in what attributes a good judge should possess, one central conclusion stands out: A few judges do not fulfill minimal standards. A few are senile, prejudiced, vindictive, tyrannical, lazy, or sometimes corrupt.

Proper judicial conduct is indispensable to people's confidence in their judiciary, confidence that itself is indispensable to the rule of law. In recent years, such confidence has been eroded by questions of judicial misconduct in a variety of states.

Judicial Independence

A critical issue in judging the judges is how to devise a system for removing unfit judges while at the same time guaranteeing **judicial independence**. At times, critics attempt to remove a judge from office not because of his or her misconduct but solely because of displeasure with the substance of the judge's decisions. Consider, for example, in *Varnum v. Brien* (2009), the Iowa Supreme Court unanimously ruled that a state law banning same-sex marriage violated the state constitution. Three justices on the court stood for retention election the following year. Opponents of marriage equality spent more than $1 million on a campaign to defeat the incumbents. Their efforts were successful; the justices were removed from office (Miller, 2013). Scholars point to this outcome as an example of how the politics of judicial elections can undermine judicial independence.

> First, one ruling in a multi-year term is weak evidence of a "justice gone rogue." Second, the gay marriage case was decided by a unanimous court comprised of justices appointed by governors from both political parties, undercutting arguments that it was an ideologically motivated usurpation of power. Third, post-election focus groups confirmed the intuitive suspicion that many voters were animated by their aversion to gay marriage, not by their assessment of the justices' constitutional analysis. (Geyh, 2012, p. 635)

Clearly, protections against unpopular court rulings constitute the hallmark of an independent judiciary. Yet judicial independence is not an end in itself. As University of Chicago law professor Philip Kurland has put it, "The provisions for securing the independence of the judiciary were not created for the benefit of the judges, but for the benefit of the judged" (quoted in Byrd, 1976, p. 267). The "Courts, Controversy, & the Administration of Justice" feature on page 243 explores the topic of whether judicial independence is being undermined.

Judicial Performance

After her retirement from the U.S. Supreme Court, Justice Sandra Day O'Connor became a passionate advocate for judicial independence. She and others have argued that judicial accountability bolsters judicial independence because the public is more likely to support the judiciary when people have confidence that judges are doing their jobs well and are accountable for the actions (Goelzhauser & Cann, 2014; O'Connor, 2009).

Proponents of judicial elections argue that they make judges accountable to the public (Bonneau & Hall, 2009; Gibson, 2012; Goelzhauser & Cann, 2014). Critics of this accountability counter that elections allow the public to vote judges out of office for making unpopular, yet legally correct decisions, rendering judicial elections a threat to judicial independence (Bam, 2013–2014; Geyh, 2012). Whatever the merits and limitations of judicial elections may be, it is clear that they are here to stay. Even in states that use merit selection initial appointments, subsequent retention elections are the norm. But do voters actually know about the judges for whom they vote? **Judicial performance evaluations (JPEs)** are an important tool for maintaining judicial accountability because they assist the public in making informed decision in retention elections (American Judicature Society, 2014b).

Most JPEs consist of questionnaires completed by an array of different respondents, including lawyers, jurors, fellow judges, court litigants, other members of the courtroom work group (Chapter 5), and even a self-assessment by the judge. Other JPE programs go beyond surveys to include "courtroom observations, videotaped proceedings, background investigations, and interviews," and even analyses "of caseload management data, disciplinary records, and health records" (White, 2002, p. 1067).

JPEs are designed to gather data about a judge's impartiality, knowledge of the law, legal reasoning abilities, clarity, timeliness in making decision, and oral and written communication skills. JPEs also examine a judge's attentiveness, preparation, control over courtroom proceedings, temperament, and demeanor—especially with regard to whether the judge is courteous, respectful, and fair (McIntyre, 2014; White, 2002).

COURTS, CONTROVERSY, & THE ADMINISTRATION OF JUSTICE

Is Judicial Independence Being Undermined?

As a candidate for the 2012 Republication nomination for president, former Speaker of the House Newt Gingrich suggested that federal law enforcement agents should arrest federal judges who make controversial decisions in order to compel the judges to justify their decisions before congressional hearings (Gardner & DeLong, 2011). Even though a number of conservatives felt that Gingrich had gone too far, it did symbolize that attacks upon "activist judges" are a recurring theme in the United States.

In an adversary system, a judge's decision often fails to find favor with the losing party. In the modern era, the losing party is often quick to label the judge an activist. The term "activist judges" has no legal meaning, but politically it stands for judges who make unpopular decisions. Some worry that in the modern era, attacks on judges seriously undermine judicial independence.

In recent years, both state and federal judges have been the subject of attack (Earley, 2013; Raftery, 2006).

- Justice Penny White of the Tennessee Supreme Court was voted off the bench in a retention election because she voted in a death penalty case to grant the defendant more leeway to present evidence that might mitigate the sentence imposed in the case (Bright, 1997).

- Jay Bybee, U.S. Court of Appeals for the Ninth Circuit, has been targeted by some for impeachment because of the legal opinions he wrote while head of President Bush's Office of Legal Counsel about harsh treatment of terrorist suspects (Justice at Stake, 2016a).

- The administration of George W. Bush harshly criticized U.S. District Judge Paul Cassell for unduly lenient sentencing even though as a law professor, Cassell was one of the leading academic critics of the Warren Court (Willing, 2003).

Attacks on the federal judiciary are hardly new. President Jefferson tried to remove Justice Samuel Chase as part of a campaign to "reform" the federal judiciary. In the 1960s, a nationwide campaign was launched by the ultraconservative John Birch Society to impeach Chief Justice Earl Warren. Not surprisingly, attacks on federal judges most often occur during election years (Earley, 2013; Segal, 2000). Thus, during the 1968 presidential election, candidate Richard Nixon attacked the Supreme Court, promising to remake the high court in his own image. But almost invariably, challenges to judicial independence fail (Friedman, 1998). Opposition campaigns are most likely to succeed when there is a clear issue that is important to a large portion of voters (Aspin, 2011).

Attacks on the judiciary, though somewhat predictable, can still exert a chilling effect on judicial independence. Former Chief Justice William Rehnquist voiced concern along these lines: "There is a wrong way and right way to go about putting a popular imprint on the judiciary" (Carelli, 1996). In the same vein, law professor Stephen Burbank (1987) reminded us that judicial independence is a means to an end rather than an end in itself. Criticism is one thing; undermining judicial independence is another. "Courts are not independent when state judges are voted off the bench because of unpopular decisions by their courts, and when federal judges reverse decisions or resign from the bench after a barrage of criticism" (Bright, 1997, p. 167). Judges are concerned that the increasing tendency to verbally attack judges appears to be related to increasing physical threats against judges. According to the U.S. Marshals Service, threats and harassment against federal judges increased 89 percent in just five years (Coyle, 2009).

Concerned that recent attacks on judges threaten to alter the delicate balance between judicial independence and judicial accountability, the American Judicature Society created the Center for Judicial Independence to respond to unwarranted attacks on the judiciary and to sponsor public education programs on relevant issues ("Issues in Judicial Independence and Accountability," 2004). Similarly, Justice at Stake (http://www.justiceatstake.org) launched a campaign to protect fair and impartial courts from outside political pressures. Some attacks on judges appear to be ideological in nature. Retired Justice Sandra Day O'Connor wrote, "What worries me is the manner in which politically motivated interest groups are attempting to interfere with justice" ("After Death Threats," 2009).

What do you think? Where do you draw the line between fair criticism of judges and intimidation?

JPEs serve two goals. First, they provide feedback to judges to improve their own performance. Second, they provide the public with information about the judge. Such information can be important in retention elections (Esterling, 1998). Some critics, however, question whether voters actually take the time to learn about a judge's performance before voting on his or her retention in judicial office in a retention election (Bam, 2013–2014; Berch & Bass, 2014). Consider, for example, that in 2012, "Illinois voters re-elected a judge who was offering an insanity defense to a misdemeanor battery charge and was barred from entering the county courthouses" (Bam, 2013–2014, p. 577).

Other critics question whether JPEs are fair to women and minority judges since survey data, in particular, might reflect unconscious gender and racial bias. Gill, Lazos, and Waters (2011) found that even when all other indicators of judicial quality were statistically controlled for, female judges in Clark County, Nevada, scored 11 points lower on quality indices than their male counterparts, and minority judges scored 14 points lower than nonminority judges. To counter problems of bias, state JPE surveys need to incorporate recent advances in scientific design of surveys (Elek, Rottman, & Cutler, 2012).

To some, surveys of practicing attorneys, although they are impressionistic and imperfect, are an indispensable and meaningful evaluation of judicial performance (Singer, 2014). Others counter that there is a pressing need to develop truly behavior-based measurements focusing not on inherent judicial traits but on judicial behavior (Elek, Rottman, & Cutler, 2014).

Judicial Misconduct

Systems for removing or disciplining unfit judges must not only strike a balance between judicial accountability and judicial independence, but they must also grapple with the wide range of misbehavior encompassed by the phrase "judicial misconduct" (Begue & Goldstein, 1987). Most directly, judicial misconduct involves corruption. In recent years, judges in big cities such as Chicago, New York, and Philadelphia have been accused of (and sometimes convicted of) criminal offenses such as taking bribes and fixing traffic tickets. But not all judicial misconduct is so venal; sometimes it involves improper or bizarre behavior on the bench (Goldschmidt, Olson, & Ekman, 2009; Wice, 1991). Exhibit 8.1 summarizes some recent cases that illustrate the range of behavior.

One of the most difficult situations involves judges of advanced years whose mental capacity has become impaired. After years of dedicated service, with exemplary conduct on the bench and no hint of scandal, a judge might become senile. Accordingly, a growing number of states impose mandatory retirement ages for judges. The Supreme Court has ruled that state laws requiring judges to retire at age 70 do not violate the federal Age Discrimination in Employment Act (*Gregory v. Ashcroft*, 1991). In another widely followed case, the nation's highest court upheld the prison sentence of David Lanier, a state judge from Dyersburg, Tennessee. Judge Lanier had been convicted in federal court of sexually attacking five women in his courthouse. He had not been prosecuted in state court, nor had the state's conduct commission taken action—many said because the judge was politically well-connected and his brother was the county prosecutor. The decision in *United States v. Lanier* (1997) strengthened federal civil rights laws. The "Key Developments" feature on page 246 summarizes some of the leading U.S. Supreme Court cases affecting judges.

Formal methods for removing unfit judges—recall elections and impeachment proceedings—are generally so cumbersome that they have seldom been used. Moreover, these techniques are better directed at corrupt judges than at those whose behavior is improper or whose advanced age has caught up with them. A more workable method for dealing with judicial misconduct is the judicial conduct commission.

State Judicial Conduct Commissions

In 1960, California became the first state to adopt a modern and practical system for disciplining its judges. In response to the mounting public clamor for accountability on the part of government officials, every state has followed California's pioneering lead (Brooks, 1985). Under the California model, a **judicial conduct commission** is created as an arm of the state's highest court. The commission, made

EXHIBIT 8.1   Examples of Errant State Judges

- Lu Ann Ballew, a magistrate in Tennessee, was removed from office for ordering, against the will of the parents, a baby's name to be change from "Messiah" to "Martin" because she believed the name to be a title that belonged exclusively to Jesus Christ (Ghianni, 2014).

- Justice Orie Melvin was convicted in 2013 of conspiracy and corruption charges stemming from having used her sister's legislative staff to help orchestrate her election to the Pennsylvania Supreme Court. She was suspended from the court immediately following her indictment. Facing removal from office after her conviction, Melvin resigned from the court (McNulty, 2013).

- In 2013, former Michigan Supreme Court Justice Diane Hathaway was convicted of bank fraud and sentenced to a year in prison. She resigned from office during her eight-year term after the state Judicial Tenure Commission had suspended her.

- A veteran town justice in upstate New York was removed from the bench for jailing five defendants without affording them due process (Stashenko, 2012).

- A Luzerne County, Pennsylvania, judge, Mark Ciavarella, Jr., was convicted of 12 criminal counts, including racketeering, receiving bribes, and conspiracy, for his involvement in a scandal that became known as "kids-for-cash." He and a fellow judge, Michael Conahan, accepted nearly $2 million in bribes from developers of juvenile detention centers and, in turn, then sentenced juvenile offenders to those facilities. Shockingly, Ciavarella sentenced thousands of teens to these centers for minor violations that almost never result in sentences of juvenile incarceration, such as a first offense for being in a schoolyard scuffle. He often did so by violating the constitutional rights of the accused teens, ranging from denying them

counsel to the right to enter a voluntary, intelligent, and knowing plea. He was sentenced to 28 years in prison in August 2011. Pennsylvania expunged more than 6,000 records of youths Ciavarella sentenced, some for crimes as small as stealing a jar of nutmeg or setting up a MySpace page mocking a school principal (Pitts, 2011).

- Chief Judge Sharon Keller of the Texas Court of Criminal Appeals was charged with incompetence, violating her duties, and casting public discredit on the judiciary for refusing to delay the closing of the clerk's office for an emergency appeal for a man facing the death penalty. The man was executed several hours later (Kovach, 2009).

- Florida fined Judge John C. Murphy $50,000 and suspended him for 120 days without pay for threatening a public defender appearing before the judge. A video of the incident revealed Murphy yelling, "You know if I had a rock, I would throw it at your [sic] right now. Stop pissing me off. Just sit down. . . . I said sit down. If you want to fight, let's go out back and I'll just beat your ass. . . . Alright you, you want to f—k with me?"

- Pennsylvania Supreme Court Justice Michael Eakin resigned from the bench when it was disclosed he had sent racist and sexist emails to judges and attorneys in the state (In re Eakin, 2016).

- Carroll County, Arkansas, District Court Judge Timothy Parker was removed from office for performing probable cause determinations for cases involving friends or former clients in which he either lowered their bail or released them on their own recognizance (Chapter 10). As of the time of this writing, Parker is facing criminal investigation for exchanging favorable judicial decisions for "sexual favors, prescription pills, and cash in a string of cases" ("AR Judge Accused…," 2017).

---

up of judges, lawyers, and prominent laypersons, investigates allegations of judicial misconduct and, when appropriate, hears testimony.

If the commission finds in favor of the judge, the investigation is closed and the matter is permanently concluded (Miller, 1991). Confidentiality is essential, lest a judge's reputation be tarnished by a crank complaint. Many complaints are issued by disgruntled litigants, whose charges amount to

simple displeasure that the judge did not rule in their favor (Gray, 2007). If the complaint has merit, the commission may recommend a sanction of private admonishment, public censure, retirement, or removal. The state supreme court retains the final power to discipline errant judges (Gardiner, 1986).

Although commissions are armed with the potent weapon of a public recommendation, they prefer to act more informally. If the information gathered suggests judicial misconduct, the commission holds a confidential conference and discusses the matter with the judge, who has an opportunity to rebut the charges. The commission may try to correct the matter; a judge with a substance-abuse problem, for example, is encouraged to enroll in a treatment program. If the problems are serious, continuous, or not immediately solvable, the commission usually seeks to force the judge's voluntary retirement. The informal pressures and the threat of bringing public proceedings are often powerful enough to force the judge in question off the bench. The complaints and investigations remain confidential unless the commission finds it necessary to seek a reprimand or removal before the state supreme court.

There is a large disparity among state judicial conduct commissions in the number of disciplinary actions they take. A recent study concludes that the larger the commission's budget, the more disciplinary actions that are taken. Somewhat surprisingly, the number of laypersons on the commission and the presence of an elected system are statistically unrelated to the number of actions taken (Abel, 2012).

Federal Conduct and Disability Act

In 1980, Congress passed the Judicial Councils Reform and Judicial Conduct and Disability Act, which lays out a precise mechanism for acting on complaints against federal judges (Remus, 2012; Scirica, 2015). Complaints are initially heard by the judicial councils (the administrative arm of each U.S. court of appeals). Most result in either a finding of no misconduct or the imposition of nonpublic sanctions. However, if substantial evidence of serious misconduct exists, the judicial council sends a written report to the Judicial Conference, which may recommend that the U.S. House of Representatives begin impeachment procedures (American Judicature Society, 2013).

KEY DEVELOPMENTS CONCERNING JUDGES	
Judicial Conduct Commission (1960)	California creates the first judicial conduct commission.
Judicial Conduct and Disability Act (1980)	Federal conduct law passed.
Gregory v. Ashcroft (1991)	State laws requiring judges to retire at 70 do not violate the federal Age Discrimination in Employment Act.
Chisom v. Roemer (1991); Houston Lawyers' Association v. Attorney General of Texas (1991)	Judicial elections are covered by the Voting Rights Act.
United states v. Lanier (1997)	State judges are covered by federal civil rights laws.
Republican Party v. White (2002)	In campaigning for a judgeship, a candidate may discuss issues.
Rules for Judicial Conduct and Judicial Disability Proceedings (2008)	Implemented the recommendations of the Breyer Commission to "provide mandatory and nationally uniform provisions" that govern how judicial misconduct proceedings are conducted in the federal circuits.
New York State Board of Elections v. Lopez Torres (2008)	It is not unconstitutional for the state of New York to allow political parties to use a judicial convention system to pick the party's judicial candidates.
Caperton v. Massey Coal (2009)	Judges must recuse themselves from cases when large campaign contributions from interested parties create the appearance of bias.
Williams v. Pennsylvania (2016)	The participation of a justice who had as the district attorney approved seeking the death penalty in the prisoner's case violated the Due Process Clause of the Fourteenth Amendment, even though the justice's failure to recuse himself may not have been decisive in the state court's 6-0 decision.

Article II of the Constitution provides for the removal of the president, vice president, or civil officers of the United States—including federal judges—for crimes of "treason, bribery, or other high crimes and misdemeanors." The House must first vote articles of impeachment specifying the specific charges. **Impeachment** does not mean conviction but rather allegations of wrongdoing—roughly equivalent to a grand jury indictment. The trial on the articles of impeachment is conducted before the Senate. Conviction requires a two-thirds vote of the senators present and carries with it **removal** from office and disqualification from holding any future office. Historically, in functioning as both judge and jury in impeachment trials, all senators observed the testimony and cross-examination of witnesses. But in the modern era, the press of legislative business makes this time-consuming process unworkable. Therefore, in 1986 the Senate made the historic decision to establish a 12-person Impeachment Committee to receive evidence and take testimony prior to the trial on the Senate floor (Heflin, 1987).

An unprecedented series of allegations of misconduct against federal judges since 1981 highlights the interlocking relationships among criminal prosecutions, impeachment, and the new statutory scheme (Exhibit 8.2). The impeachment proceedings against U.S. District Judge Alcee Hastings raised the most difficult questions: Unlike Claiborne and Nixon, he was never convicted of a criminal offense. Hastings, the first African-American federal judge ever appointed in Florida, was indicted for soliciting a $150,000 bribe from two convicted racketeers, but the jury acquitted him. Hastings argued that racial motivations lay behind the impeachment proceedings. In 1989, the Senate removed Hastings from his judicial office, but in a strange twist, Hastings was later elected to the U.S. House of Representatives.

These cases are truly exceptional. Prior to the 1980s, only four federal judges had been removed, the most recent in 1936. But these statistics obscure the fact that many misconduct and disability problems of federal judges are resolved informally by the judiciary itself. Whether the federal courts effectively police themselves, however, is open to debate.

In 2003, an attorney filed an ethical complaint under the Judicial Conduct and Disability Act against U.S. District Judge Manuel Real. The way in which the initial complaint and subsequent complaints against the judge were handled by the Ninth Circuit Court of Appeals caused the case to get the attention of the press, the Judicial Conference, and ultimately, of Congress (Bazelon, 2009). The attention paid to the handling of the allegations against Judge Real, coupled with other instances of ineffective oversight of alleged judicial misconduct, led to the formation of a commission to investigate how the Judicial Conduct and Disability Act of 1980 had been implemented. Because the commission was led by U.S. Supreme Court Justice Stephen Breyer, it came to be known as the Breyer Commission. After two years of study, which included details of the botched handling of the complaints against Judge Real, the Breyer Commission issued a 180-page report (2006). While concluding that circuit judges and judicial councils were "doing a very good overall job in handling complaints" (p. 206), the Breyer Commission found that the federal judiciary mismanaged approximately 35 percent of "high-profile complaints … filed by attorneys, court personnel, or public officials," such as the ones against Judge Real (Bazelon, 2009, p. 469). Ultimately, Judge Real was found guilty of misconduct and publicly reprimanded for having made "inaccurate and misleading" comments during the investigation of the complaints filed against him. More significantly, though, most of the recommendations of the Breyer Commission were adopted by the Judicial Conference of the United States in 2008. These changes included 29 new mandatory rules for improving the "consistency and rigor" of disciplinary processes implemented under the Judicial Conduct and Disability Act of 1980 (Bazelon, 2009, p. 474).

Judicial Ethics

Judges play a key role in enforcing legal ethics. During the course of a lawsuit, a judge may be called on to enforce rules of professional conduct. At times, hearings or trials can become heated. The judge may find that a lawyer went too far in his or her argument or was unduly nasty to

EXHIBIT 8.2   Federal Judges Who Have Faced Disciplinary Action since 1980

U.S. DISTRICT JUDGE HARRY CLAIBORNE (DISTRICT OF NEVADA)

The jury acquitted him on the charge of accepting a bribe in a criminal case over which he was presiding but convicted him of income-tax evasion. While he was serving a two-year sentence in federal prison, the Senate found Claiborne guilty on three of four impeachment articles by the required two-thirds vote and removed him from the bench (1986).

CHIEF JUDGE WALTER NIXON (SOUTHERN DISTRICT OF MISSISSIPPI)

The jury convicted him of perjury for falsely denying before a federal grand jury that he had intervened in a state narcotics case involving the son of a friend. While he was serving his sentence at Eglin Air Force Base in Florida, the Senate removed Nixon from the federal bench in 1989.

U.S. DISTRICT JUDGE ALCEE HASTINGS (SOUTHERN DISTRICT OF FLORIDA)

The jury acquitted him of the charge of soliciting a $150,000 bribe from two convicted racketeers. The Eleventh Circuit and the Judicial Conference concluded that Hastings was not guilty but also concluded that he had fabricated his defense. The Senate ousted Hastings from office in 1989, but in a strange twist, Hastings was then elected to Congress.

U.S. DISTRICT JUDGE ROBERT AGUILAR (NORTHERN DISTRICT OF CALIFORNIA)

A jury convicted him of obstruction of justice for telling a friend about a government wiretap in a racketeering investigation. The Ninth Circuit reversed, but the Supreme Court reinstated the wiretap conviction (*United States v. Aguilar*, 1995). After another conviction and yet another appellate reversal, Aguilar resigned from the bench, apparently in exchange for criminal charges being dropped.

U.S. DISTRICT JUDGE ROBERT COLLINS (EASTERN DISTRICT OF LOUISIANA)

A jury convicted him of taking a $100,000 bribe from a drug smuggler. While serving a seven-year prison sentence and facing impeachment proceedings, Collins resigned from the bench before formal Senate action was taken.

U.S. DISTRICT JUDGE BRIAN DUFF (NORTHERN DISTRICT OF ILLINOIS)

Noted for his temper and for having the highest rate of reversal in the Chicago courthouse, he stepped down amid reports of a Justice Department complaint filed with the Judicial Counsel for the Seventh Circuit. Judge Duff I cited medical problems (Robinson, 1996).

U.S. DISTRICT JUDGE EDWARD NOTTINGHAM (COLORADO)

He resigned from the bench amid allegations that he viewed an adult website on his government computer, spent $3,000 in a Denver strip club, and solicited prostitutes using his court-issued cell phone.

U.S. DISTRICT JUDGE SAMUEL KENT (SOUTHERN DISTRICT OF TEXAS)

Kent pled guilty to obstruction of justice for lying to judges who investigated sexual misconduct complaints. Sentenced to 33 months in federal prison in May 2009, Kent attempted to retire from the bench, thereby allowing him to draw his salary. The House of Representatives impeached him in June 2009. He resigned from the bench in disgrace, effectively ending his impeachment trial in the Senate.

U.S. DISTRICT JUDGE MANUEL REAL (CENTRAL DISTRICT OF CALIFORNIA)

Amid numerous allegations of bizarre behavior and also taking control of a bankruptcy case involving a friend, Real faced impeachment hearings in the House of Representatives, but the charges were later dropped. Although publicly censured, the judge who is in his late 80s continues on senior status (a form of semiretirement in which a judge may opt to hear a reduced caseload).

U.S. CIRCUIT JUDGE ALEX KOZINSKI (NINTH U.S. CIRCUIT COURT OF APPEALS)

Judge Kozinski was formally admonished in June 2009 for having sexually explicit photos and videos on his publicly accessible website. The files were stored on a personal computer at his home that was connected to the Internet using web server software. He claimed that he did not intend for the materials to be publicly available. The Judicial Council said that Kozinski had exercised "poor judgment" by failing to take safeguards to prevent the material from becoming publicly accessible, and that his carelessness was "judicially imprudent." Kozinski issued a formal apology for causing "embarrassment to the federal judiciary."

U.S. DISTRICT JUDGE THOMAS PORTEOUS (EASTERN DISTRICT OF LOUISIANA)

Accused of taking cash from lawyers with cases in his court when he was a state judge and repeatedly lying under oath, Porteous was impeached by the House and overwhelmingly convicted by the Senate in 2010.

U.S. DISTRICT JUDGE RICHARD CEBULL (DISTRICT OF MONTANA)

Judge Cebull sent racist emails involving President Barack Obama as well as hundreds of others showing his disdain for African-Americans, Indians, Hispanics, women, and liberals. Facing possible disciplinary action by the 9th U.S. Circuit Court of Appeals, he resigned from the federal bench (Volz, 2014).

U.S. DISTRICT COURT JUDGE MARK FULLER (MIDDLE DISTRICT OF ALABAMA)

Judge Fuller resigned after he was arrested and criminal charged for physically abusing his wife during their marriage. Fuller was also accused of committing perjury when he testified before a judicial ethics panel that investigated the circumstances of his arrest. A panel of federal judges investigating his case recommended that Congress impeach him even though he had already resigned from the bench, presumably to send a message to other judges that such conduct would not be tolerated. Congress, however, did not do so (Blinder, 2015).

---

opposing counsel. In such cases, the judge may find the lawyer in **contempt** of court and impose a small fine or a brief jail term. On the civil side, a lawyer may accuse opposing counsel of an ethical violation such as failing to respond in a timely fashion or unnecessarily causing additional work for the lawyer. If the judge agrees, the judge may impose a range of sanctions, including the award of attorney's fees. In other words, judges can require the lawyer responsible for misconduct to reimburse the opposing side for litigation expenses.

Because of the special role that judges occupy in the adversary system, they are subject to additional ethical constraints beyond those imposed on lawyers. The American Bar Association developed the Model Canons of Judicial Ethics, similar to the codes of legal ethics, but each state has adopted its own canons of judicial ethics. The purpose of these codes of judicial conduct is to preserve the integrity of the judicial system and to foster public confidence in the system (Gray, 2003).

A study of *A State Judicial Discipline Sanctions* by the Center for Judicial Ethics of the American Judicature Society found that the baseline cases for sanctions involve judges who drive while intoxicated or are unduly slow in issuing decisions (Gray, 2003). Overall, the study concluded that public assumptions about levels of judicial misconduct are not borne out by the evidence. But state supreme courts can do more to tackle this cynicism by providing thorough, well-reasoned opinions in judicial misconduct cases and making them readily accessible to the public. Interestingly, a failure of the judge to cooperate with the state's judicial conduct commission was a contributing factor to a judge's removal (Gray, 2003).

Accusations of improper conduct by judges often reflect a lack of understanding of the role of judges in the adversary system. Judges face public criticism for reaching decisions that the public finds unpopular. A major obstacle facing judges who are the focus of negative public comments is the judicial conduct standard prohibiting judges from commenting on cases. But some judges find ways to offer appropriate, but nonprejudicial, defenses. A case in point is Judge Arthur Hunter of New Orleans. The district attorney harshly criticized him for threatening to release defendants because the DA's office could not bring them to trial in a timely manner following Hurricane Katrina. Stressing his credentials as a former police officer, the judge wrote:

> Many people have a gross misconception of the role of judges in the criminal justice system…. Judges are like referees in a basketball game. They do not favor either side, but make sure the police, district attorney, and defense attorneys follow all the rules. Judges are not teammates with the district attorney, cheerleaders for the police, or coaches for the defense attorney. (Hunter, 2006)

Prohibition on conduct that brings the judicial office into disrepute is another requirement of canons of judicial ethics. Typically, this applies to situations in which the judge is having an extramarital affair or the like. But occasionally it involves conduct that is not personal but rather judicial. The best-known example is that of Roy Moore, who was elected chief justice of the Alabama Supreme Court. Consistent with his campaign promises, he installed a large granite monument of the Ten Commandments in the courthouse. When a federal court ordered its removal because it violated the First Amendment of the Constitution, the judge refused to comply. His refusal to obey a lawful court order was deemed to bring the judicial office into disrepute, and so he was removed from the bench (Clark, 2005). In 2012, however, Moore won another election to the Alabama Supreme Court. Then, in the wake of the U.S. Supreme Court's decision legalizing same-sex marriage (*Obergefell v. Hodges*, 2015), Justice Moore ordered the probate judges of the state of Alabama to refuse to issue marriage licenses to same-sex couples in the state in complete disregard of a federal court injunction. He was suspended without pay for the remainder of his judicial term.

The tension between electing judges and appearances of impropriety is emerging as a major issue in judicial ethics. In *Republican Party v. White* (2002), the Supreme Court allowed candidates for judicial office to discuss issues that might come before the court and to criticize past court decisions. The result has been a new dynamic in judicial elections, with some races featuring negative political ads and contentious campaigns (Fortune & White, 2008; Zuercher, 2015). Some are concerned that elections erode public perceptions of an impartial judiciary. In the words of Justice at Stake "Can two sides in a lawsuit receive equal justice when one side has spent $3 million to elect the judge deciding the case?" This issue was at the heart of *Caperton v. Massey Coal* (Justice at Stake, 2016b) in which the Supreme Court held that judges must recuse themselves from cases when large campaign contributions from interested parties create the appearance of bias.

In 2016, the Supreme Court issued another decision on the importance of judicial recusal. The case involved Terrance Williams, who had been convicted of first-degree murder and sentenced to death. At the time of his trial, Ronald Castille was the district attorney of Philadelphia. Castille had personally approved the prosecution to proceed with the case as a death penalty one. Over

the course of 26 years, various state and federal courts upheld Williams's conviction and sentence. But then a Pennsylvania court stayed Williams's execution and ordered a new sentencing hearing based on new information from a witness who had previously refused to speak with Williams's attorneys. This witness disclosed that he had informed prosecution before trial that Williams had been in a sexual relationship with the victim and that it was the real motive for the murder. But the prosecutor allegedly told the witness to give false testimony that Williams killed the victim as part of a robbery. Moreover, the witness disclosed that in exchange for the testimony, the prosecutor had promised to write a letter to the state parole board on behalf of the witness—a fact that was never disclosed to the defense as required under *Brady v. Maryland* (1963; see Chapter 11 for a discussion of *Brady*). The Commonwealth of Pennsylvania appealed to the state's supreme court, seeking to vacate the stay of execution and the order for a new sentencing hearing. The chief justice of the Pennsylvania Supreme Court at that time was former District Attorney Ronald Castille. Castille refused to recuse himself. He joined the state high court's opinion vacating the stay of execution and reinstating the death sentence. Two weeks later, Castille retired from the bench.

Williams appealed to the U.S. Supreme Court, which accepted his case. The Court held that "under the Due Process Clause there is an impermissible risk of actual bias when a judge earlier had significant, personal involvement as a prosecutor in a critical decision regarding the defendant's case" (*Williams v. Pennsylvania*, 2016). The Court reasoned as follows:

> Bias is easy to attribute to others and difficult to discern in oneself. To establish an enforceable and workable framework, the Court's precedents apply an objective standard that, in the usual case, avoids having to determine whether actual bias is present. The Court asks not whether a judge harbors an actual, subjective bias, but instead whether, as an objective matter, "the average judge in his position is 'likely' to be neutral, or whether there is an unconstitutional 'potential for bias.'" Of particular relevance to the instant case, the Court has determined that an unconstitutional potential for bias exists when the same person serves as both accuser and adjudicator in a case....

When a judge has served as an advocate for the State in the very case the court is now asked to adjudicate, a serious question arises as to whether the judge, even with the most diligent effort, could set aside any personal interest in the outcome. There is, furthermore, a risk that the judge would be so psychologically wedded to his or her previous position as a prosecutor that the judge would consciously or unconsciously avoid the appearance of having erred or changed position. In addition, the judge's own personal knowledge and impression of the case, acquired through his or her role in the prosecution, may carry far more weight with the judge than the parties' arguments to the court. (pp. 1905–06, internal quotations and citations omitted)

Notably, the Court in *Williams* also determined that the state court justice's refusal to recuse himself was not "harmless error" (see Chapter 15) that could otherwise be excused because the state high court's decision was unanimous. Rather, the court held that the due process violation was "not amenable" to the harmless error rule because:

The deliberations of an appellate panel, as a general rule, are confidential. As a result, it is neither possible nor productive to inquire whether the jurist in question might have influenced the views of his or her colleagues during the decision-making process.... [I]t does not matter whether the disqualified judge's vote was necessary to the disposition of the case. The fact that the interested judge's vote was not dispositive may mean only that the judge was successful in persuading most members of the court to accept his or her position. That outcome does not lessen the unfairness to the affected party.

A multimember court must not have its guarantee of neutrality undermined, for the appearance of bias demeans the reputation and integrity not just of one jurist, but of the larger institution of which he or she is a part. An insistence on the appearance of neutrality is not some artificial attempt to mask imperfection in the judicial process, but rather an essential means of ensuring the reality of a fair adjudication. Both the appearance and reality of impartial justice are necessary to the public legitimacy of judicial pronouncements and thus to the rule of law itself. When the objective risk of actual bias on the part of a judge rises to an unconstitutional level, the failure to recuse cannot be deemed harmless (pp. 1909–10).

Conclusion

In deciding *Caperton v. Massey Coal Company* (2009), the U.S. Supreme Court stressed that the decision addressed an "extraordinary situation": the Court stressed that the owner of Massey Coal spent over $3 million to elect his preferred candidate to the West Virginia Supreme Court, an amount three times more than any of the other candidate's supporters. By emphasizing these facts, the justices of the nation's highest court were apparently trying to separate the case from the fictional basis of the novel *The Appeal*. But where fact ends and fiction begins is always hard to tell. John Grisham is a fiction writer who excels in emphasizing extraordinary situations that, while fictional, are still based on fact. This blending of fact and fiction, life imitating art, provides another chapter in the ongoing national debate over judicial selection. Nor did interest end with the Court decision. A year after *Caperton*, a coal mine owned by Massey Energy exploded, leaving 29 dead and reopening the issue of whether the company had systematically cut corners when it came to mine safety (Tavernise, 2012).

In the modern era, displeasure with judges has led to renewed interest in how judges are selected. But no matter how we select our judges and who they are, the workaday world of the trial judge bears little resemblance to the high expectations we have about the role of the judge. The trial judge is expected to dispose of a large caseload but is often frustrated by the attorneys' lack of preparation, missing defendants, misplaced files, little time to reflect, and probably most important, insufficient control over many vital aspects of the case. For these and other reasons, judges depend on other members of the courtroom work group. Some depend heavily on the prosecutors, defense attorneys, and probation officers, feeling content to let them make the difficult decisions. Others are much more active participants and are truly leaders of the courtroom work group.

Judges are under an ethical duty to avoid misconduct and bias. Due process guarantees "an absence of actual bias" on the part of a judge. Moreover, judges are required to recuse themselves to avoid the appearance of impropriety.

CHAPTER REVIEW

LO1   1.   Discuss the role of the judge within the courtroom work group.

Judges are the most prestigious members of the courtroom work group, but they are expected to be reasonably responsive to lawyers and are also under pressure to move the docket.

LO2   2.   Name the three major ways that judges are selected in the United States.

Judges are appointed by executives (like governors and the president), elected by the voters, or appointed through a merit selection process.

LO3   3.   Analyze the consequences of different methods of judicial selection.

The various selection systems produce judges with very similar backgrounds, including local ties and past political involvement. No evidence exists that one selection system consistently produces "better" or "worse" judges than another, although research does reveal some differences in judicial approaches to decision making.

LO4   4.   Recognize major changes in the composition of the bench over the past several decades.

Over the past several decades, the composition of the bench has become more diverse, with a significant number of women and some racial and ethnic minorities being elected and appointed to the nation's courts.

LO5   5.   Describe the activities of state judicial conduct commissions.

If the state judicial conduct commissions find merit to a complaint about a judge, they often work informally to correct the problem. But if the problem is a serious one, the commission may recommend to the state supreme court that the judge be removed from office.

LO6   6.   Explain the difference between the impeachment and the removal of a federal judge.

If the House of Representatives votes articles of impeachment charging a federal judge with serious misconduct, the Senate conducts a trial and may remove the judge from the bench.

CRITICAL THINKING QUESTIONS

1.   Which method of judicial selection (election, appointment, or merit) do you think is best? What does your choice reveal about your personal attitudes? Stated another way, do you think the legal profession should have more say in judicial selection (merit) or less influence (elections)?

2.   For your state, examine judicial selection in terms of both law on the books (formal method of judicial selection) and law in action (actual practices).

3.   At what point are efforts to remove "unfit" judges really efforts to remove judges because of decisions they have made?

4.   American society has high expectations for judges, yet the actions of judges are constrained by other members of the courtroom work group. To what extent is criticism of judges, whether local or national, really criticism of the actions and inactions of prosecutors and defense attorneys?

5.   Does underrepresentation of women on the bench hurt justice? Would citizens' views of the fairness of courts improve if more nontraditional persons became judges?

KEY TERMS

FOR FURTHER READING

Baum, Lawrence. 2007. *Judges and Their Audiences: A Perspective on Judicial Behavior*. Princeton, NJ: Princeton University Press.

Carns, Teresa. 2009. "The Alaska Merit Selection System at Work, 1984–2007." *Judicature* 93: 102–108.

Epstein, Lee, and Jeffrey Segal. 2005. *Advice and Consent: The Politics of Judicial Appointments*. New York: Oxford University Press.

Geyh, Charles. 2006. *When Courts and Congress Collide: The Struggle for Control of America's Judicial System*. Ann Arbor: University of Michigan Press.

Gray, Cynthia. 2009. *Ethical Standards for Judges*. Des Moines, IA: American Judicature Society.

Hettinger, Virginia, Stefanie A. Lindquist, and Wendy L. Martinek. 2006. *Judging on a Collegial Court: Influences on Appellate Decision Making*. Charlottesville: University of Virginia Press.

Kenney, Sally. 2012. *Gender and Justice: Why Women in the Judiciary Really Matter*. New York: Routledge.

Peabody, Bruce (Ed.). 2010. *The Politics of Judicial Independence: Courts, Politics, and the Public*. Baltimore: Johns Hopkins University Press.

Peters, C. Scott. "Canons, Cost, and Competition in State Supreme Court Elections." *Judicature* 91: 27–35, 2007.

Sen, Maya. 2014. "Minority Judicial Candidates Have Changed: The ABA Ratings Gap Has Not." *Judicature* 98: 46-53.

Steigerwalt, Amy. 2010. *Battle over the Bench: Senators, Interest Groups, and Lower Court Confirmations*. Charlottesville: University of Virginia Press.

Streb, Matthew (Ed.) *Running for Judge: The Rising Political, Financial, and Legal Stakes of Judicial Elections*. New York: NYU Press, 2007.

Swanson, Rick. "Judicial Roles in State High Courts." *Judicature* 94: 168–177, 2011.

Wheat, Elizabeth, and Mark Hurwitz. "The Politics of Judicial Selection: The Case of the Michigan Supreme Court." *Judicature* 96: 178–188, 2013.

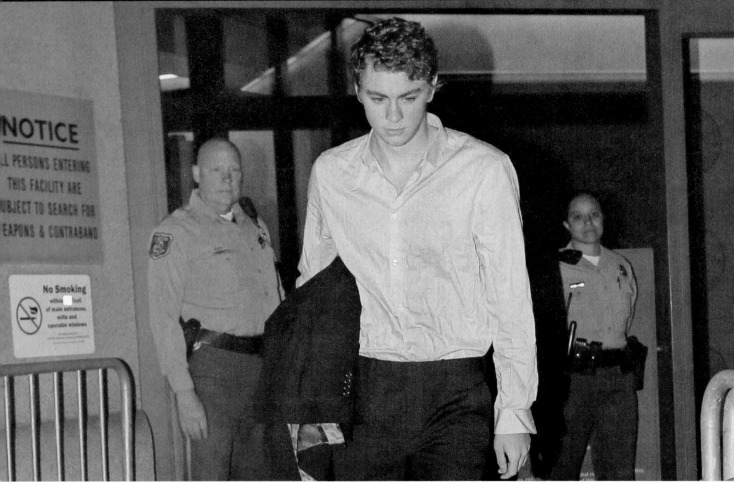

Mark Kreusch/Splash News/Newscom

After having been convicted of three felonies for sexually assaulting an unconscious woman, former Stanford University swimmer Brock Turner was sentenced to only six months in jail. This photo shows him as he was released after having served only 90 days.

Chapter Outline

In January of 2015, two graduate students from Sweden rode their bicycles across Stanford University's campus around 1:00 a.m. They noticed a young man on top of a motionless woman behind a dumpster outside of a fraternity house. They intervened, causing the young man to flee. As one of the students attended to the unconscious woman, the other chased after the man running from the scene, eventually subduing him, aided by others. Campus police arrived moments later and arrested 20-year-old Brock Turner on suspicion that he had sexually assaulted the unconscious 22-year-old victim.

Turner maintained that he and the woman he sexually assaulted had both been drinking at a fraternity party on the night in question. He claimed that the two started engaging in sexual activity consensually and that he was unaware she had passed out. The prosecution and the victim disputed Turner's version of events. A jury convicted Turner of two counts of felony sexual assault and one count of attempted rape.

Turner faced up to 14 years in prison. Prosecutors recommended a sentence of 6 years in prison. But Santa Clara County Superior Court Judge Aaron Persky sentenced Turner to six months in county jail, followed by 3 years of probation. In explaining the sentence, Judge Persky cited Turner's lack of criminal history, his expressions of remorse, and the fact that alcohol was involved, impairing Turner's judgment. Additionally, the judge said that he had taken into consideration the "severe impact" a state prison sentence would have on Turner at such a young age. Turner was expelled from Stanford and was released from jail after serving just three months (Grinberg & Shoichet, 2016).

Turner's light sentence sparked national outrage for a number of reasons. The case highlights how poorly the criminal justice system often treats the victims of crimes, especially victims of sexual assault. But the case also called attention to the way the system treats certain offenders. Brock Turner came

Learning Objectives

After reading this chapter, you should be able to:

LO1 List the three characteristics of defendants.

LO2 Describe how victims and witnesses view the court process.

LO3 Describe how court actors view victims and witnesses.

LO4 Discuss the prior relationships between defendants and victims and why this is important in domestic violence cases.

LO5 Identify three types of programs that are designed to aid victims and witnesses in coping with the criminal justice process.

LO6 Explain why some view victim programs as aiding victims whereas others view these programs as manipulating victims.

from a privileged background. The sandy blond–haired swimmer grew up in Oakwood, Ohio—a suburb of Dayton known for a high standard of living, good schools, and low crime rates. Turner began attending Stanford in the fall of 2014 on a swimming scholarship. In the aftermath of his arrest, the media frequently mentioned Turner was an athlete at Stanford and displayed a picture of him in a jacket and tie, rather than showing his mug shot. And, like Turner, the judge who presided over Turner's case had also been a student athlete at Stanford University.

The outrage that followed Turner's sentencing led to an effort to have Judge Persky recalled from the bench. That did not occur, although Persky requested not to hear any more criminal cases. He was, therefore, reassigned to the civil division of the California court system. But the plight of Brock Turner's victim caused the California state legislature to enact a new law providing a mandatory minimum three-year prison sentence for sexual assault of an unconscious or intoxicated person.

All too often, when we think about the criminal courts, our minds immediately focus on the members of the courtroom work group: prosecutors, defense attorneys, and judges. We are less likely to think about the other participants: victims, witnesses, or even defendants. Yet these other actors are also important.

Victims greatly influence workload. Courts are passive institutions. They do not seek out cases to decide; rather, they depend on others to bring matters to their attention. How many cases are filed, as well as what kinds of cases are brought to court, is determined by the decisions of others—police, victims, and those who violate the law in the first place. Thus, the courtroom work group has very little control over its workload. Second, victims, witnesses, and defendants are the consumers of the court process. Democratic governments are expected to be responsive to the wishes and demands of their citizens; victims and witnesses often complain about how the courts handle their cases. Victims and defendants are both subjects and objects of the criminal justice process. Their importance for how the courtroom work group administers justice on a day-to-day basis is the subject of this chapter.

Characteristics of Defendants

In some ways, those accused of violating the criminal law are a diverse lot. Although many defendants are economically impoverished, their numbers also include high-ranking government officials, businesspeople, and prominent local citizens. An indicator of the diversity of defendants centers on how often they are involved with the criminal justice system. At one end of the spectrum are those who are arrested once and are never involved again. At the other end are a small group of career offenders who are responsible for a disproportionate share of offenses (Tracy, Wolfgang, & Figlio, 1990; Wolfgang, Figlio, & Sellin, 1972). In fact, it is estimated that over 70 percent of all serious criminal offenses are committed by roughly 7 percent of offenders, a group commonly referred to as **career criminals** (Barnes, 2014; DeLisi, 2005; Vaughn & DeLisi, 2008). To complicate matters further, a generational effect seems to be indicated. Violent offenders are much more likely to have experienced neglect, abuse, or violence in their families (Farrington, 2006; Fox, Perez, Cass, Beglivio, & Epps, 2015; Harlow, 1999). Moreover, conviction of a parent is correlated with the likelihood of a child offending and being convicted (Farrington, 2006; Fox, Perez, Cass, Bolivia, & Epps, 2015; Roettger & Swisher, 2011; Rowe & Farrington, 1997). Whether it is possible to predict who will become a career criminal, however, is subject to extensive debate.

Aside from certain aspects of diversity, the majority of violators conform to a definite profile. Compared to the average citizen, felony defendants are significantly younger, overwhelmingly male, disproportionately members of racial minorities, more likely to come from broken homes, less educated, more likely to be unemployed, and less likely to be married (see Table 9.1). Three characteristics of defendants—sex, poverty, and race—figure prominently in discussions of crime and crime policy and therefore deserve expanded treatment.

Overwhelmingly Male

Defendants are overwhelmingly male. In fact, women account for only 17 percent of felony arrests in the 75 largest counties in the United States (Reaves, 2013) and 26.9 percent of all arrests for all crimes (Federal Bureau of Investigation, 2016). Although these percentages represent a significant increase over the past few decades, it is unclear whether women are actually committing more crimes or whether changes in the criminal justice system itself have occurred. For example, decreases in sexist and paternalistic thought processes might now lead police to arrest and prosecutors to charge female offenders at higher rates than in the past (Pollock, 2014; Pollock & Davis, 2005). According to this view, there has been no major shift in girls' or

TABLE 9.1	Profile of Felony Defendants in the 75 Largest Counties in the United States
Male	83%
Racial or ethnic minorities	70%
At least one prior arrest	75%
At least one prior conviction	60%
Younger than age 35 (Average age is 32, up from age 28 in 1990)	65%
On probation or parole at the time of arrest	18%
On pretrial release (i.e., bail) at time of arrest	29%
Charged with drug offenses	33%
Charged with property offenses	29%
Charged with violence offense	25%
Charged with public-order offenses	13%

Source: Reaves, Brian A. 2013. *Felony Defendants in Large Urban Counties, 2009.* Washington, DC: Bureau of Justice Statistics. Available online at http://www.bjs.gov/content/pub/pdf/fdluc09.pdf

women's relative violence (Lei, Simons, Simons, & Edmond, 2014; Schwartz, Steffensmeier, Zhong, & Ackerman, 2009). On the other hand, there is empirical evidence that the gap between male and female offenders in violent crimes is decreasing (Lauritsen, Heimer, & Lynch, 2009). Whatever the causes, it is clear that rates of female involvement in the justice system have been increasing in recent years, but their absolute numbers still fall well below those of males.

Mostly Underclass

Typical felony defendants possess few of the skills needed to compete successfully in an increasingly technological society. They are drawn from what sociologists call the urban underclass (Jencks & Peterson, 1991). In turn, the more poverty in a community, the higher the amount of crime (Hipp & Yates, 2011; Krivo, Bryon, Calder, Peterson, Browning, Kwan, & Lee, 2015). The association of crime with poverty helps to explain, in part, why the overwhelming number of crimes—primarily burglary, theft, and drug sale—are committed for economic motives. Although crimes of violence dominate the headlines, most defendants are not dangerous; they are charged with property or drug offenses. As for violent crimes, competing theories offer varying explanations for the fact that the "ghetto poor" are disproportionately involved in violent crime. Anderson (1999, p. 33) argued that the "street code" in such economically depressed areas leads to a subculture with norms that are "conspicuously opposed to those of mainstream society" insofar as they endorse violence as an appropriate response to disrespect (see also Bourgois, 2003).

Racial Minorities Overrepresented

Race remains a divisive issue in American politics, and nowhere is this more evident than in the area of crime. African-Americans, Hispanics, and Native-Americans are arrested, convicted, and imprisoned at significantly higher rates per capita than Whites. At the same time, it is important to stress that historically, Whites constituted the majority of those in prison, a fact conveniently ignored on some radio and TV discussions.

Why minorities are overrepresented in the criminal justice system is a topic of considerable importance (and therefore addressed in several later chapters). To some it is an indication that minorities are more likely to be poor and, therefore, more likely to commit crimes for economic advancement (Blasdell, 2015; Haynie, Weiss, & Piquero, 2008). Others counter that discrimination is the reason; minorities are more likely to be targeted by criminal justice officials and also more likely to receive a harsh sentence (Keen & Jacobs, 2009; Stolzenberg, D'Alessio, & Eitle, 2013). Whatever the cause, the impact is enormous. According to the Sentencing Project (Nellis, 2016),

- African Americans are incarcerated in state prisons at a rate that is 5.1 times the imprisonment of Whites. In five states (Iowa, Minnesota, New Jersey, Vermont, and Wisconsin), the disparity is more than 10 to 1.

- Latinos are imprisoned at a rate that is 1.4 times the rate of Whites. Hispanic/White disparities in incarceration rates are particu-

larly high in states Massachusetts (4.3 to 1), Connecticut (3.9 to 1), Pennsylvania (3.3 to 1), and New York (3.1 to 1).

(See also Carson & Golinelli, 2013; Mauer, 2011b.)

Altogether, one out of three people in the United States is a member of a racial or ethnic minority group, with Hispanics having recently become the largest minority. As explored in the "Courts, Controversy, & Racial Discrimination" feature on page 228, some question whether Latinos can get equal justice under the law.

Defendants in Court

The **defendant** is supposed to stand at the center of the criminal court drama. Yet typical felony defendants are largely powerless to control their fates; they are more objects to be acted upon than keys to what happens.

Because most defendants are poor and uneducated, they are ill equipped to deal with the technical abstractions of the criminal court process. Many are incapable of understanding even the simplest instructions about the right to bail or the presumption of innocence. Many are too inarticulate to aid their attorneys in preparing a defense. Many hold unfavorable attitudes toward the law and the criminal justice system and thus regard the judge and all other court personnel, including their defense attorneys, with hostility and distrust.

The mental competence of criminal defendants is another significant concern for the courts. Competency to stand trial concerns itself with a criminal defendant's mental state at the time of trial. If a bona fide issue regarding the defendant's competency to stand trial has been raised, the defendant must be clinically assessed. In *Ake v. Oklahoma* (1985), the Supreme Court held that an indigent criminal defendant had the right to have the state provide a psychiatric evaluation that can be used not only to determine competency to stand trial, but also may be used to help prepare and present an insanity defense, if warranted.

Even when the mental competency of a criminal defendant is not in question, the nature of the

Can Latinos Get Equal Justice under the Law?

The appointment of Sonia Sotomayor to the U.S. Supreme Court and a recent report of the U.S. Census Bureau (2011) have focused attention on race, ethnicity, and the justice system. More than one-third of our nation's population belongs to a minority group. Sotomayor is the first Hispanic, an ethnic group that constitutes the fastest-growing segment of the U.S. population, to serve on the U.S. Supreme Court. The U.S. Census Bureau reports that Hispanics now constitute nearly one in six residents, or 50.5 million people. Even more telling for the future: 44 percent of children younger than 18 years and 47 percent of children younger than 5 are now from minority families.

Hispanics (the identification adopted by the government) or Latinos (a term some in this group prefer) are diverse in terms of country of origin. Some, like Sonia Sotomayor, are from Puerto Rico, a U.S. territory. Others are Cuban, many of whose parents fled the dictatorship of Fidel Castro. Others are from Mexico, the world's 12th most populous country, with over 114 million people. Others are from other Central and South American countries. Although united by the Spanish language, the Latino population is heterogeneous in many ways.

Most importantly for American politics, Hispanics are also diverse in terms of their immigration status. No accurate counts exist of how many illegal immigrants are in the country, but many estimate about 11 million. (Some advocacy groups place the number higher.) The majority of detained immigrants do not have an attorney during their deportation hearings (California Coalition for Universal Representation, 2016; Hamblett, 2012). Immigration has become a major political issue in the United States, dividing both the American population and the nation's two major political parties. Part of this debate focuses on the role of the criminal justice system.

Hispanics share many of the same social disadvantages as African-Americans (Crutchfield, 2015; Demuth, 2003), including poverty, unemployment, living in neighborhoods with high crime rates, and a history of discrimination. But in addition, they face some unique problems surrounding language and cultural heritage. Some Latino victims/defendants speak little if any English, which makes it hard for them to understand what is happening during investigations, arrests, court appearances, and the like. Besides lacking language skills, Latino victims/defendants also often lack a basic understanding of the American justice system. Their heritage is European law, which places less emphasis on the rights of criminal defendants. Moreover, in some of their native countries, the justice system has a history of suppression, which makes them particularly fearful of governmental officials.

The social disadvantages faced by Latinos have several important consequences for the criminal justice system. For one, Latinos express the same levels of lack of confidence in the U.S. criminal justice system as Blacks (Pew Hispanic Center, 2009; Becerra, Wagaman, Androff, Messing, & Castillo, 2016). Perhaps for this reason, they are less likely to report crimes to the police. In crimes of violence such as assaults, robberies, and rapes, for example, Hispanic women report the crime

clientele can make criminal courts a depressing place to work. Judges, prosecutors, and defense attorneys seldom come away from their day's activities with a sense of accomplishment, for many of the criminal cases involve social problems—drug addiction, marital problems, lack of education, and mental illness—over which court personnel have no control. Many cases stem from disputes between people who know one another.

Court personnel have little empathy with or understanding of the types of defendants whose fates they must decide. Members of the courtroom work group are essentially middle class. Little in their backgrounds or training has equipped them to deal with violations of the law committed by the poor.

Pro Se Defendants

In spite of the legal maxim that only a fool has himself as a client, more and more court litigants elect to act *pro se*, meaning they speak on their own behalf by serving as their own attorneys. *Pro se* litigants are far more numerous in civil cases, to authorities just 35 percent of the time, as compared with 51 percent for White women, and 63 percent for Black women (Karmen, 2016). The lack of trust in governmental authorities coupled with a fear of being deported is a major reason Latinos often do not report crimes to the police. In turn, Latinos may be targeted because they are less likely to report the crime.

It is also harder for police and prosecutors to deal with crimes in which Latinos are victims or defendants. Traditionally, the Hispanic population was concentrated in states sharing a border with Mexico and a few big cities. Today, the population has spread across the nation, meaning that many police departments have few if any officers who can take an accurate police report from a Spanish speaker. The same barriers are faced by prosecutors, public defenders, and judges, with justice sometimes lost in the translation. For example, following the slaying of a Hispanic migrant worker, six Spanish-speaking witnesses were held for months in jail as material witnesses, but they had no court-appointed lawyer because no one in the public defender's office could read the letters they wrote (Alexander-Bloch, 2007).

How well or how poorly Latinos fare in the criminal justice system is hard to tell. An extensive body of research has compared White defendants with Black defendants, but relatively little is known about Latino defendants (Martinez, 2007). But we do know that after arrest, Hispanics are more likely to be detained in jail than Blacks or Whites (Demuth, 2003; Steinmetz & Henderson, 2015).

The growing Hispanic population and the issues surrounding immigration have strained the U.S. justice system in several important ways (Hsu, 2009). When an immigrant, whether in this country legally or illegally, is arrested, he or she is more likely to be detained in jail because Immigration and Customs Enforcement (ICE) puts a hold on that person for possible deportation. As a result, jail populations increase and local officials demand that the U.S. government pay for the additional costs (Bowes, 2009). Yet ironically, many undocumented immigrants convicted of a minor crime are not deported because the U.S. immigration system is overwhelmed and therefore chooses to deport only those convicted of the most serious offenses (Carroll, 2008). Several states have recently passed major anti-immigration laws that threaten to increase tensions between Latinos and the police and the criminal justice system (Becerra et al., 2016; Martinez, 2010).

The growing number of immigrants has also placed the United States at odds with the international legal community. The Vienna Convention on Consular Relations gives foreign nationals who are accused of a crime the right to talk with the consulate of their home country. The International Court of Justice found that Texas violated the treaty by not informing Jose Medellin, a Texas death row inmate, of these rights. But the Supreme Court refused to follow the decision of the world court, holding that the treaty was not binding on the United States and that rulings of the International Court of Justice are not binding when they contradict states' criminal procedures (*Medellin v. Texas*, 2008). It is also worth noting that the Mexican constitution prohibits that nation from deporting one of its citizens in death penalty cases.

especially in family law cases, largely because of the high costs of legal assistance and the general unavailability of appointed counsel in most civil cases. And although legal representation is provided free of charge to indigent criminal defendants facing incarceration (see Chapter 7), not all defendants avail themselves of this right.

Although a "right" to self-representation is not explicitly mentioned in the Sixth Amendment, in *Faretta v. California* (1975), the U.S. Supreme Court determined that the right to make one's own defense is necessarily implied by the plain language of the Amendment. To do so, however, one must be mentally competent to waive counsel and serve as one's own attorney. In *Indiana v. Edwards* (2008), the Court held that "the Constitution permits States to insist upon representation by counsel for those competent enough to stand trial . . . but who still suffer from severe mental illness to the point where they are not competent to conduct trial proceedings by themselves" (p. 178).

When a criminal defendant acts *pro se,* courts have the discretion to appoint **standby/shadow counsel** to assistant the defendant as needed.

Having a lawyer able to take over the case is desirable if the court revokes the defendant's right to self-representation either because of emerging questions of mental incompetence or if the defendant is abusive, threatening, obstructionist, or the cause of repeated, unnecessary delays. On the other hand, serving as standby counsel poses unique ethical challenges for defense attorneys.

> Standby counsel inhabits a treacherous zone of representation, directed by the court to assist a *pro se* defendant who exercises an unusual level of control and may want no assistance whatsoever. Within that relationship, counsel must respect the defendant's constitutional right to self-representation. Counsel must not undermine either the defendant's actual control of the defense or the appearance that the defendant controls the defense. But there is little guidance as to what is expected of standby counsel. Courts that appoint standby counsel express diametrically opposed understandings of the role: some direct standby counsel only to be available and provide advice if the defendant seeks it, while others expect standby counsel to be sufficiently prepared to assume representation of the defendant if the defendant abandons pro se representation. Some courts expect standby counsel to provide the court with information. Others appoint standby counsel to be a resource and support for the defendant. (Poulin, 2013, pp. 212–213)

Pro se litigants can be expensive, time consuming, and frustrating for the courts.

> *Pro se* cases increase the complexity of the duties assigned to judges, magistrates, and other court administrators and personnel and can challenge the impartiality of both judges and clerks. Pro se litigants, meanwhile, increase administrative costs, skip court proceedings or attend proceedings unprepared, and upset court routines. This development has proven to be a "fundamental challenge to many basic assumptions of our adversary system"; a system that built the roles of judges and clerks on the premise that each party is represented. (Thompson, 2010–2011, p. 610)

For example, *pro se* defendants plead "not guilty" and go to trial at significantly higher rates than do felony defendants represented by counsel (Hashimoto, 2007). And because *pro se* litigants are usually unfamiliar with the law, the rules of evidence, and the rules of criminal procedure, they can pose significant challenges for court personnel.

Yet, *pro se* criminal defendants appear to fare reasonably well in state courts. Those who do plead guilty often do so to significantly higher percentages of misdemeanors and lower numbers of felonies (47 percent and 53 percent, respectively) as compared with represented defendants, nearly 84 percent of whom plead guilty to felonies and only 16 percent to misdemeanors (Hashimoto, 2007). Of those who go to trial, acquittal rates for *pro se* defendants are generally the same as those for defendants represented by counsel. In federal courts, however, *pro se* defendants tend to garner less favorable pleas and enjoy only one-third the acquittal rate of represented defendants (Hashimoto, 2007).

The Pitfalls of Social Media for Defendants

"I could win most of my cases if it weren't for the clients. . . . They will waltz into the witness-box and blurt out things which are far better left unblurted," complained Horace Rumpole, a fictitious British defense attorney (Mortimer, 1984). Modern American defense attorneys no doubt complain that they could win a few more of their cases if their clients did not text, e-mail, tweet, or otherwise post online what was best untexted, unemailed, untweeted, or unposted. Today, many social media sites go beyond the posting of information; tags of photos, GPS locations, "check-ins," and time logs can all provide useful information in criminal investigations.

To be sure, defendants enjoy the privilege against self-incrimination, which means they cannot be forced to testify at trial. And this privilege has been extended to include police interrogation, because the police must provide suspects with *Miranda* warnings. But the privilege against self-incrimination does not apply to voluntary statements made by defendants.

- If material is publicly posted on social media sites, investigators are able to view the postings (just like anyone else can view public postings) and use whatever they find as evidence in court.
- When electronic information is posted, tweeted, or otherwise sent using certain privacy settings, law enforcement might be able to obtain the information either by posing as a

"friend" or "follower" or by accessing such posts through a cooperating witness who is a "friend" with access to the posted material (Murphy & Fontecilla, 2013).

- Law enforcement may also access social media data obscured from public view by privacy settings using traditional investigative methods such as subpoenas, search warrants, or other court orders (see Ferdico, Fradella, & Totten, 2016; Murphy & Fontecilla, 2013).

Thus, what people tweet on Twitter, send by e-mail, or post to Facebook can have major legal repercussions.

> For example, a defendant in Kentucky was jailed after he posted to Facebook a photo of himself siphoning gas from a police car. Another defendant burgled a Washington, D.C., home and then used the victim's laptop to post to the victim's Facebook page a picture of himself wearing the victim's coat and holding up the victim's cash. The photo was later used to secure a guilty plea from the defendant. (Fontecilla, 2013, p. 55)

The conviction of Dharun Ravi for hate crimes serves as another case in point. Dharun Ravi, a freshman at Rutgers University, used a webcam to spy on his gay roommate's dorm room sexual encounters and streamed the video on the Internet (Shallwani, 2012; Slane, 2015). A few days later, his roommate, Tyler Clementi, a talented young musician, committed suicide. These events quickly became the subject of intense national interest, and Ravi was charged under New Jersey law with a hate crime, invasion of privacy, witness intimidation, and bias intimidation (but not murder). The government case was based on a pixelated paper trail of Twitter feeds, Facebook posts, text messages, e-mails, and other chatter. Ravi, for example, widely publicized his actions using social media and deleted texts sent to the prosecution. In the end, the jurors decided that this overwhelming amount of social media data elevated the case from one of a teenager behaving cruelly to a person committing an insensitive crime (Halbringer & Kormanik, 2012; Slane, 2015).

It should also come as no surprise that social media communications provide strong evidence in cyberbullying cases (Grant, 2012). Additionally, social media can also pose a problem for convicted defendants at sentencing. For example,

a 22-year-old defendant had been charged with driving under the influence after crashing into another car and seriously injuring the other driver. Two weeks later, he attended a Halloween party dressed as a prisoner and wearing a sign that said, "jail bird." After another partygoer posted the photo on Facebook, prosecutors used the photo "to portray the accused as an unrepentant young man more interested in drunkenly celebrating while his seriously-injured victim recovered in the hospital. A judge agreed with the prosecutor and called the pictures 'depraved' in sentencing the young man to two years in prison" (Van Namen, 2012, pp. 566–567).

Similarly, in *People v. Binkerd* (2007), the defendant was driving home from a party when she collided with oncoming traffic, killing the friend and coworker who had been her passenger. Her blood alcohol concentration was more than twice the legal limit. At her sentencing for vehicular homicide, the probation officer had recommended a jail sentence of less than one year, a sentence the deceased victim's family supported. Yet, the judge sentenced the defendant to 64 months in state prison after seeing pictures of the defendant posted on her MySpace page wearing a t-shirt reading "I ♥ Patron" while drinking with friends after the fatal accident. The judge thought that the photos indicated the defendant lacked remorse and therefore deserved a tough sentence.

Courts Through the Eyes of Victims and Witnesses

Traditionally, victims and witnesses have been the forgotten participants in the criminal justice system. Fictional and nonfictional treatments of the court process direct attention to the criminal as victim rather than to the victim as victim (Elias, 1986). More recently, however, a growing number of studies have focused on the victim (Karmen, 2016). These studies have identified ways in which the courts, along with the rest of the criminal justice community, have ignored the interests of victims and witnesses.

Frustrations in Coping with the Process

Crime victims once played a prominent role in the criminal process. Before the American Revolution, victims were the central figures in the criminal justice drama. Criminals' fates were closely tied to their victims' wishes. When crime became viewed as an offense against the state, the victim was assigned a subordinate role. As prosecutorial dominance increased, the power of the victim declined (see Chapter 6). Victims lost control over their cases, and their role was reduced to initiating investigations by complaining to the police and testifying for the prosecution as just another piece of evidence in the state's presentation of damning facts against the accused (Karmen, 2016).

Several studies have documented the hardships victims and witnesses face while participating in the criminal court process (Cannavale & Falcon, 1976; Connick & Davis, 1983; McDonald, 1976). Although some are minor inconveniences, such as getting to the courthouse and finding a parking place, other hardships are more significant:

- Trial delays, which result in frequent travel and wasted time
- Long waits in uncomfortable surroundings
- Wages lost for time spent going to court
- Fear of the defendant or retaliation from the defendant's associates
- A sense that criminal justice personnel are indifferent to their plight

Travails of Testifying

Victims and witnesses also face major problems while testifying in court. Because few people are accustomed to testifying, lawyers must coach their witnesses ahead of time to answer only the question asked, to speak forcefully (but not belligerently), and not to become rattled by cross-examination. Even after such preparation, many witnesses are uncomfortable during cross-examination, as the defense attorney tests their memory, challenges their veracity, or even suggests that they were somehow responsible for their own victimization. After enduring cross-examination, some victims report feeling as though they, and not the offender, have been portrayed as the criminal.

Most of what we know about the ordeal of testifying in court comes from studies of rape victims (Resick, 1984) and victims of intimate partner violence (Bell, Perez, Goodman, & Dutton, 2011; Hare, 2006). Often, victims feel like they are the ones on trial, rather than the defendant. Testifying in court provokes anxiety for several months, exacerbating psychological distress (Steketee & Austin, 1989). Holmstrom and Burgess (1983), both of whom counsel rape victims at Boston City Hospital, followed the cases of 14 women who testified in court during a rape trial. They concluded that the trauma is often significant, because the victim must publicly repeat in detail how the rape occurred. The type of defense used by the defense attorney also has an impact on the victim's adjustment to the crime. A defense claim that the woman consented to sex is injurious, because it puts the victim on trial and calls into question her discouragement of the perpetrator (Steketee & Austin, 1989). Moreover, the defense often seeks to blame the victim by suggesting that she consented, did not resist, was provocatively dressed, and so on. It can take little to discredit the victim. Following the Holmstrom and Burgess study, most states have passed legislation limiting inquiry into a rape victim's past sexual conduct (Caringella, 2008).

Surprising Support for the System

Somewhat surprisingly, despite the problems and frustrations experienced, victims and witnesses still express overall support for the court process (Hagan, 1983). A study conducted in Milwaukee found that victims and witnesses were satisfied or very satisfied with the handling of their cases by the police (81 percent), district attorney (75 percent), and judge (66 percent). Less than 15 percent said that they were dissatisfied (Knudten, Meader, Knudten, & Doerner, 1976). Favorable judgments were independent of whether a victim was satisfied with the eventual outcome of the case. Since that time, courts have grown more responsive to the needs of victims and witnesses. Research suggests that increased levels of victim input into the handling of criminal cases moderately increase victims' satisfaction with the judicial system (Erez & Roberts, 2007). Such findings, however, are contingent upon a variety of factors, such as whether victims even know about their rights to participate in various processes, whether the victim was treated with dignity and respect, and whether there was an admission of guilt or an apology from the perpetrator.

Victims and Witnesses Through the Eyes of the Court

The criminal courts confront a double bind with regard to victims. On the one hand, victims are valued for the cases they bring to the system; their misfortunes become the raw material of the court process (see the "Law on the Books vs. Law in Action" feature on page 234). On the other hand, individual victims represent a potential source of irrationality in the process. The personal and often emotional involvement of victims in the crime experience can generate particular demands for case outcomes that have little to do with the public interest. Thus, at times members of the courtroom work group perceive that the victim's demands for public justice actually mask a desire for private vengeance (Hagan, 1983). Members of the courtroom work group also know that, particularly in violent and gang-related crime, the same individual may, at difference times, be a victim, a witnesses, and an offender (Dedel, 2006).

Lack of Cooperation

Many victims and witnesses are reluctant to become involved in the criminal justice process. More than half of all major crimes are never reported to the police; even when they are reported, not all victims wish to prosecute (Chapter 10). Particularly in the low-income, high-crime neighborhoods of the nation's largest cities, victims and witnesses may fail to cooperate with the police. In the words of Captain Sheilah Coley of Newark, New Jersey: "I don't know what frustrates me more. Those knuckleheads killing each other, or the residents who won't cooperate

with my officers" (quoted in Jacobs, 2007). When her officers respond to reports of gunfire, potential witnesses respond with blank looks.

Scholars often consider this lack of cooperation a function of *legal cynicism*—a cultural orientation in which law or justice system actors are viewed as illegitimate, unresponsive, and ill equipped to ensure public safety (Kirk & Matsuda, 2011). For example, youths in high-crime neighborhoods are often disinclined toward helping police as a result of their own negative encounters with law enforcement (Berg, Steward, Intravia, Warren, & Simons, 2016; Carr, Napoliatano, and Keating, 2007). This lack of cooperation is fueled by hip-hop culture's "stop snitching" mantra. Indeed hip-hop superstar B.G., known for his song "I Ain't Tellin," accepted a longer-than-normal prison term on a federal gun charge rather than snitch (McCarthy, 2011).

Some specific witness-related problems include giving the police incorrect addresses, failing to show up in court, and offering testimony that is confused, garbled, or contradicted by other facts. Witness-related problems result in a significant number of cases in which the prosecutor refuses to file charges or the case is later dismissed (Boland, Brady, Tyson, & Bassler, 1982). But when victims cooperate with the prosecution, the odds that a case will be prosecuted increase dramatically (Dawson & Dinovitzer, 2001; Ekström & Lindström, 2016).

Not all uncooperative behavior can be blamed on victims and witnesses, however; the court process can be equally at fault. In Washington, D.C., a study focusing on what it called "noncooperative" witnesses reported that 41 percent were never told that they should contact the prosecutor; 62 percent were never notified of court appearances; and 43 percent stated that the police, prosecutor, and judge all failed to explain the witnesses' rights and duties. Other reports have found that the longer the case is delayed, the more likely it is that witnesses will not appear when summoned (Cannavale & Falcon, 1976).

Witness Intimidation

One form of noncooperation involves witness intimidation. Persons who have been victims of crime, or witnessed a crime, may be pressured not

LAW ON THE BOOKS VS. LAW IN ACTION

Major Activities of Victims in the Steps of the Court Process

	Law on the Books	Law in Action
Crime	No general requirement to report crimes to the police.	Thirty-eight percent of personal and household crimes are reported to the police.
Arrest	A citizen's arrest is the taking of a person into physical custody by a person other than a law enforcement officer for the purpose of delivering the person to the custody of a law enforcement officer.	The vast majority of arrests are made by law enforcement officers. Citizen's arrests may result in injury to the victim and may also result in civil lawsuits.
Initial appearance	Open to the public.	Very unlikely for victim to be present because unlikely to know timing of the event.
Bail	VRA[a] provides that victims have a right to be heard if present and to submit a statement "to determine a release from custody."	Victims are very rarely present.
Charging	Victim has no role, and the VRA states that "nothing in this article shall provide grounds for the victim to challenge the charging decision."	Reluctance or refusal of victims to cooperate is a key reason for case dismissal.
Preliminary hearing	Besides the right to notice and to be present, the VRA is silent on the role of victims during this stage.	Victims rarely testify because hearsay evidence is admissible.
Grand jury	Grand jury can subpoena victim to testify.	In grand jury states, victim is likely to be subpoenaed to testify.
Arraignment	VRA provides that victims of crimes have the right to notice of proceedings like this.	Victims are rarely present.
Evidence	In some jurisdictions, the defense is entitled to see a copy of the victim's statement to the police.	Even if not required, some district attorneys disclose the victim's statement in hopes of inducing a guilty plea.
Plea bargaining	VRA provides that victims may be heard and may submit a statement during an acceptance of a negotiated plea.	Some jurisdictions allow victims to be heard with regard to the plea bargain, but few actually appear.
Trial	If they are to testify, victims generally cannot view the trial (wording in the VRA concerning public proceedings might change this law).	Victim's testimony is a key part of the trial.
Sentencing	VRA provides that victims may be heard and may submit a statement during sentencing.	Victims are unlikely to appear.
Appeal	Like other court proceedings, appellate argument is open to the public.	Victims are very unlikely to be present.

[a]VRA = Proposed Victims' Rights Amendment to the U.S. Constitution.

to testify. Witness intimidation may take the form of threats of violence or actual violence against the person in question or his or her friends and family members. Property damage may also be involved. Such pressures may be made by the defendant, members of the defendant's family, other associates, or even gang members (Dedel, 2006; Ewin, 2015). Witness intimidation is often a specific focus of victim/witness assistance programs, discussed later in this chapter.

Social Media and Victims

The risks of social media are not limited to defendants, as previously discussed. Victims' claims are also subject to scrutiny against their social media posts.

> In one specific case, a defense attorney used information she accessed online to dismiss the charges against her client. The particular situation involved a forcible rape claim in Oregon, where a teenager told the police she would never willingly engage in intercourse. The defense attorney viewed the "victim's" MySpace page, where she talked about parties, drinking, and engaging in sexual activity, and posted provocative pictures of herself. Thus, based on what was posted, the attorney could see how the teenage "victim" would be perceived by jurors. The defense attorney called her as a witness, and ultimately, the charge against her client was dismissed. (Van Namen, 2012, pp. 564–565)

Similarly, a New Jersey woman who accused a man of rape was forced to turn over access to her Facebook to a judge to review any comments she had made about the case. Normally courts don't force crime victims to turn over evidence, but in this situation, the defense attorney wanted to probe if she made any comments indicating that the sex was consensual (Cornfield, 2014).

Characteristics of Victims

In some ways, victims of crimes are a diverse lot, including the rich and the poor, the young and the old, and men as well as women. This diversity aside, however, crime victims are more likely to be young, non-White, male, divorced or never married, low-income, and unemployed (Elias, 1986;

Truman & Morgan, 2016). Thus, in many ways, the profile of victims matches that of defendants. Indeed, several decades of research have established that offenders and victims often possess the same characteristics and engage in many of the same behaviors (Averdijk, Gelder, Eisner, & Ribeaud, 2016; Schreck, Stewart, & Osgood, 2008). The major deviation is that rates of female victimization approach that of males.

The overlaps of offenders and their victims possess numerous problems for members of the courtroom. Indeed, it is not uncommon to find that a person who appears in court as the defendant was in the past in court in the role of victim. How a case is handled is determined by the identity of the victim as well as that of the offender. Prosecutors allocate their limited resources to the cases they believe constitute the most "trouble" (Hagan, 1983). Not surprisingly, such judgments correlate with the desire for high conviction rates. Prosecutors assume that judges and juries will find the claims of certain kinds of victims credible and acceptable, but not the claims of others (Stanko, 1981–1982). The troubles of older, white, male, employed victims are considered more worthy of public processing (Myers & Hagan, 1979). For example, legal outcomes in murder cases were related to the race, gender, and conduct of victims at the time of the incident (Baumer, Messner, & Felson, 2000; Dilks, McGrimmon, & Thye, 2015).

Prior Relationships Between Defendants and Victims

Perhaps the most important victim characteristic that influences case processing is the prior relationship between defendants and victims. The following case is illustrative.

> An auxiliary police officer watched a woman approach a man as he emerged from a liquor store. It was dark. The officer thought he saw a knife flash in her hand, and the man seemed to hand her some money. She fled, and the officer went to the aid of the victim, taking him to the hospital for treatment.

> The officer saw the woman on the street a few days later and arrested her for first-degree robbery on the victim's sworn complaint. It was presumably a "high-quality"

arrest—identification of the perpetrator by an eyewitness, not from mugshots or a lineup, but in a crowd. Yet, shortly thereafter, this apparently airtight case was dismissed on the prosecutor's motion.

What the victim had not explained to the police was that the defendant, an alcoholic, had been his girlfriend for the past five years; that they had been drinking together the night of the incident; that she had taken some money from him and got angry when he took it back; that she had flown into a fury when he then gave her only a dollar outside the liquor store; and that she had slashed at him with a pen knife in anger and run off. He had been sufficiently annoyed to have her charged with robbery, but, as the judge who dismissed the case said, "He wasn't really injured. Before it got into court they had kissed and made up." In fact, the victim actually approached the defense attorney before the hearing and asked him to prevail upon the judge and the assistant district attorney (ADA) to dismiss the charges against his girlfriend. (Vera Institute of Justice, 1981, p. xxii)

This case is one of many cited by the Vera Institute that show the importance of the prior relationship between defendants and victims.

Prior relationships between defendants and victims are more common than generally assumed. In half of all felony arrests in New York, the victim had a prior relationship with the defendant. Prior relationships were frequent in cases of homicide and assault, in which they were expected, but they were also frequent in cases of robbery, in which they were not. Other studies reach a similar conclusion. Nationwide, roughly half of all violent crimes (rape, assault, and robbery) are committed by relatives, friends, or acquaintances of the victim (Truman & Morgan, 2016). Homicides, in particular, are usually committed not by strangers but by someone the victim knows by sight; in fact, the victim and the perpetrator are strangers in only 14 to 22 percent of all murders (Cooper & Smith, 2011; Fox & Zawitz, 2007). Criminal court officials often regard crimes involving people who know one another as not very serious, viewing them as private disputes rather than offenses against the entire community.

Intimate-Partner Violence

The prior relationship between victims and defendants is most apparent in crimes against intimate partners. Women are much more likely than men to experience violence committed by an intimate partner, such as a current or former spouse, lover, or boyfriend or girlfriend, including same-sex relationships. Measuring violence between intimate partners is difficult because it often occurs in private, and victims are often reluctant to report incidents to anyone because of shame or fear of reprisal. Rates of intimate-partner violence have been declining over the past several decades but still remain a significant issue in American society (Catalano, 2013).

Intimate-Partner Violence and the Police

Historically, police officers made an arrest only as a last resort—if taking the suspect into custody seemed the only way to ensure no more violence that night. Justice system actors—including police officers, prosecutors, and judges—seemingly believed "that the importance of protecting families from interference outweighed the importance of protecting women from abuse" (Goldfarb, 2008, pp. 1495–1496; see also "Case Close-Up" on *Thurman v. Torrington*). In the late 1970s through the 1980s, however, this attitude began to change as intimate-partner violence came to be understood as a serious social problem.

Advocacy groups for intimate-partner victims have worked vigorously for policy changes designed to make the criminal justice system treat domestic violence as a serious offense. Jeffrey Fagan (1996) gave this movement a name in his aptly titled book, *The Criminalization of Domestic Violence*. As a result, there have been significant changes in how the criminal justice system responds to intimate-partner violence. The question of what constitutes the most effective criminal justice response, however, has stirred considerable controversy for decades (Maxwell, Garner, & Fagan, 2002; Messing, Ward-Lasher, Thaller, & Bagwell-Gray, 2015). The prior relationship between victim and offender causes particular problems for justice system actors (Buzawa & Buzawa, 1996).

The police have been urged to make more arrests, and prosecutors to file charges, no matter what the wishes of the victim. Mandatory-arrest policies clearly produce higher arrest rates (Hirschel,

CASE CLOSE-UP   *Thurman v. Torrington* and Domestic Violence Arrests

Between October 1982 and June 1983, Tracey Thurman repeatedly notified the police of threats made on her life and the life of her child by her estranged husband, Charles Thurman. On one of those occasions, Charles screamed threats at Tracey while she was sitting in her car. A police officer watched and did nothing until Charles broke the windshield on the car while Tracey was still inside of it. The officer then arrested Charles. He was convicted of breaching the peace and received a suspended sentence of six months. The police continued to ignore Tracey's requests each time she called. Indeed, both she and a neighbor attempted to file criminal complaints against Charles when he violated orders of protection, but police repeatedly ignored her.

On June 10, 1983, Charles appeared at the home of one of Tracey's friends, demanding to speak with Tracey, who remained indoors. The police were called with a request that Charles be picked up for violation of his probation. After about 15 minutes, Tracey went outside to speak to her husband in an effort to persuade him not to take or hurt their son. Soon thereafter Charles stabbed Tracey 13 times in the chest, neck, and throat.

Approximately 25 minutes after Tracey's call to the Torrington Police Department, and after her stabbing, a single police officer arrived on the scene. He saw Charles holding a bloody knife. Charles dropped the knife and, in the presence of the officer kicked Tracey in the head and ran into the house. Charles returned from within the residence holding their son. He dropped the child on his wounded mother and then kicked Tracey in the head a second time. Soon thereafter, three more police officers arrived on the scene, but all of them permitted Charles to wander about the crowd and to continue to threaten Tracey. Finally, upon approaching Tracey once again—this time while she was lying on a stretcher—Charles Thurman was arrested and taken into custody.

Miraculously, Tracey survived the attack, although she suffered significant injuries that left her with impaired motor function. She and her son sued the City of Torrington, Connecticut, and 24 of its police officers for their failure to arrest her violent, estranged husband. Tracey alleged that by following a policy of not arresting abusive husbands or boyfriends, Torrington police failed to provide the same protection for abused wives and children as they provided for victims of similar assaults outside a domestic relationship. The court agreed with her.

City officials and police officers are under an affirmative duty to preserve law and order and to protect the personal safety of persons in the community. This duty applies equally to women whose personal safety is threatened by individuals with whom they have or have had a domestic relationship as well as to all other persons whose personal safety is threatened, including women not involved in domestic relationships. If officials have notice of the possibility of attacks on women in domestic relationships or other persons, they are under an affirmative duty to take reasonable measures to protect the personal safety of such persons in the community.

***

[A] police officer may not knowingly refrain from interference in such violence, and may not automatically decline to make an arrest simply because the assailant and his victim are married to each other Such inaction on the part of the officer is a denial of the equal protection of the laws. (pp. 1527–1528)

Ultimately, Tracey Thurman was awarded $2.3 million in compensatory damages. But perhaps the true legacy of her story is that it prompted Connecticut to revise its domestic violence laws to include mandatory arrest provisions.

Buzawa, Pattavina, & Faggiani, 2007). Whether these mandatory-arrest policies are effective in reducing intimate-partner violence has been questioned, however (Hirschel, Hutchison, Dean, & Mills, 1992). Researchers report that arrest reduces domestic violence in some cities but increases it in others (Schmidt & Sherman, 1993). Although some exceptions exist, most studies to date indicate that criminal justice interventions deter intimate-partner violence or improve victim safety (Cosimo, 2011; Spohn, 2008).

Intimate-Partner Violence in the Courts

Arrests do not always lead to prosecutions. Many victims call the police to stop the violence but later have a change of heart and refuse to sign a complaint. In *Bronx D.A.*, Sarena Straus (2006, p. 31) expressed her frustration as a prosecutor in the sex crimes and domestic violence unit:

> I found that a large percentage of the abused women who came into the Complaint Room refused to press charges, and most of them would return time and time again. Many of these women were known to their local precincts as they were constantly calling 911 for help. . . . The story was often the same. They loved the guy. They knew he wouldn't do it again. He said he was sorry. He bought them flowers. It was their fault because they provoked him.

At times, the district attorneys would pressure the woman to file charges, but often they simply accepted defeat.

The criminalization of intimate-partner violence has also greatly increased the workload of the courts. Between 1989 and 1998, for example, the number of domestic relations cases in state courts across the nation grew by 178 percent (Ostrom & Kauder, 1999) with about a 10 percent increase in the following decade (LaFountain et al., 2008). In response to the growing awareness of domestic violence as a serious social problem, many courts in the United States have created domestic violence courts that emphasize a problem-solving approach (see Chapter 3). Evaluation of courts found significantly lower rates of re-arrests among defendants processed through the domestic violence court (Gover, MacDonald, & Alpert, 2003; Tutty & Babins-Wagner, 2016) and increased victim satisfaction with the processes that emphasized victim safety and services (Labriola, Bradley, O'Sullivan, Rempel, & Moore, 2009).

A growing number of courts rely on batterer programs as the mandate of choice. Some researchers report that batterer programs do not appear to reduce recidivism (Haggård, Freij, Danielsson, Wenander, & Långström, 2015; Labriola, Rempel, & Davis, 2008), but others argue that these programs are appropriate in most cases (Gondolf, 2012; Tutty & Babins-Wagner, 2016). However, programs involving a coordinated response that involve courts and justice agencies appear to be more effective (Visher, Harrell, Newmark, & Yahner, 2008).

Legal sanctions against domestic violence are not limited to criminal law. Victims of domestic violence may request a **civil protection order**.

Recent legislative changes in most jurisdictions now make these court orders easier to obtain. They are no longer limited to women who have filed for divorce, and they may be issued on an emergency basis without the other party present. Half of the women in five Kentucky counties who received a civil protection order experienced no violations; among the half who did experience a violation, the levels of violence and abuse declined significantly (Hawkins, 2010). However, civil protection orders are not self-enforcing; there is even a danger that a civil protection order may induce a false sense of security among some women who are at risk of continued battery from a former intimate. Conversely, some are concerned that protection orders can be abused. In the words of public defender David Feige (2006, p. 182), "Though a fine idea in principle, orders of protection are constantly abused. It is not at all uncommon for vindictive, angry partners to use orders of protection to wreak havoc on each other—using them as substitutes for eviction orders or citing them to justify ignoring child custody agreements."

In spite of the continuing shortcomings of the criminal justice system in dealing with intimate-partner violence, it is clear that these cases have dramatically altered the operation of the modern criminal justice system (see Eraz, 2002). Some of the more notable changes include:

- Better and more consistent enforcement of criminal laws against assault and battery in which perpetrators of such offenses against intimate partners are treated as having committed serious crimes
- Changes to sexual assault laws to encompass marital rape and to reduce or even eliminate the requirements of physical resistance (which previously had served to increase victimization)
- The recognition of legal defenses for victims of intimate-partner violence who fight back under circumstances that limit the applicability of the traditional defense of self-defense
- Increased police professionalism and sensitivity to intimate-partner violence such that nonintervention is no longer viewed as an acceptable response

- Increased availability of civil orders of protection and more consistent enforcement of them after issuance
- Improvement of a range of victims' services

Aiding Victims and Witnesses

For decades, reformers have urged that victims and witnesses be accorded better treatment.

- In 1931, the National Commission on Law Observance and Enforcement concluded that effective administration of public justice required willing witnesses, but testifying in court imposed unreasonable burdens on citizens.
- A 1938 American Bar Association report found that witness fees were deplorably low, courthouse accommodations were uncomfortable, and witnesses were frequently summoned to court numerous times only to have the case continued.

But it was not until the 1960s that attention was seriously devoted to the problems faced by victims and witnesses in court and to ways of improving the situation (Karmen, 2016).

- In 1967, the President's Commission on Law Enforcement and Administration of Justice highlighted a "growing concern that the average citizen identifies himself less and less with the criminal process and its officials."

A few years later, concern for victims and witnesses of crime rose to a crescendo. Crime victims received special attention from the White House.

- In 1982, the President's Task Force on Victims of Crime stressed the need for achieving a balance between the needs and rights of the victim and those of the defendant.

Public and governmental concern over the plight of victims has prompted numerous pieces of legislation (see the "Key Developments" feature on page 240). The Victim and Witness Protection Act, a federal law passed in 1982, required greater protection of victims and witnesses and also mandated guidelines for the fair treatment of victims and witnesses in federal criminal cases. The Victims of Crime Act of 1984 authorized federal funds for state victim programs. Spurred by these concerns, every state has passed comprehensive legislation protecting the interests of victims. In short, a wide variety of programs have been adopted in recent years to improve the treatment crime victims receive from the criminal justice system. The four most common types of initiatives are: (1) victim/witness assistance programs, (2) victim compensation programs, and (3) a victims' bill of rights, and (4) victim impact statements.

Victim/Witness Assistance Programs

Victim/witness assistance programs encourage cooperation in the conviction of criminals by reducing the inconvenience citizens face when appearing in court (Finn & Lee, 1988). Typical activities include providing comfortable and secure waiting areas, assisting with the prompt return of stolen property that has been recovered, and providing crisis intervention. These programs also provide victims and witnesses with a clearer understanding of the court process by distributing brochures, explaining court procedures, and notifying witnesses of upcoming court dates (Webster, 1988). Of particular concern is victim and witness intimidation. Intimidation can be either case-specific—threats or violence intended to dissuade a witness from testifying in a specific case—or communitywide—acts of gangs or drug-selling groups intended to foster a general atmosphere of fear and noncooperation within a neighborhood or community (Healey, 1995).

Today, virtually all jurisdictions of any size have established programs aimed at helping crime victims cope with the hardships of victimization and deal with the often troublesome demands of the criminal justice system. Most are based in criminal justice agencies (prosecutors', police, and sheriffs' offices). Often the program title is Victim Services. Overall, few victims use these programs, and older victims of violent crimes are more likely to use victim services than are younger victims of nonviolent crimes (Sims, Yost, & Abbott, 2005).

Evaluations of victim/witness assistance programs have yielded mixed results. In some

KEY DEVELOPMENTS IN LAW RELATING TO VICTIMS

National Crime Victims' Week (1980)	Annual event focusing on the plight of crime victims.
Victim and Witness Protection Act (1982)	Enhance and protect the necessary role of crime victims and witnesses in the criminal justice process.
Victims' Bill of Rights (1982)	California was the first state to adopt.
Victim of Crimes Act (1984)	Established Crime Victim Fund from fines, penalties, and bond forfeitures of convicted federal criminals.
***Booth v. Maryland* (1987)**	In capital cases, victim impact statements are unconstitutional because they introduce the risk of imposing the death penalty in an arbitrary and capricious manner.
***South Carolina v. Gathers* (1989)**	Characteristics of the victim are irrelevant during death penalty deliberations.
***Payne v. Tennessee* (1991)**	The Eighth Amendment creates no bar to the introduction of victim impact statements during sentencing.
***Simon & Schuster v. New York State Crime Victims Board* (1991)**	Declared unconstitutional New York's "Son of Sam" law, which sought to prevent criminals from profiting from their crimes.
Violence Against Women Act (1994)	Comprehensive law creating a variety of programs to strengthen law enforcement, prosecution, and victim services in cases involving crimes against women.
The Antiterrorism and Effective Death Penalty Act (1996)	A federal court must impose mandatory restitution, without consideration of the defendant's ability to pay.
Victims' Rights Amendment (VRA 1996)	VRA proposed in the U.S. Congress.
VRA (2000)	VRA withdrawn in face of virtually certain defeat.
Crime Victims' Rights Act (2004)	Federal legislation protecting victims in federal court that parallels the former Victims' Rights Amendment.
***Town of Castle Rock, Colorado v. Gonzales* (2005)**	A victim of domestic violence does not have the right to sue the local police department for failing to enforce a restraining order against her husband, who subsequently murdered her three children.
***Carey v. Musladin* (2009)**	A federal appeals court overstepped its authority when it granted a new trial to a murder defendant whose victim's relatives sat at the trial, in the view of the jury, wearing buttons with the victim's picture on them.

communities, a victim's willingness to cooperate in the future was positively associated with considerate treatment by criminal justice personnel (National Institute of Justice, 1982; Norton, 1983). Thus, victims and witnesses receiving help were more likely to appear when summoned than those who had not been aided. But no such impact was found in other communities (Davis, 1983; Skogan & Wycoff, 1987). Those helped by the program appeared at the same rate as those who were not aided, and there was no change in the rate of case dismissals.

Andrew Karmen (2016) suggests that one explanation for these research findings is that expectations of significant improvements in case outcomes were based on faulty assumptions. The presumption is that the adjudication process is characterized by an adversarial model. The reality is that the courtroom work group has a mutual interest in processing large numbers of cases expeditiously. Thus, whereas victims see their situations as unique events that deserve careful and individual consideration, judges, prosecutors, and defense attorneys see them as routine occurrences, to be disposed of based on "going rates."

Victim Compensation Programs

The criminal justice system in the United States is offender-oriented, focusing on the apprehension, prosecution, and punishment of wrongdoers. While emphasizing the rehabilitation of offenders, the system has done little to help victims recover from the financial and emotional problems that they suffer.

Civil lawsuits are of little relevance, because most criminal defendants have no money to pay monetary damages for personal injuries or damage to property. An increasingly common technique is restitution, in which the court orders the defendant to pay the victim for the losses suffered (see Chapter 14). But a major shortcoming of restitution is that in many crimes, no offender is convicted. Even if convicted, many defendants have little or no ability to provide adequate compensation to a victim. And once restitution is ordered, the victim's likelihood of collecting is not good (Davis, Smith, & Hillenbrand, 1992).

When restitution by the offender is inadequate or impractical, compensation by a third party (an insurance company, for example) is the only alternative. But many victims, because they are poor, do not have insurance covering medical expenses or property losses. The government is another sort of third party. Victim compensation programs rest on the premise that the government should counterbalance losses suffered by victims of criminal acts. The first compensation program in the United States began in California in 1965. Similar programs quickly emerged in a few other states.

In 1984, Congress passed the Victims of Crime Act, which established a Crime Victims Fund administered by the Office for Victims of Crimes within the U.S. Department of Justice. The fund is financed primarily from fines paid by defendants in federal court (Parent, Auerbach, & Carlson, 1992).

The federal backing has now spurred all states to enact legislation providing compensation for at least certain classes of crime victims. The staffs are small, however, and relatively few claims are filed—fewer than 100,000 during a typical year. Most programs provide for recovery of medical expenses and some lost earnings; none reimburses the victim for lost or damaged property. The maximum amount that can be paid in damages ranges from $1,000 to $50,000.

Victim compensation programs appear to provide clear benefits to victims of crime, but the actual results of such programs require careful scrutiny. Preliminary evaluations of compensation programs have yielded findings that are disappointing for administrators (Karmen, 2016). Cumbersome administrative procedures lead to added frustrations and increased alienation. Moreover, few victims of violent crimes apply for benefits, and even fewer claimants receive any money (Elias, 1986). Eligibility requirements are strict. Most states require that the victim assist in the prosecution of the offender, effectively excluding many domestic violence, child abuse, and sexual assault victims (McCormack, 1991). Similarly, most states also have a "family exclusion" clause, which makes victims living in the same household as the offender ineligible. Crime victims must also be "innocent" victims (those to whom no contributory fault can be ascribed). Indeed, in eight states, all persons with a felony conviction are ineligible for aid, even if their current problem has nothing to do with their past illegal activity (Mitchell, 2008). Overall, these programs are designed to spread the limited funds around, rather than to concentrate on a few badly injured victims.

Victims' Bill of Rights

Nowhere is the awakened concern about victims of crime more readily apparent than in proposals for a victims' bill of rights. Apart from sharing the title, however, these proposals vary markedly, reflecting different philosophies. In 1982, the President's Task Force on Victims of Crime submitted 68 separate recommendations aimed at achieving a balance between the needs and rights of the victim and those of the defendant. Also in 1982, California voters approved Proposition 8 by a 2-to-1 margin. Known as the Victims' Bill of Rights, it added 12 controversial provisions to the state constitution and the criminal code. In 2008, California voters approved Proposition 9, which granted additional rights to the victim at the expense of the defendant (Karmen, 2016). These versions of the victims' bill of rights reflect the rallying cry of the law-and-order movement, which accuses the courts of protecting the rights of defendants rather than those of victims. Premised on the notion that defendants escape too easily from the court process, these proposals stress substantive changes in the law, such as abolishing the exclusionary rule, limiting bail, restricting plea-bargaining, and imposing stiffer sentences.

Other proposed victims' bills of rights are less ideological, emphasizing improvements in court procedures to better the lot of victims and witnesses. For example, the National Conference of the Judiciary on the Rights of Victims of Crime adopted a Statement of Recommended Judicial Practices, suggesting: (1) fair treatment of victims and witnesses through better information about court procedures; (2) victim participation and input through all stages of judicial proceedings; and (3) better protection of victims and witnesses from harassment, threats, intimidation, and harm.

Efforts to protect the rights of victims began with the passage in most jurisdictions of victims'

rights legislation. These activities soon expanded to include a demand that these protections be given even greater force of law by placing them in state constitutions, and the public has responded with overwhelming support. Nearly two-thirds of the states have passed victims' rights amendments to their state constitutions (National Center for Victims of Crime, 2012). Having achieved considerable success at the state level, victims' rights groups began pressing for an amendment to the U.S. Constitution. Senator Dianne Feinstein (D-California) was a cosponsor of the proposed amendment, arguing that the Constitution protects the rights of criminal defendants but "crime victims, families, survivors have no rights at all, according to the Constitution of the United States" (Cannon, 1996).

The most fundamental concern expressed about the proposed victims' rights amendment is that its guiding assumption—that victims are being excluded from the judicial process—is patently false. Unlike many nations of the world, in the United States all steps of the criminal process (except grand jury proceedings) are mandated to be open to the public. Victims are excluded from trial only when they will be witnesses, and this is happening more often because of another facet of the victims' rights movement—victim impact statements.

Proposals to amend the U.S. Constitution are frequently offered but rarely adopted. This appears to be the fate of the proposed Victim's Rights Amendment.

Victim Impact Statements

Victim impact statements consist of written or oral information about how the crime impacted the victim and the victim's family. These emotion-filled statements are usually offered in an attempt to sway the sentencing court to impose a severe sentence on the convicted offender, although pleas for leniency do occur from time to time. Today, every state permits victim impact statements as part of the sentencing process (see Chapter 14).

Almost invariably, neither the defendant nor the defense counsel interrupt or make any after-the-fact attempt to rebut the statement. Such silence, however, should not be interpreted as acquiescence. Rather, the rules of procedure in some states prohibit the defense from challenging victim impact statements on cross-examination or otherwise. But even in the handful of states that statutorily grant an opportunity to cross-examine victim impact testimony, the defense runs the risk of alienating those in court since any "attempt by defense counsel to obstruct [a victim impact statement] will surely be met with disapproval, if not disgust, and possibly retaliation by the sentencing authority, particularly where a jury determines the sentence" (Stevens, 2000, p. 17).

Constitutionality of Victim Impact Evidence

In the late 1980s, the U.S. Supreme Court decided two cases, *Booth v. Maryland* (1987) and *South Carolina v. Gathers* (1989), in which the Court held that victim impact statements were unconstitutional in capital cases because they can create an unacceptable risk that a jury may impose the death penalty in an arbitrary and capricious manner. But this approach was short-lived.

In *Payne v. Tennessee* (1991), Pervis Tyrone Payne was convicted of two counts of first-degree murder. The trial proceeded to the penalty phase of a capital murder prosecution (see Chapter 14). The defense called four witnesses, who testified that Payne was a very caring person but had such a low score on an IQ test that he was mentally handicapped. The prosecutor countered by calling the victim's grandmother to the stand, who testified that three-year-old Nicholas (the lone survivor) kept asking why his mother didn't come home, and he cried for his sister. During closing arguments, the prosecutor made maximum use of this emotional testimony, imploring the jury to make sure that Nicholas would know later in life that justice had been done in his mother's brutal slaying. The Memphis, Tennessee, jury imposed the death penalty.

The grandmother's testimony was inadmissible by *Booth v. Maryland* (1987) and *South Carolina v. Gathers* (1989). But the membership of the Supreme Court changed with the addition of two conservatives appointed by Republican presidents. The Court in *Payne* overruled *Booth* and *Gathers* and

held that the Eighth Amendment was not a per se bar to victim impact evidence during sentencing, even in death penalty cases. Still, under some circumstances, *Payne* can serve as the basis for disallowing, on due process grounds, inflammatory and highly prejudicial victim impact evidence. For example, in *Salazar v. State* (2002), the Texas Court of Criminal Appeals invalidated the use of a 17-minute video that displayed 140 photos of the deceased victim, arranged chronologically from infancy through adulthood. The court concluded that the montage, set to the music of Enya and Celine Dion's "My Heart Will Go On," was unfairly prejudicial.

Victim Impact Evidence and Restorative Justice

The National Victim Center and other victims' groups support giving victims a voice in the process, rather than reducing them to a mere statistic. Proponents contend that, consistent with restorative justice principles (see Chapter 14), by allowing victims to vent their feelings, they are better able to get on with their lives. But critics fear that the venting of frustrations can demean the judicial process. Consider, for example, that as a certain death sentence was about to be pronounced against Richard Allen Davis for sexually molesting and then killing Polly Klaas (discussed in Chapter 14), Davis told the court that Polly's father had sexually molested her, a charge that crime-victim advocates labeled outrageous and sickening.

Incidents like this one lead critics to wonder whether victim impact statements help victims; perhaps the possibility of speaking in court at a much later date unnecessarily prolongs their grieving process. Victims are not encouraged to reach a sense of closure until they testify (or in some cases, until the defendant is actually executed). In spite of these concerns, research supports the conclusion that victim impact statements produce a beneficial effect for those making them and increase their satisfaction with both the outcomes of the case and with the criminal justice system as a whole (Alexander & Lord, 1994; Booth, 2014; Hoyle, 2011).

Effects of Victim Impact Statements on Sentences

In the states that allow for the death penalty, victim impact statements are typically allowed with few procedural restrictions. During the penalty phase of a capital trial, victim impact statements can have a very emotional impact on jurors typically eliciting punitive impulses (Manikis, 2015; Miller, Green, Dietrich, Chamberlain, & Singer, 2008). Paternoster and Deise (2011) reported that potential jurors who were shown a videotape of the penalty phase of a capital trial in which emotional victim impact evidence was presented increased their sympathy and empathy for the victim and the victim's family and their unfavorable perceptions of the offender. In turn, these emotions and perceptions increased the jurors' willingness to impose a sentence of death. In noncapital cases, research suggests that victim impact evidence has not dramatically increased defendants' sentences (Davis & Smith, 1994; Erez & Rogers, 1999). In fact, victim impact evidence appears to have little effect on overall sentence severity (Villmoare & Neto, 1987), although it can affect judicial imposition of special conductions of probation, "causing the judge to order anger-management treatment, drug and alcohol supervision, domestic violence counseling, or such" (Propen & Schuster, 2008, p. 315). Findings on the impact of victim impact statements on parole hearing outcomes is also mixed (Caplan, 2010; Hargovan, 2015; Morgan & Smith, 2005).

Aiding or Manipulating Victims?

After a long period of neglect, aiding victims has become good politics. These efforts are backed by a national movement for the rights of crime victims.

The Victims' Rights Movement

Organizing crime victims is a difficult task. Aside from having been harmed by criminals, victims as a group have very little in common (Karmen, 2016).

Despite these obstacles, victim advocacy groups have become a powerful political voice.

The emergence of the victims' rights movement reflects several parallel trends. One is the law-and-order rhetoric of the 1960s, which emphasized the harm criminals do to victims. Another is the women's rights movement, which came to take a special interest in crimes involving women. A key feature of the feminist movement is its emphasis on grassroots activism. Thus, a logical extension of the women's movement was to form local programs to aid women who had been victims of rape or spousal abuse (Weed, 1995).

The victims' rights movement involves people striking back to turn tragedy into action and rage into reform (Office for Victims of Crime, 1998). The best known of these organizations is Mothers Against Drunk Driving (MADD). Founded by Candy Lightner, whose daughter was killed by a drunk driver, MADD has become the nation's largest victim advocacy group (see Chapter 4). A search of the Internet reveals numerous other groups. Many of these groups are local, emphasizing various types of victims ranging from those harmed by drunk drivers to battered women. These grassroots operations function loosely under the national umbrella organization, the National Organization of Victim Assistance, which provides a larger focus for their specialized concerns.

Today, the victims' rights movement involves a loose coalition of local, state, and national organizations with wide-ranging interests. Their activities constitute a full-blown social movement that seeks to place the interests of crime victims into the mainstream of American political discourse. Although diverse in origins, the victims' rights movement shares a common ideology, seeking to demonstrate the triumph of good over evil. Thus, the movement resonates with a moral view of crime held by many average citizens (Weed, 1995).

Differing Goals

The victims' rights movement reflects the mutual interests of a strange set of political bedfellows, which explains why, beneath the rhetoric about aiding victims of crimes, important disagreements over goals and priorities exist (Viano, 1987). A study of a victims' rights organization in Alabama found that the membership was disproportionately White and female, with African-Americans excluded from potential membership. These results suggest that the victims' rights movement is becoming polarized, with some quite concerned about secondary victimization and others more focused on punishment of defendants (Smith & Huff, 1992). Similarly, a study in the state of Washington found that groups supporting the Community Protection Act reflected a punitive orientation toward defendants more than an effort to aid victims of sexual assault (Scheingold, Olson, & Pershing, 1994). These differing goals explain why victims' rights laws and constitutional amendments are so contradictory.

Do Victims Benefit?

Everyone agrees that victims and witnesses should be treated better during the court process. But political rhetoric should not be allowed to obscure some important issues. Although enthusiasm for helping victims is clearly growing, the willingness to pay for the necessary services is not always present. Overall, legislators and other government officials find voting for victim-oriented legislation politically advantageous, but when it comes to voting money for another "welfare program," they are much more hesitant.

Moreover, it is unclear how much aid victims and witnesses receive from these programs. Once enacted, programs do not always work as intended. Elias (1993) concluded that victim compensation laws were exercises in symbolic politics. Few claimants ever received compensation; the laws provided "political placebos," with few tangible benefits for victims (see also Erez & Roberts, 2007).

Victim/witness assistance programs appear to be important first steps in providing better services to citizens who find themselves thrust into the criminal court process, but not all agree that these programs actually benefit the victim. Sociologist William McDonald (1976, p. 35) charged that "some projects that are billed as 'assisting victims' are more accurately described as assisting the criminal justice system and extending government

control over victims. Whether the victims so controlled would regard the project as 'assisting' them is problematic." Some victims do not wish to become involved.

An important question is, at whose expense should victims be compensated? Some versions emphasize protecting the rights of victims by denying privileges and benefits to suspects, defendants, and prisoners. This type of victim's bill of rights is the most recent example of the conflict between the due process model and the crime control model (highlighted in Chapter 1). Other versions emphasize improving the welfare of victims at the expense of the privileges and options enjoyed by members of the courtroom work group (Karmen, 2016).

Overall, however, when victims have the opportunity to interact meaningfully with justice system actors, their satisfaction with the criminal justice system and its process increases. Indeed, feeling included in the process is as important to victim satisfaction as is the final outcome of a case (Regehr, Alaggia, Lambert, & Saini, 2008). Even the placement of the victim in court appears to matter. Englebrecht (2012) reported that victims who entered the "active space" of a courtroom (where they were able to face all participants in the process, including the defendant) expressed higher levels of satisfaction with their in-court participation than those who remained in the public spaces of a courtroom.

Conclusion

The future for both Brock Turner and his victim is difficult to predict. And, as of the writing of this book, Pervis Payne's future also remains in question. Payne is still on Tennessee's death row as his lawyers attempt to have his sentenced overturned on the basis that his intellectual disability should bar his execution (see Chapter 14). Predicting Nicholas's future is even more difficult. At his young age, his mind might be able to block out the memories of seeing his mother and younger sister murdered in his presence. But the chance of flashbacks and antisocial behavior is likely. It is possible that as he grows up, Nicholas will himself shift from victim to defendant. As we learned in this chapter, many defendants arrested for violent crimes were themselves the victims of violent acts as children.

The perhaps troubling future of Nicholas highlights some of the contradictions still apparent in how society reacts to victims. Today, blaming victims (particularly rape victims) for causing their own misfortune is more unusual than it was in the past. Instead, numerous groups are ready to step forward and call for helping victims. Yet some of these same voices who are quick to champion the cause of victims are just as quick to denounce what has become popularly called the "abuse excuse."

Victims and witnesses provide the raw material for the court process. The complaints they bring, the credibility of their stories, and their willingness to participate directly affect the courtroom work group's activities. But members of the courtroom work group do not respond uncritically to the demands for their services. They find some stories more believable than others and some claims more worthy than others.

The clientele shapes the criminal court process in a less obvious way. Most defendants are young, male, illiterate, impoverished members of minority groups. Many victims share similar traits. They are also poor, unversed in the ways of the courts, and disproportionately members of minority groups. As a result, in the criminal courts, victims and witnesses often exert little influence over the disposition of the cases in which they are involved.

CHAPTER REVIEW

LO1   1.   List the three characteristics of defendants.

Defendants are overwhelmingly male and mostly economically underclass, and racial minorities are overrepresented.

LO2   2.   Describe how victims and witnesses view the court process.

Victims and witnesses face frustrations in coping with the process (long waits and uncomfortable surroundings), experience travails in testifying, but overall exhibit surprising support for the system.

LO3   3.   Describe how court actors view victims and witnesses.

Members of the courtroom work group become frustrated when victims and witnesses do not cooperate and are intimidated by the defendant or the defendant's friends and family.

LO4   4.   Discuss the prior relationships between defendants and victims and why this is important in domestic violence cases.

In roughly half of the crimes of violence, the defendant and the victim had a prior relationship. Prior relationships are most notable in domestic violence cases, in which the battered woman is not always interested in criminal prosecution.

LO5   5.   Identify three types of programs that are designed to aid victims and witnesses in coping with the criminal justice process.

Victim/witness assistance programs are designed to help better navigate the court process. Victim compensation seeks to provide economic assistance for victims of crime. And the Victims' Bill of Rights seeks to provide rights for victims because defendants already have rights.

LO6   6.   Explain why some view victim programs as aiding victims whereas others view these programs as manipulating victims.

Some see the victims' movement as providing much-needed support for victims of crime. Others view the victims' movement as manipulating victims by providing symbols but no substance.

CRITICAL THINKING QUESTIONS

1. In what ways are victims and defendants similar? In what ways are they different? Is there any difference in the characteristics of victims and defendants when the victim is male as opposed to when the victim is female?

2. Many discussions of crime suggest that smart defendants are able to beat the rap by pleading insanity, slanting their testimony at the urging of the defense counsel, and exploiting legal loopholes such as the exclusionary rule (see Chapter 11). Given the profile of the typical criminal defendant, how realistic are these assumptions of a smart crook?

3. To some, the victims' rights movement is more an exercise in symbolic politics than a substantive program. Thus, some critics argue that many of these programs are really more interested in severe punishment of the defendant than in helping victims adjust socially, economically, or psychologically to their new role as victim. Which dimensions of helping victims reflect the crime control model? Which dimensions reflect the due process model?

4. Would your views on victim impact statements be different if the U.S. Supreme Court had chosen a less emotional case to consider in deciding their constitutionality? Overall, do you think victim impact statements correctly allow victims a voice in the process or just add unnecessary emotionalism?

KEY TERMS

career criminals 258

civil protection order 270

defendant 259

pro se 260

standby/shadow counsel 261

victim impact statements 274

FOR FURTHER READING

Averdijk, Margit, Jean-Louis Van Gelder, Manuel Eisner, and Denis Ribeaud. 2016. "Violence Begets Violence . . . but How? A Decision-Making Perspective on the Victim-Offender Overlap." *Criminology*, 54(2): 282–306.

Belknap, Joanne. 2015. *The Invisible Woman: Gender, Crime and Justice.* 4th ed. Stamford, CT: Cengage.

Bergelson, Vera. 2009. *Victim's Rights and Victims' Wrongs: Comparative Liability in Criminal Law.* Stanford, CA: Stanford University Press.

Cassell, Paul, Nathanael Mitchell, and Bradley Edwards. 2014. "Crime Victims' Rights During Criminal Investigations." *Journal of Criminal Law & Criminology* 104: 59–103.

Karmen, Andrew. 2016. *Crime Victims: An Introduction to Victimology.* 9th ed. Boston, MA: Cengage.

Minot, Diana. 2012. "Silenced Stories: How Victim Impact Evidence in Capital Trials Prevents the Jury from Hearing the Constitutionally Required Story of the Defendant." *Journal of Criminal Law and Criminology* 102: 227–251.

Schuster, Mary, and Amy Propen. 2011. *Victim Advocacy in the Courtroom: Persuasive Practices in Domestic Violence and Child Protection Cases.* Boston: Northeastern University Press.

Slate, Risdon, and W. Wesley Johnson. 2013. *The Criminalization of Mental Illness: Crisis and Opportunity for the Justice System.* 2nd ed. Durham, NC: Carolina Academic Press.

Walker, Samuel, Cassia Spohn, and Miriam DeLone. 2018. *The Color of Justice.* 6th ed. Boston, MA: Cengage.

@xychelsea/twitter/ZUMA Press/Newscom

Pfc. Manning was arrested in 2010 after allegedly having transferred hundreds of thousands of classified documents to WikiLeaks. Manning was accused of creating the largest breach of classified information in U.S. history. Notably, a series of violent outbursts and other behaviors caused members in Manning's unit to suspect that Manning was in serious mental distress, but nothing was done about it. Manning spent 10 months in solitary confinement even though there is no allegation that any of the material Manning is alleged to have revealed caused any harm other than embarrassment to the United States. In the last days of his presidency, Barrack Obama commuted Manning's 35-year prison sentence to six years.

Chapter Outline

After a warrantless arrest, all people have a right to have a "prompt hearing" at which a neutral judicial officer reviews the arrest to determine whether it was supported by probable cause. In Riverside County, California, arrestees were routinely taken before a judge within two days, exclusive of Saturdays, Sundays, or holidays. Thus, many of those arrested on a Friday, like Donald Lee McLaughlin, had to wait in jail at least three days before a judge was available to conduct a probable cause hearing. On holiday weekends, the wait could be even longer—four, five, or even six days. The public defender for the County argued that the U.S. Constitution requires a more prompt hearing. Not practical, countered the district attorney, stressing the realities of the contemporary criminal justice system in large urban areas—thousands of arrests, overcrowded jails, and lack of availability of judges, to say nothing of defense attorneys and prosecutors. It is in this context that the U.S. Supreme Court had to decide how prompt a "prompt hearing" needs to be. It settled on 48 hours, including weekends.

County of Riverside v. McLaughlin (1991) highlights the importance of the early stages of a felony prosecution. At first glance, the numerous preliminary stages of a prosecution seem to be of only procedural interest, with cases moving automatically from arrest to charging through preliminary hearing and grand jury before arriving at the major trial court. But a closer look indicates that at numerous stages during these early proceedings, prosecutors, judges, police officers, and victims have the option of advancing a case to the next step, seeking an alternative disposition, or dropping the case altogether. These screening decisions result in significant case attrition, with half of all felony arrests being dropped at some point after arrest and before arraignment.

This chapter examines the early stages of a criminal case, focusing on when and why case attrition occurs. The discussion begins with crimes and the arrests that sometimes follow. Our attention then shifts to events in the courthouse, including initial appearance, charging, bail, preliminary hearing, grand jury, and (for some cases) arraignment in the trial court of general jurisdiction.

Crime

Beginning in the early 1960s, the United States experienced a dramatic increase in crime. For almost two decades, the number of crimes known to the police increased much faster than the growth in population. In the early 1980s, the crime rate reached a plateau, and since the early 1990s, it has decreased considerably. The peaks and valleys of the official crime figures, however, are largely irrelevant to the general public. Rather, the public continues to perceive (no matter what the official figures say) that crime is on the increase. These fears are reinforced by extensive media coverage, particularly of violent crime.

UCR

There are two official measures of crime in the United States. The most publicized and widely used measure of crime comes from the Federal Bureau of Investigation's (FBI) **Uniform Crime Reporting (UCR)** program. Each year, policing agencies voluntarily report summary-based measures of crime within their jurisdictions to the FBI, such as the number of murders in a year. The FBI, in turn, compiles those data and disseminates statistics in a number of publications, the most comprehensive of which is their annual publication *Crime in the United States.* More than 18,000 campus, local, tribal, county, and state law enforcement agencies—representing roughly 96 percent of the U.S. population—are active in the UCR program today.

The UCR divides criminal offenses into two categories: Type I and Type II Offenses. As summarized in Table 10.1, there are eight serious **Type I offenses** that are referred to as **index crimes**; Type II offenses are less serious but more numerous. Still, Type I offenses are the crimes that produce headlines about rising crime rates. Contrary to public perceptions, most felony crimes are for nonviolent offenses involving burglary and larceny. In fact, property crimes outnumber violent offenses by a ratio of 8 to 1. The UCR program also gathers statistics on index offenses that are cleared by the police via arrest, providing a rough measure of police performance in solving crimes.

NIBRS

By the late 1970s, law enforcement recognized that more detailed crime data would be beneficial to crime prevention and analysis. After a pilot study in South Carolina, the FBI began to gather more detailed information for crimes reported to the police in 1988 called the **National Incident-Based Reporting System (NIBRS)**. NIBRS is incident-based, rather than summary-based. It tracks all of the same offenses covered in the traditional UCR Type I and Type II categories, plus a few others, such as criminal trespass and passing bad checks. A wealth of data is gathered about each incident, including

- the location of the crime
- whether the crime was completed or attempted (the traditional UCR did not differentiate between attempts and completed crimes)
- the type of weapon used (if any)
- the type and value of properly damaged or stolen
- the personal characteristics of both the offender and the victim (e.g., age, sex, race/ethnicity, marital status, and socioeconomic status)

TABLE 10.1 A Comparison of Type I and Type II UCR Offenses

	Part I: Index Crimes	Part II: Other Crimes
Violent crimes	• Murder and nonnegligent manslaughter • Forcible rape • Robbery • Aggravated assault	• Simple assault
Property crimes	• Burglary • Larceny/theft • Motor vehicle theft • Arson	• Embezzlement • Forgery and counterfeiting • Fraud • Stolen property offenses • Vandalism
Other crimes	None	• Disorderly conduct • Driving under the influence • Drug offenses • Drunkenness • Gambling • Liquor law offenses • Loitering • Prostitution • Offenses against the family (e.g., child neglect) • Sex offenses (other than forcible rape) • Vagrancy • Weapons offenses
Status offenses by juveniles	None	• Curfew and loitering offenses • Runaways

Another significant difference concerns the so-called **hierarchy rule**. If two or more crimes were committed, the traditional UCR reported the most serious of the crimes. For example, if during the commission of an armed bank robbery, the offender shoots a security guard in the foot then steals a car to escape from the bank, the UCR would count this as a robbery only since robbery is a more serious crime than aggravated assault and motor vehicle theft. NIBRS, on the other hand, would count all three crimes and gather data concerning each of the three distinct offenses.

Problems with Crime Measurement

A major weakness of both the UCR and NIBRS is that they are based only on crimes known to the police. But only a fraction of the number of crimes committed are actually reported to the police. Of the personal and household offenses measured in the National Crime Victimization Survey's yearly sample of households, only half of the violent crimes and almost two-thirds of the property crimes were not reported to the police (Langton, Berzofsky, Krebs, & Smiley-McDonald, 2012; Truman & Morgan, 2016). What this means is that the official FBI crime statistics underestimate the total amount of crime in the United States.

According to the Bureau of Justice Statistics (Langton, Berzofsky, Krebs, & Smiley-McDonald, 2012), the leading reasons why people do not report their victimization to the police include the following:

- They deal with the issue in another way, such as reporting the incident to a guard, manager, parent, school official (a prevalent response to simple assaults). Notably, 76 percent of violent victimizations that occur in schools are never reported to the police.
- They feel the incident was not important enough to report (especially prevalent for thefts).
- They feel that the police would not or could not help them (also a popular reason for not reporting a variety of thefts).
- They fear reprisal from the offender (a common response from victims of sexual assault).
- They do not want to get the offender in trouble with the law (frequently cited as the reason for not reporting intimate-partner violence or violence perpetrated by a friend or relative).

Arrest

The term *arrest* is difficult to define because it is used in different ways. In its narrow sense (sometimes called a "formal or technical arrest"), **arrest** is defined as the taking of a person into custody for the commission of an offense as the prelude to prosecuting him or her for that offense. In its broader sense, *arrest* means any seizure of a person significant enough that it becomes the functional equivalent of a formal arrest in that the person seized would reasonably not feel free to terminate the encounter (*United States v. Drayton*, 2002).

Collectively, all of the crimes cleared by police each year result in approximately 10.8 million arrests for nontraffic offenses, about 1.97 million of which are for UCR index crimes (see Figure 10.1). Other than a handful of criminal prosecutions that

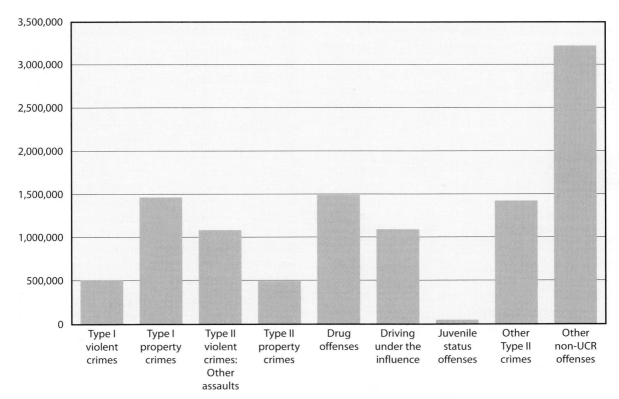

FIGURE 10.1 Criminal Arrests

Source: Federal Bureau of Investigation. 2016. *Crime in the United States—2015* (Table 29: Estimated Number of Arrests). Washington, DC: Government Printing Office.

are instituted as a result of a grand jury investigation that results in an indictment, these arrests are the overwhelming source of work for the criminal courts, since an arrest triggers the first of the steps summarized in the "Law in Action vs. Law on the Books" box on page 287.

Of the crimes known to police, the percentage that is cleared by an arrest varies greatly by the type of offense, as illustrated in Table 10.2.

Quality of Arrests

The police have a lot to do with what happens in court after arrest. The strength of the evidence police provide to prosecutors is one of the most important factors influencing whether prosecutors file criminal charges (Holleran, Beichner, & Spohn, 2009; O'Neil, Tellis, & Spohn, 2015). Thus, when police are able to secure tangible evidence and cooperative witnesses for the prosecution (while honoring suspects' constitutional rights), the prosecutor is not only more likely to file charges but is also more likely to win a conviction (Albonetti, 1987; Forst, Lucianovic, & Cox, 1977; Worrall, Ross, & McCord, 2006). Conversely, when police conduct incomplete investigations (missing important evidence or witnesses) or improperly seize, mark, or store the items they do gather, prosecutors find themselves without sufficient evidence to prosecute a case successfully, a situation that often puts stress on the relationship between police and prosecutors (Dantzker, 2005; Pattavina, Morabito, & Williams, 2015). Of course, the quality of law enforcement investigations varies greatly. Not only do individual police officers differ in particular investigatory skills, but also some police departments, as units, function better than others when conducting investigations because of differences in management, training, resources, procedures, and analytical processes (Keel, Jarvis, & Muirhead, 2009; Jarvis, Mancik, & Regoeczi, 2016).

Initial Appearance

In *Gerstein v. Pugh* (1975), the U.S. Supreme Court held that although a police officer's "on-the-scene assessment of probable cause provides legal justification for arresting a person suspected of crime, and for a brief period of detention to take the administrative steps incident to arrest[,] . . . the Fourth Amendment requires a judicial determination of probable cause as a prerequisite to extended restraint of liberty following arrest" (pp. 113–114). Thus, after a person has been arrested, a law enforcement officer must take the arrested person before a magistrate for an **initial appearance** (sometimes called a *Gerstein* hearing after the case). Statutes in different jurisdictions require that this be done promptly, using terms such as "immediately," "without unnecessary delay," "forthwith," or other similar statutory language. These statutes confer a substantial right on the arrestee and create a corresponding duty on law enforcement officers.

The reasons for requiring an initial appearance without unnecessary delay are:

- To verify that the person arrested is the person named in the complaint.

- To advise arrested persons of the charges, so that they may begin to prepare a defense.

- To advise arrested persons of their rights, such as the right to counsel, the right to remain silent, and the right to either a preliminary hearing or a grand jury indictment.

TABLE 10.2	Clearance Rates for UCR Type I Offenses		
Violent Crime Clearance Rates		**Property Crime Clearance Rates**	
Murder and nonnegligent manslaughter	61.5%	Burglary	12.9%
Forcible rape	37.8%	Larceny/theft	21.9%
Robbery	29.3%	Motor vehicle theft	13.1%
Aggravated assault	54.0%	Arson	24.9%
Overall Clearance Rate for Type I violent crimes	46.0%	Overall Clearance Rate for Type I property crimes	19.4%

Source: Federal Bureau of Investigation. 2016. *Crime in the United States—2015* (Table 25: Percent Offense Cleared by Arrest or Exceptional Means). Washington, DC: Government Printing Office.

LAW IN ACTION VS. LAW ON THE BOOKS

Steps in Pretrial Criminal Procedures

	Law on the Books	Law in Action
Crime	Any violation of the criminal law.	Property crimes outnumber violent crimes by an 8-to-1 ratio.
Arrest	The physical taking into custody of a suspected offender.	Each year, police make more than 10.8 million arrests for nontraffic offenses, about 1.97 million of which are for UCR index crimes.
Initial appearance	The accused is told of the charges and advised of his or her rights. A neutral judicial officer reviews the arrest to make sure it was supported by probable cause. Preliminary bail may be set. Date for the preliminary hearing is set, if applicable.	Occurs in lower courts. Many misdemeanor defendants plead guilty. May be combined with other judicial proceedings, such as a preliminary hearing, formal bail hearing, or an arraignment, depending on the jurisdiction.
Charging	Formal criminal charges are brought against the defendant, stating which criminal law was violated. *Information:* Formal accusation of a crime made by the prosecutor. *Complaint:* Formal accusation of a crime supported by oath or affirmation of the victim. *Arrest warrant:* An official document, signed by a judge, accusing an individual of a crime and authorizing law enforcement personnel to take the person into custody. Prosecutor is supposed to prosecute all known criminal conduct. Prosecutor controls charging decision.	From arrest to arraignment, half of felony arrests are terminated, downgraded, or diverted in some manner. Complaints very rarely used in felony prosecutions. Prosecutor exercises discretion in deciding which charges should be filed. Some prosecutors allow police input into the charging decision.
Bail	No general right to bail under the Eighth Amendment, but commonly guaranteed as a statutory right.	The average daily jail population is approximately 721,300.
Preliminary hearing	A pretrial hearing to determine whether probable cause exists to hold the accused for further proceedings. Typically used only in jurisdictions that do not require grand juries to make a probable cause determination.	In many jurisdictions, the preliminary hearing is brief, with a strong probability that the case will proceed.
Grand jury	Required for felony prosecutions in 19 states and the federal courts. Grand juries have extensive powers, not possessed by law enforcement, to investigate crimes. *Indictment:* Formal accusation of a crime, made against a person by a grand jury, upon the request of the prosecutor. *Subpoena:* Court order requiring a person to appear before the grand jury and/or produce documents.	Typically, not a major decision maker. Prosecutor dominates grand jury proceedings, deciding which cases will be presented and which charges filed. The investigatory powers of the grand jury are most likely to be used in cases involving major drug rings, governmental corruption, and significant white-collar crime.
Arraignment	Stage of the criminal process in which a defendant is formally informed of the charges pending and must enter a plea.	A significant milestone because it indicates that the evidence against the defendant is sufficient to warrant impaneling a jury for trial.

- To protect arrested persons from being abandoned in jail and forgotten by, or otherwise cut off from contact with, people who can help them.

- To prevent secret and extended interrogation of arrested persons by law enforcement officers.

- To give arrested persons an early opportunity to secure release on bail while awaiting the final outcome of the proceedings. If the person has been bailed earlier, the magistrate simply reviews that bail. Release on personal recognizance may also be granted at the initial appearance.

- To give arrested persons an opportunity to speedily conclude proceedings on charges of minor offenses by pleading guilty to the charges, paying fines, and carrying on with their lives.

- To obtain a prompt, neutral "judicial determination of probable cause as a prerequisite to extended restraint of liberty following arrest." (Ferdico, Fradella, & Totten, 2016, p. 50, quoting *Gerstein v. Pugh*, 1975, p. 114)

As a general rule, the Supreme Court expects an initial appearance to occur within 48 hours of a warrantless arrest, inclusive of weekends (*County of Riverside v. McLaughlin*, 1991). Note that in indictment jurisdictions, if a grand jury has already returned an indictment, an initial appearance is not mandated under *Gerstein v. Pugh* (1975), although some states require an initial appearance for all arrests. Not all states, however, provide for a judicial determination of probable cause at the initial appearance before a magistrate. Some states make a probable cause determination at bail hearings while other states use preliminary hearings for this purpose. But even in jurisdictions that combine an initial appearance with other pretrial proceedings, judicial probable cause determinations must generally occur within 48 hours of a warrantless arrest (see "Case Close-Up").

Most misdemeanor defendants enter a plea of guilty at their initial appearance and are sentenced immediately (see Chapter 14). In a fascinating study, Professors Alisa Smith and Sean Maddan (2011) examined a range of operations of the lower courts in the state of Florida. They found that,

- Most initial appearances (82 percent) lasted approximately three minutes, and 91 percent were completed within five minutes.

- Two-thirds of defendants appeared without counsel. Roughly one-quarter of defendants were never told of their right to counsel. Of those who were told of this right, half waived the right to counsel.

- Approximately 70 percent of misdemeanor defendants pled guilty at this early stage of criminal proceedings.

For those arrested on a felony, however, a plea is not possible because the initial appearance occurs in a trial court of limited jurisdiction, which has no authority to accept a plea. Thus, the initial appearance is typically a brief affair, as little is known about the crime or the alleged criminal. At times, suspects insist on telling their side of the story, but the judge typically cautions that anything said can be used against the defendant. Lawyers provide the same advice.

Charging

The criminal court process begins with the filing of a formal written accusation alleging that a specified person or persons committed a specific offense or offenses. The **charging document** includes a brief description of the date and location of the offense. All the essential elements (*corpus delicti*) of the crime must be specified. These accusations satisfy the Sixth Amendment provision that a defendant be given information with which to prepare a defense. Applicable state and federal laws govern technical wording, procedures for making minor amendments, and similar matters.

The four types of charging documents are complaint, information, arrest warrant, and indictment (which will be discussed later). Which one is used depends on the severity of the offense, applicable state law, and local customs.

A **complaint** must be supported by oath or affirmation of either the victim or the arresting officer. It is most commonly used in prosecuting misdemeanor offenses or city ordinance violations. An **information** is virtually identical in form to the complaint, except that it is signed by the prosecutor. It is required in felony prosecutions in most states that do not use the grand jury. In grand jury states, an information

Country of Riverside v. McLaughlin and a Prompt
Hearing Before a Magistrate

Beyond the bare fact that he was arrested in Riverside County, California, little is known about Donald Lee McLaughlin. Who he was, why he was arrested, and whatever happened to his case quickly became irrelevant. For whatever reason, the public defender's office decided that the facts of his case made him an ideal candidate to be used as a plaintiff in a suit filed in federal court. The office was prepared to challenge countywide practices; a plaintiff was needed and, at the last minute, McLaughlin's name was inserted. Thus, McLaughlin's name went first in a class action lawsuit filed on behalf of McLaughlin and all other individuals in the same situation.

McLaughlin v. County of Riverside raised the difficult question of how prompt is prompt. California law mandated a probable cause hearing for all those arrested without a warrant within 48 hours of arrest, weekends and holidays excluded. Thus, an individual arrested late in the week might in some cases be held for as long as five days before appearing before a neutral judicial official; over the Thanksgiving holiday a seven-day delay was possible. The U.S. district court agreed with part of McLaughlin's plight and ordered a probable cause hearing within 36 hours of arrest. Having lost in the trial court, the county appealed (hence the names changed place, with the county now listed as the moving party). The Ninth Circuit affirmed the district court's decision, and the county appealed to the U.S. Supreme Court, which granted certiorari.

Although *County of Riverside v. McLaughlin* appears to be a minor quibble over a few hours, the underlying issues are much more fundamental, centering on where to strike the balance between an individual's right to liberty and society's need for effective law enforcement. The Supreme Court has allowed police officers to make arrests, based on their own assessment of probable cause, without first obtaining a warrant. To counterbalance this privilege, the Court established that an individual arrested without a warrant is entitled to a prompt judicial determination of probable cause afterward. In *Gerstein v. Pugh*, they wrestled with this issue and held that the defendant was entitled to a timely determination. The Court ruled that the 30-day wait in Florida was too long, but failed to be much more specific. As a result, *Gerstein* "created a nationwide divergence in postarrest and pretrial procedures and subjected some individuals to what numerous courts and commentators believed to be unjustifiably prolonged restraints of liberty following their arrests" (Perkins & Jamieson, 1995, p. 535).

Justice Sandra Day O'Connor wrote the opinion of the Court, evidencing her ability to strike a compromise. The earlier decision in *Gerstein*, she wrote, provided flexibility to law enforcement, but not a blank check. She recognized that the standard of "prompt" has proved to be vague and therefore has not provided sufficient guidance. In the future, *prompt* shall be defined in most circumstances as 48 hours—a time period she labeled as a "practical compromise between the rights of individuals and the realities of law enforcement." A 24-hour rule would compel local governments across the nation to speed up their criminal justice mechanisms substantially, presumably by allotting local tax dollars to hire additional police officers and magistrates. What is perhaps most striking is how forthright the opinion is in recognizing that law on the books must take into account law in action.

What is most interesting about the four dissenters is their ideological mix. The three moderates agreed with the lower courts that the 36-hour standard was best. But Justice Antonin Scalia, one of the Court's most conservative members, would have fixed the time at 24 hours, a standard he says existed in the common law from the early 1800s.

is used for initiating felony charges pending grand jury action. An **arrest warrant** is issued by a judicial officer—usually a lower-court judge. On rare occasions, the warrant is issued prior to arrest, but for most street crimes, the police arrest the suspect and then apply for an arrest warrant. Some states require that the prosecutor approve the request in writing before an arrest warrant can be issued.

Law on the Books: Prosecutorial Control

Through the charging decision, the prosecutor controls the doors to the courthouse. He or she can decide whether charges should be filed and what the proper charge should be. Although the law demands prosecution for "all known criminal

Are White-Collar Criminals Underprosecuted?

Normally, Martha Stewart was at ease before television cameras as she demonstrated the latest in decorating and entertainment ideas, but she was noticeably harried as cameras caught her quick entry into the New York federal courthouse. Martha Stewart became the most recognizable person to be caught up in recent high-profile white-collar crime prosecutions. But the scope of her crime (relatively small) was soon eclipsed by Bernard Madoff, who defrauded investors (some of whom were personal friends) of $50 billion, in the largest Ponzi scheme in American history. Ponzi schemes are named after Charles Ponzi, who in 1919 and 1920 cheated investors out of $10 million. A Ponzi scheme, or pyramid scheme, is a scam in which people are persuaded to invest in a fraudulent operation that promises unusually high returns. The early investors are paid their returns out of money put in by later investors (Lavoie, 2008).

Madoff was ultimately sentenced to 150 years in prison for his crimes. Other prominent persons who have been prosecuted for white-collar crimes include the following:

- Raj Rajartnam, former hedge fund manager and billionaire founder of Galleon Group, was convicted of insider trading and sentenced to 11 years in prison, and fined over $150 million in criminal and civil penalties. The sentence is the longest ever handed out in an insider trading conviction.

- John Rigas and his son Timothy were convicted of fraud and sentenced to 10 years in prison for hiding $2.3 billion in liabilities, reporting inflated earnings, and using millions of corporate dollars for personal use while running Adelphia Communications. Notably, Rigas's other son, Michael, pled guilty to the charges and received a much lighter sentence: 10 months of home arrest and 2 years of probation.

- Sam Waksal, founder of ImClone, was sentenced to 7 years in prison for selling stock in his company the day before a negative ruling from the Food and Drug Administration.

- Ken Lay and Jeffrey Skilling, top executives of Enron, were found guilty of numerous charges of cooking the books, leading to the nation's biggest corporate collapse. (Lay died shortly thereafter, thereby making it more difficult for former employees to pursue restitution in civil court.) Skilling was sentenced to a $45 million fine and 24 years in prison. He appealed his conviction to the U.S. Supreme Court, arguing that he did not receive a fair trial in Enron's home base of Houston, Texas—an argument the high Court rejected.

- Bernie Ebbers, the former top executive at Worldcom, was found guilty of criminal activity after that company was forced into bankruptcy because of approximately $11 billion in fraudulent accounting practices. Ebbers was sentenced to 25 years in prison for his crimes.

- Jack Abramoff, a political lobbyist, was convicted of defrauding SunCruz Casinos of millions of dollars as well as bribing government officials. He was sentenced to six years in prison and ordered to pay $25 million in restitution.

- L. Dennis Kozlowski and Mark H. Swartz, chief executive and chief financial officer of Tyco International, respectively, were each convicted on multiple counts of grand larceny, conspiracy, securities fraud, and falsifying business records. Each was sentenced to $8\frac{1}{3}$–25 years in prison.

- Robert Allen Stanford was the former chairman and CEO of Stanford Financial Group. He was arrested for multiple counts of fraud and charges that his investment company was a Ponzi scheme. He was sentenced to 110 years in prison and ordered to forfeit $5.9 billion.

- Dr. Farid Fata, a hematologists-oncologist, was convicted of health care fraud whereby he submitted fraudulent claims to Medicare and administered unnecessary injections to 553 patients. He was sentenced to serve 45 years in prison.

The term *white-collar* is used because it suggests crimes committed by persons of higher economic status, as opposed to the typical street crimes most often associated with the social underclass. As such, the term encompasses a broad range of matters, ranging from crimes against consumers and the environment to securities fraud and governmental corruption (Rosoff, Pontell, & Tillman, 2014). The public, though, remains relatively indifferent to white-collar crimes. One reason is that white-collar crimes lack the drama associated with murders and bank robberies. Another is that the defendants are respectable—they don't look like criminals (whatever that might mean). In the words of David Friedrichs (2009), they are "trusted criminals." Society's contradictory assessments of white-collar criminals are most noticeable when it comes to sentencing: although the crime has negatively affected some individuals, the offenders do not present a physical threat to society. To some, draconian sentences (often amounting to effective life imprisonment) are excessive (Henning, 2015; Podgor, 2007).

Allegations that white-collar crimes are underprosecuted, however, require close scrutiny. After all, a number of major prosecutions and convictions have occurred over the years. In addition, since the Enron scandal, public attention to white-collar crimes has clearly increased, and Congress passed the Sarbanes-Oxley Act, which, among other things, sharply increased penalties for various forms of fraud ("Go Directly to Jail," 2009). At the federal level, the Justice Department and other federal regulatory agencies such as the Securities and Exchange Commission have large staffs devoted to these matters. At the local level, though, district attorneys' offices have only small staff devoted to fraud and similar crimes because the office is overwhelmed by the sheer volume of day-to-day street crimes like murder, robbery, and drug offenses. Moreover, convincing a jury to return a guilty verdict in a white-collar crime presents a difficult task to prosecutors. For one, jurors often find it difficult to follow the detailed testimony from accountants. For another, a "smoking gun" seldom points convincingly to guilty intent (Glater & Belson, 2005). But juries are increasingly returning guilty verdicts, particularly in cases like Tyco, where jurors said they did not find the defendants' stories on the witness stand to be credible (Maremont & Bray, 2005). Nor are juries any longer impressed with the "dummy defense," whereby chief executives testify that they were paid millions every year, but knew nothing about the details of their company (Norris, 2005).

On the other hand, the Transactional Records Access Clearinghouse (TRAC) at Syracuse University found that in 2011, the annual total of financial fraud prosecutions was down nearly 29 percent in 5 years and nearly 58 percent from a decade earlier even though financial institution fraud played a major role in the 2008 economic meltdown that paralyzed the U.S. economy. By 2016, white-collar crime prosecutions were down another 16.7 percent compared with 2011 (TRAC, 2016).

For several years, it appeared that corporate or banking executives would face any criminal charges for their roles in creating deceptive derivative contracts that inflated the real-estate bubble. And although only one top Wall Street banker, Kareem Serageldin, a senior trader at Credit Suisse, went prison for the financial crisis (Eisinger, 2014), *Time Magazine* reported that a number of significant criminal and civil actions occurred during the Obama administration, most stemming from banks either having sold shoddy mortgages, having bundled toxic loans for sale to unknowing investors, or for engaging in illegal foreclosure practices (Rayman, 2014). By 2014, these settlements included:

- $60 billion from Bank of America
- $13 billion from JP Morgan Chase
- $25 billion from Wells Fargo
- $7 billion from Citigroup

It took until 2016 before Goldman Sachs admitted it defrauded investors in its scheme to sell mortgage-backed securities supported by questionable loans. The investment bank settled its claims with the U.S. Department of Justice for $5.1 billion (Shen, 2016).

In addition to these large settlements, Credit Suisse (a French bank) plead guilty to federal criminal charges of helping clients avoid federal tax payments (Luckerson, 2014). And in April 2016, the special inspector general for the Troubled Assets Relief Program (TARP) reported to Congress that 35 bankers had been sentenced to prison for fraud in the use of those "bailout" funds (Isidore, 2016).

What do you think? Are white-collar crimes underprosecuted? Would white-collar crimes be better deterred by more prosecutions or more government regulations?

conduct," the courts have traditionally granted prosecutors wide discretion in deciding whether to file charges. For example, no legislative or judicial standards govern which cases merit prosecution and which should be declined. Moreover, if a prosecutor refuses to file charges, no review of this decision is possible; courts have consistently refused to order a prosecutor to proceed with a case.

Law in Action: Police Influence

Although the prosecutor has the legal authority to dominate the charging process, the police often influence the prosecutor's decision. Police and prosecutors regularly discuss cases before charges are filed. Sometimes, the police exercise considerable influence by pressuring prosecutors to overcharge defendants or to file charges even though the evidence is weak (Cole, 1970; Skolnick, 1993). Prosecutors, however, rarely need external pressure to overcharge defendants; they do so because it gives them leverage in the plea-bargaining process (see Chapter 12). But in a large number of cases, prosecutors decline to file charges against those arrested by police. In most jurisdictions, the number of police arrests that result in no criminal charges being filed varies between 20 and 50 percent (Boland, Mahanna, & Sones, 1992; Collins, 2007; Neubauer, 1974a; O'Neill, 2003).

Courts and Controversy: Charging Decisions

Police departments sometimes object when prosecutors set high standards for charging because they see case rejections as an implicit criticism of the arresting officer for making a "wrong" arrest. Prosecutorial screening can have consequences at the polls. In one jurisdiction where a district attorney refused to file charges in a significant number of arrests, the Fraternal Order of the Police forced the incumbent not to seek reelection (Flemming, Nardulli, & Eisenstein, 1992). But police and prosecutors alike can be subject to public scrutiny for how they use their resources. For example, there is much controversy surrounding whether police and prosecutors devote sufficient attention to white-collar crimes.

Bail

Bail is a guarantee. In return for being released from jail, the accused promises to return to court as needed. This promise is guaranteed by posting money or property with the court. If the defendant appears in court when requested, the security is returned. If he or she fails to appear, the security can be forfeited. The practice of allowing defendants to be released from jail pending trial originated centuries ago in England, largely as a convenience to local sheriffs. The colonists brought the concept of bail with them across the Atlantic. It eventually became embedded in the Eighth Amendment, which provides that "excessive bail shall not be required."

Law on the Books: The Monetary Bail System

A careful reading of the Eighth Amendment reveals that the Constitution does not specifically provide that all citizens have a right to bail. Rather, if bail is granted, it must not be "excessive," defined by the Supreme Court in *Stack v. Boyle* (1951), as an amount higher than reasonably calculated to ensure the defendant's presence at trial.

A right to bail, however, was recognized in common law and in statutes as early as 1789 for all those accused of committing noncapital crimes. In 1966, Congress enacted the Bail Reform Act, thereby creating a statutory presumption favoring pretrial release of federal arrestees (although amendments to that law in 1984 made it clear that judges may deny bail to arrestees they consider to pose a serious risk of danger to the community). More importantly, state statutes and state constitutions guarantee a right to bail in many types of cases. In fact, 41 states provide some form of an absolute right to bail (Hegreness, 2013; Lindermayer, 2009).

Bail Procedures

Bail procedures vary by jurisdiction and according to the seriousness of the crime. In the majority of states, those arrested for minor misdemeanors can be released fairly quickly by posting bail at the police station. In most communities, lower-court judges have adopted a fixed bail schedule (also known as an "emergency bail schedule"), which specifies an exact amount for each offense. Although bail schedules provide for quick and easy decisions regarding release after arrest, "they seem to contradict the notion that pretrial release conditions should reflect an assessment of an individual defendant's risk of failure to appear and threat to public safety" (Pepin, 2013, p. 3). Such concerns led appellate courts in Hawaii and Oklahoma to reject bail schedules on due process grounds (*Pelekai v. White*, 1993; *Clark v. Hall*, 2002). In jurisdictions that do not use bail schedules, bail determinations are made on a case-by-case basis in much the same way that bail decisions have historically been made for felonies.

Depending on the jurisdiction, bail may be set during an initial appearance, a preliminary hearing, or a separate bail hearing. Either way, the arrestee appears before a lower-court judge who must determine whether the arrestee qualifies for release on bail and, if so, what those conditions will be. Accordingly, those accused of serious crimes remain in police custody for a number of hours before they have the opportunity to make bail.

Forms of Bail

Once bail has been set, a defendant can gain pretrial release in four basic ways, outlined in Table 10.3. Because many of those arrested lack ready cash, do not own property, or lack the needed social clout, the first three options for making bail listed in Table 10.3 are only abstractions, requiring most to post a bail bond.

Preventive Detention

In the American system of monetary bail, those who are rich enough can often buy their freedom while awaiting trial. But the poor await trial in jail. On any given day, there are nearly 744,600 persons in jail (not prison), approximately 60 percent of whom have not been convicted of any crime (Minton & Zeng, 2015). "About 9 in 10 detained defendants had a bail amount set but were unable to meet the financial conditions required to secure release" (Reaves, 2013, p. 15).

Congress amended the Bail Reform Act in 1984 to make clear that when setting bail, a judge may remand arrestees to **preventive detention**, effectively holding suspects without bail if they are accused of committing a dangerous or violent

TABLE 10.3 Forms of Bail	
Release on recognizance (ROR)	Judges release a defendant from jail without monetary bail if they believe the person is not likely to flee. Such personal bonds are used most often for defendants accused of minor crimes and for those with substantial ties to the community.
Cash bond	The accused must post either the full amount of cash bail with the court or a percentage of it in the form of a cash bond. All of this money will be returned when all court appearances are satisfied. Because it requires a large amount of cash, this form of bail is seldom used. If, for example, bail is set in the amount of $10,000, most persons cannot raise that much money easily and quickly.
Property bond	Most states allow a defendant (or friends or relatives) to use a piece of property as collateral. If the defendant fails to appear in court, the property is forfeited. Property bonds are also rare, because courts generally require that the equity in the property must be double the amount of the bond. Thus, a $10,000 bond requires equity of at least $20,000.
Bail bond	The arrestee hires a bail agent (often called a bail bondsman), who posts the amount required and charges a fee for services rendered, usually 10 percent of the amount of the bond. Thus, a bail agent would normally collect $1,000 for writing a $10,000 bond; none of that money is refundable.

crime and locking them up is deemed necessary for community safety. Specifically, the Bail Reform Act of 1984 allows a suspect to be held in jail without bail for up to 90 days pending trial if the judge finds clear and convincing evidence that:

1. there is a serious risk that the person will flee;

2. the person may obstruct justice or threaten, injure, or intimidate a prospective witness or juror; or

3. the offense is one of violence or one punishable by life imprisonment or death.

The law also creates a presumption against pretrial release for major drug dealers (Berg, 1985). The Supreme Court upheld the Bail Reform Act in *United States v. Salerno* (1987), ruling that Congress enacted preventive detention not as a punishment for dangerous individuals but as a potential solution to the pressing social problem of crimes committed by persons on bail. Approximately 4 to 6 percent of all felony defendants are denied bail and held in pretrial detention, a figure that has remained remarkably consistent since the Bail Reform Act of 1984 and its state law counterparts went into effect (Cohen & Reaves, 2007; Reaves, 2013).

Law in Action: The Context of Bail Setting

Deciding whom to release and whom to detain pending trial poses critical problems for American courts. The realities of the bail system in the United States reflect an attempt to strike a balance between the legally recognized purpose of setting bail to ensure reappearance for trial and the working perception that some defendants should not be allowed out of jail until their trial.

Trial court judges have a great deal of discretion in fixing bail. Statutory law provides few specifics about how much money should be required, and appellate courts have likewise spent little time deciding what criteria should be used. Although the Eighth Amendment prohibits excessive bail, appellate courts will reduce a trial judge's bail amount only in the rare event that flagrant abuse can be proved. In practice, then, trial court judges have virtually unlimited legal discretion in determining the amount of bail. The discretion is often guided by the following factors:

- *Risk of Flight and Other Nonappearance:* Considers the suspect's "ties to the community" in terms of stable employment, property ownership, marital status, number of close, stable relationships, length of presence in the community, and such.

- *Risk to Self and Others:* Considers the suspect's mental condition, the seriousness of the crime(s) for which the suspect was arrested, and the arrestee's prior criminal history.

- *Situational Justice:* Considers factors such as how the defendant appears, acts, responds to questions, and the like. Note that the use of situational justice might lead judges to make certain judgments about defendants based on demographic characteristics, resulting in racial, ethnic, gender, and sexual orientation disparities to manifest themselves in bail decisions (Demuth, 2003; Katz & Spohn, 1995; Sacks, Sainato, & Ackerman, 2015; Schlesinger, 2005; Schnacke, 2014).

At first blush, these factors might seem straightforward. But uncertainty abounds because typically few details of the alleged crime are available shortly after a warrantless arrest. Similarly, the information about the defendant's mental status, ties to the community, and even criminal history are often in short supply. In many courts, for example, police "rap sheets" (lists of prior arrests) are available but typically do not contain information about how prior cases were eventually disposed of—dismissal, plea, or imprisonment.

Moreover, each bail decision is risky. In the face of uncertainty (often caused by a lack of complete information), judges must weigh risks such as whether a defendant released on bail will commit another crime and whether police groups, district attorneys, and the local newspapers may criticize a judge severely for granting pretrial release to defendants.

In addition, judges have to worry about jail overcrowding. If a particular arrestee is placed in pretrial detention, might that result in someone else— perhaps someone more dangerous—being released from a jail crowded beyond its capacity?

Bail Agents and Bounty Hunters

If a judge grants bail, most defendants lack the financial resources to post cash or property. Indeed, about four out of five arrestees who are released on some form of financial conditions turn to the services of commercial **bail agents**—people who, for a nonrefundable fee, post a bond with the court (Reaves, 2013). If the defendant does not appear for subsequent court proceedings, the bail agent is responsible for the full amount of the bond. For assuming this risk, he or she is permitted to charge a fee, usually 10 percent of the face amount of the bond. Rarely, however, do bail agents post cash directly with the court. Instead, they purchase a surety bond from a major insurance company, which charges 30 percent of the bail agent's fee. Thus, if the total amount of the bail is $10,000, the bail agent receives $1,000 from the client and keeps $700 of it.

As a condition of posting bail, bail agents require their clients to sign a contract waiving any protections against extradition and allowing the bail agent or a bounty hunter acting on behalf of the bail agent to retrieve the defendant from wherever he or she may have fled. These powers exceed any possessed by law enforcement officials since bail agents and bounty hunters are private actors; they are not, therefore, bound by the same constitutional constraints placed on law enforcement officers, who act under governmental authority when they seek, apprehend, detain, and transport bail jumpers. The exercise of such broad power has often led to corruption, "excessive use of force, false imprisonment, destruction of property, and arrest of innocent citizens" (Baker, Vaughn, & Topalli, 2008, p. 125). As a result, organizations like the American Bar Association and the National District Attorneys Association have recommended the abolition of commercial bail, but they have succeeded in only four states (Kentucky, Oregon, Wisconsin, and Illinois). Also, the District of Columbia, Maine, and Nebraska have little commercial bail activity (Cohen & Reaves, 2007). Yet, an estimated 14,000 commercial bail agencies nationwide secure the release of more than 2 million defendants annually (Cohen & Reaves, 2007). But things are slowly changing. Today, largely as a result of state statutory and case law changes,

Bail bond agents and bounty hunters have jurisdictional constraints placed on their actions, and they must follow the law or be subject to criminal prosecution. . . . For the most part, arbitrary, capricious, and discriminatory actions committed by bail bond agents and bounty hunters are subject to criminal prosecution, although some continue to use their extra-legal authority to flaunt the rule of law. . . . Partly as a result of the threat of criminal prosecution, many states have bail bond societies and associations that are working to professionalize the industry. More jails, and the Sheriff's Offices that run them, require bail bond agents and bounty hunters to be licensed, are using technology to establish early warning systems to monitor potential misbehavior, and require criminal background checks to detect potential wrong-doing within the industry before it spirals out of control into a major scandal. (Baker, Vaughn, & Topalli, 2008, p. 129)

Effects of the Bail System

The process of setting bail is not neutral. Defendants who have some access to money are much more likely than poor defendants to be bailed out of jail. The fact that some defendants remain in jail awaiting trial (or plea) has direct and perhaps indirect effects.

Most directly, defendants who cannot make bail face a variety of hardships. Even though defendants detained before trial are presumed innocent until proven guilty, they suffer many of the same disadvantages as those incarcerated after conviction. Economically, they often lose their jobs. Psychologically, they are subjected to stress, anxiety, and isolation. Physically, they are held in a violence-prone atmosphere. Indeed, some defendants spend time in jail during pretrial detention and are later not convicted.

More indirectly, defendants who cannot make bail may be at a disadvantage during the criminal justice process. Conversely, those who have been released may not appear in court as required. The effects of bail have been an active area of concern for the public, policymakers, and researchers alike. The topics that have received the greatest attention are jail conditions, race and ethnicity, failure to appear, and case disposition.

Jail Conditions

In an influential 1965 book *Ransom: A Critique of the American Bail System*, Ronald Goldfarb described the conditions of jails in the United States as "the ultimate ghetto." Over the past decades, jail conditions have improved greatly; Section 1983 conditions of confinement lawsuits filed in federal courts have played a role in these improvements. Nonetheless, many jails are still substandard, since efforts to improve jail conditions are typically low on the priority list of local officials, who are reluctant to spend taxpayers' dollars and do not want to appear to be coddling criminals.

Race and Ethnicity

Some studies have found clear differences between the defendants who await trial in jail and those who are released. Hispanics are the group most likely to be detained in jail, Whites are the least likely to be detained, and African-Americans are in the middle. These differences are partially the product of variation in economic status and the corresponding (in)ability to pay bail. Hispanics face a "triple disadvantage" during the bail-setting process—as a group they are least likely to qualify for ROR, have the highest bail amounts set, and are the least able to pay bail (Demuth, 2003; Sacks, Sainato, & Ackerman, 2015; Schlesinger, 2005). Higher pretrial detention rates for Hispanics may be the product of immigration holds filed by the U.S. Immigration and Customs Enforcement to detain those illegally in the country (Cohen & Reaves, 2007; Ryo, 2016).

Failure to Appear

Defendants who have gained pretrial release do not always appear in court when required. Skipping bail has several consequences. First, bail is forfeited. Second, a warrant is issued for the suspect's arrest. This warrant, termed a **bench warrant** or a *capias*, authorizes the police to take the person into custody. The person must be delivered to the judge issuing the warrant and cannot be released on bail. Finally, failure to appear often subjects the defendant to a separate criminal charge of bond jumping.

How often bailed defendants fail to appear in court is subject to considerable debate. Studies of felony defendants in large urban counties report that between 17 and 22 percent of the released defendants missed one or more court dates (Cohen & Reaves, 2007; Reaves, 2013). This estimate defined nonappearance as missing a single court date, but the problem of people absconding from bail to become fugitives from the law is real. Some studies estimate that 6 percent of released defendants were still fugitives at the end of a year, whereas other studies have reported that up to 30 percent of felony absconders will remain fugitives for at least a full year (Bornstein, Tomkins, Neeley, Herian, & Hamm, 2012; Helland & Tabarok, 2004).

Defendants who fail to appear do not always intend to miss their court dates. Failure-to-appear rates are closely related to practices within the court. A number of defendants do not show up because they were not given clear notice of the next appearance date. Another way in which courts themselves contribute to nonappearances is by lengthy delays in disposing of cases. As the time from arrest to trial increases, the rate of nonappearances rises even faster.

Case Disposition

Pretrial detention has a great impact on the legal processing of defendants:

> Viewed from the perspective of maintaining the plea-bargaining system, pretrial detention and demoralizing conditions in jails are highly functional. They discourage the defendant from bargaining too hard; they place a high price upon filing motions or demanding a trial.... This is not to argue that those in authority consciously plan rotten jails; clearly most are concerned about jail conditions. But it is to suggest that such conditions are functional, do serve the needs of the production ethic that dominates our criminal justice system. (Casper, 1972, p. 67)

The discriminatory impact of bail has been the subject of considerable research. There is widespread agreement in the literature that jailed defendants are more likely to be convicted and (once convicted) more likely to be sentenced to prison than those who have obtained pretrial release (Ares, Rankin, & Sturz, 1963; Cohen & Reaves, 2007; Phillips, 2007, 2008; Reaves, 2013; Stevenson, 2016). What is in dispute is the interpretation of these findings. Do these disparities result because the lack of pretrial release imposes additional burdens on the defendants? Or are these disparities a statistical artifact of a preselection process? Given that bail increases with the severity of the crime and the length of the prior record, one might reasonably expect that these defendants would end up disadvantaged, but for good reason.

John Goldkamp (1980) attempted to answer these difficult questions through a sophisticated analysis of more than 8,000 criminal cases in Philadelphia. Goldkamp found that jailed defendants did not differ from their bailed counterparts in terms of findings of guilt. At all the significant stages—dismissal, diversion, and trial—jailed defendants were as likely as bailed ones to receive a favorable disposition of their cases. When it came to sentencing, however, jailed defendants were more likely to be sentenced to prison, although the length of the sentence was not related to bail status. Another study (Eisenstein & Jacob, 1977) found no uniform impact of bail status on findings of guilt or on sentencing. Does bail status negatively affect the defendant's case? Perhaps the best response is provided by Goldkamp: "It depends." More recently, research in New York City found that in felony (Phillips, 2008) and nonfelony cases (Phillips, 2007), pretrial detention had a small, but statistically significant effect on the likelihood of conviction and also slightly longer sentences.

Bail Reform

Since 2005, more than 60 of all jail inmates were being held on charges pending trial (Minton & Zeng, 2016). That figure is as high as 75 percent in certain metropolitan jails (see Billings, 2016). But many of these inmates are not in pretrial detention because they pose a flight risk or because they are dangerous. Rather, between 25 and 40 percent of these inmates are in jail because they cannot afford to post bail (Justice Policy Institute, 2012; New York Civil Liberties Union, 2015). And this has serious consequences beyond the fact that those who cannot afford to pay the bail a judicial officer set for them continue to be incarcerated pending the outcome of their cases. As previously discussed, pretrial detainees "are more likely to be convicted, are less likely to have their charges reduced, and are likely to have longer sentences than those who were released before trial" (Billings, 2016, p. 1343).

Are Bail Schedules Unconstitutional?

Given the disproportionate impact the bail system has on the poor and members of racial and ethnic minorities, a strong argument can be made that contemporary bail practices—especially those based on bail schedules that do not allow judges to consider case-specific factors—are unconstitutional since they hinge on a defendant's ability to pay. Indeed, a federal district court declared that a Georgia city's bail schedule violated the Fourteenth Amendment's guarantee of equal protection of the law (*Walker v. City of Calhoun*, 2016). That case involved a man with schizophrenia who, in his mid-50s, was arrested for public drunkenness. He could not afford to pay the $160 in bail that was set for him, resulting in him spending six days in jail.

The city of Calhoun, Georgia, appealed the decision of the U.S. Court of Appeals for the Eleventh Circuit. The U.S. Department of Justice filed a brief with the court arguing the lower court's decision should be upheld because bail practices that "allow for the pretrial release of only those who can pay, without accounting for the ability to pay, unlawfully discriminate based on indigence." The American Bar Association filed a similar brief (Laird, 2016). The Eleventh Circuit vacated the district court's decision on procedural grounds, without considering the merits of the case. At the time of the writing of this book, the case remains pending on remand before a U.S. District Court Judge.

Reducing or Eliminating Commercial Bonds

Bail systems that rely heavily or exclusively on money to secure pretrial release cause defendants who are unable to afford posting bail to remain in pretrial detention even though a judge has already determined that true preventative detention is not necessary. The inability of poor defendants to pay bail costs taxpayers approximately $14 billion each year (Pretrial Justice Institute, 2017). Moreover, the system contributes to an unequal justice system in which those without financial resources to make bail sit in jail even though they may pose much little or no danger to the community or risk of flight. Additionally, as previously explained, they face numerous unfavorable outcomes in their criminal cases compared to those who successfully obtained pretrial release.

To combat these inequities, some states have enacted legislation making comprehensive changes to their systems of bail. By 2016, Wisconsin, Illinois, Oregon, Kentucky, and the District of Columbia had eliminated all use of commercial bail to secure pretrial release for the accused (Billings, 2016). In these jurisdictions, pretrial services monitor those released pending trial. And data from these jurisdictions suggest that these systems are working effectively. Consider that the Pretrial Services Agency for the District of Columbia reports that between 85 and 90 percent of arrestees are released without any financial conditions. Moreover, not only do approximately 90 percent of defendants show up for their court dates, they successfully make it through their trials without getting re-arrested (see also Wing, 2017).

Although New Jersey did not ban monetary bail for serious crimes, it largely eliminated bail for minor crimes effective in 2017. Pretrial services in the state will now assess and monitor defendants pending trial.

In 2016, voters in New Mexico approved an amendment to the state's constitution that allows judges to deny bail when prosecutors present clear and convincing evidence that defendants are too dangerous for release pending trial. But the amendment expressly prohibits the pretrial detention of defendants who are not dangerous or pose no risk of flight "solely because of financial inability" to pay bail.

Pretrial Release Services

In additional to monetary bail, all states also authorize judges to impose nonfinancial conditions of pretrial release. Such convictions usually involve travel restrictions and one or more types of court-monitored supervision. Typically, supervision programs monitor the arrestee's associations; place of residence; employment status; participation in drug, alcohol, or mental health

programs; and access to firearms. Such supervision is typically provided by **pretrial release services programs**. These programs also help combat the inequities of a purely monetary-based bail system. Indeed, as previously discussed, in the states that have restricted or eliminated bail, pretrial release services programs serve as the primary mechanism for ensuring appearance in court even in the absence of monetary bail.

Pretrial release services programs are typically comprised of at least two divisions: an investigations unit responsible for examining an arrestee's criminal history and personal background; and a case management division that conducts formal risk assessments—including substance abuse and mental health screening; coordinates the program's operations with other court staff; and supervises defendants who are released.

Risk Assessment

Pretrial release services programs seek to maximize the release of arrestees who qualify for release. This allows defendants to maintain employment and family relations and to assist their attorneys in preparing a criminal defense better than they could if they were in jail. Moreover, such programs offer the added benefit of reducing the cost to taxpayers of incarcerating people who are charged with but not convicted of any crime.

Of course, for pretrial release services programs to really be of societal benefit, they also need to serve two additional goals: reducing the failure to appear rate and decreasing the risk to the community posed by defendants who are released from pretrial custody. A number of pretrial release services programs have adopted empirically based risk assessment instruments to assist them in determining which arrestees pose a flight risk or a risk to public safety. These actuarial-style instruments offer improved predictive validity over the nonempirically based judgments of judicial officers (Kennedy, House, & Williams, 2013). Consider that in 2013, Kentucky implemented a statewide Public Safety Assessment Court that utilizes a "comprehensive, universal risk assessment" instrument that can "accurately, quickly, and efficiently assess the risk that a defendant will engage in violence, commit a new crime, or fail to come back to court" (Pretrial Justice Center for Courts, n.d., para 1). An evaluation study of that effort revealed that the actuarial assessment of arrestees resulted in a 15 percent crime reduction "among defendants on pretrial release, while at the time increasing the percentage of defendants who are released before trial" (Arnold Foundation, 2014, p. 2). The use of forensic risk assessment of pretrial defendants to determine bail eligibility has expanded beyond Kentucky to approximately 21 more U.S. jurisdictions (Dewan, 2015).

One of the problems with most pretrial risk assessment instruments is that "they combine flight risk and dangerousness into a single 'risk of pretrial failure' score" (Gouldin, 2016, p. 842). In time, risk assessment instruments will likely continue to be improved and, hopefully, will disentangle these two distinct risks to avoid overestimation of which defendants should be detained.

Pretrial Supervision

Most pretrial release services programs utilize a number of supervision strategies that are commonly used to supervise defendants who are convicted and sentenced to probation, including probation reporting (even daily, if necessary), electronic monitoring, and mandatory drug and alcohol testing (see Chapter 14 for details on such programs in the correctional supervision context). These methods appear to be successful in meeting the desired outcomes while costing much less than pretrial detention (Johnson & Baber, 2015; Tanner, Wyatt, & Yearwood, 2008), especially when they employ actuarial risk assessment instruments that have been properly validated for pretrial defendants (Cadigan, Johnson, & Lowenkamp, 2012; Cooprider, 2009; Johnson & Baber, 2015).

Preliminary Hearing

In most states, any person who has been arrested for a felony and has not been indicted by a grand jury (and, therefore, has been charged via an information or complaint or similar document filed by a prosecutor) has the right to a preliminary hearing. At the **preliminary hearing** (also called the

"preliminary examination"), the magistrate must determine whether **probable cause** exists to believe that a felony was committed and that the defendant committed it. In this context, *probable cause* means a fair probability, under the totality of the facts and circumstances known, that the person arrested committed the crime(s) charged. Usually held before a lower-court judge, the preliminary hearing is designed:

> to prevent hasty, malicious, improvident, and oppressive prosecutions, to protect the person charged from open and public accusations of crime, to avoid both for the defendant and the public the expense of a public trial, to save the defendant from the humiliation and anxiety involved in public prosecution, and to discover whether or not there are substantial grounds upon which a prosecution may be based. (*Thies v. State*, 1922, p. 541)

As stated above, the initial appearance before a magistrate may or may not include a probable cause hearing. If it does not, then a separate preliminary hearing is required unless: (1) the defendant is charged with a petty offense or misdemeanor; (2) the defendant waives the hearing; or (3) a grand jury has already determined that probable cause exists for the defendant to stand felony trial. Rule 5 of the Federal Rules of Criminal Procedure provides that, when the preliminary hearing is required, "[t]he magistrate judge must hold the preliminary hearing within a reasonable time, but no later than 10 days after the initial appearance if the defendant is in custody and no later than 20 days if not in custody."

Law on the Books: Weighing Probable Cause

The preliminary hearing is a formal adversarial proceeding conducted in open court; normally, a transcript of the proceedings is recorded. During a preliminary hearing, the state does not have to prove the defendant guilty beyond a reasonable doubt, as would be required during a trial. Rather, the prosecutor needs only to establish probable cause that a crime has been committed and that the defendant committed it. If the magistrate finds probable cause to believe that the defendant committed the offense, the magistrate **binds over** the defendant to the trial court for adjudication of the felony charges. The magistrate may admit the defendant to bail at the preliminary hearing or may continue, increase, or decrease the original bail. If the magistrate does not find probable cause, the magistrate dismisses the complaint and releases the defendant. A dismissal at this stage does not invoke the constitutional safeguard against double jeopardy. This means that the prosecution may recharge the defendant and submit new evidence at a later preliminary hearing. Nor does a dismissal prevent the prosecution from going to the grand jury and obtaining an indictment in states that have both grand jury and preliminary hearing procedures. Table 10.4 compares the preliminary hearing with grand jury proceedings.

Law in Action: Variations in Using the Preliminary Hearing

Defense attorneys weigh several factors in deciding whether to demand a preliminary hearing or waive it (Flemming, 1986b; Prosser, 2006). Practices of the local prosecutor are one important consideration. If the district attorney's files are open

TABLE 10.4 Differences in Pretrial Procedures to Determine Whether Probable Cause Exists to Make a Defendant Stand Trial in Felony Cases

Grand Jury Proceedings	Preliminary Hearing
Primary function is to determine whether probable cause exists to believe that the defendant committed the crime or crimes charged.	Primary function is to determine whether probable cause exists to believe that the defendant committed the crime or crimes charged.
If probable cause is found, the grand jury returns an indictment/"true bill" against the defendant that is signed both by the prosecutor and by the foreperson of the grand jury.	If probable cause is found, the judge binds over the defendant for the trial court for adjudication by signing an information.
Held in the grand jury room in a closed session (i.e., secret proceedings not open to the public).	Held in open court (i.e., open to the public).
Informal proceeding in which no judicial officer presides.	Formal judicial proceeding presided over by a judge or magistrate.
Nonadversarial proceeding in which the grand jury hears only evidence presented by the prosecution.	Adversarial proceeding in which both the prosecution and the defense may present evidence to the presiding judicial officer.
Defendant has no right to be present or to offer evidence.	Defendant has the right to be present, to offer evidence, and to cross-examine adverse witnesses.
Defendant has no Sixth Amendment right to counsel.	Defendant has a right to the effective assistance of counsel under the Sixth Amendment.
Grand jury has the power to investigate crimes on its own initiative.	No power to investigate crime.
Grand jury has the power to subpoena witnesses and evidence.	No subpoena power.
Grand jury has the power to grant immunity.	No power to grant immunity.

Source: John Ferdico, Henry F. Fradella, and Christopher Totten. 2016. *Criminal Procedure for the Criminal Justice Professional.* 12th ed. Belmont, CA: Wadsworth.

and plea-bargaining policies are well known, it is viewed as time consuming and redundant to hold a preliminary hearing. Second, strategic and tactical considerations are involved. Waiving the preliminary hearing may reflect an assessment that the information to be gained from holding a preliminary hearing does not outweigh the potential damage to the defendant's case (for example, the publicity that may surround a rape case). A third factor is client control. Defense attorneys sometimes insist on a preliminary hearing to impress on their client the gravity of the situation. Finally, the preliminary hearing gives the defense attorney an overview of the evidence against the client and provides the opportunity for discovery (see Chapter 11).

The tactical decision of holding or waiving the preliminary hearing highlights the complexity of the preliminary hearing from the law in action perspective. Although the legal purpose of the preliminary hearing is simple, the actual conduct of these hearings is quite complex. In some courts, they may last an hour or more; in others, they consume only a few minutes. In some jurisdictions, preliminary hearings are an important stage in the proceedings; in others, they are a perfunctory step, in which probable cause is found to exist in virtually every case.

This variability makes it difficult to generalize about the importance of the preliminary hearing, but studies do reveal four major patterns. In some jurisdictions, preliminary hearings are almost never held. In many, they are short and routine, lasting but a few minutes with the defendant almost always bound over to the grand jury (Neubauer,

1974b). In most jurisdictions, the preliminary hearing is largely ceremonial, resulting in few cases being screened out of the criminal process; but in a few courts, it is quite significant (McIntyre & Lippman, 1970; Thomas, 2014; Washburn, 2008).

Grand Jury

Grand juries make accusations; trial juries decide guilt or innocence. The **grand jury** emerged in English law in 1176, during a political struggle among King Henry II, the church, and noblemen. At first, criminal accusations originated with members of the grand jury themselves, but gradually this body came to consider accusations from outsiders as well.

After the American Revolution, the grand jury was included in the Fifth Amendment to the Constitution, which provides that "no person shall be held to answer for a capital, or otherwise infamous crime, unless on a presentment or indictment of a grand jury." The archaic phrase "otherwise infamous crime" has been interpreted to mean felonies. This provision, however, applies only to federal prosecutions. In *Hurtado v. California* (1884), the Supreme Court held that states have the option of using either an indictment or an information. Today, grand juries in every U.S. state and the District of Columbia can investigate criminal activity; in contrast, U.S. jurisdictions differ with regard to how grand jury indictments operate as explained in Table 10.5.

TABLE 10.5 Variability in State Use of Grand Juries

Grand Jury Indictments Required for Most or All Felonies (N = 24)	Grand Jury Indictments Optional for Most Felonies (N = 25)	Grand Jury Indictments Abolished (N = 2)
Alabama, Alaska, Delaware, District of Columbia, Florida, Kentucky, Louisiana, Maine, Massachusetts, Minnesota, Mississippi, Missouri, New Hampshire, New Jersey, New York, North Carolina, North Dakota, Ohio, Rhode Island, South Carolina, Tennessee, Texas, Virginia, and West Virginia	Arizona, Arkansas, California, Colorado, Georgia, Hawaii, Idaho, Illinois, Indiana, Iowa, Kansas, Maryland, Michigan, Montana, Nebraska, Nevada, New Mexico, Oklahoma, Oregon, South Dakota, Utah, Vermont, Washington, Wisconsin, and Wyoming	Connecticut, Pennsylvania

Grand juries are impaneled (formally created) for a set period of time—typically varying between 10 days and 24 months. During that time, the jurors periodically consider the cases brought to them by the prosecutor and conduct other investigations. If a grand jury is conducting a major and complex investigation, its time may be extended by the court. The size of grand juries varies greatly, from as few as 5 jurors to as many as 23, with an average size of 17. Grand jurors are normally selected randomly, in a manner similar to the selection of trial jurors. In a handful of states, however, judges, county boards, jury commissioners, or sheriffs are allowed to exercise discretion in choosing who will serve on the grand jury.

Law on the Books: Shield and Sword

The two primary functions of grand juries have been aptly summarized in the phrase "shield and sword" (Zalman & Siegel, 1997). *Shield* refers to the protections the grand jury offers, serving as a buffer between the state and its citizens and preventing the government from using the criminal process against its enemies. *Sword* refers to the investigatory powers of this body (Alpert & Petersen, 1985). If the grand jury believes grounds for holding the suspect for trial are present, they return an **indictment**, also termed a **true bill**, meaning that they find the charges to be true. Conversely, if they find the charges insufficient to justify trial, they return a no bill, or **no true bill**.

Many legal protections found elsewhere in the criminal court process are not applicable at the grand jury stage. One unique aspect of the grand jury is secrecy. Because the grand jury may find insufficient evidence to indict, it works in secret to shield those merely under investigation from adverse publicity. By contrast, the rest of the criminal court process is required to be public. Another unique aspect is that indictments are returned by a plurality vote; in most states, half to two-thirds of the votes are sufficient to hand up an indictment. Trial juries can convict only if the jurors are unanimous (or, in four states, nearly unanimous). Finally, witnesses before the grand jury have no right to representation by an attorney, whereas defendants

are entitled to have a lawyer present at all vital stages of a criminal prosecution. Nor do suspects have the right to go before the grand jury to protest their innocence or even to present their version of the facts.

In furtherance of their investigative powers, grand juries have the authority to grant **immunity** from prosecution. The Fifth Amendment protects a person against self-incrimination. In 1893, Congress passed a statute that permitted the granting of **transactional immunity**. In exchange for a witness's testimony, the prosecutor agrees not to prosecute the witness for any crimes admitted—a practice often referred to as "turning state's evidence." The Organized Crime Control Act of 1970 added a new and more limited form of immunity. Under **use immunity**, the government may not use a witness's grand jury testimony to prosecute that person. However, if the state acquires evidence of a crime independently of that testimony, the witness may be prosecuted. The Supreme Court has held that use immunity does not violate the Fifth Amendment's prohibition against self-incrimination (*Kastigar v. United States*, 1972). Use immunity gives witnesses less protection than does transactional immunity. A witness may not refuse the government's offer of immunity, and failure to testify may result in a jail term for contempt of court.

The investigative powers of the grand jury to gather evidence are also seen in its **subpoena power**. Under the court's authority, the grand jury may issue a subpoena requiring an individual to appear before the grand jury to testify and/or bring papers and other evidence for its consideration. Failure to comply with a subpoena (or offer of immunity) is punishable as **contempt**. A person found in contempt of the grand jury faces a fine or being jailed until he or she complies with the grand jury request. Thus, contempt of the grand jury is potentially open ended—as long as the grand jury is in existence and as long as the person refuses to comply, the person can sit in jail. Critics contend that some prosecutors call political dissidents to testify to find out information unrelated to criminal activity.

The contempt power can also be used for punishment. A prosecutor may call a witness, knowing that he or she will refuse to testify, and then have the witness jailed. In this way, a person can be imprisoned without a trial. This has happened mainly to newspaper reporters. In *Branzburg v. Hayes* (1972), the Supreme Court ruled that journalists must testify before a grand jury. Some journalists have gone to jail rather than reveal their confidential sources, because they believe that to do so would erode the freedom of the press protected by the First Amendment.

Law in Action: Prosecutorial Domination

The work of the grand jury is shaped by its unique relationship with the prosecutor. In theory at least, the prosecutor functions only as a legal adviser to the grand jury, but in practice, the prosecutor dominates. Grand jurors hear only the witnesses summoned by the prosecutor, and, as laypeople, they are heavily influenced by the legal advice of the prosecutor. Indeed, the high court has ruled that the government is under no obligation to disclose to the grand jury evidence that would tend to clear the defendant (*United States v. Williams*, 1992). This is one of a number of significant developments in the way criminal procedure has been shaped by the courts, as explained in the "Key Developments" feature on page 304.

The net result is that grand juries often function as a rubber stamp for the prosecutor. One study found that the average time spent per case was only 5 minutes; in 80 percent of the cases, there was no discussion by members of the grand jury; rarely did members voice a dissent; and finally, the grand jury approved virtually all of the prosecutor's recommendations (Carp, 1975). Similarly, federal grand juries rarely return no true bills. In short, grand juries generally indict whomever the prosecutor wants indicted (Gilboy, 1984; Neubauer, 1974b; Thomas, 2014; Washburn, 2008).

Courts and Controversy: Reform the Grand Jury?

The grand jury system has been the object of various criticisms. In theory, the grand jury serves as a watchdog on the prosecutor, but some portray the grand jury as "the prosecutor's darling," a "puppet," or a "rubber stamp." To William Campbell (1973), U.S. District Court judge for the Northern District of Illinois, "The grand jury is the total captive of the prosecutor who, if he is candid, will concede that he can indict anybody at any time, for almost anything, before any grand jury" (p. 174). These concerns have prompted a call for abolition of the grand jury. Early in the 20th century, judicial reformers succeeded in abolishing grand juries in some states. More recently, such abolition efforts have not been successful, however, because they require a constitutional amendment.

Today, critics call for reforming the grand jury (Brenner, 1998; Farifax, 2015; Washburn, 2008). Often these calls are based on concerns that grand jury proceedings have been misused to serve partisan political ends, harassing and punishing those who criticize the government. The leading advocate for federal grand jury reform is the National Association of Criminal Defense Lawyers (2000). This organization advocates a Citizens' Grand Jury Bill of Rights, which among other things would grant witnesses the right to counsel during testimony, require prosecutors to disclose evidence that might exonerate the target, and allow targets of investigations to testify (Lefcourt, 1998).

Arraignment

Arraignment on felony charges occurs in the trial court of general jurisdiction. During the arraignment, the defendant is formally accused of a crime (either by an information or indictment) and is called upon to enter a plea. Thus, initial appearance and arraignment are similar in that the defendant must be informed with some specificity about the alleged criminal actions. The major difference is that felony defendants are not allowed to enter a plea (either not guilty or guilty) in a lower court because that court lacks jurisdiction to take a plea and to impose sentence on felony charges.

KEY DEVELOPMENTS CONCERNING CRIMINAL PROCEDURE

Crime *Lanzetta v. New Jersey* (1939)	A law is unconstitutional if it forbids an act in terms so vague that "men of common intelligence must necessarily guess at its meaning."
Arrest *Chimel v. California* (1969)	During a search incident to arrest, the police may search only the person and the area within the immediate vicinity.
Payton v. New York (1980)	Unless the suspect gives consent or an emergency exists, an arrest warrant is necessary if an arrest requires entry into a suspect's private residence.
Arizona v. Gant (2009)	Police may search a vehicle incident to the arrest of its recent occupant after the arrest only if it is reasonable to believe that the arrestee might access the vehicle at the time of the search or that the vehicle contains evidence of the offense of the arrest.
Initial appearance **Sixth Amendment** (1791)	"In all criminal prosecutions, the accused shall enjoy the right ... to be informed of the nature and cause of the accusation."
Rothgery v. Gillespie County, Texas (2008)	Defendant's initial appearance in which he learns of the charge(s) against him and his liberty is subject to restriction, marks initiation of adversary proceedings that trigger attachment of Sixth Amendment right to counsel.
Charging **Sixth Amendment** (1791)	"In all criminal prosecutions, the accused shall enjoy the right ... to be informed of the nature and cause of the accusation."
People v. Wabash, St. Louis and Pacific Railway (1882)	Prosecutor has discretion in beginning prosecutions and may terminate them when, in his (or her) judgment, the ends of justice are satisfied.
Burns v. Reed (1991)	Prosecutor enjoys absolute immunity to civil lawsuit for all actions involving the adversarial process.
Bail **Eighth Amendment** (1791)	Excessive bail shall not be required.
Bail Reform Act of 1984	Upheld in *United States v. Salerno* (1987), this law created a statutory presumption in favor of pretrial release.
Grand jury **Fifth Amendment** (1791)	"No person shall be held to answer for a capital, or otherwise infamous crime, unless on a presentment or indictment of a grand jury."
Hurtado v. California (1884)	States are not required to use a grand jury in charging felonies.
U.S. Congress (1893)	Prosecutors may grant transactional immunity for testimony a witness is compelled to give before a grand jury.
Organized Crime Control Act (1970)	Prosecutors may grant a witness use immunity for testimony before the grand jury.
Kastigar v. United States (1972)	Use immunity does not violate the Fifth Amendment protection against self-incrimination.
Branzburg v. Hayes (1972)	Journalists have no constitutional right to maintain the confidentiality of their news sources when subpoenaed before grand juries, and are compelled to give testimony.
United States v. Williams (1992)	Prosecutors are under no obligation to present exculpatory evidence to the grand jury.
Campbell v. Louisiana (1998)	A White criminal defendant may challenge his conviction on grounds that African-Americans were discriminated against in the selection of grand jurors.
Arraignment **Sixth Amendment** (1791)	"In all criminal prosecutions, the accused shall enjoy the right . . . to be informed of the nature and cause of the accusation."

Procedurally, the arraignment provides the court the opportunity to ensure that the case is on track for disposition. The judge summons the defendant, verifying his or her name and address, and the lawyer provides formal notification to the court that he or she represents the defendant in this matter. Most important, the arraignment means that the defendant must enter a plea. Typically, defendants plead not guilty and a trial date is established. In some jurisdictions, however, a significant proportion of defendants enter a plea of guilty (Neubauer, 1996).

The arraignment is rarely a major decision-making stage in the process. Rather, its real importance is measured more indirectly. The arraignment is important because it signifies to all members of the courtroom work group that the defendant is in all probability guilty and that the likelihood of being found not guilty is now slim. Thus, from the perspective of law in action, the arraignment says something very important about case attrition.

Law in Action Perspective: Case Attrition

The law on the books perspective suggests a mechanical process—cases move almost automatically from one pretrial stage to the next. In sharp contrast, the law in action perspective emphasizes a dynamic process—cases are likely to be eliminated during these early stages.

A detailed picture of case attrition emerges in the research summarized in Figure 10.2. For every 100 arrests, 8 are diverted and 23 are dismissed by the prosecutor through a *nolle prosequi* (no prosecution). When this happens, the case is said to be "nolled," "nollied," or "nol. prossed." Overall, only 66 of the 100 arrests are carried forward to the trial stage, at which 64 are resolved by guilty pleas; only 2 go to trial. These statistics underscore the fact that decisions made during early steps of felony prosecutions are much more important in terminating

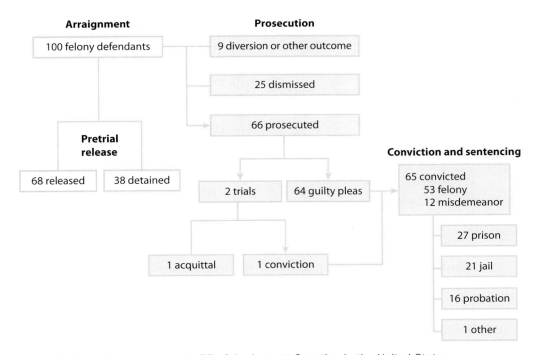

FIGURE 10.2 Case Attrition of Felony Arrests in 75 of the Largest Counties in the United States

Source: Bureau of Justice Statistics. 2013. *Felony Defendants in Large Urban Counties, 2009.* Washington, DC: Department of Justice.

cases than the later activities of judges and juries. However, important variations arise among courts in the stage at which case attrition occurs. These variations reflect differences in state law, the structure of courts, and local traditions. Thus, a critical stage for case screening and case attrition in one court may be of little importance in another jurisdiction.

Why Attrition Occurs

Case attrition is the product of a complex set of factors, including the relationships among the major actors in the criminal justice system, the patterns of informal authority within the courtroom work group, the backlog of cases on the court's docket, and community standards defining serious criminal activity. We can best examine why attrition occurs by using three facets of discretion: legal judgments, policy priorities, and personal standards of justice. As with other attempts to understand discretion, these categories are not mutually exclusive—some screening decisions are based on more than one criterion.

Legal Judgments

Legal judgments are the most important reason that cases drop by the wayside after arrest and before arraignment. Prosecutors, judges, and grand jurors begin with a basic question: Is there sufficient evidence to prove the elements of the offense? (Cole, 1970; Feeney, Dill, & Weir, 1983). One assistant district attorney phrased it this way: "When I examine the police report, I have to feel that I could go to trial with the case tomorrow. All the elements of prosecution must be present before I file charges" (Neubauer, 1974b, p. 118).

The legal-evidentiary strength of the case is the reason cited most often for prosecutors declining to prosecute cases (Albonetti, 1987; Holleran et al., 2009; Jacoby, Mellon, Ratledge, & Turner, 1982; Miller & Wright, 2008; O'Neal et al., 2015). Such problems include noncooperation by victims and witnesses; insufficient evidence to prove the elements of charged crimes; problems with the strength or credibility of witnesses' testimony; and,

on rare occasion, problems with the ways in which law enforcement obtained evidence. Lack of cooperation from victims and witnesses poses a particular problem in some urban areas (DeFrances, Smith, & van der Does, 1996; Kaiser, O'Neal, & Spohn, 2015; Miller & Wright, 2008).

Focusing on the strength of the state's case introduces an important change in evaluative standards. From an initial concern with *probable cause*, the emphasis shifts to whether it is a *prosecutable case*. At the preliminary hearing, the judge determines whether probable cause exists—that a crime has been committed and that grounds to believe that the suspect committed it are present. From the prosecutor's perspective, however, probable cause is too gross a yardstick; even though probable cause exists, a case may still be legally weak. Thus, a prosecutable case is not one that merely satisfies the probable-cause standard required of police in making an arrest and used by the judge at the preliminary hearing. Rather, it is a case that meets the standards of proof necessary to convict.

Policy Priorities

Case attrition also results from general prosecutorial policies about the priority of cases. Prosecutors devote greater resources to more serious offenses (Gilboy, 1984; Jacoby et al., 1982). At times, these case priorities are reflected in office structure; district attorneys around the nation have established priority prosecution programs that focus on major narcotics dealers, organized crime, sex offenders, and the like. Just as important, prosecutors use informal criteria that govern allocation of scarce resources. For example, some U.S. attorneys will not prosecute bank tellers who embezzle small amounts of money, get caught, and lose their jobs. The stigma of being caught and losing the job is viewed as punishment enough. Similarly, numerous local and state prosecutors have virtually decriminalized possession of small amounts of marijuana by refusing to file charges. Based on informal office policies, district attorneys are reluctant to prosecute neighborhood squabbles and noncommercial gambling. And, of course, politics also plays a role, as district attorneys are much more likely to prosecute property and drug crimes in election years than at other times (Bandyopadhyay & McCannon, 2014; Dyke, 2007).

Personal Standards of Justice

Personal standards of justice—attitudes of members of the courtroom work group about what actions should not be punished—constitute the third category of criteria that explain case attrition. Thus, some cases are dropped or reduced for reasons other than failure to establish guilt (Howell, 2014; McIntyre, 1968; Miller & Wright, 2008). Even if the evidence is strong, defendants might not be prosecuted if their conduct and background indicate that they are not a genuine threat to society. Across the nation, these reasons for rejection are referred to as "Prosecution would serve no useful purpose" or "interests of justice" (Boland, Mahanna, & Sones, 1992). Often, personal standards of justice are based on a subjective assessment on the part of the prosecutor that the case is not as serious as the legal charge suggests. In most courthouses,

officials refer to some cases as "cheap" or "garbage" cases (Rosett & Cressey, 1976). Decisions not to file charges in cheap cases reflect the effort of court officials to produce substantive justice.

The Criminal Justice Wedding Cake

The tyranny of criminal justice statistics is that they treat all cases in the same way in calculating the crime rate. Merely counting the number of criminal events gets in the way of understanding how and why court officials treat cases of murder differently from those of involuntary manslaughter, even though both are homicides. To understand case attrition, Samuel Walker (2011) suggested that it is useful to view criminal justice as a wedding cake (see Figure 10.3).

The wedding cake model is based on the observation that criminal justice officials handle different kinds of cases very differently. The cases in each layer have a high degree of consistency; the greatest disparities are found between cases in different layers.

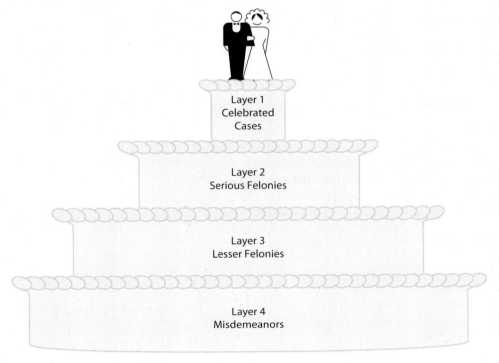

FIGURE 10.3 The Criminal Justice Wedding Cake

Source: Samuel Walker. 2015. *Sense and Nonsense about Crime, Drugs, and Communities.* 8th ed. Stamford, CT: Cengage.

An examination of these layers illuminates the paradox of American criminal justice: "The problem is not that our system is too lenient, or too severe; sadly, it is both" (Zimring, O'Malley, & Eigen, 1976).

Celebrated Cases

The top layer of the criminal justice wedding cake consists of a few celebrated cases. Every year, a few cases dominate media attention because of the number of persons killed, the bizarre nature of the crime, or the prominence of the defendant. Likewise, local communities may have a few celebrated cases, either because a local notable has been charged with a serious crime or because the crime itself was particularly heinous.

From the moment these cases begin, criminal justice officials treat them as exceptional, making sure that every last detail of the judicial process is followed. The cases are also extraordinary because they frequently involve the rarest of criminal court events—the full jury trial. To the fascination of the viewing and reading public, controversial matters are aired in public. As in morality plays of old and soap operas of today, public attention is focused on the battle between good and evil, although who is playing which role is not always obvious.

These celebrated cases are most likely to be broadcast on television, with some cable stations offering instant analysis and critique. Because of the publicity surrounding them, celebrated cases have a tremendous impact on public perceptions of criminal justice. On one level, these cases reinforce the textbook notion that defendants will receive their day in court, complete with first-rate defense counsel and an attentive jury. But on another level, celebrated cases highlight the public's worst fears—the rich often get off scot-free because they can afford an expensive attorney. All too many seem to beat the rap. People assume that the court process ordinarily functions this way, but in fact it does not. Celebrated cases are atypical; they do not reflect how the courts operate on a day-to-day basis.

Serious Felonies

The second layer of the wedding cake consists of serious felonies. The courtroom work group distinguishes between this level and the next on the basis of three main criteria: the seriousness of the crime, the criminal record of the suspect, and the relationship between the victim and the offender. The guiding question is, "How much is the case worth?" Serious cases end up in the second layer; the "not-so-serious" ones in the third. Murders, armed robberies, and most rapes are treated by all members of the courtroom work group as serious felonies, resulting in less likelihood that the suspect will be released on bail. In addition, at this level, more pretrial maneuvering means less chance that the sides can reach a plea agreement (Chapter 12), a strong likelihood of trial (Chapter 13), and eventually, an appeal (Chapter 15).

Lesser Felonies

Of course, no automatic formula dictates sorting cases into serious and not-so-serious felonies; the key is a commonsense judgment about the facts of the case. What first appears to be a serious offense might be downgraded because the victim and the offender knew one another. For example, what starts out as an armed robbery might later be viewed as essentially a private disagreement over money owed, with the criminal act a means of seeking redress outside accepted channels. On the other hand, a suspect's long criminal record might transform an otherwise ordinary felony into a serious one, at least in the eyes of the prosecuting attorney.

Analysis of the true seriousness of a case is part of the everyday language of the courthouse actors. Serious cases are routinely referred to as "heavy" cases or "real" crimes, and the less serious ones as "garbage," "bullshit," or simply not real crimes. The practical consequences are that second-layer felonies are given considerable attention, whereas third-layer crimes receive less attention and are treated in a routine and lenient manner.

The Lower Depths: Misdemeanors

The bottom layer of the criminal justice wedding cake is a world unto itself, consisting of a staggering volume of misdemeanor cases, far exceeding the number of felony cases. As discussed in

Chapter 4, about half are "public order" offenses—disorderly conduct, public drunkenness, disturbing the peace, and the like. Only about a third involve crimes against property or persons, many of which are petty thefts or physical disagreements between "friends" or acquaintances. Rarely do these defendants have any social standing. In the eyes of the courtroom work group, few of these cases are worth much, and relatively little time is devoted to their processing. They are usually handled by a different court from the one that handles felony cases and are processed in a strikingly different way. Dispositions are arrived at in a routine manner. Defendants are arraigned en masse. Guilt is rarely contested. Even more rarely are the punishments harsh.

Conclusion

The debate among the nine justices in *Country of Riverside v. McLaughlin* over what constitutes a prompt hearing may seem arcane, but it illustrates the overriding reality of the modern age: At times, the rights of individuals must be considered not just on their own merits but also in the context in which they are raised. Individually providing each defendant a probable cause hearing within 24 hours would cause no disruption to the system. But providing potentially hundreds of suspects a day such a right runs smack into logistical problems—transporting prisoners from distant jails, hiring more magistrates, making sure that police reports are available quickly, and many other issues. What is ultimately important about *County of Riverside v. McLaughlin* is that it focuses attention on what is otherwise an invisible time period in the history of a felony prosecution.

Bail is another often invisible step in the prosecution of a felony. Bail serves several purposes in the American court system, some legally sanctioned, others definitely extralegal. Bail is used to guarantee a defendant's appearance at trial, to protect society by holding those perceived to be dangerous, to punish those accused (but not yet convicted) of violating the law, and to lubricate the system by softening defendants up to enter a plea

of guilty. These varying purposes are partially the result of the tension among conflicting principles. Although the law recognizes that the only legal purpose of bail is to guarantee a suspect's future appearance at trial, court officials perceive a need to protect society. Out of these conflicting principles arise compromises.

The specific steps of criminal procedure are important because they help to ensure fairness in the process. But equally important is the substance of the decisions made. In statistical profile, the process resembles a funnel—wide at the top, narrow at the end. Fewer than half of all crimes are ever reported to the police. Only one in five of the crimes known to the police results in an arrest. Thus, most crimes never reach the courts. Of the small subset of criminal events referred to court officials, half are dropped after prosecutorial screening, preliminary hearings, or grand jury deliberations. Prosecutors and judges decline to prosecute or later dismiss charges that have been filed because the case lacks sufficient evidence, falls too low on the priority list, or is viewed as a "cheap" case. The wedding cake model highlights this sorting process. Considerable resources are devoted to serious felonies. Lesser felonies receive less attention; they are more likely to be filtered out of the system.

The decisions made at these early points set the tone of cases moving through the criminal court process. Quantitatively, the volume of cases is directly related to screening decisions. In many areas, it is common for roughly half the defendants to have their charges dismissed during these early stages. Qualitatively, screening decisions greatly influence later stages in the proceedings. Most directly, plea bargaining reflects how cases were initially screened. For instance, it is a long-standing practice in many courts for prosecutors to overcharge a defendant by filing accusations more serious than the evidence indicates, in order to give themselves leverage for later offering the defendant the opportunity to plead to a less serious charge. Thus, the important decisions about innocence or guilt are made early in the process by judges and prosecutors—not, as the adversary system projects, late in the process by lay jurors.

CHAPTER REVIEW

LO1   1.   Define the two methods of estimating the amount of crime in the United States.

In the United States the two methods of estimating the amount of crime are the Uniform Crime Reports, based on crimes reported to the police, and the National Crime Victimization Survey, based on self-reports from households.

LO2   2.   Discuss how arrests made by the police impact the criminal court process.

Arrests made by the police impact the criminal court process in two ways: (1) if the police fail to gather enough evidence, it will be difficult for the police to gain a conviction, and (2) the increase in the number of arrests has swollen the dockets of the courts.

LO3   3.   List the four ways that criminals are formally charged in court and the major actors in each of these important documents.

Defendants are formally charged in court with a violation of the criminal law by: (1) a complaint signed by the victim, (2) a bill of information filed by the prosecutor, (3) an arrest warrant prepared by the police, or (4) a true bill issued by a grand jury.

LO4   4.   List the four most common ways that defendants secure pretrial release.

The four most common ways defendants secure pretrial release are: (1) release on recognizance (ROR), (2) cash bond, (3) property bond, and (4) bail bond through the services of a commercial bail agent.

LO5   5.   Compare and contrast "law on the books" and "law in action" approaches to bail setting, including the overall effects of the bail system on criminal defendants and their cases.

Law on the books expresses a strong preference for bail unless clear and convicting evidence establishes that: (1) there is a serious risk that the person will flee; (2) the person may obstruct justice or threaten, injure, or intimidate a prospective witness or juror;

or (3) the offense is one of violence or one punishable by life imprisonment or death. **In contrast, law in action affects bail setting in terms of uncertainty, risk, jail overcrowding, and situational justice. How these factors coalesce in a bail decision affects the processing of criminal defendants in terms of jail conditions, disparate impact on racial and ethnic minorities, the failure of some defendants to appear in court as promised, and case disposition.**

LO6   6.   Explain the role bail agents play in the criminal justice system.

The bail agent provides a specialized form of insurance and makes a profit by focusing on low-risk offenders accused of less serious crimes.

LO7   7.   Contrast how the law on the books approach to criminal justice and the law in action perspective offer contrasting views of the preliminary hearing.

The law on the books approach to criminal justice emphasizes that during the preliminary hearing the judge decides whether there is probable cause to hold the defendant, while the law in action perspective emphasizes that in most jurisdictions there is a strong probability that the case will proceed.

LO8   8.   Explain why some jurisdictions use grand juries extensively and others do not.

Grand juries are used extensively in jurisdictions where the constitution requires a grand jury indictment in all felonies. In jurisdictions that do not have this constitutional requirement, grand jury indictments are required in only select offenses.

LO9   9.   Delineate the three major reasons for case attrition.

The three major reasons for case attrition are (1) legal judgments (lack of evidence), (2) policy priorities (some cases are considered too minor to be prosecuted), and

(3) personal standards of justice (attitudes of the courtroom work group about what actions should or should not be punished).

LO10 10. Describe the four layers of the criminal justice wedding cake.

From the top to the bottom, the four layers of the criminal justice cake are

(1) celebrated cases (which are very atypical), (2) serious felonies (which are treated as meriting major attention), (3) lesser felonies (which are treated as of less importance), and (4) the lower depths (which comprise the large volume of misdemeanor arrests).

CRITICAL THINKING QUESTIONS

1. How long can an arrested person be held before being brought before a neutral judicial official? Do you think it was proper for the Court to take into account law in action factors such as case volume in deciding *County of Riverside v. McLaughlin* (1991)?

2. In your community, at what stage does case attrition occur? Do you detect any public displeasure with how the process currently operates?

3. If you were the prosecutor, what arguments would you make to the police chief(s) regarding a policy of careful screening of cases soon after arrest? Conversely, what arguments do you think law enforcement officials would make?

4. In what ways do crime control model advocates approach bail differently than do backers of due process model values?

5. Examine the local papers. Have there been reports of defendants' committing crimes while out on bail? Have there been reports of poor conditions in the local jail? How might these reports affect bail setting?

6. To what extent do the issues of weeding out weak cases cut across ideological dimensions?

7. Do you know of any local crimes that fit the celebrated cases category of the criminal justice wedding cake? Why did these cases receive such attention? Are they similar to or different from cases that receive extensive coverage in the media?

KEY TERMS

arraignment   303

arrest   285

arrest warrant   289

bail   292

bail agent   295

bail bond   293

bench warrant (*capias*)   296

bind over   299

cash bond   293

charging document   288

complaint   288

contempt (of court)   302

grand jury   301

hierarchy rule   284

immunity   302

index crimes   283

indictment   302

information   288

initial appearance   286

National Incident-Based Reporting System (NIBRS)   283

nolle prosequi   305

no true bill   302

preliminary hearing   299

pretrial release services programs   298

preventive detention   293

probable cause   299

property bond   293

release on recognizance (ROR)   293

subpoena power   302

transactional immunity   302

true bill   302

Type I offenses   283

Uniform Crime Reports (UCR)   283

use immunity   302

FOR FURTHER READING

Barak, Gregg. 2012."On the Rhetoric and Reality of Fighting Financial Fraud on Wall Street." *The Criminologist* 37(4): 1–6.

Billings, Thanithia. 2016."Private Interest, Public Sphere: Eliminating the Use of Commercial Bail Bondsmen in the Criminal Justice System." *Boston College Law Review 57*: 1337–1365.

Gouldin, Lauryn P. 2016."Disentangling Flight Risk from Dangerousness." *Brigham Young University Law Review 2016*: 837–898.

Johnson, James L., and Laura M. Baber. 2015."State of the System: Federal Probation and Pretrial Services." *Federal Probation 79*(2): 34–40.

Jones, Cynthia E. 2013."'Give Us Free': Addressing Racial Disparities in Bail Determinations." *NYU Journal of Legislation and Public Policy* 16: 919–961.

Sacks, Meghan, Vincenzo A. Sainato, and Alissa R. Ackerman. 2015."Sentenced to Pretrial Detention: A Study of Bail Decisions and Outcomes." *American Journal of Criminal Justice 40*(3): 661–681.

Schnacke, Timothy R. 2014. *Fundamental of Bail: A Resource Guide for Pretrial Practitioners and a Framework for American Pretrial Reform*. Washington, DC: National Institute of Corrections.

Taibbi, Matt. 2014. *The Divide: American Injustice in the Age of the Wealth Gap*. New York: Spiegel & Grau.

11 Disclosing and Suppressing Evidence

Kim Kulish/Getty Images

A police officer reads a suspect his *Miranda* rights after arrest. *Miranda* is the best-known example of the U.S. Supreme Court's "due process revolution" that greatly changed how crimes are prosecuted. To liberals, due process limits on police power are necessary to protect the rights of all citizens, especially those who are wrongfully accused. Conservatives, however, often argue that the myriad rights enjoyed by the criminally accused often allow the guilty to go free. This philosophical debate aside, in reality, judges rarely suppress evidence in criminal cases.

Chapter Outline

Just before midnight, 18-year-old Lois Ann Jameson (not her real name) left the downtown theater where she worked and walked the two blocks to her normal bus stop. A half-hour later, she arrived in her neighborhood for her usual short walk home. The only unusual event was a strange car, which suddenly veered in front of her. A young Hispanic man got out, grabbed her with one hand, and placed the other over her mouth while dragging her into the parked car. He drove 20 minutes into the desert, where he tore off her clothes and raped her. In a strange twist of circumstances, the assailant drove Lois Ann Jameson back to her neighborhood.

Once she was home, she immediately called the police. To Detective Carroll Cooley, Jameson's story was not only somewhat contradictory but also offered few leads. Jameson couldn't provide a very good description of her attacker. The only lead was her detailed description of the car—an old model, light green, clean on the outside, and dirty brown upholstery on the inside. Moreover, in the backseat of the car was a loop of rope designed to help rear-seat passengers in pulling themselves up. This description eventually led Detective Cooley to a house on the west side of town, where he found a car exactly as described. The subsequent interrogation and conviction of Ernesto Miranda was to change the landscape of American criminal justice.

The *Miranda* warnings are the most controversial part of the Supreme Court's revolution in criminal justice. Responding to criticisms that police procedures were unfair and that the police were not adhering to the procedural requirements of the law, the Supreme Court imposed additional restrictions on police investigative techniques, such as searches, interrogations, and lineups. The Court's decisions resulted in extensive national controversy. Subsequent Courts, dominated by appointees of Republican presidents, have significantly curtailed (but not eliminated) these earlier decisions.

This chapter examines some of the diverse activities that may occur between arraignment and final disposition (either a guilty plea or a trial). The first topic will be the gathering of evidence, which is termed "discovery." Next will be a discussion of how and why some evidence is excluded from trial.

Discovery

The informal and formal exchange of information between prosecution and defense is referred to as **discovery**. Laboratory reports, statements of witnesses, defendants' confessions, and police reports are examples of information that prosecutors often gather and defense attorneys want to know about before trial.

Discovery seeks to ensure that the adversary system does not give one side an unfair advantage over the other. The guiding assumption of the adversary system is that truth will emerge after a struggle at trial. But as Justice William Brennan (1963) asked, should this struggle at trial be a sporting event or a quest for the truth? Historically, civil trials were largely sporting events, in which the outcome depended heavily on the technical skills of the lawyers. In an effort to eliminate the worst aspects of such contests, the Federal Rules of Civil Procedure were adopted in 1938, and most states have since followed the federal example. By these rules, prior to trial, every party in a civil action is entitled to the disclosure of all relevant information in the possession of any person, unless that information is privileged (Friedenthal, Kane, & Miller, 2015). These discovery rules are intended to make a trial "less a game of blind man's bluff and more a fair contest with the basic issues and facts disclosed to the fullest practicable extent" (*United States v. Procter & Gamble Co.*, 1958, p. 682). A long-standing debate, however, has been fought over the extent of pretrial discovery in criminal cases.

Law on the Books: Rules Requiring Disclosure

In contrast to the very broad power of discovery in civil proceedings, "there is no general constitutional right to discovery in a criminal case" (*Weatherford v. Bursey*, 1977, p. 559). However, a series of court decisions, statutes, and court rules provide the framework for the criminal discovery process. Courts have expressed concern that requiring too much prosecutorial disclosure might result in the defendant's taking undue advantage (*State v. Tune*, 1953). For example, the defendant, knowing of the state's case, might procure perjured testimony or might intimidate witnesses who are likely to testify (Mosteller, 2002).

Discovery in federal cases is governed primarily by sections of Rules 12, 16, and 26 of the Federal Rules of Criminal Procedure. Collectively, these rules provide a defendant, upon motion, rights to discovery concerning tangible objects; tape recordings; books, papers, and documents (including written or recorded statements made by the defendants or witnesses) that are relevant to the case; the defendant's prior criminal record, if any; the results or reports of physical examinations, scientific tests, experiments, and forensic comparisons; and summaries of any expert testimony that the government intends to offer in its case-in-chief. These materials may total only a few items and pages, or they may fill many boxes. The rules often afford the government similar reciprocal discovery upon its compliance with the request of the defendant.

In state courts, the type of information that is discoverable varies considerably from state to state. Some jurisdictions allow only limited discovery: The trial court has the discretion to order the prosecutor to disclose the defendant's confession and other physical documents, but that is all. Other jurisdictions take a middle ground: Discovery of confessions and physical evidence is a matter of right, but discovery of other items (witnesses' statements, for example) is more difficult. Finally, a few states have adopted liberal discovery rules: A presumption strongly in favor of prosecutorial disclosure exists, with only certain narrow exceptions.

Because of growing discontent with the discovery system, American courts have cautiously expanded mandatory disclosure by the prosecutor, especially with respect to disclosures of exculpatory evidence and impeachment material. **Exculpatory evidence** is any evidence that may be favorable to the defendant at trial either by tending to cast doubt on the defendant's guilt or by tending to mitigate the defendant's culpability, thereby potentially reducing the defendant's sentence.

Impeachment evidence is any evidence that would cast doubt on the credibility of a witness. The "Key Developments in Criminal Discovery Law" feature summarizes the major case and statutory law governing criminal discovery.

Discovery of Exculpatory Evidence

In *Brady v. Maryland* (1963, p. 87), the U.S. Supreme Court held that "the suppression by the prosecution of evidence favorable to an accused upon request violates due process where the evidence is material either to guilt or punishment, *irrespective of the good faith or bad faith of the prosecution*" (italics added). This is commonly referred to as the *Brady* rule.

The *Brady* rule is limited to admissible evidence. Thus, the prosecution has no obligation to provide the defense potentially exculpatory information that would not be admissible in court. For example, in *Wood v. Bartholomew* (1995), the U.S. Supreme Court held that there is no requirement to turn over the results of a polygraph examination of a witness because polygraph results are inadmissible.

Technically, the *Brady* rule applies only to exculpatory evidence that is *material*. Exculpatory evidence is material "only if there is a 'reasonable probability' that, had the evidence been disclosed to the defense, the result of the proceeding would have been different. A 'reasonable probability' is a probability sufficient to undermine confidence in the outcome" (*United States v. Bagley*, 1985, p. 682). Needless to say, this standard requires a judgment call on the part of prosecutors, and in recent years the Court has ruled that prosecutors have been too narrow in their interpretation. Indeed, in *Cone v. Bell* (2009), the Court said that

the Due Process Clause of the Fourteenth Amendment, as interpreted by *Brady*, only mandates the disclosure of material evidence, the obligation to disclose evidence favorable to the defense may arise more broadly under a prosecutor's ethical or statutory obligations. . . . [T]he prudent prosecutor will err on the side of transparency, resolving doubtful questions in favor of disclosure. (p. 470, n. 15)

In *Kyles v. Whitley* (1995), the prosecutor failed to disclose the statements of two of four witnesses and other evidence relating to Kyles's car. In a 5-to-4 decision, Justice David Souter wrote that the test was a cumulative one, looking at all the evidence that was not disclosed, not just isolated pieces. Moreover, to gain a new trial, the defense need only show a reasonable probability of a different result (not a preponderance of the evidence). "The question is not whether the defendant would more likely than not have received a different verdict with the evidence, but whether in its absence he received a fair trial, understood as a trial resulting in a verdict worthy of confidence" (p. 434). Applying this test, the Court ruled that the *Brady* rule had been violated in the case. What made the case particularly challenging, though, was that the prosecution did not know about the exculpatory evidence in the case because the police had not revealed the two witness statements to the prosecutor. According to the Court, though, prosecutors are responsible for ensuring that police communicate relevant evidence to the prosecutor's office. It is worthy to note that on retrial, three juries declined to convict Kyles, and charges were eventually dropped.

Brady does not require the prosecution to make its files available to the defendant for an open-ended "fishing expedition." Nor does *Brady* require the disclosure of inculpatory, neutral, or speculative evidence. However, prosecutors' obligations under *Brady* are not limited to situations in which the defendant specifically requests the evidence. As the "attorney for the sovereign," the prosecutor "must always be faithful to his client's overriding interest that 'justice shall be done'" (*United States v. Agurs*, 1976, pp. 110–111). Recall from Chapter 6 that prosecutors who violate their constitutional and ethical obligations in this regard may not only find their cases dismissed or overturned on appeal, but may also face disciplinary actions (like Mike Nifong) or criminal prosecution (like Ken Anderson).

Discovery of Impeachment Evidence

In *Jencks v. United States* (1957), the Supreme Court ruled that the government must disclose any prior inconsistent statements of prosecutorial witnesses so that the defense can conduct a meaningful cross-examination of such witnesses. Congress both expanded and limited the holding in *Jencks* when it enacted the Jencks Act. That law requires the prosecutor to disclose, after direct examination of a government witness and on the defendant's motion, any statement of a witness in the government's possession that relates to the subject matter of the witness's testimony. Thus, the Jencks Act requires disclosure of all prior statements of witnesses, even if the prior statements are not inconsistent with any subsequent statement by the witnesses, expanding the holding of *Jencks*. Yet, Congress placed the burden on the defense counsel to ask for the information (unlike *Brady* material, which the prosecutor has an ethical obligation to disclose even if not asked). Congress also limited the time frame for such disclosures such that it need not take place until after the direct examination of a government witness by the prosecution.

In *Giglio v. United States* (1972), the Supreme Court clarified that all impeachment evidence, even if not a prior statement by a witness, must be disclosed to the defense. Thus, *Giglio* mandated that the prosecution disclose any and all information that may be used to impeach the credibility of prosecution witnesses, including law enforcement officers. Impeachment information under *Giglio* includes information such as the prior criminal records or other acts of misconduct of prosecution witnesses, or such information as promises of leniency or immunity offered to prosecution witnesses. The prosecution even has an affirmative duty to investigate and disclose any exculpatory or impeachment evidence that is known by other governmental actors, such as investigating officers (*Kyles v. Whitley*, 1995). As with *Brady* material, the mandates of *Jencks* and *Giglio* do not require the prosecution to make its files available to the defendant for an open-ended fishing expedition.

Law in Action: Informal Prosecutorial Disclosure

Discovery rules are vitally important to defense attorneys. In states that grant defense considerable discovery rights, the lawyer can go straight to the prosecutor's files and obtain the essentials of

KEY DEVELOPMENTS IN CRIMINAL DISCOVERY LAW	
Jencks v. United States (1957)	Prior inconsistent statements of a witness must be made available to defense counsel so that the defense can conduct a meaningful cross-examination of such witnesses.
Jencks Act (1957)	Congress both expanded and limited the holding in *Jencks* by requiring the prosecutor to disclose, after direct examination of a government witness and on the defendant's motion, any statement of a witness in the government's possession that relates to the subject matter of the witness's testimony. Thus, the Jencks Act requires disclosure of all prior statements of witnesses, even if the prior statements are not inconsistent with any subsequent statement by the witnesses, expanding the holding of *Jencks*. Yet, Congress placed the burden on the defense counsel to ask for the information (unlike *Brady* material, which the prosecutor has an ethical obligation to disclose even if not asked). Congress also limited the time frame for such disclosure such that it need not take place until after the direct examination of a governmental witness by the prosecution.
Brady v. Maryland (1963)	Due process of law is violated when prosecutors either willfully or inadvertently conceal evidence that might be favorable to the defense because it is exculpatory.

(Continued)

(*Continued*)

***Williams v. Florida* (1970)**	Requiring defense to disclose an alibi defense prior to trial does not violate the defendant's privilege against self-incrimination.
***Giglio v. United States* (1972)**	All evidence that would impeach the credibility of any witnesses for the prosecution (including law enforcement officers)—even if not prior statements—must be disclosed, such as a witness's prior criminal acts or promises of leniency or immunity offered to prosecution witnesses.
***United States v. Agurs* (1976)**	*Brady* does not require the prosecution to make its files available to the defendant for an open-ended "fishing expedition." Nor does *Brady* require the disclosure of inculpatory, neutral, or speculative evidence. However, prosecutors' obligations under *Brady* are not limited to situations in which the defendant specifically requests the evidence. As the "attorney for the sovereign," the prosecutor "must always be faithful to his client's overriding interest that 'justice shall be done'" by disclosing evidence that would have been persuasive and produced reasonable doubt about guilt (pp. 110–111).
***Weatherford v. Bursey* (1977)**	There is no general constitutional right to discovery in criminal cases.
***United States v. Bagley* (1985)**	The *Brady* duty to disclose evidence that might be favorable to the defense extends to impeachment evidence (as well as exculpatory evidence).
***Kyles v. Whitley* (1995)**	A *Brady* violation occurs when the government fails to turn over evidence that is known only to police investigators—and not to the prosecutor—because prosecutors have a duty to learn of any favorable evidence known to the others acting on the government's behalf in the case, including the police. However, the test for reversing a conviction for a *Brady* violation is a cumulative one that looks at all the evidence that was not disclosed, not just isolated pieces. To gain a new trial, the defense need only show a reasonable probability of a different result (not a preponderance of the evidence). "The question is not whether the defendant would more likely than not have received a different verdict with the evidence, but whether in its absence he received a fair trial, understood as a trial resulting in a verdict worthy of confidence" (p. 434).
***Wood v. Bartholomew* (1995)**	*Brady* is limited to admissible evidence. Thus, failure of the prosecutor to turn over inadmissible polygraph evidence was not a *Brady* violation.
***Strickler v. Greene* (1999)**	To prevail on a *Brady* violation claim, a defendant must demonstrate prejudice to his or her case. Thus, even when exculpatory evidence is not disclosed in accordance with *Brady*'s mandate, there must be a reasonable probability that the conviction or sentence would have been different had the evidence been disclosed to the defense—even when there has not been a request for the information by the defense.
***United States v. Ruiz* (2002)**	A plea agreement requiring a defendant to waive the right to receive any impeachment information is valid since the Constitution does not require the prosecution to disclose impeachment material prior to entering a plea agreement with a criminal defendant.
***Banks v. Dretke* (2004)**	A *Brady* violation occurs when the prosecution fails to disclose that a key witness was a paid governmental informant.
***Youngblood v. West Virginia* (2006)**	A *Brady* violation occurs when the government fails to disclose evidence materially favorable to the accused, regardless of whether the evidence is better classified as exculpatory evidence or impeachment evidence.
***Cone v. Bell* (2009)**	A prosecutor's obligations to disclose favorable or impeaching evidence, either to guilt or punishment, "may arise more broadly under a prosecutor's ethical or statutory obligations" than under *Brady* and *Bagly*. A "prudent prosecutor" should "err on the side of transparency, resolving doubtful questions in favor of disclosure."

the state's case against the defendant. By learning the facts of the prosecutor's case, the defense attorney need not face the difficult task of trying to force his client to voluntarily disclose this information. Across the nation, "nearly all lawyers interviewed felt that clients' veracity is questionable and in need of thorough verification. This forces the attorney to devote extra hours, frequently wasted, verifying a client's version of the facts, which also puts a strain on their relationship—especially when the attorney is forced to confront the defendant with his prevarications" (Wice, 1978, p. 45; see also Sternlight & Robbennolt, 2008).

In jurisdictions that grant limited discovery rights to the defense, defense attorneys must be more resourceful in determining what actually happened. To that end, a variety of proceedings not directly designed for discovery purposes can be used. At the preliminary hearing, intended to test the sufficiency of the evidence for holding the defendant, the defense hears at least part of the story of some critical witnesses. Similarly, during a hearing on a pretrial motion to suppress evidence, the testimony of key government witnesses may yield important new facts relevant to a trial defense. But eventually, defense attorneys may be forced to confront their clients about inconsistencies (or worse) in their statements, a confrontation that can strain lawyer–client relationships (see Chapter 7).

Some prosecutors have an office policy prohibiting assistant prosecutors from disclosing any information not required by law. But it is more usual that assistant DAs voluntarily disclose certain aspects of the state's case to defense attorneys. Such informal discovery operates within the norms of cooperation of courtroom work groups. Defense attorneys who maintain good relationships with prosecutors and are viewed as trustworthy receive selected information about the case. Conversely, defense attorneys who maintain hostile relationships with the prosecutor, who represent clients who are viewed as troublemakers, or both (the two frequently go together) find the prosecutors holding the cards as tightly to the vest as the law allows.

Informal prosecutorial disclosure does not stem from sympathy for the defendant, but rather from a long-held courthouse theory that an advance glimpse at the prosecutor's case encourages a plea of guilty. From the perspective of the prosecutor, defendants often tell their lawyers only part of what happened. Therefore, the defense attorney who learns what evidence the prosecutor possesses can use it to show the defendant that contesting the matter may be hopeless. At times, though, defense attorneys are often frustrated by the prosecution's control over the discovery process, especially when the prosecution fails to disclose important information until the last possible minute—by which point it has minimal value (Medwed, 2010; Wice, 2005).

Informal prosecutorial discovery greatly encourages pleas of guilty, at least when the prosecution has a strong case. In their classic studies, Milton Heumann (1978) and Paul Wice (1978) reported that in courthouses where prosecutors emphasize closed discovery, there is often a failure to plea-bargain, and a large number of cases go to trial, frequently without a jury. In contrast, they found that in courthouses where prosecutors have adopted open discovery policies, pleas of guilty are entered sooner, resulting in a significantly smaller backlog than is found in most cities with closed discovery. More than three decades later, their findings remain the conventional wisdom, subject to the limitation that the prosecution has a strong case. If, on the other hand, the prosecution's case is weak, then open discovery may serve to embolden a defendant to take his or her chances at trial (Covey, 2007; Medwed, 2010).

Law and Controversy: Requiring Reciprocal Disclosure

Ordinarily, to obtain discoverable information, a party must make a timely motion before the court; show that the specific items sought are material to the preparation of its case; and demonstrate that its request is reasonable. Some jurisdictions, however, provide for **reciprocal disclosure**—automatic discovery for certain types of evidence, without the necessity for motions and court orders. Who must disclose what to whom, however, varies significantly, causing controversy in the criminal justice system.

Defense attorneys understandably press for broader discovery laws. But to what extent should the defense be required to disclose relevant materials in its possession to the prosecution? After all, the Constitution limits reciprocal discovery in criminal cases, unlike in civil proceedings, because criminal defendants enjoy the privilege against self-incrimination. Thus, requirements that the defense turn over to the prosecutor statements from expert witnesses that it does not intend to call at trial would probably be unconstitutional. If, however, the defendant intends to call an expert witness at trial, rules such as Federal Rule of Criminal Procedure 16 typically require the defense to disclose the expert's identity, qualifications, conclusions, and the bases for having reached those conclusions.

A few states allow the defendant access to discoverable information in the prosecution's possession without the defense having a duty to disclose any information to the prosecution. Even in such jurisdictions, however, the defense would have an obligation to disclose certain evidence in support of select affirmative defenses. For example, an **alibi defense** means that the defendant claims the crime was committed while the defendant was somewhere else and thus could not have been the perpetrator. The defense would have to disclose a list of witnesses to be called to support the alibi (Federal Rule of Criminal Procedure 12.1(a)(2); *Williams v. Florida*, 1970). Such pretrial notice enables the prosecutor to investigate the backgrounds of these witnesses and thus be prepared to undermine the defendant's contention that he or she was somewhere else when the crime was committed. Similarly, Federal Rule of Criminal Procedure 12.2 and the rules in most states mandate that the defense must disclose to the prosecution prior to trial that an insanity plea will be entered or that expert witnesses will be called.

In contrast to jurisdictions with only limited disclosure requirements for the defense, in some states "a defendant who issues a discovery request to the prosecutor thereby automatically incurs the duty to disclose information to the prosecutor. In still others, a defense discovery request gives the prosecutor the right—presumably almost certain to be exercised—to demand discovery from the defendant" (Easton & Bridges, 2008, p. 6). The state of the law governing discovery is constantly changing, but the trend appears to be in favor of broadening the right of discovery for both the defense and the prosecution. The guiding light, as articulated by prosecutors and law-and-order advocates, is that the trial should be a level playing field for all parties; both sides should be prevented from attempting to conduct a trial by ambush.

Suppressing Evidence

The most controversial of the U.S. Supreme Court's criminal justice decisions have concerned how the police gather evidence. For example, the rape conviction of Ernesto Miranda in 1966 was overturned because the police had not advised him of his constitutional right to remain silent before he confessed. In 1961, Dollree Mapp's pornography conviction was reversed because the police had illegally searched her house. In both cases, otherwise valid and trustworthy evidence was excluded from trial. These cases are applications of the *exclusionary rule*, a judicial creation that is rooted, in part, in the writings of several Framers of the U.S. Constitution (Roots, 2014).

The Exclusionary Rule

The **exclusionary rule** prohibits the prosecutor from using illegally obtained evidence during a trial. Under the common law, the seizure of evidence by illegal means did not affect its admissibility in court. Any evidence, however obtained, was admitted as long as it satisfied other evidentiary criteria for admissibility, such as relevance and trustworthiness. That changed when the exclusionary rule was first developed in *Weeks v. United States* (1914). *Weeks*, however, was limited to a prohibition on the use of evidence illegally obtained by federal law enforcement officers. Not until *Wolf v. Colorado* (1949) did the U.S. Supreme Court take the first step toward applying the exclusionary rule to the states by ruling that the Fourth Amendment was applicable to the states through the Due Process Clause of the Fourteenth Amendment. *Wolf v. Colorado*, however, left enforcement of Fourth Amendment rights to the discretion of the individual states; it did not specifically require application of the exclusionary rule. That mandate did not come until the landmark decision of *Mapp v. Ohio* (1961). With *Mapp*, the exclusionary rule became the principal method to deter Fourth Amendment violations by law enforcement officials. The rule was also supported by a normative argument: A court of law should not participate in or condone illegal conduct.

The exclusionary rule is commonly associated with the search and seizure of physical evidence under the Fourth Amendment. But the exclusionary rule is also applicable to interrogations and confessions that violate either the Fifth Amendment privilege against self-incrimination or the Sixth Amendment right to counsel. However, the rule applies differently depending on the type and severity of the underlying constitutional violation. As the U.S. Supreme Court stated in *Dickerson v. United States* (2000), "unreasonable searches under the Fourth Amendment are different from unwarned interrogation under the Fifth Amendment." Thus, for example, a failure to give *Miranda* warnings before a suspect's confession may not trigger the exclusionary rule to other, future incriminating statements by that same suspect.

Finally, it should be noted that the exclusionary rule also applies to the pretrial **confrontations** between witnesses and suspects (show-ups, photo arrays, and lineups) that were either unreliable (therefore violating due process) or that occurred in violation of the accused's Sixth Amendment right to counsel. Thus, for example, if a police lineup is improperly conducted, the identification of the suspect may be excluded from evidence during trial pursuant to the exclusionary rule.

Fruit of the Poisonous Tree

The exclusionary rule is not limited to evidence that is the direct product of illegal police behavior, such as coerced confessions, unnecessarily suggestive lineups, or seizure of items during unconstitutional searches. The rule also requires exclusion of evidence indirectly obtained as a result of a constitutional violation (this type of evidence is sometimes called **derivative evidence**). The exclusionary rule operates to exclude derivative evidence because it is considered to be **fruit of the poisonous tree**. Under this doctrine's metaphors, the poisonous tree is evidence directly obtained as a result of a constitutional violation; the fruit is the derivative evidence obtained because of knowledge gained from the first illegal search, arrest, confrontation, or interrogation. For example, assume that police illegally arrest someone without probable cause and then interrogate the suspect without first administering *Miranda* warnings. During the interrogation, the suspect confesses to a murder and tells the police the location of the body. The exclusionary rule would prevent the confession from being admitted into evidence at trial since it was obtained as a result of two constitutional violations: an illegal arrest and a Fifth Amendment self-incrimination violation. If the police then discovered the body where the suspect told them to look, the body and any evidence on it would also be inadmissible at trial since the police found the body as a result of their illegal interrogation of the suspect. The body itself would be considered fruit of the poisonous tree.

As you might imagine, judges loathe excluding derivative evidence under the exclusionary rule or the fruit of the poisonous tree doctrine. Accordingly, the courts have developed four doctrines that mitigate the harsh effects of preventing the use of both illegally obtained evidence and the fruits derived from the illegality.

First, when police act in **good faith** on warrant or statute reasonably believed to be valid, but is later determined to be a defective warrant or an unconstitutional statute, their good faith reliance on the warrant or law usually allows the evidence collected to be admissible (*United States v. Leon*, 1984; *Arizona v. Evans*, 1995). The lack of police misconduct underlies the logic of this exception to the exclusionary rule. Note, however, that police cannot be said to have acted in good faith if a warrant is obviously defective, such as if it lacks a description of the things or persons to be searched (*Groh v. Ramirez*, 2004), or if police provide deliberately or recklessly false information to obtain the warrant (*Franks v. Delaware*, 1978).

Second, if evidence is obtained through a source that is independent of any unconstitutional police actions, then the **independent source** doctrine will allow such evidence to be admitted at trial. For example, in *Segura v. United States* (1984), police obtained a valid search warrant only using information known to officers before they entered an apartment illegally. Despite an illegal trespass, the evidence collected during the search was admissible because the warrant was supported by probable cause established by information independent from the illegal entry.

Third, the **inevitable discovery** exception holds that a court may admit illegally obtained evidence if it would have been discovered anyway through independent, lawful means. For example, in *Nix v. Williams* (1984), police located a body by illegally interrogating the defendant in violation of his Sixth Amendment right to counsel. But, since a comprehensive search for the body was already under way in the area in which the body was ultimately located, the Court reasoned that the body would have inevitably been discovered anyway and, therefore, the physical evidence of the homicide was admissible.

Finally, a court may admit evidence obtained in a manner that is so far removed from a constitutional violation such that the initial illegality is deemed to be sufficiently attenuated/weakened (*Brown v. Illinois*, 1975). For example, in *Won Sun v. United States* (1963), federal agents arrested the defendant without probable cause. Several days after he was released on bail, the defendant returned to the police station and voluntarily confessed. His actions were deemed that sufficiently removed from the illegal arrest that the **attenuation** exception to the exclusionary rule applied, rendering his confession admissible.

In *Utah v. Strieff* (2016), a detective had received an anonymous tip about drug activity at a particular residence. He conducted surveillance on the property and observed a number of people making brief visits to the house, leading him to suspect the occupants of the home were dealing drugs. The officer detained Edward Strieff after observing him leave the residence. During that detention, the officer requested Strieff's identification and relayed the information to a police dispatcher, who informed him that Strieff had an outstanding arrest warrant for a traffic violation. The officer arrested Strieff based on that warrant. He then searched Strieff and found methamphetamine and drug paraphernalia.

According to the Supreme Court, the officer made "two good-faith mistakes" (p. 2063) when detaining Strieff that collectively rendered the detention unconstitutional on the basis that it lacked reasonable suspicion under *Terry v. Ohio*.

> First, he had not observed what time Strieff entered the suspected drug house, so he did not know how long Strieff had been there. [The officer] thus lacked a sufficient basis to conclude that Strieff was a short-term visitor who may have been consummating a drug transaction. Second, because he lacked confirmation that Strieff was a short-term visitor, [the officer] should have asked Strieff whether he would speak with him, instead of demanding that Strieff do so. (*Strieff*, 2016, p. 2063)

In spite of the unconstitutionality of the officer's actions in stopping Strieff, the Court held that the preexisting warrant was sufficiently attenuated from the unlawful stop such that his arrest and conviction should be upheld. The dissenting justices in the case warned that the majority of the Court eviscerated the Fourth Amendment's protections by extending the attenuation doctrine as far as it did:

> This case allows the police to stop you on the street, demand your identification, and check it for outstanding traffic warrants—even if you are doing nothing wrong. If the officer discovers a warrant for a fine you forgot to pay, courts will now excuse his illegal stop and will admit into evidence anything he happens to find by searching you after arresting you on the warrant. (p. 2064, Sotomayor, J., dissenting)

Interrogations and Confessions

Since the 1930s, the U.S. Supreme Court has struggled to place limits on how police interrogate suspects.

The Voluntariness Standard

Traditionally, English common law routinely admitted all confessions, even those produced by torture. That began to change in the mid-1700s when English courts started to examine the circumstances under which a confession was made. The rule that eventually emerged was that only confessions that were "free and voluntary" would be admitted at trial. Confessions obtained by physical coercion, such as beatings or torture, were no longer allowed into evidence because they were not trustworthy; someone in fear of a beating is likely to say what his or her antagonists want to hear. Relying on the Fourteenth Amendment's Due Process Clause, the U.S. Supreme Court adopted this approach in *Brown v. Mississippi* (1936). Since then, confessions based on physical coercion have been inadmissible in U.S. courts on due process grounds. As a result, such harsh means of interrogation by police in the United States have largely ceased. (As explained in Chapter 2, however, interrogations of "enemy combatants" under the administration of President George W. Bush were a notable departure from the trend away from physically coercive techniques.)

The Court was then confronted with the slightly different issue of confessions obtained as a result of lengthy interrogations, psychological ploys, and the like. For example, in *Ashcraft v. Tennessee* (1944), the suspect was interrogated for 36 hours with virtually no break, thereby depriving him of any rest. The Court invalidated the confession as involuntary, reasoning that confessions based on psychological coercion should be rejected just as if they were based on physical coercion, because such statements were not likely to be free and voluntary. But it is not easy to define what constitutes psychological coercion. In numerous cases, the Court sought to spell out what factors the trial court should use in deciding what constitutes psychological coercion, but the standards announced were far from precise.

The Birth of *Miranda* Warnings

In an attempt at greater precision, the Supreme Court under the leadership of Chief Justice Earl Warren adopted specific procedures for custodial police interrogations. In the path-breaking decision *Miranda v. Arizona* (1966), the Court imposed what are widely known as *Miranda* warnings. Before a suspect in custody may be lawfully interrogated, the police are required to tell the suspect:

- You have the right to remain silent.
- Anything you say can and will be used against you in a court of law.

- You have the right to talk to a lawyer and have him or her present with you while you are being questioned.
- If you cannot afford to hire a lawyer, one will be appointed to represent you before any questioning, if you wish.

In addition, the Court shifted the burden of proof from the defense, which previously had to prove that a confession was not "free and voluntary," to the police and prosecutor, who now must prove that they advised the defendant of his or her constitutional rights and that he or she knowingly and voluntarily waived those rights (see "Case Close-Up: *Miranda v. Arizona* and Police Interrogations").

Miranda is based on the Fifth Amendment's command that "No person . . . shall be compelled in any criminal case to be a witness against himself. . . ." Contrary to popular believe, law enforcement officers do not have to read *Miranda* rights to someone merely being arrested. Rather, *Miranda* rights need only be provided to a suspect who is both *in custody* and being *interrogated*. Stated differently, *Miranda* applies only to **custodial interrogations**. If someone is not "in custody" (they are talking to the police voluntarily and are free to terminate the discussion at any time), *Miranda* warnings are not necessary. Similarly, even if a suspect were in custody, if the police are not engaged in conduct designed to illicit an incriminating response, then *Miranda* is similarly inapplicable.

Given the language of the Fifth Amendment, it should come as no surprise that a criminal defendant has an "absolute right not to testify" at trial (*United States v. Patane*, 2004, p. 637). Thus, a prosecutor may not ask a jury to draw an inference of guilt from the defendant's failure to testify in his or her own defense (*Griffin v. California*, 1965). Prior to trial, however, a suspect usually must assert his or her privilege against self-incrimination to benefit from it because "the Fifth Amendment guarantees that no one may be 'compelled in any criminal case to be a witness against himself'; it does not establish an unqualified 'right to remain silent'" (*Salinas v. Texas*, 2013, p. 2177). In other words—and perhaps paradoxically, from a logical standpoint—one may

By the age of 23, Ernesto Miranda had compiled a long police record. He dropped out of Queen of Peace Grammar School in Mesa, Arizona, after the eighth grade and shortly thereafter was arrested for car theft. By age 18, his police blotter showed six arrests and four prison sentences. A stint in the military to turn his life around quickly degenerated to mirror his civilian life; after going AWOL, he was given an undesirable discharge. But at 23, he appeared to have turned the corner: his boss at the produce company described him as "one of the best workers I ever had." Indeed, on Wednesday he worked from 8:00 p.m. to 8:00 a.m. and had barely slept an hour when the police knocked on the front door:

Stating that they didn't want to talk in front of his common law wife, the police took him to a Phoenix police station. A lineup of three other Hispanics from the city jail was quickly assembled. Lois Ann Jameson viewed the four men but could state only that Miranda's build and features were similar to those of her assailant. In the interrogation room, when Miranda asked how he had done in the lineup, Detective Cooley replied, "You flunked." After two hours of questioning, he signed a written confession admitting guilt. His subsequent trial was short and perfunctory. The only prosecution exhibit was the signed confession. Needless to say, the jury quickly returned guilty verdicts for kidnapping and rape.

The interrogation of Ernesto Miranda was in most ways unremarkable. It most certainly lacked the blatant duress at the center of earlier Supreme Court decisions on the limits of police interrogation. What was missing, however, was any advice to Ernesto about his rights under the Constitution. Indeed, the police testified that they never told Miranda that he didn't have to talk to the police, nor did they advise him of his right to consult with an attorney. These facts highlighted the giant chasm between the principles of the Constitution and the realities of police stations in America.

By 1966, the Supreme Court had been grappling with the issue of confessions for three decades. Despite numerous cases, the standards for interrogating suspects were still far from clear. Chief Justice Earl Warren's opinion in *Miranda* expressed concern over the "police-dominated" atmosphere of interrogation rooms and held that warnings were required to counteract the inherently coercive nature of stationhouse questioning. But in reality, *Miranda* created no new rights. Under American law, suspects have never been required to talk to the police, and the right to counsel extends to the police station as well as the courthouse. In essence, the Court held that the Fifth Amendment privilege against self-incrimination was as applicable to interrogation by the police before trial as it was to questioning by the prosecutor during trial.

Miranda v. Arizona is the Warren Court's best known and arguably most controversial decision, extending constitutional rights to those accused of violating the criminal law. The four dissenting justices criticized the ruling on both constitutional and practical grounds. To Justice Byron White, the *Miranda* rule was "a deliberate calculus to prevent interrogation, to reduce the incidence of confessions, and to increase the number of trials." Police, prosecutors, and public officials likewise criticized the ruling, and it became a key plank in Richard Nixon's law-and-order campaign in 1968. With four Nixon-appointed justices, the Burger Court began narrowing *Miranda*, but the holding itself has not been overturned. Indeed, *Miranda* has now become settled law, deeply imbedded in the constitutional fabric of our nation.

not merely remain mute in order to invoke one's privilege against self-incrimination because the privilege "generally is not self-executing" (*Minnesota v. Murphy*, 1984, p. 425). Rather, someone who desires the protection of the Fifth Amendment's Self-Incrimination Clause must affirmatively claim it by expressly invoking the privilege at the time he or she is relying on it (*Berghuis v. Thompkins*, 2010; *Salinas v. Texas*, 2013). Although a suspect need not recite any specific phrase to invoke the privilege—like saying "I invoke my Fifth Amendment rights" or "I assert my privilege against self-incrimination"— it is clear that the suspect must say something that puts law enforcement officers on notice that he or she is refusing to answer questions.

Another limitation of the *Miranda* rule is that it applies only to "evidence of a testimonial or communicative nature" (*Schmerber v. California*, 1966, p. 761). Thus, *Miranda* warnings do not need to be given before law enforcement officers obtain nontestimonial evidence, such as breath or blood samples, handwriting exemplars, lineup participation, or fingerprints.

Interrogations and the Sixth Amendment

The Sixth Amendment provides that "[i]n all criminal prosecutions, the accused shall enjoy the right … to have the Assistance of Counsel for his defense."

> The right to counsel under the Sixth Amendment differs from the right to counsel under *Miranda* that flows from the Fifth Amendment. The sole purpose of the right under *Miranda* is to insure that a suspect's will is not overborne by coercive police interrogation tactics while the suspect is in custody. Thus, it exists to prevent compulsory self-incrimination only when a suspect is subject to custodial interrogation. In contrast, the Sixth Amendment is not concerned with compulsion in the self-incrimination context; rather, it protects those facing criminal adversarial proceedings in court. Thus, the Sixth Amendment right to counsel is triggered ("attaches") when formal criminal proceedings "have been initiated against him whether by way of formal charge, preliminary hearing, indictment, information, or arraignment." (Ferdico, Fradella, & Totten, 2016, p. 522, quoting *Fellers v. United States*, 2004, p. 560)

Once the Sixth Amendment right to counsel attaches and is invoked or asserted, authorities may not engage in any conduct that is designed to elicit an incriminating response from the defendant without the presence or waiver of counsel (*Brewer v. Williams*, 1977). This means that a defendant (whether in custody or not) may not be questioned without the defendant's lawyer being present unless a valid waiver of the Sixth Amendment right to counsel is first obtained. Thus, the Sixth Amendment bars the use of any secret investigatory techniques (such as placing an informant in a jail cell with a suspect), while the Fifth Amendment does not (*United States v. Henry*, 1980).

As with the Fifth Amendment right to counsel under *Miranda*, a defendant may waive his or her right to counsel under the Sixth Amendment. A valid waiver of *Miranda* rights for Fifth Amendment purposes also satisfies the requirements of the Sixth Amendment. Thus, *Miranda* warnings are sufficient to inform a defendant of the right to have counsel present during questioning once the Sixth Amendment right to counsel has attached, as well as the consequences of a decision to waive the Sixth Amendment right during such questioning (*Patterson v. Illinois*, 1988).

Interrogations and the Fourteenth Amendment

Neither *Miranda* nor any Sixth Amendment right to counsel cases replaced the voluntariness test; rather, the Fifth and Sixth Amendments work in conjunction with that due process requirement. "[T]he failure to provide *Miranda* warnings in and of itself does not render a confession involuntary" (*New York v. Quarles*, 1984, p. 655). However, while satisfaction of *Miranda*'s requirements is a relevant consideration in determining the voluntariness of a confession, it is not conclusive. Statements given after *Miranda* warnings may nonetheless be inadmissible if they were not given voluntarily but rather were coerced (*Berkemer v. McCarty*, 1984). In *Mincey v. Arizona* (1978), for example, the continued interrogation of an injured, depressed, and medicated suspect who was in extreme pain while being treated in a hospital intensive care unit was held to render his statements involuntary even though he had been Mirandized.

Applying the Law of Interrogation

The feature "Key Developments in Interrogation Law" summarizes some of the major cases concerning the interrogation of criminal suspects. With a handful of exceptions, such as *Minnick v. Mississippi* (1990) and *Dickerson v. United States* (2000), the Supreme Court has generally limited *Miranda*'s application under the leadership of Chief Justices Warren Burger, William Rehnquist, and John Roberts.

KEY DEVELOPMENTS IN INTERROGATION LAW

Fifth Amendment (1791)	"No person . . . shall be compelled in any criminal case to be a witness against himself. . . ."
English Common Law (19th century)	Involuntary confessions are not admissible in court.
***Brown v. Mississippi* (1936)**	Use of physical coercion to obtain confessions violates the Due Process Clause of the Fourteenth Amendment.
***Ashcraft v. Tennessee* (1944)**	Psychologically coerced confessions are not voluntary and therefore not admissible in court.
***Griffin v. California* (1965)**	If a defendant exercises his or her right to silence, the prosecutor may not ask the jury to draw an inference of guilt from the defendant's refusal to testify in his own defense.
***Miranda v. Arizona* (1966)**	Suspect's Fifth and Fourteenth Amendment rights were violated because he had not first been advised of his right to remain silent and to have an attorney present during a custodial interrogation.
***Harris v. New York* (1971)**	Voluntary statements taken in violation of *Miranda* are inadmissible only as substantive evidence in the prosecution's case-in-chief to prove the defendant's guilt. However, voluntary statements made by defendants who had not been properly warned of their *Miranda* rights may be used during trial to impeach their credibility if they take the witness stand in their own defense and contradict the earlier statements.
***Michigan v. Mosley* (1975)**	Even though *Miranda* states that the interrogation must cease when the person in custody indicates a desire to remain silent, *Miranda* did not create "a per se proscription of indefinite duration upon any further questioning by any police officer on any subject, once the person in custody has indicated a desire to remain silent" (p. 103). Thus, so long as a suspect's right to cut off questioning is "scrupulously honored" by police, a second attempt at custodial interrogation is permissible so long as a significant amount of time has passed between the first and second interrogation attempts and fresh *Miranda* warnings are administered again.
***North Carolina v. Butler* (1979)**	*Miranda* warnings must be given in language that the person can comprehend and on which the person can act intelligently. The relevant inquiry is whether the words used by the officer, in view of the language skills, age, intelligence, and demeanor of the person being interrogated, convey a clear understanding of all *Miranda* rights. If so, suspects may waive *Miranda* rights, even if they do so impliedly, rather than explicitly.
***Rhode Island v. Innis* (1980)**	A "spontaneous" statement made by a suspect in custody before being Mirandized is admissible so long as the statements were not given in response to police questioning or other conduct by the police likely to illicit an incriminating response.
***New York v. Quarles* (1984)**	Overriding considerations of public safety justified a police officer's failure to provide *Miranda* warnings before asking questions about the location of a weapon apparently abandoned just before arrest.
***Oregon v. Elstad* (1985)**	Absent deliberately coercive or improper tactics in obtaining the initial statement, when a suspect subject to custodial interrogation makes incriminating statements without having been Mirandized, but subsequently repeats those incriminating statements after having been read *Miranda* rights, defendants cannot argue that the fruit of the poisonous tree doctrine bars the admissibility of their second admission or confession as being tainted by the first if the initial statements were knowingly and voluntarily given.

Colorado v. Connelly (1986)	A suspect's personal characteristics (e.g., age; mental capacity; education level; physical or mental impairment from illness, injury, or intoxication; and experience in dealing with the police) are all relevant considerations when determining the voluntariness of an admission or confession. However, "mere examination of the confessant's state of mind can never conclude the due process inquiry.... [C]oercive police activity is a necessary predicate to the finding that a confession is not 'voluntary' within the meaning of the Due Process Clause of the Fourteenth Amendment" (p. 167).
Kuhlmann v. Wilson (1986)	Neither a defendant's Fifth nor Sixth Amendment rights are violated when someone overhears a defendant make incriminating statements and reports them to the police either voluntarily or through prior arrangement. Rather, a defendant must demonstrate that the police and their informant took some action, beyond merely listening, that was designed deliberately to elicit incriminating remarks.
Illinois v. Perkins (1990)	For Fifth Amendment purposes, a law enforcement officer can pose as a prison inmate and elicit a confession from an actual inmate, even though the officer gives no *Miranda* warnings about the inmate's constitutional rights. Note that such a practice would violate the Sixth Amendment right to counsel if formal criminal proceedings had been initiated.
Minnick v. Mississippi (1990)	Unlike an invocation of the right to remain silent, once a suspect has invoked his or her right to counsel, interrogation must cease and police may not reinitiate interrogation without counsel present—regardless of whether the accused has consulted with an attorney.
Pennsylvania v. Muniz (1990)	Routine questions asked of a suspect to determine whether he or she understands instructions on how to perform physical sobriety tests or breathalyzer tests, as well as routine booking questions regarding the suspect's name, address, eye color, weight, date of birth, and age, are not interrogation and, therefore, fall outside *Miranda*.
Arizona v. Fulminate (1991)	A coerced confession does not automatically overturn a conviction. Rather, *Miranda* violations must be reviewed for a determination of harmless or harmful error (see Chapter 15).
Davis v. United States (1994)	A suspect's assertion of *Miranda* rights must be clear and unambiguous. Thus, police do not need to stop questioning a suspect who makes an ambiguous statement about wanting to remain silent or wanting an attorney.
Dickerson v. United States (2000)	*Miranda* embodies a constitutional rule that has become embedded in police practices; the Court will not overrule it.
Texas v. Cobb (2001)	The right to counsel under the Sixth Amendment is offense specific; it does not necessarily extend to offenses that are "factually related" to those that have actually been charged. Thus, police were able to question a defendant about a murder even though his lawyer in a pending burglary case was not present during the interrogation.
Chavez v. Martinez (2003)	Suspects who are interrogated in violation of the requirements of *Miranda* may not sue police for damages under 42 U.S.C. § 1983 (see Chapter 2) for violations of their Fifth Amendment rights.
United States v. Patane (2004)	The fruit of the poisonous tree doctrine does not apply to physical evidence derived from statements made in violation of *Miranda*, so long as the suspect's unwarned statements were voluntary.

(Continued)

(Continued)

***Missouri v. Seibert* (2004)**	Deliberately questioning a suspect twice, the first time without reading the *Miranda* warnings, is usually improper.
***Florida v. Powell* (2010)**	The warnings need not be given in the exact form used in the *Miranda* decision. All that is necessary is that the words used reasonably convey to a suspect his or her *Miranda* rights.
***Maryland v. Shatzer* (2010)**	When a suspect is released from custody and returned to his normal life for at least 14 days, there is a sufficient break in custody such that the logic of *Minnick* is inapplicable. Thus, if police re-approach a suspect after this waiting period and the suspect waives his or her *Miranda* rights to counsel, the statements will be admissible.
***Berghuis v. Thompkins* (2010)**	Silence in the face of an accusation does not constitute an invocation of *Miranda* rights; a break in silence, however, may constitute a valid implied waiver of them. Thus, even though a suspect was silent during a three-hour interrogation, when he answered "yes" near the end of the interrogation when asked if he prayed to God to forgive him for the shooting, his statement was admissible.
***J.D.B. v. North Carolina* (2011)**	A suspect's age is a relevant factor in the "totality of the circumstances" when analyzing whether a minor is in custody for *Miranda* purposes (thereby triggering *Miranda* rights) or whether a "reasonable juvenile" would have felt free to terminate the interview and, therefore, was not in custody for *Miranda* purposes.
***Salinas v. Texas* (2013)**	The Fifth Amendment's privilege against self-incrimination does not extend to suspects who simply remain mute during questioning. Rather, the protections of that privilege must be expressly invoked. Thus, in the absence of an explicit invocation of the privilege, a defendant's silence in response to an incriminating question may be used as the basis of an inference of his or her guilt at trial.

Search and Seizure

The Fourth Amendment to the U.S. Constitution provides:

> The right of the people to be secure in their persons, houses, papers, and effects, against unreasonable searches and seizures, shall not be violated, and no Warrants shall issue, but upon probable cause, supported by Oath or affirmation and particularly describing the place to be searched, and the persons or things to be seized.

The first part of the Fourth Amendment is referred to as the *reasonableness clause*. A "search" occurs under the Fourth Amendment when police physically intrude onto an individual's property to obtain information or discover something (*United States v. Jones*, 2012). A "search" also occurs "when an expectation of privacy that society is prepared to consider 'reasonable' is infringed" (*United States v. Jacobsen*, 1984, 113). And, "a 'seizure' of property occurs when there is some meaningful interference with an individual's possessory interest in that property" (*United States v. Jacobsen*, 1984, p. 113). Thus, for the protections of the Fourth Amendment to apply, there must be either some governmental trespass to property or some governmental invasion of a person's actual, subjective expectation of privacy, and that expectation of privacy must be objectively reasonable by societal standards (*Katz v. Unites States*, 1967).

An **unreasonable search and seizure** occurs when law enforcement infringes upon property rights or a reasonable expectation of privacy by conducting a search or seizure without complying with the second clause of the Fourth Amendment, called the *warrants clause*. Under it, searches and seizures unsupported by probable cause are illegal. Moreover, even if there is probable cause, a warrant that describes with particularity the items police intend to search or seize is required to conduct a search and seizure unless a recognized warrant exception applies.

Although probable cause is usually necessary to conduct a search, seize evidence, or make an arrest, the U.S. Supreme Court has created several notable exceptions to this rule. The first important exception is commonly referred to as a "stop and frisk." Police are permitted to stop suspects based on reasonable suspicion of criminal activity—a lower standard of proof than probable cause. Moreover, if they have reasonable suspicion that the suspect may be armed, they may frisk the suspect for weapons (*Terry v. Ohio*, 1968).

Cursory, *Terry*-like protective sweeps of the passenger compartment of a car may be made if an officer has reasonable suspicion "that the suspect is dangerous and … may gain immediate control of weapons" (*Michigan v. Long*, 1983). The same is true for a brief protective sweep of premises (*Maryland v. Buie*, 1990).

One overarching exception to the Fourth Amendment that should be noted concerns exigent circumstances. Exigent circumstances are those "that would cause a reasonable person to believe that entry (or other relevant prompt action) was necessary to prevent physical harm to the officers or other persons, the destruction of relevant evidence, the escape of a suspect, or some other consequence improperly frustrating legitimate law enforcement efforts" (*United States v. McConney*, 1984, p. 1199). This is because the touchstone of the Fourth Amendment is reasonableness, and compliance with the usual requirements of probable cause and a warrant would be unreasonable in such emergency situations.

Search Warrants

A **search warrant** is a written document, signed by a judge or magistrate, authorizing a law enforcement officer to conduct a search. The Fourth Amendment specifies that "no Warrants shall issue, but upon probable cause, supported by Oath or affirmation, and particularly describing the place to be searched and the Persons or things to be seized." In light of the plain language of the Fourth Amendment, search warrants issued by a neutral judicial officer (usually a magistrate or judge) are the preferred mechanism for authorizing and conducting searches and seizures in the United States.

Applying for Search Warrants

Once a police officer decides that a search warrant is necessary, the officer usually goes back to the stationhouse to prepare the application, affidavit, and warrant. Three alternative procedures are used. In a few jurisdictions, search warrant applications are prepared by a deputy prosecutor on the basis of information provided by the officer. In other localities and in the federal system, the law enforcement officer prepares all the documentation and then submits them to a prosecutor, who systematically reviews them before they are presented to the magistrate. Regardless of who actually prepares the documentation, the application must provide sufficient information to a neutral judicial officer to determine that there is "a fair probability that contraband or evidence of a crime will be found in a particular place" (*Illinois v. Gates*, 1983, p. 238). This information is usually provided in an **affidavit**, a written statement of facts sworn to before the magistrate.

Next, the applicant must contact a neutral judicial officer to approve the warrant based on the application and the affidavit detailing the facts that establish probable cause. This is traditionally done in person at a courthouse. However, if court is not in session, it may occur at the home of a judge or another location. In some jurisdictions, police officers can obtain a warrant by phone, fax, e-mail, iPad, smartphones, or even using Skype (see Swingle & Thomasson, 2013). But most jurisdictions using such conveniences still require that the information provided by the police must be given under oath and recorded. Law enforcement officers must be careful to include all the relevant information on which probable cause may be based—both in their written affidavits and in oral testimony—so that a complete record exists for courts to evaluate the magistrate's decision if the warrant is challenged.

The review of a search warrant application seldom takes long. In fact, all of the few empirical studies of the search warrant process found that the process typically takes only a few minutes (Benner & Samarkos, 2000; Slobogin, 1998). But the process can be protracted and cumbersome, taking several days or even weeks, depending on both the structure of a particular jurisdiction's criminal justice system and on the type of case being investigated. For example, in some jurisdictions, search warrant applications and affidavits not only need to be in writing but also need to be reviewed by command-level police staff (e.g., such as a lieutenant or captain) or even a prosecutor. The type of case also affects the time it takes to obtain a warrant. In Phoenix, for example, police can obtain a search warrant in less than 10 minutes in cases involving suspected driving under the influence (DUI) using an "eSearch Warrant Application" that they can send electronically from their patrol cars (Chan, 2013). In other jurisdictions, it might take a skilled police officer two to three hours to prepare an affidavit summarizing his or her personal observations during a stop of a driver suspected of DUI (e.g., detailing erratic driving, bloodshot eyes, slurred speech, the smell of alcohol on the suspect's breath) and then have a judge approve the warrant. In contrast, given the requirements of particularly describing the place or person to be searched, the items to be seized, and the details necessary to establish probable cause when informants and other non-firsthand sources of information are involved, it should come as no surprise that it can take many hours—even days—to prepare search warrant applications and supporting affidavits in complex cases.

Authority to Issue a Search Warrant

Only judicial officers who have been specifically authorized to do so may issue search warrants. Most jurisdictions give this authority to judicial officers, such as magistrates, complaint justices, justices of the peace, and judges. The vesting of warrant-issuing power in a neutral and detached judicial officer stems from the Supreme Court's mandate that warrants can be issued only by people who are not involved in the "activities of law enforcement" (*Shadwick v. City of Tampa*, 1972, p. 350).

In some jurisdictions, an on-call "duty judge" or magistrate is available to issue warrants 24 hours a day, seven days per week. In other jurisdictions, finding a neutral judicial officer during off-hours can be challenging, especially if electronic procedures are not in place in a particular location.

Outright rejections of requests for search warrants are rare. A study by the National Center for State Courts reported that most police officers interviewed by the researchers could not remember having a search warrant application denied (Van Duizend, Sutton, & Carter, 1984). The authors concluded that the warrant-review process did not operate as it was intended. Research has suggested two reasons for this. Van Duizend and colleagues

concluded that the review process was largely perfunctory, as some judicial officers regarded themselves more as allies of law enforcement than as independent reviewers of evidence. And Benner and Samarkos (2000, p. 266) reported that computers have also contributed to the rubber-stamping of search warrant applications by allowing police to prepare applications by cutting-and-pasting "pre-packaged, boiler-plated affidavits [that] are produced by merely filling in a few blanks."

The Requirement of Particularity

As the text of the Fourth Amendment makes clear, warrants must describe with particularity "the place to be searched and the persons or things to be seized." This requirement means that warrants should be as detailed as possible. Thus, warrants to search premises should use specific addresses when addresses are known. Warrants to search motor vehicles should include information such as the make, body style, color, year, location, license plate number, and owner or operator of the vehicle (to the extent such information is known). Warrants to search particular people should include the person's name or, alternatively, a detailed description of a person whose name is unknown that includes the person's weight, height, age, race, clothing, address, aliases, and so forth. Finally, items to be seized must be described with sufficient particularity so that the officers executing the warrant (1) can identify the items with reasonable certainty, and (2) are left with no discretion as to which property is to be taken.

Executing Search Warrants

The final step is the execution of the warrant. The officer serves the warrant, conducts the search, and seizes evidence. Officers mainly search private residences and impound vehicles for drugs or stolen goods. Regardless of the area or persons to be searched, a few general rules must be followed during the execution of a search warrant.

1. Search warrants must be executed in a timely manner to prevent the information that established probable cause from going stale.

2. The scope of law enforcement activities during the execution of the warrant must be strictly limited to achieving the objectives that are set forth with particularity in the warrant. If officers exceed the scope of the authorized invasion

under the terms of the warrant, the evidence seized will usually be deemed inadmissible.

3. Search warrants must be executed at a reasonable time of day. This normally means that warrants must be executed during the daytime; however, courts may authorize a nighttime search if the affidavit in support of the warrant sets forth specific facts showing some need to execute the warrant at night.

4. Law enforcement officers are generally required to *knock-and-announce* their presence, authority, and purpose before entering the premises to execute a search warrant (*Wilson v. Arkansas*, 1995). Courts usually require police officers to wait at least 10 to 20 seconds after announcing their presence before entering the premises. However, police do not need to knock-and-announce their presence "if circumstances present a threat of physical violence, or if there is reason to believe that evidence would likely be destroyed if advance notice were given, or if knocking and announcing would be futile" (*Hudson v. Michigan*, 2006, pp. 589–590). In fact, if such circumstances are known in advance, many states allow for courts to issue "no knock warrants." While violations of the knock-and-announce rule may subject offending officers to civil damages, in a lawsuit brought under 42 U.S.C. § 1983, *Hudson* held that knock-and-announce violations will not result in application of the exclusionary rule to the evidence seized.

5. In light of the Fourth Amendment's command of reasonableness, courts are also concerned with the amount of time it takes law enforcement personnel to perform a search once it is initiated pursuant to a valid warrant. The police may remain on the premises only for as long as it is reasonably necessary to conduct the search. After all the objects described in a warrant have been found and seized, the authority of the warrant expires and police must leave the premises.

6. Also because of the Fourth Amendment's reasonableness requirement, officers executing a search warrant must be careful to use only a reasonable amount of force when conducting a search, such as breaking down a door. An otherwise reasonable search may be invalidated if excessive force is used.

After Search Warrants Are Executed

Once the items specified in a warrant have been found during a search and seized, the legal justification for law enforcement officers' intrusion onto premises comes to an end. They must therefore leave the premises in a timely manner. Before departing, however, Federal Rule of Criminal Procedure 41 and its state-law counterparts say that proper execution of a search warrant entails several duties after the actual search is completed. Unless the warrant provides otherwise, searching officers must inventory all the property seized and leave a copy of the warrant and inventory with the occupants or on the premises if no occupant is present. After leaving the searched premises, the warrant itself, together with a copy of the inventory, must be returned to the judicial officer designated in the warrant. Courts generally hold that these post-search duties are ministerial acts. Thus, a failure to perform them will usually not result in suppression of any evidence.

Finally, evidence seized during the execution of a search warrant must be secured in a manner that preserves the **chain of custody**. This process involves carefully collecting and labeling the evidence seized during the execution of the search warrant and then storing the evidence in a secure place—usually the evidence repository of a police department that is accessible only to designated evidence clerks. If evidence needs to be removed from secure police storage (for example, for use in court or to go to a laboratory for forensic scientific testing), then law enforcement must carefully document the dates and times at which the evidence was moved, the identity of all evidence handlers, the duration of custody and transfer, and the conditions under which evidence was stored during transfer. All people involved in handling the evidence must sign forms documenting their participation in the process to avoid subsequent allegations that the evidence was planted, unaccounted for, mishandled, or tampered with. Thus, a proper chain of custody allows the prosecution to show that evidence was scrupulously maintained in such a manner that its whereabouts can be accounted for from the moment of initial seizure until the time it is introduced into evidence in court.

Warrant Exceptions

Pursuant to the mandates of the plain text of the Constitution, **warrantless searches** "are per se unreasonable under the Fourth Amendment subject only to a few specifically established and well-delineated exceptions" (*Katz v. United States*, 1967, p. 357). Accordingly, warrants play a very important role in criminal procedure. It might therefore come as a surprise to many people that the majority of searches are conducted without a warrant under one of the recognized exceptions to the warrant requirement listed in Table 11.1.

TABLE 11.1	Exceptions to the Warrant Requirement
Doctrine and Leading Case(s)	**Fourth Amendment Holding**
Abandoned property *California v. Greenwood* (1988)	The Fourth Amendment does not prohibit the warrantless search and seizure of abandoned property, such as garbage left for collection outside a home.
Administrative searches *Donovan v. Dewey* (1981) *New York v. Burger* (1981)	Probable cause is not required to conduct administrative inspections for compliance with regulatory schemes such as fire, health, and safety codes (e.g., inspections of jetliners, mining operations, junk yards, pharmacies, gun stores, etc.).
Aerial searches *California v. Ciraolo* (1986) *Florida v. Riley* (1989)	Police do not need a warrant to conduct aerial surveillance of a suspect's property from an aircraft in public airspace, so long as they do so from a reasonable altitude.
Border searches *United States v. Ramsey* (1977) *Illinois v. Andreas* (1983) *United States v. Flores-Montano* (2004)	Searches conducted at any international border do not require a warrant, probable cause, or even reasonable suspicion that is required for *Terry* stops. This is based on the "longstanding right of the sovereign to protect itself by stopping and examining persons and property crossing into this country" (*United States v. Ramsey*, p. 616).
Consent searches *Schneckloth v. Bustamonte* (1973) *Illinois v. Rodriguez* (1990) *Fernandez v. California* (2014)	Fourth Amendment rights may be voluntarily waived. Thus, if police ask for permission to search without probable cause and/or a warrant, and permission is granted, any evidence found may be used in a criminal prosecution. The person granting consent need not actually know that s/he may refuse consent; accordingly, unlike in the *Miranda* setting, police do not have to inform people that a request to conduct a consensual search may be denied (i.e., people can refuse to give consent). Moreover, the actual owner need not be the person granting consent; warrantless searches are permitted when police have a reasonable belief that voluntary consent was obtained from a party who possesses common authority over premises—even if another party disagrees about whether police should be granted consent to enter and search premises.
Inventory searches *Colorado v. Bertine* (1987)	After lawfully taking property into custody (such as impounding a car), police may conduct a warrantless search of the property in order to protect the owner's property, protect police from potential danger, and to guard against claims of theft or loss.
Motor vehicle searches *Carroll v. United States* (1925) *California v. Acevedo* (1991) *Florida v. Jimeno* (1991) *Arizona v. Gant* (2009)	The mobility of motor vehicles justifies warrantless searches of them if there is probable cause to believe that the vehicle contains contraband. This includes any location in which the particular contraband might be found, such as the truck, the glove compartment, luggage, and other containers in the vehicle that could hold the contraband. However, police may not search the passenger compartment of a vehicle incident to a recent occupant's arrest unless it is reasonable to believe that the arrestee might access the vehicle at the time of the search or that the vehicle contains evidence of the offense of arrest.

Searches incident to lawful arrest *Chimel v. California* (1969) *Arizona v. Gant* (2009) *Riley v. California* (2014)	Police may search someone who is lawfully arrested "to remove any weapons that the latter might seek to use in order to resist arrest or effect his escape." Police may also search for and seize any evidence on the arrestee's person, or in the area within his/her immediate control, "in order to prevent its concealment or destruction." However, law enforcement officers must demonstrate an actual and continuing threat to their safety posed by an arrestee, or a need to preserve evidence related to the crime of arrest from tampering by the arrestee, in order to justify a warrantless vehicular search incident to arrest conducted after the vehicle's recent occupants have been arrested and secured. Additionally, police generally may not, without a warrant, search digital information on a cell phone seized from an individual who has been arrested.
Searches of open fields *Cady v. Dombrowski* (1973) *Oliver v. United States* (1984) *United States v. Dunn* (1987)	Because one cannot have a reasonable expectation of privacy in open areas, like fields, forests, open water, vacant lots, and the like, police do not have to comply with the Fourth Amendment's mandates of warrants and probable cause to search open areas, even if "no trespassing" signs are posted. Only those areas within the "curtilage" of one's home (i.e., the areas immediately adjacent to a home that the owner has taken steps to keep private, like a detached garage, a locked shed or barn, etc.) receive Fourth Amendment protection.
Plain view *Harris v. United States* (1968) *Washington v. Chrisman* (1982)	When a law enforcement officer is legally in a place in which s/he sees contraband or other evidence that provides probable cause to believe criminal activity is afoot, the evidence may be seized without a warrant. The plain view doctrine has been expanded to cover other senses, such as "plain smell" and "plain touch."
Special needs searches in public schools *New Jersey v. T.L.O.* (1985) *Board of Ed. of Ind. School Dist. 92, Pottawatomie County v. Earls* (2002) *Safford Unified School District v. Redding* (2009)	Although the Fourth Amendment applies to searches and seizures conducted by schoolteachers and administrators, neither probable cause nor a warrant is required. There need be only reasonable "grounds for suspecting that the search will turn up evidence that the student has violated or is violating either the law or the rules of the school" (T.L.O., 1985, p. 342). Moreover, to curb alcohol and drug abuse in schools, random drug testing of students who participate in extracurricular or athletic activities may be conducted without any individualized suspicion or a warrant. Strip searches of students, however, have been held to go too far.
Searches of public employers and/or their work spaces *O'Connor v. Ortega* (1987) *National Treasury Employees Union v. Von Raab* (1989) *Skinner v. Railway Labor Executives' Assoc.* (1989)	Neither probable cause nor a warrant is necessary for public employers to conduct searches either for work-related purposes or for investigations of work-related misconduct. This includes noninvasive seizures of bodily fluids to conduct random drug tests on public employees whose job functions make it particularly important for them to be drug-free, such as federal law enforcement agents and railroad conductors.
Searches of people under correctional supervision *Hudson v. Palmer* (1984) *Sampson v. California* (2006)	Warrantless and suspicionless searches may be conducted of jail or prison cells, as well as of the person or inmates in custody, on probation, or on parole.
Third-party disclosure *United States v. Miller* (1976) *Smith v. Maryland* (1979)	Disclosure of confidential information to third parties destroys any reasonable expectation of privacy for that information. Thus, for example, there is no reasonable expectation of privacy in bank records since they are not a person's private papers, but rather are business records of banks to which bank employees have access. Similarly, there is no reasonable expectation of privacy in the numbers dialed from a telephone since phone company employees have access to such information.

Source: Adapted from Stephen S. Owen, Henry F. Fradella, Tod W. Burke, & Jerry W. Joplin. *The Foundations of Criminal Justice* (2nd ed.). New York: Oxford University Press, 2015.

Electronic Surveillance

Searches conducted using wiretaps, bugs, or other devices to overhear conversations or obtain other kinds of information pose unique challenges for balancing privacy interests against the need for effective law enforcement in the area of electronic surveillance. On the one hand, electronic listening, tracking, and recording devices provide a very powerful tool for law enforcement officials in investigating and prosecuting crime. On the other hand, the potential for the abuse of individual rights can be far greater with electronic surveillance than with any ordinary search or seizure. The task of resolving these competing interests has fallen on state legislatures, the U.S. Congress, and ultimately, the courts.

The law governing electronic surveillance is complex. Law enforcement personnel must comply with the requirements of many pieces of legislation, the most important of which is Title III of **Omnibus Crime Control and Safe Streets Act of 1968**. That statute provides greater privacy protections than the Fourth Amendment by:

1. limiting who may apply for wiretaps;
2. requiring multiple levels of administrative and judicial review of wiretap applications;
3. mandating that the wiretap procedures minimize the interception of communications not subject to the wiretap order;
4. requiring law enforcement officers who learn information by listening to intercepted communications to keep the content of what they hear confidential; and
5. requiring that, immediately upon the expiration of a wiretap order, both the interception order and all recordings made pursuant to it be delivered to the judge who issued the order to be sealed. (Putting material *under seal* means it is not accessible to anyone without a special court order.)

Title III applies to private searches and seizures of wire, oral, or electronic communications, not just those involving governmental actors. When its mandates are violated, Title III provides its own statutory remedies, including both criminal and civil penalties for violations of its commands. Title III also provides a statutory exclusionary rule for intercepts that were illegally obtained by either government actors or private persons to which the good-faith exception to the exclusionary rule does not apply.

Eavesdropping and Consent Surveillance

If a conversation takes place in public where other parties can overhear the conversation, there is no reasonable expectation of privacy, because the participants exposed their conversation to the ears of others. Thus, any recording of such a conversation would not violate either the Fourth Amendment or Title III. Moreover, what an employer overhears while monitoring phone conversations over extensions for legitimate business reasons and what family members overhear while eavesdropping on the conversations of other family members using an extension telephone do not implicate Title III.

Title III excludes **consent surveillance** from its regulatory scheme. Therefore, when one party to a communication consents to the interception of the communication, neither Title III nor the Fourth Amendment prevents the use of the communication in court against another party to the communication. Thus, a law enforcement officer or a private citizen who is a party to a communication may intercept the communication or permit a law enforcement official to intercept the communication without violating Title III or the Fourth Amendment (*United States v. Caceres*, 1979). This exception allows a law enforcement officer or agent, an informant, an accomplice or co-conspirator, or a victim to wear a body microphone; act as an undercover agent without being wired; or eavesdrop and/or record a telephone conversation with the permission of the person receiving the call even though the person making the call has no knowledge of this activity. A private citizen, however, may not intercept a communication "for the purpose of committing any criminal or tortious act in violation of the Constitution or laws of the United States or of any State" (18 U.S.C. § 2511(2)(d)).

Electronically Stored Information

Like traditional searches for physical evidence, searches of electronically stored information (ESI) are also governed by the Fourth Amendment. Thus, ESI searches normally require a duly authorized warrant supported by probable cause. Statutory provisions in the **Stored Communications Act**, however, allow law enforcement to access stored communications older than 180 days, such as e-mail and voicemail, using either a search warrant or, after giving notice to the subscriber, a subpoena (18 U.S.C. § 2703(a)).

Computer files and programs are the most obvious sources of ESI, but ESI can also be found on servers, tablets, thumb/jump drives, CDs and DVDs, floppy disks, memory cards and sticks, tape media, external hard drives, cell phones, personal digital assistants (PDAs), and other electronic devices with data-storage capacity, such as digital cameras, iPods, voicemail systems, fax machines, and copy machines.

The U.S. Department of Justice has recommended a set of practices to ensure compliance with the particularity requirement of the Fourth Amendment when police conduct searches of ESI. The federal government recommends that an affidavit should not only list "the specific hardware to be seized and searched" but also explain "the techniques that will be used to search only for the specific files related to the investigation, and not every file on the computer" (Jekot, 2007: ¶ 2, citing U.S. Department of Justice, 2002, Part II.C.3).

There are additional requirements for law enforcement personnel who often need to use technology to monitor telephone conversations on both landlines and cell phones, e-mail communications, pager and text messages, and Internet-based communications that are beyond the scope of this book (see Ferdico, Fradella, & Totten, 2016).

Video Surveillance

Title III does not cover **video surveillance**—the use of video cameras that record only images, not sound. Thus, surreptitious video surveillance without any audio component is analyzed under state invasion of privacy laws and under the Fourth Amendment. Legal analysis under the latter, of course, depends on whether the video surveillance violated an aggrieved person's reasonable expectation of privacy. In contrast, if surveillance contains both audio and video components, then the video sections are controlled by the Fourth Amendment (and state privacy laws) and audio portions are reviewed under Title III and the Fourth Amendment.

Intelligence Surveillance

In 1978, Congress passed the **Foreign Intelligence Surveillance Act (FISA)**. FISA regulates the electronic surveillance of foreign powers and their agents within the United States where a "significant purpose" of the surveillance is to gather foreign intelligence information that cannot reasonably be obtained through normal investigative techniques. FISA also permits surveillance of "lone wolves"—any individual or group that is not linked to a foreign government but who is suspected of terrorism or sabotage.

Any federal agent may apply for a FISA warrant. However, an application must first be approved by the U.S. attorney general and either the assistant to the president for National Security Affairs or the deputy director of the Federal Bureau of Investigation. After these two layers of executive approval, judicial review of an application for a FISA warrant occurs at the Foreign Intelligence Surveillance Court (see Chapter 2). FISA permits the U.S. attorney general to authorize domestic surveillance in an emergency situation in which seeking approval of a warrant application before the Foreign Intelligence Surveillance Court would unnecessarily delay the gathering of necessary evidence.

Applying the Fourth Amendment

Historically, the gathering of physical evidence was governed by the common law rule that "if the constable blunders, the crook should not go free." This meant that if the police conducted an **illegal search and seizure** (such as a search not supported by probable cause), the evidence obtained could still be used if it was reliable, trustworthy, and relevant. How the police obtained the evidence was considered a separate issue. Thus, there were no effective controls on search and seizure; law enforcement officials who searched illegally faced no sanctions. But, as discussed earlier, the Supreme

Court modified the common law tradition when it adopted the exclusionary rule for the Fourth Amendment violations in *Weeks v. United States* (1914) and subsequently extended its application to the states in *Mapp v. Ohio* (1961).

Critics and supporters of the exclusionary rule agree on one central point: The grounds for a lawful search are complex and highly technical. Consider, for example, the cases in the "Key Developments in Search-and-Seizure Law" feature.

KEY DEVELOPMENTS IN SEARCH-AND-SEIZURE LAW

Fourth Amendment (1791)	"The right of the people to be secure in their persons, houses, paper, and effects against unreasonable searches and seizures, shall not be violated, and no Warrants shall issue, but upon probable cause, supported by Oath or affirmation, and particularly describing the place to be searched, and the persons or things to be seized."
Weeks v. United States (1914)	The exclusionary rule was established in federal prosecutions.
Wolf v. Colorado (1949)	The exclusionary rule applies to the states as well as to the federal government, but states are not required to adopt the exclusionary rule to sanction noncompliance.
Mapp v. Ohio (1961)	Both states and the federal government are required to use the exclusionary rule to sanction noncompliance with the mandates of the Fourth Amendment (overturning *Weeks* and *Wolf*).
Katz v. United States (1967)	The Fourth Amendment protects people's subjective expectations of privacy only when those expectations are objectively reasonable by societal standards.
Berger v. New York (1967)	The use of electronic devices to capture conversations is a seizure within the meaning of the Fourth Amendment.
United States v. Calandra (1974)	The exclusionary rule does not apply in grand jury proceedings.
Rakas v. Illinois (1978)	A defendant has standing to object to the admission of unconstitutionally seized evidence only if such seizure violated his own Fourth Amendment rights; a defendant may not assert another person's rights.
Dalia v. United States (1979)	Neither Title III nor the Fourth Amendment requires law enforcement officers to obtain judicial authorization to covertly enter premises to install a listening device after an inception order has been issued.
Smith v. Maryland (1979)	The installation and use of a pen register (a device that records all numbers called from a telephone line) is not a search for Fourth Amendment purposes because there is no reasonable expectation of privacy in the destination of outgoing phone calls since the telephone company routinely monitors calls to check billing, detect fraud, and prevent other violations of law.
Payton v. New York (1980)	Absent some exigent circumstances (an emergency), police may not make a warrantless entry into a suspect's home to make an arrest.
United States v. Mendenhall (1980)	A person is "seized" within the meaning of the Fourth Amendment when his or her freedom of movement is restrained by means of physical force or show of authority, and under the circumstances, a reasonable person would believe that he was not free to leave or otherwise terminate the encounter.
Illinois v. Gates (1983)	Whether probable cause exists must be examined under the "totality of the circumstances." Moreover, a trial court's ruling that probable cause exists is to be given substantial deference on appeal.

Unites States v. Knotts (1983)	The warrantless monitoring of a tracking beeper placed inside a container of chemicals did not violate the Fourth Amendment when it revealed no information that could not have been obtained through visual surveillance.
Tennessee v. Garner (1985)	The Fourth Amendment prohibits the use of deadly force to apprehend a fleeing suspect unless the pursuing officer has probable cause to believe that the suspect poses a significant threat of death or serious physical injury to the officer or others.
Winston v. Lee (1985)	A compelled surgical intrusion into an individual's body for evidence of a crime implicates expectations of privacy and security of such magnitude that it cannot be sanctioned as reasonable under the Fourth Amendment.
Illinois v. Krull (1987)	The good-faith exception applies to warrantless searches, even when the state statute authorizing a warrantless search was later found to violate the Fourth Amendment.
United States v. Sokolow (1989)	A suspect fitting a "drug courier profile" (such as using an alias; purchasing airline tickets with cash; not checking any luggage; traveling for only a short period of time to and from a city with a known, large drug distribution network; and appearing nervous) provides reasonable suspicion to stop and question the suspect.
Michigan Department of State Police v. Sitz (1990)	Sobriety roadblocks do not violate the Fourth Amendment. They are a reasonable tool for combating the problem of driving under the influence and they pose only a minimal intrusion on motorists stopped briefly at checkpoints.
United States v. Ojeda Rios (1990)	A failure to comply with Title III's sealing requirement renders intercepted communications inadmissible.
Florida v. Jimino (1991)	A suspect's consent to a search of his or her vehicle extends to closed containers found inside that can hold the object for which police are searching.
Minnesota v. Dickerson (1993)	When a police officer conducting a lawful pat-down for weapons feels something that's contour or mass makes its identity as contraband immediately apparent, the object may be seized even though it is not a weapon. However, if the nature of the object is not immediately recognizable as contraband, the officer may not manipulate the object to determine what it might be since doing so would go beyond a pat-down and into the realm of a full search.
Arizona v. Evans (1995)	The exclusionary rule does not require the suppression of evidence seized during a search incident to the arrest of a driver pursuant to a warrant that was later determined to be invalid since the officer relied in good faith on the warrant that had not been entered properly into the system by a clerk of the court.
Whren v. United States (1996)	Police officers may stop a vehicle for any violation of traffic law even if the underlying traffic offense is only a pretext to investigate other criminal activity.
Knowles v. Iowa (1998)	Issuing a speeding ticket does not give police authority to search the car.
Illinois v. Wardlow (2000)	Fleeing from the sight of police (running away) is a pertinent factor in determining whether reasonable suspicion justifies the police in stopping the runner to investigate whether criminal activity is afoot.
Bond v. United States (2000)	Bus and train passengers have a reasonable expectation of privacy in the carry-on luggage they place into overhead racks.

(Continued)

(Continued)

Florida v. J. L. (2000)	Police cannot stop and search someone solely because they have received an anonymous tip. Anonymous tips must possess a moderate level of reliability, including "predictive information" that offers police a means to test the informant's knowledge or credibility.
Kyllo v. United States (2001)	The warrantless use of thermal imaging devices to scan a building to detect the presence of high-intensity lamps used to grow marijuana violates the Fourth Amendment.
Hiibel v. Sixth Judicial District Court of Nevada (2004)	States may enact laws requiring suspects to identify themselves during police investigations without violating either the Fourth or Fifth Amendments.
Illinois v. Caballes (2005)	The Fourth Amendment permits police making a routine traffic stop to use a trained dog to sniff the car for drugs.
Georgia v. Randolph (2006)	The police must have a warrant to look for evidence in a couple's home unless both partners present agree to let them in.
Hudson v. Michigan (2006)	Although police armed with a search warrant are supposed to knock and announce their presence before they can lawfully enter homes to search for and seize evidence, a violation of the knock-and-announce rule will not give rise to the application of the exclusionary rule.
Brendlin v. California (2007)	When a police officer makes a traffic stop, both the driver of the car and his or her passengers are all "seized" within the meaning of the Fourth Amendment. Thus, a passenger may challenge the constitutionality of the stop.
Scott v. Harris (2007)	A police officer who terminated a high-speed chase of a suspect by applying his push bumper to the rear of the suspect's vehicle, causing it to leave the road and crash and rendering the suspect a quadriplegic, did not act unreasonably in using such force and therefore did not violate the motorist's Fourth Amendment right against unreasonable seizure.
Virginia v. Moore (2008)	A police officer does not violate the Fourth Amendment by making an arrest supported by probable cause for a traffic violation even though arrest is not authorized under state law for such an offense; therefore, evidence seized incident to the arrest is admissible.
United States v. Herring (2009)	The Fourth Amendment does not require the suppression of evidence seized following a search that occurred incident to an illegal arrest when the arrest was based on erroneous information negligently provided by another law enforcement agency, as long as the arresting police officer relied on the erroneous information in good faith.
United States v. Jones (2012)	Police must first obtain a warrant before attaching a GPS device to a vehicle and then monitoring the vehicle's movements.
Florida v. Jardines (2013)	Bringing a trained police dog within the curtilage of someone's home for the purposes of obtaining evidence with which to secure a search warrant constitutes a search for Fourth Amendment purposes and, therefore, requires a warrant.
Maryland v. King (2013)	When officers make an arrest supported by probable cause to hold a suspect for a serious offense and bring him to the station to be detained in custody, taking and analyzing a cheek swab of the arrestee's DNA is, like fingerprinting and photographing, a legitimate police booking procedure that is reasonable under the Fourth Amendment.

***Missouri v. McNeely* (2014)**	In routine driving under the influence investigations, the natural dissipation of alcohol in the bloodstream does not constitute an exigency that justifies a nonconsensual drawing of blood without a warrant. "When officers can reasonably obtain a warrant before having a suspect's blood drawn without significantly undermining the efficacy of the search, the Fourth Amendment mandates that they do so" (p. 1561).
***Riley v. California* (2014)**	Police may not conduct a warrantless search of a cell phone seized from a suspect incident to arrest.
***Rodriguez v. United States* (2015)**	Absent reasonable suspicion regarding the presence of contraband, the use of a K-9 unit to conduct a dog sniffing at the conclusion of an otherwise lawful traffic stop constitutes an unreasonable seizure.
***Birchfield v. North Dakota* (2016)**	Although a warrantless breadth test of a motorist lawfully arrested for drunk driving is permissible as a search incident to arrest, a warrantless blood draw is not.

The Exclusionary Rule and the Courtroom Work Group

The police must often make immediate decisions about searching or interrogating a suspect. In street arrests, officers do not have time to consult an attorney about the complex and constantly evolving law governing these areas. These on-the-spot decisions may later be challenged in court as violations of suspects' constitutional rights. Even though the exclusionary rule is directed at the police, its actual enforcement occurs in the courts, particularly the trial courts.

Pretrial Motions

A defense attorney who believes that his or her client was identified in a defective police lineup, gave a confession because of improper police activity, or was subjected to an illegal search can file a motion to suppress the evidence. Most states require that **suppression motions** be made prior to trial.

During the hearing on these pretrial motions, the defense attorney usually bears the burden of proving that the search was illegal or that the confession was coerced. The only exception involves an allegation that the *Miranda* warnings were not given, in which case the state has the burden of proof. The judge's ruling in the pretrial hearing is binding on the later trial.

Pretrial hearings on a motion to suppress evidence are best characterized as "swearing matches." As one defense attorney phrased it, "The real question in Supreme Court cases is what's going on at the police station" (Neubauer, 1974b, p. 167). Seldom is there unbiased, independent evidence of what happened. The only witnesses are the participants—police and defendant—and, not surprisingly, they give different versions. This dispute over the facts structures and apportions the roles that the police, defense attorneys, judges, and prosecutors play. Because they must search out the issues, defense attorneys are forced into a catalytic role. By virtue of their power as fact finders at hearings, judges become the supreme umpires that legal theory indicates they should be. Prosecutors, in contrast, play a relatively passive role. Although pretrial motions place prosecutors in a defensive posture, they are not at a major disadvantage, because the police are usually able to provide information indicating compliance.

Defense Attorney as Prime Mover

Because defense attorneys have the responsibility of protecting the constitutional rights of their clients, they are the prime movers in suppression matters. Unless the defense objects, it is assumed that law enforcement officials have behaved properly. Filing a pretrial motion to suppress evidence may produce benefits for the defense. If the motion is granted, the defense wins, because the prosecutor will usually dismiss the case for lack of evidence. Even if the motion is denied, the defense may be able to discover information that may later prove valuable at trial. Moreover, filing a pretrial motion keeps options open; plea bargaining remains a possible course of action.

Despite these apparent advantages, defense attorneys face major barriers in raising objections. Possible violations of *Miranda* or the Fourth Amendment do not come into the lawyer's office prepackaged, just awaiting a court hearing. Defense attorneys must frame the issue and determine whether enough facts exist to support the contention. According to many defense attorneys, the police follow proper procedures most of the time. Thus, the task of the lawyer is to separate the out-of-the-ordinary situation from the more numerous ones in which the police have not violated relevant court rulings.

In deciding whether to make a motion to suppress evidence, defense attorneys are influenced by the informal norms of the courtroom work group. Pretrial motions require extra work, not only for the defense attorney but also for the judge and prosecutor. Defense attorneys who file too many frivolous motions or use them to harass the judge, the prosecutor, or both can be given a variety of sanctions. The prosecutor may refuse to plea-bargain in a given case or may insist on a harsher-than-normal sentence.

The Defensive Posture of the Prosecutor

Suppression motions represent only liabilities for prosecutors. At a minimum, they must do extra work. At worst, they may lose the case entirely. Even if they win the suppression motion, they may have to expend extra effort defending that decision on appeal, at which time they may lose.

Despite these drawbacks, prosecutors maintain the upper hand. For once, they need only defend, because the defense attorney bears the burden of proof. Because the police control the information involved, prosecutors are generally in a favorable position to argue against excluding evidence. For example, the police are usually able to obtain the defendant's signature on the *Miranda* warning form, which indicates compliance with Supreme Court requirements. Similarly, in a search-and-seizure case, the officers are familiar enough with the law to know how to testify in order to avoid suppression of evidence. Of course, the district attorney can dismiss a case that presents potential problems, thus avoiding a public hearing on the matter.

Trial Judges as Decision Makers

The decision to suppress evidence rests with the trial judge. After hearing the witnesses and viewing the physical evidence (if any), the judge makes a ruling based on appellate court decisions. Thus, trial court judges are key policymakers in applying and implementing appellate decisions concerning confessions and search and seizure.

As noted earlier, a pretrial motion is essentially a clash over the facts. The trial court judge possesses virtually unfettered discretion in making findings of fact. Judges' backgrounds predispose them to be skeptical of defense motions to suppress. As noted in Chapter 8, many judges were once prosecutors, whose courtroom arguments supported the police. These inclinations are reinforced by the selection process. Judges are, by and large, either appointed by governors or presidents—who are often critical of appellate court restrictions on the gathering of evidence by the police—or elected by the public in campaigns that stress crime reduction. For these reasons, trial judges do not regularly grant defense motions to suppress evidence.

On appeal, higher courts examine whether the law was correctly applied by the trial judge, but they rarely scrutinize the facts to which the law was applied. Such deference is based on the trial judge's proximity to the event. Only trial judges have the opportunity to observe directly how witnesses testify—their responsiveness to questions or their attempts at concealment. Such nuances are not reflected in the trial court transcript.

Police Testimony

At the center of court hearings on police practices and defendants' rights are events that happened out in the field or in the police station. Although some jurisdictions now require police to tape interrogations, many do not (Leo, 1996b; Gershel, 2010). What is known in court, therefore, is largely the product of police testimony.

Richard Leo (1996a) observed 122 interrogations in a major urban police department and reported the following. Detectives begin by cultivating the suspect, getting him or her to make eye contact and engage in conversation. The *Miranda* warnings are useful for this purpose because they induce suspects to respond to questions. Thus, three out of four suspects waive their *Miranda* rights. Next, the detective states that his or her job is to discover the truth and typically shares with the suspect some of the evidence in the case. A two-pronged approach is being used. One is the use of negative incentives, tactics that suggest the suspect should confess because no other plausible course of action exists. The other is the use of positive incentives, tactics that suggest the suspect will in some way feel better or benefit if he or she confesses. The results were as follows:

- No incriminating statement (36 percent)
- Incriminating statement (23 percent)
- Partial admission (18 percent)
- Full confession (24 percent)

A suspect's decision to provide detectives with incriminating information was fateful. Those who incriminated themselves were more likely to be charged with a crime, more likely to enter a plea of guilty, more likely to be convicted, and likely to receive more punishment than their counterparts who did not provide incriminating statements.

Police, prosecutors, and defense attorneys often become embroiled in disputes about what occurred during interrogation. These disputes can be ended by using audio and/or video equipment to record everything that occurs during custodial interviews. By 2017, 26 states and the District of Columbia adopted some requirement that custodial interrogations be recorded (National Association of Criminal Defense Lawyers, 2017). In addition to preventing coercion (or identifying coercion if alleged), recording offers another benefit—reducing wrongful convictions that occur when someone confesses to a crime he or she did not actually commit. Such false confessions can be especially tricky for justice system actors when "innocent but vulnerable suspects, under the influence of highly suggestive interrogation tactics, come not only to capitulate in their behavior, but also to believe that they committed the crime in question" (Kassin & Gudjonsson, 2004, p. 50).

> Recording creates an objective record of any intentional or unintentional contamination during the course of an interrogation. It makes it possible for the reviewer to identify points at which an investigator may intentionally or unintentionally suggest or imply facts of the crime to the suspect. (Farrell & Farrell, 2013, pp. 5–6)

Law and Controversy: Costs of the Exclusionary Rule

A key issue in the ongoing debate over the exclusionary rule centers on its costs. In a widely cited statement, Chief Justice Burger summed up the critics' position as follows: "Some clear demonstration of the benefits and effectiveness of the exclusionary rule is required to justify it in view of the high price it exacts from society—the release of countless guilty criminals" (*Bivens v. Six Unknown Federal Narcotics Agents*, 1971, p. 416).

One study of police searches in a major American city concluded that 30 percent of the searches failed to pass constitutional muster. Even though the patrol officers knew they were being observed, they still conducted illegal searches. But only a handful of these events were documented in official records because so few resulted in arrest or citation (Gould & Mastrofski, 2004; see also Bar-Gill & Friedman, 2012). The lack of official action, therefore, makes it difficult to truly calculate the cost of the exclusionary rule at subsequent stages of the process.

Assessing the number of convictions lost because of the exclusionary rule is difficult, for reasons discussed in Chapter 10. Case attrition occurs at numerous stages of the proceedings and for

Should the Exclusionary Rule Be Abolished?

The exclusionary rule was controversial when it was adopted in 1961 and remains so today. In a 1981 speech, President Reagan's strong words expressed the views of the crime control model in opposition to the exclusionary rule:

> The exclusionary rule rests on the absurd proposition that a law enforcement error, no matter how technical, can be used to justify throwing an entire case out of court, no matter how guilty the defendant or how heinous the crime. The plain consequence of treating the wrongs equally is a grievous miscarriage of justice: The criminal goes free; the officer receives no effective reprimand; and the only ones who really suffer are the people of the community.

But to law professor Yale Kamisar (1978), illegal conduct by the police cannot be so easily ignored. Here is how he states the due process model case for the exclusionary rule: "A court which admits [illegally seized evidence] … manifests a willingness to tolerate the unconstitutional conduct which produced it."

How can the police and the citizenry be expected to "believe that the government truly meant to forbid the conduct in the first place"? A court that admits the evidence in a case involving a "run of the mill" Fourth Amendment violation demonstrates an insufficient commitment to the guarantee against unreasonable search and seizure.

While the *Mapp* decision remains controversial, the nature of the debate has changed. Initially, critics called for abolition of the exclusionary rule (Oaks, 1970; Wilkey, 1978); now, they just suggest modifications. This shift in thinking is reflected in the Reagan administration's Attorney General's Task Force on Violent Crime (1981). Although composed largely of long-standing critics of the exclusionary rule, the final report called only for its modification, not its abolition.

Among the alternatives proposed, former Chief Justice Warren Burger urged an "egregious violation standard" (*Brewer v. Williams*, 1977). Others have proposed an exception for reasonable mistakes by the police (Fyfe, 1982). To critics, modifications along these lines would reduce the number of arrests lost because of illegal searches, and the sanction would be more proportional to the seriousness of the Fourth Amendment violation. The Supreme Court, however, has recognized an "honest mistake" or a "good-faith" exception to the exclusionary rule only in extremely narrow and limited circumstances (*United States v. Leon*, 1984; *Illinois v. Krull*, 1987).

What do you think? Should the exclusionary rule be abolished outright, given "good-faith" exceptions, or kept in its present form? If one admits that there are problems in its current application, what realistic alternatives might restrain law enforcement from potentially conducting blatant and flagrant searches in violation of the Fourth Amendment?

various reasons. Several studies shed considerable light on the topic.

Exclusionary rules can lead to the freeing of apparently guilty defendants during prosecutorial screening. Prosecutors may refuse to file charges because of a search-and-seizure problem, a tainted confession, or a defective police lineup. However, this occurs very infrequently. The Comptroller General of the United States (1979) examined case rejections by U.S. attorneys and found that search and seizure was cited as the primary reason for rejection 0.4 percent of the time. Similarly, a study of seven communities reported that an average of 2 percent of the rejections were for *Mapp* or *Miranda* reasons (Boland, Brady, Tyson, & Bassler, 1982). A more controversial study

analyzed 86,033 felony cases rejected for prosecution in California. The National Institute of Justice (NIJ) report found that 4.8 percent were rejected for search-and-seizure reasons. The NIJ conclusion that these figures indicated a "major impact of the exclusionary rule" has been challenged as misleading and exaggerated (Davies, 1983). Indeed, compared to lack of evidence and witness problems, *Mapp* and *Miranda* are minor sources of case attrition.

After charges are filed, case attrition can also occur when judges grant pretrial motions to suppress. But in actuality, few pretrial motions to suppress evidence are actually filed. Nardulli (1983) reported that motions to suppress evidence were filed in fewer than 8 percent of the cases. Once filed, pretrial motions are rarely successful, although the success rate has varied significantly in the research from a low of 0.3 percent (Davies, 1983) to a high of 1.5 percent (Uchida & Bynum, 1991).

Piecing together the various stages of the criminal court process leads to the conclusion that the exclusionary rule has a marginal effect on the criminal court system (Nardulli, 1983). Examining case-attrition data from California, Davies (1983) calculated that 0.8 percent of arrests (8 of 1,000) were rejected because of *Mapp* and *Miranda.* As for cases filed, Nardulli calculated that 0.57 percent of convictions (fewer than 6 of 1,000) were lost because of exclusionary rules. Moreover, of the lost convictions, only 20 percent were for serious crimes. Weapons cases and drug cases are those most likely to involve questions about police conduct.

A special panel of the American Bar Association (1988) likewise concluded that constitutional protections of the rights of criminal defendants do not significantly handicap police and prosecutors in their efforts to arrest, prosecute, and obtain convictions for the most serious crimes. Although many people blame the failures of the criminal justice system on judges' concern for defendants' rights, the blame is misplaced. The main problem is that the criminal justice system is stretched too thin, the Association concluded.

Conclusion

In many ways, Ernesto Miranda fit the pattern of those arrested by the police—a young minority male with little education and few job prospects. But the eventual outcome of his case was hardly typical. His case was heard by the nation's highest court, and he not only won the right to a new trial but also established a new law in the process. Unlike most defendants, whose cases are quickly forgotten, his name became a code word for the rights of criminal defendants.

Although *Miranda* the legal principle endured, Miranda the man was less fortunate. Initially, his chances of gaining an acquittal during retrial looked promising indeed. After all, the state's only evidence—the signed confession—had been ruled to be inadmissible. It turned out, however, that while in jail Ernesto Miranda had admitted details of the crime to his common law wife, who by now had grown afraid of him. She testified for the state, and after an hour and a half of deliberations, the jury found Miranda guilty of rape and kidnapping a second time. After serving his prison term, Ernesto Miranda was living in Phoenix when he became involved in a barroom quarrel over small change in a poker game. A large knife ended his life. It is no small irony that the Phoenix police read Miranda's killer his *Miranda* rights when they arrested him.

This chapter has examined several important aspects of what occurs while cases are being prepared for trial. One is discovery, the formal or informal exchange of information between prosecution and defense. What information is subject to discovery varies greatly. As a rule, defense attorneys who are cooperative members of the courtroom work group receive more information than those who are not cooperative members. Another important aspect of preparing for trial centers on suppression of evidence. Confessions and physical evidence that have been illegally obtained cannot be used at trial. If the defense believes that there have been illegal actions by the police, it files a pretrial motion to suppress the evidence. Prosecutors are usually in a favorable position to show that the evidence was obtained legally.

CHAPTER REVIEW

LO1   1.   Explain the reasons why the process of discovery exists in both civil and criminal cases but is significantly curtailed in the latter.

Discovery is designed to give both parties to a legal dispute a good idea about the evidence that will be presented at trial. Not only does this exchange of information prevent surprises, but also it facilitates resolutions without trial, such as the settlement of a civil case or a plea bargain in a criminal case. Discovery, however, is limited in criminal cases, since the prosecution bears the burden of persuasion to prove a defendant guilty beyond a reasonable doubt, and the defendant is protected against being forced to incriminate himself/herself. If the defense had to disclose evidence to the prosecution, the privilege against self-incrimination would be rendered meaningless.

LO2 2.   Differentiate formal and informal discovery and the reasons why both are used in criminal cases.

Formal discovery in criminal cases concerns the exchange of information mandated either by the rules of procedure or applicable law. The crux of mandatory discovery in criminal cases concerns prosecutorial disclosure of exculpatory evidence to the defense. Informal discovery concerns the disclosure of information not mandated by law. It occurs frequently because it often facilitates a prompt resolution of a dispute without the need for trial (i.e., either the prosecutor drops the charges in light of exculpatory evidence disclosed to it by the defense, or the defendant pleads guilty once the strength of the prosecution's case becomes evident).

LO3 3.   Identify the types of evidence subject to mandatory criminal discovery.

All potentially exculpatory evidence must be disclosed to the defense. This includes any prior inconsistent statements of prosecutorial witnesses, as well as all impeachment evidence that might cast doubt on a witness's credibility.

LO4 4.   Compare and contrast the exclusionary rule and the fruit of the poisonous tree doctrine.

The exclusionary rule bars evidence from being used in the prosecution's case-in-chief if it was obtained in violation of a defendant's constitutional rights. The fruit of the poisonous tree doctrine bars derivative evidence found as a result the violation of a defendant's constitutional right from being used in the prosecution's case-in-chief unless the evidence is so far attenuated from the constitutional violation that its use would not offend due process.

LO5 5.   Summarize how the decision in *Miranda v. Arizona* regulates the process of police interrogations of suspects.

Before a suspect in police custody is interrogated, the suspect must be informed of his or her rights under the Fifth Amendment's Self-Incrimination Clause, namely that the suspect has the right to remain silent and the right to have counsel present during an interrogation. Moreover, the suspect must be told that the consequence of voluntarily waving these rights will result in the prosecution being able to use anything the suspect says at trial. If the suspect invokes his or her *Miranda* rights, questioning must stop.

LO6 6.   Explain the requirements governing the application for search warrants, the issuance of search warrants, and the execution of search warrants.

When law enforcement officers want to conduct a search for evidence, the Fourth Amendment generally requires them to seek a warrant. They apply for a warrant by swearing to the facts they know, usually in an affidavit. A magistrate then considers those facts to determine whether there is probable cause to authorize the search of a particular place or person for particular evidence connected to a specific crime. If such a warrant is issued, the police must execute the warrant quickly and in a reasonable manner.

LO7 7.   Identify the major exceptions to the Fourth Amendment's warrant requirement.

Police may conduct warrantless searches when granted consent to search by someone with actual or apparent authority to grant such consent; when incident to a lawful arrest; when items are in plain view or in open fields; when probable cause exists to search a motor vehicle; or when emergency situations make it impracticable for police to seek and obtain a warrant first.

LO8 8. Analyze the effect of the exclusionary rule on the operations of the courtroom work group.

Because pretrial motions to suppress evidence are relatively rare, the exclusionary rule does not generally impact the operations of the courtroom work group in most cases. However, when questions about the constitutionality of a search or seizure arise, the defense attorney takes charge of the situation by filing a motion to suppress. In somewhat of a role reversal, these motions have the effect of putting the prosecution on the defensive. Moreover, they ultimately cause a judge to have to rule on the credibility of testimony offered by law enforcement officers. Depending on whom the judge believes, the relationships within the courtroom work group can be significantly strained.

LO9 9. Evaluate whether the exclusionary rule should be abolished.

Supporters of the exclusionary rule argue that the rule is the only effective deterrent against police misconduct. Thus, they assert that the rule must be preserved in order to guarantee that our constitutional rights are honored. In contrast, those who want to see the exclusionary rule abolished argue that the threat of civil lawsuits should be enough to deter police misconduct. Moreover, they assert that the rule "costs" too much, in that it operates to prevent juries from considering highly relevant evidence, which, in turn, sometimes operates to allow the guilty to go free.

CRITICAL THINKING QUESTIONS

1. In civil cases, each party is entitled to all the information in the possession of the other side (unless that information is privileged). Why are discovery rules in criminal cases different?

2. To what extent do prosecutorial policies that restrict the sharing of information with defense attorneys other than what is legally required represent a contradiction in the crime control model?

3. When the Court announced its decision in *Miranda v. Arizona* in 1966, the decision sparked massive controversy and was a major issue in the 1968 presidential campaign. Yet, over time it has become much more accepted than the Court's decision in *Mapp v. Ohio* regarding search and seizure. What factors might explain this apparent shift in assessments?

4. A number of conservatives call for eliminating or restricting the exclusionary rule in street crimes. Yet some conservatives also call for a stricter rule in white-collar crimes, suggesting that the financial records of a person or a business should be given special protections under the Fourth Amendment. Are these arguments consistent or simply a case of whose ox is being gored? How would these arguments play out if a substantial citizen in the community (whose financial records are being requested) were under investigation for major drug dealings?

5. To what extent is the continuing controversy over search-and-seizure law really a debate over the war on drugs? Recall the controversy in Chapter 8 centering on judicial independence, in which a federal judge in New York suppressed a substantial amount of illegal drugs.

KEY TERMS

aerial search   334

affidavit   331

alibi defense   322

attenuation   324

chain of custody   333

confrontation   323

consent search   334

consent surveillance   336

custodial interrogation   325

derivative evidence   323

discovery   317

exclusionary rule   322

FOR FURTHER READING

Ferdico, John, Henry F. Fradella, and Chris Totten. 2016. *Criminal Procedure for the Criminal Justice Professional*, 12th ed. Belmont, CA: Cengage.

Fradella, Henry F., Weston W. Morrow, Ryan G. Fischer, and Connie E. Ireland. 2011. "Quantifying *Katz*: Empirically Measuring 'Reasonable Expectations of Privacy' in the Fourth Amendment Context." *American Journal of Criminal Law* 38(3): 289–373.

Hilton, Alicia M. 2008. "Alternatives to the Exclusionary Rule after *Hudson v. Michigan*: Preventing and Remedying Police Misconduct." *Villanova Law Review* 53: 47–82.

Howe, Scott. W. 2016. "Moving Beyond *Miranda*: Concessions for Confessions." *Northwestern University Law Review Colloquy* 110: 905–961.

Kassin, Saul M. 2012. "Why Confessions Trump Innocence." *American Psychologist* 67(6): 431–445.

Leo, Richard A. 2008. *Police Interrogation & American Justice*. Cambridge, MA: Harvard University Press.

Mialon, Hugo M., and Sue H. Mialon. 2008. "The Effects of the Fourth Amendment: An Economic Analysis." *Journal of Law, Economics, and Organization* 24: 22–44.

Roots, Roger. 2014. "The Framers' Fourth Amendment Exclusionary Rule: The Mounting Evidence." *Nevada Law Journal* 15: 42–76.

Scott-Hayward, Christine S., Henry F. Fradella, and Ryan G. Fischer. 2016. "Does Privacy Require Secrecy? Societal Expectations of Privacy in the Digital Age." *American Journal of Criminal Law* 43(1): 19–59.

Sklansky, David Alan. 2008. "Is the Exclusionary Rule Obsolete?" *Ohio State Journal of Criminal Law* 5: 567–584.

12 Negotiated Justice and the Plea of Guilty

Blend Images/Alamy Stock Photo

When members of the public think about how attorneys represent their clients, many people think of the lawyer in court, advocating before a judge or jury, rather than the scene depicted in this photo. But, as you will learn in this chapter, the overwhelming majority of cases are resolved in advance of trial via the plea bargaining process. Such agreements are a part of the normal processing of criminal cases. If trials were the norm, the system would collapse since it lacks both the time and resources to conduct trials in most cases.

Chapter Outline

Charged with two counts of felony gambling, Rudolph Santobello pled guilty to one count of a misdemeanor charge of possessing gambling records. Just as important, the prosecutor agreed to make no recommendation as to the sentence. But Santobello's sentencing hearing was delayed for several months, and in the interim the initial judge retired, and another prosecutor replaced the one who had negotiated the plea of guilty. Apparently ignorant of his colleague's commitment, the new district attorney demanded the maximum sentence, and the new judge agreed, imposing a one-year jail term. The justices of the U.S. Supreme Court were concerned about the failure of the prosecutor's office to honor the commitment it had made in inducing the guilty plea. Others were no doubt concerned about whether Santobello, who had a long and serious criminal record, should have been allowed to plead guilty with such a light sentence in the first place.

Santobello v. New York (1971) highlights the importance of guilty pleas. Although the average American equates criminal justice with trials, only a handful of defendants are ever tried. Instead, most convictions result not from a guilty verdict following a contested trial but rather from a voluntary plea by the accused. Indeed Justice Kennedy recently wrote that our criminal justice system is, "for the most part, a system of pleas, not a system of trials" (*Lafler v. Cooper*, 2012, p. 1388). The simple reality is that "ninety-seven percent of federal convictions and ninety-four percent of state convictions are the result of guilty pleas" (*Missouri v. Frye*, 2012, p. 1407). Views about this common practice differ. To some, it erodes the cornerstones of the adversary system: the presumption of innocence and the right to trial. To others, it enables the guilty to escape with a light penalty. To still others, it is a modern-day necessity if the courts are to dispose of their large caseloads. All agree, however, that it is the most important stage of the criminal court process.

Learning Objectives

After reading this chapter, you should be able to:

LO1 Distinguish between the three most common types of plea agreements.

LO2 Discuss the three major factors influencing bargaining and discretion.

LO3 Recognize the importance of *Boykin v. Alabama.*

LO4 List the major reason each of the members of the courtroom work group engages in plea bargaining.

LO5 Indicate why a few cases go to trial but most defendants plead guilty.

LO6 Explain why adherents of the crime control model of criminal justice oppose plea bargaining for different reasons from those of adherents of the due process model of criminal justice.

Law on the Books: Types of Plea Agreements

Guilty pleas are the bread and butter of the American criminal courts. Between 85 and 95 percent of all state and federal felony convictions are obtained by a defendant entering a negotiated plea of guilt (Covey, 2008; Hashimoto, 2008; United States Sentencing Commission, 2015). The data in Figure 12.1 demonstrate the pervasiveness of guilty pleas for specific types of offenses. **Plea bargaining** can best be defined as the process through which a defendant pleads guilty to a criminal charge with the expectation of receiving some consideration from the state.

Plea bargaining is hardly new. Considerable evidence shows that it became a common practice in state courts sometime after the Civil War (Alschuler, 1979; Friedman, 1979; Sanborn, 1986). In Middlesex County, Massachusetts, for example,

plea bargaining had become firmly "normalized" by the 20th century (Fisher, 2003). In federal courts, the massive number of liquor cases stemming from Prohibition led to the institutionalization of plea bargaining in the first third of the 20th century (Padgett, 1990). What is new is the amount of attention plea negotiations now receive. In an earlier era, the issue was discussed only sporadically. The crime surveys of the 1920s reported the dominance of plea bargaining (Moley, 1928), but most courts persistently denied its existence. It was not until the 1960s that plea bargaining emerged as a controversial national issue. Today, however, although specific aspects of plea bargaining may give rise to periodic controversy, the process itself is so widely accepted that it "dominates the modern American criminal process" (Covey, 2008, p. 1238; see also *Lafler v. Cooper*, 2012).

Plea bargaining is a general term that encompasses a wide range of practices. Indeed, court officials disagree about what is meant by plea bargaining. Some prosecutors refuse to admit that they engage

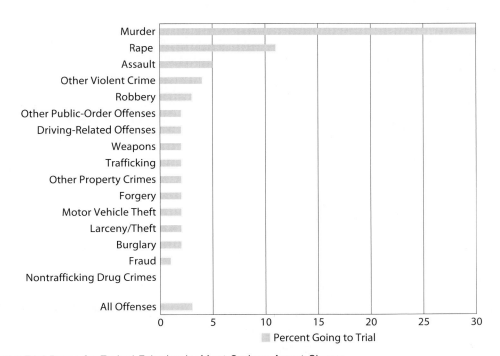

FIGURE 12.1 Trial Rates for Typical Felonies by Most Serious Arrest Charge

Source: Brian A. Reaves. 2013. *Felony Defendants in Large Urban Counties, 2009.* Washington, DC: Bureau of Justice Statistics.

in bargaining; they simply call it something else (Miller, McDonald, & Cramer, 1978). Thus, any discussion of negotiated justice must start with the recognition that important variations exist both in the types of plea agreements negotiated and the process by which such agreements are reached. Typically, plea agreements take one or more of the following three forms: charge bargaining, count bargaining, and sentence bargaining. The "Law on the Books vs. Law in Action" feature on page 355 summarizes the different types of plea bargaining.

Charge Bargaining

One type of plea agreement is termed **charge bargaining**. In return for the defendant's plea of guilty, the prosecutor allows the defendant to plead guilty to a less serious charge than the one originally filed. For example, the defendant pleads guilty to robbery rather than the original charge of armed robbery. Or the defendant enters a plea of guilty to misdemeanor theft rather than the initial accusation of felony theft. The principal effect of a plea to a less serious charge is to reduce the potential sentence.

Some offenses carry a stiff maximum sentence. A plea to a lesser charge therefore greatly reduces the possible prison term the defendant will have to serve. Bargains for reduced charges are most commonly found in jurisdictions where the state's criminal code is rigid or where prosecutors routinely overcharge to begin with. Thus, some charge reductions reflect the probability that the prosecutor would not be able to prove the original charge in a trial.

Count Bargaining

Another common type of plea agreement is called **count bargaining**. In return for the defendant's plea of guilty to one or more counts in the indictment or information, the prosecutor dismisses the remaining charges. For instance, a defendant accused of three separate burglaries pleads guilty to one burglary count, and the two remaining criminal charges are dismissed.

Like a charge-reduction agreement, a count bargain reduces the defendant's potential sentence, but in a very different way. A person charged with

multiple counts theoretically can receive a maximum sentence of something like 135 years, a figure arrived at by multiplying the number of charges by the maximum jail term for each charge and assuming that the judge will sentence the defendant to serve the sentences consecutively (one after another). Such figures are often unrealistic, because sentences are typically imposed concurrently (to run at the same time). In practice, the defendant will often receive the same penalty no matter how few (or how many) charges are involved.

Sentence Bargaining

The third common form of plea agreement is called **sentence bargaining**. A plea of guilty is entered in exchange for a promise of leniency in sentencing. There may be a promise that the defendant will be placed on probation or that the prison term will be no more than a given figure—say, five years. In a sentence bargain, the defendant typically pleads to the original charge (often termed a **plea on the nose**). In some jurisdictions, however, sentence bargaining operates in conjunction with count bargaining and charge-reduction bargaining.

In sentence bargaining, the defendant invariably receives less than the maximum penalty. To some, this is an indication that defendants get off too easily, but in fact, only defendants with long criminal records who have committed particularly heinous crimes would receive the maximum sentence anyway. In practice, courts impose sentences on the basis of normal penalties for specific crimes involving common types of defendants. In sentence bargaining, the sentence agreed to is the one typically imposed in similar cases.

Differentiating Plea Bargaining from "Straight-Up" Pleas

Sometimes, the plea bargaining process breaks down and the parties are unable to come to an agreement. Nonetheless, the defendant does not want to go to trial, often because the prosecution has a particularly strong case. In such an instance, the defendant might opt to enter a *"straight-up"* plea (also called an *open plea* or a *"plea to the sheet"*). Such pleas involve the

LAW ON THE BOOKS VS. LAW IN ACTION
Forms of Plea Bargaining

	Law on the Books	Law in Action
Plea bargaining	The process by which a defendant pleads guilty to a criminal charge with the expectation of receiving some benefit from the state.	The majority of findings of guilt occur because of plea bargaining. The proportion of pleas (as opposed to trials) varies among jurisdictions.
Charge bargaining	The defendant pleads guilty to a less serious charge than the one originally filed. Pleading to a less serious charge reduces the potential sentence the defendant faces.	Courthouse norms control allowable reductions. Some prosecutors deliberately overcharge so it appears that the defendant is getting a break.
Count bargaining	The defendant pleads guilty to some, but not all, of the counts contained in the charging document. Pleading guilty to fewer counts reduces the potential sentence the defendant faces.	Some prosecutors deliberately file additional charges so they can dismiss some later on, making it appear that the defendant got a good deal. In multiple-count charges, sentences are typically served concurrently (not consecutively), so the "sentence reduction" the defendant receives is largely illusionary.
Sentence bargaining	The defendant pleads guilty, knowing the sentence that will be imposed. The sentence in the sentence bargain is less than the maximum.	Sentences are based on normal penalties. Because the normal penalty for an offense is less than the maximum, defendants appear to get off lightly.

defendant pleading guilty to the original charges without any agreement as to sentencing and allowing the judge to determine the outcome in the case. Straight pleas essentially involve the defendant throwing himself or herself on the mercy of the court. But since the judge can impose any sentence permitted by the law (i.e., anything between the minimum and the maximum), these pleas are quite risky and are, therefore, fairly rare.

Law in Action: Bargaining and Caseloads

The common explanation for plea bargaining is that the courts have too many cases. Plea bargaining is usually portrayed as a regrettable but

necessary expedient for disposing of cases. In Chapter 5, it was argued that although this explanation contains some truth, it obscures too many important facets of what the courts do and why they do it. Certainly, the press of cases and lack of adequate resources shape the criminal court process, plea bargaining included (Worden, 1990). And because prosecutors need to move cases, they agree to more lenient pleas than they might prefer.

But the caseload hypothesis cannot explain why plea bargaining is as prevalent in courts with relatively few cases as it is in courts with heavy caseloads (Eisenstein & Jacob, 1977; Covey, 2009). A comparison of plea rates in a number of courthouses across the nation found high plea rates in suburban counties with low crime rates and below-average caseloads. The vast differences among jurisdictions in the ratio of pleas to trials primarily reflect differences in the prosecution and the police or differences in courtroom workgroup culture, not in disparities concerning crime rates or court resources (Boland & Forst, 1985; Brown, 2014; Emmelman, 2002).

A similar conclusion emerges from a study that presented the members of the courtroom work group with several hypothetical cases and asked, "Assuming that prosecution, defense, and the court have adequate resources to deal with their caseloads in a fair and expeditious manner, how do you believe this case should be resolved?" (Church, 1985, p. 474). The responses indicated that relatively few of the cases would be disposed of by a trial. Furthermore, there was little support for the notion that practitioners considered negotiated guilty pleas a necessary but illegitimate response to inadequate court system resources (see also Worden, 2015).

Law in Action: Bargaining and Discretion

The principal weakness of the excessive caseload hypothesis is that it assumes a purely mechanical process, ignoring the underlying dynamics. It seems to suggest that if only there were more judges, more prosecutors, more defense attorneys, and more courtrooms, there would be many more trials, and the penalties imposed on the guilty would also increase. Such a view ignores the discretion inherent in the criminal justice process. Plea bargaining is a response to some fundamental issues, the first of which centers on the question of guilt.

Presumption of Factual Guilt

The process of negotiated justice does not operate in isolation from the other stages of the criminal court process. What has gone before—for example, the setting of bail, the return of a grand jury indictment, and the prosecutor's evaluation of the strengths of a case—significantly affects how courts dispose of cases on a plea. The opposite is equally true. Throughout the history of a case, decisions on bail, indictment, and screening have

been premised on the knowledge that the majority of defendants end up pleading guilty (Wright & Miller, 2002).

Recall from Chapter 10 that the bulk of legally innocent defendants are removed from the criminal court process during the screening process through the preliminary hearing, the grand jury, or the prosecutor's charging decision. By the time a case reaches the trial stage, the courtroom work group presumes that the defendant is probably guilty. Survival through the prior processing means that prosecutors, defense attorneys, and judges alike perceive that trial defendants are in serious trouble.

One study estimated that about 50 percent of the cases in the major trial court were "hopeless" or devoid of triable issues of law (Schulhofer, 1984). These cases are what some court officials term a "dead bang" or a "slam dunk" case, with very strong evidence against the defendant, who has no credible explanation indicating innocence (Mather, 1974a). More recently, some courts have come to refer to these types of cases as "no-brainers" (Bowen, 2009). One district attorney summarized the strong evidence of guilt in such cases: "The pervasiveness of the facts should indicate to any competent attorney that the element of prosecution is present and a successful prosecution is forthcoming" (Neubauer, 1974b, p. 200).

No two cases are ever the same, of course. Many discussions of plea bargains leave the false impression that the attorneys haggle only over the sentence. In fact, courtroom work groups spend a lot of time discussing and analyzing how the crime was committed, the nature of the victim, the types of witnesses, and the character of the defendant (Emmelman, 2002; Maynard, 1988; Shermer & Johnson, 2010). In many cases, the likelihood that the defendant will be acquitted outright is small; however, the possibility exists that he or she might be convicted of a less serious offense. The question of what charge the facts will support is an important part of plea bargaining.

Costs and Risks of Trial

The possibility of trial greatly influences negotiations. Trials are a costly and time-consuming means of establishing guilt. For example, to try a simple burglary case typically would take from one to four days (depending on the jurisdiction) and require the presence of the judge, bailiff, clerk, defense attorney, prosecutor, and court reporter. During this period, none of them could devote much time to the numerous other cases requiring disposition. Also, each would be forced to spend time preparing for this trial. A trial would also require the presence of numerous noncourt personnel: police officers, witnesses, victims, and jurors. For each of these people, a trial represents an unwanted intrusion into their daily lives.

Based on these considerations, all members of the courtroom work group have a common interest in disposing of cases and avoiding unnecessary trials. Their reasons may differ. Judges and prosecutors want high disposition rates in order to prevent case backlogs and to present a public impression that the process is running smoothly. Public defenders prefer quick dispositions because they lack the personnel to handle the caseload. Private defense attorneys depend on a high case turnover to earn a living, because most of their clients can afford only a modest fee. In short, all members of the courtroom work group have more cases to try than the time or resources to try them.

To a large extent, then, a trial is a mutual penalty that all parties seek to avoid through plea bargaining. To be sure, not all trials are avoided. But through plea bargaining, scarce trial resources can be applied to the cases that need to be tried.

What to Do with the Guilty

The adversary proceedings of trial are designed to resolve conflict over guilt or innocence. In practice, however, it is not the issue of legal guilt that is most often in dispute, but rather what sentence to impose on the guilty. Sentencing decisions involve more than the verdict of guilt or innocence presented at trial; they incorporate difficult issues of judgment about the type of crime and the nature of the defendant. Moreover, because of the standards of evidence, information relevant to sentencing is not easily introduced at trial. Unlike a trial, plea bargaining does focus on what to do with an offender—particularly, how much leniency is appropriate.

Criminal statutes are broad; the courtroom work group is called upon to apply these broad prohibitions to specific and variable cases. The participants are concerned with adjusting the penalties to the specifics of the crime and the defendant. In the interest of fairness, they seek to individualize justice.

Consider a case with two co-defendants of unequal culpability: an armed robbery involving an experienced robber who employed a youthful accomplice as a driver. Technically, both are equally guilty, but in the interest of fairness and substantive justice, the prosecutor may legitimately decide to make a concession to the young accomplice but none to the prime mover. In short, members of the courtroom work group seek to individualize justice.

Bargaining and the Courtroom Work Group

Plea bargaining is a contest involving the prosecutor, defendant, defense counsel, and, at times, the judge. Each party has its own objectives, and each attempts to structure the situation to its own advantage by using tactics to improve its bargaining position. Each defines success in terms of its own objectives. Among the conflicting objectives, accommodations are possible, because each side can achieve its objectives only by making concessions on other matters. Plea bargaining is typical of "most bargaining situations which ultimately involve some range of possible outcomes within which each party would rather make a concession than fail to reach agreement at all" (Schelling, 1960, p. 70; see also Covey, 2016; Emmelman, 2002; Graham, 2012).

Plea bargaining typically begins informally, according to two veteran federal prosecutors. When discussing the matter with opposing counsel, prosecutors want to be reassured that the defendant is genuinely interested in pleading guilty and that a reasonable chance exists of reaching an agreement before they invest time and effort in preparing a formal plea agreement. Consistent with our earlier discussion of the courtroom work group (Chapter 5), trust is a critical component of these discussions. "If the prosecutor and the defense counsel have negotiated plea agreements with each other in the past, expect to do so in the future, and from their past dealings, respect and trust each other, these preliminary, informal discussions are likely to be candid and efficient and may quickly lead to an informal proposed agreement" (Brown & Bunnell, 2006, pp. 1065–1066; see also Bowen, 2009).

Bargaining is possible because each of the legal actors understands the realities of law in action: the presumption of guilt, the costs and uncertainties of trial, and the concern with arriving at an appropriate sentence. All these factors influence bargaining positions. Overwhelmingly, attorneys take "the view that they should work together to settle on the appropriate charge and punishment" (Bowen, 2009, p. 15).

Prosecutors

To the prosecutor, a plea bargain represents the certainty of conviction without the risks of trial. Recall that prosecutors emphasize convictions. Because they value the deterrent objectives of law enforcement, they prefer that a guilty person be convicted of some charge rather than to escape with no conviction at all.

The certainty and finality of a defendant's pleading guilty contrast sharply with the potential risks involved in a trial (Covey, 2008, 2016; Worden, 1990). During trial, a number of unexpected events can occur, most of which work to the detriment of the prosecutor. The victim may refuse to cooperate. Witnesses' testimony may differ significantly from earlier statements made in investigative reports. A mistrial—the judge ending the trial without a verdict because of a major defect in the proceedings—could be declared. Even after a jury verdict of guilty, the appellate courts may reverse, meaning that the whole process must be repeated.

In seeking a conviction through a guilty plea, the prosecutor is in a unique position to control the negotiating process (Hashimoto, 2008; Holmes, Daudistel, & Taggart, 1992). To begin with, the prosecutor proceeds from a position of strength: In most cases, the state has sufficient evidence for conviction. If, however, the case is weak, the prosecutor can avoid the embarrassment of losing a case at trial by either dismissing it altogether or offering such a good deal that the defendant cannot refuse.

To improve their bargaining position, some prosecutors deliberately overcharge. "Sure, it's a lever," said one San Francisco prosecutor, referring to his office's practice of charging every nonautomobile homicide as murder. With unusual candor, he added, "And we charge theft, burglary, and the possession of burglar's tools, because we know that if we charged only burglary there would be a trial" (Alschuler, 1968, p. 90; see also Davis, 2007).

Prosecutors, of course, control several of the forms of plea bargaining. They are in a position to offer a charge reduction or a count bargain. They can threaten to throw the book at a defendant who does not plead, or they may refuse to bargain at all. If the crime is a serious one and the defendant is viewed as very dangerous, the prosecutor may force the defendant either to plead on the nose, with no sentencing concessions, or to run the risk of trial and a harsher sentence for not having cooperated.

Defendants

If pleas give prosecutors what they want (convictions), why do defendants plead guilty? To understand plea bargaining, it is important to recognize that it is often in the defendant's best interest to give up the right to be presumed innocent at a trial. The primary benefit of a plea is the possibility of a lenient sentence.

Around the courthouse, it is a common perception that defendants who refuse to plead guilty receive harsher sentences. For example, a judge may impose a stiffer sentence because the defendant compounded the crime by lying on the witness stand or by getting some friends to perjure themselves. Or a prosecutor may agree not to invoke state "career criminal" provisions, which impose higher penalties for those with a prior felony conviction. Moreover, for defendants who are unable to post bail, a guilty plea can mean an immediate release (either on probation or for time served).

Ultimately, defendants must decide whether to go along with the plea bargain or to take their chances at trial. Few defendants are in a position to make a reasoned choice between the advantages of a plea and those of a trial; most are poor, inarticulate, and have little formal education. For these defendants, the experience in the courts is like their life on the streets: They learn to go along. Often softened up by the experience in jail awaiting trial, many defendants find that entering a plea is the best way to go along and avoid the possibility of even harsher penalties. But some question whether these motivations—some of which are quite strong—lead the innocent to plead guilty.

There can be no doubt that "sometimes the prosecutor offers such a generous discount for admitting guilt that the defendant feels he simply can't take the chance of going to trial," even if he is innocent (Leipold, 2005, p. 1154). But it is impossible to know just how many innocent defendants plead guilty. Some scholars argue the problem is minimal and therefore concerns that plea bargaining increases wrongful convictions are "exaggerated" (Tor, Gazal-Ayal, & Garcia, 2010, p. 114). Others maintain the problem is significant (Covey, 2009, 2016; Dervan, 2012). Psychological simulation studies reveal that 40 percent to 50 percent of participants were willing to falsely admit guilt in return for reduced punishments (Russano, Meissner, Narchet, & Kassin, 2005; Dervan & Edkins, 2013, p. 36).

Defense Attorneys

If the prosecutor enters negotiations from a position of strength, the opposite is true of defense attorneys, who have few bargaining chips. Over the years prosecutorial power has increased (Bowen, 2009; Rakoff, Daumier, & Case, 2014; see also Chapter 6), which in turn limits the power of defense attorneys. If the chances of winning at trial are not high—and they rarely are—defense attorneys must consider the strong possibility that after a trial conviction the defendant may be penalized with a higher prison sentence.

The decision-making process for defense attorneys involves three phases. First, the defense attorney must assess the offer for a guilty plea, weighing the potential costs of delay against the likely outcome of a trial. Second, the defense attorney negotiates the terms of a plea bargain; if the initial offer is better than average, negotiations are less intense than if it is below average. Third, the defense attorney counsels

the defendant, who may or may not accept the offer (Covey, 2016; Emmelman, 1996, 2002).

The lawyer's main resource in negotiating a plea agreement is his or her knowledge of the courtroom work group—the types of pleas the prosecutor usually enters, the length of sentence the judge normally imposes in similar cases, and so on. Defense attorneys act as classic negotiators, trying to get the best deal possible for their clients while explaining to the clients the realistic alternatives. As noted in Chapter 7, these two roles can conflict. A defense attorney may negotiate what he or she considers the best deal under the circumstances, only to have the client refuse to go along.

Convincing clients to accept a plea is not always easy. Veteran public defender David Feige (2006) recalls a lawyer and his client screaming at each other in the jail holding cell. Although other lawyers and clients were present, "No one interferes, no one tried to calm them down, and lawyer and client go on yelling at each for another four or five minutes" (p. 119). Such interactions are constant. "Overworked, underappreciated lawyers and desperate clients are a potent mix. Many lawyers see intimate client relationships as superfluous" (p. 119). As stressed in Chapter 7, some lawyers try to protect their clients from making bad decisions, but lawyers also have to deal with pressures from judges to move the docket.

Judges

Several factors limit a judge's ability to control or supervise plea bargaining. Given the division of powers in the adversary system, judges are reluctant to intrude on prosecutorial discretion. Many of the key bargaining mechanisms—specifically, the charges filed and the charges the defendant is allowed to plead to—are controlled by the prosecutor. Thus, when a prosecutor, defense attorney, and defendant have agreed either to a count bargain or a charge-reduction bargain, the judge has no legal authority to refuse to accept the plea.

Even more fundamentally, the judge knows relatively little about each case. Only the prosecutor, defendant, and defense attorney know the evidence for and against the defendant. Without knowledge of why the parties agreed to plea bargain, it is obviously difficult for a judge to reject a plea agreement. In short, the judge is dependent on the prosecutor and, to a lesser extent, the defense attorney.

Within these constraints, judges have some ability to shape the plea-bargaining process. Judicial involvement in the plea-bargaining process can have important consequences. In Essex, New Jersey, for example, trials are rare, and judges spend a great amount of time dealing with the plea-bargaining process. Indeed, "every defender interviewed recalled being coerced into returning to his client and convincing him or her of the judge's strong desire to resolve the case quickly with a plea" (Wice, 2005, p. 125).

In the federal court system, judges are prohibited from being involved in plea negotiations (Borenstein & Anderson, 2009; Covey, 2016). The extent to which judges are involved in the process in state courts varies greatly. A survey of state trial court judges (Ryan & Alfini, 1979) revealed four basic patterns:

- A few judges are actively involved in plea negotiations, offering recommendations about case disposition.

- Some judges are indirectly involved, reviewing the recommendations made by defense and prosecutor.

- A small percentage of judges attend plea discussions but do not participate.

- The majority of judges do not attend plea-negotiating sessions. Thus, their role is limited to ratifying agreements reached by others.

A review of the rules of criminal procedure across the United States reveals that these four approaches continue, although a clear preference exists for judges not to participate in the plea-bargaining process other than to ratify or reject plea agreements reached independently by the prosecution and the defense (Borenstein & Anderson, 2009). But even when judicial participation is limited to ratifying plea negotiations, judges can have an important impact on the process. Regular members of the courtroom work group know the sentence the judge is likely to impose. Therefore, they negotiate case dispositions that incorporate these sentencing expectations. On rare occasions, judges may reject a plea agreement. Such rejections serve to set a baseline for future negotiations.

Dynamics of Bargaining

Negotiating is a group activity, typically conducted in busy, noisy, public courtrooms. In such a courtroom, the initial impression is of constant talking and endless movement. While the judge is hearing a pretrial motion in one case, a prosecutor and defense attorney are engaged in an animated conversation about a charge reduction in another. Meanwhile, in more hushed tones, a public defender is briefing his client about why a continuance will be requested, and nearby a mother is talking to her son, who is being held in jail. These numerous conversations occur while other participants continually move in and out. Police officers leave after testifying in a motion to suppress, bail agents arrive to check on their clients, clerks bring in new files, and defense lawyers search for the prosecutor assigned to their case. Occasionally, the noise becomes so loud that the judge or bailiff demands silence—a request that usually produces only a temporary reduction in the decibel level.

On the surface, courtrooms appear disorganized. In fact, there is an underlying order to the diverse activities. For example, when the judge calls a case, the other participants involved in that matter are immediately expected to drop all other business and proceed to the front of the court. Decision-making norms govern the substance of the negotiations. In particular, patterns exist as to why some cases go to trial and about understandings regarding penalties for those who do go to trial.

Decision-Making Norms

Through working together on a daily basis, the members of the courtroom work group come to understand the problems and demands of the others. They develop shared conceptions of how certain types of cases and defendants should be treated. Everyone except the outsider or the novice knows these customs of the courthouse.

As we have seen, plea bargaining is a complex process, but studies in different courts reveal important similarities in shared norms. The most important consideration is the seriousness of the offense. The more serious the crime charged, the harder the prosecutor bargains (Mather, 1979; Nardulli, Flemming,

& Eisenstein, 1984; Piehl & Bushway, 2007; Ulmer & Bradley, 2006). The next most important factor is the defendant's criminal record. Those with prior convictions receive fewer concessions during bargaining (Alschuler, 1979; Kutateladze & Lawson, 2015; Nardulli, 1978; Piehl & Bushway, 2007; Smith, 1986; Springer, 1983). Another key consideration is the strength of the prosecutor's case. The stronger the evidence against the defendant, the fewer concessions are offered (Adams, 1983; Johnson, King, & Spohn, 2016; Smith, 1986).

These shared norms structure plea negotiations. In each courtroom work group, the set of allowable reductions is well understood. Based on the way the crime was committed and the background of the defendant, nighttime burglary will be reduced to daytime burglary, drunkenness to disturbing the peace, and so on. Thus, contrary to many popular fears, defendants are not allowed to plead to just any charge (Emmelman, 2002; Feeley, 1979). The crime(s) with which a defendant is charged matters during plea bargaining (Graham, 2012). If a defendant has been charged with armed robbery, the defense attorney knows that the credibility of her bargaining position will be destroyed if she suggests a plea to disturbing the peace. Such a plea would be out of line with how things are normally done.

Courtroom work groups have similar shared norms about sentencing. On the basis of these shared norms, all parties know what is open for bargaining and what is not. The shared norms provide a baseline for disposing of specific cases. Upward or downward adjustments are made, depending on the circumstances of the individual case.

Why Cases Go to Trial

Although most cases are disposed of by a guilty plea, an important 2 to 10 percent of defendants are tried (see Figure 12.1 for trial rates for leading felony cases). Cases go to trial when the parties cannot settle a case through negotiation. In large measure, the factors that shape plea bargaining—the strength of the prosecutor's case and the severity of the penalty—are the same ones that enter into the decision to go to trial. Defense attorneys recommend a trial when the risks of trial are low and the possible gains are high.

This broad calculation leads to two very different types of trial cases. In one, the possible gains for the defendant are high because of the chance of an acquittal. There may be reasonable doubt that the defendant committed any crime, or two sets of witnesses may tell conflicting versions of what happened (Neubauer, 1974b). A second category of cases going to trial involves situations in which the prison sentence will be high. Even though a judge or jury is not likely to return a verdict of not guilty, the defendant may still decide that the slim possibility of an acquittal is worth the risk of the trial penalty.

However, not all trial cases are the result of such rational calculations. Some defendants insist on a trial, no matter what. Judges, prosecutors, and defense attorneys label as irrational those defendants who refuse to recognize the realities of the criminal justice system and insist on a trial even when the state has a strong case (Bibas, 2004; Neubauer, 1974b). The net effect of these considerations is that some types of cases are more likely to go to trial than others. Property offenses (burglary and larceny) are much less likely to go to trial than homicide, sexual assault, or robbery. Mather (1974a) suggests that property crimes are least likely to go to trial because the state is apt to have a strong case (usually buttressed by the presence of indisputable physical evidence) and the prison sentence will not be long (see also Bibas, 2004). Serious crimes such as murder, rape, and robbery are much more likely to be tried. In some crimes of violence, reasonable doubt may exist because the victim may have provoked the attack. Moreover, a convicted defendant is likely to serve a long prison term and is therefore more disposed to take a chance on an outright acquittal.

Jury Trial Penalty

Although most defendants plead guilty, a significant minority of cases do go to trial. As previously indicated, it is a common assumption in courthouses around the nation that defendants who do not enter a plea of guilty can expect to receive harsher sentences. Typically called the "jury trial penalty," the notion reflects the philosophy, "He takes some of my time, I take some of his." Here, *time* refers to the hours spent hearing evidence presented to a jury (Bowen, 2009; Heumann, 1978; Kim, 2014; King, Soulé, Steen, & Weidner, 2005; Uhlman & Walker, 1980).

Several studies provide empirical documentation for these courthouse perceptions (Brereton & Casper, 1981–1982; Freiburger & Hilinski, 2013; Kim, 2014). In a major eastern city, "the cost of a jury trial for convicted defendants in Metro City is high: sentences are substantially more severe than for other defendants" (Uhlman & Walker, 1980, p. 337). Similarly in U.S. district courts across the nation, meaningful trial penalties exist after accounting for legal factors like sentencing guidelines and whether the defendant provided substantial assistance to law enforcement (Kim, 2014; Ulmer, Eisenstein, & Johnson, 2010).

Although a couple of studies have challenged these conclusions (Eisenstein & Jacob, 1977; Rhodes, 1978), more recent research finds that the magnitude of the jury trial penalty is stunningly high. In serious cases, the sentence imposed on a defendant who is found guilty after trial will often be over five times more severe than the expected sentence for the same offense for a guilty plea (Kim, 2014; King et al., 2005; McCoy, 2003; Ulmer & Bradley, 2006).

The U.S. Supreme Court clearly sanctioned the jury trial penalty in *Bordenkircher v. Hayes* (1978). That case involved a Kentucky defendant accused of forging an $88 check. He was offered a five-year prison sentence if he entered a plea of guilty. But the prosecutor indicated that if the defendant rejected the offer, the state would seek to impose life imprisonment because of the defendant's previous two felony convictions. Such stepped-up sentences for habitual criminals were allowed at that time by Kentucky law. The defendant rejected the plea, went to trial, was convicted, and was eventually sentenced to life imprisonment. The Court held, "The course of conduct engaged in by the prosecutor in this case, which no more than openly presented the defendant with the unpleasant alternative of forgoing trial or facing charges on which he was plainly subject to prosecution" did not violate constitutional protections. In dissent, however, Justice Powell noted that the offer of five years in prison "hardly could be characterized as a generous

offer." He was clearly troubled that "persons convicted of rape and murder often are not punished so severely" as the sentence ultimately imposed on the defendant in the case for check forgery. See the "Key Developments" feature for major legal developments involving plea bargaining.

Copping a Plea

"Your honor, my client wishes at this time to withdraw his previous plea of not guilty and wishes at this time to enter a plea of guilty." In phrases similar to this one, defense attorneys indicate that the case is about to end; the defendant is ready to plead. A plea of guilty is more than an admission of conduct; it is a conviction that also involves a defendant's waiver of the most vital rights of the court process: presumption of innocence, jury trial, and confrontation of witnesses (*Boykin v. Alabama*, 1969).

In an earlier era, the process of entering a plea of guilty was usually brief and informal. Because the courts and the legal process as a whole were reluctant to recognize the existence of plea bargaining, little law guided the process. Under the leadership of Chief Justice Warren Burger, however, the U.S. Supreme Court sought to set standards for the plea-bargaining process (see "Case Close-Up: *Santobello v. New York* and Honoring a Plea Agreement" on page 367).

Following *Santobello*, the plea process has become more formalized. For example, in the U.S. Attorney's Office in the District of Columbia, an initial plea agreement between opposing counsel must first be approved by a senior supervisor. Next, a plea agreement is drafted. "Over the years, written plea agreements have grown longer and more complex as successive generations of prosecutors, defense counsel and judges … have noticed or exploited ambiguities of the parties' rights and obligations. As a result, federal plea agreements in D.C. now often run ten single-spaced pages or more" (Brown & Bunnell, 2006, p. 1066). Once a plea agreement has been struck, the next step is the courtroom. A pair of recent U.S. Supreme Court opinions will likely force state courts to

KEY DEVELOPMENTS INVOLVING PLEA BARGAINING	
Boykin v. Alabama (1969)	When a defendant enters a plea of guilty, the judge must determine whether the plea is knowingly entered and completely voluntary.
Brady v. United States (1970)	Even though the defendant pled guilty to avoid the possibility of a death penalty, the plea was voluntary and intelligently made and therefore not coerced.
Alford v. North Carolina (1970)	Given the defendant's desire to avoid the death penalty and the existence of substantial evidence of guilt, the plea of guilty was valid even though the defendant denied guilt.
Santobello v. New York (1971)	When a plea rests in any significant degree on a promise or agreement of the prosecutor, so that it can be said to be a part of the inducement or consideration, such promise must be fulfilled.
Bordenkircher v. Hayes (1978)	It is not a violation of due process for a prosecutor to threaten defendants with other criminal prosecutions so long as the prosecutor has probable cause to believe that the accused has committed the offense.
Ricketts v. Adamson (1987)	The prosecutor allowed the defendant to plead guilty to second-degree murder, contingent upon his testimony against the codefendant. When the defendant refused to so testify, the DA prosecuted him for first-degree murder. The defendant was not protected by double jeopardy because he breached the plea agreement.
Alabama v. Smith (1989)	The defendant was successful in having his original guilty plea vacated. After conviction at trial, though, the judge imposed a substantially more severe sentence than had originally been negotiated in the plea agreement. The Court held that the enhanced sentence was not vindictiveness because the trial judge had more information available as a result of the trial.
United States v. Mezzanatto (1995)	Federal prosecutors may use statements made by a defendant during plea bargaining to cross-examine the defendant at trial.
United States v. Ruiz (2002)	Prior to a plea of guilty, the prosecutor does not have to disclose to the defense as much evidence as before a trial.
Iowa v. Tovar (2004)	When a defendant is *pro se* and, therefore, is acting as his or her own attorney, the court need not inform the defendant that waiving counsel's assistance in deciding whether to plead guilty risks overlooking a viable defense and forgoes the opportunity to obtain an independent opinion on the wisdom of pleading guilty.
Lafler v. Cooper (2012) and *Missouri v. Frye* (2012)	The right to effective assistance of counsel extends to plea bargaining. Thus, when an attorney provides ineffective advice that leads to the rejection of a plea agreement, the defendant is entitled to a hearing to show a reasonable possibility that the outcome of the plea process would have been different with competent advice.

formalize their plea practices along federal lines (see *Lafler v. Cooper*, 2012; *Missouri v. Frye*, 2012).

Questioning the Defendant

For years, plea negotiations were officially considered taboo. As a result, the taking of a plea was often a sham. The defendant was expected to lie and deny that a deal had been made (Casper, 1972). Today, however, to prevent the possibility of covering up plea bargaining, many courts now require that a plea agreement be placed on the record.

Most defendants plead guilty to one or more charges listed in the charging document. Before a defendant's plea of guilty can be accepted, the judge must question the defendant. This was not always the case; judges once merely accepted the attorney's statement that the defendant wanted to plead guilty. But in *Boykin v. Alabama*, the U.S. Supreme Court ruled: "It was error, for the trial judge to accept petitioner's guilty plea without an affirmative showing that it was intelligent and voluntary" (1969, p. 241).

In light of *Boykin*, Rule 11 of the Federal Rules of Criminal Procedure and similar state provisions bars courts from accepting a plea of guilty in felony proceedings unless the court is satisfied, after inquiry, that:

1. the plea is made knowingly, intelligently, and voluntarily;

2. the defendant committed the crime charged; and

3. the defendant is mentally competent to enter the plea and thereby waive important constitutional rights.

Waiver of Rights

Accordingly, Rule 11 requires a judge to "address the defendant personally in open court and determine that the plea is voluntary and did not result from force, threats, or promises (other than promises [contained] in the plea agreement)." Thus, a judge must ensure that a defendant pleading guilty has not been improperly influenced by the prosecution, law enforcement officials, or the defendant's own attorney.

At a Rule 11 hearing, the judge inquires whether the defendant understands the nature of the charge(s) and the possible penalty upon conviction; whether the defendant is satisfied with the services of defense counsel; and whether the defendant realizes that a plea waives a series of constitutional rights, including:

- the right to a trial by jury;
- the right to confront and cross-examine adverse witnesses;
- the right to compel the attendance and testimony of witnesses;
- the right to testify on one's own behalf;
- the right to be free from being forced to incriminate oneself;

- the right to be presumed innocent until proven guilty beyond a reasonable doubt; and
- the right to appeal one's conviction.

Courts often use a *Boykin* **form** to ensure that defendants have been informed of all the rights they are waiving. *Boykin* forms (a sample of which appears in Figure 12.2) also provide the added benefits of ensuring that a guilty plea reflects the defendant's own choice and that it is made with a general understanding of the charges and consequences of conviction. Finally, the questioning during a Rule 11 hearing and the completion of a *Boykin* form provide an official court record, which prevents defendants from later contending that they were forced to plead guilty or that they did not knowingly and intelligently waive their rights.

Allocution

To satisfy Rule 11's requirement that the court be satisfied that the defendant actually committed the crime charged in order for the court to accept a plea, either a law enforcement officer or the prosecutor states that if a trial were held, the evidence would show the defendant to be guilty and then proceeds to summarize the evidence sufficient to prove each of the elements of the offense. The defendant then has the opportunity to offer any corrections or additions, but must **allocute**—provide a factual basis for the plea—to each charge; in other words, the defendant, in open court, must admit to the conduct central to the criminality of crimes charged unless permission has been granted for the defendant to enter an *Alford* plea (see the following). In some jurisdictions, this Rule 11 hearing is therefore called an **allocution hearing**. This public disclosure allows defendants and attorneys to correct any misunderstandings.

Competency

Rule 11 does not specifically state that a court must ensure that a criminal defendant is competent to waive any constitutional rights. But the U.S. Supreme Court has held that because pleading guilty involves waiving the numerous rights discussed earlier, a court may not accept a guilty plea from a defendant who is not mentally competent (*Godinez v. Moran*, 1993).

STATE OF WISCONSIN, CIRCUIT COURT, _____ **COUNTY**

For Official Use

State of Wisconsin, Plaintiff
    -vs-

**Plea Questionnaire/
Waiver of Rights**

_____
          Name

Case No. _____

I am the defendant and intend to plea as follows:

Charge/Statute	Plea	Charge/Statute	Plea
	☐ Guilty ☐ No Contest		☐ Guilty ☐ No Contest
	☐ Guilty ☐ No Contest		☐ Guilty ☐ No Contest

☐ See attached sheet for additional charges.

I am _____ years old. I have completed _____ years of schooling.

I	☐ do	☐ do not	have a high school diploma, GED, of HSED.
I	☐ do	☐ do not	understand the English language.
I	☐ do	☐ do not	understand the charge(s) to which I am pleading.
I	☐ am not	☐ am	currently receiving treatment for a mental illness or disorder.
I	☐ have not	☐ have	had any alcohol, medications, or drugs within the last 24 hours.

Constitutional Rights

I understand that by entering this plea. I give up the following constitutional rights:

☐ I give up my right to a trial.
☐ I give up my right to remain silent and I understand that my silence could not be used against me at trial.
☐ I give up my right to testify and present evidence at trial.
☐ I give up my right to use subpoenas to require witnesses to come to court and testify for me at trial.
☐ I give up my right to a jury trial, where all 12 jurors would have to agree that I am either guilty or not guilty.
☐ I give up my right to confront in court the people who testify against me and cross-examine them.
☐ I give up my right to make the State prove me guilty beyond a reasonable doubt.

I understand the rights that have been checked and give them up of my own free will.

Understandings

• I understand that the crime(s) to which I am pleading has/have elements that the State would have to prove beyond a reasonable doubt if I had a trial. These elements have been explained to me by my attorney or are as follows: ☐ See Attached sheet.

_____

• I understand that the judge is not bound by any plea agreement or recommendations and may impose the maximum penalty. The maximum penalty I face upon conviction is: _____

_____

• I understand that the judge must impose the mandatory minimum penalty. If any. The mandatory minimum penalty I face upon conviction is:_____

_____

• I understand that the presumptive minimum penalty, if any. I face upon conviction is: _____

_____

The judge can impose a lesser sentence if the judge states appropriate reasons.

CR-277, 11/99 Plea Questionnaire/Waiver of Rights   §971.08, Wisconsin Statutes.

This form shall not be modified. It may be supplemented with additional material.

Page 1 of 2

FIGURE 12.2 A Typical *Boykin* Form

When a defendant has competently waived the right to counsel and, therefore, is acting as his or her own attorney, the court need not inform the defendant that waiving counsel's assistance in deciding whether to plead guilty risks overlooking a viable defense and forgoes the opportunity to obtain an independent opinion on the wisdom of pleading guilty (*Iowa v. Tovar*, 2004). In other words, the defendant who acts as his own counsel proceeds at his own peril during plea bargaining and is stuck with the consequences of that decision.

No Contest and *Alford* Pleas

There are two types of pleas that do not require a defendant to allocute by giving a factual basis for the crimes to which they are pleading because these two pleas do not involve express admissions of guilt. Rather, they amount to consent to be convicted and punished.

The first such plea is a **no contest** plea, sometimes referred to as a plea of *nolo contendere*—Latin for "I will not contest it." A *nolo contendere* plea is not an express admission of guilt by a defendant. Rather, it serves "as a consent by the defendant that he may be punished as if he were guilty and a prayer for leniency" (*North Carolina v. Alford*, 1970, p. 35 n. 8). Although a plea of *nolo contendere* has the same results in criminal proceedings as a plea of guilty, it cannot be used in a subsequent civil proceeding as a defendant's admission of guilt. Thus, this plea is usually entered when civil proceedings and liabilities may result.

The second type of plea that does not technically require allocution is an *Alford* **plea**. This plea allows a defendant to plead guilty while claiming innocence. The name of this plea stems from the case of *North Carolina v. Alford* (1970), a capital murder case. The defendant protested his innocence, but entered a plea of guilty anyway, saying, "I pleaded guilty on second-degree murder because they said there is too much evidence, but I ain't shot no man…. I just pleaded guilty because they said if I didn't they would gas me for it…. I'm not guilty but I pleaded guilty" (p. 29 n. 2). The U.S. Supreme Court held that given the defendant's desire to avoid the death penalty and the existence of substantial evidence of guilt, the plea of guilty was valid. Today, when judges accept an *Alford* plea, they usually ask, "Are you pleading because you believe it to be in your best interest?"

The only difference between a *nolo* plea and an *Alford* plea is that the defendant does not maintain he or she is innocent in a *nolo* plea, whereas innocence is asserted in *Alford* pleas. Both, however, have the same effect. They speed up the clogged judicial process by allowing the defendant to "save face," at least superficially. But for all practical purposes, both *nolo* and *Alford* plea have the same effect as a conventional guilty plea and result in roughly the same punishment.

Judges have discretion in deciding whether to accept the defendant's plea of guilty, *nolo contendere*, or *Alford* plea. Some judges refuse to accept *nolo* or *Alford* pleas since they do not require the defendant to fully admit guilt. According to Superior Court Judge Martin McKeever of Connecticut, such pleas fly "in the face of what crime and punishment should be all about." Thus, he does not accept pleas "in cases where culpability is so obvious that the public has a right to know about it" (quoted in Steinberger, 1985). Moreover, such pleas rob "the victim of the opportunity to hear the defendant acknowledge and accept responsibility" for his or her crimes, a deprivation that can impair the psychological recovery of victims (Molesworth, 2008, p. 914).

Acceptance and Withdrawal of Pleas

Even in cases in which a defendant enters a traditional plea of guilt, judges still have the discretion to reject a plea agreement if they find it does not serve the interests of justice. But, as described earlier, most judges do not reject the plea agreements negotiated between prosecutors, defense attorneys, and defendants.

To ensure fairness in negotiations between defense and prosecution, the law now gives defendants a limited right to withdraw a guilty plea. In *Santobello v. New York* (1971), Chief Justice Warren Burger wrote, "When a plea rests in any significant degree on a promise or agreement of the prosecutor, so that it can be said to be a part of the inducement or consideration, such promise must be fulfilled" (p. 262; see the "Case Close-Up" feature on page 367). Subsequent decisions likewise held that defendants must live up to their end of the plea agreement (*Ricketts v. Adamson*, 1987).

Effective Assistance of Counsel During Plea Bargaining

Decades of seeming U.S. Supreme Court indifference to plea-bargaining practices ended with two significant 2012 decisions.

Galin Edward Frye's attorney never told him of plea-bargain offers from prosecutors on charges that he was driving with a revoked license. Frye later pleaded guilty and was sentenced to three years in

CASE CLOSE-UP

Santobello v. New York and Honoring a Plea Agreement

Rudolph Santobello was indicted on two counts: promoting gambling in the first degree and possession of gambling records in the first degree, both felonies under New York law. After negotiations with the prosecutor's office in the Bronx, Santobello entered a plea to the lesser included offense of possession of gambling records in the second degree, and the prosecutor also agreed to make no recommendation as to the sentence. Santobello represented to the judge that the plea was voluntary and that the facts of the case, as described by the assistant district attorney, were true. The court accepted the plea and set a date for sentencing.

Months elapsed, though, before sentencing. A new defense attorney was hired, and he moved to suppress the evidence on grounds of an illegal search and seizure. The trial judge retired. Another assistant DA assumed control over the case (it is unclear whether his predecessor was promoted or resigned to take a job in private practice). Months later, when Santobello appeared for sentencing, the new prosecutor recommended the maximum one-year sentence, thereby breaching the terms of the plea agreement. The new judge, unaware of the terms of plea agreement, quickly imposed this sentence, leaving no doubt of his thoughts about the defendant. Reading the probation report, he said: "I have here a history of a long, long serious criminal record.... He is unamenable to supervision in the community. He is a professional criminal." The judge concluded by regretting that a one-year sentence was all he was allowed to impose.

Chief Justice Warren Burger was beginning his second term on the court. Despite being a product of the law-and-order movement, his decision begins by noting the sloppiness apparent in the DA's office. "This record represents another example of an unfortunate lapse in orderly prosecutorial procedures, in part, no doubt, because of the enormous increase in the workload of the often understaffed prosecutor's office." But, most notably, he continues the theme of workload by coming out strongly in favor of guilty pleas:

> The disposition of criminal charges by agreement between the prosecutor and the accused, sometimes loosely called "plea bargaining," is an essential component of the administration of justice. Disposition of charges after plea discussions is not only an essential part of the process but a highly desirable part.

The Court therefore vacated Santobello's sentence and remanded the case for resentencing before a different judge.

The Burger Court decision in *Santobello* in essence brought plea bargaining out of the closet. This was the Court's first look at a state non–capital punishment plea. As for the specific issue, "When a plea rests in any significant degree on a promise or agreement of the prosecutor so that it can be said to be part of the inducement or consideration, such promise must be fulfilled." The net effect was to suggest that state pleas proceed under Rule 11 of the Federal Rules of Criminal Procedure, which requires the parties to disclose in open court the nature of the plea agreement.

In hindsight, what is perhaps most notable is that a justice appointed by President Nixon as representative of his law-and-order philosophy readily embraced plea bargaining. Within just two years, Nixon's crime commission denounced the practice and called for the abolition of plea bargaining within five years—a call that was doomed to failure from the beginning. Indeed, in 2012, the Supreme Court formally recognized that since the overwhelming majority of criminal cases in the United States are disposed of by plea bargaining, the Sixth Amendment right to effective assistance of counsel applies during plea bargaining (*Lafler v. Cooper*, 2012; *Missouri v. Frye*, 2012).

---

prison. But prosecutors had offered Frye two options for plea bargains. Under the first option, Frye would plead guilty to a felony version of the driving on a revoked license charge (since he already had three misdemeanor convictions for doing so), but he would serve only 10 days of a three-year jail sentence as so-called shock time (see Chapter 14), with the balance of the three-year sentence suspended. The second offer was to reduce the charge to a misdemeanor and, if

Frye pleaded guilty to it, to recommend a 90-day sentence. Frye's defense attorney, however, never communicated these offers to him. The Court reversed Frye's conviction, ruling that his lawyer failed to provide effective assistance of counsel as guaranteed by the Sixth Amendment (Chapter 7).

Writing for a 5-to-4 majority in *Missouri v. Frye* (2012, p. 1407), Justice Kennedy stressed "In today's criminal justice system ..., the negotiation of a plea bargain, rather than the unfolding of a trial, is almost always the critical point for a defendant." Quoting from law reviews, he emphasized that "plea bargaining is not some adjunct to the criminal justice system; it *is* the criminal justice system" (p. 1407). The Court held that defense attorneys have a legal duty to communicate formal offers from the prosecution to accept a plea on terms and conditions that may be favorable to the accused.

In *Lafler v. Cooper* (2012), the Court held that the defendant had received ineffective assistance of counsel (Chapter 7) when his attorney recommended against accepting a plea agreement because the jury would not convict Lafler of murder (but it did). Lafler was therefore entitled to a hearing to determine whether there was a reasonable probability that "the outcome of the plea process would have been different with competent advice" (p. 1384).

In a sharply worded dissent, Justice Scalia wrote "the Court today opens a whole new field of constitutionalized criminal procedure: plea-bargaining law. The ordinary criminal process has become too long, too expensive, and unpredictable, in no small part as a consequence of an intricate federal Code of Criminal Procedure imposed on the States by this Court in pursuit of perfect justice" (*Lafler v. Cooper*, 2012, p. 1392).

Read together, *Lafler* and *Frye* represent the Court's recognition that the right to counsel under the Sixth Amendment is distinct from the right to a fair trial (Mallord, 2014). The majority of the Court acknowledged that future litigation would examine some details of the process. Whether future litigation results in major changes in plea-bargaining practices or some minor adjustments remains to be seen (Work, 2014).

Law in Controversy: Abolishing Plea Bargaining

Chief Justice Burger's opinion in *Santobello* supports plea bargaining because it contributes to the efficiency of the criminal justice processes. But some people find justifying plea bargaining

merely on the basis of expediency to be unconvincing. Some legitimately ask, "What of justice?" (See the feature, "Courts, Controversy, & the Administration of Justice: Who Benefits from Plea Bargaining?")

Doubts about plea bargaining have resulted in attempts in some jurisdictions to abolish or reform the practice. Such efforts conform to one of the most controversial recommendations of the National Advisory Commission on Criminal Justice Standards and Goals (1973)—abolishing plea bargaining altogether. This recommendation was prompted by the commission's view that plea bargaining produces undue leniency. The main weakness of the commission's recommendation to abolish plea bargaining is that it failed to recognize the importance of law in action. The commission seemed preoccupied with an idealized criminal law that is clear and precise and that does not have to accommodate messy disagreements.

Faced with mounting public criticism and professional concern, prosecutors and judges in a number of American communities have altered traditional plea-bargaining practices. Claims that plea bargaining has been abolished or that major reforms have been instituted require critical analysis. As a result of a growing number of studies of such efforts, some important areas of interest can be highlighted.

Are the Changes Implemented?

In analyzing the impact of changes in plea-bargaining practices, a basic question is whether the changes were indeed implemented. Written policy changes do not always alter the behavior of court actors. For example, some efforts to reform plea bargaining met with resistance from defense attorneys and others. As a result, the programs did not have their intended impact and were later dropped (Covey, 2008; Nimmer & Krauthaus, 1977). A similar pattern was observed in a Northern California county. After the grand jury publicly criticized plea bargaining for undue leniency, the prosecutor responded by trying to eliminate plea bargaining. The defense attorneys then began to take more cases to trial. After the state lost 12 out of 16 jury verdicts,

COURTS, CONTROVERSY, & THE ADMINISTRATION OF JUSTICE

Who Benefits from Plea Bargaining?

Some people within the court system are concerned that plea bargaining reduces the courthouse to a place where guilt or innocence is negotiated in the same way as one might haggle over the price of copper jugs at a Turkish bazaar (Rubin, 1976). Primarily, though, opposition to plea bargaining reflects different ideological preferences. What is particularly interesting is that civil libertarians as well as spokespersons for law and order see plea bargaining as a danger, but often for different reasons.

Supporters of the values of the due process model are concerned that plea bargaining undercuts the protections afforded individuals, may lead to the conviction of innocent defendants, and produces few tangible benefits for defendants. This view was aptly expressed by a critic of plea bargaining, law professor Albert Alschuler: "Today's guilty plea system leads even able, conscientious, and highly motivated attorneys to make decisions that are not really in their clients' interests" (1975, p. 1180; see also Covey, 2016).

A prime concern of due process adherents is that a criminal court process geared to produce guilty pleas negates the fundamental protection of the adversary system—a public trial in which the defendant is presumed innocent—because plea bargaining discourages trials by imposing a penalty on those who may lose at trial. They therefore advocate abolishing bargaining and increasing the number of trials. However, such a position ignores the reality of criminal courts: In most cases, the participants do not substantially disagree over the facts. Moreover, civil libertarian critics look to the jury as the proper forum for separating guilt from innocence. Yet, experienced trial attorneys often have grave doubts about such an approach. In the words of a Los Angeles public defender:

"If you've got an exceptional case—one which is weak and there's a good chance that the defendant may be innocent—then you don't want to take it before a jury because you never know what they'll do" (Mather, 1974a, p. 202).

If advocates of due process are worried that plea bargaining jeopardizes the rights of the individual, the backers of the crime control model express the opposite concern. They believe that plea bargaining allows defendants to avoid conviction for crimes they actually committed, results in lenient sentences, and in general gives criminal wrongdoers the impression that the courts and the law are easily manipulated. In the words of the Pima County, Arizona, prosecutor, "Plea bargains send the wrong message. When criminal offenders are permitted to plead guilty to lesser charges with lesser penalties, the credibility of the entire system is corrupted" (LaWall, 2001).

It is not a difficult task to single out individual cases in which these law enforcement criticisms of plea bargaining have merit. But the argument obscures too much. In particular, it confuses cause with effect. A bargained agreement on reduced charges, for example, may be the product of initial overcharging, of evidence problems that surface later, or both. Moreover, such criticisms suggest that in plea bargaining, anything goes—the prosecutor and judge will make any deal to dispose of a case. In reality, each court uses a more or less consistent approach to what charge or count reductions are customary, plus a set of sentencing rules of thumb.

Many of the law enforcement criticisms of plea bargaining may be reduced to an overall displeasure with the leniency of the courts. Whether sentences are too harsh or too lenient should be a separate issue from the vehicle for reaching these sentencing dispositions.

What do you think? Does plea bargaining sacrifice the rights of the defendant, or do the guilty benefit?

the prosecutor quietly returned to the old policies (Carter, 1974). Of course, not all efforts at reform are short-lived. In some jurisdictions, efforts at reforming plea bargaining have been successfully implemented (Covey, 2008; Heumann & Loftin, 1979; Nimmer & Krauthaus, 1977).

Is Discretion Eliminated or Just Moved Elsewhere?

Even when programs are successfully implemented, they may not have the impact intended. Discretion in the criminal justice system (see

Chapter 5) has been likened to a hydraulic process. Efforts to control discretion at one stage typically result in its displacement to another part of the process (Vance, 2014). Thus, the result of "abolishing" or "reforming" plea bargaining is often that the activity simply moves elsewhere. Such a hydraulic process occurred in California after the voters approved Proposition 8 in 1982. One of the key provisions of this victim's bill of rights (see Chapter 9) prohibits plea bargaining for 25 of the most serious crimes. The ban applied only to the major trial court, however. Proposition 8 did not abolish plea bargaining but rather relocated it to the lower court, where the proportion of bargained cases increased (McCoy, 1984). Indeed, the overall level of plea bargaining increased. Far from helping the victims of crime, the acceleration of plea bargaining prevented both victims and defendants from understanding the reasons for convictions and sentences (McCoy, 1993).

Alaska provides another clear example. In that state, the attorney general forbade assistant prosecutors from engaging in plea bargaining or from making sentencing recommendations to the judge. Judges complained that their responsibilities increased dramatically, meaning they had very little opportunity to give sentencing thorough consideration (Rubenstein & White, 1979, p. 277). The hydraulic process seems to explain why a later reevaluation of Alaska's plea-bargaining ban found clear evidence of both evolution and decay in the policy. For example, charge bargaining had reemerged in most of the state (Carns & Kruse, 1992).

Do Offsetting Changes Occur?

Efforts to abolish or change plea-bargaining practices may produce offsetting changes. This was the conclusion of an excellent in-depth study of a Michigan county (Church, 1976). After a law-and-order antidrug campaign, the newly elected prosecuting attorney instituted a strict policy forbidding charge-reduction plea bargaining in drug-selling cases. One result was an increased demand for trials, although it was not as great as some judges feared. But at the same time, outright dismissals because of insufficient evidence

increased. Moreover, a much greater percentage of defendants were sentenced as juveniles rather than adults so that they would not have a felony record. Most important, plea bargaining involving defense attorneys and judges continued in drug cases, and the assistant prosecutor's ability to control the disposition of the cases weakened.

Efforts to increase sentence severity by abolishing or constraining plea bargaining are not always successful. When the U.S. Coast Guard effectively eliminated plea bargains in special courts-martial, there was no increase in sentence severity (Call, England, & Talarico, 1983). In short, attempts to abolish plea bargaining often produce a number of offsetting changes because overall policies fail to consider the reasons for negotiations.

Conclusion

Most of the Supreme Court decisions highlighted in this book deal with serious crimes and punishments—quite often murder and the death penalty. Perhaps the Court decided to rule on *Santobello* because the underlying charge was a minor one. After all, establishing new rules for plea bargaining would prove less controversial if the crime was not a violent one. Nonetheless, it is still curious that Burger's opinion states so many negatives about *Santobello*, leaving little doubt that this small-time alleged member of one of New York's crime families was hardly a model citizen. As for Santobello the man, little else is known. In covering the case, the *New York Times* discussed only the legal issues, not the local man whose name is now enshrined in a major Supreme Court pronouncement.

Plea bargaining vividly illustrates the difference between law on the books and law in action. The rules of criminal procedure, decisions of appellate courts, and theories of the adversary system suggest that the trial is the principal activity of the criminal courts. Instead, plea bargaining is the predominant activity. Bargaining is best understood not as a response to the press of cases but as an adaptation to the realities of the types of cases requiring court disposition. In most cases, little question about the defendant's legal guilt exists. A trial is a costly and sometimes risky method of establishing that guilt, and it cannot wrestle with the most pressing issue: what sentence to impose on the guilty. Finally, through plea bargaining, courthouse officials are able to individualize justice. In short, it is neither necessary nor desirable that every defendant have a trial.

CHAPTER REVIEW

LO1 1. Distinguish between the three most common types of plea agreements.

The three most common types of plea agreements are charge bargaining, count bargaining, and sentence bargaining. In a charge bargain, the defendant pleads guilty to a less serious charge than the one originally specified. In a count bargain, the defendant pleads guilty to a few of the charges in the indictment or bill or information. In a sentence bargain, the defendant pleads guilty in anticipation of leniency in sentencing.

LO2 2. Discuss the three major factors influencing bargaining and discretion.

The three major factors influencing bargaining and discretion are the presumption of factual guilt, the costs and risks of trial to all parties, and the question of what sentence to impose upon the guilty.

LO3 3. Recognize the importance of *Boykin v. Alabama*.

In *Boykin*, the Court held that a plea of guilty was more than an admission of guilt and also involved the waiver of important constitutional rights. As a result, a defendant must knowingly waive his or her constitutional rights before a plea of guilty is accepted.

LO4 4. List the major reason each of the members of the courtroom work group engages in plea bargaining.

Prosecutors engage in plea bargaining because they want to gain convictions, defense attorneys seek leniency for their clients, and judges feel pressures to move cases.

LO5 5. Indicate why a few cases go to trial but most defendants plead guilty.

Defendants and their lawyers will opt for a trial if they think the case factually presents a reasonable doubt or if the prison sentence will be high.

LO6 6. Explain why adherents of the crime control model of criminal justice oppose plea bargaining for different reasons from those of adherents of the due process model of criminal justice.

Adherents of the crime control model of criminal justice oppose plea bargaining because they believe defendants get off too lightly. On the other hand, adherents of the due process model of criminal justice oppose plea bargaining because they believe that innocent defendants might be forced to plead guilty to a crime they did not commit.

CRITICAL THINKING QUESTIONS

1. Should a defendant be allowed to plead guilty without fully admitting guilt? Would you limit *Alford* pleas to situations in which the defendant wishes to avoid the death penalty? Would you allow white-collar defendants to enter *Alford* pleas? Some federal judges will not, because they perceive that high-ranking corporate officials want to end the criminal cases without accepting full responsibility for their actions.

2. What types of plea agreements were involved in *Santobello*—charge, count, or sentence?

Was the nature of the agreement implicit or explicit? How would you characterize the working relationship between the defense and the prosecution in *Santobello?*

3. Do defendants benefit from plea bargaining in terms of lower sentences, or is plea bargaining largely a shell game in which defendants are manipulated to think they are getting a good deal?

KEY TERMS

Alford plea   366

allocute/allocution hearing   364

Boykin form   364

charge bargaining   354

count bargaining   354

nolo contendere/no contest   366

plea bargaining   353

plea on the nose   354

sentence bargaining   354

FOR FURTHER READING

Brown, Darryl K. 2016. *Free Market Criminal Justice: How Democracy and Laissez Faire Undermine the Rule of Law.* New York: Oxford University Press.

Brown, Mary, and Stevan E. Bunnell. 2006. "Negotiating Justice: Prosecutorial Perspectives on Federal Plea Bargaining in the District of Columbia." *American Criminal Law Review* 43: 1063–1094.

Bushway, Shawn, and Allison Redlich. 2012. "Is Plea Bargaining in the 'Shadow of the Trial' a Mirage?" *Journal of Quantitative Criminology* 28: 437–454.

Covey, Russell D. 2016. "Plea Bargaining and Price Theory." *The George Washington Law Review* 84: 920–971.

Fisher, George. 2003. *Plea Bargaining's Triumph: A History of Plea Bargaining in America.* Stanford, CA: Stanford University Press.

Pezdek, Kathy, and Matthew O'Brien. 2014. "Plea Bargaining and Appraisals of Eyewitness Evidence by Prosecutors and Defense Attorneys." *Psychology, Crime & Law* 20: 222–241.

Vogel, Mary. 2006. *Coercion to Compromise: Plea Bargaining, the Courts, and the Making of Political Authority.* New York: Oxford University Press.

wavebreakmedia/Shutterstock.com

Each year, a number of high-profile cases like those of Dylann Roof and George Zimmerman (both discussed in Chapter 1) make the news across the country. But consistent with the "wedding cake" model of criminal justice (Chapter 10), those celebrated cases at the top the wedding cake are few and far between. Notably, high-profile cases tend to go to trial more frequently than the routine cases that are resolved by plea bargain.

Chapter Outline

The national media provided detailed accounts of high-profile trials of Jodi Arias, convicted of stabbing her boyfriend nearly 30 times, shooting him in the head, and cutting his throat; Conrad Murray, convicted of manslaughter for providing Michael Jackson with a powerful anesthetic to help Jackson sleep; and of the high-profile cases of Dylann Roof, George Zimmerman, and Casey Anthony (all discussed in Chapter 1). Local media typically offer extensive coverage of the trials of local notables, brazen murderers, and the like. The media use courtroom encounters to entertain. The importance of trials, however, extends far beyond the considerable public attention lavished on them. They are central to the entire scheme of Anglo-American law. Trials provide the ultimate forum for vindicating the innocence of the accused or the liability of the defendant. For this reason, the right to be tried by a jury of one's peers is guaranteed in several places in the Constitution.

Given the marked public interest in trials, as well as their centrality to American law, we would expect trials to be the prime ingredient in the criminal court process. They are not. Trials are relatively rare events. As Chapter 12 established, upwards of 95 percent of all felony convictions result from guilty pleas. In a fundamental sense, then, a trial represents a deviant case. But at the same time, the few cases that are tried have a major impact on the operations of the entire criminal justice system. Trials are the balance wheel of the process, determining how members of the courtroom work group bargain cases.

Learning Objectives

After reading this chapter, you should be able to:

LO1   Trace the history of trials by jury.

LO2   Analyze the scope of the right to a trial by jury in a criminal case.

LO3   Evaluate the impact of differences in jury size and unanimity requirements.

LO4   Explain how a jury is summoned and selected, including the constitutional limitations on these processes.

LO5   Discuss the function of jury consultants in the process of scientific jury selection.

LO6   Distinguish between the presumptions that apply at the start of trials and the burdens of proof applicable to overcoming them.

LO7   Summarize the basic rules of evidence concerning trustworthiness and relevance of evidence.

LO8   Analyze how special limitations on expert witnesses affect the litigation of criminal cases, especially with regard to leading types of forensic evidence.

LO9   Identify the steps in a criminal trial.

LO10   Describe the effects and implications of pretrial publicity and the solutions that courts use to prevent those effects from influencing a criminal trial.

History of Trial by Jury

The primary purpose of the jury is to prevent oppression by the government and provide the accused a "safeguard against the corrupt or over-zealous prosecutor and against the compliant, biased, or eccentric judge" (*Duncan v. Louisiana*, 1968, p. 156). Ideally, juries are made up of fair-minded citizens who represent a cross section of the local community. Once selected, their role is to judge the facts of the case. During trial, the judge rules on questions of law, but the jury decides the weight of the evidence and the credibility to give to the testimony of witnesses.

Trial juries are also called **petit juries**, to differentiate them from grand juries. The jury system represents a commitment to the role of laypeople in the administration of justice. The views and actions of judges and lawyers are constrained by a group of average citizens who are amateurs in the ways of the law (Jonakait, 2006; Kalven & Zeisel, 1966).

English Roots

The trial by jury has roots deep in Western history. Used in Athens five or six centuries B.C.E., juries were later used by the Romans. They reappeared in France during the 9th century and were transferred to England from there. The concept of the jury functioning as an impartial fact-finding body was first formalized in the Magna Carta of 1215, when English noblemen forced the king to recognize limits on the power of the Crown:

> No Freeman shall be taken or imprisoned, or be disseized of his Freehold, or Liberties, or free Customs, or be outlawed, or exiled or otherwise destroyed, nor will we pass upon him nor condemn him but by lawful judgment of his peers or by Law of the Land.

This protection applied only to nobility ("Freeman"). Its extension to the average citizen occurred several centuries later. Thus, in the centuries after the Magna Carta, the legal status of the jury continued to evolve. Early English juries often functioned more like modern-day grand juries. Only later did they become impartial bodies, selected from citizens who knew nothing of the alleged event.

Colonial Developments

By the time the U.S. Constitution was written, jury trials in criminal cases had been in existence in England for several centuries. This legal principle was transferred to the American colonies and later written into the Constitution. The pivotal role that the right to trial by jury plays in American law is underscored by the number of times it is mentioned in the Constitution.

Article III, Section 2, provides that "the trial of all crimes, except cases of impeachment shall be by jury and such trial shall be held in the state where the said crimes shall have been committed." This section not only guarantees the right to a trial by jury to persons accused by the national government of a crime but also specifies that such trials shall be held near the place of the offense. This prevents the government from harassing defendants by trying them far from home.

The Sixth Amendment guarantees that "in all criminal prosecutions, the accused shall enjoy the right to a speedy and public trial, by an impartial jury." The requirement of a public trial prohibits secret trials, a device commonly used by dictators to silence their opponents.

The Seventh Amendment provides: "In suits at common law … the right to trial by jury shall be preserved." This provision is a historical testament to the fact that the framers of the Constitution greatly distrusted the judges of the day.

Law on the Books: The Constitution and Trial by Jury

Throughout most of our nation's history, the three broad constitutional provisions dealing with trial by jury had little applicability in state courts. The U.S. Constitution applied only to trials in federal courts. These practices changed dramatically, however, when the Supreme Court decided *Duncan v. Louisiana* (1968), ruling that the jury provisions of the Sixth Amendment were incorporated by the Due Process Clause of the Fourteenth

Amendment to apply to state courts, as well. Subsequent decisions grappled with the problem of defining the precise meaning of the right to trial by jury. The most important issues concerned the scope of the right to a jury trial, the size of the jury, and unanimous versus non-unanimous verdicts. The important case law defining the right to a trial by jury is presented in the "Key Developments" feature below.

Scope of the Right to Trial by Jury

Although juries are considered "fundamental to the American scheme of justice" (*Duncan v. Louisiana*, 1968), not all persons accused of violating the criminal law are entitled to a trial by jury. Youths prosecuted as juvenile offenders have no right to have their case heard by a jury (*McKeiver v. Pennsylvania*, 1971). Similarly, adult offenders charged with petty offenses

KEY DEVELOPMENTS CONCERNING THE RIGHT TO TRIAL BY JURY AFTER THE ADOPTION OF THE BILL OF RIGHTS	
Griffin v. California (1965)	The privilege against self-incrimination prohibits the prosecutor from commenting on the defendant's failure to testify during trial.
Sheppard v. Maxwell (1966)	A criminal defendant's Sixth Amendment right to a fair trial is violated when prejudicial pretrial publicity unfairly taints the trial process.
Duncan v. Louisiana (1968)	The due process clause of the Fourteenth Amendment incorporates the Sixth Amendment's right to a jury trial.
Baldwin v. New York (1970)	Defendants accused of **petty offenses** do not have the right to a trial by jury. In this context, "no offense can be deemed 'petty' for the purposes of the right to trial by jury where imprisonment for more than six months is authorized" (*Baldwin v. New York*, 1970, p. 69). Some state constitutions, however, guarantee a jury trial to anyone facing any criminal charge whatsoever, including traffic offenses.
Williams v. Florida (1970)	State juries are not required by the U.S. Constitution to consist of 12 members.
McKeiver v. Pennsylvania (1971)	Youths prosecuted as juvenile offenders have no right to have their cases heard by a jury.
Johnson v. Louisiana (1972)	Federal criminal juries must be unanimous.
Apodaca v. Oregon (1972)	The U.S. Constitution does not require state juries to reach unanimous verdicts.
Taylor v. Louisiana (1975)	Women cannot be excluded from juries.
Ballew v. Georgia (1978)	Six is the minimum number for a jury.
Burch v. Louisiana (1979)	Six-member criminal juries must be unanimous.
Duren v. Missouri (1979)	Although neither the venire nor the actual petit jury must be "a perfect mirror of the community or accurately reflected the proportionate strength of every identifiable group," the master jury lists from which a venire is summoned must reflect a representative and impartial cross section of the community.

(Continued)

(Continued)

Chandler v. Florida (1981)	The right to a fair trial is not violated by electronic media and still photographic coverage of public judicial proceedings.
Batson v. Kentucky (1986)	The Equal Protection Clause of the Fourteenth Amendment prohibits prosecutors from exercising peremptory challenges in a racially discriminatory manner.
Powers v. Ohio (1991)	A criminal defendant may object to race-based exclusions of jurors through peremptory challenges whether or not the defendant and the excluded jurors share the same race.
Georgia v. McCollum (1992)	As with prosecutors in *Batson,* the Equal Protection Clause of the Fourteenth Amendment also prohibits the defense from exercising peremptory challenges in a racially discriminatory manner.
Daubert v. Merrell Dow Pharmaceuticals (1993)	The trial judge must ensure that any and all scientific evidence is not only relevant, but also reliable.
J.E.B. Petitioner v. Alabama (1994)	Lawyers may not exclude potential jurors from a trial because of their sex.
Victor v. Nebraska (1994)	"A reasonable doubt is an actual and substantial doubt arising from the evidence, from the facts or circumstances shown by the evidence, or from the lack of evidence on the part of the state, as distinguished from a doubt arising from mere possibility, from bare imagination, or from fanciful conjecture."
Kumho Tire v. Carmichael (1999)	*Daubert* standards for scientific testimony apply to nonscientific expert testimony as well.
United States v. Martinez-Salazar (2000)	The Court made clear that *Batson* is not limited to race, but rather also applies to ethnic origin.
Portuondo v. Agard (2000)	Prosecutors can tell jurors that the defendant's presence during trial helps them tailor their testimony to fit the evidence.
Snyder v. Louisiana (2008)	Murder conviction in a death penalty case was overturned because the judge sat idly by as prosecutors dismissed all the Blacks in the jury pool.
Warger v. Shauers (2014)	Federal Rule of Evidence 606(b), which provides that certain juror testimony about events in the jury room is not admissible "during an inquiry into the validity of a verdict," precludes a party seeking a new trial from using one juror's affidavit of what another juror said during jury deliberations to demonstrate another juror's dishonesty during the jury selection process.
Foster v. Chatman (2016)	Evidence that a prosecutor's reasons for striking a Black prospective juror apply equally to an otherwise similar non-Black prospective juror who is allowed to serve tends to suggest purposeful discrimination.

enjoy no right to be tried by a jury of their peers (Whitten, 2014). The Sixth Amendment covers only adults charged with serious offenses. In this context, "no offense can be deemed 'petty' for the purposes of the right to trial by jury where imprisonment for more than six months is authorized" (*Baldwin v. New York*, 1970). Some state constitutions, however, guarantee a jury trial to anyone facing any criminal charge whatsoever, including traffic offenses.

When there is no right to a jury trial (for example, in most traffic and petty offense cases), a **bench trial** takes place in which a judge serves as both the trier-of-law (as always) and trier-of-fact determining guilt. But bench trials are not limited to cases in which no right to a trial by jury exists. Sometimes, the parties waive the right to a trial by jury and opt for a bench trial instead. For example, a judge might appreciate subtle legal distinctions in a complicated case that a jury may neglect. Other times, either pretrial publicity or the facts of a case might motivate the parties to seek a bench trial. This is especially true in criminal cases in which the defendant has a long criminal history or is accused of a particularly heinous crime since "it may be difficult to empanel a fair and impartial jury" (Peterson, 2011, p. 458). State laws vary considerably on when the prosecution and/or defense may waive a trial by jury in criminal cases.

Jury Size

During the 14th century, the size of English juries became fixed at 12. Although some colonies experimented with smaller juries in less-important trials, the number 12 was universally accepted by the time of the American Revolution. However, in *Williams v. Florida* (1970, p. 102), the Supreme Court declared that the number 12 was a "historical accident, unnecessary to effect the purposes of the jury system and wholly without significance except to mystics" and therefore not required by the U.S. Constitution. The Court concluded that the 6-person jury used in Florida in noncapital cases was large enough to promote group deliberations and to provide a fair possibility of obtaining a representative cross section of the community. Attempts to use juries with fewer than 6 members were struck down by *Ballew v. Georgia* (1978). The defendant's misdemeanor conviction by a 5-member jury was reversed because "the purpose and functioning of the jury in a criminal trial is seriously impaired, and to a constitutional degree, by a reduction in size to below six members."

As Table 13.1 illustrates, many states have specifically authorized juries of fewer than 12 jurors, but most allow these smaller juries only in misdemeanor cases. In federal courts, defendants are entitled to a 12-person jury unless the parties agree in writing to a smaller jury, but 6-member juries in federal civil cases are quite common.

There has been a good deal of debate over whether small juries provide the defendant with a fair trial (Landsman, 2005; Luppi & Parisi, 2013; McCord, 2005; Saks, 1996). The debate stems from the fact that social science has produced inconsistent findings on the differences in the conduct of deliberations between 6- and 12-person juries. Some studies

LAW ON THE BOOKS VS. LAW IN ACTION

Going to Trial

	Law on the Books	Law in Action
Trial	The adversarial process of deciding a case through the presentation of evidence and arguments about the evidence.	Only a handful of felonies and even fewer misdemeanors are decided by trial.
Bench trial	Trial before a judge without a jury.	Defense prefers when the issues are either highly technical or very emotional.
Jury trial	A group of average citizens selected by law and sworn in to look at certain facts and determine the truth.	Introduces public standards of justice into the decision-making process.

TABLE 13.1	State Provisions of the Size of Criminal Juries
12-member juries required in felony cases	Alabama, Arkansas, California, Colorado, Delaware, District of Columbia,[a] Georgia, Hawaii, Idaho, Illinois, Iowa, Kansas, Kentucky, Maine, Maryland, Massachusetts, Michigan, Minnesota, Mississippi, Missouri, Montana, Nebraska, Nevada, New Hampshire, New Jersey,[a] New Mexico, New York, North Carolina, North Dakota, Ohio, Oklahoma, Oregon,[h] Pennsylvania,[a] Puerto Rico,[i] Rhode Island, South Carolina, South Dakota, Tennessee, Texas, Vermont, Virginia, Washington, West Virginia, Wisconsin, Wyoming
12-member juries required in misdemeanor cases	Alabama, Arkansas, California, Delaware,[a] District of Columbia,[a] Hawaii,[a] Illinois, Maine, Maryland, New Hampshire, New Jersey,[a] North Carolina, Pennsylvania, Rhode Island, South Dakota, Tennessee, Vermont, West Virginia, Wisconsin
Juries of fewer than 12 authorized for select felony cases	Arizona,[b] Connecticut,[c] Florida,[d] Indiana,[e] Louisiana,[f] Utah[g]
Juries fewer than 12 authorized for select misdemeanor cases	Alaska, Arizona,[b] Colorado, Connecticut, Florida, Georgia, Idaho, Indiana, Iowa, Kansas, Kentucky, Louisiana, Massachusetts, Michigan, Minnesota, Mississippi, Montana, Nebraska, Nevada, New Mexico, New York, North Dakota, Ohio, Oklahoma, Oregon, South Carolina, Texas, Utah, Virginia, Washington, Wyoming

Note: All verdicts must be unanimous unless specified to the contrary in these notes:

[a]The parties may stipulate to a jury that consists of fewer than 12 jurors.

[b]12-person juries required if a sentence of death or more than 30-year imprisonment is sought; otherwise, all felonies use 8-person juries. The parties may stipulate to less than 8-person jurors in misdemeanor cases. And the parties, with the consent of the court, may consent to non-unanimous verdicts in either felony or misdemeanor cases.

[c]12-person juries are used in death penalty cases unless the defendant elects to use a smaller jury.

[d]12-person juries must be used in death-penalty cases, but verdicts need not be unanimous; a 7 to 5 vote is sufficient for a death sentence. All other felonies use 6-person juries and unanimous verdicts.

[e]12-person juries are required for serious felonies or when an enhanced penalty is sought; 6-person juries are used for less series felonies.

[f]12-person juries must be used in death penalty cases and cases in which confinement at hard labor is a necessary penalty; 6-person juries are permitted when confinement at hard labor is possible, but not necessary.

[g]12-person juries must be used in capital cases; 8-member juries are used for all other felonies.

[h]Conviction permissible by 11 of 12 jurors voting for a guilty verdict.

[i]Conviction permissible by 9 of 12 jurors voting for a guilty verdict.

Source: Adapted from S. Strickland, R. Schauffler, R. LaFountain, & K. Holt, eds., 2015. *State Court Organization*. Williamsburg, VA: National Center for State Courts. Available online www.ncsc.org/sco.

have found very few differences (Pabst, 1973; Roper, 1979), while others have reported significant differences (Hastie, Penrod, & Pennington, 1983; Saks & Marti, 1997). In a review of the empirical literature on juries, Smith and Saks (2008) reported that:

- racial, ethnic, religious, and sexual minorities are represented in a smaller percentage of 6-person as compared to 12-person juries;

- larger juries deliberate longer than smaller juries;

- talking time is more evenly divided among members of smaller juries, allowing for less domination by a strong voice or two as compared with larger juries;

- members of larger juries more accurately recall evidence both during deliberation and in individual recall afterward;

- 12-person juries recall more probative information and rely on evaluative statements and nonprobative evidence less than 6-person juries;

- in the civil context, 6-person juries show more variability in their awards and, on average, give larger awards than 12-person juries; and

- jurors report more satisfaction in the deliberation process with 12-person juries than with smaller ones.

In light of these findings, it is not surprising to learn that hung juries—juries unable to reach a unanimous verdict—occur more frequently with 12-person juries than with 6-person juries (Hannaford-Agor, Hans, Mott, & Munsterman, 2002; Kalven & Zeisel, 1966). Nonetheless, increased use of smaller juries has not reduced the overall rate of hung juries. In fact, the overall rate of mistrials declared because a jury was unable to reach a verdict has not significantly changed even though smaller juries have become the norm in misdemeanor cases and certain types of civil trials (Luppi & Parisi, 2013). This may be a function of the fact that many factors other than jury size affect whether a jury hangs: "weak evidence; police credibility problems...; juror concerns about fairness; case complexity; and a dysfunctional deliberation process—a catchall phrase indicating poor interpersonal interactions among the jurors" (Hannaford-Agor et al., 2002, p. 85). Yet, the quest to reduce hung juries has resulted in some jurisdictions authorizing a controversial change in the way juries have historically functioned: non-unanimous verdicts.

Unanimity

The requirement that a jury reach a unanimous decision became a firm rule in England during the 14th century. An agreement by all of the jurors seemed to legitimize the verdict, giving the community a sense that the conclusion must be correct. However, the Supreme Court altered this assumption in a pair of 1972 decisions. It held that verdicts in federal criminal trials must be unanimous, but it affirmed state courts' findings of guilty by votes of 9 to 3 and 10 to 2 (*Johnson v. Louisiana*, 1972; *Apodaca v. Oregon*, 1972). Most state constitutions specifically require unanimous verdicts in criminal trials; only five states (Louisiana, Montana, Oregon, Oklahoma, and Texas) permit non-unanimous criminal verdicts. Of these, only Louisiana and Oregon permit non-unanimous verdicts in serious felony cases. In any case, six-member juries must be unanimous (*Burch v. Louisiana*, 1979).

Opponents of non-unanimous verdicts argue that the Supreme Court misread the history of the jury, with the result that a basic constitutional right is being sacrificed. They point out that proof beyond a reasonable doubt has not been shown if only some of the jurors vote to convict. These concerns receive some empirical support (Zeisel, 1982). A carefully controlled experiment compared unanimous with non-unanimous juries and found that non-unanimous juries tend to be hung less often, deliberate less thoroughly, and result in less-satisfied jurors (Hastie, Penrod, & Pennington, 1984; see also Smith & Saks, 2008). These findings may be explained by the fact that the deliberation process appears to differ significantly depending on whether a unanimous or majority verdict is permitted.

When juries were not required to be unanimous, they tended to be more verdict driven. That is, they were more likely to take the first formal ballot during the first 10 minutes of deliberation and to vote often until they produced a verdict. In contrast, juries that heard the same case but were required to reach a unanimous verdict tended to delay their first vote and discuss the evidence more thoroughly. These evidence-driven juries rated their deliberations as more serious and thorough (Diamond, Rose, & Murphy, 2006).

Law on the Books: Selecting a Fair and Unbiased Jury

Before the first word of testimony, trials pass through the critical stage of jury selection. Many lawyers believe that trials are won or lost on the basis of which jurors are selected. Juries are chosen in a process that combines random selection with deliberate choice.

Jury selection occurs in three stages: compiling a master list, summoning the *venire*, and conducting *voir dire*. The "Law on the Books vs. Law in Action" feature on page 383 compares perspectives on these jury selection steps. Whether these processes actually produce fair and impartial juries has been the subject of much concern.

Master Jury List

Juries are supposed to be made up of fair-minded laypeople, representatives of the community in which the defendant allegedly committed the crime. Therefore, the first step in jury selection is the development of procedures that will produce a representative cross section of the community. These sentiments are reflected in the Federal Jury Selection and Service Act of 1968, which was designed to ensure that "no citizen shall be excluded from service as a grand or petit juror in the district courts of the United States on account of race, color, religion, sex, national origin, or economic status." This act was prompted by evidence that selection of federal juries was systematically biased. Similar concerns have been expressed about jury selection at the state level (DeVoré, 2015; Fukurai, Butler, & Krooth, 1991; Re, 2007).

The first step in jury selection is the compilation of a **master jury list**. Voter registration lists are the most frequently used source for assembling this list (sometimes called a *jury wheel* or *master wheel*). Voter lists have major advantages: They are readily available, frequently updated, and collected in districts within judicial boundaries. However, basing the master jury list on voter registration tends to exclude the poor, the young, racial minorities, and the less educated (Adamakos, 2016; Kairys, Kadane, & Lehorsky, 1977; Re, 2007). Because of these limitations, many jurisdictions use other sources—telephone directories, utility customer lists, or driver's license lists—in drawing up the master list. The use of multiple sources achieves a better cross section of the community on jury panels, although it sometimes creates problems for jury administrators, who have to deal with a high number of duplicates when multiple sources are merged (Randall & Woods, 2008).

Jury panels can be challenged if master jury lists from which the venire was called fail to include racial or other minorities. The Supreme Court has ruled that master jury lists must reflect a representative and impartial cross section of the community (*Duren v. Missouri*, 1979). This does not mean, however, that either the venire or the actual petit jury must be "a perfect mirror of the community or accurately [reflect] the proportionate strength of every identifiable group" (*Swain v. Alabama* 1965, p. 208). Rather, the requirement of a representative cross section of the

---

LAW ON THE BOOKS VS. LAW IN ACTION

Jury Selection

	Law on the Books	Law in Action
Jury selection	Process of selecting a fair and impartial jury.	Each side seeks to select jurors who are biased in its favor.
Master jury list	Potential jurors are selected by chance from a list of potential jurors. The list should reflect a representative cross section of the community.	Selecting only from registered voters means that the poor, the young, and minorities are less likely to be called.
Venire	A group of citizens from which jury members are chosen (jury pool).	Judges vary in their willingness to excuse potential jurors because of hardship.
Voir dire	The process by which prospective jurors are questioned to determine whether there is cause to excuse them from the jury.	Lawyers use questioning to predispose jurors in their favor.
Peremptory challenge	Each side may exclude a set number of jurors without stating a reason.	Both sides use peremptory challenges to select a jury favorable to their side.
Challenge for cause	A judge may dismiss a potential juror if the person cannot be fair and objective.	Rarely granted.

community applies only to jury pools (*Holland v. Illinois*, 1990).

Summoning the Venire

The second step in jury selection is the drawing of the **venire** (or jury pool). Periodically, the clerk of court or jury commissioner determines how many jurors are needed for a given time. A sufficient number of names are then randomly selected from the master jury list and a **summons** is issued—a court order commanding these citizens to appear at the courthouse for jury duty. Even though people who fail to obey a jury summons can be fined or imprisoned, estimates place the nonresponse rate to jury summonses between 9 percent in some jurisdictions to as high as 66 percent in others (Bloeser, McCurley, & Mondak, 2012; Randall & Woods, 2008; Schwartz, Behrens, & Silverman, 2003). Failing to respond to a jury summons, however, is most unwise, since it can result in a warrant being issued for the scofflaw's arrest; punishments range from fines to jail sentences for contempt of court.

Venire Eligibility

Not all those summoned will actually serve on the venire. Virtually all states have laws that require jurors to be citizens of the United States, residents of the locality, of a certain minimum age, and able to understand English. Most states also disqualify people who, as a result of mental illness, are not competent to adjudicate a case. Thirty-one states also disqualify convicted felons, although that practice has been increasingly criticized as a type of disenfranchisement that disproportionately affects racial and ethnic minorities (Binnall, 2008; Campagna, Foster, Karas, Stohr, & Hemmens, 2016; Kalt, 2003; Wheelock, 2005). Persons who fail to meet these requirements are eliminated from the venire.

Others will be excused because of **statutory exemptions**. The identities of those exempted from jury duty by statute vary greatly. Historically, those statutorily excluded included government officials (especially police, firefighters, and political office-holders); medical personnel (including paramedics, physicians, nurses, and others); ministers/clergy; educators; lawyers; and full-time students. Today, however, jurisdictions have been increasingly eliminating **statutory exemptions**.

As Table 13.2 illustrates, all but three states statutorily exempt citizens with previous jury service within a prescribed period of time—usually within the past 12 to 24 months—of being summoned again. And more than half the states allow senior citizens over the ages of 65, 70, or 75 to exempt themselves from jury service. Most other statutory exemptions, however, have been eliminated in more than two-thirds of the states.

The people who show up when summoned to court and are eligible to serve on a jury usually check in with a jury administrator (or other clerk of the court staff person) who then directs them to a specific courtroom. The petit jury for a particular trial will be selected from this pool of people. The people in this jury pool, however, may be excused from serving on a jury if they convince the judge that jury duty would entail an undue hardship. People try to get excused quite frequently. As van Dyke observed in 1977, although serving on a jury is "a right and privilege of citizenship, most people consider it a nuisance" and request to be excused (p. 111). The sentiment persists today (DeVoré, 2015; Losh & Boatright, 2002; Sinclair, Behrens, & Silverman, 2003).

Voir Dire

The final step in jury selection is the **voir dire** (French legal term for "to speak the truth"), which involves the preliminary examination of a prospective juror in order to determine his or her qualifications to serve as a juror. In addition to prospective jurors' names (88.3%) and addresses (sometimes only ZIP codes), most courts "obtain preliminary voir dire information from prospective jurors, such as marital status (64%), occupation (72%), [and the] number and ages of minor children (52%)…" (Mize et al., 2007, p. 26).

The prospective jurors are questioned by the attorneys, the judge, or both about their backgrounds, familiarity with persons involved in the case

TABLE 13.2	Categories and Frequency of Statutory Exemptions from Jury Service

Exemption	Number of States
Previous jury service	47
Age (ranging from minimum of 65 to 75)	27
Political officeholder	16
Law enforcement and emergency services personnel	12
Other (most frequently clergy and teachers)	12
Judicial officers	9
Health care professionals	7
Sole caregivers of young children or incompetent adults	7
Licensed attorneys	6
Active military	5

"The median number of statutory exemption categories was three per state. Louisiana is the only state that has no exemptions whatsoever. Twelve states and the District of Columbia provide exemptions only for previous jury service. Florida provides exemptions in nine of the ten categories, the most of any state." (p. 15)

Source: Gregory E. Mize, Paula Hannaford-Agor, & Nicole L. Waters. *The State-of-the-States Survey of Jury Improvement Efforts: A Compendium Report* (Table 10). Williamsburg, VA: National Center for State Courts, 2007. Reprinted by permission.

(defendant, witness, or lawyer), attitudes about certain facts that may arise during trial, and any other matters that may reflect on their willingness and ability to judge the case fairly and impartially. In most cases, questions are posed to the venire as a group, usually with instructions to answer by raising their hands. There are then follow-up questions to individual members of the venire. Prospective jurors are often permitted to respond to sensitive voir dire questions either by written questionnaire or "in the relative privacy of a sidebar conference or in the judge's chambers" (Mize et al., 2007, p. 29).

In high-profile cases, extensive jury questionnaires may be used in an effort to screen out potential biases held by the venire—especially if jury consultants are used (see the following sections). For example, in the trial of Dr. Conrad Murray for the involuntary manslaughter of Michael Jackson, 145 venirepersons completed a 32-page questionnaire about their backgrounds, job history, and, perhaps most critically, their views of Jackson and their exposure to the media coverage of his 2009 overdose.

The Accuracy of Voir Dire

For hundreds of years, the law has considered voir dire to be an inexpensive and efficient way to select a fair and impartial jury. The process, however, may not be a particularly accurate way to detect bias (Otis, Greathouse, Kennard, & Kovera, 2014). Although the venire is sworn under oath to answer truthfully, they do not always do so. Sometimes potential jurors refuse to admit to facts or thoughts they find embarrassing to share, such as prior criminal victimization (Ferguson, 2015; Hannaford, 2001). Other reasons may be less personal but still may not be something that potential jurors want to admit in court under oath, such as a predisposition to believe the accused is guilty. Even when venirepersons are not deliberately concealing information, they may unconsciously conceal personal biases or prejudices during voir dire in an attempt to please the court and the attorneys by being "good" jurors (Borgida & Fiske, 2008; Hamilton & Zephyrhawke, 2015).

Excusing Jurors for Cause

If a potential juror's responses during questioning (whether honest or not) suggest that the person cannot fairly judge the case, the juror may be challenged for cause by either the defense or the prosecution. Both sides have an unlimited number of **challenges for cause**. The presiding judge rules on the challenge and, if it is sustained, the juror is excused. Strikes for cause generally fall into one of two categories: principal challenges and fact-partial challenges.

- *Principal challenges* involve strikes of potential jurors because they have some relationship to one of the "principals" or participants in the case. They are presumed to be partial on account of this relationship.

- *Fact-partial challenges* involve strikes of potential jurors because the subject matter of the dispute presents issues on which the potential juror is biased, prejudiced, or predisposed to a particular outcome because of their belief system or experiences.

Excusing Jurors Without Good Cause

Peremptory challenges are the second method used by the prosecution and the defense in influencing who will sit on the jury. Each side has a limited number of peremptory challenges that can be used to exclude a juror. Originally, these challenges were designed and used for a curative purpose—to correct the mistake of a judge for failing to strike a juror for cause. While they are still used in that manner today, they are primarily used to exclude people that the lawyers believe will be

hostile to their side of the case. In other words, based on hunches, prejudice, knowledge of psychology, or pseudoscience, attorneys use peremptory strikes—without having to give a reason—to eliminate the jurors they feel might not vote for their side.

Attorneys traditionally enjoyed unrestricted freedom to exercise peremptory challenges. But in *Batson v. Kentucky* (1986), the Supreme Court restricted the ability of prosecutors who used peremptory challenges to keep African-Americans off the jury in any case involving an African-American defendant (Weddell, 2013). If a prosecutor uses peremptory challenges to exclude potential jurors solely on account of their race, the prosecutor must explain his or her actions and may be ordered to change tactics. And in a move backed by prosecutors, the Court held that the defense is also prohibited from excluding jurors based on race (*Georgia v. McCollum*, 1992). Most recently, the Supreme Court has ordered new trials for several death row inmates because of racial bias during jury selection (*Foster v. Chatman*, 2016; *Miller-El v. Dretke*, 2005; *Johnson v. California*, 2005; *Snyder v. Louisiana*, 2008).

The Court extended *Batson* to cover gender jury bias, holding that lawyers may not exclude potential jurors from a trial because of their sex (*J.E.B. Petitioner v. Alabama*, 1994). The principle of nondiscrimination at the core of *Batson* and *J.E.B.* was seemingly extended to "ethnic origin" in *United States v. Martinez-Salazar* (2000, p. 315) but has not yet been extended by the U.S. Supreme Court to other categories, such as religion or sexual orientation. But some lower federal courts have done so on their own (see the following "Case Close-Up"). For example, the U.S. Court of Appeals of the Second Circuit upheld the application of *Batson* to strikes against Italian-Americans (*United States v. Biaggi*, 1988). And the U.S. Court of Appeals of the Ninth Circuit upheld the application of *Batson* to strikes against prospective jurors perceived to be gay or lesbian (*Smithkline Beecham Corp. v. Abbott Laboratories*, 2014). But as the "Case Close-Up" on *People v. Garcia* (2000) illustrates, peremptory challenges on the basis of sexual orientation have been largely to California and the federal courts within the Ninth Circuit.

Cano Garcia was charged with burglary. During his trial, it somehow became known that two members of the jury venire were lesbians. In fact, they both worked for the same gay and lesbian foundation. After the prosecution excused both women, defense counsel objected, making a *Batson*-type argument. The trial judge denied the motion, explaining, "Well, I am going to rule that sexual preference is not a cognizable group.... I don't think that your sexual preference specifically relates to them sharing a common perspective or common social or psychological outlook on human events. Lesbians or gay men vary in their social and psychological outlook on human events and I don't think they fit into this protection. So I'm going to deny your motion."

The appeals court began its analysis by stating the rule of law in California established in the wake of *Batson:* "The right under the California Constitution to a jury drawn from a 'representative cross-section of the community' is violated whenever a 'cognizable group' within that community is systematically excluded from the jury venire" (p. 1275). In concluding that lesbians and gays were such a "cognizable group," the court reasoned:

> It cannot seriously be argued ... that homosexuals do not have a common perspective—"a common social or psychological outlook on human events"—based upon their membership in that community. They share a history of persecution comparable to that of blacks and women. While there is room to argue about degree, based upon their number and the relative indiscernibility of their membership in the group, it is just that: an argument about degree. It is a matter of quantity not quality.

This is not to say that all homosexuals see the world alike. The Attorney General here derides the cognizability of this class with the rhetorical question, "[W]hat 'common perspective' is, or was, shared by Rep. Jim Kolbe (R-Ariz.), RuPaul, poet William Alexander Percy Truman Capote, and Ellen DeGeneres?" He confuses "common perspective" with "common personality." Granted, the five persons he mentions are people of diverse backgrounds and life experiences. But they certainly share the common perspective

of having spent their lives in a sexual minority either exposed to or fearful of persecution and discrimination. That perspective deserves representation in the jury venire, and people who share that perspective deserve to bear their share of the burdens and benefits of citizenship, including jury service.

The Attorney General also insists "there is no evidence that gays or lesbians have a common social or psychological outlook on human events." But this misperceives the nature of the term "common perspective." Commonality of perspective does not result in identity of opinion. That is the whole reason exclusion based upon group bias is anathema. It stereotypes. It assumes all people with the same life experience will, given a set of facts, reach the same result. Common perspective does no such thing. It affects how life experiences are seen, not how they are evaluated. And inclusion of a cognizable group in the jury venire does not assure any particular position; it assures only that the facts will be viewed from a variety of angles. It assures that as many different life views as possible will be represented in the important decisions of the judicial process. Put more elegantly the goal of the cross-section rule is to enhance the likelihood that the jury will be representative of significant community attitudes, not of groups per se.

But we cannot think of anyone who shares the perspective of the homosexual community. Outside of racial and religious minorities, we can think of no group which has suffered such "pernicious and sustained hostility and such immediate and severe opprobrium" as homosexuals.

Critique the court's reasoning in *Garcia.* Do you think the same logic should be extended to support a ban on religious discrimination during voir dire? Why or why not? What about the use of peremptory challenges to systematically excuse people on the basis of age (too young or to old) or weight (too thin or too obese)? Explain your reasoning.

As previously mentioned, in *Smithkline Beecham Corp. v. Abbott Laboratories* (2014), the Ninth Circuit held that sexual orientation is no basis for jury exclusion, citing the U.S. Supreme Court decision striking down the federal Defense of Marriage Act. Do you think this decision indicates a major shift in how courts will decide this issue in the future?

Serving on a Jury

Every year, thousands of Americans are called to serve as jurors. In addition to impaneling the requisite number of jurors (e.g., 6, 9, or 12), it is a common practice in many courts to select several **alternate jurors**, who will serve if one of the regular jurors must withdraw during the trial. Unfortunately, though, many jurors experience great frustration in the process. They are made to wait hours in barren courthouse rooms; the compensation is minimal, and not all employers pay for the time lost from work; and some potential jurors are apprehensive about criminals and courthouses. For these and other reasons, some people try to evade jury duty (Bloeser, McCurley, & Mondak, 2012; Devoré, 2015; Sams, Neal, & Brodsky, 2013).

In spite of these hardships, most citizens who actually serve on a jury express overall satisfaction with their jury service, viewing their experience as a precious opportunity of citizenship that generally bolstered their confidence in fellow citizens and public institutions (Gastil, Black, Deess, & Leighter, 2008; Pabst, 1973). Just as important, there is every indication that jurors take their job seriously.

Considerable attention is being devoted to reducing the inconvenience of jury duty. Courts in most states use a juror call-in system. In these jurisdictions, jurors can dial a number to learn whether their attendance is needed on a particular day during their term of service. In addition, an increasing number of courts are reducing the number of days a person remains in the jury pool. Traditionally, jurors were asked to serve for a full 30 days. Although only a few jurors were needed for a particular day, the entire pool had to be present in the courthouse each and every working day. Increasingly, however, jurors are asked to serve for only a few days. An approach known as the one-day/one-trial jury system requires each juror to serve either for one day or for the duration of one trial. The person is then exempt from jury duty for a year or two. The one-day/one-trial jury system is much more efficient than older practices not only because it spares many citizens the inconvenience of waiting in courthouses with no trials to hear, but also because it reduces constraints on judicial resources

(Litras & Golmant, 2006; Sinclair, Behrens, & Silverman, 2003).

As a result of some of these reforms, "more than one-third of all Americans (37.6%) are now likely to be impaneled as trial jurors sometime during their lifetime…. [Thus], American citizens have firsthand experience with jury service, due to more inclusive master jury lists, shorter terms of service, and other policies designed to make jury service more convenient and accessible for all citizens" (Mize et al., 2007, p. 8).

Law in Action: Choosing a Jury Biased in Your Favor

The National Advisory Commission (1973) has succinctly summarized the official—that is to say, the law on the books—purpose of jury selection as follows: "A defendant is entitled to an unbiased jury; he is not entitled to a jury biased in his favor" (p. 99). Members of the courtroom work group are reluctant to formally question this pious wisdom, but informally their actions are strikingly different. Particularly through selective use of peremptory challenges, lawyers for both prosecution and defense seek jurors predisposed to their side. This is the major reason why in some areas the voir dire has become a time-consuming process. Through educating jurors, trial lawyers seek decision makers who are comfortable with their approach. Through hiring jury consultants, trial lawyers aggressively seek to identify jurors who will be biased in their favor.

Educating Jurors

Attorneys use voir dire for purposes other than eliminating bias. They use the questioning of jurors to establish credibility and rapport with the panel, to educate and sell prospective jurors on their respective theories of the case, and to either highlight or neutralize potential problem areas in the case (Johnson, 2015; Voss, 2005). This, in turn, gives lawyers the opportunity to influence jurors' attitudes and perhaps later their vote.

Scientific Jury Selection: Profiling Juries Using Consultants

In recent years, jury selection has taken a scientific turn. Rather than relying on personal hunch, attorneys in a few highly publicized cases have employed social scientists to aid them in a more intelligent, systematic use of the voir dire that has come to be called "scientific jury selection" or "jury profiling."

As described in great detail by Lieberman and Sales (2006), **scientific jury selection** typically involves a small group of experts from a variety of disciplinary backgrounds, including marketing, communications, sociology, and, most especially, psychology. Teams of such **jury consultants** conduct public opinion polls and employ laypeople to participate in focus groups or mock trials. With polls and focus groups, they test which pieces of evidence, witnesses, and arguments might be most effective in convincing people to vote a particular way. With mock trials, they test their whole case and then debrief the mock jurors on why they voted as they did. These processes allow jury consultants to identify the issues in a case that are most relevant to the case outcome, as well as to formulate profiles of the juror characteristics that are likely to affect the trial outcome. In the digital era, lawyers and jury consultants may do online research of prospective jurors examining the Internet and social media sites like Facebook, Twitter, and Instagram (Browning, 2016; Hoskins, 2012). Using the information they gather, the jury consultants then design questionnaires to be administered to the potential jurors in an actual case. Once these questionnaires are compiled, the jury consultants are able to advise the lawyers in a case about which potential jurors they should want on the jury and those whom they should seek to avoid.

Trial consultants are hired most often by defense attorneys, as opposed to the prosecutors. In reality, the consultants try to deselect jurors who are likely to be adverse to their client. Whether this process actually functions any better than attorneys doing traditional jury selection using "pop psychology" and their gut instincts is still being debated both in the empirical literature and by practitioners. Two things, however, seem clear. First, jury consultants can help attorneys develop trial presentations that are clear and convincing. Second, jury consultants appear to be here to stay.

Presumptions and the Burden of Proof

Once the jury has been selected and sworn, most courts provide the jurors with some basic instructions concerning juror conduct, such as not to discuss the case until after the trial is concluded and not to form an opinion until all the evidence has been heard. Judges also typically provide an overview of both the relevant presumptions and governing burden of proof.

Starting Presumptions

The trier-of-fact must have an evidentiary starting place at the outset of a trial. In a criminal trial, that starting place usually involves two presumptions. A *presumption* is a conclusion or deduction that the law requires the trier-of-fact to make in the absence of evidence to the contrary. Criminal trials start with two presumptions: the presumption of sanity and the presumption of innocence.

The **presumption of sanity** requires that all defendants be presumed sane unless sufficient evidence of their insanity is proven. Insanity defense trials, however, are quite rare; in fact, they occur in less than one-half of 1 percent of all felony cases. But, when defendants challenge the presumption of sanity in insanity cases, considerable controversy usually follows.

The **presumption of innocence** requires the trier-of-fact to accept that the defendant is innocent unless the prosecution meets its burden to prove that the defendant is guilty beyond a reasonable doubt. This means that the state must prove all elements of the alleged crime(s); the defendant is not required to prove him- or herself innocent. This difference is a fundamental one. A moment's reflection will give an idea of how hard it would be to prove that something did not happen or that a person did not commit an alleged criminal act, for it is very difficult to rule out all possibilities. Therefore, a defendant is cloaked with the legal shield of innocence throughout all pretrial and trial processes.

Burdens of Proof

The concept of **burden of proof** actually encompasses two separate burdens, the burden of production and the burden of persuasion. If a party has the **burden of production** (often referred to as the "burden of going forward"), they must produce some evidence to put facts in issue. The **burden of persuasion** is the obligation of a party to prove a fact (or facts) to a certain level, either beyond a reasonable doubt, by clear and convincing evidence, or by a preponderance of the evidence.

In meeting its burden of persuasion in a criminal case, the prosecution is required to prove the defendant guilty beyond a reasonable doubt. **Reasonable doubt** is a legal yardstick measuring the sufficiency of the evidence. This burden of proof does not require that the state establish absolute certainty by eliminating all doubt—just reasonable doubt. *Reasonable doubt* is an amorphous term that judges have difficulty fully defining. In her concurring opinion in *Victor v. Nebraska* (1994, p. 24), Justice Ginsburg endorsed the following definition of reasonable doubt as being "clear, straightforward, and accurate":

> [T]he government has the burden of proving the defendant guilty beyond a reasonable doubt. Some of you may have served as jurors in civil cases, where you were told that it is only necessary to prove that a fact is more likely true than not true. In criminal cases, the government's proof must be more powerful than that. It must be beyond a reasonable doubt.

> Proof beyond a reasonable doubt is proof that leaves you firmly convinced of the defendant's guilt. There are very few things in this world that we know with absolute certainty, and in criminal cases the law does not require proof that overcomes every possible doubt. If, based on your consideration of the evidence, you are firmly convinced that the defendant is guilty of the crime charged, you must find him guilty. If on the other hand, you think there is a real possibility that he is not guilty, you must give him the benefit of the doubt and find him not guilty.

To meet its burden of persuasion, the prosecutor introduces evidence tending to show, either directly or indirectly, the defendant's guilt. The defense may—but is not required to—introduce evidence tending to cast doubt on the defendant's guilt. When doing so, both parties must abide by the rules of evidence.

Overview of Basic Evidence

Evidence consists of physical objects, testimony, or other things offered to prove or disprove the existence of a fact. There are several types of evidence that may be direct or circumstantial evidence, depending on how the evidence is used at trial.

Differentiating Direct and Circumstantial Evidence

Direct evidence is first-hand evidence that does not require any inferences to be drawn in order to establish a proposition of fact. The best example of direct evidence is eyewitness testimony. One need not draw any inference from a witness's testimony that she saw something. Note, however, that direct evidence does not necessarily establish truth. Witnesses can be mistaken or misleading.

Circumstantial evidence is indirect evidence. To reach a conclusion, the trier-of-fact would have to reason through the circumstantial evidence and infer the existence of some fact in dispute, such as inferring that the defendant killed the victim because the defendant's fingerprints were found on the murder weapon.

Types of Evidence

Evidence can be classified as testimonial evidence, real or physical evidence, scientific evidence, or demonstrative evidence. **Testimonial evidence** is oral testimony given under oath. **Real evidence** (also referred to as "physical evidence") consists of tangible objects such as documents, drug paraphernalia, clothing, and weapons. The scientific examination of real evidence, in a laboratory, for example, yields **scientific evidence**—the formal results of forensic investigatory and scientific techniques. **Demonstrative evidence** has no evidential value by itself. Rather, it serves as a visual or auditory aid to assist the fact-finder in understanding the evidence. Charts, maps, videos, and courtroom demonstrations are forms of demonstrative evidence.

Basic Rules of Evidence

The presentation of evidence during trial is governed by principles called **rules of evidence**. A trial is an adversarial proceeding in which the rules of evidence resemble the rules of a game, with the judge acting as an impartial umpire. Although they may seem to be a fixed set of legal rules, they are not. Like all other legal principles, they are general propositions that courts must apply to specific instances to advance the trustworthiness and reliability of the evidence used at trial. During such applications, judges use a balancing test, carefully weighing whether the trial would be fairer with or without the piece of evidence in question. Some basics of the rules of evidence are summarized in Table 13.3.

Special Rules of Evidence Governing Expert Witnesses

In contrast to lay witnesses, expert witnesses are permitted to give opinions on matters about which they have no personal knowledge. Before someone is permitted to give opinions in court, the person must be qualified as an expert witness based on their knowledge, skill, experience, training, or education. But even the opinions of properly qualified experts are not admissible unless they meet other standards for admissibility, such as those specified in Federal Rule of Evidence 702:

1. The expert's scientific, technical, or other specialized knowledge must help the trier-of-fact to understand the evidence or to determine a fact in issue;

2. The expert's testimony must be based on sufficient facts or data that they have either personally observed or been made aware of through reliable secondhand information;

3. The expert's testimony must be the product of reliable principles and methods; and

4. The expert must have reliably applied the principles and methods to the facts of the case.

Determining Reliability

For much of the 20th century, the *Frye* test governed the admissibility of scientific testimony. In *Frye v. United States* (1923), a federal appeals court refused to allow an expert to testify about the results of a lie-detector test because the instrument had not gained general acceptance in the scientific community. The purpose behind the *Frye* test was to prevent unfounded scientific principles or conclusions based on such principles from being used at trial. Shortcomings of the *Frye* test, however, caused the drafters of the federal rules of evidence to replace *Frye* with rules that the U.S. Supreme Court fleshed out in *Daubert v. Merrill-Dow Pharmaceuticals, Inc.* (1993).

Daubert established that trial court judges are supposed to act as gatekeepers who have a special obligation to ensure the reliability of scientific evidence. *Daubert* suggested several factors (that are neither exhaustive nor applicable to every case) that might be used in evaluating whether a particular scientific theory, study, or test is both valid and reliable, including whether it:

- is empirically testable and capable of replication

- has been published and/or subjected to peer review

- has a known or potential rate of error that is acceptably low

- is logical, avoids bias, and has construct validity (how well data fits into preexisting theory)

- adheres to recognized research methods and, if applicable, to proper sampling and statistical procedures for data analysis

TABLE 13.3	Summary of Select Rules of Evidence
Best-evidence rule	The best-evidence rule means that to prove the content of a writing, recording, or photograph, the original is generally required, since a copy is too easily altered.
Chain of custody	The chronological documentation of the seizure, control, transfer, analysis, and disposition of evidence before it can be admitted into evidence at trial.
Competency to testify	A witness must have personal knowledge of the matter about which he or she is testifying; must be capable of understanding the duty to tell the truth—something he or she is required to do by an oath or affirmation; must be capable of expressing himself or herself so as to be understood by the jury either directly or through an interpreter. People who cannot differentiate between truth and nontruth, such as young children and those who are affected by certain types of serious mental illnesses, generally are not competent to be witnesses in court.
Hearsay	**Hearsay** is secondhand evidence. It is testimony that is not based on personal knowledge but rather is a repetition of what another person has said: "My brother Bob told me he saw Jones enter the store that evening." The general rule is that hearsay evidence is not admissible because it is impossible to test its truthfulness; there is no way to cross-examine with regard to the truth of the matter. There are numerous exceptions to this rule, however, ranging from dying declarations and ancient writings to statements showing the speaker's state of mind.
Relevancy	Evidence is relevant if it shows the existence of any fact that is of consequence to the determination of the action by making that fact more probable or less probable than it would be without the evidence. Evidence that does not tend to prove or disprove any material fact in dispute is **irrelevant** and inadmissible. Evidence regarding the accused's motive, intent, ability, and opportunity to commit a crime would all be relevant. In contrast, information about the defendant's character, prior convictions, or a reputation would not normally be relevant and is, therefore, inadmissible.
Cumulative or unduly prejudicial evidence	Even relevant evidence may be inadmissible if its use would be a waste of time because it is cumulative (duplicative of other evidence) or if it could unfairly prejudice, confuse, or mislead the jury.
Privilege	Privileged communications protect confidential discussions in certain relationships in which we want to foster open, honest communications. The law usually recognizes privileges that include communications between attorney and client; clergy-member and penitent; physician and patient; psychotherapist and patient; and husband and wife.
Lay opinions	Since opinions are subjective beliefs, most witnesses are not permitted to give their opinions other than general opinions that are rationally based on their own common perceptions, such as whether someone acted drunk, smelled like alcohol, appeared upset, or looked tired.

- is generally accepted in the relevant scientific community (making *Frye* a part of *Daubert's* test, but not the dispositive factor)

Initially, *Daubert* applied only to scientific evidence. But in *Kumho Tire Co. v. Carmichael* (1999), the U.S. Supreme Court held that all expert testimony that involves scientific, technical, or other specialized knowledge must meet the *Daubert* test for admissibility.

Forensic Scientific Evidence in the Age of *Daubert*

Scientific evidence analyzing materials such as blood, firearms, and fingerprints has been routinely admitted into evidence for years if it met the traditional yardsticks of the rules of evidence—trustworthiness and relevance. But when the technologies for gathering and measuring these forms of evidence first emerged, their use as evidence was far from routine. Moreover, as the *Frye* case illustrated by disallowing polygraph results, not all evidence based on "science" was necessarily admissible. Results from hypnosis have similarly been excluded from evidence. But separating science from pseudoscience has never been an easy task.

Even under *Daubert*, just when a scientific principle or discovery crosses the line between the experimental and reliably demonstrable stages is difficult to define. *Daubert* has been reasonably effective at keeping "junk science" (unreliable findings, often by persons with questionable credentials) out of evidence, especially in civil cases seeking monetary compensation based on scientifically questionable claims (Buchman, 2004; Murphy, 2016). *Daubert's* impact on forensic science in criminal cases, however, has been surprisingly less dramatic (Fisher, 2008; Neufeld, 2005; Nirenberg, 2016). Indeed, forensic scientific evidence either caused or contributed to wrongful convictions in nearly half of the more than 300 post-vindication DNA exoneration cases by the Innocence Project (2014b). Troublingly, in more than a quarter of such exonerations, false or misleading testimony by forensic experts contributed to the wrongful convictions (Giannelli, 2007; Thomas, 2014).

Pseudoscience Contributes to Wrongful Convictions

Many forensic techniques—such as hair and fiber analysis, toolmark comparisons, and fingerprint analysis—rely upon matching determinations in which a forensic analyst (who may or may not be a scientist) compares a known sample to a questioned sample and makes the highly subjective determination that the two samples originated from the same source. Although lacking a true scientific foundation, these techniques play a prominent role in many cases because of the availability of trace evidence, which is easy to leave and easy to find at a crime scene. Other forensic fields, including comparative bullet lead analysis and arson investigation, rely on assumptions that are "under-researched and oversold" (Gabel & Wilkinson, 2008, p. 1002). Table 13.4 summarizes some of the problems with forensic scientific evidence that has been routinely used in criminal trials in the United States.

Due in large part to many of the shortcomings listed in Table 13.4, the National Academies of Sciences (NAS) issued a scathing report on forensic science in the United States in 2009. The report concluded that, among all existing forensic methods, "only nuclear DNA analysis has been rigorously shown to have the capacity to consistently, and with a high degree of certainty, demonstrate a connection between an evidentiary sample and a specific individual or source" (p. 100). In contrast, most other types of forensic analyses lack sufficient systematic research to even "validate the discipline's basic premises and techniques" (p. 22). Accordingly, the NAS called for the creation of an independent federal agency to oversee forensic science in the United States. That report ultimately led to the establishment of the National Commission on Forensic Science (NCFS) within the U.S. Department of Justice, and the Organization for Scientific Area Committees for Forensic Science within the National Institute of Standards and Technology (NIST). Personnel from these organizations have

TABLE 13.4	Problems with Forensic Scientific Evidence under *Daubert*
Hair microscopy	Used since the 19th century, this technique uses a microscope to compare hair samples using characteristics like color, pigment distributions, and texture. The technique has rarely been subjected to rigorous peer review or proficiency testing. Moreover, the few tests that have been performed revealed that error rates are quite high. In an FBI scientific paper entitled "Correlation of Microscopic and DNA Hair Comparisons," the authors found that even the most competent hair examiners make significant errors. In 11 percent of the cases in which the hair examiners declared two hairs to be "similar," DNA testing revealed that the hairs did not match. In some jurisdictions, hair microscopy is being phased out and replaced by the more sensitive and discriminating mitochondrial DNA typing test. Yet, many local prosecutors continue to rely on the microscope because mitochondrial DNA typing remains relatively expensive and is offered in only a few laboratories. A study of Innocence Project prisoners found nearly 22 percent of prisoners exonerated by DNA evidence had been wrongly convicted based, in large part, on hair comparisons. Yet, results of this technique are routinely used in court.
Serology	Serology is a branch of biochemistry that tests serums found in the human body (in blood, semen, and other bodily fluids). It can be reliable, yet in 40 percent of the DNA-exoneration cases, conventional serology had been used by the prosecutor to secure a conviction. The case transcripts reveal that in the vast majority of these cases, the crime lab serologist misrepresented the data to the advantage of the prosecution.
Fingerprinting	This process compares the impressions of prints from fingers or palms left at a crime scene to known impressions. Empirical studies are just starting to reveal that thousands of misidentification errors are made each year, especially because "non-mate prints can sometimes appear more similar than mate print pairs" to the FBI's automated fingerprint identification system (Cole, Welling, Dioso-Villa, & Carpenter, 2008). Wrongful convictions have also resulted from the misapplication of fingerprint identification. For example, Stephen Cowans was convicted and served six years in prison for shooting a Boston police officer. Two fingerprint experts told a jury during the trial that a thumbprint left by the perpetrator was "unique and identical" to Cowans's print because it matched at 16 points. Postconviction DNA testing excluded Cowans as the perpetrator.
Compositional analysis of bullet lead	This technique compares the quantity of various elements that comprise a lead slug recovered from a crime scene with the composition of the lead found in unused bullets seized from a suspect. In criminal cases, to say that two samples are similar can be very misleading. In fact, the National Research Council of the National Academies of Sciences (2004) concluded that variations in the manufacturing process rendered this technique "unreliable and potentially misleading" (see also NAS, 2009; PCAST, 2016). The FBI discontinued the use of this technique in 2005 accordingly, but hundreds, if not thousands, of criminal defendants may have been convicted based, in part, on this faulty pseudoscience.
Firearm, tool mark, bite mark, and forensic document comparisons	Like examinations of hair samples, these types of forensic analyses rely on an examiner to make comparisons between a crime scene sample and a known exemplar. Thus, they are subject to the same human errors based on subjective judgments as these other techniques. The reliability of these techniques is questionable in light of either unestablished or unacceptably high error rates (NAS, 2009; PCAST, 2016). For example, a classic study (Risinger, Denbeaux, & Saks, 1989) reported that forensic-document examiners were correct between 36 and 45 percent of the time, that they erred partially or completely 36 to 42 percent of the time, and were unable to draw a conclusion in 19 to 22 percent of cases. Experts have recently noted that there is little empirical evidence to support the uniqueness of teeth marks, shoeprints, or weapon markings (Moriarty, 2007). Saks and Koehler (2005) reported error rates as high as 64 percent for bite-mark comparison, a 40 percent error rate for handwriting comparison, and a 12 percent error rate for microscopic hair comparison.

Sources: Jessica D. Gabel and Margaret D. Wilkinson. 2008. "'Good' Science Gone Bad: How the Criminal Justice System Can Redress the Impact of Flawed Forensics." *Hastings Law Journal* 59: 1001–1030; Peter J. Neufeld, 2005. "The (Near) Irrelevance of *Daubert* to Criminal Justice and Some Suggestions for Reform." *American Journal of Public Health* 95: SI07–SI13.

been working together to enhance the practice and improve the reliability of forensic science. But within a few weeks of being sworn in as attorney general for the Trump administration, Jeff Sessions announced that the commission would not be renewed. At the time of this writing, it remains unclear what this means for addressing the problems with using a host of unreliable forensic scientific techniques as evidence in criminal cases.

In 2015, President Obama asked the members of the President's Council of Advisors on Science and Technology (PCAST) to assess if there were other steps that would help ensure that the U.S. legal system relies on valid scientific evidence. PCAST (2016) released a report that reviewed more than 2,000 papers on various forensic scientific techniques. Like the NAS report (2009), the PCAST report is highly critical of most of these techniques—especially those that rely on matching, such as human hair comparisons, bite-mark analysis, firearm and tool-mark comparisons, and tire or shoe-tread impression analysis. Unsurprisingly, police and prosecutors issued statements disagreeing with many of the conclusions in the PCAST report (e.g., Federal Bureau of Investigation, 2016, Sept. 20; National District Attorneys Association, 2016).

New Debates on the Validity of Forensic DNA Analysis

The NAS (2009) report stated that DNA (deoxyribonucleic acid) analysis is the gold standard of forensic science. But this statement was based on the assumption that a sizable sample of DNA from one person (blood, semen, mucus, etc.) is compared with another sizable sample of DNA from another person. This "traditional" type of DNA analysis is so well established in both science and law that prisoners and their representatives are demanding that old cases be reopened so that DNA tests (not available at the time of the original trial) can be performed. These requests are frequently identified with questions regarding the innocence of inmates on death row (see Chapter 14). However, in *District Attorney's Office v. Osborne* (2009), the U.S. Supreme Court ruled that prisoners have no constitutional right to postconviction DNA testing that might prove their innocence.

But there are some important limitations to DNA evidence. First, there must be some biological evidence that can be subjected to DNA testing. Historically, a sufficiently large sample of biological evidence was available in only about 10 percent of criminal cases (Garrett, 2008). But that is changing somewhat today because "most large crime labs most large labs have access to cutting-edge extraction kits capable of obtaining usable DNA from the smallest of samples …" (Shaer, 2016, para. 32). But these techniques have complicated DNA analysis in ways that detract from its standing as forensic science's gold standard.

When biological evidence is available, it's important to keep in mind that the evidence may have been contaminated or otherwise rendered unreliable because of mistakes by police or crime lab personnel, including mix-up of samples, deficiencies in lab-proficiency testing, and problems with or miscalculations of matching criteria—something that jurors often do not understand (Lieberman, Miethe, Carrell, & Krauss, 2008; Ritchie, 2015). Consider the 15-year hunt for the "Phantom of Heilbronn," a presumed serial killer whose DNA had been found at more than 40 crime scenes in Europe. The DNA actually belonged to a factory worker who made swabs that police used to gather samples for testing (Murphy, 2015).

The PCAST (2016) report cautioned that complex DNA mixture analysis (i.e., mixtures of DNA from three or more contributors) needs additional support to be deemed scientifically valid and reliable. This technique is especially problematic when evaluating *touch-DNA*—the very small samples of genetic material left behind from skin cells when a person touches something. The problem is that many people may have touched that same object. Because humans share 99.9 percent of their DNA in common, the more complex the sample (i.e., the more people who may have contributed touch-DNA to something being analyzed), the less reliable the analysis—especially when the sample is very small and newer techniques must be used to magnify the sample sufficiently to allow for testing. A groundbreaking study by Dror and Hampikian (2011) illustrates this point. The researchers gave a complex DNA sample to 17 different, well-trained laboratory technicians, each of whom possessed many years of experience with forensic DNA testing. Each analyst was asked whether the mixture contains DNA from a known sample, taking from a defendant in a criminal case. One of the 17 technicians concluded that the defendant could not be excluded as a contributor to the mixture; 12 said the defendant could be excluded and four said the results were inconclusive. Given how easily small amounts of DNA are transferred combined with the difficulties in interpreting complex DNA samples, scientifically speaking, "the mere presence of DNA at a crime scene" may not be sufficient anymore to support a criminal conviction (Shaer, 2016, para. 43; see also Murphy, 2015).

The CSI Effect

For many years, most of the techniques outlined in Table 13.4 were known only to scientists and criminal lawyers. But Hollywood changed that in the 1990s when dramas about crime and forensics became a staple of prime-time television. At the height of their popularity, the three different versions of *CSI: Crime Scene Investigation* (Las Vegas, Miami, and New York) each drew between 10 and 30 million viewers per week (Kelley, 2011; Shelton, 2008), with millions more watching other shows such as *NCIS, Dexter, Bones, Forensic Files, The New Detectives, Secrets of Forensic Science, Medical Detectives, Cold Case,* and *Without a Trace,* to name just a few. In these popular, although often inaccurate shows,

> lab technicians identify a suspect through analysis that isn't—or shouldn't be—possible in the real world. They match bullets to guns to gun owners, they track footprints and fingerprints in unlikely places, they match fibers from the crime scene to a car or piece of clothing. These unreliable methods usually aren't available, and when they are, they've led to wrongful convictions. Prosecutors are right to tell a jury that there's no forensic evidence rather than stretching to make a connection that isn't there (as the scientists in *CSI* might). But then they say juries are skeptical of a case without fancy forensics. (Innocence Project, 2008, para. 2)

Prosecutors insist that these television shows created the so-called **CSI effect**, in which jurors wrongfully acquit guilty defendants when no scientific evidence is presented. But research has not empirically validated their anecdotal concerns.

Jurors have come to expect sophisticated forensic evidence in even the most mundane cases (see Figure 13.1). However, these higher expectations for forensic evidence did not significantly affect conviction or acquittal voting patterns (Alejo, 2016; Shelton, Kim, & Barak, 2009). In fact, Schweitzer and Saks (2007) found that *CSI* viewers were actually more critical of the forensic evidence presented in a simulated trial, finding it less believable, than people who did not watch *CSI.* Yet, the verdicts of *CSI* viewers and nonviewers did not differ significantly (see also Podlas, 2006).

Nonetheless, it may be fair to blame *CSI*-type shows for misleading people into believing many misconceptions about forensic science. Unlike on television, crime scene investigators and forensic scientists do not engage in police activities like pursuing suspects, conducting interrogations, staging sting operations, conducting raids, and so on (Houck, 2006, para. 11). Similarly, on television, a handful of forensic personnel possess an incredible range of scientific expertise. In real crime labs, however, different types of forensic examinations are performed by specialists in the given forensic subfield.

In addition to misrepresenting the role of people involved in forensic science, television also misrepresent crime laboratories themselves. Labs on television have a dazzling array of forensic equipment and technology at their disposal. But some of the technologies that are depicted on *CSI*—upwards of 40 percent according to some experts—do not really exist (Houck, 2006). Real crime labs, on the other hand, are often understaffed, lack all of the scientific equipment they need, and cannot perform all types of forensic analyses, "whether because of cost, insufficient resources, or rare demand" (Houck, 2006, para. 12).

Most of all, television shows grossly misrepresent forensic investigative techniques and the significance of results. On *CSI,* investigators are seemingly able to lift fingerprints off of almost anything. In reality, prints can be lifted off of only certain surfaces under certain conditions. Moreover, on *CSI,* the prints are uploaded into a computer database and a screen nearly instantly appears with a photo of the person to whom the fingerprint belongs. In reality,

Percentage of Jurors Who Expect Scientific Evidence from Prosecution

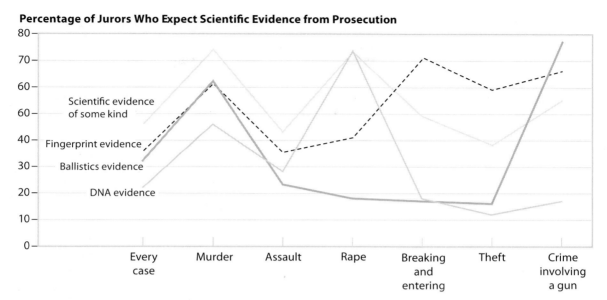

FIGURE 13.1 Juror Expectations for Forensic Evidence

Source: Donald Shelton, 2008. "The 'CSI Effect': Does It Really Exist?" *National Institute of Justice Journal* 259. Available online at http://www.nij.gov /nij/journals/259/csi-effect.htm

many latent fingerprints lifted from crime scenes are not good enough to use for identification purposes. But even when a set of prints can be run through the FBI's Integrated Automatic Fingerprint Identification System (IAFIS), the computerized database provides a list of potential matches. This process is not instantaneous; it typically takes up to two hours (Federal Bureau of Investigation, 2008). And while the IAFIS has the capacity to store and distribute photos, it does not provide pop-up photographic identifications when a set of fingerprints is potentially matched. A human trained in fingerprint comparison must then compare the latent prints with a set of known exemplars.

Similarly, shows like *CSI* routinely overstate the probative value of forensic evidence. "In one episode, for example, investigators perform a remarkable 'reverse algorithm and enhancement' of an audiotaped ransom demand. Using a spectrograph to match the sound waves from the ransom recording to those from a different voice recording, they are able to conclusively identify the kidnapper" (Tyler, 2006, p. 1070). Although this makes for great fiction, the shortcomings of voice identification are legion, as current technology simply cannot

"conclusively identify" a voice to the exclusion of others (NAS, 2009).

But blaming Hollywood for the CSI effect may be too simplistic. Television notwithstanding, the advancement of science and technology has "heightened juror expectations and demands for scientific evidence in almost every respect" (Shelton, Kim & Barak, 2009, p. 2). Forensic science on television appears to be only one factor in increasing juror expectations for scientific evidence in a wide range of criminal cases (Dysart, 2012; Hayes-Smith & Levett, 2013).

Objections to the Admission of Evidence

During trial, attorneys must always be alert, ready to make timely **objections** to the admission of evidence. After a question is asked but before the witness answers, the attorney may object if the evidence is irrelevant or hearsay. The court then rules on the objection, admitting or barring the evidence. The judge may rule immediately or may request the lawyers to argue the legal point out of the hearing of the jury (this is termed a *"sidebar conference"*).

Occasionally, inadmissible evidence will inadvertently be heard by the jury. For example, in answering a valid question, a witness may overelaborate. When this occurs and the attorney objects, the judge will instruct the jury to disregard the evidence. If the erroneous evidence is deemed so prejudicial that a warning to disregard is not sufficient, the judge may declare a **mistrial**.

Challenging Forensic Evidence

During the eight-month murder trial of O. J. Simpson in 1995, the defense team stressed the mishandling of evidence, suggesting that any subsequent analysis, no matter how precise, was not believable. This case thrust crime labs under the microscope, and the results were not always flattering.

Significant errors in laboratory testing have been documented not only at the FBI crime lab but also in numerous state and local crime labs, especially in Texas, Virginia, and West Virginia (Beety, 2015; Giannelli, 2007, 2011; Moriarty, 2007; Murphy, 2015). Part of the problem lies with workload, as crime labs have become victims of their own success with requests for scientific tests growing faster than their budgets. But negligence or outright misconduct in crime labs is clearly also to blame (Beety, 2015; Giannelli, 2011; Thompson, 2006). As a result, some cases have been dismissed, and some convictions reversed, because testimony concerning scientific evidence proved unreliable. The Supreme Court has made challenging scientific evidence easier, holding that crime laboratory reports may not be introduced as evidence unless the person responsible for creating them gives testimony and is subject to cross-examination (*Melendez-Diaz v. Massachusetts*, 2009). But, as explored in the "Courts, Controversy, & the Administration of Justice" feature, applying the rigors of *Daubert* to techniques long used for crime solving can cause quite an uproar.

Steps in the Trial Process

The order in which different components of a trial unfold differs from jurisdiction to jurisdiction (and even sometimes from courtroom to courtroom within the same courthouse). For example, some courts provide jurors with legal instructions at the start of a case; others do so at the end of the presentation of evidence but before closing arguments; and still other courts provide jury instructions after closing arguments. Such minor differences aside, most criminal trials follow the sequence outlined in the "Law on the Books vs. Law in Action" feature on page 400. Each of the steps in the trial process is explored in detail in the following sections.

Opening Statements

Once the jury has been selected and sworn, the trial begins with **opening statements** by both sides, outlining what they believe the evidence in the case will prove. The purpose of an opening statement is to advise the jury of what the attorney intends to prove. Opening statements are not evidence; the attorneys offer the jurors "road maps" to guide them through the case. It is important to note that these road maps must be limited to statements of what the attorneys actually believe will be presented as the trial progresses (*United States v. Dinitz*, 1976); an opening statement, therefore, must be rooted in some degree of fact. A detailed and well-organized opening statement presents the jury with a *schema*—a thematic framework through which to view the trial. If done well, opening statements may be case-determinative. Research has repeatedly demonstrated that even though jurors are admonished not to make up their minds until the conclusion of trial after having given fair and impartial consideration to all the evidence, many jurors make a preliminary decision with regard to the outcome of the case after hearing opening statements (Kalven & Zeisel, 1966; Spiecker & Worthington, 2003).

Prosecution's Case-in-Chief

After opening statements, the prosecutor presents the state's *case-in-chief*, calling witnesses and introducing other forms of evidence to bolster

Should Fingerprint Evidence Be Admissible?

Since *Daubert* was decided in 1993, nearly every court that has reviewed fingerprinting evidence has concluded that expert testimony using fingerprint identification is admissible. But is this the correct result? Many of the courts reviewing the "science" of fingerprinting merely cite other courts for the proposition that fingerprint identification is reliable, making it more of a judicially certified practice than one validated by science (Cole, 2010; Cooper, 2016).

The NAS report on forensic science (2009) called into question the premises upon which fingerprint identifications are based. First, although there is some scientific evidence supporting the presumption that each fingerprint is unique, this assumption has not been sufficiently empirically validated. Second, there are generally no objective standards for declaring a fingerprint to be a "match" that have been scientifically validated, especially because examiners of latent prints often receive only partial fingerprints of variable quality. The standards for fingerprint comparison under such circumstances are subjective, as are the declarations of a match. Thus, in contrast to DNA evidence, there are no generally accepted statistical models "that would permit the likelihood that two prints came from the same person to be expressed in probabilistic terms" (Mnookin, 2008, p. 129; see also, NAS, 2009, p. 139). And third, not only are the claims that fingerprint analyses have error rates near zero unsubstantiated, but they also are "not scientifically plausible" (p. 142).

Critics of fingerprint identification also point out that unlike the extensive education, training, and certification undergone by DNA analysts, most fingerprint examiners "receive the majority of their training on the job, without either a formal structure of topics covered or formal assessment of success in meeting training goals. Variation in training means that variation in the use of a method must also occur" (Haber & Haber, 2008, p. 94). Similarly, neither the reliability nor the validity of the proficiency tests used to certify analysts has ever been established. Indeed, one leading analyst referred to the prints used in the FBI proficiency test as being "so easy" that "they are a joke" (Haber & Haber, 2008, p. 95, quoting Bayle, 2002).

Collectively, these shortcomings have led leading scholars of the forensic sciences to conclude that the leading current method of fingerprint analysis (the ACE-V [accuracy, comparison, evaluation, and verification] method) is "both untested and untestable" (Haber & Haber, 2008, p. 87).

In a highly controversial ruling in 2002, a federal district judge ruled that fingerprint identification evidence did not meet the *Daubert* test and, therefore, experts could not express an opinion as to whether a particular latent fingerprint found at a crime scene could be attributed to the defendant in the case (*United States v. Llera Plaza*, 2002). The ruling caused such an outcry that the judge reversed his own decision (see Moenssens, 2002).

Latent fingerprints continue to be collected from crime scenes, and the results of their analysis play a large part in the investigation of crimes. But given the current state of scientific knowledge about fingerprint analysis, should fingerprinting analysts be permitted to testify as experts in criminal trials that the defendant's prints "match" those found at a crime scene? Most police and prosecutors answer this question with a resounding "yes" and have been quite successful in convincing courts to agree with them. But the National Academies of Science and numerous scholars with expertise in the intersection of law and forensic science cast doubt on the courts' routine acceptance of fingerprint evidence for the purposes of individualizing identifications. Where do you stand on the matter? Explain your reasoning.

the prosecution's allegation that the defendant is guilty. The prosecutor conducts a **direct examination** by asking open-ended, nonleading questions to prosecutorial witnesses, focusing on questions that get at who, what, when, where, how, and why. A fundamental tenet of the adversary system is the need to test evidence for truthfulness, and the primary means of testing the truthfulness of witnesses is **cross-examination**. Thus, the defense has the right to cross-examine any witnesses for the prosecution. Because such witnesses are presumed to be hostile to the defense, closed-ended or leading questions are permissible on cross-examination (such as, "Isn't it true that….").

Motion for Judgment of Acquittal

At the conclusion of the prosecution's case-in-chief, the defense may make a **motion for judgment of acquittal**. The court must enter such a judgment whenever the prosecution fails to introduce sufficient evidence to sustain a conviction as a matter of law. These motions are very rarely granted, since it is unusual for prosecutors to present a case that is so weak that no reasonable jury could determine that the defendant committed the crime(s) charged.

Defense's Case-in-Chief

Once the prosecutor rests, the defense must choose whether to put on its case-in-chief or to rest. Because the defendant is presumed innocent, the defense does not have to call any witnesses or introduce any evidence. But, if the defense chooses to present its side of the case to the jury, it does so following the same procedure the prosecution used: conducting direct examination of defense witnesses and introducing other forms of evidence. The prosecutor has the right to cross-examine any defense witnesses.

At times, defense attorneys present a classic defense—self-defense, intoxication, entrapment, insanity, alibi, frame-up, mistake, and so on. But more often than not, the defense instead seeks to undermine whether the prosecutor did indeed prove the defendant guilty *beyond a reasonable doubt*. But many experienced defense attorneys consider this to be the weakest kind of defense. They believe that to gain an acquittal, the defense must give the jury something to "hang their hat on." Thus, they must consider whether to let the defendant testify.

The Defendant as Witness

The Fifth Amendment protection against **self-incrimination** means that the defendant cannot be compelled to be a witness against himself or herself. If the defendant chooses not to testify, no comment or inference may be drawn from this fact.

LAW ON THE BOOKS VS. LAW IN ACTION

Steps of the Process: Trials

	Law on the Books	Law in Action
Opening statements	Lawyers discuss what the evidence will show.	Lawyers use to lead the jury to a favorable verdict.
Prosecution's case-in-chief	The main evidence offered to prove the defendant guilty beyond a reasonable doubt.	Defense suggests that the prosecution has not met its burden of proof.
Witness	A person who makes a statement under oath about the events in question.	Through cross-examination, the defense undermines the credibility of the witness.
Expert witness	A person who possesses special knowledge or experience who is allowed to testify not only about facts but also about the opinions he or she has drawn from a review of the facts.	Some expert witnesses testify only for one side or the other. Some types of forensic evidence in criminal cases may not be reliable enough to pass the *Daubert* test.
Motion for judgment of acquittal	Defense argues that no reasonable jury could convict the defendant based on the evidence presented by the prosecution.	Judges almost never grant this motion, largely because prosecutors rarely fail to present insufficient evidence to sustain a conviction.
Defense's case-in-chief	Evidence that defense may present. Because the defendant is innocent until proven guilty, the defense is not required to present evidence.	The defense may rest without calling witnesses, but jurors expect to hear reasons why they should not convict.
Defendant as witness	The defendant may waive his or her privilege against self-incrimination and testify.	Defense attorneys are reluctant to call the defendant to the stand, particularly if there is a prior conviction.

(Continued)

(Continued)

Rebuttal	Evidence that refutes or contradicts evidence given by the opposing party.	The prosecutor will call witnesses to undermine a defendant's alibi.
Renewed motion for judgment of acquittal	Defense argues that in light of the evidence presented by both sides, no jury could reasonably convict the defendant.	Trial judges almost never grant this motion.
Closing arguments	After all the evidence has been presented, each side sums up the evidence and attempts to convince the jury why their side should win.	Many trial attorneys believe that a good closing argument will win the case.
Jury instructions	Explanations by the judge informing the jury of the law applicable to the case.	Legal language difficult for average citizens to follow.
Jury deliberations	Jurors deliberate in private. Jurors select a foreperson and discuss the case. Jurors take an oath to follow the law as instructed by the judge.	Some juries introduce popular law into the decision-making process. On rare occasions, a juror might refuse to follow the law in a particular case.
Verdict	Decision that the defendant is either guilty or not guilty (acquittal).	Juries convict three out of four times. Jury verdicts often reflect a compromise.
Hung jury	Jury is unable to reach a verdict.	Defense attorneys consider a hung jury an important victory.
Postverdict motions	Motions filed by the defense after conviction and before sentencing.	Judge must accept a verdict of not guilty.
Renewed motion for judgment of acquittal	Defense argues that the jury could not have reasonably convicted the defendant based on the evidence presented.	Trial judges are very reluctant to second-guess jury verdicts and almost never grant this motion.
Motion for a new trial	Defense argues that the trial judge made mistakes and therefore a new trial should be held.	On very rare occasions, trial judges admit that an error occurred and set aside a jury verdict of guilty.

The prosecutor cannot argue before the jury, "If he is innocent, why doesn't he take the stand and say so?" (*Griffin v. California*, 1965). Nonetheless, jurors are curious about the defendant's version of what happened. They expect the defendant to profess innocence; in the secrecy of the jury room, they may ponder why the defendant refused to testify.

Defendants may, of course, waive the privilege against self-incrimination and take the stand in their own defense. In deciding whether the defendant should testify, the defense attorney must consider whether the story is believable. If it is not, the jury will probably dismiss it, thus doing more harm to the defendant's case than if he or she had not testified at all.

Like any other witness, a defendant who takes the stand is subject to cross-examination. Cross-examination usually ensures that the defendant cannot tell only a part of the story and conceal the rest. Once the defendant chooses to testify, the state can bring out all the facts surrounding the events to which the defendant testifies. Just as important, once the defendant has taken the stand, the state can **impeach** the defendant's credibility by introducing into evidence any prior felony convictions and, in some circumstances, other prior misconduct. The defense attorney must make the difficult decision about whether to arouse the jury's suspicion by not letting the accused testify or letting the defendant testify and be subjected to possibly damaging cross-examination.

"Damned if they do, damned if they don't" is the conclusion of a research project that interviewed jurors in capital murder trials. In general, jurors wanted the defendants to testify during trial and were confused when they did not. But when defendants chose to testify, jurors concluded that they were lying and showed no remorse (Antonio & Arone, 2005).

Renewed Motion for Judgment of Acquittal

At the conclusion of the defense's case-in-chief, the defense may make another motion for a judgment of acquittal, arguing that no reasonable jury could convict based upon the totality of the evidence presented. Given this high standard, these motions are very rarely granted. Moreover, most judges do not want to impinge upon the province of the jury to make a factual determination concerning the defendant's guilt.

Rebuttal

After the defense rests its case, the prosecution may call rebuttal witnesses, whose purpose is either to discredit the testimony of a previous witness or to discredit the witness. The prosecutor may call a **rebuttal** witness to show that the previous witness could not have observed what she said she did because she was somewhere else at the time. Or the prosecutor may call witnesses or otherwise present evidence to show that the previous witnesses have dishonorable reputations. The rules of evidence regarding rebuttal witnesses are complex. In general, evidence may be presented in rebuttal that could not have been used during the prosecution's main case. For example, the prosecution may legitimately inform the jury of the previous convictions of defendants who take the stand, in an attempt to impeach their credibility.

Closing Arguments

After the prosecution and defense have rested (that is, completed the introduction of evidence), each side has the opportunity to make a closing argument to the jury. **Closing arguments** allow each side to sum up the facts in its favor and indicate why it believes a verdict of guilty or not guilty is in order.

In most jurisdictions, the prosecutor goes first, carefully summing up the facts of the case and tying together into a coherent pattern what appeared during the trial to be isolated or unimportant matters. The prosecutor calls upon the jurors to do their duty and punish the defendant, who has committed the crime. The defense attorney goes next, highlighting the evidence favorable to the defendant, criticizing the witnesses for the state, and showing why they should not be believed. The defense also calls upon the jurors to do their sworn duty and return a not-guilty verdict. Because the prosecutor bears the burden of proof, he or she has the opportunity to make one last statement to the jury, refuting the defense arguments.

Closing arguments are often the most dramatic parts of the trial. However, there is a fine line between persuasiveness and unnecessary emotionalism. Jury verdicts have been reversed on appeal because the prosecutor interjected prejudicial statements into the closing argument.

Jury Instructions

Although in jury trials the jury is the sole judge of the facts of the case, the judge alone determines the law. Therefore, the court instructs the jury as to the meaning of the law applicable to the facts of the case. These **jury instructions** begin with discussions of general legal principles (innocent until proven guilty, guilty beyond a reasonable doubt, and so forth). They follow with specific instructions on the elements of the crime in the case and what specific actions the government must prove before there can be a conviction. If the defendant has raised a defense such as insanity or duress, the judge instructs the jury as to the meaning of the defense according to the law in that jurisdiction. Finally, the judge instructs the jury on possible verdicts in the case and provides a written form for each verdict of guilty and not guilty. Often juries have the option of choosing alternative forms of guilty verdicts, called *"lesser included offenses."* In a murder case, for example, the jury may find the defendant guilty of murder in the first degree, murder in the second degree, or manslaughter— or they may acquit on all charges.

The judge and the trial attorneys prepare the jury instructions during a special **charging conference** that precedes jury deliberations. Each side drafts suggested instructions, and the judge chooses the most appropriate ones. If the judge rejects a given instruction, the lawyer enters an objection on the record, thus preserving the issue for later appeal. The instructions are written out, signed by the judge, and then read to the jury. Some judges allow the jurors to take a copy of the instructions into the jury room as a guide.

Jury instructions represent a formal, detailed lecture on the law. Because faulty jury instructions are a principal basis for appellate court reversal, judges are careful in their wording. However, given the complexity of the law, juror comprehension of jury instructions is pitifully low (Ogloff & Rose, 2007; McKimmie, Antrobus, & Baguley, 2014). For example, given jury instructions stressing that a defendant is presumed innocent until proven guilty by the evidence beyond any reasonable doubt, only 50 percent of the jurors understood that the defendant did not have to present any evidence of innocence and 10 percent were still uncertain what the presumption of innocence was (Strawn & Buchanan, 1976; see also Frank & Broschard, 2006). Another study found that juror misunderstandings of the beyond a reasonable doubt burden of proof "tended to be in the direction of a more stringent standard of proof: the less jurors actually understood the standard of proof, the more convincing they believed the defense case to be" (McKimmie, Antrobus, & Baguley, 2014, p. 177).

The major difficulty in improving jury comprehension is the complexity of the law itself; it is difficult to translate into plain English the subtleties of meaning of certain legal terms and the intentional vagueness of the law, such as "reasonable person" and "recklessness" (Ogloff & Rose, 2007; Steele & Thornburg, 1991). But even when jurors understand the law contained in jury instructions, there is reason to question the true impact of the instructions. "The more jurors thought they understood the instructions . . . the more they said they relied on common sense. This suggests a less thorough consideration of the evidence ..." (McKimmie, Antrobus, & Baguley, 2014, p. 177; see also Ogloff, 1991).

Jury Deliberations

How juries decide has long fascinated lawyers and laypeople alike. There is a great deal of curiosity about what goes on behind the locked jury room door. During the trial, jurors are passive observers who are not allowed to ask questions and are usually prohibited from taking notes. But after the judge reads the jury instructions, the lawyers, judges, and defendants must wait passively, often in tense anticipation, for the jury to reach a verdict. The only hints of what is happening during **jury deliberations** occur on the rare occasions when the jurors request further instructions from the judge about the applicable law or ask to have portions of the testimony read in open court.

Sometimes juries deliberate for a significant period of time but are unable to reach a verdict. In such circumstances, a judge might opt to call the jury into the courtroom and read them an **Allen charge** (sometimes referred to as a "dynamite charge"). This strongly worded jury instruction encourages jurors to continue deliberations until a verdict is reached. If, however, the jury is unable to reach a verdict, the jury is declared *deadlocked* and the trial ends with a **hung jury**. The prosecutor then has the option of trying the defendant again. Despite recent concerns, the rate of hung juries is low and has been stable for years (Hannaford, Hans, & Munsterman, 1999). Nationwide, juries are unable to reach a decision only 6 percent of the time (National Center for State Courts, 2003).

Research demonstrates that high levels of juror participation during deliberations "are characteristic of evidence-driven deliberations, which focus on the review of case facts, evidence, and judicial instructions" (Cornwell & Hans, 2011, p. 668). Additionally, full participation by jurors of diverse backgrounds facilitates discussions that "include topics and considerations that might be missed, or even avoided by, less diverse juries"(p. 668; see also Devine, Krouse, Cavanaugh, & Basora, 2016; Sommers, 2006). But research also suggests that some jurors who may be most capable of contributing differing perspectives are also the least likely to be active participants in the deliberation process. Juror participation increases with juror educational and socio-economic status such that "upper-income and more highly educated jurors maintain a dominant presence in the jury room that may threaten the ability of lower-status jurors to advance their views" (Cornwell & Hans, 2011,

p. 690). In some instances—especially in cases involving murder, drugs, and nonviolent crimes—participation by African-American jurors appears to transcend traditional research findings, which suggested lower levels of active participation in deliberations by minority jurors (Cornwell & Hans, 2011). This finding, however, needs to be examined within the context of two caveats. First, Blacks are generally under-represented both within jury pools and on petit juries (Rose, 2005). Second, because many jurors tend to defer to the opinions of vocally participatory jurors from high-status backgrounds (in terms of education and income), it is unclear whether the viewpoints expressed by minority jurors are given full and equal consideration (Winter & Clair, 2017; York & Cornwell, 2006).

Are Juries Biased?

Juries are supposed to decided cases based on two factors: the evidence presented during a trial and the legal instructions they receive from a judge. More than a century ago, the U.S. Supreme Court stated:

> The entire effort of our trial procedure is to secure … jurors who do not know … anything of either the character [of the parties] or events [on trial]…. The zeal displayed in this effort to empty the minds of the jurors … [is a sign] that the jury … is an impartial organ of justice. (*Patterson v, Colorado*, 1907, p. 462)

The sentiment expressed in the preceding quote is known as the *tabula rasa* theory—Latin for "clean slate." Jurors are not supposed to consider any **extralegal factors**—information not admitted into evidence during a trial. But jurors do not actually come to court with an "empty mind." And if they did, would we really want them on a jury? Mark Twain commented on this paradox after he observed jury selection in a murder case. Twain noted that several intelligent potential jurors were dismissed since they had read newspaper accounts of the case even though each of them said they would be able to put aside the information they had read and decide the case fairly and impartially on the evidence. Twain concluded "ignoramuses alone could mete out unsullied justice" (1913, pp. 56–57).

Media attention is not the only factor that interferes with the *tabula rasa* theory. Even in run-of-the-mill cases that have received no media attention, jurors will inevitably still bring their own knowledge and experiences to the deliberation process. "All adults have beliefs, values, and prejudices which make impartiality in the *tabula rasa* sense impossible" (Gobert, 1988, p. 271). For example, in spite of the voir dire process,

- Jurors are less likely to convict a defendant on a charge involving conduct in which the jurors had personally engaged in the past, such as gambling or reckless driving (Kalven & Zeisel, 1966).

- Emotional arousal often based on images or descriptions of particularly gruesome bodily harm affects juror biases toward guilt (Bright & Goodman-Delahunty, 2006).

- Jurors intuitively value some types of evidence more than others. Specifically, they routinely undervalue circumstantial evidence and "overvalue direct evidence (eyewitness identifications and confessions) when making verdict choices, even though false-conviction statistics indicate that the former is normally more probative and more reliable than the latter" (Heller, 2006, p. 241). However, in cases in which DNA evidence is presented as circumstantial evidence, jurors tend to give it much greater weight than other types of evidence (Lieberman et al., 2008).

- Some jurors are inclined to credit or disregard testimony by police (Dorfman, 1999).

- The victim's or defendant's attractiveness (especially in sex-crime cases) or how sympathetic the defendant appears to the jury have both been found to be a significant factor in jurors' determinations of guilt (Kalven & Zeisel, 1966; Patry, 2008; Sigall & Ostrove, 1975).

- And demographic characteristics of the victim and defendant, including their race, gender, socio-economic class, religion, and sexual orientation, all affect juror decision making as well (see Devine, Clayton, Dunford, Seying, & Pryce, 2001; Levett et al., 2005; Miller, Maskaly, Green, & Peoples, 2011; Sommers, 2007; Williams & Burek, 2008)—especially when the race of the defendant matches the stereotypes associated with the crime for which they are on trial (Esqueda, Espinoza, & Culhane, 2008). Biases on account of race and ethnicity, whether purposeful or unconscious, have especially pronounced effects in death penalty cases (Chapter 14). McKimmie, Masters, Masser, Schuller, and Terry (2013) similarly report that being a counter-stereotypical female defendant distracts "jurors' attention away from thoroughly attending to and systematically processing the evidence presented during the trial" and refocuses their attention on the defendant herself (p. 352).

The answer to the question of whether juries are biased depends on what is meant by "biased." Most research suggests that modern juries in the United States appear to perform remarkably well on the whole, deciding cases primarily on the basis of legal factors rather than extralegal ones (Devine et al., 2016; Ford, 1986; Garvey et al., 2004; Mills & Bohannon, 1980). Even in trials involving emotional issues such as sexual assault, evidence is the primary factor in decision making. Jurors were influenced by extralegal factors, but these effects were largely limited to weak cases in which the state presented little hard evidence (Reskin & Visher, 1986). This is not to say that racism, sexism (including gender stereotypes), homophobia, and the like do not enter into juror decision making; they do. However, the effects of these biases appear to be minimal because they are significantly moderated by legal factors—especially the strength of the evidence (Devine et al., 2016; Diamond, 2006; Garvey et al., 2004; Mitchell, Haw, Pfeifer, & Meissner, 2005).

The Verdict

Once the jury informs the judge that a decision has been reached, the lawyers and the defendant gather in the courtroom. Typically, the foreperson announces the **verdict**. How often do juries convict? Given that the vast majority of cases have already been dismissed or disposed of by a plea of guilty, one might expect that the defendant's chances of winning at trial are roughly 50–50, but the real odds against acquittal are significantly

higher. In federal courts, juries convict 82 percent of the time in nondrug cases. Data from the National Center for State Courts (Ostrom, Kauder, & LaFountain, 2001) point in the same direction; juries convict about three-quarters of the time in state criminal cases.

Do juries view cases differently from judges? Harry Kalven and Hans Zeisel (1966) found that judges and juries agree more than three out of four times. When judge and jury disagree, the judge is more likely to convict and the jury to acquit. Subsequent studies have replicated these findings (Eisenberg et al., 2004). But this pattern is tied to several factors, including the severity of the charge, whether the defendant takes the stand to testify in his or her own defense and a jury learns that the defendant has no prior convictions, and whether the defense merely challenges the sufficiency of the state's case or presents its own witnesses to disprove the prosecution's version of the case (Eisenberg et al., 2004; Givelber & Farrell, 2008; Levine, 1983).

Postverdict Motions

A trial verdict of **acquittal** (not guilty) ends the case; the defendant can leave the courthouse a free person. A verdict of guilty, however, means that further proceedings will occur; the defendant must be sentenced (Chapter 14) and in all likelihood will appeal (Chapter 15).

If the jury returns a verdict of guilty, the defendant still has certain legal options remaining. A guilty defendant may file **postverdict motions**, which are heard prior to sentencing. These motions give the defense attorney the opportunity to reargue alleged mistakes made at trial. The trial judge may have a change of mind and become convinced that some ruling made against the defendant was erroneous. For example, the defense might try making another motion for a judgment of acquittal. Another common postverdict motion is the *motion for a new trial*. It asserts that serious errors were made at trial (either by the trial judge or by the prosecutor), so the guilty verdict should be set aside and a new trial granted. Postverdict motions are largely a formality; few are ever granted.

Law in Action: Trials as Balancing Wheels

Trials exert a major influence on the operation of the entire criminal court process. This process resembles a balance. A balance wheel regulates or stabilizes the motion of a mechanism. Although only a handful of cases go to trial, the possibility of trial operates as a balancing wheel on all other cases. Most important, the likelihood of conviction determines the negotiating position of lawyers during plea bargaining. Thus, jury trials must be measured not only in terms of their impact on specific cases but also on how the decisions reached affect similar cases in the future.

Popular Standards of Justice

Juries introduce the community's commonsense judgments into judicial decisions. The University of Chicago jury project (Broeder, 1959) found that popular standards of justice are by far the major reason for disagreement between judge and jury. The result is jury legislation—a jury's deliberate modification of the law to make it conform to community views of what the law ought to be (Kalven & Zeisel, 1966). A recent study also finds that judges are influenced by extralegal variables in their guilt or innocence decisions, suggesting that judge and jury disagreement is more complex than original thought (Farrell & Givelber, 2010; Spamann & Klöhn, 2016).

One example of how juries introduce popular standards into the criminal court process involves prosecutions for hunting violations. Rural juries are dubious about laws that restrict hunting privileges. Thus, federal defendants accused of shooting too many birds (and the like) have a good chance of finding friendly juries ready to come to their rescue (Levine, 1983).

The importance of juries' introducing popular standards into the justice system is associated with the concept of **jury nullification**—the right of juries to nullify or refuse to apply law in criminal cases despite facts that leave no reasonable doubt that the law was violated.

Juries can nullify for any number of reasons, but types of nullification can generally be divided into several discrete categories. "Classical" jury nullification occurs where the jury believes that the law itself is unjust, such as when a jury refuses to convict defendants for minor drug offenses. Classical nullification can also occur where the jury believes the law is just, but the punishment is excessive. "As applied" jury nullification happens when the jury does not object to the law on its face, but acquits because it believes it is being unjustly applied—for instance, when a jury refuses to convict campus protestors of trespass. "Symbolic" nullification occurs when the jury does not object to the law or its application, but acquits to send a political message to the executive or legislative apparatus, or to society. (Rubenstein, 2006, p. 962)

Some advocates of jury nullification base their ideas on a perceived need to reduce government intrusion into citizens' lives; others are motivated by concern over racial injustice (Brooks, 2004; Brown, 1997; Butler, 1995). Judges are quick to denounce jury nullification because they feel that the rule of law is undermined. But others counter that juries have been refusing to follow the law for centuries, and they have every right to send a message by not following a law they find, for whatever reason, to be flawed. Contemporary discussions focus on whether juries should be told they have the right to disregard the judge's jury instructions and substitute their own views and, if so, what the effects of doing so may be (Diamond, 2007; Dunn, 2007; Galiber et al., 1993; Horowitz, Kerr, Park, & Gockel, 2006; Rubenstein, 2006).

Uncertainty

Jury trials also affect the criminal court system by introducing uncertainty into the process. Stories about irrational juries form part of the folklore of any courthouse. Here are two examples. During jury deliberations in a drug case, two jurors announced that "only God can judge" and hung the jury by refusing to vote. After an acquittal in a burglary case, a juror put her arm around the defendant and said, "Bob, we were sure happy to find you not guilty, but don't do it again" (Neubauer, 1974b, p. 228). Legal professionals resent such intrusions into their otherwise ordered world; they seek to reduce such uncertainties by developing the norms of cooperation discussed throughout this book. Viewed in this light, plea bargaining serves to shield the system from a great deal of the uncertainty that results when lay citizens are involved in deciding important legal matters.

Prejudicial Pretrial Publicity

Two provisions of the U.S. Constitution often come into conflict in high-profile criminal cases. On the one hand, the Sixth Amendment guarantees the accused a fair trial. On the other, the First Amendment guarantees the press the ability to cover criminal trials (*Richmond Newspapers v. Virginia*, 1980). But extensive media coverage can cause **prejudicial pretrial publicity**. This term refers to the media's ability to taint the venire so that potential jurors are incapable of rendering a fair and impartial verdict based on the evidence presented in court because pretrial publicity has already shaped their opinions of the case.

Two cases in the 1960s caused the U.S. Supreme Court to overturn convictions based on prejudicial pretrial publicity having interfered with the defendants' right to a fair trial (*Irvin v. Dowd*, 1961; *Sheppard v. Maxwell*, 1966). The Sheppard case, in particular, received national attention. Dr. Sam Sheppard stood accused of bludgeoning his wife to death in her bedroom. Intensive media coverage both before and during the trial contributed to the jurors' verdict of conviction. Sheppard spent 10 years in prison before the U.S. Supreme Court ruled that the media publicity had denied Sheppard a fair trial. Prosecutors retried him and, the second time around, he was acquitted. His story was later chronicled both on television and in the movie, *The Fugitive*.

In the wake of the *Sheppard* case, trial judges attempted to preserve defendants' Sixth Amendment rights to a fair trial by imposing **gag orders** on the press. Because violations of gag orders are punishable as **contempt of court** (disobeying a judge's order), they prevented the press from reporting on pretrial criminal proceedings—or subjected them to jail time for doing so. But in *Nebraska Press Association v. Stuart* (1976), the Supreme Court ruled that such gag orders were unconstitutional violations of the First Amendment rights of the press.

Research supports the Supreme Court's reasoning that publicity does, in fact, affect jurors. In a classic study, a team of researchers provided one set of "jurors" with prejudicial news coverage of a case and a control group with "nonprejudicial" information. After listening to an identical trial involving a case in which the guilt of the defendant was greatly in doubt, the study found that the "prejudiced jurors" were more likely to convict than the "nonprejudiced jurors" (Padawer-Singer & Barton, 1975). These results have been replicated many times such that it is now widely accepted that even modest pretrial publicity can prejudice potential jurors against a defendant (Moran & Cutler, 1991; Ruva & Guenther, 2015; Ruva & LeVasseur, 2012; Studebaker & Penrod, 2007).

Historically, very few criminal trials involved prejudicial pretrial publicity. But with the advent of 24-hour cable news channels and the ease of information access through the Internet, pretrial publicity affects more cases today than ever before. Social media, in particular, can produce information overload in jurors, with the news focusing on emotional information (Taslitz, 2012). When there is extensive pretrial publicity, the jury-selection process is greatly strained. Voir dire is geared to ferreting out ordinary instances of unfairness or prejudice, not to correcting the possibility of a systematic pattern of bias. For example, if an attorney excuses all jurors who have heard something about the case at hand, he or she runs the risk of selecting a jury solely from the least attentive, least literate members of the general public. On the other hand, if an attorney accepts jurors who assert that they will judge the case solely on the basis of testimony in open court, he or she is still not certain that the juror—no matter how well intentioned—can hear the case with a truly open mind.

In trying to reconcile conflicting principles of a fair trial and freedom of the press, trial courts use (singly or in combination) three techniques: limited gag orders, change of venue, and sequestering of the jury. Each of these methods suffers from admitted drawbacks.

Limited Gag Orders

The First Amendment forbids the court from censoring what the press writes about a criminal case, but it says nothing about restricting the flow of information to the media. Thus, in cases in which it seems likely that selecting a jury may be difficult, judges now routinely issue *limited gag orders* forbidding those involved in the case—police, prosecutor, defense attorney, and defendant—from talking to the press. Since these people know the most about the case (and often have the most to gain from pretrial publicity), the net effect is to dry up news leaks. However, consistent with the First Amendment, the press is free to publish any information it discovers. The greatest difficulty is that one of the people involved in the case may secretly provide information, in violation of the judge's order. The judge can then subpoena the reporter and order disclosure of the source. Reporters believe that identifying their sources will dry up the flow of information, so they refuse to testify. They are cited for contempt and go to jail. Thus, the court may infringe on freedom of the press when its intent is simply to guarantee another Bill of Rights protection—the right to a fair trial.

Change of Venue

Recall from Chapter 2 that *venue* refers to the place where a case is tried. If the court is convinced that a case has received such extensive publicity that picking an impartial jury is impossible, the trial may be shifted to another part of the state. If a case has received statewide coverage, however, such a change is of limited use. Defense attorneys face a difficult tactical decision in deciding whether to request a **change of venue**. They must weigh the effects of prejudicial publicity against the disadvantages of having a trial in a more rural and conservative area, where citizens are hostile to big-city defendants (particularly if they are African-American). Prosecutors generally oppose such moves because they believe that the chances of conviction are greater in the local community. To justify this position, prosecutors cite the expense of moving witnesses, documents, and staff to a distant city for a long trial.

Sequestering the Jury

A prime defect in the trial of Dr. Sheppard was the failure to shield the jury from press coverage of the ongoing trial. Indeed, jurors read newspaper stories of the trial, which included inadmissible evidence. One remedy that is common in trials involving extensive media coverage is to **sequester** the jury. The jurors live in a hotel, take their meals together, and participate in weekend recreation together. Sheriff's deputies censor newspapers and shut off television news. The possibility of being in virtual quarantine for a number of weeks makes many citizens reluctant to serve. When sequestering is probable, the jury selected runs the risk of including only citizens who are willing to be separated for long periods of time from friends and family, who can afford to be off work, or who look forward to a Spartan existence. At a minimum, sequestration is a trying experience for the jurors.

Media in the Courtroom

The rise of electronic media has added a new dimension to the defendant's right to a fair trial. Trials, of course, are open to the public, and journalists are free to observe and report on courtroom proceedings. But what tools the public, journalists, and even jurors can use in the courtroom has been the subject of controversy for nearly a century. The debate is frequently framed around "cameras in the courtroom." But in this sense, the term "cameras" is used more broadly than still photography equipment; it also includes recording and broadcasting devices.

Changing Views on Cameras in the Courtroom

Since the sensational Lindbergh trial of the 1930s, radio and television coverage of the judicial process has been limited. In that case, German immigrant Bruno Hauptman was accused of kidnapping and murdering the son of the famous aviator Charles Lindbergh. Because it was perceived that the daily press coverage of the trial was excessive, rules of court came to forbid cameras or recording devices in the courthouse. Indeed, in *Estes v. Texas* (1965), the U.S. Supreme Court overturned a conviction on due process grounds when a criminal case was televised in spite of the defendant's objections. In his concurring opinion, Justice Harlan stressed the Court's reasoning: televised trials "possess such capabilities for interfering with the even course of the judicial process that they are constitutionally banned" (p. 595).

In 1978, the American Bar Association proposed allowing television coverage of courtroom proceedings when it would not be obtrusive. As a result, some states began to change their rules. Three years later, the U.S. Supreme Court changed its view when it unanimously held that electronic media and still photographic coverage of public judicial proceedings do not violate a defendant's right to a fair trial (*Chandler v. Florida*, 1981). Since then, the barriers against cameras in the courtroom have fallen in state after state. Today, all 50 states "have provisions, albeit with limitations, to allow cameras at some level of their state court system" (Marder, 2012, pp. 1491–1492).

A 2009 C-SPAN Supreme Court Survey found that 61 percent of Americans would like to see cameras in the courtroom (Penn, Schoen, & Berland Associates, 2009). But some people complain that televising trials distorts the process by encouraging the participants to play to the camera (Thaler, 1994). They also argue that by covering only sensational trials and presenting only the most dramatic moments of hours of testimony, television stations fail to portray the trial process accurately. And as recently as 2010, the U.S. Supreme Court expressed concern about the "the intimidating effect of cameras on some witnesses and jurors" (*Hollingsworth v. Perry*, 2010, p. 712).

Others argue that cameras in the courtroom have a valuable educational role, providing the public with a firsthand view of how court proceedings operate (Alexander, 1991; Raymond, 1992). As to the possibility of the camera's disrupting judicial proceedings, a detailed study in Florida concluded: "Broadcast journalists who follow state guidelines present coverage which, upon close examination by presiding judges, participating attorneys and jurors, is perceived as undistorted" (Alexander, 1991). But even if cameras do not alter courtroom proceedings, per se, research suggests that media coverage often distorts public understanding of judicial processes. "Television news in general (and trial news specifically) does not deploy imagery to reinforce public understanding, but to detract from it," thereby decreasing the civic value of such media coverage (Tilley, 2014, p. 738).

Current Broadcasting Rules

In 1996, the U.S. Judicial Conference adopted a resolution prohibiting electronic media coverage for all non-ceremonial proceedings in federal district courts but allowing each court of appeals to decide whether cameras should be allowed. As of this writing, only the Second and Ninth Circuits allow their proceedings to be broadcast. The Ninth Circuit has been at the forefront of using technology to enhance public access to the federal courts. In fact, "all 11 courtrooms in the four Ninth Circuit courthouses are video equipped" and in December 2013, the Ninth Circuit even started to stream its *en banc* hearings over the Internet (Public Information Office of the United States Courts for the Ninth Circuit, 2013, p. 2).

The Judicial Conference sponsored a pilot program starting in June 2011 that examined the use of cameras during civil proceedings in 14 district courts. In March of 2016, the Judicial Conference decided not to recommend any changes to the federal policy, although the pilot program will continue in 3 district courts within the Ninth Circuit.

Cameras are not permitted in the U.S. Supreme Court. Indeed, during the highly unusual three days of hearings that the U.S. Supreme Court devoted to reviewing President Obama's health care law, not only were television cameras banned as per the Court's usual rules, but all electronic devices were also banned, effectively preventing anyone in the courtroom from texting, e-mailing, or using social media such as Twitter or Facebook to send real-time updates about the arguments (see Ingram, 2012). However, the Court releases audio recordings of its courtroom proceedings each week and sometimes even on the same day as high-profile cases are heard.

Congress has proposed a series of bills that would allow electronic media coverage in federal judicial proceedings, but to date, none of these proposed pieces of legislation have been passed. Things are quite different, however, in state courts. Some states allow coverage of all judicial proceedings at the discretion of the presiding judge; other states allow broadcast only under certain circumstances, such as when all parties and witnesses consent; and still others limit coverage to appellate cases only (Cervantes, 2010; Marder, 2012; Patterson, 2015).

In most of the states that allow broadcast media coverage in courtrooms, there are specific restrictions designed to prevent disruptions of the proceedings. For example, the number of cameras in the courtroom is usually limited, and camera operators are prohibited from moving around the courtroom while the court is in session.

Technology Beyond "Cameras"

In May 2008, the California Supreme Court invalided state laws that limited marriage to opposite-sex couples (*In re Marriage Cases*, 2008). As a result, same-sex couples were able to be legally married in California. But in November 2008, by a 52-to-48-percent margin, voters passed Proposition 8, amending the California state constitution to prohibit the legal recognition of same-sex marriages in the state. In 2009, the constitutionality of Proposition 8 was then challenged on federal constructional law grounds. When the case came to a bench trial in January 2010, the presiding federal district judge, Vaughn R. Walker, authorized its "broadcast live via streaming audio and video to a number of federal courthouses around the country." By a 5-to-4 vote, the U.S. Supreme Court ordered Judge Walker to reverse his decision granting permission for the Proposition 8 trial to be digitally recorded and broadcast (*Hollingsworth v. Perry*, 2010). The Court found that the change in the local court rules that would have allowed for such a broadcast had occurred too quickly and without sufficient time for public comment.

Judge Walker ultimately allowed reporters to broadcast the trial through live "tweets" using Twitter. "Tweeters like '@FedCourt Junkie' were followed by more than a thousand people who wanted to stay instantly updated on the trial proceedings but who would not be able to actually go to the courtroom" (Cervantes, 2010, p. 134). Other courts have also embraced the use of Twitter as a means of increasing the transparency of the judicial process, but other courts disallow the use of all social media in their courtroom.

Misuse of Technology

Technology surely has the potential to assist the public in learning more about America's courts. But technology also poses a threat to the fairness of the trial process. Jurors are using smartphones to obtain information relevant to the case that was not actually presented or was expressly excluded from the jury (Schwartz, 2009a). In one widely reported case, a judge was forced to declare a mistrial after it was revealed that 8 of the 12 jurors used Google—some from home and some from cell phones—to conduct their own research on the defendants and the pharmaceutical medications discussed during trial. An appellate court in Maryland reversed a sexual assault conviction because a juror conducted Internet research on oppositional defiant disorder (the condition with which the defendant in the case had been diagnosed) and then shared her findings with other members of the jury (*Wardlow v. State*, 2009). To help minimize the changes of such misconduct, judges are advised to question jurors about their Internet and social media use during voir dire and to give cautionary instructions to jurors about the types of conduct in which they are prohibited from engaging. Anga (2013) advocated blocking all wireless Internet access during deliberations. Anga also suggested courts use social media to promote public service announcements that explain, in easy to understand language, "exactly what 'forbidden' use of the internet or social media means," as well as the consequences jurors face if they disregard a judge's orders regarding such Internet or social media usage.

Media Distortion

Even without any juror misconduct using technology, there is no question that media coverage of certain cases can distort the trial process (Tilley, 2014). Consider what one commentator had to say about cameras in the courtroom after the Casey Anthony trial (see Chapter 1):

> [T]he Casey Anthony case has made me realize the destructive nature of cameras in the courtroom. For months, Americans sat staring at their TV screens catching snippets of the Anthony trial. They saw only the best highlights from the arguments, the most compelling of the witness testimonies, and a host of evidence (only some of which was ever admitted in court and presented to the jury). Then Americans sat in their living rooms, pieced together everything they saw, and convicted Casey Anthony in the court of public opinion.... But twelve people sat in that courtroom for weeks and listened to every argument and heard every bit of testimony and saw only the admissible evidence. They sat and listened. Then they convened and discussed what they saw, and all of them agreed—unanimously—that they could not say beyond a reasonable doubt that Casey Anthony killed her daughter. It's pretty hard to get twelve people to agree on anything, but in this case they were all certain. They did not have enough evidence to convict Casey Anthony, even of manslaughter. (Ferguson, 2011, paras. 2–4).

Cases involving celebrities present even more challenging questions about how much information should be available to the public and what should be withheld. In 1995, the widely televised trial of O. J. Simpson clearly caused some rethinking about cameras in the courtroom. Perceptions that lawyers were playing to the cameras apparently had an impact in several highly publicized cases that followed. Ten years later, journalists complained that in the Michael Jackson child molestation case, the California judge sealed almost all of the records (Deutsch, 2004). In the rape trial of NBA star Kobe Bryant, the Colorado judge restricted inquiries into the alleged victim's prior sex life (Savage & Dolan, 2004). In short, celebrity justice cases force judges and the media to walk a fine line between full reporting and turning the case into a spectacle (Hubler, 2005).

New Technology as Evidence

Technological innovation has long shaped law enforcement. A relatively recent technological development, body-worn cameras (BWCs), has already changed modern policing in significant ways. Advocates of BWCs argue that they increase transparency and citizen views of police legitimacy, although these claims have not yet been sufficiently evaluated through empirical research (White, 2014). Advocates also assert that BWCs have a "civilizing effect" that reduces both police use of force and citizen complaints against police. This assertion is supported by several studies, although it is unclear whether these declines are "tied to improved citizen behavior, improved police officer behavior, or a combination of the two" (White, 2014, p. 6). Critics of police use of BWCs express concerns over the cost of purchasing the equipment and the resources needed for developing polices and training programs concerning the use of BWCs (see White, 2014).

Critics also cite privacy concerns for police and citizens alike. This concern is particularly palpable for victims of crimes whose contact with police may have been recorded. Concern over such footage being made public may cause victims to be unwilling to discuss their victimization with an officer who is wearing a BWC.

Lawmakers in several states have begun to address these privacy concerns in a number of ways. Some states have exempted BWC footage from public record requests; others limit the availability of footage taken in a private home or in a medical or social services facility (see Feeney, 2016). Several jurisdictions have established requirements for the storage, redaction, and eventual destruction of BWC footage, compliance with which can cost police departments millions of dollars.

BWC evidence also presents new challenges for the courts. Video evidence needs to be authenticated, and its **chain of custody** must be established. This can prove challenging if BWC footage is digitally stored, especially if stored "in the cloud," and many people have access to it (Hurley, 2016).

Even if admissibility requirements can be established, the interpretation of video evidence—including the inability to produce any such evidence because it was not recorded or it was destroyed—will undoubtedly cause problems for judges and jurors who weigh prosecutors and defense arguments about what the footage shows or would have shown (Hurley, 2016). Consider the following "negative inference" jury instruction from Arizona that may be given in a case in which BWC evidence is lost or destroyed:

> If you find that the State has lost, destroyed, or failed to preserve evidence whose contents or quality are important to the issues in this case, then you should weigh the explanation, if any, given for the loss or unavailability of the evidence. If you find that any such explanation is inadequate, then you may draw an inference unfavorable to the State, which in itself may create a reasonable doubt as to the defendant's guilt. (as cited in Hurley, 2016, p. 10)

Conclusion

After the initial screening of the venire in the case involving Michael Jackson's death, "every potential juror said they had some knowledge of the involuntary manslaughter case against Murray" (Ryan, 2011, para. 3). But an extensive questionnaire used to prescreen members of the venire led the judge to limit voir dire questioning to one minute per potential juror. In the end, the petit jury impaneled in the case took less than two days of deliberations to convict Murray, who was subsequently sentenced to imprisonment for four years.

In many ways, highly publicized jury trials for defendants like Jodi Arias, Governor Bob McDonnell, Conrad Murray, George Zimmerman, and Casey Anthony (see Chapter 1) are the high point of the judicial process. Indeed, along with Lady Justice, jury trials stand as the primary symbol of justice. In turn, many Supreme Court decisions emphasize the importance of adversarial procedures at trial. Yet, in examining the realities of trial, we are presented with two contradictory perspectives: Full-fledged trials are relatively rare, yet trials are an important dimension of the court process. Although only a smattering of cases are ever tried, the possibility of trial shapes the entire process. Thus, long after trials have declined to minimal importance in other Western nations, the institution of the jury trial remains a vital part of the American judicial process.

CHAPTER REVIEW

LO1 1. Trace the history of trials by jury.

The right to a trial by jury can be traced to the Magna Carta in 1215. This right was incorporated into Article III, Section 2, of the U.S. Constitution with respect to the federal government, and in the Sixth Amendment, with respect to the states.

LO2 2. Analyze the scope of the right to a trial by jury in a criminal case.

The right to a trial by jury applies to all nonpetty criminal offenses, usually interpreted as offenses punishable by a term of imprisonment of six months or more. The right may be waived by a defendant, who may opt for a bench trial in lieu of a jury trial.

LO3 3. Evaluate the impact of differences in jury size and unanimity requirements.

Common law juries have consisted of 12 people since the 14th century. The Supreme Court, however, authorized smaller juries in noncapital cases, but juries with less than 6 members are not permitted in criminal cases. Since that ruling, many states have specifically authorized juries of fewer than 12 jurors, but most allow these smaller juries only in misdemeanor cases. Some studies have found very few differences between 6- and 12-person juries, while others have reported significant differences.

LO4 4. Explain how a jury is summoned and selected, including the constitutional limitations on these processes.

Potential jurors are summoned to court using master jury lists. The people who are summoned, called the "venire," come

to court to participate in voir dire, a process designed to select a fair and impartial petit jury by asking members of the venire about potential biases concerning the case. Those who cannot serve as fair and impartial jurors are excused for cause. A few other members of the venire may be excused by either party using peremptory challenges so long as these challenges are not used in a discriminatory manner that violates the constitutional guarantee of equal protection.

LO5   5.   Discuss the function of jury consultants in the process of scientific jury selection.

Jury consultants use social scientific research methods to profile jurors in an attempt to help attorneys select members of the venire for petit jury service who are likely to be predisposed to their side of the case.

LO6   6.   Distinguish between the presumptions that apply at the start of trials and the burdens of proof applicable to overcoming them.

The two presumptions that apply to every criminal trial are the presumption of innocence and the presumption of sanity. It is the responsibility of the prosecution to introduce sufficient evidence over the course of a trial to overcome or rebut the presumption of innocence by proving a defendant's guilt beyond a reasonable doubt. In insanity defense cases, the defense usually must prove that the defendant was insane at the time of the commission of a crime by clear and convincing evidence.

LO7   7.   Summarize the basic rules of evidence concerning trustworthiness and relevance of evidence.

Only relevant evidence is admitted at trial—evidence that tends to prove or disprove a fact in dispute. Relevance, however, is not enough. Evidence must also be reliable. Thus, hearsay evidence, lay opinion, speculative testimony, and copies of documents (when originals are available) are generally all inadmissible.

LO8   8.   Analyze how special limitations on expert witnesses affect the litigation of criminal cases, especially with regard to leading types of forensic evidence.

Historically, and in some jurisdictions even today, expert testimony had to be based on scientific facts that were generally accepted in the relevant scientific community. However, under the *Daubert* standard, reliability is the linchpin to admissibility. Because the reliability of a number of forensic techniques is unknown, the continued use of these techniques has been called into question.

LO9   9.   Identify the steps in a criminal trial.

After a jury is selected through the voir dire process, the prosecution and then the defense usually deliver their respective opening statements. The prosecution then calls witnesses and conducts direct examination of its witnesses, some of whom will introduce physical or scientific evidence. The defense has the opportunity to cross-examine each of the prosecution's witnesses. When the prosecution rests, the defense may call its witnesses and introduce its evidence. The prosecution then has the opportunity to cross-examine the defense witnesses. At the conclusion of the trial, both parties make closing arguments. The judge instructs the jury with regard to the applicable law and then the jury deliberates until it reaches a verdict.

LO10   10. Describe the effects and implications of pretrial publicity and the solutions that courts use to prevent those effects from influencing a criminal trial.

Pretrial publicity can taint the potential jury pool by exposing them to information that is inaccurate or inadmissible as evidence. When that occurs, the defendant may be deprived of his or her Sixth Amendment right to a fair and impartial jury. To reduce the chances of the media tainting potential jurors, judges may issue limited gag orders forbidding those

involved in the case—police, prosecutor, defense attorney, and defendant—from talking to the press. But even still, venire members may have heard media reports that could have influenced their views on a case. The voir dire process is supposed to screen out potential jurors who have already been tainted. In high-profile cases, a change of venue might be necessary to find a pool of potential jurors who could render a fair and impartial verdict, free from the taint of pretrial publicity. During a trial, however, courts routinely instruct jurors not to read newspapers, magazines, or watch television news shows that may report on the trial. Sometimes, to shield jurors from such media influence, the jury may be sequestered.

CRITICAL THINKING QUESTIONS

1. What impact does the jury system have on the rest of the criminal justice system? How would criminal justice function differently if defendants had no right to a trial by a jury of their peers, which is the situation in virtually all of the non-common-law nations of the world?

2. If you are in a federal courthouse and observe a six-member jury, what type of case is being tried? How do you know this?

3. Compare two recent trials in your community. What were the similarities and differences in terms of jury selection, the prosecutor's case-in-chief, the defense strategy, and the verdict? If possible, compare a murder trial with one involving another major felony. In what ways is a murder trial different from, say, a trial for armed robbery or rape?

4. In the wake of the O. J. Simpson verdict of not guilty, many commentators spoke about the collapse of the jury system. Were these sentiments driven by the one verdict, or were there other reasons?

5. Why are some jury verdicts popular and others not? To what extent do differences of opinion over the fairness of a jury verdict reinforce notions that equate justice with winning?

KEY TERMS

acquittal   405

Allen charge   403

alternate jurors   388

bench trial   380

best-evidence rule   392

burden of persuasion   390

burden of production   390

burden of proof   390

chain of custody   411

challenge for cause   386

change of venue   408

charging conference   402

circumstantial evidence   390

closing argument   402

contempt of court   407

cross-examination   399

CSI effect   396

demonstrative evidence   391

direct evidence   390

direct examination   399

evidence   390

extralegal factors   404

gag order   407

hearsay   392

hung jury   403

impeach   401

irrelevant   392

jury consultants   389

jury deliberations   403

jury instructions   402

jury nullification   406

master jury list   383

mistrial   398

FOR FURTHER READING

Bornstein, Brian H., and Edie Greene. 2017. *The Jury Under Fire: Myth, Controversy, and Reform*. New York, NY: Oxford University Press.

Burns, Robert. 2009. *The Death of the American Trial*. Chicago, IL: University of Chicago Press.

Cherry, Michael, and Edward Imwinkelried. 2009. "Questions about the Accuracy of Fingerprint Evidence." *Judicature* 92: 158–159.

Devine, Dennis J. 2012. *Jury Decision Making: The State of the Science*. New York, NY: New York University Press.

Fisher, Jim. 2008. *Forensics under Fire: Are Bad Science and Dueling Experts Corrupting Criminal Justice?* New Brunswick, NJ: Rutgers University Press.

Kovera, Margaret Bull. 2017. *The Psychology of Juries*. Washington, DC: American Psychological Association.

Morrison, Caren Meyers. 2014. "Negotiating Peremptory Challenges." *Journal of Criminal Law & Criminology* 104: 1–58.

Murphy, Erin. 2015. *Inside the Cell: The Dark Side of Forensic DNA*. New York, NY: Nation Books.

National Academies of Sciences. 2009. *Strengthening Forensic Science in the United States: A Path Forward*. Washington, DC: National Research Council.

President's Council of Advisors on Science and Technology. 2016. Report to the President: Forensic Science in Criminal Courts: Ensuring Scientific Validity of Feature-Comparison Methods. https://obamawhitehouse.archives.gov/sites/default/files/microsites/ostp/PCAST/pcast_forensic_science_report_final.pdf

Robertson, Bernard, G. A. Vignaux, and Charles E. H. Berger. 2016. *Interpreting Evidence: Evaluating Forensic Science in the Courtroom*. West Sussex, UK: Wiley.

Russell, Brenda, Laurie Ragatz, and Shane Kraus. 2012. "Expert Testimony of the Battered Person Syndrome, Defendant Gender, and Sexual Orientation in a Case of Duress: Evaluating Legal Decisions." *Journal of Family Violence* 27: 659–670.

Ward, Frampton. 2012. "The Uneven Bulwark: How (and Why) Criminal Jury Trial Rates Vary by State." *California Law Review* 100: 183–222.

White, Michael D. 2014. *Police Officer Body Worn Cameras: Assessing the Evidence*. Washington, DC: U.S. Department of Justice, Office of Justice Programs, Diagnostic Center for Data-Driven Crime Solutions. https://www.ojpdiagnosticcenter.org/sites/default/files/spotlight/download/Police%20Officer%20Body-Worn%20Cameras.pdf

© Darrin Klimek/Jupiter Images

A man stands behind the bars of a prison cell. After prison populations reached an all-time high in the United States in 2006, many state prisons were so overcrowded that inmates won significant victories in federal courts, resulting in orders to improve the conditions of confinement on Eighth Amendment grounds.

Chapter Outline

When he was 17 years old, Christopher Simmons and a 15-year-old friend broke into a neighbor's house, hog-tied her with duct tape, and then shoved her over a railroad trestle into the Meramec River near St. Louis, Missouri. After the jury convicted Simmons of first-degree murder, it imposed the death penalty. The U.S. Supreme Court had earlier ruled that 17-year-olds could be put to death (*Stanford v. Kentucky*, 1989), but the rationale for that decision had been undermined when the Court declared that people with intellectual disabilities (formerly "mental retardation") could not be executed (*Atkins v. Virginia*, 2002). The Supreme Court ultimately reversed Simmons's sentence when it declared the Eighth Amendment prohibits the execution of offenders who were juveniles at the time they committed their crimes.

Learning Objectives

After reading this chapter, you should be able to:

LO1 Distinguish between the five major sentencing philosophies.

LO2 Describe how the three branches of government are involved in sentencing.

LO3 Recognize the main objective of changes in sentencing structure beginning in the late 1960s and the major consequences of these changes.

LO4 Outline how the U.S. Supreme Court has limited both state and federal sentencing guidelines.

LO5 Explain the law in action perspective on researching the impact of mandatory minimum sentences.

LO6 List at least three major issues related to imprisonment as a sentence in the United States.

LO7 Identify the major alternatives to imprisonment.

LO8 Summarize the two U.S. Supreme Court rulings from the 1970s on capital punishment that led to the bifurcated process for death penalty sentencing.

LO9 Indicate how the U.S. Supreme Court has narrowed the list of death-eligible cases and offenders.

LO10 Define the concept of normal penalties and indicate the two most important factors in determining normal penalties.

LO11 Distinguish between the concepts of sentencing disparities and discrimination.

Why Do We Punish?

No consensus exists on how the courts should punish the guilty, perhaps because five different philosophical principles guide sentencing in the United States: retribution, deterrence, rehabilitation, incapacitation, and restoration. These philosophies differ in important ways. Some focus on past behavior, whereas others are future oriented. Some stress that the punishment should fit the crime, whereas others emphasize that the punishment should fit the criminal.

Retribution

The idea that offenders deserve punishment lies at the heart of **retribution**. This philosophy toward criminal punishment can be traced back to ancient Babylonia in the Code of Hammurabi, one of the oldest written codifications of laws ever discovered. The code relied heavily on the principle of *lex talionis*—"an eye for an eye, a tooth for a tooth"—a revenge-based conceptualization of retributive punishment.

What is most distinctive about retribution is its focus on past behavior; the severity of the punishment is directly tied to the seriousness of the crime. This concept is based on strongly held moral principles: Individuals are held responsible for their own actions. Punishing wrongdoers in this manner reflects a desire for revenge: Because the victim has suffered, the criminal should suffer as well. But because society as a whole is punishing the criminal, individuals are not justified in taking the law into their own hands. Moreover, in applying retributive sanctions, the severity of the punishment is limited to the severity of the injury to the victim.

From biblical times through the 18th century, retribution provided the dominant justification for punishment. Beginning with the Enlightenment, however, revenge lost much of its influence as a justification for criminal punishment. In fact, criminal penalties based on revenge came to be viewed as barbaric. A new, more humane view of retribution evolved that focused on deserved punishment, or **just deserts**. It embodied two distinct but interrelated principles. First, the offender justly deserves to be punished for having wronged another person in violation of the law. Second, society has not only the right but also the obligation to punish proportionally all transgressions of the criminal law because such acts should be viewed as offenses against society as a whole (e.g., Kant, 1790). The approach to retributive punishment is alive and well in modern times (Gerber & Jackson, 2013; Wenzel & Okimoto, 2016).

The just deserts approach to retributive punishment is predicated on the notion of **proportionality**. It posits that the severity of the sanction should be proportionate to the gravity of the defendant's criminal conduct (Banks, 2009; Carlsmith, Darley, & Robinson, 2002; Wenzel & Okimoto, 2016).

Saint Augustine (c. 426) and, later, Saint Thomas Aquinas (c. 1273) and other theologians posited a third conceptualization of retribution based on **expiation**—atonement for sin through deserved suffering. In their opinion, retributive punishment should cause offenders to suffer, but not to achieve revenge or to balance the scales of justice for wrongs committed against individual victims or even society as a whole. Rather, through such

suffering, offenders would come to see the errors of their ways, repent, and, ultimately, be forgiven for their sins.

As a sentencing philosophy, retribution suffers from several limitations. Its focus on crimes of violence offers little apparent guidance for sentencing the far more numerous defendants who have committed property violations. Its moralistic emphasis on individual responsibility does not fit well with modern explanations of human behavior based on social, physical, and psychological factors (Flanders, 2014). Its emphasis on vengeance does not easily square with constitutional limits on governmental power (individual rights) that are fundamental to a representative democracy. Most important, though, it emphasizes the past behavior of the defendant and exhibits no concern for future criminal activity. Indeed, extended periods of custody may actually have unintended criminogenic effects, thereby increasing the likelihood that inmates might commit future criminal acts rather than be deterred by the sentence they received (see Austin & Hardyman, 2004). Thus, sentencing on the basis of retribution may prove to be contrary to the goal of crime reduction.

Deterrence

"Let this sentence be a warning to others." Phrases like this reflect one of the more modern and also most widely held justifications for punishment. According to **deterrence theory**, the purpose of punishment is the prevention of future crimes. Deterrence is not content to punish the given wrongdoer; rather, it seeks to prevent other potential offenders from committing crimes. Deterrence, however, does not propose to change offenders—just deter them.

Building on the work of 18th-century criminologist Cesare Beccaria (1764), Jeremy Bentham, a 19th-century British lawyer, reformer, and criminologist, articulated a coherent theory of deterrence (1830) that still influences us today. To Bentham, punishment based on retribution was pointless and counterproductive. Instead, he argued that sanctions should be used to further society's goal of preventing crime. Bentham believed that human behavior is governed by individual calculation: People seek to maximize pleasure and minimize pain—a principle he referred to as the **hedonistic calculus**. Under this utilitarian theory, the basic objective of punishment is to discourage crime by making it painful. Because people seek to minimize pain, they will refrain from activities, such as crimes, that result in painful sanctions.

Deterrence theory suggests that the criminal justice system can effectuate two types of deterrence: general and specific. The **general deterrence** goal of criminal punishment presumes that the threat of punishment will prevent the general population from engaging in the proscribed conduct. The **specific deterrence** goal of criminal punishment postulates that those for whom the general deterrent of law was insufficient to prevent them from having engaged in the proscribed conduct should be subjected to punishment so that they will be personally discouraged from engaging in the proscribed conduct again.

Much scholarly research has demonstrated that the effectiveness of law as a deterrent is dependent on three primary factors: severity, certainty, and celerity (i.e., swiftness). **Severity of punishment** is concerned with how severe the punishment is. The theory postulates that the more severe the punishment, the less likely the actor is to engage in the proscribed conduct. The **certainty of punishment** is concerned with how likely the actor is to get away with the crime as opposed to being caught. According to deterrence theory, the more likely it is that the actor is going to be caught, the less likely he or she is to engage in the conduct. Finally, the **celerity of punishment** considers the swiftness of punishment. The theory suggests that the faster the punishment is inflicted after the offense, the less likely the person is to engage in the proscribed conduct. Conversely, the later or further off the punishment, the less likely is the person to be deterred.

Notions of deterrence form the core of contemporary discussions about sentencing. In a general sense, many people refrain from committing illegal acts because they fear the consequences of being convicted. However, one of the most significant shortcomings of deterrence theory is the following: the threat of severe, certain, and swift punishment is likely to deter only those who are thinking rationally. Those who are thinking irrationally (whether due to mental illness, disability, the effects of drugs or alcohol, or other reasons) are unlikely to be deterred because their abilities to engage in the hedonistic calculus are impaired. This is particularly true for many crimes of violence that are committed on the spur of the moment or during the "heat of passion."

An extensive literature examines deterrence but reaches no firm conclusions. Some studies find a deterrent effect, and others do not (Levitt, 2006; Nagin, 1998; Webster, Doob, & Zimring, 2006). Although discussions of deterrence are usually coupled with calls for increasing the severity of sentences, some research suggests that the perceived certainty of punishment is more of a deterrent than the perceived severity of punishment (Cullen, Wright, & Blevins, 2006; Wilson, 1983). Moreover, because deterrence rests on the assumption of rational, calculating behavior, and this precondition is absent in many crimes (as described above), many observers question whether court sentences—particularly severe ones—do indeed deter.

Rehabilitation

Another modern justification for imposing punishment concerns helping offenders assume a constructive place in society through vocational, educational, or therapeutic treatment. The idea of **rehabilitation** assumes that criminal behavior is the result of social or psychological disorders, and that the treatment of such disorders should be the primary goal of corrections. Success means assessing the needs of the individual and providing a program to meet those needs. Ultimately, then, offenders are not being punished but are treated, not only for their own good but also for the benefit of society. Under rehabilitation, sentences should fit the offender rather than the offense.

The concept of rehabilitation dominated thinking about sentencing throughout much of the 20th century, providing the intellectual linchpin for important developments such as probation and parole, as well as the concept of **pretrial diversion**—an alternative to prosecution that seeks to divert certain offenders from traditional criminal justice processing into programs of supervision and rehabilitative services. Most court personnel and correctional officials have strongly favored rehabilitation. It has also enjoyed widespread public support; almost three out of four persons favor the idea that the main emphasis in prisons should be to help the offender become a productive citizen.

Starting in the mid-1970s, evidence revealed that rehabilitative programs did not substantially reduce the later criminality of their clients (Blumstein, Cohen, Martin, & Tonry, 1983; Martinson, 1974). California, for example, where the rehabilitative model had been most completely incorporated, was also marked by high rates of *recidivism* (repeat criminal behavior). To some, the key weakness of rehabilitation is that people cannot be coerced to change. Some prisoners participate in prison rehabilitation programs, such as counseling, job training, and religious services, in order to gain an early release—not because they wish to change their behavior.

More recently, though, empirical studies have found that rehabilitation can indeed be effective (see Cullen, 2005, 2013). Much of the research supporting the rehabilitative model comes from studies that have evaluated the effectiveness of different correctional interventions. An ever-growing number of modern correctional policies are being crafted in light of the empirical evidence produced by these evaluation studies, a movement called **evidence-based corrections** (MacKenzie, 2006; Robinson, 2008). As a result, resources are being put into interventions that research has demonstrated to be effective, such as "using behavioral and cognitive approaches, occurring in the offenders' natural environment, being multi-modal and intensive enough to be effective, encompassing rewards for pro-social behavior, targeting high-risk and high-criminogenic need individuals, and matching the learning styles and abilities of the offender" (Listwan, Cullen, & Latessa, 2006, p. 20). In contrast, rehabilitative strategies that have proven to be largely ineffective, such as psychodynamic therapies and "scared straight" programs, are slowly being abandoned (Cullen, Blevins, & Trager, 2005; MacKenzie, 2006).

The reemergence of rehabilitation as a viable basis for criminal punishment was also fueled by the severe economic downturn in the later part of the first decade of the 21st century. The extremely high costs of incarcerating so many people—especially nonviolent drug offenders—caused many commentators to question the sustainability of the punitive, "get tough" policies of the 1980s and 1990s (Steen & Bandy, 2007). In other words, from a cost-benefit standpoint, the harsh economic reality of the prison-industrial complex has led to a renewed focus on rehabilitative strategies (Abrams, 2013; Robinson, 2008).

Incapacitation

"Lock them up and throw away the key." Average citizens, outraged by a recent, shocking crime, often express sentiments like this. The assumption of **incapacitation** is that crime can be prevented if criminals are physically restrained. The theory of isolating current or potential criminals differs from the theory of retribution in two important ways. First, it is future oriented: the goal is to prevent future crimes, not punish past ones. Second, it focuses on the personal characteristics of the offender: the type of person committing the crime is more important than the crime committed. Unlike rehabilitation, however, incapacitation has no intention of reforming the offender. Instead, since ancient times, societies have banished or imprisoned persons who have disobeyed the rules.

As a sentencing philosophy, incapacitation suffers from important limitations. It cannot provide any standards about how long a sentence should be. Moreover, isolation without efforts directed toward rehabilitation may produce more severe criminal behavior once the offender is released. Prisons protect the community, but that protection is only temporary. Applying the incapacitation theory to the fullest would require the building of many more prisons, at great expense.

The incapacitation theory of sentencing has never been well articulated. Its assumptions about crime and criminals are simplistic. But in recent years a more focused variant, **selective incapacitation**, has received considerable attention

(Goodman-Delahunty, Forster Lee, & Forster Lee, 2007). Research has shown that a relatively small number of criminals are responsible for a large number of crimes (DeLisi, 2005; Haapanen, 1989). These findings have led to an interest in targeting dangerous offenders (Chaiken & Chaiken, 1990). Some studies estimate that sending serious offenders to prison for longer periods of time will result in a significant reduction in crime (Shinnar & Shinnar, 1975; Spelman, 2000). Not all researchers agree, however, that selective incapacitation will greatly reduce crime because predictions of who will commit crimes in the future are very unreliable (Auerhahn, 2006; Bragaric, 2014; Cunningham, Reidy, & Sorensen, 2008). "Offenders commit crimes at different rates and individuals' offending rates evolve over their life course. Therefore, estimating how many crimes are averted . . . must depend crucially on when in individuals' lives and at what point in their criminal careers the incarceration occurs" (Bhati, 2007, p. 357). Moreover, critics argue that even though some offenders may be incapacitated through imprisonment, other people on the verge of criminality are ready to take their places (Auerhahn, 1999; Visher, 1987). And still other critics argue that the costs of imprisonment typically exceed the benefits gained from preventing certain criminals from recidivating by keeping them incapacitated (Blokland & Nieuwbeerta, 2007).

Restoration

After imposing a prison sentence on a rapist, an Australian judge observed a victim who remained as upset as she had been throughout all of the judicial proceedings. So, he asked her to approach the bench. Speaking quietly, he said, "You understand that what I have done here demonstrates conclusively that *what happened was not your fault.*" Hearing these words, she burst into tears and ran from the courtroom. Several days later, he called the family and learned that his words provided a sense of "vindication for the woman; they marked the beginning of her psychological recovery. Her tears had been tears of healing" (Van Ness & Strong, 2006, p. 3).

The restorative justice movement seeks to replace retribution with **restoration**. Restorative justice is based on three distinct elements (Galaway & Hudson, 1996):

1. Crime is primarily a conflict between individuals, which results in injuries (physical and/or psychological) to victims, the community, and the offender as well. Therefore, crime is only secondarily a violation of governmental laws.

2. The principal aim of the criminal justice system should be to repair these injuries. Therefore, promoting peace and reconciling parties is much more important than punishing the guilty.

3. The criminal justice system should facilitate involvement of victims, offenders, and the community. Therefore, lay citizens should play a central role in the criminal justice system, and professionals (police, prosecutors, and probation officers, for example) should play less of a role.

Proponents of restorative justice reject retributive punishment because they view vengeance as counterproductive. Similarly, they see the rehabilitative model as being too narrow—targeting offenders but providing no healing for victims.

Skeptics voice concern that restorative justice means considerably different things to different people. Indeed, by stressing abstract concepts rather than pointing to specific programs, proponents make it somewhat difficult to discuss restorative justice because many of the examples singled out as demonstrating successful implementation are drawn from other countries.

Restorative justice programs have become increasingly common in the justice system, but relatively little is known about their effectiveness. Some of the early studies have been characterized as using weak research designs. A rigorous study of the Indianapolis Restorative Justice Experiment is important, therefore, because the results were largely positive. Youths who were assigned to family group conferences (as opposed to a control group) were less likely to be rearrested (McGarrell & Hipple, 2008).

Competing Sentencing Philosophies

Of the five major philosophies outlined above—retribution, incapacitation, deterrence, rehabilitation, and restoration—none alone is adequate; the various goals must be balanced. Therefore, elements of each of these philosophies have been incorporated into society's efforts to control crime. As a result, sentencing decisions reflect ambivalent expectations about the causes of crime, the nature of criminals, and the role of the courts in reducing crime. Moreover, debates about the morality and effectiveness of each philosophical perspective resulted in widespread sentencing reforms, many of which focus on who should have the authority to impose a sentence and what limits should be placed on that authority.

Who Should Decide the Sentence?

From the inside looking out, sentencing is a judicial function. With a few exceptions, only the judge has the legal authority to send the guilty to prison or to grant probation. From the outside looking in, however, sentencing responsibility involves all three branches of government—legislative, executive, and judicial.

Throughout most of the 20th century, sentencing was exercised within broad limits set by the legislature, which prescribed maximum sentences. The judicial branch of government had primary authority over who went to prison, and an executive agency—**parole boards**—controlled the length of the prison term. Since the mid-1970s, dramatic changes have been made in the laws under which offenders are sent to prison and in the mechanisms that control how long they stay there. Legislatures have increased their control over the sentencing process, and the judiciary and the parole boards have taken steps to formalize and regularize their exercise of discretion in applying sanctions. The result has been a significant narrowing of sentencing discretion in most states.

Legislative Sentencing Responsibility

Legislatures are initially responsible for creating sentencing options in the criminal codes they enact. Legislatures specify terms of imprisonment in different ways. Consistent with the goal of rehabilitation, which dominated correctional thinking through most of the 20th century, state legislatures adopted **indeterminate sentences** (often called *indefinite sentences*), based on the idea that correctional personnel must have discretion to release an offender when treatment has been successful. States with indeterminate sentences stipulate a minimum and maximum amount of time to be served in prison—1 to 5 years, 3 to 10 years, 20 years to life, and so on. At the time of sentencing, the offender knows the range of the sentence and knows that parole is a possibility after the minimum sentence, minus good time (discussed below), has been served. How long the person actually remains in prison is determined by the parole authority, based on its assessment of the offender's progress toward rehabilitation.

Because of the growing disillusionment with the rehabilitative model in the 1970s, along with evidence that indeterminate sentences often produced disparate sentencing outcomes for similar crimes (discussed in more detail later in this chapter), determinate sentences grew in popularity. **Determinate sentences** (sometimes called *fixed sentences*) consist of a specified number of years rather than a range of years.

Judicial Sentencing Responsibility

Although other members of the courtroom work group may recommend a criminal sentence (especially probation officers), with limited exceptions, only a judge has the authority to choose among the sentencing options provided by the legislature. Wide judicial discretion in sentencing reflects the rehabilitative model, which stresses that the punishment should fit the criminal. No two crimes or criminals are exactly alike; sentences should therefore be individualized, with judges taking these differences into account. But no agreement has been reached on what factors should increase or reduce the penalty.

By the mid-1970s, wide judicial discretion had come under attack from both ends of the political spectrum. Advocates of the due process model of criminal justice expressed concern that judicial sentencing discretion was too broad, resulting in inequities such as racial discrimination. Conversely, proponents of the crime control model expressed concern that too much judicial discretion led to unduly lenient sentences. These two political movements, although contradictory, led legislatures to greatly reduce judicial sentencing discretion. Thus, an increasing number of jurisdictions are narrowing judicial discretion over sentencing in some manner.

Executive Sentencing Responsibility

Sentences imposed by judges are typically carried out by officials of the executive branch. Of particular importance is the impact of executive officials on prison populations. How long an offender will be imprisoned depends not only on the length of the sentence imposed by the judge but also on the decisions made by governors, parole boards, and departments of corrections. Only about one-third of prisoners serve their full sentences and are then released unconditionally. The remaining two-thirds of prisoners are conditionally released from prison to serve the balance of their sentences in the community as a function of one of three early release programs: parole, good time, and (to a much lesser extent) executive clemency.

Parole is the conditional release of an inmate from incarceration, under supervision, after a portion of the prison sentence has been served. A parole officer supervises the conditions of release, and any rule violations or new crimes can result in a return to prison for the balance of the unexpired term. Parole boards, which are usually appointed by the governor, vary greatly in their discretionary authority. Approximately 870,500 persons are currently on parole in the United States (Kaeble & Bonczar, 2017).

Another way in which decisions made by the executive branch affect how long an inmate must stay in prison is **good time**; in many states, prisoners are awarded days off their minimum or maximum terms as a reward for good behavior or for participation in various vocational, educational, and treatment programs. The amount of good time that can be earned varies from 5 days a month to 45 days a month in some states. Correctional officials find these sentence-reduction provisions necessary for the maintenance of institutional order and as a mechanism to reduce overcrowding. They usually have discretion in awarding good time.

State governors, as well as the president of the United States, have the power to pardon any prisoner in their respective jurisdictions, reduce sentences, or make prisoners eligible for parole (Moore, 1989; Ruckman, 1997). **Pardons** are not a common method of prisoner release, however; only a small group of inmates receive executive clemency each year.

The failure rate for ex-prisoners, whether released on parole or after the expiration of their sentence, is dishearteningly high (Wallman, 2005). Each year more than two-thirds of the inmates who return to their communities are likely to be rearrested within three years (Mears, Wang, Hay, & Bales, 2008). Considerable attention is now being paid to prisoner reentry (James, 2015; MacKenzie, 2006; National Governors Association, 2010; Travis, 2005). Whether high failure rates are the result of bad behavior on the part of the ex-prisoners or bad public policy is an open question (Wilson, 2005).

The Courtroom Work Group and Sentencing Decisions

As the previous section should make clear, sentencing is a joint decision-making process. Although only judges possess the legal authority to impose a sentence, other members of the courtroom work group are also influential (Reitler & Frank, 2014). The extent of this influence varies from jurisdiction to jurisdiction and from judge to judge. Where sentence bargaining predominates, for example, the judge almost invariably imposes the sentence that the prosecutor and defense attorney have already agreed upon. Where count and charge bargaining are used, the actors reach agreements based on past sentencing patterns of the judge. The most significant actors in sentencing are probation officers, prosecutors, defense attorneys, and (of course) judges.

Probation Officers

Probation officers typically perform two or three critical functions in the sentencing process: conducting the presentence investigation prior to sentencing, reporting the findings of that investigation to the court, and, in some courts, making a sentencing recommendation to the judge.

The primary purpose of a **presentence investigation (PSI)** is to help the judge select an appropriate sentence by providing information about the crime and the criminal. Most often, the PSI is ordered by the court following the defendant's conviction. A date is set for sentencing the offender, and meanwhile the probation officer conducts the investigation. The presentence report is designed to give the judge, who must select the proper sentence, an appropriate database. This is particularly important when the defendant has entered a plea of guilty, because in these cases the judge knows little about the particulars of the crime or the background of the offender. Ultimately, the goal of PSIs is to allow the judge to make an informed sentencing decision that balances risk-management of the offender (the safety of the community if the defendant is not incarcerated) with rehabilitative reasons to allow the defendant to remain in the community under supervision.

In order to gather the information needed to prepare a comprehensive PSI report, probation officers need to review a variety of records and reports to obtain information on the offender's prior criminal record, financial situation, social history (education, employment history, military service, prior performance on probation or parole, marital status, family relationships, residence history, and so on), and medical and psychological history. Probation officers also conduct interviews with the defendant, the defendant's family, police, the victim, and other people in the defendant's life who might shed light on the suitability of a particular sentencing recommendation, such as friends, teachers, employers (and sometimes co-workers), and clergy members.

Some jurisdictions attempt to employ *evidence-based sentencing* by using risk assessment instruments that have been validated by empirical research to help determine whether a particular defendant would be a suitable candidate for a particular correctional rehabilitation or treatment program (Gleicher, Manchak, & Cullen, 2013; Monahan & Skeem, 2016). A few states, notably Virginia and Arizona, pioneered incorporating such risk assessment into their presentence investigation processes (Warren, 2009). A few other states have followed their lead, successfully reducing incarceration rates, recidivism, and correctional expenditures through sentencing offenders to interventions tailored to meet their rehabilitative needs (Aos, Miller, & Drake, 2006; Kimora, 2008; Warren, 2009).

In the federal court system and those of many states, PSI reports can be quite long and detailed. In other courts, short-form PSIs are commonplace, especially as sentencing systems have become more determinate. And in some states, "PSIs are no longer required at all, having been replaced by worksheets that calculate prescribed sentences under statutory or administrative guidelines" (Warren, 2009, p. 608).

Exhibit 14.1 presents a sample PSI that is quite short. In some jurisdictions, short-form PSI reports contain mostly check marks on a standardized form with even less narrative than is provided in the sample presented in Exhibit 14.1.

Beyond providing background information, many presentence reports also include a recommendation for an appropriate sentence. If probation is recommended, the report usually includes a suggested level of supervision (ranging from intensive through regular to minimal), a listing of special conditions of probation, a plan for treatment, and an assessment of community resources available to facilitate rehabilitation. In contrast, if incarceration is recommended, the PSI can assist staff in jails and prisons to classify the offender and make appropriate plans for his or her custody and rehabilitation. In making a sentencing recommendation, probation officers in some jurisdictions must

EXHIBIT 14.1	Sample PSI Report

State of New Mexico
Corrections Department
Field Service Division
Santa Fe, New Mexico 87501
Date: January 4, 2010
To: The Honorable Manuel Baca
From: Presentence Unit, Officer Brian Gaines
Re: Richard Knight

Appearing before Your Honor for sentencing is 20-year-old Richard Knight who, on November 10, 2009, pursuant to a Plea and Disposition Agreement, entered a plea of guilty to Aggravated Assault Upon a Peace Officer (Deadly Weapon) (Firearm Enhancement), as charged in Information Number 10-5736900. The terms of the agreement stipulate that the maximum period of incarceration be limited to one year, that restitution be made on all counts and charges whether dismissed or not, and that all remaining charges in the Indictment and DA Files 39780 be dismissed.

PRIOR RECORD

The defendant has no previous convictions. An arrest at age 15 for disorderly conduct was dismissed after six months of "informal probation."

EVALUATION

The defendant is an only child, born and raised in Albuquerque. He attended West Mesa High School until the 11th grade, at which time he dropped out. Richard declared that he felt school was "too difficult" and that he decided that it would be more beneficial for him to obtain steady employment rather than to complete his education. The defendant further stated that he felt it was "too late for vocational training" because of the impending one-year prison sentence he faces, due to the Firearm Enhancement penalty for his offense.

The longest period of time the defendant has held a job has been for six months with Frank's Concrete Company. He has been employed with the Madrid Construction Company since August 2008 (verified). Richard lives with his parents, who provide most of his financial support. Conflicts between his mother and himself, the defendant claimed, precipitated his recent lawless actions by causing him to "not care about anything." He stressed the fact that he is now once again "getting along" with his mother. Although the defendant contended that he doesn't abuse drugs, he later contradicted himself by declaring that he "gets drunk every weekend." He noted that he was inebriated when he committed the present offense.

In regard to the present offense, the defendant recalled that other individuals at the party attempted to stab his friend and that he and his companion left and returned with a gun in order to settle the score. Richard claimed remorse for his offense and stated that his past family problems led him to spend most of his time on the streets, where he became more prone to violent conduct. The defendant admitted being a member of the 18th Street Gang.

RECOMMENDATION

It is respectfully recommended that the defendant be sentenced to three years incarceration and that the sentence be suspended. It is further recommended that the defendant be incarcerated for one year as to the mandatory Firearm Enhancement and then placed on three years' probation under the following special conditions:

1. That restitution be made to Juan Lopez in the amount of $662.40
2. That the defendant either maintain full-time employment or obtain his GED [general equivalency diploma]
3. That the defendant discontinue fraternizing with the 18th Street Gang members and terminate his own membership in the gang

---

use a state's sentencing guidelines scores to determine if the offender is appropriate for probation or prison. More details on sentencing guidelines are presented later in this chapter.

Probation officers clearly play a significant role in the sentencing process. Judges are very likely to impose the sentence recommended in the PSI. Indeed, one study found a 95 percent rate of agreement between the judge and the probation report when probation was recommended and an 88 percent rate of agreement when the report opposed probation (Carter & Wilkins, 1967; see also Freiburger & Hilinski, 2011; Norman & Wadman, 2000). Studies have replicated these results with respect to first-time offenders, but found that probation officers recommended incarceration for recidivists almost twice as often as judges imposed it (Campbell, McCoy, & Osigweh, 1990; Hagan, 1977). Thus, although sentencing judges are not required to follow such recommendations, they usually do.

However, considerable disagreement exists over the actual influence of probation officers in the sentencing process. Some studies suggest that judges seriously consider the recommendations and use them to guide their decisions—that judges lean heavily on the professional advice of probation officers (David, 1980; Walsh, 1985). Others report that judges skim these reports and read only the sections they deem most important (Leiber, Reitzel, & Mack, 2011; Norman & Wadman, 2000; Rush & Robertson, 1987). And still other researchers argue that probation officers have little real influence on the sentencing process—that probation recommendations have been supplanted by plea bargaining (Clear, Harris, & Baird, 1992). By and large, recommendations by probation officers "do not influence judicial sentencing significantly but serve to maintain the myth that criminal courts dispense individual justice" (Rosencrance, 2004). This, however, may be changing because of the evidence-based corrections movement.

Prosecutors

Prosecutors influence the sentencing decision in several important ways. By agreeing to a count or charge bargain, prosecutors limit the maximum penalty the judge may impose. During the sentencing hearing, prosecutors can bring to the court's attention factors that are likely to increase the penalty—for example, that the victim was particularly vulnerable or that the defendant inflicted great harm on the victim. Alternatively, prosecutors can bring out factors that would lessen the penalty—for example, the defendant's cooperation with the police.

Finally, prosecutors may make a specific sentencing recommendation. If, for example, there has been a sentence bargain, the prosecutor will indicate the penalty agreed on, and the judge will usually adopt that recommendation as the sentence. When such prosecutorial recommendations are based on office policy, they can have the positive effect of muting sentencing disparities among the different judges. In some courts, however, prosecutors are not allowed to make sentencing recommendations, because sentencing is viewed solely as a judicial responsibility.

As we will discuss in detail later in this chapter, sentencing guidelines generally constrain judicial discretion in sentencing. As a result, many researchers have concluded that the sentencing discretion that was once firmly vested with judges in the sentencing phase of the criminal justice process has shifted to prosecutors at the preconviction phase, especially through the exercise of prosecutorial discretion in charging and plea bargaining decisions (e.g., McCoy, 1984; Nagel & Schulhofer, 1992; Pfaff, 2017). This power was most evident in the context of crimes that carried mandatory sentences since the charging decision all but dictated the sentence, rendering prosecutors with what Berman (2010, p. 429) called "first-look sentencers."

Empirical studies of such displacement have indeed found that prosecutorial behavior has changed as they gained more ability to control sentencing through earlier decision making in the process, but that the shift has been modest, not monumental (Miethe, 1987; Vance & Oleson, 2014; Wooldredge & Griffin, 2005). Nonetheless, there can be little doubt that prosecutors play a significant role in sentencing throughout the entirety of the criminal judicial process.

Defense Attorneys

The defense attorney's role in sentencing begins early in the history of a case. The decision whether to go to trial or to enter a guilty plea is partially based on the attorney's assessment of the sentence likely to be imposed. Based on the knowledge of what sentences have been handed out to past defendants accused of similar crimes and with similar backgrounds, the attorney must advise the client as to the probable sentence.

At the same time, the defense attorney seeks to obtain the lightest sentence possible. One way to accomplish this goal is to maneuver the case before a judge with a lenient sentencing record. Another way is to discuss the case with the prosecutor in hopes that he or she will agree to (or at least not oppose) a recommendation of probation in the presentence investigation. Defense attorneys also try to emphasize certain circumstances that make the defendant look better in the eyes of the judge, prosecutor, and probation officer. They may try to downplay the severity of the offense by stressing the defendant's minor role in the crime or the fact that the victim was not without blame; or they may have friends or employers testify about the defendant's general good character and regular employment.

Overall, though, defense attorneys are less influential than prosecutors. Judges and prosecutors typically view defense attorneys' arguments for leniency as efforts to impress their clients with the fact that they tried as hard as they could. Huck and Lee (2014) reported that judges view defense attorneys less favorably and as being less cooperative than prosecutors. Thus, judges do not value defense attorneys' "opinions or information as highly as other courtroom participants," especially at sentencing (p. 201). As a result, judges do not care as much about pleasing defense attorneys with favorable sentencing outcomes as they care about pleasing prosecutors.

Judges

Courtroom work groups impose informal limits on how judges exercise their formal legal authority to impose sentences (Walker, 2015). Judges are well aware that the disposition of cases is related to plea bargaining, which in turn depends on being able to anticipate the sentencing tendencies of judges. Judges share in a framework of understandings, expectations, and agreements that are relied on to dispose of most criminal cases. If a judge strays too far from expectations by imposing a sentence substantially more lenient or more severe than the one agreed on by the defendant, defense lawyer, and prosecutor, it becomes more difficult for the prosecutor and defense counsel to negotiate future agreements.

In working within the limits established by the consensus of the courtroom work group, judges are also constrained because the other members of the work group have more thorough knowledge about the details of the defendant and the nature of the crime. In particular, a judge's sentencing decision is restricted by the bargains struck between prosecution and defense. Indeed, judges who enjoy stable relationships with the prosecutors who practice before them are more likely to defer to those prosecutors' sentencing recommendations (see Huck & Lee, 2014).

Judges, though, are not without influence. They are the most experienced members of the courtroom team, so their views carry more weight than those of relatively inexperienced prosecutors or defense attorneys. The particular judge's attitudes about sentencing are reflected in the courtroom work group's common understanding of what sentences are appropriate.

Changing Sentencing Structures

During the late 1960s and early 1970s, an unusual (and temporary) political coalition developed between liberals and conservatives. Both sides found considerable fault in existing sentencing practices. Although their reasons reflected fundamentally different concerns, liberals and conservatives defined the problem in similar terms: The criminal laws permitted too much latitude in sentencing, providing judges with little or no guidance on how to determine the proper sentence for each individual case. This coalition therefore sought greater predictability in sentencing. The result was a fundamental change in how defendants are sentenced.

Law in Controversy: Reducing Judicial Discretion

Adherents of the due process model were concerned that excessive discretion resulted in a lack of fairness in sentencing. They perceived that criminal justice officials, ranging from police officers to parole boards, were making decisions in a discriminatory manner, especially on the basis of race. They were also concerned that judges' sentencing discretion resulted in sentencing disparities. Thus, the political left saw determinate sentences as a means of reducing individual discretion and thereby (presumably) reducing disparity and discrimination (e.g., Frankel, 1972; von Hirsch, 1976).

Adherents of the crime control model were far more concerned that excessive discretion resulted in a lack of effective crime control. They perceived that criminal justice officials were making decisions that produced undue leniency. Concern about disparity or discrimination was not part of the agenda. In particular, they viewed trial judges as all too ready to impose sentences well below the statutory maximum. They perceived that parole boards were too willing to release prisoners early; they were shocked that prisoners were back on the streets on parole well before the maximum sentence had expired. To conservatives, the essential problem was that sentencing was not reducing crime (e.g., Wilson, 1975). In an effort to make sentencing more effective, a "justice" model of sentencing came into increasing prominence. Wrongdoers should be punished on the principle of just deserts, which implies a certainty and uniformity of punishment.

Law on the Books: Variations of Determinate Sentencing Return

In response to criticisms of the rehabilitation model, with its emphasis on indeterminate sentences and discretionary parole release, a number of states returned to sentencing schemes intended to provide more legislative control over imprisonment decisions. The systems put in place are based on the assumption that judges should give offenders a specific amount of time to serve rather than an indeterminate period of incarceration between some minimum and maximum sentence. But the varying approaches to doing so use different means to accomplish the desired ends. **Structured sentencing** schemes target sentencing decisions by judges. In contrast, true **determinate sentencing** schemes control release decisions, usually by abolishing boards and requiring offenders be released after

serving the term imposed (or a high percentage of the term imposed, such as 85 percent), less any reductions through "good time" credits and similar programs (Stemen & Rengifo, 2011).

Structured Sentencing Schemes

Early efforts to impose structured sentencing suffered from a serious weakness: Legislative bodies had neither the time nor the skills to enact detailed sentencing rules. Therefore, since the 1980s, efforts to provide certainty and consistency in sentencing have taken a different form. Legislatures have created commissions to devise detailed sentencing rules, and the legislatures have then enacted these guidelines into law (Griset, 1995).

Presumptive Sentencing in the States

Under unstructured sentencing law, states typically provided a wide sentencing range for felony offenses. For example, a judge might be authorized to impose a sentence of 2 to 10 years. To reduce judicial discretion and sentencing disparities, some states opted to put in place a series of **presumptive sentences**. Under this approach, legislatures specified a presumptive term of imprisonment for a particular criminal offense. Thus, instead of an indeterminate term of 2 to 10 years, a presumptive sentence of 4 years' imprisonment would be specified for a particular felony. Judges may legally impose a term different from the recommended term only by finding aggravating or mitigating circumstances. Departures are reviewable on appeal to ensure that presumptive sentences are followed.

This approach to sentencing is based solely on the offense committed. Presumptive sentences do not take into account variations in offenders' backgrounds. This led only seven states to adopt presumptive sentencing schemes between 1975 and 2004 (Stemen & Rengifo, 2011). Many more states opted for a different approach to sentencing reform: sentencing guidelines.

State Sentencing Guidelines

Statewide **sentencing guidelines** are mentioned most frequently as the procedures for ensuring fairness and appropriate severity in sentencing. Twenty-one states adopted sentencing guidelines between 1975 and 2004 (Kauder & Ostrom, 2008), and other states seriously considered this approach (Reitz, 2001).

Sentencing guidelines direct the judge to specific actions that should be taken. The sample

Severity Level of Conviction Offense (Common offenses listed in italics)		Criminal History Score						
		0	**1**	**2**	**3**	**4**	**5**	**6 or more**
Murder, 2nd Degree (intentional murder; drive-by-shootings)	**XI**	306 261-367	326 278-391	346 295-415	366 312-439	386 329-463	406 346-480[2]	426 363-480[2]
Murder, 3rd Degree Murder, 2nd Degree (unintentional murder)	**X**	150 128-180	165 141-198	180 153-216	195 166-234	210 179-252	225 192-270	240 204-288
Assault, 1st Degree Controlled Substance Crime, 1st Degree	**IX**	86 74-103	98 84-117	110 94-132	122 104-146	134 114-160	146 125-175	158 135-189
Aggravated Robbery, 1st Degree Controlled Substance Crime, 2nd Degree	**VIII**	48 41-57	58 50-69	68 58-81	78 67-93	88 75-105	98 84-117	108 92-129
Felony DWI	**VII**	36	42	48	54 46-64	60 51-72	66 57-79	72 62-84[2]
Controlled Substance Crime, 3rd Degree	**VI**	21	27	33	39 34-46	45 39-54	51 44-61	57 49-68
Residential Burglary Simple Robbery	**V**	18	23	28	33 29-39	38 33-45	43 37-51	48 41-57
Nonresidential Burglary	**IV**	12[1]	15	18	21	24 21-28	27 23-32	30 26-36
Theft Crimes (Over $5,000)	**III**	12[1]	13	15	17	19 17-22	21 18-25	23 20-27
Theft Crimes ($5,000 or less) Check Forgery ($251-$2,500)	**II**	12[1]	12[1]	13	15	17	19	21 18-25
Sale of Simulated Controlled Substance	**I**	12[1]	12[1]	12[1]	13	15	17	19 17-22

☐ Presumptive commitment to state imprisonment. First-degree murder has a mandatory life sentence and is excluded from the guidelines by law. See Guidelines Section II.E., Mandatory Sentences, for policy regarding those sentences controlled by law.

☐ Presumptive stayed sentence; at the discretion of the judge, up to a year in jail and/or other non-jail sanctions can be imposed as conditions of probation. However, certain offenses in this section of the grid always carry a presumptive commitment to state prison. See, Guidelines Sections II.C. Presumptive Sentence and II.E. Mandatory Sentences.

FIGURE 14.1 Minnesota Sentencing Guidelines

Source: Minnesota Sentencing Guidelines Commission, 2008, p. 57.

sentencing grid in Figure 14.1 illustrates how they operate. The far-left column ranks the seriousness of the offense according to 10 categories. The top row provides a seven-category criminal history score for the defendant based on number of previous convictions, employment status, educational achievement, drug or alcohol abuse, and so on. Having determined the offense severity ranking and the criminal history score, the judge finds the recommended sentence in the cell where the applicable row and column meet. The cells below the bold black line call for sentences other than state imprisonment; these numbers specify months of supervision (that is, probation). The cells above the bold line contain the guideline sentence expressed in months of imprisonment. The single number is the recommended sentence. The range (shown below the single number) varies by plus or minus 5 to 8 percent from the guideline sentences and can be used for upward or downward adjustments.

The Continuum of Voluntary to Required Use

Of the 21 states that adopted sentencing guidelines, 11 required judges to sentence within the presumptive sentencing guidelines and 10 states made judicial compliance with sentencing guidelines voluntary (Stemen & Rengifo, 2011). But this dichotomy is a bit misleading. State sentencing guidelines are best viewed as ranging along a continuum of more voluntary on one side and more mandatory on the other (Kauder & Ostrom, 2008).

Under *voluntary sentencing guidelines*, recommended sentencing ranges were derived by empirically analyzing the sanctions judges in the jurisdiction have usually imposed in various types of cases in the past. Thus, descriptive guidelines codify past sentencing practices as standards for future cases. Once adopted, these guidelines may voluntarily be used by judges, but they are advisory only. Thus, voluntary sentencing guidelines do not have the force of law. Noncompliance by a judge creates no right to appeal a sentence. As one would expect, not all judges actually use the guidelines when imposing sentences (Miethe

& Moore, 1989). Over the years some voluntary sentencing guidelines have fallen into such disuse that it is not always clear whether a particular state's guideline system is still operational (Kauder & Ostrom, 2008).

In contrast to a voluntary compliance approach with sentencing guidelines, other states adopted *presumptive sentencing guidelines* that require judges to impose sentences in accordance with the directives in the guidelines. In most states using this approach, the legislature delegates the authority for developing detailed sentencing criteria to a sentencing commission (Kramer, Lubitz, & Kempinen, 1989). The resulting guidelines are prescriptive—that is, they express what sentence *should* be imposed, irrespective of existing practices. Once adopted, these guidelines have the force of law; they must be followed by sentencing judges. If a sentence is imposed outside the guidelines, the judge must provide reasons for the deviation. Both defendants and prosecutors have the right to have the judge's explanation reviewed by an appellate court.

The Constitutionality of State Sentencing Guidelines

Since 2000, the U.S. Supreme Court has raised serious doubts about the constitutionality of many state sentencing guidelines, holding that other than a prior conviction, any fact that increases the penalty for a crime beyond the statutory maximum must be tried before a jury (*Apprendi v. New Jersey*, 2000). Based on this reasoning, in 2004 the Court struck down sentencing guidelines in the State of Washington, holding that the Sixth Amendment gives juries (and not judges) the power to make a finding of fact beyond a reasonable doubt (*Blakely v. Washington*, 2004). The dissenters argued that the decision will serve only to increase judicial discretion and lead to less uniformity in sentencing, perhaps leading to increasing racial discrimination.

Some state high courts of last resort held that *Blakely* did not apply to their state sentencing schemes (Lankford, 2006), only to be firmly rebuffed when the U.S. Supreme Court struck down the California sentencing laws, holding that the statute gave judges authority that the U.S. Constitution places with juries (*Cunningham v. California*, 2007). Since *Cunningham*, it is clear that *Blakely* applies to state sentencing laws. But a failure to submit a sentencing factor to a jury is not "structural" error, which always invalidates a conviction. Rather, *Blakely* violations are subject to harmless error review (see Chapter 15).

Blakely limited judicial discretion in sentencing even more than mandatory sentencing guidelines did. It does not appear that the shift from judicial to jury decision making when imposing sentences more severe than those set forth in sentencing guidelines has increased sentencing disparities (Iannacchione & Ball, 2008). But it also does not appear to have reduced sentencing disparities either. Rather, extralegal factors that impact the imposition of a sentence above the maximum range of sentencing guidelines appear to affect both jury and judicial decision making, especially age and sex (Iannacchione & Ball, 2008).

Federal Sentencing Guidelines

The legal and political factors leading to the creation of state sentencing guidelines likewise led to the creation of federal sentencing guidelines, which have become more visible and also more controversial than their state counterparts. In 1984, Congress created the U.S. Sentencing Commission and charged it with developing guidelines for sentencing federal offenders. These standards became law in 1987. The Supreme Court upheld their legality in 1989 (*Mistretta v. United States*), only to rule them unconstitutional in 2005 (*United States v. Booker*).

The federal sentencing guidelines proved to be highly controversial (Stith & Cabranes, 1998). Indeed, many federal judges, probation officers, defense attorneys, and even some prosecutors resent and resist the guidelines (Tiede, 2009). According to Michael Tonry (1993), the federal sentencing guidelines "are a failure and should be radically revised or repealed." In support of this conclusion, he offers the following arguments: First, the guidelines are unduly harsh and as a result have produced a dramatic increase in the federal prison population. Second, the guidelines have failed to achieve their primary goal of reducing unwarranted disparities in federal sentencing. Indeed, the guidelines contribute to unfairness in sentencing because they are rigid and complex.

In *United States v. Booker* (2005), the U.S. Supreme Court greatly altered how federal guidelines are used. The first part of the complex opinion struck down federal sentencing guidelines as unconstitutional for the same reasons used to declare state sentencing guidelines unconstitutional—Congress improperly allowed judges and not juries to make key factual decisions in sentencing. But the second part of the opinion allows federal judges to continue to use the guidelines as advisory, and appellate courts can review for reasonableness.

The impact of *Booker* on federal sentencing practices was not as dramatic as some hoped and others feared. At the district court level, the rate of within-range sentences remained the same and average sentence lengths remained constant. There were more downward departures, but these were largely due to actions of U.S. attorneys and not the judges (Hofer, 2007). The U.S. courts of appeals varied in their approaches: Some adopted a wait-and-see attitude; others held that *Blakely* did not apply to the federal sentencing guidelines, and still others held that the guidelines were unconstitutional (Hurwitz, 2006). The Court revisited the issues, holding that sentences within the guidelines may be presumed "reasonable," but did not require appellate courts to do so (*Rita v. United States*, 2007). Amid confusion about the impact of *Rita*, the Court again considered the issues, this time making it more difficult for appeals courts to reverse a trial judge who imposes a sentence more lenient than the guideline recommendations (*Gall v. United States*, 2007). At the same time, the high court, by a vote of 7 to 2, held that trial judges may narrow the sentencing gap between crack cocaine and powder cocaine (*Kimbrough v. United States*, 2007). And three years later in *Pepper v. United States* (2011), the Court further expanded the discretion of federal judges at sentencing when it held that when a defendant's sentence has been set aside on appeal, a district court at resentencing may consider evidence of the defendant's postsentencing rehabilitation. Collectively, these decisions give federal judges the authority to consider a broad range of factors when sentencing a defendant "so long as they both begin with the Guidelines calculations, and then explicitly state their reasons for any variance from the Guidelines' range" (p. 412). "Dead Law Walking" is how one law professor described the tenacity of the federal sentencing guidelines (Bowman, 2014).

Although these decisions clearly restored some of the sentencing discretion taken away by the sentencing guidelines, they appear to have only limited impact on sentencing leniency. According to the U.S. Sentencing Commission (2012), judges in many districts are reducing the length of the imprisonment terms below the guideline recommendations for select offenses, but judges are generally reluctant to impose non-incarceration sentences.

"The empirical research on the impact of federal judges being freed from the requirement of following the federal sentencing guidelines suggests that judicially-created sentencing disparities based on extralegal factors have not increased" (Lynch & Omari, 2014, p. 440; see also Ulmer, Light, & Kramer, 2011). Scholars suggest that continued racial disparities after *Booker/Fanfan* are not a function of judicial sentencing decisions but rather appear to be a function of prosecutorial decision making in which prosecutors charge "mandatory minimum eligible crimes more in order to mitigate the uncertainties of judicial sentencing under the new 'advisory' Guidelines system" (Lynch & Omari, 2014, p. 421, citing Rehavi & Starr, 2012; see also Fischman & Schanzenbach, 2012; Hofer, 2011; Rehavi & Starr, 2012; Ulmer, Light, & Kramer, 2011).

Law in Action: Diverse Impacts

The application of sentencing guidelines is complex (Kramer & Ulmer, 2009). One major question asked by researchers and policymakers is whether structured or determinate sentencing schemes do indeed result in fairer sentences. Not surprisingly, the answer to that question might depend on one's interpretation of the data. Some adherents hoped that these laws would increase the certainty of punishment; others feared that prison populations would swell. Several studies investigated the impact of these sentencing schemes and found that the impacts were diverse. In one state, an offender's chance of receiving probation declined, but there was no change in another (Covey & Mande, 1985; McCoy, 1984). Likewise, in some states there was a projected 50 percent increase in the actual length of sentence for first offenders, yet in another jurisdiction only a modest increase was foreseen (Clarke, 1984; Clear, Hewitt, & Regoli, 1979). At least one study suggested that state presumptive guidelines were particularly useful in reducing sentencing disparities that were a function of judges' tenure on the bench, prosecutorial experience, and caseload (Wooldredge, Griffin, & Thistlethwaite, 2013).

Certain structured and determinate sentencing approaches help to reduce disparities, at least for a while. A three-state study concluded that in states that use sentencing guidelines, offenders are sentenced with more predictability, in a less discriminatory manner, and with increased transparency (Ostrom, Ostrom, Hanson, & Kleinman, 2008). Earlier studies reached similar conclusions. Racial, ethnic, and gender differences in sentencing generally decline (Kramer & Ulmer, 1996; Parent, Dunworth, McDonald, & Rhodes, 1996). Disparity reductions, though, tend to erode somewhat over time. Studies in Minnesota (Koons-Witt, 2002) and Ohio (Griffin & Wooldredge, 2006) found only short-term reductions in gender-based dispositions in felony cases. Not surprisingly, presumptive sentencing guidelines are more likely to reduce sentencing disparities than voluntary sentencing guidelines (Wang, Mears, Spohn, & Dario, 2013).

Although the specific impacts of these laws varied from state to state, the general pattern became quite clear—the overall prison populations increased. An early study in California (Casper, Brereton, & Neal, 1982) reported a significant increase in the number of prisoners incarcerated there, a finding replicated in other states as well (Carroll & Cornell, 1985; Kramer, Lubitz, & Kempinen, 1989; Tonry, 1987). By the mid-1990s, the inescapable conclusion was that changes in sentencing structure begun in the late 1960s and early 1970s resulted in major increases in the prison population across the nation (Marvell & Moody, 1996). The increase in prison populations did not begin to level off until about 2008.

By themselves, structured sentencing schemes appear to have little impact on overall incarceration rates (Stemen & Rengifo, 2011). In contrast, "determinate sentencing laws alone, through the abolition of discretionary parole release, can lead to lower incarceration rates," since they limit the ability of correctional officials to deny parole (Stemen & Rengifo, 2011, p. 194). In other words, although structured sentencing schemes limit judicial discretion, the discretion parole boards exercise can undo the intended standardization of incarceration periods by controlling release (see also, Bushway & Piehl, 2007). The combination of both presumptive sentencing guidelines and determinate sentencing schemes offers the most control over incarceration rates by impacting both sentencing and release decisions (Rengifo & Stemen, 2015; Stemen & Rengifo, 2011). But there is another factor that significantly affects incarceration rates: the increasing severity of criminal penalties.

Increasing the Severity of the Penalty

For many years, the majority of Americans have believed that prison sentences are too lenient (Cullen, Fisher, & Applegate, 2000; Krisberg, 1988; Rossi & Berk, 1997), and elected officials often express these views (Thomson & Ragona, 1987). Thus, when confronted with a crime problem, legislators responded by sounding a clarion call to get tough with criminals. Accordingly, criminal punishments grew harsher throughout the 1980s and 1990s. But the economic crisis in the late 2000s may have caused the American public to rethink its evermore-punitive stance. Opinion research finds that the public "overwhelmingly favors spending more on policing, crime prevention programs for young people, and drug treatment for nonviolent offenders," while they oppose additional funding for prisons (Gottschalk, 2009, p. 456; see also Cohen, Rust, & Steen, 2006). States have been experimenting with different sentencing formulas aimed at rehabilitation, especially for nonviolent offenders (Gottschalk, 2009; King, 2008; Porter, 2016). But there can be no doubt that the increased severity of

criminal penalties over the past 30 years or so still causes the United States to incarcerate more people per capita than any other country in the world.

Increasing the severity of penalties is premised on the notion that these harsher penalties will deter criminals and reduce crime. These ideas are more often justified by philosophical claims than by valid scientific evidence. Indeed, researchers are skeptical that this type of deterrent effect actually exists.

Law on the Books: Mandatory Minimum Sentences

Mandatory minimum sentencing laws are one method legislatures use to increase the severity of sentencing. These types of laws are typically enacted in response to allegations that lenient judges are allowing many serious offenders—particularly violent ones—to go free. The "proof" of this proposition is often limited to one or two highly publicized cases. Although fewer than half the states have adopted determinate sentencing laws, virtually all states and the federal government have enacted a particular type of determinate sentencing law mandating minimum sentences for certain offenses.

Typically, **mandatory minimum sentencing** laws require that offenders convicted of certain offenses must be sentenced to a prison term of not less than a specified period of years, and nonprison sentences (such as probation) are expressly precluded. In short, a term of imprisonment is mandated regardless of the circumstances of the offense or the background of the individual.

In recent years, the most popular mandatory minimum laws have been so-called **three strikes laws**, which supposedly target violent offenders with previous felony convictions. Through the years, legislative bodies have also enacted mandatory minimums for crimes that are particularly unpopular at the moment, including convicted felons in possession of a firearm, repeat drunk drivers, and those in possession of certain drugs (such as cocaine) with intent to sell.

In addition, some states enacted so-called **truth in sentencing laws**, which require offenders to serve a substantial portion of their prison term (often 85 percent) before release (Ditton & Wilson, 1999). Truth in sentencing laws were prompted by the 1994 Crime Act, a law that provided federal funds to help states having such a law expand their prisons to house violent offenders. But few states actually enacted such laws, and funding was discontinued in 2002 (Turner, Greenwood, Fain, & Chiesa, 2006). As a result of skyrocketing prison costs, some states, most notably Iowa, have decreased the time inmates are required to serve to facilitate earlier release through parole (Public Safety Performance Project, 2007). And other states, like California, are attempting to reduce the number of inmates in state prisons by shifting responsibility to counties for the custody, treatment, and supervision of individuals convicted of specified nonviolent, nonserious, nonsex crimes.

Law in Action: Nullification by Discretion

Sharp increases in formal penalties tend to be sidestepped by those who apply the law. At a variety of points in the application of legal sanctions—police arrest, prosecutorial discretion, jury conviction, and judicial sentencing—discretion may be exercised to offset the severity of the penalty (McCoy, 1984; Stith, 2008).

A reduction in the number of arrests is one type of discretionary reaction that may occur when the severity of the penalty is increased. This clearly occurred when Connecticut's governor tried to crack down on speeders by imposing a mandatory loss of the driver's license; arrests for speeding decreased after the severe penalties were announced, because the police and other legal officials perceived that the penalty was too severe for the offense (Campbell & Ross, 1968).

An increase in prosecutorial discretion may also compensate for an increase in the harshness of sentencing. Prosecutors often respond to new legislative actions by reducing the number of charges for that category. In 1994, Oregon voters approved Measure 11, which imposed long mandatory prison terms for 16 designated violent and sex-related offenses. This measure had fewer negative system impacts than had been anticipated by many criminal

justice administrators, largely because prosecutors exercised the discretion provided to them by the law. As a result, fewer mandatory-eligible cases were prosecuted. At the same time, more nonmandatory-sentence offenses were brought to court (Merritt, Fain, & Turner, 2006). Thus, prosecutors may choose to file charges for an offense that does not carry the most severe penalties when they anticipate that judges and juries will be reluctant to convict.

A decrease in the number of convictions may also occur when legislators increase the severity of punishment. The most commonly cited example is capital punishment in late 18th- and early 19th-century England, when most felonies were punishable by death. Judges often strained to avoid convicting defendants by inventing legal technicalities (Hall, 1952). Similarly, in New York State, after a tough drug law was passed, the number of convictions dropped.

After conviction, judges are reluctant to apply a severe penalty (Ross & Foley, 1987). When Chicago traffic court judges sought to crack down on drunk drivers by voluntarily agreeing to impose a seven-day jail term, the penalty was rarely applied (Robertson, Rich, & Ross, 1973).

Clearly, a relationship exists between punishment policy and the system that administers it. The more severe the penalty, the less likely it will be imposed when its severity exceeds what is viewed as appropriate. In other words, increasing the severity of the punishment does not increase the certainty of punishment; in fact, the threat of punishment may even be reduced by increasingly severe punishments. At this point, however, it should be clear that judicial discretion in sentencing is limited by a number of factors. Thus, the discretionary actions of police, prosecutors, and juries may be nullifying harsh penalties as much as, if not more than, discretionary decision making by judges.

Law in Controversy: Negative Side Effects

One reason legislators find raising penalties so attractive is that they appear to be fighting crime without having to increase appropriations. It is a policy apparently without costs; the public will be appeased without the painful necessity of voting for higher taxes. But a number of studies suggest that increasing the severity of the punishment produces negative side effects (referred to by economists as "hidden costs" and by others as "unanticipated consequences")—that is, harsher laws have impacts, but often not the ones intended.

One negative side effect of increasing the severity of punishments centers on the greater time, effort, and money courts must expend. Faced with severe sanctions, defendants demand more trials, which consume more court time. A backlog of cases results, delays increase, and the certainty and speed of conviction decline.

Critics are also concerned that mandatory minimum sentencing legislation results in a rigid and inflexible overreaction to problems of judicial discretion. Requiring every single defendant convicted under the same statute to serve the identical sentence threatens to create a system so automatic that it may operate in practice like a poorly programmed robot. In the words of U.S. District Court Judge Vincent Broderick, "The most frustrating aspect of mandatory minimum prison sentences is that they require routinely imposing long prison terms based on a single circumstance, when other circumstances in the case cry out for a significantly different result. The same sentence is mandated for offenders with very different criminal backgrounds and whose roles differ widely one from another" (Vincent & Hofer, 1994). Perhaps such frustrations, coupled with the high cost of mass incarceration, have led several U.S. jurisdictions to soften their three strikes laws. California voters, for example, passed a new version of Proposition 36 in 2012, limiting the imposition of a life sentence to third felony offenses that are serious or violent.

What Sentence Should Be Imposed?

What types of sentences should be imposed upon the guilty? Flogging, the stocks, exile, chopping off a hand, and branding are just a few examples of punishments historically inflicted on the guilty.

Today, such sanctions are viewed as violating the Constitution's prohibition against **cruel and unusual punishment**. In their place, we use imprisonment, probation, intermediate sanctions, fines, and restitution. Many states also make formal provisions for capital punishment, but the death penalty is rarely used. In essence, these forms of punishment are tools created under the sentencing structure to advance society's theories of punishment. They are the options from which the sentencing judge must choose.

Imprisonment

Imprisonment (incarceration) has become the dominant form of punishment only during the past two centuries. The United States imprisons a larger share of its population than any other nation. According to the Bureau of Justice Statistics (Carson & Anderson, 2015), more than 1.53 million inmates are currently housed in prisons and jails.

The high rate of imprisonment is not without its critics (Listwan, Johnson, Cullen, & Latessa, 2008). In *Big Prisons, Big Dreams*, Michael Lynch (2007) argues that the dramatic growth in our prison population has not reduced crime because we are not targeting the worst offenders. Prison populations are comprised of the poor, and many are incarcerated for nonviolent drug offenses or for relatively minor offenses. And high rates of incarceration contribute to the very social problems it is intended to solve by breaking-up families and eroding economic and social networks in economically disadvantaged communities (Clear, 2007).

One reason for this high rate of imprisonment is the length of sentences. Prison sentences in the United States are quite long as compared with those imposed in Europe, where it is rare for a defendant to be sentenced to more than 5 years.

Overcrowding

Jail and prison overcrowding has become the dominant reality of criminal justice policy. The numbers of people on probation and parole have also risen sharply. Figure 14.2 shows how the size of the correctional population has skyrocketed in recent years,

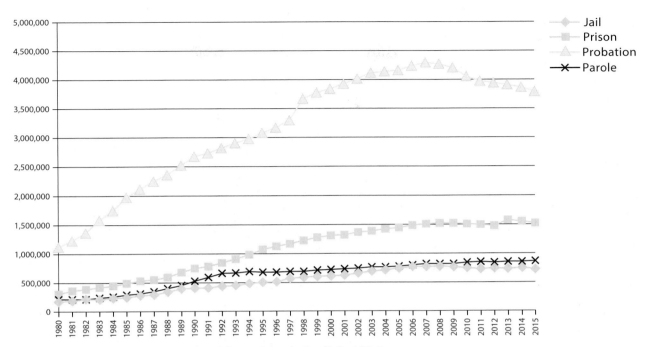

FIGURE 14.2 Adults under Correctional Supervision in the United States

Source: Kaeble, Danielle, and Lauren E. Glaze. 2016. *Correctional Populations in the United States, 2015*. Washington, DC: Bureau of Justice Statistics.

but the trend is starting to change. Record high numbers of prisoners were reported every year for nearly four decades. In 2010, though, the number of people incarcerated in U.S. prisons and jails dropped for the first time since 1972. And the downward trend in incarceration has continued since then.

California has led the nation in downsizing its prison population through its **public safety realignment** efforts. Realignment transferred the state's responsibility for nonviolent offenders to the county level. State officials hoped that county-level services could provide better rehabilitation and job-training services that might improve on the state's dismal 70 percent recidivism record. But critics feared that the lack of financial resources at the county level (including insufficient bed space in jails) would lead to more criminals being out on the street rather than incarcerated. To date, public safety realignment (in conjunction with some other criminal justice reforms) has reduced the state prison population to its lowest level in more than 20 years (Lofstrom & Martin, 2017). "To manage

jail populations, county sheriffs are increasingly using alternatives such as electronic monitoring, day reporting centers, community service, and alternative work programs. Most counties are also introducing or expanding inmate needs assessments, as well as mental health and substance abuse services, cognitive behavioral treatment, and employment and housing programs" (Lofstrom & Martin, 2017, p. 2). Although the recidivism rate has not markedly improved, crime rates did not rise. In short, these data have led researchers to conclude that prison populations can be reduced without endangering the public (Lofstrom & Raphael, 2016a, 2016b; Sundt, Salisbury, & Harmon, 2016).

Conditions of Confinement Lawsuits

Traditionally, courts followed a hands-off policy regarding correctional institutions, choosing not to interfere in their internal administration. But this policy began to change in 1964 (*Cooper v. Pate*). By the 1970s, the federal courts began to scrutinize the operations of correctional institutions to ensure compliance with the Eighth Amendment's protection against cruel and unusual punishment (DiIulio, 1990). Prisoners have sued under 42 U.S.C. § 1983 (see Chapter 2) in what are often termed **conditions of confinement lawsuits**. The lawsuits contend that local, county, or state officials have deprived them of their constitutional rights, such as adequate medical treatment, excessive force by correctional officers, and protection against violence by other inmates (Hanson & Daley, 1995). Unfortunately, though, inmates have also abused their rights to access the courts to redress legitimate grievances by suing over frivolous matters as a means of harassing correctional staff, taking revenge on the courts, or passing the time while incarcerated (Fradella, 1999). The volume of meritless suits led Congress to restrict inmates' ability to sue in 1996, when it enacted the Prison Litigation Reform Act. The law was effective in significantly reducing the number of civil rights cases filed by prisoners. Critics, however, point out that in limiting the number of frivolous lawsuits that can clog the courts, Congress may have also made it more difficult for prisoners to file and win meritorious suits (Schlanger, 2003).

Federal judges in nearly all states ordered state governments to alter dramatically the way in which they operated their prisons and jails. These court orders specified a maximum prison population, required physical conditions to be upgraded,

increased the number of prison guards, and mandated minimal medical facilities (Chilton, 1991; Crouch & Marquart, 1990; Taggart, 1989). These federal court orders have had a significant effect in transforming prison conditions (Feeley & Rubin, 1998).

It is now harder to challenge prison conditions in federal court, however. The Rehnquist Court created a new standard under the Eighth Amendment, holding that the prisoner must show "deliberate indifference" on the part of prison officials (*Wilson v. Seiter*, 1991). The Court later clarified that "deliberate indifference" requires subjective recklessness—the conscious disregard of a known risk (*Farmer v. Brennan*, 1994).

Overall, the nation's highest court has limited the conditions under which federal courts will recognize violations of a prisoner's rights (Mushlin & Galtz, 2009). And the Prison Litigation Reform Act of 1996 significantly limited the federal courts' supervisory powers over state prisons. Nonetheless, state correctional officials are aware that slipping back to old practices will result in future litigation. Consider that in *Brown v. Plata* (2011), the U.S. Supreme Court affirmed a lower court order to cap the California prison population at 137.5 percent of design capacity within two years of the decision. The case ushered in California's public safety realignment policies, as previously discussed.

KEY DEVELOPMENTS CONCERNING IMPRISONMENT

Eighth Amendment (1791)	Excessive bail shall not be required, nor excessive fines imposed, nor cruel and unusual punishments inflicted.
Ex Parte Hull (1941)	A state prison rule abridging or impairing a prisoner's right to apply to the federal courts for a writ of *habeas corpus* is invalid.
Robinson v. United States (1962)	The Eighth Amendment's prohibition against cruel and unusual punishment applies to the states as well as the federal government.
Cooper v. Pate (1964)	Prisoners can sue correctional officials in federal court under 42 U.S.C. § 1983.
Procunier v. Martinez (1974)	Prisoners retain First Amendment free speech rights while incarcerated. Restrictions on their speech must be narrowly tailored to achieve a compelling penological interest, such as maintaining security.
Wolf v. McDonnell (1974)	When facing administrative segregation or a sanction that would extend their incarcerating length, inmates have due process rights in disciplinary proceedings that include the rights to be notified of charges, to call witnesses, and to an impartial decision maker.

Estelle v. Gamble (1976)	Deliberate indifference to serious medical needs of prisoners constitutes the unnecessary and wanton infliction of pain, and thus violates the Eighth Amendment.
Bounds v. Smith (1977)	Because inmates retain a Sixth Amendment right to access the courts, correctional authorities must provide inmates access to trained legal professionals or to a law library.
Bell v. Wolfish (1979)	Correctional practices implemented in the genuine interest of institutional security, such as restrictions on reading materials and required body-cavity searches, are constitutionally permissible, even when applied to pretrial detainees.
Ruiz v. Estelle (1980)	A U.S. District Court declared a wide range of conditions of confinement in the Texas prison system unconstitutional, such as overcrowding, lack of access to health care, and abusive security practices. The court orders entered in the case led the court to oversee the Texas system for more than 25 years.
Rhodes v. Chapman (1981)	Double-celling and crowding do not necessarily constitute cruel and unusual punishment.
Smith v. Wade (1983)	Inmates are entitled to punitive damages in § 1983 cases in which the defendant's conduct involves reckless or callous indifference to the plaintiff's federally protected rights, or when it is motivated by evil motive or intent.
Hudson v. Palmer (1984)	Prisoners have no reasonable expectation of privacy in their prison cells entitling them to Fourth Amendment protection.
Whitley v. Albers (1986)	A prisoner shot in the leg during a riot does not suffer cruel and unusual punishment if the action was taken in good faith to maintain discipline rather than for the mere purpose of causing harm.
Turner v. Safely (1987)	Prisoners maintain the right to marry while incarcerated.
Wilson v. Seiter (1991)	Prisoners contesting conditions of confinement in federal court must show that prison officials acted with "deliberate indifference" to prisoner needs and living conditions.
Prison Litigation Reform Act (1996)	Congress limits the authority of federal courts to supervise the operations of correctional institutions and limits the ability of inmates to file civil rights actions.
Pennsylvania Department of Corrections v. Yeskey (1997)	Correctional institutions must abide by the mandates of the Americans with Disabilities Act by making reasonable accommodations for disabled inmates.
Miller v. French (2000)	Upheld the Prison Litigation Reform Act (PLRA), saying Congress could lawfully impose a 90-day time limit to rule on prison condition lawsuits.
Correctional Services Corp. v. Malesko (2001)	Inmates may not file *Bivens* actions for damages against private entities acting under color of federal law.
Hope v. Pelzer (2001)	Tying a prisoner to a hitching post for punitive purposes violates the Eighth Amendment.
Brown v. Plata (2011)	Federal courts may place limits on prisoner populations to remedy Eighth Amendment violations that occur due to excessive overcrowding (such as the California prison system holding nearly twice as many inmates as it was designed to accommodate).
Ross v. Blake (2016)	The PLRA requires prisoners to exhausted administrative remedies within a prison system before filing a lawsuit regardless of whether there are any "special circumstances."

High Costs

Getting tough on criminals is popular, yet public opinion polls show that spending money for more prisons is not a high priority for the general public. Prisons are costly to build and even more costly to maintain (Spelman, 2009). Estimates of the costs of constructing a single cell exceed $100,000 (Clear, Reisig, & Cole, 2016). The costs of incarcerating a prisoner (clothes, food, and guards, primarily) depend on the level of confinement and also vary from state to state, ranging from $15,000 to $60,000 per prisoner per year (Henrichson & Delaney, 2012). These costs double or even triple to house prisoners in solitary confinement—upwards of $70,000 to $92,000 annually per inmate (Solitary Watch, 2011).

Faced with swelling prison populations and federal court orders over conditions of confinement, state legislatures have been faced with spending enormous sums of money to build new prisons and upgrade existing ones. Prison construction during the 1990s was a growth industry, with 213 state and federal prisons built during the first five years, at an estimated cost of $30 billion ("In '90s, Prison," 1997). Despite large expenditures, few states have been able to build prisons fast enough to keep ahead of surging prison admissions. Across the nation, many prisons operate near or over their design capacity. During the last year for which data are available, the federal system exceeded 120 percent of its capacity, while Illinois and Nebraska reporting the highest levels of state prison overcrowding at 145 percent and 125 percent of their respective capacities (Carson & Anderson, 2015).

Some states have declared an emergency situation, thus triggering the early release of certain types of prisoners. States that fail to take such action face sanctions from federal judges. Contempt of court, hefty fines, and judicially mandated release of prisoners are some of the remedies federal judges have imposed on state and local officials who have failed to take action to solve prison overcrowding (Clear, Reisig, & Cole, 2016).

Probation

Unlike incarceration, **probation** is designed as a means of maintaining control over offenders while permitting them to live in the community (under supervision). The major justification for probation is that prisons are inappropriate places for some defendants and that limited supervision is a better way to rehabilitate criminals. Youthful or first-time offenders may only become embittered if mixed in prison with hardened criminals; they may end up learning more sophisticated criminal techniques. But most important, probation is significantly less expensive than imprisonment.

Probation is the principal alternative to imprisonment. It is also the most commonly used sanction in the United States; indeed, nearly twice as many adults are on probation as are housed in state and federal prisons (Kaeble & Bonczar, 2017; Phelps, 2017). Altogether, about 4 million adults are on probation, a number that represents a doubling in about two decades. The increasing use of probation is a direct reflection of the serious problem of prison overcrowding. Ironically, it has resulted in a significant amount of "probation crowding"—the overload of the probation system equivalent to prison overcrowding (Byrne, Lurigio, & Baird, 1989). Recall from Figure 14.2 that the number of people on probation rose almost as dramatically as the number in prison. As a result, probation officers often must handle excessive caseloads.

State and federal laws grant judges wide discretion in deciding whether to place a defendant on probation. In general, statutes allow probation when it appears that:

1. The defendant is not likely to commit another offense.
2. The public interest does not require that the defendant receive the penalty provided for the offense.
3. The rehabilitation of the defendant does not require that he or she receive the penalty provided for the offense.

Legislative provisions regarding who may be placed on probation vary considerably from state to state. Some states have statutes prohibiting certain types of offenders—typically violent offenders—from receiving probation.

Offenders placed on probation must agree to abide by certain rules and regulations prescribed by the sentencing judge. Termed "conditions of probation," these rules typically include keeping a job, supporting the family, avoiding places where alcoholic beverages are sold, reporting periodically to the probation officer, and not violating any law. Because probation is a judicial act, the judge can revoke probation and send the defendant to prison if the conditions of probation are violated.

The probation system relies on skilled probation officers who need to walk a delicate line balancing duties that are part law enforcement and part social worker. The primary job of a probation officer is to meet with the offenders assigned to him or her on a daily, weekly, or monthly basis. Additionally, the typical duties of probation officers include:

- Compiling, evaluating, and presenting the information that courts need in order to sentence a defendant

- Implementing supervision plans, including the detail of counseling plans and referrals to social service agencies

- Assisting offenders in securing or maintaining gainful employment

- Tracking offender payments of fines, restitution, supervision costs, and court costs

- Supervising probationers, ensuring that they comply with the terms of probation imposed by a court

- Maintaining awareness of offenders' lives and evaluating their activities within a framework of the social desirability for the probationer to remain on community-based supervision

- Conducting investigations on offenders who may have violated the terms of their probation, and appearing as a witness in probation revocation hearings

Fines

The imposition of a **fine** is one of the oldest and also one of the most widely used forms of punishment. Fines are used extensively for traffic offenses and minor ordinance violations, generating well over $1 billion annually for local governments (Clear, Reisig, & Cole, 2016). Judges in the lower courts impose a fine alone or in combination with other sanctions in about 86 percent of their cases. But the imposition of fines is not confined to the lower courts. In the major trial courts, a fine, either alone or together with other sanctions, is imposed in approximately 44 percent of the cases (Reaves, 2013).

The limited use of fines as punishment in felony cases contrasts sharply with practices in some Western European countries (Justice Policy Institute, 2011; Shoham, Beck, & Kett, 2007). Some countries have adopted sentencing policies that explicitly make fines the sentence of choice for many offenses, including some crimes of violence that would result in jail sentences in many American courts. In Germany, for example, a major legislative goal is to minimize the imposition of jail terms of less than six months. Instead, German courts make extensive use of **day fines**, which enable judges to set fines at amounts reflecting the gravity of the offense but also taking into account the financial means of the offender (Hillsman & Mahoney, 1988). In the United States, the day fine concept has been relabeled "structured fines" and is being recommended as a less costly sentencing option than imprisonment (Bureau of Justice Statistics, 1996; Justice Policy Institute, 2011). In some respects, structured fines reflect a "Robin Hood" approach to criminal justice—the rich pay more (DeLisi & Conis, 2012).

American judges frequently cite the poverty of offenders as an obstacle to the broader use of fines as sanctions (Gillespie, 1988–1989). Nonetheless, some courts regularly impose fines on persons whose financial resources are extremely limited and are successful in collecting those fines. Some research suggests that fines can be collected. Performance can be improved substantially if administrators systematically apply collection and enforcement techniques that already exist and have been proven effective (Cole, 1992; Klaversma, 2008; Turner & Greene, 1999).

Restitution

Restitution is the requirement that the offender provide reparation to the victim for the harm caused by the criminal offense. Requiring defendants to compensate victims (giving something back) for their losses was customary in ancient civilizations. But as the government replaced the victim as the principal party in criminal prosecution, restitution fell into decline; offenders paid fines to the government rather than restitution to the victim (Tobolowsky, 1993). Beginning in the mid-1960s, the idea of restitution became the focus of renewed interest and became touted as one of the criminal justice system's more creative responses to crime. Nearly all states have enacted laws providing for the collection and distribution of restitution funds.

Restitution efforts generally take one of two forms—direct or symbolic (Galaway, 1988). In **direct restitution**, the offender is required, as a condition of probation, to make monetary payments to the victim. As a criminal sanction, it is largely restricted to property crimes, since it has little relevance if violence figured in the commission of the offense. Since 1996, Congress has required the federal court to impose mandatory restitution, without consideration of the defendant's ability to pay. But that approach may only increase victim dissatisfaction if the offender fails to pay (Davis & Bannister, 1995). A study of the Government Accountability Office of five major white-collar cases in federal court found that only 7 percent of court-ordered payments were ever collected (Schwartz, 2007).

In **symbolic restitution**, the offender makes reparation for the harm done in the form of good works benefiting the entire community rather than the particular individual harmed. Such work is often called *community service*. This sanction is most often used when there is no direct victim of the offense—for example, in convictions for drunk driving. Community service will be discussed more fully in the next section.

Intermediate Sanctions

Concern is growing that the United States relies much too heavily on imprisonment and probation. Prison is viewed as too harsh (as well as unavailable) for many defendants, whereas high caseloads often leave too many probationers without adequate supervision. Alternative sentences that lie somewhere between prison and probation are often referred to as **intermediate sanctions**.

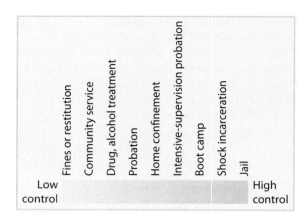

FIGURE 14.3 Continuum of Sanctions

Source: Adapted from Todd Clear, Michael Reisig, and George Cole. 2016. *American Corrections.* 11th ed. Belmont, CA: Wadsworth.

Intermediate sanctions are based on the concept of continuum of sanctions—the range of punishments vary from low control to high control (see Figure 14.3). At one end of the continuum are fines and community service, which reflect low control over the activities of the guilty person; at the other end are punishments like home confinement, intensive-supervision probation, and boot camps, which reflect high control just short of the maximum level of control—jail or prison. The importance of drug and alcohol treatment has already been stressed in Chapter 3 in the discussion of drug courts. In the following sections, we explore some of these other intermediate sanctions. It is important to note, though, that intermediate sanctions are generally not imposed in isolation; instead, they are usually imposed in conjunction with probation.

Community Service

As previously mentioned, community service is based on the theory of *symbolic restitution*—the offender has injured the community and therefore should compensate the community for that injury. Thus, a person sentenced to **community service** is required to provide a specified number of hours of free labor in some public service, such as street cleaning, repairing substandard housing, or volunteering in a hospital. In the eyes of the general public, community service is most visible when it is imposed on celebrities like actors and athletes.

Tonry (1998) suggested that community service may be the most underused sanction in the United States.

The effectiveness of community service is mixed. It does not appear to reach its major goal of reducing incarceration levels because virtually all of those sentenced to community service would have received probation (not a jail sentence). Nor does community service appear to be particularly more or less effective in reducing criminal behavior. Several studies have found, at best, only minor reductions in recidivism (when compared to terms of incarceration) that were not statistically significant (McDonald, 1986; Killias, Gilliéron, Villard, & Poglia, 2010; Muliluvuori, 2001), although a few other studies have noted lower recidivism rates that are statistically significant (e.g., Bouffard & Muftić, 2006, 2007; Caputo, 1999; Wermink, Blokland, Nieuwbeerta, Nagin, & Tollenaar, 2010). Allen and Treger (1994) noted that those who participate in community service have higher failure rates than those who receive regular supervision (Allen & Treger, 1994).

Intensive-Supervision Probation

Given the high number of persons on probation, the amount of an offender's contact with a probation officer is typically very limited—perhaps a brief meeting once a month. **Intensive-supervision probation** (ISP) involves strict reporting, with the offender required to meet with a probation officer briefly every day. ISP targets offenders who are most likely to be facing imprisonment for their next violation.

Many evaluation studies of ISP programs have found that intensive supervision aimed at increasing control, surveillance, and the threat of punishment do not reduce recidivism rates (see Gendreau, Goggin, Cullen, & Andrews, 2000; Hyatt & Barnes, 2017). At the same time, offenders on intensive-supervision probation are more likely to be found in violation of their conditions of probation largely because they are being more closely supervised. As a result, even minor violations like arrests for disorderly conduct could result in the offender being in violation of his or her probation and sent to prison. In short, contrary to their intended goals,

so-called "traditional" ISPs might actually lead to a larger prison population. In contrast, ISPs that employ a human-service philosophy while providing rehabilitative services to probationers successfully reduce rearrest rates (Drake, Aos, & Miller, 2009; Lowenkamp, Flores, Holsinger, Makarios, & Latessa, 2010).

Home Detention with Electronic Monitoring

Another alternative to incarceration that helps to reduce jail and prison overcrowding, as well as the costs of punishment, is **home detention** (sometimes referred to as *house arrest*). This punishment confines offenders to their homes under specific terms and conditions. Typically, offenders are permitted to leave their home for only explicit, pre-authorized reasons, such as to obtain health care (including court-mandated treatment), to shop for groceries and other necessities, to attend religious services, and to go to work and/or school—but only if such activities have been authorized. Home arrest is enforced by unannounced field visits (usually by probation or parole officers) at all times of the day and night. And, starting in the 1980s and growing in use to the present, enforcement has been aided by **electronic monitoring (EM)** devises that allow both computer and monitoring specialists to track offender compliance with house arrest and highly regimented, limited scheduled departures from the home that may be allowed in a particular case (DeMichele & Payne, 2009). Some EM devices can even detect alcohol consumption through skin pores.

Not surprisingly, most offenders prefer to serve their time at home rather than in jail or prison, even though they still experience incarceration in the home as punitive (Gainey & Payne, 2000; Martin, Hanrahan, & Bowers, 2009; Payne, May, & Wood, 2014). Still, most offenders under house arrest report that the combination of technological and human supervision transforms their homes into prison-like environments—places of confinement into which corrections official intrude with intense invasions of privacy that burden not only the offender but also the others living with the offender. This "creates and sustains 'a particular kind of tension between the home world and the institutional world' and uses this persistent tension 'as strategic leverage in the management of' offenders" (Staples & Decker, 2010, p. 17, quoting Goffman, 1961, p. 13).

House arrest with EM offers the benefit of access to more rehabilitative opportunities (Gainey & Payne, 2000) while avoiding the criminogenic and often dangerous environment found in many jails and prisons (Payne & Gainey, 2004; Vanhaelemeesch, Vander Beken, & Vandevelde, 2014). This in turn can lead EM participants to have lower recidivism rates than those on traditional probation with community service (Killias, Gilliéron, Kissling, & Villettaz, 2010) and those imprisoned (Bonta, Wallace-Capretta, & Rooney, 2000). That finding, however, is likely due, in part, to EM programs having lower-risk offenders. When risk is controlled for, there are no significant recidivism differences between parolees and EM offenders (see also, MacKenzie, 2006; Renzema & Mayo-Wilson, 2005). But since EM generally costs a fraction of what it would cost to incarcerate offenders in institutions (Crowe, Sydney, Bancroft, & Lawrence, 2002), its primary benefit as an alternative to incarceration may be cost savings.

GPS Monitoring

EM programs have traditionally been used with relatively low-risk offenders, such as those convicted of drug possession, driving under the influence, driving on a suspended license, petty theft, and certain white-collar crimes (Gable & Gable, 2005). But today's most sophisticated EM devices can monitor an offender's location every second of the day using global positioning satellites (GPS). The second generation of GPS-EM technology allows for greater control of higher-risk offenders, such as some sex offenders and intimate-partner violence offenders. GPS-EM can be used to monitor offenders on house arrest as an alternative to incarceration or as part of an intensive-supervision program after they are paroled (Erez & Ibarra, 2007; Payne & DeMichele, 2011). But unlike the cost-savings benefit associated with more traditional EM programs, GPS-EM can be cumbersome and expensive to operate and monitor.

Boot Camps and Shock Incarceration

To some, the deterrent effect of incarceration loses its impact after a short time, which leads some to advocate **shock incarceration**—the offender is sentenced to a brief jail or prison sentence (typically 30 to 90 days) and then released on probation, which may be combined with other intermediate sanctions, such as home detention or electronic monitoring. The assumption is that the offender will find the experience so unpleasant that he or she will be motivated to "stay clean."

The best-known example of shock incarceration is the **boot camp**, in which offenders serve a short sentence that includes a rigorous, paramilitary regimen designed to develop discipline and respect for authority. Proponents of boot camps argue that many young offenders are involved in crime because they have little discipline in their disordered lives. Thus, a relatively brief, quasi-military experience is designed to send the offender off in more productive directions. Critics, however, argue that the military-style physical training and the harshness of the program do little to overcome the problems facing inner-city youths who are in trouble with the law. Evaluations of boot camp graduates show that they do no better than other offenders after release (Cullen, Blevins, & Trager, 2005; Klenowski, Bell, & Dodson, 2010; Parent, 2003). To be effective, boot camp programs must be carefully designed, target the right types of offenders, and provide rehabilitative services (Kurlychek & Kempinen, 2006). Findings like these, coupled with the high costs, have led some state and local officials to close their boot camps.

The Death Penalty

Of all the forms of punishment, the **death penalty** is by far the most controversial, but it is also the least used; only a handful of offenders potentially face the ultimate sanction society can impose on the guilty. Since the U.S. Supreme Court ushered in the modern era of the death penalty in 1976, approximately 1,448 executions have been carried out in the United States.

Capital punishment was once almost the only penalty applied to convicted felons. By the time of the American Revolution, the English courts had defined more than 200 felonies, all of which were **capital offenses**. However, many death penalties were not carried out; instead, offenders were pardoned or banished to penal colonies. Over time, courts and legislatures began to recognize other forms of punishment, such as imprisonment and probation.

As Figure 14.4 illustrates, the number of executions in the United States fell steadily from the 1930s to the 1970s. From 1967 to 1972, an unofficial moratorium on executions existed. In 1976, the numbers increased once again, reaching a peak of 98 in 1998. Since then, however, the number of executions has been falling.

Table 14.1 presents information on the U.S. jurisdictions that have a death penalty as of this writing.

According to the Death Penalty Information Center (2017) and the U.S. Bureau of Justice Statistics (Snell, 2014), since 1976 (when then U.S. Supreme Court upheld the constitutionality of a revised approach to the punishment),

- approximately 8,618 defendants have been sentenced to death;

- approximately 16 percent of these death sentences have been carried out;
- more than 37 percent of these sentences have been overturned on appeal; and
- around 3,000 prisoners remain under sentences of death.

In the remaining cases, the prisoner either died while in custody or had his sentence commuted through executive clemency processes. As Table 14.2 makes clear, southern states account for more than 60 percent of all capital sentences and more than 81 percent of the executions.

Abolition of the death penalty has been a hot political issue. Opponents contend that it is morally wrong for the state to take a life; it has no deterrent value and is inherently discriminatory. These arguments have led all Western democracies except the United States to abolish the death penalty. Supporters counter that retribution justifies the taking of a life and that the death penalty does deter; they are generally unconcerned or unconvinced about allegations of discriminatory impact. In the United States, a series of Supreme Court opinions interpreting the Eight Amendment ushered in the modern era of death penalty jurisprudence.

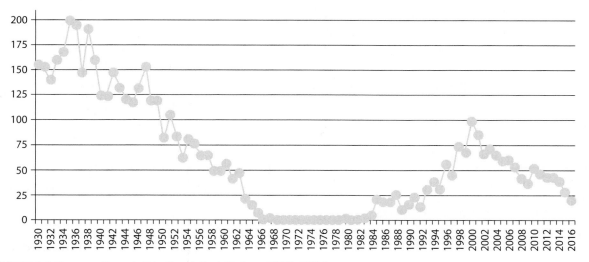

FIGURE 14.4 Persons Executed in the United States, 1930–2016

Sources: Bureau of Justice Statistics. 2014. Number of Persons Executed in the United States: Capital Punishment Statistical Tables, 1930–2013. Washington, DC: Author. Death Penalty Information Center. 2017. *Facts about the Death Penalty*. Washington, DC: Author.

TABLE 14.1	Capital Punishment Laws in the U.S. by U.S. Census Region	

Region	Death Penalty Law	No Death Penalty Law
South	N = 13 Alabama, Arkansas, Florida, Georgia, Kentucky, Louisiana, Mississippi, North Carolina, Oklahoma, South Carolina, Tennessee, Texas, and Virginia	N = 4 Delaware,[a] District of Columbia, Maryland, and West Virginia
West	N = 10 Arizona, California, Colorado,[b] Idaho, Montana, Nevada, Oregon,[b] Utah, Washington,[b] and Wyoming	N = 3 Alaska, Hawaii, and New Mexico
Midwest	N = 6 Indiana, Kansas, Missouri, Nebraska, Ohio, and South Dakota	N = 6 Illinois, Iowa, Michigan, Minnesota, North Dakota, and Wisconsin
Northeast	N = 2[a] New Hampshire and Pennsylvania[b]	N = 7 Connecticut, Maine, Massachusetts, New Jersey, New York,[a] Rhode Island, Vermont
Other	U.S. Federal Government (including the U.S. Military)	Puerto Rico

[a] Delaware and New York technically have death penalty statutes, part of which were declared unconstitutional by the highest courts in those states. Because neither state's legislature has amended their statutes to restore capital punishments, both jurisdictions are listed as not having death penalty laws.
[b] Between 2011 and 2015, the governors of Colorado, Oregon, Pennsylvania, and Washington imposed moratoria on the death penalty in their states that remain in effect as of the writing of this book.

TABLE 14.2	Executions in the United States by Region, 1976–2016

Region	Executions
South	1,178 (81.30%)
Midwest	179 (12.35%)
West	85 (5.87%)
Northeast	4 (0.28%)
Federal	3 (0.21%)
Total	1,449 (100%)

Source: Death Penalty Information Center (2017).

Eighth Amendment Standards

In *Trop v. Dulles* (1958), the U.S. Supreme Court explained that the scope of the Cruel and Unusual Punishments Clause of the Eighth Amendment to the U.S. Constitution is not static, but rather should be interpreted on the basis of "evolving standards of decency in a maturing society" (p. 101). Since that time, the Court has been repeatedly called upon to determine whether particular capital punishment laws or their application in particular cases are consistent with the Eighth Amendment as viewed from the perspective of "evolving standards of decency in a maturing society." Applying this standard in its 1972 landmark decision in *Furman v. Georgia*, the Court invalidated all 37 then-existing state death penalty statutes. The Court was deeply divided, however, with every justice writing a separate opinion.

Method of Decision Making

Furman v. Georgia raised more questions than it answered, and state legislatures attempted to write new capital punishment laws consistent with the Eighth Amendment. By 1976, a total of 37 states had enacted new legislation designed to avoid the arbitrary application of capital punishment. These laws took two forms. Some states passed mandatory death penalty laws, which removed all discretion from the process by requiring that any-one convicted of a capital offense be sentenced to death. Other states enacted guided discretion statutes, which required judges and juries to weigh various aggravating and mitigating circumstances in deciding whether or not a particular defendant should receive the death penalty (Blankenship, Luginbuhl, Cullen, & Redick, 1997).

These new laws were tested in five companion cases, collectively known as the death penalty cases (*Gregg v. Georgia*, 1976). Again, the Court was badly divided, but a seven-justice majority agreed that the death penalty did not constitute cruel and unusual punishment under all circumstances. Next, the Court considered under what circumstances the death penalty was unconstitutional. Mandatory death penalty laws in 21 states were struck down because they failed to focus on the circumstances of the case. Guided-discretion death penalty laws, on the other hand, were upheld: "The concerns expressed in *Furman* that the penalty of death not be imposed in an arbitrary or capricious manner can be met by a carefully drafted statute that ensures that the sentencing authority is given adequate information and guidance" (p. 195).

For a death penalty law to be constitutional, the high court ruled, it must provide for a **bifurcated trial** process. During the first, or guilt, phase of the trial, the jury considers only the issue of guilt or innocence. If the jury unanimously convicts for a crime carrying the death penalty, then the jury reconvenes. During the second, or penalty, phase of the trial, the jury considers aggravating and mitigating circumstances and then decides whether to impose the death penalty. If the death penalty is not imposed, the defendant is usually sentenced to life imprisonment.

Method of Execution

A variety of forms of execution have been used in the United States. Since *Gregg*, most states have used electrocution, gas poisoning, hanging, firing squad, and lethal injection. When people challenge the proposed method of their execution as cruel and unusual, the courts apply *Trop's* perspective of "evolving standards of decency in a maturing society."

KEY DEVELOPMENTS CONCERNING CAPITAL PUNISHMENT AFTER *GREGG*	
Coker v. Georgia (1977)	The imposition of the death penalty for rape is a disproportionate punishment that violates the Eighth Amendment.
Pulley v. Harris (1984)	The Eighth Amendment does not require states to compare with other cases to assess whether a sentence of death is proportional.
Lockhart v. McCree (1986)	Potential jurors may be excluded if they oppose the death penalty. Thus, a death-qualified jury was upheld.
McCleskey v. Kemp (1987)	Statistical studies about racial disparities in capital sentences do not sufficiently establish an Equal Protection Clause violation. Rather, to prevail on such claims, capital defendants must show that purposeful discrimination had a discriminatory effect in their particular trials.
Stanford v. Kentucky (1989)	It is not unconstitutional to apply the death penalty to persons who were convicted of murder when they were 17.
Simmons v. South Carolina (1994)	Defense may tell jurors that the only alternative to a death sentence is life imprisonment without parole.
Harris v. Alabama (1995)	States may give judges the power to sentence a capital defendant to death even if the jury votes not to impose the death penalty.
Ramdass v. Angelone (2000)	Even if jurors are not told that defendant is not eligible for parole if sentenced to life in prison, that does not render a death sentence unconstitutional.

(Continued)

(Continued)

***Williams v. Taylor* (2000)**	Upheld a section of the Antiterrorism and Effective Death Penalty Act intended to shorten the time between sentencing and execution.
***Ring v. Arizona* (2002)**	The Sixth Amendment entitles defendants in capital cases to a jury determination of any aggravating factors that increase their maximum punishment from life imprisonment to death.
***Atkins v. Virginia* (2002)**	The Eighth Amendment bars the execution of criminal defendants with intellectual disabilities (i.e., IQs of 70 or less).
***Roper v. Simmons* (2005)**	The Eighth Amendment forbids the imposition of the death penalty on offenders who were under age 18 when their crimes were committed, overruling *Stanford v. Kentucky.*
***Hill v. McDonough* (2006)**	Challenges to the method of execution are properly filed in federal court under 42 U.S.C. § 1983, not in *habeas corpus* proceedings.
***Kansas v. Marsh* (2006)**	Upheld Kansas law requiring that when juries find that the arguments for and against capital punishment carry equal weight, the automatic sentence must be death.
***Uttecht v. Brown* (2007)**	A juror in the capital murder trial was properly excused for cause because a reading of the transcript of the voir dire indicates he expressed reservations about the death penalty.
***Baze v. Rees* (2008)**	Because the lethal injection process is not intended to cause unnecessary pain and suffering, it does not create an "objectively intolerable risk of harm" that qualifies as cruel and unusual punishment under the Eighth Amendment.
***Kennedy v. Louisiana* (2008)**	The death penalty is unconstitutional punishment for the rape of a child.
***Hall v. Florida* (2014)**	Barring the exploration of a capital defendant's intellectual disability if his IQ score is more than 70 creates an unacceptable risk that persons with intellectual disability would be executed in violation of the Eighth Amendment.
***Glossip v. Gross* (2016)**	The use of midazolam as the initial drug in an execution protocol does not violate the Eighth Amendment's prohibition against cruel and unusual punishment, even though its use may not guarantee that the execution will be pain-free.

In *Hill v. McDonough* (2006), the Court opened the door to whether the chemicals used in lethal injections are too painful and therefore constitute an Eighth Amendment violation. In the aftermath of *Hill*, many states halted executions and sought to change their practices. In Missouri, for example, a federal judge barred executions in that state amid resistance from the medical profession over whether doctors should be involved at all in meting out lethal injections (Davey, 2006). Two years, later, however, the Court squarely addressed the issue in *Baze v. Rees* (2008). The Court upheld lethal injection, reasoning that, "Simply because an execution method may result in pain, either by accident or as an inescapable consequence of death, does not establish the sort of 'objectively intolerable risk of

harm' that qualifies as cruel and unusual" (p. 50). But few think that the issue of method of execution has been settled because many questions of state law remain (Fulkerson & Suttmoeller, 2008).

How lethal injections are carried out may be subject to renewed legal and public scrutiny as a function of the two recent developments. First, states are finding it very challenging to obtain the drugs that have been used in lethal injections. This shortage occurred due to boycotts by drug manufacturers who refuse to sell the drugs for execution purposes and by foreign countries that refuse to allow pharmaceuticals made in their nations to be exported to the United States for use in executions. Second, in April 2014, Oklahoma botched the lethal injection execution of Clayton Lockett. It took more than 43 minutes for Lockett to die of a heart attack. Ten minutes into the procedure, a doctor reported that Lockett was not unconscious. In fact, he was blinking and licking his lips even though he should have been asleep. He then had a seizure and began to mumble, nod, and move his body. Prison officials said, "something's wrong" and then the observation window was closed so that witnesses could no longer see what was transpiring. Additional botched executions led more than 20 death row inmates to challenge the use of the drug midazolam as the initial drug used in executions since it was the drug used in Clayton Lockett's execution. In *Glossip v. Gross* (2016), however, the Supreme Court denied these claims. The Court held that there was insufficient evidence that the use of midazolam as the initial drug in an execution protocol presented a substantial risk of severe pain that would violate the Eighth Amendment.

Death-Qualified Juries

One long-standing issue has been the exclusion of persons opposed to the death penalty from juries in capital cases ("Live Free and Nullify. . . , 2014). The Warren Court rejected the classic "hanging jury," holding in *Witherspoon v. Illinois* (1968) that states cannot exclude from juries in capital cases any persons who voice general objections to the death penalty or express religious scruples against its imposition. However, the more conservative Rehnquist Court limited *Witherspoon* in *Wainwright v. Witt* (1985), ruling that the Constitution does not prohibit the removal for cause of prospective jurors whose opposition to the death penalty is so strong that it would prevent or substantially impair the performance of their duties as jurors at the sentencing phase of the trial (*Lockhart v. McCree*, 1986). More recently, the Roberts Court held that a juror in a capital murder trial was properly excused for cause because a reading of the transcript of the voir dire indicated that he expressed reservations about the death penalty (*Uttecht v. Brown*, 2007). Decisions like this make it easier for prosecutors to weed out jurors who have concerns about the death penalty, meaning that juries will be more prone to convict (Levinson, Smith, & Young, 2014; Butler & Moran, 2007a, 2007b; Haney, 1984, 2005; Moran

& Comfort, 2006). In fact, a wealth of social scientific data support the notion that so-called **death-qualified juries** differ from regular juries in several important ways:

> First, death-qualified jurors are demographically unique. When compared with excludables, they are more likely to be male, Caucasian, moderately well educated, politically conservative, Catholic or Protestant, and middle-class. Second, death-qualified jurors are dispositionally unique. When compared with excludables, they are more likely to have a high belief in a just world (i.e., feel the world is a fair and just place), espouse legal authoritarian beliefs (i.e., believe the rights of the government should supersede the rights of the individual), exhibit an internal locus of control (i.e., feel that internal factors control the events in their lives), and have a low need for cognition (i.e., lack the tendency to engage in and enjoy effortful cognitive activity). Third, death-qualified jurors are attitudinally unique. When compared with excludables, they are more likely to weigh aggravating circumstances (i.e., arguments for death) more heavily than mitigating circumstances (i.e., arguments for life), evaluate ambiguous expert scientific testimony more favorably, be skeptical of defenses involving mental illness (including the insanity defense), and are more susceptible to the pretrial publicity that inevitably surrounds capital cases. [And], death-qualified jurors are more likely to believe in the infallibility of the criminal justice process and less likely to agree that even the worst criminals should be considered for mercy. Fourth, death-qualified jurors are behaviorally unique with respect to their decision-making processes. When compared with excludables, they are more likely to find capital defendants guilty as well as sentence them to death. [And fifth], death-qualified venirepersons exhibited . . . higher levels of homophobia, modern racism, and modern sexism. (Butler, 2007, pp. 857, 858–859)

Yet, in spite of these many differences, constitutional challenges to the composition of death-qualified juries have been rejected by the federal courts for decades.

Narrowing Death-Eligible Cases

Part of the national debate over capital punishment has focused on what crimes deserve the ultimate punishment. The term **death-eligible** refers to crimes that are punishable by death. Today, very few crimes are considered death-eligible, but this was not always the case. Over the years, persons were executed for committing a wide variety of

Should the Death Penalty Be Abolished?

According to the Death Penalty Information Center (2017), more than 157 death row prisoners have been exonerated since 1973; the number of innocent people who have been executed is unknown. The wrongful convictions that result in sentences of death contribute to a long-running debate over the death penalty. Not surprisingly, profound ideological differences exist on the three central issues in the death penalty debate: morality, deterrence, and fairness. To advocates of the due process model of criminal justice, the death penalty is immoral because the state should not take a life. To proponents of the crime control model, the death penalty is moral because the defendant has already taken a life.

To advocates of the due process model, the death penalty is not a deterrent, because many of those who commit murder are incapable of rational calculation. To proponents of the crime control model, the death penalty is a deterrent, because some who might murder refrain from doing so because they know they might themselves die.

To advocates of the due process model, the death penalty is unfairly administered. They stress that members of racial minorities are more likely than Whites to be executed. They also believe that in too many cases, people on death row are innocent or their trials involved procedural irregularities. To this, the proponents of the crime control model respond that the fairness of the death penalty is unimportant or unproven. They believe that African-Americans are no more likely to be executed than Whites. They also argue that the review process works because appeals have freed the few innocents who were wrongfully convicted.

What do you think? Of the three main issues in the death penalty debate—morality, deterrence, and fairness—which provides the best argument for abolishing the death penalty? Which one offers the best grounds for keeping the death penalty? Do you think that the issue of innocents on death row justifies a moratorium on the death penalty?

---

crimes besides murder, including rape, robbery, and stealing horses. Legislators have played a major role in narrowing the scope of death-eligible offenses. Today, the focus is on the U.S. Supreme Court. In the wake of *Gregg v. Georgia*, the Supreme Court has placed important limits on what types of crimes and offenders are death-eligible.

Crime Limitations

State efforts to make nonhomicide cases death-eligible have been rejected. According to the Supreme Court, rape is not a grave enough offense to justify the imposition of the death penalty (*Coker v. Georgia*, 1977). More recently, the Court ruled that the death penalty is unconstitutional as the punishment for the rape of a child (*Kennedy v. Louisiana*, 2008). Whether the Court would uphold the death penalty for treason is unclear. Under federal law, treason is also a death-eligible offense, but since no one has been sentenced to death for espionage since the 1950s, the status of this penalty has not been determined.

Developmental Limitations

The U.S. Supreme Court has also placed important developmental limitations on when the death penalty may be imposed both in terms of chronological age and mental functioning.

For many years, the minimum age varied from 12 to 18, with a few states not specifying a minimum age. In fact, George Junius Stinney, Jr., a 14-year-old African-American boy, was executed in South Carolina in 1944 after having been dubiously convicted of killing two White girls, ages 8 and 11. Jury selection to verdict took less than eight hours; the trial itself took only three hours and jury deliberations lasted only ten minutes.

In 1988, the Supreme Court applied its first age-related limitation to the death penalty when it ruled that defendants who were 15 or younger at the time they committed murder could not be executed (*Thompson v. Oklahoma*, 1988). Later, the Court refused to set aside the death penalty for defendants who were 17 at the time of the crime (*Stanford v.*

CASE CLOSE-UP   *Roper v. Simmons*: Should Juveniles Be Sentenced to Death?

The jurors in *Roper v. Simmons* (2005) wrestled with a truly difficult question: Did Christopher Simmons deserve to live or die? No doubt, his crime was heinous—he and his friend deliberately drowned a neighbor girl who had befriended them. But at 17, was he too young to truly understand the dreadful crime that he had committed?

In *Roper v. Simmons*, the Court held that the Eighth Amendment forbids the imposition of the death penalty on offenders who were under the age of 18 when their crimes were committed. The Court's decision affected 72 inmates on death row in 20 states. It also impacted untold numerous current and future murder prosecutions.

Writing for the five-judge majority, Justice Kennedy argued that capital punishment must be limited to those offenders who commit "a narrow category of the most serious crimes" and whose extreme culpability makes them "the most deserving of execution." Those under 18 cannot with reliability be classified among the worst offenders. Citing factors like juveniles' susceptibility to immature and irresponsible behavior the Court concluded: "The differences between juvenile and adult offenders are too marked and well understood to risk allowing a youthful person to receive the death penalty." In finding a national consensus opposing the execution of juveniles, the Court set the age of 18 on the basis of state legislative determinations of the age one is old enough to vote, marry, and serve on a jury (Bradley, 2006).

The decision in *Roper v. Simmons* highlights major differences of opinion over how the Constitution should be interpreted. Six of the justices expressed support for continuing to interpret the Eighth Amendment on the basis of "evolving standards of decency in a maturing society" (*Trop v. Dulles*, 1958). In short, the meaning of the Bill of Rights was not frozen when it was originally drafted but should be interpreted in a common law manner. To Justices Scalia, Rehnquist, and Thomas, the interpretation of the Bill of Rights and other provisions of the Constitution should be based on their original meaning. Doctrines like evolving standards make interpretation too subjective, they argue.

In *Atkins v. Virginia* (2002), the Court reversed its previous stance on individuals with serious developmental issues, holding that the Eighth Amendment bars persons with an IQ of 70 or lower from being executed. Then, in *Hall v. Florida* (2014), the Court invalidated the use of rigid approaches to determining a cut-off for determining intellectual disabilities. The Court held that using IQ tests alone violates the Eighth Amendment because medical professionals do not consider IQ to be the sole determinant of intellectual disability. IQ scores are imprecise and not fixed. Hence, it is essential to consider factors indicating "deficits in adaptive functioning" (p. 1994). The impact of *Hall* remains to be seen, especially since the examination of a person's adaptive functioning leaves much subjectivity in diagnosing intellectual disability—especially for people with borderline IQ scores (Fabian, 2006; Hagstrom, 2009; Stevens, 2015).

Kentucky, 1989). But in *Roper v. Simmons*, the Supreme Court ruled that evolving standards of decency required that the Eighth Amendment be interpreted as barring the execution of all juvenile offenders who were younger than age 18 at the time of their offense.

Lengthy Appeals

"Death is different" wrote Justice Thurgood Marshall about death penalty cases in general and death penalty appeals in particular (*Ford v. Wainwright*, 1986, p. 411). One way to assess how death penalty cases are different is to examine case-processing time.

The review process in death penalty cases is quite lengthy, averaging more than 12 years, mainly because of the numerous issues that federal and state courts have dealt with since *Gregg* (Snell, 2014). Like all defendants found guilty, those sentenced to death are entitled to appellate court review. In death penalty cases, however, special provisions govern appeal. In all except two states, convictions for capital cases are automatically reviewed by the state's highest appellate court (Hurwitz, 2008). In the other two, the intermediate appellate courts first hear the appeals. If state courts uphold the conviction, defendants may seek review by U.S. Supreme Court. Even though the chances of four justices voting to hear the case are not high, they are much higher than for ordinary criminal appeals. Having exhausted these appellate remedies, defendants sentenced to death often file numerous writs of *habeas corpus* in state and federal courts, although this practice changed greatly in 1996 (see Chapter 15).

Cost Concerns

After decades of debate over the morality, fairness, and effectiveness of the death penalty, a major new concern has been voiced—cost. In the words of retired California Judge Donald McCartin, who was known as "The Hanging Judge of Orange County" because he sentenced nine men to death row, "It's 10 times more expensive to kill them than to keep them alive" (quoted in Hastings, 2009). Although some might disagree with McCartin's precise cost estimates, few doubt that death penalty prosecutions and appeals are more expensive than noncapital felony prosecutions because they often require extra lawyers, and the appellate process takes years to complete. The high cost of defending capital cases has strained public defender budgets and the courts as well. Thus, within the last decade anti–death penalty advocates have placed less emphasis on the moral arguments against capital punishment, focusing more on the costs and inefficiencies of the practice (Eren, 2015; McLaughlin, 2014).

To assess how cost concerns might affect the death penalty, researchers interviewed prosecutors in South Carolina, where economic issues are particularly important because local governments, not the state, pay for prosecutions. Although local prosecutors recognized that cost might be a concern, they claimed that money issues do not influence their decisions regarding whether to file capital charges. An analysis of statistical data, however, showed a different pattern—the wealthier the county, the greater the death penalty caseloads (Douglas & Stockstill, 2008). A more recent study of 301 prosecutor's offices across 34 states reached the same conclusion: the probability of a defendant facing a death charge is higher in areas with larger budgets (Goelzhauser, 2013).

Normal Penalties and Sentencing Decisions

Making sentencing decisions is not an easy task; many judges say that sentencing is the most difficult part of their job. The frustrations of sentencing stem in part from the need to weigh the possibility of rehabilitation, the need to protect the public, popular demands for retribution, any potential deterrent value in the sentence, and restoration of the victim to the extent possible. Of course, courtroom work groups do not consider these competing perspectives in the abstract. They must sentence real defendants found guilty of actual crimes. Each defendant and crime is somewhat different. Sentences are expected to be individualized—to fit the penalty to the crime and the defendant.

In seeking individualized sentences, courtroom work groups use **normal penalties** (Spohn, 2009; Sudnow, 1965). Based on the usual manner in which crimes are committed and the typical backgrounds of the defendants who commit them, courtroom work groups develop norms of what penalties are appropriate for given categories (see Table 14.3). The normal sentences or "going rates" for typical sentences (Ulmer & Johnson, 2004) are not used mechanically; rather, they guide sentencing. It is within the context of these normal penalties that individualization occurs. Upward and downward adjustments are made. Normal penalties governing appropriate sentences for defendants take into account the seriousness of the crime, the prior criminal record, and any aggravating or mitigating circumstances.

Seriousness of the Offense

The most important factor in setting normal penalties is the seriousness of the offense (Doerner & Demuth, 2014; Kim, Spohn, & Hedberg, 2015; Spohn, 2009; Spohn & DeLone, 2000; Steffensmeier, Ulmer, & Kramer, 1998). The more serious the offense, the less likely the defendant will be granted probation. Also, the more serious the offense, the longer the prison sentence. These conclusions are hardly surprising. Society expects that convicted murderers

TABLE 14.3	Types of Sentences Imposed by Conviction Offense			

	Percent Sentenced to:			
Conviction Type	Prison	Jail	Probation	Other
All Offenses	36	37	25	3
Violent Offenses	57	27	16	1
Murder and Nonnegligent Manslaughter	98	2	0	0
Sexual Assault	84	5	8	3
Robbery	71	18	10	1
Assault	47	34	18	1
Other	47	31	21	1
Property Offenses	42	33	25	1
Burglary	53	26	20	1
Larceny/Theft	40	32	27	0
Motor vehicle theft	46	31	21	2
Forgery	29	34	36	0
Fraud	33	38	29	0
Other Property Crimes	32	46	21	1
Drug Offenses	34	37	28	1
Trafficking	45	35	19	1
Other Drug Offenses	26	39	35	1
Public-Order Offenses	46	34	20	1
Weapons Offenses	53	28	19	0
Driving-Related Crimes	44	39	16	1
Other Public-Order Crimes	42	33	24	1

Source: Brian A. Reaves. 2013. *Felony Defendants in Large Urban Counties,* 2009. Washington, DC: Department of Justice, Bureau of Justice Statistics. Available online at http://www.bjs.gov/content/pub/pdf/fdluc09.pdf

will be punished more severely than defendants found guilty of theft. What is important is how courtroom work groups go about the task of deciding what offenses are serious.

When weighing the seriousness of the offense, courtroom work groups examine the harm or loss suffered by the crime victim in what they perceive to be the "real offense" (what really happened, not the official charge). For example, by examining the prior relationship between the defendant and the victim, the courtroom work group may perceive that the underlying crime is a squabble among friends and therefore less serious than the official charge indicates (Vera Institute of Justice, 1977; Wilmot & Spohn, 2004).

Sometimes, however, the harm caused to society is misjudged by the courtroom work group. Consider that the "going rates" for white-collar crimes reflect great leniency relative to street crimes—especially those of violence, even though major fraud often victimizes hundreds or even thousands of people, whereas a typical assault case victimizes one (Maddan, Hartley, Walker, & Miller, 2012; Michel, 2016; Van Slyke & Bales, 2012).

Sentencing on the basis of seriousness is one of the principal ways courts attempt to arrive at consistent sentences. Most courts use a rank ordering that incorporates the full range of offenses—from the most serious crimes of armed robbery and rape; through middle-level crimes of domestic violence; to the lowest level of forgery, theft, and burglary. One reason that sentences appear to critics to be lenient is that most cases are ranked at the lowest of these levels.

Prior Record

After the seriousness of the offense, the next most important factor in sentencing is the defendant's prior record (Albonetti, 1997; Doerner & Demuth, 2014; Spohn, 2009; Ulmer, 1997). As the prior record increases, so does the sentence. In choosing between probation and imprisonment, the courtroom work group carefully considers the defendant's previous criminal involvement. If the decision has been made to sentence the offender to prison, the prior record also plays a role in setting the length of incarceration. In general, a previous incarceration increases the length of the sentence (Cassidy & Rydberg, 2017; Crow, 2008; DeLisi, 2001; Welch & Spohn, 1986).

How courts assess prior records varies. Some consider only previous convictions, whereas others look at arrests as well. In addition, courtroom work groups often consider the length of time between the current offense and the previous one. If there has been a significant gap, the defendant will often receive a sentence more lenient than normal. On the other hand, if the previous conviction is a recent one, this is often taken as an indication that the defendant is a "bad actor," and the severity of the punishment will increase. Finally, the prior record is assessed within the context of the severity of the crime itself. When the crime is perceived as being less serious, individual factors such as prior record seem to be given relatively more weight than when the crime is more serious.

Aggravating or Mitigating Circumstances

In passing sentence, judges and other members of the courtroom work group consider not only the formal charge but also the way the crime was committed. Prosecutors and defense counsel engage in a careful calculation of moral turpitude, examining the nature of the crime and the role of the victim. Some of the **aggravating circumstances** that lead to a higher penalty are the use of a weapon and severe injury to the victim.

Mitigating factors include lack of mental capacity and role (principal or secondary actor) in the crime. One of the most important mitigating factors is the perceived social stability of the defendant. Marital status, relationship with the family, length of employment, and prior alcohol or drug abuse are considered to be indicators of social stability or instability. Social stability is a particularly important predictor of judges' sentencing, especially when probation is being considered.

The youth of the defendant is often considered a mitigating factor. In *Graham v. Florida* (2009), the U.S. Supreme Court ruled that the Cruel and Unusual Punishment Clause of the Eighth Amendment to the U.S. Constitution does not permit a juvenile offender to be sentenced to life in prison without parole for a nonhomicide crime. Three years later, the Court invalidated the laws of 29 states when it extended this reasoning to homicide offenses carrying automatic life sentences for juveniles. Thus, as a result of *Miller v. Alabama* (2012), judges must be allowed to take a juvenile's age into account, along with other relevant circumstances, when crafting an appropriate sentence—even in murder cases.

Law in Controversy: Uncertainty and Public Opinion

Sentencing is more art than science. Judges, prosecutors, probation officers, and defense attorneys are well aware that they will make mistakes in considering the seriousness of the offense, the prior record of the defendant, aggravating or mitigating circumstances, and the stability of the defendant. Uncertainty is ingrained in the process. They may send someone to prison who should not be there or impose a prison sentence that is longer than necessary. Or they may err in the opposite direction: A defendant recently granted probation may commit a serious and well-publicized crime. Note that only the second type of error will reach public attention; mistakes of the first kind may appear, but only well after the fact.

The uncertainties inherent in sentencing are particularly important at a time when public opinion is critical of the courts and sentencing. For a long time, the majority of Americans felt that sentences were too lenient. In response, legislatures increased the severity of sentences and courts sentenced a higher proportion of defendants to prison. This caused the average sentence length in the United States to nearly double between the 1970s and the mid-2000s. By 2004, 1 out of 11 prison sentences being served in the United States was a life sentence without the possibility of parole (Mauer, King, & Young, 2004). This, in turn, led prisons to become overcrowded, adding further complexity to the difficult task of arriving at a fair and appropriate sentence.

In 2010, though, the incarceration rate in the United States fell for the first time in 40 years (see Figure 14.2). This change appears to be a function of a slow shifting in sentencing policy in response to a number of factors, including lower crime rates, the implementation of evidence-based policies, a renewed focus on rehabilitation for prisoner reentry into society, and a series of sentencing reforms that have begun to scale back some of the harsh "get tough" policies enacted in the past few decades—such as mandatory minimum sentences, as discussed next (Mauer, 2011a). And there can be no doubt that this shift has also been driven by the high costs of mass incarceration during a period of economic strain. But some changes have also been prompted by recognition of racial, ethnic, and socioeconomic differences in sentencing outcomes (Cole, 2011; Mauer, 2011b; Ulmer, Painter-Davis, & Tinik, 2016).

Differences in Sentencing Outcomes

The ideal of equal justice under the law means that all persons convicted of the same offense should receive identical sentences. But not all deviations from equality are unwarranted. The law also strives for individualized dispositions, sometimes reflecting varying degrees of seriousness of the offense, sometimes reflecting varying characteristics of the offender. What one person may perceive as unfairness, another may see as justifiable variation.

Discussions about unwarranted variation in sentencing involve two widely used terms: *disparity* and *discrimination*. Although widely used, these terms are rarely defined consistently. Moreover, the concepts overlap somewhat. Nonetheless, for our purposes they should be treated as involving distinct phenomena.

Disparity refers to inconsistencies in sentencing; the decision-making process is the principal topic of interest. **Discrimination**, on the other hand, refers to illegitimate influences on the sentencing process; defendants' attributes are the primary focus. Legal factors such as the seriousness of the offense and the prior criminal record of the defendant are considered legitimate factors that contribute to disparities. But sentencing discrimination exists when some illegitimate attribute is associated with sentencing outcomes after all other relevant variables are adequately controlled. These objectionable influences are referred to as "extralegal variables" (Walker, Spohn, & DeLone, 2017).

Imbalance Versus Discrimination

No one doubts that the criminal justice system reflects an imbalance in terms of the types of people caught in its web. Whether we examine arrests, prosecutions, convictions, or sentences, the statistical profile highlights the same imbalance—poor, young minority males are disproportionately represented.

Evidence of imbalance in outcomes, however, is not proof of discrimination. Imbalance could be the result of the legally relevant factors discussed earlier in this chapter (such as seriousness of the offense and prior record). In making claims about discrimination, researchers want to make sure they are comparing cases that are truly similar. By way of illustration, consider two defendants of different races who have received different sentences. One of the defendants is a first offender who pled guilty to burglary and received one year of probation. The other has two prior felony convictions and was convicted by a jury of simple robbery and sentenced to three years in prison. Irrespective of which offender was White or African-American, we would not conclude solely on this evidence that the sentences were discriminatory. Rather, we would want to compare a number of cases involving similar crimes and defendants with similar backgrounds.

In trying to ensure that like cases are being compared, researchers use statistical controls. A variety of statistical procedures allow researchers to compare first offenders to other first offenders, and burglars to other burglars. Only after legally relevant variables have been held constant can claims about the existence (or absence) of discrimination be made. Earlier studies often failed to incorporate appropriate statistical controls. They considered only the single variables of race and sentencing, for example, and found racial discrimination in the sentencing. When these studies were reanalyzed, Hagan (1974) found that claims of racial discrimination were not supported by the data.

Sentencing Disparities

The most commonly cited types of sentencing disparity involve geography (variations across jurisdictions) and judicial backgrounds and attitudes (variations among judges within the same jurisdiction).

The Geography of Justice

What counts against defendants is not only what they do but also where they do it. Significant variations in the sentencing patterns of judges in different judicial districts within the same political jurisdiction are referred to as the "geography of justice" or "community effects" (Fearn, 2005). The frequency of fines, probation, intermediate sanctions, or imprisonment varies not only from state to state but also from county to county within a state (e.g., Gainey, Steen, & Engen, 2005; Ulmer, Light, & Kramer, 2011; Wooldredge & Gordon, 1997). Larger, urban courts, for example, make greater use of probation and shorter prison terms than their smaller, rural counterparts (Austin, 1981; Ulmer & Johnson, 2004). The use of intermediate sanctions varies not only across judges but also across court contexts. Judges in courts with high caseloads tend to sentence offenders to probation much more than intermediate sanctions (Johnson & DiPietro, 2012). This is likely a function of judges' caseloads putting pressure on them to dispose of cases as quickly and easily as possible, rather than taking the time to craft more individualized intermediate sanctions for offenders. Johnson and DiPietro (2012) also reported that, unsurprisingly, resources matter. In areas with sufficient funding to support programs associated with a range of intermediate sanctions, judges were more likely to use such sentences. But this presents a proverbial "chicken and egg" question. Do judges use intermediate sanctions more because they are more widely available? Or are courts simply "more aggressive in obtaining funding for these programs" in jurisdictions in which judges make greater use of intermediate sanctions (Johnson & DiPietro, 2012, p. 841)?

Similar geographic variability is also found in the federal court system. For example, districts "with proportionately larger drug trafficking caseloads, and higher caseloads per judge, demonstrate somewhat more consistency in outcomes than those with fewer drug cases and smaller criminal caseloads. These factors also created downward pressure on sentence lengths, as did the median time to case resolution" (Lynch & Omari, 2014, p. 438).

Jurisdictions in the southern United States tend to sentence relatively punitively in comparison to their northeaster counterparts, where a rehabilitative orientation is more prevalent (Lynch, 2011; Lynch & Omari, 2014). Nowhere is this geographical difference in sentencing philosophies more evident than in capital sentences. Recall from Table 14.2 that death sentences and executions are concentrated in the South and the West.

Geographic sentencing patterns demonstrate that court officials, drawn as they are from the local communities, vary in their views of what offenses are the most serious as well as what penalty is appropriate (Myers & Reid, 1995; Myers & Talarico, 1986b). These geographic differences also extend to the federal courts, where the applications of the federal sentencing guidelines vary (Johnson, Ulmer, & Kramer, 2008; Tiede, 2009; Lynch & Omari, 2014). "In sum, substantial evidence exists that what kind of sentence one gets, and the factors that predict why one gets it, in significant part depends on where one is sentenced" (Ulmer, 2012, p. 14).

Judges' Backgrounds and Attitudes

What counts against defendants is not only what they do and where they do it, but also which judge imposes the sentence. Sentencing disparities among judges have fascinated social scientists for decades. A classic study of female shoplifting defendants placed on probation ranged from a low of 10 percent for one judge to a high of 62 percent for another in the same Chicago courthouse (Cameron, 1964). Similarly, downward departures in federal sentencing for certain types of offenders are routine in some districts and rare in others (Johnson, Ulmer, & Kramer, 2008; Tiede, 2009). Although such sentencing disparities are due, in part, to variations in the seriousness of the cases heard, differences in judges' backgrounds and attitudes are major contributing factors.

Variations in judges' backgrounds are associated with different perceptions of what crimes are serious as well as the relative weights to be assigned to conflicting sentencing goals. For example, judges who stress deterrence are more likely to favor longer sentences of incarceration, while judges who are more treatment oriented are more likely to impose suspended sentences or relatively shorter sentences of incarceration (Hogarth, 1971; Gibson, 1983). Such differences in judicial sentencing philosophies can be critically important attitudes to the sentence imposed in a particular case. Consider the results of study by Wooldredge (2010), which concluded that, after statistically controlling for relevant case characteristics, about 14 percent of the variation in the use of prison as a criminal sanction was attributable to judges' individual differences.

Wooldredge also found that judges differed in the weight they accorded different sentencing factors —including offender characteristics. Anderson and Spohn (2010) concluded the same thing, adding that factors like judicial caseload and prior legal experience also affect sentencing decisions.

Although the public views judges as either harsh or lenient sentencers, detailed studies indicate that the pattern is far more complex (Myers & Talarico, 1987b). It is an accepted fact that judges have different sentencing tendencies. Some have reputations for handing out stiff sentences while others are known for lenient sentences. The sentences of most judges fall somewhere in between these extremes (Partridge & Eldridge, 1974).

After statistically controlling for a wide range of factors, judges from racial and ethnic minority backgrounds were found to be a little more lenient in the sentences imposed, but female judges were not (Johnson, 2006). Subsequent research by Johnson (2014) revealed that the exercise of judicial discretion at sentencing appears to vary by the mode of conviction. "A greater proportion of variation in incarceration decisions emerged between judges for trial cases than for other dispositional outcomes. Similarly, the magnitude of between-judge differences in sentence lengths was twice as great for trials compared to pleas" (p. 176). It's important to keep in mind, however, that although sentencing outcomes differ across judges, the magnitude of these differences tend to be small—especially in jurisdictions that use sentencing guidelines. In short, who the sentencing judge is certainly matters, but overall variations between judges appear to have only a weak effect on sentencing outcomes in most cases (Steffensmeier & Hebert, 1999).

Discrimination in Noncapital Sentencing

Numerous studies have probed the extent to which a defendant's attributes, such as economic status, sex, and race, pierce the judicial blindfold when sentences are imposed. The results are provocative, not only because they raise important issues of equality before the law but also because they frequently appear to contradict one another.

Some studies find patterns of discrimination, and others do not. Clearly, sentencing discrimination involves complex issues, and researchers disagree over how best to study it. The discussion that follows examines the research concerning discrimination under the headings of economic status, sex, and race.

Economic Status

Access to economic resources makes a big difference in court processes. The poor receive significantly less preferential treatment as evidenced by the fact that they are less likely to be released on bail prior to trial and also are less likely to be able to hire a private attorney. These differences during processing carry over to sentencing: Defendants who are not released on bail or are represented by a court-appointed attorney are granted probation less often and are given longer prison sentences.

Outcome differences based on economic status are, therefore, readily apparent in sentencing. The provocative title of a book by Jeffrey Reiman (2007), *The Rich Get Richer and the Poor Get Prison*, reflects this fact. Prisons are arguably the modern equivalent of the poorhouse. Do these patterns indicate that courts discriminate against the poor in sentencing, or are they the product of other, legally permissible, factors? A number of studies yield conflicting and complex answers.

Some studies conclude that unemployment affects sentencing decisions (Chiricos & Bales, 1991; Walsh, 1987). For example, judges may assess unemployed persons as being at higher risk for reoffending (Spohn & Holleran, 2000). In contrast, other studies find that unemployment has no significant influence on sentencing (Clarke & Koch, 1976; Myers & Talarico, 1986a).

A comprehensive study comparing two cities highlights the complexity of the relationship between economic status and sentencing. In Kansas City, unemployment had a direct effect on the decision to grant probation but none on the length of imprisonment. In Chicago, on the other hand, unemployment had no effect on the decision to grant probation but directly affected sentence length. Perhaps most important, unemployment interacted with race and ethnicity. If the offender was white, unemployment status had no effect. For African-American or Hispanic young males, though, unemployment was related to harsher sentencing. Nobiling, Spohn, and DeLone (1998) concluded that certain types of unemployed offenders are perceived as "social dynamite." The term *social dynamite* is used to characterize the segment of the deviant population seen as particularly threatening and dangerous. Viewed from this perspective, economic status appears to be a dimension of social stability considered by the courtroom work group during sentencing (see also LaFrenz & Spohn, 2006).

Sex

Crime, as Chapter 9 emphasized, is predominantly (but not exclusively) a male enterprise. The marked imbalance between male and female defendants complicates efforts to examine gender-based differences in sentencing outcomes.

Some empirical research suggests that women are less likely to be incarcerated in jail or prison than men, and when they are incarcerated, women receive shorter sentences than men even when sentencing guidelines are in effect that should reduce such gender disparities (Blackwell, Holleran, & Finn, 2008; Doerner & Demuth, 2014; Tillyer, Hartley, & Ward, 2015). Other studies found that when the sexes are in similar circumstances and are charged with similar offenses, no significant gender-based differences are found (Crew, 1991; Koeppel, 2014; Spohn & Spears, 1996; Steffensmeier, Kramer, & Streifel, 1993).

Recall from Chapter 6 that *focal concerns perspective* posits that charging and sentencing decisions are shaped by three primary focal concerns: blameworthiness, protection of the community, and the practical constraints and consequences of the sentencing decision (Steffensmeier, Ulmer, & Kramer, 1998; Ulmer, 1997). As Spohn (2009) suggested, this framework helps to explain the gender-gap in sentencing: because women commit far fewer crimes than men, they are viewed as being at lower risk for recidivating and, therefore, posing less danger to the community than male defendants who are similarly situated, legally speaking. Additionally, the practical constraints and consequences concern also offers a reason for sex-based gender disparities. Women, much more than men, tend to bear much greater responsibility for family care. Thus,

judges may show more leniency to women for the benefit of their dependent children (Daly, 1994).

Regardless of the theoretical explanations, concern remains that different criteria influence the legal processing of male and female offenders. Some studies report that gender-role expectations and stereotypes guide parole decision making (Erez, 1992), and that a form of gender bias exists in capital punishment laws (Rapaport, 1991). It is important to note, however, that according to a meta-analysis study by Bontrager, Barrick, and Stupi (2013), many of the most recent studies find much less of a gender-based disparity today than existed in the past, suggesting that "sentencing outcomes may reflect the 'justice equalization' predicted [by some scholars] and signal that 'equal treatment under the law' is becoming more of a practice than an ideal"—at least insofar as sex is concerned (p. 366).

Race

More studies have been done of racial discrimination at the sentencing stage than at any other decision point in the criminal justice system. Studies conducted from the 1930s through the 1960s often reported that extralegal factors such as race were responsible for differences in sanctions. These original findings, however, have not stood up to further analysis, because they failed to use appropriate statistical techniques. When Hagan (1974) reexamined the data from early studies, he found that the relationship between the race of the offender and the sentence handed out was not statistically significant. Contemporary research using appropriate statistical techniques has produced conflicting findings.

Some researchers conclude that African-Americans are sentenced more harshly than Whites (Franklin, 2015; Spohn & Holleran, 2000; Steffensmeier, Ulmer, & Kramer, 1998; Zatz, 1984). A prominent example of this type of conclusion was based on a study of six American cities. In three southern cities, African-Americans were sentenced to prison more often than Whites. No such differences were found in northern jurisdictions (Welch, Spohn, & Gruhl, 1985). A meta-analysis of 71 studies that examined the effects of race on criminal sentencing concluded that even when legal factors (such as criminal history and severity of the offense) were statistically controlled, "on average African-Americans were sentenced more harshly than Whites," although racial differences were generally small (Mitchell, 2005, p. 462; see also Crow & Johnson, 2008; Spohn & Cederblom, 1991). More recent studies have also found racial disparities in sentencing outcomes for Hispanic offenders, especially in drug-related cases (Brennan & Spohn, 2008; Ulmer, Painter-Davis, & Tinik, 2016).

In contrast, another group of studies failed to find a link between race and sentencing (Beaver, DeLisi, Wright, Boutwell, Barnes, & Vaughn, 2013; D'Alessio & Stolzenberg, 2009; Klein, Petersilia, & Turner, 1990; Kramer & Steffensmeier, 1993; McDonald & Carlson 1993; Myers & Talarico, 1986a; Wooldredge, 2012). Research in diverse geographical locations reported the absence of consistent evidence of systematic racial discrimination in sentencing. Perhaps typical is a study of sentencing in federal courts (McDonald & Carlson, 1993), which found that from 1986 to 1988 "White, Black, and Hispanic offenders received similar sentences, on average, in Federal District Courts." After sentencing guidelines were imposed in 1989, Hispanic and African-American offenders were slightly more likely than White offenders to be sentenced to prison, but these apparent racial differences were directly attributable to characteristics of offenses and offenders.

Finally, a few studies concluded that African-Americans are sentenced more leniently than Whites (Bernstein, Kelly, & Doyle, 1977; Walker, Spohn, & DeLone, 2012).

At first blush, the findings on the studies of racial and ethnic effects on sentencing outcomes may appear to be inconsistent, making it difficult to draw firm conclusions. But the results of the most recent and methodologically sophisticated studies evidence that the contemporary sentencing process, while not characterized by "a widespread systematic pattern of discrimination" (Blumstein, Cohen, Martin, & Tonry, 1983, p. 93), is nonetheless not racially neutral.

Some research has noted that the impact of race on sentencing disparities can be mediated by the racial composition of the courtroom work group. Specifically, more racially diverse courtroom work groups— especially within prosecutors' offices—appear to reduce sentencing disparities (Ward, Farrell, & Rousseau, 2009; King, Johnson, & McGeever, 2010).

Age

Although youth under the age of 18 is generally a mitigating factor for criminal responsibility (see Chapter 4), the impact of age on sentencing outcomes is far from clear for those age 18 and older. Steffensmeier and colleagues (1995) found that the relationship between age and sentence length was best characterized by an inverted U-shaped pattern, meaning individuals who were 18 to 20 years old and those over the age of 50 received especially lenient sentences. Spohn and Holleran (2000) found no support for such a pattern. Morrow, Vickovic, and Fradella (2014) found no direct effect of youthful age mitigating sentences for offenders between 18 and 20, but did find what they termed a "senior citizen discount." Judges afford more leniency in sentencing to offenders over the age of 60 compared to their younger counterparts, regardless of gender (see also Miller, 2011). Women, however, benefit from this age discount more than men in terms of being less likely to be incarcerated and receiving shorter sentences than males in the same age group (Morrow, Vickovic, & Fradella, 2014).

The Effects of Intersectionality

Although research continues to examine the effects of specific legal and extralegal factors on sentencing decisions, most contemporary research has demonstrated that the interaction between these variables produces the most significant differences. Thus, as discussed, research has demonstrated racial and ethnic differences in sentencing outcomes; however, these disparities are magnified when other extralegal variables, such as age, gender, educational level, employment, and socioeconomic status are taken into account (Franklin & Fearn, 2008; LaFrenz & Spohn, 2006; Nowacki, 2016; Spohn & Holleran, 2000; Ulmer & Johnson, 2004; Wooldredge, 2012). As leading sentencing scholar Cassia Spohn concisely summarized, "consistent with the focal concerns perspective . . . is the combination of race, ethnicity, and sex that triggers attributions of dangerousness and threat in the minds of judges" (Spohn, 2013, p. 104). Specifically, research supports the proposition that young, poor, African-American males and Hispanic males are sentenced more harshly than any other group (Curry & Corral-Camacho, 2008; Freiburger & Hilinski, 2013; Spohn, 2013; Spohn & DeLone, 2000;

Steffensmeier et al., 1998; Ulmer, Painter-Davis, & Tinik, 2016; Warren, Chiricos, & Bales, 2012).

Discrimination and Capital Punishment

Capital punishment has figured prominently in studies of racial discrimination in sentencing. Marked racial differences in the application of the death penalty in the South provide the most obvious historical evidence of racial discrimination in sentencing. From 1930 to 1966, 72 percent of the prisoners executed in the South were African-American. This proportion is dramatically higher than the ratio of African-Americans in the overall population or the ratio of African-Americans convicted of capital offenses. The racial gap was even more pronounced in rape cases. Only the South executed rapists, and 90 percent of those executed for rape were African-American. Those most likely to be executed were African-Americans who had raped white women (Wolfgang & Riedel, 1973). Recall that in the modern era, rape is no longer a death-eligible offense. But the evolution of capital punishment law has not eliminated racial disparities in death penalty cases.

Offender–Victim Dyad

The executions in the South clearly show major racial differences (see Table 14.2). But racial disparities in outcomes do not prove discrimination. Interestingly, many studies found that the most obvious factor—race of the defendant—was not as important as the race of the offender in combination with the race of the victim. The offender–victim dyad, ordered according to the perceived seriousness of the offense, is as follows:

1. Black offender, White victim
2. White offender, White victim
3. Black offender, Black victim
4. White offender, Black victim

Research on the offender–victim dyad established that Blacks killing or raping Whites were the most likely to be executed; conversely, Whites killing or raping Blacks were the least likely to receive the death penalty. These findings have been interpreted as indicating that severe punishments were motivated by a desire to protect the White social order.

Some also argue that Black lives were not valued as much as White lives. A variety of studies indicated that the use of the death penalty in the South was racially discriminatory (Baldus, Pulaski, & Woodworth, 1983; Hindelang, 1972; Ralph, Sorensen, & Marquart, 1992). A different conclusion emerged for the North. Studies of the death penalty in northern states found no evidence of racial discrimination (Kleck, 1981).

Evidence of Discrimination since *Gregg*

Major racial differences in execution rates, together with studies finding racial discrimination in the application of the death penalty, figured prominently in the opinions of several justices when the Supreme Court struck down state death penalty laws in 1972 (*Furman v. Georgia*). The Court later upheld guided discretion statutes designed to reduce or eliminate the arbitrariness with which the death penalty is imposed. Since *Gregg v. Georgia* in 1976, several studies have reported evidence of racial discrimination in the application of post-*Gregg* death penalty laws.

Research on the use of the death penalty post-*Gregg* continue to find that the race of the defendant is rarely associated with the imposition of a death sentence (Williams, Demuth, & Holcomb, 2007). Rather, studies that find evidence of discrimination in the modern era report that Black defendants who kill White victims are more likely to receive adverse treatment than those with similarly situated cases with non-Black defendant-White victim cases (Paternoster & Brame, 2008). Conclusions like this have emerged in states as diverse as Maryland, Florida, South Carolina, Georgia, and Colorado (Spohn, 2009).

One stage in the process at which discrimination occurs, according to these studies, is the decision of the prosecutor to charge the defendant with a capital homicide, rather than a homicide that typically carries a life sentence (Radelet & Pierce, 1985; Sorensen & Wallace, 1999; Weiss, Berk, & Lee, 1996). In South Carolina, for example, the race of the victim was found to be a significant factor structuring the district attorney's decision to request capital punishment. For African-American offenders who killed White victims, the prosecutor was 40 times more likely to request the death penalty than in the case of African-American defendants accused of killing other African-Americans (Paternoster, 1984). Similarly, in Colorado, prosecutors were more likely to seek the death penalty for homicides with White female victims (regardless of the race of the defendant), and the probability of death being sought was 4.2 times higher for those who killed Whites than for those who killed Blacks (Hindson, Potter, & Radelet, 2006).

These studies also found that jurors are more likely to choose a sentence of death rather than life imprisonment during the penalty phase of the trial. Indeed, when the U.S. General Accounting Office (1990) reviewed the body of literature on racial discrimination in capital litigation in the post-*Gregg* era, it reported that in "82 percent of the studies, race of the victim was found to influence the likelihood of being charged with capital murder or receiving the death penalty, i.e., those who murdered whites were found to be more likely to be sentenced to death than those who murdered blacks" (p. 6). More recent studies have confirmed that this pattern has continued (Baldus & Woodworth, 2003; Baldus, Woodworth, Grosso, & Christ, 2002; Jacobs & Kent, 2007; Jacobs, Qian, Carmichael, & Kent, 2007; Paternoster & Brame, 2008).

Evidence of No Discrimination since *Gregg*

Findings that the application of the death penalty remain racially biased despite the apparent protections required by *Gregg* were challenged by a study of all death-eligible cases appealed to the Louisiana Supreme Court (Klemm, 1986). The initial analysis revealed the impact of extralegal variables. The chance of receiving a death sentence steadily decreased as one moved down the scale of offender–victim dyads. These findings clearly paralleled earlier ones in other states. More sophisticated analysis, however, highlighted the importance of legal variables.

Unlike previous researchers, Klemm also examined how the crime was committed. The prior relationship of the offender to the victim emerged as an important factor. *Primary homicides* are crimes of passion involving persons who knew each other. *Nonprimary homicides* occur during the commission of another felony (most typically, armed robbery), and the victim is a total stranger. Those convicted of nonprimary homicides were more likely to receive a sentence of death, regardless of the race of the offender or the race of the victim. Thus, the

chances of receiving a death sentence were greater if the victim was a stranger.

Overall, the race of the victim had only an indirect effect in Louisiana. Likewise, a study of the use of the death penalty in Texas prior to *Furman* found some remarkable parallels to the findings from Louisiana. In particular, nonprimary homicides were more likely to result in the imposition of the death penalty (Ralph, Sorensen, & Marquart, 1992).

The importance of examining not just the victim but the nature of the homicide as well emerges in recent research on victim gender. In murder cases, defendants who victimize women are punished more harshly. The three victimization factors were rape, forcing the victim to disrobe, and killing an unclothed victim (Williams et al., 2007).

McCleskey v. Kemp Rejects Social Science Evidence

The U.S. Supreme Court squarely addressed the issue of racial discrimination in capital punishment in a controversial 1987 decision, *McCleskey v. Kemp.* At issue was a study in Georgia that the application of capital punishment was related to the offender–victim dyad. Defendants convicted of killing a White victim were four times more likely to receive a sentence of death than those found guilty of slaying an African-American victim. These racial differences remained even after controls for relevant factors such as prior record and type of homicide were introduced. The authors concluded that Georgia had a dual system of capital punishment, based on the race of the victim (Baldus et al., 1983).

By a 5-to-4 vote, the majority rejected claims that statistical studies indicated that the state's death penalty law was "wanton and freakish" in application. To Justice Lewis Powell, "Disparities are an inevitable part of our criminal justice system." The opinion argued that the statistics do not prove that race enters into any capital sentencing decisions or that race was a factor in McCleskey's case. To be clear, though, the Supreme Court emphasized that racial discrimination in the imposition of the death penalty violates the Fourteenth Amendment's guarantees of due process and equal protection. However, proof of such discrimination cannot rest on statistical evidence of racially disparate sentencing outcomes. Rather, a defendant must prove that a specific state actor (or group of actors) intentionally discriminated against him or her in the specific case—a task that is often virtually impossible (Paternoster & Brame, 2008).

Overall, as the U.S. Supreme Court has become more supportive of the death penalty, it has become less inclined to consider social science evidence that might show patterns of racial discrimination (Acker, 1993; Fradella, 2004). That is not to say that statistical evidence of discrimination is inadmissible in federal or state trial courts (see Alexander, 2014). But being admissible and being convincing are two separate questions, as critics continue to point to patterns of discrimination in the application of the death penalty.

Conclusion

Although the replica of Lady Justice outside the courthouse contemplates justice in the abstract, judges inside the courthouse must pass judgment on real-life defendants, not the stereotypical villains who dominate the rhetoric of elected officials. In deciding whether to send an offender to prison or grant him or her probation, the scales of justice require the judge (and other members of the courtroom work group) to weigh the normal penalty for the offense, the seriousness of the crime, and the defendant's prior record and social stability. The resulting decisions have become the focus of heated public debate—especially when the sentence is one of death.

During the past three decades, there has been an unprecedented public debate over *why* we sentence. The previously dominant goal of rehabilitation has come under sharp attack, and many voices urge that punishment should instead be based on the principle of just deserts. After 40 years of stability, the indeterminate sentencing system has been rejected in state after state. Determinate sentencing laws, mandatory minimum sentencing provisions, and sentencing guidelines are the most prominent changes undertaken. Sentencing is likely to remain on the nation's political agenda.

For many years, members of the public and elected officials alike generally ignored the important reality of swelling prison populations. The resultant prison overcrowding caused federal courts to require major improvements in prison conditions. But improving the capacity and quality of prisons creates a political dilemma insofar as it costs large sums of tax dollars to build and improve correctional facilities. Thus, sentencing is likely to remain an important public policy issue for the foreseeable future.

CHAPTER REVIEW

LO1   1. Distinguish between the five major sentencing philosophies.

The five major sentencing philosophies are retribution, which seeks to punish wrongdoers; incapacitation, which is aimed at removing offenders from the community; deterrence, whose goal is to prevent the commission of future crimes; rehabilitation, which emphasizes restoring the offender to a constructive place in society; and restoration, which attempts to promote the victim's healing.

LO2   2. Describe how the three branches of government are involved in sentencing.

The legislative branch of government defines the range of possible punishment for a given crime. The judicial branch of government has discretion in choosing the specific sentence for the individual criminal. The executive branch of government is responsible for carrying out the actual sentence, including running prisons, pardons, and parole.

LO3   3. Recognize the main objective of changes in sentencing structure beginning in the late 1960s and the major consequences of these changes.

The main objective of changes in sentencing structure beginning in the late 1960s was a reduction in judicial discretion in sentencing. The major consequence of these changes has been a major increase

in the number of persons in prison in the United States.

LO4 4. Outline how the U.S. Supreme Court has limited both state and federal sentencing guidelines.

Beginning in 2000, the U.S. Supreme Court has raised serious constitutional doubts about the constitutionality of state sentencing guidelines. In particular, the Court held in *Apprendi v. New Jersey* (2000) that any fact which increases the penalty for a crime beyond the prescribed statutory maximum, other than the fact of a prior conviction, must be submitted to a jury and proved beyond a reasonable doubt. Put differently, juries and not judges have the authority to decide on important facts (other than prior record) that determine sentencing. Then, in *United States v. Booker* (2005), the Supreme Court held that the federal sentencing guidelines are unconstitutional but judges may use them as advisory information. In later cases, the Court held that judges may indeed sentence defendants more leniently than the guidelines prescribe.

LO5 5. Explain the law in action perspective on researching the impact of mandatory minimum sentences.

A law on the books approach to mandatory minimum sentences stresses certainty of punishment, whereas a law in action approach stresses nullification by discretion. Researchers find that at a number of stages in the process, including police arrest, prosecutorial charging, trial convictions, and judicial sentencing, discretionary changes occur in the process that nullify the impact of these laws.

LO6 6. List at least three major issues related to imprisonment as a sentence in the United States.

The three issues most directly related to the use of imprisonment as a sentence in the United States are prison overcrowding, which limits how many guilty defendants may be sentenced to prison; conditions of confinement lawsuits, which impact living conditions in prison; and the high costs of incarcerating prisoners.

LO7 7. Identify the major alternatives to institutional incarceration.

The major alternatives to imprisonment include probation, which is often used in felonies; fines, which are rarely used in felonies; restitution, which is increasingly imposed after a misdemeanor and/or felony conviction; and intermediate sanctions, such as community service, house arrest, intensive-supervision probation, boot camp, and electronic monitoring.

LO8 8. Summarize the two U.S. Supreme Court rulings from the 1970s on capital punishment that led to the bifurcated process for death penalty sentencing.

In *Furman v. Georgia* (1972), the Court declared that most U.S. death penalty laws were unconstitutional because of their arbitrary nature. In *Gregg v. Georgia* (1976), the Court upheld death penalty laws that specified aggravating and mitigating circumstances for when the death penalty may be applied and also provided for separate phases of the trial, one to determine guilt and the other to decide on the penalty.

LO9 9. Indicate how the U.S. Supreme Court has narrowed the list of death-eligible cases and offenders.

The Court has narrowed the list of death-eligible cases by striking down death penalty provisions for most crimes, such as rape—even of a child—and upholding capital punishment only in homicide cases thus far; treason remains an open question. The Court has also narrowed the list of death-eligible offenders by declaring that developmental issues, such as age less than 18 years at the time of the crime or intellectual disabilities, preclude execution.

LO10 10. Define the concept of normal crimes and indicate the two most important factors in determining normal penalties.

The concept of normal crimes refers to the group norms about the typical manner in which crimes are committed and the typical characteristics of defendants who commit those crimes. The seriousness of the offense and the prior record of the defendant are the most important factors in determining normal penalties.

LO11 11. Distinguish between the concepts of sentencing disparities and discrimination.

The concepts of disparity and discrimination highlight unwarranted variations in sentencing but point to different types of factors. *Disparities* **refer to inconsistencies resulting from the decision-making process. By contrast,** *discrimination* **refers to illegitimate influences on the sentencing process related to the characteristics of the defendant being sentenced.**

CRITICAL THINKING QUESTIONS

1. In what ways is restorative justice similar to the four dominant sentencing philosophies of retribution, incapacitation, deterrence, and rehabilitation? In what ways is restorative justice different from these four sentencing philosophies?

2. Should the punishment fit the crime, or should the punishment fit the criminal? In what ways do the four sentencing philosophies provide different answers to this question?

3. What is the mix of legislative, judicial, and executive sentencing responsibilities in your state? What changes, if any, have occurred over the past decade in the balance of sentencing responsibilities?

4. Public criticism of lenient sentencing tends to occur in a select number of violent crimes or highly unusual circumstances. In what ways do such discussions deflect attention from the question of what the appropriate sentence should be for the bulk of defendants convicted of nonviolent crimes (burglary and theft, for example) and drug-related crimes?

5. Within the courtroom work group, which actor is the most influential in sentencing decisions? Why? How might influence vary from one courtroom to the next?

6. In what ways do sentencing guidelines reflect normal penalties? In what ways do they differ?

7. How have public demands to "get tough on crimes" changed the sentencing process in the past few decades? Why do courtroom work groups resist such efforts and often subvert them?

KEY TERMS

aggravating circumstances   454

bifurcated trial   447

boot camp   444

capital offense   445

capital punishment   445

celerity of punishment   420

certainty of punishment   420

community service   442

conditions of confinement
    lawsuit   438

cruel and unusual
    punishment   436

day fine   441

death-eligible   449

death penalty   444

death-qualified juries   449

determinate sentence/determinate
    sentencing   429

deterrence theory   419

direct restitution   442

discrimination   455

disparity   455

electronic monitoring (EM)   443

evidence-based corrections   421

expiation   419

fine   441

Furman v. Georgia   446

general deterrence   420

good time   424

Gregg v. Georgia   447

hedonistic calculus   420

home detention   443

imprisonment   436

incapacitation   421

indeterminate
    sentence   423

FOR FURTHER READING

Austin, James, and John Irwin. 2011. *It's about Time: America's Imprisonment Binge*. 4th ed. Belmont, CA: Wadsworth.

Barak, Gregg, Paul Leighton, and Jeanne Flavin. 2010. *Class, Race, Gender, and Crime: The Social Realities of Justice in America*. Lanham, Maryland: Rowman and Littlefield.

Belknap, Joanne. 2014. *The Invisible Woman: Gender, Crime, and Justice*. 4th ed. Belmont, CA: Cengage.

Bryer, Stephen, and John Bessler. 2016. *Against the Death Penalty*. Washington, DC: The Brookings Institution.

Clear, Todd. 2007. *Imprisoning Communities: How Mass Incarceration Makes Disadvantaged Neighborhoods Worse*. New York: Oxford University Press.

Gabbidon, Shaun, and Helen Green. 2016. *Race and Crime*. 4th ed. Thousand Oaks, CA: Sage.

Hinton, Elizabeth. 2016. *From the War on Poverty to the War on Crime: The Making of Mass Incarceration in America*. Cambridge, MA: Harvard University Press.

Latzer, Barry. 2010. *Death Penalty Cases*. 3rd ed. Boston: Butterworth-Heineman.

Lynch, Michael. 2007. *Big Prisons, Big Dreams: Crime and the Failure of America's Penal System*. Piscataway, NJ: Rutgers University Press.

Lyon, Andrea. 2014. *The Death Penalty: What's Keeping It Alive*. New York, NY: Rowan & Littlefield.

Mandery, Evan. 2013. *A Wild Justice: The Death and Resurrection of Capital Punishment in America*. New York, NY: W.W. Norton.

Mears, Daniel P., and Joshua C. Cochran. 2015. *Prisoner Reentry in the Era of Mass Incarceration*. Thousand Oaks, CA: Sage.

O'Hear, Michael. 2017. *The Failed Promise of Sentencing Reform*. Santa Barbara, CA: Praeger.

Pfaff, John. 2017. *Locked In: The True Causes of Mass Incarceration—and How to Achieve Real Reform*. New York, NY: Basic Books.

Rice, Stephen, Danielle Dirks, and Julie Exline. 2009. "Of Guilt, and Repentance: Evidence from the Texas Death Chamber." *Justice Quarterly* 26: 295–326.

Richie, Beth. 2012. *Arrested Justice: Black Women, Violence, and Americas Prison Nation*. New York: New York University Press.

Sarat, Austin. 2014. *Gruesome Spectacles: Botched Executions and America's Death Penalty*. Stanford, CA: Stanford University Press.

Shust, Kelsey. 2014. "Extending Sentencing Mitigation for Deserving Young Adults." *Journal of Criminal Law & Criminology* 104: 667–704.

Simon, Jonathan. 2014. *Mass Incarceration on Trial: A Remarkable Court Decision and the Future of Prisons in America*. New York, NY: The Free Press.

Tonry, Michael. 2016. *Sentencing Fragments: Penal Reform in America, 1975–2025*. New York: Oxford University Press.

Tsui, Judy. 2014. "Breaking Free of the Prison Paradigm: Integrating Restorative Justice Techniques into Chicago's Juvenile Justice System." *Journal of Criminal Law & Criminology*. 104: 634–666.

Van Ness, Daniel W., and Karen Heetderks Strong. 2016. *Restoring Justice: An Introduction to Restorative Justice*. 5th ed. New York, NY: Routledge.

Vollum, Scott, Rolando del Carmen, Durant Frantzen, Claudia San Migel, and Kelley Cheeseman. 2014. *The Death Penalty: Constitutional Issues, Commentaries, and Case Briefs*. 3rd ed. New York, NY: Routledge.

The 2017 "class photo" of the justices of the U.S. Supreme Court. Seated, from left to right, are Justices Ruth Bader Ginsburg, Justice Anthony Kennedy, John Roberts, Clarence Thomas, and Stephen Breyer. Standing, from left to right, are Justices Elena Kagan; Justice Samuel Alito, Jr.; Sonia Sotomayor; and Neil Gorsuch.

Chapter Outline

For 20 years, Paul House sat on death row proclaiming his innocence. A Tennessee jury had found him guilty of murder and sentenced him to death on the basis of forensic evidence—primarily bloodstains and semen. His case had already been reviewed by numerous courts, but along the way, he and his lawyers had failed to raise key points in their earlier court papers. But then new evidence, some of it based on DNA testing, cast doubt on the jury's verdict.

Should House be entitled to yet another hearing in federal court? Proponents of the crime control model argue that *House* is a textbook example of endless appeals, and therefore he should not be allowed yet one more review.

Supporters of the due process model, on the other hand, counter that basic fairness is far more important than failure to comply with a narrow technical requirement.

House v. Bell (2006) highlights the importance of appellate court decisions. To be sure, appellate courts decide far fewer cases than the trial courts. Nonetheless, the relatively small numbers of cases decided by the appellate courts are critically important for the entire judicial process. Appellate courts subject the trial court's action to a second look, examining not a raw dispute in the course of being presented but rather a controversy already decided. This second look provides a degree of detachment by a group of judges who can examine the process to see whether mistakes were made. Appellate courts are important for a second reason: Through written opinions, appellate judges engage in significant policy making.

Ultimately, the decisions of a group of judges not only determine the results of specific cases (the fate of individual defendants like Paul House) but also, and more important, they shape the law by providing the reasons for the decisions reached. *House v. Bell* also symbolizes how a relative handful of death penalty decisions receive a disproportionate share of appellate court time and attention.

Nature of the Appellate Process

One of the few aspects of the American judicial process about which consensus exists is that everyone who loses in a trial court should have the right to appeal to a higher court. Yet, the appeals process is widely misunderstood. In the United States, an appeal is not a retrial of the case, nor is it ordinarily a reexamination of factual issues decided by a trial court. U.S. appellate courts hear no new testimony and consider no new evidence. Rather, they focus on how decisions were made in the trial court, basing their review on the appellate court record. Thus, an appellate court's function is primarily to review the questions of law presented in a case.

Appellate courts were created in part because of the belief that several heads are better than one when examining such legal questions. In essence, the decisions of a single judge on matters of the law are subjected to review by a panel of judges who are removed from the heat engendered by the trial and are consequently in a position to take a more objective view of the legal questions raised. They operate as multimember or collegial bodies, with decisions made by a group of judges. In the courts of last resort, all judges typically participate in all cases. On intermediate appellate courts, decisions are typically made using rotating three-judge panels, but in important cases, all judges may participate (this is termed an *en banc* hearing).

In unraveling the complexities of the review process, it is helpful to begin by asking why appellate courts exist and why dissatisfied litigants are permitted to appeal.

The Purposes of Appeal

The most obvious function of appellate courts is **error correction**. During trial, a significant portion of the decision making is "spur of the moment." As one trial judge phrased it, "We're where the action is. We often have to 'shoot from the hip' and hope you're doing the right thing. You can't ruminate forever every time you have to make a ruling. We'd be spending months on each case if we ever did that" (quoted in Carp & Stidham, 1990, p. 256). Fortunately, judges' quickly made decisions are often surprisingly accurate, although sometimes mistakes do occur (Guthrie, Rachlinski, & Wistrich, 2007). As reviewing bodies, appellate courts oversee the work of the lower courts, ensuring that the law was correctly interpreted. Thus, the error-correction function of appellate review protects against arbitrary, capricious, or mistaken legal decisions by a trial court judge.

The other primary function of appellate courts is **policy formulation**. The lawmaking function focuses on situations in which appellate courts fill in the gaps in existing law, clarify old doctrines, extend existing precedent to new situations, and on occasion even overrule previous decisions. Thus, through policy formulation, appellate courts shape the law in response to changing conditions in society. Stated another way, error correction is concerned primarily with the effect of the judicial process on individual litigants, whereas policy formulation involves the impact of the appellate court decision on other cases (see Cooper & Berman, 2000).

Limitations on the Right to Appellate Review

A basic principle of U.S. law is that the losing party has the **right to one appeal**. So long as the person seeking to appeal the decision of a lower court follows the rules for perfecting an appeal (such as filing a timely notice of appeal and meeting all appellate court deadlines), that initial appeal is guaranteed as a right. However, once a criminal defendant has been convicted at trial, the legal shield of innocence is gone. The individual is no longer considered innocent until proven guilty but rather now stands guilty in the eyes of the law. This has important implications for bail. Guilty defendants no longer have a right to bail; courts may set a bail amount (typically in higher amounts than prior to trial), but many defendants wait out their appeal in prison.

Although U.S. law recognizes the right to one appeal, the right to appellate review is subject to several important limits and exceptions. Appeals, for example, may be filed only by parties who have lost in the lower court. In *Kepner v. United States* (1904), the U.S. Supreme Court held that the prosecution is not permitted to appeal an acquittal. This is because the Fifth Amendment guarantees, "Nor shall any person be subject for the same offense to be twice put in jeopardy of life or limb." This provision protects citizens from **double jeopardy** (a second prosecution of the same person for the same crime by the same sovereign after the first trial). Thus, once a not-guilty verdict is returned, a prosecutor cannot appeal the acquittal, even if the original trial was littered with serious mistakes (*Sanabria v. United States*, 1978). Prosecutors may, however, appeal questions of law that would not result in a defendant being put in jeopardy again. For example, if a judge made a serious error in an evidentiary ruling, the prosecution could appeal so that there would be appellate precedent on the books; therefore, trial court judges would know not to make a similar mistake again in the future. Alternatively, if a defendant was never really in jeopardy because a trial was conducted fraudulently (for example, if the defendant bribed the judge or a juror), then double jeopardy will not prohibit a prosecutor from appeals for a new trial (*Aleman v. Judges of the Criminal Division, Circuit Court of Cook County, IL*, 1998).

Appeals are also discretionary; that is, the losing party is not required to seek appellate court review. The lone exception involves capital punishment cases; when a jury imposes a sentence of death, the case must be appealed regardless of the defendant's wishes. Typically, this automatic review is heard directly by a state court of last resort, thereby bypassing any intermediate courts of appeals a state may have. The mandatory appeal requirements in capital punishment cases aside, in all other cases, civil and criminal, appeals are discretionary.

When cases may be appealed is limited. As a general rule, the losing party may appeal only from a final judgment of the lower court. In this context,

a judgment is considered final when a final decision has been reached in the lower court. In very limited situations, however, litigants may appeal certain types of **interlocutory** (nonfinal) orders. Prosecutors may file an interlocutory appeal on certain pretrial rulings that substantially hinder the state's ability to proceed to trial. For example, if the trial court suppresses a defendant's confession or excludes physical evidence because of an illegal search and seizure, the prosecution may file an interlocutory appeal arguing that the judge's ruling was in error.

Appeals are also confined to issues properly raised in the trial court. Recall from Chapter 13 that during trial, attorneys must make timely objections to the judge's rulings on points of law or the objection will be deemed waived. This is called the **contemporaneous objection rule**. Thus, an attorney making an objection and the trial judge overruling it constitutes a disagreement over a point of law, properly preserving the issue for appeal.

Appeals in criminal cases have also historically been limited in the United States to legal rulings that led to a conviction. That is, a defendant was not able to appeal the sentence imposed as being too harsh, nor could the prosecutor appeal a sentence as being too lenient. This restriction, however, has changed slowly over time. Several states now allow defendants to appeal the sentence imposed by the trial judge. Defendants are also permitted to appeal illegally imposed sentences, such as sentences that fall outside a statutorily authorized sentencing range. And, under a string of U.S. Supreme Court rulings discussed in Chapter 14 (e.g., *Apprendi v. New Jersey*, 2000; *Blakely v. Washington*, 2004; *Cunningham v. California*, 2007; *Southern Union Company v. United States*, 2012; *Alleyne v. United States*, 2013), defendants may appeal sentences if penalty enhancements (other than those based on prior convictions) were applied by a judge without the facts underlying such aggravating factors having been proved to a jury beyond a reasonable doubt.

Finally, the right to appeal is limited to a single appeal, within which all appealable issues have to be raised. Appeals from U.S. district courts and most appeals from state courts of general jurisdiction are heard by intermediate courts of appeals. In the less-populous states, which do not have intermediate appellate bodies, the initial appeal is filed with the court of last resort (see Chapter 3). These courts have **mandatory appellate jurisdiction**, which means they must hear all properly filed appeals. But after the first reviewing body has reached a decision, the right to one appeal has been exhausted. The party that loses the appeal may request that a higher court review the case again, but such appeals are discretionary; the higher court does not have to hear the appeal. The U.S. Supreme Court and most state high courts of last resort have largely **discretionary appellate jurisdiction**, which means that they can pick and choose which cases they will hear. The overwhelming number of appeals is decided by intermediate courts of appeals; only a small fraction of appeals is heard by state courts of last resort and even fewer will be decided by the U.S. Supreme Court. Table 15.1 shows the appellate court structure of the states.

| **TABLE 15.1** | State Appellate Court Structure | | | |

Court of Last Resort Only	Court of Last Resort and One Intermediate Appellate Court		One Court of Last Resort and Two Intermediate Appellate Courts	Two Courts of Last Resort and One Intermediate Appellate Court
Delaware	Alaska	Michigan	Alabama (one civil and one criminal)	Oklahoma[a] (one civil and one criminal)
District of Columbia	Arizona	Minnesota	Indiana (one for tax cases and one for all other appeals)	Texas (one civil and one criminal)
Maine	Arkansas	Mississippi	New York[b]	
Montana	California	Missouri	Pennsylvania	
Nevada[c]	Colorado	Nebraska	Tennessee (one civil and one criminal)	
New Hampshire	Connecticut	Nevada		
Rhode Island	Florida	New Jersey		
South Dakota	Georgia	New Mexico		
Vermont	Hawaii[a]	North Carolina		
West Virginia	Idaho[a]	North Dakota[a]		
Wyoming	Illinois	Ohio		
	Iowa[a]	Oregon		
	Kansas	Puerto Rico		
	Kentucky	South Carolina[a]		
	Louisiana	Utah		
	Maryland	Virginia		
	Massachusetts	Washington		
		Wisconsin		

[a]Court of last resort assigns cases to intermediate appellate court.
[b]New York has established two intermediate appellate courts only in certain parts of the state.

Source: *State Court Structure Charts.* 2015. Williamsburg, VA: National Center for State Courts. Available at http://www.courtstatistics.org/Other-Pages/State_Court_Structure_Charts.aspx

Appellate Standards of Review

Appeals courts approach appellate decision making in different ways, depending on the types of questions presented for review on appeal. Sometimes appellate courts are very deferential to what happened in lower courts, while other times they give no deference at all. How much deference (or conversely, scrutiny) an appellate court will afford to the decisions of a judge, jury, or administrative agency in an appeal is referred to as the **standard of review**. The most frequently used standards of review in criminal cases are presented in Table 15.2.

Given these standards of review, criminal appeals rarely involve questions of fact decided by a judge or jury. Because they have not been directly exposed to the evidence, appellate courts are reluctant to second-guess findings of fact made in lower courts.

> Factual findings, whether by the trial court judge or the jury, are rarely a basis for reversal. . . . Absent certain types of error, it is improper for the reviewing court to substitute its judgment for that of the jury; having guilt or innocence decided by the community is a central tenet of the American legal system. The rationale for the principle that it is the exclusive province of the fact-finder to determine credibility is that the fact-finder had the opportunity to see the witness(es)

TABLE 15.2   Standard of Appellate Review in Criminal Cases (From Least Deferential to Most Deferential)

Type of Question Presented	Standard of Review	Level of Deference	Test	Example
Questions of law	*De novo* (anew)	None	Plenary review of a legal issue for a second time with no deference to prior decision	Whether a judge erred in interpreting a statute Whether hearsay evidence was properly admitted or excluded
Mixed questions of law and fact	Mixture of *de novo* and clear error	Moderate	Underlying factual findings are given substantial deference (reviewed for clear error), but the legal consequences of those facts are reviewed *de novo*.	Whether a suspect was subjected to "custodial interrogation" Whether a defendant knowingly, intelligently, and voluntarily waived a constitutional right
Questions of fact decided by a judge	Clear error	High	Trial court's factual findings are to be upheld unless they are so clearly erroneous that they have no support in the record.	Whether a criminal defendant is competent to stand trial Whether a criminal defendant is guilty beyond a reasonable doubt (in a bench trial)
Questions of fact decided by a jury	Reasonableness/ substantial evidence	High	Jury's decision is upheld if it is reasonable in light of the evidence in the record; support for the jury's conclusion is adequate.	Whether a criminal defendant is guilty beyond a reasonable doubt Whether a defendant has proven his/her insanity by clear and convincing evidence
Discretionary decisions by a judge	Abuse of discretion	Very high	Trial court's decision will be upheld unless arbitrary, capricious, or manifestly unfair in light of any reasonable justification under the circumstances.	Whether a judge abused his/her discretion when denying a continuance, limiting the scope of cross-examination, or refusing to dismiss a juror for cause

testify at trial, and is therefore in a much better position to determine credibility issues. Equally cogent is the idea of judicial economy—that the already over-burdened judicial system simply cannot afford to retry every case on appeal. (TerBeek, 2007, p. 36)

In contrast to the highly deferential appellate review of factual issues, questions of law are reviewed without deference on appeal. Questions of law (or mixed questions of fact and law) that are commonly raised on appeal include defects in jury selection, improper admission of evidence during the trial, and mistaken interpretations of the law. The appellant may also claim constitutional violations, including illegal search and seizure or improper questioning of the defendant by the police (see Chapter 11). Finally, some defendants who have pled guilty may seek to set aside the guilty plea because of ineffective assistance of counsel or because the plea was not voluntary.

Appellate Court Procedures

Appellate court procedures reflect numerous variations among the nation's 51 legal systems. None-theless, each judicial system uses essentially the same six steps to start an appeal from a trial court judgment. The "Law on the Books vs. Law in Action" feature summarizes the appeals process.

LAW IN ACTION VS. LAW ON THE BOOKS

Steps in the Appellate Process

	Law on the Books	Law in Action
Appeal	Legal challenge to a decision by a lower court.	Virtually certain if the defendant is convicted at trial.
Mandatory	Appellate court must hear the case.	Many appeals are "routine," which means they have little likelihood of succeeding.
Discretionary	Appellate court may accept or reject.	Appellate courts hear a very small percentage of discretionary appeal cases.
Notice of appeal	Written statement notifying the court that the defendant plans to appeal.	Standards for indigent defenders mandate that an appeal must be filed.
Appellate court record	The transcript of the trial along with relevant court documents.	Some appellate courts prefer a focused record of contested matters, whereas others want the entire record.
Appellate brief	Written statement submitted by the attorney arguing a case in court.	Defense lawyers make numerous arguments in hopes that one will be successful.
Oral argument	Lawyers for both sides argue their cases before appellate court justices, who have the opportunity to question lawyers.	Judges often complain that they learn little during oral argument. To expedite decision making, some courts limit oral argument to select cases.
Written opinion	Reasons given by appellate courts for the results they have reached.	Only appellate court opinions are considered precedent.
Disposition		
Affirmed	Appellate court decision that agrees with the lower court decision.	Seven out of eight criminal appeals are affirmed.
Remanded	Case is sent back to the lower court for a hearing on a specific issue.	Often an indication that the appellate court is troubled by the judge's action but does not wish to reverse.
Reversed	The lower court decision is set aside, and further proceedings may be held.	Defendants are very often remanded and reconvicted following retrial.

Notice of Appeal

An appeal does not follow automatically from an adverse trial court judgment. Rather, the **appellant** (the losing party in the lower court) must take affirmative action to set an appeal in motion. The first step consists of filing a **notice of appeal** with the trial court. As illustrated by Exhibit 15.1, a notice of appeal is short and simple. However, to trigger one's right to an appeal, the appellant must file a notice of appeal in a timely manner. The rules of appellate procedure in a particular jurisdiction fix the precise period—usually 10, 30, or 60 days.

Keep in mind that the filing of a notice of appeal initiates the appellate process for the first appeal—the appeal that is guaranteed as a right. In contrast, the party that loses a first appeal generally does not have a right to any subsequent appeals. Rather, the loser of a first appeal must usually seek permission to initiate any subsequent discretionary appeals. To do so, they do not file another notice of appeal. Rather, as described in Chapter 2, they file a petition for a **writ of** *certiorari*. From that point forward, the party seeking another appeal is usually known as the **petitioner**, since they are filing a petition seeking another round of appellate review.

Appellate Court Record

After the notice of appeal has been filed, the next step is preparing and transmitting the record. The **appellate court record** consists of the materials that advance to the appellate court. Many of these items—papers and exhibits—are already in the case file. A major item not in the clerk's office is the transcript of the testimony given at the trial. To include this in the record, the court reporter prepares a typewritten copy and files it with the court.

Appellate Briefs

The third step in the appeal process consists of writing briefs. An **appellate brief** is a written argument that sets forth the party's view of the facts of the case, the issues raised on appeal, and the precedents supporting their position. Many commentators have noted that the term *brief* is an oxymoron in this context because appellate briefs are usually not "brief" at all; they are usually quite long.

The length of an appellate brief notwithstanding, first, the appellant files an *opening brief*, which lists alleged errors on questions of law that were

---

EXHIBIT 15.1   Sample Notice of Appeal

Notice of Appeal to a Court of Appeals from a Judgment or Order of a District Court

File Number _____

United States of America, Plaintiff |
v. | Notice of Appeal
[Name], Defendant |
_____ |

Notice is hereby given that [insert name], the Defendant in the above named case, hereby appeals to the United States Court of Appeals for the Second Circuit from the final judgment entered in this action on the _____ day of _____, 20__.

_____
Attorney for Defendant
Address:_____

made at trial. Next, the winning party in the lower court (termed the **appellee** during the initial appeal and the **respondent** in any subsequent, discretionary appeals, since they are responding to a petition for discretionary review) files a *response brief* setting forth arguments as to why the original decision of the lower court was legally correct and should stand. The appellant then has the option of filing a *reply brief*. Briefs are arguably the most important part of the appellate process because roughly three-quarters of all appeals are decided by appeals courts based on the briefs without the benefit of oral argument.

In some cases, various nonparties may seek to influence an appellate court's decision making by seeking leave to file a brief as a "friend of the court," typically referred to in Latin as *amicus curiae*. Such *amicus* briefs are commonly filed by the American Bar Association, the American Medical Association, the American Psychological Association, and similar organizations with specialized knowledge that they feel might help an appellate court make a decision in a case.

Oral Argument

Oral argument provides an opportunity for face-to-face contact between the appellate judges and lawyers. The lawyers for both parties are allotted a limited time to argue their side of the case before the appellate court panel. The appellant's oral argument, for example, briefly discusses the facts on which the cause of action is based, traces the history of the case through the lower courts, and presents legal arguments as to why the decision of the trial court was erroneous. In this phase, judges typically ask lawyers questions about particular issues in the case.

Many judges view oral arguments as not particularly helpful in deciding routine cases (Hellman, 2006; Wasby, 1982). Thus, some courts have eliminated oral arguments altogether in straightforward cases. By ruling solely on the basis of the appellate court record and the briefs, judges can decide cases more quickly. In some states, however, the litigants are entitled to oral arguments before an appeals court either if requested in a timely manner by one

of the parties or by rule in certain types of cases (Binford et al., 2007; Levy, 2013).

Written Opinion

After the case has been argued, the court recesses to engage in group deliberations. Decisions are made in private conference, with one judge in the majority assigned the task of writing the opinion, which summarizes the facts of the case and discusses the legal issues raised on appeal. If the case is an easy one, the **opinion** of the court may be short, perhaps no more than a page or two. But if the legal issues are important or complex, the court's opinion may run dozens of pages. The decisions of appellate courts are compiled and published in books of reported court decisions, which can be found in law libraries. Attorneys and judges use these reported decisions as authorities for arguing and deciding future cases that raise issues similar to those already decided.

Some decisions are *per curium* **opinions**, those written "by the court" without attribution to a specific judicial author. But most of the time, judges sign their opinions. Judges who disagree with the majority often write **dissenting opinions**, explaining why they believe their fellow judges reached the wrong conclusions. In some cases, judges who agree with the case outcome on appeal might elect to write a **concurring opinion**. Judges who write concurring opinions may do so to emphasize particular points, or they may express disagreement with a portion of the rationale expressed in the majority decision. In courts of last resort, where multiple appellate judges review a case, sometimes so many judges write concurring opinions that a true majority cannot be reached. For example, assume that six justices on the U.S. Supreme Court believe that a defendant petitioning to have his conviction reversed should win. Of those six votes, three justices sign a concurring opinion expressing their reasoning, and three others sign a separate concurring opinion expressing different reasons why they think the conviction should be overturned (leaving three justices in the dissent). In such cases with no majority decision, the decision is called a **plurality opinion**. Although a plurality decision may resolve a particular case, it generally has limited or no precedential value. In other words, the rationale expressed in a plurality decision has no *stare decisis* effect.

Opinion preparation consumes more of appellate judges' time than any other activity, and for this reason the opinion-writing process is a prime candidate for increasing the efficiency of appellate courts. Some appellate courts are therefore deciding some cases by summary affirmation, in which the court affirms the decision of the lower court without providing a written opinion and often without granting oral argument (Binford et al., 2007; Neubauer, 1985).

Many courts are reluctant to take the drastic step of not writing opinions, even in selected cases. Therefore, a more common practice is curtailing opinion publication; the litigants are given written reasons for the decision reached, but the opinion is not published. Unpublished opinions are used in error-correction cases when the court is applying existing law (Songer, 1990). They save considerable judicial time because unpublished opinions need not be as polished as published opinions. Because unpublished opinions have limited precedential authority since they merely apply existing law, a number of courts prohibited citation to unpublished cases as precedent for many years. But the Judicial Conference of the United States banned this practice in the federal courts when it enacted Federal Rule of Appellate Procedure 32.1(a), prohibiting courts from restricting the citation of persuasive precedential authority after January 1, 2007. Although roughly half of the states do not allow citation to unpublished cases, the modern trend is clearly away from such bans and toward the new federal rule that allows citation to all available precedents regardless of whether or not the opinion was formally published (Payne, 2008; Wood, 2016).

Disposition

The court's opinion ends with a disposition of the case. The appellate court may **affirm** (uphold) the judgment of the lower court. Or the court may *modify* the lower court ruling by changing it in part but not totally reversing it. Alternatively, the previous decision may be **reversed** (set aside) with no further court action required. A disposition of **reversed and remanded** means that the decision of the lower court is overturned and the case is sent back to the lower court for further proceedings, which may include holding a hearing or conducting a new trial. Often the defendant is tried a second time, but not always. Finally, the case may be **remanded** to the lower court with instructions for further proceedings. What the ultimate disposition of a case will be on appeal will turn on whether a majority (or plurality) of the appellate judges hearing the case find a reversible error under the applicable standard of review.

Reversible vs. Harmless Error

Appellate courts modify, reverse, remand, or reverse and remand only if they find **error**—that is, a mistake made during the trial. If the error is substantial, it is called **reversible error** by the higher court. If the error is minor, it is called **harmless error**. This distinction means that an appellate court may find error but may nonetheless affirm the lower court decision anyway if the mistake was not significant enough to have had a prejudicial effect on the ultimate outcome of the case.

Recall that the contemporaneous objection rule bars an appellate court from considering any claim on appeal to which a timely objection was not made. However, one exception to this rule is for mistakes that constitute **plain error**. Plain errors are defects that seriously affect substantial rights that are so prejudicial to a jury's deliberations "as to undermine the fundamental fairness of the trial and bring about a miscarriage of justice" (*United States v. Polowichak*, 1986, p. 416).

On the other hand, even when an appellant preserves a claim by timely objection and the appellate court finds that the trial court erred, the appellate court may still affirm the conviction if it finds that the error was harmless. This harmless error rule avoids the "setting aside of convictions for small errors or defects that have little, if any, likelihood of having changed the result of the trial" (*Chapman v. California*, 1967, p. 22). If the error was of constitutional dimensions, the appellate court must determine "beyond a reasonable doubt that the error complained of did not contribute to the verdict obtained" (p. 23). If the error was not of constitutional dimensions, the appellate court must determine with "fair assurance after pondering all that happened without stripping the erroneous action from the whole that the judgment was not substantially swayed by the error" (*Kotteakos v. United States*, 1946, p. 765).

Most types of error are subject to harmless error analysis, including classic trial errors involving the erroneous admission of evidence (*Arizona v. Fulminante*, 1991). Some types of error, however, involve rights so basic to a fair trial that they can never be considered harmless, such as conflicts of interest in representation (*Holloway v. Arkansas*, 1978); denial of the right to an impartial judge (*Chapman v. California*, 1967); racial, ethnic, or sex discrimination in grand jury or petit jury selection (*Vasquez v. Hillery*, 1986; *Batson v. Kentucky*, 1986; *J.E.B. v. Alabama ex rel. T.B.*, 1994); and a failure to inquire whether a defendant's guilty plea is voluntary (*United States v. Gonzalez*, 1987).

Rising Caseloads and Expedited Appeals

In recent years, traditional appellate court procedures have been modified because of exponential increases in appellate court filings. Appellate court caseloads have been increasing more rapidly than those of the trial courts. By way of illustration, appeals filed in the U.S. courts of appeals increased by a whopping 705 percent from 1961 through 1983 and then increased another 131 percent from 1983 through 2005, a year in which a record high of more than 68,400 cases were filed in federal appellate courts. That caseload began to drop slightly in 2006 and 2007 and by 2013, then total number of appeals in federal appellate courts was down to 42,703 (Administrative Office of the U.S. Courts, 2014). The federal appellate caseload, however, then began to rise again such that 54,244 appeals were filed in 2015 (Administrative Office of the U.S. Courts, 2016).

Appeals in state courts also grew rapidly between the 1960s and early 2000s. But in the decade between 2006 and 2015, "[i]ncoming caseloads in courts of last resort have fallen by 18 percent, from approximately 92,000 cases in 2006 to a little less than 75,000 cases in 2015. Intermediate appellate courts saw caseloads decline from almost 192,000 cases in 2006 to just over 185,000 cases in 2015" (Schauffler, LaFountain, Strickland, Holt, & Genthon, 2016, p. 18). Thus, according to the most up-to-date data available, roughly 260,000 appeals are filed in state appellate courts every year. To accommodate this volume of appeals, reviewing bodies now often use expedited processing for some cases, such as shortening the period for submitting briefs, waiving the submission of formal briefs, denying extensions of time, and eliminating oral argument (Binford et al., 2007).

Criminal Appeals

The bulk of trial court filings are never appealed because the case is settled without a trial—civil cases are negotiated and criminal cases are plea-bargained. As a result, only a small percentage of state trial court cases are reviewed by higher courts. The majority of appeals involve civil cases, but the number of criminal appeals has increased dramatically since the 1960s.

Law on the Books: Expanded Opportunity to Appeal Criminal Convictions

For decades, most defendants found guilty by judge or jury did not appeal because they could not afford the expense. This pattern changed significantly in the early 1960s. A series of important Warren Court decisions held that economically impoverished defendants cannot be barred from effective appellate review. Indigent defendants, therefore, are entitled to a free trial court transcript (*Griffin v. Illinois*, 1956) and a court-appointed lawyer (*Douglas v. California*, 1963). Indigents, however, are not normally provided free legal service to pursue discretionary appeals (*Ross v. Moffitt*, 1974).

As a result of these rulings, it is now rare for a convicted defendant not to appeal a trial verdict of guilty. Indeed, indigent defendants have everything to gain and nothing to lose by filing an appeal. For example, if the appeal is successful but the defendant is reconvicted following a new trial, the sentencing judge cannot increase the sentence out of vindictiveness (*North Carolina v. Pearce*, 1969; *Texas v. McCullough*, 1986). However, if a convicted defendant's lawyer fails to file a timely appeal, that does not necessarily violate the Sixth Amendment right to effective assistance of counsel (*Roe v. Flores-Ortega*, 2000).

Law in Action: Defendants Rarely Win on Appeal

For many years, criminal appeals were drawn from a fairly narrow stratum of the most serious criminal convictions in the trial courts (Davies, 1982). For example, more than half the criminal appeals contested convictions for crimes of violence (primarily homicides and armed robberies). Moreover, these appeals cases often involved substantial sentences

(Chapper & Hanson, 1990). In short, criminal appeals were fairly atypical of crimes prosecuted in the trial courts. However, over the past 30 years or so, penalties for all sorts of crimes have increased, especially for drug offenses, as penal social control has been increasingly used to incapacitate criminal offenders (Tonry, 2004). This has led to a broader range of criminal cases being appealed, as illustrated by Figure 15.1, which shows a recent distribution of the types of criminal cases appealed in the federal system.

Criminal appeals are generally routine because they seldom raise meritorious issues (Primus, 2007; Wold & Caldeira, 1980). Current standards of effective assistance of counsel often force lawyers to appeal, no matter how slight the odds of appellate court reversal. As a result, a significant number of criminal appeals lack substantial merit. According to one intermediate appellate court judge, "If 90 percent of this stuff were in the United States Post Office, it would be classified as junk mail" (Wold, 1978). Although this quote is more than 35 years

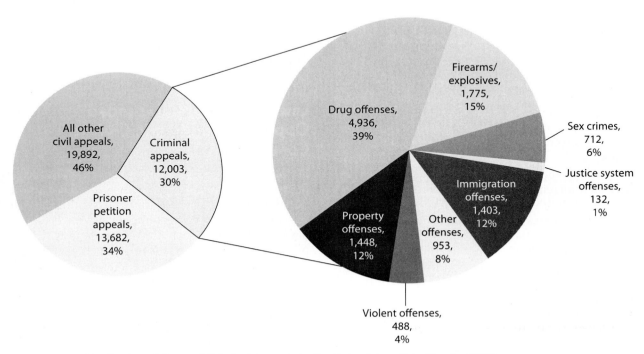

FIGURE 15.1 Distribution of Types of Criminal Appeals in the Federal Appellate Courts, 2016

Source: Administrative Office of the U.S. Courts. 2017. *Federal Judicial Statistics*, 2016. Washington, DC: Author. Available online at http://www.uscourts.gov/statistics-reports/federal-judicial-caseload-statistics-2016

old, the sentiment expressed appears to be valid today (see Miner, 1999; Stogel, 2002). Consider, for example, that of the roughly 10,000 written dispositions in criminal appeals filed by defendants in the California Court of Appeals in between 2013 and 2014, the court reversed only about 880 (9 percent) convictions (Judicial Council of California, 2015).

Why do criminal appeals rarely succeed? The answer is twofold. First, as illustrated in Table 15.2, the appellate standards of review applicable to most decision making during criminal trials are highly deferential to trial court outcomes (Primus, 2007). Thus, the rules of appeals are designed not to disturb the results of a criminal trial unless a serious, reversible error has occurred (see *Parker v. Matthews*, 2012). Second, appellate courts often find that no reversible error was committed during the trial court proceedings. That is due, in large part, to the harmless error doctrine. Accordingly, the vast majority of criminal appeals affirm the conviction.

Roughly speaking, defendants win cases on appeal less than 10 percent of the time. A closer look, though, indicates that an appellate court reversal often produces only minor victories for many criminal defendants. For example, some "reversals" produce a modification but do not otherwise disturb the conviction or even order a new trial (Burke-Robertson, 2008; Neubauer, 1992). Moreover, if the appellate court reverses and remands the case to the lower court for a new trial, many defendants will be convicted a second time. In fact, the few studies that have examined retrials following successful appeals found that roughly half resulted in reconviction (Neubauer, 1991, 1992; Roper & Melone, 1981).

The types of cases in which reversals occur are also interesting. Neubauer (1991) found that defendants convicted of nonviolent offenses and who received a relatively lenient sentence were the most likely to win on appeal; conversely, defendants convicted of violent offenses and sentenced to lengthy prison terms were the least likely to win on appeal. He concluded that this pattern of winners and losers is far from random. Rather, the appellate court justices strained to find ways to affirm convictions for crimes such as murder and armed robbery when the defendant had a long criminal record.

Postconviction Review

After the appellate process has been exhausted, state as well as federal prisoners may challenge their convictions in federal courts on certain limited grounds. These postconviction remedies are termed **collateral attacks**, because they are attempts to avoid the effects of a prior court decision by bringing a different (collateral) action in new court proceedings. Although they are filed by prisoners who have been convicted of a criminal offense, they are technically civil matters. Thus, they are usually filed against a prison warden or the chief administrator of a state's department of corrections. The "Case Close-Up: *House v. Bell* and Federal Court Scrutiny of State Death Row Inmates" illustrates this point. When Paul House appealed, the case title was *House v. State of Tennessee*. But after the right to appeal had been exhausted, he later filed a *habeas* petition in federal court, and the case was captioned *House v. Bell*. The warden, Ricky Bell, is considered a nominal respondent because no actions on his part are at issue. Bell is merely a stand-in; the defendant contends he is being illegally detained because of the actions of the trial judge.

How Postconviction Remedies Differ from Appeals

Postconviction remedies differ from appeals in several ways that have important implications for the criminal justice system. First, they may be filed only by those actually in custody. Second, they may raise only constitutional defects, not technical ones. Third, they may be somewhat broader than appeals, which are usually limited to objections made by the defense during the trial absent plain error. Postconviction petitions can bring up issues not raised during trial, as well as assert constitutional protections that have developed since the original trial under certain circumstances. Finally, many state court systems allow unlimited postconviction remedies; thus, a prisoner could file numerous petitions in state court as well as seek postconviction relief in the various levels of the federal court system.

Carolyn Muncey disappeared from her rural Tennessee home on Saturday night, July 3, 1984. The next day, two local residents found her body concealed amid brush and tree branches roughly 100 yards from her house. The police later arrested Paul House, a convicted sex offender who lived in the area. During House's 1985 capital murder trial, several witnesses testified about Mrs. Muncey's disappearance and discovery, but no one could directly link House to the murder. Central to the state's case was what FBI testing showed (or seemed to show). Lab experts testified that the semen found on her nightgown and panties was consistent with House's blood type and that small bloodstains on House's blue jeans were consistent with Carolyn Muncey's blood type. The jury convicted House and sentenced him to death.

On appeal, the Tennessee Supreme Court concluded the evidence was circumstantial but "quite strong." The U.S. Supreme Court refused to grant *certiorari*, thus ending House's appeals. His lawyers then filed successive writs of *habeas corpus* in both state and federal courts. At a key point in these protracted legal proceedings, House procedurally defaulted, that is, he failed to properly preserve issues for *habeas corpus* review. He now faced a very high legal hurdle —to proceed further he had to prove actual innocence before a federal court would grant his *habeas corpus* petition seeking a new trial (*Schlup v. Delo*, 1995).

Since House's 1985 conviction, DNA evidence has increasingly been introduced during trial (Chapter 13) and also used to overturn convictions on appeal and/or during postconviction relief (see the discussion in this chapter). No such testing had been done for the original trial because DNA testing did not exist then. But was it relevant in House's case? A majority of the U.S. Supreme Court said yes.

Justice Kennedy, often the "swing vote" on the Roberts Court, wrote the opinion of the court stressing that DNA testing showed that the semen found on Mrs. Muncey did not come from the defendant. Similarly, the testimony based on bloodstains was suspect because of poor evidence control

by the state crime lab—the samples were not properly preserved and were possibly contaminated during testing. The court's opinion also emphasized that not only did the new evidence tend to undermine the state's claim of guilt, but it also seemed to point to a different suspect—Carolyn Muncey's husband. The court concluded that "this is the rare case where—had the jury heard all the conflicting testimony—it is more likely than not that no reasonable jury viewing the record as a whole would lack reasonable doubt" (p. 554).

Chief Justice Roberts concurred in the judgment in part and dissented in part. He was joined by the other two conservatives, but Justice Alito did not participate because the case was argued before he was confirmed. The dissenters were unconvinced that the newly discovered DNA evidence was as important as the majority concluded, arguing "the case against House remains substantially unaltered from the case presented to the jury" (p. 566). As a result, Roberts wrote, "I do not find it probable that no reasonable juror would vote to convict him" (p. 556). In short, the threshold for federal review of state court convictions in matters like this should remain high.

In the end, the Court sided with House, but the holding is a narrow one. Future appellants will continue to face a high hurdle in convincing a reviewing court that they are actually innocent and therefore are entitled to federal court relief when they procedurally default in state court. Perhaps what is most important about this case is that for the first time the Supreme Court dealt with postconviction appeals based on DNA testing. For this reason, death penalty opponents view the case as a major victory. Peter Neufeld, co-director of the Innocence Project, concluded that *House* "recognizes that scientific advances have transformed our criminal justice system and must be weighed heavily in determining whether innocent people have been wrongly convicted" (quoted in Mauro, 2006).

As for Paul House, after 22 years in prison, he was released and the district attorney eventually declined a second trial, based on DNA tests which suggested an unknown suspect was involved.

House v. Bell illustrates these factors. House was eligible to file because he was in prison. Second, his postconviction relief petitions raised issues that had not been properly preserved at trial or on direct appeal. Finally, the petition had been filed in two state courts and the U.S. District Court for the Eastern District of Tennessee, had been reviewed by the Sixth Circuit Court of Appeals, and was now being considered by yet another federal court—the U.S. Supreme Court.

The most common type of postconviction relief is ***habeas corpus*** (Latin for "you have the body"). Protected by the U.S. Constitution, it is a judicial order to someone holding a person to bring that person immediately before the court. Article provides that "the Privilege of the Writ of Habeas Corpus shall not be suspended unless when in Cases of Rebellion or Invasion the public Safety may require it." This provision traces its roots to 17th-century England, when the king's officers often detained citizens without ever filing charges. The writ of *habeas corpus* has been described as the "great writ," because it prevents the government from jailing citizens without ever filing charges. Many totalitarian regimes have no such protections; even some Western democracies allow the police or prosecutors to detain a person suspected of a crime for up to a year without formally accusing the person of any wrongdoing. Note that a state prisoner who challenges the conditions of confinement or attempts to obtain damages for violations of constitutional rights should seek relief by means of a civil action under 42 U.S.C. § 1983, not by filing a petition for a writ of *habeas corpus*.

Originally, *habeas corpus* was regarded as an extraordinary means to determine the legality of detention prior to trial. But the great writ of liberty has undergone considerable transformation in recent decades. See "Courts, Controversy, & the Administration of Justice: Should Federal Courthouse Doors Be Closed to State Prisoners?"

Judicial Expansion and Contraction of *Habeas* Access for State Prisoners

In the 1950s and 1960s, the U.S. Supreme Court greatly expanded the application of *habeas corpus*, making it much easier for state prisoners to seek judicial relief in the federal courts (see "Key Developments in Federal *Habeas Corpus* Law, 1953–1996"). These decisions opened the floodgate for federal review, dramatically increasing the number of *habeas corpus* petitions filed in federal courts. But the more conservative Burger, Rehnquist, and Roberts Supreme Courts have narrowed the scope of federal *habeas* relief.

Congress Greatly Restricts *Habeas* Access in 1996

For more than two decades Congress considered proposed changes in *habeas corpus* proceedings (Smith, 1995). This inconclusive debate was shattered by the Oklahoma City bombing in 1995. Victims were anxious to channel their grief into tangible reform, and one avenue was *habeas corpus* reform (Gest, 1996). Thus, as the 1996 elections loomed, Congress passed the Antiterrorism and Effective Death Penalty Act. In terms of *habeas corpus* actions filed in federal courts, the act:

- Imposed a strict deadline for filing a *habeas* petition within one year of the underlying state court judgment becoming final
- Limited successive petitions
- Restricted the review of petitions by state prisoners if the claim was adjudicated on the merits in state courts
- Required a "certificate of appealability" before a *habeas* petition could be appealed to a federal court of appeals
- Provided that decisions of a federal appellate panel are not appealable by writ of *certiorari* to the Supreme Court

Moving with unusual speed, the U.S. Supreme Court agreed to hear a challenge to the new law within two months of its passage. A unanimous Court held that the law was constitutional in *Felker v. Turpin* (1996).

Violations of state law are not valid grounds for a *habeas* action unless such violations are of constitutional magnitude. For example, *Brown v. Sanders* (2006) held that *habeas* relief was unavailable when a jury had considered a state sentencing guideline that was later invalidated by a state high court of last resort because the claim did not present any violation of a constitutional right.

Prisoners must exhaust available state remedies before a federal court will consider their constitutional claim on *habeas corpus*. This rule means that if an appeal or other procedure to hear a claim is still available by right in the state court system, the prisoner must pursue that procedure before a federal *habeas corpus* application will be considered. Federal

Should Federal Courthouse Doors Be Closed to State Prisoners?

The right of convicted offenders to seek review through *habeas corpus* proceedings has sparked a heated debate. Some people would keep the doors of the federal courts wide open to state prisoners; others would slam the doors firmly shut in most cases.

Some proposals to restrict *habeas corpus* relief are based on problems of judicial administration. Postconviction petitions contribute to the heavy caseload of the federal courts, are sometimes frivolous, and undermine the value of a final determination of guilt.

But most restrictive efforts are anticrime proposals. Typical is the letter President Reagan wrote to Congress urging passage of remedial legislation: "As a result of judicial expansion of the habeas corpus remedy, state prisoners are now free to relitigate their convictions and sentences endlessly in the lower federal courts" (quoted in Remington, 1988). Conservatives stress that a criminal trial is a procedure that determines the defendant's guilt or innocence, not a game in which the accused may elude justice for any imperfection (Fein, 1994).

Writs of *habeas corpus* play a particularly important role in capital punishment cases. After exhausting appellate remedies, defendants engage in lengthy challenges to the sentence of death by filing multiple writs of *habeas corpus* in various state and federal courts. Chief Justice William Rehnquist criticized his colleagues for providing capital offenders with "numerous procedural protections unheard of for other crimes" and "for allowing endlessly drawn out legal proceedings" (*Coleman v. Balkcom*, 1981, pp. 958, 960, Rehnquist, J., dissenting).

Others counter that the death penalty is qualitatively different from other types of sanctions, so multiple scrutiny of such cases is more than justified. The argument for keeping the federal courthouse doors open was forcefully stated by Justice John Paul Stevens, who noted that federal *habeas* proceedings reveal deficiencies in 60 to 70 percent of the capital cases (*Murray v. Giarratano*, 1989). Advocates of this policy also argue that not only should there be no rush to judgment but also that death row inmates should have access to legal assistance, yet often they do not. The majority of postconviction cases are *pro se*—the prisoner is appearing on his or her own behalf. Recall from Chapter 7 that the Court has held that defendants have no right to counsel after the first appeal has been exhausted. Many death row defendants must rely on overworked volunteer attorneys (Applebome, 1992).

The Antiterrorism and Effective Death Penalty Act of 1996 restricted both the time periods during which prisoners must file *habeas corpus* petitions and the number of petitions they may file. Nearly 20,000 such petitions were filed in 2015, comprising approximately 7 percent of the civil docket of federal district courts (Administrative Office of the U.S. Courts, 2016). This marks a dramatic decrease in *habeas* access at roughly the same time as national attention began to focus on innocents on death row. Thus, some now question whether the law went too far in denying federal court access to inmates—particularly death row inmates—who may be innocent.

Justices of the U.S. Supreme Court have expressed increasing concern that the lower federal courts have become too cursory in reviewing death penalty appeals (Greenhouse, 2004). Justice Kennedy said that while Congress has instructed the federal courts to accord greater deference to state-court decisions, "deference does not imply abandonment or abdication of judicial review" (*Miller-El v. Cockrell*, 2003, p. 340). In particular, the Court has often been critical of the Fifth Circuit Court of Appeals (which oversees much of the South) for being too willing to uphold death penalty cases. Overall, the court has shown a willingness in recent years to reverse death penalty cases on the basis of ineffective assistance of counsel (Chapter 7), failure of prosecutors to disclose exculpatory evidence to the defense Chapter 11), bias in jury selection (Chapter 13), and DNA evidence (this chapter).

What do you think? Should the federal courthouse doors be reopened to state prisoners, particularly those on death row, to ensure that justice is not short-circuited? Or should the federal courthouse doors remain as they are now, with only one federal review (unless the case presents an extraordinary issue)? Asked another way, where should the line be drawn between the interests of justice (ensuring that only the truly guilty are executed) and the need for finality (many of the *habeas* petitions raise issues that are very unlikely to succeed)?

KEY DEVELOPMENTS IN FEDERAL *HABEAS CORPUS* LAW, 1953–1996

Brown v. Allen (1953)	Established *de novo* standard of review for federal courts conducting *habeas* review of state court convictions.
Fay v. Noia (1963)	Although the doctrine of *procedural default* requires petitioners to have presented *habeas* claims to state courts on direct appellate review first before having those claims reviewed in federal *habeas* proceedings, the federal courts may waive the doctrine of procedural default to grant *habeas* relief if the facts of a case establish that a conviction was obtained unconstitutionally.
Townsend v. Sain (1963)	*Habeas* courts may "receive evidence and try the facts anew."
Sanders v. United States (1963)	*Habeas* courts may consider previously rejected claims if doing so serves "the ends of justice."
Stone v. Powell (1976)	Removed all claims of Fourth Amendment search and seizure violations from the scope of federal *habeas* review.
Wainwright v. Sykes (1977)	Overruled *Fay v. Noia* by holding that petitioners must show good cause and actual prejudice to his or her case for not complying with state procedural rules.
Patton v. Yount (1984)	Overruled *Brown v. Allen* by requiring federal courts to afford deference to state court findings of fact.
Kimmelman v. Morrison (1986)	*Stone v. Powell* does not bar a Sixth Amendment ineffective assistance of counsel *habeas* claim based on mishandling or failing to raise a valid Fourth Amendment issue.
Teague v. Lane (1989)	An individual may not seek to enforce a new rule of law in federal *habeas corpus* proceedings if the new rule was announced after the petitioner's conviction became final or if the petitioner is seeking to establish a wholly new rule or to apply a settled precedent in a novel way that would result in the creation of a new rule.
Coleman v. Thompson (1991)	Elaborating on *Wainwright v. Sykes*, federal *habeas* courts generally may not review a state court's denial of a state prisoner's federal constitutional claim if the state court's decision rests on a state procedural default that is independent of the federal question and adequate to support the prisoner's continued custody.
McCleskey v. Zant (1991)	A *habeas* court must honor state procedural default rules unless the petitioner can show cause and prejudice for his or her procedural default.
Keeney v. Tamayo-Reyes (1992)	Overruled *Townsend v. Sain* by holding that *habeas* courts may not try facts anew but rather may consider facts not presented in state court proceedings only if the petition can establish good cause and prejudice for not having fully developed the facts in state court.
Herrera v. Collins (1993)	Claims of actual innocence are not valid *habeas* actions unless there is an independent constitutional violation in the underlying criminal proceedings that led to the state prisoner's wrongful conviction. However, a "truly persuasive demonstration of 'actual innocence' made after trial" can render the execution of an innocent defendant unconstitutional.
Schlup v. Delo (1995)	A petitioner establishes actual innocence by making a showing that, in light of all the evidence, "it is more likely than not that no reasonable juror would have convicted."
Murray v. Carrier (1996)	An innocent petitioner's failure to show cause and prejudice for procedural default should not prevent a court from granting a writ.

habeas corpus review may likewise be barred if a defendant is unable to show cause for noncompliance with a state procedural rule and to show some actual prejudice resulting from the alleged constitutional violation (*McCleskey v. Zant*, 1991; *Dretke v. Haley*, 2004). And, finally, the timing of filing is of the utmost importance. A prisoner seeking *habeas corpus* review must file his or her petition within one year of the date on which the underlying judgment became final in state courts either by the conclusion of direct appellate review or by the expiration of the deadline for seeking such appellate review (*Gonzalez v. Thaler*, 2012). As with many other judicial processes, however, if a prisoner's petition is filed after the one-year deadline has expired, then a state must affirmatively raise the issue of the petition's untimeliness with the reviewing court, or else the state's procedural defense to a *habeas corpus* petition will be deemed waived (*Wood v. Milyard*, 2012).

Habeas Corpus Relief for Federal Prisoners

In 1948, Congress enacted a statute that was designed to serve as a substitute for *habeas corpus* for federal prisoners. The primary purpose of the statute was to shift the jurisdictions of the courts hearing *habeas corpus* applications. The statute did not change the basic scope of the remedy that had been available to federal prisoners by *habeas corpus*. That statute, 28 U.S.C. § 2255, provides, in relevant part:

> Federal custody; remedies on motion attacking sentence. A prisoner in custody under sentence of a court established by Act of Congress claiming the right to be released upon the ground that the sentence was imposed in violation of the Constitution or laws of the United States, or that the court was without jurisdiction to impose such sentence, or that the sentence was in excess of the maximum authorized by law, or is otherwise subject to collateral attack, may move the court which imposed the sentence to vacate, set aside, or correct the sentence.

> ***

> An application for a writ of habeas corpus in behalf of a prisoner who is authorized to apply for relief by motion pursuant to this section, shall not be entertained if it appears that the applicant has failed to apply for relief, by motion, to the court which sentenced him, or that such court has denied him relief, unless it also appears that the remedy by motion is inadequate or ineffective to test the legality of his detention.

A Section 2255 motion is, therefore, the correct mechanism for a federal prisoner to challenge the validity of a federal criminal conviction. The statute recognizes four grounds upon which an inmate in federal custody may seek relief:

1. that the sentence was imposed in violation of the Constitution or laws of the United States
2. that the court was without jurisdiction to impose such sentence
3. that the sentence was in excess of the maximum authorized by law
4. that the sentence is "otherwise subject to collateral attack."

Although the final criterion may appear broad, Section 2255 relief may be granted under it only if a violation of federal law caused a "fundamental defect which inherently results in a complete miscarriage of justice [or] an omission inconsistent with the rudimentary demands of fair procedure" (*Davis v. United States*, 1974, p. 346).

Section 2255 is similar in many respects to the *habeas* remedy for state prisoners, including in terms of time limitations. Section 2255 motions, for example, must usually be filed within one year of the date on which a judgment of conviction becomes final, such as the day after the deadline for filing a petition for *certiorari* or when such a petition is denied. There are, however, some significant distinctions between state and federal *habeas*-type relief that are beyond the scope of this text.

Wrongful Convictions

In spite of the many procedural protections afforded to the criminally accused prior to and during trial, it is clear that some defendants are wrongfully convicted of crimes they did not actually commit. Paul House's case is just one example. One might think that the appeals and postconviction review processes would routinely correct situations in which a defendant was wrongfully convicted, but that is clearly not the case.

Up until the mid-1990s, public perception was that criminal defendants had gained too many rights during the Warren era, and, that as a result, far too many criminal defendants escaped criminal punishment on technicalities (Uphoff, 2006). Such perceptions led many—including judges and several U.S. Supreme Court justices—to deny that wrongful convictions were a major problem (see *Herrera v. Collins*, 1993). Moreover, such sentiments caused legislators to sharply curtail "the avenues available to convicted defendants to challenge their convictions," including appellate review after a certain period (Rosen, 2006, pp. 237–238). And the Antiterrorism and Effective Death Penalty Act's curtailment of *habeas corpus* review further complicated defendants' pursuit of judicial remedies for alleged wrongful convictions.

How Many Wrongful Convictions Are There?

It is impossible to get an accurate count of the number of innocent people who are wrongfully convicted each year. In 2014, a study published in the prestigious *Proceedings of the National Academy of Sciences* concluded that 4.1 percent of defendants who are sentenced to death in the United States are later shown to be innocent; that translates into a shocking ratio of 1 in 25 (Gross, O'Brien, Hu, & Kennedy, 2014). But capital cases are generally much better documented than other cases, so it is difficult to extrapolate the overall rate of wrongful criminal convictions from a study of death penalty cases.

Using different methods (each with their own limitations), estimates range between a low of 0.5 percent and a high of 15 percent, with between 1 percent and 3 percent being the estimate with the most empirical support (Zalman, Smith, & Kiger, 2008; Zalman, 2012). But it should be noted that most of what we know about wrongful convictions comes from exoneration cases, 95 percent of which occur in murder and rape cases (Gross & O'Brien, 2008). Since murder and rape cases account for only 2 percent of all felony convictions, exoneration cases are treated "as an imperfect proxy for a subset of likely wrongful convictions" (Gould & Leo, 2010, p. 826).

DNA Exonerations

Since 1989, over 349 inmates have been exonerated by DNA evidence, largely due to the efforts of the Innocence Project and similar organizations (Innocence Project, 2016a, 2016b; see also Zalman, Smith, & Kiger, 2008). As a result of these exonerations—and media portrayals of them—all 50 states have changed their laws to allow for appellate or postconviction review on the grounds of actual innocence supported by new DNA evidence (Innocence Project, 2016b, 2016c). The federal government similarly enacted the Innocence Protection Act of 2004, which expands judicial review of convictions on the basis of evidence that tends to exonerate. Some of the state laws, however, place significant hurdles to presenting actual innocence claims, including limited access to DNA, bans on petitions in cases in which pleas were entered, and inadequate preservation of evidence to allow for DNA testing (Innocence Project, 2016c).

Other Exonerations

Most people associate exonerations with DNA evidence. But DNA exonerations account for approximately 442 of the 1,994 exonerations (22 percent) in the National Registry of Exonerations (2017). In fact, in 2016 alone, 166 people were exonerated for crimes they did not commit, but only 17 of these exonerations were based on DNA evidence. The 166 exonerations in 2016 set a record for the third year in a row. According to the National Registry (2017), "We now average more than three exonerations a week" (p. 3). Of the exonerations in 2016,

- 70 (42.1 percent) involved official misconduct by criminal justice system actors, most frequently police or prosecutors concealing exculpatory evidence.

- 74 (45 percent) occurred in cases in which defendants had pled guilty even though they were innocent, mostly to avoid detention in pretrial custody for months and to avoid having to "risk years in prison if convicted, especially since many had undoubtedly been told that the substance they had been carrying had field-tested positive for illicit drugs already" (p. 9).

- 94 (56.6 percent) occurred in cases in which no crime actually occurred, such as in cases involving claims of child abuse that were subsequently determined to be false or in cases in which presumptive drug tests incorrectly identified something as a controlled substance that subsequent, confirmatory laboratory testing revealed was not, in fact, an illicit drug.

Why Do Wrongful Convictions Occur?

One of our leading sources of knowledge about wrongful convictions comes from the work of the Innocence Project. Since it first started operations in 1989, the Innocence Project has exonerated more than 349 wrongfully convicted defendants using DNA, including 20 who had erroneously been sentenced to death (Innocence Project, 2016a). An examination of these cases and of the results of several leading empirical studies of wrongful convictions reveals much about how and why they occur.

Mistaken Eyewitness Identifications

According to the Innocence Project (2016d), eyewitness misidentification is *the* leading cause of wrongful convictions, playing a role in approximately 71 percent of the DNA exonerations to date. However, as Wells and Quinlivan (2009) explain,

> There are several reasons why the true numbers would have to be dramatically higher. . . . First, in a large percentage of the old cases (in which convicted persons claim to have been misidentified) the biological evidence for DNA testing has deteriorated, has been lost, or has been destroyed. Moreover, virtually all DNA exoneration cases involved sexual assault because those are the cases for which definitive biological evidence (contained in semen) is available to trump the mistaken identification. Such biological evidence is almost never available for murders, robberies, drive-by shootings, and other common crimes that have relied on eyewitness identification evidence. A study of lineups in Illinois indicates that only 5% of lineups conducted in Chicago, Evanston, and Joliet were sexual assault cases (Mecklenburg, 2006). Most lineup identifications were for non-sexual assaults, robberies, and murders for which there is almost no chance that DNA would be available to trump a mistaken identification. In addition, we would normally expect sexual assault victims to be among the most

> reliable of eyewitnesses because sexual assault victims usually have a longer and closer look at the culprit than other crime witnesses (compared to robberies, for instance). For these reasons, the DNA exoneration cases can only represent a fraction, probably a very small fraction, of the people who have been convicted based on mistaken eyewitness identification. (p. 2; see also Gross et al., 2005)

Flowe, Mehta, and Ebbesen (2011) empirically confirmed Wells and Quinlivan's intuitive logic. They examined a random sample of 725 felony cases from the archives of a district attorney's office in a large, southwestern U.S. city. They found that one out of every three suspects had positive ID evidence in their case. Moreover, eyewitness identifications by both strangers and acquaintances was associated with increased odds of prosecution.

> Misidentifications can be caused by a number of natural psychological errors in human judgment that involve the complex interplay of perception and memory (see Fradella, 2007b). Yet, "despite its inherent unreliability, much eyewitness identification evidence has a powerful impact on juries. . . . All evidence points rather strikingly to the conclusion that there is almost nothing more convincing than a live human being who takes the stand, points a finger at the defendant, and says, 'That's the one!'" (*Watkins v. Sowders*, 1981, p. 352)

Given the powerful effect eyewitness identifications have on jurors, perhaps it is not surprising that mistaken identifications are the leading cause of wrongful convictions (Huff, Rattner, & Sagarin, 2003; Innocence Project, 2016d).

Improper Forensic Evidence

Recall from Chapter 13 that DNA testing is the "gold standard" of forensic science because it was developed by leading scientists and subjected to rigorous, peer-reviewed empirical validation. In contrast, many other forensic techniques, such as hair and fiber analysis, toolmark comparisons, and fingerprint analysis, rely on subjective determinations that the two samples are consistent with having originated from the same source, and comparative bullet lead analysis and many arson investigation techniques have been disproven. And even forensic analyses that have been scientifically validated can be improperly conducted, due to shoddy laboratory practices, or conducted on contaminated samples, due to shoddy police work (see Garret & Neufeld, 2009). Collectively, invalidated and improper forensic evidence contribute to roughly 46 percent of wrongful convictions (Innocence Project, 2016e).

False Confessions

False confessions occur when people confess to crimes they did not commit. At first blush, it may seem unfathomable that someone would incriminate themselves in this manner, but both empirical research and police practice demonstrate that the phenomenon is actually fairly common. In fact, false confessions contributed to approximately 27 percent of the wrongful convictions identified through the Innocence Project's DNA exonerations (Innocence Project, 2016f). Many false confessions occur as a result of psychologically coercive police interrogation tactics (Ofshe & Leo, 1997; Leo, 2008).

> In a candid 2008 op-ed piece for the *Los Angeles Times*, D.C. Police Detective Jim Trainum detailed how he unwittingly coaxed a false confession out of a 34-year-old woman he suspected of murder. She even revealed details about the crime that could only have been known to police investigators and the killer. But Trainum later discovered that the woman couldn't possibly have committed the crime. When he reviewed video of his interrogation, he realized that he had inadvertently provided the woman with those very specific details, which she then repeated back to him when she was ready to confess. (Balko, 2011, para. 44)

The Innocence Project (2016f, para. 4) summarized the leading factors that contribute to false confessions as follows:

- duress
- coercion
- intoxication
- diminished capacity
- mental impairment
- ignorance of the law
- fear of violence
- the actual infliction of harm
- the threat of a harsh sentence
- misunderstanding the situation

Unreliable Informants

People who are not in law enforcement but provide information to law enforcement are called **informants**. One particularly unreliable type of informant is commonly known as the *jailhouse snitch*. These jailhouse informants are criminals who, while in custody, claim to overhear incriminating information from a fellow inmate and then pass that information along to police and prosecutors, often in the hopes that it will help their own situations. But these informants are notoriously unreliable. "With little or nothing to lose, and everything to gain, cunning and unscrupulous jail-house snitches invent narratives and crime details that mislead law enforcement officers and contribute to appalling miscarriages of justice" (The Justice Project, 2007, p. 1). As a result, jailhouse informants are one of the leading contributors to wrongful convictions.

Fabricated testimony by unreliable informants accounted for 33.4 percent of wrongful convictions in a classic study (Bedau & Radelet, 1987), 21 percent in another study (Dwyer, Neufeld, & Scheck, 2000), and 45.9 percent in another (Warden, 2004). In a particularly comprehensive study of 340 exonerations in the United States from 1989 through 2003, Gross and his colleagues (2005, pp. 543–544) reported that "the real criminal lied under oath to get the defendant convicted" in 5.6 percent of cases, and in 28.5 percent of exonerations, "a civilian witness who did not claim to be directly involved in the crime committed perjury—usually a jailhouse snitch or another witness who stood to gain from the false testimony." Cases involving misleading informants account for approximately 15 percent of all DNA exonerations to date (Innocence Project, 2016g).

Tunnel Vision and Misconduct by Justice Professionals

The more police, prosecutors, and forensic analysts become convinced of a conclusion, such as the guilt of a particular suspect, the more likely they are to focus only on factors that support that conclusion while conversely, the less likely they are to consider alternative explanations. This process is commonly referred to as **tunnel vision**. It occurs at both conscious and unconscious levels when justice professionals "select and filter the evidence that will 'build a case' for conviction, while ignoring or suppressing evidence that points away from guilt" (Findley & Scott, 2006, p. 292).

Tunnel vision is exacerbated by the emphasis the criminal justice system places on obtaining convictions, especially for police who are evaluated by their clearance rates through arrests and prosecutors whose performance is evaluated by their conviction rates (see Chapter 6).

> [P]rosecutors may engage in overly suggestive witness coaching, offer inappropriate and incendiary closing arguments, or fail to disclose critical evidence to the defense, all of which may raise the prospect of a wrongful conviction. In research on wrongful convictions, the most commonly established transgression is the prosecution's failure to turn over exculpatory evidence. Sometimes police officers do not provide prosecutors with this evidence in order to make it available to the defense, or prosecutors may not be aware that they have such information in their files. In other cases, though, the misdeeds are intentional. (Gould & Leo, 2010, pp. 854–855)

Recall from Chapter 6 that prosecutors are absolutely immune from civil liability for their misconduct when prosecuting a case. Of course, they may be subject to criminal liability and professional sanctions for misconduct, but either type of sanction is quite rare. Consider that Ridolfi and Possley identified 782 acts of prosecutorial misconduct in 707 California criminal cases between 1997 and 2009—"on average, about one case a week" (2010, p. 2). The types of misconduct they uncovered included intimidating witnesses, presenting false evidence, illegally discriminating during jury selection, violating a defendant's Fifth Amendment privilege against self-incrimination, failing to disclose exculpatory or impeachment evidence, and conducting improper direct or cross examinations during judicial proceedings. Only six of these cases resulted in the state bar taking any disciplinary action against the at-fault prosecutors.

One might assume that appellate courts would take steps to fix the problems caused by any type of governmental misconduct that may have tainted a verdict. But two factors already discussed in this chapter limit the effectiveness of appeals in doing so. First, the clearly erroneous standard of review governs appellate evaluations of factual determinations at trial. Thus, appeals courts rarely second-guess a jury's determination based on the evidence in a criminal case. Second, governmental misconduct is often dismissed as harmless error on appeal, especially when other factors implicating the defendant's guilt are present, even though those factors may be highly suspect themselves (such as invalid forensic evidence or unreliable eyewitness identifications). Consider, for example, that convictions were upheld on appeal under the harmless error rule in 548 (77.5 percent) of the 707 misconduct cases Ridolfi and Possley identified. Garrett (2008) found that of the first 200 DNA exoneration cases, only 18 convictions had been reversed by appellate courts.

As explained in Chapter 13, misconduct by forensic scientific personnel has been well documented. Sometimes this misconduct takes the form of sloppy, improperly conducted forensic analyses (Giannelli, 2007). Other times, it takes the form of inaccurate or misleading trial testimony (Garrett & Neufeld, 2009). And, in rare but egregious cases, forensic analysts have outright fabricated results (Garrett & Neufeld, 2009). All of these types of forensic misconduct contribute to wrongful convictions.

Inadequate Defense Representation

As detailed in Chapter 7, upwards of 80 percent of all criminal defendants are represented by court-appointed defense attorneys. Many of these lawyers are chronically overworked and do not have the resources to perform their duties effectively. Bad lawyering clearly contributes to wrongful convictions. In fact, a leading study of capital appeals found that "ineffective defense lawyering was the biggest contributing factor to the wrongful conviction or death sentence of criminal defendants in capital cases over a 23-year period" (Gould & Leo, 2010, p. 855, citing Liebman, Fagan, & West, 2000).

Reducing Wrongful Convictions

Traditional wisdom held that the courts can do only so much to combat wrongful convictions. After all, courts make decisions based on the evidence presented. Neither participants in a trial nor judges in an appellate court may be aware of problems with faulty evidence. Thus, the most significant ways to combat wrongful convictions lie with reforms in other areas of the criminal justice system. These include changing the ways in which pretrial identifications are conducted to minimize the risk of misidentification; videotaping interrogations of criminal suspects to help reduce the incidence of false confessions; and improving the collection, handling, preservation, and analysis of forensic evidence (National Academies of Science, 2009; Rosen, 2006; Uphoff, 2006). But conventional wisdom is slowly giving way to select policy recommendation that could help the courts reduce the number of wrongful convictions.

1. In light of the National Academies of Science (2009) report on forensics, courts should rigorously apply *Daubert* to exclude or limit the use of unreliable forensic techniques (see Chapter 13; see also Giannelli, 2011).

2. As Fradella (2007b) argued, rather than just relying on cross-examination and jury instructions, judges should admit expert testimony from witnesses who specialize in the ways in which memory, perception, and even a variety of crime scene variables can affect the reliability of eyewitness identifications (see *State v. Clopten*, 2009).

3. Attorney discipline is the province of the courts. State high courts of last resort should be more active in disciplining attorneys who engage in misconduct in the course of criminal prosecutions in both state and federal courts.

4. The courts have recognized the inherent unreliability of snitches who testify in exchange for reduced sentences or other such consideration. Even the U.S. Supreme Court has stated, "[t]he use of informers, accessories, accomplices, false friends, or any of the other betrayals which are 'dirty business' may raise serious questions of credibility" (*On Lee v. United States*, 1952, p. 757). At least 18 states now require that "snitch" testimony from an alleged accomplice be corroborated by other evidence (American Bar Association, 2005). But no such corroboration is required for jailhouse informants. Without such corroboration, courts should exclude such testimony as unreliable and unduly prejudicial under Rule 403 of the Federal Rules of Evidence and its state-law counterparts.

5. Finally, appellate courts need to be more aware of the ways in which the leading causes of wrongful conviction interact with each other—especially when applying the harmless error rule. Specifically, when examining whether any particular type of mistake in a criminal case constitutes harmless or prejudicial error, appeals courts should be hesitant to rely on any other factor that contributes to wrongful convictions.

State Courts of Last Resort

No typical state court of last resort exists. While some are referred to as state supreme courts, some go by other names, such as the *state court of appeals*, *supreme judicial court*, *court of criminal appeals*, or *supreme court of appeals*. More important, the role that state high courts play is affected by the control these judicial bodies exercise over their dockets. Perhaps just as important is the exact wording of the state constitution. But these legal factors only partially explain the policy-making role of state supreme courts. Perhaps nowhere is this more obvious than in death penalty appeals.

Law on the Books: State High Courts and Discretionary Dockets

In states that have not created intermediate courts of appeals, the responsibility for appellate review falls directly on the state court of last resort. In such circumstances, the state's highest court finds itself relegated to dealing with a succession of relatively minor disputes, devoting its energies to error correction rather than to more time-consuming efforts to shape the law of the state.

By contrast, in the District of Columbia and in the 40 or so states that have created intermediate courts of appeals, it is the intermediate appellate courts that are primarily concerned with error correction. This leaves the state's highest court free to devote more attention to cases that raise important policy questions (Scott, 2006; Tarr & Porter, 1988). This high level of discretion not only yields low caseloads but also transforms the nature of the judicial process. The high court is no longer merely reacting to disputes brought to it by disgruntled litigants; that is the job of the intermediate court of appeals. Rather, the high court exercises its considerable discretion to carefully select disputes in which it chooses to participate, usually for reasons of advancing public policy. In sum, the architecture of the system tells the judges of the top court to be creative (Carrington, Meador, & Rosenberg, 1976; Scott, 2006).

Law in Action: State High Courts as Policymakers

In recent years, state high courts have become important policymakers in a number of contentious areas, such as tort reform, same-sex marriages, and parental rights in divorce cases. No wonder that elections for state high court judgeships have become nastier, noisier, and costlier (Neubauer & Meinhold, 2013).

Applying U.S. Supreme Court decisions is one way that state high courts participate in policy making. Although in theory federal law is supreme over conflicting state law, in practice state courts of last resort do not invariably follow authoritative pronouncements of the nation's highest court (Bloom, 2008; Tarr, 1982). For example, noncompliance was pronounced in race relations cases, with southern state high courts often aiding and abetting their states' massive resistance to desegregation (Garrow, 2008; Tarr & Porter, 1988). Noncompliance has also occurred in a variety of states in areas such as the constitutionality of executing juveniles (*State ex rel Simmons v. Roper*, 2003); the constitutionality of executing a rapist (*State v. Kennedy*, 2007); the scope of Fourth Amendment search-and-seizure requirements (*State v. Kimbro*, 1985; see also Comparato & McClurg, 2007); the role the doctrine of proportionality plays in limiting criminal sentencing (*Andrade v. Attorney General of State of California*, 2001); school districts' responses to school prayer decisions (*Murray v. Curlett*, 1962; see also Abel & Hacker, 2006); and how warning requirements for

interrogation announced in *Miranda* would be applied (*Alvord v. State*, 1975; see also Epstein, Cameron, Segal, & Westerland, 2006; Gruhl, 1981).

Interpretation of state constitutional provisions is another way that state supreme high courts act as important government policymakers. The phrase **new judicial federalism** refers to the movement in the state supreme courts to reinvigorate state constitutions as sources of individual rights over and above the rights granted by the U.S. Constitution. New judicial federalism occurred partially as a response to the Burger Court's unwillingness to continue the Warren Court's understanding of civil liberties (Friedman, 2000; Galie, 1987). Just as important, though, new judicial federalism reflects the growing understanding that the federal Constitution establishes minimum guarantees of individual rights rather than maximum protections (Emmert & Traut, 1992; Friedman, 2000). In some instances, for example, state high courts have interpreted provisions regarding criminal procedures in the state's bill of rights more expansively than the equivalent sections of the U.S. Bill of Rights. Researchers have identified hundreds of state high-court decisions that interpret state charters as more rights-generous than their federal counterpart (Bloom & Massey, 2008; Fino, 1987). For example, reasoning that garbage was abandoned property, the U.S. Supreme Court ruled in *California v. Greenwood* (1988) that the Fourth Amendment to the U.S. Constitution does not require law enforcement to obtain a search warrant before searching someone's garbage. The high courts of New Jersey and Washington State, however, held that search warrants were required for police to search garbage in those states because their state constitutions afforded more privacy rights than the Fourth Amendment (*State v. Hempele*, 1990; *State v. Boland*, 1990).

Law in Controversy: State High Courts and Death Penalty Cases

State courts of last resort reveal pronounced differences in their handling of death penalty cases. For example, before New Jersey abolished the death penalty in 2007, the state had not executed anyone since 1963, partially because the New Jersey

Supreme Court had invalidated 27 of the 28 death sentences it had reviewed (Bienen, 2008). At the other extreme, the high courts of Texas and Virginia routinely uphold the imposition of death sentences (Smith, 2008). Consider, for example, that the Texas Court of Criminal Appeals upheld a death sentence for a criminal defendant whose lawyer slept through major portions of the trial, ruling that such behavior did not rise to the level of ineffective assistance of counsel (*Ex parte McFarland*, 2005). Other states fit somewhere in between. Illinois and the Carolinas, for example, have thrown out roughly half of the sentences of death they reviewed while upholding the other half (Liebman et al., 2000).

Differences in how state courts of last resort respond to death penalty appeals is not random. Justices on high courts in states with competitive judicial elections are more likely to uphold death sentences (Brace & Hall, 1997; Brooks & Raphael, 2003). In particular, liberal justices facing reelection with possibly close margins of victory are more likely to conceal their opposition to the death penalty; they cast votes reflecting their constituents' opinions.

The U.S. Supreme Court and Criminal Justice Policy

"I'll appeal all the way to the Supreme Court" is a familiar phrase. Alas, it is not very realistic. The jurisdiction of the U.S. Supreme Court is almost exclusively discretionary; that is, it can pick and choose the cases it wishes to decide. Most of the time, it decides not to decide. Of the roughly 92 million lawsuits filed in the United States every year, only between 7,500 and 9,300 are appealed to the nation's highest court; and from this small number, the justices select a mere handful, between 80 and 90 in recent years. Of these, most are civil cases, as the Supreme Court tends to review only between 20 and 35 criminal cases each year. Even though the number of cases filed with the Supreme Court has increased over the decades, the total amount of time a case is in the system has remained stable (McLauchlan & Waltenburg, 2014).

Scholars refer to Court eras according to the chief justice. Thus, the Warren Court refers to the

period from 1953 to 1969, when Earl Warren (a former Republican governor of California appointed by President Eisenhower) was chief justice. Because the associate justices change, however, these references provide only informal guides to the dominant thinking of the Court. Nonetheless, an examination of the Warren Court, Burger Court, Rehnquist Court, and now the Roberts Court offers a useful summary of major differences in the direction of criminal justice policy.

We begin with the Warren Court because it decided so many cases that shaped contemporary criminal justice policy in the United States, such as the extension of the exclusionary rule to the states in *Mapp v. Ohio* (1961). It should be noted, though, that earlier Supreme Courts decided many key cases that affected subsequent Courts. For example, *Mapp*'s exclusionary rule holding was based largely on *Weeks v. United States* (1914). *Brown v. Mississippi* (1936), *Chambers v. Florida* (1940), and *Ashcraft v. Tennessee* (1944) prohibited the use of confessions obtained through coercion, laying the groundwork for *Miranda*. *Johnson v. Zerbst* (1938) made clear that the Sixth Amendment entitled a person charged with crime in a federal court to appointed defense counsel, laying the groundwork for *Gideon v. Wainwright*, which in 1963 extended the right to counsel to state felony trials. The scope of First Amendment right to free speech is still greatly affected today by the fighting words doctrine announced in *Chaplinsky v. New Hampshire* (1942). The foundations of the right to privacy were formed in *Meyer v. Nebraska* (1923) and *Pierce v. Society of Sisters* (1925). Even before the historic *Brown v. Board of Education* (1954) case, earlier Courts began to whittle away at legalized racial discrimination on equal protection grounds (e.g., *Shelley v. Kraemer*, 1948). And the power of judicial review—the ability of courts to review the constitutionality of acts by the executive and legislative branches of government—dates back to *Marbury v. Madison* in 1803.

The Warren Court (1953–1969)

The **Warren Court** (1953–1969) commands attention because in the areas of civil liberties and civil rights, it remains the benchmark against which subsequent periods of the Supreme Court are measured. The Warren Court revolutionized constitutional law and American society as well, giving to minorities victories they had not been able to obtain from reluctant legislatures and recalcitrant executives.

The Warren Court first captured national attention with its highly controversial 1954 decision invalidating racial segregation in the public schools (*Brown v. Board of Education*, 1954). In addition, the Court first confronted the difficult problem of defining obscenity and considerably narrowed the grounds for prosecution of obscene material (*Roth v. United States*, 1957). What produced the greatest controversy, however, was the adoption of a series of broad rules protecting criminal defendants.

During the 1960s, the Supreme Court for the first time attempted to exercise strong policy control over the administration of criminal justice. The nation's highest court began to apply to state courts some of the more specific requirements of the Bill of Rights. Earlier opinions enunciating vague standards of "due process" were replaced by decisions specifying precise rules. The Bill of Rights was seemingly transformed from a collection of general constitutional principles into a code of criminal procedure. These sweeping changes in constitutional interpretation have been called the "due process revolution." Many of the leading cases of the due process revolution have been covered throughout this book.

The Burger Court (1969–1986)

Many of the Warren Court's criminal justice decisions were far from popular. The Supreme Court's attempt to nationalize and constitutionalize the criminal justice system came at a time of increasing crime in the streets, riots in big cities, political violence protesting the Vietnam War, and most tragically of all, assassinations of American leaders. To the public, there appeared to be a connection between the new trends of what was seen as judicial permissiveness and the breakdown of law and order. Supreme Court justices were accused of "coddling criminals" and "handcuffing the

police." This controversy became the focus of national debate.

During the 1968 presidential campaign, Republican candidate Richard Nixon made the Warren Court's decisions on criminal procedure a major issue. He promised to appoint "strict constructionists" to the Court, and after his election he made good on this promise. With his four appointments, Nixon achieved remarkable success in remodeling the Court. After Warren Burger, Harry Blackmun, Lewis Powell, and William Rehnquist took the bench, support for civil liberties quickly began to diminish (Segal & Spaeth, 1989).

Although on balance the **Burger Court** (1969–1986) was more conservative than its predecessor, there was no constitutional counterrevolution, only modest adjustment. The withdrawal from Warren Court decisions was most apparent in criminal justice. *Miranda* was weakened, but not overturned. Similarly, despite clamor by conservatives, *Mapp* was not overruled, although the Court began creating "good faith" exceptions to the exclusionary rule (see Chapter 11). To be sure, the death penalty was reinstated, but overall the Burger Court did not cut back on Warren Court criminal procedure rulings as much as had been expected.

The Rehnquist Court (1986–2005)

Presidents Ronald Reagan and George H. W. Bush continued the Republican policy of appointing conservatives to the court. The **Rehnquist Court** (1986–2005) officially began when William Rehnquist was elevated from associate justice to chief justice. Unofficially, it can be dated from the 1988 appointment of Anthony Kennedy, who provided a conservative vote far more dependably than did his predecessor Lewis Powell. Thus, it was during the 1988 term that the Rehnquist Court seemed to come of conservative age by cutting back abortion rights, condoning mandatory drug testing, and permitting capital punishment for juveniles and developmentally impaired persons who were convicted of murder. And as emphasized in this chapter, it significantly curtailed *habeas corpus* relief.

But other Rehnquist Court decisions cannot be so easily categorized as conservative. For example, the Court announced a new constitutional right grounded in the Eighth Amendment's prohibitions against excessive fines; these limits place brakes on the government's aggressive use of its authority under the drug forfeiture laws.

The retirement of Byron White gave President Clinton the opportunity to become the first Democratic president in 26 years to make an appointment to the Supreme Court. He chose Ruth Bader Ginsburg. With his second appointment, he elevated Stephen Breyer to the high court. Both have been moderately liberal and have often forged an alliance with the centrist justices.

Decisions reflect shifting alliances of the justices. Firmly on the right were Antonin Scalia, Clarence Thomas, and William Rehnquist, with Anthony Kennedy often joining them. Arrayed more to the left were John Paul Stevens, Ruth Bader Ginsburg, Stephen Breyer, and David Souter. It was Sandra Day O'Connor who often held the balance of power. These shifting alliances were reflected in two controversial 2003 decisions in which the Court declared unconstitutional a state law prohibiting intimate sexual conduct between persons of the same sex (*Lawrence v. Texas*) and upheld some types of race-based diversity programs in university admissions (*Grutter v. Bollinger*).

For 11 years, the same nine justices sat on the Supreme Court, but this changed quickly in the summer of 2005. First, Sandra Day O'Connor announced her retirement, followed two months later by the death of the chief justice. Amid considerable public attention, President George W. Bush had his long-anticipated opportunity to try to move the Court further to the right (Neubauer & Meinhold, 2013).

The Roberts Court (2005–)

The **Roberts Court** (2005–) began on the first Monday in October 2005, when John Roberts officially assumed his duties as the nation's 17th chief justice. In selecting Roberts, President George W. Bush clearly stated his desire to make the Court more conservative. Although some Democrats viewed Roberts as too conservative, he was confirmed. But all eyes were on the next nominee. Bush eventually nominated Samuel Alito to replace O'Connor. Alito's record as a conservative appellate judge caused some Democrats to consider filibustering his nomination. But Alito was eventually confirmed by the Senate by a relatively narrow margin of 58 to 42.

Democratic President Barack Obama made two appointments to the U.S. Supreme Court. Sonia Sotomayor, the nation's first Latina justice, replaced Justice David Souter when he retired in 2009. And Elena Kagan, the first female Dean of Harvard Law School and the first female solicitor general, replaced Justice John Paul Stevens when he retired in 2010.

Because both Souter and Stevens were largely considered to be liberal, their replacements by Sotomayor and Kagan did not change the balance of power significantly on the Supreme Court. When conservative Justice Antonin Scalia died during Obama's last year in office, he nominated centrist U.S. Court of Appeals Judge Merrick Garland to replace Scalia. But for the first time in U.S. history, the U.S. Senate refused to hold confirmation hearings on Garland's nomination. The Republican-controlled Senate wanted to wait until after the 2016 election in the hopes of a Republican president being able to nominate Scalia's successor, thereby maintaining the Court's presumed balance of power. After his election, President Donald Trump nominated Neil Gorsuch to fill the seat that had been empty for more than a year after Scalia's death. After Republicans changed the filibuster rules (Chapter 8) to get Gorsuch approved without significant support from Democrats, Gorsuch was narrowly confirmed. Table 15.3 presents information about the justices on the Supreme Court as of the publication of this book.

To date, the Roberts Court appears to be slightly more conservative than the Rehnquist Court, but how much more conservative still remains to be seen. "Empirical scrutiny of the Court's voting patterns reveals no significant distinctions between the Rehnquist and Roberts Courts" thus far; rather, the Court appears to be in a state of "relative

| TABLE 15.3 | Supreme Court Justices in Order of Seniority | | | | | |

Name	Year of Birth	Home State	Religion	Year of Appointment	Appointed	Senate Vote
John Roberts	1955	Indiana	Catholic	2005	George W. Bush	78–22
Anthony Kennedy	1936	California	Catholic	1988	Ronald Reagan	97–0
Clarence Thomas	1948	Georgia	Catholic	1991	George H. W. Bush	52–48
Ruth Bader Ginsburg	1933	New York	Jewish	1993	Bill Clinton	96–3
Stephen Breyer	1938	Massachusetts	Jewish	1994	Bill Clinton	87–9
Samuel Alito, Jr.	1950	New Jersey	Catholic	2006	George W. Bush	58–42
Sonia Sotomayor	1954	New York	Catholic	2009	Barack Obama	68–31
Elena Kagan	1960	New York	Jewish	2010	Barack Obama	63–37
Neil Gorsuch	1967	Denver	Catholic or Episcopal[a]	2017	Donald Trump	54–45

[a]Gorsuch was raised Roman Catholic, but he is registered as a congregant of an Episcopal church. If he considers himself to be a Protestant, he would be the first Protestant confirmed to sit on the U.S. Supreme Court since President George H. Bush nominated David Souter, another Episcopalian, in 1990.

continuity" rather than dramatic change (Epstein, Martin, Quinn, & Segal, 2008, pp. 651–652). The difference, however, is that Justice Kennedy has replaced Justice Sandra Day O'Connor as the Court's key swing vote.

The current Court is highly polarized (Liptak, 2014b). Until Antonin Scalia's death in 2016, the conservative bloc consisted of four justices appointed by Republican presidents—Justices Roberts, Alito, Scalia, and Thomas. And the liberal bloc consisted of four justices appointed by Democratic presidents—Justices Ginsburg, Breyer, Sotomayor, and Kagan. Justice Kennedy, who was appointed by Republican president Ronald Reagan, is most often in the middle, casting the deciding vote. For example, Justice Kennedy was the key fifth vote in *Boumediene v. Bush* (2008). This important case held that the "enemy combatants" being held as prisoners by the U.S. government at the U.S. Naval Station at Guantanamo Bay, Cuba, on suspicion of involvement in terrorist activities had the right to challenge their detention in civilian courts in *habeas corpus* proceedings even though Congress had enacted laws to prevent the

prisoners from doing so. Justice Kennedy also sided with the Court's "liberal wing" in holding that defendants have the right to effective assistance of counsel during plea bargaining (*Lafler v. Cooper*, 2012; *Missouri v. Frye*, 2012). Conversely, Justice Kennedy sided with the four conservative justices in *Hudson v. Michigan* (2006) when the Court ruled that the exclusionary rule was not an appropriate remedy for violations of the requirement that police officers knock and announce their presence before executing a search warrant (see Chapter 11). Overall, Justice Kennedy is often a voice of pragmatism in debates with the conservative justices (Bibas, 2013).

In some closely watched death penalty cases, Justice Kennedy has sided with both ideological factions of the Court (see Carter, 2013). On the so-called liberal side, Kennedy wrote the majority opinion that allowed a Tennessee death row inmate to use DNA evidence in a federal *habeas corpus* hearing (see "Case Close-Up: *House v. Bell* and Federal Court Scrutiny of State Death Row Inmates" on page 480). He also joined with the "liberal" branch of the Court in invalidating the use of capital punishment against a child rapist (*Kennedy v. Louisiana*, 2008). Yet, he sided with conservatives in several other death penalty cases. With Justice Kennedy writing for the majority in *Ayers v. Belmontes* (2006), the Court ruled that juries need not consider forward-looking mitigating circumstances during death-sentence deliberations. Justice Kennedy also provided the key votes in *Schriro v. Landrigan* (2007), which upheld a death sentence over an ineffective assistance of counsel claim; *Uttecht v. Brown* (2006), which upheld a trial court's dismissal of three venirepersons because they were opposed to the death penalty over an objection that such dismissals violated the right to an impartial jury guaranteed by the Sixth and Fourteenth Amendments; and *James v. United States* (2007), which held that an attempted burglary qualified as a "violent felony" for triggering a 15-year mandatory sentence under the federal Armed Career Criminal Act. The future direction of the Court will depend on the political balance between the president and the U.S. Senate.

The Supreme Court in Broad Perspective

Newspaper coverage of the Supreme Court tends to resemble the play-by-play commentary for an athletic event, with each decision in the term described as a "victory" or "defeat" for conservatives or liberals. Unfortunately, what gets lost in this commentary is the broader perspective.

Overall, the decisions of the U.S. Supreme Court swing back and forth much like a pendulum. Far from being random, however, these swings reflect major political movements in the nation. Most directly, this occurs because of the swing of electoral politics; presidential appointments control the composition of the bench and may temper the speed, if not shift the direction, of the Court. More indirectly, public opinion also affects the justices' lives and may serve to curb them when they threaten to go too far or too fast in their rulings. "But changes in the direction of the Court are ultimately moderated by its

functioning as a collegial body, in which all nine justices share power and compete for influence" (O'Brien, 1988, p. 13; see also Devins, 2008). The Court thus generally shifts direction gradually, incorporating and accommodating the views of new appointees. Ultimately, these long-term trends, more than individual decisions, have the most influence.

Conclusion

"This is not a case of conclusive exoneration," wrote Justice Kennedy. Paul House was entitled to another hearing in federal district court, but with no guarantee as to the outcome of that hearing. In the end, the prosecutor chose not to retry the case. As a result, Paul House was released after spending 24 years on death row. Whether this decision will offer much hope to other inmates sitting on death row remains to be seen. But *House v. Bell* only adds a new chapter to the long-running debate over federal review of state court convictions, particularly federal court review of state death penalty cases. To some, allowing multiple reviews only introduces unnecessary complexities into the process, thus eroding the deterrent value of punishment. To others, though, allowing multiple reviews properly introduces multiple perspectives, thus ensuring that justice is done.

The right to one appeal is being increasingly used. Appellate court caseloads have grown dramatically in recent years. The explosive growth in appellate court caseloads not only reflects the greater willingness of litigants to ask reviewing bodies to correct errors but also represents the greater role appellate courts play in policy making. U.S. Supreme Court decisions have important impacts on the criminal justice system. But the nine justices are often as divided over the correct answer to a legal problem as is society. Thus, predicting specific case outcomes is difficult; indeed, the conservative Rehnquist Court did not always rule in a predictably conservative manner, and it remains to be seen whether the Roberts Court will consistently rule as conservatively as predicted.

CHAPTER REVIEW

LO1   1. Explain how appeals and appellate processes differ from trials and trial processes.

Unlike trial courts, appeals courts do not
hear evidence at trials. Thus, witnesses do
not provide testimony at appeals. Rather,
lawyers for both sides appear before a
panel of judges to argue about the law
applicable to the case.

LO2   2. Describe the two primary functions
of appeals.

The two primary functions of appeals are
error correction and policy formation.

LO3   3. Explain how double jeopardy limits
appeals by the prosecution in criminal cases.

Although the prosecution can file an
appeal over a question of law, the Double
Jeopardy Clause of the Fifth Amendment
to the U.S. Constitution prevents the
prosecution from seeking to have a "not
guilty" verdict overturned on appeal.

LO4   4. Define the contemporaneous objection
rule and explain its impact on appeals.

When lawyers think an error is being
made at trial, they must object in order to
give the trial court judge the opportunity
to correct the error. If the attorneys fail
to object, then their objection is deemed
waived and, therefore, cannot form the
basis of a legal argument on appeal.

LO5   5. Differentiate between mandatory and
discretionary appellate jurisdiction.

Mandatory appellate jurisdiction concerns the cases that an appeals court must
hear. Discretionary appellate jurisdiction
concerns the cases that an appeals court
may elect to hear but is not required to
adjudicate.

LO6   6. Identify the different appellate standards of review and evaluate their impact
on the criminal appeals.

Questions of law are reviewed *de novo*,
questions of fact are reviewed for clear

error, and discretionary rulings by judges
are reviewed for an abuse of discretion.
The *de novo* standard allows an appellate
court to consider any legal question without regard or deference to the decision
made by a lower court. The other standards of review require appellate courts
to give deference to the decisions of a
trial court.

LO7   7. Describe the six customary phases in the
appeals process.

Appeals are started by the appellant's
filing a notice of appeal. The parties then
designate the record on appeal and the
trial court transmits the designated materials to an appellate court. The parties then
brief their cases. The appeals court may
then opt to hear oral arguments. The decision of the appellate court is memorialized
in a written opinion that concludes with
an order disposing of the case.

LO8   8. Compare and contrast plain error,
reversible error, and harmless error.

Plain errors are severe defects in trial proceedings that require reversal of a conviction and remand for a new trial in order
to avoid a miscarriage of justice. All other
errors are subject to the harmless error
rule. If the mistakes are minor such that
they probably did not affect the outcome
of the case, they are deemed "harmless"
and therefore do not provide grounds for
the reversal of a conviction on appeal. In
contrast, if the errors likely contributed to
a defendant being convicted, then they are
deemed prejudicial and therefore require
that a conviction be reversed.

LO9   9. Analyze the reasons why most criminal appeals result in convictions being
affirmed.

Most criminal cases are affirmed on
appeal because of the harmless error rule
and the standards of review applied by
appellate courts.

LO10 10. Compare and contrast appeals and postconviction review processes.

So long as criminal defendants file a notice of appeal within the specified time limits, they are guaranteed the right to have an appellate court directly examine their convictions for all types of alleged errors. Postconviction reviews, however, collaterally attack convictions in civil court. The grounds for such postconviction reviews are usually much narrower than the grounds that can form the basis of a direct appeal.

LO11 11. Identify the leading causes of wrongful convictions.

The leading causes of wrongful convictions include mistaken identifications, improper forensic evidence, false confessions, unreliable informants, tunnel vision and misconduct by justice professionals, and inadequate defense representation.

LO12 12. Analyze how state courts of last resort and the U.S. Supreme Court exercise their discretion to set justice policy.

High courts of last resort help to set justice policy through their exercise of their discretionary appellate jurisdiction. They accept only cases that present significant public policy questions while rejecting petitions that merely allege the need for error correction.

CRITICAL THINKING QUESTIONS

1. In the public's mind, at least, appeals drag on endlessly and result in a lack of finality in the process. Do you think this is a significant problem, or is it merely one of appearance?

2. How does the appeal-and-review process in a capital murder case differ from the appeal-and-review process in a serious felony?

3. Why are most findings of guilt at the trial level not appealed? In what ways are appellate cases unrepresentative of trial court cases?

4. Based on material in this chapter and earlier ones, what have been the significant differences in decisions among the Warren Court, the Burger Court, the Rehnquist Court, and now the Roberts Court? In particular, consider Court decisions related to right to counsel (Chapter 7), bail (Chapter 10), right to trial (Chapter 13), the death penalty (Chapter 14), and *habeas corpus* (this chapter).

KEY TERMS

affirm   476

amicus curiae   475

appellant   474

appellate brief   474

appellate court record   474

appellee   475

Burger Court   492

collateral attack   479

concurring opinion   475

contemporaneous objection rule   470

discretionary appellate jurisdiction   471

dissenting opinion   475

double jeopardy   470

en banc   469

error   476

error correction   469

habeas corpus   481

harmless error   476

informants   487

interlocutory   470

mandatory appellate jurisdiction   471

new judicial federalism   490

notice of appeal   474

opinion   475

oral argument   475

per curium opinion   475

petitioner   474

plain error   476

plurality opinion   475

policy formulation   469

FOR FURTHER READING

Acker, James. 2013. "The Flipside Injustice of Wrongful Convictions: When the Guilty go Free." *Albany Law Review* 76: 1629–1712.

Acker, James, and Allison Redlich. 2011. *Wrongful Conviction: Law, Science, and Policy.* Durham, NC: Carolina Academic Press.

Benforado, Adam. 2016. *Unfair: The New Science of Criminal Injustice.* New York, NY: Penguin/Random House.

Bowie, Jennifer Barnes, Donald R. Songer, and John Szmer. 2014. The *View from the Bench and Chambers: Examining Judicial Process and Decision Making on the U.S. Courts of Appeals.* Charlottesville: University of Virginia Press.

Chemerinsky, Erwin. 2017. *Closing the Courthouse Door: How Your Constitutional Rights Became Unenforceable.* New Haven, CT: Yale University Press.

Ferak, John. 2016. *Failure of Justice: A Brutal Murder, An Obsessed Cop, Six Wrongful Convictions.* Denver, CO: Wildblue Press.

Garrett, Brandon. 2011. *Convicting the Innocent: Where Criminal Prosecutions Go Wrong.* Cambridge, MA: Harvard University Press.

Hughes, Emily. 2013. "Investigating *Gideon*'s Legacy in the U.S. Courts of Appeals." *Yale Law Journal* 122: 2376–2393.

Keys, David. 2014. *Unbearable Burden: Wrongful Convictions and the Crisis in American Justice.* Las Cruces, NM: Levine Riordan.

King, Nancy, and Joseph Hoffman. 2011. *Habeas for the Twenty-First Century: Uses, Abuses, and the Future of the Great Writ.* Chicago, IL: University of Chicago Press.

O'Brien, David. 2017. *Storm Center: The Supreme Court in American Politics.* 11th ed. New York, NY: Norton.

Redlich, Allison, James Acker, Robert Norris, and Catherine Bonventre (Eds.). 2014. *Examining Wrongful Convictions: Stepping Back, Moving Forward.* Durham, NC: Carolina Academic Press.

Richman, William M., and William L. Reynolds. 2013. *Injustice on Appeal: The United States Courts of Appeals in Crisis.* New York, NY: Oxford University Press.

Simon, Dan. 2012. *In Doubt: The Psychology of the Criminal Justice Process.* Boston: Harvard University Press.

Smith, Christopher, and April Sanford. 2013. "The Roberts Court and Wrongful Convictions." *St. Louis University Public Law Review* 32: 307–328.

Time, The Editors of. 2017. *Innocent: The Fight Against Wrongful Convictions. Time Magazine*: Special edition.

Zalman, Marvin, and Julia Carrano. 2014. *Wrongful Conviction and Criminal Justice Reform: Making Justice.* New York, NY: Routledge

APPENDIX A

Overview of the Constitution of the United States

Note: Portions in **bold type** are especially important to criminal courts and judicial processes.

Preamble

We the people of the United States, in order to form a more perfect union, establish justice, insure domestic tranquility, provide for the common defense, promote the general welfare, and secure the blessings of liberty to ourselves and our posterity, do ordain and establish this Constitution for the United States of America.

Article I—The Legislative Branch

Section 1   Vests legislative power in a bicameral (two-part) Congress

Section 2   House of Representatives—minimum age 25; 2-year terms; representation by state to be proportional to population; members elect their own Speaker; sole power of impeachment

Section 3   Senate—minimum age 30; 6-year terms; two senators per state; tries all impeachments

Section 4   Elections of Senators and Representatives

Section 5   Rules of House and Senate

Section 6   Compensation and Privileges of Members

Section 7   Passage of Bills

Section 8   Scope of Legislative Power

Section 9   Limits on Legislative Power

Section 10   Limits on States

Article II—The Presidency

Section 1   Election, Installation, Removal

Section 2   Presidential Power

Section 3   State of the Union, Receive Ambassadors, Laws Faithfully Executed, Commission Officers

Section 4   Impeachment

Article III—The Judiciary

Section 1. The judicial Power of the United States, shall be vested in one supreme Court, and in such inferior Courts as the Congress may from time to time ordain and establish. The Judges, both of the supreme and inferior Courts, shall hold their Offices during good Behavior, and shall, at stated Times, receive for their Services a Compensation which shall not be diminished during their Continuance in Office.

Section 2. *Clause 1:* The judicial Power shall extend to all Cases, in Law and Equity, arising under this Constitution, the Laws of the United States, and Treaties made, or which shall be made, under their Authority; to all Cases affecting Ambassadors, other public Ministers and Consuls; to all Cases of admiralty and maritime Jurisdiction; to Controversies to which the United States shall be a Party; to Controversies between two or more States; between a State and Citizens of another State; between Citizens of different States; between Citizens of the same State claiming Lands under Grants of different States, and between a State, or the Citizens thereof, and foreign States, Citizens or Subjects. (This section was modified, in part, by Amendment XI.)

Clause 2:   In all Cases affecting Ambassadors, other public Ministers and Consuls, and those in which a State shall be Party, the supreme Court shall have original Jurisdiction. In all the other Cases before mentioned, the supreme Court shall have appellate Jurisdiction, both as to Law and Fact, with such Exceptions, and under such Regulations as the Congress shall make.

Clause 3:   The Trial of all Crimes, except in Cases of Impeachment, shall be by Jury; and such Trial shall be held in the State where the said Crimes shall have been committed; but when not committed within any State, the Trial shall be at such Place or Places as the Congress may by Law have directed.

Section 3.   Treason against the United States, shall consist only in levying War against them, or in adhering to their Enemies, giving them Aid and Comfort. No Person shall be convicted of Treason unless on the Testimony of two Witnesses to the same overt Act, or on Confession in open Court.

The Congress shall have power to declare the Punishment of Treason, but no Attainder of Treason shall work Corruption of Blood, or Forfeiture except during the Life of the Person attainted.

Article IV—The States

Section 1	Full Faith and Credit
Section 2	Privileges and Immunities, Extradition, Fugitive Slaves
Section 3	Admission of States
Section 4	Guarantees to States

Article V—The Amendment Process

Article VI—Legal Status of the Constitution

Clause 1:   All Debts contracted and Engagements entered into, before the Adoption of this Constitution, shall be as valid against the United States under this Constitution, as under the Confederation.

Clause 2:   This Constitution, and the Laws of the United States which shall be made in Pursuance thereof; and all Treaties made, or which shall be made, under the Authority of the United States, shall be the supreme Law of the Land; and the Judges in every State shall be bound thereby, any Thing in the Constitution or Laws of any State to the Contrary notwithstanding.

Clause 3:   The Senators and Representatives before mentioned, and the Members of the several State Legislatures, and all executive and judicial Officers, both of the United States and of the several States, shall be bound by Oath or Affirmation, to support this Constitution; but no religious Test shall ever be required as a Qualification to any Office or public Trust under the United States.

Article VII—Ratification

Amendment I

"Congress shall make no law respecting an establishment of religion, or prohibiting the free exercise thereof; or abridging the freedom of speech, or of the press; or the right of the people peaceably to assemble, and to petition the Government for a redress of grievances" (1791).

Amendment II

"A well regulated Militia, being necessary to the security of a free State, the right of the people to keep and bear Arms, shall not be infringed" (1791).

Amendment III

"No Soldier shall, in time of peace be quartered in any house, without the consent of the Owner, nor in time of war, but in a manner to be prescribed by law" (1791).

Amendment IV

"The right of the people to be secure in their persons, houses, papers, and effects, against unreasonable searches and seizures, shall not be violated, and no Warrants shall issue, but upon probable cause, supported by Oath or affirmation, and particularly describing the place to be searched, and the persons or things to be seized" (1791).

Amendment V

"No person shall be held to answer for a capital, or otherwise infamous crime, unless on a presentment or indictment of a Grand Jury, except in cases arising in the land or naval forces, or in the Militia, when in actual service in time of War or public danger; nor shall any person be subject for the same offense to be twice put in jeopardy of life or limb; nor shall be compelled in any criminal case to be a witness against himself, nor be deprived of life, liberty, or property, without due process of law; nor shall private property be taken for public use, without just compensation" (1791).

Amendment VI

"In all criminal prosecutions, the accused shall enjoy the right to a speedy and public trial, by an impartial jury of the State and district wherein the crime shall have been committed, which district shall have been previously ascertained by law, and to be informed of the nature and cause of the accusation; to be confronted with the witnesses against him; to have compulsory process for obtaining witnesses in his favor, and to have the Assistance of Counsel for his defence" (1791).

Amendment VII

"In Suits at common law, where the value in controversy shall exceed twenty dollars, the right of trial by jury shall be preserved, and no fact tried by a jury, shall be otherwise re-examined in any Court of the United States, than according to the rules of the common law" (1791).

Amendment VIII

"Excessive bail shall not be required, nor excessive fines imposed, nor cruel and unusual punishments inflicted" (1791).

Amendment IX

"The enumeration in the Constitution, of certain rights, shall not be construed to deny or disparage others retained by the people" (1791).

Amendment X

"The powers not delegated to the United States by the Constitution, nor prohibited by it to the States, are reserved to the States respectively, or to the people" (1791).

Amendment XI

"The Judicial power of the United States shall not be construed to extend to any suit in law or equity, commenced or prosecuted against one of the United States by Citizens of another State, or by Citizens or Subjects of any Foreign State" (1795).

Amendment XII

Election of President and Vice-President (1804).

Amendment XIII

Abolition of Slavery (1865).

Amendment XIV

Section 1. All persons born or naturalized in the United States, and subject to the jurisdiction thereof, are citizens of the United States and of the State wherein they reside. No State shall make or enforce any law which shall abridge the privileges or immunities of citizens of the United States; nor shall any State deprive any person of life, liberty, or property, without due process of law; nor deny to any person within its jurisdiction the equal protection of the laws.

Section 5.   The Congress shall have power to enforce, by appropriate legislation, the provisions of this article (1868).

Amendment XV

Rights Not to Be Denied on Account of Race (1870).

Amendment XVI

Income Tax (1913).

Amendment XVII

Election of Senators (1913).

Amendment XVIII

Prohibition (1919).

Amendment XIX

Women's Right to Vote (1920).

Amendment XX

Presidential Term and Succession (1933).

Amendment XXI

Repeal of Prohibition (1933).

Amendment XXII

Two Term Limit on President (1951).

Amendment XXIII

Presidential Vote in D.C. (1961).

Amendment XXIV

Poll Tax (1964).

Amendment XXV

Presidential Succession (1967).

Amendment XXVI

Right to Vote at Age 18 (1971).

Amendment XXVII

Compensation of Members of Congress (1992).

We the People of the United States, in Order to form a more perfect Union, establish Justice, insure domestic Tranquility, provide for the common defence, promote the general Welfare, and secure the Blessings of Liberty to ourselves and our Posterity, do ordain and establish this Constitution for the United States of America.

Article I

Section 1. All legislative Powers herein granted shall be vested in a Congress of the United States, which shall consist of a Senate and House of Representatives.

Section 2. The House of Representatives shall be composed of Members chosen every second Year by the People of the several States, and the Electors in each State shall have the Qualifications requisite for Electors of the most numerous Branch of the State Legislature.

No Person shall be a Representative who shall not have attained to the age of twenty five Years, and been seven Years a Citizen of the United States, and who shall not, when elected, be an Inhabitant of that State in which he shall be chosen.

Representatives and direct Taxes shall be apportioned among the several States which may be included within this Union, according to their respective Numbers, which shall be determined by adding to the whole Number of free Persons, including those bound to Service for a Term of Years, and excluding Indians not taxed, three fifths of all other Persons. The actual Enumeration shall be made within three Years after the first Meeting of the Congress of the United States, and within every subsequent Term of ten Years, in such Manner as they shall by Law direct. The Number of Representatives shall not exceed one for every thirty Thousand, but each State shall have at Least one

Representative; and until such enumeration shall be made, the State of New Hampshire shall be entitled to choose three, Massachusetts eight, Rhode-Island and Providence Plantations one, Connecticut five, New-York six, New Jersey four, Pennsylvania eight, Delaware one, Maryland six, Virginia ten, North Carolina five, South Carolina five, and Georgia three.

When vacancies happen in the Representation from any State, the Executive Authority thereof shall issue Writs of Election to fill such Vacancies.

The House of Representatives shall choose their Speaker and other Officers; and shall have the sole Power of Impeachment.

Section 3. The Senate of the United States shall be composed of two Senators from each State, chosen by the Legislature t+hereof, for six Years; and each Senator shall have one Vote.

Immediately after they shall be assembled in Consequence of the first Election, they shall be divided as equally as may be into three Classes. The Seats of the Senators of the first Class shall be vacated at the Expiration of the second Year, of the second Class at the Expiration of the fourth Year, and the third Class at the Expiration of the sixth Year, so that one third may be chosen every second Year; and if Vacancies happen by Resignation, or otherwise, during the Recess of the Legislature of any State, the Executive thereof may make temporary Appointments until the next Meeting of the Legislature, which shall then fill such Vacancies.

No Person shall be a Senator who shall not have attained to the Age of thirty Years, and been nine Years a Citizen of the United States and who shall not, when elected, be an Inhabitant of that State for which he shall be chosen.

The Vice President of the United States shall be President of the Senate, but shall have no Vote, unless they be equally divided.

The Senate shall choose their other Officers, and also a President pro tempore, in the Absence of the Vice President, or when he shall exercise the Office of President of the United States.

The Senate shall have the sole Power to try all Impeachments. When sitting for that Purpose, they shall be on Oath or Affirmation. When the President of the United States is tried, the Chief Justice shall preside: And no Person shall be convicted without the Concurrence of two thirds of the Members present.

Judgment in Cases of Impeachment shall not extend further than to removal from Office, and disqualification to hold and enjoy any Office of Honor, Trust or Profit under the United States: but the Party convicted shall nevertheless be liable and subject to Indictment, Trial, Judgment and Punishment, according to Law.

Section 4. The Times, Places and Manner of holding Elections for Senators and Representatives, shall be prescribed in each State by the Legislature thereof; but the Congress may at any time by Law make or alter such Regulations, except as to the Places of choosing Senators.

The Congress shall assemble at least once in every Year, and such Meeting shall be on the first Monday in December, unless they shall by Law appoint a different Day.

Section 5. Each House shall be the Judge of the Elections, Returns and Qualifications of its own Members, and a Majority of each shall constitute a Quorum to do Business; but a smaller Number may adjourn from day to day, and may be authorized to compel the Attendance of absent Members, in such Manner, and under such Penalties as each House may provide.

Each House may determine the Rules of its Proceedings, punish its Members for disorderly Behaviour, and, with the Concurrence of two thirds, expel a Member.

Each House shall keep a Journal of its Proceedings, and from time to time publish the same, excepting such Parts as may in their Judgment require Secrecy; and the Yeas and Nays of the Members of either House on any question shall, at the Desire of one fifth of those Present, be entered on the Journal.

Neither House, during the Session of Congress, shall, without the Consent of the other, adjourn for more than three days, nor to any other Place than that in which the two Houses shall be sitting.

Section 6. The Senators and Representatives shall receive a Compensation for their Services, to be ascertained by Law, and paid out of the Treasury of the United States. They shall in all Cases, except Treason, Felony and Breach of the Peace, be privileged from Arrest during their Attendance at the Session of their respective Houses, and in going to and returning from the same; and for any Speech or Debate in either House, they shall not be questioned in any other Place.

No Senator or Representative shall, during the Time for which he was elected, be appointed to any civil Office under the Authority of the United States, which shall have been created, or the Emoluments whereof shall have been increased during such time: and no Person holding any Office under the United States, shall be a Member of either House during his Continuance in Office.

Section 7. All Bills for raising Revenue shall originate in the House of Representatives; but the Senate may propose or concur with Amendments as on other Bills.

Every Bill which shall have passed the House of Representatives and the Senate, shall, before it become a Law, be presented to the President of the United States; if he approve he shall sign it, but if not he shall return it, with his Objections to that House in which it shall have originated, who shall enter the Objections at large on their Journal, and proceed to reconsider it. If after such Reconsideration two thirds of that House shall agree to pass the Bill, it shall be sent, together with the Objections, to the other House, by which it shall likewise be reconsidered, and if approved by two thirds of that House, it shall become a Law. But in all such Cases the Votes of both Houses shall be determined by Yeas and Nays, and the Names of the Persons voting for and against the Bill shall be entered on the Journal of each House respectively. If any Bill shall not be returned by the President within ten Days (Sundays excepted) after it shall have been presented to him, the Same shall be a Law, in like Manner as if he had signed it, unless the Congress by their Adjournment prevent its Return, in which Case it shall not be a Law.

Every Order, Resolution, or Vote to which the Concurrence of the Senate and House of Representatives may be necessary (except on a question of Adjournment) shall be presented to the President of the United States; and before the Same shall take Effect, shall be approved by him, or being disapproved by him, shall be repassed by two thirds of the Senate and House of Representatives, according to the Rules and Limitations prescribed in the Case of a Bill.

Section 8. The Congress shall have Power To lay and collect Taxes, Duties, Imposts and Excises, to pay the Debts and provide for the common Defence and general Welfare of the United States; but all Duties, Imposts and Excises shall be uniform throughout the United States;

To borrow Money on the credit of the United States;

To regulate Commerce with foreign Nations, and among the several States, and with the Indian Tribes;

To establish a uniform Rule of Naturalization, and uniform Laws on the subject of Bankruptcies throughout the United States;

To coin Money, regulate the Value thereof, and of foreign Coin, and fix the Standard of Weights and Measures;

To provide for the Punishment of counterfeiting the Securities and current Coin of the United States;

To establish Post Offices and post Roads;

To promote the Progress of Science and useful Arts, by securing for limited Times to Authors and Inventors the exclusive Right to their respective Writings and Discoveries;

To constitute Tribunals inferior to the Supreme Court;

To define and punish Piracies and Felonies committed on the high Seas, and Offences against the Law of Nations;

To declare War, grant Letters of Marque and Reprisal, and make Rules concerning Captures on Land and Water;

To raise and support Armies, but no Appropriation of Money to that Use shall be for a longer Term than two Years;

To provide and maintain a Navy;

To make Rules for the Government and Regulation of the land and naval Forces;

To provide for calling forth the Militia to execute the Laws of the Union, suppress Insurrections and repel Invasions;

To provide for organizing, arming, and disciplining, the Militia, and for governing such Part of them as may be employed in the Service of the United States, reserving to the States respectively, the Appointment of the Officers, and the Authority of training the Militia according to the discipline prescribed by Congress;

To exercise exclusive Legislation in all Cases whatsoever, over such District (not exceeding ten Miles square) as may, by Cession of particular States, and the Acceptance of Congress, become the Seat of the Government of the United States, and to exercise like Authority over all Places purchased by the Consent of the Legislature of the State in which the Same shall be, for the Erection of Forts, Magazines, Arsenals, dock-Yards, and other needful Buildings;—And

To make all Laws which shall be necessary and proper for carrying into Execution the foregoing Powers, and all other Powers vested by this Constitution in the Government of the United States, or in any Department or Officer thereof.

Section 9. The Migration or Importation of such Persons as any of the States now existing shall think proper to admit, shall not be prohibited by the Congress prior to the Year one thousand eight hundred and eight, but a Tax or duty may be imposed on such Importation, not exceeding ten dollars for each Person.

The Privilege of the Writ of Habeas Corpus shall not be suspended, unless when in Cases of Rebellion or Invasion the public Safety may require it.

No Bill of Attainder or ex post facto Law shall be passed.

No Capitation, or other direct, Tax shall be laid, unless in Proportion to the Census or Enumeration herein before directed to be taken.

No Tax or Duty shall be laid on Articles exported from any State.

No Preference shall be given by any Regulation of Commerce or Revenue to the Ports of one State over those of another: nor shall Vessels bound to, or from, one State, be obliged to enter, clear or pay Duties in another.

No Money shall be drawn from the Treasury, but in Consequence of Appropriations made by Law; and a regular Statement and Account of Receipts and Expenditures of all public Money shall be published from time to time.

No Title of Nobility shall be granted by the United States: And no Person holding any Office of Profit or Trust under them, shall, without the Consent of the Congress, accept of any present, Emolument, Office, or Title, of any kind whatever, from any King, Prince, or foreign State.

Section 10. No State shall enter into any Treaty, Alliance, or Confederation; grant Letters of Marque and

Reprisal; coin Money; emit Bills of Credit; make any Thing but gold and silver Coin a Tender in Payment of Debts; pass any Bill of Attainder, ex post facto Law, or Law impairing the Obligation of Contracts, or grant any Title of Nobility.

No State shall, without the Consent of the Congress, lay any Imposts or Duties on Imports or Exports, except what may be absolutely necessary for executing its inspection Laws: and the net Produce of all Duties and Imposts, laid by any State on Imports or Exports, shall be for the Use of the Treasury of the United States; and all such Laws shall be subject to the Revision and Control of the Congress.

No State shall, without the Consent of Congress, lay any Duty of Tonnage, keep Troops, or Ships of War in time of Peace, enter into any Agreement or Compact with another State, or with a foreign Power, or engage in War, unless actually invaded, or in such imminent Danger as will not admit of delay.

Article II

Section 1. The executive Power shall be vested in a President of the United States of America. He shall hold his Office during the Term of four Years, and, together with the Vice President, chosen for the same Term, be elected, as follows:

Each State shall appoint, in such Manner as the Legislature thereof may direct, a Number of Electors, equal to the whole Number of Senators and Representatives to which the State may be entitled in the Congress: but no Senator or Representative, or Person holding an Office of Trust or Profit under the United States, shall be appointed an Elector.

The Electors shall meet in their respective States, and vote by Ballot for two Persons, of whom one at least shall not be an Inhabitant of the same State with themselves. And they shall make a List of all the Persons voted for, and of the Number of Votes for each; which List they shall sign and certify, and transmit sealed to the Seat of the Government of the United States, directed to the President of the Senate. The President of the Senate shall, in the Presence of the Senate and House of Representatives, open all the Certificates, and the Votes shall then be counted. The Person having the greatest Number of Votes shall be the President, if such Number be a Majority of the whole Number of Electors appointed; and if there be more than one who have

such Majority, and have an equal Number of Votes, then the House of Representatives shall immediately choose by Ballot one of them for President; and if no Person have a Majority, then from the five highest on the List the said House shall in like Manner choose the President. But in choosing the President, the Votes shall be taken by States, the Representation from each State having one Vote; A quorum for this Purpose shall consist of a Member or Members from two thirds of the States, and a Majority of all the States shall be necessary to a Choice. In every Case, after the Choice of the President, the Person having the greatest Number of Votes of the Electors shall be the Vice President. But if there should remain two or more who have equal Votes, the Senate shall choose from them by Ballot the Vice President.

The Congress may determine the Time of choosing the Electors, and the Day on which they shall give their Votes; which Day shall be the same throughout the United States.

No Person except a natural born Citizen, or a Citizen of the United States, at the time of the Adoption of this Constitution, shall be eligible to the Office of President; neither shall any Person be eligible to that Office who shall not have attained to the Age of thirty five Years, and been fourteen Years a Resident within the United States.

In Case of the Removal of the President from Office, or of his Death, Resignation, or Inability to discharge the Powers and Duties of the said Office, the Same shall devolve on the Vice President, and the Congress may by Law provide for the Case of Removal, Death, Resignation or Inability, both of the President and Vice President, declaring what Officer shall then act as President, and such Officer shall act accordingly, until the Disability be removed, or a President shall be elected.

The President shall, at stated Times, receive for his Services, a Compensation, which shall neither be increased nor diminished during the Period for which he shall have been elected, and he shall not receive within that Period any other Emolument from the United States, or any of them.

Before he enter on the Execution of his Office, he shall take the following Oath or Affirmation:—"I do solemnly swear (or affirm) that I will faithfully execute the Office of President of the United States, and will to the best of my Ability, preserve, protect and defend the Constitution of the United States."

Section 2. The President shall be Commander in Chief of the Army and Navy of the United States, and of the Militia of the several States, when called into the actual Service of the United States; he may require the Opinion, in writing, of the principal Officer in each of the executive Departments, upon any Subject relating to the Duties of their respective Offices, and he shall have Power to grant Reprieves and Pardons for Offences against the United States, except in Cases of Impeachment.

He shall have Power, by and with the Advice and Consent of the Senate, to make Treaties, provided two thirds of the Senators present concur; and he shall nominate, and by and with the Advice and Consent of the Senate, shall appoint Ambassadors, other public Ministers and Consuls, Judges of the supreme Court, and all other Officers of the United States, whose Appointments are not herein otherwise provided for, and which shall be established by Law: but the Congress may by Law vest the Appointment of such inferior Officers, as they think proper, in the President alone, in the Courts of Law, or in the Heads of Departments.

The President shall have Power to fill up all Vacancies that may happen during the Recess of the Senate, by granting Commissions which shall expire at the End of their next Session.

Section 3. He shall from time to time give to the Congress Information of the State of the Union, and recommend to their Consideration such Measures as he shall judge necessary and expedient; he may, on extraordinary Occasions, convene both Houses, or either of them, and in Case of Disagreement between them, with Respect to the Time of Adjournment, he may adjourn them to such Time as he shall think proper; he shall receive Ambassadors and other public Ministers; he shall take Care that the Laws be faithfully executed, and shall Commission all the Officers of the United States.

Section 4. The President, Vice President and all civil Officers of the United States, shall be removed from Office on Impeachment for, and Conviction of, Treason, Bribery, or other high Crimes and Misdemeanors.

Article III

Section 1. The judicial Power of the United States, shall be vested in one supreme Court, and in such inferior Courts as the Congress may from time to time ordain and establish. The Judges, both of the supreme and

inferior Courts, shall hold their Offices during good Behaviour, and shall, at stated Times, receive for their Services, a Compensation, which shall not be diminished during their Continuance in Office.

Section 2. The judicial Power shall extend to all Cases, in Law and Equity, arising under this Constitution, the Laws of the United States, and Treaties made, or which shall be made, under their Authority;—to all Cases affecting Ambassadors, other public Ministers and Consuls;—to all Cases of admiralty and maritime Jurisdiction;—to Controversies to which the United States shall be a Party;—to Controversies between two or more States;—between a State and Citizens of another State;—between Citizens of different States;— between Citizens of the same State claiming Lands under Grants of different States, and between a State, or the Citizens thereof, and foreign States, Citizens or Subjects.

In all Cases affecting Ambassadors, other public Ministers and Consuls, and those in which a State shall be Party, the supreme Court shall have original Jurisdiction. In all the other Cases before mentioned, the supreme Court shall have appellate Jurisdiction, both as to Law and Fact, with such Exceptions, and under such Regulations as the Congress shall make.

The Trial of all Crimes, except in Cases of Impeachment, shall be by Jury; and such Trial shall be held in the State where the said Crimes shall have been committed; but when not committed within any State, the Trial shall be at such Place or Places as the Congress may by Law have directed.

Section 3. Treason against the United States, shall consist only in levying War against them, or in adhering to their Enemies, giving them Aid and Comfort. No Person shall be convicted of Treason unless on the Testimony of two Witnesses to the same overt Act, or on Confession in open Court.

The Congress shall have Power to declare the Punishment of Treason, but no Attainder of Treason shall work Corruption of Blood, or Forfeiture except during the Life of the Person attainted.

Article IV

Section 1. Full Faith and Credit shall be given in each State to the public Acts, Records, and judicial Proceedings of every other State. And the Congress may by general Laws prescribe the Manner in which such

Acts, Records, and Proceedings shall be proved, and the Effect thereof.

Section 2. The Citizens of each State shall be entitled to all Privileges and Immunities of Citizens in the several States.

A Person charged in any State with Treason, Felony, or other Crime, who shall flee from Justice, and be found in another State, shall on Demand of the executive Authority of the State from which he fled, be delivered up, to be removed to the State having Jurisdiction of the Crime.

No Person held to Service or Labour in one State, under the Laws thereof, escaping into another, shall, in Consequence of any Law or Regulation therein, be discharged from such Service or Labour, but shall be delivered up on Claim of the Party to whom such Service or Labour may be due.

Section 3. New States may be admitted by the Congress into this Union; but no new States shall be formed or erected within the Jurisdiction of any other State; nor any State be formed by the Junction of two or more States, or Parts of States, without the Consent of the Legislatures of the States concerned as well as of the Congress.

The Congress shall have Power to dispose of and make all needful Rules and Regulations respecting the Territory or other Property belonging to the United States; and nothing in this Constitution shall be so construed as to Prejudice any Claims of the United States, or of any particular State.

Section 4. The United States shall guarantee to every State in this Union a Republican Form of Government, and shall protect each of them against Invasion; and on Application of the Legislature, or of the Executive (when the Legislature cannot be convened) against domestic Violence.

Article V

The Congress, whenever two thirds of both Houses shall deem it necessary, shall propose Amendments to this Constitution, or, on the Application of the Legislatures of two thirds of the several States, shall call a Convention for proposing Amendments, which, in either Case, shall be valid to all Intents and Purposes, as Part of this Constitution, when ratified by the Legislatures of three fourths of the several States, or by Conventions in three fourths thereof, as the one or the other Mode of Ratification may be proposed by the Congress; Provided that no Amendment which may be made prior to the Year One thousand eight hundred and eight shall in any Manner affect the first and fourth Clauses in the Ninth Section of the first Article; and that no State, without its Consent, shall be deprived of its equal Suffrage in the Senate.

Article VI

All Debts contracted and Engagements entered into, before the Adoption of this Constitution, shall be as valid against the United States under this Constitution, as under the Confederation.

This Constitution, and the Laws of the United States which shall be made in Pursuance thereof; and all Treaties made, or which shall be made, under the Authority of the United States, shall be the supreme Law of the Land; and the Judges in every State shall be bound thereby, any Thing in the Constitution or Laws of any State to the Contrary notwithstanding.

The Senators and Representatives before mentioned, and the Members of the several State Legislatures, and all executive and judicial Officers, both of the United States and of the several States, shall be bound by Oath or Affirmation, to support this Constitution; but no religious Test shall ever be required as a Qualification to any Office or public Trust under the United States.

Article VII

The Ratification of the Conventions of nine States, shall be sufficient for the Establishment of this Constitution between the States so ratifying the Same.

Done in Convention by the Unanimous Consent of the States present the Seventeenth Day of September in the Year of our Lord one thousand seven hundred and Eighty seven and of the Independence of the United States of America the Twelfth

In witness whereof, We have hereunto subscribed our Names,

George Washington—President and deputy from Virginia

New Hampshire: John Langdon, Nicholas Gilman

Massachusetts: Nathaniel Gorham, Rufus King

Connecticut: William Samuel Johnson, Roger Sherman

New York: Alexander Hamilton

New Jersey: William Livingston, David Brearly, William Paterson, Jonathan Dayton

Pennsylvania: Benjamin Franklin, Thomas Mifflin, Robert Morris, George Clymer, Thomas FitzSimons, Jared Ingersoll, James Wilson, Gouverneur Morris

Delaware: George Read, Gunning Bedford, Jr., John Dickinson, Richard Bassett, Jacob Broom

Maryland: James McHenry, Daniel of Saint Thomas Jenifer, Daniel Carroll

Virginia: John Blair, James Madison, Jr.

North Carolina: William Blount, Richard Dobbs Spaight, Hugh Williamson

South Carolina: John Rutledge, Charles Cotesworth Pinckney, Charles Pinckney, Pierce Butler

Georgia: William Few, Abraham Baldwin

Amendment I

Congress shall make no law respecting an establishment of religion, or prohibiting the free exercise thereof; or abridging the freedom of speech, or of the press; or the right of the people peaceably to assemble, and to petition the Government for a redress of grievances.

Amendment II

A well regulated Militia, being necessary to the security of a free State, the right of the people to keep and bear Arms, shall not be infringed.

Amendment III

No Soldier shall, in time of peace be quartered in any house, without the consent of the Owner, nor in time of war, but in a manner to be prescribed by law.

Amendment IV

The right of the people to be secure in their persons, houses, papers, and effects, against unreasonable searches and seizures, shall not be violated, and no Warrants shall issue, but upon probable cause, supported by Oath or affirmation, and particularly describing the place to be searched, and the persons or things to be seized.

Amendment V

No person shall be held to answer for a capital, or otherwise infamous crime, unless on a presentment or indictment of a Grand Jury, except in cases arising in the land or naval forces, or in the Militia, when in actual service in time of War or public danger; nor shall any person be subject for the same offence to be twice put in jeopardy of life or limb; nor shall be compelled in any criminal case to be a witness against himself, nor be deprived of life, liberty, or property, without due process of law; nor shall private property be taken for public use, without just compensation.

Amendment VI

In all criminal prosecutions, the accused shall enjoy the right to a speedy and public trial, by an impartial jury of the State and district wherein the crime shall have been committed, which district shall have been previously ascertained by law, and to be informed of the nature and cause of the accusation; to be confronted with the witnesses against him; to have compulsory process for obtaining witnesses in his favor, and to have the Assistance of Counsel for his defence.

Amendment VII

In Suits at common law, where the value in controversy shall exceed twenty dollars, the right of trial by jury shall be preserved, and no fact tried by a jury, shall be otherwise re-examined in any Court of the United States, than according to the rules of the common law.

Amendment VIII

Excessive bail shall not be required, nor excessive fines imposed, nor cruel and unusual punishments inflicted.

Amendment IX

The enumeration in the Constitution, of certain rights, shall not be construed to deny or disparage others retained by the people.

Amendment X

The powers not delegated to the United States by the Constitution, nor prohibited by it to the States, are reserved to the States respectively, or to the people.

Amendment XI

The Judicial power of the United States shall not be construed to extend to any suit in law or equity, commenced or prosecuted against one of the United States by Citizens of another State, or by Citizens or Subjects of any Foreign State.

Amendment XII

The Electors shall meet in their respective states, and vote by ballot for President and Vice-President, one of whom, at least, shall not be an inhabitant of the same state with themselves; they shall name in their ballots the person voted for as President, and in distinct ballots the person voted for as Vice-President, and they shall make distinct lists of all persons voted for as President, and of all persons voted for as Vice-President, and of the number of votes for each, which lists they shall sign and certify, and transmit sealed to the seat of the government of the United States, directed to the President of the Senate;—The President of the Senate shall, in the presence of the Senate and House of Representatives, open all the certificates and the votes shall then be counted;—The person having the greatest number of votes for President, shall be the President, if such number be a majority of the whole number of Electors appointed; and if no person have such majority, then from the persons having the highest numbers not exceeding three on the list of those voted for as President, the House of Representatives shall choose immediately, by ballot, the President. But in choosing the President, the votes shall be taken by states, the representation from each state having one vote; a quorum for this purpose shall consist of a member or members from two-thirds of the states, and a majority of all the states shall be necessary to a choice. And if the House of Representatives shall not choose a President whenever the right of choice shall devolve upon them, before the fourth day of March next following, then the Vice-President shall act as President, as in the case of the death or other constitutional disability of the President. The person having the greatest number of votes as Vice-President, shall be the Vice-President, if such number be a majority of the whole number of Electors appointed, and if no person have a majority, then from the two highest numbers on the list, the Senate shall choose the Vice-President; a quorum for the purpose shall consist of two-thirds of the whole number of Senators, and a majority of the whole number shall be necessary to a choice. But no person constitutionally ineligible to the office of President shall be eligible to that of Vice-President of the United States.

Amendment XIII

Neither slavery nor involuntary servitude, except as a punishment for crime whereof the party shall have been duly convicted, shall exist within the United States, or any place subject to their jurisdiction.

Congress shall have power to enforce this article by appropriate legislation.

Amendment XIV

Section 1. All persons born or naturalized in the United States, and subject to the jurisdiction thereof, are citizens of the United States and of the State wherein they reside. No State shall make or enforce any law which shall abridge the privileges or immunities of citizens of the United States; nor shall any State deprive any person of life, liberty, or property, without due process of law; nor deny to any person within its jurisdiction the equal protection of the laws.

Section 2. Representatives shall be apportioned among the several States according to their respective numbers, counting the whole number of persons in each State, excluding Indians not taxed. But when the right to vote at any election for the choice of electors for President and Vice President of the United States, Representatives in Congress, the Executive and Judicial officers of a State, or the members of the Legislature thereof, is denied to any of the male inhabitants of such State, being twenty-one years of age, and citizens of the United States, or in any way abridged, except for participation in rebellion, or other crime, the basis of representation therein shall be reduced in the proportion which the number of such male citizens shall bear to the whole number of male citizens twenty-one years of age in such State.

Section 3. No person shall be a Senator or Representative in Congress, or elector of President and Vice

President, or hold any office, civil or military, under the United States, or under any State, who, having previously taken an oath, as a member of Congress, or as an officer of the United States, or as a member of any State legislature, or as an executive or judicial officer of any State, to support the Constitution of the United States, shall have engaged in insurrection or rebellion against the same, or given aid or comfort to the enemies thereof. But Congress may by a vote of two-thirds of each House, remove such disability.

Section 4. The validity of the public debt of the United States, authorized by law, including debts incurred for payment of pensions and bounties for services in suppressing insurrection or rebellion, shall not be questioned. But neither the United States nor any State shall assume or pay any debt or obligation incurred in aid of insurrection or rebellion against the United States, or any claim for the loss or emancipation of any slave; but all such debts, obligations and claims shall be held illegal and void.

Section 5. The Congress shall have power to enforce, by appropriate legislation, the provisions of this article.

Amendment XV

The right of citizens of the United States to vote shall not be denied or abridged by the United States or by any State on account of race, color, or previous condition of servitude.

The Congress shall have power to enforce this article by appropriate legislation.

Amendment XVI

The Congress shall have power to lay and collect taxes on incomes, from whatever source derived, without apportionment among the several States, and without regard to any census or enumeration.

Amendment XVII

The Senate of the United States shall be composed of two Senators from each State, elected by the people thereof, for six years; and each Senator shall have one vote. The electors in each State shall have the qualifications requisite for electors of the most numerous branch of the State legislatures.

When vacancies happen in the representation of any State in the Senate, the executive authority of such State shall issue writs of election to fill such vacancies: Provided, That the legislature of any State may empower the executive thereof to make temporary appointments until the people fill the vacancies by election as the legislature may direct.

This amendment shall not be so construed as to affect the election or term of any Senator chosen before it becomes valid as part of the Constitution.

Amendment XVIII

Section 1. After one year from the ratification of this article the manufacture, sale, or transportation of intoxicating liquors within, the importation thereof into, or the exportation thereof from the United States and all territory subject to the jurisdiction thereof for beverage purposes is hereby prohibited.

Section 2. The Congress and the several States shall have concurrent power to enforce this article by appropriate legislation.

Section 3. This article shall be inoperative unless it shall have been ratified as an amendment to the Constitution by the legislatures of the several States, as provided in the Constitution, within seven years from the date of the submission hereof to the States by the Congress.

Amendment XIX

The right of citizens of the United States to vote shall not be denied or abridged by the United States or by any State on account of sex.

Congress shall have power to enforce this article by appropriate legislation.

Amendment XX

Section 1. The terms of the President and Vice President shall end at noon on the 20th day of January, and the terms of Senators and Representatives at noon on the 3d day of January, of the years in which such terms would have ended if this article had not been ratified; and the terms of their successors shall then begin.

Section 2. The Congress shall assemble at least once in every year, and such meeting shall begin at noon on the 3d day of January, unless they shall by law appoint a different day.

Section 3. If, at the time fixed for the beginning of the term of the President, the President elect shall have died, the Vice President elect shall become President. If a President shall not have been chosen before the time fixed for the beginning of his term, or if the President elect shall have failed to qualify, then the Vice President elect shall act as President until a President shall have qualified; and the Congress may by law provide for the case wherein neither a President elect nor a Vice President elect shall have qualified, declaring who shall then act as President, or the manner in which one who is to act shall be selected, and such person shall act accordingly until a President or Vice President shall have qualified.

Section 4. The Congress may by law provide for the case of the death of any of the persons from whom the House of Representatives may choose a President whenever the right of choice shall have devolved upon them, and for the case of the death of any of the persons from whom the Senate may choose a Vice President whenever the right of choice shall have devolved upon them.

Section 5. Sections 1 and 2 shall take effect on the 15th day of October following the ratification of this article.

Section 6. This article shall be inoperative unless it shall have been ratified as an amendment to the Constitution by the legislatures of three-fourths of the several States within seven years from the date of its submission.

Amendment XXI

Section 1. The eighteenth article of amendment to the Constitution of the United States is hereby repealed.

Section 2. The transportation or importation into any State, Territory, or possession of the United States for delivery or use therein of intoxicating liquors, in violation of the laws thereof, is hereby prohibited.

Section 3. This article shall be inoperative unless it shall have been ratified as an amendment to the Constitution by conventions in the several States, as provided in the Constitution, within seven years from the date of the submission hereof to the States by the Congress.

Amendment XXII

Section 1. No person shall be elected to the office of the President more than twice, and no person who has held the office of President, or acted as President, for more than two years of a term to which some other person was elected President shall be elected to the office of the President more than once. But this article shall not apply to any person holding the office of President when this article was proposed by the Congress, and shall not prevent any person who may be holding the office of President, or acting as President, during the term within which this article becomes operative from holding the office of President or acting as President during the remainder of such term.

Section 2. This article shall be inoperative unless it shall have been ratified as an amendment to the Constitution by the legislatures of three-fourths of the several states within seven years from the date of its submission to the states by the Congress.

Amendment XXIII

Section 1. The District constituting the seat of government of the United States shall appoint in such manner as the Congress may direct: A number of electors of President and Vice President equal to the whole number of Senators and Representatives in Congress to which the District would be entitled if it were a state, but in no event more than the least populous state; they shall be in addition to those appointed by the states, but they shall be considered, for the purposes of the election of President and Vice President, to be electors appointed by a state; and they shall meet in the District and perform such duties as provided by the twelfth article of amendment.

Section 2. The Congress shall have power to enforce this article by appropriate legislation.

Amendment XXIV

Section 1. The right of citizens of the United States to vote in any primary or other election for President or Vice President, for electors for President or Vice President, or for Senator or Representative in Congress, shall not be denied or abridged by the United States or any state by reason of failure to pay any poll tax or other tax.

Section 2. The Congress shall have power to enforce this article by appropriate legislation.

Amendment XXV

Section 1. In case of the removal of the President from office or of his death or resignation, the Vice President shall become President.

Section 2. Whenever there is a vacancy in the office of the Vice President, the President shall nominate a Vice President who shall take office upon confirmation by a majority vote of both Houses of Congress.

Section 3. Whenever the President transmits to the President pro tempore of the Senate and the Speaker of the House of Representatives his written declaration that he is unable to discharge the powers and duties of his office, and until he transmits to them a written declaration to the contrary, such powers and duties shall be discharged by the Vice President as Acting President.

Section 4. Whenever the Vice President and a majority of either the principal officers of the executive departments or of such other body as Congress may by law provide, transmit to the President pro tempore of the Senate and the Speaker of the House of Representatives their written declaration that the President is unable to discharge the powers and duties of his office, the Vice President shall immediately assume the powers and duties of the office as Acting President.

Thereafter, when the President transmits to the President pro tempore of the Senate and the Speaker of the House of Representatives his written declaration that no inability exists, he shall resume the powers and duties of his office unless the Vice President and a majority of either the principal officers of the executive department or of such other body as Congress may by law provide, transmit within four days

to the President pro tempore of the Senate and the Speaker of the House of Representatives their written declaration that the President is unable to discharge the powers and duties of his office. Thereupon Congress shall decide the issue, assembling within forty-eight hours for that purpose if not in session. If the Congress, within twenty-one days after receipt of the latter written declaration, or, if Congress is not in session, within twenty-one days after Congress is required to assemble, determines by two-thirds vote of both Houses that the President is unable to discharge the powers and duties of his office, the Vice President shall continue to discharge the same as Acting President; otherwise, the President shall resume the powers and duties of his office.

Amendment XXVI

Section 1. The right of citizens of the United States, who are 18 years of age or older, to vote, shall not be denied or abridged by the United States or any state on account of age.

Section 2. The Congress shall have the power to enforce this article by appropriate legislation.

Amendment XXVII

No law varying the compensation for the services of the Senators and Representatives shall take effect until an election of Representatives shall have intervened.

APPENDIX

C Legal Reasoning

Adjudication is the formal process by which legal disputes are judicially resolved in courts of law. Adjudication involves numerous processes, some of which are procedural in nature and some of which are mental insofar as they involve decision making. Collectively, the mental components of adjudication are commonly referred to as **legal reasoning**.

Legal reasoning is a complicated process. In its most broad sense, it represents the ways in which judges (and sometimes jurors) make decisions in legal cases. Those decisions tend to involve three distinct types of rational thought processes: analogical, inductive, and deductive reasoning. But, to be sure, legal reasoning is not limited to the use of these logical forms of reasoning. Legal reasoning is more complicated than using logic to resolve factual disputes under the law. It also must take into account other elements of persuasion, such as current events and contemporary morals and values (Carter & Burke, 2007).

Types of Logical Reasoning

Reasoning by Analogy

Reasoning by analogy, or **analogical reasoning**, is a type of inductive reasoning that involves comparing and contrasting things to find key similarities. An analogy is usually expressed in the form of one thing being like another (X is like Y; A is similar to B). You are probably most familiar with analogies used on standardized exams that test vocabulary. Here is a simple example:

Dolphin is to ocean as…
A. Ant is to jungle   B. Salami is to lunch
C. Camel is to desert   D. Pencil is to lead

The correct answer would be "C"—camel is to desert. This is because a dolphin lives in the ocean like a camel

lives in the desert. Ants may be found in jungles but also live in many other places. Salami does not "live" anywhere; it may be eaten for lunch, but it may be eaten for other meals as well. And pencils may contain lead, but pencils do not "live" in lead. In this example, where the dolphin lives is what makes it most similar to the camel living in the desert. Selecting where the animal lives is the logical connection from which we draw the analogy. It is important to note, though, that there are other similarities upon which we could base a logical connection. For example, a dolphin and camel are both animals, whereas an ant is an insect, salami is a type of food, and a pencil is an inanimate object.

Let's try a slightly more complex analogy. Is an apple more like an orange or a banana? While all three are fruit, there are a number of characteristics upon which these fruits may be compared and contrasted.

Using the information in Table C.1, we find that apples and oranges are alike on only two of our selected dimensions: neither has edible seeds and both are round. Similarly, we find that apples and bananas are alike in only one way under our selected criteria for comparison: neither fruit is a member of the citrus family. Since apples and oranges are alike in two ways while apples and bananas are alike in only one, it would be a valid conclusion to say that apples are more like oranges than bananas. But what is critical to the analogy here is that we have selected six characteristics for comparison, one of which—color when ripe—is of no help whatsoever in comparing apples to the other two fruits. This illustrates one of the major shortcomings of analogical reasoning. It is dependent upon the criteria used for comparison.

Let's now apply this analogy in a legal framework. Suppose that a state prohibited the importation of "oranges and similar fruits" but allowed "bananas and similar fruits" to be imported into the state. Can apples be imported into this state? If you use shape as the basis

| TABLE C.1 | An Example of Reasoning by Analogy |

Characteristics for Comparison	Apple	Orange	Banana
Edible seeds	No	No	Yes
Shape	Round	Round	Oblong
Edible skin	Yes	No	No
Peelable without a knife	No	Yes	Yes
Citrus family	No	Yes	No
Color when ripe	Variable (red, orange, yellow, green)	Orange	Yellow

Source: Adapted from Edward C. Martin (n.d.). *Thinking like a lawyer.* http://www.samford.edu/schools/netlaw/dh2/logic

for comparison, apples may not be imported. But if you use the criterion of whether the fruit belongs to the citrus family, then apples may be imported into the state. Both outcomes would be equally valid from the standpoint of logic. But only one outcome is likely to be correct under the law. Given the ambiguity in the statutory law of this state, it would likely fall on the courts to figure out whether apples could be legally imported into the state. To make that determination, the courts would consider the arguments by analogy offered by the lawyers in the case and try to make as logical a ruling as possible.

In summary, analogical reasoning allows us to make comparisons. The validity of those comparisons depends upon the criteria or characteristics selected as the basis for the comparisons. In the end, though, analogical reasoning does not allow us to declare any general conclusions that may be used to support other arguments. That is where inductive and deductive reasoning come into play.

Inductive Reasoning

Inductive reasoning is the process of forming a generalization from a list of similar examples. The generalization is called a "conjecture."

The process of inductive reasoning begins by assembling a series of examples from a necessarily limited number of observations (because it is not possible to observe every example on the planet). This process uses analogical reasoning in order to group similar examples together. For example, suppose you observed the following types of fruit: apples, oranges, grapes, plums, tangerines, grapefruits, cranberries, cherries, coconuts, and lemons. From this limited set of

examples, what generalization might you make about fruit? If you said, "all fruit are round," that would be an excellent conjecture based on the limited number of examples you had available to you. However, as you know, not all fruits are, in fact, round. Bananas, for example, are oblong. So, your conjecture, although logical in light of your list of examples, would not be valid. This example illustrates the importance of having a sufficient number of examples that are drawn from a representative sample—something that is key to the scientific method. Determining whether the sample is representative is dependent, in part, on there being a sufficient number of examples that are comparable. Whether the examples are sufficiently alike as to warrant a logical comparison is dependent upon the criteria used to compare them. As discussed above, that comparison process involves analogical reasoning.

What color are swans? For thousands of years, all examples of swans in Europe led people to conclude that all swans were white. But they learned that all swans were not white when black swans were discovered in Australia in the late 1600s (Taleb, 2007). These Australian counter-examples demonstrated that the conjecture "all swans are white" was not true. But it took going to a distant continent after centuries of firsthand observations to invalidate a conjecture that was assumed to be valid for centuries.

Let's examine an inductive argument as applied to legal reasoning. Suppose that you examined the facts and outcomes of a series of 20 murder cases from a single state in a given year (State A). In each case, the defendant intentionally killed the victim without the victim having done anything to provoke the killing.

And, in each case of the 20 cases, the defendant was convicted. From this limited set of 20 examples, a good conjecture would be: "All people who intentionally kill another human being without any provocation will be convicted of murder."

Suppose you then studied 80 more murder cases—20 from each of four other states (States B, C, D, and E) that occurred in the same year from which you drew your sample of 20 cases in State A. In all 80 of these cases, the defendant intentionally killed the victim without the victim having done anything to provoke the killing. Again, in each case of these 80 cases, the defendant was convicted. When added to the 20 murder cases from State A, you would be justified in having more confidence in your conjecture at this point because you not only examined more examples, but you diversified the representativeness of your sample by studying cases from four additional states. At this point, your conjecture could be called a **legal precept**—a generalized legal conclusion drawn from a reasonably representative list of examples. But your legal precept could not yet be considered a **rule of law** because it has not yet been established over time in a sufficient number of cases. For that to occur, you would need to examine many more murder cases from more states from a variety of years. See Exhibit C.1 for

---

EXHIBIT C.1   Flowchart of Inductive Reasoning in the Law

Inductive Reasoning

Observations
The observations must be made from representative examples. The representativeness of the examples is judged by using *analogical reasoning*. The strength of the analogy is based on the number of instances, the variety of instances, the number of similarities, the number of differences, the relevance of the observations, and the modesty of the conclusion.

↓

Pattern
Continuing to use analogical reasoning, similarities among and differences between the examples are noted until a pattern is discerned.

↓

Tentative Hypothesis/Conjecture
A logical generalization called a *conjecture* is made that links the similarities together. In legal reasoning, this conjecture is called a *legal precept*.

↓

Theory
Over time, as more and more representative observations are added, the tentative hypothesis/conjecture is refined into a theory. In legal reasoning, this process of refinement allows a legal precept to evolve into a *rule of law*. The rule of law can then serve as the major premise of a deductive argument.

an illustration of the process of inductive reasoning as it applies within a legal framework.

Suppose, for example, that you studied a random sample of 200 cases drawn from 20 different states over a 50-year period of time. In all 200 cases, the defendant intentionally killed the victim without the victim having done anything to provoke the killing. Again, in each case of these 200 cases, the defendant was convicted (either by a jury or through a guilty plea). At this point, you may feel comfortable saying that your legal precept is a rule of law because the conjecture you made from your study of more than 200 cases was formed from a large number of examples drawn from a cross section of states over a long period of time. In spite of these facts, though, you would be mistaken if you were to conclude that "All people who kill another human being without any provocation will be convicted of murder."

Assume that you continued to gather data by looking at more cases in more states from different years. In one of the cases in State J, the defendant intentionally killed the victim without the victim having done anything to provoke the killing. However, the defendant in that case was not convicted because he was determined to be legally insane. Your conjecture/legal precept is now invalidated by this single counterexample. Therefore, the alleged "rule of law" must also be invalid as currently phrased. As you do more research, you find more cases in which mentally ill people were not convicted of murder for the intentional killing of another human being, some of which involved acquittals on the basis of insanity, others of which involved convictions of less serious forms of homicide after a determination of diminished capacity. You would have to refine your legal precept to take into account these examples. You might do so by forming the following inductive conjecture/legal precept: "All people who intentionally kill another human being without any provocation or legally recognized excuse will be convicted of murder."

Deductive Reasoning

In contrast to inductive reasoning, which goes from specific examples to a generalization, **deductive reasoning** goes from a generalization to a specific conclusion. The most simple and logically sound deductive argument takes the form of a "deductive syllogism." The syllogism allows us to compare the logical

relationship between two arguments if arranged in a particular form. This form is as follows:

Major Premise	A generalized statement formed through induction.
Minor Premise	A statement capturing the essence of a particular example that relates to the generalization in the major premise.
Conclusion	A statement that is logically consistent with both the major and minor premises.

Here is a classic example of a deductive syllogism:

Major Premise	All men are mortal.
Minor Premise	Socrates is a man.
Conclusion	Socrates is mortal.

The form of the deductive syllogism is key to the validity of its conclusion. There are a number of rules that must be met in order for a deductive syllogism to be validly formed[1] that are beyond the scope of this appendix. For our purposes, it is sufficient to say that a properly formed deductive syllogism guarantees the accuracy of the conclusion, assuming the truth of its premises. Recall, for example, the belief regarding the color of swans.

Major Premise	All swans are white.
Minor Premise	Daphne is a swan.
Conclusion	Daphne is white.

If, however, Daphne was one of the black swans discovered in Australia, then the logical form of the deductive syllogism is useless in providing a valid conclusion because one of the premises is false.

Let's apply the deductive syllogism to a legal example. Recall from the section above on inductive reasoning the generalization that we formed after examining murder cases in many states across a

---

[1]E.g., there must be three and only three terms; at least one of the terms must be distributed using a universal term (like "all" or "none"); the conclusion cannot contain any term that is not distributed by a universal statement in one of the premises; if a negative universal term (like "none") is used to distribute one premise, then the other premise cannot also be phrased using a negative distributor; if either premise is negative, the conclusion must also be negative; and a syllogism with two universal premises cannot have a particular conclusion. For more information, see Martin (n.d.).

number of years. We eventually refined our inductive conjecture into a rule of law. That rule of law would serve as the major premise in a deductive syllogism.

Major Premise	All people who intentionally kill another human being without any provocation or legally recognized excuse will be convicted of murder.
Minor Premise	John intentionally killed another human being without any provocation or legally recognized excuse.
Conclusion	John will be convicted of murder.

There are two limitations to using deductive reasoning in the law that should be obvious at this point. First, as mentioned above, the conclusion will be invalid if either one of the premises is invalid. Thus, if it is not true that all people who intentionally kill other human beings without any provocation or legally recognized excuse will be convicted of murder, then we cannot know whether or not John will be convicted. Similarly, if John did not kill without provocation or legally recognized excuse, again we cannot form a valid conclusion about the outcome of his trial using the form of the deductive syllogism.

Second, the law rarely presents situations that can be reduced to the form of a pure deductive syllogism. There are clearly rules of law, but most of those rules have exceptions, and some of those exceptions have even more specialized exceptions. Thus, it becomes quite difficult to form universal legal statements that can serve as the major premise of a deductive argument. Take, for example, the major premise concerning murder liability that we have been using in this appendix. "A person who intentionally kills another human being without any provocation or legally recognized excuse will be convicted of murder." This statement is fairly close to being an accurate statement of the law. But the problem is that we cannot say that all such people "will be convicted." Some people will be acquitted due to lack of evidence; others may be acquitted due to the sympathies of the jury; others may never even be caught and put on trial. Simply put, legal syllogisms are rarely, if ever, based upon absolute truths. Legal reasoning, therefore, is more complicated than the rules of logic.

Logic as Part of Legal Reasoning

Analogical, inductive, and deductive reasoning all play important roles in the process of legal reasoning.

But, as stated above, legal reasoning involves more than these forms of logic. The process of legal reasoning rests upon an important principle in law known as *stare decisis*—Latin for "to stand by decided matters." This principle stands for the proposition that prior cases should serve as **precedent** for deciding future cases that are factually and legal similar. This is especially important in the hierarchy of court structure. A decision of a higher court serves as binding precedent on a lower court within a particular jurisdiction. Thus, for example, a decision of the Supreme Court of Texas is binding on the lower appellate and trial courts of that state. That decision, however, is not binding on the courts of any other state. In our federal system, the decisions of the U.S. Supreme Court are binding on all lower courts, both state and federal, when it comes to interpretations of federal law (especially constitutional law). But state courts are free to interpret their state laws differently so long as they do not infringe upon the minimal baselines of federal constitutional protections as interpreted by the U.S. Supreme Court.

Given the roles of precedent and the principle of *stare decisis*, legal reasoning in the U.S. common law tradition brings a certain amount of stability to the law. It helps us organize cases, using analogical reasoning, into legal precepts because we assume that the result in prior similar cases should guide the result in future similar cases. Moreover, the stability of law that *stare decisis* facilitates allows us to refine legal precepts over time into rules of law. These rules of law may then be deductively applied in new cases to produce reasonably predictable outcomes. The results in these cases then are added to the body of precedent to serve as even more examples to which analogies may be made in subsequent cases. This circular process is graphically represented in Figure C.1.

While stability in law is one of the benefits of reasoning from precedent within the principle of *stare decisis*, that stability can also have a downside. Because lower courts are bound to follow the precedents of higher courts, "bad precedent" must be overruled by the court that established it. It usually takes many years before courts recognize that one of its decisions was poor (or wrong) and, therefore, should not be retained as valid precedent. Part of what transpires over those years may be shifts in social conscience. After all, social norms evolve with time. For example, it took the Supreme Court nearly 60 years to overrule its decision in *Plessy v. Ferguson* (1896), which upheld the racial segregation on the "separate but equal"

FIGURE C.1 The Circular Process of Legal Reasoning

principle. By the time the Court declared the "separate but equal" unconstitutional in *Brown v. Board of Education of Topeka* (1954), much had changed about the ways race was perceived in the United States.

Similarly, in 2003, the Supreme Court invalidated the nation's sodomy laws (i.e., laws criminalizing consensual oral or anal sex) on due process grounds when it decided *Lawrence v. Texas*. But only 17 years earlier, the Court had upheld the constitutionality of sodomy laws over a due process challenge in *Bowers v. Hardwick* (1986). Certainly, social mores and values had changed over those 17 years, especially with regard to views on homosexuality. That shift in social thought certainly had an impact on the Court's reasoning in *Lawrence* (see Fradella, 2003).

Sometimes the passage of time is not enough; perhaps there needs to be a change in the judicial composition of court such that new judicial officials bring a different philosophy of decision making to

subsequent cases. Consider, for example, that several of the justices who had voted to uphold sodomy laws in *Bowers* had left the Supreme Court by the time *Lawrence* was decided and were replaced by justices who saw things differently, perhaps due in part to different judicial philosophies (see below).

These examples illustrate that although the principle of stare decisis brings stability to the law, it does not necessarily mean that the law is stagnant. Other factors such as current events and evolving social norms and values also play an important role in legal reasoning (Carter & Burke, 2007). This brings a certain amount of uncertainty to the law. You can never be quite sure how a court will rule in a case—especially when the case involves a complex question of constitutional law. This uncertainty is especially prominent when cases go to high courts, like the U.S. Supreme Court, since it is not bound by its own precedents. In light of such uncertainty, the politics of judicial decision making is frequently an issue when governors and the president select judges or justices.

Jurisprudence and Legal Reasoning

There are many different theories of jurisprudence that collectively form the philosophy of law (see Table C.2).

A judge's belief in one of these schools of jurisprudential thought over another may have a significant effect on the outcome of case. But as Table C.2 should make clear, other factors clearly enter into the decision-making process. Carter and Burke (2007) posit that the decision in a given case is a product of a judge's views on (1) the law governing a particular type of dispute (L); (2) the relevant facts of a case (F); (3) current events (E); and (4) widely shared contemporary morals and values (V).

$$L + F + E + V \longmapsto D$$

While these four factors clearly form the basis for most legal reasoning as illustrated in Table C.2, it is important to keep in mind that the particular judicial philosophy (P) of any judge can significantly influence his or her interpretation of any other variable.

TABLE C.2	Major Schools of Jurisprudential Thought		
School	**Summary of Major Beliefs**	**Descriptors**	**Equation Analogy**
Natural Law	Human/Positive law (L) ought to reflect the law of nature or "nature law" which some would consider to be "God's Law." Decisions (D) should be a function (f) of moral principles (M) that are universally applied to promote human life, knowledge, community, friendship, and faith. Ambiguities in law must be resolved to harmonize positive law with natural law.	Static Infallible Humanistic	$f\,[EP(L + F)] \longmapsto D$
Legal Formalism	Judges apply the relevant positive law (L) to the pertinent facts of a case (F) and arrive at the correct legal decision (D). Normative or policy considerations are irrelevant. Thus, judges should be guided by the plain meaning of the words in a law, not by their interpretation of what the law should be. Ambiguities in the law should be resolved in accordance with the original meaning of the words and, if known, the intent of those who wrote the words.	Static Fallible Logical	$L + F \longmapsto D$
Legal Realism	Law (L) is indeterminate. Law cannot be applied to the facts of a case (F) to reach a result without judges drawing on other extralegal considerations (ELC), especially the judge's personal experiences. ELC may go unstated in a legal opinion but most often manifest themselves as part of the process of analogical reasoning process when judges decide which cases present the best "fit" to be followed as precedent.	Flexible Fallible Somewhat Idiosyncratic	$L + F + ELC \longmapsto D$
Legal Process	Procedural consistency must guide legal reasoning. Decisions are a function (f) of applying positive law (L) to the facts of a case in accordance with certain neutral principles (NP) that restrain the discretion of any individual judge such as deference to legislative and/or executive intent, or widely shared ethical principles of societal goals as expressed in the plain language of positive law. Ambiguities in law should be interpreted in light of which neutral principle (NP) is consistently applied in such cases.	Somewhat Flexible Fallible Consistent	$f\,[NP(L + F)] \longmapsto D$

(Continued)

TABLE C.2	Major Schools of Jurisprudential Thought (*Continued*)			
School	**Summary of Major Beliefs**	**Descriptors**	**Equation Analogy**	
Law and Economics	Legal decisions (D) should be a function (*f*) of laissez faire economic principles (EP) being applied to the facts of the case (F) and the governing law. Ambiguities in law should be resolved to promote economic efficiency and maximize wealth.	Somewhat Flexible Fallible Consistent	$f\,[EP(L + F)] \longmapsto D$	
Rights-Based Jurisprudence	Legal decisions (D) should be a function (*f*) of interpreting the facts of a case (F) and the applicable law (L) in ways that produce just outcomes and fair public policies. Ambiguities in law should be resolved to maximize individual rights and liberties (R) while simultaneously promoting social justice (J) and equality (E).	Highly Flexible Fallible Pragmatic and Humanistic	$f\,[(R + J + E)\,(L + F)]$ $\longmapsto D$	
Critical Legal Studies and Postmodern Jurisprudence	Law (L) represents a political and hegemonic device (i.e., it perpetuates the status quo) that is used to promote social stratification in a manner that, overall, benefits certain groups of people over others. Indeed, judges interpret both the facts of a case (F) and the law as a function (*f*) of their indoctrination into ideologies that promotion deeply ingrained structural inequalities (SI) in society on the basis of socio-economic status, race (critical race theory), sex (feminist jurisprudence), and sexual identify (queer legal theory).	Somewhat Static Flawed Hegemonic and Illegitimate	$f\,[SI(L + F)] \longmapsto D$	

One judge might find a particular fact to be the legally operative fact in the case, while another judge may view that same fact as being less important. And, as presented in Table C.2, judges also clearly differ with respect to how to interpret the law, especially ambiguities in the law. And, finally, most of us recognize that current events and contemporary morals and values are all subject to different interpretations. Accordingly, judicial philosophy that judges bring with them to the bench clearly will have some effect on how they legally reason through a particular case. Collectively, these principles of legal reasoning may be represented by the equation:

$$f\,[P(L) + P(F) + P(E) + P(V)] \longmapsto D$$

Finally, how the judge perceives his or her own role also plays an important role in the legal reasoning process. While perceptions of the judicial role are related, to a certain degree, to a certain jurisprudential schools of thought, they are distinct, as we shall now explore.

Judicial Philosophies and Legal Reasoning

One of the most salient philosophical distinctions in legal reasoning stems from how a judge perceives his

or her own role. Some judges believe that they should avoid making law through the common law process and instead restrict themselves to narrow questions of law presented in the cases they adjudicate. This philosophy, most frequently associated with socially conservative judges, is referred to as **judicial restraint** (Carter & Burke, 2007). Those who subscribe to judicial restraint generally believe that judges ought to focus on the original intent of a constitution or a statute. In doing so, they tend to strictly construe a legal provision by focusing on the actual meaning of the words used in a constitution or statute. Judges who subscribe to this point of view tend to be uncomfortable with the courts being used as agents of social change. Instead, they prefer for changes in the law to occur as a result of legislative actions.

In contrast, other judges see their roles as facilitating social change. They feel that they should make new laws in accordance with the changing needs of society. This philosophy, most commonly associated with liberal or moderate judges, is often referred to as **judicial activism**. Judges who subscribe to this perspective tend to view the language of constitutions and statutes as lenses through which interpretations can be made. To them, the law is as an evolving framework for courts to solve social problems that the other branches of government have neglected or refused to address.

It should be noted that the differences between the philosophies of judicial restraint and judicial activism might produce some false dichotomies, especially with respect to liberals and conservatives. Indeed, in their book *Battle Supreme*, Neubauer and Meinhold (2005) say that perceptions of judicial activism depend on whose ox is being gored.

> Historically, conservatives have tended to interpret legal doctrines quite flexibly, or actively, when it suited their purposes—for example, to extend more power to the executive branch, the police, and employers. Liberals have tended to read the Constitution quite strictly, or with restraint, when an amendment in is line with their beliefs—for example, the First Amendment stipulation that Congress make no law restricting freedom of speech. (Friedrichs, 2006, p. 58)

Consider, for example the Supreme Court's decision in *District of Columbia v. Heller* (2008). In that case, four conservative justices (Scalia, Roberts, Thomas, and Alito) were joined by one moderate justice (Kennedy) when they ruled that the Second Amendment to the U.S. Constitution grants an individual person the right to possess and use a firearm for lawful purposes, such as self-defense within the home. The Second Amendment provides: "A well regulated Militia, being necessary to the security of a free State, the right of the people to keep and bear Arms, shall not be infringed." They gave the Second Amendment an expansive (liberal?) reading when they decided that the introductory phrase regarding a militia was nothing more than a "prefatory clause" that in no way limited the "operative clause" of the Amendment—the one concerning the right to bear arms. In contrast, four liberal to moderate justices (Stevens, Breyer, Ginsburg, and Souter) dissented in the case by giving the Second Amendment a narrow, strict constructionist (conservative?) reading. They asserted the language used in the text of prefatory clause to the Amendment, as well as the original intent of the Framers, evidenced that the Amendment provided for the right of military and police use of firearms, not any right of private citizens to have and use such weapons. Since the outcome of the case was not in accordance with usual liberal/conservative principles of judicial decision making, that tells us something about the role of judicial philosophy in the constitutional adjudication process. In short, legal reasoning is more complex than a reductionist label. Rather, it is a function of judicial philosophies, jurisprudential theories, current events, morals, and values as they collectively apply to the facts of a particular case and the interpretation of laws which, all too frequently, leave room for disagreement as to their meaning.

BOX C.1	An Exercise in Legal Reasoning

Assume that you and your friend Tom are in a bar together. Tom makes eye contact with an attractive young woman who, unbeknownst to him, is Scott's girlfriend. Scott, a very jealous person, sees this and immediately comes over to Tom and hits him over the head with a beer bottle without saying a word. As a result, Tom sustains a concussion and needs ten stitches to repair his injuries. And, for the first time in his life, Tom also starts to suffer severe headaches as a result of the injuries inflicted by Scott. Both you and Tom want Scott brought to justice. In light of your knowledge of criminal justice, Tom asks you what you think will happen to Scott. To answer Tom, you decide to go to a law library in search of some answers.

First, you would need to determine which body of precedent to consult in order to find guiding legal precepts and binding rules of law. In doing so, you would disregard contract disputes, child custody cases, cases involving the probate of wills, and so on. Instead, you would be looking for criminal law cases.

Thus, the type of legal dispute would be the organizing characteristic upon which we separate cases using analogical reasoning.

Once you identified criminal law as the subfield you needed to research, you would then need to engage in more analogical reasoning to find cases most similar to Tom's. Accordingly, you would not likely concern yourself with reading cases concerning homicides, thefts, or sexual assaults. Rather, you would look for cases involving the crime of battery—cases in which the victim sustained physical injuries without being killed.

Once you found a group of cases concerning battery, you would want to locate the ones with facts that are most similar to Tom's case. Again, this process would use analogical reasoning. Ideally, you would hope to find a case in which someone had been hit over the head with a beer bottle while in a bar. If you found such a case, you would be excited because the facts

(Continued)

(Continued)

of that case would be nearly identical to yours. Unfortunately, you are unable to find such a case. However, you do find several cases that you think will help you answer Tom's questions.

Case 1: During an argument, the defendant hit the victim over the head with a tire iron, causing the victim to sustain permanent brain damage. The incident took place in an auto repair shop. That defendant was convicted of aggravated battery and sentenced to 8 years in prison.

Case 2: During an argument, the defendant used a chainsaw to sever the arm of the victim. The incident took place in the street in a residential neighborhood. The defendant was convicted of mayhem and sentenced to 12 years in prison.

Case 3: After walking into his own bedroom to find a friend of his in bed with his wife, the defendant shot both his wife and his friend. Both victims lived but required surgery to save their lives. The defendant was acquitted of attempted voluntary manslaughter but was convicted of two counts of aggravated battery with a deadly weapon. He was sentenced to 5 years in prison.

Case 4: During an argument that occurred in a bar, the defendant punched the victim in the face, breaking his nose. The defendant was convicted of battery and sentenced to 6 months in jail.

Case 5: The defendant slapped the victim across the face during an argument that occurred in a university dining hall. The defendant was suspended from school and was also criminally convicted of battery for which the defendant was placed on 6 months of probation.

- Which case is most like the one involving Tom and Scott? Why?
- Which case is most unlike the one involving Tom and Scott? Why?
- After reviewing these and other cases, you feel confident that Scott committed either a battery or an aggravated battery.
- Which crime do you think Scott committed? Explain your answer. What types of reasoning did you use to arrive at this answer?

You then look up the statute in your state governing the crimes of battery and aggravated battery. You find that simple battery is punishable by a term of probation to a maximum of 12 months in jail. The crime of aggravated battery, however, is punishable by a term of 5 to 10 years in prison.

- Based upon the case law and statutory research you did as summarized above, what do you think is the most likely outcome of the criminal case against Scott? Will he be convicted of a crime? If so, which one? What do you think the most likely sentence will be?
- As you no doubt surmised, you had to consider other factors in addition to the technical definition of the crimes of battery and aggravated battery in order to make a prediction about the likely outcome of Scott's case and the sentence he is likely to receive. What were those factors?

Glossary

A

absolute immunity Complete immunity from civil lawsuits. In the case of prosecutors, absolute immunity shields them from all civil liability for actions taken in connection with the traditional role of courtroom advocacy on behalf of the government.

acquittal The decision of the judge or jury that the defendant is not guilty.

actus reus **(guilty act)** Requirement that, for an act to be considered criminal, the individual must have committed a voluntary act, omission, or state of knowing possession prohibited by the criminal law. See *elements of a crime.*

adjudicated Judicial determination (judgment) that a youth is a delinquent or status offender.

adjudicatory hearing Court hearing to determine whether a youth is responsible for an offense and therefore should be adjudicated a delinquent.

administrative regulations Rules and regulations, adopted by administrative agencies, that have the force of law.

adversary system A proceeding in which the opposing sides have the opportunity to present their evidence and arguments.

aerial search A search conducted from an aircraft, usually a helicopter or a small, low-flying plane.

affidavit A written statement of facts, which the signer swears under oath are true.

affirm In an appellate court, to reach a decision that agrees with the result reached in the case by the lower court.

affirmative defense A defense in which the defendant bears the burden of production and/or persuasion to prove that extenuating or mitigating circumstances, such as insanity, self-defense, or entrapment, should result in a not-guilty verdict.

aggravating circumstances Factors that increase the seriousness of a crime and therefore tend to increase the severity of the sentence imposed.

Alford **plea** A plea that allows a defendant to plead guilty while nonetheless maintaining his or her innocence.

alibi defense A defense alleging that the defendant was elsewhere at the time that the crime with which he or she is charged was committed.

Allen **charge** A type of jury instruction in which a judge strongly encourages deadlocked jurors to continue deliberations until a verdict is reached.

allocute/allocution hearing (1) The statement made by a defendant at the time he or she admits to the commission of a crime as a condition of the court accepting a guilty plea. (2) The statement made by a defendant at his/her sentencing hearing.

alternate jurors Jurors chosen in excess of the minimum number needed, in case one or more jurors is unable to serve for the entire trial.

alternative dispute resolution (ADR) Less adversarial means of settling disputes that may or may not involve a court.

American Bar Association (ABA) The largest voluntary organization of lawyers in the United States.

amicus curiae Latin for "friend of the court," the term used to refer to an advocacy brief filed in court by a non-party urging a particular outcome and/or rationale.

Anglo-American law The American legal system. See *common law.*

appellant (petitioner) The party, usually the losing one, that seeks to overturn the decision of a lower court by appealing to a higher court.

appellate brief A formal document submitted to an appellate court setting forth the legal arguments in support of a party's case on appeal. When a brief is filed in support of a motion at the trial court level, it is sometimes referred to as a "memorandum of points and authorities."

appellate court A court that hears appeals from trial courts on points of law.

appellate court record Papers, documents, and exhibits, as well as the transcript of the trial, that are submitted to the appellate court for review.

appellate jurisdiction The authority of a court to hear, determine, and render judgment in an action on appeal from an inferior court.

appellee (respondent) A party, usually the winning party, against whom a case is appealed.

arbitration A form of *alternative dispute resolution (ADR)* for resolving legal disputes outside the courts in which arbitrators generally act similarly to judges, making decisions that can be binding or nonbinding.

arraignment The stage of the criminal process in which the defendant is formally told the charges and allowed to enter a plea.

arrest The act of depriving a person of his or her liberty, most frequently accomplished by physically taking the arrestee into police custody for a suspected violation of criminal law.

arrest warrant A document issued by a judicial officer authorizing the arrest of a specific person.

Article I Section of the U.S. Constitution concerning the legislative branch of the national government.

Article III Section of the U.S. Constitution concerning the judicial branch of the national government.

assembly-line justice The operation of any segment of the criminal justice system in which excessive workloads result in decisions being made with such speed and impersonality that defendants are treated as objects to be processed rather than as individuals.

assigned counsel system Arrangement that provides attorneys for persons who are accused of crimes and are unable to hire their own lawyers. The judge assigns a member of the bar to provide counsel to a particular defendant.

attempt An act done with the specific intent to commit a crime; an overt act toward the commission of a crime, the failure to complete the crime, and the apparent possibility of committing it.

attendant (accompanying) circumstances Conditions surrounding a criminal act—for example, the amount of money stolen in a theft.

attenuation doctrine An exception to the fruit of the poisonous tree doctrine that allows the admission of tainted evidence if that evidence was obtained in a manner that is sufficiently removed or "attenuated" from unconstitutional search or seizure, thereby rendering the evidence admissible at trial.

automatic waiver Premised on the notion of "once an adult, always an adult," automatic waiver laws require adult criminal courts to handle all subsequent offenses allegedly committed by a juvenile after an initial transfer to adult court.

B

bail The security (money or bail bond) given as a guarantee that a released prisoner will appear at trial.

bail agent (bail bondsperson) A person whose business it is to effect release on bail for persons held in custody by pledging to pay a sum of money if a defendant fails to appear in court as required.

bail bond A bond for the amount of bail set by a court that is posted by a bail agent to secure the pretrial release of a defendant in exchange for a fee the defendant pays.

bankruptcy judge Judicial officer who presides over the legal procedure under federal law by which a person is relieved of all debts after placing all property under the court's authority. An organization may be reorganized or terminated by the court in order to pay off creditors.

bench trial Trial before a judge without a jury.

bench warrant (*capias*) An order issued by the court itself, or from the bench, for the arrest of a person; it is not based, as is an arrest warrant, on a probable cause showing that a person has committed a crime, but only on the person's failure to appear in court as directed.

best-evidence rule Rule requiring that someone coming into court must bring the best available original evidence to prove the questions involved in the case.

beyond a reasonable doubt Proof that leaves jurors firmly convinced of the defendant's guilt in a criminal case.

bifurcated trial A trial split into two phases, such as the guilty and penalty phases of a capital prosecution.

Bill of Rights The first ten amendments to the U.S. Constitution, guaranteeing certain rights and liberties to the people.

bind over If at the preliminary hearing the judge believes that sufficient probable cause exists to hold a criminal defendant, the accused is said to be bound over for trial.

***Bivens* actions** The class of civil lawsuits that may be filed against federal officials for an alleged deprivation of one's constitutional rights.

blended sentencing A sentencing scheme that allows criminal court judges to impose juvenile dispositions on youthful offenders transferred to criminal court under certain circumstances, rather than imposing standard criminal sentences.

boot camp A physically rigorous, disciplined, and demanding regimen emphasizing conditioning, education, and job training, typically designed for young offenders.

***Boykin* form** Document intended to show that the defendant entered a guilty plea voluntarily and intelligently, understanding the charges and consequences of conviction (*Boykin v. Alabama* 1969).

brief See *appellate brief*.

burden of persuasion The level or quantum of evidence necessary to convince a judge or jury of the existence of some fact in dispute. In a criminal case, the prosecution bears the burden of persuasion to prove each and every element of a crime beyond a reasonable doubt.

burden of production The responsibility of a party in a legal action to introduce sufficient evidence in support of an assertion such that a factual decision needs to be made at a trial or hearing to determine the truth of the assertion, as opposed to having a court summarily reject the assertion on the grounds of insufficient proof.

burden of proof The requirement to introduce evidence to prove an alleged fact or set of facts. See *burden of persuasion* and *burden of production*.

Burger Court The Supreme Court under the leadership of Chief Justice Warren Burger (1969–1986).

C

capital offense Any crime punishable by death.

capital punishment Use of the death penalty as the punishment for the commission of a particular crime.

career criminals Those people who commit a sequence of delinquent and criminal acts across the lifespan from childhood through adolescence and into adulthood.

cash bond Requirement that money be posted to secure pretrial release.

celerity of punishment The swiftness with which punishment is imposed on a criminal offender. Celerity is a central component of deterrence theory, such that the more swift the punishment, the more the threatened punishment should deter the violation of law.

centralized administration The state supreme court, working through court administrators, provides leadership for the state court system.

centralized judicial budgeting The state judicial administrator (who reports to the state supreme court) has the authority to prepare a single budget for the entire state judiciary and send it directly to the legislature.

centralized rule making The power of the state supreme court to adopt uniform rules to be followed by all courts in the state.

certainty of punishment A core concept of deterrence theory that posits that the more certain it is that an offender will be caught, convicted, and punished, the less likely would-be offenders are to violate the law.

chain of custody The chronological documentation of the seizure, control, transfer, analysis, and disposition of evidence.

challenge for cause Method for excusing a potential juror because of specific reasons such as bias or prejudgment; can be granted only by the judge.

chambers The private office of a judge.

change of venue The removal of a case from one jurisdiction to another. It is usually granted if the court believes that, due to prejudice, a defendant cannot receive a fair trial in the area where the crime occurred.

charge bargaining In return for the defendant's plea of guilty, the prosecutor allows the defendant to plead guilty to a less-serious charge than the one originally filed.

charging conference Meeting attended by judge, prosecutor, and defense attorney during which the judge's instructions to the jury are discussed.

charging document An information, indictment, or complaint that states the formal criminal charge against a named defendant.

child-victims See *children in need of supervision.*

children in need of supervision A type of juvenile court case involving a child who has been abused and/or neglected by parents or legal guardians.

circuit justice The justice of the U.S. Supreme Court assigned to issue temporary rulings for a judicial circuit until such time as the full court can decide whether to grant a stay or enter another type of judicial order.

circumstantial evidence An indirect method of proving the material facts of a case; testimony that is not based on the witness's personal observation of the material events.

civil law Law governing private parties; other than criminal law.

civil protection order Court order requiring a person to stay away from another person.

clear and convincing evidence A more exacting level of proof than preponderance of the evidence, but less demanding than proof beyond a reasonable doubt. This level of proof leaves the trier-of-fact reasonably satisfied as to the existence of a fact, yet there may be some doubts.

clerk of court An elected or appointed court officer responsible for maintaining the written records of the court and for supervising or performing the clerical tasks necessary to conduct judicial business.

closing argument Statement made by an attorney at the end of the presentation of evidence in which the attorney summarizes the case for the jury.

collateral attack An attempt to overturn the outcome of a court case by challenging it in a different proceeding or court.

common law Law developed in England by judges who made legal decisions in the absence of written law. Such decisions served as precedents and became "common" to all of England. Common law is judge-made, it uses precedent, and it is found in multiple sources.

community courts Neighborhood-focused, problem-solving courts that deal with local crime and safety concerns.

community service Compensation for injury to society, by the performance of service in the community.

competency The mental capacity of an individual to participate in legal proceedings.

complaint In civil law, the first paper filed in a lawsuit. In criminal law, a charge signed by the victim that a person named has committed a specified offense.

concurrent jurisdiction When two courts (e.g., both state and federal courts or both state criminal courts and juvenile courts) share some judicial powers to adjudicate certain types of cases.

concurring opinion A written opinion in which a judge agrees with the outcome of a case on appeal but wishes to emphasize different points or rationales than those used by the judges who sign on to the majority decision.

conditions of confinement lawsuit Lawsuit brought by a prisoner contesting prison conditions.

conference Juvenile court proceeding roughly equivalent to a preliminary hearing, in which the suspect is informed of his or her rights and a disposition decision may be reached.

confrontation A process by which a witness "confronts" a suspect in a lineup, a photo array, or even in person (i.e., a show-up) for the purpose of attempting to identify a suspect.

consent search A person, place, or movables may be lawfully searched by an officer of the law if the owner gives free and voluntary consent.

consent surveillance A situation in which one or more parties to a communication consents to the interception of the communication. Neither Title III nor the Fourth Amendment prevents the use of such communications in court against a nonconsenting party to the communication.

constitution The fundamental rules that determine how those who govern are selected, the procedures by which they operate, and the limits to their powers.

constitutional courts Federal courts created by Congress by virtue of its power under Article III of the Constitution to create courts inferior to the Supreme Court.

contemporaneous objection rule The requirement that an objection be made at a hearing or trial at the time of the alleged error in order for the mistake to qualify as the basis for an appeal.

contempt (of court) The failure or refusal to obey a court order; may be punished by a fine or imprisonment.

contract A legally enforceable agreement between two or more parties.

contract system Method of providing counsel for indigents under which the government contracts with a law firm to represent all indigents for the year in return for a set fee.

corpus delicti The body or substance of a crime, composed of two elements—the act and the criminal agency producing it.

count bargaining The defendant pleads guilty to some, but not all, of the counts contained in the charging document, which reduces the potential sentence.

courtroom work group The regular participants in the day-to-day activities of a particular courtroom; judge, prosecutor, and defense attorney interacting on the basis of shared norms.

crime control model A perspective on the criminal justice process based on the proposition that the most important function of criminal justice is the repression of crime, focusing on efficiency as a principal measure.

criminal defense Legally recognized justification for illegal actions, or acceptance that individuals were not legally responsible for their actions.

criminal justice system Agencies and institutions directly involved in the implementation of public policy concerning crime, mainly the law enforcement agencies, courts, and corrections.

criminal law Laws passed by government that define and prohibit antisocial behavior.

cross-examination At trial, the questions of one attorney put to a witness called by the opposing attorney.

cruel and unusual punishment Governmental punishment that is prohibited by the Eighth Amendment.

CSI effect The phenomenon in which technology has heightened juror expectations and demands for scientific evidence. Anecdotal evidence suggests that this effect causes jurors to wrongfully acquit guilty defendants when no scientific evidence is presented, a claim not supported by empirical research.

custodial interrogation Any questioning (or its functional equivalent) by law enforcement officers after a suspect has been arrested or otherwise deprived of his or her freedom in any significant way, thereby requiring that the suspect be informed of his or her Fifth Amendment rights as set forth in *Miranda*.

D

day fine A type of graduated fine structure that is based, in part, on the offender's ability to pay as a function of daily personal income.

death-eligible Crimes that are punishable by death.

death penalty Capital punishment, or executions by the state for purposes of social defense.

death-qualified juries Juries that sit in judgment of a defendant in a capital trial and are comprised of members (selected through the *voir dire* process) who are not morally opposed to voting to impose the death penalty.

defendant The person or party against whom a lawsuit or prosecution is brought.

defenses of excuse Criminal defenses that excuse criminal conduct because of some impairment, such as youthful age or insanity, that significantly mitigates criminal responsibility.

defenses of justification Criminal defenses that justify the use of force under limited circumstances, such as defending oneself or another person.

delay Postponement or adjournment of proceedings in a case; lag in case-processing time.

delinquency An act committed by a juvenile that would require an adult to be prosecuted in a criminal court. Because the act is committed by a juvenile, it falls within the jurisdiction of the juvenile court. Delinquent acts include crimes against persons or property, drug offenses, and crimes against public order.

demonstrative evidence Evidence created for demonstration purposes at trial, such as photos, maps, and computer simulations.

derivative evidence Secondary evidence derived from primary evidence obtained as a result of an illegal search or seizure.

detention Holding a youth in custody before case disposition.

determinate sentence A term of imprisonment, imposed by a judge, that has a specific number of years.

deterrence theory The view that certain, severe, and swift punishment will discourage others from similar illegal acts.

direct evidence Evidence derived from one or more of the five senses.

direct examination The questioning of witnesses, using primarily open-ended questions, to adduce evidence as part of a party's case-in-chief.

direct restitution The defendant pays money directly to the victim of the crime.

discovery Pretrial procedure in which parties to a lawsuit ask for and receive information such as testimony, records, or other evidence from each other.

discretion The lawful ability of an agent of government to exercise choice in making a decision.

discretionary appellate jurisdiction Jurisdiction that a court may accept or reject particular cases. The Supreme Court has discretionary jurisdiction over most cases that come to it.

discrimination Illegitimate influences in the sentencing process based on the characteristics of the defendants.

dismissal Cases terminated (including those warned, counseled, and released) with no further disposition anticipated.

disparity Unequal sentences resulting from the sentencing process itself.

disposition A court decision about what will happen to a youth who has not been found innocent.

dissenting opinion An opinion written by a judge of an appellate court in which the judge states the reasons for disagreeing with the majority decision.

diversity of citizenship When parties on the opposite sides of a federal lawsuit come from different states, the jurisdiction of the U.S. district courts can be invoked if the case involves a controversy concerning $75,000 or more in value.

domestic relations Relating to the home; the law of divorce, custody, support, adoption, and so on.

double jeopardy Fifth Amendment prohibition against a second prosecution after a first trial for the same offense.

drug courts Specialty courts with jurisdiction over cases involving illegal substances. Drug courts typically stress treatment rather than punishment.

dual court system A court system consisting of a separate judicial structure for each state in addition to a national structure. Each case is tried in a court of the same jurisdiction as that of the law or laws involved.

due process model A philosophy of criminal justice based on the assumption that an individual is innocent until proven guilty and has a right to protection from arbitrary power of the state.

due process of law A right guaranteed in the Fifth and Fourteenth Amendments of the U.S. Constitution and generally understood to mean the due course of legal proceedings according to the rules and forms established for the protection of private rights.

E

electronic monitoring The use of technologies to surveil and control offenders, including wrist and ankle bracelets, field monitoring devices, alcohol testing devices, and voice verification systems.

elements of a crime Five principles of a crime that are critical to the statutory definition of crimes: guilty act, guilty intent, relationship between guilty act and guilty intent, attendant circumstances, and results.

en banc French term referring to the session of an appellate court in which all the judges of the court participate, as opposed to a session presided over by three judges.

enemy combatants People the United States regards as unlawful combatants, a category of persons who do not qualify for prisoner-of-war status under the Geneva Conventions.

error A mistake made by a judge in the procedures used at trial, or in making legal rulings during the trial, that allows one side in a lawsuit to ask a higher court to review the case.

error correction Appellate courts seek to correct legal errors made in lower courts.

evidence Any kind of proof offered to establish the existence or nonexistence of a fact in dispute—for example, testimony, writings, other material objects, or demonstrations.

evidence-based corrections The use of rehabilitative programs, practices, and techniques in correctional settings that have been empirically evaluated and determined to be effective interventions.

exclusionary rule A rule created by judicial decisions holding that evidence obtained through violations of the constitutional rights of the criminal defendant must be excluded from the trial.

exculpatory evidence Evidence that casts doubt on the guilt of a criminally accused person.

expiation Atoning for sin through deserved suffering.

extradition Legal process whereby officials of one state or country surrender an alleged criminal offender to officials of the state or country in which the crime is alleged to have been committed.

extralegal factors Factors, such as race, ethnicity, sex, and socioeconomic status, that are associated with differential treatment by the criminal justice system even though they are not supposed to affect case processing, outcomes, and sentences.

F

federal question Case that contains a major issue involving the U.S. Constitution or U.S. laws or treaties.

felony The more serious of the two basic types of criminal behavior, usually bearing a possible penalty of one year or more in prison.

fine A sum of money to be paid to the state by a convicted person as punishment for an offense. See also *day fine*.

focal concerns theory A theoretical perspective that seeks to explain sentencing disparities on the basis of three primary *focal concerns*: blameworthiness, protection of the community, and the practical constraints and consequences of the sentencing decision.

Foreign Intelligence Surveillance Act (FISA) A federal statute that regulates the electronic surveillance of foreign powers and their agents within the United States where a "significant purpose" of the surveillance is to gather foreign intelligence information that cannot reasonably be obtained through normal investigative techniques. FISA also permits surveillance of "lone wolves"—any individual or group that is not linked to a foreign government but who is suspected of terrorism or sabotage.

fruit of the poisonous tree The poisonous tree is evidence directly obtained as a result of a constitutional violation; the fruit is the derivative evidence obtained because of knowledge gained from the first illegal search, arrest, confrontation, or interrogation.

Furman v. Georgia Supreme Court ruling that statutes leaving arbitrary and discriminatory discretion to juries in imposing death sentences are in violation of the Eighth Amendment.

G

gag order A judge's order that lawyers, witnesses, or members of law enforcement not discuss the trial with outsiders.

general deterrence The theory that posits that rational, self-interested people will be deterred from committing crimes by the threat of certain, severe, and swift punishment.

geographical jurisdiction Geographical area over which courts can hear and decide disputes.

good faith exception An exception to the exclusionary rule that allows illegally seized evidence to be admitted at trial if law enforcement officers acted in good faith, relying on a defective search warrant or a law subsequently determined to be unconstitutional.

good time A reduction of the time served in prison as a reward for not violating prison rules.

GPS monitoring A particular type of electronic monitoring that uses ground positioning satellites to monitor the location of an offender or to surveil a vehicle, suspect, or item.

grand jury A group of citizens who decide whether persons accused of crimes should be indicted (true bill) or not (no true bill).

Gregg v. Georgia Supreme Court ruling that: (1) the death penalty is not, in itself, cruel and unusual punishment, and (2) a two-part proceeding—one for the determination of innocence or guilt and the other for determination of the sentence—is constitutional and meets the objections noted in *Furman v. Georgia*.

gubernatorial appointment Method of judicial selection in which the governor appoints a person to a judicial vacancy without an election.

guilty act See *actus reus*.

H

habeas corpus Latin phrase meaning "you have the body"; a writ inquiring of an official who has custody of a person whether that person is being lawfully imprisoned or detained.

habeas corpus **petition** The petition a person in custody files with a court, seeking the court to order his or her release by granting a writ of *habeas corpus* on the grounds that the continued detention of the person violates the constitution.

harmless error An error made at trial that is insufficient grounds for reversing a judgment on appeal.

hearsay An out-of-court assertion or statement, made by someone other than the testifying witness, which is offered to prove the truth of testimony. Hearsay evidence is excluded from trials unless it falls within one of the recognized exceptions and does not otherwise violate the Sixth Amendment's Confrontation Clause.

hedonistic calculus A principle of utilitarian philosophy that posits that humans seek pleasure and avoid pain. This principle plays an important role in deterrence theory insofar as rational thinkers will seek to avoid the pain that criminal punishment will inflict upon them by avoiding lawbreaking behaviors if and only if the pain of punishment outweighs the pleasure that would be gained through the commission of crime.

hierarchical jurisdiction Refers to differences in the functions of courts and involves original as opposed to appellate jurisdiction.

hierarchy rule A UCR rule that records only the most serious crime to occur during an event in which two or more crimes were committed, rather than recording each crime.

home detention An intermediate sanction that confines offenders to their homes under specific terms and conditions. It may be used independently or in combination with *electronic monitoring*.

hung jury A jury that is unable to reach a verdict.

I

illegal search and seizure See *unreasonable search and seizure*.

immunity A grant of exemption from prosecution in return for evidence or testimony.

impeach To question the truthfulness of a witness's testimony.

impeachment Official accusation against a public official brought by a legislative body seeking his or her removal.

impeachment evidence Any evidence that would cast doubt on the credibility of a witness.

imprisonment Placing a person in a prison, jail, or similar correctional facility as punishment for committing a crime.

incapacitation Sentencing philosophy that stresses crime prevention through isolating wrongdoers from society.

independent source doctrine An exception to the fruit of the poisonous tree doctrine that allows the admission of tainted evidence if that evidence was also obtained through a source wholly independent of the primary constitutional violation.

indeterminate sentence A sentence that has both a minimum and a maximum term of imprisonment, the actual length to be determined by a parole board.

index crimes The specific crimes used by the FBI when reporting the incidence of crime in the United States in the *Uniform Crime Reports;* also called "Type I offenses."

indictment A formal accusation of a criminal offense made against a person by a grand jury.

indigents Defendants who are too poor to pay a lawyer and therefore are entitled to a lawyer for free.

inevitable discovery doctrine A variation of the independent source doctrine allowing the admission of tainted evidence if it would inevitably have been discovered in the normal course of events. Under this exception, the prosecution must establish by a preponderance of the evidence that, even though the evidence was actually discovered as the result of a constitutional violation, the evidence would ultimately or inevitably have been discovered by lawful means, for example, as the result of the predictable and routine behavior of a law enforcement agency, some other agency, or a private person.

infancy A criminal defense based on the young age of an offender, preventing the formation of *mens rea*.

inference A logical conclusion that the trier-of-fact may make in light of the evidence.

inferior court (lower court) Term for a trial court of limited jurisdiction; also may refer to any court lower in the judicial hierarchy.

informants People who are not in law enforcement but provide information to law enforcement personnel.

information A formal accusation charging someone with the commission of a crime, signed by a prosecuting attorney, which has the effect of bringing the person to trial.

inheritance Property received from a dead person, either by effect of intestacy or through a will.

initial appearance Shortly after arrest, the suspect is brought before a judicial official, who informs the person of the reason for the arrest and makes an initial determination about whether there was probable cause for the arrest. In some jurisdictions, a preliminary determination regarding bail may also be made.

initial hearing In juvenile court, an often informal hearing during which an intake decision is made.

injunction A court order directing someone to do something or to refrain from doing something.

insanity defense A criminal defense that excuses criminal conduct if a severe mental disease or defect substantially impaired the defendant's ability to appreciate the wrongfulness of his or her conduct.

intake decision The decision made by a juvenile court that results in the case being handled either informally at the intake level or more formally by petition and scheduled for an adjudicatory or transfer hearing.

intensive-supervision probation (ISP) Probation granted under conditions of strict reporting to a probation officer with a limited caseload.

interlocutory Provisional; temporary; while a lawsuit is still going on.

intermediate courts of appeals (ICAs) Judicial bodies falling between the highest, or supreme, tribunal and the trial court; created to relieve the jurisdiction's highest court of hearing a large number of cases.

intermediate sanctions Variety of sanctions that lie somewhere between prison and probation.

irrelevant Testimony that has no bearing on the issue of a trial.

J

judge-made law The common law as developed in form and content by judges or judicial decisions.

judgment The official decision of a court concerning a legal matter.

judicial conduct commission An official body whose function is to investigate allegations of misconduct by judges.

judicial election Method of judicial selection in which the voters choose judicial candidates in a partisan or nonpartisan election.

judicial independence Normative value that stresses a judge should be free from outside pressure in making a decision.

judicial performance evaluations (JPEs) The mechanisms used to assess how judges perform their jobs, often using a combination of ratings from lawyers assessing competency, fairness, and temperament, as well as objective metrics, like caseload processing.

judicial waiver Laws that permit—and sometimes even require—juvenile court judges to transfer jurisdiction over a juvenile delinquency case to adult court for criminal prosecution.

jurisdiction The power of a court to hear and adjudicate a case.

jury consultants Professionals who assist lawyers in selecting juries through the use of behavioral scientific principles and techniques.

jury deliberations The action of a jury in determining the guilt or innocence, or the sentence, of a defendant.

jury instructions Directions given by a judge to the members of the jury informing them of the law applicable to the case.

jury nullification The idea that juries have the right to refuse to apply the law in criminal cases despite facts that leave no reasonable doubt that the law was violated.

just deserts Punishment for criminal wrongdoing should be proportionate to the severity of the offense.

justice of the peace (JP) A low-level judge, sometimes without legal training, typically found in rural areas of some states, empowered to try petty civil and criminal cases and to conduct the preliminary stages of felony cases.

juvenile Youth at or below the upper age of juvenile court jurisdiction.

juvenile court Any court that has jurisdiction over matters involving juveniles.

juvenile delinquency An act committed by a juvenile for which an adult could be prosecuted in a criminal court.

L

law Body of rules enacted by public officials in a legitimate manner and backed by the force of the state.

legal ethics Codes of conduct governing how lawyers practice law and how judges administer justice.

legislative courts Judicial bodies created by Congress under Article I (legislative article) and not Article III (judicial article).

legislative waiver See *statutory waiver.*

lex talionis Latin for "the law of retaliation," this is the philosophical principle that punishments should be equal to the harm caused by the commission of a crime as embodied in the phrase, "an eye for an eye; a tooth for a tooth; an arm for an arm; a life for a life."

local prosecutors General term for lawyers who represent local governments (cities and counties, for example) in the lower courts; often called "city attorneys" or "solicitors."

lower age of jurisdiction Minimum age at which a youth may be transferred to adult court.

M

mandamus petitions A type of lawsuit in which a plaintiff seeks a court order commanding someone to perform an act or duty imposed by law as an obligation.

mandatory appellate jurisdiction Jurisdiction that a court must accept. Cases falling under a court's mandatory jurisdiction must be decided officially on their merits, though a court may avoid giving them full consideration.

mandatory minimum sentencing Minimum required penalty specified for a certain crime.

master jury list A list of potential jurors in a court's district, from which a representative cross section of the community in which a crime allegedly was committed can be selected for a trial. It is usually compiled from multiple sources, such as voter registration lists, driver's license lists, utility customer lists, and telephone directories. Also called "jury wheel" or "master wheel."

mediation A form of *alternative dispute resolution (ADR)* in which a mediator acts, not as a judge, but rather as someone who facilitate discussion and resolution of the dispute.

mens rea **(guilty intent)** Latin for "evil mind," it refers to the mental state of intent required for a crime.

misdemeanor Lesser of the two basic types of crime, usually punishable by no more than one year in jail.

Missouri Bar Plan The name given to a method of judicial selection combining merit selection and popular control in retention elections.

mistake of fact A criminal defense asserting that the defendant was mistaken about a fact that, if honest and reasonable, negates the *mens rea* for the crime charged.

mistrial Invalid trial.

mitigating factors Factors that mitigate the seriousness of a crime and therefore tend to reduce the severity of the sentence imposed.

Model Rules of Professional Conduct The American Bar Association's set of model rules that impose ethical obligations on lawyers to their clients and to the courts. Some variations of these rules have been adopted in all 50 states.

monetary damage Compensatory damages—payment for actual losses suffered by a plaintiff. Punitive damages—money awarded by a court to a person who has been harmed in a malicious or willful way.

motion for judgment of acquittal A motion made by a criminal defendant at the close of the government's case (or at the close of all evidence) that asks a judge to enter a verdict of "not guilty" because no legally sufficient evidentiary basis has been established on which a reasonable jury could return a guilty verdict.

motions to vacate sentences Filings by prisoners who seek to have their sentences set aside or changed on the grounds that the sentence was imposed in violation of the Constitution or laws of the United States.

motor vehicle searches The warrantless search of a motor vehicle when there is probable cause to believe that the vehicle contains contraband or evidence of a crime.

municipal court A trial court of limited jurisdiction created by a local unit of government.

municipal ordinance Law passed by a local unit of government.

N

National Incident-Based Reporting System (NIBRS) An incident-based, rather than summary-based, system for tracking criminal offenses with significantly more detail than the UCR.

necessity A criminal defense in which the defendant asserts that in an emergency situation not caused by the defendant, he or she had no choice but to break the law in order to avoid more serious harm than that caused by the commission of the crime.

new judicial federalism Movement in state supreme courts to reinvigorate states' constitutions as sources of individual rights over and above the rights granted by the U.S. Constitution.

no true bill The decision of a grand jury not to indict a person for a crime.

nolle prosequi The ending of a criminal case because the prosecutor decides or agrees to stop prosecuting. When this happens, the case is "nollied," "nolled," or "nol. prossed."

nolo contendere/**no contest** Latin phrase meaning "I will not contest it." A plea of "no contest" in a criminal case means that the defendant does not directly admit guilt but submits to sentencing or other punishment.

nonpetitioned case A case handled informally by duly authorized court personnel.

normal crime Categorization of crime based on the typical manner in which it is committed, the type of defendant who typically commits it, and the typical penalty to be applied.

normal penalties Norms for proper sentencing based on the crime committed and the defendant's prior record.

notice of appeal Written document filed with the clerk of court stating that the defendant in the criminal case plans to appeal.

O

objection The act of taking exception to a statement or procedure during a trial.

officer of the court Lawyers are officers of the court and, as such, must obey court rules, be truthful in court, and generally serve the needs of justice.

Omnibus Crime Control and Safe Streets Act of 1968 A federal statute, Title III of which provides greater privacy protections than the Fourth Amendment by regulating both law enforcing and private searches and seizures of wire, oral, or electronic communications.

open fields The doctrine that allows law enforcement to search open lands without a warrant.

opening statement Address made by attorneys for both parties at the beginning of a trial in which they outline for the jury what they intend to prove in their case.

opinion The reasons given for the decision reached by an appellate court.

oral argument The part of the appellate court decision-making process in which lawyers for both parties plead their case in person before the court.

ordinance A law enacted by a local government body for the regulation of some activity within the community.

original jurisdiction Jurisdiction in the first instance; commonly used to refer to trial jurisdiction as opposed to appellate jurisdiction. Appellate courts, however, have limited original jurisdiction.

other dispositions Miscellaneous dispositions, including fines, restitution, community service, and referrals outside the court for services, with minimal or no further court involvement anticipated.

P

pardon An act of executive clemency that has the effect of releasing an inmate from prison and/or removing certain legal disabilities from persons convicted of crimes.

parens patriae The state as parent; the state as guardian and protector of all citizens (such as juveniles) who are unable to protect themselves.

parole Early release from prison on the condition of good behavior.

parole board An administrative body whose members are chosen by the governor to review the cases of prisoners eligible for release on parole. The board has the authority to release such persons and to return them to prison for violating the conditions of parole.

per curium **opinion** Latin for "by the court," a decision by an appellate court that is not attributed to a specific author.

peremptory challenge Method for excusing a potential juror without cause, so long as the reasons for doing so are not based on racial or gender discrimination.

personal jurisdiction The power of a court over a particular person or legal entity (such as a partnership or corporation).

petit jury A trial jury, as distinguished from a grand jury.

petition A document filed in juvenile court alleging that a juvenile is a delinquent or a status offender and asking that the court assume jurisdiction over the juvenile or that an alleged delinquent be transferred to criminal court for prosecution as an adult.

petitioner The party filing a petition in a court of law. It is most commonly used to refer to the party seeking discretionary appellate review through filing a petition for a writ of *certiorari*.

petty offense A minor criminal offense that does not entitle the defendant to a trial by jury.

placement Cases in which youths are placed in a residential facility or otherwise removed from their homes and placed elsewhere.

plain error An exception to the contemporary objection rule in which a highly prejudicial error substantially affects the rights of the accused such that a failure to correct the error on appeal, even if an objection was not made at the hearing or trial at the time of the alleged error, would result in a miscarriage of justice.

plain view If police happen to come across something while acting within their lawful duty, that item may be used as evidence in a criminal trial, even if the police did not have a search warrant.

plaintiff The person or party who initiates a lawsuit.

plea bargaining The process by which a defendant pleads guilty to a criminal charge with the expectation of receiving some benefit from the state.

plea on the nose The defendant pleads guilty to the charges contained in the indictment or bill of information.

plurality opinion A decision, usually of an appellate court, in which no single opinion received the support of a majority of the court.

policy formulation Function of appellate courts to make new law and adjust existing law to changing circumstances.

postverdict motions Various motions made by the defense after a jury conviction in hopes of gaining a new trial.

precedent A case previously decided that serves as a legal guide for the resolution of subsequent cases.

prejudicial pretrial publicity Prejudicial information, often inadmissible at trial, that is circulated by the news media before a trial and that reduces the defendant's chances of a trial before an impartial jury.

preliminary hearing A pretrial hearing to determine whether there is probable cause to bind a defendant over for felony trial.

preponderance of the evidence In civil law, the standard of proof required to prevail at trial. To win, the plaintiff must show that the greater weight, or preponderance, of the evidence supports his or her version of the facts.

presentence investigation (PSI) Investigation by a probation department into circumstances surrounding a crime in order to help judges make appropriate sentencing decisions.

presumption A conclusion that the law requires the trier-of-fact to accept as true.

presumption of innocence Presumption that whenever a person is charged with a crime, he or she is innocent until proved guilty. The defendant is presumed to be innocent, and the burden is on the state to prove guilt beyond a reasonable doubt.

presumption of sanity The rebuttable presumption that a criminal defendant was legally sane at the time of the commission of the crime(s) for which he or she is charged. To overcome this presumption, most U.S. jurisdictions require the defense to prove that the defendant was insane by clear and convincing evidence.

presumptive sentencing A required structured sentencing system that provides a single recommended prison term within a wider statutory sentence range for each felony offense, with the recommended term based solely on the offense committed.

presumptive sentencing guidelines A required structured sentencing system of multiple recommended sentences and dispositions for each offense class determined by both the severity of the offense and the prior criminal history of the offender.

pretrial diversion An alternative to prosecution that seeks to divert certain offenders from traditional criminal justice processing into a program of supervision and services, especially ones run by a department of probation.

pretrial release services programs Units within court systems whose employees collect and evaluate information that judges use to determine the suitability of defendants for release from custody while criminal charges are pending. Many units also employ officers who supervise defendants who are granted pretrial release.

preventive detention Holding a defendant in custody pending trial in the belief that he or she is likely to commit further criminal acts or flee the jurisdiction.

prisoner petition Civil lawsuit filed by a prisoner alleging violations of his or her rights during trial or while in prison.

privileged communication A recognized right to keep certain communications confidential or private.

pro se Acting as one's own attorney in court; representing oneself.

probable cause Standard used to determine whether a crime has been committed and whether there is sufficient evidence to believe a specific individual committed it.

probation Punishment for a crime that allows the offender to remain in the community without incarceration but subject to certain conditions.

probation officer Employee of probation agency, responsible for supervision of convicted offenders who have been released to the community under certain conditions of good behavior.

procedural defenses Defenses for crimes that are not concerned with factual guilt, but rather are rooted in violations of the rules or processes of the criminal justice system, such as the right to a speedy trial.

procedural law Law that outlines the legal processes to be followed in starting, conducting, and finishing a lawsuit.

property Legal right to use or dispose of particular things or subjects.

property bond Use of property as collateral for pretrial release.

proportionality A philosophical principle positing that criminal punishment should be proportional to the harm caused by the offense committed.

prosecutor A public official who represents the state in a criminal action.

prosecutorial waiver Laws granting prosecutors the discretion to file delinquency petitions in juvenile court or file criminal charges in adult court.

public defender An attorney employed by the government to represent indigent defendants.

public safety realignment A shift of correctional resources, primarily associated with California, in which the state's responsibility for lower-level drug offenders, thieves, and other nonviolent convicts is transferred to the county level, where services might better provide for rehabilitation and job training services that reduce recidivism.

Q

qualified immunity A justice actor's partial immunity from civil liability for acts within the scope of their professional duties and sanctioned by law. For prosecutors, such immunity applies only when they are acting in good faith that they are not violating any law or ethical rule of which a reasonable person in the prosecutor's position would be aware.

R

real evidence Objects, such as fingerprints, seen by the jury.

reasonable, articulable suspicion The reasons a law enforcement officer is able to articulate for being suspicious of criminal activity. It is the level of proof necessary to conduct a brief, limited investigative detention (also known as a "*Terry* stop").

reasonable doubt The state of mind of jurors when they are not firmly convinced of a defendant's guilt because they think there is a real possibility that he or she is not guilty.

rebuttal The introduction of contradictory evidence.

reciprocal disclosure Automatic discovery for certain types of evidence, without the necessity for motions and court orders.

referral A request by a law enforcement agency, governmental agency, parent, or individual that a juvenile court take jurisdiction of a youth. A referral initiates court processing.

rehabilitation The notion that punishment is intended to restore offenders to a constructive role in society; based on the assumption that criminal behavior is a treatable disorder caused by social or psychological ailments.

Rehnquist Court The Supreme Court under the leadership of Chief Justice William Rehnquist (1986–2005).

release on recognizance (ROR) The release of an accused person from jail on his or her own obligation rather than on a monetary bond.

remand In an appellate court, to send a case back to the court from which it came for further action.

remedy Vindication of a claim of right; a legal procedure by which a right is enforced or the violation of a right is prevented or compensated.

removal To dismiss a person from holding office.

respondent The party responding to a petition. It is most commonly used to refer to the party responding to the filing of a petition for a writ of *certiorari*.

restitution To restore or to make good on something—for example, to return or pay for a stolen item.

restoration/restorative justice A philosophy of justice positing that the principal aim of the criminal justice system should be to repair the various physical, psychological, and community harms caused by crime. Promoting peace and reconciling parties is, therefore, considered to be more important than punishing the guilty.

result A consequence; an outcome.

retention election An election in which voters decide if a sitting state court judge should be retained on the bench or relieved of judicial office.

retribution A concept that implies the payment of a debt to society and thus the expiation of one's offense.

reverse In an appellate court, to reach a decision that disagrees with the result reached in the case by the lower court.

reverse waiver A process that allows a juvenile to petition a criminal court to transfer jurisdiction over an offense to a juvenile court.

reversed and remanded Decision of an appellate court that the guilty verdict of the lower court be set aside and the case be retried.

reversible error An error made at trial serious enough to warrant a new trial.

right to counsel Right of the accused to the services of a lawyer paid for by the government, established by the Sixth Amendment and extended by the Warren Court (*Gideon v. Wainwright*) to indigent defendants in felony cases.

right to one appeal U.S. law generally grants the loser in trial court the right to a single appeal, which the upper court must hear.

Roberts Court The Supreme Court under the leadership of Chief Justice John Roberts (2005–).

routine administration A matter that presents the court with no disputes over law or fact.

rule of four The rule that four of the nine justices on the U.S. Supreme Court must vote in favor of granting a petition for a writ of *certiorari* in order for the Court to actually issue the writ, thereby accepting discretionary jurisdiction over an appeal.

rules of evidence Rules that govern whether, when, how, and for what purposes certain forms of proof may be placed before the trier-of-fact for consideration at a hearing or trial.

S

scientific evidence The formal results of forensic investigatory and scientific techniques.

scientific jury selection The use of social scientific techniques and expertise to select venirepersons to serve as petit jurors who are likely to be favorably disposed to one's side of a case.

search incident to lawful arrest The ability of law enforcement to conduct a warrantless search of a person and the area around the arrestee's immediate control when making a lawful arrest.

search warrant A written order, issued by judicial authority, directing a law enforcement officer to search for personal property and, if found, to bring it before the court.

Section 1983 The shorthand way of referring to 42 U.S.C. § 1983, a statute that allows a person to sue someone acting under color of state law for an alleged deprivation of constitutional rights.

selective incapacitation Sentencing philosophy that stresses targeting dangerous offenders for lengthy prison sentences.

selective incorporation An approach to constitutional law that posits that select rights guaranteed by Bill of Rights to the U.S. Constitution are so fundamental to the concept of liberty that they are incorporated into the Fourteenth Amendment's due process clause and therefore are applicable to the states.

self-defense The right to use physical force against another person who is committing a felony, threatening the use of physical force, or using physical force.

self-incrimination Forcing a suspect to provide evidence against himself or herself; prohibited by the Fifth Amendment.

sentence bargaining The defendant pleads guilty knowing the sentence that will be imposed; the sentence in the sentence bargain is less than the maximum.

sentencing guidelines Sentences based on the severity of the crime and the defendant's prior record in an attempt to ensure fair and consistent sentencing. The structure of sentencing guidelines varies on a continuum from voluntary (meaning that they merely recommend a sentence) to presumptive to mandatory.

sequester To isolate members of a jury from the community until they have reached a final verdict.

severity of punishment A key component of deterrence theory concerned with how severe a criminal sentence may be. The theory posits that the more severe the punishment, the less likely people are to violate the law.

shock incarceration A short period of incarceration (the "shock"), followed by a sentence reduction.

simplified court structure A simple, uniform court structure for the entire state.

small claims court A lower-level court whose jurisdiction is limited to a specific dollar amount—for example, damages not exceeding $1,500.

socialization As used in the court setting, the process in which new members of the courtroom work group learn the norms, values, behaviors, and skills expected of them in a professional position.

specific deterrence The notion that the experience of criminal punishment should be unpleasant enough to deter an offender from committing future criminal acts.

speedy-trial laws Federal or state statutes that specify time limits for bringing a case to trial after arrest. Some speedy-trial laws specify precise time standards for periods from arrest to arraignment, trial, and/or sentencing.

standard of review The amount of deference an appellate court gives to the determinations made by a lower court.

standby/shadow counsel The lawyer appointed by a court to shadow a *pro se* defendant. The defendant may consult with the lawyer while representing himself or herself. The lawyer may also take over the case if the court revokes the defendant's right to self-representation either because of emerging questions of mental incompetence or if the defendant is abusive, threatening, obstructionist, or the cause of repeated, unnecessary delays.

stare decisis Latin phrase meaning "let the decision stand." The doctrine that principles of law established in earlier judicial decisions should be accepted as authoritative in similar subsequent cases.

state attorney general The chief legal officer of a state, representing that state in civil and, under certain circumstances, criminal cases.

state high court of last resort General term for the highest court in a state.

statewide financing Courts financed by the state government as opposed to local government.

status offense Behavior that is considered an offense only when committed by a juvenile—for example, running away from home.

statute A written law enacted by a legislature.

statutory exemptions Rules adopted by legislatures exempting certain types of persons or occupations from jury duty.

statutory/legislative waivers Laws that grant exclusive jurisdiction over certain offenses to adult criminal courts regardless of the age of the offender.

stay The temporary suspension of a case or of specific proceedings within a case.

Stored Communications Act A federal statute that governs law enforcement access to stored communications, such as those in e-mail, voice mail, computer files, and cell phones.

structured sentencing Sentencing schemes that seek to curtail judicial discretion in sentencing by classifying offenders on the basis of the severity of the crime committed and on the extent and gravity of their prior criminal record.

subject matter jurisdiction Types of cases that courts have been authorized to hear and decide.

subpoena (power) An order from a court directing a person to appear before the court and to give testimony about a cause of action pending before it.

substantive law Law that deals with the content or substance of the law—for example, the legal grounds for divorce.

summons A legal document ordering an individual to appear in court at a certain time on a certain date.

suppression motion Request that a court of law prohibit specific statements, documents, or objects from being introduced into evidence in a trial.

symbolic restitution The defendant performs community service.

T

tabula rasa Latin for "blank slate," it is a largely discredited view of jury decision making that posits that jurors come to trials without any preconceived notions that would interfere with their abilities to deliberate to a verdict based solely on the evidence presented in court.

testimonial evidence The giving of evidence by a witness under oath.

therapeutic jurisprudence Judicial bodies such as drug courts that stress helping defendants in trouble through nonadversarial proceedings.

three strikes laws Statutes that mandate increased sentences for repeat offenders, often requiring a mandatory sentence of 20 years or more in prison for those convicted of a third qualifying felony.

tort A private or civil wrong, not arising as the result of a breach of contract, in which the defendant's actions cause injury to the plaintiff or to property.

traffic offenses A group of offenses, including infractions and minor misdemeanors, relating to the operation of self-propelled motor vehicles.

transactional immunity Absolute protection against prosecution for any event or transaction about which a witness is compelled to give testimony or furnish evidence.

transfer to criminal court A case is moved to a criminal court because of a waiver or transfer hearing in the juvenile court.

trial court Judicial body with primarily original jurisdiction in civil or criminal cases. Juries are used, and evidence is presented.

trial court of general jurisdiction A trial court responsible for major criminal and civil cases.

trial court of limited jurisdiction A lower-level state court, such as a justice of the peace court, whose jurisdiction is limited to minor civil disputes or misdemeanors.

trial *de novo* A new trial at a higher level of court.

true bill A bill of indictment by a grand jury.

truth in sentencing laws Laws that require offenders to serve a substantial portion of their prison terms (often 85 percent) before release.

tunnel vision The conscious and unconscious process through which justice professionals select and filter evidence to build a case for conviction against a particular suspect while ignoring or suppressing exculpatory evidence.

Type I offenses Serious crimes of homicide, rape, arson, aggravated assault, robbery, burglary, auto theft, and larceny, according to the FBI's *Uniform Crime Reports;* also called "index crimes."

U

unified court system A simplified state trial court structure with rule making centered in the supreme court, system governance authority vested in the chief justice of the supreme court, and state funding of the judicial system under a statewide judicial budget.

Uniform Crime Reports A program conceived in 1929 by the International Association of Chiefs of Police to meet a need for reliable, uniform crime statistics for the nation. Today, the FBI collects and compiles several annual statistical publications produced from the data collected from law enforcement agencies across the United States.

unreasonable search and seizure The Fourth Amendment provides for protection against unreasonable searches and seizures or the illegal gathering of evidence, but it was not very effective until the adoption of the exclusionary rule, barring the use of evidence so obtained (*Mapp v. Ohio*, 1961).

upper age of jurisdiction The oldest age at which a juvenile court has original jurisdiction over an individual for behavior that violates the law.

U.S. attorney general Head of the Department of Justice; nominated by the president and confirmed by the Senate.

U.S. attorneys Officials responsible for the prosecution of crimes that violate the laws of the United States; appointed by the president and assigned to a U.S. district court.

U.S. courts of appeals Intermediate appellate courts in the federal judicial system.

U.S. district courts Trial courts established in the respective judicial districts into which the United States is divided. These courts are established for the purpose of hearing and deciding cases in the limited districts to which their jurisdiction is confined.

U.S. magistrate judges Judicial officers appointed by the U.S. district courts to perform the duties formerly performed by U.S. commissioners and to assist the court by serving as special masters in civil actions, conducting pretrial or discovery proceedings, and conducting preliminary review of applications for post-trial relief made by individuals convicted of criminal offenses.

U.S. solicitor general Third-ranking official in the U.S. Department of Justice; conducts and supervises government litigation before the Supreme Court.

U.S. Supreme Court The nation's highest court, composed of nine justices nominated by the president and confirmed by the Senate.

use immunity A witness may not be prosecuted based on grand jury testimony he or she provides but may be prosecuted based on evidence acquired independently of that testimony.

V

venire A group of citizens from which members of the jury are chosen.

venue The geographic location of a trial, which is determined by constitutional or statutory provisions.

verdict The decision of a trial court.

victim impact statement Written or oral statements communicating information about how a crime impacted the victim and the victim's family.

video surveillance The use of video cameras that record only images, not sound and, therefore, is beyond the reach of Title III of the Omnibus Crime Control and Safe Streets Act of 1968.

violations Minor criminal offenses that are punishable by fine, probation, or a short jail term, typically less than 30 days.

voir dire French legal phrase meaning "to speak the truth." The process by which prospective jurors are questioned to determine whether there is cause to excuse them from the jury.

voluntary sentencing guidelines A recommended structured sentencing system of multiple recommended sentences and dispositions for each offense class determined by both the severity of the offense and the prior criminal history of the offender.

W

warrantless search Search without a search warrant.

Warren Court The Supreme Court under the leadership of Chief Justice Earl Warren (1953–1969).

writ of *certiorari* Order issued by an appellate court for the purpose of obtaining from a lower court the record of its proceedings in a particular case.

writ of *certiorari*, petition for The petition a party files asking an appellate court to exercise its discretionary appellate jurisdiction to review a case.

References

Abel, C. F., and Hans J. Hacker. 2006. "Local Compliance with Supreme Court Decisions: Making Space for Religious Expression in Public Schools." *Journal of Church and State* 48: 355–378.

Abel, Jonathan. 2012. "Testing Three Commonsense Intuitions about Judicial Conduct Commissions." *Stanford Law Review* 64: 1021–1078.

Aberbach, Joel D., and Mark A. Peterson. 2006. *The Executive Branch.* New York: Oxford University Press.

Abrams, David. 2013. "The Imprisoner's Dilemma: A Cost-Benefit Approach to Incarceration." *Iowa Law Review* 98: 905–969.

AbuDagga, Azza, Sidney Wolfe, Michael Carome, Amanda Phatdouang, and E. Fuller Torrey. 2016. "Individuals with Serious Mental Illnesses in County Jails: A Survey of Jail Staff's Perspectives." *Public Citizen and Treatment Advocacy Center.* Available online at http://www.citizen.org/documents/2330.pdf

Acker, James. 1993. "A Different Agenda: The Supreme Court, Empirical Research Evidence, and Capital Punishment Decisions, 1986–1989." *Law and Society Review* 27: 65–86.

Acker, James R. 2007. "Impose an Immediate Moratorium on Executions." *Criminology & Public Policy* 6: 641–650.

Adamakos, Stephanie. 2016. "Race and the Jury: How the Law Is Keeping Minorities Off the Jury." *Washington University Undergraduate Law Review* 1(2): 2–23.

Adams, Benjamin, and Sean Addie. 2011. *Delinquency Cases Waived to Criminal Court, 2008.* Washington, DC: Department of Justice, Office of Justice Programs.

Adams, Kenneth. 1983. "The Effect of Evidentiary Factors on Charge Reduction." *Journal of Criminal Justice* 11: 525–538.

Administrative Office of the U.S. Courts. 2014. *Federal Judicial Caseload Statistics: 2013.* Washington, DC: Author. Available online at http://www.uscourts.gov/statistics-reports/federal-judicial-caseload-statistics-2013

Administrative Office of the U.S. Courts. 2016. *Federal Judicial Statistics, 2015.* Washington, DC. Retrieved from http://www.uscourts.gov/statistics-reports/federal-judicial-caseload-statistics-2015.

"After Death Threats, O'Connor Responds to GOP Attacks on Judges." 2009. Available online at http://www.perrspectives.com/blog/archives/001415.htm

Agnew-Brune, Christine, Kathryn E. Moracco, Cara J. Person, and J. Michael Bowling. 2015. "Domestic Violence Protective Orders: A Qualitative Examination of Judges'

Decision-Making Processes." *Journal of Interpersonal Violence*: 1–22.

Aikman, Alexander B. 2006. *The Art and Practice of Court Administration.* Boca Raton, FL: CRC Press.

Albonetti, Celesta. 1997. "Sentencing under the Federal Sentencing Guideline: Effects of Defendant Characteristics, Guilty Pleas, and Departures on Sentence Outcomes for Drug Offenses, 1991–1992." *Law and Society Review* 31: 789–822.

Albonetti, Celesta A. 1986. "Criminality, Prosecutorial Screening, and Uncertainty: Toward a Theory of Discretionary Decision Making in Felony Case Processings." *Criminology* 24(4): 623–644.

Albonetti, Celesta A. 1987. "Prosecutorial Discretion: The Effects of Uncertainty." *Law & Society Review* 21: 291–313.

Albonetti, Celesta A. 1991. "An Integration of Theories to Explain Judicial Discretion." *Social Problems* 38(2): 247–266.

Albonetti, Celesta A., and John R. Hepburn. 1996. "Prosecutorial Discretion to Defer Criminalization: The Effects of Defendant's Ascribed and Achieved Status Characteristics." *Journal of Quantitative Criminology* 12: 63–81.

Alejo, Kavita. 2016. "The CSI Effect: Fact or Fiction?" *Themis: Research Journal of Justice Studies and Forensic Science* 4(1): 1–20.

Alexander, Ellen, and Janice Harris Lord. 1994. *Impact Statements—A Victim's Right to Speak . . . A Nation's Responsibility to Listen.* Arlington, VA: National Center for Victims.

Alexander, Rees. 2014. "A Model State Racial Justice Act: Fighting Racial Bias without Killing the Death Penalty." *George Mason University Civil Rights Law Journal* 24: 113–157.

Alexander, S. L. 1991. "Cameras in the Courtroom: A Case Study." *Judicature* 74: 307–313.

Alexander-Bloch, Benjamin. 2007. "Justice Can Be Lost in Translation." *Times-Picayune*, December 2.

Alkon, Cynthia. 2016. "Plea Bargain Negotiations: Defining Competence Beyond *Lafler* and *Frye*." *American Criminal Law Review* 53: 377–515.

Allen, G. Frederick, and Harvey Treger. 1994. "Fines and Restitution Orders: Probationers' Perceptions." *Federal Probation* 58: 34–38.

Allison, Junius L. 1976. "Relationship between the Office of Public Defender and the Assigned Counsel System." *Valparaiso Law Review* 10(3): 399–422.

Alpert, Geoffrey P., and Donald A. Hicks. 1977. "Prisoners' Attitudes toward Components of the Legal and Judicial Systems." *Criminology* 14: 461–482.

Alpert, Geoffrey P., and Thomas Petersen. 1985. "The Grand Jury Report: A Magic Lantern or an Agent of Social Control?" *Justice Quarterly* 2: 23–50.

Alschuler, Albert. 1968. "The Prosecutor's Role in Plea Bargaining." *University of Chicago Law Review* 36: 50–112.

Alschuler, Albert. 1975. "The Defense Attorney's Role in Plea Bargaining." *Yale Law Journal* 84: 1179–1314.

Alschuler, Albert. 1979. "Plea Bargaining and Its History." *Law and Society Review* 13: 211–246.

Alvarez, Alex. 2011. "Nancy Grace Blasts Her Critics." July 8. Available online at http://www.mediaite.com/online /nancy-grace-blasts-her-critics-i-suggest-if-they-dont -like-my-coverage-then-dont-watch-it

Alvarez, Lizette, and Cara Buckley. 2013. "Zimmerman Is Acquitted in Trayvon Martin Killing." *New York Times*, July 13, A1. Available online at http://www.nytimes .com/2013/07/14/us/george-zimmerman-verdict -trayvon-martin.html?pagewanted=all&_r=0

Amendola, Andrew. 2010. "New Perspectives in Negotiation: A Therapeutic Jurisprudence Approach." *Harvard Negotiation Law Review* 15. Available online at http://www.hnlr .org/2010/01/new-perspectives-in-negotiation-a -therapeutic-jurisprudence-approach

American Bar Association. 2005. *Section on Criminal Justice, Report to the House of Delegates*. Chicago: Author.

American Bar Association. 2012. *ABA Criminal Justice Standards*. Chicago: American Bar Association. Available online at: https://www.americanbar.org/groups /criminal_justice/standards.html

American Civil Liberties Union. 2008. "A Call to Action for Juvenile Justice." Available online at http://www.aclu.org /images/asset_upload_file183_37705.pdf

American Civil Liberties Union. 2013, Dec. 5. *Federal Court Finds Public Defense System Violates Constitutional Rights of Indigent Defendants*. Retrieved from https://www.aclu.org/news/federal-court-finds-public -defense-system-violates-constitutional-rights -indigent-defendants

American Judicature Society. 2013a. *Federal Judicial Conduct*. Formerly available online at https://www.ajs.org /judicial-ethics/judicial-conduct-commissions /federal-judicial-conduct/

American Judicature Society. 2013b. *Judicial Selection in the States: Appellate and General Jurisdiction Courts: Initial Selection, Retention, and Term Length*. Des Moines, IA: Author. Available online at http://www .judicialselection.us/uploads/documents/Judicial _Selection_Charts_1196376173077.pdf

American Judicature Society. 2014a. *Diversity on the Bench*. http://www.judicialselection.us/judicial_selection/bench _diversity/index.cfm?state=

American Judicature Society. 2014b. "Judicial Performance Evaluation: A Symposium." *Judicature* 98(1): 11–53.

American Judicature Society. n.d. "Merit Selection: The Best Way to Choose the Best Judge." Formerly available online at http://judicialselection. com/uploads/documents /ms_descrip_1185462202120.pdf

Anderson, Amy L., and Cassia C. Spohn. 2010. "Lawlessness in the Federal Sentencing Process: A Test for Uniformity and Consistency in Sentence Outcomes." *Justice Quarterly* 27: 362–393.

Anderson, Elijah. 1999. *Code of the Street: Decency, Violence, and the Moral Life of the Inner City*. New York: Norton.

Anderson, James, and Paul Heaton. 2012. "How Much Difference Does the Lawyer Make? The Effect of Defense Counsel on Murder Cases Outcomes." *Yale Law Journal* 122: 154–217.

Anderson, John. 2010. "Film Reviews: Dog Pound." *Variety*. April 5.

Anderson, Krista M. 2013. "Twelve Years Post *Morrison*: State Civil Remedies and a Proposed Government Subsidy to Incentivize Claims by Rape Survivors." *Harvard Journal of Law & Gender* 36: 223–268.

Anderson, Lawrence O. 2007. "United States Magistrate Judge: The Utility Fielder of the Federal Courts." *Arizona Attorney* 43: 10–14.

Anderson, Seth. (2004). "Examining the Decline in Support for Merit Selection in the States." *Albany Law Review* 67, 793–802.

Anderson, Seth (Moderator). 2009. "Anatomy of a Merit Selection Victory." *Judicature* 93: 6–13.

Anga, Ahunanya. 2013. "Jury Misconduct: Can Courts Enforce a Social Media and Internet Free Process? We 'Tweet,' Not." *Journal of Technology Law & Policy* 18: 265–287.

Antonio, Michael, and Nicole Arone. 2005. "Damned If They Do, Damned If They Don't: Jurors' Reaction to Defendant Testimony or Silence During a Capital Trial." *Judicature* 89: 60–66.

Aos, Steve, Marna Miller, and Elizabeth Drake. 2006. *Evidence-Based Adult Corrections Programs: What Works and What Does Not*. Olympia: Washington State Institute for Public Policy.

Applebome, Peter. 1992. "Indigent Defendants, Overworked Lawyers." *New York Times*, September 18.

Applegate, Brandon, Francis Cullen, Bruce Link, Pamela Richards, and Lonn Lanza-Kaduce. 1996. "Determinants of Public Punitiveness toward Drunk Driving: A Factorial Survey Approach." *Justice Quarterly* 13: 57–79.

Applegate, Brandon, Michael Turner, Joseph Sanborn, Edward Latessa, and Melissa Moon. 2000. "Individualization, Criminalization, or Problem Resolution: A Factorial

Survey of Juvenile Court Judges' Decisions to Incarcerate Youthful Felony Offenders." *Justice Quarterly* 17: 309–332.

Applegate, Brandon K., and Shannon Santana. 2000. "Intervening with Youthful Substance Abusers: A Preliminary Analysis of a Juvenile Drug Court." *The Juvenile Justice System Journal* 21: 281–300.

Appleton, Mike. 2011. "*Connick v. Thompson* and Prosecutorial Immunity." Guest blog published on JonathanTurley .org, April 10. Available online at http://jonathanturley.org /2011/04/10/connick-v-thompson-and-prosecutorial -impunity

Aquinas, Thomas. c. 1273. *Summa Theologica*. Fathers of the English Dominican Province (transl.). Notre Dame, IN: Christian Classics.

Arbor, Brian, and Mark McKenzie. 2011. "Campaign Messages in Lower-Court Elections after Republican Party of Minnesota vs. White." *Justice System Journal* 32: 1–23.

Ares, Charles, Ann Rankin, and Herbert Sturz. 1963. "The Manhattan Bail Project: An Interim Report on the Use of Pretrial Parole." *New York University Law Review* 38: 67–92.

"AR Judge Accused of Sex with Defendants." 2017, January 3. *ArkansasMatters.com*, http://www .arkansasmatters.com/news/local-news/ar-judge-accused -of-sex-with-defendants/635284138

Armstrong, Gaylene, and Nancy Rodriguez. 2005. "Effects of Individual and Contextual Characteristics in Preadjudication Detention of Juvenile Delinquents." *Justice Quarterly* 22: 521–538.

Arnold Foundation. 2014. *Results from the First Six Months of the Public Safety Assessment—Court in Kentucky*, http:// www.arnoldfoundation.org/wp-content/uploads/2014/02 /PSA-Court-Kentucky-6-Month-Report.pdf

Ashman, Allan. 1975. *Courts of Limited Jurisdiction: A National Survey*. Chicago: American Judicature Society.

Ashman, Allan, and Pat Chapin. 1976. "Is the Bell Tolling for Nonlawyer Judges?" *Judicature* 59: 417–421.

Aspin, Larry. 2011. "The 2010 Judicial Retention Elections in Perspective: Continuity and Change from 1964 to 2010." *Judicature* 94: 218–232.

Aspin, Larry, William Hall, Jean Bax, and Celeste Montoya. 2000. "Thirty Years of Judicial Retention Elections: An Update." *Social Science Journal* 37: 1.

Associated Press. 2014, July 23. "Montana Supreme Court Reprimands Judge for Rape Comments." Retrieved from http://missoulian.com/news/state-and-regional/montana -supreme-court-reprimands-judge-for-rape-comments /article_76974ae4-11b2-11e4-9bbc-001a4bcf887a.html

Atherton, Susie. 2015. "Community Courts to Address Youth Offending: A Lost Opportunity?" *British Journal of Community Justice* 13(2): 111–124.

Atkins, Burton M., and Emily W. Boyle. 1976. "Prisoner Satisfaction with Defense Counsel." *Criminal Law Bulletin* 12(4): 427–450

Attorney General's Task Force on Violent Crime. 1981. *Final Report*. Washington, DC: Department of Justice.

Auerhahn, Kathleen. 1999. "Selective Incapacitation and the Problem of Prediction." *Criminology* 37: 703–734.

Augustine. c. 426. *The City of God*. R.W. Dyson (transl.) Cambridge, United Kingdom: Cambridge University Press, 1998.

Austin, James, and Patricia L. Hardyman. 2004. "The Risks and Needs of the Returning Prisoner Population." *Review of Policy Research* 21: 13–29.

Austin, Thomas. 1981. "The Influence of Court Location on Types of Criminal Sentences: The Rural–Urban Factor." *Journal of Criminal Justice* 9: 305–316.

Averdijk, Margit, Jean-Louis Van Gelder, Manuel Eisner, and Denis Ribeaud. 2016. "Violence Begets Violence… But How? A Decision-Making Perspective on the Victim-Offender Overlap." *Criminology* 54(2): 282–306.

Baar, Carl. 1980. "The Scope and Limits of Court Reform." *Justice System Journal* 5: 274–290.

Bainbridge, Stephen. 2011. "Musing on Nancy Grace." *Stephen Bainbridge's Journal of Law, Politics, and Culture*. July 6. Available online at http://www.professorbainbridge.com /professorbainbridgecom/2011/07/musing-on-nancy -grace.html

Baker, Mark. 1999. *D.A.: Prosecutors in Their Own Words*. New York: Simon & Shuster.

Baker, Shannon M., Michael S. Vaughn, and Volkan Topalli. 2008. "A Review of the Powers of Bail Bond Agents and Bounty Hunters: Exploring Legalities and Illegalities of Quasi-Criminal Justice Officials." *Aggression and Violent Behavior* 13: 124–130.

Baldus, David, Charles Pulaski, and George Woodworth. 1983. "Comparative Review of Death Sentences: An Empirical Study of the Georgia Experience." *Journal of Criminal Law and Criminology* 74: 661–753.

Baldus, David C., and George Woodworth. 2003. "Race Discrimination in the Administration of the Death Penalty: An Overview of the Empirical Evidence with Special Emphasis on the Post-1990 Research." *Criminal Law Bulletin* 39: 194–226.

Baldus, David C., George A. Woodworth, Catherine M. Grosso, and Aaron M. Christ. 2002. "Arbitrariness and Discrimination in the Administration of the Death Penalty: A Legal and Empirical Analysis of the Nebraska Experience (1973–1999)." *Nebraska Law Review* 81: 486–754.

Balko, Radley. 2011. "Wrongful Convictions: How Many Innocent Americans Are Behind Bars?" *Reason*. Available online at http://reason.com/archives/2011/06/07/wrongful-convictions.

Bam, Dmitry. 2013–2014. "Voter Ignorance and Judicial Elections." *Kentucky Law Journal* 102: 553–599.

Banks, Cyndi. 2009. *Criminal Justice Ethics: Theory and Practice.* Thousand Oaks, CA: Sage.

Banks, Duren, and Denise Gottfredson. 2004. "Participation in Drug Treatment Court and Time to Rearrest." *Justice Quarterly* 21: 637–658.

Bannon, Alicia. 2016. *Rethinking Judicial Selection in State Courts.* New York: Brennan Center for Justice at New York University School of Law.

Bannon, Alicia, Mitali Nagrecha, and Rebekah Diller. 2010. *Criminal Justice Debt: A Barrier to Reentry.* New York: Brenan Center.

Bard, Jennifer S. 2011. "Practicing Medicine and Studying Law: How Medical Schools Used to Have the Same Problems We Do and What We Can Learn from Their Efforts to Solve Them." *Seattle Journal for Social Justice* 10: 135–209.

Bar-Gill, Oren, and Barry Friedman. 2012. "Taking Warrants Seriously." *Northwestern University Law Review* 106: 1609–1674.

Barnes, Brooks. 2009. *"American Violet* to Premier in Texas Town Where Story Occurred." *The Carpetbagger: The Hollywood Blog of the New York Times* (March 12). Available online at http://carpetbagger.blogs.nytimes.com/2009/03/12/american-violet-to-premier-in-texas-town-where-story-occurred/#more-3725

Barnes, Carole Wolff, and Rodney Kingsnorth. 1996. "Race, Drug, and Criminal Sentencing: Hidden Effects of the Criminal Law." *Journal of Criminal Justice* 24(1): 39–56.

Barnes, J. C. 2014. "Catching the Really Bad Guys: An Assessment of the Efficacy of the U.S. Criminal Justice System." *Journal of Criminal Justice* 42(4): 338–346.

Barnes, Robert. 2007. "Judicial Races Now Rife with Politics." *Washington Post*, October 28.

Bartol, Anne. 1996. "Structures and Roles of Rural Courts." In Thomas McDonald, Robert Wood, and Melissa Pflug (Eds.), *Rural Criminal Justice: Conditions, Constraints, and Challenges* (pp. 79–92). Salem, WI: Sheffield.

Barton, Benjamin H. 2012. "An Empirical Study of Supreme Court Justice Pre-Appointment Experience." *Florida Law Review* 64: 1137–1187.

Bass, Alison. 1995. "Youth Violence Explosion Likely to Worsen." *Times-Picayune*, July 2, p. A14.

Battelle Memorial Institute Law and Justice Center. 1977. *Forcible Rape: A National Survey of the Response by Prosecutors.* National Institute on Law Enforcement and Criminal Justice. Washington, DC: Government Printing Office.

Baum, Lawrence. 2011. *Specializing the Courts.* Chicago: University of Chicago Press.

Baumer, Eric, Steven Messner, and Richard Felson. 2000. "The Role of Victim Characteristics in the Disposition of Murder Cases." *Justice Quarterly* 17: 281–308.

Baxter, Heather. 2012. Too Many Clients, Too Little Time: How States Are Forcing Public Defenders to Violate Their Ethical Obligations. *Federal Sentencing Reporter* 25(2): 91–102.

Baxter, Heather. 2014. "Too Many Clients, Too Little Time: How States are Forcing Public Defers to Violate their Ethical Obligations." *Federal Sentencing Reporter* 25: 91–102.

Bayle, Allan. (2002). Testimony in *United States v. Llera Plaza,* 188, R. Suppl. 2d, *Daubert* Hearing.

Bazelon, Lara A. 2009. "Putting the Mice in Charge of the Cheese: Why Federal Judges Cannot Always Be Trusted to Police Themselves and What Congress Can Do about It." *Kentucky Law Journal* 97: 439–503.

Becerra, David, M. Alex Wagaman, David Androff, Jill Messing, and Jason Castillo. 2016. "Policing Immigrants: Fear of Deportations and Perceptions of Law Enforcement and Criminal Justice." *Journal of Social Work.* Advanced online publication. doi: 10.1177/1468017316651995

Beccaria, Cesare. 1764. "On Crimes and Punishments." In Aaron Thomas (Ed. and transl.), *On Crimes and Punishments and Other Writings.* Toronto, ON: University of Toronto Press, 2008.

Bedau, Hugo Adam, and Michael L. Radelet. 1987. "Miscarriages of Justice in Potentially Capital Cases." *Stanford Law Review* 40: 21–173.

Beety, Valena E. 2015. "Cops in Lab Coats and Forensics in the Courtroom." *Ohio State Journal of Criminal Law* 13(2): 543–565.

Begue, Yvette, and Candace Goldstein. 1987. "How Judges Get into Trouble." *Judges Journal* 26: 8.

Beichner, Dawn, and Cassia C. Spohn. 2005. "Prosecutorial Charging Decisions in Sexual Assault Cases: Examining the Impact of a Specialized Prosecution Unit." *Criminal Justice Policy Review* 16: 461–498.

Belenko, Steven. 2001. *Research on Drug Courts: A Critical Review: 2001 Update.* New York: National Center on Addiction and Substance Abuse at Columbia University.

Belenko, Steven, and Richard Dembo. 2003. "Treating Adolescent Substance Abuse Problems in the Juvenile Drug Court." *Journal of Law and Psychiatry* 26: 87–110.

Belknap, Joanne. 2007. *The Invisible Woman: Gender, Crime, and Justice.* 2nd ed. Belmont, CA: Wadsworth.

Belknap, Joanne, Jennifer Hartman, and Victoria L. Lippen. 2010. "Misdemeanor Domestic Violence Cases in the Courts." In Vanessa Garcia and Janice Clifford (Eds.),

Female Victims of Crime: Reality Reconsidered (pp. 259–278). Columbus, OH: Prentice Hall.

Bell, Griffin. 1993. "Appointing United States Attorneys." *Journal of Law and Politics* 9: 247–256.

Bell, Laura Cohen. 2002. *Warring Factions: Interest Groups, Money, and the New Politics of Senate Confirmation.* Columbus: Ohio State University Press.

Bell, Margret E., Sara Perez, Lisa A. Goodman, and Mary Ann Dutton. 2011. "Battered Women's Perceptions of Civil and Criminal Court Helpfulness: The Role of Court Outcome and Process." *Violence Against Women* 17(1): 71–88.

Benesh, Sara. 2013. "Judicial Elections: Directions in the Study of Institutional Legitimacy." *Judicature* 96: 204–208.

Benner, Laurence A., and Charles T. Samarkos. 2000. "Searching for Narcotics in San Diego: Preliminary Findings from the San Diego Search Warrant Project." *California Western Law Review* 36: 221–266.

Benson, Sara R. 2016. "Assisting Rural Domestic Violence Victims: The Local Librarian's Role." *Law Library Journal* 108(2): 237–250.

Bentham, Jeremy. 1830. "Principles of Penal Law: Rationale of Punishment." In John Bowring (Ed.), *The Works of Jeremy Bentham*, Vol. 1 (pp. 365–398). Edinburgh, Scotland: W. Tait (published 1843).

Berch, Rebecca White, and Erin Norris Bass. 2014. "Judicial Performance Review in Arizona: A Critical Assessment." *Oñati Socio-legal Series* 4(5): 927–952.

Berg, Kenneth. 1985. "The Bail Reform Act of 1984." *Emory Law Journal* 34: 687–740.

Berg, Mark T., and Janet L. Lauritsen. 2016. "Telling a Similar Story Twice? NCVS/UCR Convergence in Serious Violent Crime Rates in Rural, Suburban, and Urban Places, 1973-2010." *Journal of Quantitative Criminology* 32(1): 61–87.

Berg, Mark T., Erica A. Steward, Jonathan Intravia, Patricia Y. Warren, and Ronald L. Simons. 2016. "Cynical Streets: Neighborhood Social Processes and Perceptions of Criminal Injustice." *Criminology* 54(3): 1–28.

Berkson, Larry, and Susan Carbon. 1978. *Court Unification: History, Politics, and Implementation.* Washington, DC: National Institute of Law Enforcement and Criminal Justice.

Berman, Douglas A. 2010. "Afternoon Keynote Address: Encouraging (and Even Requiring) Prosecutors to Be Second-Look Sentencers." *Temple Political & Civil Rights Law Review* 19: 249–441.

Berman, Greg, and John Feinblatt. 2015. "McJustice." In *Good Courts: The Case for Problem-Solving Justice* (Chapter 1). New Orleans: Quid Pro Books.

Bernstein, Ilene Nagel, William R. Kelly, and Patricia A. Doyle. 1977. "Societal Reaction to Deviants: The Case of Criminal Defendants." *American Sociological Review* 42(5): 743–755.

Bertram, Eva, et al. 1996. *Drug War Politics: The Price of Denial.* Berkeley: University of California Press.

Bessler, John D. 1994. "The Public Interest and the Unconstitutionality of Private Prosecutors." *Arkansas Law Review* 47: 511–602.

Bhati, Avinash Singh. 2007. "Estimating the Number of Crimes Averted by Incapacitation: An Information Theoretic Approach." *Journal of Quantitative Criminology* 23: 355–375.

Bibas, Stephanos. 2004. "Plea Bargaining Outside the Shadow of Trial." *Harvard Law Review* 117: 2463–2547.

Bibas, Stephanos. 2013. "Justice Kennedy's Sixth Amendment Pragmatism." *McGeorge Law Review* 44: 211–227.

Bienen, L. B. 2008. "Anomalies: Ritual and Language in Lethal Injection Regulations." *Fordham Urban Law Journal* 35: 857–881.

Bijlsma-Frankema, Katinka, Sim B. Sitkin, and Antoinette Weibel. 2015. "Distrust in the Balance: The Emergence and Development of Intergroup Distrust in a Court of Law." *Organization Science* 26(4): 1018–1039.

Billings, Thanithia. 2016. "Private Interest, Public Sphere: Eliminating the Use of Commercial Bail Bondsmen in the Criminal Justice System." *Boston College Law Review* 57: 1337–1365.

Binder, Sarah, and Forest Maltzman. 2004. "The Limits of Senatorial Courtesy." *Legislative Studies Quarterly* 29: 5–22.

Binford, W. Warren H., Preston C. Greene, Maria C. Schmidlkofer, Robert M. Wilsey, and Hillary A. Taylor. 2007. "Seeking Best Practices among Intermediate Courts of Appeal: A Nascent Journey." *Journal of Appellate Practice and Process* 9: 37–119.

Binnall, James M. 2008. "EG1900 . . . The Number They Gave Me When They Revoked My Citizenship: Perverse Consequences of Ex-Felon Civic Exile." *Willamette Law Review* 44: 667–697.

Bisceglia, Joseph. 2007. "CSI, Judge Judy and Civic Education." *Illinois Bar Journal* 95: 508.

Biskupic, Joan. 1993. "Congress Cool to Proposals to Ease Load on Courts." *Congressional Quarterly* (April 7): 1073–1075.

Blackwell, Brenda Sims, David Holleran, and Mary A. Finn. 2008. "The Impact of the Pennsylvania Sentencing Guidelines on Sex Differences in Sentencing." *Journal of Contemporary Criminal Justice* 24: 399–418.

Blankenship, Michael, James Luginbuhl, Francis Cullen, and William Redick. 1997. "Juror Comprehension of Sentencing Instructions: A Test of Tennessee's Death Penalty Process." *Justice Quarterly* 14: 325–357.

Blasdell, Raleigh. 2015. "The Intersection of Race, Gender, and Class in Routine Activities: A Proposed Criminological Model of Victimization and Offending." *Race, Gender & Class* 22(3/4): 260–273.

Blinder, Alan. 2015, September 18. "Mark Fuller, Former Federal District Court Judge, Could Be Impeached." *New York Times*, https://www.nytimes.com/2015/09/19/us/mark-e-fuller-former-judge-could-be-impeached.html?_r=0

Bloeser, Andrew, Carl McCurley, and Jeffery Mondak. 2012. "Jury Service as Civic Engagement: Determinants of Jury Summons Compliance." *American Politics Research* 40: 179–204.

Blokland, Argan A. J., and Paul Nieuwbeerta. 2007. "Selectively Incapacitating Frequent Offenders: Costs and Benefits of Various Penal Scenarios." *Journal of Quantitative Criminology* 23: 327–353.

Bloom, Frederic M. 2008. "State Courts Unbound." *Cornell Law Review* 93: 501–554.

Bloom, Robert M., and Hillary J. Massey. 2008. "Accounting for Federalism in State Courts: Exclusion of Evidence Obtained Lawfully by Federal Agents." *University of Colorado Law Review* 79: 381–420.

Blumberg, Abraham. 1967a. *Criminal Justice*. Chicago: Quadrangle Books.

Blumberg, Abraham. 1967b. "The Practice of Law as a Confidence Game." *Law and Society Review* 1: 15–39.

Blumberg, Abraham. 1970. *Criminal Justice*. New York: Quadrangle Books.

Blumstein, Alfred, Jacqueline Cohen, Susan Martin, and Michael Tonry (Eds.). 1983. *Research on Sentencing: The Search for Reform*. Washington, DC: National Academies Press.

Boland, Barbara. 1996. "What Is Community Prosecution?" *National Institute of Justice Journal* 231: 35–40.

Boland, Barbara, Elizabeth Brady, Herbert Tyson, and John Bassler. 1982. *The Prosecution of Felony Arrests*. Washington, DC: Institute for Law and Social Research.

Boland, Barbara, and Brian Forst. 1985. "Prosecutors Don't Always Aim to Pleas." *Federal Probation* 49: 10–15.

Boland, Barbara, Paul Mahanna, and Ronald Sones. 1992. *The Prosecution of Felony Arrests, 1988*. Washington, DC: U.S. Department of Justice, Bureau of Justice Statistics.

Boldt, Richard C. 2014. "Problem Solving Courts and Pragmatism." *Maryland Law Review* 73(4): 1120–1172.

Bonneau, Chris. 2007. "The Effects of Campaign Spending in State Supreme Court Elections." *Political Research Quarterly* 60: 489.

Bonneau, Chris W. 2001. "The Composition of State Supreme Courts." *Judicature* 85: 26–31.

Bonneau, Chris W., and Melinda Gann Hall. 2003. "Predicting Challengers in State Supreme Court Elections: Context and Politics of Institutional Design." *Political Research Quarterly* 56: 337–349.

Bonneau, Chris W., and Melinda Gann Hall. 2009. *In Defense of Judicial Elections*. New York: Routledge.

Bonnie, Richard, Norman Poythress, Steven Hoge, John Monahan, and Marlene Eisenberg. 1996. "Decision-Making in Criminal Defense: An Empirical Study of Insanity Pleas and the Impact of Doubted Client Competence." *Journal of Criminal Law and Criminology* 87: 48–77.

Bonta, James, Suzanne Wallace-Capretta, and Jenniffer Rooney. 2000. "Can Electronic Monitoring Make a Difference? An Evaluation of Three Canadian Programs." *Crime and Delinquency* 46(2): 61–75.

Bontrager, Stephanie, Kelle Barrick, and Elizabeth Stupi. 2013. "Gender and Sentencing: A Meta-Analysis of Contemporary Research." *Journal of Gender, Race & Justice* 16(2): 349–372.

Booth, Tracey. 2014. "The Restorative Capacities of Victim Impact Statements: An Analysis of the Victim–Judge Communication Dyad in the Sentencing of Homicide Offenders." *Restorative Justice* 2(3): 302–326.

Borenstein, Isaac and Erin J. Anderson. 2009. "Judicial Participation in Plea Negotiations: The Elephant in Chambers." *Suffolk Journal of Trial and Appellate Advocacy* 14: 1–34.

Borgida, Eugene, and Susan T. Fiske. 2008. *Beyond Common Sense: Psychological Science in the Courtroom*. Oxford, UK: Wiley-Blackwell.

Boritch, Helen. 1992. "Gender and Criminal Court Outcomes: An Historical Analysis." *Criminology* 30: 293–317.

Bornstein, Brian H., Alan J. Tomkins, Elizabeth M. Neeley, Mitchel N. Herian, and Joseph A. Hamm. 2012. "Reducing Courts' Failure-to-Appear Rate by Written Reminders." *Psychology, Public Policy, and Law* 19(1): 70–91.

Borys, Bryan, Cynthia Banks, and Darrel Parker. 1999. "Enlisting the Justice Community in Court Improvement." *Judicature* 82: 176–185.

Bouffard, Jeffrey A., and Lisa R. Muftic. 2006. "Program Completion and Recidivism Outcomes among Adult Offenders Ordered to Complete a Community Service Sentence." *Journal of Offender Rehabilitation* 43(2): 1–33.

Bouffard, Jeffrey A., and Lisa R. Muftic. 2007. "The Effectiveness of Community Service Sentences Compared to Traditional Fines for Low-Level Offenders." *The Prison Journal* 87(2): 171–194.

Bouffard, Jeffrey A., and Katie Richardson. 2007. "The Effectiveness of Drug Court Programming for Specific Kinds of Offenders: Methamphetamine- and DWI-Offenders versus Other Drug-Involved Offenders." *Criminal Justice Policy Review* 18: 274–293.

Bouffard, Jeffrey A., Katie Richardson, and Travis Franklin. 2010. "Drug Courts for DWI Offenders? The Effectiveness of Two Hybrid Drug Courts on DWI Offenders." *Journal of Criminal Justice* 38: 25–33.

Bourgois, Philippe. 2003. *In Search of Respect: Selling Crack in El Barrio*. 2nd ed. New York: Cambridge University Press.

Bowden, Deborah. 2011. "Social Media's Effect on the Casey Anthony Trial." *Fox 13 News*, July 19.

Bowen, Deirdre. 2009. "Calling Your Bluff: How Prosecutors and Defense Attorneys Adapt Plea Bargaining Strategies to Increased Formalization." *Justice Quarterly* 26: 1–29.

Bowes, Mark. 2009. "Localities Recoup Incarceration Costs." *Richmond Times-Dispatch*, January 12.

Bowman, Frank. 2014. "Dead Law Walking: The Surprising Tenacity of the Federal Sentencing Guidelines." *Houston Law Review* 51: 1227–1270.

Boyd, Christina, Lee Epstein, and Andrew Martin. 2010. "Untangling the Casual Effects of Sex on Judging." *American Journal of Political Science* 54: 389–411.

Brace, Paul, and Brent D. Boyea. 2007. "Judicial Selection Methods and Capital Punishment in the American States." In Matthew Justin Streb (Ed.), *Running for Judge: The Rising Political, Financial, and Legal Stakes of Judicial Elections* (pp. 186–203). New York: New York University Press.

Brace, Paul, and Melinda Gann Hall. 1997. "The Interplay of Preferences, Case Facts, Context, and Rules in the Politics of Judicial Choice." *Journal of Politics* 59: 1206–1241.

Bradley, Craig. 2006. "The Right Decision on the Juvenile Death Penalty." *Judicature* 89: 302–303.

Bagaric, Mirko. 2014. "The Punishment Should Fit the Crime—Not the Prior Convictions of the Person That Committed the Crime: An Argument for Less Impact Being Accorded to Previous Convictions in Sentencing." *San Diego Law Review* 51: 343–417.

Bandyopadhyay, Siddhartha, and Bryan C. McCannon. 2014. "The Effect of the Election of Prosecutors on Criminal Trials." *Public Choice* 161(1–2): 141–156.

Braun, Stephen. 2013. "Former FISA Judge Says Secret Court Flawed." *Associated Press*. July 9. https://www.yahoo.com/news/former-fisa-judge-says-secret-court-flawed-201422173.html

Brennan, Carrie Dvorak. 2015. "Public Defender System: A Comparative Analysis." *The Indiana International & Comparative Law Review* 25: 237–268.

Brennan, Pauline K., and Cassia Spohn. 2008. "Race/Ethnicity and Sentencing Outcomes among Drug Offenders in North Carolina." *Journal of Contemporary Criminal Justice* 24: 371–398.

Brennan, William. 1963. "The Criminal Prosecution: Sporting Event or Quest for Truth?" *Washington University Law Quarterly* 279–294.

Brenner, Susan. 1998. "Is the Grand Jury Worth Keeping?" *Judicature* 81: 190–199.

Brereton, David, and Jonathan Casper. 1981–1982. "Does It Pay to Plead Guilty? Differential Sentencing and the Functioning of Criminal Courts." *Law and Society Review* 16: 45–70.

Breyer, Stephen, et al. 2006. "Implementation of the Judicial Conduct and Disability Act of 1980: A Report to the Chief Justice." Washington, DC: The Judicial Conduct and Disability Act Study Committee. Available online at http://www.supremecourtus.gov/publicinfo/breyercommitteereport.pdf

Bright, David A., and Jane Goodman-Delahunty. 2006. "Gruesome Evidence and Emotion: Anger, Blame, and Jury Decision-Making." *Law and Human Behavior* 30: 183–202.

Bright, Stephen. 1997. "Political Attacks on the Judiciary." *Judicature* 80: 165–173.

Britto, Sarah, Tycy Hughes, Kurt Saltzman, and Colin Stroh. 2007. "Does 'Special' Mean Young, White and Female? Deconstructing the Meaning of 'Special' in *Law & Order: Special Victims Unit*." *Journal of Criminal Justice and Popular Culture* 14(1): 39–57.

Broccolina, Frank, and Richard Zorza. 2008. "En$uring Access to Ju$tice in Tough Economic Times." *Judicature* 92(3): 124–128.

Brody, David C. 2008. "The Use of Judicial Performance Evaluation to Enhance Judicial Accountability, Judicial Independence, and Public Trust." *Denver University Law Review* 86: 115–156.

Broeder, D. W. 1959. "The University of Chicago Jury Project." *Nebraska Law Review* 38: 744–760.

Brooks, Daniel. 1985. "Penalizing Judges Who Appeal Disciplinary Sanctions: The Unconstitutionality of 'Upping the Ante.'" *Judicature* 69: 95–102.

Brooks, Richard R. W., and Stephen Raphael. 2003. "Life Terms or Death Sentences: The Uneasy Relationship between Judicial Elections and Capital Punishment." *Journal of Criminal Law and Criminology* 92: 609–640.

Brooks, Thom. 2004. "A Defence of Jury Nullification." *Res Publica* 10: 401–423.

Brown, Brian, and Greg Jolivette. 2005. *A Primer: Three Strikes—The Impact after More Than a Decade*. Sacramento: California Legislative Analyst's Office.

Brown, Darryl. 1997. "Jury Nullification within the Rule of Law." *Minnesota Law Review* 81: 1149–1200.

Brown, Darryl K. 2014. "The Perverse Effects of Efficiency in Criminal Process." *Virginia Law Review* 100(1): 183–223.

Brown, Gina. 2005. "A Community of Court ADR Programs: How Court-Based ADR Programs Help Each Other Survive and Thrive." *Justice System Journal* 26: 327–341.

Brown, Joe M., and Jon R. Sorensen. 2014. "Legal and Extra-Legal Factors Related to the Imposition of Blended Sentences." *Criminal Justice Policy Review* 25(2): 227–241.

Brown, Mary, and Steven Bunnell. 2006. "Negotiated Justice: Prosecutorial Perspectives on Federal Plea Bargaining in the District of Columbia." *American Criminal Law Review* 43: 1063.

Browning, John G. 2016. "Voir Dire Becomes Voir Google: Ethical Concerns of 21st Century Jury Selection." *The Brief* 45(2): 40–50.

Bublick, Ellen M. 2006. "Tort Suits Filed by Rape and Sexual Assault Victims in Civil Courts: Lessons for Courts, Classrooms, and Constituencies." *Southern Methodist University Law Review* 59: 55–122.

Buchanan, John. 1989. "Police–Prosecutor Teams: Innovations in Several Jurisdictions." *NIJ Reports* 214: 2–8.

Buchman, Jeremy. 2004. "The Legal Model and *Daubert's* Effect on Trial Judges' Decisions to Admit Scientific Testimony." Paper presented at the annual meeting of the Midwest Political Science Association, Chicago.

Buller, Tyler J. (2015). Public Defenders and Appointed Counsel in Criminal Appeals: The Iowa Experience. *Journal of Appellate Practice and Process* 16(2): 183–255.

Bulman, Philip. 2009. "Increasing Sexual Assault Prosecution Rates." *NIJ Journal* 264, November.

Burbank, Stephen. 1987. "Politics and Progress in Implementing the Federal Judicial Discipline Act." *Judicature* 71: 13–28.

Bureau of Justice Statistics. 1990. *Juvenile and Adult Records: One System, One Record?* Washington, DC: Department of Justice.

Bureau of Justice Statistics. 1996. *How to Use Structured Fines (Day Fines) as an Intermediate Sanction.* Washington, DC: Government Printing Office.

Bureau of Justice Statistics. 2011. "Justice Expenditure and Employment Extracts Series." Available online at https://www.bjs.gov/index.cfm?ty=dcdetail&iid=286

Bureau of Justice Statistics. 2012. *Indigent Defense Systems.* Washington, DC: Department of Justice, Bureau of Justice Statistics. Available online at https://www.bjs.gov/index.cfm?ty=tp&tid=28

Bureau of Justice Statistics. 2014. Number of Persons Executed in the United States: Capital Punishment Statistical Tables, 1930–2013. Washington, DC: Author.

Burke-Robertson, C. 2008. "Judging Jury Verdicts." *Tulane Law Review* 83: 157–218.

Burruss, George, and Kimberly Kempf-Leonard. 2002. "The Questionable Advantage of Defense Counsel in Juvenile Court." *Justice Quarterly* 19: 37–68.

Bushway, Shawn D., and Brian Forst. 2013. "Studying Discretion in the Processes That Generate Criminal Justice Sanctions." *Justice Quarterly* 30(2): 199–222.

Bushway, Shawn D., and Anne Morrison Piehl. 2007. "Social Science Research and the Legal Threat to Presumptive Sentencing Guidelines." *Criminology and Public Policy* 6: 461–482.

Butler, Brooke. 2007. "Death Qualification and Prejudice: The Effect of Implicit Racism, Sexism, and Homophobia on Capital Defendants' Right to Due Process." *Behavioral Sciences and the Law* 25: 857–867.

Butler, Brooke, and Gary Moran. 2007a. "The Impact of Death Qualification, Belief in a Just World, Legal Authoritarianism, and Locus of Control on Venirepersons' Evaluations of Aggravating and Mitigating Circumstances in Capital Trials." *Behavioral Sciences and the Law* 25: 57–68.

Butler, Brooke, and Gary Moran. 2007b. "The Role of Death Qualification and Need for Cognition in Venirepersons' Evaluations of Expert Scientific Testimony in Capital Trials." *Behavioral Sciences and the Law* 25: 561–571.

Butler, Paul. 1995. "Racially Based Jury Nullification: Black Power in the Criminal Justice System." *Yale Law Journal* 105: 677–725.

Butterfield, Fox. 1997. "Justice Besieged: With Juvenile Courts in Chaos, Critics Propose Their Demise." *New York Times*, July 21.

Buzawa, Eve, and Carl Buzawa. 1996. *Domestic Violence: The Criminal Justice Response.* 2nd ed. Thousand Oaks, CA: Sage.

Byrd, Harry. 1976. "Has Life Tenure Outlived Its Time?" *Judicature* 59: 266–277.

Byrne, James, Arthur Lurigio, and Christopher Baird. 1989. "The Effectiveness of the New Intensive Supervision Programs." *Research in Corrections* 2: 1–15.

Cadigan, Timothy P., James L. Johnson, and Christopher T. Lowenkamp. 2012. "The Re-validation of the Federal Pretrial Services Risk Assessment (PTRA)." *Federal Probation* 76(2): 3–9.

Caher, John, and Andrew Keshner. 2011. "Deep Overtime Cuts Bring Delay, Rethinking of Case Presentation." *New York Law Journal*, November 28.

California Coalition for Universal Representation. 2016. *California's Due Process Crisis: Access to Legal Counsel for Detained Immigrants.* Available at http://centrolegal.org/wp-content/uploads/2016/06/Californias-Representation-Crisis.pdf.

Call, Jack, David England, and Susette Talarico. 1983. "Abolition of Plea Bargaining in the Coast Guard." *Journal of Criminal Justice* 11: 351–358.

Cameron, Mary. 1964. *The Booster and the Snitch.* Glencoe, IL: Free Press.

Campagna, Michael, Cheyenne Foster, Stephanie Karas, Mary K. Stohr, and Craig Hemmens. 2016. "Restrictions on the Citizenship Rights of Felons: Barriers to Successful Reintegration." *Journal of Law and Criminal Justice* 4(1): 22–39.

Campbell, Curtis, Candace McCoy, and Chimezie Osigweh. 1990. "The Influence of Probation Recommendations on Sentencing Decisions and Their Predictive Accuracy." *Federal Probation* 54: 13–21.

Campbell, Donald, and H. Laurence Ross. 1968. "The Connecticut Crackdown on Speeding: Time-Series Data in Quasi-Experimental Analysis." *Law and Society Review* 3: 33–54.

Campbell, Rebecca, Deborah Bybee, Stephanie M. Townsend, Jessica Shaw, Nidal Karim, and Jenifer Markowitz. 2014. "The Impact of Sexual Assault Nurse Examiner Programs on Criminal Justice Case Outcomes: A Multisite Replication Study." *Violence Against Women* 20(5): 607–625.

Campbell, William. 1973. "Eliminate the Grand Jury." *Journal of Criminal Law and Criminology* 64: 174–182.

Cannavale, F., and W. Falcon. 1976. *Witness Cooperation*. Lexington, MA: Heath.

Cannon, Angie. 1996. "Bill Spells Out Rights of Victims." *Times-Picayune*, April 23.

Cannon, Angie. 1997. "Violent Teen Crime Rate Drops Two Years in a Row." *Times-Picayune*, October 3.

Capers, I. Bennett. 2009. "Legal Outsiders in American Film: Notes on Minority Report." *Suffolk University Law Review* 42: 795–807.

Caplan, Joel M. 2010." Parole Release Decisions: Impact of Positive and Negative Victim and Nonvictim Input on a Representative Sample of Parole-Eligible Inmates." *Violence and Victims* 25: 224–242.

Caplan, Lincoln. 1988. *The Tenth Justice: The Solicitor General and the Rule of Law*. New York: Vintage.

Caputo, Gail. 1999. *Evaluation of CAES CSP Program*. New York: Vera Institute of Justice.

Carbon, Susan. 1984. "Women in the Judiciary." *Judicature* 65: 285.

Carelli, Richard. 1996. "Independent Judiciary Vital, Rehnquist Says." *Times-Picayune*, April 27.

Carey, Shannon M., Michael W. Finigan, and Kimberly Pukstas. 2008. *Exploring the Key Components of Drug Courts: A Comparative Study of 18 Adult Drug Courts on Practices, Outcomes and Costs*. Portland, OR: NPC Research.

Caringella, Susan. 2008. *Addressing Rape Reform in Law and Practice*. New York: Columbia University Press.

Carlsmith, Kevin, John Darley, and Paul Robinson. 2002. "Why Do We Punish? Deterrence and Just Deserts as Motives for Punishment." *Journal of Personality and Social Psychology* 83: 284–299.

Carns, Teresa White, and John Kruse. 1992. "Alaska's Ban on Plea Bargaining Reevaluated." *Judicature* 75: 310–317.

Carp, Robert. 1975. "The Behavior of Grand Juries: Acquiescence or Justice?" *Social Science Quarterly* 55(4): 855–870.

Carp, Robert, Kenneth Manning, and Ronald Stidham. 2013. "A First Term Assessment: The Ideology of Barrack Obama's District Court Appointees." *Judicature* 97: 128–136.

Carp, Robert, and Ronald Stidham. 1990. *Judicial Process in America*. Washington, DC: Congressional Quarterly Press.

Carr, Patrick, Laura Napolitano, and Jessica Keating. 2007. "We Never Call the Cops and Here Is Why: A Qualitative Examination of Legal Cynicism in Three Philadelphia Neighborhoods." *Criminology* 45: 445.

Carrington, Paul, Daniel Meador, and Maurice Rosenberg. 1976. *Justice on Appeal*. St. Paul, MN: West.

Carroll, Leo, and Claire Cornell. 1985. "Racial Composition, Sentencing Reforms, and Rates of Incarceration, 1970–1980." *Justice Quarterly* 2: 473–490.

Carroll, Susan. 2008. "A System's Fatal Flaws." *Houston Chronicle*, November 16.

Carson, E. Ann, and Daniela Golinelli. 2013. *Prisoners in 2012*. Washington, DC: Bureau of Justice Statistics.

Carson, E. Anne, and Elizabeth Anderson. 2016. *Prisoners in 2015*. Washington, DC: Bureau of Justice Statistics.

Carter, Lief. 1974. *The Limits of Order*. Lexington, MA: Heath.

Carter, Lief H., and Tom F. Burke. 2007. *Reason in Law*. 7th ed. Upper Saddle River, NJ: Pearson/Longman.

Carter, Linda. 2013. "The Evolution of Justice Kennedy's Eighth Amendment Jurisprudence on Categorical Bars in Capital Cases." *McGeorge Law Review* 44: 229–246.

Carter, Robert, and Leslie Wilkins. 1967. "Some Factors in Sentencing Policy." *Journal of Criminal Law, Criminology and Police Science* 58: 503–514.

Casey, Pamela, and David Rottman. 2004. *Problem-Solving Courts: Models and Trends*. Williamsburg, VA: National.

Casper, Jonathan. 1972. *American Criminal Justice: The Defendant's Perspective*. Englewood Cliffs, NJ: Prentice Hall.

Casper, Jonathan D. 1970–1971. "Did You Have a Lawyer When You Went to Court? No, I Had a Public Defender." *Yale Review of Law and Society in Action* 1: 4–9.

Casper, Jonathan D., David Brereton, and David Neal. 1982. *The Implementation of the California Determinate Sentencing Law*. Washington, DC: Department of Justice.

Cass, Ronald A. 2015. *Power Failures: Prosecution, Discretion, and the Demise of Official Constraint*. No. 05-2015. ICER-International Centre for Economic Research.

Cassata, Donna. 2014. "Senate Blocks Change to Military Sex Assault Cases." *Associated Press*, March 7.

Cassidy, Michael, and Jason Rydberg. 2017. "Analyzing Variation in Prior Record Penalties Across Conviction Offenses." Advanced online publican. *Crime & Delinquency*. doi: 10.1177/0011128717693215

Catalano, Shannan. 2013. *Intimate Partner Violence: Attributes of Victimization, 1993–2011*. Washington, DC: Bureau of Justice Statistics.

Cauchon, Dennis. 1999. "Indigents' Lawyers: Low Pay Hurts Justice?" *USA Today*, February 3.

Cauthen, James, and Barry Latzer. 2008. "Why So Long? Explaining Processing Time in Capital Appeals." *Justice System Journal* 29: 298–312.

Center for Children's Law and Policy. 2012. "Models for Change." Washington, DC: Author.

Center for Court Innovation. 2009. "Manhattan Community Court." Available online at http://www.courtinnovation.org

Center for Court Innovation. 2016. "Community Court." Available online at http://www.courtinnovation.org/topic/community-court

Center for Court Innovation. 2012b. "Community Prosecution." Available online at http://www.courtinnovation.org/topic/community-prosecution

Center for Court Innovation. 2014. "Domestic Violence Courts." Available online at http://www.courtinnovation.org/project/domestic-violence-courts

Cervantes, Adriana C. 2010. "Will Twitter Be Following You in the Courtroom?: Why Reporters Should Be Allowed to Broadcast During Courtroom Proceedings." *Hastings Communications and Entertainment Law Journal* 33: 133–157.

Chabot, Christine Kexel. 2013. "A Long View of the Senate's Influence Over Supreme Court Appointments." *Hastings Law Journal* 64: 1229–1272.

Chaiken, Marcia, and Jan Chaiken. 1990. *Redefining the Career Criminal: Priority Prosecution of High-Rate Dangerous Offenders*. Washington, DC: Department of Justice.

Champion, Dean J. 2007. *Sentencing: A Reference Handbook*. Santa Barbara, CA: ABC-CLIO.

Chan, Cecilia (2013, April 11). Search-warrant process in DUIs faster for Phoenix police. *Arizona Republic*. Retrieved from http://www.azcentral.com/community/phoenix/articles/20130410phoenix-police-search-warrant-process-duis-faster-brk.html

Chapper, Joy, and Roger Hanson. 1990. "Understanding Reversible Error in Criminal Appeals." *State Court Journal* 14: 16–24.

Chassin, Laurie. 2008. "Juvenile Justice and Substance Use." *Juvenile Justice: The Future of Children* 18(2): 165–183.

Cheesman, Fred L., Scott E. Graves, Kathryn Holt, Tara L. Kunkel, Cynthia G. Lee, and Michelle T. White. 2016. "Drug Court Effectiveness and Efficiency: Findings for Virginia." *Alcoholism Treatment Quarterly* 32(2): 143–169.

Chen, Elsa Y. 2014. "In the Furtherance of Justice, Injustice, or Both? A Multilevel Analysis of Courtroom Context and the Implementation of Three Strikes." *Justice Quarterly* 31(2): 257–286.

Chilton, Bradley. 1991. *Prisons under the Gavel: The Federal Takeover of Georgia Prisons*. Columbus: Ohio State University Press.

Chiricos, Theodore, and William Bales. 1991. "Unemployment and Punishment: An Empirical Assessment." *Criminology* 29: 701–724.

Choi, Stephen J., G. Mitu Gulati, and Eric A. Posner. 2008. "Professionals or Politicians: The Uncertain Empirical Case for an Elected Rather Than Appointed Judiciary." *Journal of Law, Economics, and Organization* 26(2): 290–336.

Chokshi, Niraj. 2014. "Nearly a Million Dollars Has Been Spent Ahead of Thursday's Tennessee Judicial Election." *Washington Post*, August 6. Retrieved from http://www.washingtonpost.com/blogs/govbeat/wp/2014/08/06/nearly-a-million-dollars-has-been-spent-on-thursdays-tennessee-judicial-election/

Christopher, Russell. 2014. "Penalizing and Chilling an Indigent's Exercise of the Right to Appointed Counsel for Misdemeanors." *Iowa Law Review* 99: 1905–1927.

Christy, Annette, Norman G. Poythress, Roger A. Boothroyd, John Petrila, Shabnam Mehra. 2005. "Evaluating the Efficiency and Community Safety Goals of the Broward County Mental Health Court." *Behavioral Sciences and the Law* 22: 227–243.

Church, Thomas. 1976. "Plea Bargains, Concessions and the Courts: Analysis of a Quasi-Experiment." *Law and Society Review* 10: 377–389.

Church, Thomas. 1982. "The 'Old' and the 'New' Conventional Wisdom of Court Delay." *Justice System Journal* 7: 395–412.

Church, Thomas. 1985. "Examining Local Legal Culture." *American Bar Foundation Research Journal* 449–518.

Church, Thomas, Alan Carlson, Jo-Lynne Lee, and Teresa Tan. 1978. *Justice Delayed: The Pace of Litigation in Urban Trial Courts*. Williamsburg, VA: National Center for State Courts.

Church, Thomas, and Virginia McConnell. 1978. *Pretrial Delay: A Review and Bibliography*. Williamsburg, VA: National Center for State Courts.

Clark, John, James Austin, and D. Alan Henry. 1997. "*Three Strikes and You're Out*": A Review of State Legislation. Washington, DC: National Institute of Justice.

Clark, John, James Austin, and D. Alan Henry. 1998. "'Three Strikes and You're Out': Are Repeat Offender Laws Having Their Anticipated Effects?" *Judicature* 81: 144–154.

Clark, Tom. 2005. "A Note on the Moore Case and Judicial Administration." *The Justice System Journal* 26: 355–361.

Clarke, Stevens. 1984. "North Carolina's Determinate Sentencing Legislation." *Judicature* 68: 140–152.

Clarke, Stevens, and Gary Koch. 1976. "The Influence of Income and Other Factors on Whether Criminal Defendants Go to Prison." *Law and Society Review* 11: 57–92.

Clear, Todd. 2007. *Imprisoning Communities: How Mass Incarceration Makes Disadvantaged Neighborhoods Worse*. New York: Oxford University Press.

Clear, Todd R., John R. Hamilton, Jr., and Eric Cadora. 2011. *Community Justice*. 2nd ed. Belmont, CA: Wadsworth.

Clear, Todd R., Patria M. Harris, and S. Christopher Baird. 1992. "Probationer Violations and Officer Response." *Journal of Criminal Justice* 20: 1–12.

Clear, Todd R., John Hewitt, and Robert Regoli. 1979. "Discretion and the Determinate Sentence: Its Distribution, Control and Effect on Time Served." *Crime and Delinquency* 24: 428–445.

Clear, Todd R., Michael D. Reisig, and George F. Cole. 2016. *American Corrections*. 11th ed. Belmont, CA: Wadsworth.

Cloud, John. 2011. "The Troubled Life of Jarod Loughner." *Time*, January 24.

Clynch, Edward, and David Neubauer. 1981. "Trial Courts as Organizations: A Critique and Synthesis." *Law and Policy Quarterly* 3: 69–94.

CNN. 2008. "Is 'American Gangster' Really All That 'True'?"

CNN. 2010. The Evidence against Amanda Knox. June 11. Available online at http://www.cnn.com/2010/CRIME/06/11/amanda.knox.evidence/index.html.

CNN. 2011, September 14. "Police Shoot Arkansas Courthouse Gunman Dead." Available online at http://articles.cnn.com/2011-09-14/justice/arkansas.courthouse.shooting_1_fort-smith-police-metal-detectors-arkansas?_s=PM:CRIME

Cochran, Joshua C., and Daniel P. Mears. 2014. "Race, Ethnic, and Gender Divides in Juvenile Court Sanctioning and Rehabilitative Intervention." *Journal of Research in Crime and Delinquency* 52(2): 181–212.

Cohen, Mark A., Roland T. Rust, and Sara Steen. 2006. "Prevention, Crime Control or Cash? Public Preferences towards Criminal Justice Spending Priorities." *Justice Quarterly* 23: 317–335.

Cohen, Robyn. 1992. *Drunk Driving: 1989 Survey of Inmates of Local Jails*. Washington, DC: Bureau of Justice Statistics.

Cohen, Thomas. 2014. "Who's Better at Defending Criminals? Does Type of Defense Attorney Matter in Terms of Producing Favorable Case Outcomes." *Criminal Justice Policy Review* 25(1): 29–58.

Cohen, Thomas, and Brian Reaves. 2007. *Pretrial Release of Felony Defendants in State Courts*. Washington, DC: Bureau of Justice Statistics.

Cohen, Thomas H., and Tracey Kyckelhahn. 2010. *Felony Defendants in Large Urban Counties, 2006*. Washington, DC: Bureau of Justice Statistics. Available at http://www.bjs.gov/content/pub/pdf/fdluc06.pdf

Cohn, Adam. 2005. "Want Social Condemnation with Your Justice? Tune in Judge Judy." *New York Times*, October 9.

Colburn, Jamison E. 2006. "Localism's Ecology: Protecting and Restoring Habitat in the Suburban Nation." *Ecology Law Quarterly* 33: 945–1014.

Cole, David. 2011. "Turning the Corner on Mass Incarceration." *Ohio State Journal of Criminal Law* 9: 27–51.

Cole, George. 1970. "The Decision to Prosecute." *Law and Society Review* 4: 313–343.

Cole, George. 1992. "Using Civil and Administrative Remedies to Collect Fines and Fees." *State Court Journal* 16: 4–10.

Cole, Simon A. 2010. "Who Speaks for Science? A Response to the National Academies of Science Report on Forensic Science." *Law, Probability & Risk* 9: 25–46.

Cole, Simon A., Max Welling, Rachel Dioso-Villa, and Robert Carpenter. 2008. "Beyond the Individuality of Fingerprints: A Measure of Simulated Computer Latent Print Source Attribution Accuracy." *Law, Probability, & Risk* 7: 165–189.

Coles, C. (2000). "Community Prosecution, Problem Solving, and Public Accountability: The Evolving Strategy of the American Prosecutor." *Program in Criminal Justice Policy and Management of the Malcolm Wiener Center for Social Policy, John F. Kennedy School of Government, Harvard University, October, 2.*

Coles, Catherine, and George Kelling. 1999. "Prevention Through Community Prosecution." *The Public Interest* 36: 69.

Collins, Reed. 2007. "Strolling While Poor: How Broken-Windows Policing Created a New Crime in Baltimore." *Georgetown Journal on Poverty Law and Policy* 14: 419–439.

Coltri, Laurie. 2009. *Alternative Dispute Resolution: A Conflict Approach*. 2nd ed. Upper Saddle River, NJ: Pearson.

Comparato, Scott A., and Scott D. McClurg. 2007. "A Neo-Institutional Explanation of State Supreme Court Responses in Search and Seizure Cases." *American Politics Research* 35(5): 726–754.

Connick, Elizabeth, and Robert Davis. 1983. "Examining the Problems of Witness Intimidation." *Judicature* 66: 438–447.

Coontz, Phyllis. 2000. "Gender and Judicial Decisions: Do Female Judges Decide Cases Differently Than Male Judges?" *Gender Issues* 18(4): 59–73.

Cooper, Alexia, and Erica L. Smith. 2011. *Homicide Trends in the United States: Annual Rates for 2009 and 2010*. Washington, DC: Bureau of Justice Statistics.

Cooper, Caroline. 2003. "Rural Drug Courts." Washington, DC: American University, Bureau of Justice Assistance Drug

Court Clearinghouse. Available online at http://www1 .spa.american.edu/justice/documents/2014.pdf

Cooper, Caroline S. 2001. "Juvenile Drug Court Programs." *Juvenile Accountability Incentive Block Grants Program Bulletin*. Washington, DC: Office of Juvenile Justice and Delinquency Prevention.

Cooper, Jeffrey O., and Douglas A. Berman. 2000. "Passive Virtues and Casual Vices on the Federal Courts of Appeals." *Brooklyn Law Review* 66: 712–754.

Cooper, Sarah Lucy. 2016. "Challenges to Fingerprint Identification Evidence: Why the Courts Need a New Approach to Finality." *Hamline Law Review* 42(2): 756–790.

Cooprider, Keith. 2009. "Pretrial Risk Assessment and Case Classification: A Case Study." *Federal Probation* 73(1): 12–15.

Corman, Hope, and Naci Mocan. 2005. "Carrots, Sticks, and Broken Windows." *The Journal of Law and Economics* 48: 235–266.

Cornfield, Josh. 2014. "Judge to Review Facebook Posts of Rape Accuser." *Associated Press*, August 9. Retrieved from http://bigstory.ap.org/article /rape-case-judge-review-victims-facebook-posts

Cornwell, Erin York, and Valerie P. Hans. 2011. "Representation through Participation: A Multilevel Analysis of Jury Deliberations." *Law & Society Review* 45(3): 667–698.

Cosden, Merith, Jeffrey Ellens, Jeffrey Schnell, and Yasmeen Yamini-Diouf. 2005. "Efficacy of a Mental Health Treatment Court with Assertive Community Treatment." *Behavioral Sciences and the Law* 23: 199–214.

Cose, Ellis. 2009. "Closing the Gap: Obama Could Fix Cocaine Sentencing." *Newsweek*, July 20.

Cosimo, S. Deborah. 2011. *Domestic Violence: Legal Sanctions and Recidivism Rates among Male Perpetrators*. El Paso, TX: LFB Scholarly.

Costello, Margaret. 2014. "Fulfilling the Unfulfilled Promise of *Gideon*: Litigation as a Viable Strategic Tool." *Iowa Law Review* 99: 1951–1978.

Council of Economic Advisers. (2015). *Fines, Fees, and Bail: Payments in the Criminal Justice System that Disproportionately Impact the Poor*. Washington, DC: U.S. Executive Office of The President.

Council of State Governments Justice Center. 2008. *Mental Health Courts: A Primer for Policymakers and Practitioners*. New York: Author. Available online at https://csgjusticecenter.org /wp-content/uploads/2012/12/mhc-primer.pdf

Council of State Governments Justice Center. 2012. *Mental Health Consensus Project*. Available online at http:// consensusproject.org

Covarrubias, Rebecca J. 2009. "Lives in Defense Counsel's Hands: The Problems and Responsibilities of Defense Counsel Representing Mentally Ill or Mentally Retarded Capital Defendants." *Scholar* 11: 413–468.

Covey, Herbert, and Mary Mande. 1985. "Determinate Sentencing in Colorado." *Justice Quarterly* 2: 259–270.

Covey, Russell. 2007. Reconsidering the Relationship between Cognitive Psychology and Plea Bargaining." *Marquette Law Review* 91: 213–247.

Covey, Russell D. 2008. "Fixed Justice: Reforming Plea Bargaining with Plea-Based Ceilings." *Tulane Law Review* 82: 1237–1290.

Covey, Russell D. 2009. "Signaling and Plea Bargaining's Innocence Problem." *Washington and Lee Law Review* 66: 73–130.

Covey, Russell D. 2016. "Plea Bargaining and Price Theory." *The George Washington Law Review* 84: 920–971.

Cox, Gail. 1993. "Hellish Clients, Big Trouble." *National Law Journal* 15: 1.

Coyle, Marcia. 2009. "Written, Verbal Threats to Federal Judges Jump." *The National Law Journal*. Available online at http://www.law.com/jsp/nlj/PubArticleNLJ .jsp?id=1202429189887

Crew, B. Keith. 1991. "Sex Differences in Criminal Sentencing: Chivalry or Patriarchy?" *Justice Quarterly* 8: 59–84.

Crouch, Ben, and James Marquart. 1990. "Resolving the Paradox of Reform: Litigation, Prisoner Violence, and Perceptions of Risk." *Justice Quarterly* 7: 103–123.

Crow, Matthew S. 2008. "The Complexities of Prior Record, Race, Ethnicity, and Policy Interactive Effects in Sentencing." *Criminal Justice Review* 33: 502–523.

Crow, Matthew S., and Katherine A. Johnson. 2008. "Race, Ethnicity, and Habitual-Offender Sentencing: A Multilevel Analysis of Individual Contextual Threat." *Criminal Justice Policy Review* 19: 63–83.

Crowe, Ann H., Linda Sydney, Pat Bancroft, and Beverly Lawrence. 2002. *Offender Supervision with Electronic Technology: A User's Guide*. Lexington, KY: American Probation and Parole Association. Available online at http://www .ncjrs.gov/pdffiles1/nij/grants/197102.pdf

Crutchfield, Robert D. 2015. "From Slavery to Social Class to Disadvantage: An Intellectual History of the Use of Class to Explain Racial Differences in Criminal Involvement." *Crime & Justice: A Review of Research* 44(1): 1–47.

Cullen, Francis T. 2005. "The Twelve People Who Saved Rehabilitation: How the Science of Criminology Made a Difference." *Criminology* 43: 1–42.

Cullen, Francis T. 2013. "Rehabilitation: Beyond Nothing Works." *Crime and Justice* 42(1): 299–376.

Cullen, Francis T., Kristie R. Blevins, and Jennifer S. Trager. 2005. "The Rise and Fall of Boot Camp: A Case Study in Common-Sense Corrections." *Journal of Offender Rehabilitation* 40: 53–70.

Cullen, Francis, Bonnie Fisher, and Brandon Applegate. 2000. "Public Opinion about Punishment and Corrections." *Crime and Justice* 27: 1–79.

Cullen, Francis T., John Paul Wright, and Kristie R. Blevins. 2006. *Taking Stock: The Status of Criminological Theory.* Edison, NJ: Transaction.

Cunningham, Mark D., Thomas J. Reidy, and Jon R. Sorensen. 2008. "Assertions of 'Future Dangerousness' at Federal Capital Sentencing: Rates and Correlates of Subsequent Prison Misconduct and Violence." *Law and Human Behavior* 32: 46–63.

Currie, Elliot. 1985. *Confronting Crime: An American Challenge.* New York: Pantheon.

Currie, Elliot. 1989. "Confronting Crime: Looking toward the Twenty-First Century." *Justice Quarterly* 6: 5–15.

Curry, Theodore R., and Guadalupe Corral-Camacho. 2008. "Sentencing Young Minority Males for Drug Offenses: Testing for Conditional Effects Between Race/Ethnicity, Gender and Age During the U.S. War on Drugs." *Punishment and Society* 10: 253–276.

Curry, Todd A. 2015. "A Look at the Bureaucratic Nature of the Office of the Solicitor General." *The Justice System Journal* 36(2): 180–191.

D'Alessio, Stewart, and Lisa Stolzenberg. 2009. "Racial Animosity and Interracial Crime." *Criminology* 47: 269–296.

Daly, Kathleen. 1994. *Gender, Crime, and Punishment.* New Haven, CT: Yale University Press.

Dancey, Logan, Kjersten Nelson, and Eve Ringsmuth. 2011. "'Strict Scrutiny': The Content of Senate Judicial Confirmation Hearings During the George W. Bush Administration." *Judicature* 95: 126–135.

Dantzker, M. L. 2005. *Understanding Today's Police.* Monsey, NY: Criminal Justice Press.

Davey, Monica. 2006. "Missouri Says It Can't Hire Doctor for Executions." *New York Times*, July 15.

David, James R. 1980. *The Sentencing Dispositions of New York City Lower Court Criminal Judges.* Ph.D. dissertation, New York University.

Davies, Thomas. 1982. "Affirmed: A Study of Criminal Appeals and Decision-Making Norms in a California Court of Appeal." *American Bar Foundation Research Journal* 7(3): 543–648.

Davies, Thomas. 1983. "A Hard Look at What We Know (and Still Need to Learn) about the 'Costs' of the Exclusionary Rule: The NIJ Study and Other Studies of 'Lost Arrests.'" *American Bar Foundation Research Journal* 8(3): 611–690.

Davis, Angela J. 2009. *Arbitrary Justice: The Power of the American Prosecutor.* New York: Oxford University Press.

Davis, Robert C. 1983. "Victim/Witness Noncooperation: A Second Look at a Persistent Phenomenon." *Journal of Criminal Justice* 11: 287–299.

Davis, Robert C., and Tanya Bannister. 1995. "Improving Collection of Court-Ordered Restitution." *Judicature* 79: 30–33.

Davis, Robert, C., and Barbara E. Smith, 1994. "The Effects of Victim Impact Statements on Sentencing Decisions: A Test in an Urban Setting." *Justice Quarterly* 11: 453–469.

Davis, Robert C., Barbara Smith, and Susan Hillenbrand. 1992. "Restitution: The Victim's Viewpoint." *Justice System Journal* 15: 746–758.

Davis, Sue. 1993. "The Voice of Sandra Day O'Connor." *Judicature* 77: 134–139.

Davoli, Joanmarie Ilaria. 2012. "You Have the Right to an Attorney; If You Cannot Afford One, Then the Government Will Underpay an Overworked Attorney Who Must Also Be an Expert in Psychiatry and Immigration Law." *Michigan State Law Review* 2012: 1149–1187.

Dawson, Myrna, and Ronit Dinovitzer. 2001. "Victim Cooperation and the Prosecution of Domestic Violence in a Specialized Court." *Justice Quarterly* 18: 593–649.

Death Penalty Information Center. 2009. "Prominent Conservative Calls for Death Penalty Moratorium." Available online at http://www.deathpenaltyinfo.org/new-voices-prominent-conservative-calls-death-penalty-moratorium

Death Penalty Information Center. 2014. *Execution Facts: Modern Era.* http://www.deathpenaltyinfo.org/executions-united-states

Dedel, Kelly. 2006. *Witness Intimidation.* Washington, DC: U.S. Department of Justice, Office of Community Oriented Policing Services.

DeFrances, Carol. 2001. "State-Funded Indigent Defense Services, 1999." *Special Report.* Washington, DC: Bureau of Justice Statistics.

DeFrances, Carol, Steven Smith, and Louise van der Does. 1996. "Prosecutors in State Courts, 1994." *Bulletin.* Washington, DC: Bureau of Justice Statistics.

DeLisi, Matt. 2001. "Extreme Career Criminals." *American Journal of Criminal Justice* 25: 239–252.

DeLisi, Matt. 2005. *Career Criminals in Society.* Thousand Oaks, CA: Sage.

DeLisi, Matt, and Peter Conis. 2010. *American Corrections.* Sudbury, MA: Jones and Bartlett.

DeLisi, Matt, and Peter J. Conis. 2012. *American Corrections: Theory, Research, Policy and Practice*, 2nd ed. Sudbury, MA: Jones and Bartlett Learning

Delsohn, Gary. 2003a. *The Prosecutors: Kidnap, Rape, Murder, Justice: One Year behind the Scenes in a Big-City DA's Office.* New York: Plume.

Delsohn, Gary. 2003b. The Prosecutors: *A Year in the Life a District Attorney's Office.* New York: Dutton/Penguin.

DeMichele, Matthew, and Brian Payne. 2009. "Using Technology to Monitor Offenders: A Community Corrections Perspective." *Corrections Today*, August.

Dempsey, John. 2003. "Wolf Pack Leads Cable with 'Law and Order.'" *Variety*, October 6, p. 26.

Demuth, Stephen. 2003. "Racial and Ethnic Differences in Pretrial Release Decisions and Outcomes: A Comparison of Hispanic, Black, and White Felony Arrestees." *Criminology* 41: 873–907.

Dervan, Lucian E. 2012. "Bargained Justice: Plea Bargaining's Innocence Problem and the *Brady* Safety-Valve." *Utah Law Review* 2012: 51–97.

Dervan, Lucian E., and Vanessa A. Edkins. 2013. "The Innocent Defendant's Dilemma: An Innovative Empirical Study of Plea Bargaining's Innocence Problem." *Journal of Criminal Law & Criminology* 103(1): 1–48.

Deutsch, Linda. 2004. "Two-Tiered Justice Favors Famous." Associated Press, July 25.

Devine, Dennis J., Laura D. Clayton, Benjamin B. Dunford, Rasmy Seying, and Jennifer Pryce. 2001. "Jury Decision Making: 45 Years of Empirical Research and Deliberating Groups." *Psychology, Public Policy, and Law* 7: 622–727.

Devine, Dennis J., Paige C. Krouse, Caitlin M. Cavanaugh, and Jaime Colon Basora. 2016. "Evidentiary, Extraevidentiary, and Deliberation Process Predictors of Real Jury Verdicts." *Law and Human Behavior* 40(6): 670–682.

Devins, Neal. 2008. "Ideological Cohesion and Precedent (Or Why the Court Only Cares about Precedent When Most Justices Agree with Each Other)." *North Carolina Law Review* 86: 1399–1442.

DeVoré, Summer M. 2015. "California Juries: How the Overuse of Undue Hardship as an Excuse by Potential Jurors in Order to Be Excused from Jury Duty Means You May No Longer Be Afforded the Right of Having a Trial with a Jury of Your Community." *Western State Law Review* 43(2): 249–274.

Dewan, Shaila. 2015, June 26. "Judges Replacing Conjecture with Formula for Bail." *NY Times*, http://www.nytimes.com/2015/06/27/us/turning-the-granting-of-bail-into-a-science.html

Diamond, Shari Seidman. 2006. "Beyond Fantasy and Nightmare: A Portrait of the Jury." *Buffalo Law Review* 54: 717–763.

Diamond, Shari Seidman. 2007. "Dispensing with Deception, Curing with Care." *Judicature* 91: 20–25.

Diamond, Shari Seidman, Mary R. Rose, and Beth Murphy. 2006. "Revisiting the Unanimity Requirement: The Behavior of the Non-Unanimous Civil Jury." *Northwestern University Law Review* 100: 201–230.

Diascro, Jennifer Segal, and Rorie Spill Solberg. 2009. "George W. Bush's Legacy on the Federal Bench: Policy in the Face of Diversity." *Judicature* 92: 289–301.

Dilks, Lisa M., Tucker S. McGrimmon, and Shane R. Thye. 2015. "Status, Emotional Displays, and the Relationally-Based Evaluation of Criminals and Their Behavior." *Social Science Research* 50: 246–263.

DiIulio, John (Ed.). 1990. *Courts, Corrections, and the Constitution: The Impact of Judicial Intervention on Prisons and Jails*. New York: Oxford University Press.

DiPietro, Susanne. 2008. "From the Benches and Trenches: Evaluating the Court Process for Alaska's Children in Need of Aid." *Justice System Journal* 29: 187–208.

Dirks-Linhorst, P. Ann, and Donald M. Linhorst. 2012. "Recidivism Outcomes for Suburban Mental Health Court Defendants." *American Journal of Criminal Justice* 37: 76–91.

Ditton, Paula, and Doris Wilson. 1999. *Truth in Sentencing in State Prisons*. Washington, DC: Bureau of Justice Statistics.

Dixon, Herbert. 2011. "The Evolution of a High-Technology Courtroom." Williamsburg, VA: National Center for State Courts. Available online at http://ncsc.contentdm.oclc.org/cdm/ref/collection/tech/id/769

Dolan, Maura, and Victoria Kim. 2011. "Budget Cuts to Worsen California Court Delays, Officials Say." *Los Angeles Times*, July 20.

Doerner, Jill K., and Stephen Demuth. 2014. "Gender and Sentencing in the Federal Courts: Are Women Treated More Leniently?" *Criminal Justice Policy Review* 25(2): 242–269.

Dorfman, David N. 1999. "Proving the Lie: Litigating Police Credibility." *American Journal of Criminal Law* 26: 455–503.

Dougherty, Joyce. 1988. "Negotiating Justice in the Juvenile Justice System: A Comparison of Adult Plea Bargaining and Juvenile Intake." *Federal Probation* 52: 72–80.

Douglas, James, and Helen Stockstill. 2008. "Starving the Death Penalty: Do Financial Considerations Limit Its Use?" *Justice System Journal* 29: 326–337.

Downey, P. Mitchell, and John K. Roman. 2010. *A Bayesian Meta-Analysis of Drug Court Cost-Effectiveness*. Washington DC: The Urban Institute.

Doyle, Michael. 2013. "Hold Calls for Curbs on Drug Sentencing." *McClatchy News*, August 13.

Drake, Elizabeth K., Steve Aos, and Marna G. Miller. 2009. "Evidence-Based Public Policy Options to Reduce Crime and Criminal Justice Costs: Implications in Washington State." *Victims and Offenders* 4: 170–196.

Dror, Itiel E., and Greg Hampikian. (2011). "Subjectivity and Bias in Forensic DNA Mixture Interpretation." *Science & Justice* 51(4): 204–208.

Dubois, Philip. 1980. *From Ballot to Bench: Judicial Elections and the Quest for Accountability*. Austin: University of Texas Press.

Dubois, Philip. 1984. "Voting Cues in Nonpartisan Trial Court Elections: A Multivariate Assessment." *Law and Society Review* 18: 395–436.

Dunkelberger, Lloyd. 2009. "Fast Lane Offers Financial Fast Fix." *Sarasota Herald Tribune*, January 10.

Dunn, B. Michael. 2007. "'Must Find the Defendant Guilty' Jury Instructions Violate the Sixth Amendment." *Judicature* 91: 12–19.

DuPont-Morales, M. A., Michael Hooper, and Judy H. Schmidt. *Handbook of Criminal Justice Administration.* Boca Raton, FL: CRC Press.

Dwyer, Jim, Peter Neufeld, and Barry Scheck. 2000. *Actual Innocence: Five Days to Execution and Other Dispatches from the Wrongly Convicted.* New York: Doubleday.

Dyke, Andrew. 2007. "Electoral Cycles in the Administration of Criminal Justice." *Public Choice* 133: 417–437.

Dysart, Katie. 2012. "Managing the CSI Effect in Jurors." Trial Evidence Committee, American Bar Association http://apps.americanbar.org/litigation/committees/trialevidence/articles/winterspring2012-0512-csi-effect-jurors.html

Dzienkowski, John, and Amon Burton. 2006. *Ethical Dilemmas in the Practice of Law.* St. Paul, MN: Thomson/West.

Earley, David W. 2013. When Bathtub Crocodiles Attack: The Timing and Propriety of Campaigning by Judicial Retention Election Candidates. *NYU Annual Survey of American Law* 68: 239–288.

Easton, Stephen D., and Kaitlin A. Bridges. 2008. "Peeking behind the Wizard's Curtain: Expert Discovery and Disclosure in Criminal Cases." *American Journal of Trial Advocacy* 32: 1–56.

Eavis, Petr, and Michael Corkery. 2014. "Bank of America's $16 Billion Mortgage Settlement Less Painful than it Looks." *New York Times*, August 21. Retrieved from http://dealbook.nytimes.com/2014/08/21/bank-of-america-reaches-16-65-billion-mortgage-settlement/?_php=true&_type=blogs&_r=0

Eckberg, Deborah A., and David Squier Jones. 2015. "I'll Just Do My Time: The Role of Motivation in the Rejection of the DWI Court Model." *The Qualitative Report* 20(1): 130–147.

Eckholm, Erik. 2008. "Public Defenders' Offices Refuse to Take New Cases." *New York Times*, November 9.

Eckholm, Erik. 2014. "Outside Spending Enters Arena of Judicial Races." *New York Times*, May 5. Retrieved from http://www.nytimes.com/2014/05/06/us/politics/outside-spending-transforms-supreme-court-election-in-north-carolina.html

Eisenberg, Theodore, Paula Hannaford-Agor, Valarie Hans, Nicole Mott, G. Thomas Munsterman, Stewart Schwab, and Martin Wells. 2004. "Judge-Jury Agreement in Criminal Cases: A Partial Replication of Kalven and Zeisel's *The American Jury.*" *Journal of Empirical Legal Studies* 2: 171–207.

Eisinger, Jesse. 2014, April 30. "Why Only One Top Banker Went to Jail for the Financial Crisis." *New York Times Magazine*, https://www.nytimes.com/2014/05/04/magazine/only-one-top-banker-jail-financial-crisis.html

Eisenstein, James. 1978. *Counsel for the United States: U.S. Attorneys in the Political and Legal System.* Baltimore: Johns Hopkins University Press.

Eisenstein, James, Roy Flemming, and Peter Nardulli. 1988. *The Contours of Justice: Communities and Their Courts.* Boston: Little, Brown.

Eisenstein, James, and Herbert Jacob. 1977. *Felony Justice: An Organizational Analysis of Criminal Courts.* Boston: Little, Brown.

Ekström, Veronica, and Peter Lindström. 2016. "In the Service of Justice: Will Social Support to Victims of Domestic Violence Increase Prosecution?" *International Review of Victimology* 22(3): 257–267.

Elek, Jennifer, David Rottman, and Brian Cutler. 2012. "Judicial Performance Evaluation: Steps to Improve Survey Process and Measurement." *Judicature* 96: 65–75.

Elek, Jennifer, David Rottman, and Brian Cutler. 2012. "Judicial Performance Evaluation in the States: A Re-Examination." *Judicature* 98: 12–19.

Elias, Paul. 2014. "Arizona Execution Renews Debate over Methods." *Associate Press*, July 26.

Elias, Robert. 1986. *The Politics of Victimization: Victims, Victimology and Human Rights.* New York: Oxford University Press.

Elias, Robert. 1993. *Victims Still: The Political Manipulation of Crime Victims.* Thousand Oaks, CA: Sage.

Elliott-Engel, Amaris. 2008. "Judge Charged with Misconduct after YouTube Video Shows Him Soliciting Campaign Funds." *The Legal Intelligencer*, June 20.

Ellis, Michael. 2012. "The Origins of the Elected Prosecutor." *Yale Law Journal* 121: 1528–1569.

Emmelman, Debra. 1996. "Trial by Plea Bargain: Case Settlement as a Product of Recursive Decision Making." *Law and Society Review* 30: 335–360.

Emmelman, Debra S. 2002. "Trial by Plea Bargain: Case Settlement as a Product of Recursive Decision-Making." In Mark Pogrebin (Ed.), *Qualitative Approaches to Criminal Justice* (pp. 219–236). Thousand Oaks, CA: Sage.

Emmert, Craig, and Henry Glick. 1987. "Selection Systems and Judicial Characteristics: The Recruitment of State Supreme Court Judges." *Judicature* 70: 228–235.

Emmert, Craig, and Carol Ann Traut. 1992. "State Supreme Courts, State Constitutions, and Judicial Policymaking." *Justice System Journal* 16: 37–48.

Englebrecht, Christine M. 2012. "Where Do I Stand?: An Exploration of the Rules That Regulate Victim Participation in the Criminal Justice System." *Victims and Offenders* 7: 161–184.

Engstrom, Richard. 1971. "Political Ambitions and the Prosecutorial Office." *Journal of Politics* 33: 190.

Engstrom, Richard. 1989. "When Blacks Run for Judge: Racial Divisions in the Candidate Preferences of Louisiana Voters." *Judicature* 73: 87–89.

Epstein, Lee, Charles M. Cameron, Jeffrey Segal, and Chad Westerland. 2006. "Lower Court Defiance of (Compliance with) the U.S. Supreme Court." Available online at http://ssrn.com/abstract=929018

Epstein, Lee, Jack Knight, and Olga Shvetsova. 2002. "Selecting Selection Systems." In Stephen B. Burbank and Barry Friedman (Eds.), *Judicial Independence at the Crossroads: An Interdisciplinary Approach*. Philadelphia: American Academy of Political and Social Science/Sage.

Epstein, Lee, Andrew D. Martin, Kevin M. Quinn, and Jeffrey A. Segal. 2008. "The Bush Imprint on the Supreme Court: Why Conservatives Should Continue to Yearn and Liberals Should Not Fear." *Tulsa Law Review* 43: 651–671.

Epstein, Robert A. 2015. "Trial Court Found to Have Denied Due Process Rights to Pro Se Litigant in Domestic Violence Matter." *NJ Family Legal Blog*, Aug, 27.

Eren, Colleen. 2015. "The Right Anti-Death Penalty Movement? Framing Abolitionism for the Twenty-First Century." *New Politics* 15(2): 95–100.

Erez, Edna. 1992. "Dangerous Men, Evil Women: Gender and Parole Decision-Making." *Justice Quarterly* 9: 105–126.

Erez, Edna. 2002. "Domestic Violence and the Criminal Justice System: An Overview." *The Online Journal of Issues in Nursing* 7(1), Manuscript 3. Available online at http://www.nursingworld.org/MainMenuCategories/ANAMarketplace/ANAPeriodicals/OJIN/TableofContents/Volume72002/No1Jan2002/DomesticViolenceandCriminalJustice.html

Erez, Edna, and Peter R. Ibarra. 2007. "Making Your Home a Shelter." *British Journal of Criminology* 47: 100–120.

Erez, Edna, and Julian Roberts. 2007. "Victim Participation in the Criminal Justice Systems." In Robert Carl Davis, Arthur J. Lurigio, and Susan Herman (Eds.), *Victims of Crime*. Thousand Oaks, CA: Sage.

Erez, Edna, and Linda Rogers. 1999. "Victim Impact Statements and Sentencing Outcomes and Processes. The Perspectives of Legal Professionals." *British Journal of Criminology*, 39(2): 216–239.

Ericson, J. 2014. April 30. "Botched Execution Shows Perils of Lethal Injection Drug Shortage." *Newsweek*. Retrieved from http://www.newsweek.com/2014/05/16/states-go-great-lengths-find-lethal-injection-drugs-249154.html

Esterling, Kevin M. 1998. "Judicial Accountability the Right Way." *Judicature* 82: 206–215.

Esqueda, Cynthia Willis, Russ K. E. Espinoza, and Scott E. Culhane. 2008. "The Effects of Ethnicity, SES, and Crime Status on Juror Decision Making: A Crosscultural Examination of European American and Mexican American Mock Jurors." *Hispanic Journal of Behavioral Sciences* 30(2): 181–199.

Everett, Burgess, and Seung Min Kim. 2015. April 20. "The Senate's 'Nuclear' Fallout: The GOP Slow-Walks Obama's Nominees in the Wake of Changes to Filibuster Rules." *Politico*. http://www.politico.com/story/2015/04/republican-senate-obama-nominees-117128.html

Ewin, Rob. 2015. "The Vulnerable and Intimidated Witness; a Socio-Legal Analysis of Special Measures." *Journal of Applied Psychology and Social Science* 1(2): 31–54.

Executive Office for Immigration Review. 2014a. *2013 Statistics Year Book*. Available online at http://www.justice.gov/eoir/statspub/fy13syb.pdf

Executive Office for Immigration Review. 2014b. *EOIR at a Glance*. Available online at http://www.justice.gov/eoir/eoir-at-a-glance

Fabian, John M. 2006. "State Supreme Court Responses to *Atkins v. Virginia*: Adaptive Functioning Assessment in Light of Purposeful Planning, Premeditation, and the Behavioral Context of the Homicide." *Journal of Forensic Psychology Practice* 6: 1–25.

Fader, Jamie, Philip Harris, Peter Jones, and Mary Poulin. 2001. "Factors Involved in Decisions on Commitment to Delinquency Programs for First-Time Juvenile Offenders." *Justice Quarterly* 18: 323–341.

Fagan, Jeffrey. 1996. *The Criminalization of Domestic Violence: Promises and Limits*. Washington, DC: National Institute of Justice.

Fairfax, Roger A., Jr. 2009. "Delegation of the Criminal Prosecution Function to Private Actors." *U.C. Davis Law Review* 43: 411–456.

Fang, Songying, Timothy R. Johnson, and Jason M. Roberts. 2007. "Will of the Minority: Rule of Four on the United States Supreme Court." (July 5, 2007) Available online at SSRN: http://papers.ssrn.com/sol3/papers.cfm?abstract_id=998492

Farifax, Roger A., Jr. 2015. "Thinking Outside the Jury Box: Deploying the Grand Jury in the Guilty Plea Process." *William & Mary Law Review* 57(4): 1395–1413.

Farole, Donald, and Lynn Langton. 2010. *County-based and Local Public Defender Offices, 2007*. Washington, DC: Department of Justice, Bureau of Justice Statistics.

Farrell, Amy, and Daniel Givelber. 2010. "Liberation Reconsidered: Understanding Why Judges and Juries Disagree about Guilt." *Journal of Criminal Law & Criminology* 100: 1549–1586.

Farrell, Brian R., and Sara K. Farrell. 2013. "Watching the Detectives: Electronic Recording of Custodial Interrogations in Iowa." *Iowa Law Review Bulletin* 99: 1–16.

Farrington, David P. 2006. "Family Background and Psychopathy." In C. J. Patrick (Ed.), *Handbook of Psychopathy* (pp. 229–250). New York: Guilford.

Fautsko, T. F. 2013. *Status of Court Security in State Courts: A National Perspective*. Williamsburg, VA: National Center for State Courts.

Fearn, Noelle. 2005. "A Multilevel Analysis of Community Effects on Criminal Sentencing." *Justice Quarterly* 22: 452–486.

Federal Bureau of Investigation. 2008. *Integrated Automated Fingerprint Identification System*. Available online at http://www.fbi.gov/hq/cjisd/iafis.htm.

Federal Bureau of Investigation. 2011. *Crime in the United States: 2010*. Washington, DC: Author. Available online at http://www.fbi.gov/aboutus/cjis/ucr/crimeintheu.s/2010/crimeintheu.s.2010.

Federal Bureau of Investigation. 2014. *Crime in the United States, 2013*, Table 29. Retrieved from http://www.fbi.gov/about-us/cjis/ucr/crime-in-the-u.s/2013/crime-in-the-u.s.-2013/tables/table-29/table_29_estimated_number_of_arrests_united_states_2013.xls

Federal Bureau of Investigation. 2015. *Crime in the United States: 2015*. Washington, DC: Author. Available online at https://ucr.fbi.gov/crime-in-the-u.s/2015/crime-in-the-u.s.-2015

Federal Bureau of Investigation. (2016, Sept. 20). "Comments on President's Council of Advisors on Science and Technology's Report to the President: Forensic Science in Criminal Courts: Ensuring Scientific Validity of Feature-Comparison Methods." Available online at https://www.fbi.gov/file-repository/fbi-pcast-response.pdf/view

Federal Bureau of Investigation. 2016. *Crime in the United States: 2015*. Washington, DC: Author. Available online at https://ucr.fbi.gov/crime-in-the-u.s/2016/preliminary-semiannual-uniform-crime-report-januaryjune-2016

Federal Judicial Center. *Caseload Statistics 2013*, Table D-2. Washington, DC: Administrative Office of the U.S. Courts.

Federal Judicial Center. 2012. *Caseload Statistics 2011*. Washington, DC: Administrative Office of the U.S. Courts.

Federal Judicial Center. 2017. *Judges of the United States Courts*. Available online at http://www.fjc.gov/

Feeley, Malcolm. 1979. *The Process Is the Punishment: Handling Cases in a Lower Criminal Court*. New York: Russell Sage Foundation.

Feeley, Malcolm, and Sam Kamin. 1996. "The Effect of 'Three Strikes and You're Out' on the Courts: Looking Back to See the Future." In David Shichor and Dale Sechrest (Eds.), *Three Strikes and You're Out: Vengeance as Public Policy*. Thousand Oaks, CA: Sage.

Feeley, Malcolm, and Edward Rubin. 1998. *Judicial Policy Making and the Modern State: How the Courts Reformed America's Prisons*. New York: Cambridge University Press.

Feeney, Floyd, Forrest Dill, and Adrianne Weir. 1983. *Arrests without Conviction: How Often They Occur and Why*. Washington, DC: Department of Justice, National Institute of Justice.

Feeney, Matthew. (2016). National Police Misconduct Reporting Project: Police Body Cameras. Washington, DC: The Cato Institute. https://www.policemisconduct.net/explainers/police-body-cameras

Feige, David. 2006. *Indefensible: One Lawyer's Journey into the Inferno of American Justice*. New York: Little, Brown.

Fein, Bruce. 1994. "Don't Play Criminals' Game." *USA Today*, April 15, p. 11.

Feld, Barry, and Shelly Schaefer. 2010. "The Right to Counsel in Juvenile Court: The Conundrum of Attorneys as an Aggravating Factor at Disposition." *Justice Quarterly* 27: 713–740.

Ferdico, John, Henry F. Fradella, and Christopher Totten. 2016. *Criminal Procedure for the Criminal Justice Professional*. 12th ed. Belmont, CA: Wadsworth.

Ferguson, Andrew Guthrie. 2015. "The Big Data Jury." *Notre Dame Law Review* 91(3): 935–1006.

Ferguson, Russ. 2011. "Cameras in the Courtroom." *The American Spectator*. July 19. Available online at https://spectator.org/37258_cameras-courtroom/

Ferrand, Casey. 2016 (March 30). "Lawsuit Claims New Orleans Traffic Cameras Illegal, Suing to Stop Program and Reclaim Money." *WDSU News*, http://www.wdsu.com/news/local-news/new-orleans/Lawsuit-claims-New-Orleans-traffic-cameras-illegal-suing-to-stop-program-and-reclaim-money/38776002

Fidell, Eugene R., Elizabeth Lutes Hillman, and Dwight Hall Sullivan. 2012. *Military Justice: Cases and Materials*. 2d ed. Cincinnati, OH: Lexis-Nexis.

Financial Express. 2010. "Rape Remains Underprosecuted in U.S. Agencies." September 15.

Findley, Keith, and Michael Scott. 2006. "The Multiple Dimensions of Tunnel Vision in Criminal Cases." *Wisconsin Law Review* 2006: 291–397.

Finn, Peter, and Beverley Lee. 1988. *Establishing and Expanding Victim–Witness Assistance Programs*. Washington, DC: National Institute of Justice.

Fino, Susan. 1987. *The Role of State Supreme Courts in the New Judicial Federalism*. Westport, CT: Greenwood.

Fischman, Joshua B., and Max M. Schanzenbach. 2012. "Racial Disparities under the Federal Sentencing Guidelines: The

Role of Judicial Discretion and Mandatory Minimums." *Journal of Empirical Legal Studies* 9: 729–764.

Fisher, George. 2003. *Plea Bargaining's Triumph: A History of Plea Bargaining in America*. Stanford, CA: Stanford University Press.

Fisher, Jim. 2008. *Forensics under Fire: Are Bad Science and Dueling Experts Corrupting Criminal Justice*. New Brunswick, NJ: Rutgers University Press.

Flanders, Chad. 2014. "Can Retributivism Be Saved?" *Brigham Young University Law Review* 2014: 309–362.

Flanders, Steven. 1991. "Court Administration and Diverse Judiciaries: Complementarities and Conflicts." *Justice System Journal* 15: 640–651.

Flango, Victor. 1994. "Court Unification and Quality of State Courts." *Justice System Journal* 16: 33–56.

Flango, Victor Eugene, and Craig Ducat. 1979. "What Differences Does Method of Judicial Selection Make? Selection Procedures in State Courts of Last Resort." *Justice System Journal* 5: 25–44.

Flanzer, Jerry. 2005. "The Status of Health Services Research on Adjudicated Drug-Abusing Juveniles: Selected Findings and Remaining Questions." *Substance Use and Misuse* 40: 887–911.

Flemming, Roy. 1986a. "Client Games: Defense Attorney Perspectives on Their Relations with Criminal Clients." *American Bar Foundation Research Journal* 253–277.

Flemming, Roy. 1986b. "Elements of the Defense Attorney's Craft: An Adaptive Expectations Model of the Preliminary Hearing Decision." *Law and Policy* 8: 33–57.

Flemming, Roy. 1989. "If You Pay the Piper, Do You Call the Tune? Public Defenders in America's Criminal Courts." *Law and Social Inquiry* 14: 393–405.

Flemming, Roy. 1990. "The Political Styles and Organizational Strategies of American Prosecutors: Examples from Nine Courthouse Communities." *Law and Policy* 12: 25.

Flemming, Roy, Peter Nardulli, and James Eisenstein. 1992. *The Craft of Justice: Politics and Work in Criminal Court Communities*. Philadelphia: University of Pennsylvania Press.

Flemming, Roy B., Peter F. Nardulli, and James Eisenstein. 1987. "The Timing of Justice in Felony Trial Courts." *Law & Policy* 9(2): 179–206.

Flowe, Heather D., Amrita Mehta, and Ebbe B. Ebbesen. 2011. "The Role of Eyewitness Identification Evidence in Felony Case Dispositions." *Psychology, Public Policy, and Law* 17: 140–159.

Fontecilla, Adrian. 2013. "The Ascendance of Social Media as Evidence." *Criminal Justice* 28(1): 55–57.

Ford, Marilyn. 1986. "The Role of Extralegal Factors in Jury Verdicts." *Justice System Journal* 11: 16–39.

Forst, Brian, J. Lucianovic, and S. Cox. 1977. *What Happens after Arrest? A Court Perspective of Police Operations in the District of Columbia*. Washington, DC: Law Enforcement Assistance Administration.

Fortune, William, and Penny White. 2008. "Judicial Campaign Oversight Committees' Complaint Handling in the 2006 Elections: Survey and Recommendations." *Judicature* 91: 232–237.

Fox, Bryanna Hahn, Nicholas Perez, Elizabeth Cass, Michael T. Baglivio, and Nathan Epps. 2015. "Trauma Changes Everything: Examining the Relationship Between Adverse Childhood Experiences and Serious, Violent, and Chronic Juvenile Offenders." *Child Abuse & Neglect* 46: 163–173.

Fox, James Alan, and Marianne W. Zawitz. 2007. *Homicide Trends in the United States*. Washington, DC: Bureau of Justice Statistics.

Fradella, Henry F. 1999. "In Search of Meritorious Claims: A Study of the Processing of Prisoner Civil Rights Cases in a Federal District Court." *Justice Systems Journal* 21: 23–55.

Fradella, Henry F. 2000. "Minimum Mandatory Sentences: Arizona's Ineffective Tool for the Social Control of DUI." *Criminal Justice Policy Review* 11: 113–135.

Fradella, Henry F. 2003. *Lawrence v. Texas*: Genuine or illusory progress for gay rights in America? *Criminal Law Bulletin* 39: 597–607.

Fradella, Henry F. 2004. "A Content Analysis of Federal Judicial Views of the Social Science 'Researcher's Black Arts.'" *Rutgers Law Journal* 35: 103–170.

Fradella, Henry F. 2007a. *Mental Illness and Criminal Defenses of Excuse in Contemporary American Law*. Bethesda, MD: Academica Press.

Fradella, Henry F. 2007b. "Why Judges Should Admit Expert Testimony on the Unreliability of Eyewitness Identifications." *Federal Courts Law Review* 2(1): 2–25.

Fradella, Henry F. 2013. "Thoughts on the *State v. Zimmerman* Verdict." *The Western Criminologist* (Fall): 5–8.

Fradella, Henry F., Ryan G. Fischer, Christine Kleinpeter, and Jeffrey Koob. 2009. "Latino Youth in the Juvenile Drug Court of Orange County, CA." *Journal of Ethnicity in Criminal Justice* 7: 271–292.

Frank, Mitchell J., and Dawn Broschard. 2006. "The Silent Criminal Defendant and the Presumption of Innocence: In the Hands of Real Jurors, Is Either of Them Safe?" *Lewis and Clark Law Review* 10: 237–285.

Frankel, Marvin E. 1972. *Criminal Sentences: Law without Order*. New York: Hill and Wang.

Franklin, Cortney A., and Noelle E. Fearn. 2008. "Gender, Race, and Formal Court Decision-Making Outcomes: Chivalry/Paternalism, Conflict Theory or Gender Conflict?" *Journal of Criminal Justice* 36: 279–290.

Franklin, Malcolm. 2008, Fall. "Ensuring the Personal Security of Judges." *California Courts Review*, 18–21. Available online at http://www.courts.ca.gov/documents/CCR_08fall.pdf

Franklin, Travis W. 2010. "The Intersection of Defendants' Race, Gender, and Age in Prosecutorial Decision Making." *Journal of Criminal Justice* 38(2): 185–192.

Franklin, Travis W. 2015. "Race and Ethnicity Effects in Federal Sentencing: A Propensity Score Analysis." *Justice Quarterly* 32(4): 653–679.

Frase, Richard S. 2005. "Punishment Purposes." *Stanford Law Review* 58: 67–83.

Freeman, Donald. 2007. "Drunk Driving Legislation and Traffic Fatalities: New Evidence on BAC 08 Laws." *Contemporary Economic Policy* 25: 293–310.

Freiburger, Tina L., and Carly M. Hilinski. 2011. "Probation Officers' Recommendations and Final Sentencing Outcomes." *Journal of Crime & Justice* 34(1): 45–61.

Freiburger, Tina L., and Carly M. Hilinski. 2013. "An Examination of the Interactions of Race and Gender on Sentencing Decisions Using a Trichotomous Dependent Variable." *Crime & Delinquency* 59(1): 59–86.

Friedenthal, Jack H., Mary Kay Kane, and Arthur R. Miller. 2015. *Civil Procedure, Hornbook Series*. 5th ed. Eagan, MN: West.

Friedman, Barry. 1998. "Attacks on Judges: Why They Fail." *Judicature* 81: 150–156.

Friedman, Lawrence. 1979. "Plea Bargaining in Historical Perspective." *Law and Society Review* 13: 247–259.

Friedman, Lawrence. 1984. *American Law: An Introduction*. New York: Norton.

Friedman, Lawrence. 2000. "The Constitutional Value of Dialogue and the New Judicial Federalism." *Hastings Constitutional Law Quarterly* 28: 93–144.

Friedman, Lawrence, and Robert Percival. 1976. "A Tale of Two Courts: Litigation in Alameda and San Benito Counties." *Law and Society Review* 10: 267–302.

Friedrichs, David. 2006. *Law in Our Lives: An Introduction*. 2nd ed. Los Angeles, CA: Roxbury.

Friedrichs, David. 2009. *Trusted Criminals: White Collar Crime in Contemporary Society*. Belmont, CA: Wadsworth.

Frohmann, Lisa. 1997. "Convictability and Discordant Locales: Reproducing Race, Class, and Gender Ideologies in Prosecutorial Decision-Making." *Law and Society Review* 31: 531–556.

Fukurai, Hiroshi, Edgar Butler, and Richard Krooth. 1991. "Cross-Sectional Jury Representation or Systematic Jury Representation? Simple Random and Cluster Sampling Strategies in Jury Selection." *Journal of Criminal Justice* 19: 31–48.

Fulkerson, Andrew, and Michael Suttmoeller. 2008. "Current Issues Involving Lethal Injection." *Criminal Justice Studies* 21: 271–282.

Fyfe, James. 1982. "In Search of the 'Bad Faith' Search." *Criminal Law Bulletin* 18: 260–265.

Gabel, Jessica D., and Margaret D. Wilkinson. 2008. "'Good' Science Gone Bad: How the Criminal Justice System Can Redress the Impact of Flawed Forensics." *Hastings Law Journal* 59: 1001–1030.

Gable, Ralph Kirkland, and Robert S. Gable. 2005. "Electronic Monitoring: Positive Intervention Strategies." *Federal Probation* 69(1): 21–25.

Gabriel, Trip. 2014. "Former Governor in Virginia Guilty in Bribery Case." *New York Times*, September 14.

Gainey, Randy R., and Brian K. Payne. 2000. "Understanding the Experience of House Arrest with Electronic Monitoring: An Analysis of Quantitative and Qualitative Data." *International Journal of Offender Therapy and Comparative Criminology* 44(1): 84–96.

Gainey, Randy R., Sara Steen, and Rodney L. Engen. 2005. "Exercising Options: An Assessment of the Use of Alternative Sanctions for Drug Offenders." *Justice Quarterly* 22: 488–520.

Galanter, Marc. 1988. "The Life and Times of the Big Six: or, The Federal Courts since the Good Old Days." Working Paper 9:2. Madison: University of Wisconsin, Institute for Legal Studies.

Galaway, Burt. 1988. "Restitution as Innovation or Unfilled Promise?" *Federal Probation* 52: 3–14.

Galaway, Burt, and Joe Hudson (Eds.). 1996. *Restorative Justice: International Perspectives*. Monsey, NY: Criminal Justice Press.

Galiber, Joseph, Barry Latzer, Mark Dwyer, Jack Litman, H. Richard Uviller, and G. Roger McDonald. 1993. "Law, Justice, and Jury Nullification: A Debate." *Criminal Law Bulletin* 29: 40–69.

Galie, Peter. 1987. "State Supreme Courts, Judicial Federalism and the Other Constitutions." *Judicature* 71: 100–110.

Gallagher, John R., Anne Nordberg, and Teneisha Kennard. 2015. "A Qualitative Study Assessing the Effectiveness of the Key Components of a Drug Court." *Alcoholism Treatment Quarterly* 33: 64–81.

Gallas, Geoff. 1976. "The Conventional Wisdom of State Court Administration: A Critical Assessment and an Alternative Approach." *Justice System Journal* 2: 35.

Gardiner, John. 1986. "Preventing Judicial Misconduct: Defining the Role of Conduct Organizations." *Judicature* 70: 113–121.

Gardner, Amy, and Matt DeLong. 2011. "Newt Gingrich's Assault on 'Activist Judges' Draws Criticism, Even from the Right." *Washington Post*, December 18.

Garner, Joel. 1987. "Delay Reduction in the Federal Courts: Rule 50(b) and the Federal Speedy Trial Act of 1974." *Journal of Quantitative Criminology* 3: 229–250.

Garrett, Brandon L. 2008. "Judging Innocence." *Columbia Law Review* 108: 55–142.

Garrett, Brandon L., and Peter J. Neufeld. 2009. "Invalid Forensic Science Testimony and Wrongful Convictions." *Virginia Law Review* 95: 1–97.

Garrow, David J. 2008. "Bad Behavior Makes Big Law: Southern Malfeasance and the Expansion of Federal Judicial Power, 1954–1968." *Saint John's Law Review* 82: 1–38.

Garvey, Stephen P., Paula Hannaford-Agor, Valerie P. Hans, Nicole L. Mott, G. Thomas Munsterman, and Martin T. Wells. 2004. "Juror First Votes in Criminal Trials in Four Major Metropolitan Jurisdictions." *Journal of Empirical Legal Studies* 1: 371–398.

Garvin, Glenn. 2011. "Casey Anthony's Acquittal Prompts Critics to Blame the Media." *Miami Herald*, July 7.

Gastil, John, Laura W. Black, E. Pierre Deess, and Jay Leighter. 2008. "From Group Member to Democratic Citizen: How Deliberating with Fellow Jurors Reshapes Civic Attitudes." *Human Communication Research* 34: 137–169.

Gendreau, P., C. Goggin, F. T. Cullen, and D. A. Andrews. 2000. "The Effects of Community Sanctions and Incarceration on Recidivism." *Forum on Corrections Research* 12(2): 10–13.

Gendreau, Paul, Claire Goggin, and Betsy Fulton. 2000. "Intensive Supervision in Probation and Parole." In Clive R. Hollin (Ed.), *Handbook of Offender Assessment and Treatment* (pp. 195–204). Chichester, UK: John Wiley.

George, Tracey E., and Albert H. Yoon. 2016. *The Gavel Gap: Who Sits in Judgment on State Courts?* American Constitution Society for Law and Policy. Available online at http://gavelgap.org/pdf/gavel-gap-report.pdf

Georgetown Law Journal. 2007. "The Judicial Nomination Process Over Time: Some Historic Background." *Georgetown Law Journal* 95: 1028–1039.

Gerber, Monica, and Jonathan Jackson. 2013. "Retribution as Revenge and Retribution as Just Deserts." *Social Justice Research* 26: 61–80.

Gerhardt, Michael J., and Michael Ashley Stein. 2014. "The Politics of Early Justice: Federal Judicial Selection, 1789–1861." *Iowa Law Review* 100(2): 551–615.

Gershel, Alan M. 2010. "A Review of the Law in Jurisdictions Requiring Electronic Recording of Custodial Interrogations." *Richmond Journal of Law & Technology* 16(3), art. 9, 1–43. Retrieved from http://jolt.richmond.edu/v16i3/article9.pdf

Gershman, Bennett L. 2011. "Prosecutorial Decisionmaking and Discretion in the Charging Decision." *Hastings Law Journal* 62: 1259–1283.

Gershman, Bennett L. 2013. "Overcharging George Zimmerman with Murder." *Huffington Post: The Blog*, July 1 Available online at http://www.huffingtonpost.com/bennett-l-gershman/george-zimmerman-charges_b_3529636.html

Gest, Ted. 1996. "The Law That Grief Built." *U.S. News & World Report*, April 29, p. 58.

Geyh, Charles Gardner. 2012. "Judicial Selection Reconsidered: A Plea for Radical Moderation." *Harvard Journal of Law & Public Policy* 35(3): 623–642.

Ghianni, Tim. 2014. "Tennessee Judge Who Ordered Name Change for Baby Messiah Fired." *Reuters: U.S. Edition*, Feb. 4. Available online at http://www.reuters.com/article/2014/02/04/us-usa-tennessee-judge-idUSBREA131UE20140204

Giannelli, Paul C. 2007. "Wrongful Convictions and Forensic Science: The Need to Regulate Crime Labs." *North Carolina Law Review* 86: 163–235.

Giannelli, Paul C. 2011. "Daubert and Forensic Science: The Pitfalls of Law Enforcement Control of Scientific Research." *University of Illinois Law Review* 2011: 53–90.

Gibson, James L. 1983. "From Simplicity to Complexity: The Development of Theory in the Study of Judicial Behavior." *Political Behavior* 5: 7–50.

Gibson, James L. 2012. *Electing Judges: The Surprising Effects of Campaigning on Judicial Legitimacy*. Chicago: University of Chicago Press.

Gilboy, Janet. 1984. "Prosecutors' Discretionary Use of the Grand Jury to Initiate or to Reinitiate Prosecution." *American Bar Foundation Research Journal* 1–81.

Gill, Rebecca D., Sylvia R. Lazos, and Mallory M. Waters. 2011. "Are Judicial Performance Evaluations Fair to Women and Minorities? A Cautionary Tale from Clark County, Nevada." *Law & Society Review* 45(3): 731–759.

Gillespie, Robert. 1988–1989. "Criminal Fines: Do They Pay?" *Justice System Journal* 13: 365–378.

Gilmore, Amna Saddick, Nancy Rodriguez, and Vincent J. Webb. 2005. "Substance Abuse and Drug Courts: The Role of Social Bonds in Juvenile Drug Courts." *Youth Violence and Juvenile Justice* 3: 287–315.

Givelber, Daniel, and Amy Farrell. 2008. "Judges and Juries: The Defense Case and Differences in Acquittal Rates." *Law and Social Inquiry* 33: 31–52.

Glaberson, William. 2006. "In Tiny Courts of N.Y., Abuses of Law and Power." *New York Times*, September 25.

Glater, Jonathan, and Ken Belson. 2005. "In White-Collar Crimes, Few Smoking Guns." *New York Times*, March 12.

Glaze, Lauren E., and Erinn J. Herberman. 2013. *Correctional Population of the United States, 2012*. Washington, DC: Department of Justice, Bureau of Justice Statistics.

Gleicher, Lily, Sarah Manchak, and Francis Cullen, 2013. "Creating a Supervision Tool Kit: How to Improve Probation and Parole." *Federal Probation* 77: 1–8.

Glick, Henry, and Kenneth Vines. 1973. *State Court Systems*. Englewood Cliffs, NJ: Prentice Hall.

Global Courts. 2012. "Electronic Courtrooms." Formerly available online at http://www.globalcourts.com/text /e_courtrooms.html

Go Directly to Jail: White Collar Sentencing after the Sarbanes–Oxley Act. 2009. *Harvard Law Review* 122: 1728.

Gobert, James J. 1988. "In Search of the Impartial Jury." *Journal of Criminal Law and Criminology* 79: 269–327.

Goehner, Amy, Lina Lofaro, and Kate Novack. 2004. "Where *CSI* Meets Real Law and Order." *Time*, November 8, p. 69.

Goelzhauser, Greg. 2013. "Prosecutorial Discretion under Resource Constraints: Budget Allocations and Local Death-Charging Decisions." *Judicature* 96: 161–168.

Goelzhauser, Greg, and Damon M. Cann. 2014. Judicial Independence and Opinion Clarity on State Supreme Courts. *States, Politics, and Policy Quarterly* 14(2): 123–141.

Goffman, Ervin. 1961. *Asylums: Essays on the Social Situation of Mental Patients and Other Inmates*. Garden City, NY: Anchor.

Goldberg, Deborah, Craig Holman, and Samantha Sanchez. 2002. "The New Politics of Judicial Elections." Available online at http://www.justiceatstake.org/files /JASMoneyReport.pdf.

Goldberg, Stephen, Frank Sander, Nancy Rogers, and Sarah Cole. 2012. *Dispute Resolution: Negotiation, Mediation, and Other Processes*. 6th ed. New York: Aspen.

Goldfarb, Sally F. 2008. "Reconceiving Civil Protection Orders for Domestic Violence: Can Law Help End the Abuse Without Ending the Relationship?" *Cardozo Law Review* 29: 1487–1551.

Goldkamp, John. 1980. "The Effects of Detention on Judicial Decisions: A Closer Look." *Justice System Journal* 5: 234–257.

Goldkamp, John. 2002. "The Importance of Drug Courts: Lessons from Measuring Impact." Paper presented at the American Society of Criminology, Chicago.

Goldkamp, John, Cheryl Irons-Guynn, and Doris Weiland. 2002. *Community Prosecution Strategies: Measuring Impact*. Washington, DC: Bureau of Justice Assistance.

Goldkamp, John, and Doris Weiland. 1993. "Assessing the Impact of Dade County's Felony Drug Court." *National Institute of Justice Research in Brief*. Washington, DC: Department of Justice.

Goldkamp, J. S., M. D. White, and J.B. Robinson. 2001. "Do Drug Courts Work? Getting Inside the Drug Court Black Box." *Journal of Drug Issues* 31(1): 27–72.

Goldman, Sheldon. 1997. *Picking Federal Judges: Lower Court Selection from Roosevelt through Reagan*. New Haven, CT: Yale University Press.

Goldman, Sheldon, and Matthew Saronson. 1994. "Clinton's Nontraditional Judges: Creating a More Representative Bench." *Judicature* 78: 68–73.

Goldman, Sheldon, and Elliot Slotnick. 1999. "Clinton's Second Term Judiciary: Picking Judges under Fire." *Judicature* 82: 264–285.

Goldman, Sheldon, Elliot Slotnick, Gerard Gryski, and Sara Schiavoni. 2007. "Picking Judges in a Time of Turmoil: W. Bush's Judiciary during the 109th Congress. *Judicature* 90: 252–283.

Goldman, Sheldon, Elliot Slotnick, and Sara Schiavoni. 2011. "The Confirmation Drama Continues." *Judicature* 94: 262–303.

Goldman, Sheldon, Elliot Slotnick, and Sara Schiavoni. 2013. "Obama's First Term Judiciary: Picking Judges in the Minefield of Obstruction." *Judicature* 97: 7–47.

Goldschmidt, Jona, David Olson, and Margaret Ekman. 2009. "The Relationship between Method of Judicial Selection and Judicial Misconduct." *Widener Law Journal* 18: 455–481.

Gondolf, Edward. 2012. *The Future of Batterer Programs: Reassessing Evidence-Based Practice*. Boston: Northeastern University Press.

Goodman-Delahunty, Jane, Lynee Forster Lee, and Robert Forster Lee. 2007. "Dealing with Guilty Offenders." In Neil Brewer and Kipling Williams (Eds.), *Psychology and the Law: An Empirical Perspective*. New York: Guilford Press.

Gordon, Corey, and William Brill. 1996. *The Expanding Role of Crime Prevention through Environmental Design in Premises Liability*. Washington, DC: National Institute of Justice.

Gorman, Sean. 2009. "Bedford Judge Admonished for Doling Out Excessive Traffic Fines." *LoHud.com* (New York's Lower Hudson Valley), July 30.

Gottfredson, Denise, Stacy Najaka, and Brook Kearley. 2003. "Effectiveness of Drug Treatment Courts: Evidence from a Randomized Trial." *Criminology and Public Policy* 2: 171–196.

Gottfredson, Michael R., and Don M. Gottfredson. 1988. *Decision Making in Criminal Justice: Toward the Rational Exercise of Discretion*. New York: Plenum.

Gottschalk, Marie. 2009. "The Long Reach of the Carceral State: The Politics of Crime, Mass Imprisonment, and Penal Reform in the United States and Abroad." *Law and Social Inquiry* 34: 439–472.

Gottsfield, Robert L., and Marianne Alcorn. 2009. "The Capital Case Crisis in Maricopa County: What (Little) We Can Do about It." *Arizona Attorney* 45: 22–30.

Gould, Jon. 2008. "Justice Delayed or Justice Denied? A Contemporary Review of Capital Habeas Corpus." *Justice System Journal* 29: 273–287.

Gould, Jon, and Stephen Mastrofski. 2004. "Suspect Searches: Assessing Police Behavior under the U.S. Constitution." *Criminology and Public Policy* 3: 315–362.

Gould, Jon B., and Richard A. Leo. 2010. "One Hundred Years Later: Wrongful Convictions After a Century of Research." *Journal of Criminal Law and Criminology* 100: 825–868.

Gouldin, Lauryn P. 2016. "Disentangling Flight Risk from Dangerousness." *Brigham Young University Law Review* 2016: 837–898.

Gourevitch, Philip. 2001. "The Crime Lover." *The New Yorker*, February 19, pp. 160–173.

Gover, Angela, John MacDonald, and Geoffrey Alpert. 2003. "Combating Domestic Violence: Findings from an Evaluation of a Local Domestic Violence Court." *Criminology and Public Policy* 3: 109–132.

Graham, Barbara Luck. 1990. "Do Judicial Selection Systems Matter? A Study of Black Representation on State Courts." *American Politics Quarterly* 18: 316–336.

Graham, Kyle. 2012. "Crimes, Widgets, and Plea Bargaining: An Analysis of Charge, Content, Pleas, and Trials." *California Law Review* 100(6): 1573–1630.

Grant, Nicole P. 2012. "Mean Girls and Boys: The Intersection of Cyberbullying and Privacy Law and Its Social-Political Implications." *Howard Law Journal* 56: 169–206.

Gray, Cynthia. 2003. "State Supreme Courts Play Key Role in Judicial Discipline." *Judicature* 86: 267–268.

Gray, Cynthia. 2007. "How Judicial Conduct Commissions Work." *The Justice System Journal* 28: 405–418.

Green, Bruce A. 2012. "The Community Prosecutor: Questions of Professional Discretion." *Wake Forest Law Review* 47(285): 12–14.

Greenhouse, Linda. 2004. "Death Sentence Overturned in Texas." *New York Times*, February 25.

Greenwood, Peter, C. Peter Rydell, Allan Abrahamse, Jonathan Caulkins, James Chiesa, Karyn Model, and Stephen Klein. 1996. "Estimated Benefits and Costs of California's New Mandatory Sentencing Law." In David Shichor and Dale Sechrest (Eds.), *Three Strikes and You're Out: Vengeance as Public Policy*. Thousand Oaks, CA: Sage.

Gresko, Jennifer. 2011. "New Crack Cocaine Sentencing Guidelines May Apply to Old Cases." *Huffington Post*, May 31.

Griffin, Patrick, Sean Addie, Benjamin Adams, and Kathy Firestine. 2011. "Trying Juveniles as Adults: An Analysis of State Transfer Laws and Reporting." Washington, DC: Department of Justice, Office of Juvenile Justice and Delinquency Prevention.

Griffin, Timothy, and John Wooldredge. 2006. "Sex-Based Disparities in Felony Dispositions before versus after Sentencing Reform in Ohio." *Criminology* 44: 893–923.

Grinberg, Emanuella, and Catherine E. Shoichet. 2016, September 2. "Brock Turner Released from Jail After Serving 3 Months for Sexual Assault." *CNN.com*, http://www.cnn.com/2016/09/02/us/brock-turner-release-jail/

Griset, Pamala. 1995. "Determinate Sentencing and Agenda Building: A Case Study of the Failure of a Reform." *Journal of Criminal Justice* 23: 349–362.

Grisham, John. 2008. *The Appeal*. New York: Doubleday.

Grisso, Thomas. 1981. *Juveniles' Waiver of Rights*. New York: Plenum.

Gross, John P. 2013. "Rationing Justice: The Underfunding of Assigned Counsel Systems: A 50-State Survey of Trial Court Assigned Counsel Rates." In John P. Gross (Ed.), *Gideon at 50: A Three-Part Examination of Indigent Defense in America*. Washington, DC: National Association of Criminal Defense Lawyers.

Gross, Samuel R., Kristen Jacoby, Daniel J. Matheson, Nicholas Montgomery, and Sujata Patil. 2005. Exonerations in the United States 1989 through 2003." *Journal of Criminal Law and Criminology* 95: 523–560.

Gross, Samuel R., and Barbara O'Brien. 2008. "Frequency and Predictors of False Conviction: Why We Know So Little, and New Data on Capital Cases." *Journal of Empirical Legal Studies* 5(4): 927–962.

Gross, Samuel R., Barbara O'Brien, Chen Hu, and Edward H. Kennedy. 2014. "Rate of False Conviction of Criminal Defendants Who Are Sentenced to Death." *Proceedings of the National Academy of Sciences* 111(20): 7230–7235.

Grubb, Amy Rose, and Julie Harrower. 2009. "Understanding Attribution of Blame in Cases of Rape: An Analysis of Participant Gender, Type of Rape and Perceived Similarity to the Victim." *Journal of Sexual Aggression* 15(1): 63–81.

Gruhl, John. 1981. "State Supreme Courts and the U.S. Supreme Court's Post-*Miranda* Rulings." *Journal of Criminal Law and Criminology* 72: 886–913.

Gryski, Gerard S., Eleanor C. Main, and William J. Dixon. 1986 "Models of State High Court Decision Making in Sex Discrimination Cases." *Journal of Politics* 48: 143–155.

Guevara, Lori, Denis Herz, and Cassia Spohn. 2008. "Race, Gender, and Legal Counsel: Differential Outcomes in Two Juvenile Courts." *Youth Violence and Juvenile Justice* 6: 83–104.

Gupta, Sanjay. 2011. "Rx Drug Deaths Triple in Decade." *The Chart*, November 1. Available online at http://thechart.blogs.cnn.com/2011/11/01/40-die-daily-in-rx-drug-epidemic-cdc-says/?iref=allsearch

Gusfield, Joseph. 1981. *The Culture of Public Problems: Drinking-Driving and the Symbolic Order*. Chicago: University of Chicago Press.

Guthrie, C., J. J. Rachlinski, and A. J. Wistrich. 2007. "Blinking on the Bench: How Judges Decide Cases." *Cornell Law Review* 93: 1–43.

Guzik, Keith. 2007. "The Forces of Conviction: The Power and Practice of Mandatory Prosecution upon Misdemeanor Domestic Battery Suspects." *Law and Social Inquiry* 32: 41–74.

Haapanen, Rudy. 1989. *Selective Incapacitation and the Serious Offender: A Longitudinal Study of Criminal Career Patterns*. New York: Springer.

Haber, Lyn, and Ralph Normal Haber. 2008. "Scientific Validation of Fingerprint Evidence under *Daubert*." *Law, Probability & Risk* 7: 87–109.

Hagan, John. 1974. "Extra-Legal Attributes and Criminal Sentencing: An Assessment of a Sociological Viewpoint." *Law and Society Review* 8: 357–381.

Hagan, John. 1977. "Criminal Justice in Rural and Urban Communities: A Study of the Bureaucratization of Justice." *Social Forces* 55: 597–612.

Hagan, John. 1983. *Victims before the Law: The Organizational Domination of Criminal Law*. Toronto: Butterworth's.

Haggård, Ulrika, Ingrid Freij, Maria Danielsson, Diana Wenander, and Niklas Långström. 2015. "Effectiveness of the IDAP Treatment Program for Male Perpetrators of Intimate Partner Violence: A Controlled Study of Criminal Recidivism." *Journal of Interpersonal Violence*: 1–17.

Hagstrom, Anna M. 2009. "*Atkins v. Virginia*: An Empty Holding Devoid of Justice for the Mentally Retarded." *Law and Inequality: A Journal of Theory and Practice* 27: 241–276.

Haire, Susan, Barry Edwards, and David Hughes. 2013. "Presidents and Courts of Appeals: The Voting Behavior of Obama's Appointees." *Judicature* 97: 137–143.

Hakim, Simon, George Rengert, and Yochanan Shachmurove. 1996. "Estimation of Net Social Benefits of Electronic Security." *Justice Quarterly* 13: 153–170.

Halbringer, David, and Beth Kormanik. 2012. "In Digital Record, Jurors Say, They Found Reasons to Convict." *New York Times*, March 17.

Hall, Jerome. 1952. *Theft, Law and Society*. Indianapolis: Bobbs-Merrill.

Hall, Melinda. 2014. *Attacking Judges: How Campaigning Advertising Influences State Supreme Court Elections*. Stanford, CA: Stanford University Press.

Haller, Mark. 1979. "Plea Bargaining: The Nineteenth-Century Context." *Law and Society Review* 13: 273–280.

Hallinan, Joe. 1993. "Violent Children Straining Limit of Justice System." *Times-Picayune*, October 31, p. A24.

Hamblett, Mark. 2012. "Summit Participants Discuss Efforts to Find Competent Lawyers for Poor N.Y. Immigrants." *New York Law Journal*, January 30.

Hamburg, Daniel. 2015. "A Broken Clock: Fixing New York's Speedy Trial Statute." *Columbia Journal of Law and Social Problems* 48: 223–264.

Hamilton, Mykol C., and Kate Zephyrhawke. 2015. "Revealing Juror Bias Without Biasing Your Juror: Experimental Evidence for Best Practice Survey and Voir Dire Questions." *The Jury Expert* 27(4): 1–7.

Haney, Craig. 1984. "On the Selection of Capital Juries: The Biasing Effects of the Death-Qualification Process." *Law and Human Behavior* 8: 121–132.

Haney, Craig. 2005. *Death by Design: Capital Punishment as a Social Psychological System*. New York: Oxford University Press.

Hannaford, Paula L. 2001. "Safeguarding Juror Privacy: A New Framework for Court Policies and Procedures." *Judicature* 85: 18–25.

Hannaford, Paula, Valerie Hans, and G. Thomas Munsterman. 1999. "How Much Justice Hangs in the Balance? A New Look at Hung Jury Rates." *Judicature* 83: 59–67.

Hannaford-Agor, Paula L., Valerie P. Hans, Nicole L. Mott, and G. Thomas Munsterman. 2002. *Are Hung Juries a Problem?* Washington, DC: The National Center for State Courts.

Hanson, Roger, and Henry Daley. 1995. *Challenging the Conditions of Prisons and Jails*. Washington, DC: Department of Justice, Bureau of Justice Statistics.

Hanson, Roger, William Hewitt, and Brian Ostrom. 1992. "Are the Critics of Indigent Defense Counsel Correct?" *State Court Journal* (Summer): 20–29.

Hare, Sara C. 2006. "What Do Battered Women Want? Victims' Opinions on Prosecution." *Violence and Victims* 21: 611–628.

Hargovan, Hema. 2015. "Violence, Victimization and Parole: Reconciling Restorative Justice and Victim Participation." *SA Crime Quarterly* 54: 55–64

Harlow, Caroline. 1999. *Prior Abuse Reported by Inmates and Probationers*. NCJ 172879. Washington, DC: Department of Justice, Office of Justice Programs.

Harrell, Adele, Shannon Cavanagh, and John Roman. 2000. *Evaluation of the D.C. Superior Court Drug Intervention Programs*. Washington, DC: National Institute of Justice.

Harris, David. 2011. "The Interaction and Relationship between Prosecutors and Police Officers in the U.S., and How This Affects Police Reform Efforts." In Erik Luna and Marianne Wad (Eds.), *The Prosecutor in Transnational Perspective*. New York: Oxford University Press.

Harris, John, and Paul Jesilow. 2000. "It's Not the Old Ball Game: Three Strikes and the Courtroom Workgroup." *Justice Quarterly* 17: 185–204.

Hashimoto, Erica. 2007. "Defending the Right to Self-Representation: An Empirical Look at the Pro Se Felony Defendant." *North Carolina Law Review* 85: 423–487.

Hashimoto, Erica. 2008. "Toward Ethical Plea Bargaining." *Cardozo Law Review* 30: 949–963.

Hashimoto, Erica J. 2013. *Assessing the Indigent Defense System*. Washington, DC: The American Constitution Society for Law and Policy.

Hashimoto, Erica J. 2015. "Protecting the Constitutional Right to Counsel for Indigents Charged with Misdemeanors—Testimony of Erica J. Hashimoto before the U.S. Senate." *Presentations and Speeches* 37. Available online at http://digitalcommons.law.uga.edu/fac_presp/37

Hastie, Reid, Steven Penrod, and Nancy Pennington. 1984. *Inside the Jury*. Cambridge, MA: Harvard University Press.

Hastings, Deborah. 2009. "Money May Decide Execution Debate." Associated Press, March 8.

Hartley, Richard, Holly Miller, and Cassia Spohn. 2010. "Do You Get What You Pay for? Type of Counsel and Its Effect on Criminal Court Outcomes." *Journal of Criminal Justice* 38: 1063–1070.

Hawkins, Nikki. 2010. "Perspectives on Civil Protective Orders in a Domestic Violence Cases: The Rural and Urban Divide." *NIJ Journal* 266: 4–8.

Hayes-Smith, Rebecca M., and Lora M. Levett. 2013. "The Jury's Still Out: How Television and Crime Show Viewing Influences Jurors' Evaluation of Evidence." *Applied Psychology in Criminal Justice* 7(1): 29–46.

Haynes, Stacy Hoskins, Barry Ruback, and Gretchen Ruth Cusick. 2010. "Courtroom Workgroups and Sentencing: The Effects of Similarity, Proximity, and Stabilty." *Crime & Delinquency* 56(1): 126–161.

Haynie, Dana, Harald Weiss, and Alex Piquero. 2008. "Race, the Economic Maturity Gap, and Criminal Offending in Young Childhood." *Justice Quarterly* 25: 595–622.

Healey, Kerry. 1995. *Victim and Witness Intimidation: New Developments and Emerging Responses*. Washington, DC: National Institute of Justice.

Health, Brad and Kevin McCoy. 2010, Sept. 23. "Prosecutors' Conduct Can Tip Justice Scales." *USA Today*, http://usatoday30.usatoday.com/news/washington/judicial/2010-09-22-federal-prosecutors-reform_N.htm

Heflin, Howell. 1987. "The Impeachment Process: Modernizing an Archaic System." *Judicature* 71: 123–125.

Hegreness, Matthew J. 2013. "America's Fundamental and Vanishing Right to Bail." *Arizona Law Review* 55: 909–969.

Heinz, John, and Edward Laumann. 1982. *Chicago Lawyers: The Social Structure of the Bar*. New York: Russell Sage Foundation.

Heinz, John, Robert Nelson, Rebecca Sandefur, and Edward Laumann. 2005. *Urban Lawyers: The New Social Structure of the Bar*. Chicago: University of Chicago Press.

Helland, Eric, and Alexander Tabarrok. 2002. "The Effect of Electoral Institutions on Tort Awards." *American Law and Economics Review* 4: 341–370.

Helland, Eric, and Alexander Tabarrok. 2004. "The Fugitive: Evidence on Public Versus Private Law Enforcement from Bail Jumping." *Journal of Law and Economics* 47: 93–122.

Heller, Kevin Jon. 2006. "The Cognitive Psychology of Circumstantial Evidence." *Michigan Law Review* 105: 241–305.

Hellman, Arthur D. 2006. "The View from the Trenches: A Report on the Breakout Sessions at the 2005 National Conference on Appellate Justice." *Journal of Appellate Practice and Process* 8(1): 141–205.

Helms, Ronald, and David Jacobs. 2002. "The Political Context of Sentencing: An Analysis of Community and Individual Determinants." *Social Forces* 81: 577–604.

Hemmens, Craig, Kristin Strom, and Elicia Schlegel. 1997. "Gender Bias in the Courts: A Review of the Literature." Paper presented at the Academy of Criminal Justice Sciences, Louisville, KY.

Henggler, Scott W., Michael R. McCart, Phillippe B. Cunningham, and Jason E. Chapman. 2012. "Enhancing the Effectiveness of Juvenile Drug Courts by Integrating Evidence-Base Practices." *Journal of Consulting and Clinical Psychology* 80(2): 264–275.

Henning, Peter J. 2015. "Is Deterrence Relevant in Sentencing White-Collar Criminals?" *Wayne Law Review* 61(1): 27–59.

Henrichson, Christian, and Ruth Delaney. 2012. *The Price of Prisons: What Incarceration Costs Taxpayers*. New York: Vera Institute of Justice.

Herinckx Heidi A., Sandra C. Swart, Shane M. Ama, Cheri D. Dolezal, and Steve King. 2005. "Rearrest and Linkage to Mental Health Services among Defendants of the Clark County Mental Health Court Program." *Psychiatric Services* 56(7): 853–857.

Herman, Susan N., and Erwin Chemerinsky. 2006. *The Right to a Speedy and Public Trial: A Reference Guide to the United States Constitution*. Westport, CT: Greenwood.

Heumann, Milton. 1975. "A Note on Plea Bargaining and Case Pressure." *Law and Society Review* 9: 515–528.

Heumann, Milton. 1978. *Plea Bargaining: The Experience of Prosecutors, Judges, and Defense Attorneys*. Chicago: University of Chicago Press.

Heumann, Milton, and Colin Loftin. 1979. "Mandatory Sentencing and the Abolition of Plea Bargaining: The Michigan Felony Firearm Statute." *Law and Society Review* 13: 393–430.

Hiday, Virginia Aldige, Bradley Ray, and Heathcote Wales. 2015. "Longer-Term Impacts of Mental Health Courts: Recidivism Two Years After Exit." *Psychiatric Services* 67(4): 378–383.

Higgins, George E., Melissa L. Ricketts, James D. Griffith, and Stephanie A. Jirard. 2013. "Race and Juvenile Incarceration: A Propensity Score Matching Examination." *American Journal of Criminal Justice* 38(1): 1–12.

Hillsman, Sally, and Barry Mahoney. 1988. "Collecting and Enforcing Criminal Fines: A Review of Court Processes, Practices, and Problems." *Justice System Journal* 13: 17–36.

Hindelang, Michael. 1972. "Equality under the Law." In Charles Reasons and Jack Kuykendall (Eds.), *Race, Crime and Justice* (pp. 312–323). Pacific Palisades, CA: Goodyear.

Hindson, Stephanie, Hillary Potter, and Michael Radelet. 2006. "Race, Gender, Region, and Death Sentencing in Colorado, 1980-1999." *Colorado Law Review* 77: 549–574.

Hingson, Ralph, Timothy Heeren, and Erika Edwards. 2008. "Age at Drinking Onset, Alcohol Dependence, and Their Relation to Drug Use and Dependence, Driving under the Influence of Drugs, and Motor-Vehicle Crash Involvement Because of Drugs." *Journal of Studies on Alcohol and Drugs* 69: 192–201.

Hipp, John, and Daniel K. Yates. 2011. "Ghettos, Thresholds, and Crime: Does Concentrated Poverty Really Have an Accelerating Increase Effect on Crime?" *Criminology* 49: 955–990.

Hirschel, David, Eve Buzawa, April Pattavina, and Don Faggiani. 2007. "Domestic Violence and Mandatory Arrest Laws: To What Extent Do They Influence Police Arrest Decisions?" *Journal of Criminal Law and Criminology* 98: 255.

Hirschel, J. David, Ira Hutchison, Charles Dean, and Anne-Marie Mills. 1992. "Review Essay on the Law Enforcement Response to Spouse Abuse: Past, Present and Future." *Justice Quarterly* 9: 247–284.

HLN. 2012. Formerly available online at http://nancygrace.blogs.cnn.com

Hockenberry, Sarah, Melissa Sickmund, and Anthony Sladky. 2011. "Juvenile Residential Facility Census, 2008: Selected Findings." Washington, DC: Department of Justice, Office of Juvenile Justice and Delinquency Prevention.

Hofer, Paul J. 2007. "*United States v. Booker* as a Natural Experiment: Using Empirical Research to Inform the Federal Sentencing Debate." *Criminology and Public Policy* 6: 433–460.

Hofer, Paul J. 2011. "Has *Booker* Restored Balance? A Look at Data on Plea Bargaining and Sentencing." *Federal Sentencing Reporter* 23: 326-332.

Hoffman, Richard. 1991. "Beyond the Team: Renegotiating the Judge–Administrator Partnership." *Justice System Journal* 15: 652–666.

Hogarth, John. 1971. *Sentencing as a Human Process*. Toronto: University of Toronto Press.

Holbrook, R. Andrew, and Timothy Hill. 2005. "Agenda-Setting and Priming in Prime Time Television: Crime Dramas as Political Cues." *Political Communication* 22: 277–295.

Holleran, David, Dawn Beichner, and Cassia Spohn. 2009. "Examining Charging Agreement between Police and Prosecutors in Rape Cases." *Crime and Delinquency* 56: 385–413.

Holmes, Lisa, and Elisha Savchak. 2003. "Judicial Appointment Politics in the 107th Congress." *Judicature* 86: 240–250.

Holmes, Lisa M., and Jolly A. Emrey. 2006. "Court Diversification: Staffing the State Courts of Last Resort through Interim Appointments." *Justice Systems Journal* 27: 1–12.

Holmes, Malcolm, Howard Daudistel, and William Taggart. 1992. "Plea Bargaining and State District Court Caseloads: An Interrupted Time Series Analysis." *Law and Society Review* 26: 139–160.

Holmes, Oliver Wendell, Jr. 1881. *The Common Law*. Boston: Little, Brown.

Holmes, Oliver Wendell. 1920. *Collected Legal Papers*. Boston: Harcourt.

Holmstrom, Lynda, and Ana Burgess. 1983. *The Victim of Rape: Institutional Reactions*. New Brunswick, NJ: Transaction.

Homel, Ross. 1988. *Policing and Punishing the Drinking Driver: A Study of General and Specific Deterrence*. New York: Springer-Verlag.

Hoover, Eric. 2008. "For MADD, the Legal Drinking Age Is Not for Debate." *The Chronicle of Higher Education* 55(11).

Horney, Julie, and Cassia Spohn. 1996. "The Influence of Blame and Believability Factors on the Processing of Simple versus Aggravated Rape Cases." *Criminology* 34: 135–162.

Horowitz, Irwin A., Norbert L. Kerr, Ernest S. Park, and Christine Gockel. 2006. "Chaos in the Courtroom Reconsidered: Emotional Bias and Juror Nullification." *Law and Human Behavior* 30: 163–181.

Hoskins, Adam. 2012. "Armchair Jury Consultants: The Legal Implications and Benefits of Online Research of Prospective Jurors in the Facebook Era." *Minnesota Law Review* 96: 1100–1122.

Houck, Max M. 2006. "CSI: Reality." *Scientific American* 295: 84–89.

Houck, Max M., and Bruce Budowle. 2002. "Correlation of Microscopic and Mitochondrial DNA Hair Comparisons." *Journal of Forensic Science* 47(5): 964–967.

House, Rebecca. 2013. "Seen but Not Heard: Using Judicial Waiver to Save the Juvenile Justice System and Our Kids." *University of Toledo Law Review* 45: 149–179.

Howell, K. Babe. 2014. "Prosecutorial Discretion and the Duty to Seek Justice in an Overburdened Criminal Justice System." *Georgetown Journal of Legal Ethics* 27: 285–334.

Hoyle, Carolyn. 2011. "Empowerment through Emotion: The Use and Abuse of Victim Impact Evidence." In Edna Erez, Michael Kilching, and Joanne Wemmers (Eds.), *Therapeutic Jurisprudence and Victim Participation in Justice: International Perspectives*. Durham, NC: Carolina Academic Press.

Hsu, Spencer. 2009. "U.S. to Expand Immigration Checks to all Local Jails." *Washington Post*, May 19.

Hubler, Shawn. 2005. "Spectacle Supplants Law as Focus of Jackson Trial." *Los Angeles Times*, June 13.

Huck, Jennifer L., and Daniel R. Lee. 2014. "The Creation of Sentencing Decisions: Judicial Situated Identities." *Criminal Justice Policy Review* 25(2): 185–207.

Huddleston, West, and Douglas Marlowe. 2011. *Painting the Current Picture: A National Report on Drug Courts and Other Problem-Solving Court Programs in the United States*. New York: National Drug Court Institute.

Huebner, Beth M., and Timohy S. Bynum. 2008. The role of race and ethnicity in parole decisions. *Criminology* 46(4): 907–938.

Huff, C. Ronald, Arye Rattner, and Edward Sagarin, 2003. *Convicted but Innocent: Wrongful Conviction and Public Policy*. Thousand Oaks, CA: Sage.

Hunter, Arthur. 2006. "Judges Are Like Referees, Guarding Citizen Rights." *Times-Picayune*, July 20.

Hurley, Greg. (2016). *Body Worn Cameras and the Courts*. Williamsburg, VA: National Center for State Courts.

Hurwitz, Mark. 2006. "Much Ado about Sentencing: The Influence of *Apprendi*, *Blakely*, and *Booker* in the U.S. Courts of Appeals." *Justice System Journal* 27: 81–94.

Hurwitz, Mark. 2008. "Give Him a Fair Trial, Then Hang Him: The Supreme Court's Modern Death Penalty Jurisprudence." *Justice System Journal* 29: 243–256.

Hurwitz, Mark, and Drew Noble Lanier. 2012. "Judicial Diversity in Federal Courts." *Judicature* 96: 76–83.

Hurwitz, Mark S., and Dew Noble Lanier. 2003. "Explaining Judicial Diversity: The Differential Ability of Women and Minorities to Attain Seats on State Supreme and Appellate Courts." *State Politics and Policy Quarterly* 3: 329–352.

Husak, Douglas N. 2008. *Overcriminalization: The Limits of the Criminal Law*. New York: Oxford University Press.

Hyatt, Jordan M., and Geoffrey C. Barnes. 2017. "An Experimental Evaluation of the Impact of Intensive Supervision on the Recidivism of High-Risk Probationers." *Crime and Delinquency* 63(1): 3-38.

Iannacchione, Brian, and Jeremy D. Ball. 2008. "The Effect of *Blakely v. Washington* on Upward Departures in a Sentencing Guideline State." *Journal of Contemporary Criminal Justice* 24(4): 419–436.

"In '90s, Prison Building by States and U.S. Government Surged." 1997. *New York Times*, July 24, p. A14.

Ingram, David. 2012. "Twitter Coverage of US Court Gets Stuck Down." *Reuters Online: U.S. Edition*. March 27. Available online at: http://www.reuters.com/article/2012/03/27/usa-healthcare-twitter-idUSL2E8ERWED20120327

Innocence Project. 2004. "Issues in Judicial Independence and Accountability." *Judicature* 88: 114–121.

Innocence Project. 2008. "Innocence Blog: The 'CSI Effect' on Both Sides of the Courtroom." June 20. Available online at https://www.innocenceproject.org/the-csi-effect-on-both-sides-of-the-courtroom/

Innocence Project. 2014. *False Confessions & Recording of Custodial Interrogations*. http://www.innocenceproject.org/free-innocent/improve-the-law/fact-sheets/false-confessions-recording-of-custodial-interrogations

Innocence Project, 2016a. *Exonerate the Innocent*. Retrieved from https://www.innocenceproject.org/exonerate/

Innocence Project. 2016b. *DNA Exonerations in the United States*. Retrieved from https://www.innocenceproject.org/dna-exonerations-in-the-united-states/

Innocence Project. 2016c. *Access to Post-Conviction DNA Testing*. Retrieved from https://www.innocenceproject.org/access-post-conviction-dna-testing/

Innocence Project. 2016d. *Eyewitness Identification Reform*. Retrieved from https://www.innocenceproject.org/eyewitness-identification-reform/

Innocence Project. 2016e. *Misapplication of Forensic Science*. Retrieved from https://www.innocenceproject.org/causes/misapplication-forensic-science/

Innocence Project. 2016f. False Confessions or Admissions. Retrieved from https://www.innocenceproject.org/causes/false-confessions-admissions/

Innocence Project. 2016g. Incentivized Informants. Retrieved from https://www.innocenceproject.org/causes/incentivized-informants/

Isidore, Chris. 2016, April 28. "35 Bankers Were Sent to Prison for Financial Crisis Crimes." *CNN Money*, http://money.cnn.com/2016/04/28/news/companies/bankers-prison/

Iyengar, Radha. 2007. *An Analysis of the Performance of Federal Indigent Defense Counsel*. Cambridge, MA: National Bureau of Economic Research, Harvard University.

Jackson, Donald. 1974. *Judges*. New York: Atheneum.

Jackson, Robert H. 1940. "The Federal Prosecutor—His Temptations." *Journal of the American Judicature Society* 24: 18–25.

Jacob, Herbert. 1966. "Judicial Insulation: Elections, Direct Participation, and Public Attention to the Courts in Wisconsin." *Wisconsin Law Review* 812.

Jacob, Herbert. 1984. *Justice in America*. 4th ed. Boston: Little, Brown.

Jacob, Herbert. 1991. "Decision Making in Trial Courts." In John Gates and Charles Johnson (Eds.), *The American Courts: A Critical Assessment* (pp. 211–233). Washington, DC: CQ Press.

Jacob, Herbert. 1997. "Governance by Trial Court Judges." *Law and Science Review* 31: 3–37.

Jacobs, Andrew. 2007. "Newark Battles Murder and Its Accomplice, Silence." *New York Times*, May 29.

Jacobs, David, and Stephanie Kent. 2007. "The Determinants of Execution Since 1951: How Politics, Protests, Public Opinion and Social Divisions Shape Capital Punishment." *Social Problems* 54: 297–318.

Jacobs, David, Zhenchao Qian, Jason Carmichael, and Stephanie Kent. 2007. "Who Survives on Death Row? An Individual and Contextual Analysis." *American Sociological Review* 72: 610–362.

Jacobson, Michael. 2005. *Downsizing Prisons: How to Reduce Crime and End Mass Incarceration*. New York: NYU Press.

Jacoby, Joan. 1980. *The American Prosecutor: A Search for Identity*. Lexington, MA: Heath.

Jacoby, Joan. 1995. "Pushing the Envelope: Leadership in Prosecution." *Justice System Journal* 17: 291–308.

Jacoby, Joan, Leonard Mellon, Edward Ratledge, and Stanley Turner. 1982. *Prosecutorial Decisionmaking: A National Study*. Washington, DC: Department of Justice, National Institute of Justice.

James, Nathan. 2015. *Offender Reentry: Correctional Statistics, Reintegration into the Community, and Recidivism* [Report RL34287]. Washington, DC: Library of Congress, Congressional Research Service. Retrieved from https://fas.org/sgp/crs/misc/RL34287.pdf

James, Veronyka J., and Daniel R. Lee. 2015. "Through the Looking Glass: Exploring How College Students' Perceptions of the Police Influence Sexual Assault Victimization Reporting." *Journal of Interpersonal Violence* 30(14): 2447–2469.

Jarvis, John P., Ashley Mancik, and Wendy C. Regoeczi. 2017. "Police Responses to Violent Crime: Reconsidering the Mobilization of Law." *Criminal Justice Review* 42(1): 5–25.

Jefferson, David. 2005. "America's Most Dangerous Drug." *Newsweek*, August 8, pp. 40–48.

Jehle, Jörg-Martin, and Marianne Wade. 2006. *Coping with Overloaded Criminal Justice Systems*. New York: Springer.

Jekot, Wayne. 2007. "Computer Forensics, Search Strategies, and the Particularity Requirement." *University of Pittsburgh Journal of Technology Law and Policy* 12(2): 2–48.

Jencks, Christopher, and Paul Peterson, eds. 1991. *The Urban Underclass*. Washington, DC: Brookings Institution.

Jensen, Jennifer. 2011. "Career Satisfaction and State Trial Court Judges' Plans to Leave the Bench." *Judicature* 95: 116–125.

Johnsen, Diane M. 2016. "Building a Bench: A Close Look at State Appellate Courts Constructed by the Respective Methods of Judicial Selection." *San Diego Law Review* 54: 831–900.

Johnson, Brian D. 2006. "The Multilevel Context of Criminal Sentencing: Integrating Judge- and County-Level Influences." *Criminology* 44: 259–298.

Johnson, Brian D. 2014. "Judges on Trial: A Reexamination of Judicial Race and Gender Effects Across Modes of Conviction." *Criminal Justice Policy Review* 25(2): 159–184.

Johnson, Brian D., and Sara Betsinger. 2009. Punishing the "Model Minority": Asian-American Criminal Sentencing Outcomes in Federal District Courts. *Criminology* 47(4): 1045–1090.

Johnson, Brian D., and Stephanie DiPietro. 2012. "The Power of Diversion: Intermediate Sanctions and Sentencing Disparity under Presumptive Guidelines." *Criminology* 50(3): 811–850.

Johnson, Brian D., Ryan D. King, and Cassia C. Spohn. 2016. "Sociolegal Approaches to the Study of Guilty Pleas and Prosecution." *Annual Review of Law and Social Science* 12(1): 479–495.

Johnson, Brian, Jeffrey Ulmer, and John Kramer. 2008. "The Social Context of Guidelines Circumvention: The Case of Federal District Courts." *Criminology* 46: 737–783.

Johnson, Chris. 2014. "Black Gay Judicial Nominees Confirmed to Federal Court." *Washington Blade*, June 17. Available online at http://www.washingtonblade.com/2014/06/17/black-gay-judicial-nominees-confirmed-to-federal-court/

Johnson, Gene. 2013. "Public Defenders Warn of Dire Cuts." *Associated Press*. July 2.

Johnson, James, and Philip Secret. 1995. "The Effects of Court Structure on Juvenile Court Decisonmaking." *Journal of Criminal Justice* 23: 63–82.

Johnson, James L., and Laura M. Baber. 2015. "State of the System: Federal Probation and Pretrial Services." *Federal Probation* 79(2): 34–40.

Johnson, Kevin. 2010. "Imposing Fees." *USA Today*, October 31.

Johnson, Richard R., Charles F. Klahm, and Harrison G. Maddox. 2015. "An Exploratory Analysis of Time Lapses in Serving Arrest Warrants: A Focal Concerns and

Disproportionate Contact Approach." *Criminal Justice Review* 40(4): 470–487.

Johnson, Vida B. 2015. "Presumed Fair? Voir Dire on the Fundamentals of Our Criminal Justice System." *Seton Hall Law Review* 45: 545–580.

Jonakait, Randolph N. 2006. *The American Jury System.* New Haven: Yale University Press.

Jones, David. 1994. "Prosecutorial Tenure in Wisconsin." Paper presented at the Midwest Criminal Justice Association Meeting, Chicago.

Jones, David. 2001. "Toward a Prosecutorial 'Civil Service': A Wisconsin Case Study." Paper presented at the annual meeting of the American Society of Criminology, Atlanta.

Judicial Council of California. 2015. *2015 Court Statistics Report: Statewide Case Trends through 2013–2014.* San Francisco: California Administrative Office of the Courts.

"Judicial Firsts Under Obama." 2015, April/May. *The Advocate,* p. 14.

Justice at Stake. 2016a. "Bybee Invited to Testify by Leahy." April 30. Available online at http://www.gavelgrab .org/?cat=8

Justice at Stake. 2016b. "*Caperton v. Massey* Resource Page." Available online at http://www.justiceatstake .org/resources/in_depth_issues_guides/caperton _resource_page

Justice Policy Institute. 2011. *Finding Direction: Expanding Criminal Justice Options by Considering Policies of Other Nations.* Washington, DC: Author. Available online at http://www.justicepolicy.org/uploads/justicepolicy /documents/sentencing.pdf

Justice Policy Institute. 2012. *Bail Fail: Why the U.S. Should End the Practice of Using Money for Bail*: www.justicepolicy.org /uploads/justicepolicy/documents/bailfail.pdf

The Justice Project. 2007. *Jailhouse Snitch Testimony: A Policy Review.* Washington, DC: Author.

Kaeble, Danielle, and Thomas P. Bonczar. 2017. *Probation and Parole in the United States, 2015.* Washington, DC: Bureau of Justice Statistics.

Kairys, David, Joseph Kadane, and John Lehorsky. 1977. "Jury Representativeness: A Mandate for Multiple Source Lists." *California Law Review* 65: 776–827.

Kaiser, Kimberly A., Eryn N. O'Neal, and Cassia Spohn. 2015. "'Victim Refuses to Cooperate': A Focal Concerns Analysis of Victim Cooperation in Sexual Assault Cases." *Victims & Offenders*: 1–26.

Kalt, Brian C. 2003. "The Exclusion of Felons from Jury Service." *American University Law Review* 53: 65–189.

Kalven, Harry, and Hans Zeisel. 1966. *The American Jury.* Boston: Little, Brown.

Kamisar, Yale. 1978. "Is the Exclusionary Rule an 'Illogical' or 'Unnatural' Interpretation of the Fourth Amendment?" *Judicature* 78: 83–84.

Kant, Immanuel. 1790. *The Science of Right.* (W. Hastie, trans.). Available online at http://philosophy.eserver.org/kant /science-of-right.txt

Kanter, Lois H. 2005. "Invisible Clients: Exploring Our Failure to Provide Civil Legal Services to Rape Victims." *Suffolk University Law Review* 38: 253–289.

Karatekin, Canan, Richard Gehrman, and Jamie Lawler, 2014. "A Study of Mistreated Children and their Families in Juvenile Court: Court Performance Measures." Children and Youth Services Review 41: 62–74.

Karmen, Andrew. 2016. *Crime Victims: An Introduction to Victimology.* 9th ed. Boston: Cengage.

Kassin, Saul M., and Gisli H. Gudjonsson. 2004. "The Psychology of False Confessions: A Review of the Literature and Issues." *Psychological Science in the Public Interest* 5(2): 33–67.

Katz, Charles M., and Cassia C. Spohn. 1995. "The Effect of Race and Gender on Bail Outcomes: A Test of an Interactive Model." *American Journal of Criminal Justice* 19: 161–184.

Kauder, Neal, and Brian Ostrom. 2008. *State Sentencing Guidelines: Profiles and Continuum.* Williamsburg, VA: National Center for State Courts.

Keel, Timothy G., John P. Jarvis, and Yvonne E. Muirhead. 2009. "An Exploratory Analysis of Factors Affecting Homicide Investigations: Examining the Dynamics of Murder Clearance Rates." *Homicide Studies* 13: 50–68.

Keen, Bradley, and David Jacobs. 2009. "Racial Threat, Partisan Politics, and Racial Disparities in Prison Admissions: A Panel Analysis." *Criminology* 47: 209–238.

Keenan, David, Deborah Jane Cooper, David Lebowitz, and Tamar Lerer. 2011. "The Myth of Prosecutorial Accountability after *Connick v. Thompson*: Why Existing Professional Responsibility Measures Cannot Protect against Prosecutorial Misconduct." *Yale Law Journal Online* 121: 203–265.

Kenney, Sally. 2012. *Gender and Justice: Why Women in the Judiciary Really Matter.* New York: Routledge.

Kelley, Matt. 2011. "Innocence Blog: Is the 'CSI Effect' Real?" Innocence Project, June 24. Available online at https:// www.innocenceproject.org/is-the-csi-effect-real/

Kennedy, Darlene. 1997. "Let's Hold Juveniles Responsible for Their Crimes." National Center for Public Policy Research. Available online at http://www.nationalcenter.org /NPA166.html

Kennedy, Spurgeon, Laura House, & Michael Williams. 2013. "Using Research to Improve Pretrial Justice and Public

Safety: Results from PSA's Risk Assessment Validation Project." *Federal Probation* 77(1): 28–32.

Kerr, Orin S. 2008. "Criminal Law in Virtual Worlds." University of Chicago Legal Forum, 2008: 415–442, GWU Law School Public Law Research Paper No. 391. Available online at http://ssrn.com/abstract=1097392

Kerrigan, Tim. 2008. "No Money? No Problem. Legal Aid Lawyers Find Innovative Ways to Serve the Rural Poor." *Public Interest Law Reporter* 13: 133–139.

Kerstetter, Wayne A. 1990. "Gateway to Justice: Police and Prosecutorial Response to Sexual Assaults Against Women." *Journal of Criminal Law and Criminology* 81: 267–313.

Killias, Martin, Gwladys Gilliéron, Françoise Villard, and Clara Poglia. 2010. "How Damaging Is Imprisonment in the Long-Term? A Controlled Experiment Comparing Long-Term Effects of Community Service and Short Custodial Sentences on Re-Offending and Social Integration." *Journal of Experimental Criminology* 6(2): 115–130.

Killias, Martin, Gwladys Gilliéron, Izumi Kissling, and Patrice Villettaz. 2010. "Community Service versus Electronic Monitoring—What Works Better?" *British Journal of Criminology* 50: 1155–1170.

Kim, Andrew Chongseh. 2014. "Underestimating the Trial Penalty: An Empirical Analysis of the Federal Trial Penalty and Critique of the Abrams Study." *Mississippi Law Journal* 84: 1195–1256.

Kim, Byungbae, Cassia C. Spohn, and Eric C. Hedberg. 2015. "Federal Sentencing as a Complex Collaborative Process: Judges, Prosecutors, Judge–Prosecutor Dyads, and Disparity in Sentencing." *Criminology* 53(4): 597–623.

Kimora. 2008. "The Emerging Paradigm in Probation and Parole in the United States." *Journal of Offender Rehabilitation* 46: 1–11.

King, Nancy J., David A. Soulé, Sara Steen, and Robert R. Weidner. 2005. "When Process Affects Punishment: Differences in Sentences after Guilty Plea, Bench Trial, and Jury Trial in Five Guidelines States." *Columbia Law Review* 105: 959–1009.

King, Ryan S. 2008. *The State of Sentencing 2007: Developments in Policy and Practice*. Washington, DC: The Sentencing Project.

King, Ryan D., Kecia R. Johnson, and Kelly McGeever. 2010. "Demography of the Legal Profession and Racial Disparities in Sentencing." *Law & Society Review* 44(1): 1–32.

Kingsnorth, Rodney, Carole Barnes, and Paul Coonley. 1990. "Driving under the Influence: The Role of Legal and Extralegal Factors in Court Processing and Sentencing Practices." Unpublished manuscript, Department of Sociology, California State University, Sacramento.

Kingsnorth, Rodney, and Louis Rizzo. 1979. "Decision-Making in the Criminal Courts: Continuities and Discontinuities." *Criminology* 17: 3–14.

Kilpatrick, Dean G., Heidi S. Resnick, Kenneth J. Ruggiero, Lauren M. Conoscenti, and Jenna McCauley. 2007. *Drug-facilitated, Incapacitated, and Forcible Rape: A National Study*. Charleston, SC: National Crime Victims Research & Treatment Center. Available online at http://www.ncjrs.gov/pdffiles1/nij/grants/219181.pdf

Kirk, David S., and Mauri Matsuda. 2011. "Legal Cynicism, Collective Efficacy, and the Ecology of Arrest." *Criminology* 49: 443–472.

Klaversma, Laura. 2008. *Courts and Collections*. Williamsburg, VA: National Center for State Courts.

Kleck, Gary. 1981. "Racial Discrimination in Criminal Sentencing: A Critical Evaluation of the Evidence with Additional Data on the Death Penalty." *American Sociological Review* 46: 783–805.

Klein, Stephen, Joan Petersilia, and Susan Turner. 1990. "Race and Imprisonment Decisions in California." *Science* 247: 812–816.

Klemm, Margaret. 1986. "The Determinants of Capital Sentencing in Louisiana, 1979–1984." Unpublished doctoral dissertation, University of New Orleans.

Klenowski, Paul M., Keith J. Bell, and Kimberly D. Dodson. 2010. "An Empirical Evaluation of Juvenile Awareness Programs in the United States: Can Juveniles Be 'Scared Straight'?" *Journal of Offender Rehabilitation* 49(4): 254–272.

Knudten, Richard, Anthony Meader, Mary Knudten, and William Doerner. 1976. "The Victim in the Administration of Criminal Justice: Problems and Perceptions." In William McDonald (Ed.), *Criminal Justice and the Victim* (pp. 115–146). Newbury Park, CA: Sage.

Koeppel, Maria D. H. 2014. "Gender Sentencing of Rural Property Offenders in Iowa." *Criminal Justice Policy Review* 25(2): 208–226.

Koons-Witt, Barbara. 2002. "The Effect of Gender on the Decision to Incarcerate before and after the Introduction of Sentencing Guidelines." *Criminology* 40: 297–328.

Koshan, Jennifer. (2014). "Investigating Integrated Domestic Violence Courts: Lessons from New York." *Osgoode Hall Law Journal* 51(3): 989–1036.

Koss, Mary P. 2000. *Blame, Shame, and Community: Justice Responses to Violence Against Women*. St. Paul: Minnesota Center Against Violence and Abuse. Available online at http://www.mincava.umn.edu/documents/koss/koss.html

Kovach, Gretel. 2009. "Mixed Opinions of a Judge Accused of Misconduct." *New York Times*, March 8.

Kramer, John, Robin Lubitz, and Cynthia Kempinen. 1989. "Sentencing Guidelines: A Quantitative Comparison of Sentencing Politics in Minnesota, Pennsylvania, and Washington." *Justice Quarterly* 6: 565–587.

Kramer, John, and Darrell Steffensmeier. 1993. "Race and Imprisonment Decisions." *Sociological Quarterly* 34: 357–376.

Kramer, John, and Jeffrey Ulmer. 1996. "Sentencing Disparity and Departures from Guidelines." *Justice Quarterly* 13: 81–106.

Kramer, John, and Jeffrey Ulmer. 2009. *Sentencing Guidelines: Lessons from Pennsylvania*. Boulder, CO: Lynne Rienner.

Krisberg, Barry. 1988. "Public Attitudes about Criminal Sanctions." *Criminologist* 13: 1–21.

Krisberg, Barry, and James Austin. 1993. *Reinventing Juvenile Justice*. Newbury Park, CA: Sage.

Krisberg, Barry, and Eleanor Taylor-Nicholson. 2011. *Research Brief: Criminal Justice Realignment: A Bold New Era in California Corrections*. Berkeley, CA: The Chief Justice Earl Warren Institute on Law and Social Policy.

Krivo, Lauren J., Reginald A. Byron, Catherine A. Calder, Ruth D. Peterson, Christopher R. Browning, Mei-Po Kwan, and Jae Young Lee. (2015). "Patterns of Local Segregation: Do They Matter for Neighborhood Crime?" *Social Science Research* 54: 303–318.

Kruger, Karen J. 2007. "Pregnancy & Policing: Are They Compatible? Pushing the Legal Limits on Behalf of Equal Employment Opportunities." *Wisconsin Women's Law Journal* 22: 61–89.

Kupchik, Aaron. 2006. *Judging Juveniles: Prosecuting Adolescents in Adult and Juvenile Courts*. New York: New York University Press.

Kurland, Philip B., and Dennis J. Hutchinson. 1983. "The Business of the Supreme Court, O.T. 1982." *University of Chicago Law Review* 50: 628–651.

Kurlychek, Megan, and Cynthia Kempinen. 2006. "Beyond Boot Camp: The Impact of Aftercare on Offender Reentry." *Criminology and Public Policy* 2: 363–388.

Kutateladze, Besiki Luka, and Victoria Z. Lawson. 2015. "How Bad Arrests Lead to Bad Prosecution: Exploring the Impact of Prior Arrests on Plea Bargaining." *Cardozo Law Review* 37: 973–993.

Labriola, Melissa, Sarah Bradley, Chris O'Sullivan, Michael Rempel, and Samantha Moore. 2009. *A National Portrait of Domestic Violence Courts*. New York: Center for Court Innovation.

Labriola, Melissa, Michael Rempel, and Robert Davis. 2008. "Do Batterer Programs Reduce Recidivism? Results from a Randomized Trial in the Bronx." *Justice Quarterly* 25: 251–282.

Lacey, Marc. 2011. "Police Officers Find That Dissent on Drug Laws May Come with a Price." *New York Times*, December 2, p. A11.

Lacks, Robyn Diehl. 2007. "The 'Real' *CSI*: Designing and Teaching a Violent Crime Scene Class in an Undergraduate Setting." *Journal of Criminal Justice Education* 18: 2.

LaCroix, Alison L. 2007. "The New Wheel in the Federal Machine: From Sovereignty to Jurisdiction in the Early Republic." *Supreme Court Review* 2007: 345–394.

LaFave, Wayne. 1965. *Arrest: The Decision to Take a Suspect into Custody*. Boston: Little, Brown.

LaFountain, Robert C., Richard Y. Schauffler, Shauna M. Strickland, Sarah A. Gibson, and Ashley N. Mason. 2011. *Examining the Work of State Courts: An Analysis of 2009 State Court Caseloads*. Williamsburg, VA: National Center for State Courts.

LaFountain, Robert C., Richard Y. Schauffler, Shauna M. Strickland, and Katherine A. Holt. 2012. *Examining the Work of State Courts: An Analysis of 2010 State Court Caseloads*. Williamsburg, VA: National Center for State Courts.

LaFountain, Robert, Richard Schauffler, Shauna Strickland, William Raftery, Chantal Bromage, Cynthia Lee, and Sarah Gibson. 2008. *Examining the Work of State Courts, 2007*. Williamsburg, VA: National Center for State Courts.

LaFree. Gary D. 1980. "The Effect of Sexual Stratification by Race on Official Reactions to Rape." *American Sociological Review* 45(5): 842–854.

LaFrenz, C. D., and Cassia Spohn. 2006. "Who Is Punished More Harshly in Federal Court? The Interaction of Race/Ethnicity, Gender, Age, and Employment Status in the Sentencing of Drug Offenders." *Justice Research and Policy* 8: 25–56.

Lagos, Marisa. 2015. "Cutbacks Still Felt Deeply in California Civil Courts." *KQED News*, March 11. https://ww2.kqed.org/news/2015/03/12/court-budget-cuts-delay-justice/

Lain, Corinna Barrett. 2013. "Death Penalty Drugs: A Prescription That's Getting Hard to Fill." *Richmond Law* Summer 2013. http://scholarship.richmond.edu/cgi/viewcontent.cgi?article=1279&context=law-faculty-publications

Laird, Lorelei. 2016, August 22. "Bail Schedules Are Unconstitutional and Bad Public Policy, DOJ Says." *ABA Journal*, http://www.abajournal.com/news/article/justice_department_files_amicus_brief_in_challenge_to_use_of_bail_schedules

Lamber, Julia, and Mary Luskin. 1992. "Court Reform: A View from the Bottom." *Judicature* 75: 295–299.

Landsberg, Brian. 1993. "The Role of Civil Service Attorneys and Political Appointees in Making Policy in the Civil Rights Division of the U.S. Department of Justice." *Journal of Law and Politics* 9: 275–289.

Landsman, Stephan. 2005. "In Defense of the Jury of 12 and the Unanimous Decision Rule." *Judicature* 88: 301–305.

Langton, Lynn, Marcus Berzofsky, Christopher Krebs, and Hope Smiley-McDonald. 2012. *Victimizations Not Reported* to the Police, 2006–2010. Washington, DC: Department of Justice, Bureau of Justice Statistics. Available online at http://www.bjs.gov/content/pub/pdf/vnrp0610.pdf.

Langton, Lynn, and Donald Farole. 2010. *State Public Defender Programs, 2007.* Washington, DC: Department of Justice, Bureau of Justice Statistics.

Lankford, Jefferson. 2006. "The Effect of *Blakely* v. *Washington* on State Sentencing." *Justice System Journal* 27: 96–104.

Lauritsen, Janet, Karen Heimer, and James Lynch. 2009. "Trends in the Gender Gap in Violent Offending: New Evidence from the National Crime Victimization Survey." *Criminology* 47: 361–400.

Lavoie, Denise. 2008. "Successful Schemers Know How to Charm Their Victims." *Times-Picayune*, December 20.

LaWall, Barbara. 2001. "Should Plea Bargaining Be Banned in Pima County?" Pima County (Arizona) Attorney's Office.

Law Enforcement Against Prohibition. 2012. "Welcome to Law Enforcement Against Prohibition." Available online at: http://www.leap.cc

Lawler, Jamie M., Richard Gehman, and Canan Karatekin. 2016. "Maltreated Children and Their Families in Juvenile Dependency Court II: Maltreatment Recidivism." *Journal of Public Child Welfare* 10(2): 215–236.

Lawson, Harry, and Dennis Howard. 1991. "Development of the Profession of Court Management: A History with Commentary." *Justice System Journal* 15: 580–605.

"LDF Applauds Supreme Court Decision in *Kimbrough v. United States*." 2007. *US Newswire*, December 10.

Lee, David W. 2011. *Handbook of Section 1983 Litigation, 2011 Edition.* Frederick, MD: Wolters Kluwer Law & Business.

Lee, Matthew. 2008. "Civic Community in the Hinterland: Toward a Theory of Rural Social Structure and Violence." *Criminology* 46: 447–463.

Lee, Monica. 1992. "Indigent Defense: Determination of Indigency in the Nation's State Courts." *State Court Journal* (Spring): 16–23.

Lefcourt, Gerald. 1998. "Curbing the Abuse of the Grand Jury." *Judicature* 81: 196–197.

Lefstein, Norman. 2011. *Securing Reasonable Caseloads: Ethics and Law in Public Defense.* Chicago: American Bar Association.

Lehmann, Peter S., Ted Chiricos, and William D. Bales. 2017. "Sentencing Transferred Juveniles in the Adult Criminal Court the Direct and Interactive Effects of Race and Ethnicity." *Youth Violence and Juvenile Justice* 15(2): 172–190.

Lei, Man-Kit, Ronald L. Simons, Leslie Gordon Simons, and Mary Bond Edmond. 2014. "Gender Equality and Violent Behavior: How Neighborhood Gender Equality Influences the Gender Gap in Violence." *Violence and Victims* 29(1): 89–108.

Leiber, Michael J. 2013. "Race, Pre- and Postdetention, and Juvenile Justice Decision Making." *Crime & Delinquency* 59(3): 396–418.

Leiber, Michael J., John Reitzel, and Kristin Mack. 2011. "Probation Officer Recommendations for Sentencing Relative to Judicial Practice: The Implications for African Americans." *Criminal Justice Policy Review* 22: 301–329.

Leipold, Andrew D. 2005. "How the Pretrial Process Contributes to Wrongful Convictions." *American Criminal Law Review*, 42(4): 1123–1166.

Lens, Vicki. 2015. "Judge or Bureaucrat? Examining how Administrative Law Judges Exercise their Discretion in Public Welfare Bureaucracies." *Social Service Review* 86(2): 269–293.

Leo, Richard. 1996a. "Inside the Interrogation Room." *Journal of Criminal Law and Criminology* 86: 266–303.

Leo, Richard. 1996b. "The Impact of *Miranda* Revisited." *Journal of Criminal Law and Criminology* 86: 621–692.

Leo, Richard A. 2008. *Police Interrogation and American Justice.* Cambridge, MA: Harvard University Press.

Leonnig, Carol D. 2013. "Court: Ability to Police U.S. Spying Program Limited." *Washington Post*, August 15. Available online at http://www.washingtonpost.com/politics/court-ability-to-police-us-spying-program-limited/2013/08/15/4a8c8c44-05cd-11e3-a07f-49ddc7417125_story.html

Levett, Lora M., et al. 2005. "The Psychology of Jury and Juror Decision Making." In Neil Brewer and Kipling D. Williams (Eds.), *Psychology and Law: An Empirical Perspective* (pp. 365–406). Guilford, NC: The Guilford Press.

Levine, James. 1983. "Using Jury Verdict Forecasts in Criminal Defense Strategy." *Judicature* 66: 448–461.

Levinson, Justin, Robert Smith, and Danielle Young. 2014. "Devaluing Death: An Empirical Study of Implicit Racial Bias on Jury-Eligible Citizens in Six Death Penalty States." *New York University Law Review* 89: 513–581.

Levitt, Steven. 2006. "The Case of the Critics Who Missed the Point: A Reply to Webster et al." *Criminology and Public Policy* 5: 449–460.

Levy, Marin K. 2013. "Judicial Attention as a Scarce Resource: A Preliminary Defense of How Judges Allocate Time Across Cases in the Federal Courts of Appeals." *The George Washington Law Review* 81: 401–447.

Lewis, Anthony. 1964. *Gideon's Trumpet.* New York: Vintage Books/Random House.

Lewis, Anthony. 1989. *Gideon's Trumpet.* New York: Vintage Books. (Original work published 1964.)

Lewis, Neil. 2006. "Moussaoui Given Life Term by Jury over Link to 9/11." *New York Times*, May 4.

Lichtblau, Eric. 2013. "In Secret, Courts Vastly Broadens Powers of N.S.A." *New York Times*, July 6, A1.

Lichtenstein, Michael. 1984. "Public Defenders: Dimensions of Cooperation." *Justice System Journal* 9: 102–110.

Lieberman, Joel D., and Bruce Dennis Sales. 2006. *Scientific Jury Selection*. Washington, DC: American Psychological Association.

Lieberman, Joel D., Terance D. Miethe, Courtney A. Carrell, and Daniel A. Krauss. 2008. "Gold versus Platinum: Do Jurors Recognize the Superiority and Limitations of DNA Evidence Compared to Other Types of Forensic Evidence?" *Psychology, Public Policy, and Law* 14: 27–62.

Liebman, James S., Jeffrey Fagan, and Valerie West. 2000. "Capital Attrition: Error Rates in Capital Cases, 1973–1995." *Texas Law Review* 78: 1839–1865.

Lim, Claire S. H. 2013. "Preferences and Incentives of Appointed and Elected Public Officials: Evidence from State Trial Court Judges." *American Economic Review* 103(4): 1360–1397.

Linderman, Juliet. 2013. "Federal Public Defender Fires Herself Amid Budget Cuts." *New Orleans Times-Picayune*, September 8.

Lindermayer, Ariana. 2009. "What the Right Hand Gives: Prohibitive Interpretations of the State Constitutional Right to Bail." *Fordham Law Review* 78: 267–310.

Lininger, Tim. 2008. "Is It Wrong to Sue for Rape?" *Duke Law Journal* 57: 1557–1640.

Liptak, Adam. 2003. "County Says It's Too Poor to Defend the Poor." *New York Times*, April 15.

Liptak, Adam. 2005. "New Trial for a Mother Who Drowned 5 Children." *New York Times*, January 7.

Liptak, Adam. 2007. "Given the Latitude to Show Leniency, Judges May Not." *New York Times*, December 11.

Liptak, Adam. 2014. "The Polarized Court." *New York Times*, May 16.

Liptak, Adam. 2017, March 31. "White House Ends Bar Association's Role in Vetting Judges." *New York Times*. https://www.nytimes.com/2017/03/31/us/politics/white-house-american-bar-association-judges.html

Listwan, Shelley, Francis T. Cullen, and Edward Latessa. 2006. "How to Prevent Prison Re-entry Programs from Failing: Insights from Evidence-Based Corrections." *Federal Probation* 70: 19–25.

Listwan, Shelley, Cheryl Johnson, Francis Cullen, and Edward Latessa. 2008. "Cracks in the Penal Harm Movement: Evidence from the Field." *Criminology and Public Policy* 7: 423–465.

Litras, Marika, and John R. Golmant. 2006. "A Comparative Study of Juror Utilization in U.S. District Courts." *Journal of Empirical Legal Studies* 3: 99–120.

"Live Free and Nullify: Against Purging Capital Juries of Death Penalty Opponents." 2014. *Harvard Law Review* 127: 2092–2113.

Lofstrom, Magnus, and Brandon Martin. 2017. *California's Future: Corrections*. San Francisco, CA: Public Policy Institute of California. Retrieved from http://www.ppic.org/content/pubs/report/R_117MLR.pdf

Lofstrom, Magnus, and Steven Raphael. 2016a. "Incarceration and Crime Evidence from California's Public Safety Realignment Reform." *The ANNALS of the American Academy of Political and Social Science* 664(1): 196–220.

Lofstrom, Magnus, and Steven Raphael. 2016b. "Prison Downsizing and Public Safety: Evidence from California." *Criminology & Public Policy* 15(2): 349–365.

Logan, T. K., William H. Hoyt, Kathryn E. McCollister, Michael T. French, Carl Leukefeld, and Lisa Minton. 2004. "Economic Evaluation of Drug Court: Methodology, Results, and Policy Implications." *Evaluation and Program Planning*, 27(4): 381–396.

Losh, Susan C., and Robert G. Boatright. 2002. "Life-Cycle Factors, Status, and Civil Engagement: Issues of Age and Attitudes toward Jury Service." *Justice System Journal* 23: 221–234.

Lowenkamp, Christopher T., Anthony W. Flores, Alexander M. Holsinger, Matthew D. Makarios, and Edward J. Latessa. 2010. "Intensive Supervision Programs: Does Program Philosophy and the Principles of Effective Intervention Matter?" *Journal of Criminal Justice* 38(4): 368–375.

Lowy, Joan. 2009. "Summit to Focus on Driver Phone Use." *Times-Picayune*, August 5.

Luckerson, Victor. 2014. "U.S. Charges Credit Suisse over Tax-Fraud Scheme." *Time*, May 19.

Luna, Erik. 2005. "The Overcriminalization Phenomenon." *American University Law Review* 54: 703–746.

Luppi, Barbara, and Francesco Parisi. 2013. "Jury Size and the Hung-Jury Paradox." *Journal of Legal Studies* 42: 399–422.

Lurigio, Arthur, David Olson, and Jessica Snowden. 2009. "The Effects of Setting, Analyses and Probation Status." *Corrections Compendium* 34: 1–16.

Lushing, Peter. 1992. "The Fall and Rise of the Criminal Contingent Fee." *Journal of Criminal Law and Criminology* 82: 498–568.

Lynch, David. 1994. "The Impropriety of Plea Agreements: A Tale of Two Counties." *Law & Social Inquiry* 19: 115–134.

Lynch, David R., and T. David Evans. 2002. "Attributes of Highly Effective Criminal Defense Negotiators." *Journal of Criminal Justice* 30: 387–396.

Lynch, Michael. 2007. *Big Prisons, Big Dreams: Crime and the Failure of America's Penal System*. Piscataway, NJ: Rutgers University Press.

Lynch, Mona. 2011. "Mass Incarceration, Legal Change and Locale: Understanding and Remediating American Penal Overindulgence." *Criminology and Public Policy* 10: 671–698.

Lynch, Mona, and Marisa Omori. 2014. "Legal Change and Sentencing Norms in the Wake of *Booker*: The Impact of Time and Place on Drug Trafficking Cases in Federal Court." *Law & Society Review* 48(2): 411–445.

Mack, Kathy, and Sharyn Roach Anleu. 2007. "'Getting Through the List': Judgecraft and Legitimacy in the Lower Courts." *Social Legal Studies* 16: 341–361.

MacKenzie, Doris L. 2006. *What Works in Corrections: Reducing the Criminal Activities of Offenders and Delinquents.* New York: Cambridge University Press.

MADD. 2009. "Support Ignition Interlocks for all Convicted Drunk Drivers." Available online at https://secure2 .convio.net/madd/site/Advocacy?JServSessionIdr004 =08v7ubeh61.app7a& pagename=homepage& id=477

MADD. 2015. Support Ignition Interlocks for all Convicted Drunk Drivers. Available online http://www.madd.org /drunk-driving/ignition-interlocks/take-action-interlocks .html

Maddan, Sean, Richard D. Hartley, Jeffery T. Walker, and J. Mitchell Miller. 2012. "Sympathy for the Devil: An Exploration of Federal Judicial Discretion in the Processing of White-Collar Offenders." *American Journal of Criminal Justice* 37(1): 4–18.

Maggi, Laura. 2011, March 29. U.S. Supreme Court rejects $14 million judgment against New Orleans district attorney's office. *The Times-Picayune*. Retrieved from http:// www.nola.com/crime/index.ssf/2011/03/us_supreme _court_rejects_14_mi.html

Mahoney, Barry, with Alexander Aikman, Pamela Casey, Victor Flango, Geoff Gallas, Thomas Henderson, Jeanne Ito, David Steelman, and Steven Weller. 1988. *Changing Times in Trial Courts.* Williamsburg, VA: National Center for State Courts.

Mallord, Joel. 2014. "Putting Plea Bargaining on the Record." *University of Pennsylvania Law Review* 162: 683–718.

Manfredi, Christopher. 1998. *The Supreme Court and Juvenile Justice.* Lawrence: University Press of Kansas.

Manikis, Marie. 2015. "Victim Impact Statements at Sentencing: Towards a Clearer Understanding of Their Aims." *The University of Toronto Law Journal* 65(2): 85–123.

Mann, Jim. 2011. "Delivering Justice to the Mentally Ill: Characteristics of Mental Health Courts." *Southwest Journal of Criminal Justice* 8(1): 44–58.

Mansfield, Cathy Lesser. 1999. "Disorder in the Court: Rethinking the Role of Non-Lawyer Judges in Limited Jurisdiction Court Civil Cases." *New Mexico Law Review* 29: 119–174.

Marceau, Justin F. 2012. "Embracing a New Era of Ineffective Assistance of Counsel." *University of Pennsylvania Journal of Constitutional Law* 14: 1161–1217.

Marder, Nancy S. 2012. "The Conundrum of Cameras in the Courtroom." *Arizona State Law Journal* 44: 1489–1574.

Maremont, Mark, and Chad Bray. 2005. "Tyco Trial Jurors Say Defendants Weren't Credible." *Wall Street Journal*, June 20.

Marlowe, Douglas B. 2016. "Drug Courts and Drug Policy." In Thomas G. Bloomberg, Julie Mestre Brancale, Kevin M. Beaver, and William D. Bales (Eds.), *Advancing Criminology and Criminal Justice Policy* (pp. 203–216). New York: Routledge.

Martin, Edward C. (n.d.) Tutorial on the Basics of Legal Analysis. Available online at http://omnilearn.net/LOGIC /index.html Martin, Elaine. 1993. "Women on the Bench: A Different Voice?" *Judicature* 77: 126–128.

Martin, Jamie S., Kate Hanrahan, and James H. Bowers, Jr. 2009. "Offenders' Perceptions of House Arrest and Electronic Monitoring." *Journal of Offender Rehabilitation* 48: 547–570.

Martinez, Ramiro. 2007. "Incorporating Latinos and Immigrants into Policing Research." *Criminology and Public Policy* 6: 57–64.

Martinez, Ramiro. 2010. "Economic Conditions and Racial/ Ethnic Variations in Violence: Immigration, the Latino Paradox, and Future Research." *Criminology and Public Policy* 9: 707–714.

Martinson, Robert. 1974. "What Works? Questions and Answers about Prison Reform." *Public Interest* 35: 22–54.

Marvell, Thomas, and Mary Luskin. 1991. "The Impact of Speedy Trial Laws in Connecticut and North Carolina." *Justice System Journal* 14: 343–357.

Marvell, Thomas, and Carlisle Moody. 1996. "Determinate Sentencing and Abolishing Parole: The Long-Term Impacts on Prisons and Crime." *Criminology* 34: 107–128.

Mastrofski, Stephen, and R. Richard Ritti. 1996. "Police Training and the Effects of Organization on Drunk Driving Enforcement." *Justice Quarterly* 13: 291–320.

Mather, Lynn. 1974a. "Some Determinants of the Method of Case Disposition: Decision-Making by Public Defenders in Los Angeles." *Law and Society Review* 8: 187–216.

Mather, Lynn. 1974b. "The Outsider in the Courtroom: An Alternative Role for the Defense." In Herbert Jacob (Ed.), *The Potential for Reform of Criminal Justice.* Newbury Park, CA: Sage.

Mather, Lynn. 1979. *Plea Bargaining or Trial?* Lexington, MA: Heath.

Mather, Lynn, and Leslie Levin. 2012. "Why Context Matters." In Leslie Levin and Lynn Mather (Eds.), *Lawyers in Practice: Ethical Decision Making in Context.* Chicago: University of Chicago Press.

Mauer, Marc. 2011a. "Sentencing Reform Amid Mass Incarcerations—Guarded Optimism." *Criminal Justice* 26(1): 27–36.

Mauer, Marc. 2011b. "Addressing Racial Disparities in Incarceration." *The Prison Journal* 91(3): 87S–101S.

Mauer, Marc, Ryan S. King, and Malcolm C. Young. 2004. *The Meaning of "Life": Long Prison Sentences in Context*. Washington, DC: The Sentencing Project.

Mauro, Tony. 2006. "Court Backs Death Row Inmates." *Legal Times*, June 19.

Maxwell, Christopher, Joel Garner, and Jeffrey Fagan. 2002. "The Preventive Effects of Arrest on Intimate Partner Violence: Research, Policy, and Theory." *Criminology and Public Policy* 2: 51–80.

Mayer, Martin. 2007. *The Judges*. New York: Macmillan.

Maynard, Douglas. 1988. "Narratives and Narrative Structure in Plea Bargaining." *Law and Society Review* 22: 449–481.

Mays, G. Larry, and William Taggart. 1986. "Court Clerks, Court Administrators, and Judges: Conflict in Managing the Courts." *Journal of Criminal Justice* 14: 1–7.

McCahill, Thomas W., Linda C. Meyer, Arthur M. Fischman. 1979. *The Aftermath of Rape*. Lexington, VA: Lexington Books.

McCampbell, Robert. 1995. "Parallel Civil and Criminal Proceedings: Six Legal Pitfalls." *Criminal Law Bulletin* 31: 483–501.

McCarthy, Brendan, 2011. "B.G. Pleads Guilty While Refusing to 'Snitch.'" *The Times-Picayune*, December 8.

McCord, David. 2005. "Juries Should Not Be Required to Have 12 Members or to Render Unanimous Verdicts." *Judicature* 88: 301–305.

McCormack, Robert. 1991. "Compensating Victims of Violent Crime." *Justice Quarterly* 8: 329–346.

McCormick, John. 1999. "Coming Two Days Shy of Martyrdom." *Newsweek*, February 15.

McCoy, Candace. 1984. "Determinate Sentencing, Plea Bargaining Bans, and Hydraulic Discretion in California." *Justice System Journal* 9: 256–275.

McCoy, Candace. 1993. *Politics and Plea Bargaining: Victim's Rights in California*. Philadelphia: University of Pennsylvania Press.

McCoy, Candace. 2003. "Bargaining under the Hammer: The Trial Penalty in the USA." In Douglas Koski (Ed.), *The Criminal Jury Trial in America*. Raleigh, NC: Carolina Academic Press.

McDonald, Douglas Corry. 1986. *Punishment Without Walls: Community Service Sentences in New York City*. New Brunswick, NJ: Rutgers University Press.

McDonald, Douglas Corry, and Kenneth Carlson. 1993. *Sentencing in the Federal Courts: Does Race Matter? The Transition to Sentencing Guidelines, 1986–1990*. Washington, DC: Bureau of Justice Statistics.

McDonald, Thomas, Robert Wood, and Melissa Pflug (Eds.). 1996. *Rural Criminal Justice: Conditions, Constraints, and Challenges*. Salem, WI: Sheffield.

McDonald, William (Ed.). 1976. *Criminal Justice and the Victim*. Newbury Park, CA: Sage.

McDonald, William. 1979. "The Prosecutor's Domain." In William McDonald (Ed.), *The Prosecutor*. Newbury Park, CA: Sage.

McDonough, Molly. 2008. "Judge Dismisses Nifong from Duke Player's Civil Suit, for Now." *ABA Journal*, January 30.

McGarrell, Edmund, and Natalie Kroovand Hipple. 2008. "Family Group Conferencing and Re-Offending among First-Time Juvenile Offenders: The Indianapolis Experiment." *Justice Quarterly* 24: 221–246.

McGlone, Tim. 2007a. "Judge's Stand on Norfolk Man's Sentencing Heads to Supreme Court." *The Virginian-Pilot*, September 29.

McGlone, Tim. 2007b. "Supreme Court Hears Case on Norfolk Drug Sentencing." *The Virginian-Pilot*, October 3.

McIntyre, Donald. 1968. "A Study of Judicial Dominance of the Charging Decision." *Journal of Criminal Law, Criminology and Police Science* 59: 463–490.

McIntyre, Donald, and David Lippman. 1970. "Prosecutors and Disposition of Felony Cases." *American Bar Association Journal* 56: 154–1159.

McIntyre, Joe. 2014. "Evaluating Judicial Performance Evaluations: A Conceptual Analysis." *Oñati Socio-legal Series* 4(5): 898–926.

McIntyre, Lisa. 1987. *The Public Defender: The Practice of Law in the Shadows of Repute*. Chicago: University of Chicago Press.

McKeon, John C., and David G. Rice. 2009. "Administering Justice in Montana's Rural Courts." *Montana Law Review* 70: 201–220.

McKimmie, Blake M., Emma Antrobus, and Chantelle Baguley. 2014. "Objective and Subjective Comprehension of Jury Instructions in Criminal Trials." *New Criminal Law Review* 17: 163–183.

McKimmie, Blake M., Jane M. Masters, Barbara M. Masser, Regina A. Schuller, and Deborah J. Terry. 2013. "Stereotypical and Counterstereotypical Defendants: Who Is He and What Was the Case Against Her?" *Psychology, Public Policy, and Law* 19: 343–354.

McLauchlan, William, and Eric Waltenburg. 2014. "Crossing the Finish Line: An Analysis of the Work of the Supreme Court." *Judicature* 97: 257–264.

McLaughlin, Jolie. 2014. "The Price of Justice: Interest-Convergence, Cost, and the Anti-Death Penalty Movement." *Northwestern University Law Review* 108: 675–710.

McNiel Dale E., and Renée L. Binder. 2007. "Effectiveness of a Mental Health Court in Reducing Criminal Recidivism and Violence." *American Journal of Psychiatry* 164(9): 1395–1403.

McNulty, Timothy. 2013. "Convicted Orie Melvin Resigns from Pennsylvania Supreme Court. *Pittsburgh Post-Gazette*, March 25. Available online at http://www.post-gazette .com/news/state/2013/03/25/Convicted-Orie-Melvin -resigns-from-Pennsylvania-Supreme-Court /stories/201303250171#ixzz34vPfuqyR

McQuiston, J. T. 1995. "In the Bizarre L.I.R.R. Trial, Equally Bizarre Confrontations." *New York Times*, February 5.

Mears, Bill. 2012. "Justices Rule for Death Row Inmate after Legal Mistakes." *CNN* January 18. Available online at http://www.cnn.com/2012/01/18/justice/scotus -alabama-inmate/index.html

Mears, Daniel, Joshua Cochran, Brian Stults, Sarah Greenman, Avinash Bhati, and Mark Greenwald. 2014. "The 'True' Juvenile Offender: Age Effects and Juvenile Court Sanctioning." *Criminology* 52: 169–194.

Mears, Daniel, Zia Wang, Carter Hay, and William Bales. 2008. "Social Ecology and Recidivism: Implications for Prisoner Reentry." *Criminology* 46: 301–348.

Mears, Daniel P., Carter Hay, Marc Gertz, and Christina Mancini. 2007. "Public Opinion and the Foundation of the Juvenile Court." *Criminology* 45: 223–257.

Mecklenburg, Sheri. 2006. "Addendum to the Report to the Legislature of the State of Illinois: The Illinois Pilot Program on Sequential Double-Blind Identification Procedures." Springfield, IL: Illinois State Police. Available online at http://eyewitness.utep.edu/Documents /IllinoisPilotStudyOnEyewitnessIDAddendum.pdf

Medwed, Daniel S. 2010. "*Brady*'s Bunch of Flaws." *Washington and Lee Law Review* 67: 1533–1567.

Megale, Elizabeth. 2013. "Zimmerman's Acquittal: A Race-Neutral Verdict for a Racially-Charged Crime." *JURIST* - Forum, July 19. Available online at http://jurist.org /forum/2013/07/elizabeth-megale-zimmerman-acquittal .php

Meinhold, Stephen, and Steven Shull. 1993. "Policy Congruence between the President and the Solicitor General." Paper presented at the annual meeting of the Midwest Political Science Association, Chicago.

Melcarne, Alessandro, and Giovanni B. Ramello. 2015. Judicial Independence, Judges' Incentives and Efficiency. *Review of Law & Economics* 11(2): 149–169.

Mental Health America. 2012. *Position Statement 53: Mental Health Courts*. Available online at http://www.mental-healthamerica.net/positions/mental-health-courts

Merritt, Nancy, Terry Fain, and Susan Turner. 2006. "Oregon's Get Tough Sentencing Reform: A Lesson in Justice System Adaptation." *Criminology and Public Policy* 5: 5–36.

Messing, Jill Theresa, Allison Ward-Lasher, Jonel Thaller, and Meredith E. Bagwell-Gray. 2015. "The State of Intimate Partner Violence Intervention: Progress and Continuing Challenges." *Social Work* 60(4): 305–313.

Metcalfe, Christi. 2016. "The Role of Courtroom Workgroups in Felony Case Dispositions: An Analysis of Workgroup Familiarity and Similarity." *Law & Society Review* 50(3): 637–673.

Meyer, Jon'a, and Paul Jesilow. 1997. *Doing Justice in the People's Court: Sentencing by Municipal Court Judges*. Albany: State University of New York Press.

Meyers, David. 2005. *Boys among Men: Trying and Sentencing Juveniles as Adults*. Westport, CT: Praeger.

Michel, Cedric. 2016. "Violent Street Crime versus Harmful White-Collar Crime: A Comparison of Perceived Seriousness and Punitiveness." *Critical Criminology* 24(1): 127–143.

Miethe, Terance D. 1987. "Charging and plea bargaining practices under determinate sentencing: An investigation of the hydraulic displacement of discretion. *Journal of Criminal Law & Criminology* 78: 155–176.

Miethe, Terance D., and Charles Moore. 1989. "Sentencing Guidelines: Their Effect in Minnesota." Washington, DC: Department of Justice, Bureau of Justice Statistics.

Miles, Thomas J. 2013. "Does the "Community Prosecution" Strategy Reduce Crime? A Test of Chicago's Experience." *American Law and Economics Review* 2–27.

Mileski, Maureen. 1971. "Courtroom Encounters: An Observation Study of a Lower Criminal Court." *Law and Society Review* 5: 473–538.

Miller, Benjamin. 1991. "Assessing the Functions of Judicial Conduct Organizations." *Judicature* 75: 16–19.

Miller, Dawn. 2011. "Sentencing Elderly Criminal Offenders." *NAELA Journal* 7: 221–247.

Miller, Herbert, William McDonald, and James Cramer. 1978. *Plea Bargaining in the United States*. Washington, DC: National Institute of Law Enforcement and Criminal Justice.

Miller, J. Mitchell, Holly Ventura-Miller, and J. C. Barnes. 2007. "The Effect of Demeanor on Drug Court Admission." *Criminal Justice Policy Review* 18: 246–259.

Miller, Kenneth P. 2013. "Defining Rights in the States: Judicial Activism and Popular Response." *Albany Law Review* 76: 2061–2103.

Miller, Marc L., and Ronald Wright. 2008. "The Black Box." *Iowa Law Review* 94: 125–196.

Miller, Monica K., Edie Greene, Hannah Dietrich, Jared Chamberlain, and Julie A. Singer. 2008. "How Emotion Affects the Trial Process." *Judicature* 92: 56–64.

Miller, Monica K., Jonathan Maskaly, Morgan Green, and Clayton D. Peoples. 2011. "The Effects of Deliberations and Religious Identity on Mock Jurors' Verdicts." *Group Processes Intergroup Relations* 14(4): 517–532.

Miller, Susan L., and Shana L. Maier. 2008. "Moving Beyond Numbers: What Female Judges Say about Different Judicial Voices." *Journal of Women, Politics & Policy* 29: 527–559.

Mills, Carol, and Wayne Bohannon. 1980. "Jury Characteristics: To What Extent Are They Related to Jury Verdicts?" *Judicature* 64: 22–31.

Miner, Roger J. 1999. "Professional Responsibility in Appellate Practice: A View from the Bench." *Pace Law Review* 19: 323–344.

Minton, Michelle. 2013. "The Legal Drinking Age Has Not Been Effective." In Stefan Kiesbye (Ed.), *Should the Legal Drinking Age Be Lowered?* Detroit: Greenhaven Press.

Minton, Todd D. 2013. *Jail Inmates at Midyear—2012* [Statistical Tables]. Washington, DC: Bureau of Justice Statistics. Retrieved from http://www.bjs.gov/content/pub/pdf/jim12st.pdf

Minton, Tom D., and Zhen Zeng. 2015. *Jail Inmates at Midyear—2014*. Washington, DC: Department of Justice, Bureau of Justice Statistics.

Misner, Robert. 1996. "Recasting Prosecutorial Discretion." *Journal of Criminal Law and Criminology* 86: 717–758.

Mitchell, Josh. 2008. "Victims Fund Assists Felons." *Baltimore Sun*, March 16.

Mitchell, Ojmarrh. 2005. "A Meta-Analysis of Race and Sentencing Research: Explaining the Inconsistencies." *Journal of Quantitative Criminology* 21: 439–466.

Mitchell, Tara L., Ryann M. Haw, Jeffrey E. Pfeifer, and Christian A. Meissner. 2005. "Racial Bias in Mock Juror Decision-Making: A Meta-Analytic Review of Defendant Treatment." *Law and Human Behavior* 29: 621–637.

Mize, Gregory E., Paula Hannaford-Agor, and Nicole L. Waters. 2007. *The State-of-the States Survey of Jury Improvement Efforts: A Compendium Report*. Williamsburg, VA: National Center for State Courts. Available online at http://www.ncsconline.org/D_Research/cjs/pdf/SOSCompendiumFinal.pdf

Mnookin, Jennifer L. 2008. "The Validity of Latent Fingerprint Identification: Confessions of a Fingerprinting Moderate." *Law, Probability & Risk* 7: 127–141.

Moenssens, André. 2002. "The Reliability of Fingerprint Identification: A Case Report." Available online at http://onin.com/fp/reliability_of_fp_ident.html

Molesworth, Claire L. 2008. "Knowledge versus Acknowledgment: Rethinking the *Alford* Plea in Sexual Assault Cases." *Seattle Journal for Social Justice* 6: 907–942.

Moley, Raymond. 1928. "The Vanishing Jury." *Southern California Law Review* 2: 97.

Monahan, John, and Jennifer L. Skeem. 2016. "Risk Assessment in Criminal Sentencing." *Annual Review of Clinical Psychology* 12: 489–513.

"Montana Judge Censured Over Rape Comments." 2014. *Associated Press*, July 22.

Moore, Kathleen Dean. 1989. *Pardons: Justice, Mercy and the Public Interest*. New York: Oxford University Press.

Moore Marlee E., and Virgina Aldigé Hiday. 2006. "Mental Health Court Outcomes: A Comparison of Re-Arrest and Re-Arrest Severity Between Mental Health Court and Treatment Court Participants." *Law and Human Behavior* 30: 659–674.

Morabito, Melissa Schaefer, April Pattavina, and Linda M. Williams. 2016. "It All Just Piles Up: Challenges to Victim Credibility Accumulate to Influence Sexual Assault Case Processing." *Journal of Interpersonal Violence*. Advanced online publication. doi: 10.1177/0886260516669164

Moran, Gary, and John C. Comfort. 1986. "Neither 'Tentative' nor 'Fragmentary': Verdict Preference of Impaneled Felony Jurors as a Function of Attitude toward Capital Punishment." *Journal of Applied Psychology* 71: 146–155.

Moran, Gary, and Brian Cutler. 1991. "The Prejudicial Impact of Pretrial Publicity." *Journal of Applied Social Psychology* 21: 345–367.

Morgan, Kathryn, and Brent Smith. 2005. "Victims, Punishment, and Parole: The Effects of Victim Participation on Parole Hearings." *Criminology and Public Policy* 4: 333–360.

Moriarty, Jane Campbell. 2007. "'Misconvictions,' Science, and the Ministers of Justice." *Nebraska Law Review* 86: 1–42.

Moriearty, Perry L. 2008. "Combating the Color-Coded Confinement of Kids: An Equal Protection Remedy." *New York University Review of Law and Social Change* 32: 285–343.

Morris, Norval, and Michael Tonry. 1990. *Between Prison and Probation: Intermediate Punishments in a Rational Sentencing System*. New York: Oxford University Press.

Morrow, Weston, Samuel G. Vickovic, and Henry F. Fradella. 2014. "Examining the Prevalence and Correlates of a 'Senior Citizen Discount' in U.S. Federal Courts." *Criminal Justice Studies* 27(4): 362–386.

Mortimer, John. 1984. "Rumpole and the Confession of Guilt." *Rumpole for the Defence*. New York: Penguin Books.

Mosteller, Robert P. 2002. "Discovery in Criminal Cases." *Encyclopedia of Crime and Justice*. Farmington Hills, MI: Gale/Cengage.

Mosteller, Robert P. 2007. "The Duke Lacrosee Case, Innocence, and False Identifications: A Fundamental Failure to 'Do Justice.'" *Fordham Law Review* 76: 1337–1412.

Müeller-Johnson, Katrin U., and Mandeep K. Dhami. 2009. "Effects of Offenders' Age and Health on Sentencing Decisions." *The Journal of Social Psychology* 150(1): 77–97.

Muliluvuori, Marja-Liisa. (2001). "Recidivism among People Sentenced to Community Service in Finland." *Journal of Scandinavian Studies in Criminology and Crime Prevention* 2(1): 72–82.

Murphy, Erin. (2015). *Inside the Cell: The Dark Side of Forensic DNA*. New York: Nation Books.

Murphy, Erin. 2016. "Neuroscience and the Civil/Criminal Daubert Divide." *Fordham Law Review* 85: 619–639.

Murphy, Justin P., and Adrian Fontecilla. 2013. "Social Media Evidence in Government Investigations and Criminal Proceedings: A Frontier of New Legal Issues." *Richmond Journal of Law and Technology* 19: 11–33.

Mushlin, Michael, and Naomi Galtz. 2009. "Getting Real about Race and Prisoner Rights." *Fordham Urban Law Journal* 36: 27–53.

Myers, Laura, and Sue Titus Reid. 1995. "The Importance of County Context in the Measurement of Sentencing Disparity: The Search for Routinization." *Journal of Criminal Justice* 23: 233–241.

Myers, Martha, and John Hagan. 1979. "Private and Public Trouble: Prosecutors and the Allocation of Court Resources." *Social Problems* 26: 439–451.

Myers, Martha, and Susette Talarico. 1986b. "Urban Justice, Rural Injustice? Urbanization and Its Effect on Sentencing." *Criminology* 24: 367–391.

Nader, Laura. 1992. "Trading Justice for Harmony." *National Institute for Dispute Resolution Forum* (Winter): 12–14.

Nagel, Irene, and John Hagan. 1983. "Gender and Crime: Offense Patterns and Criminal Court Sanctions." In Michael Tonry and Norval Morris (Eds.), *Crime and Justice: An Annual Review of Research* (vol. 4, pp. 91–144). Chicago: University of Chicago Press.

Nagel, Irene, H., and Schulhofer, Stephen J. 1992. "A Tale of Three Cities: An Empirical Study of Charging and Bargaining Practices under the Federal Sentencing Guidelines. *Southern California Law Review* 66: 501–566.

Nagin, Daniel. 1998. "Criminal Deterrence Research at the Outset of the Twenty-First Century." In Michael Tonry (Ed.), *Crime and Justice: A Review of Research*. Vol. 23. Chicago: University of Chicago Press.

Nardulli, Peter. 1978. *The Courtroom Elite: An Organizational Perspective on Criminal Justice*. Cambridge, MA: Ballinger.

Nardulli, Peter. 1979. "The Caseload Controversy and the Study of Criminal Courts." *Journal of Criminal Law and Criminology* 70: 89–101.

Nardulli, Peter. 1983. "The Societal Cost of the Exclusionary Rule: An Empirical Assessment." *American Bar Foundation Research Journal* 8(3): 585–609.

Nardulli, Peter. 1986. "'Insider' Justice: Defense Attorneys and the Handling of Felony Cases." *Journal of Criminal Law and Criminology* 77: 379–417.

Nardulli, Peter, Roy Flemming, and James Eisenstein. 1984. "Unraveling the Complexities of Decision Making in Face-to-Face Groups: A Contextual Analysis of Plea-Bargained Sentences." *American Political Science Review* 78: 912–928.

National Academies of Sciences. 2009. *Strengthening Forensic Science in the United States: A Path Forward*. Washington, DC: National Research Council.

National Advisory Commission on Criminal Justice Standards and Goals. 1973. *Report on Courts*. Washington, DC: Government Printing Office.

National Association of Criminal Defense Lawyers. 2000. "Citizens Grand Jury Bill of Rights." Available online at http://www.criminaljustice.org

National Association of Criminal Defense Lawyers. 2009. *Minor Crimes, Massive Waste: The Terrible Toll of America's Broken Misdemeanor Courts*. Washington, DC: Author.

National Association of Criminal Defense Lawyers. 2017. *Criminal Defense Issue: Custodial Interrogation Recording*. Available at https://www.nacdl.org/usmap/crim/30262/48121/d

National Association of Women Judges. 2016. "2016 Representation of United State Court Women Judges." Available online at https://www.nawj.org/statistics/2016-us-state-court-women-judges

National Center for State Courts. 2003. "A Profile of Hung Juries." *Caseload Highlights* 9: 1.

National Center for State Courts. 2010. "Guidelines for Implementing Best Practices in Court Building Security Costs, Priorities, Funding Strategies, and Accountability." Available online at http://contentdm.ncsconline.org/cgibin/showfile.exe?CISOROOT=/facilities&CISOPTR=153

National Center for State Courts. n.d. "Technology in the Courts: Resource Guide." Available online at http://www.ncsc.org/topics/technology/technology-in-the-courts/resource-guide.aspx

National Center for State Courts. 2016. *Survey of Judicial Salaries* 40(2).

National Center for State Courts. 2014. "101 Personal Safety Tips for Judges and Court Staff." Retrieved from https://www.courts.state.wy.us/Documents/SecCom/CourtSecurityPersonalSafetyTipsforJudgesandCourtStaff2014.pdf

National Center for State Courts. 2015. *Methods of Judicial Selection*. Retrieved from http://www.judicialselection.us/judicial_selection/methods/selection_of_judges.cfm?state

National Center for Victims of Crime. 2012. "Issues: Victims' Bill of Rights." Available online at http://www.ncvc.org

National Center for Victims of Crime. 2015. *NCVRW Resource Guide: Urban and Rural Crime*. Washington, DC: U.S. Department of Justice, Office of Justice Programs, Office for Victims of Crime.

National District Attorneys Association. 2007. "Statement in Response to the Proposed Resolution Concerning Sentence Mitigation for Youthful Offenders." Available online at http://www.ndaa.org

National District Attorneys Association. (2016, Sept. 30). "Response to the Report Forensic Science in Criminal Courts: Ensuring Scientific Validity of Feature-Comparison Methods." Available online at http://www.crime-scene-investigator.net /national-district-attorneys-association-response-to-the -report-forensic-science-in-criminal-courts-ensuring -scientific-validity-of-feature-comparison-methods.html

National Drug Court Resource Center. 2014. "How Many Drug Courts Are There?"

National Governors Association. 2010. "Prisoner Reentry Policy." Washington, DC: Author.

National Institute of Justice. 1982. *Exemplary Projects: Focus for 1982—Projects to Combat Violent Crime*. Washington, DC: Department of Justice.

National Institute of Justice, Office of Justice Programs. 2017. *Specialized Courts*. Available online at https://www.nij.gov /topics/courts/pages/specialized-courts.aspx

National Law Enforcement and Corrections Technology Center. 1999. *Keeping Track of Electronic Monitoring*. Available online at https://www.justnet.org/InteractiveTechBeat /Winter-1999.pdf

National Registry of Exonerations. 2017. *Exonerations in 2016*. Irvine, CA: University of California Irvine.

National Research Council, Committee on Scientific Assessment of Bullet Lead Elemental Composition Comparison. 2004. *Forensic Analysis: Weighing Bullet Lead Evidence*. Washington, DC: National Academies Press.

National Right to Counsel Committee. 2009. *Justice Denied: America's Continuing Neglect of Our Constitutional Right to Counsel*. Washington, DC: The Constitution Project.

National Sheriffs' Association. 2011. "History of Court Security." Available online at http://www.sheriffs.org /publications/brief-history-of-court-security

National Sheriffs' Association. 2012. "NSA Statement on the Neighborhood Watch Tragedy in FL."

Nellis, Ashley. 2016. *The Color of Justice: Racial and Ethnic Disparity in State Prisons*. Washington, DC: The Sentencing Project.

Nelson, Michael. 2011. "Uncontested and Unaccountable? Rates of Contestations in Trial Court Elections." *Judicature* 94: 208–217.

Neubauer, David. 1974a. "After the Arrest: The Charging Decision in Prairie City." *Law and Society Review* 8: 495–517.

Neubauer, David. 1974b. *Criminal Justice in Middle America*. Morristown, NJ: General Learning Press.

Neubauer, David. 1983. "Improving the Analysis and Presentation of Data on Case Processing Time." *Journal of Criminal Law and Criminology* 74: 1589–1607.

Neubauer, David. 1985. "Published Opinions versus Summary Affirmations: Criminal Appeals in Louisiana." *Justice System Journal* 10: 173–189.

Neubauer, David. 1991. "Winners and Losers before the Louisiana Supreme Court: The Case of Criminal Appeals." *Justice Quarterly* 8: 85–106.

Neubauer, David. 1992. "A Polychotomous Measure of Appellate Court Outcomes: The Case of Criminal Appeals." *Justice System Journal* 16: 75–87.

Neubauer, David. 1996. "A Tale of Two Cities: A Comparison of Orleans and Jefferson Parish, Louisiana." Paper presented at the annual meeting of the Academy of Criminal Justice Sciences, Louisville, KY.

Neubauer, David. 2001. *Debating Crime: Rhetoric and Reality*. Belmont, CA: Wadsworth.

Neubauer, David, Marcia Lipetz, Mary Luskin, and John Paul Ryan. 1981. *Managing the Pace of Justice: An Evaluation of LEAA's Court Delay Reduction Programs*. Washington, DC: Government Printing Office.

Neubauer, David, and Stephen Meinhold. 2006. *Battle Supreme: The Confirmation of Chief Justice John Roberts and the Future of the Supreme Court*. Belmont, CA: Wadsworth.

Neubauer, David W., and Stephen S. Meinhold. 2013. *Judicial Process: Law, Courts, and Politics in the United States*. 6th ed. Belmont, CA: Wadsworth.

Neufeld, Peter J. 2005. "The (Near) Irrelevance of *Daubert* to Criminal Justice and Some Suggestions for Reform." *American Journal of Public Health* 95: S107–S113.

Newton, Samuel P., Teresa L. Welch, and Neal G. Hamilton. 2012. "No Justice in Utah's Justice Courts: Constitutional Issues, Systemic Problems, and the Failure to Protect Defendants in Utah's Infamous Local Courts." *Utah Law Review OnLaw* 27: 27–72.

New York Times Editorial Board. 2013, November 8. "A Prosecutor Is Punished." http://www.nytimes.com/2013/11/09 /opinion/a-prosecutor-is-punished.html

Nimmer, Raymond. 1978. *The Nature of System Change: Reform Impact in the Criminal Courts*. Chicago: American Bar Foundation.

Nimmer, Raymond, and Patricia Krauthaus. 1977. "Plea Bargaining Reform in Two Cities." *Justice System Journal* 3: 6–21.

Nirenberg, Michael. 2016. "Meeting a Forensic Podiatry Admissibility Challenge: A Daubert Case Study." *Journal of Forensic Sciences* 61(3): 833–841.

Nobiling, Tracy, Cassia Spohn, and Miriam DeLone. 1998. "A Tale of Two Counties: Unemployment and Sentence Severity." *Justice Quarterly* 15: 459–485.

Nolan-Haley, Jacqueline. 2013. *Alternative Dispute Resolution in a Nutshell.* 4th ed. St. Paul, MN: West.

NOLO. 2015. "50-State Chart of Small Claims Court Dollar Limits." Available online at http://www.nolo.com

Norman, Michael D., and Robert C. Wadman. 2000. "Utah Presentence Investigation Reports: User Group Perceptions of Quality and Effectiveness." *Federal Probation* 64: 7–12.

Norris, Floyd. 2005. "Chief Executive Was Paid Millions, and He Never Noticed the Fraud?" *New York Times*, January 7.

Norton, Lee. 1983. "Witness Involvement in the Criminal Justice System and Intention to Cooperate in Future Prosecutions." *Journal of Criminal Justice* 11: 143–152.

Novak, Lisa. 2003. "Federal Courts Adapt for Maximum Security." *The Judges' Journal* 42: 22–24.

Nowacki, Jeffery. 2017. "An Intersectional Approach to Race/Ethnicity, Sex, and Age Disparity in Federal Sentencing Outcomes: An Examination of Policy Across Time Periods." *Criminology & Criminal Justice* 17(1): 97–116.

Nugent, Hugh, and Thomas McEwen. 1988. *Prosecutor's National Assessment of Needs.* Washington, DC: Department of Justice, National Institute of Justice.

Nugent-Borakove, Elaine, Barry Mahoney, and Debra Whitcomb. "Strengthening Rural Courts: Challenges and Progress." National Center for State Courts. Available online http://ncsc.contentdm.oclc.org/cdm/ref/collection/ctadmin/id/1843

N.Y. Civil Liberties Union. 2015. *Press Release: New York City Takes Important Step Toward Ending Destructive Cash Bail System,* http://www.nyclu.org/news/new-york-city-takes-important-step-toward-ending-destructive-cash-bail-system

Oaks, Dallin. 1970. "Studying the Exclusionary Rule in Search and Seizure." *University of Chicago Law Review* 37: 665–753.

O'Brien, David. 1988. "The Supreme Court: From Warren to Burger to Rehnquist." *Political Science* 20: 13.

O'Brien, Stewart, Steven Pheterson, Michael Wright, and Carl Hostica. 1977. "The Criminal Lawyer: The Defendant's Perspective." *American Journal of Criminal Law* 5(3): 283–312.

O'Connor, Sandra Day. 2009. "Judicial Independence and Civic Education." *Utah Bar Journal* 22: 10–19.

Office for Victims of Crime. 1998. *From Pain to Power: Crime Victims Take Action.* Washington, DC: Department of Justice.

Office of Juvenile Justice and Delinquency Prevention. 1996. *Female Offenders in the Juvenile Justice System.* Washington, DC: Department of Justice.

Office of Juvenile Justice and Delinquency Prevention. 2014. *OJJDP Statistical Briefing Book, 2013.* Available online at http://www.ojjdp.gov/ojstatbb/

Ofshe, Richard J., and Richard A. Leo. 1997. "The Social Psychology of Police Interrogation: The Theory and Classification of True and False Confessions." *Studies in Law, Politics, and Society* 16: 189–254.

Ogletree, Charles J., Jr., and Yoav Sapir. 2004. "Keeping *Gideon*'s Promise: A Comparison of the American and Israeli Public Defender Experiences." *New York University Review of Law and Social Change* 29: 203–235.

Ogloff, J. R. P. (1991). "A Comparison of Insanity Defense Standards on Juror Decision Making." *Law and Human Behavior* 15(5): 509–531.

Ogloff, James R. P., and V. Gordon Rose. 2007. "The Comprehension of Judicial Instructions." In Neil Brewer and Kipling D. Williams (Eds.), *Psychology and Law: An Empirical Perspective.* New York: Guildford Press.

OJJDP. 2015. Juveniles Tried as Adults. In *Statistical Briefing Book* [Online]. Available at https://www.ojjdp.gov/ojstatbb/structure_process/qa04115.asp?qaDate=2014

Oldenburg, Ann. 2011. "Lindsay Lohan Ordered to 30 Days in Jail." *USA Today*, November 2.

Oran, Daniel. 2000. *Law Dictionary for Nonlawyers.* 3rd ed. St. Paul, MN: West.

Oran, Daniel. 2000. *Law Dictionary for Nonlawyers.* 4th ed. Belmont, CA: Cengage Learning.

O'Neal, Eryn Nicole, and Cassia Spohn. 2016. "When the Perpetrator Is a Partner: Arrest and Charging Decisions in Intimate Partner Sexual Assault Cases—A Focal Concerns Analysis." *Violence Against Women* 23(6): 707–729.

O'Neal, Eryn Nicole, Katharine Tellis, and Cassia Spohn. 2015. "Prosecuting Intimate Partner Sexual Assault: Legal and Extra-Legal Factors That Influence Charging Decisions." *Violence Against Women* 21(10): 1237–1258.

O'Neill, Michael Edmund. 2003. "When Prosecutors Don't: Trends in Federal Prosecutorial Declinations." *Notre Dame Law Review* 79: 221–290.

O'Neill-Shermer, Lauren, and Brian D. Johnson. 2010. "Criminal Prosecutions: Examining Prosecutorial Discretion and Charge Reductions in U.S. Federal District Courts." *Justice Quarterly* 27(3): 394–430.

Osborn, Elizabeth Hervey. 2008. "What Happened to 'Paul's Law'?: Insights on Advocating for Better Training and Better Outcomes in Encounters Between Law Enforcement and Persons with Autism Spectrum Disorders." *University of Colorado Law Review* 79: 333–397.

Ostrom, Brian, and Neal Kauder. 1999. *Examining the Work of State Courts, 1998.* Williamsburg, VA: National Center for State Courts.

Ostrom, Brian, Charles Ostrom, Jr., Roger Hanson, and Matthew Kleiman. 2007. *Trial Courts as Organizations*. Philadelphia: Temple University Press.

Ostrom, Brian, Charles Ostrom, Roger Hanson, and Matthew Kleinman. 2008. *Assessing Consistency and Fairness in Sentencing: A Comparative Study in three States*. Williamsburg, VA: National Center for State Courts.

Ostrom, Brian J., Neal B. Kauder, and Robert C. LaFountain. 2001. *Examining the Work of State Courts, 2001: A National Perspective from the Court Statistics Project*. Washington, DC: National Center for State Courts.

Otis, Caroline Crocker, Sarah M. Greathouse, Julia Busso Kennard, and Margaret Bull Kovera. 2014. "Hypothesis Testing in Attorney-Conducted Voir Dire." *Law & Human Behavior* 38(4): 392–404.

Owen, Stephen S., Henry F. Fradella, Tod W. Burke, and Jerry Joplin. 2015. *The Foundations of Criminal Justice*. New York: Oxford University Press.

Owens, Stephen D., Elizabeth Accetta, Jennifer J. Charles, and Samantha E. Shoemaker. 2015. *Indigent Defense Services in the United States, FY 2008–2012—Updated*. U.S. Department of Justice (NCJ 246683). Retrieved from https://www.bjs.gov/content/pub/pdf/idsus0812.pdf

Pabst, William. 1973. "What Do Six-Member Juries Really Save?" *Judicature* 57: 6–11.

Packer, Herbert. 1968. *The Limits of the Criminal Sanction*. Palo Alto, CA: Stanford University Press.

Padawer-Singer, Alice, and Alice Barton. 1975. "The Impact of Pretrial Publicity on Jurors'Verdicts." In Rita James Simon (Ed.), *The Jury System in America: A Critical Overview*. Beverly Hills, CA: Sage.

Padgett, John. 1990. "Plea Bargaining and Prohibition in the Federal Courts, 1908–1934." *Law and Society Review* 24: 413–450.

Padgett, Kathy G., William D. Bales, and Thomas G. Blomberg. 2006. "Under Surveillance: An Empirical Test of the Effectiveness and Consequences of Electronic Monitoring." *Criminology and Public Policy* 5(1): 61–92.

Palmer, Barbara. 2001. "Women in the American Judiciary: Their Influence and Impact." *Women and Politics* 23: 89.

Parent, Dale. 2003. *Correctional Boot Camps: Lessons from a Decade of Research.* Washington, DC: Department of Justice.

Parent, Dale, Barbara Auerbach, and Kenneth Carlson. 1992. *Compensating Crime Victims: A Summary of Policies and Practices.* Washington, DC: Department of Justice, National Institute of Justice.

Parent, Dale, Terence Dunworth, Douglas McDonald, and William Rhodes. 1996. *The Impact of Sentencing Guidelines.* Washington, DC: National Institute of Justice.

Partridge, Anthony, and William Eldridge. 1974. *The Second Circuit Sentencing Study: A Report to the Judges of the Second Circuit.* Washington, DC: Federal Judicial Center.

Passon, Doug. 2010. "Using Mitigation Videos to Bridge the Cultural Gap at Sentencing." Chapter 23 of *Cultural Issues in Criminal Justice*. Huntington, NY: Juris.

Paternoster, Raymond. 1984. "Prosecutorial Discretion in Requesting the Death Penalty: A Case of Victim-Based Racial Discrimination." *Law and Society Review* 18: 437–478.

Paternoster, Raymond, and Robert Brame. 2008. "Reassessing Race Disparities in Maryland Capital Cases." *Criminology* 46: 971–1007.

Paternoster, Raymond, and Jerome Deise. 2011. "A Heavy Thumb on the Scale: The Effect of Victim Impact Evidence on Capital Decision Making." *Criminology* 49: 129–161.

Patry, Marc W. 2008. "Attractive but Guilty: Deliberation and the Physical Attractiveness Bias." *Psychological Reports* 102: 727–733.

Pattavina, April, Melissa Morabito, and Linda M. Williams. 2015. "Examining Connections Between the Police and Prosecution in Sexual Assault Case Processing: Does the Use of Exceptional Clearance Facilitate a Downstream Orientation? *Victims & Offenders* 11(2): 315–334.

Patterson, Paul A. 2015. "Sixth Amendment, Televising Trials, and *Chandler v. Florida.*" *Akron Law Review* 15(1): 183–190.

Payne, Brian, and Randy R. Gainey. 2004. "The Electronic Monitoring of Offenders Released from Jail or Prison: Safety, Control, and Comparisons to the Incarceration Experience." *The Prison Journal* 84: 413–435.

Payne, Brian K., and Matthew DeMichele. 2011. "Probation Philosophies and Workload Considerations." *American Journal of Criminal Justice* 36: 29–43.

Payne, Brian K., David C. May, and Peter B. Wood. 2014. "The 'Pains' of Electronic Monitoring: A Slap on the Wrist or Just as Bad as Prison?" *Criminal Justice Studies* 27(2): 133–148.

Payne, Shenoa L. 2008. "The Ethical Conundrums of Unpublished Opinions." *Willamette Law Review* 44: 723–760.

Penn, Schoen, and Berland Associates. 2012. "C-SPAN Supreme Court Survey." *C-Span*, July 9. Available online at http://static.c-span.org/files/pressCenter/CSPAN-HCR-SCOTUS-Poll.pdf

Penney, Steven. 1998. "Theories of Confession Admissibility: A Historical Overview." *American Journal of Criminal Law* 25: 309–383.

Pepin, Arthur W. 2013. *Evidence-Based Pretrial Release*. Williamsburg, VA: National Center for State Courts, Conference of State Court Administrators.

Perkins, David, and Jay Jamieson. 1995. "Judicial Probable Cause Determinations after *County of Riverside v. McLaughlin.*" *Criminal Law Bulletin* 31: 534–546.

Perlstein, Michael. 1990. "DA's Office Suffers as Prosecutors Flee to Better Pay, Hours." *Times-Picayune*, July 22, p. B1.

Perry, Barbara. 2016, February 29. "One-Third of All U.S. Presidents Appointed a Supreme Court Justice in an Election Year." *Washington Post*, https://www.washingtonpost.com/news/monkey-cage/wp/2016/02/29/one-third-of-all-u-s-presidents-appointed-a-supreme-court-justice-in-an-election-year/?utm_term=.034250c63190

Perry, Steven. 2006. *Prosecutors in State Courts*, 2005. Washington, DC: Bureau of Justice Statistics, National Institute of Justice.

Perry, Steven W., and Duren Banks. 2011. *Prosecutors in State Courts, 2007—Statistical Tables*. Washington, DC: Bureau of Justice Statistics, National Institute of Justice.

Peters, C. Scott. 2009. "Canons of Ethics and Accountability in State Supreme Court Elections." *State Politics & Policy Quarterly* 9(1): 24–55.

Peterson, Richard. 2004. "Manhattan's Specialized Domestic Violence Court." *Research Brief No. 7*. New York: New York City Criminal Justice Agency.

Peterson, Richard L. 2011. "Unintelligent Jury Waivers: A Call to Amend Federal Rule of Criminal Procedure 23A." *George Mason University Civil Rights Law Journal* 21: 441–470.

Petrucci, Carrie. J. 2002. "Respect as a Component in the Judge-Defendant Interaction in a Specialized Domestic Violence Court That Utilizes Therapeutic Jurisprudence." *Criminal Law Bulletin* 38(2): 263–295.

Petrucci, Carrie J. 2010. "A Descriptive Study of a California Domestic Violence Court: Program Completion and Recidivism." *Victims and Offenders* 5: 130–160.

Pew Hispanic Center. 2009. "Hispanics and the Criminal Justice System: Low Confidence, High Exposure." Available online at http://pewresearch.org/pubs/1182/hispanic-confidence-in-criminal-justice-system-low

Pew Research Center. 2013, July 22. *Big Racial Divide over Zimmerman Verdict*. Retrieved from http://www.people-press.org/2013/07/22/big-racial-divide-over-zimmerman-verdict/2/

Pfaff, John. 2017. *Locked In: The True Causes of Mass Incarceration—and How to Achieve Real Reform*. New York: Basic Books.

Phelps, Michelle S. 2017. "Mass Probation: Toward a More Robust Theory of State Variation in Punishment." *Punishment & Society* 19(1): 53–73.

Phillips, Joshua Daniel, and Rachel Alicia Griffin. 2015. "Crystal Mangum as Hypervisible Object and Invisible Subject: Black Feminist Thought, Sexual Violence, and the Pedagogical Repercussions of the Duke Lacrosse Rape Case." *Women's Studies in Communication* 36: 36–56.

Phillips, Mary. 2007. "Bail, Detention and Nonfelony Case Outcomes." *Research Brief #14*. New York: New York City Criminal Justice Agency.

Phillips, Mary. 2008. "Bail, Detention and Felony Case Outcomes." *Research Brief #18*. New York: New York City Criminal Justice Agency.

Phillips, Thomas R. 2009. "The Merits of Merit Selection." *Harvard Journal of Law and Public Policy* 32: 67–96.

Piehl, Anne Morrison, and Shawn D. Bushway. 2007. "Measuring and Explaining Charge Bargaining." *Journal of Quantitative Criminology* 23: 105–125.

Pinello, Daniel. 1995. *The Impact of Judicial-Selection Method of State-Supreme-Court Policy: Innovation, Reaction and Atrophy*. Westport, CT: Greenwood Press.

Pinto, Nick. 2011. "DUI Laws ARE Discriminatory and Do Not Prevent Drunk Driving." *Drunk Driving*. Ed. Stefan Kiesbye. Detroit: Greenhaven Press.

Pitts, Leonard, Jr. 2011. "Justice for an Awful Judge." *The Stump*, February 28. Available online at http://www.oregonlive.com/opinion/index.ssf/2011/02/justice_for_an_awful_judge.html

Pitts, Wayne, Eugena Givens, and Susan McNeeley. 2009. "The Need for a Holistic Approach to Specialized Domestic Violence Court Programming: Evaluating Offender Rehabilitation Needs and Recidivism." *Juvenile and Family Court Journal* 60(3): 1–21.

Platt, Anthony. 1969. *The Child Savers: The Invention of Delinquency*. Chicago: University of Chicago Press.

Platt, Anthony, and Randi Pollock. 1974. "Channeling Lawyers: The Careers of Public Defenders." In Herbert Jacob (Ed.), *The Potential for Reform of Criminal Justice*. Newbury Park, CA: Sage.

Podgor, Ellen. 2007. "The Challenge of White Collar Sentencing." *Journal of Criminal Law and Criminology* 97: 731.

Podlas, Kimberlianne. 2002. "Should We Blame Judge Judy? The Messages TV Courtrooms Send Viewers." *Judicature* 86: 38–43.

Podlas, Kimberlianne. 2006. "'The CSI Effect': Exposing the Media Myth." *Fordham Intellectual Property, Media & Entertainment Law Journal* 16(429): 429–465.

Pollock, Joycelyn M. 2012. *Ethical Dilemmas and Decisions in Criminal Justice*. 7th ed. Belmont, CA: Wadsworth.

Pollock, Joycelyn M. 2014. *Women's Crimes, Criminology, and Corrections*. Long Grove, IL: Waveland Press.

Pollock Joycelyn M., and Sareta M. Davis. 2005. "The Continuing Myth of the Violent Female Offender." *Criminal Justice Review* 30: 5–29.

Porter, Nicole D. 2016. *The State of Sentencing—2015: Developments in Policy and Practice*. Washington, DC: The Sentencing Project.

Porter, Rachael. 2011. *Choosing Performance Indicators for Your Community Prosecution Initiative*. Washington, DC: Association of Prosecuting Attorneys. Available online at http://www.courtinnovation.org/sites/default/files /documents/Choosing_Performance_Indicators.pdf

Pou, Charles. 2005. "Scissors Cut Paper: A 'Guildhall' Helps Maryland's Mediators Sharpen Their Skills." *Justice System Journal* 26: 307–325.

Poulin, Anne Bowen. 2013. "Ethical Guidance for Standby Counsel in Criminal Cases: A Far Cry from Counsel?" *American Criminal Law Review* 50: 211–245.

Powers-Jarvis, Robin S. 2013. "Putting Together "Shattered Dreams": A Program to Reduce Alcohol-Related and Districted Driving-Related Car Crashes Among Adolescents." *Journal of Emergency Nursing* 40(1): 82–83.

President's Commission on Law Enforcement and Administration of Justice. 1967. *Task Force Report: The Courts*. Washington, DC: Government Printing Office.

President's Council of Advisors on Science and Technology (2016). *Report to the President: Forensic Science in Criminal Courts: Ensuring Scientific Validity of Feature-Comparison Methods*. https://obamawhitehouse.archives.gov/sites /default/files/microsites/ostp/PCAST/pcast_forensic _science_report_final.pdf

Pretrial Justice Center for Courts. n.d. *Public Safety Assessment-Court (PSA-Court)*, http://www.ncsc.org/Microsites /PJCC/Home/Tools/Pretrial-Risk-Assessment/PSA-Court .aspx

Pretrial Justice Institute. 2017. "Pretrial Justice: How Much Does It Cost?" https://university.pretrial.org /HigherLogic/System/DownloadDocumentFile .ashx?DocumentFileKey=4c666992-0b1b-632a-13cb -b4ddc66fadcd&forceDialog=1

Priehs, Richard. 1999. "Appointed Counsel for Indigent Criminal Appellants: Does Compensation Influence Effort?" *Justice System Journal* 21: 57–79.

Primus, Eve B. 2007. "Structural Reform in Criminal Defense: Relocating Ineffective Assistance of Counsel Claims." *Cornell Law Review* 92: 679–732.

Priumu, Eve Brensike. (2016). Culture as a Structural Problem in Indigent Defense. *Minnesota Law Review* 100: 1769–1821.

Propen, Amy and Mary Lay Schuster. 2008. "Making Academic Work Advocacy Work: Technologies of Power in the Public Arena." *Journal of Business and Technical Communications* 22: 299–329.

Prosser, Mary. 2006. "Reforming Criminal Discovery: Why Old Objections Must Yield to New Realities." *Wisconsin Law Review* 2006: 541–614.

Provine, Doris Marie. 2007. *Unequal Under Law: Race and the War on Drugs*. Chicago: University of Chicago Press.

Pruitt, Lisa R. 2006. "Rural Rhetoric." *Connecticut Law Review* 39: 159–240.

Pruitt, Lisa R. 2008. "Gender, Geography, and Rural Justice." *Berkeley Journal of Gender, Law & Justice* 23: 338–391.

Pruitt, Lisa R., Cliff McKinney II, Juliana Fehrenbacher, and Amy Dunn Johnson. 2015. "Access to Justice in Rural Arkansas." *Arkansas Access to Justice Commission*. Available online http://www.arkansasjustice.org/sites /default/files/file%20attachments/AATJPolicyBrief 2015-0420.pdf.

Pruitt, Lisa R., and Bradley Showman. 2014. "Law Stretched Thin: Access to Justice in Rural America." *South Dakota Law Review* 59(3): 466–528.

Public Information Office of the United States Courts for the Ninth Circuit. 2013. "Courts of Appeals to Open En Banc Proceedings to Internet Viewing." Available online at http://cdn.ca9.uscourts.gov/datastore/uploads /calendar/641-En_Banc_Streaming.pdf

Public Safety Performance Project. 2007. *Public Safety, Public Spending: Forecasting America's Prison Population 2007–2011*. Washington, DC: The Pew Charitable Trust.

Puritz, Patricia, S. Burrell, R. Schwartz, M. Soler, and L. Warboys. 1995. *A Call for Justice: An Assessment of Access to Counsel and Quality of Representation in Delinquency Proceedings*. Washington, DC: American Bar Association.

Puzzanchera, Charles, and Benjamin Adams. 2011. *Juvenile Arrests 2009*. Washington, DC: Department of Justice, Office of Justice Programs.

Puzzanchera, Charles, Benjamin Adams, and Melissa Sickmund. 2011. *Juvenile Court Statistics, 2008*. Pittsburgh, PA: National Center for Juvenile Justice.

Puzzanchera, Charles, and Sarah Hockenberry. 2013. *Juvenile Court Statistics, 2010*. Pittsburgh, PA: National Center for Juvenile Justice.

Quinn, Mae. 2014. "Giving Kids Their Due: Theorizing a Modern Fourteenth Amendment Framework for Juvenile Defense Representation." *Iowa Law Review* 99: 2185–2217.

Radelet, Michael, and Glenn Pierce. 1985. "Race and Prosecutorial Discretion in Homicide Cases." *Law and Society Review* 19: 587–621.

Raftery, William. 2006. "The Legislatures, the Ballot Boxes and the Courts." *Court Review* 4: 102–107.

Ragland, James. 2009. "*American Violet* Tells Story of Ill-Fated Hearne Drug Raids." *Dallas Morning News* (March 13).

Ragona, Anthony, and John Paul Ryan. 1983. "Misdemeanor Courts and the Choice of Sanctions: A Comparative View." *Justice System Journal* 8: 199–221.

Rakoff, Jed S., Honoré Daumier, and A Criminal Case. 2014. "Why Innocent People Plead Guilty." *The New York Review of Books* 61(18): 1–12.

Ralph, Paige, Jonathan Sorensen, and James Marquart. 1992. "A Comparison of Death-Sentenced and Incarcerated Murderers in Pre-*Furman* Texas." *Justice Quarterly* 9: 185–209.

Randall, Ronald, and James A. Woods. 2008. "Racial Representativeness of Juries: An Analysis of Source List and Administrative Effects on the Jury Pool." *Justice System Journal* 29: 71–82.

Rapaport, Elizabeth. 1991. "The Death Penalty and Gender Discrimination." *Law and Society Review* 25: 367–384.

Rayman, Noah. 2014, August 21."Here's How Much the Banks Have Paid Out Since the Financial Crisis." *Time*, http://time.com/3154590/bank-payouts-since-financial-crisis/

Raymond, Paul. 1992. "The Impact of a Televised Trial on Individuals' Information and Attitudes." *Judicature* 75: 204–209.

Re, Richard M. 2007. "Re-Justifying the Fair Cross-Section Requirement: Equal Representation and Enfranchisement in the American Criminal Jury." *Yale Law Journal* 116: 1568–1614.

Reaves, Brian A. 2013. *Felony Defendants in Large Urban Counties, 2009*. Washington, DC: Bureau of Justice Statistics.

Reddick, Malia. 2010. "Judging the Quality of Judicial Selection Methods: Merit Selection, Elections, and Judicial Discipline." Nashville, TN: American Judicature Society. Available online at http://judicialselection.com/uploads/documents/Judging_the_Quality_of_Judicial_Sel_8EF0DC3806ED8.pdf

Redding, Richard. 2008. "Juvenile Transfer Laws: An Effective Deterrent to Delinquency?" Washington, DC: Department of Justice, Office of Justice Programs.

Regehr, C., Alaggia, R., Lambert, L., and Saini, M. (2008). "Victims of Sexual Violence in the Canadian Criminal Courts." *Victims and Offenders* 3: 99–113.

Rehavi, M. Marit, and Sonia Starr. 2012. "Racial Disparity in Federal Criminal Charging and Its Sentencing Consequences." University of Michigan Law & Economics, Empirical Legal Studies Center Paper No. 12-002. Available online at SSRN: http://ssrn.com/abstract=1985377

Reiman, Jeffrey. 2007. *The Rich Get Richer and the Poor Get Prison: Ideology, Class, and Criminal Justice*. 8th ed. Boston: Pearson/Allyn & Bacon.

Reitler, Angela K., and James Frank, 2014. "Interdistrict Variation in the Implementation of the Crack Retroactivity." *Criminal Justice Policy Review* 25(1): 105–130.

Reitz, Kevin. 2001. "The Status of Sentencing Guidelines Reforms in the United States." In Michael Tonry (Ed.), *Penal Reform in Overcrowded Times*. New York: Oxford University Press.

Remington, Frank. 1988. "Post-Conviction Review: What State Trial Courts Can Do to Reduce Problems." *Judicature* 72: 53–57.

Remus, Dana. 2012. "The Institutional Politics of Federal Judicial Conduct Regulation." *Yale Law & Policy Review* 31: 33–78.

Rengifo, Andres F., and Don Stemen. 2015. "The Unintended Effects of Penal Reform: African American Presence, Incarceration, and the Abolition of Discretionary Parole in the United States." *Crime & Delinquency* 61(5): 719–741.

Renzema, Marc, and Evan Mayo-Wilson. 2005. "Can Electronic Monitoring Reduce Crime for Moderate to High-Risk Offenders?" *Journal of Experimental Criminology* 1: 215–237.

Resick, Patricia. 1984. "The Trauma of Rape and the Criminal Justice System." *Justice System Journal* 9: 52–61.

Reskin, Barbara, and Christine Visher. 1986. "The Impacts of Evidence and Extralegal Factors in Jurors' Decisions." *Law and Society Review* 20: 423–439.

Resnik, Judith. 2006. "Whither and Whether Adjudication?" *Boston University Law Review* 86: 1101–1154.

Rhodes, William. 1978. *Plea Bargaining: Who Gains? Who Loses?* Washington, DC: Institute for Law and Social Research.

Ribovich, Donald J., and Anthony Martino. 2007. "Technology, Crime Control, and the Private Sector in the 21st Century." In James Michael Byrne and Donald J. Ribovich (Eds.), *New Technology of Crime, Law and Social Control*, (pp. 49–79). Monsey, NY: Criminal Justice Press.

Richardson, Richard, and Kenneth Vines. 1970. *The Politics of Federal Courts*. Boston: Little, Brown.

Richmond, Todd. 2010. "Many States Closing Their Juvenile Jails." Associated Press, June 7.

Ridolf, Kathleen and Maurice Possley. 2010. Preventable Error: A Report on Prosecutorial Misconduct in California 1997–2009. *Northern California Innocence Project Publications. Book 2*. http://digitalcommons.law.scu.edu/ncippubs/2

Ringhand, Lori A., and Paul M. Collins, Jr. 2011. "May It Please the Senate: An Empirical Analysis of the Senate Judiciary Committee Hearings of Supreme Court Nominees, 1939–2009." *American University Law Review* 60(3): 589–641.

Risinger, D. Michael, Mark P. Denbeaux, and Michael J. Saks. 1989. "Exorcism of Ignorance as a Proxy for Rational Knowledge: The Lessons of Handwriting Identification 'Expertise.'" *University of Pennsylvania Law Review* 137(3): 731–792.

Ritchie, Jessica. 2015. "Probabilistic DNA Evidence: The Laypersons Interpretation." *Australian Journal of Forensic Sciences* 47(4): 440–449.

Rivera, Jenny. 2015. "Diversity and the Law." *Hofstra Law Review* 44: 1271–1285.

Roach, Michael. 2010. "Explaining the Outcome Gap between Different Types of Indigent Defense Counsel: Adverse Selection and Moral Hazard Effects." Available online at http://ssrn.com/abstract=1839651

Roach-Anleu, Sharyn L. 2009. *Law and Social Change*. 2nd ed. Thousand Oaks, CA: Sage.

Roberts, John G., Jr. 2008. *Year-End Report on the Federal Judiciary*. Available online at https://www.supremecourt.gov/publicinfo/year-end/2008year-endreport.pdf

Roberts, Paul Craig, and Lawrence M. Stratton. 2008. *The Tyranny of Good Intentions: How Prosecutors and Law Enforcement Are Trampling the Constitution in the Name of Justice*. New York: Three Rivers Press/Random House.

Robertson, Leon, Robert Rich, and H. Laurence Ross. 1973. "Jail Sentences for Driving While Intoxicated in Chicago: A Judicial Action That Failed." *Law and Society Review* 8: 55–68.

Robinson, Gwen. 2008. "Late-Modern Rehabilitation: The Evolution of a Penal Strategy." *Punishment and Society* 10: 429–445.

Robinson, Mike. 1996. "Abrasive, Erratic Judge Sidelined." *Times-Picayune*, October 12.

Rodriguez, Nancy, Hilary Smith, and Marjorie Zatz. 2009. "'Youth Is Enmeshed in a Highly Dysfunctional Family System': Exploring the Relationship among Dysfunctional Families, Parental Incarceration, and Juvenile Court Decision Making." *Criminology* 47: 177–206.

Roesler, Richard. 2009. "Drivers Sue 19 Cities over Traffic Camera Fines." *Spokesman-Review*, June 24.

Roettger, Michael, and Raymond Swisher. 2011. "Association of Father's History of Incarceration with Sons' Delinquency and Arrest among Black, White and Hispanic Males in the United States." *Criminology* 49(4): 1109–1147.

Roots, Roger. 2014. "The Framers' Fourth Amendment Exclusionary Rule: The Mounting Evidence." *Nevada Law Journal* 15: 42–76.

Roper, Robert. 1979. "Jury Size: Impact on Verdict's Correctness." *American Politics Quarterly* 7: 438–452.

Roper, Robert, and Albert Melone. 1981. "Does Procedural Due Process Make a Difference? A Study of Second Trials." *Judicature* 65: 136–141.

Rose, Mary R. 2005. "A Dutiful Voice: Justice in the Distribution of Jury Service," *Law & Society Review* 39: 601–634.

Rosen, Ellen. 1987. "The Nation's Judges: No Unanimous Opinion." *Court Review* 24: 5.

Rosen, Richard A. 2006. "Reflections on Innocence." *Wisconsin Law Review* 2006: 237–290.

Rosencrance, John. 2004. "Maintaining the Myth of Individualized Justice: Probation Presentence Reports." In George Cole, Mark Gertz, and Amy Bunger (Eds.), *The Criminal Justice System: Politics and Policies*. 9th ed. Belmont, CA: Wadsworth.

Rosenmerkel, Sean, Matthew Durose, and Donald Farole. 2010. *Felony Sentences in State Courts, 2006*. Washington, DC: Department of Justice, Bureau of Justice Statistics.

Rosenthal, John. 2002. "Therapeutic Jurisprudence and Drug Treatment Courts: Integrating Law and Science." In James Nolan (Ed.), *Drug Courts in Theory and Practice*. Hawthorne, NY: de Gruyter.

Rosett, Arthur, and Donald Cressey. 1976. *Justice by Consent: Plea Bargaining in the American Courthouse*. Philadelphia: Lippincott.

Rosoff, Stephen, Henry Pontell, and Robert Tillman. 2007. *Profit without Honor: White-Collar Crime and the Looting of America*. 4th ed. Upper Saddle River, NJ: Prentice Hall.

Ross, H. Laurence, and James Foley. 1987. "Judicial Disobedience of the Mandate to Imprison Drunk Drivers." *Law and Society Review* 21: 315–323.

Ross, H. Laurence. 1992. "The Law and Drunk Driving." *Law and Society Review* 26: 219–230.

Rossi, Peter, and Richard Berk. 1997. *Public Opinion on Sentencing Federal Crimes*. Washington, DC: United States Sentencing Commission.

Rossman, Shelli B., Janeen Buck Willison, Kamala Mallik-Kane, KiDeuk Kim, Sara Debus-Sherrill, and P. Mitchell Downey. 2012. *Criminal Justice Interventions for Offenders with Mental Illness: Evaluation of Mental Health Courts in Bronx and Brooklyn, New York: Final Report*. Available online at http://www.courtinnovation.org/sites/default/files/documents/Criminal_Justice_Interventions.pdf

Rosoff, Stephen, Henry Pontell, and Robert Tillman. 2014. *Profit without Honor: White-Collar Crime and the Looting of America*. 6th ed. New York: Pearson.

Rothwax, Harold J. 1996. Guilty: *The Collapse of Criminal Justice*. New York: Random House.

Rottman, David, and Pamela Casey. 1999. "Therapeutic Jurisprudence and the Emergence of Problem-Solving Courts." *National Institute of Justice Journal* July: 12–19.

Rowden, Emma, and Diane Jones. 2015. "Design, Dignity and Due Process: The Construction of the Coffs Harbour Courthouse." *Law, Culture, and the Humanities*. Advanced online publication. doi: 10.1177/1743872115612954

Rowe, Brenda I. 2015. "Predictions of Texas Police Chiefs' Satisfaction with Police–Prosecutor Relationships." *American Journal of Criminal Justice* 1–23.

Rowe, David C., and David P. Farrington. 1997. "The Familial Transmission of Criminal Convictions." *Criminology* 35: 177–201.

Rubenstein, Ari M. 2006. "Verdicts of Conscience: Nullification and the Modern Jury Trial." *Columbia Law Review* 106(4): 959–993.

Rubenstein, Michael, and Teresa White. 1979. "Plea Bargaining: Can Alaska Live without It?" *Judicature* 62: 266–279.

Rubin, Alvin. 1976. "How We Can Improve Judicial Treatment of Individual Cases without Sacrificing Individual Rights:

The Problems of the Criminal Law." *Federal Rules of Decisions* 70: 176.

Rubin, H. Ted. 1989. "The Juvenile Court Landscape." In Albert Roberts (Eds.), *Juvenile Justice: Policies, Programs and Services*. Chicago: Irwin.

Ruckman, P. S. 1997. "Executive Clemency in the United States: Origins, Development, and Analysis (1900–1993)." *Presidential Studies Quarterly* 27: 251–271.

Rush, Christina, and Jeremy Robertson. 1987. "Presentence Reports: The Utility of Information to the Sentencing Decision." *Law and Human Behavior* 11: 147–155.

Russano, Melissa B., Christian A. Meissner, Fadia M. Narchet, and Saul M. Kassin. 2005. "Investigating True and False Confessions with a Novel Experimental Design." *Psychological Science* 16: 481–486.

Russell, Brenda L., Debra L. Oswald, and Shane W. Kraus. 2011. "Evaluations of Sexual Assault: Perceptions of Guilt and Legal Elements for Male and Female Aggressors Using Various Coercive." *Violence & Victims* 26(6): 799–815.

Ruva, Christine L., and Michelle A. LeVasseur. 2012. "Behind Closed Doors: The Effect of Pretrial Publicity on Jury Deliberations." *Psychology, Crime & Law* 18(5): 431–452.

Ruva, Christine L., and Christina C. Guenther. 2015. "From the Shadows into the Light: How Pretrial Publicity and Deliberation Affect Mock Jurors' Decisions, Impressions, and Memory." *Law and Human Behavior* 39(3): 294–310.

Ryan, Harriet. 2011, September 23. "Conrad Murray Jury Selection Will Be Quick." *Los Angeles Times*. Retrieved from http://articles.latimes.com/2011/sep/23/local/la-me-0923-conrad-murray-20110924

Ryan, Joan. 2002. "Do We Count Strikes or Justice?" *San Francisco Chronicle*, November 5.

Ryan, John Paul, and James Alfini. 1979. "Trial Judges' Participation in Plea Bargaining: An Empirical Perspective." *Law and Society Review* 13: 479–507.

Ryo, Emily. 2016. "Detained: A Study of Immigration Bond Hearings." *Law & Society Review* 50(1): 117–153.

Sacks, Meghan, Vincenzo A. Sainato, and Alissa R. Ackerman. 2015. "Sentenced to Pretrial Detention: A Study of Bail Decisions and Outcomes." *American Journal of Criminal Justice* 40(3): 661–681.

Sahoo, Smita. 2006. "Exploring Transient Security: A Case Study of the Alachua County Courthouse Entrance Lobby in Gainesville, Florida." Master's Thesis, University of Florida, Gainesville.

Saini, Michael. 2016. "Understanding Pathways to Family Dispute Resolution and Justice Reforms: Ontario Court File Analysis & Survey of Professionals." *Family Court Review* 54(3): 382–397.

Saks, Michael. 1996. "The Smaller the Jury, the Greater the Unpredictability." *Judicature* 79: 263–265.

Saks, Michael J., and Mollie Weighner Marti. 1997. "A Meta-analysis of the Effects of Jury Size." *Law and Human Behavior* 21: 451–467.

Sams, David, Tess Neal, and Stanley Brodsky. 2013. "Avoiding Jury Duty: Psychological and Legal Perspectives." *Jury Expert* 25: 4–8.

Samuels, Diana. 2016. "Latest Court Challenge to Redflex Traffic Cameras is in Gretna." NOLA.com The Times-Picayune, April 27.

Sanborn, Joseph. 1986. "A Historical Sketch of Plea Bargaining." *Justice Quarterly* 3: 111–138.

Sanborn, Joseph. 1993. "The Right to a Public Jury Trial: A Need for Today's Juvenile Court." *Judicature* 76: 230–238.

Sanborn, Joseph. 1994. "The Juvenile, the Court, or the Community: Whose Best Interests Are Currently Being Promoted in Juvenile Court?" *Justice System Journal* 17: 249–266.

Sapien, Joaquin, and Sergio Hernandez. 2013, April 3. "Who Polices Prosecutors Who Abuse Their Authority? Usually Nobody." *ProPublica*, https://www.propublica.org/article/who-polices-prosecutors-who-abuse-their-authority-usually-nobody

Sarat, Austin, and Conor Clarke. 2008. "Beyond Discretion: Prosecution, the Logic of Sovereignty, and the Limits of Law." *Law and Social Inquiry* 33: 387–416.

Sarat, Austin, and William Felstiner. 1995. *Divorce Lawyers and Their Clients: Power and Meaning in the Legal Process*. New York: Oxford University Press.

Saslow, Eli. 2014. "In a Crowded Immigration Court, Seven Minutes to Decide a Family's Future." *Washington Post*, February 2. Available online at http://www.washingtonpost.com/national/in-a-crowded-immigration-court-seven-minutes-to-decide-a-familys-future/2014/02/02/518c3e3e-8798-11e3-a5bd-844629433ba3_story.html

Savage, Charlie. 2013. "Roberts's Picks Reshaping Secret Surveillance Court." *New York Times*, July 25, A1.

Savage, David G., and Maura Dolan. 2004. "New Media Struggle to Keep Ground Rules from Changing." *Los Angeles Times*, August 2.

Savage, David G., and Michael Muskal. 2013. "Zimmerman Verdict: Legal Experts Say Prosecutors Overreached." *Los Angeles Times*, July 14.

Schammert, William. 2015. "Some OK Towns Using Traffic Tickets to Fund up to 1/3 of Budget." Fox 25, November 5.

Schauffler, R., R. LaFountain, S. Strickland, K. Holt, and K. Genthon. 2016. *Examining the Work of State Courts: An Overview of 2015 State Court Caseloads*. Williamsburg, VA:

National Center for State Courts. Retrieved from http://www.courtstatistics.org/~/media/Microsites/Files/CSP/EWSC%202015.ashx

Scheingold, Stuart, Toska Olson, and Jana Pershing. 1994. "Sexual Violence, Victim Advocacy, and Republican Criminology: Washington State's Community Protection Act." *Law and Society Review* 28: 729–763.

Schelling, Thomas. 1960. *The Strategy of Conflict*. Cambridge, MA: Harvard University Press.

Scherer, Nancy. 2005. *Scoring Points: Politicians, Political Activists and the Lower Federal Court Appointment Process*. Stanford, CA: Stanford University Press.

Scherer, Nancy, Brandon Bartels, and Amy Steigerwalt. 2008. "Sounding the Fire Alarm: The Role of Interest Groups in the Lower Federal Court Confirmation Process." *The Journal of Politics* 70: 1026–1039.

Schlanger, Margo. 2003. "Inmate Litigation." *Harvard Law Review* 116: 1555–1706.

Schlesinger, Traci. 2005. "Racial and Ethnic Disparity in Pretrial Criminal Processing." *Justice Quarterly* 22: 170–192.

Schmidt, Janell, and Lawrence Sherman. 1993. "Does Arrest Deter Domestic Violence?" *American Behavioral Scientist* 36: 601–615.

Schmidt, Janell, and Ellen H. Steury. 1989. "Prosecutorial Discretion in Filing Charges in Domestic Violence Cases." *Criminology* 27: 487–510.

Schnacke, Timothy R. 2014. *Fundamentals of Bail: A Resource Guide for Pretrial Practitioners and a Framework for American Pretrial Reform*. Washington, DC: National Institute of Corrections. Retrieved from http://www.pretrial.org/download/research/Fundamentals%20of%20Bail%20-%20NIC%202014.pdf

Schotland, Roy. 1998. "Comment." *Law and Contemporary Problems* 61: 149–150.

Schoenfeld, Heather. 2005. "Violated Trust: Conceptualizing Prosecutorial Misconduct." *Journal of Contemporary Criminal Justice* 21: 250–271.

Schreck, Christopher, Eric Stewart, and D. Wayne Osgood. 2008. "A Reappraisal of the Overlap of Violent Offenders and Victims." *Criminology* 46: 871–906.

Schulhofer, Stephen. 1984. "Is Plea Bargaining Inevitable?" *Harvard Law Review* 97: 1037–1107.

Schultz, David. 2000. "No Joy in Mudville Tonight: The Impact of 'Three Strike' Laws…." *Cornell Journal of Law and Public Policy* 9: 557.

Schwartz, Emma. 2007. "A Debt Hard to Collect: Only 7 Percent of Restitution Orders Get Paid." *U.S. News & World Report*, December 24, 143: 29.

Schwartz, Jennifer, Darrell Steffensmeier, Hua Zhong, and Jeff Ackerman. 2009. "Trends in the Gender Gap in Violence: Reevaluating NCVS and other Evidence." *Criminology* 47: 401–425.

Schwartz, John. 2009a. "As Jurors Turn to Google and Twitter, Mistrials Are Popping Up." *New York Times*, March 18.

Schwartz, John. 2009b. "Pinched Courts Push to Collect Fees and Fines." *New York Times*, April 7.

Schwartz, John. 2011. "Critics Say Budget Cuts for Courts Risk Rights." *New York Times*, November 26, p. A18.

Schwartz, Victor E., Mark A. Behrens, and Cary Silverman. 2003. *The Jury Patriotism Act: Making Jury Service More Appealing and Rewarding to Citizens*. Washington, DC: American Legislative Exchange Council.

Schweitzer, N. J., and Michael J. Saks. 2007. "The 'CSI-effect': Popular Fiction about Forensic Science Affects the Public's Expectations about Real Forensic Science." *Jurimetric* 47: 357–364.

Scirica, Anthony J. 2015. "Judicial Governance and Judicial Independence." *New York University Law Review* 90(3): 779–801.

Scott, Kevin M. 2006. "Understanding Judicial Hierarchy: Reversals and the Behavior of Intermediate Appellate Judges." *Law and Society Review* 40: 163–191.

Scruggs, Anna, Jean-Claude Mazzola, and Mary Zaug. 1995. "Recent Voting Rights Act Challenges to Judicial Elections." *Judicature* 79: 34–41.

Secret, Mos. 2011. "States Prosecute Fewer Teenagers in Adult Courts." *New York Times*, March 5.

Segal, Jeffrey, and Harold Spaeth. 1989. "Decisional Trends on the Warren and Burger Courts: Results from the Supreme Court Data Base Project." *Judicature* 73: 103–107.

Segal, Jeffrey, and Harold Spaeth. 2002. *The Supreme Court and the Attitudinal Model Revisited*. Cambridge, UK: Cambridge University Press.

Segal, Jennifer. 2000. "Judicial Decision Making and the Impact of Election Year Rhetoric." *Judicature* 84: 26–33.

Serrano, Richard. 2006. "With Case Closed, Moussaoui Silenced." *Times-Picayune*, May 5.

Shaer, Matthew. (2016, June). The False Promise of DNA Testing. *The Atlantic*. https://www.theatlantic.com/magazine/archive/2016/06/a-reasonable-doubt/480747/

Shaffer, Deborah Koetzle. 2006. *Reconsidering Drug Court Effectiveness: A Meta-Analytic Review*. Doctoral dissertation, University of Cincinnati, Cincinnati.

Shaffner, Laurie. 2006. *Girls in Trouble with the Law*. Piscataway, NJ: Rutgers University Press.

Shallwani, Pervaiz. 2012. "Hate-Crimes Conviction." *The Wall Street Journal*, March 17, at A.17 (Greater New York edition).

Shaw, Michelle, and Kenneth Robinson. 1998. "Summary and Analysis of the First Juvenile Drug Court Evaluations: The Santa Clara County Drug Treatment Court and the Delaware Juvenile Drug Court Diversion Program." *National Drug Court Institute Review* 1(1): 73–85.

Sheindlin, Judy. 1996. *Don't Pee on My Leg and Tell Me It's Raining: America's Toughest Family Court Judge Speaks Out.* New York: HarperCollins.

Sheindlin, Judy. 1999. *Beauty Fades, Dumb Is Forever.* New York: HarperCollins.

Sheindlin, Judy. 2000. *Keep It Simple, Stupid: You're Smarter Than You Look.* New York: Cliff Street Books/ HarperCollins.

Sheindlin, Judy. 2000. *Win or Lose by How You Choose.* New York: HarperCollins.

Sheindlin, Judy. 2001. *You Can't Judge a Book by Its Cover: Cool Rules for School.* New York. HarperCollins.

Shelton, Donald E. 2008. "The 'CSI Effect': Does It Really Exist?" *National Institute of Justice Journal* 259. Available online at https://www.ncjrs.gov/pdffiles1/nij/221501.pdf

Shelton, Donald E., Young S. Kim, and Gregg Barak. 2009. "An Indirect-Effects Model of Mediated Adjudication: The CSI Myth, the Tech Effect, and Metropolitan Jurors' Expectations for Scientific Evidence." *Vanderbilt Journal of Entertainment and Technology Law* 12(1): 1–43.

Shen, Lucinda. 2016, April 12. "Goldman Sachs Finally Admits It Defrauded Investors During the Financial Crisis." *Fortune,* http://fortune.com/2016/04/11 /goldman-sachs-doj-settlement/

Shepherd, Robert E., Jr. 2003. "Still Seeking the Promise of Gault: Juveniles and the Right to Counsel." *Criminal Justice* 18: 22–27.

Shine, James, and Dwight Price. 1992. "Prosecutors and Juvenile Justice: New Roles and Perspectives." In Ira Schwartz (Ed.), *Juvenile Justice and Public Policy: Toward a National Agenda.* New York: Lexington Books.

Shinnar, Shlomo, and Reuel Shinnar. 1975. "The Effects of the Criminal Justice System on the Control of Crime: A Quantitative Approach." *Law and Society Review* 9: 581–611.

Shoham, S. Giora, Ori Beck, and Martin Kett. 2007. *International Handbook of Penology and Criminal Justice.* Boca Raton, FL: CRC Press.

Shomade, Salmon. 2012. "Sentencing Patterns: Drug Court Judges Serving in Conventional Criminal Courts." *Judicature* 96: 36–44.

Shook, Jeffrey. 2014. "Looking Back and Thinking Forward: Examining the Consequences of Policies and Practices that Treat Juveniles as Adults." *Journal of Evidence-Based Social Work* 11: 392–403.

Sickmund, Melissa, and Charles Puzzanchera. 2014. *Juvenile Offenders and Victims: 2014 National Report.* Washington, DC: Department of Justice, Office of Juvenile Justice and Delinquency Prevention.

Sickmund, Melissa, Anthony J. Sladky, Wei Kang, and Charles Puzzanchera. 2013. "Easy Access to the Census of Juveniles in Residential Placement." Pittsburgh, PA: National Center for Juvenile Justice. Available online at http://www .ojjdp.gov/ojstatbb/ezacjrp/

Sigall, Harold, and Nancy Ostrove. 1975. "Beautiful but Dangerous: Effects of Offender Attractiveness and Nature of the Crime on Juridic Judgment." *Journal of Personality and Social Psychology* 31(3): 410–414.

Silva, Lahny. 2014a. "The Best Interest is the Child: A Historical Philosophy for Modern Issues." *BYU Journal of Public Law* 28: 415–470.

Silva, Lahny. 2014b. "Right to Counsel and Plea Bargaining: *Gideon*'s Legacy Continues." *Iowa Law Review* 99: 2219–2244.

Silverstein, Lee. 1965. *Defense of the Poor.* Chicago: American Bar Foundation.

Sims, Barbara, Berwood Yost, and Christina Abbott. 2005. "Use and Nonuse of Victim Services Programs: Implications from a Statewide Survey of Crime Victims." *Criminology and Public Policy* 4: 361–384.

Sinclair, J. Walter, Mark A. Behrens, and Cary Silverman. 2003. "Making Jury Duty a Little Friendlier." *Advocate* 46: 23–26.

Singer, Jordan. 2014. "Attorney Surveys of Judicial Performance: Impressionistic, Imperfect, Indispensable." *Judicature* 98: 20–25.

Sisk, Gregory C., Michael F. Noone, John Montague Steadman, and Urban A. Lester. 2006. *Litigation with the Federal Government.* 4th ed. Chicago: ALI-ABA.

Sitomer, Curtis. 1985. "Rural Justice Affects Many, but May Serve Few." *Christian Science Monitor,* May 28, p. 23.

Sklansky, David Alan. 2016. "The Nature and Function of Prosecutorial Power." *Journal of Criminal Law and Criminology* 106: 473–520.

Skogan, Wesley, and Mary Ann Wycoff. 1987. "Some Unexpected Effects of a Police Service for Victims." *Crime and Delinquency* 33: 490–501.

Skolnick, Jerome. 1967. "Social Control in the Adversary System." *Journal of Conflict Resolution* 11: 52–70.

Skolnick, Jerome H., and James J. Fyfe. 1993. *Above the Law: Police and the Excessive Use of Force.* New York: Free Press.

Slane, Andrea. (2015). "Motion to Dismiss: Bias Crime, Online Communication, and the Sex Lives of Others in *NJ v. Ravi.*" In Valerie Steeves and Jane Bailey (Eds.), *eGirls, eCitizens: Putting Technology, Theory and Policy into Dialogue with Girls' and Young Women's Voices* (pp. 253–280). Ottawa, Ontario: University of Ottawa Press.

Slobogin, Christopher. 1998. *Criminal Procedure: Regulation of Police Investigation*, Charlottesville, VA: Lexis.

Slocum, R. W. 2009. "The Dilemma of the Vengeful Client: A Prescriptive Framework for Cooling the Flames of Anger." *Marquette Law Review* 92: 481–549.

Smelcer, Susan Navarro. 2010. "Supreme Court Justices: Demographic Characteristics, Professional Experience, and Legal Education, 1789–2010." Washington, DC: Congressional Research Service.

Smelcer, Susan Navarro, Amy Steigerwalt, and Richard Vining, Jr. 2014. "Where One Sits Affects Where Others Stand: Bias, the Bar, and Nominees to Federal District Courts." *Judicature* 98: 35–45.

Smith, Alisa, and Sean Maddan. 2011. *Three Minute Justice: Haste and Waste in Florida's Misdemeanor Courts*. Washington, DC: National Association of Criminal Defense Lawyers.

Smith, Alisa, and Michael J. Saks. 2008. "The Case for Overturning *Williams v. Florida* and the Six-Person Jury: History, Law, and Empirical Evidence." *Florida Law Review* 60: 441–470.

Smith, Brent, and C. Ronald Huff. 1992. "From Victim to Political Activist: An Empirical Examination of a Statewide Victims' Rights Movement." *Journal of Criminal Justice* 20: 201–215.

Smith, Christopher. 1995. "Federal Habeas Corpus Reform: The State's Perspective." *Justice System Journal* 18: 1–11.

Smith, Douglas. 1986. "The Plea Bargaining Controversy." *Journal of Criminal Law and Criminology* 77: 949–957.

Smith, Nancy, and Julie Garmel. 1992. "Judicial Election and Selection Procedures Challenged under the Voting Rights Act." *Judicature* 76: 154–155.

Smith, S. F. 2008. "The Supreme Court and the Politics of Death." *Virginia Law Review* 94: 283–383.

Smith-Spark, Laura. 2011. "Strauss-Kahn Case: What Next for Accuser and Accused?" *CNN World News*, August 24. Available online at http://www.cnn.com/2011/WORLD /europe/08/24/us.france.dsk.case/index.html

Smitts, Todd. 2004. "Plot Summary for *Boston Legal*." *Internet Movie Database*. Available online at http://www.imdb.com /title/tt0402711/plotsummary

Snell, Tracy L. 2014. *Capital Punishment, 2012 Statistical Tables*. Washington, DC: Bureau of Justice Statistics.

Snell, Tracy L. 2014. *Capital Punishment, 2013—Statistical Tables*. Washington, DC: Bureau of Justice Statistics.

Sobel, Russell S., and Joshua C. Hall. 2007. "The Effect of Judicial Selection Processes on Judicial Quality: The Role of Partisan Politics." *Cato Journal* 27: 69–82.

Solberg, Rorie Spill. 2005. "Diversity and George W. Bush's Judicial Appointments: Serving Two Masters." *Judicature* 88: 276–283.

Solitary Watch. 2011. *Fact Sheet: The High Cost of Solitary Confinement*. Washington, DC: Author. Available online at http://solitarywatch.com/wp-content/uploads/2011/06 /fact-sheet-the-high-cost-of-solitary-confinement.pdf

Sommer, Udi, and Quan Li. 2011. "Judicial Decision Making in Times of Financial Crises." *Judicature* 95: 68–77.

Sommers, Samuel. 2007. "Race and the Decision Making of Juries." *Legal and Criminological Psychology* 12: 171–187.

Sommers, Samuel R. 2006. "On Racial Diversity and Group Decision Making: Identifying Multiple Effects of Racial Composition on Jury Deliberations." *Journal of Personality and Social Psychology* 90: 597–612.

Songer, Donald. 1990. "Criteria for Publication of Opinions in the U.S. Courts of Appeals: Formal Rules versus Empirical Reality." *Judicature* 73: 307–313.

Sorensen, Jon R., and Donald Wallace. 1999. "Prosecutorial Discretion in Seeking Death: An Analysis of Racial Disparity in the Pretrial Stages of Case Processing in a Midwestern County." *Justice Quarterly* 16: 559–578.

Sosin, Michael. 1978. "Parens Patriae and Dispositions in Juvenile Courts." Madison, WI: Institute for Research on Poverty.

Spamann, Holger, and Lars Klöhn. 2016. "Justice Is Less Blind, and Less Legalistic Than We Thought: Evidence from an Experiment with Real Judges." *The Journal of Legal Studies* 45(2): 255–280.

Spangenberg Group. 2000. *Contracting for Indigent Defense Services: A Special Report*. Washington, DC: Bureau of Justice Statistics.

Spangenberg, Robert, and Marea Beeman 1995. "Indigent Defense Systems in the United States." *Law and Contemporary Problems* 58: 31–50.

Spangenberg, Robert, Richard Wilson, Patricia Smith, and Beverly Lee. 1986. *Containing the Cost of Indigent Defense Programs: Eligibility Screening and Cost Recovery Procedures*. Washington, DC: Department of Justice, National Institute of Justice.

Spears, Jeffrey, and Cassia Spohn. 1997. "The Effect of Evidence Factors and Victim Characteristics on Prosecutors' Charging Decisions in Sexual Assault Cases." *Justice Quarterly* 14: 501–524.

Spelman, William. 2000. "What Recent Studies Do (and Don't) Tell Us about Imprisonment and Crime. *Crime and Justice* 27: 419–494.

Spelman, William. 2009. "Crime, Cash, and Limited Options: Explaining the Prison Boom." *Criminology and Public Policy* 8: 29–77.

Spiecker, Shelley C., and Debra L. Worthington. 2003. "The Influence of Opening Statement/Closing Argument Organizational Strategy on Juror Verdict and Damage Awards." *Law and Human Behavior* 27: 437–456.

Spill, Rorie, and Kathleen Bratton. 2001. "Clinton and Diversification of the Federal Judiciary." *Judicature* 84: 256–261.

Spohn, Cassia C. 2008. "Editorial Introduction to Coordinated Community Response to Intimate Partner Violence." *Criminology & Public Policy* 7(4): 489–493.

Spohn, Cassia C. 2009. *How Do Judges Decide?* 2nd ed. Thousand Oaks, CA: Sage.

Spohn, Cassia C. 2013. "The Effects of the Offender's Race, Ethnicity, and Sex on Federal Sentencing Outcomes in the Guidelines Era." *Law & Contemporary Problems* 76(1): 75–104.

Spohn, Cassia C., Dawn Beichner, Erika Davis Frenzel, and David Holleran. 2002. *Prosecutors' Charging Decisions in Sexual Assault Cases: A Multi-Site Study, Final Report to the National Institute of Justice.* Available online at https://www.ncjrs.gov/pdffiles1/nij/grants/197048.pdf

Spohn, Cassia C., and Jerry Cederblom. 1991. "Race and Disparities in Sentencing: A Test of the Liberation Hypothesis." *Justice Quarterly* 8: 305–328.

Spohn, Cassia C., and Miriam DeLone. 2000. "When Does Race Matter? An Analysis of the Conditions under Which Race Affects Sentence Severity." *Sociology of Crime, Law and Deviance* 2: 3–37.

Spohn, Cassia C., John Gruhl, and Susan Welch. 1987. "The Impact of the Ethnicity and Gender of Defendants on the Decision to Reject or Dismiss Felony Charges." *Criminology* 25: 175–191.

Spohn, Cassia C., and David Holleran. 2000. "The Imprisonment Penalty Paid by Young, Unemployed Black and Hispanic Male Offenders." *Criminology* 38: 281–307.

Spohn, Cassia C., and David Holleran. 2001. "Prosecuting Sexual Assault: A Comparison of Charging Decisions in Sexual Assault Cases Involving Strangers, Acquaintances, and Intimate Partners." *Justice Quarterly* 18(3): 651–688.

Spohn, Cassia C., and Jeffrey Spears. 1996. "The Effect of Offender and Victim Characteristics on Sexual Assault Case Processing Decisions." *Justice Quarterly* 13: 649–679.

Springer, Charles. 1986. *Justice for Juveniles.* Washington, DC: Office of Juvenile Justice and Delinquency Prevention.

Springer, D. W., and A. R. Roberts. Eds. 2007. *Handbook of Forensic Mental Health with Victims and Offenders: Assessment, Treatment, and Research.* New York: Springer.

Springer, J. Fred. 1983. "Burglary and Robbery Plea Bargaining in California: An Organizational Perspective." *Justice System Journal* 8: 157–185.

Stanko, Elizabeth. 1981. "The Arrest versus the Case." *Urban Life* 9: 295–414.

Stanko, Elizabeth. 1981–1982. "The Impact of Victim Assessment on Prosecutors' Screening Decisions: The Case of the New York County District Attorney's Office." *Law and Society Review* 16: 225–239.

Stanko, Elizabeth. 1988. "The Impact of Victim Assessment on Prosecutor's Screening Decisions: The Case of the New York County District Attorney's Office." In G. Cole (Ed.), *Criminal Justice: Law and Politics.* Pacific Grove, CA: Brooks-Cole.

Staples, William G., and Stephanie K. Decker. 2010. "Between the 'Home' and 'Institutional' Worlds: Tensions and Contradictions in the Practice of House Arrest." *Critical Criminology* 18: 1–20.

Statistical Briefing Book. 2009. "Juvenile Arrests Rates for All Crimes, 1980–2007." Washington, DC: Office of Juvenile Justice and Delinquency Prevention.

Steadman Henry J, Fred C. Osher, Pamela Clark Robbins, Brian Case, and Steven Samuels. 2009. "Prevalence of Serious Mental Illness among Jail Inmates." *Psychiatric Services* 60(6): 761–765.

Stashenko, Joel. 2012. "Commission Backs Removal of Justice in Last Days of Term." *New York Law Journal*, February 14.

Steele, Walter, and Elizabeth Thornburg. 1991. "Jury Instructions: A Persistent Failure to Communicate." *Judicature* 74: 249–254.

Steelman, David C. 1997. "What Have We Learned about Court Delay, 'Local Legal Culture,' and Caseflow Management Since the Late 1970s?" *Justice Systems Journal* 19: 145–161.

Steen, Sara, and Rachel Bandy. 2007. "When the Policy Becomes the Problem: Criminal Justice in the New Millennium." *Punishment & Society* 9: 5–26.

Steffensmeier, Darrell J. 1980. "Assessing the Impact of the Women's Movement on Sex-Based Differences on the Handling of Adult Criminal Defendants." *Criminology* 26: 344–357.

Steffensmeier, Darrell J., and Chris Hebert. 1999. "Women and Men Policymakers: Does the Judge's Gender Affect the Sentencing of Criminal Defendants?" *Social Forces* 77: 1163.

Steffensmeier, Darrell J., John H. Kramer, and Cathy Streifel. 1993. "Gender and Imprisonment Decisions." *Criminology* 31: 411–446.

Steffensmeier, Darrell J., John H. Kramer, and Jeffrey T. Ulmer. 1995. "Age Differences in Sentencing." *Justice Quarterly* 12: 701–719.

Steffensmeier, Darrell J., Jeffrey T. Ulmer, and John H. Kramer. 1998. "The Interaction of Race, Gender, and Age in

Criminal Sentencing: The Punishment Cost of Being Young, Black, and Male." *Criminology* 36: 763–798.

Steigerwalt, Amy. 2010. *Battle over the Bench: Senators, Interest Groups, and Lower Court Confirmations*. Charlottesville: University of Virginia Press.

Steiker, Carol. 2013. "Raising the Bar: *Maples v. Thomas* and the Sixth Amendment Right to Counsel." *Harvard Law Review* 127: 468–472.

Steinberger, Barbara. 1985. "*Alford* Doctrine Popular in State's Courts." *New Haven Register*, June 9.

Steiner, Benjamin. 2009. "The Effects of Juvenile Transfer to Criminal Courts on Incarceration Decisions." *Justice Quarterly* 26: 77–106.

Steinmetz, Kevin F., and Howard Henderson. 2015. "On the Precipice of Intersectionality: The Influence of Race, Gender, and Offense Severity Interactions on Probation Outcomes." *Criminal Justice Review* 40(3): 361–377.

Steketee, Gail, and Anne Austin. 1989. "Rape Victims and the Justice System: Utilization and Impact." *Social Service Review* 63: 285–303.

Stemen, Don, and Andres F. Rengifo. 2011. "Policies and Imprisonment: The Impact of Structured Sentencing and Determinate Sentencing on State Incarceration Rates, 1978–2004." *Justice Quarterly* 28(1): 174–201.

Stemen, Don, and Bruce Frederick. 2013. "Rules, Resources, and Relationships: Contextual Constraints on Prosecutorial Decision Making." *Quinnipiac Law Review* 31(1): 1–84.

Stern, Andrew. 2000. "Illinois Governor Halts Executions Pending Review." Reuters, January 23.

Sternlight, Jean R., and Jennifer Robbennolt. 2008. "Good Lawyers Should Be Good Psychologists: Insights for Interviewing and Counseling Clients." *Ohio State Journal on Dispute Resolution* 23: 437–548.

Stevens, Mark. 2000. "Victim Impact Statements Considered in Sentencing: Constitutional Concerns." *California Criminal Law Review*, 3. Available online at http://www.boalt.org/CCLR/v2/v2stevensnf.htm

Stevens, Ruthie. 2015. "Are Intellectually Disabled Individuals Still at Risk of Capital Punishment After Hall V. Florida—the Need for a Totality-of-the-Evidence Test to Protect Human Rights in Determining Intellectual Disability." *Oklahoma Law Review* 68: 411–432.

Stevens, Sally, Josephine D. Korchmaros, Alison Greene, Monica Davis, Pamela Baumer, Michael L. Dennis, John Carnevale, Erika Ostile, Raanan Kagan, and Kathryn McCollister. 2016. "National Cross-Site Evaluation: Juvenile Drug Courts and Reclaiming Futures: Final Report: 7/1/2011-6/30/2015." *The University of Arizona - Southwest Institute for Research on Women*. Available online https://www.ncjrs.gov/pdffiles1/ojjdp/grants/249744.pdf

Stevenson, Megan. 2016. "Distortion of Justice: How Inability to Pay Bail Affects Case Outcomes." Available online at https://papers.ssrn.com/sol3/papers.cfm?abstract_id=2777615

Stidham, Ronald, and Robert Carp. 1997. "Judges' Gender and Federal District Court Decisions." Paper presented at the Southwestern Political Science Association, New Orleans.

Stith, Kate. 2008. "The Arc of the Pendulum: Judges, Prosecutors, and the Exercise of Discretion." *Yale Law Journal* 117: 1420–1496.

Stith, Kate, and Jose Cabranes. 1998. *Fear of Judging: Sentencing Guidelines in the Federal Courts*. Chicago: University of Chicago Press.

Stogel, Christopher. 2002. "Note, *Smith v. Robbins*: Appointed Criminal Appellate Counsel Should Watch for the *Wende* in Their Hair." *Southwestern University Law Review* 31: 281–304.

Stolzenberg, Lisa, Steward J. D'Alessio, and David Eitle. 2013. "Race and Cumulative Discrimination in the Prosecution of Criminal Defendants." *Race & Justice* 3(4): 275–299.

Stone, Geoffrey R. 2010. "Understanding Supreme Court Confirmations." *Supreme Court Review* 2010: 381–467.

Stott, E. Keith. 1982. "The Judicial Executive: Toward Greater Congruence in an Emerging Profession." *Justice System Journal* 7: 152–179.

Straus, Sarena. 2006. *Bronx D.A.: True Stories from the Sex Crimes and Domestic Violence Unit*. Fort Lee, NJ: Barricade Books.

Strawn, David, and Raymond Buchanan. 1976. "Jury Confusion: A Threat to Justice." *Judicature* 59: 478–483.

Streb, Matthew, Brian Frederick, and Casey Lafrance. 2007. "Contestation, Competition, and Potential for Accountability in Intermediate Appellate Court Elections." *Judicature* 91: 71–78.

Streb, Matthew J. 2007. *Running for Judge: The Rising Political, Financial, and Legal Stakes of Judicial Elections*. New York: New York University Press.

Streb, Matthew J. 2013. "Gibson's *Electing Judges*: What We Know and What We Need to Know about the Effects of Politicized Judicial Campaigns." *Judicature* 96: 223–237.

Strickland, Shauna M., Richard Y. Schauffler, Robert C. LaFountain, and Kathryn A. Holt. 2014. *State Court Organization*. Williamsburg, VA: National Center for State Courts. Available online at http://www.ncsc.org/sco

Studebaker, Christina A., and Steven D. Penrod. 2007. "Pretrial Publicity and Its Influence on Juror Decision Making." In Neil Brewer and Kipling D. Williams (Ed.), *Psychology and Law: An Empirical Perspective*. New York: Guildford Press.

Sudnow, David. 1965. "Normal Crimes: Sociological Features of the Penal Codes in a Public Defender Office." *Social Problems* 12: 254–264.

Sullivan, Christopher J., Lesil Blair, Edward Latessa, and Carrie Coen Sullivan. "Juvenile Drug Courts and Recidivism: Results from a Multisite Outcome Study." *Justice Quarterly* 33(2): 291–318.

Sundt, Jody, Emily J. Salisbury, and Mark G. Harmon. 2016. "Is Downsizing Prisons Dangerous? The Effect of California's Realignment Act on Public Safety." *Criminology & Public Policy* 15(2): 315–341.

Surette, Ray. 1996. "News from Nowhere, Policy to Follow: Media and the Social Construction of 'Three Strikes and You're Out.'" In David Shichor and Dale Sechrest (Eds.), *Three Strikes and You're Out: Vengeance as Public Policy*. Thousand Oaks, CA: Sage.

Surette, Ray. 2010. *Media, Crime, and Criminal Justice: Images and Realities.* 4th ed. Belmont, CA: Wadsworth, Cengage.

Sutton, John R. 2013. "Symbol and Substance: Effects of California's Three Strikes Law on Felony Sentencing." *Law & Society Review* 47(1): 37–72.

Swingle, H. Morley, and Lane P. Thomasson. (2013). Beam Me Up: Upgrading Search Warrants with Technology. *Journal of the Missouri Bar* 69: 16–20.

Taggart, William. 1989. "Redefining the Power of the Federal Judiciary: The Impact of Court-Ordered Prison Reform on State Expenditures for Corrections." *Law and Society Review* 23: 241–272.

Taleb, Nassim Nicholas. 2007. *The Black Swan: The Impact of the Highly Improbable*. Crawfordsville, IN: Random House Inc.

Tanner, Melinda, Dillon Wyatt, and Douglas L. Yearwood. 2008. "Evaluation Pretrial Services Programs in North Carolina." *Federal Probation* 72(1): 18–27.

Tarr, G. Alan. 1982. "State Supreme Courts and the U.S. Supreme Court: The Problem of Compliance." In Mary Cornelia Porter and G. Alan Tarr (Eds.), *State Supreme Courts: Policymakers in the Federal System*. Westport, CT: Greenwood.

Tarr, G. Alan, and Mary Cornelia Porter. 1988. *State Supreme Courts in State and Nation*. New Haven, CT: Yale University Press.

Task Force on Judicial Budget Cuts. 2014. "Courts in Crisis." New York County Lawyers' Association. Available online at http://www.nycla.org/siteFiles/Publications /Publications1666_0.pdf.

Taslitz, Andrew. 2012. "Information Overload, Multi-Tasking, and the Socially Networked Jury: Why Prosecutors Should Approach the Media Gingerly." *Journal of the Legal Profession* 37: 8–138.

Tavernise, Sabrina. 2012. "Mine Superintendent Charged in 2010 Disaster." *New York Times*, February 22.

Taxin, Amy. 2014. "Backlogged Immigration Courts Face New Deluge." *Associated Press*, July 13.

Taylor, Clifford W. 2009. "Merit Selection: Choosing Judges Based on their Politics under the Veil of a Disarming Name." *Harvard Journal of Law and Public Policy* 32: 97–101.

TerBeek, Calvin. 2007. "A Call for Precedential Heads: Why the Supreme Court's Eyewitness Identification Jurisprudence Is Anachronistic and Out-of-Step with the Empirical Reality." *Law and Psychology Review* 31: 21–51.

Thaler, Paul. 1994. *The Watchful Eye: American Justice in the Age of the Television Trial*. Westport, CT: Praeger.

Thomas, Sabra. 2014. "Addressing Wrongful Convictions: An Examination of Texas's New Junk Science Writ and Other Measures for Protecting the Innocent." *Houston Law Review* 53: 1037–1066.

Thomas, Suja A. 2014. "Blackstone's Curse: The Fall of the Criminal, Civil, and Grand Juries and the Rise of the Executive, the Legislature, the Judiciary, and the States." *William & Mary Law Review* 55(3): 1195–1239.

Thompson, Kevin. 1996. "The Nature and Scope of Rural Crime." In Thomas McDonald, Robert Wood, and Melissa Pflug (Eds.), *Rural Criminal Justice: Conditions, Constraints, and Challenges* (pp. 3–18). Salem, WI: Sheffield.

Thompson, Timothy D. 2010–2011. "Non-Prisoner Pro Se Litigation in the United States District Court for the Eastern District of Kentucky: Analyzing 2004 and 2007 Cases from Filing to Termination." *Kentucky Law Journal* 99(3): 601–635.

Thompson, William C. 2006. "Tarnish on the 'Gold Standard': Recent Problems in Forensic DNA Testing." *The Champion* 30: 10–16.

Thomson, Douglas, and Anthony Ragona. 1987. "Popular Moderation versus Governmental Authoritarianism: An Interactionist View of Public Sentiments toward Criminal Sanctions." *Crime and Delinquency* 33: 337–357.

Tiede, Lydia. 2009. "The Impact of the Federal Sentencing Guidelines and Reform: A Comparative Analysis." *Justice System Journal* 30: 34–49.

Tilley, Cristina Carmody. 2014. "I Am a Camera: Scrutinizing the Assumption That Cameras in the Courtroom Furnish Public Value by Operating as a Proxy for the Public." *University of Pennsylvania Journal of Constitutional Law* 16: 697–738.

Tillyer, Rob, Richard D. Hartley, and Jeffrey T. Ward. 2015. "Does Criminal History Moderate the Effect of Gender on Sentence Length in Federal Narcotics Cases?" *Criminal Justice and Behavior* 42(7): 703–721.

Tjaden, Patricia, and Nancy Thoennes. 2006. *Extent, Nature, and Consequences of Rape Victimization: Findings from the National Violence Against Women Survey*. Washington, DC: National Institute of Justice.

Tobias, Carl W. 2015. "Judicial Selection in Congress' Lame Duck Session." *Indian Law Journal Supplement* 90(5): 52–62.

Tobias, Carl W. 2016. "Fixing the Federal Judicial Selection Process." *Emory Law Journal Online* 65: 2051–2059.

Tobolowsky, Peggy. 1993. "Restitution in the Federal Criminal Justice System." *Judicature* 77: 90–95.

Tonry, Michael H. 1987. *Sentencing Reform Impacts*. Washington, DC: Government Printing Office.

Tonry, Michael H. 1993. "The Failure of the U.S. Sentencing Commission's Guidelines." *Crime and Delinquency* 39: 131–149.

Tonry, Michael H. 1998. *Sentencing Matters*. New York Oxford University Press.

Tonry, Michael H. 2004. *Thinking about Crime: Sense and Sensibility in American Penal Culture*. New York: Oxford University Press.

Toone, Robert E. 2015. "The Absence of Agency in Indigent Defense." *American Criminal Law Review* 52(25): 25–72.

Tor, Avishalom, Oren Gazal-Ayal, and Stephen M. Garcia. 2010. "Fairness and the Willingness to Accept Plea Bargain Offers." *Journal of Empirical Legal Studies* 7(1): 97–116.

Torbet, Patricia, Patrick Griffin, Hunter Hurst, and Lynn MacKenzie. 2000. *Juveniles Facing Criminal Sanctions: Three States That Changed the Rules*. Washington, DC: Department of Justice, Office of Juvenile Justice and Delinquency Prevention.

Torpy, Bill, and Bill Rankin. 2010. "Off the Bench, in Disgrace." *The Atlanta Journal-Constitution*, August 22.

Torres, Sam, and Elizabeth Piper Deschenes. 1997. "Changing the System and Making It Work: The Process of Implementing Drug Courts in Los Angeles County." *Justice System Journal* 19: 267–290.

Tracy, Paul E., Marvin E. Wolfgang, and Robert M. Figlio. 1990. *Delinquency Careers in Two Birth Cohorts*. New York: Plenum.

Trahan, Adam, and Daniel M. Stewart. 2011. "Examining Capital Jurors' Impressions of Attorneys' Personal Characteristics and Their Impact on Sentencing Outcomes." *Applied Psychology in Criminal Justice* 7(2): 93–105.

Transactional Records Access Clearinghouse (TRAC). 2016, April 7. "White Collar Crime Convictions Continue to Decline." Syracuse University, http://trac.syr.edu/whatsnew/email.160407.html

Travis, Jeremy. 2005. *But They All Come Back: Facing the Challenges of Prisoner Reentry*. Washington, DC: Urban Institute Press.

Treatment Advocacy Center. 2014. "How Many Individuals with Serious Mental Illness are in Jails and Prisons?" Available online at http://www.treatmentadvocacycenter.org/storage/documents/backgrounders/how%20many%20individuals%20with%20serious%20mental%20illness%20are%20in%20jails%20and%20prisons%20final.pdf

Truman, Jennifer L. 2011. *Criminal Victimization*, 2010. Washington, DC: Bureau of Justice Statistics.

Truman, Jennifer L., and Lynn Langton. 2014. *Criminal Victimization, 2013*. Washington, DC: Bureau of Justice Statistics. Available online at http://www.bjs.gov/content/pub/pdf/cv13.pdf

Truman, Jennifer L., and Rachel E. Morgan. 2016. *Criminal Victimization, 2015*. Washington, DC: Bureau of Justice Statistics.

Trupin Eric, and Henry Richards. 2003. "Seattle's Mental Health Courts: Early Indicators of Effectiveness." *International Journal of Law and Psychiatry* 26(1): 33–53.

Tucker, Eric. 2014a. "Citigroup to Pay $7B in Subprime Mortgages Probe." *Associated Press*, July 14.

Tucker, Eric. 2014b. "U.S. Weighs Clemency for Inmates Jailed for 10 Years." *Associated Press*, April 23.

Turley, Jonathan. 2012. "Huguely's Failure to Speak." *USA Today*, February 29.

Turner, Susan, and Judith Greene. 1999. "The FARE Probation Experiment: Implementation and Outcomes of Day Fines for Felony Offenders in Maricopa County." *Justice System Journal* 21: 1–21.

Turner, Susan, Peter W. Greenwood, Terry Fain, and James R. Chiesa. 2006. "An Evaluation of the Federal Government's Violent Offender Incarceration and Truth-in-Sentencing Incentive Grants." *Prison Journal* 86: 364–385.

Tutty, Leslie M., and Robbie Babins-Wagner. 2016. "Outcomes and Recidivism in Mandated Batterer Intervention Before and After Introducing a Specialized Domestic Violence Court." *Journal of Interpersonal Violence*. Advanced online publication. doi: 10.1177/0886260516647005

Tyler, Tom R. 2006. "Viewing CSI and the Threshold of Guilt: Managing Truth and Justice in Reality and Fiction." *Yale Law Journal* 115: 1050–1085.

U.S. Census Bureau. 2011. "The Hispanic Population: 2010." Available online at www.census.gov/prod/cen2010/briefs/c2010br-04.pdf

U.S. General Accounting Office. 1990. "Death Penalty Sentencing: Research Indicated a Pattern of Racial Disparities." Gaithersburg, MD: Author. Available online at http://archive.gao.gov/t2pbat11/140845.pdf

U.S. Government Accountability Office. 2005. *Adult Drug Courts: Evidence Indicates Recidivism Reductions and Mixed Results for Other Outcomes*. Available online at: http://www.gao.gov/new.items/d05219.pdf

U.S. Joint Service Committee on Military Justice. 2008. *Manual for Courts-Martial-United States*. Washington, DC: U.S. Department of Defense.

Uchida, Craig, and Timothy Bynum. 1991. "Search Warrants, Motions to Suppress and 'Lost Cases': The Effects of the

Exclusionary Rule in Seven Jurisdictions." *Journal of Criminal Law and Criminology* 81: 1034–1066.

Uhlman, Thomas, and Darlene Walker. 1980. "'He Takes Some of My Time: I Take Some of His': An Analysis of Judicial Sentencing Patterns in Jury Cases." *Law and Society Review* 14: 323–342.

Ulmer, Jeffrey. 1997. *Social Worlds of Sentencing: Court Communities under Sentencing Guidelines*. Albany: State University of New York Press.

Ulmer, Jeffrey, and Mindy Bradley. 2006. "Variations in Trial Penalties among Serious Violent Offenses." *Criminology* 44: 631–658.

Ulmer, Jeffery, James Eisenstein, and Brian Johnson. 2010. "Trial Penalties in Federal Sentencing: Extra-Guidelines Factors and District Variation." *Justice Quarterly* 27: 560–592.

Ulmer, Jeffery, and Brian D. Johnson. 2004. "Sentencing in Context: A Multilevel Analysis." *Criminology* 42: 137–177.

Ulmer, Jeffery, Noah Painter-Davis, and Leigh Tinik. 2016. "Disproportional Imprisonment of Black and Hispanic Males: Sentencing Discretion, Processing Outcomes, and Policy Structures." *Justice Quarterly* 33(4): 642–681.

Ulmer, Jeffery T. 2012. "Recent Developments and New Directions in Sentencing Research." *Justice Quarterly* 29(1): 1–40.

Ulmer, Jeffrey T., Megan C. Kurlychek, and John H. Kramer. 2007. "Prosecutorial Discretion and the Imposition of Mandatory Minimum Sentences." *Journal of Research in Crime and Delinquency* 44: 427–458.

Ulmer, Jeffery T., Michael T. Light, and John Kramer. 2011. "The 'Liberation' of Federal Judges' Discretion in the Wake of the Booker/Fanfan Decision: Is There Increased Disparity and Divergence between Courts?" *Justice Quarterly* 28(6): 799–837.

Underwood, James. M. 2006. "The Late, Great Diversity Jurisdiction." *Case Western Reserve Law Review* 57: 179–222.

United States Sentencing Commission. 2015. *U.S. Sentencing Commission's 2015 Sourcebook of Federal Sentencing Statistics*. Available online at http://www.ussc.gov /research/sourcebook-2015

Uphoff, R. 2006. "Convicting the Innocent: Aberration or Systemic Problem?" *Wisconsin Law Review* 2006: 739–842.

Utz, Pamela. 1979. "Two Models of Prosecutorial Professionalism." In William McDonald (Ed.), *The Prosecutor*. CA: Sage.

Vance, Stephen E. 2014. "Displaced Discretion: The Effects of Sentencing Guidelines on Prosecutors' Charge Bargaining in the District of Columbia Superior Court." *Criminal Justice Policy Review* 25: 347–377.

Vance, Stephen E., and J. C. Oleson. 2014. "Displaced Discretion: The Effects of Sentencing Guidelines on Prosecutors'

Charge Bargaining in the District of Columbia Superior Court." *Criminal Justice Policy Review* 25(3): 347–377.

Van Duizend, Richard, David Steelman and Lee Suskin. 2011. *Model Time Standards for State Trial Courts*. Williamsburg, VA: National Center for State Courts.

Van Duizend, Richard, L. Paul Sutton, and Charlotte Carter. 1984. *The Search Warrant Process*. Williamsburg, VA: National Center for State Courts.

van Dyke, Jon. 1977. *Jury Selection Procedures: Our Uncertain Commitment to Representative Panels*. Cambridge, MA: Ballinger.

Vanhaelemeesch, Delphine, Tom Vander Beken, and Stijn Vandevelde. 2014. "Punishment at home: Offenders' Experiences with Electronic Monitoring." *European Journal of Criminology* 11(3): 273–287.

Van Namen, Kathryn Kinnison. 2012. "Facebook Facts and Twitter Tips—Prosecutors and Social Media: An Analysis of the Implications Associated with the Use of Social Media in the Prosecution Function." *Mississippi Law Journal* 81: 549–587.

von Hirsch, Andrew. 1976. *Doing Justice: The Choice of Punishment*. New York: Hill and Wang.

Van Ness, Daniel, and Karen Heetderks Strong. 2006. *Restoring Justice*. 3rd ed. Cincinnati: Anderson.

Van Slyke, Shanna, and William D. Bales. 2012. "A Contemporary Study of the Decision to Incarcerate White-Collar and Street Property Offenders." *Punishment & Society* 14: 217–246.

Vaughn, Michael G., and Matt DeLisi. 2008. "Were Wolfgang's Chronic Offenders Psychopaths? On the Convergent Validity between Psychopathy and Career Criminality." *Journal of Criminal Justice* 36: 33–42.

Vera Institute of Justice. 1977. *Felony Arrests: Their Prosecution and Disposition in New York City's Courts*. New York: Author.

Vera Institute of Justice. 1981. *Felony Arrests: Their Prosecution and Disposition in New York City's Courts*. Rev. ed. New York: Longman.

Vermont Center for Justice Research. 1995. "DUI Adjudication and BAC Level: An Assessment." *Data-Line: The Justice Research Bulletin* 4 (May).

Verrecchia, Philip. 2011. "The Effect of Transfer Mechanism from Juvenile Court on Conviction on a Target Offense: Criminal Court." *Contemporary Justice Review* 14: 189–201.

Viano, Emilio. 1987. "Victim's Rights and the Constitution: Reflections on a Bicentennial." *Crime and Delinquency* 33: 438–451.

Villmoore, Edwin, and Virginia N. Neto. 1987. "Executive Summary, Victim Appearances at Sentencing Hearings under the California Victims' Bill of Rights." Washington, DC: National Institute of Justice, Department of Justice.

Vincent, Barbara, and Paul Hofer J. 1994. *The Consequences of Mandatory Minimum Prison Terms: A Summary of Recent Findings*. Washington, DC: Federal Judicial Center.

Visher, Christy. 1987. "Incapacitation and Crime Control: Does a 'Lock 'Em Up' Strategy Reduce Crime?" *Justice Quarterly* 4: 513–544.

Visher, Christy, Adele Harrell, Lisa Newmark, and Jennifer Yahner. 2008. "Reducing Intimate Partner Violence: An Evaluation of a Comprehensive Justice System-Community Collaboration." *Criminology and Public Policy* 7: 495–524.

Volz, Matt. 2014. "Judge Sent Hundreds of Bigoted Emails." *Associated Press*, January 17.

Voss, Jansen. 2005. "The Science of Persuasion: An Exploration of Advocacy and the Science Behind the Art of Persuasion in the Courtroom." *Law and Psychology Review* 29: 301–327.

Wald, Matthew. 2006. "A New Strategy to Discourage Driving Drunk." *New York Times*, November 19.

Waldron, Jeremy. 2008. "Lucky in Your Judge." *Theoretical Inquiries in Law* 9: 185–216.

Walker, Samuel. 2015. *Sense and Nonsense about Crime and Drugs: A Policy Guide*. 8th ed. Belmont, CA: Wadsworth.

Walker, Samuel, Cassia Spohn, and Miriam DeLone. 2017. *The Color of Justice: Race, Ethnicity, and Crime in America*. 6th ed. Belmont, CA: Wadsworth.

Waller, Mark. 2008. "Officials Say Jefferson's Traffic Cameras Increase Safety, but Critics Say the Red-Light System Is All about Seeing Green." *Times-Picayune*, December 10.

Wallman, Joel. 2005. "Unpacking Recidivism." *Criminology and Public Policy* 4: 479–484.

Walsh, Anthony. 1985. "The Role of the Probation Officer in the Sentencing Process." *Criminal Justice and Behavior* 12: 289–303.

Walsh, Anthony. 1987. "The Sexual Stratification Hypothesis and Sexual Assault in Light of the Changing Conceptions of Race." *Criminology* 25: 153–173.

Walsh, Colleen. 2010. "Film Explores Military Tribunal." *Harvard Gazette*, May 6. Available online at http://news.harvard.edu/gazette/story/2010/05/film-explores-military-tribunal

Wandall, Rasmus H. 2016. *Decisions to Imprison: Court Decision-Making Inside and Outside the Law*. New York: Routledge.

Wang. Xia, Daniel P. Mears, Cassia Spohn. and Lisa Dario. 2013. "Assessing the Differential Effects of Race and Ethnicity on Sentence Outcomes under Different Sentencing Systems." *Crime & Delinquency* 59(1): 87–114.

Ward, Geoff, Amy Farrell, and Danielle Rousseau. 2009. "Does Racial Balance in Workforce Representation Yield Equal Justice? Race Relations of Sentencing in Federal Court Organizations." *Law & Society Review* 43(4): 757–806.

Ward, Jeffrey T., Richard D. Hartley, and Rob Tillyer. 2016. "Unpacking Gender and Racial/Ethnic Biases in the Federal Sentencing of Drug Offenders: A Causal Mediation Approach." *Journal of Criminal Justice* 46: 196–206.

Warden, Rob. 2004. *The Snitch System: How Snitch Testimony Sent Randy Steidl and Other Innocent Americans to Death Row*. Chicago: Northwestern University School of Law, Center on Wrongful Convictions.

Warren, Patricia, Ted Chiricos, and William D. Bales. 2012. "The Imprisonment Penalty for Young Black and Hispanic Males: A Crime-Specific Analysis." *Journal of Research in Crime and Delinquency* 49: 56–80.

Warren, Roger K. 2009. "Evidence-Based Sentencing: The Application of Principles of Evidence-Based Practice to State Sentencing Practice and Policy." *University of San Francisco Law Review* 43: 585–634.

Wasby, Stephen. 1982. "The Functions and Importance of Appellate Oral Argument: Some Views of Lawyers and Federal Judges." *Judicature* 65: 340–353.

Washburn, Kevin K. 2008. "Restoring the Grand Jury." *Fordham Law Review* 76: 2333–2388.

Watkins, Matthew. 2009. "Screening Stirs Community." (March 17). Available online at http://www.theeagle.com/news/local/screening-stirs-community/article_55676854-fed1-5091-8ee7-ca54b62ba965.html

Watson, Richard, and Ronald Downing. 1969. *The Politics of the Bench and Bar: Judicial Selection under the Missouri Nonpartisan Court Plan*. New York: Wiley.

Webster, Barbara. 1988. *Victim Assistance Programs Report Increased Workloads*. Washington, DC: National Institute of Justice.

Webster, Cheryl, Anthony Doob, and Franklin Zimring. 2006. "Proposition 8 and Crime Rates in California: The Case of the Disappearing Deterrent." *Criminology and Public Policy* 5: 417–448.

Weddell, Hilary. 2013. "A Jury of Whose Peers? Eliminating Racial Discrimination in Jury Selection Procedures." *Boston College Journal of Law & Social Justice* 33: 453–486.

Weed, Frank. 1995. *Certainty of Justice: Reform in the Crime Victim Movement*. New York: Aldine de Gruyter.

Weisheit, Ralph, David Falcone, and L. Edward Wells. 2006. *Crime and Policing in Rural and Small-Town America*. Long Grove, IL: Waveland Press.

Weisheit, Ralph, and Sue Mahan. 1988. *Women, Crime and Criminal Justice*. Cincinnati: Anderson.

Weiss, Karen G. 2010. "Too Ashamed to Report: Deconstructing the Shame of Sexual Assault." *Feminist Criminology* 5: 286–310.

Weiss, Michael. 2005. *Public Defenders: Pragmatic and Political Motivations to Represent the Indigent.* New York: LFB Scholarly.

Weiss, Robert, Richard Berk, and Catherine Lee. 1996. "Assessing the Capriciousness of Death Penalty Charging." *Law and Society Review* 30: 607–638.

Welch, Susan, and Cassia Spohn. 1986. "Evaluating the Impact of Prior Record on Judges' Sentencing Decisions: A Seven-City Comparison." *Justice Quarterly* 3: 389–408.

Welch, Susan, Cassia Spohn, and John Gruhl. 1985. "Convicting and Sentencing Differences among Black, Hispanic and White Males in Six Localities." *Justice Quarterly* 2: 67–80.

Wells, Gary. L., and Deah S. Quinlivan. 2009. "Suggestive Eyewitness Identification Procedures and the Supreme Court's Reliability Test in Light of Eyewitness Science: 30 Years Later." *Law and Human Behavior* 33(1):1–24.

Wemple, Erik. 2013. "Zimmerman Lawyer to Move 'ASAP' against NBC News." *The Washington Post*, July 14. Retrieved from http://www.washingtonpost.com/blogs/erik-wemple/wp/2013/07/14/zimmerman-lawyer-to-move-asap-against-nbc-news/

Wenzel, Michael, and Tyler G. Okimoto. 2016. "Retributive Justice." In C. Sabbagh and M. Schmitt (Eds.), *Handbook of Social Justice Theory and Research* (pp. 237–256). New York: Springer.

Wermink, Hilde, Arjan Blokland, Paul Nieuwbeerta, Daniel Nagin, and Nikolaj Tollenaar. 2010. "Comparing the Effects of Community Service and Short-Term Imprisonment on Recidivism: A Matched Samples Approach." *Journal of Experimental Criminology* 6(3): 325–349.

Wessell, Todd. 2016. "From Red, Seeing Green: How Much 2 Towns Haul from Traffic Cameras." Journal and Topics Online, Jan 27.

Wexler, David B., and Bruce J. Winick (Eds.). 1996. *Law in a Therapeutic Key: Developments in Therapeutic Jurisprudence.* Durham, NC: Carolina Academic Press.

Wheeler, Russell. 2003. *A New Judge's Introduction to Federal Judicial Administration.* Washington, DC: Federal Judicial Center.

Wheeler, Russell. 2012. *Judicial Nominations and Confirmations after Three Years—Where Do Things Stand?* Washington, DC: Brookings Institute.

Wheeler, Russell, and Cynthia Harrison. 1994. *Creating the Federal Judicial System.* 2nd ed. Washington, DC: Federal Judicial Center, p. 26.

Wheelock, Darren. 2005. "Collateral Consequences and Racial Inequality: Felon Status Restrictions as a System of Disadvantage." *Journal of Contemporary Criminal Justice* 21: 82–90.

White, John Valery. 2008. "A Time for Change." *Nevada Lawyer* 16: 38.

White, M. D., and H. F. Fradella. (2016). *Pat-Down: Examining the Role of "Stop, Question, and Frisk" Practices in American Policing.* New York: New York University Press.

White, Michael D. (2014). *Police Officer Body Worn Cameras: Assessing the Evidence.* Washington, DC: U.S. Department of Justice, Office of Justice Programs, Diagnostic Center for Data-Driven Crime Solutions.

White, Penny J. 2002. "Judging Judges: Securing Judicial Independence by Use of Judicial Performance Evaluations." *Fordham Urban Law Journal* 29: 1053–1077.

Whitten, Taylor. 2014. "Under the Guise of Reform: How Marijuana Possession Is Exposing the Flaws in the Criminal Justice System's Guarantee of a Right to a Jury Trial." *Iowa Law Review* 99: 919–937.

Wice, Paul. 1978. *Criminal Lawyers: An Endangered Species.* Newbury Park, CA: Sage.

Wice, Paul B. 1985. *Chaos in the Courthouse: The Inner Workings of the Urban Criminal Courts.* New York: Praeger.

Wice, Paul. 1991. *Judges and Lawyers: The Human Side of Justice.* New York: Harper-Collins.

Wice, Paul. 2005. *Public Defenders and the American Justice System.* Westport, CT: Praeger.

Wickersham Commission. 1931. National Commission on Law Observance and Enforcement, Publication no. 11, Report on Lawlessness in Law Enforcement.

Wilkey, Malcolm. 1978. "The Exclusionary Rule: Why Suppress Valid Evidence?" *Judicature* 62: 214–232.

Wilkins, David. 2012. "Some Realism about Legal Realism for Lawyers: Assessing the Role of Context in Legal Ethics." In Leslie Levin and Lynn Mather (Eds.), *Lawyers in Practice: Ethical Decision Making in Context.* Chicago: University of Chicago Press.

Williams, Frank V. 2007. "Reinventing the Courts: The Frontiers of Judicial Activism in the State Courts." *Campbell Law Review* 29: 591–735.

Williams, Jimmy. 1995. "Type of Counsel and the Outcome of Criminal Appeals: A Research Note." *American Journal of Criminal Justice* 19: 275–285.

Williams, Marian R. 2013. "The Effectiveness of Public Defenders in Four Florida Counties." *Journal of Criminal Justice* 41: 205–212.

Williams, Marian R., and Melissa W. Burek. 2008. "Justice, Juries, and Convictions: The Relevance of Race in Jury Verdicts." *Journal of Crime & Justice* 31(1): 149–169.

Williams, Marian R., Stephen Demuth, and Jefferson E. Holcomb. 2007. "Understanding the Influence of Victim Gender in Death Penalty Cases: The Importance of Victim Race, Sex-Related Victimization, and Jury Decision Making." *Criminology* 45: 865–891.

Williams, Marian R., and Jefferson E. Holcomb. 2004. "The Interactive Effects of Victim Race and Gender on Death Sentence Disparity Findings." *Homicide Studies* 8: 350–376.

Williams, Paige. 2014. "Witnesses to a Botched Execution." *The New Yorker*, April 30, http://www.newyorker.com/online/blogs/newsdesk/2014/04/witnesses-to-a-botched-execution.html

Williams, R. Seth, and Will Steward. 2013. *"Implementing a Geographic Community-Based Prosecution Model in Philadelphia."* Washington, DC: Association of Prosecuting Attorneys.

Willing, Richard. 2003. "Judges Go Softer on Sentences More Often." *USA Today*, August 28, p. 1.

Wilmot, Keith Alan, and Cassia Spohn. 2004. "Prosecutorial Discretion and Real-Offense Sentencing: An Analysis of Relevant Conduct under the Federal Sentencing Guidelines." *Criminal Justice Policy Review* 15: 324–343.

Wilson, James. 2005. "Bad Behavior or Bad Policy? An Examination of Tennessee Release Cohorts, 1993–2001." *Criminology and Public Policy* 4: 485–518.

Wilson, James Q. 1973. "If Every Criminal Knew He Would Be Punished if Caught." *New York Times Magazine*, January 28.

Wilson, James Q. 1975. *Thinking about Crime*. New York: Basic.

Wilson, James Q. 1983. *Thinking about Crime: A Policy Guide*. 2nd ed. New York: Basic Books.

Wing, Nick. 2017, January 4. "How a State Bail Reform Measure Lost the Support of Bail Reformers." *Huffington Post*, http://www.huffingtonpost.com/entry/new-mexico-bail-reform_us_580a7885e4b0cdea3d8784e5

Winick, Bruce J. 2013. "Problem Solving Courts: Therapeutic Jurisprudence in Practice." In Richard L. Wiener and Eve M. Brank (Eds.), *Problem Solving Courts: Social Science and Legal Perspectives* (pp. 211–236). New York: Springer.

Winter, Alix S., and Matthew Clair. 2017. "Jurors' Subjective Experiences of Deliberation in Criminal Cases." *Law & Social Inquiry*. Advance online publication. doi: 10.1111/Isi.12288.

Wiseman, Jacqueline. 1970. *Stations of the Lost: The Treatment of Skid Row Alcoholics*. Englewood Cliffs, NJ: Prentice Hall.

Wold, John. 1978. "Going through the Motions: The Monotony of Appellate Court Decisionmaking." *Judicature* 62: 58–65.

Wold, John, and Greg Caldeira. 1980. "Perceptions of 'Routine' Decision-Making in Five California Courts of Appeal." *Polity* 13: 334–347.

Wolf, Robert V. 2007. *Principles of Problem-Solving Justice*. New York: Center for Court Innovation.

Wolfe, Scott E., Kyle McLean, and Travis C. Pratt. 2017. "I Learned it by Watching You: Legal Socialization and the Intergenerational Transmission of Legitimacy Attitudes." *British Journal of Criminology* 57(5): 1123–1143.

Wolfgang, Marvin E., Robert M. Figlio, and Thorsten Sellin. 1972. *Delinquency in a Birth Cohort*. Chicago: University of Chicago Press.

Wolfgang, Marvin, and Marc Riedel. 1973. "Race, Judicial Discretion, and the Death Penalty." *Annals of the American Academy of Political and Social Science* 407: 119–133.

Wolfram, Charles. 1986. *Modern Legal Ethics*. St. Paul, MN: Thomson/West.

Womer, Denise. 2016. "High Tech Courtrooms." *Law Enforcement Today*, Aug 29.

Wood, Lauren S. 2016. "Out of Cite, Out of Mind: Navigating the Labyrinth That Is State Appellate Courts' Unpublished Opinion Practices." *University of Baltimore Law Review* 45(3): 561–604.

Woods, Andrea. 2014. "The Undersigned Attorney Herby Certifies: Ensuring Reasonable Caseloads for Washington Defenders and Clients." *Washington Law Review* 89: 217–255.

Wooldredge, J. 2010. "Judges' Unequal Contributions to Extralegal Disparities in Imprisonment." *Criminology* 48(2): 539–567.

Wooldredge, John. 2012. "Distinguishing Race Effects on Pre-Trial Release and Sentencing Decisions." *Justice Quarterly* 29(1): 41–75.

Wooldredge, John, and Jill Gordon. 1997. "Predicting the Estimated Use of Alternatives to Incarceration." *Journal of Quantitative Criminology* 13: 121–142.

Wooldredge, John, and Timothy Griffin. 2005. "Displaced Discretion under Ohio Sentencing Guidelines." *Journal of Criminal Justice* 33: 301–316.

Wooldredge, John, Timothy Griffin, and Amy Thistlethwaite. 2013. "Comparing Between-Judge Disparities in Imprisonment Decisions Across Sentencing Regimes in Ohio." *Justice System Journal* 34(3): 345–368.

Worden, Alissa Pollitz. 1990. "Policymaking by Prosecutors: The Uses of Discretion in Regulating Plea Bargaining." *Judicature* 73: 335–340.

Worden, Alissa Pollitz. 1991. "Privatizing Due Process: Issues in the Comparison of Assigned Counsel, Public Defender, and Contracted Indigent Defense Systems." *Justice System Journal* 14: 390–418.

Worden, Alissa Pollitz. 1993. "Counsel for the Poor: An Evaluation of Contracting for Indigent Criminal Defense." *Justice Quarterly* 10: 613–637.

Worden, Alissa Pollitz. 2008. "Courts and Communities: Toward a Theoretical Synthesis." In David Duffee and Edward R. Maguire (Eds.), *Criminal Justice Theory* (pp. 181–222). New York: Routledge.

Worden, Alissa Pollitz. 2015. "Courts and Communities: Towards a Theoretical Synthesis." In David Duffee and Edward R. Maguire (Eds.), *Criminal Justice Theory* (pp. 243–286). New York: Routledge.

Worden, Alissa Pollitz, and Robert Worden. 1989. "Local Politics and the Provision of Indigent Defense Counsel." *Law and Policy* 11: 401–424.

Work, Mike. 2014. "Creating Constitutional Procedure: *Frye, Lafler,* and Plea Bargaining Reform." *Journal of Criminal Law & Criminology* 104: 457–487.

Worrall, John, and Tomislav Kovandzic. 2008. "Is Policing for Profit? Answers from Asset Forfeiture." *Criminology and Public Policy* 2: 219–244.

Worrall, John, and M. Elaine Nugent-Borakove (Eds.). 2008. *The Changing Role of the American Prosecutor*. Albany, NY: SUNY Press.

Worrall, John L. 2008. "Asset Forfeiture." *Problem-Oriented Guides for Policy Response Guides Series No. 7*. Washington, DC: Department of Justice, Office of Community Oriented Policing Services. Available online at http://www.cops.usdoj.gov/files/RIC/Publications/e1108-Asset-Forfeiture.pdf.

Worrall, John L., Jay W. Ross, and Eric S. McCord. 2006. "Modeling Prosecutors' Charging Decisions in Domestic Violence Cases." *Crime & Delinquency* 52: 472–503.

Wright, Ronald F., and Kay L. Levine. 2014. "The Cure for Young Prosecutors' Syndrome." Emory Legal Studies Research Paper No. 14-277; Wake Forest University Legal Studies Paper No. 2405137. Available online at http://ssrn.com/abstract=2405137

Wright, Ronald F., and Marc Miller. 2002. "The Screening/Bargaining Tradeoff." *Stanford Law Review* 55: 29–118.

York, Erin, and Benjamin Cornwell. 2006 "Status on Trial: Social Characteristics and Influence in the Jury Room." *Social Forces* 85: 455–477.

Young, Malcolm. 2000. "Providing Effective Representation for Youth Prosecuted as Adults." Washington, DC: Department of Justice, Bureau of Justice Assistance Bulletin.

Zahn, Margaret, Stephanie Hawkins, Janet Chiancone, and Ariel Whitworth. 2008. *The Girls Study Group—Charting the Way to Delinquency Prevention for Girls*. Washington, DC: Department of Justice, Office of Justice Programs.

Zalman, Marvin. 2012. "Qualitatively Estimating the Incidence of Wrongful Convictions." *Criminal Law Bulletin* 48(2): 221–279.

Zalman, Marvin, and Larry Siegel. 1997. *Criminal Procedure: Constitution and Society*. 2nd ed. Belmont, CA: Wadsworth.

Zalman, Marvin, Brad Smith, and Amy Kiger. 2008. "Officials' Estimates of the Incidence of 'Actual Innocence' Convictions." *Justice Quarterly* 25(1): 72–100.

Zaruba, John E. 2007. "Courthouse Security: A Direction or a Destination?" *Justice System Journal* 28(1): 46–49.

Zatz, Marjorie. 1984. "Race, Ethnicity, and Determinate Sentencing: A New Dimension to an Old Controversy." *Criminology* 22: 147–171.

Zeisel, Hans. 1982. "The Verdict of Five Out of Six Civil Jurors: Constitutional Problems." *American Bar Foundation Research Journal* 141–156.

Zimring, Franklin, Sheila O'Malley, and Joel Eigen. 1976. "Punishing Homicide in Philadelphia: Perspectives on the Death Penalty." *University of Chicago Law Review* 43: 227–252.

Ziv, Stan. 2015 (August 17). "U.S. Traffic Deaths, Injuries, and Related Costs Up in 2015." *Newsweek*, http://www.newsweek.com/us-traffic-deaths-injuries-and-related-costs-2015-363602.

Zubeck, Pam. 2009. "El Paso County Reaps Bonanza in Traffic Fines." *Gazette*, July 20.

Zuercher, Robert J. 2015. "Campaigning for Judicial Office, 2015." Unpublished doctoral dissertation, University of Kentucky.

Case Index

Italic page numbers indicate material in exhibits, figures, or tables.

Index

Italic page numbers indicate material in exhibits, figures, or tables.